Psychology Applied to Teaching

Eleventh Edition

Jack Snowman
Southern Illinois University

Robert Biehler

Houghton Mifflin Company
Boston   New York

Editor in Chief: Patricia A. Coryell
Senior Sponsoring Editor: Sue Pulvermacher-Alt
Senior Development Editor: Lisa Mafrici
Senior Project Editor: Florence Kilgo
Editorial Assistant: Kristen Truncellito
Art and Design Coordinator: Jill Haber
Photo Editor: Jennifer Meyer-Dare
Composition Buyer: Sarah Ambrose
Manufacturing Coordinator: Chuck Dutton
Marketing Manager: Jane Potter
Marketing Assistant: Erin Lane

Cover image: © Pate Eng

Text and photo credits appear on the last pages of this book, which constitute an extension of the copyright page.

Copyright © 2006 by Houghton Mifflin Company. All rights reserved.

No part of this work may be reproduced or transmitted in any form or by any means, electronic or mechanical, including photocopying and recording, or by any information storage or retrieval system without the prior written permission of Houghton Mifflin Company unless such copying is expressly permitted by federal copyright law. Address inquiries to College Permissions, Houghton Mifflin Company, 222 Berkeley Street, Boston, MA 02116-3764.

Printed in the U.S.A.

Library of Congress Control Number: 2004114225

ISBN: 0-618-47397-1

1 2 3 4 5 6 7 8 9-WEB-08 07 06 05 04

Brief Contents

Contents

Part I Student Characteristics

3   **Age-Level Characteristics**   67

Part II   Learning and Instruction

7   Behavioral Learning Theory: Operant Conditioning   211

8 Information-Processing Theory 237

9   Social Cognitive Theory   276

Part III Creating a Positive Learning Environment

Part IV Assessment of Students

14 Assessment of Classroom Learning 455

15   Understanding and Using Standardized Tests   491

Preface to the Eleventh Edition

This edition of *Psychology Applied to Teaching*, like those that preceded it, can be characterized by two words: change and continuity. Although these two terms carry opposing meanings, in the context of this book they complement each other.

Change is inescapable in educational psychology for several reasons. First, the theories on which this field rests are relatively young and so are still evolving. Second, new types of research and new ways of conducting research continue to be formulated. Third, new issues that affect and concern educators continually come to the fore. We have done our best to address each of these changes and hope, as a result, that students will be better able to understand the forces that shape contemporary education.

Yet, in the face of these changes, this book has been dedicated, ever since its first edition, to the same basic goal: providing a practical, student-oriented approach to educational psychology. The book is written to be used in three ways: (1) as a text that provides basic information, organized and presented so that it will be understood, remembered, and applied; (2) as a source of practical ideas about instructional techniques for student teachers and beginning teachers; and (3) as a means for teachers to improve their effectiveness as they gain experience in the classroom.

Major Features of This Edition

Because of its central role in American society, education is a dynamic enterprise. Tens of thousands of people—including classroom teachers, school administrators, state education officials, politicians, and educational and psychological researchers—are constantly searching for and trying out new ideas to increase student learning and achievement. This is especially true of educational and psychological researchers. Since the last edition of this text many new developments have occurred in social, emotional, and cognitive development; learning processes; motivation; classroom assesssment and management; standardized testing; bilingual education; inclusion of students with disabilities; and the use of computer-based technology to support student learning and achievement. The Eleventh Edition of *Psychology Applied to Teaching* is extensively revised and updated, incorporating new developments in all its domains. Almost half (48 percent) of the references were published since the year 2000, and 71 percent date from 1995 or later.

Noteworthy themes of this edition include:

- **Advances in social cognitive theory**—the subject of a *brand-new chapter*. Because of the many recent developments in cognitive research, this edition devotes a full chapter (Chapter 9) to social cognitive theory. The chapter gives particular attention to the twin concepts of self-regulation and self-efficacy.
- **Debate on critical issues** in educational psychology in the new *Take a Stand! feature*. All the editions of *Psychology Applied to Teaching* have framed the crucial issues in contemporary education in ways that encourage students to consider the research and make informed judgments. This edition goes a step further with a feature called "Take a Stand!" Later in this preface we describe this feature in more detail.
- **Emphasis on educational technology.** Each chapter contains at least one section, and sometimes several, on how technology can be used to address the main themes and concepts of that chapter. For example, the reader will find discussions of how such technology tools as multimedia, hypermedia, tutorial programs, simulation programs, telecommunications, and the World Wide Web can be used to foster cognitive development, address individual differences, promote

greater multicultural understanding, make learning easier for students with disabilities, promote learning and problem solving for all students, increase motivation for learning, help teachers manage their classroom, and aid in assessment of students. In addition, all chapters provide addresses for World Wide Web sites that contain useful supplementary information and links to other relevant sites. Marginal icons direct readers to the textbook's own web site, which provides connections to extended web resources.

- **Emphasis on classroom applications.** *Psychology Applied to Teaching* was the first educational psychology textbook to provide numerous specific examples and guidelines for applying psychological concepts and research findings to classroom teaching. That orientation not only continues but is augmented by Chapter 11, "Approaches to Instruction," which links the writing of instructional objectives with five approaches to instruction that flow from different conceptions of learning.
- **Emphasis on diverse learners.** To help prospective and new teachers understand and cope with the wide range of student diversity they will almost certainly face, we provide extensive treatment of this issue in two chapters: Chapter 4, "Understanding Student Differences," and Chapter 5, "Addressing Cultural and Socioeconomic Diversity." In addition, and where appropriate, we discuss aspects of student diversity in other chapters.
- **Emphasis on real-life contexts.** The Case in Print feature offers newspaper articles about actual classrooms, illustrating the relationship between chapter content and real-life classroom practices. Because of this feature's popularity with both students and instructors, we have included it in every chapter of this edition.
- **Reflective teaching.** The concept of reflective teaching, its importance, and the role that a personal journal can play in helping one become a more reflective teacher are introduced in Chapter 1. This theme is picked up again in Chapter 16, where students learn how to construct a personal journal and how useful this activity is to practicing teachers.

The following lists explain some, though not all, of the major changes made to each chapter.

Chapter 1: Applying Psychology to Teaching

- A new section that correlates the content of *Psychology Applied to Teaching* with the content of the Praxis II, a standardized exam often required for teacher certification, and with the standards for teacher preparation of the Interstate New Teacher Assessment and Support Consortium (INTASC).
- Attention to the increased national emphasis on using scientific research to inform educational practice: for example, the requirement of the No Child Left Behind Act that schools receiving federal funds create and maintain programs on the basis of scientific research; the suggestions of the Task Force on Psychology and Education of the American Psychological Association (APA) for using research to improve teaching and learning; and the APA's publication of standards to strengthen the relationship between educational psychology and teacher education.
- Description of current research that demonstrates the greater effectiveness of certified versus noncertified teachers.
- A new section that describes how the complexity of teaching and learning affects educational research.
- A new Case in Print profiling an award-winning teacher.

Chapter 2: Theories of Psychosocial and Cognitive Development

- Additional criticisms of Erikson's theory of psychosocial development.
- Additional criticisms of Kohlberg's theory of moral development.
- New research on the percentages of adolescents in each identity status, the acceleration of cognitive development through science instruction, the use of

technology to foster cognitive development, and the effectiveness of character education programs.
- New Case in Print on character education.

Chapter 3: Age-Level Characteristics
- New findings on gender differences in physical development, motor skill proficiency, play preferences, and gender typing among preschool and kindergarten children.
- Additional material on primary grade children's use of language to aid cognition.
- Research on meeting the cognitive and emotional needs of middle school students.
- Updated discussion of sexual activity, after-school employment, and incidence of depression and suicide among high school students.
- Discussion of the similarities and differences of the concepts of self-description, self-esteem, and self-concept.
- New Case in Print on middle school anxieties.

Chapter 4: Understanding Student Differences
- Recent refinements of and research on Sternberg's triarchic theory.
- New research on how technology affects intelligence and cognitive style, the cross-cultural validity of Sternberg's mental self-government styles of learning, gender differences in cognitive skills and academic performance, and the effects of gender bias.

Chapter 5: Addressing Cultural and Socioeconomic Diversity
- Suggestions for Teaching in Your Classroom expanded from one section to three.
- Reorganized, revised, and expanded section on ethnicity and social class that includes new material on native Hawaiian and Native American children's preferences for particular instructional formats and processes, Japanese versus Western children's preferences for particular learning processes, and the effect of social class on learning.
- Recent developments in bilingual education.
- New Case in Print on attempts to address the achievement gap between minority and white students.

Chapter 6: Accommodating Student Variability
- Current data on the implementation of IDEA.
- New section on identifying students with learning disabilities.
- New material on characteristics of—and treatment options for—students with attention-deficit/hyperactivity disorder (ADHD).
- New research on ability grouping and its effects on students of low socioeconomic status; on improving reading skills of students with learning disabilities; on methods of identifying gifted and talented students; and on uses of technology for students with disabilities.
- New Case in Print on apparent ethnic/racial biases in special education.

Chapter 7: Behavioral Learning Theory: Operant Conditioning
- New research on the effect of computer-based instruction on learning and the effect of token economies, extinction, and time-out on behavior.
- New material on the debate about corporal punishment.
- New Case in Print on one school's successful behavior management program.
- Material on social learning theory transferred to a new chapter (9) on social cognitive theory.

Chapter 8: Information-Processing Theory
- Suggestions for Teaching in Your Classroom expanded from one section to two.
- New material on relationship between neurological functioning as measured by PET scans and performance on memory tasks.

- New table summarizing instructional implications of the control processes of short-term memory.
- New research on the role of working memory in learning, visual forms of encoding, students' spontaneous use of learning strategies, the effect of mnemonics on essay-test performance, and the use of technology to help students process information more efficiently and effectively.

Chapter 9: Social Cognitive Theory

- This is a *new* chapter, based on the latest developments in social cognitive theory. Anchored in Albert Bandura's triadic reciprocal causation model, it highlights the effect on learning of two of the theory's central variables—self-regulation and self-efficacy—and summarizes the self-regulatory model proposed by social cognitive theorist Barry Zimmerman.
- The chapter also describes how self-regulation is applied to academic achievement, the conditions that make it possible for students to become self-regulated learners, new research that bears on the validity of social cognitive theory, and how technology can be used to promote self-regulated learning.
- As with the other chapters in *Psychology Applied to Teaching*, this chapter offers specific classroom applications through its Suggestions for Teaching in Your Classroom section, Case in Print feature, and the many examples that appear in its different sections.

Chapter 10: Constructivist Learning Theory, Problem Solving, and Transfer

- New Table 10.2 that describes the characteristics of a constructivist classroom.
- New material in Suggestions for Teaching that illustrates how to teach from a constructivist perspective and also satisfy state learning standards.
- New section on the nature of near and far transfer.
- New material on how such technology as multimedia simulations, virtual reality environments, and the Jasper Woodbury series can be used to promote the goals of constructivist learning theory. Several web sites that offer constructivist-oriented activities are described.
- New research on factors that influence the extent to which teachers adopt a constructivist approach to teaching and on when to use worked examples to help students become better problem solvers.

Chapter 11: Approaches to Instruction

- New figure that compares objectives written according to Mager's guidelines with those that follow Gronlund's model.
- New sections on encouraging students to become self-directed learners and the challenges facing teachers who wish to adopt a constructivist approach to teaching.
- New material on how technology can facilitate a cognitive approach to teaching, including problem- and project-based learning.
- New research on the effectiveness of direct instruction, the value of a humanistic approach to teaching, and uses of technology to support cooperative learning.

Chapter 12: Motivation

- New figure that summarizes recent research on the effect of extrinsic rewards on intrinsic motivation.
- New section on the social cognitive view of motivation that draws extensively from the work of Albert Bandura, Dale Schunk, and Barry Zimmerman.
- Suggestions for Teaching in Your Classroom expanded into two parts: "Motivating Students to Learn" and "Satisfying Deficiency Needs and Strengthening Self-Perceptions."
- Revised table (Table 12.2) comparing and illustrating the related concepts of self-description, self-esteem (also known as self-worth), self-concept, and self-efficacy.

- New research on the effect of interest on motivation, the role of academic self-concept in motivation and learning, and the use of technology to motivate students.
- New Case in Print describing one school's innovative approach to increasing students' interest in literature.

Chapter 13: Classroom Management

- New material on the role of integrated learning systems in classroom management.
- Updated statistics on school safety.
- Additional material on biological, gender-related, and psychosocial reasons for school violence.
- New research on classroom interventions and schoolwide programs to reduce violence and improve discipline.
- New Case in Print on a school anger management program.

Chapter 14: Assessment of Classroom Learning

- New material on criteria for constructing a useful classroom test, the benefits of scoring rubrics, potential disadvantages and shortcomings of performance tests, a mastery approach to grading, and using technology to aid classroom assessment.
- New research on the validity of performance assessments.

Chapter 15: Understanding and Using Standardized Tests

- The section on high-stakes testing has been rewritten in response to the No Child Left Behind Act and the spirited reaction by educators to its features, consequences, and implications. This new section describes the main features of NCLB, problems with its implementation, arguments about its actual and likely effects, research findings to date, and recommendations for improving high-stakes testing.
- The technology section has also been extensively rewritten to reflect recent developments in using computer-based technology to prepare students for high-stakes assessments and to administer and score standardized tests (such as computer scoring of essays and computer adaptive testing).
- The new Case in Print focuses on various effects of NCLB.

Chapter 16: Becoming a Better Teacher by Becoming a Reflective Teacher

- The section on student evaluations has been expanded to include discussion of the Constructivist Learning Environment Survey (CLES), a relatively new instrument that assesses the extent to which students believe the classroom environment adheres to constructivist learning principles. Figure 16.2 contains the 25 items that make up the instrument.
- The section on classroom observation schedules has been revised to include a discussion and examples of checklists.
- We have added a new section on the effectiveness of reflective teaching techniques.

Special Features of the Text

The pedagogic features introduced in earlier editions have been improved and augmented to make this Eleventh Edition even more useful and effective.

New **Take a Stand!** In this era of accountability, teachers are frequently criticized and called upon to defend their profession and their practices. Although many veteran teachers do this quite confidently and effectively, the novice teacher often feels ill prepared to engage the public. To provide students with a brief model of how one can articulate a compelling position on an educational issue, we have created the new feature called Take a Stand! In Chapters 2 through 15, the senior author draws on his thirty years of experience and knowledge of the research literature to take a strong but supportable stand on an issue that relates to the chapter content. Further, the feature encourages students to do the same—to articulate and discuss their own opinions on key issues. At the textbook web site this feature is extended with additional resources and pedagogy. For users of our Eduspace course this feature will be integrated with the discussion board.

Key Points   At the beginning of each chapter, Key Points are listed under major headings. They also appear in the margins of pages opposite sections in which each point is discussed. The Key Points call attention to sections of the text that are considered to be of special significance to teachers and thus serve as instructional objectives.

Suggestions for Teaching in Your Classroom   Most chapters include summaries of research findings and principles relating to a particular topic. These are followed by detailed descriptions of various ways in which the information and concepts might be applied in classrooms. Numerous examples of applications at different grade levels are supplied, and readers are urged to select applications that will fit their own particular personality, style, and teaching situation and record their ideas in a Reflective Journal. The Suggestions for Teaching are intended to be read while the book is used as a text and referred to by future teachers and in-service teachers after they have completed coursework. For ease in reference, these suggestions are printed on a colored background.

Case in Print   This feature, which uses recent news articles to demonstrate how a basic idea or technique in a chapter is being applied by educators from the primary grades through high school, has proven to be extremely popular with users. Following each article are several open-ended questions designed to encourage the student to think more deeply about the issue in question. The purpose of the Case in Print feature is to illustrate to preservice teachers that the psychological theory and research that their instructors require them to learn does have real-world relevance. A Case in Print can be found in every chapter, and eleven of the sixteen are new to this edition. Additional Cases in Print can be found on the textbook web site.

Pause and Reflect   Knowing how difficult it is for students to meaningfully grasp the abstract concepts that make up educational psychology, we have added a new feature to help students make connections between one idea and another and between theory and actual classroom practice. As students read each chapter, they will encounter several Pause and Reflect headings that ask them to stop and think about a concept or issue raised in the chapter or consider how their own experiences relate to what they are reading.

Journal Entries   This feature is intended to help students prepare and use a Reflective Journal when they teach. Readers are urged to use the journal entries, which appear in the margins, to prepare a personal set of guidelines for reference before and during the student teaching experience and during the first years of teaching. A guide for setting up and using a Reflective Journal is included in Chapter 16, "Becoming a Better Teacher by Becoming a Reflective Teacher."

Links to the Textbook Web Site   Because a wealth of material is available on the web site that supplements the text, this edition includes marginal icons to suggest points at which the reader may want to refer to the web site.

Resources for Further Investigation   At the end of each chapter, an annotated bibliography is presented, offering sources of information on the major topics covered in the chapter. Internet addresses for World Wide Web sites that provide additional useful information are also listed in this section. Please note that the web sites were active at the time we prepared the text, but we, of course, are not responsible for their continued presence. Readers can access the textbook's web site for live, recently updated links.

Summary A numbered set of summary statements appears after the Resources for Further Investigation. This feature is intended to help students review the main points of a chapter for upcoming examinations or class discussions.

Key Terms Also appearing at the end of each chapter is a list of key concepts discussed in the chapter. Understanding these topics is an essential part of understanding the chapter as a whole. To facilitate use of this feature, the page where each term is initially defined and discussed appears in parentheses.

Glossary A glossary of key terms and concepts is provided at the back of the book as an aid in reviewing for examinations or classroom discussion.

Instructional Components That Accompany the Text

Houghton Mifflin Video Cases Available online and organized by topic, each "case" is a 3- to 5-minute module consisting of video and audio files presenting actual classroom scenarios that depict the complex problems and opportunities teachers face every day. The video and audio clips are accompanied by "artifacts" to provide background information and allow preservice teachers to experience true classroom dilemmas in their multiple dimensions.

Instructor's Resource Manual This teaching aid provides for each chapter a detailed lecture outline with supplementary teaching suggestions, coverage of Key Points, supplementary discussion topics, student activities, extra references, listings of films, videotapes, software and Internet resources, and "Approaches to Teaching Educational Psychology," a compendium of teaching tactics from professors across the country.

Test Bank The Test Bank has been thoroughly revised by Jack Snowman. It includes test items consisting of multiple-choice items in alternate forms, short-answer questions, and essay questions. Consistent with this text's long-standing emphasis on mastery, each multiple-choice and short-answer question reflects a Key Point and either the Knowledge, Comprehension, Application, or Analysis level of Bloom's taxonomy. Feedback booklets allow instructors to point out misconceptions in students' reasoning.

HM Class Prep CD-ROM with HM Testing This product offers resources for instructors, including much of the Instructor's Resource Manual in electronic format for easy customization, PowerPoint slides, videos on key topics on diversity and teacher decision-making, and an interactive computerized version of the Test Bank.

Eduspace For instructors who teach the course online, Houghton Mifflin's new Eduspace course offers a convenient format. Eduspace is Houghton Mifflin's proprietary version of Blackboard. In addition to its handy gradebook and other course management tools, Eduspace includes special interactive components such as videos, a discussion board, reflective journal questions, test items, and additional materials to aid students in studying and reflecting on what they have learned.

Dedicated Web Site Helping today's instructors and students learn how to use technology meaningfully is a primary strength of this text. As a corollary, a dedicated, interactive web site for both instructors and students is available; it can be accessed from **http://education.college.hmco.com.** The site, updated by Gary and Katrina Daytner of Western Illinois University, offers a wide variety of study aids (including ACE practice tests and interactive glossary flashcards), project ideas, technology links, site-based cases, lesson plans, and more. Although the marginal icons in the text remind students to use the web site, we cannot possibly cross-reference all of our online material. We hope that both instructors and students will explore the web site and make full use of it.

Houghton Mifflin Teacher Education Web Site   Houghton Mifflin's general education web site for students (go to **http://education.college.hmco.com/students**) provides additional pedagogic support and resources for beginning and experienced professionals in education, including the unique Project-Based Learning Space. This page links to five extended problem-based projects and provides background theory about project-based learning.

Acknowledgments

While the content of a textbook is mostly the product of an author's knowledge, judgment, and communication skill, the suggestions of others play a significant role in shaping its final form. A number of reviewers made constructive suggestions and provided thoughtful reactions at various stages in the development of this edition. Thanks go out to the following individuals for their help:

Valerie Amber, Brenda Czech,
Norman O. Douglass, and
Mark Ryan
   National University
Kent Chrisman
   Shippensburg University
Henry T. Clark
   Arizona University
Frank Gault
   The University of Texas at
   Arlington

Joseph E. Gillespie
   Neumann College
William G. Huitt
   Valdosta State University
Dale H. Schunk
   University of North Carolina at
   Greensboro
Jean Schwisow-Thatcher
   Texas Tech University
Jina Yoon
   Wayne State University

1 Applying Psychology to Teaching

As you begin to read this book, you may be asking yourself, "What will this book tell me about teaching that I don't already know?" The answer to that question depends on several factors, including your previous experiences with teaching and the number of psychology courses you have taken. Because you have been actively engaged in the process of formal education for a number of years, you already know a great deal about learning and teaching. You have had abundant opportunities to observe and react to more than one hundred teachers. You have probably read several hundred texts, finished all kinds of assignments, used a variety of software programs, and taken hundreds of examinations. Undoubtedly, you have also established strong likes and dislikes for certain subjects and approaches to teaching.

Yet despite your familiarity with education from the student's point of view, you probably have had limited experience with education from the teacher's point of view. Therefore, a major purpose of this book is to help you take the first steps in what will be a long journey to becoming an expert teacher.

Throughout this book, we will describe many different psychological theories, concepts, and principles and illustrate how you might apply them to teaching. The branch of psychology that specializes in understanding how different factors affect the classroom behavior of both teachers and students is **educational psychology.** In the next several sections, we will briefly describe the nature of this field of study and highlight the features of this book that will help you understand psychological principles and apply them in your classroom.

WHAT IS EDUCATIONAL PSYCHOLOGY?

● Educational psychologists study how students learn in classrooms

Most educational psychologists, us included, would define their field as a scientific discipline that is concerned with understanding and improving how students acquire a variety of capabilities through formal instruction in classroom settings. According to Nathaniel Gage and David Berliner (1998), for example, "Psychology is the study of the thoughts and actions of individuals and groups. Educational psychology is the study of those thoughts and actions as they relate to how we teach and learn, particularly in school settings" (p. 3). This description of educational psychology suggests that to become the most effective teacher possible, you will need to understand such aspects of the learner as physical, social, emotional, and cognitive development; cultural, social, emotional, and intellectual differences; learning and problem-solving processes; self-esteem; motivation; testing; and measurement.

This book's web site offers many helpful resources, such as quick links to web pages mentioned in the text. Go to **http://education.college.hmco.com/students** and select the Snowman textbook site. Be sure to bookmark it for later use.

The importance of these topics to classroom learning has been underscored by the American Psychological Association (APA). In November 1997, the APA's Board of Educational Affairs proposed that efforts to improve education be based on a set of fourteen learner-centered psychological principles. These principles, which were derived from decades of research and practice, highlight the importance of learning processes, motivation, development, social processes, individual differences, and instructional practices in classroom learning. These are the same topics and principles that have long been emphasized by *Psychology Applied to Teaching*. A description of and rationale for each principle can be found on the following APA web site: **www.apa.org/ed/lcp2/**.

We recognize that you may have some doubts right now both about your ability to master all of this material and about the necessity to do so. To help you learn as much of this material as possible, we have incorporated into each chapter a number of helpful features that are described at the end of this chapter. But first let's examine why the learning you will do in educational psychology is a worthwhile goal.

The information in this book can help you be a better teacher for three reasons: teaching is a complex activity that requires a broad knowledge base; many instructional practices are supported by research; and teachers who are knowledgeable about that research are better teachers.

HOW WILL LEARNING ABOUT EDUCATIONAL PSYCHOLOGY HELP YOU BE A BETTER TEACHER?

There's no question that knowledge of psychological concepts and their application to educational settings has the potential to help you be a better teacher. Whether that potential is ever fulfilled depends on how willing you are to maintain an open mind and a positive attitude. We say this because many prospective and practicing teachers have anything but a positive attitude when it comes to using psychological knowledge in the classroom. One teacher, for example, notes that "educational psychology and research are relatively useless because they rarely examine learning in authentic classroom contexts" (Burch, 1993). As you read through the next few paragraphs, as well as the subsequent chapters, you will see that criticisms like this are easily rebutted. We will offer a three-pronged argument to explain how educational psychology can help you be a better teacher, whether you plan to teach in an elementary school, a middle school, or a high school.

Teaching Is a Complex Enterprise

The first part of our argument is that teaching is not the simple, straightforward enterprise some people imagine it to be; in fact, it ranks in the top quartile on complexity for all occupations (Rowan, 1994). There are many reasons for this complexity. In increasing ways, teachers have daily responsibility for diverse populations of students with varied and sometimes contradictory needs. But perhaps most fundamental, the complexity of teaching derives from its decision-making nature. Teachers are constantly making decisions—before and after instruction as well as on the spot. To be informed and effective, these decisions should be based on a deep reservoir of knowledge and a wide range of skills.

● Teaching is complex work because it requires a wide range of knowledge and skills

The view that teaching is a complex activity that requires in-depth knowledge in a number of areas has been recognized by the National Board for Professional Teaching Standards **(www.nbpts.org/)**. This is an independent, nonprofit organization of educators, administrators, and political and business leaders whose mission is to establish clear and measurable standards for what accomplished teachers should know and be able to do and to identify those teachers through a voluntary system of certification. The board's standards are based on the following five propositions (National Board for Professional Teaching Standards, 2003):

1. Teachers are committed to students and their learning.
2. Teachers know the subjects they teach and how to teach those subjects to students.
3. Teachers are responsible for managing and monitoring student learning.
4. Teachers think systematically about their practice and learn from experience.
5. Teachers are members of learning communities.

In general, the standards require teachers to be knowledgeable about learning and development, individual differences, motivation, self-concept, assessment, classroom management, and various approaches to instruction, all of which are covered in this textbook. Although the complexity inherent in teaching makes it a difficult profession to master, making progress toward that goal is also one of teaching's greatest rewards.

To help you prepare to take on such challenges and become an effective teacher, educational psychology offers many useful ideas. It does not, in most cases, provide specific prescriptions about how to handle particular problems; rather, it gives you general principles that you can use in a flexible manner. Fortunately, the research literature contains a wealth of these ideas.

Research That Informs Teachers

● Research in educational psychology offers many useful ideas for improving classroom instruction

The second part of our argument pertains to the potential usefulness of educational psychology research. Contrary to the opinion ventured by the anonymous teacher quoted previously, the research literature contains numerous studies that were conducted under realistic classroom conditions and offer useful ideas for improving instruction. There is consistent classroom-based support for the following instructional practices (Berliner & Casanova, 1996; Cruickshank, 1990; Marzano, Pickering, & Pollock, 2001), all of which are discussed in later chapters of this text:

1. Using more advanced students to tutor less advanced students
2. Giving positive reinforcement to students whose performance meets or exceeds the teacher's objectives and giving corrective feedback to students whose performance falls short of the teacher's objectives
3. Communicating to students what is expected of them and why
4. Requiring students to respond to higher-order questions
5. Providing students with cues about the nature of upcoming tasks by giving them introductory information and telling them what constitutes satisfactory performance
6. Teaching students how to monitor and improve their own learning efforts and offering them structured opportunities to practice independent learning activities
7. Knowing the misconceptions that students bring to the classroom that will likely interfere with their learning of a particular subject matter

8. Creating learning situations in which students are expected to organize information in new ways and formulate problems for themselves
9. Accepting responsibility for student outcomes rather than seeing students as solely responsible for what they learn and how they behave
10. Showing students how to work in small cooperative learning groups

The federal government has acknowledged the importance of applying research on learning and learning-related issues to teaching. As part of the No Child Left Behind Act of 2001 (a revision of the earlier Elementary and Secondary Education Act), all schools that receive federal funds to create and maintain programs (such as safe and drug-free schools and Title I) must document how those programs are supported by scientifically based research. This legislation also authorizes the National Science Foundation to create a network of Science of Learning Centers. These centers will have an interdisciplinary focus, combining, for example, the work of researchers in psychology, education, computer science, linguistics, and sociology on various learning-related issues. The knowledge gained from these efforts will then be used to shape curriculum development and assessment (Azar, 2002).

In addition to the federal government's initiatives, the American Psychological Association has created a Task Force on Psychology and Education that will use research findings to suggest how teaching and learning can be improved. The Educational Psychology Division of APA will publish standards that strengthen the relationship between educational psychology and teacher education (Murray, 2002).

Coursework and Competence

The third part of our argument that educational psychology can help you be a better teacher concerns the courses you are currently taking, particularly this educational psychology course. Many researchers have asked, "How do the courses teachers take as students relate to how capable they perceive themselves to be as teachers?" One means that researchers have used to determine the answer has been to ask beginning teachers to rate how prepared they feel to handle a variety of classroom tasks.

On the plus side, studies of beginning teachers (e.g., Maloch, Fine, & Flint, 2002/2003; Ruhland & Bremer, 2002) report that most believe that their teacher education programs adequately have prepared them to deal with most classroom challenges, and they are confident of their ability to be effective teachers. On the negative side, many teachers have reported that they feel uncomfortable in areas such as motivating students to learn, working with culturally diverse students, teaching exceptional students, managing the classroom, and teaching students how to use computers (e.g., Houston & Williamson, 1992/1993; Leyser, Frankiewicz, & Vaughn, 1992; Ruhland & Bremer, 2002; Scales, 1993). In fact, a recent survey conducted for the U.S. Department of Education's National Center for Education Statistics found that only 20 to 30 percent of teachers felt very well prepared to meet the needs of students with disabilities, use performance assessment techniques, and integrate educational technology into classroom instruction (Lewis et al., 1999). This textbook will address all of these issues, with special emphasis on most of those about which teachers have reported discomfort. Our belief is that this course and this book will be one important means for helping you feel prepared to enter your first classroom.

Another way to gauge the value of teacher-education coursework is to look at the effectiveness of certified versus noncertified teachers. Several studies (see Darling-Hammond & Youngs, 2002; Laczko-Kerr & Berliner, 2003; Wayne & Youngs, 2003; and Wilson, Floden, & Ferrini-Mundy, 2002 for summaries of this research) found that the students of certified teachers scored higher on standardized achievement tests than did the students of noncertified teachers even though the noncertified teachers were judged to have had a good understanding of their subject matter.

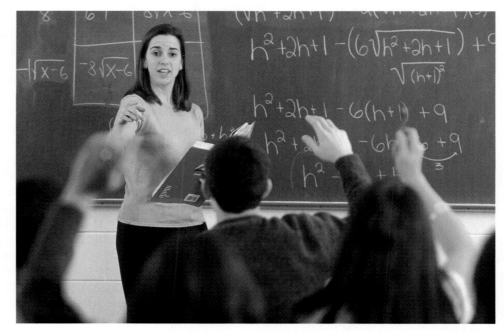

The students of teachers who were trained in teacher education programs and certified by their states score higher on standardized achievement tests than do the students of noncertified teachers.

● Teachers who have had professional training are generally more effective

Case studies of individual teachers have produced similar findings. Linda Valli (1993) describes one student who stopped working on his bachelor's degree in mathematics to teach full-time at a parochial high school. After one year of teaching, in which he described his classes as "basically out of control," he quit teaching, returned to college, and completed a teacher-education program in high school mathematics. Recalling the contributions of his educational psychology course, he judged his next teaching job as much more successful than his first.

THE NATURE AND VALUES OF SCIENCE

The primary purpose of this book is to offer suggestions on how psychology (the scientific study of behavior and mental processes) might be applied to teaching. This text is based on the premise that information reported by scientists can be especially useful for those who plan to teach. Some of the reasons for this conviction become apparent when the characteristics of science are examined and compared with the limitations of casual observation.

Limitations of Unsystematic Observation

● Unsystematic observation may lead to false conclusions

Those who make unsystematic observations of human behavior may be easily misled into drawing false conclusions. For instance, they may treat the first plausible explanation that comes to mind as the only possible explanation. Or they may mistakenly apply a generalization about a single episode to superficially similar situations. In the process, they may fail to realize that an individual's reactions in a given situation are due primarily to unrecognized idiosyncratic factors that may never occur again or that the behavior of one person under certain circumstances may not resemble that of other persons in the same circumstances. In short, unsystematic observers are especially prone to noting only evidence that fits their expectations and ignoring evidence that does not.

● Grade retention policies are influenced by unsystematic observation

A clear example of the limitations of unsystematic observation is the practice of retaining children for a second year in a given grade because of poor achievement. Grade retention has long been used as a way of dealing with individual differences in learning rate, emotional development, and socialization skills. The average retention rate for students in kindergarten through eighth grade in the United States is estimated to be about 6 percent. Across school districts, rates vary from 0 percent to 40 percent. Retention is an expensive tactic, since the average school spends about $4,000–$5,000 per year per student (Allington & McGill-Franzen, 1995; Dyer & Binkney, 1995). To some extent, retention rates are related to the growth of state learning standards and high-stakes testing programs (which we discuss in our chapter on standardized tests); school districts are often required to retain students whose test scores fall below a certain level.

This widespread and expensive use of retention continues even though most research clearly shows that it has negative effects. Retained students are 40 to 50 percent more likely to drop out of school than nonretained students. Moreover, low-achieving children who are promoted learn more the following year, have a stronger self-concept, and are better adjusted emotionally than similar children who are retained, even when the retention occurs as early as kindergarten (Haberman & Dill, 1993; Jimerson, 2001; Jimerson & Kaufman, 2003; Jimerson, Anderson, & Whipple, 2002; Meisels & Liaw, 1993; Roderick, 1995; Rodney, Crafter, Rodney, & Mupier, 1999). Yet grade retention continues to be recommended by some parents, schools, administrators, and teachers because "common sense" suggests that repeating a grade should be beneficial to a student, and people tend to overgeneralize from the exceptional case in which the outcome was positive (Graue & DiPerna, 2000; Owings & Kaplan, 2001; Thomas, 2000).

The best way to minimize, if not avoid, the use of retention is to provide developmentally, cognitively, and culturally appropriate forms of instruction (Darling-Hammond & Falk, 1997). The major goal of this text is to help you become the kind of teacher who knows how to provide such instruction.

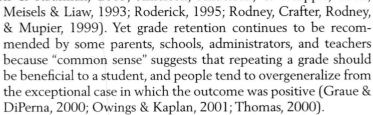

Imagine that you are a second-grade teacher. Your principal suggests that one of your students, who performed poorly this year, repeat second grade next year. Given what you know about the research on retention, how would you respond?

Strengths of Scientific Observation

Those who study behavior and mental processes scientifically are more likely to acquire trustworthy information than a casual observer is, and they are likely to apply what they learn more effectively because they follow the scientific procedures of sampling, control, objectivity, publication, and replication. In most cases, researchers study a representative sample of subjects so that individual idiosyncrasies are canceled out. An effort is made to note all plausible hypotheses to explain a given type of behavior, and each hypothesis is tested under controlled conditions. If all factors but one can be held constant in an experiment, the researcher may be able to trace the impact of a given condition by comparing the behaviors of those who have been exposed to it and those who have not.

● Scientific methods: sampling, control, objectivity, publication, replication

Scientific observers make special efforts to be objective and to guard against being misled by predetermined ideas, wishful thinking, or selected evidence. Observations are made in a carefully prescribed, systematic manner, which makes it possible for different observers to compare reactions.

Complete reports of experiments—including descriptions of subjects, methods, results, and conclusions—are published in professional journals. This dissemination allows other experimenters to replicate a study to discover if they obtain the same results. The existence of reports of thousands of experiments makes it possible to discover what others have done. This knowledge can then serve as a starting point for one's own speculations.

COMPLICATING FACTORS IN THE STUDY OF BEHAVIOR AND THOUGHT PROCESSES

Although the use of scientific methods makes it possible to overcome many of the limitations of unscientific observation, the application of knowledge acquired in a scientific manner to classroom settings is subject to several complicating factors. We want you to be aware of these so that you do not think we are insisting that science can cure all your classroom problems.

The Limited Focus of Research

Human behavior is complex, changes with age, and has many causes. A student may perform poorly on a history exam, for example, for one or more of the following reasons: poorly developed study skills, inattentiveness in class, low interest in the subject, a poorly written text, low motivation to achieve high grades, vaguely worded exam questions, and difficulty with a particular type of exam question (compare-and-contrast essays, for example).

● Research focuses on a few aspects of a problem

To understand how these factors affect performance on school-related tasks, research psychologists study at most only a few of them at a time under conditions that may not be entirely realistic. Imagine that a researcher is interested in comparing simulation software with drill or tutorial software in terms of their effect on conceptual understanding. The researcher may recruit subjects who are equivalent in terms of social class, prior knowledge of the topic of the reading passage, and age; randomly assign them to one of two experimental groups; give them either a simulation program or a drill program to use; and then examine each group's responses to several types of comprehension items. As a consequence of such focused approaches, most research studies provide specific information about a particular aspect of behavior. More comprehensive knowledge, however, is acquired by combining and interrelating separate studies that have looked at different aspects of a common problem.

The Complexity of Teaching and Learning

David Berliner (2002), a leading educational researcher, considers the scientific study of education to be "the hardest-to-do science of them all" for at least two reasons. First, it is difficult to implement research findings and programs uniformly because schools and classrooms differ from one another along such lines as quality and quantity of personnel, teaching methods, budget, leadership, and community support. Thus, a program or technique may work just as the research says it should in one district or teacher's class, but not in other classes or districts.

● Complexity of teaching and learning limits uniform outcomes

Second, the outcomes of schooling that teachers, students, and parents typically value are the result of complex interactions among numerous variables. This is true for both cognitive (thinking) outcomes and affective (emotional) outcomes. Achievement may, for example, be the result of interactions among student characteristics (such as prior knowledge, interests, and socioeconomic levels), teacher characteristics (type of training, ideas about learning, interests, and values, for example), curriculum materials, socioeconomic status of the community, and peer influences. Consequently, students exposed to the same materials and teaching methods are likely to vary in how much and what they learn.

Such differences in student outcomes are largely a result of the fact that ideas are not given from one person to another like so many packages but rather are actively *constructed* by each person (Brooks & Brooks, 2001; Schifter, 1996; Wheatley, 1991). Because different factors come into play for different people and the same factors affect people differently, two people can read the same passage yet construct entirely different interpretations of its meaning. This concept, known as *constructivism*, is so

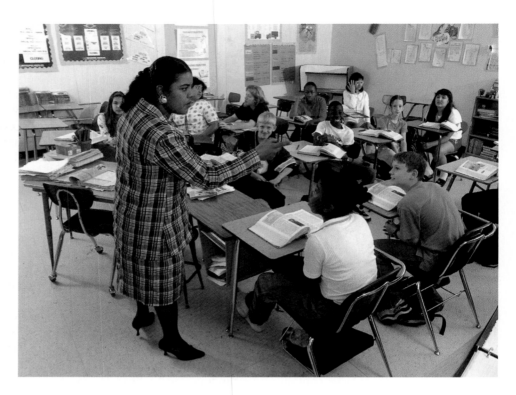

The constructivist view of learning holds that individual differences in such factors as age, gender, race, and ethnic background lead to differences in what people perceive and how they form ideas.

fundamental to human behavior and to learning that we will return to it again and again in this text.

Because of these differences in context and individual characteristics, researchers rarely find that a particular instructional technique, program, or set of learning materials produces the same effect for all students. Consequently, the most useful research findings are those that stem from such questions as these:

- Who (males or females; high-, average-, or low-achieving students; ethnic minority or majority students; younger or older students) is likely to benefit most from this technique, program, or type of material?
- Under what conditions are the strongest results likely to be obtained?
- For what types of outcomes (such as multiple-choice tests, essay tests, performance tests) are the strongest results likely to be obtained?

Selection and Interpretation of Data

● Differences of opinion result from selection and interpretation of data

The amount of scientific information available on behavior and mental processes is so extensive that no individual could examine or interpret all of it. Accordingly, researchers learn to be highly selective in their reading. In addition, conclusions about the meaning of scientific results vary from one researcher to another. As you read this book, you will discover that there are differences of opinion among psychologists regarding certain aspects of development, motivation, and intelligence. Opposing views may be based on equally scientific evidence, but the way in which the evidence is selected and interpreted will vary. The fact that a topic is studied scientifically does not necessarily mean that opinions about interpretations of the data will be unanimous.

New Findings Mean Revised Ideas

Scientific information is not only voluminous and subject to different interpretations; it is also constantly being revised. A series of experiments may lead to the development of a new concept or pedagogical technique that is highly successful when

● Accumulated knowledge leads
researchers to revise original ideas

it is first tried out. Subsequent studies, however, may reveal that the original research was incomplete, or repeated applications of a technique may show that it is less effective once the novelty has worn off. But frequent shifts of emphasis in education also reflect the basic nature of science. A quality of science that sets it apart from other intellectual processes is that the discoveries by one generation of scientists set the stage for more complete and far-reaching discoveries by the next. More researchers are studying aspects of psychology and education now than at any previous time in history. And thousands of reports of scientific research are published every month.

As our knowledge accumulates, it is inevitable that interpretations of how children learn and how we should teach will continue to change. We know more about development, learning, and teaching today than ever before, but because of the nature of some of the factors just discussed and the complexity of human behavior, our answers are tentative and incomplete.

You should be aware, of course, that fads occur in education (just as they occur in other fields). Occasionally, national or international events cause changes in our political and social climate that often result in pressures on education to "do something." And when large numbers of educators embrace a new practice without waiting for or paying attention to research findings, fads develop. One of our objectives in writing this text is to demonstrate the importance of basing your practices on principles that have some research support. If you do so, you can avoid contributing to fads.

Think of a popular instructional practice. Would you classify it as a fad or as the outgrowth of scientific knowledge? Why? How can you tell the difference?

Over the past few pages, we have asked you to consider some of the values of science, the strengths of scientific observation, and a few of the factors that complicate the scientific study of behavior and lead to frequent changes of emphasis in teaching techniques. These considerations help explain why this book stresses how psychology might be applied to teaching; they also support the position that information reported by scientists can be especially valuable for those who plan to teach. At the same time, our intention has been to acquaint you with a few of the limitations and sometimes unsettling by-products of science.

The science of psychology has much to offer educators, but a scientific approach to teaching does have its limits. Because teaching is a dynamic *decision-making process*, you will be greatly aided by a systematic, objective framework for making your decisions. Research on teaching and learning can give you that framework. But for the reasons just cited, research cannot give you a prescription or a set of rules that specify how you should handle every situation. Often you will have to make on-the-spot, subjective decisions about how to present a lesson, explain a concept, handle mass boredom, or reprimand a student. This contrast between an objective, systematic approach to planning instruction and the need to make immediate (yet appropriate) applications and modifications of those plans calls attention to a question that has been debated for years: Is teaching primarily an art or a science—or a combination of both?

GOOD TEACHING IS PARTLY AN ART AND PARTLY A SCIENCE

Some educators have argued that teaching is an art that cannot be practiced or even studied in an objective or scientific manner because of its inherent unpredictability (Eisner, 2002; Flinders, 1989; Hansgen, 1991; Rubin, 1985). Selma Wasserman (1999), who taught public school and college for many years, recounts how her teacher-education program prepared her for her first day as a public school teacher:

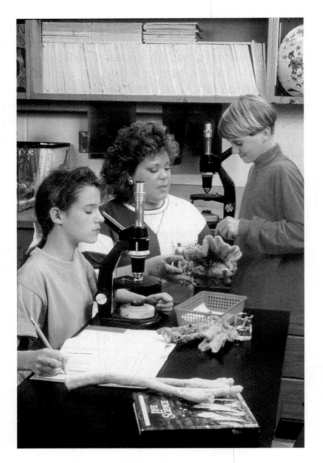

Part of the art of teaching is knowing when to introduce an unusual assignment or activity that captures students' interest.

Learning the "correct answers" not only had not equipped me for the complex and confusing world of the classroom but, even worse, had led me down the garden path. Implicit in what I had learned was that teaching was merely a matter of stockpiling certain pieces of information about teaching. If I only knew what the answers were, I would be prepared to face the overwhelming and exhausting human dilemmas that make up life in classrooms. Unfortunately, I had been swindled. My training in learning the answers was as useless as yesterday's pizza. I was entering a profession in which there are few, if any, clear-cut answers, a profession riddled with ambiguity and moral dilemmas that would make Solomon weep. Even more of a handicap was that I became desperate in my search for the answers—certain that they were out there, somewhere, if only I could find them. (p. 466)

Wasserman's account suggests that there are no authoritative sources that will provide teachers with fail-safe prescriptions for the myriad problems they will face. Good teaching is as much the result of one's beliefs, values, and emotions as of one's formal knowledge. A few examples of beliefs that support good teaching are that teaching is one of society's most valuable and rewarding activities, that teaching must be done as well as possible every day, that it is important to get students excited about learning, and that there is no such thing as an unteachable student. The Case in Print: "Teaching Can Be a Rewarding Experience" tells the story of a high school math teacher who obviously subscribes to these beliefs and was handsomely rewarded for her efforts.

When Wasserman states that teaching is not a matter of clear-cut answers, she is urging teachers to be flexible. Flexibility, which can be thought of as a "feel" for doing the right thing at the right time, can take many forms. First, it means being able to choose from among all the techniques and information at your disposal to formulate effective lesson plans that take the diverse needs and interests of all your students into consideration. It means knowing, for example, when to present a formal lesson and when to let students discover things for themselves, when to be demanding and when to make few demands, when and to whom to give direct help and when and to whom to give indirect help.

Second, flexibility entails the communication of emotions and interest in a variety of ways. David Flinders (1989) describes a teacher who, when talking to students, would lean or step in their direction and maintain eye contact. At various times, she would raise her eyebrows, nod her head, smile, and bring the index finger of her right hand to her lips, indicating serious consideration of the student's comments. In their book *Acting Lessons for Teachers: Using Performance Skills in the Classroom* (1994), Robert Tauber and Cathy Sargent Mester describe the importance for successful teaching of such acting skills as voice animation (variations in pitch, volume, voice quality, and rate), body animation (facial expressions, gestures), and use of classroom space. A nice example of capturing students' attention by the unorthodox use of space can be seen in the 1989 film *Dead Poets Society* when the teacher (played by Robin Williams) stands on his desk to lecture.

pause & reflect

The effective teacher as artist communicates enthusiasm. At some point, however, you may be asked to teach a grade level or subject for which you have little enthusiasm, or you may grow bored teaching the same grade level or subject year after year. How will you fulfill the role of teacher-artist if faced with these conditions?

Third, flexibility includes the ability to improvise. When a lesson plan falls flat, the flexible teacher immediately thinks of an alternative presentation that recaptures the students' interest. Expert teachers actually plan improvisation into their lessons. Instead of writing out what they intend to do in great detail, they formulate general mental plans and wait to see how the students react before filling in such details as pacing, timing, and number of examples (Moshavi, 2001; Westerman, 1991). Obviously, this type of high-wire act requires a great deal of experience and confidence.

Fourth, flexibility involves the willingness and resourcefulness to work around impediments. Teaching does not always occur under ideal circumstances, and teachers must sometimes cope with inadequate facilities, insufficient materials, interruptions, and other difficulties.

● Teaching as an art: beliefs, emotions, values, flexibility

Teacher educator Sharon Feiman-Nemser (2003) underscored the importance of flexibility to the art of teaching by noting what experienced educators said when asked what beginning teachers most needed to learn. One recommended that new teachers focus on helping students understand the essence of each lesson, even if that means going beyond or ignoring guidelines in a teacher's manual. Another noted that because teachers are essentially on stage, they need to develop a performing self that they are comfortable with. A third observation was that new teachers need to learn how to size up situations and think on their feet. In sum, **teaching as an art** involves beliefs, emotions, values, and flexibility. Because these characteristics are intangible, they can be very difficult, if not impossible, to teach. Teachers must find these qualities within themselves.

The argument for **teaching as a science** is equally persuasive. Although many educational psychologists agree that the science of teaching, as such, does not exist, they contend that it is possible and desirable to have a scientific basis for the art of teaching (e.g., Gage & Berliner, 1998; Hiebert, Gallimore, & Stigler, 2002; Kosunen & Mikkola, 2002). By drawing on established research findings, both prospective and practicing teachers can be taught many of the prerequisites that make artistic teaching possible. Also, as Robert Slavin (1989) persuasively argues, working from a scientific basis helps teachers avoid the pitfall of subscribing to the latest fad.

● Research provides a scientific basis for "artistic" teaching

The case for teaching as a science rests on the existence of a usable body of research findings. Research has identified dozens of instructional practices that improve student achievement. For example, at least twenty-four separate studies have found that giving teachers more instructional time—that is, giving students more time to learn—leads to higher achievement (Walberg, 1990 Wang, Haertel, & Walberg, 1993). (This finding is often used to support proposals for a longer school year.) Other studies have demonstrated the benefits of alerting students to important

Teaching Can Be a Rewarding Experience

Good teaching is as much the result of one's beliefs, values, and emotions as of one's formal knowledge. A few examples of beliefs that support good teaching are that teaching is one of society's most valuable and rewarding activities, that teaching must be done as well as possible every day, that it is important to get students excited about learning, and that there is no such thing as an unteachable student. (p. 10)

Dedication, Innovation Add Up to Prize for Teacher

ALEXA AGUILAR
St. Louis Post-Dispatch, 11/15/03

No one at O'Fallon High School had a clue why they had convened for a special assembly in the gym Tuesday afternoon. The buzz was that a dignitary from California would be on hand for a special announcement, and the predominant theory in the hallways was that Arnold Schwarzenegger was coming.

It wasn't Arnold. But it was Lowell Milken, a philanthropist from Los Angeles who hands out $25,000 checks to 100 teachers and principals a year for outstanding work. With a drumroll and a dramatic pause, Milken told the crowd he came to bestow one of the coveted awards on one of their very own.

Twenty or so bleacher rows up, Kelly Wamser sat among her students, looking around, wondering who it could be. When Milken announced that Wamser had received the $25,000—no strings attached—she sat stupefied. Then the tears came.

"Oh my God," said the geometry and algebra teacher, a nine-year employee at the high school. "Can someone wake me up right now?"

That's how Milken presents his annual gifts, by surprise, in front of school assemblies. Milken, who started the Milken Family Foundation in 1985, wanted to reward teachers and principals in a dramatic way, with a prize attached. So far, the foundation has awarded nearly $50 million to about 2,000 teachers and principals. In Missouri on Tuesday, Karen LaFever, an eighth-grade science teacher at Parkway Central Middle School, also won one of the awards.

Wamser, who mentors teachers and recently traveled to Japan to observe teaching methods, is known as a teacher who puts in long hours to make her classroom engaging and exciting. In Wamser's geometry class, students design and build houses or replicas of the Leaning Tower of Pisa to learn the real-life applications of math.

"She definitely deserves it," said Kristin Strubhart, a fellow teacher. "She's one of the first ones here in the morning, working on special projects."

All the attention left Wamser embarrassed.

"I'm just trying to figure out why they picked me," she said, shaking her head in disbelief.

Her mother, Norma Anderson, said through tears that Wamser wanted to be a teacher from an early age, when she would follow her now-deceased father, James Wamser, to his own math classroom when he worked late preparing lessons for the next day.

"She's following in his footsteps. Kelly would do problems on the board when he would be there late," she said. "He would put in the long hours. She's the same way."

As a few stragglers mingled at the cookie-and-soda reception, a student hesitantly approached her. Zach McCarter, a sophomore, apologized for bothering her, but he was having trouble with his detour proofs. Could he ask her a quick question?

Wamser smiled, left her group and spent the next five minutes with pen in hand, helping Zach navigate his assignment. After he walked away, question answered, and the room was near-empty, she turned to her mother and let out a huge sigh.

"Wow," she said softly.

Questions and Activities

1. Kelly Wamser, the math teacher in this story, is obviously internally motivated, creative, and hardworking. Do you think these are characteristics that people are born with or that develop with experience? If you think such characteristics are at least partly learnable and if you think you might be lacking in one or more of these areas, what can you do to improve your levels of motivation, creativity, and leadership?

2. Good teachers spend a considerable amount of time preparing for class so that students are not bored or turned off. In this chapter and in the final chapter, we describe how to create a Reflective Journal as a way to help you plan, revise, and refine your instruction. If you would like to be as dynamic and effective as the teacher in this story, resolve to begin a Reflective Journal this semester and to add to it in the coming years.

3. This story illustrates that good teachers are internally motivated and committed to all aspects of their role. One way to start down the road to being this kind of teacher is to make a list of the special knowledge and talents you possess and then to think about the various school-related activities in which you could participate that would allow you to use those capabilities.

material through the use of objectives and pretests, engaging students in a task through the use of questions and homework, and providing corrective feedback and reinforcement with written comments, verbal explanations, and praise.

As useful as the scientific literature is, there is at least one other major contributor to a teacher's knowledge base: classroom experience. Although the knowledge that teachers gain from teaching actual lessons often lacks the broad generalizability that is characteristic of scientific knowledge, it does have the following advantages:

- It is linked to a particular task and goal (such as teaching students how to discover the various themes embedded in a reading passage).
- It is sufficiently detailed, concrete, and specific that other teachers can use the same techniques with the same or highly similar material.
- It typically combines knowledge of the task, knowledge of teaching methods, and knowledge of students' characteristics (Hiebert et al., 2002).

● Good teachers combine "artistic" and "scientific" characteristics

Look back at the heading of this section. Notice that it reads "Good Teaching Is Partly an Art and Partly a Science," not "Teaching as an Art Versus Teaching as a Science." Our choice of wording indicates our belief that good teaching is a skillful blend of artistic and scientific elements. The teacher who attempts to base every action on scientific evidence is likely to come across as rigid and mechanical—perhaps even indecisive (when the scientific evidence is lacking or unclear). The teacher who ignores scientific knowledge about teaching and learning and makes arbitrary decisions runs the risk of using methods that are ineffective.

pause & reflect

How do good teachers strike a balance between the art and the science of teaching? Are they born with the right personality? Are they the products of good teacher-education programs? If both factors play a role, which is more important?

REFLECTIVE TEACHING: A PROCESS TO HELP YOU GROW FROM NOVICE TO EXPERT

● Reflective teachers think about what they do and why

The blending of artistic and scientific elements can be seen in discussions of what is called **reflective teaching** (see, for example, Eby, Herrell, & Hicks, 2002; Ellis, 2001; Henderson, 2001; and McEntee et al., 2003). Reflective teachers are constantly engaged in thoughtful observation and analysis of their actions in the classroom before, during, and after interactions with their students.

Prior to instruction, reflective teachers may think about such things as the types of knowledge and skills students in a democratic society need to learn, the kind of classroom atmosphere and teaching techniques that are most likely to produce this learning, and the kinds of assessments that will provide clear evidence that these goals are being accomplished (a topic that we discuss at some length in the chapters on assessment and testing). Jere Brophy and Janet Alleman (1991) illustrate the importance of thinking about long-range goals by pointing out how the choice of goals affects content coverage and how content coverage affects teachers' choice of classroom activities. If, for example, one goal is for students to acquire problem-solving skills, students would likely be engaged in activities that call for inquiring, reasoning, and decision making. Debates, simulations, and laboratory experiments are just three examples of activities that might be used to meet such a goal. If the goal is for students to memorize facts and information, students will likely be given activities that call for isolated memorization and recall. Worksheets and drill-and-practice exercises are typically used to meet this type of goal. The point here is that effective teachers are reflective: they think about these issues as a basis for drawing up lesson plans.

As they interact with students, reflective teachers are highly aware of how students are responding to what they are doing and are prepared to make minor but significant changes to keep a lesson moving toward its predetermined goal. Consider an elementary school classroom in which some students are having difficulty understanding the relationship between the orbits of the planets around the sun and their position in the night sky. The teacher knows there is a problem: some students have a puzzled expression on their faces, and others cannot describe this phenomenon in their own words. Realizing that some students think in more concrete terms than others, the teacher decides to push the desks to the sides of the room and have the students simulate the planets by walking through their orbits. All in the moment, this teacher engages in thoughtful observation, spontaneous analysis, and flexible, resourceful problem solving.

For events that cannot be handled on the spot, some period of after-school time should be set aside for reflection. This is the time to assess how well a particular lesson met its objective, to wonder why some students rarely participate in class discussions, to ponder the pros and cons of grouping students by ability, and to formulate plans for dealing with these concerns.

To become a reflective teacher, you will need to acquire several attitudes and abilities. Three of the most important attitudes are an introspective orientation, an open-minded but questioning attitude about educational theories and practices, and the willingness to take responsibility for your decisions and actions. These attitudes need to be combined with the ability to view situations from the perspectives of others (students, parents, principal, other teachers), the ability to find information that allows an alternative explanation of classroom events and produces more effective instructional methods, and the ability to use compelling evidence in support of a decision (Eby et al., 2002; Ross et al., 1993). We hasten to add that although reflection is largely a solitary activity, you should discuss your concerns with colleagues, friends, students, and parents to get different perspectives on the nature of a problem and possible alternative courses of action.

As you can probably see from this brief discussion, the reflection process is likely to work well when teachers have command of a wide range of knowledge about the nature of students, the learning process, and the instructional process. By mastering much of the content of this text, you will be that much more prepared than your less knowledgeable peers to make productive use of the time you devote to reflection.

Another factor that has been shown to contribute to teacher reflectivity is journal writing. Keeping a written journal forces you to express with some clarity your thoughts and beliefs about the causes of classroom events, how you feel about those events, and what you might do about them (Bennett & Pye, 2000; Good & Whang, 2002; McVarish & Solloway, 2002). Thus, one potentially helpful way you might begin developing this reflective capacity is to follow our suggestion for compiling a Reflective

● Reflective teachers have particular attitudes and abilities

pause & reflect

The reflective teacher sets aside regular blocks of time to think about teaching activities and to make new plans. Most teachers complain about having insufficient time to reflect and plan. What would you do to make more time available?

Reflective teachers set aside time to think about what they do in class, why they do it, and how their methods affect student performance.

Journal. In the final chapter of this book, we describe how you might set up this journal.

SPECIAL FEATURES OF THIS BOOK

This book has several distinctive features that are intended to be used in rather specialized ways: Key Points, Suggestions for Teaching in Your Classroom, Take a Stand!, Case in Print, one or more sections of every chapter that are devoted to discussing applications of technology to teaching, references to numerous web sites that relate to various aspects of teaching and learning, Resources for Further Investigation, Pause and Reflect questions, and Journal Entries. In addition, your compilation of a separate component to accompany this book—the Reflective Journal—is recommended. This journal makes use of the text's Journal Entries and the Suggestions for Teaching.

Key Points

The textbook web site includes additional study aids, such as Thought Questions and Interactive Flashcards for glossary terms.

At the beginning of each chapter, you will find a list of *Key Points*. The Key Points also appear within the body of the chapter, printed in the margins. These points have been selected to help you learn and remember sections of each chapter that are of special significance to teachers. (These sections may be stressed on exams, but they were originally selected because they are important, not because they can serve as the basis for test items.) To grasp the nature of the Key Points, turn back to the opening page of this chapter, which lists points stressed under the chapter's major headings. Then flip through the chapter to see how the appearance of the Key Points in the margins calls attention to significant sections of the text.

Suggestions for Teaching in Your Classroom

In most of the chapters, you will find summaries of research that serve as the basis for related principles or conclusions. These sets of principles or conclusions are the foundation for *Suggestions for Teaching in Your Classroom*. Suggestions are usually followed by examples illustrating how they might be applied. In most cases, examples are provided for both elementary and secondary grades because there usually are differences in the way a principle might be applied in dealing with younger and with older students.

Many research articles and textbooks provide only vague guidelines for classroom use and no concrete examples. But when new research-based ideas are presented in a concrete and usable form, teachers are much more likely to try them out (Gersten & Brengelman, 1996). This is why *Psychology Applied to Teaching* places so much emphasis on concrete suggestions for teaching. But as useful as our suggestions might be, you cannot use them as prescriptions. Every school building and every group of students is different. You have to learn how to adapt the suggestions in this book and any other books that you will read to the particular dynamics of each class. This is the essence of being a reflective teacher.

Take a Stand!

Earlier in this chapter we discussed why the scientific study of behavior and thought processes in a classroom setting is a complex undertaking. Such factors as the limited focus of research, the complexity of teaching and learning, and the revision of ideas due to new findings make it difficult at times to draw definitive conclusions about why students behave as they do and how teachers might respond. But there are other instances when the evidence is sufficiently deep and consistent, or the logic so compelling, that we feel confident taking a stand on an issue and believe you can as well, be it publicly or privately.

For each of the following chapters we identify one of these instances with the Take a Stand! label, and we state our beliefs succinctly. You may, of course, disagree with our conclusion and decide to take either no stand or a different stand. That's fine, and we commend you for being an independent and critical thinker so long as your decision is based on additional evidence and logical thinking.

On the textbook web site, one section is devoted to the issues highlighted in the Take a Stand! features. Here, you can find additional material related to these important topics. We invite you to take advantage of this resource, because exploring a controversial issue is a good way to both broaden and sharpen your thinking.

 At the textbook web site (accessible from **http://education.college.hmco. com/students**), the Take a Stand! section can help you develop your own positions on major issues.

Case in Print

This feature in each chapter presents a recent article that either elaborates on an idea or technique described in the chapter or shows how public school educators have applied an idea. The focus is on real-life settings, where you can see the practical effect of ideas you read about in the text.

 If you find the Cases in Print interesting and useful, look for additional ones on the textbook web site.

Emphasis on the Role of Technology in Learning and Instruction

Throughout this book, we discuss the role of technology in relation to all the major aspects of learning and instruction. In addition, the textbook web site that accompanies this book (accessible from **http://education.college.hmco.com/students**) provides many technology-oriented resources as well as other useful material for developing your skills as a teacher.

When we use the term *technology*, we are referring to devices that extend and amplify people's ability to store, transform, retrieve, and communicate information.

Although this broad definition encompasses a wide array of devices (such as calculators, slide and movie projectors, videocassette and audiotape recorders, videodisc players, and computers), our focus will be largely on computers because of their widespread use and potential to transform teaching and learning.

Having access to a computer in a classroom is no longer a novelty. By 2002, the number of students per school computer was 3.8, the number of students per Internet-connected computer was 5.6, and approximately 90 percent of schools had Internet access from one or more classrooms ("Access to Technology," 2003). Access continues to improve every year.

In our discussions of computer-based technology that involve links to other computers beyond one's classroom or school, we follow popular usage, employing the terms *Internet* and *World Wide Web* interchangeably. But they do refer to different things. The **Internet** is a system of computers from around the world that are connected to one another via telephone lines, cable lines, and satellites. The **World Wide Web** refers to any part of the Internet that can be accessed using an address called a uniform resource locator, or URL; we typically refer to such parts of the Internet as web sites (Smith, 2003). So when you exchange e-mail or use an instant messaging program, you are using the Internet but not the web. But when you type **http://education.college.hmco.com/students** into your web browser and find the web site for this text, you're using the World Wide Web.

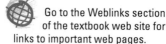
Go to the Weblinks section of the textbook web site for links to important web pages.

A good place to begin your exploration of what the web has to offer is the web page Teacher Resources from the Cheney School District in Washington State (**www.cheneysd.org/websites.htm**). Here you will find links to web sites that will aid your professional development, arranged in five categories (Top Ten Educational Websites, K–12 Reference Sites, K–8 Curriculum Sites, 9–12 Curriculum Sites, Free Pictures and Clip Art, and Assessment Links). Some sites provide materials and ideas for lessons, and others make it possible for you to exchange teaching tips with and solicit opinions from other teachers about how to solve various instructional and classroom management problems. In the final chapter, we provide our own list of web sites that have discussion forums or chatrooms for preservice and practicing teachers.

As with any other instructional method, material, or medium that has been enthusiastically received, however, you should strive to keep things in proper perspective. There is no doubt about the computer's ability to help students and teachers analyze, sort, transform, and present information in a variety of formats or about the ability of the World Wide Web to connect students to other individuals and information sources. But as Richard Mayer (2001), a leading educational psychology researcher, has noted, educational technology is simply a medium of instruction, not a method of instruction. It is Mayer's belief, and ours, that teachers should embed technology within a learner-centered approach to teaching—that is, within an approach based on an understanding of how students develop and learn.

Mayer's view of technology as a medium rather than a method is supported by a two-year study of how three teachers used laptop computers in their classrooms (Windschitl & Sahl, 2002). The findings indicated that the teachers used the computers in very different ways. Of the three teachers, only one had a preexisting commitment to a student-centered, constructivist approach to teaching. She was more inclined than the other teachers, for example, to allow students to choose and explore specific issues within a broad topic area. She saw laptop computers as a way for students to access the same world of information used by adults and as a tool to help them formulate sophisticated ideas. One of the other teachers was more strongly committed to a teacher-centered philosophy and used technology only to support that approach. Because she believed that her role was to help students acquire basic skills, her use of computers was more limited, revolving around drill-and-practice exercises. In essence, she saw computer technology as a way to present one's work rather than as a way to further one's learning.

As you examine the technology resources and ideas mentioned in this book, you should be thinking about the ways in which they might enhance the learning environment of your own classroom. To help you do this, we encourage you to examine the National Educational Technology Standards that have been proposed for four grade levels by the International Society for Technology in Education (ISTE, 2000). For each grade level, Table 1.1 lists two of the six standards and their respective competencies. The complete list of technology standards and competencies for students as well as standards for teachers and administrators, and a list of states that have adopted the standards, can be found on the ISTE web site (**www.cnets.iste.org/**).

Resources for Further Investigation

 For additional online resources keyed to each chapter, use the Weblinks section at the textbook web site.

Despite this book's attempt to provide at least partial solutions to the most common difficulties that teachers face, you are bound, sooner or later, to become aware of problems that are not discussed in these pages. You may want additional data on some aspects of teaching, either while you are taking this course or afterward. For this reason, we provide an annotated bibliography at the end of each chapter. *Resources for Further Investigation* lists articles, books, and online (Internet) sources you might consult.

Two important points should be mentioned regarding Internet sources of information. First, all the databases and resources listed or described throughout this book have been checked for accuracy as of the book's publication date. The world of online information, however, is in constant flux: databases are updated, moved, renamed, or deleted from the Internet network every day. If you are unable to find one of the resources mentioned, we recommend that you consult your school's computer support person or your colleagues (because the most current information is often passed by word of mouth).

This brings up the second important point about online information: it is no more reliable (and in some cases is definitely less reliable) than what you may find in print. In particular, newsgroups and discussion groups are notorious for participants' distribution of incorrect, incomplete, or misleading advice or information. Our recommendation to you is to treat online information as you would print: try to stay with publishers or databases that are maintained by reputable sources, such as education or psychology departments of universities, major educational associations, and the U.S. government. Double-check the information you gather online. Never assume that because it appears on a computer it is accurate! And remember that participating in a newsgroup discussion is most useful for generating new ideas or potential directions that you can pursue further on your own or with a group of classmates.

Pause and Reflect

As you have seen several times in this chapter, from time to time we pose a question that invites you to think about issues raised in the text and how you will handle them in your own teaching. You can use these questions either for personal reflection or for discussion with classmates and practicing teachers.

Journal Entries

You can find additional Reflective Journal Questions at the textbook web site.

Within the margins of each chapter, you will find numerous instances of the phrase *Journal Entry*. These marginal headings are related to the material just opposite in the text. They are intended to serve as suggested wordings for the headings of pages in a Reflective Journal that we strongly encourage you to keep. In the final chapter, we describe the beneficial effects of reflection and journal writing on teaching, and we describe how you can use the suggested Journal Entries to organize your first Reflective Journal. If you do not have time to begin your journal while taking the course, we hope you will go through the book a second time, after you finish this course, for the purpose of developing a custom-designed journal.

Table 1.1	Examples of Technology Standards and Competencies for Students	
Grade Level	**Standards**	**Competencies**
PreK–2	Basic Operations and Concepts	Use input devices (e.g., mouse, keyboard, remote control) and output devices (e.g., monitor, printer) to successfully operate computers, VCRs, audiotapes, and other technologies.
	Technology Communications Tools	Gather information and communicate with others using telecommunications, with support from teachers, family members, or student partners.
3–5	Social, Ethical, and Human Issues	Discuss common uses of technology in daily life and the advantages and disadvantages those uses provide.
	Technology Problem-Solving and Decision-Making Tools	Evaluate the accuracy, relevance, appropriateness, comprehensiveness, and bias of electronic information sources.
6–8	Technology Productivity Tools	Use content-specific tools, software, and simulations (e.g., environmental probes, graphing calculators, exploratory environments, web tools) to support learning and research.
	Technology Research Tools	Select and use appropriate tools and technology resources to accomplish a variety of tasks and solve problems.
9–12	Social, Ethical, and Human Issues	Identify capabilities and limitations of contemporary and emerging technology resources and assess the potential of these systems and services to address personal, lifelong learning, and workplace needs.
	Technology Productivity Tools	Investigate and apply expert systems, intelligent agents, and simulations in real-world situations.

International Society for Technology in Education (2000).

HOW THIS BOOK WILL HELP PREPARE YOU TO MEET INSTRUCTIONAL STANDARDS

 To review this chapter's content and help yourself prepare for licensing exams, see the ACE practice tests and PowerPoint slides on the textbook web site.

We live in an age of standards and accountability, particularly in education. Just as students, teachers, and administrators are held accountable for students' meeting various learning standards, prospective and beginning teachers are increasingly expected to demonstrate that they have met a set of knowledge standards that are believed to be the foundation of high-quality instruction. Among the standards that govern the preparation and licensing of teachers, two that are particularly prominent are the Praxis II, a standardized test, and a set of ten instructional principles and related standards called the INTASC standards (after the Interstate New Teacher Assessment and Support Consortium). In this book's section, we will briefly discuss the content of the Praxis II and the INTASC standards and show you how *Psychology Applied to Teaching* will help prepare you to meet the standards.

Praxis II and *Psychology Applied to Teaching*

As part of recent educational reform efforts, many state boards of education and teacher education programs require that, as a condition for licensure, beginning teachers demonstrate that they are knowledgeable about the psychological and educational factors that are likely to affect how well their students will perform in the classroom. A popular instrument used for this purpose is the Praxis II, published by the Educational Testing Service (ETS). The Principles of Learning and Teaching section of the Praxis II assesses a beginning teacher's knowledge of topics that are typically covered in an educational psychology course.

Because *Psychology Applied to Teaching* (PAT) is closely aligned with the Principles of Teaching and Learning section of the Praxis II and emphasizes classroom applications, we believe PAT will help prepare you to do well on this important assessment. On this book's front endpapers, you will find a table that lists the topics and subtopics covered by the Principles of Learning and Teaching test (also available on the ETS web site at **www.ets.org/praxis/**) along with the chapter numbers and pages in PAT where discussions of these topics can be found.

INTASC and *Psychology Applied to Teaching*

In the early 1990s, the Interstate New Teacher Assessment and Support Consortium (INTASC) published a set of ten principles and related standards to guide the preparation of beginning teachers. These principles and standards represent the core knowledge, dispositions, and skills that INTASC believes are essential for all beginning teachers, regardless of their specialty or grade level. The INTASC standards are also designed to be compatible with the certification program for highly skilled veteran teachers developed by the National Board for Professional Teaching Standards.

An important part of the philosophy behind the INTASC standards is the belief that well-trained teachers have the knowledge, dispositions, and skills to help all students achieve at acceptable levels. That notion has also been a major part of the philosophy of *Psychology Applied to Teaching*. To help you see how the content of *Psychology Applied to Teaching* corresponds to the INTASC knowledge standards, we have included a correlation table on the book's back endpapers.

Resources for Further Investigation

● The Art and Science of Teaching

Louis J. Rubin examines teaching as art and teaching as theater in *Artistry in Teaching* (1985). In *Acting Lessons for Teachers: Using Performance Skills in the Classroom* (1994), Robert Tauber and Cathy Sargent Mester provide additional insights into the art of teaching. They discuss how such theatrical skills as gesture, body movement, voice pitch, role playing, use of props, and suspense contribute to teacher enthusiasm and student achievement. Don't overlook Appendix II, which contains testimonials from eighteen award-winning college professors about the value of acting skills in the classroom.

Borrowing from the writings of ancient Greek philosophers and the early twentieth-century philosopher John Dewey, James Garrison describes teaching as a creative calling that involves such factors as emotions, intuition, values, and practical wisdom in *Dewey and Eros: Wisdom and Desire in the Art of Teaching* (1997). In Chapter 1 of *Researching the Art of Teaching: Ethnography for Educational Use* (1996), Peter Woods summarizes the various arguments that have been made for teaching as an art, as a science, and as an activity that combines both art and science. Using a letter format, Vito Perrone covers such topics as deciding what to teach, engaging students, valuing differences, empowering teachers, and refining the craft of teaching in *A Letter to Teachers: Reflections on Schooling and the Art of Teaching* (1991).

To learn about the scientific knowledge base that underlies teaching, you might want to look at *Putting Research to Work in Your School* (1996), by David Berliner and Ursula Casanova. In each of six sections (teaching, instructional strategies, learning, motivation, school and society, and testing), they point out how a research study has shed light on such relevant issues as how to make cross-age tutoring work, teaching memory skills to students, and motivating students through project-based learning. A similar book is *Classroom Instruction That Works: Research-Based Strategies for Increasing Student Achievement* (2001), by Robert Marzano, Debra Pickering, and Jane Pollock.

Several handbooks provide excellent analyses of research on various aspects of teaching. Part 8 of the *Handbook of Research on Teaching* (4th ed., 2001), edited by Virginia Richardson, contains articles on connecting instruction to learning, the role of classroom assessment in teaching and learning, the influence of theory and research on teaching, and teaching in middle schools. Part V of the *Handbook of Research on Teacher Education* (2nd ed., 1996), edited by John Sikula, discusses the problems of beginning teachers, among other topics. Part IV of the *Handbook of Educational Psychology* (1996), edited by David C. Berliner and Robert C. Calfee, contains seven chapters that deal with such issues as learning to teach, the beliefs and knowledge base of teachers, and teaching and learning in a classroom context. Section I, Part A of the *Handbook of Education and Human Development* (1996), edited by David R. Olson and Nancy Torrance, deals with the psychological foundations of teaching.

● Reflective Teaching

Several books explain what it means to be a reflective teacher and describe the benefits that this approach to teaching can produce. The briefest of these books, at seventy-eight pages, is *Reflective Teaching: An Introduction* (1996), by Kenneth M. Zeichner and Daniel P. Liston. Other books you might consult are *Reflective Planning, Teaching, and Evaluation: K-12* (3rd ed., 2002), by Judy Eby, Adrienne Herrell, and James Hicks; *Teaching, Learning, and Assessment Together: The Reflective Classroom* (2001), by Arthur Ellis; *Reflective Teaching: Professional Artistry Through Inquiry* (3rd ed., 2001), by James Henderson; and *At the Heart of Teaching: A Guide to Reflective Practice* (2003), edited by Grace Hall McEntee.

Summary

1. Educational psychology is a scientific discipline that seeks to understand and improve how students learn from instruction in classroom settings.

2. Learning about the research findings and principles of educational psychology can help you be a better teacher because (a) teaching is complex work that requires a wide range of knowledge and skills, (b) the research literature contains numerous useful ideas for improving your instruction, and (c) teachers who have had professional training are often more effective than those who have not had such training.

3. Unsystematic observations of students may lead teachers to draw false conclusions because of limited cases, unrecognized or unusual factors, and a tendency to ignore contrary evidence. As an example, although scientific evidence does not support the practice of grade retention, it remains popular among teachers, parents, and educational policy makers, partly because of unsystematic observations about its effectiveness.

4. Scientifically gathered evidence is more trustworthy than casual observation because it involves sampling, control, objectivity, publication, and replication.

5. The scientific study of education is complicated by the limited focus of research, debates about which type of research is most useful, the complexity of teaching and learning, the inability of researchers to keep up with all published research, different interpretations of findings, and the ongoing accumulation of new knowledge.

6. Research on teaching and learning provides a systematic, objective basis for making instructional decisions, but it cannot specify how to handle every classroom situation. Many classroom decisions must be made on the spot. This contrast represents the science and the art of teaching.

7. Those who argue that teaching is an art point to communication of emotions, values and beliefs, and flexibility as qualities that good teachers must possess but that are not easily taught. In contrast, other scholars contend that there is a scientific basis for teaching that can be learned.

8. Good teachers strike a balance between the art and the science of teaching.

9. Reflective teachers constantly think about such issues as the goals they are trying to achieve, the types of teaching methods they use and how effective those methods are, and the extent to which their methods and goals are supported by scientific evidence.

Key Terms

educational psychology *(1)*
teaching as an art *(11)*

teaching as a science *(11)*
reflective teaching *(13)*

Internet *(17)*
World Wide Web *(17)*

2 Theories of Psychosocial and Cognitive Development

KEY POINTS

These key points will help you learn the important information in this chapter. To help you study, they also appear in the margins of the pages, next to the text where they are discussed.

Erikson: Psychosocial Development

- Erikson's theory encompasses the life span, highlights the role of the person and culture in development
- Personality development based on epigenetic principle
- Personality grows out of successful resolution of psychosocial crises
- 2 to 3 years: autonomy vs. shame and doubt
- 4 to 5 years: initiative vs. guilt
- 6 to 11 years: industry vs. inferiority
- 12 to 18 years: identity vs. role confusion
- Role confusion: uncertainty as to what behaviors others will react to favorably
- Students' sense of industry hampered by unhealthy competition for grades
- Identity: accepting one's body, having goals, getting recognition
- Psychosocial moratorium delays commitment
- Adolescents exhibit a particular process, called an identity status, for establishing an identity
- Individuals in identity diffusion avoid thinking about jobs, roles, values
- Individuals in foreclosure unquestioningly endorse parents' goals and values
- Individuals in moratorium uncertain about identity
- Individuals who have reached identity achievement status have made their own commitments
- Criticisms of Erikson's theory: based largely on personal experience, not applicable to many cultures, gender-biased

Piaget: Cognitive Development

- Organization: tendency to systematize processes
- Adaptation: tendency to adjust to environment
- Scheme: organized pattern of behavior or thought
- Assimilation: new experience is fitted into existing scheme
- Accommodation: scheme is created or revised to fit new experience
- Equilibration: tendency to organize schemes to allow better understanding of experiences
- Sensorimotor stage: schemes reflect sensory and motor experiences
- Preoperational stage: child forms many new schemes but does not think logically
- Perceptual centration, irreversibility, egocentrism: barriers to logical thought
- Egocentrism: assumption that others see things the same way
- Concrete operational stage: child is capable of mentally reversing actions but generalizes only from concrete experiences
- Formal operational stage: child is able to deal with abstractions, form hypotheses, engage in mental manipulations
- Adolescent egocentrism: adolescents preoccupied with their own view of the world and how they appear to others
- Piaget: cognitive development more strongly influenced by peers than by adults
- Instruction can accelerate development of schemes that have begun to form
- Piaget's theory underestimates children's abilities
- Most adolescents are not formal operational thinkers
- Sequence of stages uniform across cultures but rate of development varies

Key Points continued on next page.

In the opening chapter, we pointed out that individuals vary in how they perceive and think about the world around them. This commonplace observation implies that you need to be aware of the major ways in which students differ from one another in order to design potentially effective lessons. What may work well for one part of your class may not work quite so well for another part. The lesson that was a huge success with last year's class may be a disaster with this year's group if you fail to take into account critical differences between the two classes. The five chapters in this part of the book will introduce you to how students may differ from one another in psychosocial development, cognitive development, age, mental ability, thinking style, achievement, ethnic background, and social class. You will also discover how those differences affect classroom learning.

Human development is a complex topic to discuss because, in addition to analyzing many different forms of behavior, we must trace the way each type of behavior changes as a child matures. Authors of books on development have adopted different strategies for coping with this problem. Some have described theories that outline stages in the emergence of particular forms of behavior. Others have summarized significant types of behavior at successive age levels. Still others have examined specific types of behavior, noting age changes for every topic. Each approach has advantages and disadvantages.

Developmental theories call attention to the overall sequence, continuity, and interrelatedness of aspects of development, but they typically account for only limited facets of behavior. Texts organized in terms of age levels make readers aware of varied aspects of children's behavior at a given age but sometimes tend to obscure how particular types of behavior emerge and change. And although texts organized according to types of behavior do not have the limitation of the age-level approach, they may make it difficult for the reader to grasp the overall pattern of behavior at a particular stage of development.

Vygotsky: Cognitive Development

- How we think influenced by current social forces and historical cultural forces
- Psychological tools aid and change thought processes
- Cognitive development strongly influenced by those more intellectually advanced
- Teachers should help students learn how to use psychological tools
- Cognitive development promoted by instruction in zone of proximal development
- Scaffolding techniques support student learning

Using Technology to Promote Cognitive Development

- Computer-based simulations promote exploration and visual representations of abstract ideas, and correct misconceptions
- Computer programs can act as expert collaborative partners

Piaget, Kohlberg, and Gilligan: Moral Development

- Morality of constraint (moral realism): rules are sacred, consequences determine guilt
- Morality of cooperation (moral relativism): rules are flexible, intent important in determining guilt
- Preconventional morality: avoid punishment, receive benefits in return
- Conventional morality: impress others, respect authority
- Postconventional morality: mutual agreements, consistent principles
- Criticisms of Kohlberg's theory: moral development difficult to accelerate, moral dilemmas not relevant to daily life, relies on macromoral issues, ignores characteristics other than moral reasoning
- Males and females may use different approaches to resolve real-life moral dilemmas
- Moral knowledge does not always result in moral behavior

psychosocial stages, Jean Piaget's cognitive stages, and Lev Vygotsky's views on the role of social interaction. It also describes Piaget's ideas about moral development, Lawrence Kohlberg's extension of Piaget's work, and Carol Gilligan's criticism and modification of Kohlberg's theory. The next chapter describes age-level characteristics of students at five levels: preschool, primary school, elementary school, middle school, and high school. Discussion at each age level focuses on four types of behavior: physical, social, emotional, and cognitive. The information in these chapters will help you adapt teaching techniques to the students who are in the age range that you expect to teach. The patterns of behavior described in these chapters are ones exhibited by typical children and adolescents.

The following three chapters are devoted to individual differences and how to deal with them. The chapter "Understanding Student Differences" discusses the nature of variability and how students vary with respect to gender, mental ability, and cognitive style. The chapter titled "Addressing Cultural and Socioeconomic Diversity" describes the characteristics of students from different ethnic and social-class backgrounds. And the chapter "Accommodating Student Variability" describes types of students who vary from their classmates to such an extent that they may require special kinds of education.

In an effort to profit from the advantages and to minimize the disadvantages of each approach, this chapter and the next present discussions of development that combine all three. This chapter focuses on Erik Erikson's

---

ERIKSON: PSYCHOSOCIAL DEVELOPMENT

To preview this chapter's basic concepts, read the Chapter Themes on the Snowman textbook web site, accessible from **http://education.college.hmco.com/students**.

Of all the developmental theories that we could have chosen to discuss, why did we decide to open this chapter with Erik Erikson's theory of psychosocial development? There are several reasons for this choice:

- Erikson described psychological growth from infancy through old age. Thus, one can draw out instructional implications for every level of education from preschool through adult education.
- Erikson's theory portrays people as playing an active role in their own psychological development through their attempts to understand, organize, and integrate their everyday experiences.
- This theory highlights the important role that cultural goals, aspirations, expectations, requirements, and opportunities play in personal growth (a theme we will discuss in the chapter "Understanding Student Differences") (Newman & Newman, 2003).

● Erikson's theory encompasses the life span, highlights the role of the person and culture in development

Although Erikson (1902–1994) studied with Sigmund Freud, he concluded that Freud's tendency to stay in Vienna and interact with only a small and very select group of individuals prevented the founder of psychoanalysis from fully appreciating how social and cultural factors (for example, values, attitudes, beliefs, and customs) influence behavior, perception, and thinking. Erikson decided to formulate a theory of development based on psychoanalytic principles but taking into account such influences.

Basic Principles of Erikson's Theory

● Personality development based on epigenetic principle

Epigenetic Principle   Erikson based his description of personality development on the **epigenetic principle,** which states that in fetal development, certain organs of the body appear at certain specified times and eventually "combine" to form a child. Erikson hypothesized that just as the parts of the body develop in interrelated ways in a human fetus, so the personality of an individual forms as the ego progresses through a series of interrelated stages. All of these ego stages exist in some form from the very beginning, but each has a critical period of development.

● Personality grows out of successful resolution of psychosocial crises

Psychosocial Crisis   In Erikson's view, personality development occurs as one successfully resolves a series of turning points, or psychosocial crises. Although the word *crisis* typically refers to an extraordinary event that threatens our well-being, Erikson had a more benign meaning in mind. Crises occur when people feel compelled to adjust to the normal guidelines and expectations that society has for them but are not altogether certain that they are prepared to carry out these demands fully. For example, Western societies expect children of elementary and middle school age to develop a basic sense of industry, mostly through success in school. Adolescents are expected to come to terms with such questions as, "Who am I?" and "Where am I going?" (Newman & Newman, 2003).

As you will see in the next section, Erikson described these crises in terms of opposing qualities that individuals typically develop. For each crisis, there is a desirable quality that can emerge and a corresponding unfavorable characteristic. Yet Erikson did not mean to imply that a healthy individual develops only the positive qualities. He emphasized that people are best able to adapt to their world when they possess both the positive and negative qualities of a particular stage, provided the positive quality is significantly stronger than the negative quality. In the first stage, for example, it is important that the child learn trust, but a person who never experienced a bit of mistrust would struggle to understand the world. In Erikson's view, difficulties in development and adjustment arise only when the negative quality outweighs the positive for any given stage or when the outcome for most stages is negative (Newman & Newman, 2003).

As you read through the following brief descriptions of the stages of psychosocial development, keep in mind that a positive resolution of the issue for each stage depends on how well the issue of the previous stage was resolved. An adolescent who strongly doubts her own capabilities, for example, may have trouble making the commitments required for identity development in adulthood (Marcia, 1991).

Stages of Psychosocial Development

The following designations, age ranges, and essential characteristics of the stages of personality development are proposed by Erikson in *Childhood and Society* (1963).[1]

Trust Versus Mistrust (Birth to One Year)   The basic psychosocial attitude for infants to learn is that they can trust their world. Trust is fostered by "consistency, continuity, and sameness of experience" in the satisfaction by the parents of the infant's basic needs. Such an environment will permit children to think of their world as safe

---

[1] All quotations in "Stages of Psychosocial Development" are drawn from Chapter 7 of *Childhood and Society.*

and dependable. Conversely, children whose care is inadequate, inconsistent, or negative will approach the world with fear and suspicion.

● 2 to 3 years: autonomy vs. shame and doubt

Autonomy Versus Shame and Doubt (Two to Three Years; Preschool) Just when children have learned to trust (or mistrust) their parents, they must exert a degree of independence. If toddlers are permitted and encouraged to do what they are capable of doing at their own pace and in their own way—and with judicious supervision by parents and teachers—they will develop a sense of autonomy (willingness and ability to direct one's behavior). But if parents and teachers are impatient and do too many things for young children or shame young children for unacceptable behavior, these children will develop feelings of self-doubt.

● 4 to 5 years: initiative vs. guilt

Initiative Versus Guilt (Four to Five Years; Preschool to Kindergarten) The ability to participate in many physical activities and to use language sets the stage for initiative, which "adds to autonomy the quality of undertaking, planning, and 'attacking' a task for the sake of being active and on the move." If four- and five-year-olds are given freedom to explore and experiment and if parents and teachers take time to answer questions, tendencies toward initiative will be encouraged. Conversely, if children of this age are restricted and made to feel that their activities and questions have no point or are a nuisance to adults and older siblings, they will feel guilty about acting on their own.

● 6 to 11 years: industry vs. inferiority

Industry Versus Inferiority (Six to Eleven Years; Elementary to Middle School) A child entering school is at a point in development when behavior is dominated by intellectual curiosity and performance. "He now learns to win recognition by producing things. . . . He develops a sense of industry." If the child is encouraged to make and do things well, helped to persevere, allowed to finish tasks, and praised for trying, industry results. If the child's efforts are unsuccessful or if he is derided or treated as bothersome, a feeling of inferiority results. Children who feel inferior may never learn to enjoy intellectual work and take pride in doing at least one kind of thing really well. At worst, they may believe they will never excel at anything.

● 12 to 18 years: identity vs. role confusion

● Role confusion: uncertainty as to what behaviors others will react to favorably

Identity Versus Role Confusion (Twelve to Eighteen Years; Middle Through High School) The goal at this stage is development of the roles and skills that will prepare adolescents to take a meaningful place in adult society. The danger at this stage is **role confusion:** having no clear conception of appropriate types of behavior that others will react to favorably. If adolescents succeed (as reflected by the reactions of others) in integrating roles in different situations to the point of experiencing continuity in their perception of self, identity develops. In common terms, they know who they are. If they are unable to establish a sense of stability in various aspects of their lives, role confusion results.

Intimacy Versus Isolation (Young Adulthood) To experience satisfying development at this stage, the young adult needs to establish close and committed intimate relationships and partnerships with other people. The hallmark of intimacy is the "ethical strength to abide by such commitments, even though they may call for significant sacrifices and compromises." Failure to do so will lead to a sense of isolation.

Generativity Versus Stagnation (Middle Age) "Generativity . . . is primarily the concern of establishing and guiding the next generation." Erikson's use of the term *generativity* is purposely broad. It refers, of course, to having children and raising them. In addition, it refers to the productive and creative efforts in which adults take part (for example, teaching) that have a positive effect on younger generations. Those unable or unwilling to "establish" and "guide" the next generation become victims of stagnation and self-absorption.

Integrity Versus Despair (Old Age)   Integrity is "the acceptance of one's one and only life cycle as something that had to be and that, by necessity, permitted of no substitutions. . . . Despair expresses the feeling that the time is now short, too short for the attempt to start another life and to try out alternate roads to integrity."

Of Erikson's eight stages, the two you should pay particular attention to are industry versus inferiority and identity versus role confusion, because they are the primary psychosocial issues that students must resolve during their elementary, middle school, and high school years. If you are committed to helping students learn as much as possible, you need to have a basic understanding of these two stages so that your lesson plans and instructional approaches help students achieve a strong sense of industry and identity. The next two sections will briefly describe the major factors that contribute to students' sense of industry and their grasp of who they are and what they might become.

Helping Students Develop a Sense of Industry

Between kindergarten and sixth grade, most children are eager to demonstrate that they can learn new skills and successfully accomplish assigned tasks. One factor that has long been known to have a detrimental effect on one's sense of industry is competition for a limited number of rewards. If you have ever taken a class where the teacher graded exams or projects "on a curve," you are familiar with the most common form that such competition takes in schools. What the teacher does is compare each student's score with the score of every other student in that class. The few students who achieve the highest scores receive the top grade, regardless of the actual level of their scores. Then a predetermined number of B's, C's, D's, and F's are awarded. Because the resulting distribution of grades looks something like the outline of a bell, it is often referred to as a "bell-shaped curve" (which explains the origin of the term "grading on the curve").

There are at least two reasons that this practice may damage a student's sense of industry:

1. Grading on the curve limits the top rewards to a relatively small number of students regardless of each student's actual level of performance. If the quality of instruction is good and students learn most of what has been assigned, the range of scores will be relatively small. Consider the impact to your sense of industry if you respond correctly to 85 percent of the questions on an exam but earn only a grade of C. The same problem exists when, for whatever reasons, all students perform poorly. How much pride can you have in a grade of A or B when you know it is based on a low success rate? The senior author of this book endured a college chemistry class in which the top grade on an exam went to a student who answered only 48 percent of the questions correctly.

2. Curve grading also guarantees that some students have to receive failing grades regardless of their actual level of performance. Students who are forced into this unhealthy type of competition (there are acceptable forms of competition, which we describe in the chapter titled "Approaches to Instruction") may develop a sense of inadequacy and inferiority that will hamper them for the rest of their school career.

● Students' sense of industry hampered by unhealthy competition for grades

The solution to this problem is to base grades on realistic and attainable standards that are worked out ahead of time and communicated to the students. In our chapter on assessment, we describe how to do this. Also, in the chapter "Approaches to Instruction," we describe several instructional approaches that will likely have a beneficial impact on students' sense of industry

pause & reflect

Suppose you were an elementary school teacher. What kinds of things would you do to help your students attain a sense of industry rather than inferiority? How would you help them feel more capable and productive? What things would you avoid doing?

Take a Stand!

Promote Industry, Stamp Out Inferiority

For some educators, parents, and educational policymakers, an important purpose of education is to sort children into ability categories by forcing them to compete for a limited number of top grades. We strongly oppose such an approach and urge you to do the same because it promotes a sense of inferiority in most students by interfering with the development of such important characteristics as self-efficacy, self-worth, self-regulated learning skills, and intrinsic motivation. The evidence in support of this stand can be found in most of the subsequent chapters in this book. Instead, emphasize to students and others that a more relevant and useful goal is to help all students develop those attitudes, values, and cognitive skills that lead to high levels of meaningful learning.

What are your own views on this subject? Go to the textbook web site (accessible from **http://education.college.hmco.com/students**) and select the Take a Stand! section to find out more about this and other controversial issues.

because they all promote learning and a sense of accomplishment. In general, they involve establishing a classroom atmosphere in which students feel accepted for who they are and understand that the teacher is as interested in their success as they are. These goals are accomplished by providing clear expectations as to what students should be able to do after a unit of instruction, designing lessons that are logical and meaningful, and using teaching methods that support effective learning processes.

Helping Students Formulate an Identity

● Identity: accepting one's body, having goals, getting recognition

The most complex of Erikson's stages is identity versus role confusion; he wrote more extensively about this stage than any other. Because this stage is often misunderstood, let's use Erikson's own words to describe the concept of **identity:** "An optimal sense of identity . . . is experienced merely as a sense of psychosocial well-being. Its most obvious concomitants are a feeling of being at home in one's body, a sense of 'knowing where one is going' and an inner assuredness of anticipated recognition from those who count" (1968, p. 165). As you may know from your own experience or the experiences of others, the process of identity formation is not always smooth, and it does not always follow the same path. But by being aware of the problems and uncertainties that adolescents may experience as they try to develop a sense of who they are, you can help them positively resolve this major developmental milestone.

pause & reflect

American high schools are often criticized for not helping adolescents resolve identity problems. Do you agree? Why? How could schools improve?

Taking a Psychosocial Moratorium   One aspect of identity formation that often causes difficulty for adolescents is defining the kind of work they want to do—in other words, choosing a career. For individuals who are unprepared to make a career choice, Erikson suggested the possibility of a **psychosocial moratorium.** This is a period marked by a delay of commitment. Such a postponement occurred in Erikson's own life: after leaving high school, he spent several years wandering around Europe without making any firm decision about the sort of job he would seek. Under ideal circumstances, a psychosocial moratorium should be a period of adventure and exploration, having a positive, or at least neutral, impact on the individual and society.

● Psychosocial moratorium delays commitment

Adolescent Identity Statuses

● Adolescents exhibit a particular process, called an identity status, for establishing an identity

Erikson's observations on identity formation have been usefully extended by James Marcia's notion of **identity statuses** (1966, 1980, 1991). Identity statuses, of which there are four, are styles or processes "for handling the psychosocial task of establishing a sense of identity" (Waterman & Archer, 1990, p. 35). Marcia (1980) developed this idea as a way to test scientifically the validity of Erikson's notions about identity.

Marcia established the four identity statuses after he had conducted semistructured interviews with a selected sample of male youths. The interviewees were asked their thoughts about a career, their personal value system, their sexual attitudes, and

Identity, as Erikson defines it, involves acceptance of one's body, knowing where one is going, and recognition from those who count. A high school graduate who is pleased with his or her appearance, who has already decided on a college major, and who is admired by parents, relatives, and friends is likely to experience a sense of psychosocial well-being.

their religious beliefs. Marcia proposed that attainment of a mature identity depends on two variables: crisis and commitment. "Crisis refers to times during adolescence when the individual seems to be actively involved in choosing among alternative occupations and beliefs. Commitment refers to the degree of personal investment the individual expresses in an occupation or belief" (1967, p. 119). Subsequent research has shown that exploring and making commitments to interpersonal relationships also contributes to identity formation (Allison & Schultz, 2001; Marcia, 2001).

After analyzing interview records with these two criteria in mind, Marcia established four identity statuses, described in Table 2.1, that vary in their degree of crisis and commitment:

- Identity diffusion
- Foreclosure
- Moratorium
- Identity achievement

The moratorium and identity achievement statuses are generally thought to be more developmentally mature than the foreclosure and identity diffusion statuses because individuals exhibiting moratorium and identity achievement have either evaluated alternatives and made a commitment or are actively involved in obtaining and evaluating information in preparation for a commitment (Marcia, 2001). Support for the hypothesized superiority of the identity achievement status was provided by Anne Wallace-Broscious, Felicisima Serafica, and Samuel Osipow (1994). They found that high school students who had attained the identity achievement status scored higher on measures of career planning and career certainty than did students in the moratorium or diffusion statuses.

As you read the brief descriptions of each identity type in Table 2.1, keep a few points in mind. First, the more mature identity statuses are slow to evolve and are found in a relatively small percentage of individuals. Among one sample of sixth, seventh, and eighth graders, 12 percent were in the moratorium status and 9 percent had reached the identity achievement status (Allison & Schultz, 2001). Among adults, only about 33 percent undergo the exploration and identity construction process that characterizes the achievement status (Marcia, 1999).

Table 2.1	James Marcia's Identity Statuses		
Identity Status	**Crisis**	**Commitment**	**Characteristics**
Identity diffusion	Not yet experienced. Little serious thought given to occupation, gender roles, values.	Weak. Ideas about occupation, gender roles, values are easily changed as a result of positive and negative feedback.	Not self-directed; disorganized, impulsive, low self-esteem, alienated from parents; avoids getting involved in school work and interpersonal relationships.
Foreclosure	Not experienced. May never suffer doubts about identity issues.	Strong. Has accepted and endorsed the values of his or her parents.	Close-minded, authoritarian, low in anxiety; has difficulty solving problems under stress; feels superior to peers; strong identification with and more dependent on parents and other authority figures for guidance and approval than in other statuses.
Moratorium	Partially experienced. Has given some thought to identity-related questions.	Weak. Has not achieved satisfactory answers.	Anxious, dissatisfied with school; changes major often, daydreams, engages in intense but short-lived relationships; may temporarily reject parental and societal values.
Identity achievement	Fully experienced. Has considered and explored alternative positions regarding occupation, gender roles, values.	Strong. Has made self-chosen commitments to at least some aspects of identity.	Introspective; more planful, rational, and logical in decision making than in other identity statuses; high self-esteem; works effectively under stress; likely to form close interpersonal relationships. Usually the last identity status to emerge.

SOURCES: Bilsker & Marcia (1991); Cramer (2001); Hoegh & Bourgeois (2002); Kroger (1996); MacKinnon & Marcia (2002); Marcia (1999); Vondracek, Schulenberg, Skorikov, Gillespie, & Wahlheim (1995).

● Individuals in identity diffusion avoid thinking about jobs, roles, values

● Individuals in foreclosure unquestioningly endorse parents' goals and values

● Individuals in moratorium uncertain about identity

● Individuals who have reached identity achievement status have made their own commitments

Second, an identity status is not a once-and-for-all accomplishment. If an ego-shattering event (loss of a job, divorce) occurs later in life, individuals who have reached identity achievement, for example, may find themselves uncertain about old values and behavior patterns and once again in crisis. But for most individuals, a new view of oneself is eventually created. This cycling between certainty and doubt as to who one is and where one fits in society may well occur in each of the last three of Erikson's stages and is often referred to as a MAMA (moratorium-achievement-moratorium-achievement) cycle (Marcia, 1999, 2001).

Finally, because identity is an amalgam of commitments from a number of different domains, only a small percentage (about 20 percent) of adolescents will experience a triumphant sense of having "put it all together." To cite just one example, an adolescent is more likely to have made a firm occupational choice than to be decisive about gender role or religious values (Waterman, 1988).

Cultural, Ethnic, and Gender Factors in Identity Status   Although the foreclosure status is the historical norm for adolescents in Western societies, things can and do change. For example, individuals in moratorium were more numerous during the 1960s and 1970s than during the 1980s. This was a time of great social and cultural upheaval (opposition to the war in Vietnam, civil rights demonstrations, the women's movement), and many adolescents reacted to the uncertainty produced by these changes by not making a commitment to occupational, sexual, and political values (Scarr, Weinberg, & Levine, 1986; Waterman, 1988). Also, recent evidence indicates that African American adolescents are now more likely to be in a moratorium status or an identity achievement status, or in transition between these two statuses, than in the foreclosure status common to earlier generations (Branch & Boothe, 2002; Forbes & Ashton, 1998; Watson & Protinsky, 1991).

Gender differences in identity status are most apparent in the areas of political ideology, family and career priorities, and sexuality. With respect to political beliefs, males are more likely to exhibit a foreclosure process and females a diffusion process. With respect to family and career priorities and sexuality, males are likely to be foreclosed or diffuse, whereas females are likely to express an identity achievement or a moratorium status. These findings indicate that female adolescents are more likely than males to make developmentally advanced decisions in the areas of family and career roles and sexuality. A likely explanation has to do with how the female gender role has and has not changed over the past twenty years. Although most females now work outside the home, they are still expected to have primary responsibility for child rearing (Archer, 1991).

A relevant question to ask about Marcia's identity statuses, particularly if you plan to teach in a foreign country or to instruct students with different cultural backgrounds, is whether these identity statuses occur only in the United States. The answer appears to be no. Researchers in such diverse countries as Korea, India, Nigeria, Japan, Denmark, Holland, Colombia, and Haiti report finding all four statuses, although the percentage of adolescents and young adults in each status does vary by culture (Portes, Dunham, & Del Castillo, 2000; Scarr et al., 1986).

Criticisms of Erikson's Theory

Although Erikson's theory has, in general, been supported by research (Steinberg & Morris, 2001), several aspects have been criticized. For example, although Erikson occasionally carried out research investigations, most of his conclusions were based on personal and subjective interpretations that have been only partly substantiated by controlled investigations of the type that most psychologists value. As a result, there have been only limited checks on Erikson's tendency to generalize from limited experiences. Some of his observations on identity, for example, reflect his own indecision about occupational choice (Sorell & Montgomery, 2001).

Other criticisms focus on Erikson's contention that one's identity is achieved by actively exploring alternatives regarding one's career, ideological beliefs, and interpersonal relationships and then making choices. This is not, in all likelihood, a universal practice. In some societies and cultures, these decisions are, for the most part, made by adults and imposed on adolescents (Marcia, 1999, 2001; Sorell & Montgomery, 2001). There appear to be two basic societal conditions that make it possible for individuals to explore and construct an identity: the willingness to tolerate an extended

● Criticisms of Erikson's theory: based largely on personal experience, not applicable to many cultures, gender-biased

Suggestions for Teaching in Your Classroom

Applying Erikson's Theory of Psychosocial Development

1 **Keep in mind that certain types of behaviors and relationships may be of special significance at different age levels.**

JOURNAL ENTRY

Ways to Apply Erikson's Theory
(Preschool and Kindergarten)

2 **With younger preschool children, allow plenty of opportunities for free play and experimentation to encourage the development of autonomy, but provide guidance to reduce the possibility that children will experience doubt. Also avoid shaming children for unacceptable behavior.**

3 **With older preschool children, encourage activities that permit the use of initiative and provide a sense of accomplishment. Avoid making children feel guilty about well-motivated but inconvenient (to you) questions or actions.**

JOURNAL ENTRY

Ways to Apply Erikson's Theory
(Elementary Grades)

4 **During the elementary and middle school years, help children experience a sense of industry by presenting tasks that they can complete successfully.**

Arrange such tasks so that students will know they have been successful. To limit feelings of inferiority, play down comparisons and encourage cooperation and self-competition. Also try to help jealous children gain satisfaction from their own behavior. (Specific ways to accomplish these goals will be described in several later chapters.)

JOURNAL ENTRY

Ways to Apply Erikson's Theory
(Secondary Grades)

5 **At the secondary school level, keep in mind the significance of each student's search for a sense of identity.**

The components of identity that Erikson stressed are acceptance of one's appearance, recognition from those who count, and knowledge about where one is going. Role confusion is most frequently caused by failure to formulate clear ideas about gender roles and by indecision about occupational choice.

The American school system, particularly at the high school level, has been described as a place where individual differences are either ignored or discouraged and where negative feedback greatly outweighs positive feedback (Johnson, Farkas, & Bers, 1997; Steinberg, 1996; Toch, 2003). Because you are important to your students, you can contribute to their sense of positive identity by recognizing them as individuals and praising them for their accomplishments. If you become aware that particular students lack recognition from peers because of abrasive qualities or ineptness and if you have the time and opportunity, you might also attempt to encourage social skills.

You might be able to reduce identity problems resulting from indecisiveness about gender roles by having class discussions (for example, in social science courses) centering on changes in attitudes regarding masculinity, femininity, and family responsibilities. You can, for example, encourage boys to become more sensitive to the needs of others and girls to be more achievement oriented. This approach to gender-role development that combines traditional "masculine" and "feminine" behaviors is called **psychological androgyny** (Karniol, Gabay, Ochion, & Harari, 1998; Steinberg, 2002).

Another forum for such discussion is an on-line bulletin board or class web site. On-line writing can be conducive to explorations of sensitive issues because it provides a slightly slower, more thoughtful pace and also allows an equal voice to male and female students, even those who feel shy about speaking out loud in class. An online discussion that is carefully moderated by an experienced teacher can both model and explore the territory of psychological androgyny.

Working with your school counselor, you may in some cases be able to help students make decisions about occupational choice by providing them with information (gleaned from classroom performance and standardized test results) about their intellectual capabilities, personality traits, interests, and values. Or you may be able to help students decide whether to apply for admission to college instead of entering the job market after high school graduation.

6 **Remember that the aimlessness of some students may be evidence that they are engaging in a psychosocial moratorium. If possible, encourage such individuals to focus on short-term goals while they continue to search for long-term goals.**

There are many ways to enable students to work toward short-term goals, particularly in your classroom. These will be described in detail in later chapters that deal with approaches to instruction and motivation.

7 **Remain aware that adolescents may exhibit characteristics of different identity status types.**

Some may drift aimlessly; others may be distressed because they realize they lack goals and values. A few high school students may have arrived at self-chosen commitments; others may have accepted the goals and values of their parents.

If you become aware that certain students seem depressed or bothered because they are unable to develop a satisfactory set of personal values, consult your school psychologist or counselor. In addition, you might use the techniques just summarized to help these students experience at least a degree of identity achievement. Perhaps the main value of the identity status concept is that it calls attention to individual differences in the formation of identity. Because students in the foreclosure status will pose few, if any, classroom problems, you must keep in mind that foreclosure is not necessarily desirable for the individual student. Those experiencing identity diffusion or moratorium may be so bothered by role confusion that they are unwilling to carry out even simple assignments—unless you supply support and incentives.

adolescence that makes a minimal contribution to society and a certain level of societal wealth. In addition, individuals need to have developed secure attachments to parents and other influential individuals (successful resolution of the trust versus mistrust stage) and a high level of cognitive development (Hoegh & Bourgeois, 2002; Marcia, 1999). The absence of these last two conditions may account for the fact that by adulthood only about 33 percent of individuals have undergone the exploration and construction processes that characterize the moratorium and achievement statuses.

Some critics, such as Carol Gilligan (1982, 1988), argue that Erikson's stages reflect the personality development of males more accurately than that of females. Gilligan believes that the process and timing of identity formation are different for each gender. Beginning in about fourth grade (the industry versus inferiority stage), girls are as concerned with the nature of interpersonal relationships as they are with achievement, whereas boys focus mainly on achievement. And during adolescence, many young women seem to work through the crises of identity *and* intimacy simultaneously, whereas most young men follow the sequence that Erikson described: identity versus role confusion, then intimacy versus isolation (Gilligan, 1982; Ochse & Plug, 1986; Sorrell & Montgomery, 2001).

If you keep these reservations in mind, you are likely to discover that Erikson's observations (as well as the identity statuses that Marcia described) will clarify important aspects of development. Suggestions for Teaching that draw on Erikson's observations follow. (These suggestions might also serve as the nucleus of a section in your Reflective Journal. Possible journal entries are indicated in the margins, and more can be found on the book's web site.)

PIAGET: COGNITIVE DEVELOPMENT

Basic Principles of Piaget's Theory

- Organization: tendency to systematize processes

Jean Piaget's conception of intellectual development reflected his basic interest in biology as well as knowledge. Piaget (1896–1980) postulated that human beings inherit two basic tendencies: **organization** (the tendency to systematize and combine processes into coherent general systems) and **adaptation** (the tendency to adjust to the environment). For Piaget, these tendencies governed both physiological and mental functioning. Just as the biological process of digestion transforms food into a form that the body can use, so intellectual processes transform experiences into a form that the child can use in dealing with new situations. And just as biological processes must be kept in a state of balance (through homeostasis), intellectual processes seek a balance through the process of equilibration (a form of self-regulation that all individuals use to bring coherence and stability to their conception of the world).

- Adaptation: tendency to adjust to environment

Organization   As we just stated, *organization* refers to the tendency of all individuals to systematize or combine processes into coherent (logically interrelated) systems. When we think of tulips and roses as subcategories of the more general category *flowers*, instead of as two unrelated categories, we are using organization to aid our thinking process. This organizational capacity makes thinking processes efficient and powerful and allows for a better fit, or adaptation, of the individual to the environment.

- Scheme: organized pattern of behavior or thought

Schemes   Children formulate organized patterns of behavior or thought, known as **schemes,** as they interact with their environment, parents, teachers, and age-mates. Schemes can be behavioral (throwing a ball) or cognitive (realizing that there are many different kinds of balls). Whenever a child encounters a new experience that does not easily fit into an existing scheme, adaptation is necessary.

Adaptation   The process of creating a good fit or match between one's conception of reality (one's schemes) and the real-life experiences one encounters is called adaptation. According to Piaget, adaptation is accomplished by two subprocesses: **assimilation** and **accommodation.** A child may adapt either by interpreting an experience so that it fits an existing scheme (assimilation) or by changing an existing scheme to incorporate the experience (accommodation).

- Assimilation: new experience is fitted into existing scheme

Imagine a six-year-old who goes to an aquarium for the first time and calls the minnows "little fish" and the whales "big fish." In both cases, the child is assimilating—attempting to fit a new experience into an existing scheme (in this case, the conception that all creatures that live in the water are fish). When her parents point out that even though whales live in the water, they are mammals, not fish, the six-year-old begins to accommodate—to modify her existing scheme to fit the new experience she has encountered. Gradually (accommodations are made slowly, over repeated experiences), a new scheme forms that contains nonfish creatures that live in the water.

- Accommodation: scheme is created or revised to fit new experience

Relationships Among Organization, Adaptation, and Schemes   To give you a basic understanding of Piaget's ideas, we have talked about them as distinct elements. But the concepts of organization, adaptation, and schemes are all related. In their drive to be organized, individuals try to have a place for everything (accommodation) so they can put everything in its place (assimilation). The product of organization and adaptation is the creation of new schemes that allow individuals to organize at a higher level and adapt more effectively.

- Equilibration: tendency to organize schemes to allow better understanding of experiences

Equilibration, Disequilibrium, and Learning   Piaget believed that people are driven to organize their schemes in order to achieve the best possible adaptation to their environment. He called this process **equilibration.** But what motivates people's drive

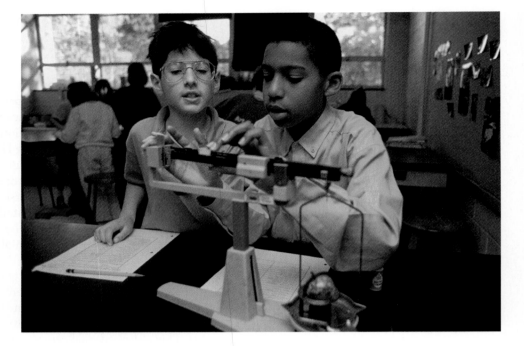

Activities that encourage children to create new ideas or schemes through experimentation, questioning, discussion, and discovery often produce meaningful learning because of the inherent drive toward equilibration.

toward equilibration? It is a state of *disequilibrium*, or a perceived discrepancy between an existing scheme and something new. In other words, when people encounter something that is inconsistent with or contradicts what they already know or believe, this experience produces a disequilibrium that they are driven to eliminate (assuming they are sufficiently interested in the new experience to begin with).

A student may wonder why, for example, tomatoes and cucumbers are referred to as fruits in a science text since she has always referred to them as vegetables and has distinguished fruits from vegetables on the basis of sweetness. This discrepancy may cause the student to read the text carefully or to ask the teacher for further explanation. Gradually, the student reorganizes her thinking about the classification of fruits and vegetables in terms of edible plant roots, stems, leaves, and ovaries so that it is more consistent with the expert view. These processes are two sides of the learning coin: for equilibration to occur, disequilibrium must already have occurred. Disequilibrium can occur spontaneously within an individual through maturation and experience, or it can be stimulated by someone else (such as a teacher).

Constructing Knowledge   Meaningful learning, then, occurs when people *create* new ideas, or knowledge (rules and hypotheses that explain things), from existing information (for example, facts, concepts, and procedures). To solve a problem, we have to search our memory for information that can be used to fashion a solution. Using information can mean experimenting, questioning, reflecting, discovering, inventing, and discussing. This process of creating knowledge to solve a problem and eliminate a disequilibrium is referred to by Piagetian psychologists and educators as **constructivism** (Brooks & Brooks, 2001; Haney & McArthur, 2002; Yager, 2000). It is a powerful notion that will reappear in later chapters and in other forms. (The Pause and Reflect features in each chapter are intended to stimulate constructivist thinking, as is the manner in which we encourage you to set up and use your journal for reflective thinking and teaching.)

Stages of Cognitive Development

Organization and adaptation are what Piaget called *invariant functions*. This means that these thought processes function the same way for infants, children, adolescents, and adults. Schemes, however, are not invariant. They undergo systematic change at particular points in time. As a result, there are real differences between the ways younger children and older children think and between the ways children and adults think. The schemes of infants and toddlers, for example, are sensory and motor in nature. They are often referred to as *habits* or *reflexes*. In early childhood, schemes gradually become more mental in nature; during this period, they are called *concepts* or *categories*. Finally, by late adolescence or early adulthood, schemes are very complex and result in what we call *strategic* or *planful* behavior.

On the basis of his studies, Piaget concluded that schemes evolve through four stages. The *rate* at which a particular child proceeds through these stages varies, but Piaget believed the *sequence* is the same in all children.

Piaget's four stages are described in the following sections. To help you grasp the sequence of these stages, Table 2.2 briefly outlines the range of ages to which they generally apply and their distinguishing characteristics.

Although Piaget used this "stage" or stair-step metaphor to describe the pattern of cognitive development, don't be misled into thinking that children "jump" from one stage to the next. In trying to understand certain concepts or solve certain problems, children may on some occasions use a more advanced kind of thinking but on other occasions revert to an earlier, less sophisticated form. Over time, the more advanced concepts and strategies supplant the less sophisticated ones. Because of this variability in how children think, some developmental psychologists (e.g., Siegler, 1996) prefer to use the metaphor of overlapping waves rather than stages to characterize the nature of cognitive development. But because Piaget spoke in terms of stages, we will as well.

- Sensorimotor stage: schemes reflect sensory and motor experiences

Sensorimotor Stage (Infants and Toddlers)   Up to the age of two, children acquire understanding primarily through sensory impressions and motor activities. Therefore, Piaget called this the *sensorimotor stage*. Because infants are unable to move around much on their own during the first months of postnatal existence, they develop schemes primarily by exploring their own bodies and senses. After toddlers learn to walk and manipulate things, however, they get into everything and build up a sizable repertoire of schemes involving external objects and situations.

An important cognitive development milestone, *object permanence*, occurs between the fourth and eighth months of this stage. Prior to this point, the phrase "out of sight, out of mind" is literally true. Infants treat objects that leave their field of vision as if they no longer exist. When they drop an object from their hands or when an object at which they are looking is covered, for example, they do not search for it. As object permanence develops, children's intentional search behaviors become increasingly apparent.

Most children under age two are able to use schemes they have mastered to engage in mental as well as physical trial-and-error behavior. By age two, toddlers' schemes have become more mental in nature. You can see this in the way toddlers imitate the behavior of others. They imitate people they have not previously observed, they imitate the behavior of animals, and, most important, they imitate even when the model is no longer present (this is called *deferred imitation*). These types of imitative behaviors show toddlers' increasing ability to think in terms of symbols.

- Preoperational stage: child forms many new schemes but does not think logically

Preoperational Stage (Preschool and Primary Grades)   The thinking of preschool and primary grade children (roughly two to seven years old) centers on mastery of symbols (such as words), which permits them to benefit much more from past experiences. Piaget believed that many symbols are derived from mental imitation and involve both visual images and bodily sensations (notice how the schemes of this stage incorporate and build on the schemes of the previous stage). Although the thinking at this stage is much more sophisticated than that of one- and two-year-olds, preschool children are limited in their ability to use their new symbol-oriented schemes. From an adult perspective, their thinking and behavior are illogical.

Table 2.2	Piaget's Stages of Cognitive Development	
Stage	**Age Range**	**Characteristics**
Sensorimotor	Birth to two years	Develops schemes primarily through sense and motor activities. Recognizes permanence of objects not seen.
Preoperational	Two to seven years	Gradually acquires ability to conserve and decenter but not capable of operations and unable to mentally reverse actions.
Concrete operational	Seven to eleven years	Capable of operations but solves problems by generalizing from concrete experiences. Not able to manipulate conditions mentally unless they have been experienced.
Formal operational	Eleven years and older	Able to deal with abstractions, form hypotheses, solve problems systematically, engage in mental manipulations.

● Perceptual centration, irreversibility, egocentrism: barriers to logical thought

When Piaget used the term *operation*, he meant an action carried out through logical thinking. *Preoperational*, then, means prelogical. The main impediments to logical thinking that preschoolers have to overcome are *perceptual centration*, *irreversibility*, and *egocentrism*. You can see these impediments at work most clearly when children attempt to solve **conservation** problems—those that test their ability to recognize that certain properties stay the same despite a change in appearance or position.

One of the best-known conservation problems is conservation of continuous quantity. A child is taken to a quiet place by an experimenter, who then pours water (or juice or beans or whatever else) into identical short glasses until the child agrees that each contains an equal amount. Then the water is poured from one of these glasses into a tall, thin glass. At that point the child is asked, "Is there more water in this glass [the experimenter points to the tall glass] or this one [the short glass]?" Immediately after the child answers, the experimenter asks, "Why do you think so?" If the child's response is evasive or vague, the experimenter continues to probe until the child's underlying thought processes become clear.

In carrying out this experiment (and many others similar to it) with children of different ages, Piaget discovered that children below the age of six or so maintain that there is more water in the tall, thin glass than in the short, squat glass. Although they agree at the beginning of the experiment that the water in the two identical glasses is equal, young children stoutly insist that after the water has been poured, the taller glass contains more. When asked, "Why do you think so?" many preschool children immediately and confidently reply, "Because it's taller." Children over the age of six or so, by contrast, are more likely to reply, "Well, it *looks* as if there's more water in this one because it's taller, but they're really the same."

One reason preoperational stage children have difficulty solving conservation problems (as well as other problems that require logical thinking) is **perceptual centration**. This is the very strong tendency to focus attention on only one characteristic of an object or aspect of a problem or event at a time. The young child focuses only on the height of the water in the two containers and ignores the differences in width and volume. Another way to put this is to say that the child has not yet mastered **decentration**—the ability to think of more than one quality at a time—and is therefore not inclined to contemplate alternatives.

● Egocentrism: assumption that others see things the same way

The second impediment to logical thinking is **irreversibility.** This means that young children cannot mentally pour the water from the tall, thin glass back into the short, squat one (thereby proving to themselves that the glasses contain the same amount of water). For the same reason, these youngsters do not understand the logic behind simple mathematical reversals (4 + 5 = 9; 9 – 5 = 4).

The third major impediment is **egocentrism.** When applied to preschool children, *egocentric* does not mean selfish or conceited. It means that youngsters find it difficult, if not impossible, to take another person's point of view. In their conversations and in experimental situations in which they are asked to describe how something would look if viewed by someone else, preschool children reveal that they often have difficulty seeing things from another person's perspective (Piaget & Inhelder, 1956). They seem to assume that others see things the same way they see them. As a result, attempts to explain the logic behind conservation are usually met with quizzical looks and the insistence (some would mistakenly call it stubbornness) that the tall, thin glass contains more water.

Concrete Operational Stage (Elementary to Early Middle School) Through formal instruction, informal experiences, social contact, and maturation, children over the age of seven gradually become less influenced by perceptual centration, irreversibility, and egocentrism (DeVries, 1997). Schemes are developing that allow a greater understanding of such logic-based tasks as conservation (matter is neither created nor destroyed but simply changes shape or form or position), class inclusion (the construction of hierarchical relationships among related classes of items), and seriation (the arrangement of items in a particular order).

● Concrete operational stage: child is capable of mentally reversing actions but generalizes only from concrete experiences

But operational thinking is limited to objects that are actually present or that children have experienced concretely and directly. For this reason, Piaget described the stage from approximately seven to eleven years as that of *concrete operations.* The nature of the concrete operational stage can be illustrated by the child's mastery of different kinds of conservation.

By the age of seven, most children are able to explain correctly that water poured from a short, squat glass into a tall, thin glass is still the same amount of water. Being able to solve the water-pouring problem, however, does not guarantee that a seven-year-old will be able to solve a similar problem involving two balls of clay. A child who has just explained why a tall glass of water contains the same amount as a short one may inconsistently maintain a few moments later that rolling one of two equally sized balls of clay into an elongated shape causes the rolled one to appear as if it contains more clay.

Children in the primary and early elementary grades tend to react to each situation in terms of concrete experiences. The tendency to solve problems by generalizing from one situation to a similar situation does not occur with any degree of consistency until the end of the elementary school years.

Nevertheless, children in the concrete operational stage are often more capable of learning advanced concepts than most people realize. Kathleen Metz (1995) argues that Piaget's theory has been improperly interpreted as suggesting that formal science education should be delayed until children have started to demonstrate the capacity for formal operational reasoning. She provides evidence in support of the view that such abstract concepts as *theory, evidence,* and *hypothesis* begin to emerge during the elementary school years and are sufficiently understood by children that they should be included in science education programs.

Because most elementary grade students are in the concrete operational stage of development, science educators have concluded that children cannot think in hypothetical-deductive terms (e.g., "What if . . ." and "If I do such and such, then such and such should occur") but are limited to hands-on activities and to such descriptive forms of reasoning as observation, assigning objects to categories (class inclusion), and arranging objects in serial order (seriation). Metz cites evidence that preschool children begin to think in terms of simple categories and that most sixth graders can distinguish between theory and evidence. She also argues that Piaget's work with elementary school children indicates that although their thinking is based on concrete objects, they can construct from these experiences simple forms of such abstract concepts as time, speed, and probability. Consequently, she believes that elementary grade children can understand and carry out, in a simplified form, such advanced elements of scientific inquiry as posing questions, gathering and interpreting data, and revising one's theory on the basis of the data.

Although some Piagetian scholars (e.g., Kuhn, 1997) agree with Metz that children have the potential to design and carry out scientific inquiries, they caution that most elementary grade children will be unable truly to understand the nature of scientific inquiry (such as changing one's beliefs in the light of contradictory evidence, drawing only conclusions that are supported by existing evidence, recalling and accurately summarizing the evidence that support one's conclusions, using the same methods and logic from one inquiry to another) and use this understanding to regulate their subsequent behavior. If, for example, you told a student at the concrete operational stage to assume that a feather could break a piece of glass and then asked him whether the deduction "If one hits the glass with a feather, then the glass will break" is true or false, he would likely respond that it is false because in his experience, feathers do not break glass (Overton & Byrnes, 1991).

pause & reflect

From Piaget's point of view, why is it wrong to think of children as "small adults"?

The science education standards for students in grades K–4 that have been formulated by the National Research Council (1996) reflect the conclusions of both Metz (1995) and Kuhn (1997). Balancing the abilities and limitations of students at this stage, the standards state:

> In elementary grades, students begin to develop the physical and intellectual capabilities of scientific inquiry. They can design investigations to try things to see what happens—they tend to focus on concrete results of tests and will entertain the idea of a "fair" test (a test in which only one variable at a time is changed). However, children in K–4 have difficulty with experimentation as a process of testing ideas and the logic of using evidence to formulate explanations. (p. 122)

● Formal operational stage: child is able to deal with abstractions, form hypotheses, engage in mental manipulations

Formal Operational Stage (Middle School, High School, and Beyond)   When children *do* reach the point of being able to generalize and to engage in mental trial and error by thinking up hypotheses and testing them in their heads, they are at the stage of *formal operations*, according to Piaget. The term *formal* reflects the ability to respond to the *form* of a problem rather than its content and to *form* hypotheses. For example, the formal operational thinker can read the analogies "5 is to 15 as 1 is to 3" and "penny is to dollar as year is to century" and realize that despite the different content, the form of the two problems is identical (both analogies are based on ratios). In the same way, the formal thinker can understand and use complex language forms: proverbs ("Strike while the iron is hot"), metaphor ("Procrastination is the thief of time"), sarcasm, and satire.

We can see the nature of formal operational thinking and how it differs from concrete operational thinking by looking at a simplified version of Piaget's rod-bending experiment. Adolescents are given a basin filled with water, a set of metal rods of varying lengths, and a set of weights. The rods are attached to the edge of the basin and the weights to the ends of the rods. The subject's task is to figure out how much weight is required to bend a rod just enough to touch the water. Let's say that our hypothetical subject picks out the longest rod in the set (which is 9 inches long), attaches it to the edge of the basin, and puts just enough weight on the end of it to get it to touch the water. This observation is then recorded. Successively shorter rods are selected, and the same procedure is carried out. At some point, the subject comes to the 4-inch rod. This rod does not touch the water even when all of the weights have been attached to it. There are, however, three more rods, all of which are shorter than the last one tested.

Students who are within Piaget's formal operational stage of cognitive development are capable of solving problems by systematically using abstract symbols to represent real objects.

This is where the formal and concrete operators part company. The formal operational thinker reasons that if all of the available weights are not sufficient to bend the 4-inch rod enough to touch the water, the same will be true of the remaining rods. In essence, the rest of the experiment is done mentally and symbolically. The concrete operational thinker, however, continues trying out each rod and recording each observation independent of the others. Although both subjects reach the same conclusion, the formal operator does so through a more powerful and efficient process.

But remember that new schemes develop gradually. Although adolescents can sometimes deal with mental abstractions representing concrete objects, most twelve-year-olds solve problems haphazardly, using trial and error. It is not until the end of the high school years that adolescents are likely to attack a problem by forming hypotheses, mentally sorting out solutions, and systematically testing the most promising leads.

Some interpreters of Piaget (e.g., Wadsworth, 1996) note that a significant aspect of formal thought is that it causes the adolescent to concentrate more on possibilities than on realities. This is the ability that Erikson and others (e.g., Kalbaugh & Haviland, 1991) suggest is instrumental in the emergence of the identity crisis. At the point when older adolescents can become aware of all the factors that have to be considered in choosing a career and can imagine what it might be like to be employed, some may feel so threatened and confused that they postpone the final choice. Yet the same capability can also help resolve the identity crisis because adolescents can reason about possibilities in a logical manner. An adolescent girl, for example, may consider working as a pediatrician, teacher, or child psychologist in an underprivileged environment because she has always enjoyed and sought out activities that allowed her to interact with children and has also been concerned with the effects of deprivation on development.

Although mastery of formal thought equips the older adolescent with impressive intellectual skills, it may also lead to a tendency for the burgeoning formal thinker to become preoccupied with abstract and theoretical matters. Barry Wadsworth makes this point in the following way:

> If motivated to do so, and if in possession of the necessary content, adolescents with formal reasoning can reason as logically as adults. The tools for an evaluation of intellectual arguments are formed and fully functional. One of the major affective

> differences between the thought of the adolescent and that of the adult is that, initially in their use of formal operations, adolescents apply a criterion of pure logic in evaluating reasoning about human events. If it is logical it is good, right, and so on. This is the nature of their egocentrism. Adolescents lack a full appreciation of the way in which the world is ordered. With the capability for generating endless hypotheses, an adolescent believes that what is best is what is logical. He or she does not yet differentiate between the logical world as she thinks it to be and the "real" world. (1996, p. 124)

● Adolescent egocentrism: adolescents preoccupied with their own view of the world and how they appear to others

This inability to differentiate between the world as the adolescent thinks it should be and the world as it actually is was referred to by David Elkind (1968) as **adolescent egocentrism.** This occurs when high school students use their emerging formal operational capabilities to think about themselves and the thinking of others. Because adolescents are preoccupied with themselves and how they appear to others, they assume that peers and adults are equally interested in what they think and do. This is why, in Elkind's view, the typical adolescent is so self-conscious. The major difference between the egocentrism of childhood and that of adolescence is summed up in Elkind's observation: "The child is egocentric in the sense that he is unable to take another person's point of view. The adolescent, on the other hand, takes the other person's point of view to an extreme degree" (1968, p. 153).

Elkind believes that adolescent egocentrism also explains why the peer group becomes such a potent force in high school:

> Adolescent egocentrism . . . accounts, in part, for the power of the peer group during this period. The adolescent is so concerned with the reactions of others toward him, particularly his peers, that he is willing to do many things which are opposed to all of his previous training and to his own best interests. At the same time, this egocentric impression that he is always on stage may help to account for the many and varied adolescent attention-getting maneuvers. (1968, p. 154)

Although the concept of adolescent egocentrism is widely accepted among researchers, ascribing its cause to formal operational thinking gets mixed support. Some studies have found a relationship while other studies have not (Rycek, Stuhr, & McDermott, 1998; Vartanian, 2000).

The Role of Social Interaction and Instruction in Cognitive Development

● Piaget: cognitive development more strongly influenced by peers than by adults

How Social Interaction Affects Cognitive Development   When it comes to social experiences, Piaget clearly believed that peer interactions do more to spur cognitive development than do interactions with adults. The reason is that children are more likely to discuss, analyze, and debate the merits of another child's view of some issue (such as who should have which toy or what the rules of a game should be) than they are to take serious issue with an adult. The balance of power between children and adults is simply too unequal. Not only are most children quickly taught that adults know more and use superior reasoning, but also the adult always gets to have the last word: argue too long, and it's off to bed with no dessert. But when children interact with one another, the outcome is more dependent on how well each child uses her wits (Light & Littleton, 1999).

It is the need to understand the ideas of a peer or playmate in order to formulate responses to those ideas that leads to less egocentrism and the development of new, more complex mental schemes. Put another way, a strongly felt sense of cognitive conflict automatically impels the child to strive for a higher level of equilibrium. Formal instruction by an adult expert simply does not have the same impact regardless of how well designed it might be. That is why parents and teachers are often surprised to find children agreeing on some issue after having rejected an adult's explanation of the very same thing. Thus, educational programs that are patterned after Piaget's ideas usually provide many opportunities for children to interact socially and to discover through these interactions basic ideas about how the world works (Crain, 2000; Rogoff, 1990; Tudge & Winterhoff, 1993). In our chapter on approaches to instruction we describe in detail a systematic way to accomplish this goal—cooperative learning. Proof of the feasibility of this approach can be found in several summaries and analyses of the effects of cooperative learning (see, for example, Johnson & Johnson, 1995; Qin, Johnson, & Johnson, 1995; and Slavin, 1995).

How Instruction Affects Cognitive Development   Although Piaget believed that formal instruction by expert adults will not significantly stimulate cognitive development, not all psychologists have been willing to accept this conclusion at face value. Over the past thirty years, dozens of experiments have been conducted to determine whether it is possible to teach preoperational stage children to understand and use concrete operational schemes or to teach students in the concrete operational stage to grasp formal operational reasoning.

The typical conclusion of psychologists who have analyzed and evaluated this body of research ranges from uncertainty to cautious optimism (see, e.g., Case, 1975; Good & Brophy, 1995; Nagy & Griffiths, 1982; Sprinthall, Sprinthall, & Oja, 1998). The uncertainty results from shortcomings in the way some studies were carried out and disagreements about what constitutes evidence of true concrete operational thinking or formal operational thinking.

The cautious optimism comes from the work of Michael Shayer and others (Adey, Shayer, & Yates, 2001; Shayer, 1999) in England. They found that schools that participated in a science instruction program called CASE (Cognitive Acceleration through Science Education), which combined aspects of the cognitive developmental theories of Piaget and Vygotsky, had a much greater percentage of thirteen- and fourteen-year-olds at or above the early formal operational stage than did non-CASE schools. Furthermore, after two years in the program, CASE students scored higher on national tests of mathematics, science, and English than did students in the non-CASE schools. CASE programs have also been implemented to help preoperational stage children acquire concrete operational schemes (Robertson, 2001) and to help teachers accelerate the cognitive development of students with various learning impediments (Simon, 2002).

● Instruction can accelerate development of schemes that have begun to form

The safest conclusion that can be drawn from this literature (see, for example, Sigelman & Shaffer, 1991; Sprinthall et al., 1998) is that children who are in the process of developing the schemes that will govern the next stage of cognitive functioning can, with good-quality instruction, be helped to refine those schemes a bit faster than would normally be the case. For example, teachers can teach the principle of conservation by using simple explanations and concrete materials and by allowing children to manipulate the materials. This means that teachers should nurture the process of cognitive growth at any particular stage by presenting lessons in a form that is consistent with but slightly more advanced than the students' existing schemes. The objective here is to help students assimilate and accommodate new and different experiences as efficiently as possible.

Criticisms of Piaget's Theory

Underestimating Children's Capabilities   Among the thousands of articles that have been published in response to Piaget's findings are many that offer critiques of his work. Some psychologists argue that Piaget underestimated children's abilities not only because he imposed stringent criteria for inferring the presence of particular cognitive abilities, but also because the tasks he used were often complex and far removed from children's real-life experiences (Case, 1999). The term *preoperational*, for instance, stresses what is absent rather than what is present. Over the past two decades, researchers have focused more on what preoperational children *can* do. The results (summarized by Kamii, 2000; Siegler, 1998) suggest that preschoolers' cognitive abilities are more advanced in some areas than Piaget's work suggests.

● Piaget's theory underestimates children's abilities

● Most adolescents are not formal operational thinkers

Overestimating Adolescents' Capabilities   Other evidence suggests that Piaget may have overestimated the formal thinking capabilities of adolescents. Norman Sprinthall and Richard Sprinthall (1987) reported that only 33 percent of a group of high school seniors could apply formal operational reasoning to scientific problem solving. Research summarized by Michael Shayer (1997) indicates that only 20 percent of children exhibit well-developed formal operational thinking by the end of adolescence. According to these studies, formal reasoning seems to be the exception, not the rule, throughout adolescence.

A study of French adolescents (Flieller, 1999) reported similar percentages but also sought to determine if the pattern has changed in recent years. Of a group of ten- to twelve-year-olds who were tested on formal operational tasks in 1972, only 9 percent were at the beginning of that stage and only 1 percent were mature formal operators. The percentages for a group of ten- to twelve-year-olds tested in 1993 were just slightly higher, at 13 percent and 3 percent, respectively. Significantly larger differences were noted, however, between two groups of thirteen- to fifteen-year-olds. Among those tested in 1967, 26 percent were early formal operators and 9 percent were mature formal operators. But among those tested in 1996, 40 percent were early formal operators and 15 percent were mature formal operators. The author of this study suggested that the increase in formal operational thinking among thirteen- to fifteen-year-olds may be attributable in part to teaching practices (such as creating tables to display information and using tree diagrams to clarify grammatical structure) that foster the development of formal operational schemes.

Vague Explanations for Cognitive Growth   Piaget's theory has also been criticized for its vagueness in specifying the factors that are responsible for cognitive growth. Why, for example, do children give up conserving responses in favor of nonconserving responses at a particular age?

On the basis of recent research, Robert Siegler (1996) has suggested an explanation. He believes that variability in children's thinking plays an influential role. For example, it is not uncommon to hear children use on successive occasions different forms of a given verb, as in "I ate it," "I eated it," and "I ated it." Similar variability has been found in the use of memory strategies (five-year-old and eight-year-old children do not always rehearse information they want to remember), addition rules, time-telling rules, and block-building tasks. Siegler's explanation is that variability gives the child a range of plausible options about how to deal with a particular problem. The child then tries them out in an attempt to see which one produces the best adaptation. Note the use of the qualifying word *plausible*. Most children do not try out any and all possible solutions to a problem. Instead, they stick to possibilities that are consistent with the underlying principles of a problem.

● Sequence of stages uniform across cultures but rate of development varies

Cultural Differences   Questions have also been raised as to whether children from different cultures develop intellectually in the manner Piaget described. The answer at this point is both yes and no. The sequence of stages appears to be universal, but the rate of development may vary from one culture to another (Dasen & Heron, 1981; Hughes & Noppe, 1991; Leadbeater, 1991; Rogoff & Chavajay, 1995).

The average Eskimo child acquires the spatial concept of horizontalness faster than the average West African child. But many West African children (around the age of twelve or thirteen) understand conservation of quantity, weight, and volume sooner than Eskimo children do (Dasen & Heron, 1981). Although children in Western, industrialized societies (like ours) usually are not given baby-sitting responsibilities until they are at least ten years old because their high level of egocentrism prevents them from considering the needs of the other child, Mayan children in Mexican villages as young as age five play this role because their culture stresses the development of cooperative behavior (Sameroff & McDonough, 1994).

Research conducted during the 1970s found that individuals living in non-Western cultures who had little formal education did not engage in formal operational thinking. Although these same people used concrete operational schemes when tested with the kinds of tasks Piaget used, they usually did so at a later age than the Swiss children Piaget originally studied. This result was attributed to their lack of schooling, which left them unfamiliar with the language and conventions of formal testing. When concrete operational tasks were conducted with materials that were part of these people's everyday lives (such as asking children from Zambia to reproduce a pattern with strips of wire rather than with paper and pencil), they performed as well as Western children who drew the patterns on paper (Rogoff & Chavajay, 1995).

Noting that American schoolchildren score lower than many European and Asian children on standardized achievement tests, critics argue that U.S. formal schooling should begin earlier than age five and should focus on basic reading and math skills. In light of research on Piaget's theories, what do you think of this proposal?

Now that you are familiar with Piaget's theory of cognitive development, you can formulate specific classroom applications. You might use the Suggestions for Teaching for the grade level you expect to teach as the basis for a section in your journal.

Suggestions for Teaching in Your Classroom

Applying Piaget's Theory of Cognitive Development

GENERAL GUIDELINES

1 **Focus on what children at each stage can do and avoid what they cannot meaningfully understand.**

This implication must be interpreted carefully, as recent research has shown that children at the preoperational and concrete operational levels can do more than Piaget believed. In general, however, it is safe to say that since preoperational stage children (preschoolers, kindergartners, most first and some second graders) can use language and other symbols to stand for objects, they should be given many opportunities to describe and explain things through the use of speech, artwork, body movement, role play, and musical performance. Although the concepts of conservation, seriation, class inclusion, time, space, and number can be introduced, attempts at mastering them should probably be postponed until children are in the concrete operational stage.

Concrete operational stage children (grades 3–6) can be given opportunities to master such mental processes as ordering, seriating, classifying, reversing, multiplying, dividing, subtracting, and adding by manipulating concrete objects or symbols. Although a few fifth and sixth graders may be capable of dealing with abstractions, most exercises that involve theorizing, hypothesizing, or generalizing should be done with concrete objects or symbols.

Formal operational stage children (grades 7 through high school) can be given activities that require hypothetical-deductive reasoning, reflective thinking, analysis, synthesis, and evaluation.

2 Because individuals differ in their rates of intellectual growth, gear instructional materials and activities to each student's developmental level.

3 Because intellectual growth occurs when individuals attempt to eliminate a disequilibrium, instructional lessons and materials that introduce new concepts should provoke interest and curiosity and be moderately challenging in order to maximize assimilation and accommodation.

4 Although information (facts, concepts, procedures) can be efficiently transmitted from teacher to student through direct instruction, knowledge (rules and hypotheses) is best created by each student through the mental and physical manipulation of information.

Accordingly, lesson plans should include opportunities for activity, manipulation, exploration, discussion, and application of information. Small-group science projects are one example of how to implement this goal.

5 Because students' schemes at any given time are an outgrowth of earlier schemes, point out to them how new ideas relate to their old ideas and extend their understanding. Memorization of information for its own sake should be avoided.

6 Begin lessons with concrete objects or ideas, and gradually shift explanations to a more abstract and general level.

PRESCHOOL, ELEMENTARY, AND MIDDLE SCHOOL GRADES[2]

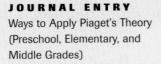

JOURNAL ENTRY
Ways to Apply Piaget's Theory
(Preschool, Elementary, and
Middle Grades)

1 Become thoroughly familiar with Piaget's theory so that you will be aware of how your students organize and synthesize ideas. You may gain extra insight if you analyze your own thinking, since you are likely to discover that in some situations, you operate at a concrete, rather than an abstract, level.

2 If possible, assess the level and the type of thinking of each child in your class. Ask individual children to perform some of Piaget's experiments, and spend most of your time listening to each child explain her reactions.

3 Remember that learning through activity and direct experience is essential. Provide plenty of materials and opportunities for children to learn on their own.

4 Arrange situations to permit social interaction, so that children can learn from one another.

Hearing others explain their views is a natural way for students to learn that not everyone sees things the same way. The placement of a few advanced thinkers with less mature thinkers is more likely to facilitate this process than is homogeneous grouping.

5 Plan learning experiences to take into account the level of thinking attained by an individual or group.

Encourage children to classify things on the basis of a single attribute before you expose them to problems that involve relationships among two or more attributes. Ask many questions, and give your students many opportunities to explain their interpretations of experiences so that you can remain aware of their level of thinking.

---

[2] These guidelines are adapted from Elkind (1989); Ginsburg and Opper (1988); Kamii (2000); Singer and Revenson (1996); and Wadsworth (1996).

6 **Keep in mind the possibility that students may be influenced by egocentric speech and thought.**

Allow for the possibility that each child may assume that everyone else has the same conception of a word that he has. If confusion becomes apparent or if a child becomes impatient about failure to communicate, request an explanation in different terms. Or ask several children to explain their conception of an object or a situation.

MIDDLE SCHOOL AND SECONDARY GRADES[3]

JOURNAL ENTRY
Ways to Apply Piaget's Theory (Middle School and Secondary Grades)

1 **Become well acquainted with the nature of concrete operational thinking and formal thought so that you can recognize when your students are resorting to either type or to a combination of the two.**

2 **To become aware of the type of thinking that individual students use, ask them to explain how they arrived at solutions to problems. Do this either as part of your classroom curriculum or in response to experimental situations similar to those devised by Piaget.**

3 **Teach students how to solve problems more systematically (suggestions for doing this will be provided in later chapters) and provide opportunities for hands-on science experiments.**

4 **Keep in mind that some high school students may be more interested in possibilities than in realities.**

If class discussions become unrealistically theoretical and hypothetical, call attention to facts and practical difficulties. If students are contemptuous of unsuccessful attempts by adults to solve school, local, national, and international problems, point out the complexity of many situations involving conflicts of interest, perhaps by summarizing arguments from both sides.

 If you would like more suggestions for your journal, check the Reflective Journal Questions on the textbook web site.

5 **Allow for the possibility that younger adolescents may go through a period of egocentrism that will cause them to act as if they are always on stage and to be extremely concerned about the reactions of peers.**

---

[3] Many of these suggestions are derived from points made in Chapter 2 of *Adolescence* (Steinberg, 2002).

VYGOTSKY: COGNITIVE DEVELOPMENT

From the time Piaget's work first became known to large numbers of American psychologists in the early 1960s until the 1980s, it was the dominant explanation of cognitive development. Not that Piaget didn't have his critics. As the previous section made clear, many psychologists challenged one aspect or another of his work. But there were no competing explanations of cognitive development. Beginning in the early 1980s, however, the ideas of Russian psychologist Lev Vygotsky began to appear in the psychological literature with increasing frequency. A contemporary of Piaget who died prematurely from tuberculosis in 1934, Vygotsky had very different views about the major forces that shape learning and thinking, particularly with respect to the roles of culture, social interaction, and formal instruction.

How One's Culture Affects Cognitive Development

● How we think influenced by current social forces and historical cultural forces

Vygotsky's theory of cognitive development is often referred to as a sociocultural theory because it maintains that how we think is a function of both social and cultural forces. If, for example, you were given a list of nouns (such as *plate, box, peach, knife, apple, hoe, cup,* and *potato*) and told to create groupings, you would probably put *plate, knife,* and *cup* in a group labeled utensils and *peach, apple,* and *potato* in a group labeled food. Why? Is there something inherently compelling about those groupings? Not really.

We could just as logically have put *plate, knife,* and *apple* in a group, because we can use the first two to eat the third. But we are more likely to put objects in taxonomic categories than in functional categories because we have been taught by others who organize ideas taxonomically most of the time. And why do *they* think that way? Because they are the product of a culture that prizes the ability of its members to think at the most abstract levels (which is why Piaget saw formal operations as the most advanced stage of thinking).

Typically, then, parents and schools will shape children's thought processes to reflect that which the culture values. So even when individuals are by themselves, what they think and do is the result of cultural values and practices, some of which may stretch back over hundreds or thousands of years, as well as recent social contacts (Wertsch & Tulviste, 1996).

The Importance of Psychological Tools   Vygotsky believed that the most important things a culture passes on to its members (and their descendants) are what he called *psychological tools.* These are the cognitive devices and procedures with which we communicate and explore the world around us. They both aid and change our mental functioning. Speech, writing, gestures, diagrams, numbers, chemical formulas, musical notation, rules, and memory techniques are some examples of common psychological tools.

● Psychological tools aid and change thought processes

Early explorers, for example, created maps to help them represent where they had been, communicate that knowledge to others, and plan future trips. Today we use the same type of tool to navigate efficiently over long distances or within relatively compact but complex environments (like large cities). Another example is the use of multiplication. If asked to solve the multiplication problem 343 × 822, you would, in all likelihood, quickly and easily come up with the answer, 281,946, by using the following procedure:

$$
\begin{array}{r}
343 \\
\times\ 822 \\
\hline
686 \\
686\ \ \ \\
2744\ \ \ \ \ \\
\hline
281{,}946
\end{array}
$$

But you could have produced the same answer by adding 343 to itself 821 times. Why would you automatically opt for the first procedure? Because the culture in which you operate has, through the medium of formal instruction, provided you with a psychological tool called multiplication as a means of more efficiently and accurately solving certain types of complex mathematical problems (Wertsch, 1998).

Children are first introduced to a culture's major psychological tools through social interactions with their parents and later through more formal interactions with classroom teachers. Eventually these social interactions are internalized as cognitive processes that are autonomously invoked. As Vygotsky so elegantly put it, "through others we become ourselves" (Tudge & Scrimsher, 2003, p. 218).

How Social Interaction Affects Cognitive Development

The difference between Vygotsky's views on the origin and development of cognitive processes and those of other cognitive developmental psychologists is something like the old question, "Which came first: the chicken or the egg?" Influenced by Piaget, many developmental psychologists argue that as children overcome cognitive conflict through the internal processes of assimilation, accommodation, and equilibration, they become more capable of higher-level thinking, and so come to understand better the nature of the world in which they live and their place in it. In other words, cognitive development makes social development possible (see our discussion of Robert Selman's work on the social development of children in the next chapter).

● Cognitive development strongly influenced by those more intellectually advanced

Vygotsky, however, believed that just the opposite was true. He saw social inter-action as the primary cause of cognitive development. Unlike Piaget, Vygotsky be-lieved that children gain significantly from the knowledge and conceptual tools handed down to them by those who are more intellectually advanced, whether they are same-age peers, older children, or adults.

Consider, for example, a simple concept like grandmother. In the absence of for-mal instruction, a primary grade child's concept of grandmother is likely to be very narrow in scope because it is based on personal experience ("My grandmother is sev-enty years old, has gray hair, wears glasses, and makes the best apple pie"). But when children are helped to understand the basic nature of the concept with such instruc-tional tools as family tree diagrams, they understand the notion of grandmother (and other types of relatives) on a broader and more general basis. They can then use this concept to compare family structures with friends and, later, to do genealogical research (Tappan, 1998; Tudge & Scrimsher, 2003).

In order for social interactions to produce advances in cognitive development, Vygotsky argued, they have to contain a process called *mediation*. Mediation occurs when a more knowledgeable individual interprets a child's behavior and helps trans-form it into an internal and symbolic representation that means the same thing to the child as to others (Light & Littleton, 1999; Tudge & Winterhoff, 1993; Wertsch & Tulviste, 1996). Perhaps the following example will help clarify this point: Imagine a child who reaches out to grasp an object that is beyond her reach. A nearby parent thinks the child is pointing at the object and says, "Oh, you want the box of crayons," and retrieves the item for the child. Over time, what began as a grasping action becomes transformed, through the mediation of an adult, into an internalized sign ("I want you to give that object to me") that means the same thing to the child as it does to the adult (Driscoll, 2000). Thus, a child's potential level of mental de-velopment can be brought about only by introducing the more advanced thought processes of another person.

How Instruction Affects Cognitive Development

Vygotsky drew a distinction between the type of information that preschool children learn and the type of information that children who attend school learn (or should learn). During early childhood, children acquire what Vygotsky called **spontaneous concepts.** That is, they learn various facts and concepts and rules (such as how to speak one's native language and how to classify objects in one's environment), but they do so for the most part as a by-product of such other activities as engaging in play and communicating with parents and playmates. This kind of knowledge is un-systematic, unconscious, and directed at the child's everyday concrete experiences. Hence, Vygotsky's use of the term *spontaneous*.

● Teachers should help students learn how to use psychological tools

Schooling, however, should be directed to the learning of what Vygotsky called **scientific concepts.** Scientific concepts are the psychological tools mentioned earlier that allow us to manipulate our environment consciously and systematically. Vygotsky believed that the proper development of a child's mind depended on learning how to use these psychological tools, and this would occur only if classroom instruction was properly designed. This meant providing students with explicit and clear verbal definitions as a first step. The basic purpose of instruction, then, is not simply to add one piece of knowledge to another like pennies in a piggy bank but to stimulate and guide cognitive development (Crain, 2000; Rogoff, 1990).

Contemporary Russian psychologists have extended Vygotsky's notions of spon-taneous and scientific concepts. They use the term **empirical learning** to refer to the

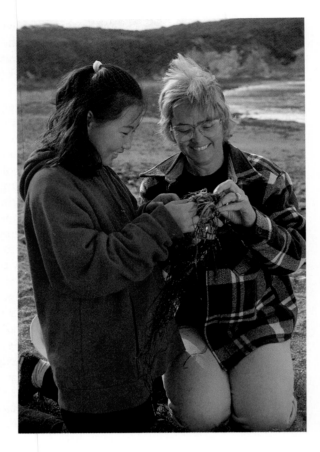

Jean Piaget believes that children's schemes develop more quickly when children interact with one another than when they interact with adults. But Lev Vygotsky believes that children learn more from the instructional interactions they have with those who are more intellectually advanced, particularly if the instruction is designed to fall within the child's zone of proximal development.

way in which young children acquire spontaneous concepts. The hallmark of empirical learning is that the most observable characteristics of objects and events are noticed and used as a basis for forming general concepts. The main limitation of this approach is that salient characteristics are not necessarily critical or defining characteristics, and it is the latter that form the basis of correct concept formation. For example, in the absence of formal instruction, children come to believe that any utterance that has two or more words is a sentence, that whales are fish, and that bamboo is not a type of grass.

Theoretical learning, on the other hand, involves using psychological tools to learn scientific concepts. As these general tools are used repeatedly with a variety of problems, they are gradually internalized and generalized to a wide variety of settings and problem types. Good-quality instruction, in this view, is aimed at helping children move from the very practical empirical learning to the more general theoretical learning and from using psychological tools overtly, with the aid of an adult, to using these tools mentally, without outside assistance (Karpov & Bransford, 1995).

Here's an example that compares the efficacy of the empirical and theoretical approaches: Two groups of six-year-old children were taught how to write the twenty-two letters of the Russian alphabet. Group 1 was taught using the empirical approach. The teacher gave the students a model of each letter, showed them how to write each one, and also gave a verbal explanation of how to write each letter. The students then copied each letter under the teacher's supervision. When they produced an acceptable copy of a letter, they were taught the next letter. Group 2 was taught using the theoretical approach. First, students were taught to analyze the shape of each letter so they could identify where the direction of the contour of each line changed. Then they were to place dots in those locations outlining the change in contour. Finally, they were to reproduce the pattern of dots on another part of the page and connect the dots with a pencil.

The speed with which the children in each group learned to produce the letters of the alphabet accurately differed by quite a large margin. The average student in the empirical group needed about 170 trials to learn the first letter and about 20 trials to write the last letter. The number of trials taken to learn all twenty-two letters was about 1,230. The average student in the theoretical group required only about fourteen trials to learn how to write the first letter correctly, and from the eighth letter on needed only one trial per letter. The number of trials needed to learn all twenty-two letters for the second group was about 60. Furthermore, these students were able to use the general method they were taught to help them learn to write the letters of the Latin and Arabic alphabets (Karpov & Bransford, 1995).

Instruction and the Zone of Proximal Development   This discussion of empirical and theoretical learning illustrates Vygotsky's belief that well-designed instruction is like a magnet. If it is aimed slightly ahead of what children know and can do at the present time, it will pull them along, helping them master things they cannot learn on their own. We can illustrate this idea with an experiment that Vygotsky (1986) described. He gave two eight-year-olds of average ability problems that were a bit too difficult for them to solve on their own. (Although Vygotsky did not specify what types of problems they were, imagine that they were math problems.) He then tried to help the children solve the problems by giving them leading questions and hints. He found that one child, with this aid, was able to solve problems designed for twelve-year-olds, whereas the other child could reach only a nine-year-old level.

Vygotsky referred to the difference between what a child can do on his own and what can be accomplished with some assistance as the **zone of proximal development (ZPD).** The size of the first eight-year-old's zone is 4 (that is, the eight-year-old could, with help, solve the problem designed for a child four years older), whereas the second child has a zone of 1 (he could solve the problem designed for a child one year older). According to Vygotsky, students with wider zones are likely to experience greater cognitive development when instruction is pitched just above the lower limit of their ZPD than will students with narrower zones because the former are in a better position to capitalize on the instruction. The ZPD, then, encompasses those abilities, attitudes, and patterns of thinking that are in the process of maturing and can be refined only with assistance (Tappan, 1998; Tudge & Scrimsher, 2003).

Helping students answer difficult questions or solve problems by giving them hints or asking leading questions is an example of a technique called **scaffolding.** Just as construction workers use external scaffolding to support their building efforts, Vygotsky recommended that teachers similarly support learning in its early phases. The purpose of scaffolding is to help students acquire knowledge and skills they would not have learned on their own. As the student demonstrates mastery over the content in question, the learning aids are faded and removed. Scaffolding techniques that are likely to help students traverse their ZPD include prompts, suggestions, checklists, modeling, rewards, feedback, cognitive structuring (using such devices as theories, categories, labels, and rules for helping students organize and understand ideas), and questioning (Gallimore & Tharp, 1990; Ratner, 1991). As students approach the upper limit of their ZPD, their behavior becomes smoother, more internalized, and more automatized. Any assistance offered at this level they are likely to perceive as disruptive and irritating.

Mark Tappan (1998) has proposed the following four-component model that teachers can use to optimize the effects of their scaffolding efforts and help students move through their ZPD:

1. *Model desired academic behaviors.* Children can imitate many behaviors that they do not have the capability to exhibit independently, and such experiences stimulate students to act this way on their own.
2. *Create a dialogue with the student.* A child's understanding of concepts, procedures, and principles becomes more systematic and organized as a result

● Cognitive development promoted by instruction in zone of proximal development

● Scaffolding techniques support student learning

of the exchange of questions, explanations, and feedback between teacher and child within the child's ZPD. As with modeling, the effectiveness of this dialogue is determined, at least in part, by the extent to which the teacher and student are committed to creating and maintaining a relationship in which each makes an honest effort to satisfy the needs of the other.

3. *Practice.* Practice speeds up the internalizing of thinking skills that students observe and discuss with others.

4. *Confirmation.* To confirm others is to bring out the best in them by focusing on what they can do with some assistance, and this process helps create a trusting and mutually supportive relationship between teacher and student. For example, you might say to a student, "I know this assignment seems difficult right now and that you have had some problems in the past with similar assignments, but with the help I'm willing to offer, I'm certain you'll do good-quality work."

Vygotsky's notion of producing cognitive development by embedding instruction within a student's ZPD is an attractive one and has many implications for instruction. In the chapter on information-processing theory, for example, we will describe how this notion was used to improve the reading comprehension skills of low-achieving seventh graders.

USING TECHNOLOGY TO PROMOTE COGNITIVE DEVELOPMENT

Piaget and Vygotsky believed that people use physical, mental, and social experiences to construct personal conceptions (schemes) of what the world is like. Although there are numerous opportunities throughout the course of each day to watch what other people do, try out ideas, and interact with others, we are normally limited to the physical and social stimuli that make up our immediate environment. Factors such as distance, time, and cost keep us from wider-ranging interactions. Technology, however, greatly reduces these limitations and thus has the potential to expand the range of our experiences.

Technology Applied to Piaget

There are at least two main ways in which technology can be used in schools to support Piaget's original ideas about the cognitive development of young children: (1) as a simulation tool, or microworld, for displaying knowledge and repairing misconceptions and errors in thinking, and (2) as a source for same-age peers to debate issues, thereby fostering cognitive conflict and disequilibrium.

- Computer-based simulations promote exploration and visual representations of abstract ideas, and correct misconceptions

Computers provide many routes to knowledge and can help restructure common student misconceptions (for example, that the seasons are caused by the closeness of the earth to the sun or that electrical current is equal in all parts of a circuit). One way technology can overcome such misconceptions is to create explorable **microworlds,** or simulated learning environments, that allow students to get a sense of how things work in the real world (Healy & Hoyles, 2001; Kordaki & Potari, 2002). One such microworld, the Geometer's Sketchpad, allows students to transform objects with unusual shapes into squares so their areas can be calculated and directly compared. In one eighth-grade classroom students used the Sketchpad to calculate in square miles the areas of the 50 states and create formulas to express relationships among them (such as AK = TX + OK + NM + CO, meaning Alaska is as big as Texas, Oklahoma, New Mexico, and Colorado combined) (Bay, Bledsoe, & Reys, 1998). Another microworld, the Conservation of Area and Its Measurement (C.AR.ME), provides a set of geometric tools to help students create different ways to represent

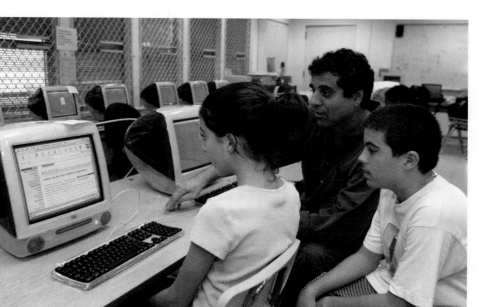

Computer-based technology can be used to promote cognitive development in ways that are consistent with both Piaget's and Vygotsky's views.

To explore microworlds, see the Weblinks for this chapter at the textbook web site.

the concept of area measurement. A group of high school students created eleven ways to represent the measurement of area using C.AR.ME (Kordaki & Potari, 2002). A third microworld, Probability Explorer, allows students to design probability experiments that relate to such real-world activities as weather forecasting; it is intended to help students refine their intuitive understanding of chance (Drier, 2001). As these examples illustrate, microworlds foster cognitive development by encouraging student exploration, student control, and visual representation of abstract ideas.

A **microcomputer-based laboratory (MBL)** can also be used to build on existing knowledge and to correct misconceptions. In an MBL, one or more sensors are attached to a microcomputer to generate graphs of such physical phenomena as temperature, sound, motion, and electromotive force (Peña & Alessi, 1999; Trumper & Gelbman, 2000, 2002). The following anecdote illustrates how helpful an MBL can be. When seventh- and eighth-grade students were asked to draw a graph depicting how fast a bicyclist travels uphill, downhill, and on flat stretches, their products represented the hills and valleys rather than the bicyclist's speed. That is, they drew an ascending line to represent the bicyclist's speed going uphill without realizing that such a line represented the downhill portion of the journey since it indicated increasing speed. In effect, they drew pictures that represented the exact opposite of what they were asked to represent. The students' graph-interpretation skills were significantly improved by having them work with an MBL. As the student applied a source of energy to one of the sensors—heating up and allowing to cool down a beaker of water, for example—a corresponding graphic representation was instantly created on the computer's screen (Kozma, 1991).

In a review of twenty MBL studies, Mary Nakhleh (1994) found that MBL applications show promise in altering or restructuring students' faulty understandings of key science concepts. Because MBLs provide an immediate link between a hands-on, concrete experience and a symbolic representation of that experience (a graph), their use may facilitate the shift from concrete to formal operational thinking (Trumper & Gelbman, 2000).

A second fundamental way to put Piaget's ideas into practice is to use technology to promote cognitive conflict. Remember that, according to Piaget, cognitive development is contingent on students' confronting others who have contradictory thoughts and claims, thereby creating internal tension and conflict. When students notice a discrepancy or a contradiction of what they believe, they are motivated to find more information and move back to a state of equilibrium. One way to accomplish this goal is to have students debate with peers over a computer network. Curt Bonk and Jack Cummings (1998), for example, discuss how World Wide Web–based debates can be used to get students to reflect on the different positions people take on controversial issues. Students are also encouraged to consult the original source material that their opponents use. Such a technique, Bonk and Cummings argue, enhances the quality of student rebuttals and reaction papers. The advantage of a computer network is that the peers one debates can be students in the class down the hall, in another school district, in another state, or even in another country. This kind of easy access to others greatly increases the probability that students will encounter people who hold truly divergent views on issues.

Technology Applied to Vygotsky

As with Piaget, there are at least two ways to link educational technology with the ideas of Vygotsky: (1) using the computer as an expert peer or collaborative partner to support skills and strategies that can be internalized by the learner and (2) using the computer as a tool to link learners to more knowledgeable peers and experts, who establish a master-novice apprenticeship and scaffold the student's learning.

● Computer programs can act as expert collaborative partners

As you'll recall, Vygotsky believed that children gain significantly from the knowledge and conceptual tools handed down to them by those who are more intellectually advanced. Roy Pea (1985) and Gavriel Salomon (1988) were among the first to suggest that the computer might play the same role as more capable tutors with such tasks as writing an essay and reading a book. Basically, the computer is programmed to provide prompts and expert guidance during reading and writing tasks. These supports, or scaffolds, are gradually faded as students become more competent at regulating their own behavior. According to some researchers (Cotterall & Cohen, 2003; Donovan & Smolkin, 2002), such support is vital in writing, because young children often lack the cognitive resources and skills to move beyond simple knowledge telling in their compositions. Salomon, who helped develop both the Reading Partner and Writing Partner software tools, found that they improved children's reading comprehension, essay writing, effort, and awareness of useful self-questioning strategies (Salomon, Globerson, & Guterman, 1989; Zellermayer, Salomon, Globerson, & Givon, 1991). Other studies, however, have not always reported such positive results (Bonk & Reynolds, 1992; Daiute, 1985; Reynolds & Bonk, 1996).

The second technology-based technique that has been derived from Vygotsky's view of cognitive development is the **cognitive apprenticeship** (Bonk & Cunningham, 1998; Brown, Collins, & Duguid, 1989). Like the traditional master-apprentice relationship in the skilled crafts and trades, a mentor works closely with a learner to develop the learner's cognitive skills. Also like the traditional apprenticeship, mentors provide students with real-life tasks to perform under realistic conditions. The learner moves from newcomer to expert by first observing the mentor and then participating in some tasks. Gradually, there is a shift in responsibility for solving the task from the expert or teacher to the student as the student moves from the fringes of the community to a more central role within it. As that happens, new skills are tested and, it is hoped, internalized.

When this master-apprentice relationship occurs on a computer network, it is typically called **telementoring** (Duff, 2000; Rea, 2001). The education and technology literature is filled with examples of telementoring in K–12 education. For instance, international weather projects such as the Kids as Global Scientists project (Mistler-Jackson & Songer, 2000), the Collaborative Visualization project (Edelson, Pea, & Gomez, 1996), and the Global Learning and Observations to Benefit the Environment program (Singletary & Jordan, 1996) all involve students in genuine scientific data collection and reporting. The collaborative relationships that students establish with peers and mentors create in students a strong sense of participation in what is called a community of practice. The web site of the International

Telementor Program (**www.telementor.org/**) provides volunteer mentors from around the world to teachers and students.

Richard Ruopp et al. (1993) documented how an electronic community of physics teachers, in a project called Labnet, was able to use MBLs to get students to share and compare their experimental findings across sites, while simultaneously providing a vehicle for teacher pooling of talents and discussion of lesson plans. Such a project is a prime example of two-tiered scaffolding (Gaffney & Anderson, 1991): consultants and experts scaffolded teachers, who in turn scaffolded students. With the rise in telecommunications and collaborative technologies for the Internet, the possibilities for working online with specialists, practitioners, or content experts continue to increase.

PIAGET, KOHLBERG, AND GILLIGAN: MORAL DEVELOPMENT

Piaget's Analysis of the Moral Judgment of the Child

Because he was intrigued by all aspects of children's thinking, Piaget became interested in moral development. He began his study of morality by observing how children played marbles. (He first learned the game himself, so that he would be able to understand the subtleties of the conception.) Piaget discovered that interpretations of rules followed by participants in marble games changed with age.

Age Changes in Interpretation of Rules   Four- to seven-year-olds just learning the game seemed to view rules as interesting examples of the social behavior of older children. They did not understand the rules but tried to go along with them. Seven- to ten-year-olds regarded rules as sacred pronouncements handed down by older children or adults. At about the age of eleven or twelve, children began to see rules as agreements reached by mutual consent. Piaget concluded that younger children see rules as absolute and external.

Although children ranging from the age of four to about ten do not question rules, they may frequently break them because they do not understand rules completely. After the age of eleven or so, children become increasingly capable of grasping why rules are necessary. At that point, Piaget concluded, they tend to lose interest in adult-imposed regulations and take delight in formulating their own variations of rules to fit a particular situation. Piaget illustrated this point by describing how a group of ten- and eleven-year-old boys prepared for a snowball fight (1965, p. 50). They divided themselves into teams, elected officers, decided on rules to govern the distances from which the snowballs could be thrown, and agreed on a system of punishments for those who violated the rules. Although they spent a substantial amount of playtime engaging in such preliminary discussions, they seemed to thoroughly enjoy their newly discovered ability to make up rules to supplant those that previously had been imposed on them by their elders.

Moral Realism Versus Moral Relativism   The way children of different ages responded to rules so intrigued Piaget that he decided to use the interview method to obtain more systematic information about moral development. He made up pairs of stories and asked children of different ages to discuss them. Here is a typical pair of stories:

> A: There was a little boy called Julian. His father had gone out and Julian thought it would be fun to play with father's ink-pot. First he played with the pen, and then he made a little blot on the table cloth.

Table 2.3	Morality of Constraint Versus Morality of Cooperation
Morality of Constraint	**Morality of Cooperation**
(Typical of Six-Year-Olds)	**(Typical of Twelve-Year-Olds)**
Holds single, absolute moral perspective (behavior is right or wrong)	Is aware of different viewpoints regarding rules
Believes rules are unchangeable	Believes rules are flexible
Determines extent of guilt by amount of damage	Considers the wrongdoers' intentions when evaluating guilt
Defines moral wrongness in terms of what is forbidden or punished	Defines moral wrongness in terms of violation of spirit of cooperation
(Notice that these first four differences call attention to the tendency for children below the age of ten or so to think of rules as sacred pronouncements handed down by external authority.)	
Believes punishment should stress atonement and does not need to "fit the crime"	Believes punishment should involve either restitution or suffering the same fate as one's victim
Believes peer aggression should be punished by an external authority	Believes peer aggression should be punished by retaliatory behavior on the part of the victim*
Believes children should obey rules because they are established by those in authority	Believes children should obey rules because of mutual concerns for rights of others
(Notice how these last three differences call attention to the tendency for children above the age of ten or so to see rules as mutual agreements among equals.)	

* Beyond the age of twelve, adolescents increasingly affirm that reciprocal reactions, or "getting back," should be a response to good behavior, not bad.

SOURCES: Freely adapted from interpretations of Piaget (1932) by Kohlberg (1969) and Lickona (1976).

B: A little boy who was called Augustus once noticed that his father's ink-pot was empty. One day that his father was away he thought of filling the ink-pot so as to help his father, and so that he should find it full when he came home. But while he was opening the ink-bottle he made a big blot on the table cloth. (1965, p. 122)

After reading these stories, Piaget asked, "Are these children equally guilty? Which of the two is naughtier, and why?" As was the case with interpretations of rules, Piaget found that younger children reacted to these stories differently from older children. The younger children maintained that Augustus was more guilty than Julian because he had made a bigger inkblot on the tablecloth. They took no account of the fact that Julian was misbehaving and that Augustus was trying to help his father. Older children, however, were more likely to base their judgment of guilt on the intent of each child.

● Morality of constraint (moral realism): rules are sacred, consequences determine guilt

Piaget referred to the moral thinking of children up to the age of ten or so as the **morality of constraint,** but he also called it *moral realism*. (Remember our definition of *decentration* in the earlier discussion of Piaget's theory. How do you think the young child's lack of decentration might affect her moral reasoning?) The thinking of children of eleven or older Piaget called the **morality of cooperation.** He also occa-

● Morality of cooperation (moral relativism): rules are flexible, intent important in determining guilt

sionally used the term *moral relativism*. Piaget concluded that the two basic types of moral reasoning differ in several ways. We summarize these differences in Table 2.3.

Kohlberg's Description of Moral Development

Just as James Marcia elaborated Erikson's concept of identity formation, Lawrence Kohlberg elaborated Piaget's ideas on moral thinking. Kohlberg believed that (1) moral reasoning proceeds through fixed stages, and (2) moral development can be accelerated through instruction.

Kohlberg's Use of Moral Dilemmas   As a graduate student at the University of Chicago in the 1950s, Lawrence Kohlberg became fascinated by Piaget's studies of moral development. He decided to expand on Piaget's original research by making up stories involving moral dilemmas that would be more appropriate for older children. Here is the story that is most often mentioned in discussions of his work:

> In Europe a woman was near death from cancer. One drug might save her, a form of radium that a druggist in the same town had recently discovered. The druggist was charging $2,000, ten times what the drug cost him to make. The sick woman's husband, Heinz, went to everyone he knew to borrow the money, but he could only get together about half of what it cost. He told the druggist that his wife was dying and asked him to sell it cheaper or let him pay later, but the druggist said "No." The husband got desperate and broke into the man's store to steal the drug for his wife. Should the husband have done that? Why? (1969, p. 376)

For an interactive exploration of Kohlberg's moral dilemmas, see the Netlabs at the textbook web site.

Kohlberg's Six Stages of Moral Reasoning   After analyzing the responses of ten- to sixteen-year-olds to this and similar moral dilemmas, Kohlberg (1963) eventually developed a description of six stages of moral reasoning. Be forewarned, however, that Kohlberg later revised some of his original stage designations and that descriptions of the stages have also been modified since he first proposed them. In different discussions of his stages, therefore, you may encounter varying descriptions. The outline presented in Table 2.4 is a composite summary of the sequence of moral development as described by Kohlberg, but you should expect to find differences if you read other accounts of his theory.

The scoring system Kohlberg developed to evaluate a response to a moral dilemma is extremely complex. Furthermore, the responses of subjects are lengthy and may feature arguments about a particular decision. To help you understand a bit more about each Kohlberg stage, the following list offers simplified examples of responses to a dilemma such as that faced by Heinz. For maximum clarity, only brief typical responses to the question "Why shouldn't you steal from a store?" are mentioned.

● Preconventional morality: avoid punishment, receive benefits in return

Stage 1: punishment-obedience orientation. "You might get caught." (The physical consequences of an action determine goodness or badness.)

Stage 2: instrumental relativist orientation. "You shouldn't steal something from a store, and the store owner shouldn't steal things that belong to you." (Obedience to laws should involve an even exchange.)

● Conventional morality: impress others, respect authority

Stage 3: good boy–nice girl orientation. "Your parents will be proud of you if you are honest." (The right action is one that will impress others.)

Stage 4: law-and-order orientation. "It's against the law, and if we don't obey laws, our whole society might fall apart." (To maintain the social order, fixed rules must be obeyed.)

● Postconventional morality: mutual agreements, consistent principles

Stage 5: social contract orientation. "Under certain circumstances laws may have to be disregarded—if a person's life depends on breaking a law, for instance." (Rules should involve mutual agreements; the rights of the individual should be protected.)

Stage 6: universal ethical principle orientation. "You need to weigh all the factors and then try to make the most appropriate decision in a given situation. Sometimes it would be morally wrong *not* to steal." (Moral decisions should be based on consistent applications of self-chosen ethical principles.)

Table 2.4	Kohlberg's Stages of Moral Reasoning

LEVEL 1: PRECONVENTIONAL MORALITY. (Typical of children up to the age of nine. Called *preconventional* because young children do not really understand the conventions or rules of a society.)

Stage 1   Punishment-obedience orientation. The physical consequences of an action determine goodness or badness. Those in authority have superior power and should be obeyed. Punishment should be avoided by staying out of trouble.

Stage 2   Instrumental relativist orientation. An action is judged to be right if it is instrumental in satisfying one's own needs or involves an even exchange. Obeying rules should bring some sort of benefit in return.

LEVEL 2: CONVENTIONAL MORALITY. (Typical of nine- to twenty-year-olds. Called *conventional* since most nine- to twenty-year-olds conform to the conventions of society because they are the rules of a society.)

Stage 3   Good boy–nice girl orientation. The right action is one that would be carried out by someone whose behavior is likely to please or impress others.

Stage 4   Law-and-order orientation. To maintain the social order, fixed rules must be established and obeyed. It is essential to respect authority.

LEVEL 3: POSTCONVENTIONAL MORALITY. (Usually reached only after the age of twenty and only by a small proportion of adults. Called *postconventional* because the moral principles that underlie the conventions of a society are understood.)

Stage 5   Social contract orientation. Rules needed to maintain the social order should be based not on blind obedience to authority but on mutual agreement. At the same time, the rights of the individual should be protected.

Stage 6   Universal ethical principle orientation. Moral decisions should be made in terms of self-chosen ethical principles. Once principles are chosen, they should be applied in consistent ways.*

* In an article published in 1978, several years after Kohlberg had originally described the six stages, he described the last stage as an essentially theoretical ideal that is rarely encountered in real life.

SOURCE: Based on descriptions in Kohlberg (1969, 1976, 1978).

Criticisms and Evaluations of Kohlberg's Theory   Is Kohlberg's contention that moral reasoning proceeds through a fixed universal sequence of stages accurate? Based on analysis of research on moral development, Martin Hoffman (1980) believes that although Kohlberg's sequence of stages may not be true of every individual in every culture, it may provide a useful general description of how moral reasoning develops in American society. Carol Gilligan (1979), whose position we will discuss in detail later, has proposed two somewhat different sequences that reflect differences in male and female socialization.

What about Kohlberg's view that moral development can be accelerated through direct instruction? Is this another "mission impossible," as some critics contend? Alan Lockwood (1978), after summarizing the findings of almost a dozen studies on acceleration of moral reasoning, concludes that the strongest effects (about half a stage increase in reasoning) occurred among individuals whose reasoning reflected stages 2 and 3. The effect of the instruction varied considerably from one subject to another. Some individuals showed substantial increases in reasoning; others showed no change. A comprehensive review of research on this topic by Andre Schlaefli, James Rest, and Stephen Thoma (1985) revealed similar conclusions. The authors found that moral education programs produced modest positive effects. They also found that the strongest effects were obtained with adult subjects.

Paul Vitz (1990) criticizes Kohlberg's use of moral dilemmas on the grounds that they are too far removed from the kinds of everyday social interactions in which children and adolescents engage. He prefers instead the use of narrative stories, both fictional and real accounts of others, because they portray such basic moral values as honesty, compassion, fairness, and hard work in an understandable context. Others (e.g., Rest, Narvaez, Bebeau, & Thoma, 1999) have criticized the fact that Kohlberg relied on the ability of his participants to explain clearly how they solved such hypothetical dilemmas as Heinz's. Individuals not adept at self-reflection or without the vocabulary to express their thoughts clearly either would not be recruited into such studies or would have little to contribute.

● Criticisms of Kohlberg's theory: moral development difficult to accelerate, moral dilemmas not relevant to daily life, relies on macromoral issues, ignores characteristics other than moral reasoning

Another criticism concerns the type of moral issue that most interested Kohlberg. Kohlberg's theory deals primarily with what are called macromoral issues. These are broad social issues such as civil rights, free speech, the women's movement, and wilderness preservation. The focus is on how the behavior of individuals affects the structure of society and public policy. At this level, a moral person is one who attempts to influence laws and regulations because of a deeply held principle. For some psychologists (for example, Rest et al., 1999), a limitation of Kohlberg's theory is that it does not adequately address micromoral issues. Micromoral issues concern personal interactions in everyday situations, examples of which include courtesy (not interrupting someone before that person has finished speaking), helpfulness (giving up your seat on a crowded bus or train to an elderly person), remembering significant events of friends and family, and being punctual for appointments. For micromoral issues, a moral person is one who is loyal, dedicated, and cares about particular people.

Finally, Kohlberg's work has also been criticized because it places such a strong emphasis on the role of reasoning in moral behavior but says little about the nature of people who behave in moral ways. Studies of adolescents who exhibit high levels of moral commitment and action (such as volunteering to work for social service agencies and community soup kitchens) show that these individuals have a self-concept that distinguishes them from other adolescents. They describe themselves in terms of moral characteristics and goals, have a greater sense of stability, and emphasize the importance of personal beliefs and personal philosophy. Yet these same adolescents did not differ from their peers on measures of moral judgment—their scores ranged from stage 3 to stage 5. It appears that advanced levels of moral reasoning may be only weakly related to moral behavior (Arnold, 2000).

Educational Implications of Kohlberg's Theory Carol Harding and Kenneth Snyder (1991) believe that teachers can make productive use of contemporary films to illustrate moral dilemmas. Film is an attractive medium to students, and several types of moral dilemmas are often portrayed in the space of about two hours. To highlight the dilemma of the rights of the individual versus the rights of others in a community, Harding and Snyder recommend the films *Platoon* and *Wall Street*. *Platoon* is a story about the Vietnam War and contains scenes of American soldiers burning villages and abusing villagers who are suspected of having ties to or of being the enemy. In response to such scenes, students can be asked such questions as, "Should the enemy in war be granted certain rights, or is personal survival more important?" *Wall Street* is a story about a corporate raider who uses borrowed money to take control of public companies and then sells off the assets (thereby eliminating people's jobs) to enrich himself.

The Tom Snyder educational software company offers a series of computer-based programs titled Decisions, Decisions, in which students identify and discuss moral dilemmas such as protecting the environment or using drugs. Students discuss each situation and as a group choose a response. Each response is stored by the program and in turn affects the development and outcome of the following situations to illustrate that events do not occur in isolation and that all decisions have consequences.

If films or computer programs are not available but you occasionally wish to engage your students in a discussion of moral dilemmas, the daily newspaper is an excellent source of material. Biology teachers, for example, can point to stories of the conflicts produced by machines that keep comatose patients alive or by medical

How would you respond to a parent or colleague who argued that students have better things to do in class than discuss ways of resolving moral dilemmas?

practices based on genetic engineering. Other science teachers might bring in articles that describe the moral dilemma produced by the debate over nuclear power versus fossil fuel. Civics or government teachers could use news items that reflect the dilemma that arises when freedom of speech conflicts with the need to curtail racism.

Gilligan's View of Identity and Moral Development

Carol Gilligan (1982, 1988) argues that Erikson's view of identity development and Kohlberg's view of moral development more accurately describe what occurs with adolescent males than with adolescent females. In her view, Erikson's and Kohlberg's ideas emphasize separation from parental authority and societal conventions. Instead of remaining loyal to adult authority, individuals as they mature shift their loyalty to abstract principles (for example, self-reliance, independence, justice, and fairness). This process of detachment allows adolescents to assume a more equal status with adults. It's almost as if adolescents are saying, "You have your life, and I have mine; you don't intrude on mine, and I won't intrude on yours."

But, Gilligan argues, many adolescent females have a different primary concern. They care less about separation and independence and more about remaining loyal to others through expressions of caring, understanding, and sharing of experiences. Detachment for these female adolescents is a moral problem rather than a sought-after developmental milestone. The problem for them is how to become autonomous while also being caring and connected.

Given this view, Gilligan believes that adolescent females are more likely to resolve Erikson's identity versus role confusion and intimacy versus isolation crises concurrently rather than consecutively. The results of at least one study (Ochse & Plug, 1986) support this view. With respect to Kohlberg's theory, Gilligan argues that because females are socialized to value more highly the qualities of understanding, helping, and cooperation with others than that of preserving individual rights, and because this latter orientation is reflected most strongly in Kohlberg's two conventional stages, females are more likely to be judged to be at a lower level of moral development than males.

Stephen Thoma (1986) has offered a partial answer to Gilligan's criticism. After reviewing more than fifty studies on gender differences in moral development, he drew three conclusions:

- First, the effect of gender on scores from the Defining Issues Test (the DIT is a device that uses responses to moral dilemmas to determine level of moral reasoning) was very small. Less than one-half of 1 percent of the differences in DIT scores was due to gender differences.
- Second, females almost always scored higher. This slight superiority for females appeared in every age group studied (middle school, high school, college, adults).
- Third, differences in DIT scores were strongly associated with differences in age and level of education. That is, individuals who were older and who had graduated from college were more likely to score at the postconventional level than those who were younger and had less education.

Thoma's findings suggest that females are just as likely as males to use justice and fairness concepts in their reasoning about *hypothetical* moral dilemmas.

● Males and females may use different approaches to resolve real-life moral dilemmas

But there is one aspect of Gilligan's criticism that cannot be answered by Thoma's analysis of existing research. She argues that when females are faced with their own real-life moral dilemmas (abortion, civil rights, environmental pollution) rather than hypothetical ones, they are more likely to favor a caring-helping-cooperation orientation than a justice-fairness-individual rights orientation. Perhaps the best approach that educators can take when they involve students in discussions of moral issues is to emphasize the utility of *both* orientations.

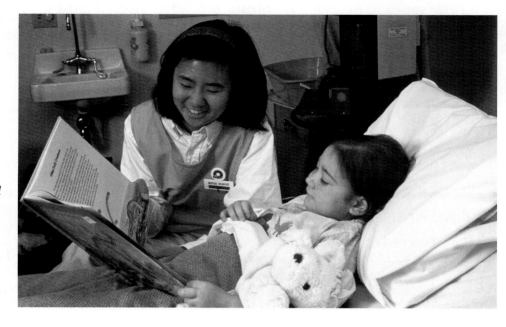

Carol Gilligan believes that Erikson's theory of identity development and Kohlberg's theory of moral development do not accurately describe the course of identity formation and moral reasoning in females. She believes that adolescent females place a higher value on caring, understanding, and sharing of experiences than they do on independence, self-reliance, and justice.

Does Moral Thinking Lead to Moral Behavior?

The Hartshorne and May Studies　Hugh Hartshorne and Mark May (1929, 1930a, 1930b) observed thousands of children at different age levels reacting in situations that revealed their actual moral behavior. The researchers also asked the children to respond to questions about hypothetical situations to reveal how much they understood about right and wrong behavior. Elementary school children, for example, were allowed to correct their own papers or record their own scores on measures of athletic skill without being aware that accurate measures were being made independently by adult observers. The children were also asked what they *thought* was the right thing to do in similar situations.

● Moral knowledge does not always result in moral behavior

　　A comparison of the two sets of data made it possible to determine, among other things, whether children practiced what they preached. What Hartshorne and May discovered was that many children who were able to describe right kinds of behavior in hypothetical situations indulged in wrong behavior in real-life situations. Children reacted in specific, rather than consistent, ways to situations that called for moral judgment. Even a child who was rated as among the most honest in a group would behave in a dishonest way under certain circumstances. A boy who was an excellent student but an indifferent athlete, for example, would not cheat when asked to correct his own paper, but he *would* inflate scores on sports skills.

　　Another significant, and dismaying, discovery that Hartshorne and May made was that children who went to Sunday school or who belonged to such organizations as the Boy Scouts or Girl Scouts were just as dishonest as children who were not exposed to the kind of moral instruction provided by such organizations. Hartshorne and May concluded that one explanation for the ineffectiveness of moral instruction in the 1920s was that too much stress was placed on having children memorize values such as the Ten Commandments or the Boy Scout oath and law. The two researchers suggested that it would be more effective to invite children to discuss real-life moral situations as they occurred. Instead of having children chant, "Honesty is the best policy," for example, Hartshorne and May urged teachers to call attention to the positive consequences of honest acts. If a student in a school reported that she had found money belonging to someone else, the teacher might praise the child and ask everyone in the class to think about how relieved the person who had lost the money would be to get it back.

Teaching Students to Be Good Characters

Many parents, educators, and political leaders believe that today's students lack the moral values possessed by previous generations. Concerned adults cite violence in schools and widespread drug abuse, among other problems, as evidence of such a decline. One commonly voiced solution to these problems is for the schools to institute moral education programs (also called character education programs). (p. 61)

Reading, Writing, and Character Education

CAROLYN BOWER
St. Louis Post-Dispatch 11/28/03

A blue banner over the entrance to Ridgewood Middle School in Arnold reads "Character under construction."

Similar banners appear in the halls and gym. Once a week students take a half-hour to focus on a character education activity. Recently, Justin Schweiss, 12, and Conan Morrison, 14, dusted the lockers. A half-dozen other seventh-graders gathered paper from classroom bins to recycle. Some students wrote messages about what they could do to promote peace.

"We don't have too many fights at this school," said Jacob Brydels, 14, an eighth-grade member of the Student Council. "We all get along."

Ridgewood, with about 530 students in grades seven and eight, is often singled out as an example of a school where character education works. Since focusing on character education a little more than three years ago, Ridgewood Principal Tim Crutchley has watched state test scores rise and discipline referrals drop by nearly 70 percent.

Hundreds of schools across the country use character education, defined as any initiative intended to develop student character. Missouri is one of 47 states that have received federal money for character education. Ridgewood is one of 111 school districts in Missouri and Illinois—and one of 38 in the St. Louis region—that take part in CHARACTERplus, a character education program.

Character education can improve academic achievement, behavior and attitudes, according to a study by Marvin Berkowitz and Melinda Bier, both at the University of Missouri at St. Louis. Berkowitz is the Sanford N. McDonnell Endowed Professor in Education at the university and Bier is an affiliate assistant professor.

The study was presented last month at a national forum of the Character Education Partnership, a nonpartisan coalition devoted to improving children's civic virtue and morals. The John Templeton Foundation financed the research.

Berkowitz found effective character education usually includes a number of strategies, requires staff training and needs parent and community involvement.

"We as a society have allowed an erosion of respect," Berkowitz said.

Students who act rudely to each other or cheat on tests reflect what has happened elsewhere in society with high profile scandals such as corporation executives cheating people of their money or celebrities cheating on their wives.

"In families we are not teaching or modeling how to treat other people with respect," Berkowitz said. "In schools we are not standing up to kids and saying, 'Look, this is the norm of civility in society.'"

At Jefferson Elementary School in Belleville, Principal Mark Eichenlaub began a push last year to involve parents and the community in character education.

Jefferson's 343 students in kindergarten through sixth grade have a reputation for strong academic achievement. But Eichenlaub wanted to make sure students, parents and those at the school were on the same page as far as intangible values.

The school adopted one rule for all students: "Be in the right place, at the right time, doing the right thing."

"There is no canned program," Eichenlaub said. "But creating a climate of character has to be the backbone of a school."

At Ridgewood, teachers study books such as Clifton Taulbert's "Eight Habits of the Heart," and talk about nurturing attitudes.

"The staff has to model good behavior, not just talk about it," said Kristen Pelster, assistant principal at Ridgewood. "Kids can't learn respect and responsibility by someone putting those words on paper on a wall. Character education is not a program. It is a way of life."

Questions and Activities

1. Just on the basis of the information provided in the article, what factors might account for the success of the character education program at Ridgewood Middle School? What other factors might have played a role but were not mentioned?

2. Ridgewood Middle School has been identified as "a school where character education works" because test scores increased and discipline referrals decreased. If you were responsible for designing and evaluating a character education program, would you be satisfied with these two outcomes as a basis for claiming that the program works? If not, what other outcomes would you want to measure? Why?

3. Professor Marvin Berkowitz, a character education researcher mentioned in the article, believes that there has been an erosion of respect in our society and that the cause is at least partly due to many parents' not teaching or modeling for their children how to treat other people with respect. Do you believe that people, including children, are unnecessarily rude toward and inconsiderate of others? If so, what other causes might there be besides parents who do a poor job of teaching their children?

4. Kristen Pelster, the assistant principal at Ridgewood Middle School, maintains that the teaching and administrative staff have to model good character and not just talk about it. How might you do that as a teacher?

Recent research shows that Hartshorne and May's basic finding is still valid. Approximately 90 percent of high school students and 60 percent of college students admitted to engaging in academic cheating. At both grade levels, males cheated more often than females. Moreover, cheating was judged to be more or less acceptable depending on the reason. Cheating was deemed more justifiable if it resulted in passing a class and getting a job that would help one's family. It was also seen as more justifiable if it was done to avoid disappointing one's parents, to avoid academic probation, or because the instructor had treated the student unfairly (Jensen, Arnett, Feldman, & Cauffman, 2002).

Research on Character Education Programs Many parents, educators, and political leaders believe that today's students lack the moral values possessed by previous generations. Concerned adults cite violence in schools and widespread drug abuse, among other problems, as evidence of such a decline.

One commonly voiced solution to these problems is for the schools to institute moral education programs (also called character education programs). As the Case in Print: "Teaching Students to be Good Characters" demonstrates, these programs are becoming increasingly popular. After reviewing the research on the effectiveness of character education programs, James Leming (1993) drew the following conclusions:

- Telling students what they should or should not do, through either slogans ("Just say no") or conduct codes, is unlikely to have significant or lasting effects on character.
- Helping students think about how to resolve moral dilemmas in higher-level ways does not automatically result in increases in morally acceptable behavior.
- An individual's social environment plays an important role in the learning and exhibiting of virtuous behavior. When students have clear rules with which to guide their behavior, when they accept those rules as appropriate and worthwhile, and when they are rewarded for complying with those rules, they are more likely to exhibit morally acceptable behavior.
- Producing changes in moral behavior requires a commitment to a well-conceived, long-term program.

As part of character education programs or as an independent activity, many social critics recommend that children either read or have read to them stories with a moral theme (sometimes called virtue stories). Being exposed to such stories is supposed to help children develop a strong set of traditional moral values, such as honesty, trustworthiness, responsibility, and loyalty. Darcia Narvaez (2002) points out that such a claim, whether or not its advocates realize it, rests on five assumptions that are not supported by contemporary research findings on learning. Let's briefly examine each of these assumptions.

Assumption 1: Reading Is a Passive Activity   The picture that emerges from thousands of research studies is that reading comprehension is not passive. Rather, it is the result of considerable cognitive activity. Children attempt to create a coherent, meaningful representation of a text by integrating the information in a text with prior knowledge.

Assumption 2: All Readers Extract the Same Information from a Text   Because of individual differences in prior knowledge, interests, and reading skills, each reader constructs a somewhat unique representation of what a text is about. Furthermore, texts with unfamiliar ideas are likely to be recalled less well and have more distortions than texts with more familiar ideas.

Assumption 3: All Readers Understand the Author's Point   Once again, because of individual differences in prior knowledge, interests, and familiarity with the ideas presented in a text, some readers will "get" an author's point while others will construct something entirely different. (If you have ever argued with someone about the point of a movie or novel, you can appreciate this phenomenon.) Research on summarizing text passages shows that before the age of ten children can accurately recount much of what they read but have great difficulty synthesizing that information to identify the author's main point.

Assumption 4: Moral Themes Are Readily Accessible to Readers   Because children have different conceptions (moral schemas, or prior moral knowledge) of how to get along with others and why such behavior is important, moral themes in a text are not necessarily accessible. As we noted earlier, people may base moral judgments on a variety of criteria, including personal interests (morally correct behavior is that which benefits me), maintaining norms (morally correct behavior is that which fosters law and order), and ideals (morally correct behavior is that which is consistent with higher-order principles). Older or more intellectually advanced children are more likely to grasp moral themes that reflect maintenance of norms and ideals than are younger or less advanced children. A recent study (Williams et al., 2002), although not done with morality stories, reinforces this point. Second and third graders who were trained to identify and comprehend story themes did better than noninstructed children, but they were unable to apply these themes to real-life situations or to identify and apply themes for which they received no instruction.

Assumption 5: Moral Themes Are Just Another Type of Information Conveyed by a Text   Because moral themes vary in their complexity and abstractness, and because children's comprehension of such themes develops through predictable stages, moral themes cannot be treated as the equivalent to fact-based information.

Despite the fact that character education programs have not received strong support in the research literature (probably because many programs are poorly designed and/or implemented), they are popular among parents and educators, and some appear to produce positive effects.

Whether or not your school has a character education program, there are certainly ways you can influence the moral development of your students. The following section of Suggestions for Teaching in Your Classroom provides several ideas. But before you use any techniques of moral education in your classes, it is wise to check with your principal. In some communities, parents have insisted that they, not teachers, should take the responsibility for moral instruction.

Suggestions for Teaching in Your Classroom

JOURNAL ENTRY
Ways to Encourage Moral
Development

 For additional journal entries,
see the Reflective Journal
Questions on the textbook web
site.

Encouraging Moral Development

1 **Recognize that younger children respond to moral conflicts differently from older children.**

2 **Try to take the perspective of students, and stimulate their perspective-taking abilities.**

3 **Develop an awareness of moral issues by discussing a variety of real and hypothetical moral dilemmas and by using daily opportunities in the classroom to heighten moral awareness. (Moral education should be an integral part of the curriculum; it should not take place during a "moral education period.")**

Here is a hypothetical moral dilemma that a first-grade teacher presented to her class:

> Mark was going to the movies when he met his friend Steven. Although Steven wanted to go to the movie with Mark, he had spent all of his allowance and wouldn't be getting any more until after the movie left town. Both boys were 12 years old but looked much younger. If they lied about their ages, they could both see the movie for the amount of money that Mark had. Mark was unsure if he should lie about his age. Steven said, "It's your money, so it's your decision." What should Mark do?

The responses of the students illustrate both the punishment-obedience orientation (stage 1) and the instrumental relativist orientation (stage 2) of Kohlberg's preconventional level of morality:

MS. KITTLE: *Okay, what do you think Mark should do?*
JOHN: *Him and Steven should tell them how old they are.*
EMILY: *They shouldn't lie about their age.*
MS. KITTLE: *Why do you think they shouldn't lie?*
TINA: *Because if they did lie, they'd get a spanking.*
JOHN: *Mark shouldn't lie about his age because it leads to a mess.*
MS. KITTLE: *What kind of mess?*
JOHN: *His mother might find out.*
SARA: *The father too.*
ERIN: *They'd get punished.*
MS. KITTLE: *So you all think Mark and Steven shouldn't lie because they might get caught and be punished. What if no one catches them—would it be right to lie then?*
MOST: *Yes!*
BILLY: *No, it's not. The manager of the show might catch them.*
MS. KITTLE: *But what if no one catches them?*
BILLY: *Then it's all right.*
MS. KITTLE: *Who thinks it would still be wrong to lie, even if Mark and Steven wouldn't get caught? (Five children raised their hands.)*
TROY: *They'd still get in a mixed-up mess.*
MS. KITTLE: *How?*
TROY: *Somebody might tell somebody that they lied.*
MS. KITTLE: *He might, that's true. But would it still be wrong even if Steven didn't tell anybody?*
TROY: *Yes.*
MS. KITTLE: *Why, Troy?*
TROY: *I don't know—but it is.*
EMILY: *It's not nice to lie.*
TROY (IN A RUSH): *Yeah, and it's not fair to other people, either!*
MS. KITTLE: *Who wouldn't it be fair to?*

TROY: *The others in the show. They had to pay full price.*
MS. KITTLE: *You mean if other 12-year-old kids had to pay the full price for their tickets, then it's not fair for Mark and Steven to get in cheaper?*
TROY: *Right. (Lickona, 1998)*

4 **Create a classroom atmosphere that will enhance open discussion. For example, arrange face-to-face groupings, be an accepting model, foster listening and communication skills, and encourage student-to-student interaction.**

Richard Hersh, Diana Paolitto, and Joseph Reimer (1979) offer the following specific suggestions for supervising classroom discussions:

- *Highlight the moral issue to be discussed.* Example: Describe a specific real or hypothetical moral dilemma.
- *Ask "why?" questions.* Example: After asking students what they would do if they were faced with the moral dilemma under discussion, ask them to explain why they would act that way.
- *Complicate the circumstances.* Example: After students have responded to the original dilemma, mention a factor that might complicate matters—for example, the involvement of a best friend in the dilemma.
- *Use personal and naturalistic examples.* Example: Invite students to put themselves in the position of individuals who are confronted by moral dilemmas described in newspapers or depicted on television.

To solidify your understanding of this chapter, use the ACE practice tests and PowerPoint slides on the textbook web site.

Resources for Further Investigation

● Erikson's Description of Development

Erik Erikson's books are of considerable significance for their speculations about development and education. In the first six chapters of *Childhood and Society* (2nd ed., 1963), he describes how studying Native Americans and observing patients in treatment led him to develop the Eight Ages of Man (described in Chapter 7 of the book). In the final chapters of this book, Erikson uses his conception of development to analyze the lives of Hitler and Maxim Gorky (a Russian novelist of the late 1800s and early 1900s). *Identity: Youth and Crisis* (1968) features a revised description of the eight stages of development, with emphasis on identity and role confusion. Erikson comments on many aspects of his work in an interview with Richard Evans, published as *Dialogue with Erik Erikson* (1967). Laurence Steinberg provides an overview of Erikson's theory and related research in (6th ed., 2002).

● Piaget's Theory of Cognitive Development

Jean Piaget has probably exerted more influence on theoretical discussions of development and on educational practices than any other recent psychologist. Of his own books, you might wish to consult *The Language and Thought of the Child* (1952a), *The Origins of Intelligence in Children* (1952b), and *The Psychology of the Child* (1969), the last of which was written in collaboration with Barbel Inhelder. Howard Gruber and Jacques Vonèche have edited *The Essential Piaget: An Interpretive Reference and Guide* (1977), which Piaget describes in the foreword as "the best and most complete of all anthologies of my work." An inexpensive paperback that provides a biography of Piaget and an analysis of his work is

Piaget's Theory of Intellectual Development (3rd ed., 1988), by Herbert Ginsburg and Sylvia Opper. Other books about Piaget are *Piaget for Teachers* (1970), by Hans Furth; *Piaget's Theory of Cognitive and Affective Development* (5th ed., 1996), by Barry Wadsworth; *Theories of Developmental Psychology* (4th ed., 2002), by Patricia Miller; and *Piaget's Theory: Prospects and Possibilities* (1992), edited by Harry Beilin and Peter Pufall.

An online source of information and relevant publications for Piaget is the Jean Piaget Society database, located at **www.piaget.org/**. It contains information about journals and conferences and is dedicated to "the presentation and discussion of scholarly work on issues related to human knowledge and its development."

● Vygotsky's Theory of Cognitive Development

Comprehensive descriptions and analyses of Lev Vygotsky's ideas about cognitive development can be found in *Vygotsky and Education: Instructional Implications and Applications of Sociohistorical Psychology* (1990), edited by Luis Moll; *Vygotsky's Sociohistorical Psychology and Its Contemporary Application* (1991), by Carl Ratner; and *Lev Vygotsky: Revolutionary* (1993), by Fred Newman and Lois Holzman. An overview of the theories of Erikson, Piaget, and Vygotsky can be found in *Theories of Childhood* (2000), by Carol Garhart Mooney.

● Piaget's Description of Moral Development

Piaget describes his observations on moral development in *The Moral Judgment of the Child* (1965). Thomas Lickona summarizes research investigations stimulated by Piaget's conclusions in "Research on Piaget's Theory of Moral Development," in *Moral Development and Behavior: Theory, Research, and Social Issues* (1976), an excellent compilation of articles on all aspects of morality, which Lickona edited.

● Kohlberg's Stages of Moral Development

If you would like to read Kohlberg's own account of the stages of moral development, examine "Moral Stages and Moralization: The Cognitive-Developmental Approach," in *Moral Development and Behavior: Theory, Research, and Social Issues* (1976), edited by Thomas Lickona. Kohlberg discusses changes in his theory in "Revisions in the Theory and Practice of Moral Development," in *New Directions for Child Development: Moral Development* (1978), edited by William Damon. In *Postconventional Moral Thinking: A Neo-Kohlbergian Approach* (1999), James Rest, Darcia Narvaez, Muriel Bebeau, and Stephen Thoma describe an approach to studying postconventional moral thinking that is based on but differs from Kohlberg's theory. Chapter 1 offers a brief (eight pages) overview of their approach, and Chapter 6 provides a concise (ten pages) discussion of why the authors have replaced Kohlberg's use of the stages concept with that of schemas.

● Gilligan's Analysis of Adolescent Development

If you would like to know more about the basis of Carol Gilligan's critique of Erikson's and Kohlberg's theories and her arguments for a broader view of adolescent development, start with her widely cited book *In a Different Voice: Psychological Theory and Women's Development* (1982). Briefer and more recent analyses of this issue are "Adolescent Development Reconsidered," a chapter in *Adolescent Social Behavior and Health* (1987), edited by Charles Irwin, Jr.; and "Exit Voice Dilemmas in Adolescent Development," a chapter in *Mapping the Moral Domain: A Contribution of Women's Thinking to Psychological Theory and Education* (1988), edited by Carol Gilligan, Janie Ward, Jill Taylor, and Betty Bardige.

● Character Education Programs

The Character Education Partnership (CEP) is a coalition of organizations and individuals who are dedicated to the implementation of character education programs in schools. Its web site (**www.character.org/**) contains a discussion of eleven principles that schools can use to design and evaluate their own character education programs (CEP, 2000). Character Counts is a coalition of schools, communities, and nonprofit organizations that promotes teaching the six pillars of character. You can find out what the six pillars are and obtain more information about the organization on its web site, **www.charactercounts.org/**.

Summary

1. Erikson's theory of psychosocial development is notable because it covers the life span, describes people as playing an active role in their own psychological development as opposed to passively responding to external forces, and emphasizes the role played by cultural norms and goals.

2. Erikson's theory is based on the epigenetic principle of biology. Just as certain parts of the fetus are formed at certain times and combine to produce a biologically whole individual at birth, certain aspects of personality develop at certain times and combine to form a psychologically whole individual.

3. Erikson's theory describes eight stages, from birth through old age. The stages that deal with the personality development of school-age children are initiative versus guilt (four to five years), industry versus inferiority (six to eleven years), and identity versus role confusion (twelve to eighteen years).

4. Forcing students to compete with one another for grades is likely to have a negative effect on their sense of industry.

5. Individuals with a strong sense of identity are comfortable with their physical selves, have a sense of purpose and direction, and know they will be recognized by others.

6. When faced with making an occupational choice, some adolescents declare a psychosocial moratorium.

7. Erikson's observations about identity were extended by Marcia, who described four identity statuses: identity diffusion, foreclosure, moratorium, and identity achievement.

8. Erikson's theory has been criticized for its heavy reliance on his personal experience, its lack of applicability to other cultures, and its inaccuracies in terms of female personality development.

9. Piaget believed that individuals inherit two basic intellectual tendencies: organization (the tendency to combine mental processes into more general systems) and adaptation (the tendency to adjust to the environment).

10. Adaptation occurs through the processes of assimilation (fitting an experience into an existing scheme) and accommodation (changing a scheme or creating a new one to incorporate a new experience).

11. A scheme is an organized pattern of behavior or thought that guides what we see, think, and do.

12. Equilibration is the process of trying to organize a system of schemes that allows us to adapt to current environmental conditions. Equilibration is produced by a state of disequilibrium.

13. Piaget concluded on the basis of his studies that schemes evolve through four stages: sensorimotor (birth to two years), preoperational (two to seven years), concrete operational (seven to eleven years), and formal operational (eleven years and older).

14. During the sensorimotor stage, the infant and toddler use senses and motor skills to explore and understand the environment.

15. In the preoperational stage, the child masters symbol systems but cannot manipulate symbols logically.

16. In the concrete operational stage, the child is capable of logical thinking, but only with ideas with which he has had firsthand experience.

17. During the formal operational stage, the individual is capable of hypothetical reasoning, dealing with abstractions, and engaging in mental manipulations. Although some adolescents are capable of formal operational reasoning, adolescent egocentrism restricts its range and power.

18. Piaget believed that social interactions among peers on the same level of development would do more to stimulate cognitive development than social interactions between children and adults because interactions among intellectual equals are more likely to lead to fruitful discussions, analyses, and debates.

19. Systematic instruction may have modest positive effects on the rate of cognitive development as long as the schemes that will govern the next stage have already begun to develop.

20. Piaget's theory has been criticized for underestimating children's abilities, for overestimating the capability of adolescents to engage in formal operational thinking, for vague explanations of how individuals move from stage to stage, and for not addressing cultural differences.

21. Vygotsky believed that cognitive development is shaped by both the interactions children have with others, particularly adults, and historical cultural forces. Parents and teachers help children acquire those psychological tools (such as language skills, concepts, and procedures) that their culture has come to value.

22. For Vygotsky, social interactions between children and more intellectually advanced individuals, such as peers, older siblings, and adults, are primarily responsible for advances in cognitive development, provided those interactions are based on mediation of external behaviors into internal signs.

23. Vygotsky believed that cognitive development is aided by explicitly teaching students how to use cognitive tools to acquire basic concepts and by teaching within a student's zone of proximal development.

24. Computer-based technology can be used to support Piaget's view of cognitive development through programs that help students explore and construct knowledge, formulate concrete representations of abstract ideas, and understand the ideas of others.

25. Computer-based technology can be used to support Vygotsky's view of cognitive development through programs that play the role of an expert tutor who provides a high degree of support and structure that is gradually withdrawn (scaffolding), through online mentoring programs, and through computer links that allow students to participate in actual scientific studies.

26. Piaget identified two types of moral reasoning in children: morality of constraint (rules are inflexible and external) and morality of cooperation (rules are flexible and internal).

27. Kohlberg defined six stages in the development of moral reasoning: punishment-obedience, instrumental relativist, good boy–nice girl, law and order, social contract, and universal ethical principle.

28. Structured discussions based on moral dilemmas may have some positive effects on the rate of development of moral reasoning.

29. Kohlberg's theory has been criticized because it is not applicable to other cultures, because its promise that moral development can be accelerated through direct instruction has received only limited support, because Kohlberg's moral dilemmas are not relevant to everyday social settings, because the theory relies too much on macromoral issues, and because it ignores the effect of characteristics other than moral reasoning on moral behavior.

30. Gilligan maintains that Erikson's theory of identity development and Kohlberg's theory of moral development more accurately describe male development than female development.

31. Studies show that children's moral behavior varies in different circumstances and that moral education is a complex process.

Key Terms

epigenetic principle *(24)*
role confusion *(25)*
identity *(27)*
psychosocial moratorium *(27)*
identity statuses *(27)*
psychological androgyny *(31)*
organization *(33)*
adaptation *(33)*
schemes *(33)*
assimilation *(33)*
accommodation *(33)*

equilibration *(33)*
constructivism *(34)*
conservation *(36)*
perceptual centration *(36)*
decentration *(36)*
irreversibility *(37)*
egocentrism *(37)*
adolescent egocentrism *(40)*
spontaneous concepts *(47)*
scientific concepts *(47)*
empirical learning *(47)*

theoretical learning *(48)*
zone of proximal development (ZPD) *(49)*
scaffolding *(49)*
microworlds *(50)*
microcomputer-based laboratory (MBL) *(51)*
cognitive apprenticeship *(52)*
telementoring *(52)*
morality of constraint *(54)*
morality of cooperation *(54)*

3

Age-Level Characteristics

KEY POINTS

These key points will help you learn the important information in this chapter. To help you study, they also appear in the margins of the pages, next to the text where they are discussed.

Preschool and Kindergarten (Three, Four, and Five Years)

- Large-muscle control better established than small-muscle control and eye-hand coordination
- Play patterns vary as a function of social class, gender, and age
- Gender differences in toy preferences and play activities noticeable by kindergarten
- By age four, children have a theory of mind: aware of own mental processes and that others may think differently
- Young children overgeneralize language rules

Primary Grades (1, 2, 3; Six, Seven, and Eight Years)

- Primary grade children have difficulty focusing on small print
- Accident rate peaks in third grade because of confidence in physical skills
- Rigid interpretation of rules in primary grades
- To encourage industry, use praise, avoid criticism
- Awareness of cognitive processes begins to emerge

Elementary Grades (4 and 5; Nine and Ten Years)

- Boys slightly better at sports-related motor skills; girls better at flexibility, balance, rhythmic motor skills
- Peer group norms for behavior begin to replace adult norms
- Self-image becomes more generalized and stable; is based primarily on comparisons with peers
- Delinquents have few friends, are easily distracted, are not

interested in schoolwork, lack basic skills
- Elementary grade students reason logically but concretely

Middle School (Grades 6, 7, and 8; Eleven, Twelve, and Thirteen Years)

- Girls' growth spurt occurs earlier, and so they look older than boys of same age
- Early-maturing boys likely to draw favorable responses
- Late-maturing boys may feel inadequate
- Early-maturing girls may suffer low self-esteem
- Late-maturing girls likely to be popular and carefree
- Average age of puberty: girls, eleven; boys, fourteen
- Discussion of controversial issues may be difficult because of strong desire to conform to peer norms
- Teenagers experience different degrees of emotional turmoil
- Environment of middle schools does not meet needs of adolescents, leading to lower levels of learning
- Self-efficacy beliefs for academic and social tasks become strong influences on behavior

High School (Grades 9, 10, 11, and 12; Fourteen, Fifteen, Sixteen, and Seventeen Years)

- Factors related to initiation of sexual activity vary by gender, race
- Parents influence values, plans; peers influence immediate status
- Girls more likely than boys to experience anxiety about friendships
- Depression most common among females, minorities
- Depression may be caused by negative cognitive set, learned helplessness, sense of loss

Key Points continued on next page.

The theories described in the preceding chapter call attention to the course of psychosocial, cognitive, and moral development. Although these types of behavior are important, they represent only a small part of the behavior repertoire of a child or adolescent. This chapter, which is organized by age and grade levels, will present an overview of types of behavior that are not directly related to any particular theory. In selecting points for emphasis, we used one basic criterion: Does this information about development have potential significance for teachers?

To organize the points to be discussed, we have divided the developmental span into five levels, corresponding to common grade groupings in schools:

Preschool and kindergarten. Ages three through five
Primary grades. Grades 1 through 3; ages six through eight
Elementary grades. Grades 4 and 5; ages nine and ten
Middle school. Grades 6 through 8; ages eleven through thirteen
High school. Grades 9 through 12; ages fourteen through seventeen

Because the way grades are grouped varies, you may find yourself teaching in a school system where the arrangement described in this chapter is not followed. In that case, simply refer to the appropriate age-level designations and, if necessary, concentrate on two levels rather than one.

You should read all of the chapter with care. Even though you now anticipate that you will teach a particular grade level, you may at some point teach younger or older students. You may also gain awareness of continuities of development and come to realize how some aspects of the behavior of older children were influenced by their earlier experiences. Indeed, although a particular type of behavior is discussed at a level where it is considered to be of special significance, that behavior may be important at any age level.

● Depression and unstable family situation place adolescents at risk for suicide

Political thinking becomes more abstract, less authoritarian, more knowledgeable

nitive characteristics. Following each characteristic are implications for teachers. To help you establish a general conception of what children are like at each level, brief summaries of the types of behavior stressed by the theorists discussed in the preceding chapter are listed in a table near the beginning of each section (Tables 3.1, 3.2, 3.3, 3.4, and 3.7). ●

At each of the five levels, behaviors are discussed under four headings: physical, social, emotional, and cog-

PRESCHOOL AND KINDERGARTEN (THREE, FOUR, AND FIVE YEARS)

Physical Characteristics: Preschool and Kindergarten

JOURNAL ENTRY
Active Games

1. *Preschool children are extremely active. They have good control of their bodies and enjoy activity for its own sake.* Provide plenty of opportunities for the children to run, climb, and jump. Arrange these activities, as much as possible, so that they are under your control. If you follow a policy of complete freedom, you may discover that thirty improvising three- to five-year-olds can be a frightening thing. In your Reflective Journal, you might note some specific games and activities that you could use to achieve semicontrolled play.

JOURNAL ENTRY
Riot-Stopping Signals and Activities

2. *Because of an inclination toward bursts of activity, kindergartners need frequent rest periods. They themselves often don't recognize the need to slow down.* Schedule quiet activities after strenuous ones. Have rest time. Realize that excitement may build up to a riot level if the attention of "catalytic agents" and their followers is not diverted. In your journal, you might list some signals for calling a halt to a melee (for example, playing the opening chords of Beethoven's Fifth Symphony on the piano) or for diverting wild action into more or less controlled activity (marching around the room to a brisk rendition of "Stars and Stripes Forever").

JOURNAL ENTRY
Allowing for Large-Muscle Control

3. *Preschoolers' large muscles are more developed than those that control fingers and hands. Therefore, preschoolers may be quite clumsy at, or physically incapable of, such skills as tying shoes and buttoning coats.* Avoid too many small-motor activities, such as pasting paper chains. Provide big brushes, crayons, and tools. In your journal, you might note other activities or items of king-sized equipment that would be appropriate for the children's level of muscular development.

● Large-muscle control better established than small-muscle control and eye-hand coordination

4. *Young children find it difficult to focus their eyes on small objects. Therefore, their eye-hand coordination may be imperfect.* If possible, minimize the necessity for the children to look at small things. (Incomplete eye development is the reason for large print in children's books.) This is also important to keep in mind if you are planning to use computers or software programs; highly graphic programs requiring a simple point-and-click response are most appropriate for very young students.

5. *Although children's bodies are flexible and resilient, the bones that protect the brain are still soft.* Be extremely wary of blows to the head in games or fights between children. If you notice an activity involving such a blow, intervene immediately; warn the class that this is dangerous and explain why.

6. Gender differences in physical development and motor skill proficiency are usually not noticeable until kindergarten and are fairly small in magnitude. Differences that do manifest themselves are due in part to biological endowment and in part to differences in socialization (Seifert & Hoffnung, 2000). Consequently, you may

Table 3.1	Applying Theories of Development to the Preschool and Kindergarten Years

Psychosocial development: initiative vs. guilt. Children need opportunities for free play and experimentation as well as experiences that give them a sense of accomplishment.

Cognitive development: preoperational thought. Children gradually acquire the ability to conserve and decenter but are not capable of operational thinking and are unable to mentally reverse operations.

Moral development: morality of constraint, preconventional. Rules are viewed as unchangeable edicts handed down by those in authority. Punishment-obedience orientation focuses on physical consequences rather than on intentions.

General factors to keep in mind: Children are having their first experiences with school routine and interactions with more than a few peers and are preparing for initial academic experiences in group settings. They need to learn to follow directions and get along with others.

want to encourage all children to participate in tasks that emphasize gross motor skills and tasks that emphasize fine motor skills.

Social Characteristics: Preschool and Kindergarten

1. *Most children have one or two best friends, but these friendships may change rapidly. Preschoolers tend to be quite flexible socially; they are usually willing and able to play with most of the other children in the class. Favorite friends tend to be of the same gender, but many friendships between boys and girls develop.* Young children are quite adept at figuring out which social and linguistic skills elicit responses from playmates. Typical gambits include inviting a peer to engage in rough-and-tumble play, offering an object to a playmate, offering to exchange objects with a playmate, sticking to the topic of a conversation, moving close to the person to whom one is speaking, and asking a question or giving a command (Guralnick, 1986). You might make a habit of noticing whether some children seem to lack the ability or confidence to join others. In some cases, a child may prefer to be an observer. But if you sense that a child really wants to get to know others, you might provide some assistance.

2. *Younger children exhibit different types of play behavior.* Mildred Parten (1932) observed the free play of children in a preschool and noted the types of social behavior they engaged in. Eventually, she was able to write quite precise descriptions of six types of **play behavior:**

   Unoccupied behavior. Children do not really play at all. They either stand around and look at others for a time or engage in aimless activities.

   Solitary play. Children play alone with toys that are different from those used by other children within speaking distance of them. They make no attempt to interact with others.

   Onlooker behavior. Children spend most of their time watching others. They may kibitz and make comments about the play of others, but they do not attempt to join in.

   Parallel play. Children play beside but not really with other children. They use the same toys in close proximity to others but in an independent way.

   Associative play. Children engage in rather disorganized play with other children. There is no assignment of activities or roles; individual children play in their own ways.

   Cooperative play. Children engage in an organized form of play in which leadership and other roles are assigned. The members of the group may cooperate in creating some project, dramatize some situation, or engage in some sort of coordinated enterprise.

3. *Play patterns may vary as a function of social class and gender.* Kenneth Rubin, Terence Maioni, and Margaret Hornung (1976) observed and classified the free play of preschoolers according to their level of social and cognitive participation. The four levels of social participation they observed (solitary, parallel, associative,

Young children engage in a variety of types of play. These play patterns may vary as a function of social class and gender.

● Play patterns vary as a function of social class, gender, and age

and cooperative) were taken from the work of Parten. The four levels of cognitive participation they observed were taken from the work of Sara Smilansky (1968), who based them on Piaget's work, and are as follows:

Functional play. Making simple, repetitive muscle movements with or without objects
Constructive play. Manipulating objects to construct or create something
Dramatic play. Using an imaginary situation
Games with rules. Using prearranged rules to play a game

The Parten and Rubin et al. studies found that children of lower socioeconomic status (SES) engaged in more parallel and functional play than their middle-class peers, whereas middle-class children displayed more associative, cooperative, and constructive play. Girls engaged in more solitary- and parallel-constructive play and in less dramatic play than did the boys. Boys engaged in more solitary-functional and associative-dramatic play than did girls.

These studies call attention to the variety of play activities common to preschool children. This knowledge may help you determine if a child *prefers* solitary play or plays alone because of shyness or lack of skills for joining in associative or cooperative play.

4. *Preschool and kindergarten children show definite preferences for gender of play peers and for pair versus group play.* A three-year study (Fabes, Martin, & Hanish, 2003) of more than two hundred preschool children (average age 4.25 years) found the following play preferences:

• Same-sex play occurred more often than mixed-sex play.
• Girls were more likely than boys to play in pairs rather than groups, and boys were more likely than girls to play in groups rather than pairs. When girls did play in groups, they were more likely than boys to play in a group in which they were not the only member of their sex.
• When boys played with each other, whether in pairs or groups, they were more likely than girls who played with each other to engage in active-forceful play. This tendency was less apparent when a boy played in a group that was otherwise all girls. But when a girl played in a group whose other members were boys, her level of active-forceful play tended to increase.

● Gender differences in toy preferences and play activities noticeable by kindergarten

Want to try an interactive quiz on gender roles? Go to the Netlabs section of the textbook web site, accessible from **http://education.college.hmco. com/students.**

JOURNAL ENTRY
Encouraging Girls to Achieve, Boys to Be Sensitive

5. *Awareness of gender roles and gender typing is evident.* By the time children enter kindergarten, most of them have developed an awareness of gender differences and of masculine and feminine roles (Wynn & Fletcher, 1987). This awareness of **gender roles** shows up very clearly in the toys and activities that boys and girls prefer. Boys are more likely than girls to play outdoors, to engage in rough-and-tumble play, and to behave aggressively. Boys play with toy vehicles and construction toys, and they engage in action games (such as football). Girls prefer art activities, doll play, and dancing (Carter, 1987). By age six, some children associate job titles that are considered to be gender neutral, such as doctor, librarian, and waiter, with either males (in the case of doctors) or females (in the case of librarians and waiters) (Liben, Bigler, & Krogh, 2002). Such strong gender typing in play activities occurs in many cultures, including non-Western ones, and is often reinforced by the way parents behave: they model what their culture has defined as gender-appropriate roles and encourage boys to be active and independent and girls to be more docile (Lancey, 2002). Peers may also reinforce these tendencies. A boy or girl may notice that other children are more willing to play when he or she selects a gender-appropriate toy.

Therefore, if you teach preschool children, you may have to guard against a tendency to respond too soon when little girls ask for help. If they *need* assistance, of course you should supply it; but if preschool girls can carry out tasks on their own, you should urge them to do so. You might also remind yourself that girls often need to be encouraged to become more achievement oriented and boys to become more sensitive to the needs of others.

Emotional Characteristics: Preschool and Kindergarten

1. *Kindergarten children tend to express their emotions freely and openly. Anger outbursts are frequent.* It is probably desirable to let children at this age level express their feelings openly, at least within broad limits, so that they can recognize and face their emotions. In *Between Parent and Child* (1965; Ginott, Ginott, & Goddard, 2003) and *Teacher and Child* (1972), Haim Ginott offers some specific suggestions on how a parent or teacher can help children develop awareness of their feelings. His books may help you work out your own philosophy and techniques for dealing with emotional outbursts.

Suppose, for example, that a boy who was wildly waving his hand to be called on during share-and-tell time later knocks down a block tower built by a girl who monopolized sharing time with a spellbinding story of a kitten rescued by firefighters. When you go over to break up the incipient fight, the boy angrily pushes you away. In such a situation, Ginott suggests you take the boy to a quiet corner and engage in a dialogue such as this:

You: It looks as if you are unhappy about something, Connor.

Boy: Yes, I am.

You: Are you angry about something that happened this morning?

Boy: Yes.

You: Tell me about it.

Boy: I wanted to tell the class about something at sharing time, and Lily talked for three hours, and you wouldn't let me say anything.

You: And that made you mad at Lily and at me?

Boy: Yes.

You: Well, I can understand why you are disappointed and angry. But Lily had an exciting story to tell, and we didn't have time for anyone else to tell what they had to say. You can be the very first one to share something tomorrow morning. Now how about doing an easel painting? You always do such interesting paintings.

● By age four, children have a
theory of mind: aware of own
mental processes and that others
may think differently

Ginott suggests that when children are encouraged to analyze their own behavior, they are more likely to become aware of the causes of their feelings. This awareness, in turn, may help them learn to accept and control their feelings and find more acceptable means of expressing them. But because these children are likely to be in Piaget's preoperational stage of intellectual development, bear in mind that this approach may not be successful with all of them. The egocentric orientation of four- to five-year-olds makes it difficult for them to reflect on the thoughts of self or others. Anger outbursts are more likely to occur when children are tired, hungry, or exposed to too much adult interference. If you take such conditions into account and try to alleviate them (by providing a nap or a snack, for example), temper tantrums may be minimized.

2. *Jealousy among classmates is likely to be fairly common at this age since kindergarten children have much affection for the teacher and actively seek approval. When there are thirty individuals competing for the affection and attention of just one teacher, some jealousy is inevitable.* Try to spread your attention around as equitably as possible, and when you praise particular children, do it in a private or casual way. If one child is given lavish public recognition, it is only natural for the other children to feel resentful. Think back to how you felt about teachers' pets during your own school years. If you have observed or can think of other techniques for minimizing jealousy, jot them down in your journal.

Cognitive Characteristics: Preschool and Kindergarten

1. *By age four, many children begin to develop a theory of mind.* Children's **theory of mind** concerns the ability of children around the age of four to be aware of the difference between thinking about something and experiencing that same thing and to predict the thoughts of others. Being able to make this distinction is critical to understanding such aspects of social life as surprises, secrets, tricks, mistakes, and lies.

By three years of age, most children realize the difference between thinking about something and actually experiencing that same something. But a significant change occurs around age four when children begin to realize that thoughts may be false. In one study described by Janet Astington (1998), a box that children knew normally contained candy was filled instead with pencils. When three-year-olds opened the box and discovered the pencils, they were asked what a friend would think was in the box before it was opened. They replied that the friend would know (just as they now did) that there were pencils inside. When they were asked later what they thought was in the box before it was opened, they replied "pencils" rather than "candy," indicating an inability to recall that their belief had changed. But four-year-olds understood that the friend would be misled by the fact that pencils had replaced the candy. The four-year-olds also remembered that they themselves had expected the box to contain candy. So, beginning at age four, children start to realize that the actions of people are based on how they *think* the world is.

Talking about different viewpoints will help children understand that people have beliefs about the world, that different people believe different things, and that beliefs may change when new information is acquired. Astington (1998) offers the following example of how teachers can foster the development of children's theory of mind:

> In a 1st-grade classroom that I recently observed, the teacher often talked about her own thought processes, saying, for example, "I just learned something new" when she found out that one student had a pet rabbit at home. When she was surprised or made a mistake, she talked about her own wrong beliefs, and at storytime, she had the children talk about the motivations and beliefs of story characters. Her style of talk helped the class focus not just on the thought content, but also on the thinking process—yet the term *theory of mind* was unknown to this teacher. (p. 48)

JOURNAL ENTRY
Handling Sharing

● Young children overgeneralize language rules

JOURNAL ENTRY
Encouraging Competence

2. *Kindergartners are quite skillful with language. Most of them like to talk, especially in front of a group.* Providing a sharing time gives children a natural opportunity for talking, but many will need help in becoming good listeners. Some sort of rotation scheme is usually necessary to divide talking opportunities between the gabby and the silent extremes. You might provide activities or experiences for less confident children to talk about, such as a field trip, a book, or a film. In your journal, you might note some comments to use if students start to share the wrong thing (such as a vivid account of a fight between their parents) or if they try to one-up classmates (for example, "Your cat may have had five kittens, but *our* cat had a *hundred* kittens"). For titillating topics, you might say, "There are some things that are private, and it's better not to talk about them to others."

3. *Preschoolers may overgeneralize rules in using language.* One of the most intriguing aspects of early language development is the phenomenon of **overgeneralization.** This occurs when children consistently misapply the rule of adding "ed" to the ends of words to make them past tense and "s" to nouns to make them plural, even after being corrected (Bjorklund, 2000). This tendency is so strong that Roger Brown (1973) concludes that efforts by parents and teachers to speed up acquisition of correct speech may not always be successful. Evidence to back up this conclusion is provided in an ingenious study by Jean Berko (1958). Berko found that when four-year-olds were shown pictures and told, for example, "Here is a goose, and here are two geese" and were then asked to complete the sentence "There are two _____," most said, "Gooses."

   Given this strong tendency of children to use their own rules of grammar, you should probably limit any attempts at grammar instruction to modeling the correct forms. The possibility of getting youngsters to use adult forms of grammar is outweighed by the risk of inhibiting their spontaneous use of language. Direct and systematic instruction in grammar should be delayed until second or third grade.

4. *Competence is encouraged by interaction, interest, opportunities, urging, limits, admiration, and signs of affection.* Studies of young children rated as highly competent (Burchinal, Peisner-Feinberg, Pianta, & Howes, 2002; Clawson & Robila, 2001; Schweinhart, Weikart, & Hohmann, 2002) show that to encourage preschoolers to make the most of their abilities, adults should

   Interact with the child often and in a variety of ways.
   Show interest in what the child does and says.
   Provide opportunities for the child to investigate and experience many things.
   Permit and encourage the child to do many things.
   Urge the child to try to achieve mature and skilled types of behavior.
   Establish firm and consistent limits regarding unacceptable forms of behavior, explain the reasons for these as soon as the child is able to understand, listen to complaints if the child feels the restrictions are too confining, and give additional reasons if the limits are still to be maintained as originally stated.
   Show that the child's achievements are admired and appreciated.
   Communicate love in a warm and sincere way.

   Diana Baumrind's (1971, 1991a) analysis of four types of child-rearing approaches shows why such techniques contribute to competence in children. Baumrind found that parents of competent children are **authoritative parents.** They have confidence in their abilities as parents and therefore provide a model of competence for their children to imitate. When they establish limits and explain reasons for restrictions, they encourage their children to set standards for themselves and to think about why certain procedures should be followed. And because these parents are warm and affectionate, children value their positive responses as rewards for mature behavior. The children of authoritative parents tend to be self-motivated. They stand up for what they believe, yet are able to work productively with others.

Authoritarian parents, by contrast, make demands and wield power, but their failure to take into account the child's point of view and their lack of warmth lead to resentment and insecurity on the part of the child. Children of authoritarian parents may do as they are told, but they are likely to do so out of compliance or fear, not out of a desire to earn love or approval. They also tend to be other-directed rather than inner-directed.

Permissive parents, as defined by Baumrind, are disorganized, inconsistent, and lack confidence, and their children are likely to imitate such behavior. Permissive parents make few demands of their children, allow them to make many of their own decisions, do not require them to exhibit mature behavior, and tend to avoid confrontations with their children. As a result, such children are markedly less assertive and intellectually skilled than are children from authoritative homes.

Finally, **rejecting-neglecting parents** do not make demands on their children or respond to their emotional needs. They do not structure the home environment, are not supportive of their children's goals and activities, and may actively reject or neglect their child-rearing responsibilities. Children of rejecting-neglecting parents are the least socially and intellectually competent of the four types.

You might refer to these observations not only when you plan how to encourage competence but also when you think about the kind of classroom atmosphere you hope to establish.

pause & reflect

Given the characteristics of preschool and kindergarten children, what classroom atmosphere and instructional tactics would you use to foster learning and enjoyment of school?

PRIMARY GRADES
(1, 2, AND 3; SIX, SEVEN, AND EIGHT YEARS)

Physical Characteristics: Primary Grades

1. *Primary grade children are still extremely active. Because they are frequently required to participate in sedentary pursuits, energy is often released in the form of nervous habits—for example, pencil chewing, fingernail biting, and general fidgeting.* You will have to decide what noise and activity level should prevail during work periods. A few teachers insist on absolute quiet, but such a rule can make children work so hard at remaining quiet that they cannot devote much effort to their lessons. The majority of teachers allow a certain amount of moving about and talking. Whatever you decide, be on the alert for the point of diminishing returns—whether from too much or too little restriction.

    To minimize fidgeting, avoid situations in which your students must stay glued to their desks for long periods. Have frequent breaks, and try to work activity (such as bringing papers to your desk) into the lessons themselves. When children use computer software that contains sound effects, distribute headphones to ensure that they concentrate on their own work and minimize distractions from others.

2. *Children at these grade levels still need rest periods; they become fatigued easily as a result of physical and mental exertion.* Schedule quiet activities after strenuous ones (story time after recess, for example) and relaxing activities after periods of mental concentration (art after spelling or math).

3. *Large-muscle control is still superior to fine coordination. Many children, especially boys, have difficulty manipulating a pencil.* Try not to schedule too much writing at one time. If drill periods are too long, skill may deteriorate, and children may develop a negative attitude toward writing or toward school in general.

4. *Many primary grade students may have difficulty focusing on small print or objects. Quite a few children may be farsighted because of the shallow shape of the eye.* Try not to require too much reading at one stretch. Be on the alert for rubbing the eyes or blinking, signs of eye fatigue. When you are preparing class handouts, be

JOURNAL ENTRY
Building Activity into Classwork

● Primary grade children have difficulty focusing on small print

Table 3.2	Applying Theories of Development to the Primary Grade Years

Psychosocial development: industry vs. inferiority. Students need to experience a sense of industry through successful completion of tasks. Try to minimize and correct failures to prevent development of feelings of inferiority.

Cognitive development: transition from preoperational to concrete operational stage. Students gradually acquire the ability to solve problems by generalizing from concrete experiences.

Moral development: morality of constraint, preconventional. Rules are viewed as edicts handed down by authority. Focus is on physical consequences, meaning that obeying rules should bring benefit in return.

General factors to keep in mind: Students are having first experiences with school learning, are eager to learn how to read and write, and are likely to be upset by lack of progress. Initial attitudes toward schooling are being established. Initial roles in a group are being formed, roles that may establish a lasting pattern (for example, leader, follower, loner, athlete, or underachiever).

sure to print in large letters or use a primary grade typewriter. Until the lens of the eye can be easily focused, young children have trouble looking back and forth from near to far objects.

Another vision problem that preschool and primary grade children encounter is amblyopia, or "lazy eye." In normal vision, the muscles of the two eyes work together to fuse their two images into one. If the eye muscles are not coordinated, however, children may experience double vision. In their efforts to cope with this problem, children may try to eliminate one image by closing one eye, tilting their heads, or blinking or rubbing their eyes. You should watch for signs of amblyopia, and let the parents know if you detect any.

Although many children at this age have had extensive exposure to computer games and video games and therefore have begun to develop greater eye-hand coordination with images on-screen, it's still appropriate to select software programs that incorporate easy-to-see graphics and easy-to-click buttons to avoid frustration.

● Accident rate peaks in third grade because of confidence in physical skills

5. *At this age children tend to be extreme in their physical activities. They have excellent control of their bodies and develop considerable confidence in their skills. As a result, they often underestimate the danger involved in their more daring exploits. The accident rate is at a peak in the third grade.* You might check on school procedures for handling injuries, but also try to prevent reckless play. During recess, for example, encourage class participation in "wild" but essentially safe games (such as relay races involving stunts) to help the children get devil-may-care tendencies out of their systems. In your journal, you might list other games to use for this purpose.

JOURNAL ENTRY
Safe But Strenuous Games

6. *Bone growth is not yet complete. Therefore, bones and ligaments can't stand heavy pressure.* If you notice students indulging in strenuous tests of strength (punching each other on the arm until one person can't retaliate, for example), you might suggest that they switch to competition involving coordinated skills. During team games, rotate players in especially tiring positions (for example, the pitcher in baseball).

Social Characteristics: Primary Grades

The characteristics noted here are typical of both primary and elementary grade students and underlie the elementary-level characteristics described in the next section.

1. *Children become somewhat more selective in their choice of friends and are likely to have a more or less permanent best friend.* Friendships are typically same-sex relationships marked by mutual understanding, loyalty, cooperation, and sharing.

Competition between friends should be discouraged because it can become intense and increase their dissatisfaction with each other. Although friends disagree with each other more often than with nonfriends, their conflicts are shorter, less heated, and less likely to lead to a dissolving of the relationship (Hartup, 1989).

You might use a device called a *sociogram* to identify friendships, cliques, and children who are social isolates and then give tentative assistance to children who have difficulty in attracting friends. Also, be on the alert for feuds, which can develop beyond good-natured quarreling and teasing. For detailed information on how to construct and use sociograms, consult *Sociometry in the Classroom*, by Norman Gronlund (1959), or "Sociometrics: Peer-Referenced Measures and the Assessment of Social Competence," by Scott McConnell and Samuel Odom (1986).

2. *Children during this age span often like organized games in small groups, but they may be overly concerned with rules or get carried away by team spirit.* Keep in mind that, according to Piaget, children at this age practice the morality of constraint: they find it difficult to understand how and why rules should be adjusted to special situations. When you divide a class into teams, you may be amazed at the amount of rivalry that develops (and the noise level generated). One way to reduce both the rivalry and the noise is to promote the idea that games should be fun. Another technique is to rotate team membership frequently. If you know any especially good but not excessively competitive team games, note them in your journal. You might also consult *Cooperative Learning: Theory, Research, and Practice* (2nd ed., 1995), by Robert Slavin, for descriptions of several team learning games that emphasize cooperation.

3. *Quarrels are still frequent. Words are used more often than physical aggression, but many boys (in particular) may indulge in punching, wrestling, and shoving.* Occasional fights are to be expected. If certain children, especially the same pair, seem to be involved in one long battle, you should probably try to effect a truce. But when you can, give children a chance to work out their own solutions to disagreements; social conflict is effective in spurring cognitive growth (Howe, Rinaldi, Jennings, & Petrakos, 2002; Murphy & Eisenberg, 2002; Tudge & Rogoff, 1989).

Emotional Characteristics: Primary Grades

1. *Primary grade students are sensitive to criticism and ridicule and may have difficulty adjusting to failure.* Young children need frequent praise and recognition. Because they tend to admire or even worship their teachers, they may be crushed by criticism. Provide positive reinforcement as frequently as possible, and reserve your negative reactions for nonacademic misbehavior. Scrupulously avoid sarcasm and ridicule. Remember that this is the stage of industry versus inferiority; if you make a child feel inferior, you may prevent the development of industry.

2. *Most primary grade children are eager to please the teacher.* They like to help, enjoy responsibility, and want to do well in their schoolwork. The time-honored technique for satisfying the urge to help is to assign jobs (eraser cleaner, wastebasket emptier, paper distributor, and the like) on a rotating basis. In your journal, you might note other techniques—for example, were there any particular responsibilities you enjoyed as a student?

3. *Children of this age are becoming sensitive to the feelings of others.* Unfortunately, this permits them to hurt others deeply by attacking a sensitive spot without realizing how devastating their attack really is. It sometimes happens that teasing a particular child who has reacted to a gibe becomes a group pastime. Be on the alert for such situations. If you are able to make a private and personal appeal to the ringleaders, you may be able to prevent an escalation of the teasing, which may make a tremendous difference in the way the victim feels about school.

JOURNAL ENTRY
Using Sociometric Techniques

● Rigid interpretation of rules in primary grades

JOURNAL ENTRY
Enjoyable Team Games

JOURNAL ENTRY
Handling Feuds and Fights

● To encourage industry, use praise, avoid criticism

JOURNAL ENTRY
Spreading Around Responsibilities

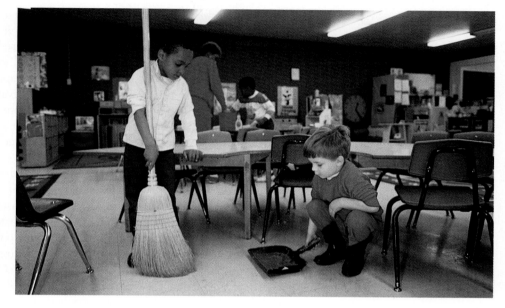

Most primary grade students eagerly strive to obtain "helping" jobs around the classroom. Accordingly, you may wish to arrange a rotating schedule for such jobs.

Cognitive Characteristics: Primary Grades

1. *Primary grade children understand that there are different ways to know things and that some ways are better than others.* When an observation can be explained with either a possible (that is, a theoretical) explanation or an evidence-based explanation, preschoolers fail to see one as more compelling than the other, but primary grade children usually prefer the explanation based on evidence. In one study described by Deanna Kuhn (1999), preschoolers viewed a set of pictures depicting two individuals running a race. They were asked to indicate who won the race and to explain what led them to that conclusion. One of the runners was wearing a fancier running shoe, and some of the children said that was the reason he beat his opponent. But because this same individual was also holding a trophy and exhibiting a wide grin in the last picture, some children cited that fact as evidence that the boy won the race. By the time they reach the primary grades, virtually all children understand that a fact-based explanation is superior to a theory-based explanation and so point to the second picture as the reason for their conclusion.

● Awareness of cognitive processes begins to emerge

2. *Primary grade children begin to understand that learning and recall are caused by particular cognitive processes that they can control.* Not until children are about seven or eight years of age do they begin to realize that learning and memory stem from cognitive processes that are under their conscious control. When learning words, for example, younger children may need to be prompted or directed to group the words by category because they do not realize that such a technique aids recall. Likewise, they may not recognize their lack of comprehension when they read difficult or unfamiliar material and may need to be prompted to think about how well they are understanding what they read. By the primary grades, this awareness and monitoring of one's learning processes, called metacognition, begins to emerge. We will return to the subject in the chapter on information-processing theory.

JOURNAL ENTRY
Assigning Short and Varied Tasks

3. *Because of continuing neurological development and limited experience with formal learning tasks, primary grade children do not learn as efficiently as older children do.* Therefore, you should assign primary grade children relatively short tasks and switch periodically from cognitively demanding activities to less demanding ones. Providing youngsters with periodic breaks, such as recess, increases their ability to attend to and perform well on subsequent classroom tasks. The nature of the recess activity does not seem to be important. It can be physical activity in a schoolyard or playing games in class (Pellegrini & Bjorklund, 1997).

4. *Talking aloud to oneself reaches a peak between the ages of six and seven and then rapidly declines.* Don't be surprised or concerned if you observe primary grade students talking to themselves, either when they are by themselves or when they are with classmates. This is a well-documented phenomenon that Vygotsky called private speech. Vygotsky described private speech as a transition between speaking with others and thinking to oneself. Private speech is first noticeable around age three and may constitute anywhere from 20 to 60 percent of a child's utterances between the ages of six and seven. By age eight, however, it all but disappears and is replaced by silent, or inner, speech (Berk, 1994; Feigenbaum, 2002).

As its name implies, private speech is not intended to communicate a message to someone else, nor does it always take the form of complete sentences. One important purpose of private speech, which may consist of single words or phrases, is to help children clarify their thinking and solve difficult problems, such as those that arise in the course of doing math problems or reading unfamiliar material. For example, a child may count on her fingers out loud while working on a math problem and then say, "The answer's ten." Observations of first and second graders found that those who talked to themselves while doing math problems did better at math the following year than did students who exhibited little private speech. Another interesting finding is that students who exhibit the greatest use of self-guiding private speech are more likely to have authoritative mothers (Berk, 1994).

ELEMENTARY GRADES (4 AND 5; NINE AND TEN YEARS)

Physical Characteristics: Elementary Grades

1. *Both boys and girls become leaner and stronger.* In general, there is a decrease in the growth of fatty tissue and an increase in bone and muscle development. In a year's time, the average child of this age will grow about 2 to 3 inches and gain about 5 to 7 pounds. As a result, the typical child will tend to have a lean and gangly look. Although the average nine-year-old boy is slightly taller and heavier than the average nine-year-old girl, this difference all but disappears a year later. And from age eleven until about fourteen and a half, girls are slightly heavier and taller than boys. Because secondary sex characteristics have not yet appeared, boys and girls can be mistaken for one another. This is particularly likely to happen when girls have close-cropped hair, boys have very long hair, and both genders wear gender-neutral clothing (Hetherington & Parke, 1993; LeFrançois, 2001; Mitchell, 1990).

2. *Obesity can become a problem for some children of this age group.* Because nine- and ten-year-olds have more control over their eating habits than younger children do, there is a greater tendency for them to overeat, particularly junk food (foods high in calories and fat but low in nutritional value). When this eating pattern is coupled with a relatively low level of physical activity (mainly because of television watching) and a genetic predisposition toward obesity, children become mildly to severely overweight. In the last half of the 1970s, 6.5 percent of children from six to eleven years of age were judged to be overweight. By 1999, the percentage doubled to 13 percent. Not only do overweight children put themselves at risk for cardiovascular problems and Type II diabetes later in life, but they also become targets for ridicule and ostracism in the present from peers (Eberstadt, 2003; Kelly & Moag-Stahlberg, 2002; National Center for Health Statistics, 2002; Sweeting & West, 2001).

■ **Table 3.3**	Applying Theories of Development to the Elementary Grade Years

Psychosocial development: industry vs. inferiority. Keep students constructively busy; try to play down comparisons between best and worse learners.

Cognitive development: concrete operational. Except for the most intellectually advanced students, most will need to generalize from concrete experiences.

Moral development: morality of constraint; transition from preconventional to conventional. A shift to viewing rules as mutual agreements is occurring, but "official" rules are obeyed out of respect for authority or out of a desire to impress others.

General factors to keep in mind: Initial enthusiasm for learning may fade as the novelty wears off and as the process of perfecting skills becomes more difficult. Differences in knowledge and skills of fastest and slowest learners become more noticeable. "Automatic" respect for teachers tends to diminish. Peer group influences become strong.

● Boys slightly better at sports-related motor skills; girls better at flexibility, balance, rhythmic motor skills

---

JOURNAL ENTRY
Minimizing Gender Differences in Motor Skill Performance

3. *Although small in magnitude, gender differences in motor skill performance are apparent.* Boys tend to outperform girls on tasks that involve kicking, throwing, catching, running, broad jumping, and batting. Girls surpass boys on tasks that require muscular flexibility, balance, and rhythmic movements. These differences may be due in part to gender-role stereotyping. That is, because of socialization differences, girls are more likely to play hopscotch and jump rope, whereas boys are more likely to play baseball and basketball.

One benefit of attaining mastery over large and small muscles is a relatively orderly classroom. Fourth and fifth graders can sit quietly for extended periods and concentrate on whatever intellectual task is at hand (Hetherington & Parke, 1993; Mitchell, 1990). Another benefit is that children enjoy arts and crafts and musical activities.

4. *This is a period of relative calm and predictability in physical development.* Growth in height and weight tends to be consistent and moderate, hormonal imbalances are absent, disease occurs less frequently than at any other period, and bodily coordination is relatively stable (Hetherington & Parke, 1993; Mitchell, 1990).

Social Characteristics: Elementary Grades

● Peer group norms for behavior begin to replace adult norms

1. *The peer group becomes powerful and begins to replace adults as the major source of behavior standards and recognition of achievement.* During the early school years, parents and teachers set standards of conduct, and most children try to live up to them. But by grades 4 and 5, children are more interested in getting along with one another without adult supervision. Consequently, children come to realize that the rules for behavior within the peer group are not quite the same as the rules for behavior within the family or the classroom.

JOURNAL ENTRY
Moderating the Power of Peer Group Norms

This newfound freedom can have a down side. Because children of this age typically want to be accepted by their peers, have a relatively naive view of right and wrong, and do not have enough self-assurance to oppose group norms, they may engage in behaviors (shoplifting, fighting, prejudice against outsiders) that they would not exhibit at home or in the classroom (Mitchell, 1990).

2. *Friendships become more selective and gender based.* Elementary grade children become even more discriminating than primary grade children in the selection of friends and playmates. Most children choose a best friend, usually of the same gender. These relationships, based usually on common ideas, outlooks, and impressions of the world, may last through adolescence. Although children of this age will rarely refuse to interact with members of the opposite sex when directed to do so by parents and teachers, they will avoid the opposite sex when left to their own devices (Mitchell, 1990).

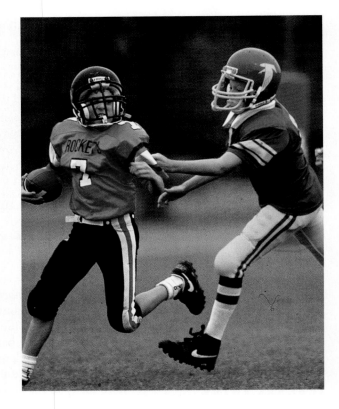

Elementary grade boys tend to be better than girls on motor skill tasks that involve large muscle movement, while elementary grade girls tend to perform better than boys on motor skill tasks that involve muscular flexibility, balance, and rhythmic movements.

Emotional Characteristics: Elementary Grades

1. *During this period, children develop a more global, integrated, and complex self-image.* Researchers who study self-perceptions (e.g., Harter, 1990, 1999; Marsh & Hattie, 1996) distinguish among the concepts of self-description, self-esteem, and self-concept:

   - A **self-description** is simply the way in which people describe themselves to others. Self-descriptive statements are largely, but not entirely, free of evaluative judgments. Examples of self-descriptions are "I am eleven years old," "I am tall for my age," and "I am an outgoing person."
   - **Self-esteem** (or self-worth, as it is sometimes called) refers to the overall or global evaluation people make of themselves, and it is indicated by such statements as "I believe that I am a worthwhile person" and "I am pretty happy with myself."
   - **Self-concept** refers to the evaluative judgments people make of themselves in specific domains, such as academic performance, social interactions, athletic performance, and physical appearance. It is indicated by such statements as "I have a good head for math," "I have a hard time making friends," and "My big nose makes me look ugly."

   Taken together, self-descriptions, self-esteem, and self-concept constitute a person's **self-image** or self-portrait. By middle childhood each of these aspects of self-image is present; children can make an accurate self-description, construct a global evaluation of themselves, and specify their positive and negative attributes in specific domains.

   There are several important facts to keep in mind about the formulation of a child's self-image. First, in the elementary grades it is more generalized or integrated than is the case for primary grade children because it is based on information gained over time, tasks, and settings. A child may think of herself as socially adept not just because she is popular at school but because she has always been well liked and gets along well with adults as well as peers in a variety

● Self-image becomes more generalized and stable; is based primarily on comparisons with peers

JOURNAL ENTRY
Ways to Improve Students' Self-Image

pause & reflect

The primary and elementary years correspond to Erikson's stage of industry versus inferiority. The implication is that educators should encourage a sense of industry and competence in each student. On a scale of 1 to 10, how well do you think schools accomplish this goal? What major factors account for your rating?

● Delinquents have few friends, are easily distracted, are not interested in schoolwork, lack basic skills

● Elementary grade students reason logically but concretely

of situations. It is this generalized quality that helps make self-portraits relatively stable.

Second, comparison with others is the fundamental basis of a self-image during the elementary grades. This orientation is due in part to the fact that children are not as egocentric as they were a few years earlier and are developing the capability to think in terms of multiple categories. It is also due to the fact that competition and individualism are highly prized values in many Western cultures. Consequently, children will naturally compare themselves to one another ("I'm taller than my friend") as well as to broad-based norms ("I'm tall for my age") in an effort to determine who they are. This social comparison process can have detrimental effects on a student's academic self-image when most of his classmates are more able learners (Marsh & Craven, 2002). But as William Damon and Daniel Hart (1988) point out, comparison is a less important basis for building a self-image in cultures where competition and individualism are downplayed.

Third, in the elementary grades the self is described for the first time in terms of emotions (pride, shame, worry, anger, happiness) and how well they can be controlled. Fourth, a child's sense of self is influenced by the information and attitudes that are communicated by such significant others as parents, teachers, and friends and by how competent the child feels in areas where success is important. The implications of this fact will be discussed in many of the remaining chapters of the text.

Because major developmental changes usually do not occur during the elementary grades, a child's self-image will remain fairly stable for a few years if there are no major changes in the child's home or social environment. But as you will see later in this chapter, the developmental changes that typically occur during the middle school and high school grades often produce dramatic changes in the sense of self (Alasker & Olweus, 2002).

2. *Disruptive family relationships, social rejection, and school failure may lead to delinquent behavior.* Gerald Patterson, Barbara DeBarsyshe, and Elizabeth Ramsey (1989) marshal a wide array of evidence to support their belief that delinquent behavior is the result of a causal chain of events that originates with dysfunctional parent-child relationships. In their view, poor parent-child relationships lead to behavior problems, which lead to peer rejection and academic failure, which lead to identification with a deviant peer group, which results in delinquent behavior. Parents of such children administer harsh and inconsistent punishment, provide little positive reinforcement, and do little monitoring and supervising of each child's activities.

Because these children have not learned to follow adult rules and regulations but have learned how to satisfy their needs through coercive behavior, they are rejected by their peers, are easily distracted when doing schoolwork, show little interest in the subjects they study, and do not master many of the basic academic skills necessary for subsequent achievement. Attempts at short-circuiting this chain of events stand a greater chance of success if they begin early and are multifaceted. In addition to counseling and parent training, mastery of basic academic skills is important.

Cognitive Characteristics: Elementary Grades

1. *The elementary grade child can think logically, although such thinking is constrained and inconsistent.* In terms of Piaget's stages, upper elementary grade children are concrete operational stage thinkers. Most will have attained enough mastery of logical schemes that they can understand and solve tasks that involve such processes as class inclusion (understanding the superordinate-subordinate relationships that make up hierarchies), seriation, conservation, and symbolic representation

Although elementary grade children understand the logical basis for tasks such as classification, seriation, and conservation, they can solve such tasks only if they are based on concrete objects and ideas.

(reading maps, for example), provided that the content of the task refers to real, tangible ideas that the child has either experienced or can imagine. But general and abstract ideas often escape the elementary-age child. For example, sarcasm, metaphor, and allegory are usually lost on concrete stage thinkers.

The knowledge base of fourth- and fifth-grade children contains many misconceptions, and these children may behave illogically. To prove a point or win a debate with a classmate or playmate, the upper elementary child may reel off a string of facts, some of which reflect authoritative sources, some of which are exaggerations, and some of which are invented on the spot. A ten-year-old may believe, for example, that people can live for several months without eating and that vacant houses are haunted. As John Mitchell (1990) humorously put it, "Many kids possess a gift for compressing the largest number of words into the smallest amount of thought" (p. 213).

2. *On tasks that call for simple memory skills, elementary grade children often perform about as well as adolescents or adults. But on tasks that require more complex memory skills, their performance is more limited.* When tasks call for recognizing previously learned information, such as vocabulary words or facts about a person or event, or for rehearsing several items for immediate use, elementary grade children can perform about as well as older students. Relatively simple memory processes like recognition or rote repetition approach their maximum levels by this point in cognitive development. But the same is not true for tasks that require such advanced memory processes as elaboration and organization. When asked to sort a set of pictures into categories, for example, elementary grade children create fewer and more idiosyncratic categories (which are generally less effective for later recall of the items in the category) than do older children or

adults. Similarly, fewer than half of a group of ten-year-olds in one study devised a way to help them remember to take a batch of cupcakes out of an oven after thirty minutes had elapsed, whereas 75 percent of a group of fourteen-year-olds did (Kail, 1990).

MIDDLE SCHOOL (GRADES 6, 7, AND 8; ELEVEN, TWELVE, AND THIRTEEN YEARS)

In this section, we use the term *adolescent* for the first time. Although it may strike you as odd to think of eleven- and twelve-year-olds as adolescents, developmental psychologists typically apply this term to individuals as young as ten years of age. The reason they do is that the onset of puberty is taken as the primary characteristic that defines the passage from middle childhood to adolescence (Balk, 1995; Steinberg, 2002). Although a variety of terms are used to denote the initial period of change that marks the adolescent years (ages ten to fourteen), we use two of the more popular: *early adolescent* and *emerging adolescent*.

Physical Characteristics: Middle School

1. *Physical growth tends to be both rapid and uneven.* During the middle school years, the average child will grow 2 to 4 inches per year and gain 8 to 10 pounds per year. But some parts of the body, particularly the hands and feet, grow faster than others. Consequently, middle school children tend to look gangly and clumsy (Steinberg, 2002). Because girls mature more rapidly than boys, their **growth spurt** begins at about age ten and a half, reaches a peak at about age twelve, and is generally complete by age fourteen. The growth spurt for boys begins on average at about age twelve and a half, peaks at about age fourteen, and is generally complete by age sixteen (Dusek, 1996). The result of this timing difference in the growth spurt is that many middle school girls look considerably older than boys of the same age. After the growth spurt, however, the muscles in the average boy's body are larger, as are the heart and lungs (Steinberg, 2002).

    If you notice that students are upset about sudden growth (or lack of it), you might try to help them accept the situation by explaining that things will eventually even out. To reduce the unhappiness that arises from conflicts between

● Girls' growth spurt occurs earlier, and so they look older than boys of same age

JOURNAL ENTRY
Helping Students Adjust to the Growth Spurt

Table 3.4	Applying Theories of Development to the Middle School Years

Psychosocial development: transition from industry vs. inferiority to identity vs. role confusion. Growing independence leads to initial thoughts about identity. There is greater concern about appearance and gender roles than about occupational choice.

Cognitive development: beginning of formal operational thought for some. There is increasing ability to engage in mental manipulations and test hypotheses.

Moral development: transition to morality of cooperation, conventional level. There is increasing willingness to think of rules as flexible mutual agreements; yet "official" rules are still likely to be obeyed out of respect for authority or out of a desire to impress others.

General factors to keep in mind: A growth spurt and puberty influence many aspects of behavior. An abrupt switch occurs (for sixth graders) from being the oldest, biggest, most sophisticated students in elementary school to being the youngest, smallest, least knowledgeable students in middle school. Acceptance by peers is extremely important. Students who do poor schoolwork begin to feel bitter, resentful, and restless. Awareness grows of a need to make personal value decisions regarding dress, premarital sex, and code of ethics.

● Early-maturing boys likely to draw favorable responses

physical attributes and gender roles, you might try to persuade students that being male or female should not in itself determine what a person does.

After reviewing research on early and later maturation, Laurence Steinberg (2002) concludes that differences in physical maturation are likely to produce specific differences in later behavior (see Table 3.5). Because of their more adultlike appearance, **early-maturing boys** are likely to be more popular with peers, have a more positive self-concept, and have more friends among older peers. But friendships with older adolescents put early-maturing boys at greater risk for delinquency, drug and alcohol abuse, truancy, and increased sexual activity. As adults, early maturers were more likely to be responsible, cooperative, self-controlled, conforming, and conventional. **Late-maturing boys,** by contrast, are likely to have relatively lower self-esteem and stronger feelings of inadequacy. But later in adolescence, they show higher levels of intellectual curiosity, exploratory behavior, and social initiative. As adults, late-maturing boys are more impulsive, assertive, insightful, and inventive.

● Late-maturing boys may feel inadequate

Because **early-maturing girls** are taller and heavier than their peers and don't have a thin and "leggy" fashion model look, they are likely to have lower self-esteem and are more likely to suffer from depression, anxiety, eating disorders, and panic attacks. They are more likely to be popular with boys, particularly older boys, and experience more pressure to date and become sexually active than their more normally developing peers. **Late-maturing girls**, whose growth spurt is less abrupt and whose size and appearance more closely reflect the feminine stereotype mentioned, share many of the characteristics (positive self-concept, popular) of the early-maturing boy. Late-maturing girls are more likely to be seen by peers as attractive, sociable, and expressive.

● Early-maturing girls may suffer low self-esteem

● Late-maturing girls likely to be popular and carefree

If late-maturing boys in your classes appear driven to seek attention or inclined to brood about their immaturity, you might try to give them extra opportunities to gain status and self-confidence by succeeding in schoolwork or other nonathletic activities. If you notice that early-maturing girls seem insecure, you might try to bolster their self-esteem by giving them extra attention and by recognizing their achievements.

JOURNAL ENTRY

Helping Early and Late Maturers Cope

2. *Pubertal development is evident in practically all girls and in many boys.* From ages eleven through thirteen, most girls develop sparse pubic and underarm hair and exhibit breast enlargement. In boys, the testes and scrotum begin to grow, and lightly pigmented pubic hair appears (McDevitt & Ormrod, 2002).

Table 3.5	The Impact of Early and Late Maturation	
Maturational Stage	**Characteristics as Adolescents**	**Characteristics as Adults**
Early-maturing boys	Self-confident, high in self-esteem, likely to be chosen as leaders (but leadership tendencies more likely in low-SES boys than in middle-class boys)	Self-confident, responsible, cooperative, sociable. But also rigid, moralistic, humorless, and conforming
Late-maturing boys	Energetic, bouncy, given to attention-getting behavior, not popular, lower aspirations for educational achievement	Impulsive and assertive. But also insightful, perceptive, creatively playful, able to cope with new situations
Early-maturing girls	Not popular or likely to be leaders, indifferent in social situations, lacking in poise (but middle-class girls more confident than those from low-SES groups), more likely to date, smoke, and drink earlier	Self-possessed, self-directed, able to cope, likely to score high in ratings of psychological health
Late-maturing girls	Confident, outgoing, assured, popular, likely to be chosen as leaders	Likely to experience difficulty adapting to stress, likely to score low in ratings of overall psychological health

SOURCES: Hetherington & Parke (1993); Livson & Peskin (1980); Peterson & Taylor (1980); Steinberg (2002).

● Average age of puberty: girls, eleven; boys, fourteen

3. *Concern and curiosity about sex are almost universal, especially among girls.* The average age of puberty for girls in the United States is eleven years (Dusek, 1996); the range is from eight to eighteen years. For boys, the average age of puberty is fourteen years; the range is from ten to eighteen years. Since sexual maturation involves drastic biological and psychological adjustments, children are concerned and curious. It seems obvious that accurate, unemotional answers to questions about sex are desirable. However, for your own protection, you should find out about the sex education policy at your school. Many school districts have formal programs approved by community representatives and led by designated educators. Informal spur-of-the-moment class discussions may create more problems than they solve.

Social Characteristics: Middle School

1. *The development of interpersonal reasoning leads to greater understanding of the feelings of others.* Robert L. Selman (1980) has studied the development of **interpersonal reasoning** in children. Interpersonal reasoning is the ability to understand the relationship between motives and behavior among a group of people. The results of Selman's research are summarized in Table 3.6. The stages outlined there reveal that during the elementary school years, children gradually grasp the fact that a person's overt actions or words do not always reflect inner feelings. They also come to comprehend that a person's reaction to a distressing situation can have many facets. Toward the end of the elementary school years and increasingly during adolescence, children become capable of taking a somewhat detached and analytical view of their own behavior as well as the behavior of others.

Not surprisingly, a child's interpersonal sensitivity and maturity seem to have an impact on relationships with others. Selman (1980) compared the responses of seven- to twelve-year-old boys who were attending schools for children with learning and interpersonal problems with the responses of a matched group of boys attending regular schools. The boys attending special schools were below average for their age in understanding the feelings of others.

JOURNAL ENTRY
Ways to Promote Social Sensitivity

Selman believes that teachers and therapists might be able to aid children who are not as advanced in role-taking skills as their age-mates by helping them become more sensitive to the feelings of others. If an eight-year-old boy is still functioning at the egocentric level, for example, he may fail to interpret the behavior of classmates properly and become a social isolate. Selman describes how

Table 3.6	Stages of Interpersonal Reasoning Described by Selman

Stage 0: egocentric level (about ages four to six). Children do not recognize that other persons may interpret the same social event or course of action differently from the way they do. They do not reflect on the thoughts of self and others. They can label the overtly expressed feelings of others but do not comprehend cause-and-effect relations of social actions.

Stage 1: social information role taking (about ages six to eight). Children are able in limited ways to differentiate between their own interpretations of social interactions and the interpretation of others. But they cannot simultaneously think of their own view and those of others.

Stage 2: self-reflective role taking (about ages eight to ten). Interpersonal relations are interpreted in specific situations whereby each person understands the expectations of the other in that particular context. Children are not yet able to view the two perspectives at once, however.

Stage 3: multiple role taking (about ages ten to twelve). Children become capable of taking a third-person view, which permits them to understand the expectations of themselves and of others in a variety of situations as if they were spectators.

Stage 4: social and conventional system taking (about ages twelve to over fifteen). Each individual involved in a relationship with another understands many of the subtleties of the interactions involved. In addition, a societal perspective begins to develop. That is, actions are judged by how they might influence *all* individuals, not just those who are immediately concerned.

SOURCE: Adapted from discussions in Selman (1980).

one such boy was encouraged to think continually about the reasons behind his social actions and those of others and acquired sufficient social sensitivity to learn to get along with others.

Discussion techniques Selman recommends can be introduced in a natural, rather than a formal, way. If you see a boy react with physical or verbal abuse when jostled by a playmate, for example, you might say, "You know, people don't always intentionally bump into others. Unless you are absolutely sure that someone has hurt you on purpose, it can be a lot pleasanter for all concerned if you don't make a big deal out of it."

2. *The desire to conform reaches a peak during the middle school years.* Early adolescents find it reassuring to dress and behave like others, and they are likely to alter their own opinions to coincide with those of a group. When you encourage student participation in class discussions, you may need to be alert to the tendency for students at these grade levels to be reluctant to voice minority opinions. If you want them to think about controversial issues, it may be preferable to invite them to write their opinions anonymously rather than voice them in front of the rest of the class.

Because early adolescents are often so concerned with receiving social approval from their peers, they may adapt their explanations of school performance to suit this purpose. This tendency was demonstrated by Jaana Juvonen (2000) in a study of fourth, sixth, and eighth graders. These students were asked to imagine that they had received a low score on an important exam and then to indicate how they would explain their performance to teachers and peers. The results may surprise you. The fourth and sixth graders were willing to explain their poor performance to both teachers and peers as being due to low ability rather than to low effort, whereas the eighth graders were much more likely to offer that explanation to their peers than to their teacher. This seems counterintuitive. Why would adolescents want to portray themselves to their peers as being dumb (to put it crudely)? The answer is that ability is seen by many adolescents as something beyond their control (see our account of Carol Dweck's work along this line in the chapter on motivation). They therefore conclude that ascribing poor performance to low ability rather than low effort will result in expressions of sympathy rather than contempt ("It wasn't Matthew's fault that he got a low grade on the last math exam; he just doesn't have a head for numbers").

● Discussion of controversial issues may be difficult because of strong desire to conform to peer norms

pause & reflect

During the middle school years, the peer group becomes the general source for rules of behavior. Why? What advantages and disadvantages does this create?

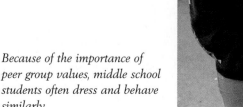

Because of the importance of peer group values, middle school students often dress and behave similarly.

Emotional Characteristics: Middle School

1. *The view of early adolescence as a period of "storm and stress" appears to be an exaggeration.* Starting with G. Stanley Hall, who wrote a pioneering two-volume text on adolescence in 1904, some theorists have described adolescence as a period of turmoil. Feelings of confusion, anxiety, and depression; extreme mood swings; and low levels of self-confidence are felt to be typical of this age group. Some of the reasons cited for this turbulence are rapid changes in height, weight, and body proportions; increases in hormone production; the task of identity formation; increased academic responsibilities; and the development of formal operational reasoning (Jackson & Bosma, 1990; Peterson, 1988; Susman, 1991).

   ● Teenagers experience different degrees of emotional turmoil

   Since the 1970s, however, a number of psychologists have questioned whether turmoil is universal during the emerging adolescent (and later) years (for example, see Jackson & Bosma, 1990; Peterson, 1988; Steinberg & Morris, 2001). Current evidence suggests that although many adolescents have social and emotional problems from time to time and experiment with risky behavior, most do not develop significant social, emotional, or behavioral difficulties. For example, while most adolescents will have been drunk at least once before high school graduation, relatively few will develop drinking problems or allow alcohol to adversely affect their academic or social lives. Those adolescents who do exhibit a consistent pattern of delinquency, substance abuse, and depression are likely to have exhibited these behaviors as children. In other words, problems displayed *during* adolescence are not necessarily problems *of* adolescence (Steinberg & Morris, 2001).

   Some gender differences in psychological adjustment have been documented. Boys who exhibit problems during adolescence are more likely to have had similar problems in childhood, whereas girls are more likely to exhibit problems initially in adolescence. Achievement situations are more likely to produce anxiety responses in boys, whereas girls are more likely to become anxious in interpersonal situations. Finally, girls are more likely than boys to exhibit signs of depression. Although this last gender difference is well established and several explanations for it have been offered (hormonal changes and the prevalence of stressful life events, for example), there is not yet enough evidence to identify the cause or causes with any degree of certainty (Steinberg & Morris, 2001).

2. *As a result of the continued influence of egocentric thought, middle school students are typically self-conscious and self-centered.* Because emerging adolescents are acutely aware of the physical and emotional changes that are taking place within them, they assume that everyone else is just as interested in, and is constantly evaluating, their appearance, feelings, and behavior. Consequently, they are deeply concerned about such matters as what type of clothing to wear for special occasions, with whom they should and should not be seen in public (they should never be seen with their parents at the mall, for example), and how they greet and talk with various people.

   Another manifestation of adolescent egocentrism is the assumption that adults do not, indeed cannot, understand the thoughts and feelings of early adolescence. It's as if the early adolescent believes she is experiencing things no one else has ever experienced before. Hence, a teen or preteen will likely say to a parent, "You just don't know what it feels like to be in love" (Wiles & Bondi, 2001).

Cognitive Characteristics: Middle School

1. *Because of the psychological demands of early adolescence, middle school students need a classroom environment that is open, supportive, and intellectually stimulating.* Early adolescence is an unsettling time for students because of changes in their physical development, social roles, cognitive development, and sexuality. Another source of stress is coping with the transition from the elementary grades to a middle school (which often begins in sixth grade) or junior high (which typically begins

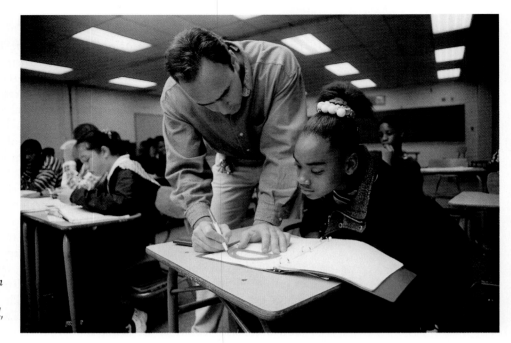

Early adolescents are faced with several developmental challenges. Consequently, middle school teachers should make a special effort to establish a supportive classroom atmosphere in which students can meet their social, emotional, and cognitive needs.

● Environment of middle schools does not meet needs of adolescents, leading to lower levels of learning

in seventh grade). Partly because of these personal and environmental stresses, the self-concept, academic motivation, and achievement levels of adolescents decline, sometimes drastically. Are schools at all to blame for these problems? Perhaps they are. Several researchers (e.g., Clements & Seidman, 2002; Midgley, 2001; Roeser & Lau, 2002; Wigfield & Eccles, 2002a) provide persuasive evidence that these negative changes are due in part, perhaps in large part, to the fact that the typical school environment does not meet the needs of developing adolescents.

Their argument is based on an analysis of the psychological needs of early adolescence and the kinds of changes that take place in classroom organization, instruction, and climate as one moves from the last of the elementary grades to the first of the middle school or junior high grades. Although the typical middle school classroom is much improved in meeting students' needs for a sense of community, acceptance, and belonging (our Case in Print for this chapter describes how several schools accomplish this goal), the environment continues to be largely incompatible with students' intellectual needs (Gentry, Gable, & Rizza, 2002; Midgley, 2001; Midgley, Middleton, Gheen, & Kumar, 2002; Wigfield & Eccles, 2002a). Common problems include these:

- Instead of providing students with opportunities to make decisions about such things as classroom rules, seating arrangements, homework assignments, and time spent on various tasks, teachers impose most of the requirements and limit the choices students can make. In one study, most middle school students (grades 6 through 8) characterized their classroom activities as less interesting and enjoyable, and as providing fewer opportunities for choice, than did students in grades 3 through 5 (Gentry et al., 2002).
- Competition and social comparisons among students are increased as a result of such practices as whole-class instruction, ability grouping, normative grading (also called grading on the curve, a practice we discuss in our chapter on classroom assessment), and public evaluations of one's work. Small-group instruction is infrequent, and individualized instruction almost never occurs.
- Many classroom tasks in middle school or junior high involve low-level seatwork, verbatim recall of information, and little opportunity for discussion or group work. In one study of eleven junior high school science classes, the most frequent activity was copying information from the board or textbook onto

Take a Stand!

Meeting the Intellectual Needs of Middle School Students

Research from developmental and cognitive psychologists paints a consistent picture of middle school students. They can handle more abstract and complex tasks and work more independently of the teacher, and they have strong needs for both autonomy and social contact. Consequently, middle school teachers ought to minimize the use of lecture, independent seatwork, and competition for grades. Instead, teachers should design lessons around constructivist learning principles. For example, teachers should create assignments that relate to the issues and experiences adolescents are familiar with and care about, let students work cooperatively in small groups, provide whatever intellectual and emotional support students need to complete assignments, and foster the perception that the purpose of education is personal growth rather than competition for grades. Teachers who fail to provide this kind of environment may be doing more harm than good.

Do you agree that middle school teaching practices often leave much to be desired? As you consider this issue, check the additional resources available in the Take a Stand! section of the textbook web site, which you can access from **http://education.college.hmco.com/students.**

worksheets. This emphasis on rote learning and recall has unfortunately been intensified in recent years by the growth of statewide learning standards, standardized testing, and accountability. We say "unfortunately" because this type of testing and approach to accountability discourages teachers from using instructional methods that foster meaningful learning.

- Students perceive their relationships with their teachers as being less friendly, supportive, and caring than those in earlier grades.

When middle schools fail to provide students with an intellectually challenging yet emotionally safe classroom environment, one negative consequence is an effect on motivation. Theorists like Carol Dweck describe achievement goals as being either *mastery* or *performance* in nature. Students who subscribe to a mastery goal are primarily interested in understanding ideas and their interrelationships, acquiring new skills, and refining them over time. Students who subscribe to a performance goal are primarily interested in demonstrating their ability to finish first (however that is defined) and avoiding situations where a relative lack of ability would be apparent. Mastery goals have been associated with positive feelings about one's ability, potential, the subject matter, and school, and with the use of effective learning strategies (which we describe in the chapter on information-processing theory).

The most recent evidence suggests that as students move from the elementary grades to the middle grades, there is a shift in their values and practices that leads to more of an emphasis on performance goals. Some researchers blame this change on teaching practices. For example, middle grade teachers are more inclined to post papers and exams with the highest scores, grade on a curve, accord special privileges to high achievers, and remind students of the importance of getting high grades and producing mistake-free papers. Such an environment tells students that meaningful learning is not necessarily expected and that support of learning will not be provided (Midgley, 2001). Students then are motivated to focus on their scores and grades rather than on what they can learn.

2. *Self-efficacy becomes an important influence on intellectual and social behavior.* As we mentioned in point 1 of social characteristics, middle school children become capable of analyzing both their own view of an interpersonal interaction and that of the other person. This newfound analytic ability is also turned inward, resulting in evaluations of one's intellectual and social capabilities. Albert Bandura (1986), a learning theorist whom we will discuss later in the book, coined the term **self-efficacy** to refer to how capable people believe they are at dealing with one type of task or another. Thus, a student may have a very strong sense of self-efficacy for math ("I know I can solve most any algebraic equation"), a moderate degree of self-efficacy for certain athletic activities ("I think I play baseball and basketball about as well as most other kids my age"), and a low sense of self-efficacy for interpersonal relationships ("I'm just no good at making friends").

● Self-efficacy beliefs for academic and social tasks become strong influences on behavior

These self-evaluative beliefs influence what activities students choose and for how long they will persist at a given task, particularly when progress becomes difficult. Students with a moderate to strong sense of self-efficacy will persist at

Case in Print

Middle School Anxieties

Early adolescence is an unsettling time for students because of changes in their physical development, social roles, cognitive development, and sexuality. Another source of stress is coping with the transition from the elementary grades to a middle school (which often begins in sixth grade) or junior high (which typically begins in seventh grade). Partly because of these personal and environmental stresses, the self-concept, academic motivation, and achievement levels of adolescents decline, sometimes drastically. (p. 87–88)

Middle Ground

CAROLYN BOWER
St. Louis Post-Dispatch 5/29/2002

Getting lost. Not being able to open the combination lock to your locker. More homework. Less recess. Taunts from eighth-graders.

Those are among the fears some sixth-graders said they had when they first came to middle school from elementary school.

"Last year you got the advantage of being the oldest, but now you are the youngest," said Sara Klarfeld, a sixth-grader at Parkway Northeast Middle School in Creve Coeur. "Now you have to sit in the front of the bus. After a while you get used to it."

Sara and other students in Peggy Flynn's class recently wrote letters that Flynn will share with students entering sixth grade at Parkway Northeast in August. "I asked my students to give the new students advice about what it takes to survive in the sixth grade," Flynn said.

More than 88 percent of public school students nationwide change schools when they enter sixth grade. Some principals say that transition is one of the biggest of a student's school career.

From having one teacher and one classroom in elementary school, many middle-schoolers will change classes and have several teachers. And it's up to the student to find out what work to make up after an absence.

Flynn said teachers in middle school expect a lot of responsibility, independence and time management—things some students have not had to deal with.

"A comparable situation for an adult is changing jobs after working six years in the same place with the same people," said Jack Berckemeyer, assistant executive director of the National Middle School Association based in Columbus, Ohio.

Earlier this year, the middle school association and the National Association of Elementary School Principals issued a paper urging principals, teachers, and parents to help ease the transition to middle school. Adults can help new middle school students recover that sense of belonging so common in elementary school, the groups said.

"When students feel more comfortable, they are more likely to perform well," said Nathan Bailey, principal at Ladue Middle School. Like principals in many area middle schools, Bailey meets with fifth-graders in the spring to answer their questions and give them a tour.

Triad Middle School Principal Max Pigg said fifth-graders in that district are invited to visit and to share classrooms with sixth-graders. "It seems to ease the anxiety," Pigg said.

In Parkway, at least one Parkway summer school offers a course in how to survive middle school.

Some of Flynn's students could teach that class.

"Future sixth-graders should never give out the combination to the lock on their locker because people will turn it upside down or take things and put them where you can't find them," Michael Holloran said.

Britt Banaszynski advised future sixth-graders to "get to classes on time, have your books and materials so you don't get in trouble."

"Teachers will say something if your shorts are too short or if you wear pajama pants," Claire Latham wrote to future sixth-graders.

Certain supplies are essential. Mike Caraffa, 12, recommends a calculator, a ruler, and "a focused mind."

Alena Armstrong said: "Let those butterflies out of your stomach and take a deep breath. Wish for the best. Be yourself, and don't try to impress others. It's really not that scary."

1. If the middle school years are especially challenging for eleven- to thirteen-year-olds and their parents, then they certainly will be for teachers as well. What characteristics of this age group should you keep uppermost in mind, and what general approaches to instruction should you seek to implement?

2. Peggy Flynn, the sixth-grade teacher mentioned in this article, said that middle school teachers expect students to be more responsible and independent than they were in the elementary grades, yet suggests that some students may have not had much experience or instruction in these capabilities. What steps can you take, as either an elementary grade or a middle school teacher, to help students learn to be more responsible and independent?

3. To find out for yourself what middle school students are like, arrange to visit several middle school classrooms and then interview some students and teachers.

a task long enough to obtain the success or corrective feedback that leads to expectations of future success. Students with a low sense of self-efficacy, however, tend to abandon tasks at the first sign of difficulty, thereby establishing a pattern of failure, low expectations of future success, and task avoidance. Because self-efficacy beliefs grow out of personal performance, observation of other people doing the same thing, and verbal persuasion, you can help students develop strong feelings of self-efficacy by following the suggestions we will make in later chapters about modeling and imitation, learning strategies, and effective forms of instruction.

HIGH SCHOOL (GRADES 9, 10, 11, AND 12; FOURTEEN, FIFTEEN, SIXTEEN, AND SEVENTEEN YEARS)

Physical Characteristics: High School

1. *Most students reach physical maturity, and virtually all attain puberty.* Although almost all girls reach their ultimate height, some boys may continue to grow even after graduation from high school. Tremendous variation exists in height and weight and in rate of maturation. As noted earlier, late-maturing boys seem to have considerable difficulty adjusting to their slower rate of growth. There is

---

Table 3.7	Applying Theories of Development to the High School Years

Psychosocial development: identity vs. role confusion. Concerns arise about gender roles and occupational choice. Different identity statuses become apparent.

Cognitive development: formal operational thought for many students. There is increasing ability to engage in mental manipulations, understand abstractions, and test hypotheses.

Moral development: morality of cooperation, conventional level. There is increasing willingness to think of rules as mutual agreements and to allow for intentions and extenuating circumstances.

General factors to keep in mind: Achievement of sexual maturity has a profound effect on many aspects of behavior. Peer group and reactions of friends are extremely important. There is concern about what will happen after graduation, particularly for students who do not intend to continue their education. Awareness grows of the significance of academic ability and importance of grades for certain career patterns. There is a need to make personal value decisions regarding use of drugs, premarital sex, and code of ethics.

Table 3.8	Trends in Sexual Activity Among High School Students	
	Percentage Who Reported Having Sexual Intercourse	
	1991	**2001**
Gender		
Females	50.8	42.9
Males	57.4	48.5
Grade levels		
Ninth grade	39	34.4
Tenth grade	48.2	40.8
Eleventh grade	62.4	51.9
Twelfth grade	66.7	60.5
Ethnic groups		
African American	81.4	60.8
Hispanic	53.1	48.4
White	50	43.2

SOURCE: Centers for Disease Control (2002a).

still concern about appearance, although it may not be as strong as during the middle school years. Glandular changes leading to acne may be a source of worry and self-consciousness to some students. The most significant glandular change accompanying puberty is arousal of the sex drive.

2. *Many adolescents become sexually active, although the long-term trend is down.* From 1991 through 2001 sexual intercourse among high school students decreased across the board, as shown in Table 3.8. Still, in the latter year, more than 60 percent of students reported having engaged in sexual intercourse by the end of grade 12.

● Factors related to initiation of sexual activity vary by gender, race

The factors that are significantly related to initiation of sexual activity among high school students vary by gender and race. White males and females with low educational goals and below-average grades are more likely to have sexual intercourse at an earlier age as compared with peers who have higher goals and grades. The factors that were most strongly related to initiation of sexual activity for African American female students were having a mother with twelve or more years of education (presumably, mothers with more education spend less time at home caring for their children), spending less time with one's mother, and being uninvolved in church activities. The factors that predicted onset of sexual activity for African American male students were low grade-point average, living in a one-parent family, limited contact with the father, and lack of participation in family decision making. In addition, the onset of sexual activity is associated with subsequent declines in educational goals and achievement and an increased risk of substance abuse (Hallfors et al., 2002; Ramirez-Valles, Zimmerman, & Juarez, 2002; Schvaneveldt, Miller, Berry, & Lee, 2001).

These findings illustrate the pressing need for sex education during the high school years. In particular, adolescents need to understand the distinction between sex and mature love. A major characteristic of mature love is that "the well-being of the other person is just a little bit more important than the well-being of the self" (Gordon & Gilgun, 1987, p. 180).

pause & reflect

What are the advantages and disadvantages of sex education in school? For help with your answer, visit the web sites of the National Campaign to Prevent Teen Pregnancy (**www.teenpregnancy.org/**) and the Sexuality Information and Education Council of the United States (**www.siecus.org/**).

3. *Although the birthrate for unmarried adolescents has fallen in recent years, it remains unacceptably high, as is the rate of sexually transmitted diseases.* From an all-time high in 1957 of 96 births per 1,000 women of ages fifteen to nineteen, the birthrate for this group fell to an all-time low of 49 per 1,000 in 2000. This trend has occurred among teens of all ages and races. Pregnancy rates for teens fifteen to nineteen years old have also declined. In 1990 the pregnancy rate was 117 per 1,000, but it slid to 93 per 1,000 in 1997. This decline is attributed to a combination of increased abstinence and contraception. Even so, pregnancy rates and birthrates in the United States are considerably higher than in Canada and many European countries because American teens are less likely than their Canadian and European counterparts to use contraception (Boonstra, 2002). Among the many factors related to these trends in adolescent sexual behavior, one has clear educational implications: Adolescents who were retained at least once and were behind schedule in their schooling were more likely to have unprotected sex than adolescents who had not been retained (Abma & Sonenstein, 2001).

Because many adolescents are sexually active, there is a strong need for sex education in the schools.

● Parents influence values, plans; peers influence immediate status

The relatively high levels of sexual activity and low levels of regular contraception among adolescents are particularly worrisome because they put adolescents at risk for contracting **sexually transmitted diseases (STDs).** According to one report (Panchaud, Singh, Feivelson, & Darroch, 2000), STDs among adolescents in the United States are considerably more prevalent than in most other developed countries. The rates for syphilis, gonorrhea, and chlamydia, for example, are 6.4 per 100,000 adolescents, 571.8 per 100,000, and 1,138 per 100,000, respectively.

The worst of the STDs is, of course, acquired immune deficiency syndrome (AIDS) because there is no known cure. Although the number of AIDS cases among adolescents is currently low, it will rise in the future, potentially becoming a major problem. The percentage of adolescents who test positive for human immunodeficiency virus (HIV, the viral cause of AIDS) ranges from about 2 percent to 6 percent (MacKay, Fingerhut, & Duran, 2000). Because HIV has a long incubation period, AIDS symptoms may not show up for several years. Consequently, the proportion of today's teens who will be diagnosed with AIDS in their twenties will be more than the 2 percent to 6 percent figure just cited.

Social Characteristics: High School

1. *Parents and other adults are likely to influence long-range plans; peers are likely to influence immediate status.* When adolescents look for models and advice on such social matters as dress, hairstyle, speech patterns, friendships, and leisure activities, the peer group is likely to have the greatest influence (as a visit to any high school will reveal). Peer values can also influence academic performance (Dornbusch & Kaufman, 2001). When the issues are which courses to take in school and what different careers are like, teachers, guidance counselors, and parents are likely to have more influence over decision making than peers. For questions about values, ethics, and future plans, the views of parents are usually sought. The influence of peer groups is strongest during early and middle childhood (Steinberg, 2002).

Not surprisingly, most conflicts between parents and their adolescent children are about such peer-influenced issues as personal appearance, friends, dating, hours, and eating habits (Hill, 1987). This general pattern may be modified, however, by type of parenting style. The adolescents of parents who have an authoritarian style (see Diana Baumrind's work on parenting styles in the section on the cognitive characteristics of preschool and kindergarten children) have a stronger tendency than other adolescents to make decisions that are consistent with peer group advice. The adolescents of parents who have an authoritative style, on the other hand, are more likely to make decisions that are consistent with parental advice (Steinberg & Morris, 2001). Perhaps this is why the influence of parents appears to be greatest when there are mutual affection and respect between parent and child (Baumrind, 1991b; Hill, 1987).

● Girls more likely than boys to experience anxiety about friendships

2. *Girls seem to experience greater anxiety about friendships than boys do.* Factors that cause girls to become concerned about the reactions of others were summarized in the preceding chapter. Adolescent girls tend to seek intimacy in friendships. Boys, in contrast, often stress skills and interests when they form friendships, and their tendencies to be competitive and self-reliant may work against the formation of close relationships with male companions. Because adolescent girls often wish to form an intimate relationship with another girl, they are more likely than boys to experience anxiety, jealousy, and conflicts regarding friendships with same-sex peers. You should not be surprised, therefore, if secondary school girls are much more preoccupied with positive and negative aspects of friendships than boys are (Hardy, Bukowski, & Sippola, 2002; Pleydon, & Schner, 2001; Steinberg, 2002).

3. *Many high school students are employed after school.* During the school months of 1999–2000, 68.2 percent of sixteen-year-olds worked part-time at some point during the school year. For seventeen- and eighteen-year-olds the percentages increased to 78.9 and 84.8, respectively. Some students may have worked for only a week or two, but the average number of weeks worked was 23.4 for sixteen-year-olds, 33.8 for seventeen-year-olds, and 34.2 for eighteen-year-olds (Bureau of Labor Statistics, 2003).

The pros and cons of after-school employment have been vigorously debated. On the positive side, it is thought to enhance self-discipline, a sense of responsibility, self-confidence, and attitudes toward work. On the negative side, part-time employment leaves less time for homework, participation in extracurricular activities, and development of friendships; it may also lead to increased stress, lower grades, and lower career aspirations. Most experts agree that students who work more than 20 hours per week are likely to have lower grades than students who work less or not at all (Steinberg, 2002).

Emotional Characteristics: High School

1. *Many psychiatric disorders either appear or become prominent during adolescence. Included among these are eating disorders, substance abuse, schizophrenia, depression, and suicide.* Eating disorders are much more common in females than in males. *Anorexia nervosa* is an eating disorder characterized by a preoccupation with body weight and food, behavior directed toward losing weight, peculiar patterns of handling food, weight loss, intense fear of gaining weight, and a distorted perception of one's body. This disorder occurs predominantly in females (more than 90 percent of the cases) and usually appears between the ages of fourteen and seventeen (APA, 2000).

Bulimia nervosa is a disorder in which binge eating (uncontrolled rapid eating of large quantities of food over a short period of time), followed by self-induced vomiting, is the predominant behavior. Binges are typically followed by feelings of guilt, depression, self-disgust, and fasting. As with anorexia, over 90 percent of individuals with bulimia are female (APA, 2000).

 How well do you understand adolescent drinking behavior? Try the interactive quiz in the Netlabs section of the textbook web site.

Adolescents who engage in *substance abuse* (tobacco, alcohol, and controlled substances such as marijuana and cocaine) not only jeopardize their physical and emotional health but increase their risk of doing poorly in school or of dropping out of school. A 1999 survey of high school students found that:

• More than one-third reported smoking on one or more of the previous thirty days, and about 17 percent reported smoking on twenty or more of the previous thirty days.

• About one-half reported drinking in the previous thirty days. Twenty-eight percent of female students and 35 percent of male students engaged in binge drinking.

- Forty-seven percent had used marijuana at least once during their lifetime, and 27 percent had used marijuana one or more times in the past thirty days.
- Ten percent reported using some form of cocaine at least once during their lifetime, and 4 percent reported using cocaine in the past thirty days (MacKay et al., 2000).

Schizophrenia, a thinking disorder characterized by illogical and unrealistic thinking, delusions, and hallucinations, is relatively rare among adolescents, affecting less than 0.25 percent of all thirteen- to nineteen-year-olds. Yet it is the most frequently occurring psychotic disorder, and the number of cases diagnosed between the ages of twelve and eighteen is steadily increasing. Early symptoms include odd, unpredictable behavior; difficulty communicating with others; social withdrawal; and rejection by peers (Beiser, Erickson, Fleming, & Iacono, 1993; Conger & Galambos, 1997; Gilberg, 2001).

2. *The most common type of emotional disorder during adolescence is depression.* The most common forms of **depression,** from least to most serious, are *depressed mood, depressive syndrome,* and *clinical depression.* Depressed mood is primarily characterized by feelings of sadness or unhappiness, although emotions such as anxiety, fear, guilt, anger, and contempt are frequently present as well (Peterson et al., 1993). In 2001, 34.5 percent of high school females and 21.6 percent of high school males reported feeling so sad and hopeless almost every day for two or more weeks in a row that they stopped engaging in some usual activities. The percentages of white, African American, and Hispanic students who gave this response were 26.5, 28.8, and 34, respectively (Centers for Disease Control, 2003). As you can see from these data, more girls than boys report having emotional responses indicative of depression, as do minority students, particularly those of Hispanic origin.

● Depression most common among females, minorities

Common symptoms of depression include feelings of worthlessness, crying spells, and suicidal thoughts, threats, and attempts. Additional symptoms are moodiness, social isolation, fatigue, hypochondria, and difficulty in concentrating (Cicchetti & Toth, 1998; Peterson et al., 1993). Depression in adolescents often precedes substance abuse (MacKay et al., 2000). High school students who experience such symptoms typically try to ward off their depression through restless activity or flight to or from others. They may also engage in problem behavior or delinquent acts carried out in ways that make it clear they are appealing for help. (A depressed fifteen-year-old boy may carry out an act of vandalism, for instance, at a time when a school authority or police officer is sure to observe the incident.)

● Depression may be caused by negative cognitive set, learned helplessness, sense of loss

Aaron Beck (1972) suggests that depression consists of a *cognitive set* made up of negative views of oneself, the world, and the future. Martin Seligman (1975) proposes that depression is caused by *learned helplessness,* which leads to feelings of having no control over one's life. Irving Weiner (1975) emphasizes that depression typically involves a *sense of loss* that may have many causes. Depression may stem from the abrupt end of a personal relationship through death, separation, or broken friendship. An individual may undergo a sharp drop in self-esteem as a result of failure or guilt. Or a person may experience a loss of bodily integrity following illness, incapacitation, or disfigurement.

Although many techniques exist for changing a negative self-concept to a positive view of self, one effective approach to minimizing depression is to help as many of your students as possible to experience success as they learn. Techniques to accomplish that goal will be discussed in following chapters of this book.

JOURNAL ENTRY
Helping Students Overcome
Depression

3. *If depression becomes severe, suicide may be contemplated.* In 2001, 19 percent of high school students had seriously considered attempting suicide during the previous twelve months, and 8.8 percent had made one or more attempts. Many more females than males consider attempting suicide (23.6 percent versus 14.2 percent) and make one or more attempts (11.2 percent versus 6.2 percent).

Many high school students, girls in particular, experience periods of depression, loneliness, and anxiety. Because severe depression often precedes a suicide attempt, teachers should refer students they believe to be depressed to the school counselor.

● Depression and unstable family situation place adolescents at risk for suicide

White teens are more likely to consider a suicide attempt, while Hispanic teens are more likely to make an attempt. While the percentage of teens who seriously considered attempting suicide declined from 29 to 19 between 1991 and 2001, the percentage who made one or more attempts rose from 7.3 to 8.8 (Centers for Disease Control, 2003). In 2000, among teens fifteen through nineteen years of age, about 8 per 100,000 actually committed suicide, meaning that suicide accounted for 12 percent of total deaths in that age group—the third-leading cause of death, behind accidental deaths and homicides (Centers for Disease Control, 2002b).

Although the suicide rate for Native Americans is higher than for any other ethnic group, there is considerable variation across tribes. The rate for Navajos is close to the national average (12 per 100,000), while the rate among some Apache tribes is as high as 43 per 100,000 (Garland & Zigler, 1993).

The single most important signal of a youth at risk for suicide is depression. Along with the common symptoms noted earlier under point 2, signs of depression include poor appetite, weight loss, changes in sleeping patterns, difficulty in concentrating, academic problems, poor self-concept, few friends, and feelings of loneliness. These symptoms take on added significance when accompanied by a family history of suicide or parents who commit abuse or use drugs and alcohol excessively. The factors that usually trigger a suicide include a shameful or humiliating experience, such as perceived failure at school or rejection by a romantic partner or parent (Field, Diego, & Sanders, 2001; Perkins & Hartless, 2002).

If you notice that a student in one of your classes seems extremely depressed, take the trouble to ask if there is anything you can do to provide support, and seek the advice of the school counselor. Your interest and sympathy may prevent a suicide attempt. Also, be aware that recent prevention efforts include school-based programs. These programs, which are run by a mental health professional or an educator (or both), are typically directed to high school students, their parents, and their teachers. They usually include a review of suicide statistics, a list of warning signs, a list of community mental health resources and how to contact them, and a discussion of how to refer a student or peer to counseling. Unfortunately, there is as yet too little research to know how effective such programs are in reducing the adolescent suicide rate (Breton et al., 2002; Garland & Zigler, 1993; Gould & Kramer, 2001).

Cognitive Characteristics: High School

1. *High school students become increasingly capable of engaging in formal thought, but they may not use this capability.* These students are more likely than younger students to grasp relationships, mentally plan a course of action before proceeding, and test hypotheses systematically. Without supervision and guidance, however, they may not use such capabilities consistently. Accordingly, you might take advantage of opportunities to show students at these grade levels how they can function as formal thinkers. Call attention to relationships and to ways that previously acquired knowledge can be applied to new situations. Provide specific instruction in techniques of problem solving. (Ways you might do this will be discussed in the chapter on constructivist theory and problem solving.) Although your advice may be ignored by some students, others will probably take it more seriously. Despite the constant attempts of adolescents to appear totally self-sufficient and independent, they still view parents and teachers as knowledgeable authority figures when it comes to school achievement (Amiram, Bar-Tal, Alona, & Peleg, 1990).

● Political thinking becomes more abstract, less authoritarian, more knowledgeable

2. *Between the ages of twelve and sixteen, political thinking becomes more abstract, liberal, and knowledgeable.* Joseph Adelson (1972, 1986) used an interview approach to obtain information about the development of political thought during the adolescent years. At the start of the interviews, the subjects were requested to imagine that one thousand people had ventured to an island in the Pacific for the purpose of establishing a new society. The respondents were then asked to explain how these people might establish a political order; devise a legal system; establish a balance among rights, responsibilities, personal liberty, and the common good; and deal with other problems of public policy.

   The analysis of the interview responses showed no significant gender differences in the understanding of political concepts and no significant differences attributable to intelligence and social class, although brighter students were better able to deal with abstract ideas and upper-class students were less likely to be authoritarian. The most striking and consistent finding was the degree to which the political thinking of the adolescent changed in the years between ages twelve and sixteen. Adelson concluded that the most significant changes were (1) an increase in the ability to deal with such abstractions as freedom of speech, equal justice under law, and the concept of community; (2) a decline in authoritarian views; (3) an increase in the ability to imagine the consequences of current actions; and (4) an increase in political knowledge.

   Increased ability to deal with abstractions is a function of the shift from concrete to formal operational thought. When thirteen-year-olds were asked, "What is the purpose of laws?" a typical answer was, "So people don't steal or kill" (Adelson, 1972, p. 108). A fifteen- or sixteen-year-old, by contrast, was more likely to say, "To ensure safety and enforce the government" (p. 108).

   When considering punishment for crimes, younger children (Piaget's moral realists) hold the conviction that laws are immutable and that punishment should be stern. But by age fourteen and fifteen, the adolescents whom Adelson interviewed were more likely to consider circumstances and individual rights and to recommend rehabilitation rather than punishment.

   If you will be teaching courses in social studies, you may find this information useful in lesson planning. It may also help you understand why students may respond to discussions of political or other abstract matters in different ways.

SELECTING TECHNOLOGIES FOR DIFFERENT AGE LEVELS

As this chapter and the preceding one indicate, your teaching approaches will be influenced by the developmental level of your students. Your incorporation of educational technology will be no different. For kindergarten and primary grade teachers, tools to enhance student literacy are likely to be a priority. Elementary, middle school, and high school teachers will be more interested in tools that promote thinking, problem solving, and communication.

Technology and Literacy

Technology and literacy have always been intertwined. In most societies, spoken language resulted in the development of various media (stone, wood, and paper, for example) with which to record, store, and transmit ideas. As written information became more widely available and as societies became more technological, the need for increasing numbers of literate people grew. With the availability of word processors today, ideas can be swiftly recorded, rearranged, modified, and copied. Writing technologies have emerged during the past three decades to help young children prewrite and rewrite their text, publish their stories, write reactions to stories they have read, and store data banks of words they are learning (Castellani & Jeffs, 2001; Maslin & Nelson, 2002; Sistek-Chandler, 2002). In addition, voice synthesis or feedback allows students to hear how their stories sound, thereby building their phonemic awareness and assisting in the transition from listening and speaking to reading and writing (Forgrave, 2002; MacArthur, 1998a, 1998b). There are also numerous software tools to help children learn such vital reading skills as differentiating phonics sounds and letter blends, sounding out words, and recognizing rhyming patterns.

One computer program for developing literacy skills of young children, Bubble Dialogue, provides an environment resembling a cartoon strip in which young students can create a dialogue between characters (Jones & Selby, 1997). Bubble Dialogue supports dialogue and role play between pairs of students by using "thought" and "speech" bubbles to foster student expression of ideas and interaction. Students work on their writing skills by inserting text into the empty comic strip balloons. The theoretical basis of this tool is Vygotsky's belief, mentioned in the last chapter, that language development needs to take place first in the social world so as to provide a meaningful basis for internalizing the rules of language use. Research by Charoula Angeli and Donald Cunningham (1998) indicates that Bubble Dialogue promotes student articulation of ideas, development of thought processes and word meanings, and acquisition of sentence structure awareness. The Bubble Dialogue software can be downloaded for free from **http://www.dialogbox.org.uk/BubbleDiagogue.htm.**

For quick links to featured web sites, use the Weblinks section of the textbook web site.

Because there is a natural distancing effect in Bubble Dialogue (characters rather than the child do the talking and thinking), this tool is useful for exploring controversial topics and sensitive issues (Eakin, 1997). For instance, it can be used as a therapeutic tool for adopted or foster children as well as those suffering from abuse (Jones & Selby, 1997).

Using Technology to Reduce Egocentrism

As we pointed out in the preceding chapter, primary to elementary grade children are limited by egocentrism in their ability to think logically. Egocentrism, as you may recall, is the inability to understand the world from any perspective but your own. According to Jean Piaget, who first proposed the concept, the main factor that contributes to the decline of egocentrism is exposure to different points of view through social interaction. Because these interactions do not have to be face-to-face, it is quite possible that sharing experiences and points of view by computer may produce the same result.

Judi Harris (1998) notes that World Wide Web networking activities can be structured to foster six different types of interpersonal exchanges:

1. *Keypals.* Students from two or more locations are matched as e-mail pals.
2. *Global classrooms.* Two or more classrooms anywhere in the world study a common topic together.
3. *Electronic "appearances."* Famous people interact with students over a web site, or electronic commemorations of important historical events are staged on the Web.
4. *Telementoring.* In telementoring, as we mentioned in an earlier chapter, subject matter experts use e-mail or the Web to help learners understand a concept or complete a task.
5. *Question-and-answer services.* Web sites such as Ask-a-Geologist provide answers to students' questions.
6. *Impersonation projects.* Participants communicate as someone else, often a famous historical figure.

Kidlink (**www.kidlink.org/**) is a nonprofit organization that helps teachers arrange keypal exchanges. More than a hundred thousand students from over one hundred countries participate in keypal programs arranged through Kidlink. Joyce Burtch, a middle school teacher, has described how she created a keypal program through Kidlink for her students, including three students with moderate neurological and physical impairments (Burtch, 1999).

The Virtual Classroom Program at J. Percy Page High School in Edmonton, Canada, illustrates both the global classroom and the telementoring concepts. Through the use of Canada's high-speed communications network, students from Page High School have participated in real-time videoconferences with students from other parts of Canada as well as Switzerland, Ireland, and Germany on such topics as the global water crisis, technology and privacy, cultural differences and world conflict, and gene technology. During these videoconferences, students at one school make presentations, often accompanied by slide shows or film, and engage in discussion and debate with students from the other school (or schools, since more than two classrooms at a time can participate). In addition, students can listen to and ask questions of prominent professionals from a wide range of disciplines (Andrews & Marshall, 2000).

Effect of Technology on Cognitive and Interpersonal Reasoning

Electronic conferencing, by allowing students to assume roles, can promote the development of interpersonal reasoning. For instance, middle school and high school students who assume the role of famous historical characters on sensitive environmental issues exhibit higher levels of dialogue and interpersonal reasoning than would be expected by Selman's (1980) developmental scheme (Bonk & Sugar, 1998).

Another type of program that allows students to interact electronically with experts and explorers around the world is **adventure learning.** For instance, students from various schools might get together for virtual field trips to places like the Statue of Liberty for insights on immigration policies or the Civil War battlefield at Gettysburg for demonstrations of military tactics (Siegel & Kirkley, 1998). They also might communicate electronically with explorers traversing the Arctic tundra or the Amazon rain forest. While on virtual field trips, students are electronically transported to the actual site to view historical reenactments, listen to experts, ask questions, and electronically correspond with peers across the nation.

Adventure-learning explorations can be incorporated into the problem-based learning (PBL) approach, a technique that promotes formal operational thought by emphasizing real-world problem solving. We discuss PBL in our chapter on approaches to instruction. Two adventure-learning web sites that you might want to take a look at are the Global Online Adventure Learning Site at **www.goals.com/** and ThinkQuest's Ocean AdVENTure site at **library.thinkquest.org/18828/.**

 For reviewing this chapter, try the ACE practice tests and PowerPoint slides on the textbook web site.

Resources for Further Investigation

How Children Develop

Helen Bee and Denise Boyd describe how children develop physically, socially, emotionally, and cognitively in *The Developing Child* (10th ed., 2004). Robert V. Kail does the same in *Children and Their Development* (2nd ed., 2001).

Children's Play Behavior

In *Children, Play, and Development* (3rd ed., 1999), Fergus Hughes discusses the history of play in the Western world; different theories of play; cultural differences in play behaviors; patterns of play among toddlers, preschoolers, school-age children, and adolescents; gender differences in play; and the play behaviors of children with disabilities. Sandra Heidemann and Deborah Hewitt (1992), in *Pathways to Play*, describe the play categories of Mildred Parten and the proper conditions for children's play (such as time, space, and props), give a checklist for observing play behaviors, and explain how to use the results of the checklist for teaching children different play skills.

Cognitive Development

A basic but comprehensive treatment of cognitive development can be found in *Cognitive Development* (4th ed., 2002), by John Flavell, Patricia Miller, and Scott Miller. Specialized treatments of cognitive development in infancy, early childhood, and childhood, as well as atypical cognitive development and models of development, appear in the *Blackwell Handbook of Childhood Cognitive Development* (2002), edited by Usha Goswami.

Teaching the Middle School Grades

Turning Points 2000: Educating Adolescents in the 21st Century (2000), by Anthony W. Jackson and Gayle A. Davis, provides a comprehensive, research-based discussion of the type of school atmosphere and instruction that leads to high-quality outcomes. In *Changing Middle Schools: How to Make Schools Work for Young Adolescents* (1994), Nancy Ames and Edward Miller describe the experiences of four urban Indiana middle schools that were part of a restructuring program called the Middle Grades Improvement Program. Carol Midgley provides specific recommendations for encouraging students to adopt mastery goals rather than performance goals in Chapter Two of *Adolescence and Education* (Vol. 1, 2001).

Several foundations and organizations are committed to helping educators make education in the middle grades more consistent with what is known about the characteristics of early adolescence. For example, the web site of the National Forum to Accelerate Middle-Grades Reform (**www.mgforum. org/**) contains a Schools to Watch page that specifies a set of criteria that middle schools must meet if they are to be judged as having an exemplary program. The page also describes award-winning schools that were judged to have met those criteria.

The web site of MiddleWeb (**www.middleweb.com/**) includes the latest news and updates on middle school reform, as well as a resource page with links about such topics as assessment and evaluation, teaching strategies, parents and the public, student and school life, and teacher professional development.

Characteristics of Adolescence

For a good overall treatment of the major developmental changes that occur during adolescence—biological, cognitive, moral reasoning, self-concept and self-esteem, identity, gender-role socialization, sexuality, vocational choice—consult the sixth edition of *Adolescence* (2002), by Laurence Steinberg.

If you expect to be teaching adolescents, you should read *Puberty, Sexuality, and the Self: Boys and Girls at Adolescence* (1996) by Karin A. Martin. Based on extensive interviews with teenage boys and girls, this highly readable narrative describes the role of puberty and sexuality in teens' self-concept and behavior. In addition to the author's analysis, each chapter contains many interesting and revealing quotes from the interviewees.

In *Adolescent Stress* (1991), edited by Mary Ellen Colten and Susan Gore, fourteen authors discuss such sources of adolescent stress as negative emotions, conflicts with parents, drug use, pregnancy, and abuse at home and how adolescents try to cope with them. Robert D. Ketterlinus and Michael E. Lamb (1994), in *Adolescent Problem Behaviors: Issues and Research*, describe how such factors as sexual behavior, delinquency, risk taking, and childhood victimization give rise to troublesome behaviors among adolescents.

Summary

1. Preschool and kindergarten children are quite active and enjoy physical activity. Their incomplete muscle and motor development limits what they can accomplish on tasks that require fine motor skills, eye-hand coordination, and visual focusing.

2. The social behavior of preschool and kindergarten children is marked by rapidly changing friendships and play groups, a variety of types of play, short quarrels, and a growing awareness of gender roles.

3. Kindergartners openly display their emotions. Anger and jealousy are common.

4. By age four, children are aware of their own mental activity and the fact that others may think about the world differently.

5. Kindergartners like to talk and are reasonably skilled at using language. Preschoolers tend to apply their own rules of grammar. An authoritative approach by parents is more likely to produce competent preschoolers than is an authoritarian, permissive, or rejecting-neglecting approach.

6. Primary grade children exhibit many of the same physical characteristics as preschool and kindergarten children

(high activity level, incomplete muscle and motor development, frequent periods of fatigue). Most accidents occur among third graders because they overestimate their physical skills and underestimate the dangers in their activities.

7. Primary grade children's friendships are typically same sex and are made on a more selective basis than among younger children. Quarrels among peers typically involve verbal arguments, although boys may engage in punching, wrestling, and shoving.

8. Primary grade students are becoming more emotionally sensitive. As a result, they are more easily hurt by criticism, respond strongly to praise, and are more likely to hurt another child's feelings during a quarrel.

9. Primary grade children recognize that fact-based explanations are superior to theory-based explanations and are beginning to realize that their cognitive processes are under their control. They learn best when tasks are relatively short and when less cognitively demanding tasks occasionally follow more cognitively demanding tasks.

10. Elementary grade boys and girls become leaner and stronger and tend to have a gangly look. But some run the risk of becoming overweight because of poor eating habits and lack of exercise. Boys usually outperform girls on such sports-related motor skills as kicking, throwing, catching, running, and jumping, whereas girls often surpass boys on such play-related motor skills as flexibility, balance, and rhythm.

11. The peer group becomes a strong influence on the norms that govern the behavior of elementary grade children.

12. Friendships in the elementary grades become even more selective and gender based than they were in the primary grades.

13. A child's self-image (the combination of self-descriptions, self-concept, and self-esteem) becomes more stable and generalized during the elementary grades. As a result of the decline of egocentric thought and the competitive nature of American society, self-image is based primarily on comparisons with peers.

14. Delinquency occurs more frequently among elementary grade children than at earlier ages and is associated with dysfunctional parent-child relationships and academic failure.

15. The thinking of elementary grade children, although more logical, can be wildly inconsistent and is constrained by the limitations of Piaget's concrete operational stage.

16. Although most children grow rapidly during the middle school years, girls grow more quickly and begin puberty earlier than boys. Early versus late maturation in boys and girls may affect subsequent personality development.

17. The social behavior of middle school children is increasingly influenced by peer group norms and the development of interpersonal reasoning. Children are now capable of understanding why they behave as they do toward others and vice versa.

18. Because the peer group is the primary source for rules of acceptable behavior, conformity and concern about what peers think reach a peak during the middle school years.

19. Although anxiety, worry, and concern about self-esteem, physical appearance, academic success, and acceptance by peers are prominent emotions among many adolescents, some cope with these emotions better than others.

20. Although middle schools are doing a better job of meeting the social and emotional needs of early adolescents than they did in the past, the intellectual needs of these youngsters are still largely unmet.

21. Self-efficacy beliefs, or how competent one feels at carrying out a particular task, begin to stabilize during the middle school years and influence the willingness of students to take on and persist at various academic and social tasks.

22. Physical development during the high school years is marked by physical maturity for most students and by puberty for virtually all. Sexual activity increases.

23. The long-range goals, beliefs, and values of adolescents are likely to be influenced by parents, whereas immediate status is likely to be influenced by peers. Many teens have part-time, after-school employment.

24. Eating disorders, substance abuse, schizophrenia, depression, and suicide are prominent emotional disorders among adolescents. Depression is the most common emotional disorder during adolescence. Depression coupled with an unstable family situation places adolescents at risk for suicide.

25. Cognitively, high school students become increasingly capable of formal operational thought, although they may function at the concrete operational level a good deal of the time. The influence of formal operational reasoning can be seen in political thinking, which becomes more abstract and knowledgeable.

26. Technologies that aid student learning and development are available for every age level, ranging from beginning reading and writing programs for primary and elementary grade children to complex problem-solving and collaborative programs for high school students.

Key Terms

play behavior *(69)*

gender roles *(71)*

theory of mind *(72)*

overgeneralization *(73)*

authoritative parents *(73)*

authoritarian parents *(74)*

permissive parents *(74)*

rejecting-neglecting parents *(74)*

self-description *(80)*

self-esteem *(80)*

self-concept *(80)*

self-image *(80)*

growth spurt *(83)*

early-maturing boys *(84)*

late-maturing boys *(84)*

early-maturing girls *(84)*

late-maturing girls *(84)*

interpersonal reasoning *(85)*

self-efficacy *(89)*

sexually transmitted diseases
(STDs) *(93)*

depression *(95)*

adventure learning *(99)*

KEY POINTS

These key points will help you learn the important information in this chapter. To help you study, they also appear in the margins of the pages, next to the text where they are discussed.

The Nature and Measurement of Intelligence

- Intelligence test scores most closely related to school success, not job success, marital happiness, or life happiness
- IQ scores can change with experience, training
- Intelligence involves more than what intelligence tests measure
- Triarchic theory: part of intelligence is ability to achieve personal goals
- Multiple intelligences theory: intelligence composed of eight distinct forms of intelligence
- Individuals with a high level of a particular intelligence may use it in different ways
- Factors other than high levels of a particular intelligence influence interests, college major, career choice

Using the New Views of Intelligence to Guide Instruction

- Triarchic theory suggests that instruction and assessment should emphasize all types of ability
- Various technology tools may strengthen different intelligences

Learning Styles

- Learning styles are preferences for dealing with intellectual tasks in a particular way

- Impulsive students prefer quick action; reflective students prefer to collect and analyze information before acting
- Field-independent students prefer their own structure; field-dependent students prefer to work within existing structure
- Legislative style prefers to create and plan; executive style prefers to follow explicit rules; judicial style prefers to evaluate and judge
- Teachers should use various instructional methods to engage all styles of learning at one time or another
- Teachers should use various test formats to measure accurately what students with various styles have learned

Gender Differences and Gender Bias

- Boys score higher on tests of visual-spatial ability, math reasoning; girls score higher on tests of memory, language skills
- Gender bias: responding differently to male and female students without having sound educational reasons for doing so
- Gender bias can affect course selection, career choice, and class participation of male and female students
- Academic success, encouragement, models influence women to choose careers in science, math
- Loss of voice: students suppress true beliefs about various topics in the presence of parents, teachers, and classmates of opposite sex
- Females and males have equal access to computers, but small differences exist in how they are used

Sit back for a few minutes, and think about some of your friends and classmates over the past twelve years. Make a list of their physical characteristics (height, weight, visual acuity, and athletic skill, for example), social characteristics (outgoing, reserved, cooperative, sensitive to the needs of others, assertive), emotional characteristics (self-assured, optimistic, pessimistic, egotistical), and intellectual characteristics (methodical, creative, impulsive, good with numbers, terrible at organizing ideas). Now analyze your descriptions in terms of similarities and differences. In all likelihood, they point to many ways in which your friends and classmates have been alike, but to even more ways in which they have differed from one another. Indeed, although human beings share many important characteristics, they also differ from one another in significant ways (and we tend to notice the differences more readily than the similarities).

Now imagine yourself a few years from now, when your job as a teacher is to help every student learn as much as possible despite all the ways in which students differ from one another. By fourth grade, for example, the range of achievement in some classes is greater than four grade levels. Some children's reading or math skills may be at the second-grade level, while other children may be functioning at the sixth-grade level. By sixth grade, about one-third of all children will be working one grade level or more below the average student in class (Biemiller, 1993). In one study of a group of first graders from a suburban school district, the number of words correctly read from a list of one hundred words ranged from 0 to 100. By the middle grades, the least capable students will have read about a hundred thousand words, the average student will have read about one million words, and the most capable students will have read between ten and fifty million words (Roller, 2002).

The variability among any group of students is one reason that teaching is both interesting and challenging. Richard Snow, who has written extensively about individual differences in education, has summarized this challenge as follows:

> At the outset of instruction in any topic, students of any age and in any culture will differ from one another in various intellectual and psychomotor abilities and skills, in both general and specialized prior knowledge, in interests and motives, and in personal styles of thought and work during learning. These differences, in turn, appear directly related to differences in the students' learning progress. (1986, p. 1029)

Although it usually will be essential for you to plan lessons, assignments, and teaching techniques by taking into account typical characteristics, you will also have to expect and make allowances for differences among students. The practice of using different learning materials, instructional tactics, and learning activities with students who vary along such dimensions as intelligence, learning style, gender, ethnicity, and social class is commonly referred to as *differentiated instruction* (see, e.g., Benjamin, 2002; Gregory & Chapman, 2002). The aim is for all students to meet the same goals.

Over the next two chapters, we examine five broad characteristics that distinguish one group of students from another and have a demonstrated effect on learning. In this chapter, we focus on differences in mental ability (usually referred to as *intelligence*), learning styles, and gender. In the next chapter, we explore two related characteristics that are becoming more important every year: cultural and socioeconomic background. Teachers and researchers have demonstrated a strong interest in all five characteristics in recent years, and much has been written about them. ●

THE NATURE AND MEASUREMENT OF INTELLIGENCE

The Origin of Intelligence Testing

 As study aids for this chapter, read the Chapter Themes on the textbook site, accessible from **http:// education. college.hmco .com/students.**

The form and content of contemporary intelligence tests owe much to the pioneering work of French psychologist Alfred Binet. In 1904, Binet was appointed to a commission of experts charged by the minister of public instruction for the Paris school system with figuring out an accurate and objective way of distinguishing between children who could profit from normal classroom instruction and those who required special education. Since the point of this project was to predict degree of future academic success, Binet created a set of questions and tasks that reflected the same cognitive processes as those demanded by everyday classroom activities. Thus, Binet's first scale measured such processes as memory, attention, comprehension, discrimination, and reasoning.

In 1916, Lewis Terman of Stanford University published an extensive revision of Binet's test. This revision, which came to be known as the Stanford-Binet, proved to be extremely popular. One reason for its popularity was that Terman, following the 1912 suggestion of a German psychologist named William Stern, expressed a child's level of performance as a global figure called an intelligence quotient (IQ). Stern's original formula divided a child's mental age, which was determined by performance on the test, by the child's chronological age and multiplied the resulting figure by 100 to eliminate fractional values (Seagoe, 1975).

We have provided this abbreviated history lesson to illustrate two important points:

● Intelligence test scores most closely related to school success, not job success, marital happiness, or life happiness

1. The form and function of contemporary intelligence tests have been directly influenced by the task Binet was given a century ago. Intelligence test items are still selected on the basis of their relationship to school success. Thus, predictions about job success, marital bliss, happiness in life, or anything else made on the basis of an IQ score are attempts to make the test do something for which it was not designed. As some psychologists have pointed out, this type of test might

Individually administered intelligence tests (such as the one shown here) are usually given to determine eligibility for a special class. They were designed to predict, and are moderately good predictors of, academic performance.

Do you want to take a sample intelligence test? Go to the textbook web site (accessible from **http://education.college.hmco .com/students)** and see the Netlabs for this chapter.

better have been called a test of scholastic aptitude or school ability rather than a test of intelligence.

2. Stern and Terman's use of the IQ as a quantitative summary of a child's performance was not endorsed by Binet, who worried that educators would use a summary score as an excuse to ignore or get rid of uninterested or troublesome students. Binet's intent was "to identify in order to help and improve, not to label in order to limit" (Gould, 1981, p. 152).

Later in this section, we will see that Binet's concern was well placed. First, however, we will turn to a more detailed consideration of what intelligence tests do and do not measure.

What Traditional Intelligence Tests Measure

In 1904, British psychologist Charles Spearman noticed that children given a battery of intellectual tests (such as the memory, reasoning, and comprehension tests that Binet and Terman used) showed a strong tendency to rank consistently from test to test: children who scored high (or average or below average) on memory tests tended to score high (or average or below average) on reasoning and comprehension tests. Our use of the words *tendency* and *tended* indicates, of course, that the rankings were not identical. Some children scored well on some tests but performed more poorly on others.

Spearman explained this pattern by saying that intelligence is made up of two types of factors: a general factor (abbreviated as *g*) that affected performance on all intellectual tests and a set of specific factors (abbreviated as *s*) that affected performance on only specific intellectual tests. Spearman ascribed to the *g* factor the tendency for score rankings to remain constant over tests. That the rankings varied somewhat from test to test, he said, resulted from individual differences in specific factors. Not surprisingly, Spearman's explanation is called the *two-factor theory of intelligence*.

When you examine such contemporary intelligence tests as the Stanford-Binet Intelligence Scale IV (Thorndike, Hagen, & Sattler, 1986), the Wechsler Intelligence Scale for Children–IV (Wechsler, 2003), and the Wechsler Adult Intelligence Scale–II (Wechsler, 1997), you will notice that the items in the various subtests differ greatly from one another. They may involve performing mental arithmetic, explaining the meanings of words, describing how two things are alike, repeating a spoken sequence of letters and numbers, reproducing a pictured geometric design with blocks, or selecting from a larger set three pictures that share a common characteristic and form a group. These varied items are included because, despite their apparent differences, they relate strongly to one another and to performance in the classroom. In other words, intelligence tests still reflect Binet's original goal and Spearman's two-factor theory. In practice, the examiner can combine the scores from each subtest into a global index (the IQ score), offer a prediction about the tested individual's degree of academic success for the next year or so, and make some judgments about specific strengths and weaknesses.

Limitations of Intelligence Tests

So where does all this leave us in terms of trying to decide what traditional intelligence tests do and do not measure? Four points seem to be in order:

1. The appraisal of intelligence is limited by the fact that it cannot be measured directly. Our efforts are confined to measuring the overt manifestations (responses to test items) of what is ultimately based on brain function and experience.
2. The intelligence we test is a sample of intellectual capabilities that relate to classroom achievement better than they relate to anything else. That is why, as stated earlier, many psychologists prefer the terms *test of scholastic aptitude* or *test of school ability*.

● IQ scores can change with experience, training

3. Since current research demonstrates that the cognitive abilities measured by intelligence tests can be improved with systematic instruction (Sternberg, 2002a, 2002b, 2003), intelligence test scores should not be viewed as absolute measures of ability. Many people—parents, especially—fail to grasp this fact. An IQ score is not a once-and-for-all judgment of how bright a child is. It is merely an estimate of how successful a child is in handling certain kinds of problems at a particular time on a particular test as compared with other children of the same age.

4. Since IQ tests are designed to predict academic success, anything that enhances classroom performance (such as a wider range of factual information or more effective learning skills) will likely have a positive effect on intelligence test performance. This means that IQ scores are not necessarily permanent. Research on the stability of IQ scores shows that although they do not change significantly for most people, they can change dramatically for given individuals, and changes are most likely to occur among individuals who were first tested as preschoolers (Weinert & Hany, 2003). This last point is often used to support early intervention programs like Head Start and Follow-Through.

Imagine a colleague tells you about one of her students, who has a C+ average and received an IQ score of 92 (low average) on a recent test. Your colleague says that since the student is working up to his ability level, he should not be encouraged to set higher goals because that would only lead to frustration. Your colleague then asks for your opinion. How do you respond?

Because traditional theories of intelligence and their associated IQ tests view intelligence as being composed of a relatively small set of cognitive skills that relate best to academic success, and because the results of such tests are used primarily to place students in special programs, contemporary theorists have proposed broader conceptions of intelligence that have more useful implications for classroom instruction.

Contemporary Views of Intelligence

David Wechsler's Global Capacity View   As David Wechsler (1975) persuasively points out, intelligence is not simply the sum of one's tested abilities. Wechsler defines **intelligence** as the global capacity of the individual to act purposefully, think rationally, and deal effectively with the environment. Given this definition, which many psychologists endorse, an IQ score reflects just one facet of a person's global capacity: the ability to act purposefully, rationally, and effectively on academic tasks in a *classroom* environment. However, people display intelligent behavior in other settings (at work, home, and play, for example), and other characteristics contribute to intelligent behavior (such as persistence, realistic goal setting, the productive use of corrective feedback, creativity, and moral and aesthetic values). A true assessment of intelligence would take into account behavior related to these other settings and characteristics.

● Intelligence involves more than what intelligence tests measure

In fact, recent research (Perkins, Tishman, Ritchhart, Donis, & Andrade, 2000) has shown that in everyday settings, intelligent behavior is related to the ability to recognize occasions that call for various capabilities and the motivation actually to use those capabilities. For example, in a situation that had the potential to become confrontational and hostile, intelligence might involve being open-minded and using a sense of humor. If this sounds to you like a description of the well-known concept of wisdom, Robert Sternberg, a leading intelligence theorist and researcher whose work we describe in the next section, would agree. He defines wisdom as the use of one's abilities for the benefit of oneself and others by either adapting to one's environment, shaping it to better suit one's needs, or selecting a more compatible environment in which to function (Keane & Shaughnessy, 2002).

Assessment of intelligence in everyday settings would be highly subjective and take a great deal of time. That is one reason current intelligence tests assess only a small sample of cognitive abilities. But if recent formulations of intelligence by Robert Sternberg and Howard Gardner become widely accepted, future intelligence tests may be broader in scope than those in use today. Even before such tests are devised, these theories serve a useful purpose by reminding us that intelligence is multifaceted and can be expressed in many ways.

Robert Sternberg's Triarchic Theory Like David Wechsler, Robert Sternberg (2002a, 2002b, 2003) believes that most of the research evidence supports the view that intelligence has many facets, or dimensions, and that traditional mental ability tests measure just a few of these facets. Sternberg's **triarchic theory of intelligence** (which he also refers to as the theory of successful intelligence) has, as its name suggests, three main parts (see Figure 4.1):

- *Practical ability* involves applying knowledge to everyday situations, using knowledge and tools, and seeking relevance.
- *Creative ability* involves inventing, discovering, imagining, and supposing.
- *Analytical ability* involves breaking ideas and products into their component parts, making judgments, evaluating, comparing and contrasting, and critiquing.

Because these abilities need information on which to operate, memory ability underlies each of them (Grigorenko, Jarvin, & Sternberg, 2002).

Sternberg's work is a break with tradition in two respects. First, it includes an aspect of intelligence that has been—and still is—largely overlooked: how people use practical intelligence to adapt to their environment. Second, Sternberg believes that each of these abilities can be improved through instruction and that students learn best when all three are called into play.

● Triarchic theory: part of intelligence is ability to achieve personal goals

In describing the nature of practical intelligence, Sternberg argues that part of what makes an individual intelligent is the ability to achieve personal goals (for example, graduating from high school or college with honors, working for a particular company in a particular capacity, or having a successful marriage). One way to accomplish personal goals is to understand and adapt to the values that govern behavior in a particular setting. For example, if most teachers in a particular school (or executives in a particular company) place a high value on conformity and cooperation, the person who persistently challenges authority, suggests new ideas without being asked, or operates without consulting others will, in all likelihood, receive fewer rewards than those who are more willing to conform and cooperate. According to Sternberg's theory, this person would be less intelligent.

Figure 4.1 The Three Components of Sternberg's Triarchic Theory

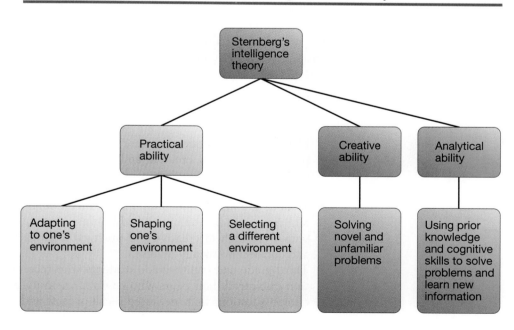

SOURCE: Adapted from Sternberg (1985); Sternberg, Ferrari, Clinkenbeard, & Grigorenko (1996).

Robert Sternberg's theory maintains that intelligence is composed of practical ability, creative ability, and analytical ability.

Where a mismatch exists and the individual cannot adapt to the values of the majority, the intelligent person explores ways to make the values of others more consistent with his own values and skills. An enterprising student may try to convince her teacher, for example, that short-answer questions are better measures of achievement than essay questions or that effort and classroom participation should count just as much toward a grade as test scores. Finally, where all attempts at adapting or attempting to change the views of others fail, the intelligent person seeks out a setting where his behaviors are more consistent with those of others. For instance, many gifted and talented students will seek out private alternative schools where their particular abilities are more highly prized.

Sternberg's basic point is that intelligence should be viewed as a broad characteristic of people that is evidenced not only by how well they answer a particular set of test questions but also by how well they function in different settings. The individual with average test scores who knows how to get people to do what she wants is, in this view, at least as intelligent as the person who scores at the 99th percentile of a science test.

Early evaluations of the triarchic model (Sternberg et al., 1996; Sternberg, Torff, & Grigorenko, 1998) found the following:

- High school students who were taught and tested in a way that matched their profile of analytical, creative, and practical abilities performed significantly better on homework assignments, midterm exams, and final exams than students who were mismatched.
- Most of the high school students who were high in analytical ability were white and from middle- to upper-middle-class homes, whereas most of the students who were high in creative and practical abilities were more racially, ethnically, and socioeconomically diverse.
- Third-grade and eighth-grade students who received triarchically based instruction outscored their peers who received memory-based instruction on multiple-choice questions that measured recall of facts and on open-ended questions that measured analytical, creative, and practical thinking.

More recently, Elena Grigorenko, Linda Jarvin, and Robert Sternberg (2002) conducted three experiments to test the educational applicability of the triarchic theory. In each study, instructional lessons and materials were designed to improve the analytical, creative, and practical thinking skills of middle and high school students as well as their vocabulary and reading comprehension skills. As an example of an analytical task, students read a story about a pioneer family and then drew a family tree diagram to show how the characters were related and a timeline to show when key events occurred. As an example of a creative task, students looked for examples in another story of how the author appealed to the human senses and then tried to describe what one would hear, see, and smell in such settings as a park, a pizza restaurant, and a zoo. As an example of a practical task, after reading a story about a family's Christmas celebration, students discussed all the steps involved in preparing a meal for a large group of people and how you might solve such problems as overcooking the main course.

The first study was done with two sets of inner-city fifth graders in each of two consecutive years. For each group, the study lasted about five months. Half the students in each set were exposed to triarchically based instruction and half were exposed to instruction that emphasized the learning and recall of factual information. Using stories from their basal reader, students in the experimental (triarchic) group completed classroom and homework tasks that emphasized the use of analytical, creative, and practical abilities. Students in the control group completed tasks that emphasized recall. As predicted, the experimental students significantly outscored the control students on tests of vocabulary and reading comprehension skills that tapped analytical, creative, and practical thinking skills as well as on a standardized reading test.

The second study investigated the effect of a six-week triarchic reading program on high-achieving, low-SES, inner-city sixth graders. As in the first study, the triarchic and control groups read passages both in class and at home and answered questions that emphasized analytical, creative, and practical thinking skills. On the posttest, the triarchic group outscored the control group on analytical, creative, and practical measures.

The third study investigated the effect of a six-week triarchic program on inner-city high school students' analytical, creative, and practical vocabulary and comprehension skills. Unlike the second study, which was a standalone reading program, the triarchic instruction in this study was integrated into students' English, social sciences, French, physical sciences, history, and art classes. Although students in the triarchic group scored higher on the vocabulary and comprehension skills posttest, their scores and those of the control group were not significantly different. Despite this one disappointing result, the research to date indicates that triarchically based instruction produces significant gains in students' vocabulary and reading comprehension skills as well as their analytical, creative, and practical thinking skills.

Howard Gardner's Multiple Intelligences Theory   Howard Gardner's conception of intelligence, like Sternberg's, is broader than traditional conceptions. It is different from Sternberg's, however, in that it describes eight separate types of intelligence. Accordingly, Gardner's work is referred to as the **theory of multiple intelligences** (or MI theory). The intelligences that Gardner describes are logical-mathematical, linguistic, musical, spatial, bodily-kinesthetic, interpersonal (understanding of others), intrapersonal (understanding of self), and naturalist (the ability to notice the characteristics that distinguish one plant, mineral, or animal from another and to create useful classification schemes called taxonomies) (Gardner, 1999). Table 4.1 describes each of these intelligences and provides examples of the kind of person who best represents each one.

Because these intelligences are presumed to be independent of one another, an individual would likely exhibit different levels of skill in each of these domains. One student, for example, may show evidence of becoming an outstanding trial lawyer, novelist, or journalist because his linguistic intelligence produces a facility for vividly describing, explaining, or persuading. Another student may be able to manipulate

● Multiple intelligences theory: intelligence composed of eight distinct forms of intelligence

Table 4.1	Gardner's Eight Intelligences	
Intelligence	**Core Components**	**End States**
Logical-mathematical	Sensitivity to, and capacity to discern, logical or numerical patterns; ability to handle long chains of reasoning	Scientist Mathematician
Linguistic	Sensitivity to the sounds, rhythms, and meanings of words; sensitivity to the different functions of language	Poet Journalist
Musical	Abilities to produce and appreciate rhythm, pitch, and timbre; appreciation of the forms of musical expression	Violinist Composer
Spatial	Capacities to perceive the visual-spatial world accurately and to perform transformations on one's initial perceptions	Sculptor Navigator
Bodily-kinesthetic	Abilities to control one's body movements and handle objects skillfully	Dancer Athlete
Interpersonal	Capacities to discern and respond appropriately to the moods, temperaments, motivations, and desires of other people	Therapist Salesperson
Intrapersonal	Access to one's own feelings and the ability to discriminate among them and draw on them to guide behavior; knowledge of one's own strengths, weaknesses, desires, and intelligences	Person with detailed, accurate self-knowledge
Naturalist	Ability to recognize and classify the numerous plants and animals of one's environment and their relationships on a logical, justifiable basis; talent of caring for, taming, and interacting with various living creatures	Botanist Entomologist

SOURCE: Gardner (1999); Gardner & Hatch (1989).

aspects of sound (such as pitch, rhythm, and timbre) to produce musical experiences that people find highly pleasing. And the student who is adept at understanding her own and others' feelings and how those feelings relate to behavior would be exhibiting high intrapersonal and interpersonal intelligence. Like Sternberg's work, Gardner's theory cautions us against focusing on the results of IQ tests to the exclusion of other worthwhile behaviors.

Gardner's MI theory has become extremely popular among educators. As usually happens with such ideas, they are often misinterpreted. A number of misconceptions have arisen:

1. *Misconception: A person who has a strength in a particular intelligence will excel on all tasks within that domain.* Not so. A student with a high level of linguistic intelligence may be quite good at writing insightful essays on various topics but be unable to produce a good poem. Another student may excel at the kind of direct, fact-oriented style of writing that characterizes good newspaper reporting but be limited in her ability to write a long, highly analytical essay.

● Individuals with a high level of a particular intelligence may use it in different ways

   Instead of focusing on how much intelligence students have, we need to attend to the different ways in which students make the most of their intelligences. For example, Thomas Hatch (1997), an associate of Gardner, describes how three children, all of whom were judged to have a high level of interpersonal intelligence, used that ability in different ways. One child was very adept at organizing the classroom activities of his classmates. The second was able to resolve conflicts among his classmates far better than anybody else in that class. The third child shunned leadership and was sometimes excluded from group activities, but excelled at forming friendships among his peers. He was so good at this that he was able to make friends with one of the least popular students in class.

2. *Misconception: Ability is destiny.* If a child exhibits a high level of linguistic intelligence, she will not necessarily choose to major in English or journalism or seek a job as a writer. Not only do intelligences change over time in how they are used, but decisions about a college major and career are influenced by many other factors. The student who wrote such interesting stories as a child may grow

● Factors other than high levels of a particular intelligence influence interests, college major, career choice

Contemporary theories typically view intelligence as being composed of several types of capabilities. Howard Gardner's theory of multiple intelligences, for example, describes several different ways of expressing intelligent behavior.

up to be a college professor who excels at writing journal articles and textbooks or a noted politician or a successful business leader (Hatch, 1997).

3. *Misconception: Every child should be taught every subject in eight different ways in order to develop all of the intelligences.* MI theory does not indicate or even suggest that such a step is necessary in order for learning to occur. In fact, it may be counter-productive if students are turned off by lessons that appear forced and contrived. And as a practical matter, there simply isn't enough time in the day to teach every lesson eight ways (Gardner, 1999; Hatch, 1997).

Although there have been no systematic evaluations to date of Gardner's theory, a fair amount of anecdotal evidence exists. An elementary school in Turkey, for example, has designed its curriculum around MI theory. One part involves "explorato-ries." On Friday afternoons students spend one hour in an area of the classroom where they can engage in an activity that draws on their strongest intelligence. They then spend a second hour in one of five other exploratory areas. Over the course of five weeks they rotate through all of the exploratory areas, thereby developing their weaker intelligences (Saban, 2002).

Karen Rubado (2002), a middle grades alternative school teacher, describes how she used MI theory to improve the self-concept and achievement of students who had failed in regular classes and had given up. Through a variety of activities (such as questionnaires, using each intelligence in practice exercises, clas-sifying school activities according to each intelligence), she helped these students understand that they could be smart in different ways and that, in varying degrees, they possessed all eight intel-ligences. There were noticeable increases in students' motivation, self-esteem, and achievement.

Assuming Robert Sternberg and Howard Gardner are correct in thinking that people can be intelligent in ways other than the traditional analytical, linguistic, and logical-mathematical modes, why do you think schools have been so reluctant to address other abilities?

USING THE NEW VIEWS OF INTELLIGENCE TO GUIDE INSTRUCTION

The various theories of intelligence that were formulated during the first half of the twentieth century are of limited value to educators because they do not allow teach-ers to match instructional approaches and learning assessments to abilities. For ex-ample, because traditional intelligence tests, like the Stanford-Binet or the Wechsler Intelligence Scale for Children–IV, are designed to rank students according to how they score rather than to assess how they think, their basic educational use is to de-termine eligibility for programs for the gifted and talented, learning disabled, and mentally disabled. What sets the theories of Sternberg and Gardner apart is their belief in a broad view of intelligence that can inform instructional practice and improve student performance. As we have shown, the preliminary evidence suggests that these beliefs have merit. What follows are a few illustrations of how you can use their ideas in your classroom.

Sternberg's Triarchic Theory   Based on his triarchic theory, Sternberg proposes a teaching and assessment model (Sternberg, 1996, 1997a; Sternberg, et al., 1996). He suggests that for any grade level and for any subject, teaching and testing can be designed to emphasize the three abilities in his triarchic theory—analytical, creative, and practical—as well as memory. (As we pointed out, although memory is not an explicit part of Sternberg's theory, some memorization of factual information is necessary in any classroom.) To take into account individual differences, instruction and testing should involve all four abilities. At some point, each student has an opportunity to excel because the task and related test match the student's ability. Table 4.2 shows how language arts, mathematics, social studies, and science can be taught so as to emphasize all four of these abilities. Notice that Sternberg does not suggest that *all* instruction and assessment match a student's dominant ability. Some attempts need to be made to strengthen abilities that are relatively weak.

● Triarchic theory suggests that instruction and assessment should emphasize all types of ability

Gardner's Multiple Intelligences Theory   Gardner's general recommendation for applying MI theory in the classroom is essentially the same as Sternberg's. He believes that teachers should use MI theory as a framework for devising alternative ways to teach subject matter. Some children learn a subject best when it is presented in a particular format or emphasizes a particular type of ability, whereas other children learn well when the subject is taught under different conditions (Checkley, 1997).

MI theory should lead to increased transfer of learning to out-of-school settings. Because MI theory helps students mentally represent ideas in multiple ways, they are likely to develop a better understanding of the topic and be able to use that knowledge in everyday life.

Because MI theory stresses different ways of learning and expressing one's understanding, it fits well with the current emphasis on performance assessment (described in the later chapters on assessment and testing). For example, instead of using just multiple-choice questions to measure linguistic competence, teachers can ask students to play the role of newspaper editor and write an editorial in response to a current issue.

As we mentioned earlier, it is a mistake to think that every lesson has to be designed to involve all eight intelligences. But with a little thought, many lessons can be designed to include two or three. For example, a high school algebra teacher combined kinesthetic and logical-mathematical abilities to teach a lesson on graphing. Instead of using in-class paper-and-pencil exercises, this teacher took the students outside to the school's courtyard. Using the large cement pavement squares as a grid and the grooves between the squares as X and Y coordinates, she had the students stand at various junctures and plot their own location. Similarly, as part of a primary grade lesson on birds and their nesting habits, students designed and built birdhouses and then noted whether the birds used them, thereby using spatial, bodily-kinesthetic, and logical-mathematical abilities (Campbell, 1997).

Using Technology to Develop Intelligence

Because contemporary theories view intelligence as being made up of modifiable cognitive skills, you shouldn't be overly surprised that there are technology implications for the development of intelligence. Robert Sternberg (1997c), author of the triarchic theory, expressed that sentiment when he said, "Technology can enable people to better develop their intelligence—no question about it" (p. 13). The following study (Howard, McGee, Shin, & Shia, 2001) provides one example

Table 4.2	Teaching Different Subjects from a Triarchic Perspective			
	Memory	**Analysis**	**Creativity**	**Practicality**
Language arts	Remember the name of Tom Sawyer's aunt.	Compare the personality of Tom Sawyer to that of Huckleberry Finn.	Write a very short story with Tom Sawyer as a character.	Describe how you could use Tom Sawyer's power of persuasion.
Mathematics	Remember the mathematical formula Distance = Rate × Time.	Solve a mathematical word problem using the $D = R \times T$ formula.	Create your own mathematical word problem using the $D = R \times T$ formula.	Show how to use the $D = R \times T$ formula to estimate driving time from one city to another.
Social studies	Remember a list of factors that led up to the U.S. Civil War.	Compare, contrast, and evaluate the arguments of those who supported slavery versus those who opposed it.	Write a page of a journal from the viewpoint of either a Confederate or a Union soldier.	Discuss the applicability of the lessons of the Civil War to countries today.
Science	Name the main types of bacteria.	Analyze the means the immune system uses to fight bacterial infections.	Suggest ways to cope with the increasing immunity bacteria are showing to antibiotic drugs.	Suggest three steps that individuals might take to reduce the chances of bacterial infection.

SOURCE: Adapted from Sternberg (1997a).

of how technology can facilitate certain aspects of intelligence from a triarchic perspective.

Ninth-grade students were administered the Sternberg Triarchic Abilities Test and classified as being relatively stronger either in analytical, creative, or practical thinking. They then learned how to conduct and communicate the results of scientific research by working in groups of three with a computer simulation program called Astronomy Village (modeled after the famous Kitt Peak Observatory in Arizona). To assess both their understanding of the content and their problem-solving ability, students were given scenarios and related questions to answer like the following:

Scenario: You are a member of a research team that has been asked to calculate the distance to a particular star. A famous astronomer has suggested that the star is relatively close to Earth (within 25 light years).

Content comprehension question: Put an X in the boxes next to the five concepts that are most important to finding the distance to that star.

Problem-solving question: You have been asked to meet with the press to discuss how the team will proceed with this research. Assume that the people who will be reading your explanation have little or no knowledge of astronomy. Write your explanation so that it is easy enough for anyone to understand. Make sure you provide specific details of the procedures you will follow to measure the distance. You may want to use drawings to illustrate your thinking.

As expected, students who had relatively strong analytical or practical abilities scored significantly higher on the content comprehension questions than did students who were relatively strong in creative ability. The explanation given by the authors was that analytically oriented students did well because this is the type of question they are most used to seeing in school and have the most success answering. Students high in practical ability did well because the simulation appealed to their preference for real-life tasks. But a different pattern emerged for the problem-solving items. Students who had relatively strong creative or practical ability scored significantly higher on these items than did students who were relatively strong in analytical ability. Presumably, the unfamiliarity of the astronomy problems provided students high in creative ability an opportunity to use this form of thinking. Since students with high practical ability did well on both types of questions, simulation types of computer programs appear to be a particularly good match for them.

Like Robert Sternberg, Howard Gardner believes that technology has a role to play in fostering the development of intelligence (or, from his perspective, intelligences). For example, he notes that computer programs allow students who cannot read music or play an instrument to create musical compositions, and CD-ROMs, videodiscs, and hypermedia can engage several intelligences (Weiss, 2000). **Hypermedia** is a marriage of **multimedia** (a communication format integrating several types of media such as text, graphics, animation, sound, images, and video) and **hypertext** (a system of linking text in a nonlinear way, thereby enabling users to jump from one section of text to another section of the same document or to other documents, often through highlighted words). With hypermedia, the learner can explore facts, concepts, or knowledge domains and immediately traverse to interesting links or appealing presentation formats. Most web sites use hypermedia, and so do computerized encyclopedias and many other types of educational software.

● Various technology tools may strengthen different intelligences

For many educators, technology holds great promise in addressing the MI theory promoted by Gardner (McKenzie, 2002). For instance, web-based conferencing might promote students' interpersonal intelligence. Programs that make it easy to do concept mapping, flowcharting, photo editing, and three-dimensional imaging are closely tied to visual-spatial intelligence (Lach, Little, & Nazzaro, 2003; McKenzie, 2002). Idea generation and prewriting software tools, like Sunbuddy Writer, Imagination Express, and Inspiration, can assist verbal intelligence (Quenneville, 2001). Computer programming with tools like LOGO might help students' problem solving and logical-mathematical intelligence (Gillespie & Beisser, 2001; Suomala & Alajaaski, 2002). Other software addresses musical intelligence (for instance, by enabling students to see musical scores as the notes are played) and bodily-kinesthetic intelligence (by offering a visual breakdown of an athletic skill such as a tennis swing). Clearly, there are technology tools for all the aspects of intelligence that Sternberg and Gardner described.

As a teacher, these tools allow you a great deal of flexibility. With the many options that hypermedia applications offer, you can allow students to choose ways of learning that match their own strongest abilities, or you can have students use software that helps them improve in areas where they are weak.

LEARNING STYLES

Whether one conceives of intelligence as having one major component or several, psychologists agree that it is an *ability*. Typically it is better to have more of an ability than less of it. In recent years, psychologists have also studied how students use their abilities, and this line of research has led to the concept of a learning style. Unlike abilities, styles are value neutral—that is, all styles are adaptive under the right circumstances.

● Learning styles are preferences for dealing with intellectual tasks in a particular way

A **learning style** can be defined as a consistent preference over time and subject matter for perceiving, thinking about, and organizing information in a particular way (Sternberg & Grigorenko, 2001). Some students, for example, prefer to think about the nature of a task, collect relevant information, and formulate a detailed plan before taking any action, while others prefer to run with the first idea they have and see where it leads. Some students prefer to work on several aspects of a task simultaneously, while others prefer to work on one aspect at a time in a logical sequence.

Notice that styles are referred to as *preferences*. They are not fixed modes of behavior that we are locked into. When the situation warrants, we can, at least

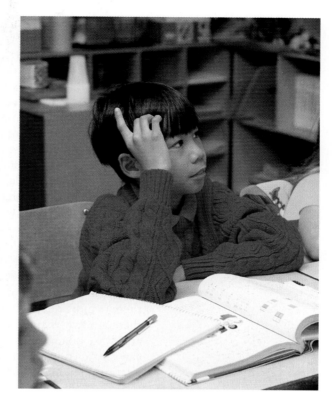

During the elementary years it becomes very apparent that students approach tasks in different ways. This preference for doing things in a particular way is often referred to as a cognitive style. Some students, for example, are impulsive thinkers who tend to react quickly when asked a question; other students are reflective thinkers who prefer to mull over things before answering.

temporarily, adopt different styles, although some people are better than others at switching styles.

In the psychological literature on styles, a distinction is drawn between cognitive styles and learning styles. Because learning style is considered to be the more inclusive concept and because the implications for instruction are the same, we will use the term *learning style* throughout this section. Among the many learning style dimensions that have been investigated, we will examine three. Two of these (reflectivity-impulsivity and field dependence–field independence) were formulated over forty years ago and have a long history of research. The third (mental self-government) is more recent in origin and contains some original elements, but also includes styles that have been the subject of much research.

Reflectivity and Impulsivity

● Impulsive students prefer quick action; reflective students prefer to collect and analyze information before acting

One of the first learning style dimensions to be investigated was reflectivity-impulsivity. During the early 1960s, Jerome Kagan (1964a, 1964b) found that some students seem to be characteristically **impulsive,** whereas others are characteristically **reflective.** Impulsive students are said to have a fast conceptual tempo. When faced with a task for which there is no ready solution or a question for which the answer is uncertain, the impulsive student responds more quickly than students who are more reflective. In problem-solving situations, the impulsive student collects less information, does so less systematically, and gives less thought to various solutions than do more reflective students. Reflective students, in contrast, prefer to spend more time collecting information (which means searching one's memory as well as external sources) and analyzing its relevance to the solution before offering a response (Morgan, 1997).

Kagan discovered that when tests of reading and inductive reasoning were administered in the first and second grades, impulsive students made more errors than reflective students did. He also found that impulsiveness is a general trait; it appears early in a person's life and is consistently revealed in a great variety of situations.

Field Dependence and Field Independence

Another very popular learning style dimension, known as field dependence–field independence, was proposed by Herbert Witkin (Witkin, Moore, Goodenough, & Cox, 1977) and refers to the extent to which a person's perception and thinking about a particular piece of information are influenced by the surrounding context. For example, when some individuals are shown a set of simple geometric figures and asked to locate each one (by outlining it with a pencil) within a larger and more complex display of intersecting lines, those with a **field-dependent style** take significantly longer to respond and identify fewer of the figures than individuals with a **field-independent style**. The former are labeled field dependent because their perception is strongly influenced by the prevailing field. The latter are called field independent because they are more successful in isolating target information despite the fact that it is embedded within a larger and more complex context. As one practical example, individuals who are field independent will probably be better than field-dependent individuals at locating insects that have the same coloration as the surrounding branches and leaves on which they sit.

When we talk about individuals who have a field-dependent style and compare them to individuals who have a field-independent style, we do not mean to imply that there are two distinctly different types of individuals. That is like saying that people are either tall or short. Just as people's heights range over a measured span, students can vary in the extent to which they are field dependent or field independent. In fact, relatively few individuals exhibit a pure field-dependent or field-independent style (Morgan, 1997).

● Field-independent students prefer their own structure; field-dependent students prefer to work within existing structure

In school, the notes that field-dependent students take are more likely to reflect the structure and sequence of ideas as presented by the teacher or textbook author, whereas the notes of field-independent students are more likely to reflect their own ideas about structure and sequence. When reading, field-independent students are more likely than field-dependent students to analyze the structure of the story. The significance of this difference in approach is clearly seen with materials and tasks that are poorly structured. Field-independent students usually perform better in these situations because of their willingness to create a more meaningful structure.

The positive effect of field independence on achievement is particularly noticeable in the sciences because of their emphasis on analyzing objects and ideas into their component parts, reorganizing ideas into new configurations, and identifying potential new uses of that information. Biology students, for example, need to be able to identify tissues, organs, and systems that are difficult to see at first glance because they are embedded in the surrounding tissue of an organism.

In social situations, field-dependent people, in comparison to field-independent people, spend more time looking directly at the faces of others; are more aware of prevailing attitudes, values, and behaviors; prefer to be in the company of other people; and are generally thought of as more tactful, considerate, socially outgoing, and affectionate than field-independent individuals (Fehrenbach, 1994; Morgan, 1997; Witkin et al., 1977). Not surprisingly, in one study kindergarten children gave field-dependent teachers higher ratings than field-independent teachers. They also preferred teachers whose styles matched their own (Saracho, 2001).

Mental Self-Government Styles

Robert Sternberg (1994), whose ideas on intelligence we discussed earlier in this chapter, has proposed an interesting learning style theory that is roughly modeled on the different functions and forms of civil government. Sternberg's **styles of mental self-government** theory describes thirteen styles that fall into one of five categories (functions, forms, levels, scope, and leaning). There are legislative, executive, and judicial functions; monarchic, hierarchic, oligarchic, and anarchic forms; global and local levels; internal and external scopes; and liberal and conservative leanings. Most individuals have a preference for one style within each category.

● Legislative style prefers to create and plan; executive style prefers to follow explicit rules; judicial style prefers to evaluate and judge

In Table 4.3 we briefly describe the main characteristics of each style and suggest an instructional activity consistent with it. If you are wondering how to identify these styles, Sternberg offers a simple solution: Teachers can simply note the type of instruction that various students prefer and the test types on which they perform best.

Evidence that these styles can apply to various cultures comes from Hong Kong, where instructional methods tend to emphasize rote learning and be more regimented than is the case in many U.S. schools. High school students in Hong Kong who expressed a preference for the legislative, liberal, and judicial styles tended to have lower grades than did students who preferred the conservative and executive styles (Zhang & Sternberg, 2001).

Table 4.3	Matching Instructional Activities to Sternberg's Mental Self-Government Styles	
Styles	**Characteristics**	**Instructional Activities**
Legislative	Prefers to formulate rules and plans, imagine possibilities, and create ideas and products.	Require students to design science projects, write stories, imagine how historical figures might have done things differently, organize work groups.
Executive	Prefers to follow rules and guidelines.	Present well-organized lectures, require students to prepare book reports, work out answers to problems.
Judicial	Prefers to compare things and make evaluations about quality, worth, effectiveness.	Require students to compare literary characters, critique an article, evaluate effectiveness of a program.
Monarchic	Prefers to work on one task at a time or to use a particular approach to tasks.	Assign one project, reading assignment, or homework assignment at a time. Allow ample time to complete all aspects of the assignment before assigning another.
Hierarchic	Prefers to have several tasks to work on, deciding which one to do first, second, and so on, and for how long.	Assign several tasks that vary in length, difficulty, and point value and are due at various times over several weeks.
Oligarchic	Prefers to have several tasks to work on, all of which are treated equally.	Assign several tasks that are equivalent in length, difficulty, and point value.
Anarchic	Prefers an unstructured, random approach to learning that is devoid of rules, procedures, or guidelines.	Assign tasks and problems that require non-conventional thinking and methods, self-directed form of study.
Global	Prefers to have an overall view of a task before beginning work.	Require students to scan a reading assignment to identify major topics, create an outline before writing, formulate a plan before beginning a complex task.
Local	Prefers to identify and work on the details of a particular part of a task before moving to another part.	Present a detailed outline or overview of a lecture or project. Require students to identify and interrelate particular details of each part of a reading assignment.
Internal	Prefers to work alone.	Require seatwork, projects, and assignments that do not depend on others for completion.
External	Prefers to work with others.	Assign group projects or reports, encourage study groups, create discussion groups.
Liberal	Prefers to work out own solution to problems.	Assign projects for which students must work out solution procedures. For example, identify and report on proposed legislation that concerns the environment.
Conservative	Prefers to do things according to established procedures.	Assign homework or projects that specify the steps, procedures, or rules for accomplishing the task.

SOURCE: Adapted from Sternberg (1994).

Using Awareness of Learning Styles to Guide Instruction

● Teachers should use various instructional methods to engage all styles of learning at one time or another

Because the typical classroom contains two dozen or more students who collectively exhibit several styles, teachers must be flexible and learn to use a variety of teaching and assessment methods so that at some point, every student's style is addressed (recall our discussion of the teacher-as-artist earlier in the book). An impulsive boy, for example, may disrupt a class discussion by blurting out the first thing that pops into his head, thereby upstaging the reflective types, who are still in the process of formulating more searching answers. To minimize this possibility, you may want to have an informal rotation scheme for recitation or sometimes require that everyone sit and think about a question for two or three minutes before answering. To give the impulsive style its place in the sun, you might schedule speed drills or question-and-answer sessions covering previously learned basic material.

To motivate students with a legislative style, have them describe what might have happened if a famous historical figure had acted differently than he or she did. For example, how might World War II have ended if President Harry Truman had decided *not* to drop the atomic bomb on Japan? To motivate students with a judicial style, have them compare and contrast the literary characters Tom Sawyer (from Mark Twain's novel of the same name) and Holden Caulfield (from J. D. Salinger's novel *Catcher in the Rye*).

● Teachers should use various test formats to measure accurately what students with various styles have learned

When you design your classroom assessments, keep in mind that multiple-choice tests, for example, match up nicely with the executive and conservative styles, while students with a legislative style are more likely to perform better on projects and performances. Try to use a variety of assessment methods on each test and across all the tests given during a term. You may also want to consider letting students choose the type of assessment they prefer. Another reason for using various teaching techniques and testing formats is that it may stimulate students to expand their own repertoire of learning styles (Sternberg, 1994). You might want to peruse Table 4.3 again to review which methods of instruction are most likely to fit which styles.

Using Technology to Accommodate Learning Styles

Just as technology can be used to strengthen different forms of intelligence, so can it target different learning styles. For example, students with an impulsive cognitive style often perform at lower than desirable levels because they don't always follow directions or fully attend to a model's behavior. Although teachers are limited in how much time they can spend reteaching material, computers are not. Consequently, a computer program called VISPRO (for Visualizing Processes) was designed to model the writing of letters and numbers for preschool and kindergarten children who have an impulsive cognitive style. The child clicks on one of several letters at the bottom of the screen, the program draws the letter, and the image remains on the screen for two or three seconds for the child to study. The child then writes the letter on paper using the direction and shape modeled by the program. The child can study the formation of a particular letter as often as desired by simply clicking on its icon at the bottom of the screen (Bornas, Servera, & Llabrés, 1997).

pause & reflect

Analyze yourself in terms of the learning styles discussed in this chapter. Recall classroom situations that made you comfortable because they fit your style(s) and classroom situations where you were uncomfortable because of a mismatch of style. Now imagine the students who will fill your classroom. Should you even try to design your lessons and assessments so they match the styles of most students at least some of the time? If so, how will you do that?

GENDER DIFFERENCES AND GENDER BIAS

At the beginning of this chapter, we asked you to think about the ways in which friends and classmates over the past twelve or so years may have differed from one another. In all likelihood, you thought about how those people differed cognitively, socially, and emotionally. And with good reason. As we have seen so far in this chapter and in preceding ones, students' academic performance is strongly influenced by their cognitive, social, and emotional characteristics. But there is another major characteristic you may have ignored: gender. Although it may not be obvious, there are noticeable differences in the achievement patterns of males and females and in how they are taught. As Myra Sadker and David Sadker (1994) point out, "Sitting in the same classroom, reading the same textbook, listening to the same teacher, boys and girls receive very different educations" (p. 1). Just how different is the subject of the next few sections.

Gender Differences in Cognition and Achievement

Although there are reliable gender differences in cognitive functioning and achievement, they do not always favor one sex. On some tests, boys outscore girls, and on other tests girls have the upper hand (Halpern & LeMay, 2000; Marsh & Yeung, 1998; Royer, Tronsky, Chan, Jackson, & Marchant III, 1999; Wigfield, Battle, Keller, & Eccles, 2002). Although these differences are statistically significant (meaning they are probably not due to chance), they tend to be modest in size—about 10 to 15 percentile ranks.

Males tend to outscore females on the following tests:

● Boys score higher on tests of visual-spatial ability, math reasoning; girls score higher on tests of memory, language skills

- *Visual-spatial ability.* This category includes tests of spatial perception, mental rotation, spatial visualization, and generation and maintenance of a spatial image. Male superiority in visual-spatial ability appears during the preschool years and persists throughout the life span.
- *Mathematical reasoning.* This difference may be related to males' superior visual-spatial skill and, after fourth grade for high-scoring males, faster retrieval of math facts from long-term memory.
- *College entrance.* Tests like the Scholastic Achievement Test (SAT) are designed to predict grade-point average after the freshman year of college. The superiority of males in this category may be related to differences in mathematical reasoning.

Females tend to outscore males on the following tests:

- *Memory.* This is a broad category that includes memory for words from word lists, working memory (the number of pieces of information that one is aware of and that are available for immediate use), name-face associations, first-last name associations, memory for spatial locations, and episodic memory (memories for the events in one's own life). This difference appears to persist throughout the life span.
- *Language use.* This is another broad category that encompasses tests of spelling, reading comprehension, writing, onset of speech, and rate of vocabulary growth. Gender differences in language use appear anywhere between one and five years of age and grow larger over time. For example, the average difference in the size of males' and females' vocabulary at sixteen, twenty, and twenty-four months of age is 13, 51, and 115 words, respectively. On tests of reading comprehension, the gender gap also grows larger over time. By the senior year of high school, girls outscore boys by almost 10 percentile ranks. The superior scores that girls get on tests of writing are due in large part to the fact that their essays are better organized, more grammatically correct, and more logical. It is worth noting that although these writing skills would strike most people as being reflective of intelligence, they are not part of standardized tests of intelligence.

Just as there are gender differences on tests of cognitive skills, there are differences in academic performance. A 1999 study of mathematics achievement among eighth graders in thirty-eight countries concluded that most of the participating countries, including the United States, were making progress toward gender equity in mathematics education, but the study found a few notable differences between the genders (Mullis et al., 2001). Among the major findings were the following:

- In most countries, the mathematics achievement differences between boys and girls were statistically nonsignificant. Boys significantly outscored girls in only four countries: Israel, Czech Republic, Iran, and Tunisia.
- There was, however, a modest overall significant difference in favor of boys.
- A slightly higher percentage of boys had scores above the median (the midpoint of a distribution) and above the 75th percentile.

Why do gender differences in cognition and achievement exist? No one knows for sure, although hormonal differences, differences in brain structure, differences in cognitive processes, and socialization differences are all thought to play a role. Despite increased awareness of how society reinforces gender-role stereotyping and measures taken to ensure greater gender equity, girls and boys continue to receive different messages about what is considered to be appropriate behavior. One source of influence that is being intensively studied is the peer group. During the middle childhood years (roughly ages six through nine), boys and girls are often under more pressure from their peers to exhibit gender-typed behaviors, in order to maintain the group's identity, than they are from their parents. But these observations do not answer the question of causation. Are gender differences the result of social pressures to participate in some activities and not others, or are socialization patterns the result of biological differences, or do both factors play a role? We simply do not know yet.

In addition to gender differences on tests of cognitive skills and in academic performance, there are differences in students' emotional reactions to grades. A study of more than nine hundred fourth-, fifth-, and sixth-grade children (Pomerantz, 2002) showed that the girls on average received higher grades than the boys in language arts, social studies, science, and mathematics. But, somewhat perversely, girls expressed greater worry about academic performance, higher levels of general anxiety, and higher levels of depression. The girls' perceived self-competence was lower than that of the boys for social studies, science, and math. The difference between boys and girls in levels of internal distress was smaller among students who received A's and B's and larger among students who received C's and D's. To put this picture in stark terms, girls achieve higher grades than boys but don't seem to be able to enjoy the fruits of their labors as much. Why this is the case is not clear. One possibility is that girls are more concerned than boys with pleasing teachers and parents. Thus, failure or lower-than-expected achievement is interpreted as disappointing those on whom they depend for approval. Another possibility is that girls are more likely than boys to use academic performance as an indicator of their abilities, spurring them to higher levels of learning as well as higher levels of internal distress because of the possibility of failure. Boys may be better able to maintain higher levels of self-confidence by denying the link between performance and ability.

Although you should be aware of the gender differences we have mentioned and should take steps to try to reduce them, you should also keep the following points in mind. First, there are many tasks for which differences do not exist. Second, some differences do not appear until later in development. For example, boys and girls have similar scores on tests of mathematical problem solving until adolescence, when boys begin to pull ahead. Third, what is true in general is not true of all individuals. Some boys score higher than most girls on tests of language use, and some girls score higher than most boys on tests of mathematical reasoning (Halpern, 1997; Wigfield et al., 2002). Finally, as Robert Sternberg and Howard Gardner have argued, virtually all cognitive skills can be improved to some degree with the aid of well-designed instruction.

Gender Bias

If you asked your class a question and some students answered without waiting to be called on, how do you think you would react? Do you think you would react differently to male students than to female students? Do not be so sure that you would

● Gender bias: responding differently to male and female students without having sound educational reasons for doing so

not. Studies have found that teachers are more willing to listen to and accept the spontaneous answers of male students than female students. Female students are often reminded that they are to raise their hand and be recognized by the teacher before answering. Boys also receive more extensive feedback than do girls, but are punished more severely than girls for the same infraction. These consistent differences in response to male and female students when there is no sound educational reason for doing so are the essence of **gender bias.**

Why do teachers react so differently to males and females? Probably because they are operating from traditional gender-role stereotypes: they expect boys to be more impulsive and unruly and girls to be more orderly and obedient (American Association of University Women, 1999; Matthews, Binkley, Crisp, & Gregg, 1998).

Exposure to gender bias apparently begins early in a child's school life. Most preschool programs stress the importance of following directions and rules (impulse control) and contain many activities that facilitate small-muscle development and language skills. Because girls are typically better than boys in these areas before they go to preschool, the typical preschool experience does not help girls acquire new academically related skills and attitudes. For example, preschool-age girls are usually not as competent as boys at large-motor activities (such as jumping, climbing, throwing, and digging) or investigatory activities (such as turning over rocks or pieces of wood to see what is under them). Lest you think that climbing, digging, and investigating one's environment are trivial behaviors, bear in mind that they are critical to the work of scientists who do field research (for example, botanists, geologists, anthropologists, and oceanographers), occupations in which women are significantly underrepresented. Perhaps the designers of preschool curricula should make a greater effort to include these more male-oriented activities (American Association of University Women, 1999).

Other students can be the source of gender bias as easily as the teacher can be. The authors of one study (Matthews et al., 1998) observed a fifth-grade classroom for four months and made the following observations:

- The class was divided into six small groups to work on ideas for a drug prevention program. Five of the groups chose a boy to deliver their report.
- On another occasion, the students worked in groups to create a machine that would produce both sounds and action. After each group demonstrated its machine, they called on other students to provide a name for it. Boys were called on thirty-one times, while girls were called on thirteen times.
- After a science lab, a girl complained that the boys said that the way in which the girls were weighing items and comparing the weights was wrong. Another girl remarked that the boys did not want the girls to touch any of the equipment. On hearing this, one of the boys said that he thought the girls might drop or damage something.
- Boys were more likely than girls to name a boy as the best student in mathematics and science, while the girls usually named a girl as the best in English.
- Boys usually named another boy as the one who contributed most to class discussions, while girls named both boys and girls.

How Gender Bias Affects Students

● Gender bias can affect course selection, career choice, and class participation of male and female students

Gender bias can affect students in at least three ways: the courses they choose to take, the careers they consider, and the extent to which they participate in class activities and discussions.

Course Selection   There are modest but noticeable differences in the percentage of high school boys and girls who take math and science courses. In 1998, a larger percentage of girls than boys took algebra II (63.7 versus 59.8 percent) and trigonometry (9.7 versus 8.2 percent). Although there was no difference in the percentages of boys and girls who took geometry and precalculus, slightly more boys than girls took calculus (11.2 versus 10.6 percent). The pattern for science courses was similar. A larger percentage of girls than boys took biology (94.1 versus 91.4 percent), Advanced Placement or honors biology (18 versus 14.5 percent), and chemistry (63.5 versus 57.1 percent), while more boys than girls took physics (31.7 versus 26.2 percent) and engineering (7.1 versus 6.5 percent) (Bae, Choy, Geddes, Sable, & Snyder, 2000).

Career Choice   As you may be aware because of numerous stories in the media, relatively few girls choose careers in science or mathematics. As of 1998, a much smaller percentage of women than men held positions in such math- and science-oriented professions as chemistry and biological science (about 31 percent), engineering (about 18 percent), computer systems analyst (about 27 percent), and drafting/surveying/mapping (about 17 percent). On the other hand, a much greater percentage of women than men were found in such nonmath and nonscience fields as educational administration (63 percent), educational and vocational counseling (69 percent), social work (68 percent), and public relations (68 percent) (Wigfield et al., 2002).

Can you recall any instances of gender bias from teachers or friends? If so, do you think it had any effect on your choice of career?

Several factors are thought to influence the choice male and female students make to pursue a career in science or engineering. One is familiarity with and interest in the tools of science. In one study of middle school science classes that emphasized hands-on experiences by instructors who were committed to increasing girls' active participation, gender differences were noted. Boys spent more time than girls manipulating the equipment, thereby forcing girls to participate in more passive ways (Jovanovic & King, 1998).

A second factor is perceived self-efficacy (how confident one feels in being able to meet the demands of a task). In the middle school science classes just mentioned (Jovanovic & King, 1998), even though end-of-year science grades were equal for girls and boys, only girls showed a significant decrease in their perception of their science ability over the school year. A 1996 survey found that although fourth-grade boys and girls were equally confident about their math abilities, by twelfth grade only 47 percent of girls were confident about their math skills as compared to 59 percent of the boys (Bae et al., 2000).

A third factor is the competence-related beliefs and expectations communicated by parents and teachers. Girls who believe they have the ability to succeed in male-dominated fields were encouraged to adopt these beliefs by parents and teachers (Wigfield et al., 2002). The Case in Print describes how one school district is trying to interest more girls in computer science and related careers.

Supporting evidence that factors such as self-efficacy influence career choice comes from a recent study of fifteen women with established careers in math, science, or technology. Because there have always been women who have successfully carved out careers in math or science, Amy Zeldin and Frank Pajares (2000) wanted to know what sets them apart from equally qualified women who choose other fields. Zeldin and Pajares found that these fifteen women had very high levels of self-efficacy for math and science that could be traced to three sources: (1) early and consistent academic success, (2) encouragement to pursue math and science careers from such influential others as parents and teachers, and (3) the availability of respected models (both male and female) whom they could observe and model themselves after. All three sources working in concert appear necessary to persuade women to consider a career in math, science, or technology.

● Academic success, encouragement, models influence women to choose careers in science, math

Class Participation   As we pointed out earlier, many children tend to adopt the gender role that society portrays as the more appropriate and acceptable. Through the influence of parenting practices, advertising, peer norms, textbooks, and teaching practices, girls are reinforced for being polite, helpful, obedient, nonassertive, quiet,

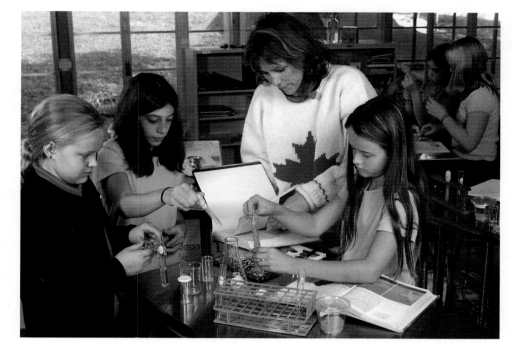

Women who choose a career in math or science are likely to be those who do well in science classes, are encouraged to pursue math or science careers by parents or teachers, and have respected models available to emulate.

● Loss of voice: students suppress true beliefs about various topics in the presence of parents, teachers, and classmates of opposite sex

and aware of and responsive to the needs of others. Boys are reinforced for being assertive, independent, aggressive, competitive, intellectually curious, and achievement oriented. When females look at the world around them, they see relatively few women in positions of power and influence, relatively few women interviewed by the media for their opinion or expertise on various issues, and boys either ignoring or not taking seriously the suggestions and opinions offered by girls. The result, according to Carol Gilligan and others, is that adolescent girls learn to suppress their true personality and beliefs. Instead of saying what they really think about a topic, they say either that they have no opinion or what they think others want to hear. Gilligan refers to this behavior as **loss of voice** (Harter, Waters, & Whitesell, 1997).

To measure the extent of loss of voice in different contexts, Susan Harter, Patricia Waters, and Nancy Whitesell gave questionnaires to several hundred students of both genders in grades 6 through 12. The questionnaire items asked students to rate how honestly they voiced their ideas when they were in the presence of teachers, male classmates, female classmates, parents, and close friends. Their main findings were as follows:

- Males and females are most likely to speak their mind when they are with close friends and classmates of the same gender and are less likely to do so when they are in the presence of members of the opposite gender, parents, and teachers.
- Loss of voice did not increase between grades 6 and 12.
- Equal numbers of males and females reported suppressing their true thoughts in certain circumstances.
- Girls who strongly identified with the stereotypical female gender role were more likely than androgynous females (those who exhibit behaviors that are characteristic of both gender roles) to suppress their true thoughts when interacting with their teachers and male classmates. This difference between feminine and androgynous females disappeared with close friends and parents.
- Androgynous males and females who said they were frequently encouraged and supported by teachers for expressing their views were most likely to speak their mind in classroom and other settings.

These findings have major implications for the way in which teachers address female students, particularly those who have adopted a strong feminine gender role,

Case in Print

Correcting Gender Bias

Gender bias can affect students in at least three ways: the courses they choose to take, the careers they consider, and the extent to which they participate in class activities and discussions. . . . As you may be aware because of numerous stories in the media, relatively few girls choose careers in science or mathematics. . . . Several factors are thought to influence the choice male and female students make to pursue a career in science or engineering. One is familiarity with and interest in the tools of science. (p. 121–122)

Girl-Powered

CAROLYN BOWER
St. Louis Post-Dispatch 12/1/2000

Eighteen girls meet once a week at Sappington Elementary School, just west of Grant's Farm in southwest St. Louis County, to discuss binary codes, circuits and computer chips.

The girls, all fifth-graders, come from public and parochial schools throughout the Lindbergh School District. One recent afternoon, they took apart six computers and put them back together, installing CD-ROMs, sound cards and network cards. In a few weeks, they plan to assemble more computers. Then they'll begin to design web pages.

Laurice Badino, a gifted-education teacher at Sappington, 11011 Gravois Road, began the after-school class this fall as a way to interest girls in technology and computer science.

"With such a focus on technology in our world and in schools, you would think girls would continue to pursue this as they get older, but they don't," Badino said.

Federal statistics indicate that women hold only 28 percent of technical jobs, even though the number of women in the work force approaches 50 percent. Less than one in every five people who took Advanced Placement computer science tests last year was a woman. Women also made up less than a third of workers in computer and math jobs, according to the U.S. Bureau of Labor Statistics. Yet information technology jobs are among the fastest-growing occupations.

Badino has taught off and on for twenty years, the past four in the Lindbergh district.

At a recent class, she instructed the girls to hook up power supplies to hard drives. "It only goes in one way, so don't force it," Badino said.

The girls worked in teams of two or three to a computer.

Riley Krus, ten, had come to the class from St. Justin the Martyr School, where she attends fifth grade.

"Two weeks ago, we learned about binary boards and ASCII," she said. "They're both fun."

Students have learned to format hard drives and discs. They also learned about components of circuits, such as microprocessors, capacitors and light-emitting diodes. They learned that an example of a light-emitting diode is when a light signals the use of a computer hard drive.

At the other end of a table from Riley, Ariana Black, ten, a fifth-grader at Truman Elementary School, used a screwdriver and easily installed a CD-ROM in the computer. But Ariana cautioned she was not quite ready to take apart her home computer, which runs Windows 98.

Lindbergh school Superintendent James Sandfort said the girls' focus, concentration and technical skill impressed him.

"We hope that as these girls move up through the grades, they will move toward technical programs rather than away from them," Sandfort said. "When my computer shuts down, I know where to bring it now. These girls have no fear."

Badino would like to see some of her students become CEOs of computer companies some day—or at least be open to taking computer courses in high school and college.

"Now they can tell the boys how things work," Badino said.

Kara Jacquin, eleven, who also attends Truman, said she was intrigued by how the separate parts of a computer flow together.

"I wouldn't mind being smarter than the boys," Kara added.

Questions and Activities

1. This article describes several environmental influences on learning and classroom behavior and at least one innate factor. List these various influences and factors. Then describe how they might interact with one another to affect your students' learning differently depending on their gender. Is your description consistent with your own experience as a student? Why or why not?

2. The program described in this article indicates that girls can be successful at and enjoy science and technology activities if certain classroom conditions are established. Is a girls-only program the only way to meet this goal? If not, is it the best way? On what evidence or experience (or both) do you base your conclusion?

3. Kara Jacquin, the eleven-year-old girl quoted at the end of the article, said that she "wouldn't mind being smarter than the boys." Why do you think she, and presumably many of the other girls in her class, believe that boys are smarter than girls with respect to computer science? In addition to programs like the one described in this article, what other ideas can you come up with to ensure that girls think of themselves as equal in ability to boys in math and science?

Take a Stand!

Eliminate Gender Bias

Gender bias, or treating male students differently from female students when such differences are neither warranted nor desirable, should have no place in any teacher's classroom. Because such biases are typically based on stereotypes and prejudices (the type of nonsystematic data we criticized in the book's opening chapter), they are likely to have the negative impact on students' attitudes toward school, motivation for learning, classroom participation, course selection, and career choice that researchers have documented.

One way to avoid this undesirable practice is to think about the normally unconscious assumptions you make about the capabilities, motives, and interests of males and females, perhaps because of your own socialization. And when students, colleagues, or parents make broad-based, stereotypical statements like "Girls aren't interested in electronics" or "Boys don't like to display their emotions," respond by saying, "Oh, which girl [or boy]?" to get across the point that any given individual can deviate from whatever average trends might exist.

Do you believe that all teachers need to take specific steps to combat gender stereotypes? Look into the additional resources on this issue at the Take a Stand! section of the textbook web site.

and for the use of constructivist approaches to teaching (discussed in detail in the chapter "Approaches to Instruction"). Because constructivism relies heavily on free and open discussion to produce its effects, teachers need to monitor carefully the verbal exchanges that occur among students and to intervene when necessary to ensure that all students feel that their opinions are getting a fair and respectful hearing.

Working Toward Gender Equity in the Classroom

Although much of the literature on gender bias highlights the classroom obstacles that make it difficult for girls to take full advantage of their talents, gender equity is about producing an educational experience that will be equally meaningful for students of both genders. Several authors (Bailey, 1996; Jobe, 2002/2003; Taylor & Lorimer, 2002/2003) suggest the following techniques to benefit both genders:

1. Use work arrangements and reward systems that will encourage all students to value a thorough understanding of a subject or task and that emphasize group success as well as individual accomplishment. In the chapter "Approaches to Instruction," we will describe how a technique called cooperative learning does just this.
2. Emphasize concrete, hands-on science, math, and technology activities.
3. Incorporate math, science, and technology concepts into such other subjects as music, history, art, and social studies.
4. Talk about the practical, everyday applications of math and science. Although girls seem more interested in science when they understand how such knowl-

edge transfers to everyday life, so do many boys. Nobody suffers when the curriculum is made more meaningful and relevant.

5. Emphasize materials that highlight the accomplishments and characteristics of women (such as Hillary Rodham Clinton, Oprah Winfrey, and Sandra Day O'Connor) and women's groups.

6. From the titles listed on the web site **www.guysread.com,** create a reading list that appeals to boys.

Charles Rop (1998) describes how Anna Kasov, a veteran high school teacher, teaches introductory chemistry. In high school and college, Kasov found science to be a male-dominated profession that did not go out of its way to make women students feel comfortable or accepted. Consequently, her goal as a teacher is to combat the message that chemistry is not women's work and that interesting women are not scientists by creating a supportive atmosphere in her classroom. To accomplish her goal, Kasov (1) models how scientists think (formulate hypotheses about chemical processes, conduct experiments, use that evidence to support your hypotheses) and encourages students to do the same, (2) requires that students treat each others' ideas with respect, and (3) attends to how frequently girls and boys contribute to class discussions and to the nature of the contributions.

As Kasov and others have pointed out, science becomes more interesting for all students, but for girls in particular, when they understand its relevance. The following quotation from Kasov about her own college experience is instructive:

> One of the things that I vividly remember is sitting in this lecture going through these biochemical cycles. I wondered where this happens—in the cell, in the nucleus, in the mitochondria? The guy didn't even bother to tell us. We were counting ATPs somewhere and I thought, "This is so stupid. I have no idea what this has to do with anything." (p. 60)

Consequently, Kasov recommends giving girls opportunities to manipulate technology, deemphasizing competition in favor of collaborative problem solving, showing how the products of chemical research affect the everyday lives of people, and integrating chemical concepts with other subjects, such as history, literature, and the arts.

Gender Differences and Technology: Overcoming the Gap

In the 1980s, when desktop computers first started appearing in classrooms, surveys showed that females were less likely than males to use a computer at both school and home. That difference has now disappeared. A 2001 national survey of children and adolescents between the ages of five and seventeen found that about 80 percent of males and females reported using a computer at school and about 65 percent of both sexes reported using a computer at home (DeBell & Chapman, 2003).

Although there is no overall difference between males and females in computer use, small gender differences still exist for the ways in which computers are used. Among students who actually use computers at home, more females than males use computers for word processing (52.8 versus 46.8 percent), e-mail (55 versus 50.5 percent), and to complete school assignments (69.2 versus 66.5 percent). The largest difference in favor of the males was for the category of playing games (92.7 versus 88.8 percent) (DeBell & Chapman, 2003).

Males are also more likely to have appropriate computer-using role models than females, for at least two reasons. First, female teachers express less confidence in using computers in the classroom than do male teachers. Second, about 80 percent of computer coordinators at the secondary level are men. In the primary and elementary grades, about 75 percent of computer coordinators are women (Volman & van Eck, 2001).

● Females and males have equal access to computers, but small differences exist in how they are used

What can be done to continue reducing the gender gap? Several steps have been recommended (Duff, 2000; Gipson, 1997; Koch, 1994; Nicholson et al., 1998; Sanders, 1985):

- Because the research literature indicates that early positive experiences with computers are central to later success, teachers' attitudes and actions must demonstrate that the computer is equally important to both genders.
- As computer technology expands in schools, teachers and administrators should try to embed it in reading, writing, history, and literature curricula, not just in math and science.
- Girls need more role models of female computer users in their schools and the workplace.
- Schools should establish a telementoring program that puts female students in touch with women professionals, especially in occupations where women are underrepresented. Carole Duff (2000) describes how Ursuline Academy, a private high school in Dallas, Texas, created and runs just such a program.
- Parents may need training in raising their mathematical and technological expectations of their female children, as well as advice on the role of computer technology in the home.
- Some scholars recommend computer camps, programs, and classes just for girls to interest them in science and technology careers.
- Because males tend to dominate open computer workstations during free choice time, teachers might increase access time or require turn-taking practices on the computer.
- Schools and teachers need to establish policies on software, thereby avoiding purchase of the more violent and insulting or demeaning products. They might choose to select new software games with female main characters and computer tools that appeal to girls.

The Suggestions for Teaching that follow will help you better respond to differences in intelligence, learning styles, and gender.

Suggestions for Teaching in Your Classroom

Addressing Student Differences

1 Design lessons and test items that call for memory, analytical, creative, and practical abilities

Robert Sternberg (1997a) has pointed out that many teachers tend to emphasize memory and analytical abilities, which is fine for students who are good at memorizing facts or breaking things down into their component parts and explaining how the parts relate to each other. But students whose abilities are in the creative or practical areas may appear to be less capable than they really are. You can get a better idea of each student's strengths and weaknesses and how well students have learned the subject matter you just taught by using a variety of instructional cues and test items.

To emphasize students' memory abilities when you teach and test, use prompts such as:

"Who said . . . ?"
"Summarize the ideas of . . ."
"Who did . . . ?"
"When did . . . ?"
"How did . . . ?"
"Describe . . ."

To emphasize students' analytical abilities, use prompts like:

"Why in your judgment . . . ?"
"Explain why . . ."
"Explain what caused . . ."
"Critique . . ."

To emphasize creative abilities, use prompts like:

"Imagine . . ."
"Design . . ."
"Suppose that . . ."
"What would happen if . . . ?"

To emphasize practical thinking, ask students to:

"Show how you can use . . ."
"Implement . . ."
"Demonstrate how in the real world . . ."

JOURNAL ENTRY
Encouraging the Development of
Multiple Intelligences

2 Design lessons that emphasize different intelligences.

As Howard Gardner and others point out, most of the tasks that we ask students to master reflect the linguistic and logical-mathematical forms of intelligence. But there are other ways that students can come to know things and demonstrate what they have learned. Potentially, lesson plans for any subject can be designed that incorporate each of Gardner's eight intelligences. Here are a few examples suggested by Thomas Armstrong (1994) and David Lazear (1992).

Elementary Grades: Punctuation Marks

Bodily-kinesthetic: Students use their bodies to mimic the shape of various punctuation marks.

Musical: Students make up different sounds or songs for each punctuation mark.

Interpersonal: In small groups of four to six, students teach and test one another on proper punctuation usage.

Middle School Grades: American History

Linguistic: Students debate the pros and cons of key historical decisions (such as Abraham Lincoln's decision to use military force to prevent the Confederate states from seceding from the Union, the Supreme Court decision in *Plessy v. Ferguson* that allowed separate facilities for African Americans and whites, or President Harry Truman's decision to drop the atomic bomb on Japan).

Musical: Students learn about and sing some of the songs that were popular at a particular point in the country's history.

Spatial: Students draw murals that tell the story of a historical period.

High School Grades: Boyle's Law (Physics)

Logical-mathematical: Students solve problems that require the use of Boyle's law: for a fixed mass and temperature of gas, the pressure is inversely proportional to the volume, or $P \times V = K$.

Bodily-kinesthetic: Students breathe air into their mouths, move it to one side of their mouths (so that one cheek is puffed out), indicate whether the pressure goes up or down, distribute it to both sides of their mouths, and indicate again whether the pressure goes up or down.

Intrapersonal: Students describe times in their lives when they felt they were either under a lot of psychological pressure or little pressure and whether they felt as if they had either a lot of or a little psychological space.

3 **Recognize that different styles of learning call for different methods of instruction.**

JOURNAL ENTRY
Allowing for Differences in Cognitive Style

Robert Sternberg's work on styles of mental self-government calls for the same approach to instruction and testing as does his work on intellectual abilities: use a variety of instructional methods and testing formats. Not only will you have a more accurate picture of what students know, but you will be helping them learn how to shift styles to adapt to changing conditions. For example, students with a judicial style have a preference for "why" questions (for example, Why did the United States go to war with Iraq in 2003?), whereas students with a legislative style have a preference for "suppose" or "what if" questions (for example, If you were President George W. Bush, would you have gone to war with Iraq?). Table 4.3 indicates which of Sternberg's learning styles are most compatible with particular methods of instruction.

4 **Help students become aware of the existence of gender bias.**

JOURNAL ENTRY
Taking Steps to Eliminate Gender Bias

The following techniques have all been used by teachers to demonstrate that males often receive preferential treatment in our society in somewhat subtle ways (Bailey, 1996; Rop, 1998; Rutledge, 1997):

- Have students count how often in the space of a month male and female athletes are mentioned in the sports section of the local paper, and have the students create a graph depicting the difference.
- Have students survey similar-aged friends and classmates about the size of their allowance and report the results by gender.
- Have students review several textbooks and record how often men and women are mentioned.
- Have students keep a record of who participates in class discussions, how often they speak, for how long, and how they respond to comments made by male versus female classmates.

5 **Encourage girls to consider pursuing a career in science.**

JOURNAL ENTRY
Encouraging Girls to Excel in Math and Science

Anna Kasov, the high school chemistry teacher we mentioned earlier, offers the following suggestions to teachers interested in encouraging adolescent girls to consider a career in science:

- Invite female scientists to class to talk about science as a career, or arrange for an electronic exchange through e-mail.
- Have students read articles written by female scientists, contact the authors with questions about the articles, and report the findings to the class.
- Contact recent female graduates who are majoring in science in college, and ask them to talk to the class about their experiences.

6 **Recognize that you will not be able to address the various abilities and cognitive styles of all of your students all of the time.**

Although this chapter has described three major ways in which students differ from one another and explained why it is important to gear instruction to these differences (the goal of differentiated instruction), we do not want you to get the impression that you should strive to accommodate the unique needs of each student every minute of the day. When you have twenty-five or more students in a class, such a goal is nearly

For additional suggestions for your journal, see the Reflective Journal Questions on the textbook web site

To solidify your understanding of this chapter, go to this book's web site and use the ACE practice tests and PowerPoint slides.

impossible. But that does not mean you should make no attempt to get to know and work with students as individuals either. You might, for example, adopt the practice of Lori Tukey (2002), a sixth-grade teacher. She allowed students themselves to provide basic instruction on various aspects of writing. Each student listed aspects of writing, such as spelling, punctuation, and organization, that he or she wanted to improve. Then those who were proficient at one or more of these aspects were identified as "experts" to whom other students could go for help. This tactic gave the teacher enough extra time to work individually with each student twice a month.

Resources for Further Investigation

● The New Views of Intelligence

In *Teaching for Thinking* (1996), Robert Sternberg and Louise Spear-Swerling use Sternberg's triarchic theory to illustrate the nature of good thinking, how various teaching techniques can be used to promote good thinking, and how teachers can evaluate the thinking of their students.

Evangeline Stefanakis describes how to teach and assess children through portfolios from a multiple intelligences perspective in *Multiple Intelligences and Portfolios* (2002). Each chapter contains anecdotes from teachers about how they used MI theory to help them individualize their instruction, create student portfolios, and assess student progress.

● Learning Styles and Classroom Instruction

Rita and Kenneth Dunn describe and illustrate in the following two books dozens of teaching techniques designed to be compatible with a variety of learning styles: *Teaching Elementary Students Through Their Individual Learning Styles* (1992) and *Teaching Secondary Students Through Their Individual Learning Styles* (1993). In *Thinking Styles* (1997b), Robert J. Sternberg provides a very readable and detailed description of his theory of mental self-government styles, the factors that affect their development, and how teachers can use this knowledge to improve the classroom performance of students. The first chapter contains an interesting account of how Sternberg did poorly in his first psychology course and temporarily abandoned psychology as a college major because of a mismatch between his thinking style and that of his instructor. To discover your own learning style, go to the Index of Learning Styles web site at **www2.ncsu.edu/unity/lockers/users/f/felder/public/ILSpage.html.**

● The Impact of Gender Bias on Students

The research literature on sex differences in cognition is very complex and can easily be misinterpreted. A useful aid to reading this literature is the chapter "Causes, Correlates, and Caveats: Understanding the Development of Sex Differences in Cognition" by Diane Halpern and Simay Ikier in *Biology, Society, and Behavior: The Development of Sex Differences in*

Cognition (2002), edited by Anne McGillicuddy-De Lisi and Richard De Lisi.

In *Boys and Girls Learn Differently!* (2001), Michael Gurian and Patricia Henley describe the physical, social, emotional, and intellectual differences between boys and girls and provide a wealth of ideas for creating a classroom that facilitates the development of both genders. Part I covers differences in brain structure and function and how those differences affect classroom performance. Part II covers how to create what the authors call the "ultimate classroom" for boys and girls at the preschool/kindergarten, elementary, middle school, and high school grade levels.

The issue of gender bias in education is taken up in a different way by Frances Maher and Janie Victoria Ward in *Gender and Teaching* (2002). Part I contains four case histories about different aspects of gender bias (such as sexism in the classroom and the effect of teacher expectations), Part II summarizes the arguments made by public figures from different parts of the political spectrum, and Part III provides suggestions and resources for further reflection.

The web site of the Gender, Diversities, and Technology Institute (**www2.edc.org/GDI/**) offers online weekend workshops and courses on such gender equity–related topics as instruction and achievement, assessment, raising and educating boys, and engaging middle school girls in math and science. Click on the Professional Development tab at the top of the web site's home page to learn more about these offerings.

● Differentiated Instruction

If you intend to teach either at the middle or high school level and are interested in the concept of differentiated instruction, consult *Differentiated Instruction: A Guide for Middle and High School Teachers* (2002), by Amy Benjamin. The author is a veteran English teacher who has taught at all levels. In Chapter 1, she explains what differentiated instruction is and is not by discussing seven myths about the concept. In Chapters 4–9 she describes how to practice differentiated instruction for a variety of subjects. Chapter 10 contains fourteen case studies that illustrate how differentiated instruction can be used at the high school level.

Summary

1. The extent to which students differ from one another can be substantial, even in the primary grades. By fourth grade, the range of achievement can vary by four or more grade levels.

2. The first practical test of intelligence was devised by Alfred Binet to identify students who would be best served in a special education program.

3. Because they were designed to predict academic success, intelligence tests predict that outcome better than they predict other outcomes, such as job success, marital happiness, or life satisfaction.

4. Traditional intelligence tests seem to measure a general intellectual factor and a factor specific to the particular test being taken.

5. Traditional intelligence tests measure a relatively small sample of cognitive skills that can change over time as additional knowledge and skills are acquired.

6. Intelligence, broadly defined, is the global capacity of the individual to act purposefully, think rationally, and deal effectively with the environment.

7. Sternberg's triarchic theory of intelligence is composed of analytical, creative, and practical abilities. The practical component, which includes the ability to adapt to one's environment in order to achieve personal goals, has been ignored by traditional theories.

8. Research has shown that students learn more when learning tasks require them to use all three of Sternberg's types of abilities: analytical, creative, and practical.

9. Gardner's multiple intelligences theory holds that each person has eight distinct intelligences, some of them more well developed than others.

10. Several misconceptions exist about Gardner's multiple intelligences theory. Individuals who have a high level of a particular intelligence should not be expected to excel on all tasks involving that intelligence or to choose a career that calls for that intelligence. Because of other factors, students may use their skills in different ways. Also, it is not necessary, and may be counterproductive, to try to teach every subject in eight different ways.

11. Sternberg's triarchic theory implies that instruction and testing should be designed to involve memory, analytical, creative, and practical abilities.

12. To accommodate the different profiles of intelligences that exist in a typical classroom, Gardner recommends that teachers use MI theory as a framework for devising alternative ways of teaching subject matter.

13. Technology tools, such as multimedia and hypermedia simulations, web-based conferencing, and concept mapping, can strengthen the different aspects of intelligence that Sternberg and Gardner described.

14. A learning style is a consistent preference students have for perceiving, thinking about, and organizing information.

15. When faced with a question or a problem for which the answer is uncertain, students with an impulsive learning style spend less time than classmates with a reflective style collecting and analyzing information before making a response.

16. Students with a strong field-dependent learning style prefer to work in situations where the procedures are clear and well defined because they take their cue for acceptable behavior from the context in which they work. Students with a strong field-independent style prefer to work in situations where they can impose their own structure and procedures on a task. Most students exhibit both field-dependent and field-independent behaviors to some degree, depending on the nature of the task.

17. Sternberg has proposed a theory of mental self-government that is modeled after the structure and functions of civil government and contains thirteen learning styles.

18. Boys tend to outscore girls on tests of visual spatial ability (such as spatial perception, mental rotation, and generation and maintenance of a spatial image) and mathematical reasoning, whereas girls tend to outscore boys on tests of memory and language skills (such as spelling, reading comprehension, and writing).

19. International comparisons of mathematics achievement among eighth graders reveal that overall, boys score significantly higher than girls, but that girls and boys score at about the same level in many countries.

20. Although late elementary grade and middle school girls tend to receive higher grades than boys in language arts, social studies, science, and math, they experience higher levels of worry and depression over their academic performance.

21. Gender bias is the consistent differential response (both positive and negative) to male and female students when there is no sound educational reason for doing so.

22. The likely source of gender bias, which is communicated by both teachers and students, is a belief in traditional gender-role stereotypes.

23. The persistent exposure of students to gender bias is thought to play a role, particularly for females, in the courses that students select in high school, the career choices they make, and the extent to which they participate in class discussions.

24. Females who choose careers in science or mathematics have a high level of self-efficacy for science and math that was the result of early and consistent academic success, encouragement to pursue a career in science or math from significant others, and the availability of respected models in the math and science areas.

25. Both adolescent males and females have a tendency not to express their true beliefs and opinions when in the company of teachers, parents, and members of the opposite sex. This phenomenon is called *loss of voice*.

26. Among children between the ages of five and seventeen, the same percentage of males and females use computers at school and at home. Small differences (three to five percentage points) still exist, however, in how males and females use computers. More females than males use computers for word processing, e-mail, and to complete homework assignments, while more males use computers to play games. Suggestions for maintaining females' interest in computers include early positive experiences with computers; computer applications for subjects girls prefer, such as reading, writing, history, and literature; access to female role models who use technology; and telementoring programs in which girls exchange e-mails with professional women.

Key Terms

intelligence *(106)*
triarchic theory of intelligence *(107)*
theory of multiple intelligences *(109)*
hypermedia *(114)*
multimedia *(114)*

hypertext *(114)*
learning style *(114)*
impulsive *(115)*
reflective *(115)*
field-dependent style *(116)*

field-independent style *(116)*
styles of mental self-government *(116)*
gender bias *(121)*
loss of voice *(123)*

5 Addressing Cultural and Socioeconomic Diversity

These key points will help you learn the important information in this chapter. To help you study, they also appear in the margins of the pages, next to the text where they are discussed.

The Rise of Multiculturalism

- Cultural pluralism assumes societies should maintain different cultures, every culture within a society should be respected, individuals have right to participate in society without giving up cultural identity

- U.S. becoming more culturally diverse because of changes in immigration, birthrates

Ethnicity and Social Class

- Ethnocentrism: belief that one's own culture is superior to other cultures

- Culture: how a group of people perceives, believes, thinks, behaves

- Ethnic group members differ in verbal and nonverbal communication patterns

- Ethnic group members may hold different values

- Ethnic group members may favor different learning arrangements and processes

- Poverty rates higher for ethnic families of color than for whites

- Minority children often score lower on tests, drop out of school sooner

- Achievement gap between low-SES minority students and white students due to living conditions, family environment, characteristics of the student, and classroom environment

- Low-SES children more likely to live in stressful environment that interferes with studying

- Classroom atmosphere, teachers' approaches connected with achievement levels of low-SES students

- Teacher expectancy (Pygmalion) effect: impact of teacher expectations leads to self-fulfilling prophecy

- Limited effect of teacher expectancy on IQ scores

- Strong effect of teacher expectancy on achievement, participation

- Teacher expectancies influenced by social class, ethnic background, achievement, attractiveness, gender

Multicultural Education Programs

- Multicultural programs aim to promote respect for diversity, reduction of ethnocentrism and stereotypes, improved learning

- Multicultural education can be approached in different ways

- Multicultural lessons organized around key concepts

- Peer tutoring improves achievement

- Cooperative learning: students work together in small groups

- Cooperative learning fosters better understanding among ethnically diverse students

- Mastery learning: all students can master the curriculum

- Multicultural understanding can be promoted by electronically linking students from different cultural backgrounds

Bilingual Education

- Transition programs focus on rapid shift to English proficiency

- Maintenance programs focus on maintaining native-language competence

- Two-way bilingual education programs feature instruction in both languages

- Bilingual education programs produce moderate learning gains

reviously in this text, we pointed out that if your instructional plans are to be effective, they have to take into account what your students are like. (The term *entering behavior* is typically used to refer to the characteristics students bring with them to class.) In previous chapters, we described students in terms of their age-related differences in psychosocial, cognitive, and moral development, and we discussed how students typically are similar to and different from one another in terms of physical, social, and cognitive characteristics. In this chapter, we will turn to two other important ways in which students differ: cultural background and language.

Culture is a term that describes how a group of people perceives the world; formulates beliefs; evaluates objects, ideas, and experiences; and behaves. It can be thought of as a blueprint that guides the ways in which individuals within a group do such important things as communicate with others (both verbally and nonverbally), handle time and space, express emotions, and approach work and play. The concept of culture typically includes ethnic group but can also encompass religious beliefs and socioeconomic status (Gollnick & Chinn, 2002).

Different groups of people vary in their beliefs, attitudes, values, and behavior patterns because of differences in cultural norms. (By *norms,* we mean the perceptions, beliefs, and behaviors that characterize most members of a group.) Students who were raised with mainstream American values, for example, find acceptable the practice of working individually and competing with others for academic rewards. Most Native Americans and Asians, in contrast, have been taught to de-emphasize competition and individual accomplishment in favor of cooperation and group solidarity (Sadker & Sadker, 2000).

To provide the appropriate classroom and school conditions that will help your students from different cultural backgrounds master a common curriculum, you must come to understand and take into account your students' differing cultural backgrounds. A culturally aware teacher will emphasize the way in which American society has been enriched by the contributions of many different ethnic groups (and place special emphasis on those ethnic groups to which the students belong) and will not schedule a major exam or field trip for a day when certain students are likely to be out of school in observance of a religious holiday.

The approach to teaching and learning that we will describe in this chapter, one that seeks to foster an understanding of and mutual respect for the values, beliefs, and practices of different cultural groups, is typically referred to as **multicultural education.** Because culturally diverse children often come to school with different language backgrounds, another related issue is bilingual education, described at the end of this chapter. ●

THE RISE OF MULTICULTURALISM

From Melting Pot to Cultural Pluralism

 To preview this chapter's basic concepts, read the Chapter Themes on the textbook web site, accessible from **http://education.college.hmco .com/students.**

More than most other countries, the United States is made up of numerous ethnic groups with widely diverse histories, cultural backgrounds, and values. In addition to the hundreds of thousands of African Americans who were brought to the United States as slaves, the United States was peopled by many waves of immigrants, mostly from Europe but also from Asia and Latin America. Throughout the eighteenth and nineteenth centuries, the United States needed large numbers of people to settle its western frontier, build its railroads, harvest its natural resources, and work in its growing factories. As Table 5.1 indicates, approximately 33 million people immigrated to the United States between 1820 and 1920.

Throughout this period, the basic view of American society toward immigrants was that they should divest themselves of their old customs, views, allegiances, and rivalries as soon as possible and adopt English as their primary language along with mainstream American ideals, values, and customs. This assimilation of diverse ethnic groups into one national mainstream was known as the **melting pot** phenomenon, a term and viewpoint popularized in a 1909 play by Israel Zangwill, *The Melting Pot.* The main institution responsible for bringing about this assimilation was the public school (Ornstein & Levine, 2003).

The notion of America as a great melting pot was generally accepted until the social unrest of the late 1960s and early 1970s. As an outgrowth of urban riots and the civil rights movement, minority ethnic groups argued not only for bilingual education

Table 5.1	Number of Immigrants to the United States, by Decade		
Years	**Number**	**Years**	**Number**
1820–1830	151,824	1911–1920	5,735,811
1831–1840	599,125	1921–1930	4,107,209
1841–1850	1,713,251	1931–1940	528,431
1851–1860	2,598,214	1941–1950	1,035,039
1861–1870	2,314,824	1951–1960	2,515,479
1871–1880	2,812,191	1961–1970	3,321,677
1881–1890	5,246,613	1971–1980	4,493,314
1891–1900	3,687,564	1981–1990	7,338,062
1901–1910	8,795,386	1991–2000	9,095,417
		Total	66,089,431

SOURCE: U.S. Office of Immigration Statistics (2003).

programs in public schools but also for ethnic studies. It might be said that many minority group members realized that they did not wish to fit the white Anglo-Saxon Protestant mold of a "traditional American" and began to express a desire to be Americans who have different characteristics. Michael Novak (1971) refers to this movement as the "rise of the unmeltable ethnics." Since the early 1970s, factors such as discrimination, the desire to maintain culturally specific ideas and practices, and continued immigration from different parts of the world have served to maintain, if not accelerate, this trend toward cultural diversity—or **cultural pluralism,** to use the preferred term. Cultural pluralism rests on three beliefs: (1) a society should strive to maintain the different cultures that reside within it; (2) each culture within a society should be respected by others; and (3) individuals within a society have the right to participate in all aspects of that society without having to give up their cultural identity (Sleeter & Grant, 2003).

● Cultural pluralism assumes societies should maintain different cultures, every culture within a society should be respected, individuals have the right to participate in society without giving up cultural identity

The Changing Face of the United States

Given recent changes in birthrates and immigration patterns and population projections for the next thirty to fifty years, one could argue that the decline of the melting pot philosophy and the rise of cultural pluralism and multicultural education will only accelerate in the years ahead. Consider the following statistics.

Between 1991 and 2002, 84 percent of legal immigrants to the United States came from non-European countries. Most of these immigrants came from Asia (principally the Philippine Islands, China, and India) and the Americas (principally Mexico and South America) and settled in the major cities of California, New York, Texas, and Florida. In the ten-year period from 1991 to 2000, about 9.1 million legal immigrants arrived in the United States, an all-time U.S. immigration record for a decade (U.S. Office of Immigration Statistics, 2003). Adding to the change produced by immigration itself is the fact that immigrant mothers have a higher average birthrate than native-born mothers. As of 2000, native-born women averaged 61.5 births per 1,000, while foreign-born women averaged 85.4 per 1,000 (U.S. Bureau of the Census, 2001).

These immigration and birthrate patterns are expected to have a significant effect over the next two decades on the makeup of the school-age population (see Figure 5.1).

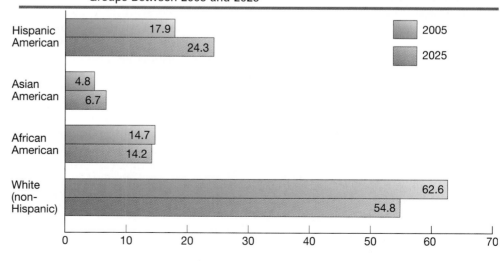

Figure 5.1 Projected Change in Percentage of School-Age Children for Four Ethnic Groups Between 2005 and 2025

Percentage of children between 5 and 18 years of age

SOURCE: U.S. Bureau of the Census (2000).
*Because of rounding errors, percentages for 2001 do not add up to exactly 100 percent.

● U.S. becoming more culturally diverse because of changes in immigration, birthrates

According to Census Bureau projections, the populations of Hispanic American and Asian American schoolchildren will increase rapidly, raising their combined percentage of the school-age population to about 31 percent. African American school-age children will also increase in numbers, although their proportion of the overall school population will remain at 14 to 15 percent. The proportion of white non-Hispanic school children will fall from 63 percent to just under 55 percent. As these figures make clear, not only is the United States rapidly on its way to becoming an even more ethnically diverse nation than ever before, but certain areas of the country (for example, southern California, Texas, southern Florida, New York) already have very large minority populations.

Much of the rest of this chapter will focus on characteristics of certain groups of students. But for you and your students to benefit from your knowledge of cultural diversity, you must view it in the proper perspective. The perspective we encourage you to adopt has three aspects, which are described in the following Suggestions for Teaching in Your Classroom.

Suggestions for Teaching in Your Classroom

Taking Account of Your Students' Cultural Differences

1 **Recognize that differences are not necessarily deficits.**

● Ethnocentrism: belief that one's own culture is superior to other cultures

JOURNAL ENTRY
Minimizing Ethnocentric Tendencies

Students who subscribe to different value systems and exhibit different communication patterns, time orientations, learning modes, motives, and aspirations should not be viewed as incapable (García, 2002). Looking on ethnic and social class differences as deficits usually stems from an attitude called *ethnocentrism*. This is the tendency of people to think of their own culture as superior to the culture of other groups. You may be able to moderate your ethnocentric tendencies and motivate your students to learn by consciously using instructional tactics that are congruent with the different cultural backgrounds of your students.

2 **Recognize that the groups we and others describe with a general label are frequently made up of subgroups with somewhat different characteristics.**

These subgroups, in fact, may use different labels to refer to themselves. Among Native Americans, for example, Navajos differ from the Hopi in physical appearance, dress, and hairstyle. Individuals who are called Hispanic often refer to themselves as either Chicano, Latino, Mexicano, of Mexican descent, or of Spanish descent (P. Schmidt, 2003). Learn as much as you can about the subgroups your students come from, and keep these specific qualities in mind as you teach.

3 **Above all, remember that each student is a unique person. Although descriptions of various ethnic groups and subgroups may accurately portray some general tendencies of a large group of people, they may apply only partly or not at all to given individuals.**

How can you use the concept of constructivism (discussed earlier in this book) to help students overcome any ethnocentrism they may have and understand the beliefs and practices of other cultures?

Rather than thinking of culture as a set of perceptions, thoughts, beliefs, and actions that are inherent in all individuals who nominally belong to a culture (perhaps because of surname or country of origin), you will be far better served in working with students and their parents if you take the time to understand the extent to which individuals participate in the practices of their cultural communities. For example, some Hispanic American students may prefer cooperative learning arrangements because such behavior is the norm at home and in their community, whereas others may prefer to work independently because that behavior is more typical for them (Gutiérrez & Rogoff, 2003).

ETHNICITY AND SOCIAL CLASS

● Culture: how a group of people perceives, believes, thinks, behaves

As we pointed out in the opening paragraphs of this chapter, culture refers to the way in which a group of people perceives, thinks about, and interacts with the world. It provides a set of norms that guide what we say and how we say it, what we feel, and what we do in various situations. Two significant factors that most readily distinguish one culture from another are ethnicity and social class.

The Effect of Ethnicity on Learning

An **ethnic group** is a collection of people who identify with one another on the basis of one or more of the following characteristics: country from which one's ancestors came, race, religion, language, values, political interests, economic interests, and behavior patterns (Banks, 2001; Gollnick & Chinn, 2002). Viewed separately, the ethnic groups in the United States, particularly those of color, are numerical minorities; collectively, however, they constitute a considerable portion of American society (Banks, 2001). Most Americans identify with some ethnic group (Irish Americans, German Americans, Italian Americans, African Americans, Chinese Americans, and Hispanic Americans, to name but a few). As a teacher, you need to know how your students' ethnicity can affect student-teacher relationships.

Christine Bennett (2003) identifies five aspects of ethnicity that are potential sources of student-student and student-teacher misunderstanding: verbal communication, nonverbal communication, time orientation, social values, and instructional formats and learning processes.

Verbal Communication Patterns   Problems with verbal communication can occur in a number of ways. Verbal exchanges in the classroom typically take the following form: the teacher elicits a comment from a student by either making a request or asking a question, the student responds, and the teacher makes some sort of evaluative comment. But the conversations that occur between many Mexican American parents and their children often lack the evaluative component. As a result, Mexican American students may be unsure of what to do with corrective feedback or may misinterpret its intent (Losey, 1995). An easy solution, and one that will benefit all of your students, is to explain the purpose of corrective feedback.

Second, classroom discussions may not go as planned if teachers have students who do not understand—or feel overly confined by—the mainstream convention of "you take a turn and then somebody else takes a turn." For example, in Hispanic families in which there are several siblings and the parenting style is authoritarian, children may be reluctant to enter into a teacher-led discussion in class. Because teachers, like parents, are viewed as authority figures, many children consider it disrespectful to offer their opinions. They are there to learn what the teacher tells them.

But as with their siblings at home, they may be quite active in small-group discussions composed entirely of peers (García, 2002).

Finally, because of differences in cultural experiences, some students may be reluctant to speak or perform in public, whereas others may prefer exchanges that resemble a free-for-all shouting match. Some Native American children, for example, prefer to work on ideas and skills in private. A public performance is given only after an acceptable degree of mastery is attained (Bennett, 2003; Vasquez, 1990). This practice is not as unique to Native American culture as it might seem at first glance. Music lessons and practices are typically done in private, and public performances are not given until a piece or program is mastered.

Nonverbal Communication   A form of nonverbal communication that mainstream American culture highly values is direct eye contact. Most people are taught to look directly at the person to whom they are speaking, as this behavior signifies honesty on the part of the speaker and interest on the part of the listener. Among certain Native American, Hispanic, and Asian cultures, however, averting one's eyes is a sign of deference to and respect for the other person, whereas looking at someone directly while being corrected is a sign of defiance. Thus, an Asian American, Hispanic American, or Native American student who looks down or away when being questioned or corrected about something is not necessarily trying to hide guilt or ignorance or to communicate lack of interest (Bennett, 2003; Howe, 1994; Pewewardy, 2002).

Time Orientation   Mainstream American culture is very time oriented, and people who know how to organize their time and work efficiently are praised and rewarded. We teach our children to value such statements as "Time is money" and "Never put off until tomorrow what you can do today." Nowhere else is this time orientation more evident than in our schools. Classes begin and end at a specified time regardless of whether one is interested in starting a project, pursuing a discussion, or finishing an experiment. But for students whose ethnic cultures are not so time bound (Hispanic Americans and Native Americans, for example), such a rigid approach to learning may be upsetting. Indeed, it may also be upsetting to some students who reflect the mainstream culture (Bennett, 2003; Pewewardy, 2002).

Social Values   Two values that lie at the heart of mainstream American society are competition ("Competition brings out the best in people") and rugged individualism ("People's accomplishments should reflect their own efforts"). Because schools tend to reflect mainstream beliefs, many classroom activities are competitive and done on one's own for one's personal benefit. However, students of some ethnic groups, such as Mexican Americans, are more likely to have been taught to value cooperative relationships and family loyalty. These students may thus prefer group projects; they may also respond more positively to praise that emphasizes family pride rather than individual glory (Bennett, 2003; Vasquez, 1990).

Instructional Formats and Learning Processes   Finally, ethnic groups may differ in terms of the instructional formats and learning processes they prefer. According to research summarized by Christine Sleeter and Carl Grant (2003), most elementary teachers use a teacher-centered, large-group approach to instruction in which all students work from the same text, workbook, and worksheets. At the high school and middle school levels, the typical classroom arrangement is rows of chairs facing the front of the room and a teacher who governs exchanges with students by talking, asking questions, and listening to answers. This approach to teaching may be somewhat incompatible with the learning conditions that students from other cultural backgrounds favor. For example, native Hawaiian children's achievement improved when teachers switched from whole-class instruction and independent seatwork to small-group learning centers because the latter approach was more similar to the children's

● Ethnic group members differ in verbal and nonverbal communication patterns

● Ethnic group members may hold different values

● Ethnic group members may favor different learning arrangements and processes

out-of-school social structure (Okagaki, 2001). African American students also seem to favor cooperative arrangements, as well as discussion and hands-on learning. One way of teaching math to students with these preferences might be to engage them with problems that involve buying, trading, or borrowing (Sleeter & Grant, 2003).

Aspects of Native American culture also call for flexibility in instructional formats and processes. Because longer periods of silence between speakers are more customary in Navajo than in Anglo culture, teachers need to wait longer for students to answer questions (Okagaki, 2001). Furthermore, because Navajo students are taught by their culture to treat serious learning as private, they may not fully participate in such traditionally Western activities as tests, debates, and contests (Okagaki, 2001; Sleeter & Grant, 2003; Soldier, 1997). Choctaw children are less likely than other children to speak individually in class, and speak in shorter sentences when they do speak, but they are more likely to participate in choral responding (two or more students respond to the teacher simultaneously) because of their cultural emphasis on group processes (Okagaki, 2001).

With respect to learning processes, some researchers have found that many Native Americans prefer visual imagery and drawing rather than verbal propositions as a way to represent knowledge mentally, and many have a preference for the field-dependent and reflective cognitive styles (Guild, 1994; Pewewardy, 2002). Additional evidence that the cultural background of students influences the learning process they use comes from the work of Nola Purdie and John Hattie (1996). They sought to determine if there is any truth to the common perception that Japanese students tend to be literal learners who emphasize memorizing at the expense of their own views and interpretations. People who believe this description attribute it to the emphasis in Japanese culture on subordination of individual viewpoints to the group's perceptions and goals.

Purdie and Hattie found that the Japanese students they interviewed chose memorizing as their preferred learning process, while a similar group of Australian students gave it a very low preference rating (eighteenth out of twenty-four options). A group of Japanese students who had been living in Australia for almost three years at the time of the study were in between these two extremes. These differences in learning processes may be related to differences in attitudes toward learning. Western students place a higher value on working independently, competing with others, and completing tasks efficiently (and Australian students can be considered Western in these respects). Japanese students, by contrast, place a higher value on working cooperatively with others, complying with authority, and being thorough in their approach to tasks (Li, 2002).

Students from different ethnic groups often prefer different instructional formats and learning processes. African American students, for example, may favor cooperative learning over lecture/recitation, while Native American students may dislike debates and contests.

These findings suggest that although cultural background does influence choice of learning activity, the effects of culture seem to diminish as one becomes more accustomed to and comfortable with the values and practices of another culture.

The Effect of Social Class on Learning

The social class from which a student comes plays an influential role in behavior. **Social class** is an indicator of an individual's or a family's relative standing in society. It is determined by such factors as annual income, occupation, amount of education, place of residence, types of organizations to which family members belong, manner of dress, and material possessions. The first three factors are used by the federal government to determine the closely related concept of **socioeconomic status (SES).** The influence of social class is such that the members of working-class Hispanic American and Irish American families may have more in common than the members of an upper-middle-class Hispanic American family and those of a working-class Hispanic American family (Gollnick & Chinn, 2002).

Because of the severe and long-lasting historic pattern of discrimination experienced by ethnic groups of color in the United States, many members of these groups have fewer years of education, a less prestigious occupation, and a lower income than the average white person. In 2001, 15.8 percent of American children under age eighteen lived in families with incomes below the poverty level. Although most such children are white (meaning of European ancestry), Figure 5.2 shows that the poverty rates among African American, Native American, and Hispanic American families are usually about three times higher than that for white children (U.S. Bureau of the Census, 2002).

How do such differences in social class influence learning and performance in school? One major effect is that significantly fewer African American, Hispanic American, and Native American adolescents graduate from high school than do whites, thereby shortening their years of education and earning potential. Whereas

● Poverty rates higher for ethnic families of color than for whites

Figure 5.2 Percentage of Families Within Ethnic Groups Living Below Poverty Level in 2001

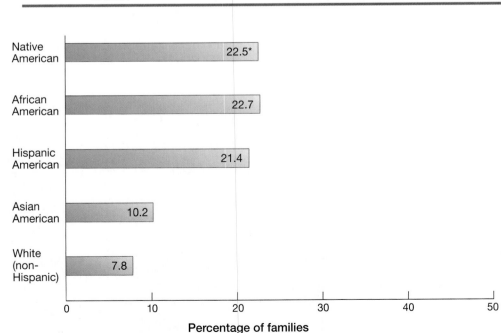

SOURCE: U.S. Bureau of Census (2002).
*The average from 2000 and 2001.

74.9 percent of whites graduate from high school, only 50.2 percent of African Americans, 53.2 percent of Hispanic Americans, and 51.1 percent of Native Americans do so (Swanson, 2004). Investigations into the reasons that minority students fail to complete school have found that social class factors, economic factors, school environment factors, and individual factors may all play a role. Compared with white students who graduate, minority students have lower levels of motivation, lower self-esteem, and weaker academic skills; they are also more impulsive. In addition, students who do not graduate nearly always report a sense of alienation from school because of low teacher expectations, expressions of racial or ethnic group prejudice from teachers and students, and unfair discrimination. Students required to repeat grades (recall our discussion of this topic earlier in the text) are among the most likely to drop out of school and not graduate.

pause & reflect

What steps might you take to reduce or eliminate the sense of alienation that causes many minority students to drop out of school?

• Minority children often score lower on tests, drop out of school sooner

During their time in school, many minority students achieve at significantly lower levels than do white students. Compared with white high school sophomores and seniors, African American, Hispanic American, and Native American students score lower on standardized tests of vocabulary, reading, writing, mathematics, and science (Ornstein & Levine, 2003). These differences appear early. Results from the National Assessment of Educational Progress reveal that the reading, writing, mathematics, and science skills of African American and Hispanic American children are substantially below those of white children as early as the fourth grade (Donahue, Finnegan, Lutkus, Allen, & Campbell, 2001; Greenwald, Persky, Campbell, & Mazzeo, 1999; O'Sullivan, Reese, & Mazzeo, 1997; Reese, Miller, Mazzeo, & Dossey, 1997).

The long-standing achievement gap between low-SES (and some middle-SES) minority students and their white classmates is perhaps the most researched and discussed effect of social class on learning (e.g., Alson, 2002/2003; Bell, 2002/2003; Denbo, 2002; Hrabowski, 2002/2003; Ladson-Billings, 2002; Lee, 2002; Nieto, 2002/2003; Singham, 2003). Our Case in Print describes how several school districts in the suburbs of Philadelphia are addressing this problem. The exact reasons for the gap relate to a number of interweaving factors, including living conditions, family environment, characteristics of the student, and classroom environment. As you read the following sections about these factors, think about how they combine and reinforce one another—and about what you as a teacher can do to minimize their effect.

• Achievement gap between low-SES minority students and white students due to living conditions, family environment, characteristics of the student, and classroom environment

Health and Living Conditions   Many low-SES Americans do not receive satisfactory health care (Stinson, 2003). For example, African American women have a high level of such pregnancy complications as toxemia, hemorrhage, hypertension, heart disease, infection, and diabetes. In addition, inadequate diets during pregnancy and low-birth-weight babies are common (Sanders-Phillips, 1989; Swartz, 2003; Umar, 2003). As a consequence, there is a greater incidence of premature births, birth defects, and infant mortality among low-SES children as compared with middle-class children (Umar, 2003). Because poor children do not receive medical or dental care regularly, accurate statistics on general health are difficult to compile. It seems reasonable to assume, however, that the same inadequate nutrition and health care that leads to elevated infant mortality rates probably also leads to higher rates of illness in later years. In other words, low-SES children probably continue to suffer from untreated illnesses at a rate that may be at least twice that of middle-class children (Sanders-Phillips, 1989).

Another health-related factor in the development and intellectual performance of low-SES children is lead poisoning. Because many of these children live in homes that were painted prior to the discontinuation of lead-based paint, their ingestion of paint dust and chips leads to elevated levels of lead in the blood. Exposure to lead, even in small amounts, is associated with low standardized test scores, attention deficits, and disruptive behavior in children. Almost 37 percent of African American

Case in Print

Bridging the Achievement Gap

The long-standing achievement gap between low-SES (and some middle-SES) minority students and their white classmates is perhaps the most researched and discussed effect of social class on learning. . . . The exact reasons for the gap relate to a number of interweaving factors, including living conditions, family environment, characteristics of the student, and classroom environment. (p. 141)

Minority Students Trail in Suburbs

CONNIE LANGLAND AND ALLETTA EMENO
Philadelphia Inquirer, 12/14/03

Across the Pennsylvania suburbs, high-achieving and well-funded schools are facing sizeable gaps in achievement between white and minority students.

The racial learning divide exists in 84 percent of the 204 suburban schools with minority students, an *Inquirer* analysis of state math and reading test results shows.

This achievement gap, with black and Latino students falling behind white students, persists even in such high-performing districts as Abington, Lower Merion, Downingtown, West Chester, Tredyffrin-Easttown and Wallingford-Swarthmore.

The problem also exists in a fourth of Philadelphia schools.

The gap emerges from new data, released as part of the federal No Child Left Behind law, which seeks to identify areas of poor student performance. States must report grade-level proficiency scores for racial and ethnic minorities, poor and special-education students. New Jersey plans to release similar data in February.

Harvard economist Ron Ferguson, who specializes in the achievement gap, said the new rules made disparities "more difficult to sweep under the rug." In the past, he said, districts could mask poor minority student performance behind high overall school achievement.

Rogers Vaughn, the West Chester board president, said that districts traditionally have "dealt with averages, compared themselves with other districts and, if they did well, patted themselves on the back."

The *Inquirer* analyzed Pennsylvania System of School Assessment test results for grades 5, 8 and 11 for 2003. In the 204 suburban schools with minority students, 84 percent showed them performing at least 10 percentage points below whites in reading and math.

In addition, the analysis found that:

In 89 percent of the 162 suburban schools with black students, those students scored lower than whites in math; in 83 percent of the schools, blacks scored lower in reading.

Half of suburban schools with black students missed state goals because not enough black students passed the reading test.

In 91 percent of suburban schools with Latino students, those students scored lower than whites in math; in 80 percent of schools, Latinos scored lower in reading.

Going against the trend, blacks outperformed whites in about a dozen suburban schools; Asians outperformed whites in nearly 80 percent of schools they attended.

The data did not indicate whether the underperforming minority students were also poor or in special education.

Advocates for minority children last week expressed dismay at the disparities.

"You look at the numbers and look at the group and have to ask, what is going on here?" asked Diana Robertson, president of the Main Line NAACP. "And what are you going to do about it? The system has to be responsible for the education of all children."

While the details are new to the public, school officials have known for about two years that they are obligated to pay attention to the performance of students in the subgroups; many are addressing it.

The West Chester school district—where six of its 15 schools show black students lagging white students—two years ago set up a minority achievement committee and has hired extra reading specialists to work with struggling students.

In the high-performing Lower Merion school district, the achievement gap exists in five of its 10 schools. "We think any subgroup of children not achieving proficiency or above at high levels needs our attention," said Thomas Tobin, assistant superintendent.

Philadelphia, which has long faced low scores and an achievement gap, has seen results with innovative curriculum in math and reading.

Nationwide, "there's been a tendency to dummy down the curriculum particularly for poor minority children," said Paul Vallas, chief executive officer of the Philadelphia School District. "The effect of that has been to institutionalize poor achievement. The way to close the gap is to teach to high standards."

Philadelphia has less of a performance gap than the suburbs. In fact, in 27 percent of schools with both black and white students, black students scored better in either math or reading.

Vallas said that breaking out test scores for minority and ethnic groups "is long overdue. It's one of the strongest features of No Child Left Behind."

School officials are scrambling to improve student results and identify the causes of disparities.

The North Penn district, for instance, held a two-day retreat in August to identify trends in 2003 test data.

Lower Merion has added reading and math specialists in its elementary schools.

Colonial is among districts that have set up after-school and summer programs for students with weak skills.

Norristown has opened all-day kindergartens—also planned next year in Colonial.

Hatboro-Horsham credits a 96 percent attendance rate for black students as helping close a reading gap. "Time on task is important. You cannot learn when you are not in school," said assistant superintendent Curtis Griffin.

In William Penn's Penn Wood East Junior High School, where a third of new students last year were transfers, new students are tested to catch those who are lagging in skills.

West Chester has begun sensitivity training for new hires. "I think there's still a stigma with minorities and disadvantaged students," said Debora Sahijwani, the district's assessment supervisor. "People make assumptions about their ability to learn. I think it's unconscious, but it's there."

Why this disparity exists is complex and stems from a variety of factors including poverty, early learning of reading and math skills, teacher-student interaction and home learning.

In high-achieving suburban districts, it is harder to pinpoint reasons for persistent gaps, said Robert Floden, who directs a teaching institute at Michigan State University.

"Sometimes it's still poverty-related," he said. "Part of it is just puzzling. People are trying to sort out what's due to family background and what's due to things that go on in the schools."

Edmund Gordon, a founder of Head Start and director of Columbia University's Institute for Urban and Minority Education, is now focusing on "supplemental education"—what happens outside of school.

He said many African Americans believe that only schools are responsible for providing education. "We're trying to convince people that what happens outside of school is an important adjunct," he said.

Ferguson, the Harvard economist, found that teacher attitudes play a role. "It is a challenge to get teachers to acknowledge that they can do things much differently," he said. "Many of them believe strongly that 'I am doing the best with the kids I have.'"

Questions and Activities

1. Paul Vallas, the head of the Philadelphia School District, is quoted as saying, "The way to close the gap is to teach to high standards." This is a phrase that educators and policymakers frequently use but rarely define. What do you think it means? How would you define high standards? What instructional materials, instructional techniques, classroom conditions, and school conditions would make teaching to high standards a feasible goal?

2. The article mentions steps that several school districts are taking to raise the achievement levels and test scores of low-SES minority students, such as hiring math and reading specialists, creating after-school and summer programs, opening all-day kindergartens, and raising attendance rates. If you were to construct a list of activities that might accomplish this goal, where (upper part of the list, in the middle, toward the bottom) would you place the ones mentioned in the article? Why? What other steps would you suggest?

3. Deborah Sahijwani, the assessment supervisor of the West Chester School District, states that people make unconscious assumptions about low-SES minority students' ability to learn. This phenomenon has a formal name and has been discussed in this chapter. What is its name, and how can it be overcome?

4. One of the puzzling aspects of the achievement gap is that in some suburban and city schools, African American students outperform white students. If you were going to study this phenomenon, what factors would you investigate first? Why?

On average, ethnic minority and low-SES students do not perform as well as other groups in school because of such factors as poor health care, an unstable family environment, low motivation, negative attitudes toward school, and negative classroom environments.

● Low-SES children more likely to live in stressful environment that interferes with studying

children and 17 percent of Mexican American children between the ages of one and five have lead levels in their blood that are associated with cognitive impairments and behavioral problems. These impairments need not be permanent, however: medication can reduce the level of lead in the blood, leading to an improvement in the children's academic performance (Jackson, 1999).

Furthermore, many low-SES students, especially those in urban areas, live in relatively small, and sometimes overcrowded, apartments. Adequate study space is often nonexistent, and parental supervision is spotty or absent. In their neighborhoods, street crime is a constant threat (Levine & Levine, 1996).

Family Environment   Low-SES students are more likely than middle-class students to grow up in one-parent families (the father usually being the missing parent). Like many other risk factors, the effect of a one-parent family on the academic performance of a child is not straightforward. It depends on such factors as the duration and cause of the separation, the age and sex of the child, and the type of interactions the child has with the remaining parent. But although one-parent families may not negatively affect a child's performance in school, two-parent families are likely to be more effective because both parents have the potential to exert a positive influence (Levine & Levine, 1996).

Some studies show that parents' support for their children's schooling varies by social class and ethnic group. For example, white and Asian American adolescents are more likely than Latino or African American adolescents to get support for academic achievement from parents as well as friends (Okagaki, 2001).

Moreover, compared with the parents of low-SES children, the parents of middle-class children in the United States expose their children to a wider variety of experiences. They tend to buy their children more books, educational toys, and games and take them on more trips that expand their knowledge of the world. These experiences accumulate and make school learning more familiar and easy than it would otherwise be. A child who has not had such experiences is likely to be at a disadvantage when placed in competitive academic situations (Levine & Levine, 1996). Furthermore, there has been increasing concern about the development of a technological underclass of children whose families cannot afford to provide access to computers and online services at home.

Overall, the interactions that occur between low-SES parents and their children tend to lack the characteristic of mediation (a concept we introduced earlier in the book in connection with Vygotsky's theory of cognitive development). When mediation occurs, someone who is more intellectually advanced than the learner presents, explains, and interprets stimuli in a way that produces a more meaningful understanding than the learner could have obtained working alone. A parent or older sibling, for example, may mediate by discussing objects, ideas, or events that are separated in time or space and pointing out their similarities and differences; presenting a set of seemingly different objects and explaining how they all belong to the same category; and providing some sort of context for an idea that allows the child to connect that idea to his or her life.

To illustrate this process, imagine a child walking alone through a hands-on science museum looking at the various exhibits, occasionally pushing the buttons of interactive displays, and listening to some of the prerecorded messages. What the child learns from this experience is likely to be a haphazard collection of isolated fragments of information that are not meaningful. Now imagine another child of the same age looking at and interacting with the same exhibits but accompanied by a parent or older sibling who wants this to be a meaningful learning experience. The parent or sibling points out specific aspects of the displays, names them, describes their purpose, and explains how they work. This child is more likely than the first child to construct a set of cohesive, interrelated, and meaningful knowledge structures (Ben-Hur, 1998).

Students' Motivation, Beliefs, and Attitudes   Many low-SES students may not be strongly motivated to do well in school because of lower levels of a characteristic called *need for achievement*. A need for achievement (which is discussed more fully in our chapter on motivation) is a drive to accomplish tasks and is thought to be one of the main reasons that people vary in their willingness to invest time and energy in the achievement of a goal. Recent research suggests that low-SES African American students score lower than comparable groups of white students on tests of need for achievement, but this racial difference is considerably smaller among middle-class samples (Cooper & Dorr, 1995).

Other studies have found that some minority students, especially males, tend to develop beliefs and attitudes that inhibit strong academic performance:

- African American and Latino adolescents are more likely than Asian American or white adolescents to believe that they can get a good job without first getting a good education. Asian American, white, and Latino adolescents who are doing well in school, on the other hand, see getting a good education as a prerequisite to getting a good job (Okagaki, 2001).
- Ethnic and racial minority middle school females appear to place a higher value on academic achievement than do ethnic and racial minority males. When ethnic and racial minority females from a low-income urban elementary and middle school were asked to identify classmates whom they admired, respected, and wanted to be like, about 60 percent of second- and fourth-grade students and 66 percent of seventh-grade students selected a high-achieving classmate. Ethnic and racial minority males from the same schools responded similarly, but only through fourth grade. Whereas 51 percent of second graders and 52 percent of fourth graders chose a high-achieving classmate, only 21 percent of seventh-grade males made that choice. Average achievers were selected by about 56 percent of seventh-grade males, and low achievers by about 23 percent. Data from other studies indicate that while African American males recognize the importance of working hard, many of them adopt an indifferent attitude toward high levels of school achievement.

This decline in achievement-related values on the part of minority male adolescents was corroborated by the observations of teachers, who made such comments as "They can do the work but they just don't seem to care" and "In the peer culture, one risks rejection by exerting effort in school (Graham & Taylor, 2002).

This inability to establish what might be called an academic identity appears related to a sense that one is not part of the larger school community, that school does not meet one's needs, that one is incapable of meeting academic demands, and that schoolwork is not part of who one wants to be (Jackson, 2003).

Elaine Kaplan (1999) conducted in-depth interviews with thirty-nine inner-city African American and Latino adolescent students who were participating in a pre-college academic tutorial program. She noted that before the students became involved in the program, they were doing poorly in school and were influenced by a peer group that did not value educational achievement. The students discussed the difficulty of leaving the old peer group and learning to accept the idea that they could be successful in school.

The frustration that is created by peers who do not share one's academic values was described by an African American female student who was attending a student conference of the Minority Student Achievement Network:

> I'm a member from Amherst, Massachusetts, and it is predominantly White. . . . I'm able to get along with the White kids, but it's the Black kids that I find I have a hard time relating to. . . . In class, they're always thinking, "There goes that girl, trying to be smart, trying to 'act white.'" It seems like I can't relate to them, and I'm Black myself. How is that supposed to make me feel? I'm trying to fit in both worlds, and it's like I have no place. (Ash, 2000, p. 6)

Given such peer group influences, it is not surprising that educationally disadvantaged students may have no definite career plans after leaving school and may be limited to low-paying, dead-end jobs, resulting in low self-esteem (Pollard, 1993).

A clear and chilling example of factors like these is offered by Marc Elrich (1994), a sixth-grade teacher in a Maryland school district just outside Washington, D.C. His class of twenty-nine students was composed almost entirely of African American and Hispanic American low-SES youths who saw no value in education and who exhibited low self-esteem and low expectations. To prompt a discussion of self-esteem, he showed them a film based on a Langston Hughes story about an African American youth who attempts to steal the purse of an elderly African American woman. He fails, and the woman takes him into her home, where she tries to change his attitudes and behavior. The message of the film is that with love, we all learn that we have it within ourselves to be better people. When Elrich asked for reactions to the film, this exchange occurred:

Student: As soon as you see a black boy, you know he's gonna do something bad.

Teacher: Just because he's black, he's bad?

Student: Everybody knows that black people are bad. That's the way we are. (p. 12)

When Elrich asked who else agreed with that assessment, twenty-four students raised their hands. Further discussion revealed that most of the students agreed with the following statements:

- Blacks are poor and stay poor because they're dumber than whites (and Asians).
- Black people don't like to work hard.
- Black men make women pregnant and leave.
- Black boys expect to die young and unnaturally.
- White people are smart and have money.
- Asians are smart and have money.
- Asians don't like blacks or Hispanics.
- Hispanics are more like blacks than whites. They can't be white so they try to be black.
- Hispanics are poor and don't try hard because, like blacks, they know it doesn't matter. They will be like blacks because when you're poor, you have to be bad to survive. (p. 13)

According to Elrich (1994), his students' view of the world was that

> hard work does not equal success in their world; instead, it means that parents are gone and children take care of children, they told us. The people who have the material goods that reflect the good life get their money through guns and drugs. Wimps die young and live in fear. Tough guys die young but are proud. Bosses are white and workers are black, and black people don't do important things, except in school books. In their world, few aspire to be doctors, scientists, or lawyers. (p. 14)

During the course of the year, Elrich prompted discussions of slavery, racism, and class. In an attempt to help his students understand that the effects of bigotry and racism are not necessarily permanent, he pointed out that two hundred years ago, life for most whites was harsh and not terribly free, especially in Europe, and that ideas about race and class were taught and promoted in the interest of a few—primarily very wealthy and privileged—white men. But over time and with persistent effort, many of these barriers to personal advancement were either eliminated or drastically reduced. Therefore, his students could influence what they became if they worked at doing so.

The relationship of low self-esteem to low achievement is dramatic but not always simple. In one recent study (van Laar, 2000), many African American high school and college students scored as high on measures of self-esteem as did whites even though the African American students had lower levels of achievement. This seeming paradox results from minority students' belief that because of discrimination, they will not have available to them the same opportunities for employment and career advancement that are available to white students. Being able to blame the environment rather than oneself allows one to maintain a healthy sense of self-esteem. This perception may also play a role in minorities' lower need for achievement, the characteristic we discussed at the beginning of this section.

Classroom Environment Although teachers cannot work magical changes in a student's social class, health, family, or peer group, they can do a great deal to encourage learning among students of all social classes. Marc Elrich's efforts are just one example.

A recent study involved observations of, interviews with, and questionnaire responses from urban, low-SES African American students in grades 3 through 5. The study revealed that a positive attitude toward school was strongly related to classroom atmosphere. Students who liked school the most and found their classroom experiences to be the most satisfying described their relationship with their teacher as a caring and supportive one. Supportive teachers showed an interest in students by talking with them about their personal problems and providing emotional support (Baker, 1999).

● Classroom atmosphere, teachers' approaches connected with achievement levels of low-SES students

High levels of achievement for low-SES students have also been associated with the following attitudes and approaches among teachers:

- Teachers' high but realistic expectations for their students
- Mastery goals (an approach discussed later in this chapter)
- Never accepting low-quality work
- The use of scaffolded instruction (Denbo, 2002; Rolón, 2002/2003)

Teachers' expectations for their students are so important that we devote the next section to this subject.

The Effect of Ethnicity and Social Class on Teachers' Expectations

So far we have described how students' ethnic and social class backgrounds influence their approach to and success with various learning tasks. Now we would like to tell you how those and other characteristics often affect (consciously and unconsciously) the expectations that teachers have for student performance and how those

● Teacher expectancy (Pygmalion) effect: impact of teacher expectations leads to self-fulfilling prophecy

expectations affect the quantity and quality of work that students exhibit. This phenomenon has been extensively studied since 1968 and is known variously as the *Pygmalion effect*, the *self-fulfilling prophecy*, and the **teacher expectancy effect**. By becoming aware of the major factors that influence teachers' perceptions of and actions toward students, you may be able to reduce subjectivity to a minimum, particularly with students whose cultural backgrounds are very different from your own.

The teacher expectancy effect basically works as follows:

1. On the basis of such characteristics as race, SES, ethnic background, dress, speech pattern, and test scores, teachers form expectancies about how various students will perform in class.
2. They subtly communicate those expectancies to the students in a variety of ways.
3. Students come to behave in a way that is consistent with what the teacher expects.

This phenomenon was first proposed by Robert Rosenthal and Lenore Jacobson in their 1968 book, *Pygmalion in the Classroom*. They described an experiment in which first- through sixth-grade teachers were led to believe that certain children had untapped potential and were "likely to show unusual intellectual gains in the year ahead" because of their scores on a new kind of ability test. In fact, the test was

pause & reflect

How have your experiences with members of ethnic or racial minority groups been similar to or different from what you have heard and read about those groups? Which source (personal experience or ideas derived from others) most affects your expectations for minority students?

composed of standard items, and the designated students were chosen at random. Nevertheless, Rosenthal and Jacobson reported that the students who were labeled potential achievers showed significant gains in intelligence quotient (IQ) and that the reason for these gains was that their teachers expected more of these students. The authors referred to this phenomenon as the Pygmalion effect because they felt that teacher expectations had influenced the students to become intelligent in the same way that the expectations of the mythical Greek sculptor Pygmalion caused a statue he had carved to come to life.

● Limited effect of teacher expectancy on IQ scores

● Strong effect of teacher expectancy on achievement, participation

Research on the Effects of Teachers' Expectancies   Given the obvious implications of the teacher expectancy effect for shaping student behavior, researchers wasted no time investigating its validity and limits (see Spitz, 1999, for an excellent summary and analysis of the original and subsequent research, and Rosenthal, 2002, for the views of the senior author of *Pygmalion* on the original study). Despite the dramatic results that Rosenthal and Jacobson reported, subsequent research showed that the effect of teacher expectancy on IQ scores was essentially limited to first- and second-grade students, was moderate in strength at those grade levels, and occurred only when it was induced within the first two weeks of the school year (Raudenbush, 1984). Apparently, once teachers have had an opportunity to observe and interact with their students, they view these experiences as more credible and informative than the results of a mental ability test.

But research that has investigated the effect of teacher expectancy on classroom achievement and participation has generally found sizable positive *and* negative effects (for example, Braun, 1976; Brophy, 1983; Cooper, 1979; Good & Nicholls, 2001; Rosenthal, 1985). In addition, it appears that teacher expectations are more likely to maintain already existing tendencies than to alter well-established behaviors drastically. For example, primary grade teachers react differently to students in the fast-track reading group than to students in the slow-track group. When working with the more proficient readers, teachers tend to smile, lean toward the students, and establish eye contact more often, and they tend to give criticism in friendlier, gentler tones than they use in the slow-track group. They often overlook the oral reading errors of proficient readers, and when they give corrections, they do so at the end of the sentence or other meaningful unit rather than in the middle of such units. And they ask comprehension questions more often than factual questions as a means of monitoring students' attention to the reading selection.

In contrast, teachers correct less proficient readers more often and in places that interrupt meaningful processing of the text, give these students less time to decode difficult words or to correct themselves, and ask low-level factual questions as a way of checking on students' attention. Teachers' body posture is often characterized by frowning, pursing the lips, shaking the head, pointing a finger, and sitting erect. In sum, through a variety of subtle ways, teachers communicate to students that they expect them to perform well or poorly and then create a situation that is consistent with the expectation. As a result, initial differences between good and poor readers either remain or widen over the course of the school career (Wuthrick, 1990).

Factors That Help Create Expectancies   In addition to documenting the existence of teacher expectancy effects and the conditions under which they occur, researchers have sought to identify the factors that might create high or low teacher expectations. Here are some important factors taken from analyses by Carl Braun (1976), Thomas Good and Sharon Nicholls (2001), Gloria Ladson-Billings (1994), Vonnie McLoyd (1998), and Sonia Nieto (2004):

● Teacher expectancies influenced by social class, ethnic background, achievement, attractiveness, gender

- Middle-class students are expected to receive higher grades than low-SES students, even when their IQ scores and achievement test scores are similar.
- African American students are given less attention and are expected to learn less than white students, even when both groups have the same ability.
- Teachers tend to perceive children from poor homes as less mature, less capable of following directions, and less capable of working independently than children from more advantaged homes.
- Teachers who think of intelligence as a fixed and stable capacity are more likely to formulate negative and positive expectations of students than are teachers who think of intelligence as a collection of skills that can be shaped.
- Teachers are more influenced by negative information about students (for example, low test scores) than they are by neutral or positive information.
- High-achieving students receive more praise than low-achieving ones.
- Attractive children are often perceived by teachers to be brighter, more capable, and more social than unattractive children.
- Teachers tend to approve of girls' behavior more frequently than they approve of boys' behavior.

It is important to bear in mind that these factors (plus others such as ethnic background, knowledge of siblings, and impressions of parents) usually operate in concert to produce an expectancy. The following Suggestions for Teaching in Your Classroom will give you some ideas for combating the damaging effects of teacher expectancies as well as other problems often faced by low-SES and minority students.

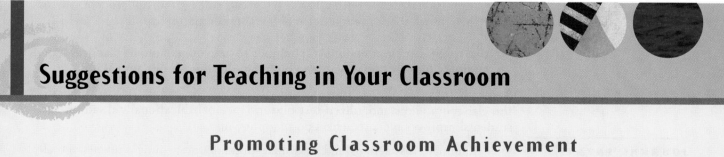

Suggestions for Teaching in Your Classroom

Promoting Classroom Achievement for All Students

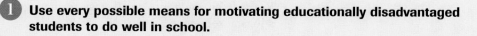

1 **Use every possible means for motivating educationally disadvantaged students to do well in school.**

Because of the factors we mentioned earlier in the chapter that serve to depress the motivation and performance of many low-SES and ethnic minority students, they require the highest-quality instruction in order to meet district and state learning standards. A good place to start in thinking about how to teach such students is with the opinions of the students themselves. According to the responses of almost four hundred low-income, inner-city middle school and high school students, good teachers do the following:

- Push students to learn by such actions as not accepting excuses for missed or late work, constantly checking homework, giving rewards, and keeping parents informed.
- Maintain an orderly and well-run classroom in which disruptions are kept to a minimum. (You will find more detailed information on how to create such an environment in our chapter on classroom management.)
- Are always available to provide a student with help in whatever form the student prefers. Some students, for example, want help after school, some during class, some individually, some by working with peers, and some through whole-class question-and-answer sessions. Some students may ask for help only if they are sure that no one besides the teacher knows they are receiving it.
- Strive to have all students understand the material by not rushing through lessons and by offering explanations in a clear step-by-step fashion and in various ways.
- Use a variety of instructional tactics such as group work, lecture, textbook reading, worksheets, whole-class instruction, and hands-on activities.
- Make an effort to understand students' behavior by trying to understand the personalities and after-school lives of students (Corbett & Wilson, 2002).

The perceptions of these students are remarkably consistent with a set of five teaching standards that is based on Vygotsky's theory of cognitive development and was designed with low-SES, ethnic minority students in mind (Doherty, Hilberg, Epaloose, & Tharp, 2002; Tharp, Estrada, Dalton, & Yamauchi, 2000). The five standards are as follows:

- *Joint Productive Activity:* The teacher works with small groups of students on a joint project, modeling language, skills, and problem-solving strategies.
- *Language and Literacy Development:* The teacher designs activities that involve extended language use and development of content vocabulary and assists students through questioning, rephrasing, and modeling.
- *Contextualization:* The teacher relates new information to what students already know by situating problems and issues in familiar home and community contexts.
- *Challenging Activities:* The teacher gives students challenging objectives to master and provides feedback about their progress.
- *Instructional Conversation:* The teacher and small groups of students discuss their views about the relevance of learning certain topics.

2 **Use a variety of instructional techniques to help educationally disadvantaged students master both basic and higher-order knowledge and skills.**

Research from the 1970s (for example, Brophy & Evertson, 1976) found that the classroom and standardized test performance of educationally disadvantaged students improves when teachers do the following:

JOURNAL ENTRY
Using Productive Techniques
of Teaching

- Eliminate distractions and maximize the amount of time students actually spend working on a task
- Establish high expectations and a classroom climate that supports achievement
- Break tasks down into small, easy-to-manage pieces, and arrange the pieces in a logical sequence
- Have students work on specific exercises in small groups

- Ask direct questions that have direct answers
- Provide frequent opportunities for practice and review
- Provide timely corrective feedback

Designing classroom instruction along these guidelines has both benefits and costs. The benefits are that students spend more time on-task, success tends to be more consistent, and more students reach a higher level of mastery of content knowledge and skills. The main cost is the lack of transfer that usually occurs when knowledge and skills are learned as isolated segments in a nonmeaningful context. A second cost is that students have few opportunities to interact with one another.

If teachers combine the seven guidelines just mentioned with current learning theory and research (see, for example, Gordon, Rogers, Comfort, Gavula, & McGee, 2001; Knapp & Shields, 1990; Knapp, Shields, & Turnbull, 1995; Means & Knapp, 1991; as well as later chapters of this book), they may be able to raise the basic skill level of educationally disadvantaged students *and* improve their ability to transfer what they have learned to meaningful and realistic contexts. To accomplish this goal, a teacher should also do the following:

- Provide opportunities for students to apply ideas and skills to real-life or realistic situations in order to make the lesson more meaningful. For example, after collecting and analyzing information, students might write letters to the mayor or city council requesting more streetlights for increased safety at night or improvements to basketball courts and baseball fields.
- Allow students the opportunity to discuss among themselves the meaning of ideas and their potential applications. In making a request of a government official, students should be encouraged to discuss which arguments are likely to be most effective and how they would respond should the official turn their proposal down.
- Embed basic skills instruction within the context of complex and realistic tasks. Letter-writing campaigns, for example, can be used to practice such basic English skills as vocabulary acquisition, spelling, punctuation, and grammar. Science projects can be used to practice a variety of mathematics skills.
- Point out how classroom tasks relate to students' out-of-school experiences. One example is to draw attention to the basic similarities between poetry and rap music.
- Model for and explain to students the various thinking processes that are activated and used when one engages in a complex task. As you will see when you read the chapter on information-processing theory, effective learners approach tasks strategically, which is to say they analyze the task, formulate a plan for dealing with it, use a variety of specific learning skills, and monitor their progress. These are fundamental learning processes that are almost never made explicit to students.
- Gradually ease students into the process of dealing with complex and realistic tasks. There is no question that the approach described in this list carries with it more risk for failure than was the case for the structured, small-scale approach of the 1970s. But much of this risk can be minimized by *scaffolding*, which we described in the chapter on stage theories of development. As you may recall, in scaffolding, the teacher initially provides a considerable amount of support through explanations, demonstrations, and prompts of various types. As students demonstrate their ability to carry out more of a task independently, the scaffolding is withdrawn.

 Be alert to the potential dangers of labeling. Concentrate on individuals while guarding against the impact of stereotyping.

Myrna Gantner (1997), an eighth-grade teacher in an inner-city middle school near the Mexican border, learned the following lessons about treating her Hispanic students as individuals:

- Treat Hispanic students the same as you would treat any other student. When teachers believe that inner-city Hispanic students are less capable than other students, they tend to give them less time and attention. Students quickly notice these differences and may respond with lower-quality work and more disruptive behavior.
- Don't prejudge students. If you believe that most Hispanic children use drugs, belong to gangs, or have limited academic ability, students will eventually become aware of your prejudice and act accordingly. Gantner's students said they were most appreciative of teachers who were interested in them as individuals, had high expectations for them, and showed them how to achieve their goals.
- Don't ridicule or make fun of students' limited English proficiency. The best way to acquire proficiency in a second language is to use it frequently. Students will be less inclined to do so if they think teachers and other students will laugh at their mistakes.

4   **Remember that in addition to being a skilled teacher, you are also a human being who may at times react subjectively to students.**

JOURNAL ENTRY
Ways to Minimize Subjectivity

Try to control the influence of such factors as name, ethnic background, gender, physical characteristics, knowledge of siblings or parents, grades, and test scores. If you think you can be honest with yourself, you might attempt to describe your prejudices so that you will be in a position to guard against them. (Do you tend to be annoyed when you read descriptions of the exploits of members of a particular religious or ethnic group, for example?) Try to think of a student independently of her siblings and parents.

MULTICULTURAL EDUCATION PROGRAMS

The concept of multicultural education has been around for some time. Many of the elements that constitute contemporary programs were devised seventy to eighty years ago as part of a then-current emphasis on international education (Gollnick & Chinn, 2002). In this section, we will give you some idea of what it might be like to teach today from a multicultural perspective by describing the basic goals, assumptions, and characteristics of modern programs.

Assumptions and Goals

The various arguments in favor of multicultural education that are made by its proponents (for example, Banks, 1994, 2002; Bennett, 2003; García, 2002; Gollnick & Chinn, 2002; Ogbu, 1992; Singer, 1994) stem from several assumptions. These assumptions and the goals that flow from them appear in Table 5.2.

Basic Approaches and Concepts

Approaches   James Banks (2001, 2002), a noted authority on multicultural education, describes four approaches to multicultural education. Most multicultural programs, particularly those in the primary grades, adopt what he calls the *contributions approach*. Here, ethnic historical figures whose values and behaviors are consistent with American mainstream culture (for example, Booker T. Washington, Sacajawea) are studied, whereas individuals who have challenged the dominant view (such as W. E. B. Du Bois, Geronimo) are ignored.

● Multicultural education can be approached in different ways

Table 5.2	Common Assumptions and Goals of Multicultural Education Programs
Assumptions of Multicultural Education	**Goals of Multicultural Education**
U.S. culture has been formed by the contributions of different cultural groups	Promote understanding of the origins and lack of validity of ethnic stereotypes (e.g., African Americans are violent, Jews are stingy, Asian Americans excel at math and science, Hispanic Americans are hot tempered)
Individuals must have self-esteem and group esteem to work productively with people from other cultures	Teachers should give all students a sense of being valued and accepted by expressing positive attitudes, using appropriate instructional methods, and formulating fair disciplinary policies and practices
Learning about the achievements of one's cultural group will raise self- and group esteem	Promote self-acceptance and respect for other cultures by studying the impact ethnic groups have had on American society
American society benefits from positive interactions among members of different cultural groups	Reduce ethnocentrism and increase positive relationships among members of different ethnic groups by understanding the viewpoints and products of these groups
Academic performance is enhanced when teachers incorporate various cultural values and experiences into instructional lessons	Help students master basic reading, writing, and computation skills by embedding them in a personally meaningful (i.e., ethnically related) context

● Multicultural programs aim to promote respect for diversity, reduction of ethnocentrism and stereotypes, improved learning

A second approach, which incorporates the first, is called the *ethnic additive approach*. Here, an instructional unit composed of concepts, themes, points of view, and individual accomplishments is simply added to the curriculum. The perspective from which an ethnic group's contributions are viewed, however, tends to be that of the mainstream.

In a third approach, which Banks calls the *transformation approach*, the assumption is that there is no one valid way of understanding people, events, concepts, and themes. Rather, there are multiple views, and each has something of value to offer.

pause & *reflect*

Think about the four approaches to multicultural education described in this section. What advantages and disadvantages do you see for each approach? Which approach would you use? Why?

For example, the view of the early pioneers who settled the American West could be summed up by such phrases as "How the West Was Won" and "The Westward Movement." But the Native American tribes who had lived there for thousands of years may well have referred to the same event as "How the West Was Taken" or "The Westward Plague." You may recognize that the transformation approach is based on the principle of constructivism (discussed in earlier chapters). Because this approach requires the concrete operational schemes described in our chapter on stage theories of development, it is typically introduced at the middle school level.

Finally, there is the *decision making and social action approach*. It incorporates all of the components of the previous approaches and adds the requirement that students make decisions and take actions concerning a concept, issue, or problem being studied.

● Multicultural lessons organized around key concepts

Concepts   Regardless of which approach you use, Banks (2002) suggests that multicultural units and lessons be organized around a set of key concepts that incorporate a range of facts, generalizations, and subject-matter disciplines. These concepts

In order for children to understand and appreciate different cultural values and experiences, those values and experiences have to be integrated into the curriculum and rewarded by the teacher.

can be used to analyze a particular ethnic group or to compare and contrast groups. The following set of key concepts and associated questions illustrates what Banks has in mind:

> *Immigration:* From what country or countries did this group originate? When and in what numbers did this group immigrate to the United States?
>
> *Culture:* What ethnic elements (for example, values, customs, perspectives) are present in the group's culture today? How is the group's culture reflected in its music, literature, and art?
>
> *Identity:* To what extent does the group see itself as separate and apart from other groups in society because of its unique history?
>
> *Perspectives:* To what extent do most members of the group hold the same view on an issue of importance to it?
>
> *Ethnic institutions:* What educational, commercial, religious, and social organizations were formed by members of the group to help satisfy its needs?
>
> *Demographic, social, political, and economic status:* How can the current status of the group be described in terms of numbers, political influence, and income?
>
> *Racism and discrimination:* In what ways has this group been subjected to racism and discrimination?
>
> *Intraethnic diversity:* How do members of the group differ from each other in terms of such major characteristics as geographical location, social class, religion, and political affiliation?
>
> *Acculturation:* To what extent has the group influenced and been influenced by the mainstream society?

pause & reflect

Why are these concepts so important that Banks labels them key concepts?

Characteristics of Effective Multicultural Teachers

Although Banks's ideas about how to structure multicultural education programs are well conceived, they require the efforts of effective teachers for their potential benefits to be realized. Eugene García (2002), on the basis of his own research and that of others, identifies several characteristics that contribute to the success some teachers have in teaching students from culturally diverse backgrounds. Briefly stated, the effective multicultural teacher does the following:

Advocates of multicultural education believe that ethnic minority students learn more effectively when some of their learning materials and assignments contain ethnically related content.

1. Provides students with clear objectives.
2. Continuously communicates high expectations to the student.
3. Monitors student progress and provides immediate feedback.
4. Has several years of experience in teaching culturally diverse students.
5. Can clearly explain why she uses specific instructional techniques (like the ones described in the next section).
6. Strives to embed instruction in a meaningful context. For example, a topic from one subject, such as controlling crop-damaging insects with insecticide, could be extended to other subjects (examining the effects of insecticide on human health, graphing crop yields sprayed with various types and amounts of insecticides).
7. Provides opportunities for active learning through small-group work and hands-on activities. One teacher, for example, created writing workshops in which students wrote, revised, edited, and published their products for others to read.
8. Exhibits a high level of dedication. Effective multicultural teachers are among the first to arrive at school and among the last to leave, work weekends, buy supplies with their own money, and are constantly looking for opportunities to improve their instructional practices.
9. Enhances students' self-esteem by having classroom materials and practices reflect students' cultural and linguistic backgrounds.
10. Has a strong affinity for the students. Effective multicultural teachers describe their culturally diverse students in such terms as "I love these children like my own" and "We are a family here."

Instructional Goals, Methods, and Materials

Instructional Goals   Teachers whose classes have a high percentage of children from ethnic minority and low-SES backgrounds often assume that they need to emphasize mastery of basic skills (such as computation, spelling, grammar, and word decoding) because minority and low-SES students are often deficient in those skills. Although this approach does improve children's performance on tests of basic skills, some educators argue that it does so at the expense of learning higher-level skills and that it is possible for students from poverty backgrounds to acquire both basic and higher-level skills.

Michael Knapp, Patrick Shields, and Brenda Turnbull (1995) conducted a study to investigate this issue. They examined the teaching practices of almost 140 first-through sixth-grade classrooms in fifteen elementary schools that served large numbers of children from low-SES families to determine if the assumption that low-SES children can acquire both basic and higher-level skills is true. Over a two-year period, these authors studied classrooms where the learning of basic skills was paramount, as well as classrooms that emphasized higher-level and more meaningful outcomes. Teachers in the first group made extensive use of drill and practice, tasks that were limited in their demands, and tasks that could be completed quickly. Teachers in the second group used classroom discussions to let students work out the reasons behind mathematical procedures or explore alternative solutions to math problems, required students to read longer passages and gave them opportunities to discuss what they had read, taught them reading comprehension strategies, and gave them more extended writing assignments.

Knapp and his colleagues found that children whose instruction emphasized conceptual understanding and problem solving performed better on mathematics, reading comprehension, and writing test items that measured advanced skills than their counterparts whose instruction focused on mastery of basic skills. And their performance on basic skill items was either no worse or better than that of students whose teachers emphasized the learning of basic skills.

Instructional Methods   The three instructional tactics that are recommended most often by proponents of multicultural education are peer tutoring, cooperative learning, and mastery learning. Although each of these techniques can be used with any group of students and for almost any purpose, they are so well suited to the goals of multicultural education that the phrase "culturally responsive teaching" has been used to describe them (Wlodkowski & Ginsberg, 1995).

Peer Tutoring   As its name implies, **peer tutoring** involves the teaching of one student by another. The students may be similar in age or separated by one or more years. (The latter arrangement is usually referred to as cross-age tutoring.) The theoretical basis of peer tutoring comes from Jean Piaget's notions about cognitive development. Recall from our discussion of Piaget earlier in the book that cognitive growth depends on the presence of a disequilibrating stimulus that the learner is motivated to eliminate. When children with different cognitive schemes (because of differences in age, knowledge, or cultural background) are forced to interact with each other, cognitive conflict results. Growth occurs when children try to resolve this conflict by comparing and contrasting each other's views.

● Peer tutoring improves achievement

Researchers have consistently found that peer tutoring (also referred to as peer-assisted learning) aids achievement for a wide range of students and subject matters. An analysis of eighty-one studies published between 1974 and 2000 found that on average students who received peer tutoring scored at the 63rd percentile on a measure of achievement whereas students who did not receive peer tutoring scored at the 50th percentile. The strongest effects were obtained for younger students (grades 1–3), urban students, ethnic minority students, and low-SES students. Also, stronger effects were produced by studies in which students rather than teachers were responsible for such self-management behaviors as setting goals, selecting rewards, and administering rewards (Rohrbeck, Ginsburg-Block, Fantuzzo, & Miller, 2003). Because peer tutoring involves working cooperatively either in pairs or small groups, Native American and Hispanic American students are particularly likely to be comfortable with its use.

● Cooperative learning: students work together in small groups

Cooperative Learning   Closely related to peer tutoring is cooperative learning. The general idea behind **cooperative learning** is that by working in small, heterogeneous groups (of four or five students total) and by helping one another master the various aspects of a particular task, students will be more motivated to learn, will learn more than if they had to work independently, and will forge stronger interpersonal relationships than they would by working alone.

David Johnson and Roger Johnson (1998), who have been researching the effects of cooperative learning for over twenty-five years, make a basic observation about the relevance of cooperative learning to the goals of multicultural education programs:

● Cooperative learning fosters better understanding among ethnically diverse students

students cannot learn everything they need to know about cultural diversity from reading books and articles. A deeper understanding of the nature and value of diversity is gained by learning how to work cooperatively with individuals from different cultural backgrounds.

There are several forms of cooperative learning, one of which is student team learning. Student team learning techniques are built on the concepts of team reward, individual accountability, and equal opportunities for success. *Team reward* means that teams are not in competition with one another for limited rewards. All of the teams, some of them, or none of them may earn whatever rewards are made available depending on how well the team's performance matches a predetermined standard. *Individual accountability* means that each member of the team must perform at a certain level (on a quiz, for example) for the team's effort to be judged successful. It is not permissible for one team member's above-average performance to compensate for another team member's below-average performance. Finally, *equal opportunities for success* allow students of all ability levels to contribute to their team's success by improving on their own past performances (Slavin, 1995).

Robert Slavin (1995), a leading exponent of cooperative learning, reports that cooperative learning produced significantly higher levels of achievement than did non-cooperative arrangements in sixty-three of ninety-nine studies (64 percent). The results for the student team learning programs have been the most consistently positive. Of particular relevance to this chapter are the findings that students who cooperate in learning are more likely to list as friends peers from different ethnic groups and are better able to take the perspective of a classmate than are students who do not work in cooperative groups.

Cooperative learning is a generally effective instructional tactic that it is likely to be particularly useful with Hispanic American, African American, and Native American students. These cultures value a communal orientation that emphasizes cooperation and sharing. Thus, these students may be more prepared than other individuals to work productively as part of a group by carrying out their own responsibilities as well as helping others do the same (Bennett, 2003; Nieto, 2004; Soldier, 1989). One study found that small groups of African American fifth-grade students who were told that they had to help one another learn a reading passage recalled more of the text than did similar students who worked either in pairs or individually (Dill & Boykin, 2000).

The power of students working cooperatively in small groups has also been demonstrated by a college mathematics professor. Curious as to why African American and Hispanic students performed so poorly in mathematics classes while Asian students excelled, despite the fact that each group was similar in terms of quality of high school education and family background, a University of California mathematics professor interviewed students from each group and uncovered a critical difference: the Asian students studied in cooperative groups. They worked together to analyze the text material and class notes, shared both successful and unsuccessful strategies for problem solving, and made sure each member of the group was prepared for the next exam. The African American students, by contrast, tended to study individually. To close the gap between these two groups, the instructor created workshops in which diverse groups of students (different ethnic backgrounds and levels of achievement) worked cooperatively. The result was that the African American students' performance improved by as much as one letter grade (Singham, 1998). We will have more to say about cooperative learning and its effects on learning in the chapter "Approaches to Instruction."

● Mastery learning: all students can master the curriculum

Mastery Learning   The third frequently recommended instructional tactic, **mastery learning,** is an approach to teaching and learning that assumes most students can master the curriculum if certain conditions are established: students (1) have sufficient aptitude to learn a particular task, (2) have sufficient ability to understand instruction, (3) are willing to persevere until they attain a certain level of mastery, (4) are allowed whatever time is necessary to attain mastery, and (5) are provided with good-quality instruction.

Mastery learning proponents assume that all of these conditions can be created if they are not already present. Aptitude, for example, is seen as being partly determined by how well prerequisite knowledge and skills have been learned. And perseverance can be strengthened by the deft use of creative teaching methods and various forms of reward for successful performance. The basic mastery learning approach is to specify clearly what is to be learned, organize the content into a sequence of relatively short units, use a variety of instructional methods and materials, allow students to progress through the material at their own rate, monitor student progress in order to identify budding problems and provide corrective feedback, and allow students to relearn and retest on each unit until mastery is attained (Block, Efthim, & Burns, 1989; Gentile & Lalley, 2003).

Like the research on peer tutoring and cooperative learning, the research on mastery learning has generally been positive. On the basis of a comprehensive review of this literature, Chen-Lin Kulik, James Kulik, and Robert Bangert-Drowns (1990) conclude that mastery learning programs produce moderately strong effects on achievement. The average student in a mastery learning class scored at the 70th percentile on a classroom examination, whereas the average student in a conventional class scored at the 50th percentile. The positive effect of mastery learning was slightly more pronounced for lower-ability students. As compared to students in conventional classes, those in mastery classes had more positive feelings about the subjects they studied and the way in which they were taught.

Textbooks   Let's assume that you have decided to incorporate a multicultural orientation into your classroom lessons. Can you count on the history or social studies textbook that your school district has chosen to provide adequate coverage of this topic? Probably not. Jesus Garcia (1993) examined how various ethnic groups have been portrayed in elementary and high school social studies and history textbooks. Although contemporary textbooks provide broader coverage of various ethnic groups than did earlier textbooks, Garcia concludes that their coverage is still superficial. Discussions of African Americans, for example, include such topics as slavery, Reconstruction, the civil rights movement, black organizations, free blacks in colonial America, and the development of black churches. But none of these topics is discussed in great depth. The same conclusion was drawn about the treatments of Irish, Italian, Jewish, and Polish Americans.

The implication for teachers who believe that their classroom should have a strong multicultural emphasis is that their school's textbooks should probably be viewed as just a starting point. The teacher who is committed to providing students a strong multicultural experience will have to seek out high-quality supplementary materials. Our Resources for Further Investigation at the end of the chapter is a good place to start.

A Rationale for Multicultural Education

Some people seem to believe that multicultural education programs represent a rejection of basic American values and that this opposition to traditional values is the only rationale behind such programs. We feel this belief is mistaken on both counts. We see multicultural programs as being consistent with basic American values (such as tolerance of differences and equality of opportunity) and consider them to be justified in several ways.

1. *Multicultural programs foster teaching practices that are effective in general as well as for members of a particular group.* For example, expressing an interest in a student through occasional touching and smiling and allowing the child to tutor a younger student are practices likely to benefit most students, not just those of Hispanic American origin.

2. *All students may profit from understanding different cultural values.* For example, the respect for elders that characterizes Native American and Asian American cultures is likely to become increasingly desirable as the percentage of elderly Americans increases over the years. Similarly, learning the Native American value of living in harmony with nature may come to be essential as we run out of natural resources and attempt to alleviate environmental pollution (Triandis, 1986).

3. *The United States is becoming an increasingly multicultural society (because of the immigration and birthrate trends mentioned earlier), and students thus need to understand and know how to work with people of cultures different from their own.*

4. *Multicultural education programs expose students to the idea that "truth" is very much in the eye of the beholder.* From a European perspective, Christopher Columbus did indeed discover a new world. But from the perspective of the Arawak Indians who were native to the Caribbean, Columbus invaded territories that they had occupied for thousands of years. Similarly, one can describe the history of the United States as one in which continual progress toward democratic ideals has been made or as one in which progress has been interrupted by conflict, struggle, violence, and exclusion (Banks, 1993).

5. *Multicultural programs can encourage student motivation and learning.* These programs demonstrate respect for a child's culture and teach about the contributions that the student's group has made to American society. Proponents argue that these features both personalize education and make it more meaningful. Conversely, when children perceive disrespect for their cultural background, the result can be disastrous. Consider the following comment by a Mexican-American student who realized for the first time that his teachers viewed him as both different and inferior:

   > One recreation period, when we were playing our usual game of soccer, I took time out to search for a rest room. I spotted a building on the north side of the playground and ran for it. As I was about to enter, a teacher blew her whistle very loudly, freezing me on the spot. She approached me and demanded to know where I was going, who I was, and what I was doing on that side of the playground. I was dumbfounded and afraid to respond, so she took me by the ear and escorted me back across the playground to the south side. Her parting remark was a stern admonition not to cross the line and to stay with all the other Mexicans.
   >
   > At that very moment I stopped, turned, and looked at the school as if for the first time. I saw a white line painted across the playground. On one side were the white children playing; on my side were the Mexicans. Then I looked at the building, which was divided in half. The office was in the center, with two wings spreading north and south—one wing for whites and the other for Mexicans. I was overwhelmed with emotions that I could not understand. I was hurt, disappointed, and frustrated. But more than anything else, I was profoundly angry. (Mendoza, 1994, p. 294)

6. *The rationale for multicultural education that we have provided has been reinforced by numerous studies that document the disappointing academic performance of a significant number of minority-group students.* As we mentioned earlier, African American, Hispanic American, and Native American students tend to score lower than white students on standardized tests of vocabulary, reading, writing, mathematics, and science (Ornstein & Levine, 2003), and these differences appear as early as the fourth grade. Although such problems are not easy to solve, the inclusion of ethnically related content and activities in the curriculum helps make classroom assignments more meaningful and encourages minority students to master reading, writing, computational, and reasoning skills (Banks, 2002; Vasquez, 1990).

Bridging the Cultural and SES Gap with Technology

As we stated earlier, a basic purpose of multicultural education is to give students the opportunity to learn about the characteristics of people from different cultures

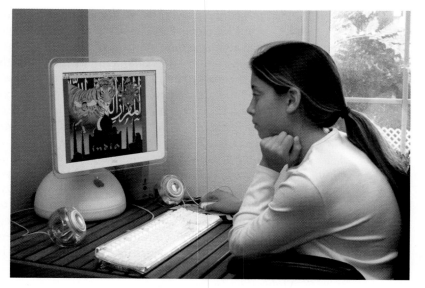

Computer-based technology helps students learn more about other cultures and social classes by providing access to various reference sources and individuals from almost anywhere in the world.

and to try to understand how those individuals view the world. For schools that draw from an ethnically, racially, and socioeconomically diverse population, acquiring firsthand experience about the history, beliefs, and practices of different cultures is not likely to be a major problem. But schools that draw from more homogeneous populations have traditionally been limited to such resources as books, magazines, and videotapes. This limitation on multicultural education is being surmounted, however, by the ability of technology to bring the world to the student, and in a very real sense.

● Multicultural understanding can be promoted by electronically linking students from different cultural backgrounds

Telecommunication projects allow students from different places and varied backgrounds to interact with one another, sharing ideas and experiences and learning new points of view. These exchanges can lead to a greater respect for diversity (Kontos & Mizell, 1997; Salmon & Akaran, 2001). Kerry Freedman and Meihui Liu (1996), for instance, found that despite clear differences in attitudes and communication patterns, telecommunication projects among nonnative Asian American students, Native American students on a reservation, and white rural students encouraged more questioning and interaction than occurred in face-to-face settings. A similar project in Connecticut attempted to increase respect and tolerance for other cultures through videoconferences between an urban and a suburban school. Discussions of lifestyle, local stores, city services, handgun problems, and explorations of the concept of diversity were eye-opening for these students. Michaele Salmon and Susan Akaran (2001) describe an e-mail exchange program between kindergarten students from New Jersey and first-grade Eskimo children from Alaska that produced greater respect and understanding of each other's culture.

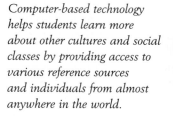

For quick links to relevant web sites, go to the Weblinks section of the textbook web site, which you can access from **http://education.college .hmco.com/students.**

Another noteworthy program is the International Education and Resource Network (iEARN; **www.iearn.org/**), which developed from the AT&T Learning Network (Riel, 1993, 1996). iEARN is a nonprofit organization, made up of more than fifteen thousand schools in a hundred different countries, that allows teachers and students to work together online on various education projects. One way for students and teachers to work on a common project is through Interactive Forums. In these electronic spaces, teachers and students meet other participants and get involved in ongoing projects. Another feature for accomplishing this goal is Learning Circles—interactive, project-based partnerships among a small number of schools located around the world. Each Learning Circle session lasts fourteen weeks.

These types of electronic networking tools open up unique possibilities for cross-class or cross-cultural collaboration and mentoring (Riel, 1996). Imagine if one of the Learning Circle partners for your students was located in the Middle East during a period of intense conflict there. What if you received daily eyewitness reports from such locations right in your classroom, as one teacher's high school classes in Seattle did (Golub, 1994)? What an incredible opportunity for students to gain access to new information, analyze and evaluate it, and communicate their own insights and ideas.

The 4Directions Project is another significant example. Developed by a consortium of nineteen Native American schools in ten states and eleven public and private universities and organizations, the project allows isolated far-flung members of Native American schools to share local customs and values with other Native American tribes around the country. The students display their projects and achievements and participate in virtual communities through Internet teleconferencing. Although the 4Directions web site (**http://4directions.org/**) was created to facilitate communication among Native American communities, the project welcomes other schools to participate in the project or use its resources (Allen et al., 1999).

Earlier in this chapter, we indicated that many students from low-SES homes are considered to be at risk for educational failure because of adverse conditions surrounding their physical, social, emotional, and cognitive development. Creative technology products may be able to reduce the numbers of at-risk students who perform at low levels or drop out of school altogether. One multimedia environment, MOST (Multimedia Environments That Organize and Support Learning Through Technology), was designed to engage at-risk middle school and high school students in authentic tasks that develop their literacy skills (Bransford et al., 1996; Cognition and Technology Group at Vanderbilt, 1994). Students create interesting multimedia products that teach their parents, teachers, peers, and others about important life concepts and issues such as drug abuse, AIDS, and driving safety, all while working on their literacy skills. Technological supports, or scaffolds, are embedded in MOST environments to foster student reading comprehension, listening, communication, and information-generation skills. Besides engaging students in a meaningful learning context, MOST environments attempt to build on student strengths and connect to out-of-school experiences.

Integrating technology into the classrooms of schools with high percentages of low-SES students does seem to produce modest but statistically significant improvements in achievement over classrooms that lack computer-based technology. In one study (Page, 2002), half of the third- and fifth-grade low-SES students in five schools worked in technology-enriched classrooms while the other students worked on the same lessons without the aid of technology. For a unit on the planets and constellations within the Milky Way galaxy, for example, students in the technology-enriched classrooms would gather information for a report from science software or the World Wide Web and then prepare a slide show presentation using PowerPoint. For other lessons they might have videoconferences with same-grade students from other schools. Although there were no differences between the two groups on a standardized test of reading, students in the technology-enriched classes did score higher than their nontechnology peers on a standardized test of mathematical skills and a test of self-esteem. In addition, there was considerably more student-to-student interaction and less teacher-to-student interaction in the technology-enriched classes.

Bear in mind, however, that access to technology is not equal across school districts. In 2002, the number of students per Internet-connected computer for all schools was 5.6, whereas the number of students per Internet-connected computer for schools with high minority enrollments was 6.7 ("Access to Technology," 2003). In some schools, lack of technology resources may hinder the efforts we have described in this section.

Now that you are familiar with the nature and goals of multicultural education programs and some of the instructional tools that are available to you, the following Suggestions for Teaching should help you get started.

Promoting Multicultural Understanding and Classroom Achievement

1 Use culturally relevant teaching methods.

To fulfill the goals of multicultural education, teachers should practice what is referred to as either culturally relevant pedagogy (Ladson-Billings, 2002) or culturally responsive pedagogy (Nieto, 2002/2003). This approach to instruction is based on two premises. First, all students, regardless of their ethnic, racial, and social class backgrounds, have assets they can use to aid their learning. Second, teachers need to be aware of and meet students' academic needs in any number of ways. In other words, simply adopting a multicultural basal reader is not culturally responsive pedagogy. In addition to adopting multicultural reading material, you should do everything possible to help all students learn to read. For example, successful teachers of Latino students in Arizona and California have high expectations for students, make their expectations clear, never accept low-quality work, scaffold students' learning, and use Spanish for instruction or allow students to speak Spanish among themselves when working in pairs or groups (Rolón, 2002/2003).

Gloria Ladson-Billings (2002), who has written extensively about working with minority and at-risk students, provides several examples of culturally relevant or responsive teaching. A second-grade teacher allowed her students to bring in lyrics from rap songs that both she and the students deemed to be nonoffensive. The students performed the songs, and the teacher and students discussed the literal and figurative meanings of the words and such aspects of poetry as rhyme scheme, alliteration, and onomatopoeia. The students acquired an understanding of poetry that exceeded both the state's and school district's learning standards. Another teacher invited the parents of her students to conduct "seminars" in class for two to four days, one to two hours at a time. One parent who was famous for the quality of her sweet potato pie taught the students how to make one. In addition, the students were required to complete such related projects as a written report on George Washington Carver's research on the sweet potato, a marketing plan for selling pies, and a statement of the kind of education and experience one needed to become a cook or chef. Similar seminars were done by a carpenter, a former professional basketball player, a licensed practical nurse, and a church musician, all of whom were parents or relatives of the students.

2 Help make students aware of the contributions that specific ethnic groups have made to the development of the United States and the rest of the world.

JOURNAL ENTRY
Ways to Promote Awareness of Contributions of Ethnic Minorities

The first principle suggested by Nicholas Appleton (1983) for implementing a multicultural education program is that students should examine their own ethnic backgrounds before examining the backgrounds of others. Appleton's rationale is that racism in the United States has had a negative impact on the self-concepts of ethnic minority children. Because self-concept is related to achievement, it is important to help students develop positive attitudes about their ethnic heritage. One suggestion for accomplishing this goal is to invite family members of students (and other local residents) of different ethnic backgrounds to the classroom. Ask them to describe the values subscribed to by members of their group and explain how those values have contributed to life in the United States and the rest of the world.

3 Use instructional techniques and classroom activities that are consistent with the value system of students who share a particular cultural background and that encourage students to learn from and about one another's cultures.

Students from Latino cultures (such as those whose families emigrated from Mexico, Central America, and South America) place a high value on the concept of collectivism, or the interdependence of family members. From an early age, children are taught to think first about fostering the success of any group to which they belong by seeking to work cooperatively with others (Rothstein-Fisch, Greenfield, & Trumbull, 1999). To capitalize on this value, consider doing some or all of the following:

- Assign two or three children rather than just one to a classroom task, such as cleaning up after an art period, and allow them to help one another if necessary.
- Increase the use of choral reading with students whose English proficiency is limited so they can practice their decoding and pronunciation skills without being the center of attention.
- After distributing a homework assignment, allow students to discuss the questions but not write down the answers. Those who are more proficient in English and have better-developed intellectual skills can help their less skilled classmates better understand the task. One third-grade teacher who used this technique was surprised to find that every student completed the assignment.

Another opportunity for cultural interaction is provided by the Internet. For example, a web site begun by St. Olaf College in Minneapolis, Minnesota, is dedicated to facilitating e-mail exchanges between students around the globe. Such exchanges can promote shared cultural knowledge and understanding, especially in schools whose populations are relatively homogeneous. The Intercultural E-Mail Classroom Connections web site is now located at **www.teaching.com/iecc/**.

4 **At the secondary level, involve students in activities that explore cultural differences in perceptions, beliefs, and values.**

A well-conceived multicultural education program cannot, and should not, avoid or minimize the issue of cultural conflict. There are at least two reasons for helping students examine this issue. One is that conflict has been a constant and salient aspect of relationships among cultural groups. Another is that cultural conflicts often produce changes that benefit all members of a society (a prime example is the civil rights movement of the 1960s with its boycotts, marches, and demonstrations).

Cultural conflicts arise from differences in perceptions, beliefs, and values. American culture, for example, places great value on self-reliance. Americans generally respect and praise individuals who, through their own initiative, persistence, and ingenuity, achieve substantial personal goals, and they tend to look down on individuals who are dependent on others for their welfare. Consequently, American parents who are financially dependent on their children, even though the children may be prosperous enough to support them, would probably feel ashamed enough to hide the fact. The same situation in China would likely elicit a different reaction because of different values about self-reliance and family responsibilities. Chinese parents who are unable to provide for themselves in their old age but have children successful enough to support them might well brag about it to others (Appleton, 1983).

One technique for exploring cultural conflict is to have students search through newspapers and news magazines for articles that describe clashes. Ask them to identify the source of the conflict and how it might be positively resolved. Another technique is to involve students in games that simulate group conflict. Class members can, for example, play the role of state legislators who represent the interests of diverse ethnic groups and have been lobbied to change the school funding formula so that poorer school districts receive more money (Appleton, 1983). The use of both simulations and the discussion of newspaper articles will probably work best at the high school level because adolescents are better able than younger students to understand the abstract concepts involved in these activities.

JOURNAL ENTRY
Ways to Help Students Explore
Conflicts Between Cultures

⑤ Involve students, especially at the secondary level, in community service activities.

Service-learning programs, found in many school systems, serve several purposes. First, they afford students the opportunity to broaden the knowledge they acquire in school by working to solve real problems in a community setting. Second, they help students develop a sense of civic and social responsibility. Third, they help students become more knowledgeable about career options. And fourth, they provide a useful and needed service to the community (Billig, 2000). To cite one example of a service-learning program with a multicultural perspective, a group of college students advocated and helped draft legislation that would address the needs of poor Hispanic female heads of households (Weah, Simmons, & Hall, 2000). More detailed information about service-learning programs and organizations can be found on the web site of the Corporation for National and Community Service (**www.learnandserve.org/**).

⑥ Make every effort to contact and work with the parents of ethnic minority students.

Would you like more suggestions for your journal? See the Reflective Journal Questions at the textbook web site.

Linda Holman (1997) is the principal of an elementary school in El Paso, Texas. In her school, 43 percent of the 700 students have limited English proficiency and are recent immigrants to the United States. To help students and their parents make a successful transition to a new country and school system, Holman makes the following suggestions:

- During the first week of the school year, hold parent-teacher-child conferences. Be willing to hold these meetings in the parents' home and during the evening hours if necessary.
- Recruit bilingual parent volunteers to help teachers and staff members talk with parents and students.
- In discussing classroom tasks and student performance with parents, avoid technical terminology and acronyms. Not only does this result in fewer misunderstandings, but it lessens the sense of inferiority that some parents feel.
- Encourage parents to work with their children in their native language in order to build a strong foundation for second-language learning.

Lee Little Soldier (1997) makes the same recommendation about meeting with parents of Native American students. He states that parents may at first be intimidated by the atmosphere of the school. Offering to work with them in the comfort of their home indicates the school's interest in the family as well as the child.

BILINGUAL EDUCATION

As we mentioned earlier, the 1990s set a U.S. record for the number of immigrants during a decade. Just over 11 million legal immigrants arrived in the United States between 1991 and 2002. Not surprisingly, many of the school-age children of these families have either limited or no English proficiency. For the 1999–2000 school year, there were just over 4.1 million limited-English-proficient (LEP) students in grades K–12, about 73 percent of whom spoke Spanish as their primary language. This was an increase in LEP students of 104 percent over the 1989–1990 school year (Haver, 2003).

To address the needs of these students, the federal government provides financial support for the establishment of bilingual education programs. Because language is viewed as an important part of a group's culture, many school districts integrate bilingual education with multicultural education. In this section, we will examine the nature and effectiveness of bilingual education programs.

Before we consider different approaches to bilingual education, there are three general points we would like you to keep in mind.

1. Bilingual programs have become an emotionally charged and politicized topic (see, for example, Macedo, 2000; Porter, 2000; Rothstein, 1998; Thompson, DiCerbo, Mahoney, & MacSwan, 2002). Educators, parents, and legislators have strong opinions regarding what time and resources should be devoted to helping students master native-language skills and whether such programs should include cultural awareness goals. Some people favor moving students into all-English classes as quickly as possible, while others believe that students should have a firm grasp of their native language *and* English before attempting to make the transition to regular classes. Although research on this issue is helpful because it informs us about what is, such research cannot tell us what we should do about what we know.

2. Some language-minority students may suffer from problems that bilingual education alone cannot solve, such as the multiple difficulties associated with low SES.

3. No one approach to bilingual education is likely to be equally effective for all language-minority students. What works well for some low-SES Puerto Rican children may not work well for middle-class Cuban children and vice versa.

Goals and Approaches

Most bilingual education programs have a common long-term goal, but they differ in their approach to that goal. The goal is to help minority-language students acquire as efficiently as possible the English skills they will need to succeed in school and society. The approaches to that goal usually fall into one of three categories: *transition, maintenance,* or *two-way bilingual.*

● Transition programs focus on rapid shift to English proficiency

Transition Programs Programs that have a transition approach teach students wholly (in the case of non-English-proficient students) or partly (in the case of limited-English-proficient students) in their native language so as not to retard their acade-

Some bilingual education programs emphasize using the student's native language competence to help the student learn English as quickly as possible. Other programs emphasize the maintenance or improvement of both the student's native language and English.

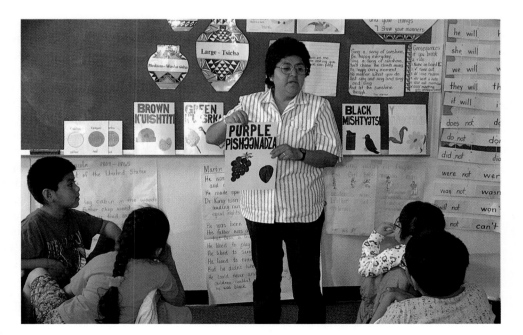

mic progress, but only until they can function adequately in English. At that point, they are placed in regular classes, where all of the instruction is in English. To make the transition time as brief as possible, some programs add an English as a second language (ESL) component. ESL programs typically involve pulling students out of their regular classes and providing them with full-time intensive instruction in English (Gersten, 1999; Mora, Wink, & Wink, 2001; Thomas & Collier, 1999).

● Maintenance programs focus on maintaining native-language competence

Maintenance Programs   Programs that have a maintenance approach try to maintain or improve students' native-language skills. Instruction in the students' native language continues for a significant time before transition to English. Supporters of maintenance programs point to the results of psychological and linguistic studies that suggest that a strong native-language foundation supports the subsequent learning of both English and subject-matter knowledge. In addition, many proponents of multicultural education favor a maintenance approach because they see language as an important part of a group's cultural heritage (Mora et al., 2001; Robledo & Cortez, 2002).

● Two-way bilingual education programs feature instruction in both languages

Two-Way Bilingual Programs   Some bilingual education scholars (e.g., Calderón & Minaya-Rowe, 2003; Thomas & Collier, 1997/1998, 1999) are critical of both transitional and maintenance bilingual education programs because they are remedial in nature, and students who participate in such programs tend to be perceived as inferior in some respect. These educators favor what is generally known as **two-way bilingual (TWB) education** (although the terms *bilingual immersion* and *dual language* are also used). In a TWB program, subject-matter instruction is provided in two languages to all students. This approach is typically used when English is the primary language of about half the students in a school and the other language (usually Spanish) is the primary language of the other half of the students.

TWB programs are used in 271 schools in twenty-four states in the United States (Center for Applied Linguistics, 2003). Although most of these programs are English-Spanish, other programs include Korean, French, Cantonese, Navajo, Japanese, Arabic, Portuguese, Russian, and Mandarin Chinese as the minority language. TWB programs differ from traditional transition and ESL programs in that they begin as early as kindergarten and continue throughout the elementary school years in order to maintain facility in the student's native language while building facility in the nonnative language.

Canada and Miami, Florida, have two of the oldest and largest TWB programs. Canada has always had a large French-speaking population, mostly in the province of Québec. Because many parents wanted their children to be proficient in both English and French, Canadian schools in the 1960s began a K–12 program. In kindergarten and first grade, 90 percent of the instruction is in French and the remaining 10 percent is in English. From grade 2 through grade 5, the proportion gradually shifts to 50/50. By grade 6, most students can work equally well on any subject matter in either language.

The impetus for a TWB program in the Miami area was the large number of residents who emigrated from Cuba. As with all other two-way programs, students whose primary language is Spanish *and* students whose primary language is English participate in the program together. Unlike the Canadian model, which has a strong immersion component in the early grades (80 to 90 percent of the instruction is in French), teachers in Miami's program teach in Spanish for half the day and in English for the other half of the day at all grade levels.

TWB programs typically include the following features:

- At least six years of bilingual instruction
- High-quality instruction in both languages
- Separation of the two languages for instruction (for example, by time of day, day of the week, or even by week)

- Use of the minority language for teaching and classroom discussion at least 50 percent of the time
- A roughly balanced percentage of students for whom each language is primary
- Use of peer tutoring

Despite the growth and success of TWB programs, some states have eliminated all bilingual education programs. In 1998, Californians voted to eliminate their state's bilingual education program and provide instead a one-year English immersion program, in which language-minority students are taught only in English. In 2000, voters in Arizona approved a similar proposition (Thompson et al., 2002). An English immersion program was approved in Massachusetts in 2002 but was later amended to allow TWB programs to continue to operate (Saltzman, 2003).

Research Findings

The question of whether bilingual education programs facilitate the learning of non-English-speaking students is one that has been vigorously debated (see, for example, Baker, 1998; Beaumont, de Valenzuela, & Trumbull, 2002; Cummins, 1999; Krashen, 1999; Meier, 1999). Nevertheless, the weight of the evidence to date seems to support the following conclusions:

● Bilingual education programs produce moderate learning gains

- In comparison to immersion (English-only) programs, participation in bilingual education programs produces small to moderate gains in reading, language skills, mathematics, and total achievement when measured by tests in English. When measured by tests administered in the student's native language, participation in bilingual education leads to significantly better performance on tests of listening comprehension, reading, writing, total language, mathematics, social studies, and attitudes toward school and self. Thus, increasing the amount of time devoted to instruction in English (as is done in immersion programs) does not necessarily lead to higher levels of achievement (Cummins, 1999; Willig, 1985). Early analysis of California's immersion program indicates that although LEP students improved their scores on the Stanford-9 (a standardized achievement test), the scores of non-LEP students increased by a similar amount. Consequently, the achievement gap between LEP and non-LEP students remained unchanged (Thompson et al., 2002).
- ESL programs appear to have positive effects on reading comprehension skills and grade-point average. ESL students recognize cognate vocabulary (related words) fairly well (although there is a wide range of proficiency for this outcome), demonstrate the ability to monitor their comprehension, and use prior knowledge to help them understand and remember what they read (Fitzgerald, 1995). Also, Mexican American students who had more years of ESL/bilingual education than their peers had higher grades (Padilla & Gonzalez, 2001).
- Students who participate in TWB programs score at or above grade level on subject-matter tests and score higher on reading and mathematics tests than LEP students who are taught only in English. Perhaps because of this reason, the bilingual-immersion program in New York City became so popular that students who wanted to participate had to be selected by lottery (Genesee & Cloud, 1998; Thomas & Collier, 1997/1998).

Technology and Bilingual Education

Multimedia, hypermedia, and other technologies are enhancing opportunities for bilingual students and LEP students to learn mathematics (Kinard & Bitter, 1997) as well as the English language (Heath, 1996). With some technology tools, students can hear the pronunciation of a word, see how it is used in context, see a picture of the word if appropriate, explore links to definitions and related words,

Take a Stand!

Bilingual Education: Plus les choses changent, plus elles restent les mêmes

The preceding French phrase translates to "The more things change, the more they remain the same." So it is with the current dispute over the goals and methods of bilingual education. In the early part of the twentieth century, prior to World War I, bilingual public schools were not uncommon, particularly in areas with large numbers of German immigrants. After the war, however, public financing of bilingual schools was abruptly withdrawn, partly as a reaction against Germany (which lost the war and was seen as the aggressor) and partly because of increasing nationalism and isolationism. American society strongly endorsed a one country/one culture policy and stressed once again the idea of America as a melting pot. As a result, English immersion programs for immigrant students became the norm.

But during and after World War II, as now, American students' deficiencies in foreign language fluency became noticeable and a source of concern. This situation contributed to the first Bilingual Education Act in 1965, which emphasized the maintenance of one's native language as well as mastery of English.

As a future educator whose decisions will rest partly on scientific evidence, we suggest you ignore as much as possible both the pro and con arguments about bilingual education that appear to be based on biases and political beliefs. Focus instead on what the research has to say. Our reading of the current research leads us to conclude that bilingual education, particularly in the form of two-way bilingual programs, benefits both limited-English-proficient and native English-speaking students. Given the ease with which technology allows students from different countries to communicate and work collaboratively, as well as the trend toward international commerce, programs that increase students' bilingual fluency should be encouraged and strongly supported.

Have you ever taken part in bilingual education? What is your position on expanding its use in U.S. schools? For more material on this subject, go to the Take a Stand! section of the textbook web site.

discover the origin of the word, and construct personal glossaries (Liu, 1994). There are now "books on disk" for young children and second-language learners that allow them to see the story (for example, *The Tale of Peter Rabbit*) as it is being read. Not only do students see the words highlighted as they are pronounced, but in some of these packages, when they click on an object, the word for it is simultaneously pronounced and displayed on the screen. Importantly, students control the pace, style, and amount of interaction and repetition (Fabris, 1992/1993).

Web resources for bilingual education are also expanding rapidly. For example, the web site La Clase Mágica (**communication.ucsd.edu/LCM/**) is written partly in English and partly in Spanish and contains an electronic wizard (el Maga) that survives by eating the words in the messages that children type to el Maga. The web site Science Fair Assistant (**www.iteachilearn.com/teach/tech/science.htm**), written in both English and Spanish, is designed to

 To review this chapter, go to the ACE practice tests and PowerPoint slides on the textbook web site.

help children in grades K–8 find experiments and ideas for a science project. A number of publications describe how to use web sites for creating lessons to improve LEP students' listening, oral proficiency, reading comprehension, and writing skills (e.g., Feyten et al., 2002).

Resources for Further Investigation

● Multicultural Education: Theory and Practice

James Banks offers a brief introduction to multicultural education in *An Introduction to Multicultural Education* (3rd ed., 2002). A more detailed discussion can be found in his *Teaching Strategies for Ethnic Studies* (7th ed., 2003). Part 1 discusses goals for multicultural programs, key concepts, and planning a multicultural curriculum. Parts 2 through 5 provide background information about ten ethnic groups and strategies for teaching about each group. The book concludes with such useful appendixes as a list of videotapes and films on U.S. ethnic groups, a bibliography of books about women of color, and a chronology of key events concerning ethnic groups in U.S. history.

Another practical book is *Comprehensive Multicultural Education: Theory and Practice* (5th ed., 2003), by Christine Bennett. Part 1 of this book (Chapters 1 to 5) presents the case for multicultural education. Part 2 (Chapters 6, 7, and 8) describes culturally based individual differences that affect teaching and learning. Part 3 (Chapter 9) presents a model for multicultural curriculum development, guidelines for instruction, and a set of twenty-five illustrative lessons written by classroom teachers. The lessons include statements of goals and objectives, a description of the instructional sequence, a list of needed materials, and a means for evaluating how well the objectives were met.

Paul Gorski outlines how teachers can use the Internet to help them meet their multicultural goals and provides a wealth of online resources in *Multicultural Education and the Internet: Intersections and Integrations* (2001). Among the many web sites mentioned throughout the book is his own, the Multicultural Pavilion (**www.edchange.org/multicultural/**). Some of the features of this site are a teacher's corner, and education research room, community forums, an index of related web sites, and a multicultural awareness quiz.

Another phrase for what we have called culturally relevant pedagogy is "culturally proficient instruction." In the book *Culturally Proficient Instruction* (2002), Kikanza Nuri Robins, Randall B. Lindsey, Delores B. Lindsey, and Raymond D. Terrell discuss the elements of this method and provide readers with an opportunity to reflect on and record their answers to a set of directions or questions that relate to this approach to teaching. On page 59, for example, the authors pose the following direction and provide space for the reader to write in a response: "List aspects of culture—yours and your learners'—that affect how your lessons are received." On page 61 they ask the question, "What works for the dominant culture of your organization or school that may not work for all its employees or students?"

A large number of multicultural resources are available on the Internet. Several good starting points include:

Multicultural Education Resources:
www.education.gsw.edu/johnson/MulticulturalEducation.htm

Multicultural Pavilion:
www.edchange.org/multicultural/

National Association for Multicultural Education:
www.nameorg.org/

Center for Multicultural Education:
depts.washington.edu/centerme/

Intercultural E-Mail Classroom Connections:
www.teaching.com/iecc/

● Bilingual Education

Judith Lessow-Hurley offers a readable introduction to bilingual education in *The Foundations of Dual Language Instruction* (2000). *Bilingual Education: A Reference Handbook* (2002), by Rosa Castro Feinberg, is an everything-you-wanted-to-know-about-bilingual-education type of book. This book provides useful chapters on state policies, federal law, and the political issues that affect bilingual education. Chapter 7 discusses agencies and organizations that are associated with bilingual education, and Chapter 8 describes print and nonprint resources.

Margarita Espino Calderón and Liliana Minaya-Rowe describe how to plan, design, and implement a two-way bilingual program in *Designing and Implementing Two-Way Bilingual Programs* (2003). Chapter 1 notes what two-way bilingual programs are and are not, lists the benefits of two-way programs, and provides reasons why schools should develop and support such programs.

For those interested in English immersion programs or who teach in states where immersion programs are mandated (such as Arizona and California), *Structured English Immersion: A Step-by-Step Guide for K–6 Teachers and Administrators* (2003), by Johanna Haver, is a useful resource. Ms. Haver, a retired teacher with thirty-two years of classroom experience, discusses the characteristics of structured English immersion programs and provides concrete examples of SEI teaching methods for K–6 teachers and administrators.

An excellent resource for information on bilingual education is the web site of the Center for Applied Linguistics (**www.cal.org/**). It provides, for example, a directory of two-way bilingual programs and a set of online articles about two-way programs.

Summary

1. Culture refers to the perceptions, emotions, beliefs, ideas, experiences, and behavior patterns that a group of people have in common.

2. Beginning in the 1960s, the notion of the United States as a cultural melting pot became less popular, and the concept of cultural diversity, or cultural pluralism, increased in popularity. As the latter became more widely accepted, calls were made for the establishment of multicultural education programs in American public schools.

3. The concept of cultural pluralism is based on three beliefs: (a) societies should strive to maintain different cultures, (b) each culture within a society should be respected by others, and (c) individuals within a society have the right to participate in all aspects of that society without having to give up their cultural identity.

4. Because of immigration patterns and high birthrates in some ethnic groups, the United States is becoming an increasingly diverse country.

5. Two important factors that distinguish one culture from another are ethnicity and social class.

6. People of the same ethnic group typically share many of the following characteristics: ancestral country of origin, race, religion, values, political interests, economic interests, and behavior patterns.

7. Ethnic differences in communication patterns and preferences, time orientation, values, and instructional format and learning process preferences can lead to misunderstandings among students and between students and teachers.

8. Social class indicates an individual's or a family's relative position in society in terms of such factors as income, occupation, level of education, place of residence, and material possessions. Socioeconomic status (SES) is a somewhat narrower concept that focuses on the first three of these factors.

9. Low-SES students, especially those from minority groups, tend to achieve at significantly lower levels than white, middle-class children for a variety of reasons. They are more likely than middle-class students to grow up in one-parent households in which the father is the missing parent. Often, too, they receive irregular health care, live in urban areas in small apartments that lack adequate study space, are not exposed to a wide variety of experiences, have low career and academic aspirations, and face classroom environments that are less than fully supportive.

10. The teacher expectancy effect, also known as the self-fulfilling prophecy or the Pygmalion effect, occurs when teachers communicate a particular expectation about how a student will perform and the student's behavior changes so as to be consistent with that expectation.

11. Although the effect of teacher expectancy on IQ scores originally reported by Rosenthal and Jacobson has never been fully replicated, research has demonstrated that teacher expectancy strongly affects classroom achievement and participation in both positive and negative ways.

12. Factors that seem to play a strong role in producing a teacher expectancy effect are a student's social class, ethnic background, gender, achievement, attractiveness, and teachers' conception of the nature of intelligence.

13. Multicultural education programs assume that minority students will learn more and have a stronger self-concept if teachers understand, accept, and reward the thinking and behavior patterns characteristic of the students' culture.

14. Effective multicultural teachers use such proven instructional techniques as providing clear objectives, communicating high expectations, monitoring progress, providing immediate feedback, and making lessons meaningful. In addition, they have experience in teaching culturally diverse classes, exhibit a high level of dedication, and have a strong affinity for their students.

15. Peer tutoring, cooperative learning, and mastery learning are three generally effective instructional tactics that are particularly well suited to multicultural education programs.

16. Calls for multicultural education were stimulated by changing immigration and birthrate patterns, low levels of school achievement by many ethnic minority children, and students' need to work productively with members of other cultures.

17. For students who live in culturally homogeneous communities, an increased understanding of the characteristics of students from different cultural backgrounds and the problems they face can be gained by using such technological tools as videoconferencing and electronic communities.

18. Most bilingual education programs reflect a transition goal, a maintenance goal, or a two-way bilingual goal. Transition programs teach students in their native language only until they speak and understand English well enough to be placed in a regular classroom. Maintenance programs try to maintain or improve students' native-language skills. Two-way programs provide subject-matter instruction in both the majority and minority languages in roughly equal proportions to all students and are growing in popularity.

19. A few states have eliminated their bilingual education programs in favor of one-year English immersion programs.

Key Terms

culture *(133)*
multicultural education *(134)*
melting pot *(134)*
cultural pluralism *(135)*
ethnic group *(137)*

social class *(140)*
socioeconomic status (SES) *(140)*
teacher expectancy effect *(148)*
peer tutoring *(156)*

cooperative learning *(156)*
mastery learning *(157)*
two-way bilingual (TWB) education *(166)*

6 Accommodating Student Variability

These key points will help you learn the important information in this chapter. To help you study, they also appear in the margins of the pages, next to the text where they are discussed.

Ability Grouping

● Ability grouping assumes intelligence is inherited, reflected by IQ, unchangeable, and instruction will be superior

● No research support for between-class ability grouping

● Joplin Plan and within-class ability grouping for math and science produce moderate increases in learning

● Between-class ability grouping negatively influences teaching goals and methods

● Joplin Plan and within-class ability grouping may allow for better-quality instruction

The Individuals with Disabilities Education Act (IDEA)

● Before placement, student must be given complete, valid, and appropriate evaluation

● IEP must include objectives, services to be provided, criteria for determining achievement

● Students with disabilities must be educated in least restrictive environment

● Mainstreaming: policy of placing students with disabilities in regular classes

● Procedural safeguards intended to protect rights of students and parents

● Inclusion policy aims to keep students with disabilities in regular classroom for entire day

● Students who are learning disabled, speech impaired, mentally retarded, or emotionally disturbed most likely to be served under IDEA

● Multidisciplinary assessment team determines if student needs special services

● Classroom teacher, parents, several specialists prepare IEP

Students with Mental Retardation

● Students with mild retardation may frustrate easily, lack confidence and self-esteem

● Students with mild retardation tend to oversimplify, have difficulty generalizing

● Give students with mild retardation short assignments that can be completed quickly

Students with Learning Disabilities

● Learning disabilities: disorders in basic processes that lead to learning problems not due to other causes

● Students with learning disabilities have problems with perception, attention, memory, metacognition

● Symptoms of ADHD include inattention, hyperactivity, and impulsivity

● Help students with learning disabilities to reduce distractions, attend to important information

Students with Emotional Disturbance

● Emotional disturbance: poor relationships, inappropriate behavior, depression, fears

● Term *behavior disorder* focuses on behavior that needs to be changed, objective assessment

● Students with behavior disorders tend to be either aggressive or withdrawn

● Foster interpersonal contact among withdrawn students

● Use techniques to forestall aggressive or antisocial behavior

Gifted and Talented Students

● Gifted and talented students show high performance in one or more areas

Key Points continued on next page.

rior to the twentieth century, few educators had to deal with the challenge of teaching extremely diverse groups of students. Most communities were fairly small, and students in a given school tended to come from similar backgrounds. Many children, especially those of low socioeconomic status (SES), attended school irregularly or not at all. In 1900, for example, only 8.5 percent of eligible students attended high school (Boyer, 1983), and these students were almost entirely from the upper and middle classes (Gutek, 1992). In addition, children with mental, emotional, or physical disabilities were sent to special schools, educated at home, or not educated at all. In comparison with today's schools, earlier student populations were considerably less diverse.

In the preceding chapter, you read about the varieties of cultural and socioeconomic diversity among today's students. This chapter focuses on another dimension of diversity: the twin (but often somewhat fuzzy) concepts of ability and disability. Before explaining how educators attempt to meet the needs of diverse students, we take a brief look at historical developments that helped shape current educational practices. ●

● Minorities underrepresented in
gifted classes because of over-
reliance on test scores

● Gifted and talented students
differ from their nongifted peers
intellectually and emotionally

● Separate classes for gifted and
talented students aid achievement but may lower academic
self-concept of some students

**Using Technology to Assist
Exceptional Students**

● Federal legislation has led to the
development of various assistive
technologies

HISTORICAL DEVELOPMENTS

The Growth of Public Education and Age-Graded Classrooms

To understand this chapter's structure, see the Chapter Themes on the textbook web site, accessible from **http:// education.college. hmco .com/students.**

By 1920, public education in the United States was no longer a small-scale and optional enterprise, largely because of three developments. First, by 1918, all states
had passed compulsory attendance laws. Second, child labor laws had been enacted
by many states, as well as by Congress in 1916, to eliminate the hiring of children
and adolescents in mines and factories. Third, large numbers of immigrant children
arrived in the United States from 1901 through 1920. The result was a vast increase
in the number and diversity of children attending elementary and high school.

Educators initially dealt with this growth in student variability by forming age-
graded classrooms. Introduced in the Quincy, Massachusetts, schools in the mid-1800s,
these classrooms grouped all students of a particular age together each year to master a certain portion of the school's curriculum (Gutek, 1992). The main assumptions behind this approach were that teachers could be more effective in helping
students learn and that students would have more positive attitudes toward themselves and school when classrooms were more homogeneous than heterogeneous
(Oakes, 1985; Peltier, 1991). Regardless of whether these assumptions were well
founded (an issue we will address shortly), they were (and still are) so widely
held by educators that two additional approaches to creating even more homogeneous groups were eventually implemented: ability grouping and special class
placement.

Ability-Grouped Classrooms

Ability grouping involved the use of standardized mental ability or achievement tests
to create groups of students who were considered very similar to each other in learning ability. In elementary and middle schools, students typically were (and frequently
still are) placed in low-, average-, or high-ability groups. At the high school level,
students were placed into different tracks that were geared toward such different
post–high school goals as college, secretarial work, and vocational school.

Ability grouping was another means for school authorities to deal with the large
influx of immigrant students. Because many of these children were not fluent in
English and had had limited amounts of education in their native countries, they
scored low on standardized tests when compared to American test norms. In addition, many of these children came from poor homes and were in poor health. At the
time, their assignment to a low-ability group seemed both logical and appropriate
(Wheelock, 1994).

In the next major part of this chapter, we will look at current applications of ability
grouping, which now takes several forms and is still used to reduce the normal range
of variability in cognitive ability and achievement found in the typical classroom.

Special Education

For more or less normal children, age grading and ability testing were seen as workable approaches to creating more homogeneous classes. But compulsory attendance laws also brought to school many children with mild to severe mental and physical disabilities. These students were deemed incapable of profiting from any type of normal classroom instruction and so were assigned to special schools. Unfortunately, as Alfred Binet feared, the labeling of a student as mentally retarded or physically disabled often resulted in a vastly inferior education. Early in the twentieth century, special schools served as convenient dumping grounds for all kinds of children who could not adapt to the regular classroom (Vallecorsa, deBettencourt, & Zigmond, 2000).

In the latter two-thirds of this chapter, we will detail the varied types and degrees of special class placement for children whose intellectual, social, emotional, or physical development falls outside (above as well as below) the range of normal variation. In discussing this approach, we pay particular attention to Public Law (PL) 101-476, the Individuals with Disabilities Education Act (IDEA), which was enacted to counter past excesses of special class placement and to encourage the placement of children with disabilities in regular classes.

ABILITY GROUPING

Ability grouping is a widespread practice (for example, Brewer, Rees, & Argys, 1995; Dornbusch & Kaufman, 2001; Loveless, 1998). In the elementary grades, virtually all teachers form separate groups within their classrooms for instruction in reading, and many do so for mathematics as well. At the middle school level, approximately two-thirds to three-fourths of schools assign students to different self-contained classes in one or more subjects on the basis of standardized test scores. This proportion rises to about 85 percent at the high school level, where students are assigned to different classes (e.g., honors, college preparatory, basic) on a subject-by-subject basis (Dornbusch & Kaufman, 2001). At the middle and high school levels, the term *tracking* rather than *ability grouping* is typically used. In this section, we will describe the most common ways in which teachers group students by ability, examine the assumptions that provide the rationale for this practice, summarize research findings on the effectiveness of ability grouping, and look at alternative courses of action.

Types of Ability Groups

Four approaches to ability grouping are popular among educators today: between-class ability grouping, regrouping, the Joplin Plan, and within-class grouping. You may be able to recall a few classes in which one or another of these techniques was used. If not, you will no doubt encounter at least one of them during your first year of teaching.

Between-Class Ability Grouping   The goal of **between-class ability grouping** is for each class to be made up of students who are homogeneous in standardized intelligence or achievement test scores. Three levels of classes are usually formed: high, average, and low. Students in one ability group typically have little or no contact with students in others during the school day. Although each group covers the same subjects, a higher group does so in greater depth and breadth than lower groups. At the high school level, as we mentioned, this approach is often called *tracking*. Traditionally, high school tracks have been labeled academic (or college preparatory), vocational, and general. These terms have been increasingly replaced by such designations as advanced (or honors), regular, and basic (Hallinan, 1994).

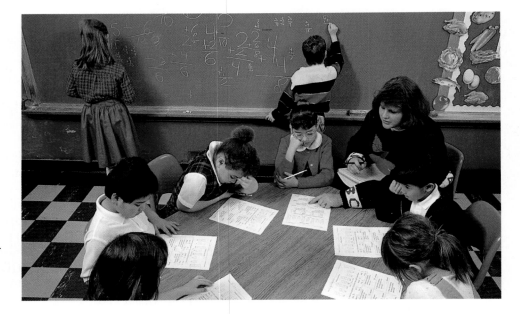

In ability grouping, students are selected and placed in homogeneous groups with other students who are considered to have very similar learning abilities.

Regrouping   The groups formed under a **regrouping** plan are more flexible in assignments and narrower in scope than between-class groups. Students of the same age, ability, and grade but from different classrooms come together for instruction in a specific subject, usually reading or mathematics. If a student begins to outperform the other members of the group significantly, a change of group assignment is easier since it involves just that particular subject.

Regrouping has two major disadvantages, however. First, it requires a certain degree of planning and cooperation among the teachers involved. They must agree, for example, to schedule reading and arithmetic during the same periods. Second, many teachers are uncomfortable working with children whom they see only once a day for an hour or so.

Joplin Plan   The **Joplin Plan** is a variation of regrouping. The main difference is that regroupings take place across grade levels. For example, all third, fourth, and fifth graders whose grade-equivalent scores in reading are 4.6 (fourth grade, sixth month) would come together for reading instruction. The same would be done for mathematics. The Joplin Plan has the same advantages and disadvantages as simple regrouping, and it is the basis for a successful reading program called Success for All (Kulik, 2003).

You probably experienced ability grouping in one form or another at the elementary and secondary levels. Think about whether it might have been between-class grouping, regrouping, the Joplin Plan, or within-class grouping. Could you tell which group you were in? Did you have feelings about being in that group?

Within-Class Ability Grouping   The most popular form of ability grouping, occurring in almost all elementary school classes, **within-class ability grouping** involves the division of a single class of students into two or three groups for reading and math instruction. Like regrouping and the Joplin Plan, within-class ability grouping has the advantages of being flexible in terms of group assignments and being restricted to one or two subjects. In addition, it eliminates the need for cooperative scheduling. One disadvantage of this approach is that the teacher needs to be skilled at keeping the other students in the class productively occupied while working with a particular group.

Assumptions Underlying Ability Grouping

When ability grouping was initiated early in the twentieth century, much less was known about the various factors that affect classroom learning. Consequently,

● Ability grouping assumes intelligence is inherited, reflected by IQ, unchangeable, and instruction will be superior

educators simply assumed certain things to be true. One of those assumptions was that intelligence, which affects the capacity to learn, was a fixed, inherited trait and that little could be done to change the learning capacity of individuals. A second assumption was that intelligence was adequately reflected by an intelligence quotient (IQ) score. A third assumption was that all students would learn best when grouped with those of similar ability (Hallinan, 1994; Marsh & Raywid, 1994; Ornstein & Levine, 2003). Although many educators still believe these assumptions are true, the research evidence summarized here and elsewhere in this book casts doubt on their validity.

Evaluations of Ability Grouping

Because ability grouping occurs in virtually all school districts, its effects have been intensively studied (for example, Abrami, Lou, Chambers, Poulsen, & Spence, 2000; Applebee, Langer, Nystrand, & Gamoran, 2003; Hoffer, 1992; Kulik, 2003; Lloyd, 1999; Lou, Abrami, & Spence, 2000; Marsh & Raywid, 1994; Raudenbush, Rowan, & Cheong, 1993; Yonezawa, Wells, & Serna, 2002). The main findings of these analyses are as follows:

● No research support for between-class ability grouping

1. There is little to no support for between-class ability grouping. Students assigned to low-ability classes generally performed worse than comparable students in heterogeneous classes. Students assigned to average-ability classes performed at about the same level as their nongrouped peers. High-ability students sometimes performed slightly better in homogeneous classes than in heterogeneous classes. A report by the Carnegie Corporation on educating adolescents (Jackson & Davis, 2000) noted: "Instruction in tracked classes thus falls short on measures of both equity and excellence. Tracking affects students unequally, both by grouping minorities and economically disadvantaged students in lower tracks and by providing unequal educational opportunities to students. Instruction in lower-track classes is typically far from excellent, often depending on rote memorization and recall, isolated facts, worksheets, and a slow pace" (p. 66).

2. Research on the effect of regrouping for reading or mathematics is inconclusive. Some of the relatively few studies that have been done on this form of ability grouping suggest that it can be effective if the instructional pace and level of the text match the student's actual achievement level rather than the student's nominal grade level. In other words, a fifth grader who scores at the fourth-grade level on a reading test should be reading out of a fourth-grade reading book.

● Joplin Plan and within-class ability grouping for math and science produce moderate increases in learning

3. The Joplin Plan yields moderately positive effects compared with instruction in heterogeneous classes.

4. Within-class ability grouping in mathematics and science in grades 1 through 12 has produced modestly positive results (about eight percentile ranks) compared with whole-class instruction and an even smaller positive effect (about four percentile ranks) when compared with mixed-ability groups. Average-achieving students benefit most from being placed in homogeneous-ability groups, while low-achieving students benefit most from being placed in mixed-ability groups. Because within-class ability grouping for reading is an almost universal practice at every grade level, researchers have not had the opportunity to compare its effectiveness with whole-class reading instruction. Nevertheless, it would be reasonable to expect much the same results for reading as were found for mathematics and science.

   Research also shows that some within-class grouping practices are more effective than others. The largest positive effects were found in classrooms that had the following two conditions: (1) students were assigned to groups not only on the basis of ability, but also on the basis of other factors that contributed to group cohesiveness, and (2) cooperative learning techniques were used that included the features of positive interdependence and individual accountability (Abrami et al., 2000; Lou et al., 2000). (See our chapter "Approaches to Instruction" for a discussion of these and other features of cooperative learning.)

5. Students in homogeneously grouped classes scored the same as students in heterogeneously grouped classes on measures of self-esteem.

6. Students in high-ability classes had more positive attitudes about school and higher educational aspirations than did students in low-ability classrooms.

7. Between-class ability grouping affected the quality of instruction received by students in several ways:

   a. The best teachers were often assigned to teach the highest tracks, whereas the least experienced or weakest teachers were assigned to teach the lowest tracks.

   b. Teachers of high-ability classes stressed critical thinking, self-direction, creativity, and active participation, whereas teachers of low-ability classes stressed working quietly, following rules, and getting along with classmates. This effect was particularly noticeable in math and science.

   c. Teachers of low-ability groups covered less material and simpler material than did teachers of high-ability groups.

   d. Teachers of low-ability students expected and demanded less of them than did teachers of high-ability students.

● Between-class ability grouping negatively influences teaching goals and methods

Despite the evidence against between-class ability grouping, ethnic minority and low-SES students are frequently assigned to the lowest tracks, where they fall further behind white, middle-class students. This situation has prompted accusations of discrimination, and some districts have responded by adopting policies that specifically allow low-track minority students to enroll in honors courses. However, this technique (sometimes called a freedom of choice program) does not necessarily increase minority students' participation in higher-level courses. An examination of this practice in four middle schools and six high schools indicates that it is largely ineffective in encouraging ethnic minority/low-SES students to enroll in honors classes (Yonezawa et al., 2002). The major reasons for the failure of freedom of choice programs are as follows:

a. In some of the schools studied, low-track students (who were mostly low-income and minority students) were not always informed that they could request honors classes.

b. In some cases, the requests of low-track students were delayed by such tactics as not being able to get an appointment with a counselor. In fact, some counselors tried to dissuade students from taking an honors or high-track class.

c. Only after requesting a high-track class did students learn that they needed to have taken prerequisite courses or had to have a minimum grade-point average. In one case, a counselor administered an abbreviated reading comprehension test before allowing students to enroll in advanced courses.

d. Because of their previous academic placement and history, low-track students felt they did not have the ability or confidence to succeed in advanced classes. They had, in essence, come to identify themselves as "low-track" or "slow."

e. Some students were uninterested in advanced classes because that action would have separated them from their friends and a familiar culture. Others believed that they simply would not be accepted by the other (mostly white, middle-class) students.

To Group or Not to Group?

The findings just summarized suggest three courses of action. The first course is to discontinue the use of full-day, between-class ability groups or tracks. Despite the fact that most middle and high schools continue to use this form of ability grouping, students do not learn more or feel more positively about themselves and school. This is a case in which even widely held beliefs must be modified or eliminated

Take a Stand!

Ability Grouping and Tracking: A Practice That Fails to Deliver What It Promises

At the beginning of this book, we stated that an advantage of using scientific methods to study education was that it helped us avoid drawing false conclusions about an idea or practice because of subjective and unsystematic thinking. When people substitute personal values and experience for systematic research findings, educational decisions that are detrimental to students are usually the result. So it is with between-class ability grouping and rigid tracking systems at the middle school and high school levels. Many educators fervently believe that teachers are more effective and students learn more when classrooms are more homogeneous in ability than heterogeneous. But almost all of the research conducted on ability grouping and tracking over the past several decades refutes these beliefs. Consequently, this is a practice that should rarely, if ever, be used.

Among other detriments, it destroys the motivation of students and stunts their intellectual growth.

We believe that teachers should speak out forcefully against between-class ability grouping and in favor of the effective instructional practices that can be used with all students, especially cooperative learning and peer tutoring. When the opportunity arises, let your colleagues know that the assumptions they carry about the benefits of ability grouping are not supported by the scientific literature.

Do you share the authors' opposition to ability grouping and tracking? Do you think such practices aided or hindered your own educational progress? Explore this subject further at the Take a Stand! section of the textbook web site, accessible from **http://education.college.hmco.com/students.**

● Joplin Plan and within-class ability grouping may allow for better-quality instruction

when the weight of evidence goes against them.

The second course of action is to use only those forms of ability grouping that produce positive results: within-class grouping and the Joplin Plan, especially for reading and mathematics. We do not know why these forms of ability grouping work. It is assumed that the increase in group homogeneity allows for more appropriate and potent forms of instruction (for example, greater effort by the teacher to bring lower-achieving groups up to the level of higher-achieving groups). If this assumption is correct, within-class ability grouping and the Joplin Plan must be carried out in such a way that homogeneous groups are guaranteed to result. The best way to achieve similarity in cognitive ability among students is to group them on the basis of past classroom performance, standardized achievement test scores, or both. The least desirable (but most frequently used) approach is to base the assignments solely on IQ scores.

The third course of action is to dispense with all forms of ability grouping. But bear in mind that unless teachers make a concerted effort to meet the educational needs of all students, detracking (the term often used to denote the elimination of ability groups, particularly at the middle school and high school levels) may lead to slightly lower performance of average and above-average students (Loveless, 1999).

In keeping with the concept of differentiated instruction mentioned earlier in the book, teachers can use a variety of organizational and instructional techniques that will allow them to cope with a heterogeneous class, or they can use these same techniques in conjunction with the Joplin Plan or within-class grouping. For instance, you might use with all students instructional techniques that are associated with high achievement. These would include:

- Making clear presentations
- Displaying a high level of enthusiasm
- Reinforcing students for correct responses
- Providing sufficient time for students to formulate answers to questions
- Prompting correct responses
- Providing detailed feedback about the accuracy of responses
- Requiring a high level of work and effort
- Organizing students into small, heterogeneous learning groups and using the cooperative learning techniques that we discuss in detail in the chapter on approaches to instruction

Other ideas include optional honors activities, pullout (meaning programs that occur outside the classroom) challenge classes that are available to all students, study skills classes for low-achieving students, and small-group projects (Oakes & Wells, 1998).

THE INDIVIDUALS WITH DISABILITIES EDUCATION ACT (IDEA)

Many of the criticisms and arguments marshaled against ability grouping have come to be applied as well to special classes for students with disabilities. In addition, the elimination of racially segregated schools by the U.S. Supreme Court in the case of *Brown v. Board of Education* (1954) established a precedent for providing students with disabilities an equal opportunity for a free and appropriate education (Ornstein & Levine, 2003). As a result, influential members of Congress were persuaded in the early 1970s that it was time for the federal government to take steps to correct the perceived inequities and deficiencies in our educational system. The result was a landmark piece of legislation, Public Law 94-142, the Education for All Handicapped Children Act of 1975. This law was revised and expanded in 1986 as the Handicapped Children's Protection Act (PL 99-457) and again in 1990 as the Individuals with Disabilities Education Act (IDEA, PL 101-476).

IDEA was then amended in 1997 to broaden and clarify a number of its provisions ("Individuals with Disabilities," 1997). The 1990 version of IDEA, for example, said nothing about the participation of children with disabilities in standardized testing programs. The 1997 amendment, however, states that children with disabilities must be provided with whatever modifications are necessary (for instance, large print for children who have visual impairments, extended time limits for children with a learning disability) to allow them to take part in state- and districtwide assessments. If a child with a disability does not participate in a standardized assessment, school district officials must explain why they feel such an assessment is inappropriate and how that child will be assessed (Ysseldyke, Algozzine, & Thurlow, 2000).

Major Provisions of IDEA

A Free and Appropriate Public Education   The basic purpose of IDEA is to ensure that all individuals from birth through age twenty-one who have an identifiable disability, regardless of how severe, receive at public expense supervised special education and related services that meet their unique educational needs. These services can be delivered in a classroom, at home, in a hospital, or in a specialized institution and may include physical education and vocational education, as well as instruction in the typical academic subjects ("Individuals with Disabilities," 1997).

● Before placement, student must be given complete, valid, and appropriate evaluation

Preplacement Evaluation   Before a child with a disability can be placed in a program that provides special education services, "a full and individual evaluation of the child's educational needs" must be conducted. Such an evaluation must conform to the following rules:

1. Tests must be administered in the child's native language.
2. A test must be valid for the specific purpose for which it is used.
3. Tests must be administered by trained individuals according to the instructions provided by the test publisher.
4. Tests administered to students who have impaired sensory, manual, or speaking skills must reflect aptitude or achievement rather than the impairment.
5. No single procedure (such as an IQ test) can be the sole basis for determining an appropriate educational program. Data should be collected from such nontest sources as observations by other professionals (such as the classroom teacher), medical records, and parental interviews.
6. Evaluations must be made by a multidisciplinary team that contains at least one teacher or other specialist with knowledge in the area of the suspected disability.
7. The child must be assessed in all areas related to the suspected disability ("Individuals with Disabilities," 1997).

When you deal with students whose first language is not English, it is important to realize that standardized tests are designed to reflect cultural experiences common to the United States and that English words and phrases may not mean quite the same thing when translated. Therefore, these tests may not be measuring what they were developed to measure. In other words, they may not be valid. The results of such assessments should therefore be interpreted very cautiously (Kubiszyn & Borich, 2003).

Individualized Education Program   Every child who is identified as having a disability and who receives special education services must have an **individualized education program (IEP)** prepared. The IEP is a written statement that describes the educational program that has been designed to meet the child's unique needs. The IEP must include the following elements:

1. A statement of the child's existing levels of educational performance
2. A statement of annual goals, including short-term instructional objectives
3. A statement of the specific special education and related services to be provided to the child and the extent to which the child will be able to participate in regular educational programs
4. The projected dates for initiation of services and the anticipated duration of the services
5. Appropriate objective criteria and evaluation procedures and schedules for determining, on at least an annual basis, whether short-term objectives are being achieved ("Individuals with Disabilities," 1997)

The IEP is to be planned by a multidisciplinary team composed of the student's classroom teacher in collaboration with a person qualified in special education, one or both of the student's parents, the student (when appropriate), and other individuals at the discretion of the parents or school. (An example of an IEP is depicted later in this chapter in Figure 6.1.)

Least Restrictive Environment   According to the 1994 Code of Federal Regulations that governs the implementation of IDEA, educational services must be provided

● IEP must include objectives, services to be provided, criteria for determining achievement

● Students with disabilities must be educated in least restrictive environment

The least restrictive environment provision of IDEA has led to mainstreaming—the policy that children with disabilities should attend regular classes to the maximum extent possible. Some special education proponents argue that full-time regular classroom placement should be the only option for such students.

to children with disabilities in the **least restrictive environment** that their disability will allow. A school district must identify a continuum of increasingly restrictive placements (instruction in regular classes, special classes, home instruction, instruction in hospitals and institutions) and, on the basis of the multidisciplinary team's evaluation, select the least restrictive setting that will best meet the student's special educational needs. This provision is often referred to as **mainstreaming** because the goal of the law is to have as many children with disabilities as possible, regardless of the severity of the disability, enter the mainstream of education by attending regular classes with nondisabled students. In recent years, mainstreaming has frequently evolved into *inclusion*, a practice we discuss later in this chapter. The Case in Print describes the type of controversy that arises when mainstreaming is applied unequally to different ethnic groups.

● Mainstreaming: policy of placing students with disabilities in regular classes

Procedural Safeguards   The basic purpose of the various procedural safeguards that were written into IDEA is to make sure that parents are fully informed about the actions a school district intends to take to classify their child as having a disability, protect the legal rights of parents and their child, and provide a way to resolve disputes about any aspect of the process. Among other rights, parents have the right to inspect their child's education records; obtain an independent assessment of their child; obtain written prior notice of identification, assessment, and placement procedures; request a due process hearing; appeal the results of a due process hearing; or file a lawsuit in state or federal court. A due process hearing is a fact-finding procedure that is intended to resolve disagreements between the school district and the parents of a child with a disability. Such hearings include a hearing officer, the parents of the disabled child, school district personnel (such as the classroom teacher, the principal, and the school psychologist), and attorneys for the parents and the school district.

● Procedural safeguards intended to protect rights of students and parents

The Policy of Inclusion

Although IDEA calls for children with disabilities to be placed in the least restrictive environment, the law clearly allows for more restrictive placements than those of the regular classroom "when the nature or severity of the disability is such that education in regular classes with the use of supplementary aids and services cannot be achieved satisfactorily" ("Individuals with Disabilities," 1997, p. 61). Nevertheless, there has been a movement in recent years to eliminate this option. Known as **inclusion** or **full inclusion,** this extension of the mainstreaming provision has become one of the most controversial outgrowths of IDEA.

● Inclusion policy aims to keep students with disabilities in regular classroom for entire day

As most proponents use the term, *inclusion* means keeping special education students in regular classrooms and bringing support services to the children rather than the other way around. *Full inclusion* refers to the practice of eliminating all pullout programs *and* special education teachers and of providing regular classroom teachers with training in teaching special-needs students so that they can teach these students in the regular classroom (Kirk, Gallagher, & Anastasiow, 2003; Smelter, Rasch, & Yudewitz, 1994; Smith, 2004).

The Debate About Inclusion   The proponents of inclusion and full inclusion often raise three arguments to support their position:

1. Research suggests that special-needs students who are segregated from regular students perform more poorly academically and socially than comparable students who are mainstreamed (Kavale, 2002).
2. Given the substantial body of evidence demonstrating the propensity of children to observe and imitate more competent children (see, for example, Schunk, 1987), it can be assumed that students with disabilities will learn more by interacting with nondisabled students than by attending homogeneous classes (Sapon-Shevin, 1996).

3. The Supreme Court in *Brown v. Board of Education* declared the doctrine of separate but equal to be unconstitutional. Therefore, pullout programs are a violation of the civil rights of children with special needs because these programs segregate them from their nondisabled peers in programs that are assumed to be separate but equal (Kavale, 2002; Mock & Kauffman, 2002; Skrtic, Sailor, & Gee, 1996).

The opponents of inclusion often cite cases of students who fail to learn basic skills, students whose disabilities interrupt the normal flow of instruction, or teachers who are ill prepared to adequately assist the various special-needs students who are placed in their classes (for example, Fox & Ysseldyke, 1997; Kavale, 2002; MacMillan, Gresham, & Forness, 1996; Mock & Kauffman, 2002).

Research Findings   The evidence that bears on the inclusion issue is a combination of anecdotes (reports about individual cases) and experiments that compare inclusive to noninclusive practices for special-needs students. It seems to indicate, at least for now, that inclusion works well for some students but produces modest or no benefits for others. On the basis of this evidence (for example, Kavale, 2002; MacMillan et al., 1996; Mock & Kauffman, 2002; Raison, Hanson, Hall, & Reynolds, 1995; Stevens & Slavin, 1995; Zigmond et al., 1995), three conclusions seem warranted:

1. Inclusion may not be an appropriate course of action for every child with a disability.
2. Inclusion will likely work best when the presence of a disabled student stimulates the teacher to improve the general quality of classroom instruction and well-trained support staff, such as teacher aides and inclusion facilitators, are available (see, for example, Choate 2003; Ruder, 2000).
3. For students who are mainstreamed, IEPs should be written so as to reflect better what a given student probably can and cannot accomplish.

It also seems that successful inclusion programs may take many years to implement. For example, two researchers (McLeskey & Waldron, 2002) who helped an elementary school district institute an inclusion program found that students with disabilities made at least as much academic progress in regular classes as they did in special education classes, and that teachers, administrators, and parents were satisfied with the inclusive program. But the transformation required a considerable amount of effort and about twelve years to accomplish.

What IDEA Means to Regular Classroom Teachers

By the time you begin your teaching career, the original legislation governing the delivery of educational services to the disabled, PL 94-142, will have been in effect for about thirty years. Each state was required to have established laws and policies for implementing the various provisions by 1978. The first guiding principle to follow, therefore, is, *find out what the local ground rules are.* You will probably be told during orientation meetings about the ways IDEA is being put into effect in your state and local school district. But if such a presentation is not given or is incomplete, it would be wise to ask about guidelines you should follow. Your second guiding principle, then, should be, *when in doubt, ask.* With these two caveats in mind, consider some questions you may be asking yourself about the impact of IDEA as you approach your first teaching job.

What Kinds of Disabling Conditions Are Included Under IDEA?   According to the U.S. Department of Education (2001a), during the 1999–2000 academic year, 5.38 million children and youths from ages six through seventeen (about 11.4 percent of the total number of individuals in this age group) received special education services under IDEA.

Who Swims in the Mainstream?

*A school district must identify a continuum of increasingly restrictive placements (instruction in regular classes, special classes, home instruction, instruction in hospitals and institutions) and, on the basis of the multidisciplinary team's evaluation, select the least restrictive setting that will best meet the student's special educational needs. This provision is often referred to as **mainstreaming** because the goal of the law is to have as many children with disabilities as possible, regardless of the severity of the disability, enter the mainstream of education by attending regular classes with nondisabled students. (p. 180)*

Study Finds Special Ed Disparities

LINDA PERLSTEIN
Washington Post, 12/18/03

African American and Hispanic students in special education were far more likely than white and Asian students in recent years to be educated in special classrooms instead of integrated into the general population, according to a study of special education in Montgomery County Public Schools.

The study also found that students who live in poverty were almost 2½ times more likely than higher-income students to be labeled emotionally disturbed, and African Americans were almost three times more likely than whites to be identified as mentally retarded, a ratio that lowers only slightly when controlling for income.

The report was prepared by Margaret J. McLaughlin and Sandra Embler of the University of Maryland School of Education under the auspices of the county's Continuous Improvement Team. The Board of Education had directed the team to come up with a set of indicators for measuring the status of special education in the county. The report was completed in the summer but presented to the board last week as part of an update on special education services.

"Most of it was anticipated, but to get anything done you have to have a baseline for improvement," said Ricki Sabia, a co-chairman of the Continuous Improvement Team. "The whole point of the report was to bring up these issues, and the next step is to drill down what to do about it."

The research, conducted from 2000 to 2002, found that black and Hispanic special education students were more likely than other disabled students to be taught in segregated settings instead of regular classrooms. State guidelines require the county to increase the number of special education students integrated into regular classrooms.

Black students received an average of 16.8 hours of special education services in total weekly compared with 14.8 for Hispanics and 12.4 hours for whites.

Low-income students received 16.3 hours weekly, compared with 12 hours for the rest of the population.

For students with and without disabilities, a gap in academic performance exists by race and by income. Brian Bartels, Montgomery County's director of special education, said this correlation may partially explain why black, Hispanic and low-income disabled students are receiving more intensive services in less integrated environments, not just in Montgomery County but elsewhere in the state as well.

Educators may recommend more intensive services—not necessarily in separate settings—because of the greater instructional needs of students with lower achievement levels, Bartels said.

Attendance rates for special education students were, depending on school level, from 1 percentage point to 3 percentage points lower than rates for students in regular programs. Disparity in absences was greatest in high schools. Students with emotional disabilities and low-income students were most likely to have many absences.

Bartels said depression and behavioral problems may be keeping some emotionally disturbed students home, though he also said the attendance rate may have been skewed by a small number of students with very large numbers of absences.

Regardless of income, Asian American students were less likely than those in any other racial or ethnic group to receive special education services. They were, however, more likely to receive assistance in speech and language.

Thirteen percent of students with disabilities received no scores on the Comprehensive Test of Basic Skills. The CTBS is not used to comply with the federal No Child Left Behind Act, but test participation is a concern because the law requires that 95 percent of students in any group, including special education, take standardized tests.

Of the students who took the test, 70 percent received extra time to complete it, and more than 50 percent of sixth-graders and 25 percent of second-graders used a calculator—both permitted accommodations.

In surveys, special education teachers said parents do not support them in discipline or instruction or recognize their accomplishments, while parents and special education teachers felt that teachers in regular classrooms have low expectations for disabled students.

Questions and Activities

1. The study of special education placements in the Montgomery County (Maryland) school system that is described in this article replicates the findings of other studies: compared with white, middle-income students, a larger percentage of ethnic minority, racial minority, and low-income students are placed in special education classes. What factors, one of which was mentioned in the article, might account for this difference?

2. Assuming for the moment that all of these students met IDEA guidelines for receiving special education services, how likely is it that a special education class is the most appropriate placement (that is, the least restrictive environment) for all or most of these students? Why?

3. Another finding from this study is that attendance rates for students in special education classes were a few percentage points lower than for students in regular classes. What other disadvantages might there be for placing students in segregated special education classes?

4. The last paragraph of the article indicates that special education teachers, regular education teachers, and parents of students with disabilities are not in agreement about how to handle students with disabilities. Form your own opinion by talking to individuals from these three groups about their views on special education class placement versus mainstreaming. If there are differences, try to identify their basis.

For individuals between the ages of three and twenty, IDEA recognizes twelve categories of disability. A thirteenth category, developmental delay, applies only to children from ages three through nine and is optional for state programs. The first twelve categories described in the legislation are listed as follows in alphabetical order, with brief definitions of each type:

Autism. Significant difficulty in verbal and nonverbal communication and social interaction that adversely affects educational performance.

Deaf-blindness. Impairments of both hearing and vision, the combination of which causes severe communication, developmental, and educational problems. The combination of these impairments is such that a child's educational and physical needs cannot be adequately met by programs designed for only deaf children or only blind children.

Hearing impairment. Permanent or fluctuating difficulty in understanding speech that adversely affects educational performance.

Mental retardation. Significant subaverage general intellectual functioning accompanied by deficits in adaptive behavior (how well a person functions in social environments).

Multiple disabilities. Two or more impairments (such as mental retardation–blindness and mental retardation–orthopedic, but not deaf-blindness) that cause such severe educational problems that a child's needs cannot be adequately met by programs designed solely for one of the impairments.

Orthopedic impairments. Impairment in a child's ability to use arms, legs, hands, or feet that significantly affects that child's educational performance.

Other health impairments. Conditions such as asthma, hemophilia, sickle cell anemia, epilepsy, heart disease, and diabetes that so limit the strength, vitality, or alertness of a child that educational performance is significantly affected.

Emotional disturbance. Personal and social problems exhibited in an extreme degree over a period of time that adversely affect a child's ability to learn and get along with others (prior to the 1997 amendments to IDEA, this category was called "serious emotional disturbance").

Specific learning disability. A disorder in one or more of the basic psychological processes involved in understanding or using language that leads to learning problems not traceable to physical disabilities, mental retardation, emotional disturbance, or cultural-economic disadvantage.

Speech or language impairment. A communication disorder such as stuttering, impaired articulation, or a language or voice impairment that adversely affects educational performance.

Traumatic brain injury. A brain injury due to an accident that causes cognitive or psychosocial impairments that adversely affect a child's educational performance.

Visual impairment including blindness. A visual impairment so severe that even with corrective lenses, a child's educational performance is adversely affected.

● Students who are learning disabled, speech impaired, mentally retarded, or emotionally disturbed most likely to be served under IDEA

The percentages of each type of student who received special educational services during the 1999–2000 school year are indicated in Table 6.1. As you can see, the most common types of children with disabilities receiving services (89.3 percent of the total) were those classified as having a specific learning disability, a speech or language impairment, mental retardation, or an emotional disturbance.

What Are the Regular Classroom Teacher's Responsibilities Under IDEA? Regular classroom teachers may be involved in activities required directly or indirectly by IDEA in four possible ways: referral, assessment, preparation of the IEP, and implementation and evaluation of the IEP.

Table 6.1	Students Receiving Special Education Services, 1999–2000	
Disabling Condition	**Percentage of Total School Enrollment**[a]	**Percentage of Students with Disabilities Served**
Specific learning disabilities	5.73	50.6
Speech or language impairments	2.28	20.2
Mental retardation	1.15	10.2
Emotional disturbance	0.94	8.3
Other health impairments	0.52	4.6
Multiple disabilities	0.21	1.8
Hearing impairments	0.14	1.2
Orthopedic impairments	0.14	1.2
Autism	0.13	1.1
Visual impairments	0.05	0.4
Traumatic brain injury	0.03	0.2
Deaf-blindness	0.00	0.0
Total	11.32	99.8[b]

[a]Percentages are based on children with disabilities ages 6–17 as a percentage of total school enrollment for kindergarten through twelfth grade.

[b]Percentages do not add to 100 percent because of rounding.

SOURCE: U.S. Department of Education (2001).

The decision as to whether a child qualifies for special education services under IDEA is made largely on the basis of information supplied by the multidisciplinary assessment team. Classroom teachers typically contribute information about the child's academic and social behavior.

Referral Most referrals for assessment and possible special instruction are made by a child's teacher or his or her parents because they are the ones most familiar with the quality of the child's daily work and progress as compared to other children.

Assessment The initial assessment procedures, which must be approved by the child's parents, are usually carried out by school psychologists who are certified to administer tests. If the initial conclusions of the school psychologist support the teacher's or parents' perception that the student needs special services, the **multidisciplinary assessment team** required under IDEA will be formed. Because the 1997 amendment of IDEA requires that classroom teachers be part of the multidisciplinary assessment team, you should be prepared to provide such information as the quality of the child's homework and test scores, ability to understand and use language, ability to perform various motor functions, alertness at different times of the day, and interpersonal relationships with classmates (Kubiszyn & Borich, 2003; Smith, 2004).

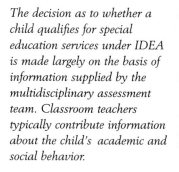

● Multidisciplinary assessment team determines if student needs special services

Preparation of the IEP At least some, if not all, of the members of the assessment team work with the teacher (and the parents) in preparing the IEP. The necessary components of an IEP were described earlier, and they are illustrated in Figure 6.1.

● Classroom teacher, parents, several specialists prepare IEP

Implementation and Evaluation of the IEP Depending on the nature and severity of the disability, the student may spend part or all of the school day in a regular classroom or be placed in a separate class or school. If the student stays in a regular classroom, the teacher will be expected to put into practice the various instructional techniques listed in the IEP. Because the IEP is planned by a multidisciplinary team, you will be given direction and support in providing regular class instruction for students who have a disabling condition as defined under IDEA. The classroom teacher may also be expected to determine if the listed objectives are being met and to furnish evidence of attainment. Various techniques of instruction as well as approaches to evaluation that stress student mastery of individualized assignments will be discussed in several of the chapters that follow.

pause & reflect

Many teachers say that although they agree with the philosophy behind IDEA, they feel that their training has not adequately prepared them for meeting the needs of students with disabling conditions. Would you say the same about your teacher education program? Why? What might you do to prepare yourself better?

Figure 6.1 Example of an Individualized Education Program (IEP)

INDIVIDUAL EDUCATIONAL PLAN *11/2004*	Description of Services to Be Provided

The types of atypical students you will sometimes be expected to teach in your classroom will vary. Some will be special education students who are being mainstreamed for part of the school day. Others, although different from typical students in some noticeable respect, will not qualify for special education services under IDEA. The remainder of this chapter will describe students from both categories and techniques for teaching them. Students with mental retardation, learning disabilities, and emotional disturbance often require special forms of instruction, and we will focus on these categories. In addition, though not mentioned in IDEA, students who are gifted and talented require special forms of instruction, as we will also discuss.

STUDENTS WITH MENTAL RETARDATION

Definition of Mental Retardation

The American Association on Mental Retardation (AAMR) defines **mental retardation** as "a disability characterized by significant limitations both in intellectual functioning and in adaptive behavior as expressed in conceptual, social, and practical adaptive skills. This disability originates before age 18" (American Association on Mental Retardation, 2002).

An individual whose score is two or more standard deviations below the mean (a score of 70 to 75 or below) on a standardized test of intelligence is considered to have a significant limitation in intellectual functioning. If you're not sure what a standard deviation is, take a look now at the chapter on standardized tests, where we discuss this statistical concept. As with intellectual functioning, a significant limitation in adaptive behavior is said to exist when an individual scores at least two standard deviations below the mean on standardized tests of adaptive skills.

As a result of legal challenges to IQ testing and special class placement, as well as to the trend toward mainstreaming, students classified as "mildly" retarded who were once separated are more likely now to be placed in regular classes. You probably will not encounter a great many mainstreamed children classified as "moderately" or "severely" retarded because of the specialized forms of care and instruction they need. You may, however, be asked to teach one or more of the higher-scoring children with mild retardation for at least part of the day.

Characteristics of Children with Mild Retardation

Students who have below-average IQ scores follow the same general developmental pattern as their peers with higher IQ scores, but they differ in the rate and degree of development.[1] Accordingly, students with low IQ scores may possess characteristics typical of students with average IQ scores who are younger than they are. One general characteristic of such students, therefore, is that they often appear immature compared with their age-mates. Immature students are likely to experience frustration frequently when they find they are unable to do things their classmates can do, and many students with mild retardation tend to have a low tolerance for frustration and a tendency toward low self-esteem, low confidence, and low motivation. These feelings, in conjunction with the cognitive deficits outlined in the next paragraph, sometimes make it difficult for the child with mild retardation to make friends and get along with peers of average ability.

● Students with mild retardation may frustrate easily, lack confidence and self-esteem

The cognitive characteristics of children with mild retardation include a tendency to oversimplify concepts, limited ability to generalize, smaller memory capacity, shorter attention span, the inclination to concentrate on only one aspect of a learning situation and to ignore other relevant features, the inability to formulate learning strategies that fit particular situations, and delayed language development. These children also show a limited amount of *metacognition*, that is, knowledge about how one learns and the factors that affect learning. (This concept will be discussed more fully in the chapter on information-processing theory.)

● Students with mild retardation tend to oversimplify, have difficulty generalizing

Several of these cognitive deficits often operate in concert to produce or contribute to the learning problems of students with mild retardation. Consider, for example, the problem of generalization (also known as transfer). This refers to the ability of a learner to take something that has been learned in one context, such as paper-and-pencil arithmetic skills, and use it to deal with a similar but different task, such as knowing whether one has received the correct change after making a purchase at a store. Students with mild mental retardation may not spontaneously exhibit transfer because (1) their metacognitive deficits limit their tendency to look for signs of similarity between two tasks, (2) their relatively short attention span prevents them from noticing similarities, and (3) their limited memory capacity and skills lessen their ability to recall relevant knowledge.

These characteristics can be understood more completely if they are related to Jean Piaget's description of cognitive development. Middle and high school students

---

[1] Many of the points in this section are based on a discussion of characteristics of mentally retarded children in *Exceptional Children and Youth* (2002), by Nancy Hunt and Kathleen Marshall; *Exceptional Children: An Introduction to Special Education* (2003), by William L. Heward; *Educating Exceptional Children* (2003), by Samuel Kirk, James Gallagher, and Nicholas Anastasiow; and *Introduction to Special Education* (2004), by Deborah Deutsch Smith.

with mild retardation may never move beyond the level of concrete operations. They may be able to deal with concrete situations but find it difficult to grasp abstractions, generalize from one situation to another, or state and test hypotheses. Younger children with retardation tend to classify things in terms of a single feature.

The following Suggestions for Teaching take into account the characteristics just described, as well as points made by Nancy Hunt and Kathleen Marshall (2003, pp. 188–195); William L. Heward (2003, pp. 220–226); Samuel Kirk, James Gallagher, and Nicholas Anastasiow (2003, pp. 186–198); and Deborah Deutsch Smith (2004, pp. 206–212).

Suggestions for Teaching in Your Classroom

Instructing Students with Mild Retardation

1 **As much as possible, try to avoid placing students with mild retardation in situations that are likely to lead to their frustration. When, despite your efforts, such students indicate that they are close to their limit of frustration tolerance, encourage them to engage in relaxing change-of-pace pursuits or in physical activities.**

JOURNAL ENTRY
Helping Students with Mild
Retardation Deal with Frustration

Because children with retardation are more likely to experience frustration than their more capable peers, try to minimize the frequency of such experiences in the classroom. Probably the most effective way to do this is to give students with mild retardation individual assignments so that they are not placed in situations where their work is compared with that of others. No matter how hard you try, however, you will not be able to eliminate frustrating experiences, partly because you will have to schedule some all-class activities and partly because even individual assignments may be difficult for a child with mild retardation to handle. If you notice that such a student appears to be getting more and more bothered by an inability to complete a task, you might try to divert attention to a less demanding form of activity or allow the student to take a short break by sharpening pencils or going for a drink of water.

2 **Do everything possible to encourage a sense of self-esteem.**

Children with mild retardation are prone to devalue themselves because they are aware that they are less capable than their classmates at doing many things. One way to combat this tendency toward self-devaluation is to make a point of showing that you have positive feelings about less capable students. You might, for example, say something like "I'm so glad you're here today. You make the classroom a nicer place to be in." If you indicate that you have positive feelings about an individual, that person is likely to acquire similar feelings about herself.

JOURNAL ENTRY
Combating the Tendency to
Communicate Low Expectations

As you saw in the preceding chapter, many teachers, usually inadvertently, tend to communicate low expectations to some of their students. To avoid committing the same error, you might do one or more of the following: make it clear that you will allow plenty of time for all students to come up with an answer to a question, repeat the question and give a clue before asking a different question, remind yourself to give frequent personal attention to students with mild retardation, or try to convey to these students the expectation that they *can* learn. Perhaps the best overall strategy to use in building self-esteem is to help children with retardation successfully complete learning tasks. Suggestions 3 through 5 offer ideas you might use.

JOURNAL ENTRY
Giving Students with Mild
Retardation Simple Assignments

3 **Present learning tasks that contain a small number of elements, at least some of them familiar to students, and that can be completed in a short period of time.**

Because students with retardation tend to oversimplify concepts, try to provide learning tasks that contain only a few elements, at least some of which they have previously learned. For example, you might ask middle or secondary school social studies students with mild retardation to prepare a report on the work of a single police officer, as opposed to preparing an analysis of law enforcement agencies (which might be an appropriate topic for the most capable student in the class). Also, because students with retardation tend to have a short attention span, short assignments are preferable to long ones.

● Give students with mild
retardation short assignments
that can be completed quickly

4 **Try to arrange what is to be learned into a series of small steps, each of which leads to immediate feedback.**

Again because of their short attention span, students with retardation may become distracted or discouraged if they are asked to concentrate on demanding tasks that lead to a delayed payoff. Therefore, it is better to give a series of short activities that produce immediate feedback than to use any sort of contract approach or the equivalent in which the student is expected to engage in self-directed effort leading to a remote goal.

Students who lack confidence, tend to think of one thing at a time, are unable to generalize, and have a short memory and attention span usually respond quite positively to programmed instruction and certain forms of computer-assisted instruction (described more completely in the chapter on behavioral learning theory). Some computer programs offer a systematic step-by-step procedure that emphasizes only one specific idea per step or frame. They also offer immediate feedback. These characteristics closely fit the needs of children who are mildly retarded. You might look for computer programs in the subject or subjects you teach or develop your own materials, perhaps in the form of a workbook of some kind.

5 **Teach simple techniques for improving memory, and consistently point out how use of these techniques leads to more accurate recall.**

In our chapter on information-processing theory, we describe a set of memory aids called mnemonic devices. Used for thousands of years by scholars and teachers in different countries, most are fairly simple devices that help a learner organize information, encode it meaningfully, and generate cues that allow it to be retrieved from memory when needed. The simplest mnemonic devices are rhymes, first-letter mnemonics (also known as acronyms), and sentence mnemonics. For example, a first-letter mnemonic or acronym for the Great Lakes is *HOMES: H*uron, *O*ntario, *M*ichigan, *E*rie, *S*uperior.

6 **Devise and use record-keeping techniques that make it clear that students have completed assignments successfully and are making progress.**

JOURNAL ENTRY
Giving Students with Mild
Retardation Proof of Progress

Students who are experiencing difficulties in learning are especially in need of tangible proof of progress. When, for instance, they correctly fill in blanks in a programmed workbook and discover that their answers are correct, they are encouraged to go on to the next question. You might use the same basic approach in more general ways by having students with retardation keep their own records showing their progress. (This technique might be used with all students in a class.) For example, you could make individual charts for primary grade students. As they successfully complete assignments, have them color in marked-off sections, paste on gold stars or the equivalent, or trace the movement of animal figures, rockets, or something else toward a destination.

STUDENTS WITH LEARNING DISABILITIES

By far the greatest number of students who qualify for special education under IDEA are those classified as having **learning disabilities.** According to the U.S. Department of Education (2001a) figures, the number of students identified as learning disabled increased from approximately 800,000 in 1976–1977 to 2,716,655 in 1999–2000. In the 1976–1977 school year, students with learning disabilities accounted for about 24 percent of the disabled population. By the 1999–2000 school year, that estimate had grown to almost 51 percent. Especially because so many students are now classified as learning disabled, it is important to define and explore the characteristics of students with learning disabilities.

Characteristics of Students with Learning Disabilities

According to IDEA, an individual who has a specific learning disability can be described as follows:

● Learning disabilities: disorders in basic processes that lead to learning problems not due to other causes

1. The individual has a *disorder in one or more of the basic psychological processes.* These processes refer to intrinsic prerequisite abilities such as memory, auditory perception, and visual perception.
2. The individual has *difficulty in learning,* specifically in the areas of speaking, listening, writing, reading (word recognition skills and comprehension), spelling, and mathematics (calculation and reasoning).
3. The problem is *not due primarily to other causes,* such as visual or hearing impairments, motor disabilities, mental retardation, emotional disturbance, or economic, environmental, or cultural disadvantage.

In addition to problems with cognitive processing and learning, many students with a learning disability (as well as students with mild mental retardation and students with emotional disturbance) have more poorly developed social skills than their nondisabled peers. Such students are more likely to ignore the teacher's directions, cheat, use profane language, disturb other students, disrupt group activities, and start fights. Consequently, they are often rejected by the rest of the class, which contributes to lowered self-esteem and poor academic performance (Gresham & MacMillan, 1997).

Some people dismiss the notion of a learning disability as a fiction because, they say, everyone at one time or another has misread numbers, letters, and words; confused pronunciations of words and letters; and suffered embarrassing lapses of attention and memory. But students with learning disabilities really are different from others—mostly in degree rather than in kind. Although the nondisabled individual may occasionally exhibit lapses in basic information processing, the learning disabled individual does so consistently and with little hope of self-correction. The important point to keep in mind is that you need to know what a student with a learning disability (as well as a low-achieving non–learning disabled student) can and cannot do so that you can effectively remediate those weaknesses (Spear-Swerling & Sternberg, 1998).

Identifying Students with Learning Disabilities

The major criterion used by most school districts to identify children with a learning disability is at least an average score on a standardized test of intelligence and a significantly below average score (one standard deviation or more) on a standardized achievement test. In other words, districts typically look for a discrepancy between achievement and IQ scores.

Since about 80 percent of children with a learning disability have difficulty with reading (Meyer, 2000), a considerable amount of research has been done to determine if a discrepancy between IQ and reading comprehension scores is a valid in-

Students with a learning disability learn more slowly than other students because of deficits in perception, attention, and memory.

dicator of a learning disability. One approach to this problem has been to compare children who exhibit the discrepancy we just described with children whose IQ and reading scores are *both* below average. Researchers often refer to students in the first group as IQ-discrepant and students in the second group as IQ-consistent. Two analyses of almost four dozen studies that have examined this issue (Meyer, 2000; Steubing et al., 2002) conclude that IQ-consistent students are indistinguishable from IQ-discrepant students in terms of reading skills (such as phonological awareness and word naming) and behavior (such as social skills and fine motor skills).

This research casts doubt on the usefulness of the discrepancy criterion. Learning disabilities certainly exist, but educators may need to develop a more sophisticated means of identifying them.

Problems with Basic Psychological Processes

● Students with learning disabilities have problems with perception, attention, memory, metacognition

The fundamental problem that underlies a learning disability is, as the law states, "a disorder in one or more basic psychological processes." Although this phrase is somewhat vague, it generally refers to problems with how students receive information, process it, and express what they have learned. Specifically, many students with learning disabilities have deficits in perception, attention, memory encoding and storage, and metacognition.

Some students with learning disabilities have great difficulty perceiving the difference between certain sounds (*f* and *v*, *m* and *n*, for example) or letters (*m* and *n*, or *b*, *p*, and *d*, for example). As a result, words that begin with one letter (such as *v*ase) are sometimes perceived and pronounced as if they begin with another letter (as in *f*ase). As you can no doubt appreciate from this simple example, this type of deficit makes learning to read and reading with comprehension long and frustrating for some students.

Many students with learning disabilities also have difficulty with attention and impulse control: focusing on a task, noticing important cues and ideas, and staying with the task until it is completed. The source of the distraction may be objects and activities in the classroom, or it may be unrelated thoughts. In either case, the student misses much of what the teacher says or what is on a page of text or misinterprets directions.

Because so many students with learning disabilities have problems with perception and attention, they also have problems with accurate recall of information. Accurate recall is heavily dependent on what gets stored in memory in the first place and where in memory information is stored (Hunt & Marshall, 2002), so students who encode partial, incorrect, or unimportant information have memory problems.

Like students with mild retardation, many students with learning disabilities have a deficit in metacognitive skills (Hunt & Marshall, 2002). As a result, their learning activities are chaotic, like those of young children. For example, they may begin a task before they have thought through all of the steps.

Students with learning disabilities tend to be characterized as passive and disorganized: passive in the sense that they take few active steps to attend to relevant information, store it effectively in memory, and retrieve it when needed; and disorganized in the sense that their learning activities are often unplanned and subject to whatever happens to capture their attention at the moment.

Given these problems with basic processes, researchers have studied ways to help students structure the way they learn. For example, one approach to improving the reading skills of students with a learning disability that shows some promise is teaching students how to use reading comprehension strategies (see, for example, Gersten, Fuchs, Williams, and Baker, 2001). One such program that was tested on middle school students with a reading disability (Bryant et al., 2000) contained the following components:

1. *Word identification:* Students used a first-letter mnemonic to help them recall the seven steps involved in decoding multisyllabic words.
2. *Partner reading:* To improve reading fluency (reading whole words in text accurately and at an appropriate speed), pairs of students modeled fluent reading for one another and helped each other decode unfamiliar words.
3. *Collaborative strategic reading:* This technique is aimed at improving reading comprehension and combines two proven instructional techniques, reciprocal teaching and cooperative learning (we discuss both techniques in detail in later chapters). Students first learn how to use the four comprehension-aiding techniques that are part of reciprocal teaching: (a) previewing a reading passage to help students make predictions about what they will read and already know about the topic, (b) monitoring reading to identify and fix comprehension failures, (c) identifying main ideas, and (d) asking questions and reviewing. Students then apply the techniques by working either in pairs or small cooperative groups.

Compared with pretest scores, students achieved higher posttest scores on word identification, reading fluency, and reading comprehension tests. The differences for word identification and reading fluency were statistically significant (meaning they were not likely due to chance).

Attention-Deficit/Hyperactivity Disorder

Many children who have a learning disability are also diagnosed as having **attention-deficit/hyperactivity disorder (ADHD).** Estimates of the extent to which these two conditions co-occur range from 25 to 40 percent (Lerner, 2003). Approximately 3.3 percent of six- to eleven-year-old children have ADHD alone, with boys outnumbering girls by at least three to one (Bowman, 2002). In addition, some studies have found that as many as 30 percent of children with ADHD exhibit aggressive behaviors (such as fighting, stealing, lying, and vandalism) that are consistent with the psychiatric diagnosis of conduct disorder (Connor, 2002). The co-occurrence of ADHD and conduct disorder (called comorbidity) is seen more frequently among children from urban homes than middle-class suburban homes and is associated with significant social, behavioral, and academic problems (Bloomquist & Schnell, 2002).

The American Psychiatric Association recognizes three types of ADHD: children who are predominantly inattentive, children who are predominantly hyperactive and impulsive, and children who exhibit a combination of all three behaviors. For a student to be judged as having ADHD, the symptoms have to appear before the age of seven; they have to be displayed in several settings, such as at home, at school, and at play; and they have to persist over time (American Psychiatric Association, 2000). Although ADHD is not mentioned in IDEA as a separate disability category, services for children with ADHD can be funded under the "specific learning dis-

● Symptoms of ADHD include inattention, hyperactivity, and impulsivity

abilities" category, the "emotionally disturbed" category, or the "other health impaired" category of IDEA (Lerner, 2003).

In general, the treatments for ADHD fall into one of the following three categories (Lerner, 2003; Purdie, Hattie, & Carroll, 2002):

1. *Prescribed stimulant medication:* The most popular class of drugs prescribed for children with ADHD is psychostimulants. The psychostimulants that are prescribed most often are Ritalin, Dexedrine, Cylert, and Adderall. The effect of these medications is highly specific. Some children do better on one drug, others on another, while still others do not respond to any of them.

2. *School-based psychological/educational programs:* These programs typically involve either behavior management, cognitive behavioral therapy, or classroom environment restructuring. Behavior management programs (which we describe in more detail in the chapter on behavioral learning theory) involve the systematic use of reinforcement and punishment to increase the frequency of desired behaviors and decrease the frequency of undesired behaviors. Cognitive behavior therapy programs involve teaching students to remind themselves to use effective learning skills, monitor their progress, and reinforce themselves. Classroom environment restructuring programs use such techniques as reducing classroom noise, assigning students permanent seats, seating ADHD students at the front of the class, and providing frequent breaks between tasks.

3. *Multimodal programs:* Multimodal programs are combinations of one or more of the above treatments, typically stimulant medications and cognitive behavioral programs.

An analysis of seventy-four research studies (Purdie et al., 2002) found, not surprisingly, that an overall best treatment for ADHD does not exist. Rather, different treatments had stronger effects depending on the outcome that was being examined. For example, stimulant medications were more effective than other treatments in minimizing impulsivity, hyperactivity, and attentional deficits; multimodal programs were most effective in reducing dislike by classmates and fostering more effective prosocial skills and positive peer interactions; and school-based programs were most effective in aiding the growth of cognitive skills.

The following Suggestions for Teaching will give you some ideas about how to help students with learning disabilities and ADHD improve their learning skills and feel better about themselves.

Suggestions for Teaching in Your Classroom

Instructing Students with Learning Disabilities

1   **Structure learning tasks to help students with learning disabilities and ADHD compensate for weaknesses in psychological processes.**

JOURNAL ENTRY
Helping Students with Learning
Disabilities Improve Basic
Learning Processes

Because of their weaknesses in basic psychological processes, students with learning disabilities and ADHD are often distractible, impulsive, forgetful, disorganized, poor at comprehension, and unaware of the factors that affect learning. Research findings indicate that the most effective instructional approach in such cases is one that combines direct instruction with strategy instruction (both methods are described in the chapter "Approaches to Instruction"). This combined approach has produced substantial improvements in reading comprehension, vocabulary, word recognition, memory, writing, cognitive processing, and self-concept (Swanson & Hoskyn, 1998).

The following examples are consistent with an instructional approach that is based on both direct instruction and strategy instruction.

EXAMPLES

- For students who have difficulty distinguishing between similar-looking or -sounding stimuli (such as letters, words, or phrases), point out and highlight their distinguishing characteristics. For example, highlight the circular part of the letters *b, p,* and *d* and place a directional arrow at the end of the straight segment to emphasize that they have the same shape but differ in their spatial orientation. Or highlight the letters *t* and *r* in the words *though, thought,* and *through* to emphasize that they differ from each other by the absence or presence of one letter.

- For students who are easily distracted, instruct them to place only the materials being used on top of the desk or within sight.

- For students who seem unable to attend to important stimuli such as significant sections of a text page, show them how to underline or outline in an effort to distinguish between important and unimportant material. Or suggest that they use a ruler or pointing device under each line as they read so that they can evaluate one sentence at a time. To help them attend to important parts of directions, highlight or write key-words and phrases in all capitals. For especially important tasks, you might want to ask students to paraphrase or repeat directions verbatim.

- For students who have a short attention span, give brief assignments, and divide complex material into smaller segments. After each short lesson segment, provide both immediate positive feedback and tangible evidence of progress. (Many sets of published materials prepared for use with students with learning disabilities are designed in this way.)

● Help students with learning disabilities to reduce distractions, attend to important information

- To improve students' memory and comprehension of information, teach memorization skills and how to relate new information to existing knowledge schemes to improve long-term storage and retrieval. Also, make frequent use of simple, concrete analogies and examples to explain and illustrate complex, abstract ideas. (We will describe several techniques for enhancing memory and comprehension in the chapter on information-processing theory.)

- To improve organization, suggest that students use a notebook to keep a record of homework assignments, a checklist of materials needed for class, and a list of books and materials they need to take home for studying and homework.

- To improve general awareness of the learning process, emphasize the importance of thinking about the factors that could affect one's performance on a particular task, of forming a plan before actually starting to work, and of monitoring the effectiveness of learning activities.

- Consider the variety of learning environments available through multimedia software programs. Some students with learning disabilities may respond better to a combination of visual and auditory information, while others may learn best in a hands-on setting. Multimedia programs provide options to address these different styles and also allow the student to control the direction and pace of learning. Examples of such programs can be found on the Special Needs page of the web site of the Educational Software Directory (**www.educational-software-directory.net/**).

● For additional journal suggestions, see the Reflective Journal Questions on the textbook web site.

② Capitalize on the resources in your classroom to help students with learning disabilities improve academically, socially, and emotionally.

Although you and the resource teacher will be the main sources of instruction and support for mainstreamed students, recognize that other sources of classroom support are almost always available. The other students in your class, for example, can supplement your instructional efforts. As we pointed out in the previous chapter, peer tutoring typically produces gains in achievement and improvements in interpersonal relationships and attitudes toward subject matter. These effects have been documented for students with a learning disability as well as low-achieving students without a learning disability (Fuchs, Fuchs, Mathes, & Simmons, 1997). And do not overlook the benefits of having students with learning disabilities play the role of tutor. Giving students with disabilities the opportunity to tutor either a low-achieving classmate in a subject that is not affected by the student's disability or a younger student in a lower grade can produce a noticeable increase in self-esteem.

Another way to make use of the other students in your class is through cooperative learning. This technique was described in the last chapter and is explored in more detail in the chapter on approaches to instruction. Like peer tutoring, which it incorporates, it also produces gains in achievement, interpersonal relationships, and self-esteem.

Finally, make use of the various ways in which information can be presented to students and in which students can respond. In addition to text material and lecturing, you can use films, computer-based presentations, picture charts, diagrams, and demonstrations. In addition to having students demonstrate what they have learned through paper-and-pencil tests and other written products, you can have them make oral presentations, produce pictorial products, create an actual product, or give a performance. Hands-on activities are particularly useful for students with ADHD.

STUDENTS WITH EMOTIONAL DISTURBANCE

Estimates of Emotional Disturbance

In the 2001 report to Congress on the implementation of IDEA, the Department of Education noted that 443,143 students between the ages of six and seventeen were classified as emotionally disturbed for the 1999–2000 school year. This figure accounted for 8.3 percent of all schoolchildren classified as disabled and slightly less than 1 percent of the general school-age population. Not everyone agrees that these figures accurately reflect the scope of the problem. Other scholars believe that 3 to 5 percent of all school-age children qualify for special education services under IDEA's emotional disturbance criteria (Heward, 2003).

Definitions of Emotional Disturbance

Two reasons that estimates of **emotional disturbance** vary are the lack of clear descriptions of such forms of behavior and different interpretations of the descriptions that do exist. Children with *emotional disturbance* are defined in IDEA in this way:

● Emotional disturbance: poor relationships, inappropriate behavior, depression, fears

(I) The term means a condition exhibiting one or more of the following characteristics over a long period of time and to a marked degree that adversely affects a child's educational performance:
   (A) An inability to learn that cannot be explained by intellectual, sensory, or health factors;
   (B) An inability to build or maintain satisfactory interpersonal relationships with peers and teachers;
   (C) Inappropriate types of behavior or feelings under normal circumstances;
   (D) A general pervasive mood of unhappiness or depression; or
   (E) A tendency to develop physical symptoms or fears associated with personal or school problems.
(II) The term includes schizophrenia. The term does not apply to children who are socially maladjusted, unless it is determined that they have a serious emotional disturbance. (Office of the Federal Register, 1994, pp. 13–14)

Several special education scholars (for example, Kirk et al., 2003, pp. 253–255; Heward, 2003, p. 284; Smith, 2004, pp. 260–261) point out the difficulties caused by vague terminology in distinguishing between students who have emotional disturbance and students who are normal. The phrase *a long period of time*, for example, is not defined in the law (although many special education experts use six months as a rough rule of thumb). Indicators such as *satisfactory interpersonal relationships*, *a general pervasive mood*, and *inappropriate types of behavior or feelings under normal circumstances* are difficult to measure objectively and can often be observed in normal individuals. Because long-term observation of behavior is often critical in making a correct diagnosis of emotional disturbance, you can aid the multidisciplinary assessment team in this task by keeping a behavioral log of a child you suspect may have this disorder.

● Term *behavior disorder* focuses on behavior that needs to be changed, objective assessment

That many educators and psychologists use such terms as *emotionally disturbed*, *socially maladjusted*, and *behavior disordered* synonymously makes matters even more confusing. The term **behavior disorder** has many adherents and has been adopted by several states for two basic reasons. One reason is that it calls attention to the actual behavior that is disordered and needs to be changed. The second reason is that behaviors can be directly and objectively assessed. Although there are subtle differences between the terms *emotionally disturbed* and *behavior disorder*, they are essentially interchangeable, and you can probably assume that those who use them are referring to children who share similar characteristics. Because of the nature of bureaucracies, however, it may be necessary for anyone hoping to obtain special assistance for a child with what many contemporary psychologists would call a behavior disorder to refer to that child as *emotionally disturbed* since that is the label used in IDEA.

Characteristics of Students with an Emotional Disturbance

The most frequently used classification system of emotional disturbance (or behavior disorder) involves two basic patterns: externalizing and internalizing (see, for example, Heward, 2003; Wicks-Nelson & Israel, 2003).

● Students with behavior disorders tend to be either aggressive or withdrawn

- *Externalizing* students are often aggressive, uncooperative, restless, and negativistic. They tend to lie and steal, defy teachers, and be hostile to authority figures. Sometimes they are cruel and malicious.

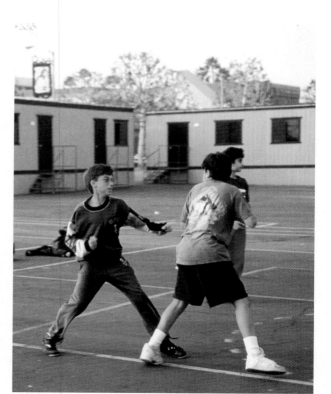

Students who have an emotional disturbance tend to be either aggressive or withdrawn. Because aggressive students disrupt classroom routines, teachers need to focus on classroom design features and employ behavior management techniques to reduce the probability of such behaviors.

- *Internalizing* students, by contrast, are typically shy, timid, anxious, and fearful. They are often depressed and lack self-confidence.

Teachers tend to be more aware of students who display aggressive disorders because their behavior often stimulates or forces reactions. The withdrawn student, however, may be more likely to develop serious emotional problems such as depression and may even be at risk of suicide during the adolescent years. The following Suggestions for Teaching will help you teach both the withdrawn student and the aggressive student.

Suggestions for Teaching in Your Classroom

Instructing Students with Emotional Disturbance

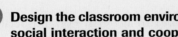 **Design the classroom environment and formulate lesson plans to encourage social interaction and cooperation.[2]**

● Foster interpersonal contact among withdrawn students

Students whose emotional disturbance manifests itself as social withdrawal may stay away from others on purpose (perhaps because they find social contacts threatening), or they may find that others stay away from them (perhaps because they have poorly developed social skills). Regardless of the cause, the classroom environment and your instructional activities can be designed to foster appropriate interpersonal contact.

EXAMPLES

JOURNAL ENTRY
Activities and Materials That
Encourage Cooperation

● Preschool and elementary school teachers can use toys and materials as well as organized games and sports that encourage cooperative play and have a reduced focus on individual performance. Activities might include dress-up games or puppet plays; games might include soccer, variations of It (such as tag), and kickball or softball modified such that everyone on the team gets a turn to kick or bat before the team plays in the field.

● Elementary and middle school teachers can use one or more of several team-oriented learning activities. *Cooperative Learning* (2nd ed., 1995), by Robert Slavin, provides details on using such activities as student teams–achievement divisions, jigsaw, and team-accelerated instruction.

2 **Prompt and reinforce appropriate social interactions.**

Prompting and positive reinforcement are basic learning principles that will be discussed in the chapter on behavioral learning theory. Essentially, a prompt is a stimulus that draws out a desired response, and positive reinforcement involves giving the student a positive reinforcer (something the student wants) immediately after a desired behavior. The aim is to get the student to behave that way again. Typical reinforcers are verbal praise, stickers (with pictures of gold stars and smiley faces, for instance), and small prizes (such as a pencil with the child's name printed on it).

---

[2] Most of these suggestions are derived from points made in Chapters 6, 7, and 8 of *Strategies for Addressing Behavior Problems in the Classroom* (4th ed., 2002), by Mary Margaret Kerr and C. Michael Nelson.

EXAMPLE

- You can set up a cooperative task or activity: "Marc, I would like you to help Carol and Raquel paint the scenery for next week's play. You can paint the trees and flowers, Carol will paint the grass, and Raquel will do the people." After several minutes, say something like, "That's good work. I am really pleased at how well the three of you are working together." Similar comments can be made at intervals as the interaction continues.

3 Train other students to initiate social interaction.

In all likelihood, you will have too many classroom responsibilities to spend a great deal of time working directly with a withdrawn child. It may be possible, however, using the steps that follow, to train other students to initiate contact with withdrawn students.

EXAMPLE

- First, choose a student as a helper who interacts freely and well, can follow your instructions, and can concentrate on the training task for at least ten minutes. Second, explain that the goal is to get the withdrawn child to work or play with the helping student but that the helper should expect rejection, particularly at first. Role-play the actions of a withdrawn child so that the helper understands what you mean by rejection. Emphasize the importance of making periodic attempts at interaction. Third, instruct the helper to suggest games or activities that appeal to the withdrawn student. Fourth, reinforce the helper's attempts to interact with the withdrawn child.

4 Design the classroom environment to reduce the probability of disruptive behavior.

The best way to deal with aggressive or antisocial behavior is to nip it in the bud. This strategy has at least three related benefits. One benefit of fewer disruptions is that you can better accomplish what you had planned for the day. A second benefit is that you are likely to be in a more positive frame of mind than if you spend half the day acting as a referee. A third benefit is that because of fewer disruptions and a more positive attitude, you may be less inclined to resort to permissible or even impermissible forms of physical punishment (which often produces undesirable side effects).

EXAMPLES

- With student input, formulate rules for classroom behavior and penalties for infractions of rules. Remind all students of the penalties, particularly when a disruptive incident seems about to occur, and consistently apply the penalties when the rules are broken.
- Place valued objects and materials out of reach when they are not needed or in use.
- Minimize the aggressive student's frustration with learning by using some of the same techniques you would use for a child with mild retardation: break tasks down into small, easy-to-manage pieces; provide clear directions; and reinforce correct responses.

5 Reinforce appropriate behavior, and, if necessary, punish inappropriate behavior.

In suggestion 2, we described the use of positive reinforcement to encourage desired behavior. Reinforcement has the dual effect of teaching the aggressive student which behavior is appropriate and reducing the frequency of inappropriate behavior as it is replaced by desired behavior. Disruptive behavior will still occur, however. Three effective techniques for suppressing it while reinforcing desired behaviors are contingency contracts, token economies and fines, and time-out. Each of these techniques will be described in the chapter on behavioral learning theory.

6 Use group contingency-management techniques.

You may want to reward the entire class when the aggressive student behaves appropriately for a certain period of time. Such rewards, which may be free time, special classroom events, or certain privileges, should make the aggressive student the hero and foster better peer relationships.

JOURNAL ENTRY
Getting Students to Initiate Interaction with a Withdrawn Child

- Use techniques to forestall aggressive or antisocial behavior

GIFTED AND TALENTED STUDENTS

Students who learn at a significantly faster rate than their peers or who possess superior talent in one or more areas also need to be taught in special ways if they are to make the most of their abilities. Unlike students with mental retardation, learning disabilities, and emotional disturbance, however, students with superior capabilities are not covered by IDEA. Instead, the federal government provides technical assistance to states and local school districts for establishing programs for superior students. Although most states have such programs, some experts in special education (for example, Colangelo & Davis, 2003b; Gallagher, 2003) feel that they are not given the resources they need to meet the needs of all gifted and talented students adequately. The Suggestions for Teaching that follow a bit later reflect this situation. All of the suggestions are inexpensive to implement and require few additional personnel.

A definition of the term **gifted and talented** was part of a bill passed by Congress in 1988:

● Gifted and talented students show high performance in one or more areas

> The term *gifted and talented children and youth* means children and youth who give evidence of high performance capability in areas such as intellectual, creative, artistic, or leadership capacity, or in specific academic fields, and who require services or activities not ordinarily provided by the school in order to fully develop such capabilities.

Identification of Gifted and Talented Students

Eligibility for gifted and talented programs has traditionally been based on standardized test scores, particularly IQ tests. It was not uncommon in years past for students to have to achieve an IQ score of at least 130 to be admitted to such programs. But criticisms about the narrow range of skills covered by such tests (and their heavy reliance on multiple-choice items) have led most states to de-emphasize or eliminate the use of traditional intelligence tests and a numerical cutoff score for identification (Reid, Romanoff, & Algozzine, 2000; Renzulli, 2002).

Evidence that alternative assessments can do a better job of identifying gifted and talented children does exist. In one study (Reid et al., 2000), 434 second-grade students who were recommended for a gifted education program were tested with both traditional and nontraditional measures. The traditional assessment was a nonverbal test of analogical reasoning. The nontraditional assessment, which combined aspects of both Gardner's and Sternberg's theories of intelligence, was a set of linguistic, logical-mathematical, and spatial problem-solving tasks that called for analytic, synthetic, and practical thinking. For example, students were given a bag of small items, each of which had to be used as the basis of a five-minute story. For another task, students were given a set of colored cardboard pieces and told to make a variety of objects, such as an animal, a building, something that moves, and whatever they wanted. On the basis of analogical reasoning scores, about 17 percent of the sample would have been recommended for placement in the gifted program. That percentage rose to 40 percent when scores from the problem-solving assessment were used. Another interesting statistic was that almost 70 percent of the students recommended on the basis of their problem-solving performance would not have been recommended on the basis of their analogical reasoning score.

Joseph Renzulli (2002), a leading researcher of giftedness and gifted education, believes that the concept of giftedness should be expanded beyond the dimensions examined in the study we just described to include students who can channel their assets into constructive social actions that benefit others. As an example, he describes Melanie, a fifth-grade girl, who befriended Tony, a visually impaired first-grade boy who was ignored by most other students and teased by a few others. Melanie persuaded some of the school's most popular students to sit with Tony in the lunchroom, and she recruited other students to create and illustrate large-print books on topics of interest to Tony. Over the course of several months, Tony was accepted by many of the school's students, and his attitude toward school markedly improved. According to Howard Gardner's multiple intelligences theory, Melanie's gift likely stems from an above-average interpersonal (and possibly intrapersonal) intelligence. In the adult world, two examples of this type of person are Mother Teresa and Martin Luther King Jr.—and, as Renzulli points out, no one really cares what their test scores or grade-point averages were.

● Minorities underrepresented in gifted classes because of over-reliance on test scores

Broadening the definition and instruments used to assess giftedness will serve diversity goals as well. Students from many minority cultures are underrepresented in programs for the gifted and talented. In fact, there is a general ignorance of characteristics that are more highly valued by a minority culture than by the majority culture. Some Native American tribes, for example, de-emphasize the concept of giftedness because it runs counter to their belief that the welfare and cohesion of the group are more important than celebrating and nurturing the talents of any individual. The members of other tribes may place as much value on a child's knowledge of tribal traditions, storytelling ability, and artistic ability as they do on problem-solving ability and scientific reasoning (Callahan & McIntire, 1994). A child's giftedness may therefore be evident only when examined from the perspective of a particular culture. This may explain why only 2 percent of Native Americans can be found in classes for the gifted and talented (Winner, 1997).

Characteristics of Gifted and Talented Students

In one sense, gifted and talented students are like any other group of students. Some are healthy and well coordinated, whereas others are not. Some are extremely popular and well liked, but others are not. Some are well adjusted; others are not (Kirk et al., 2003). Some formulate a strong identity (Marcia's identity achievement status) and are successful later in life, while others are not (Zuo & Cramond, 2001). But as a group, gifted and talented students are often noticeably different (see, for example, discussions by Dai, Moon, & Feldhusen, 1998; Piechowski, 1997; and Winner, 1997). Here are some of the main characteristics that many gifted and talented students share:

● Gifted and talented students differ from their nongifted peers intellectually and emotionally

- They excel on tasks that involve language, abstract logical thinking, and mathematics.
- They are faster at encoding information and retrieving it from memory.
- They are highly aware of how they learn and the various conditions that affect their learning. As a result, they excel at transferring previously learned information and skills to new problems and settings.
- They exhibit such high levels of motivation and task persistence that the phrase "rage to master" is sometimes used to describe their behavior. Their motivation to learn is partly due to high levels of self-efficacy and appropriate attributions. That is, they believe they have the capability to master those tasks and subject matters they choose to tackle and that their success is the result of both high ability and hard work.
- They tend to be more solitary and introverted than average children.
- They tend to have very intense emotional lives. They react with intense feelings, such as joy, regret, or sorrow, to a story, a piece of music, or a social encounter. They also tend to be emotionally sensitive and sometimes surpass adults in their ability to notice and identify with the feelings of others.

For the most part, gifted and talented students see themselves as they were just described. In comparison to intellectually average students, they have a moderately stronger academic self-concept but score at about the same level on measures of physical and social self-concepts (Hoge & Renzulli, 1993).

Researchers who favor broadening the traditional definition of giftedness add other characteristics to the mix. Joseph Renzulli (2002), for example, believes that people like Melanie (the student who befriended an unpopular boy) possess the following characteristics:

- *Optimism:* Expecting that the future will be largely beneficial for oneself and others.
- *Courage:* The willingness to overcome physical, psychological, and moral fears and face difficulties or danger. We typically refer to such people as having integrity and strength of character.
- *Passionate involvement with a topic or discipline:* Being so emotionally committed to a topic that one can be said to have, in essence, fallen in love with it.
- *Sensitivity to human concerns:* The ability to understand the feelings of others and to communicate that understanding through acts of altruism and empathy.
- *Physical/mental energy:* The willingness to work hard over an extended period of time on a problem or an issue.
- *Vision/sense of destiny:* Visualizing a more desirable future and believing that one has been chosen to play a role in bringing that vision to reality.

Instructional Options

Gifted and talented students constantly challenge a teacher's skill, ingenuity, and classroom resources. While trying to instruct the class as a whole, the teacher is faced with the need to provide more and more interesting and challenging materials and ideas to gifted students. In this section, we will examine three possible ways to engage these students.

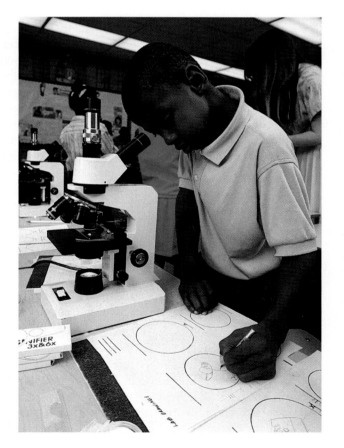

Because gifted and talented students understand and integrate abstract ideas more quickly than do their nongifted classmates, they are capable of successfully completing tasks that older students routinely carry out.

Accelerated Instruction   Accelerated instruction is often suggested as one way to meet the academic needs of gifted and talented students. For many people, the phrase *accelerated instruction* means allowing the student to skip one or more grades, which, while not as common as in years past, does occasionally occur. But there are at least three other ways of accomplishing the same goal: (1) the curriculum can be compressed, allowing gifted and talented students to complete the work for more than one grade during the regular school year; (2) the school year can be extended by the use of summer sessions; and (3) students can take college courses while still in high school.

Whatever the form of accelerated instruction, this is always a hotly debated topic, with pros and cons on each side. Two often quoted advantages for giving gifted students the opportunity to work on complex tasks are that it keeps them from becoming bored with school, and it produces more positive attitudes toward learning. On the negative side, two frequent arguments are that a gifted student may have trouble with the social and emotional demands of acceleration, and acceleration produces an undesirable sense of elitism among gifted students. Research evidence supports the presumed academic benefits of acceleration and fails to confirm the predicted negative social and emotional outcomes (Gallagher, 2003; Kulik, 2003). As with all other informed educational decisions, the unique needs of the individual and the situation must be considered before the best course of action can be determined.

Gifted and Talented Classes and Schools   Some public school districts offer separate classes for gifted and talented students as either an alternative to accelerated instruction or something that follows accelerated instruction. In addition, so-called magnet schools are composed of students whose average level of ability is higher than that found in a typical elementary, middle, or high school. Finally, many states sponsor high-ability high schools, particularly in mathematics and science.

● Separate classes for gifted and talented students aid achievement but may lower academic self-concept of some students

Recent findings suggest that such placements do not produce uniformly positive results and should be made only after the characteristics of the student and the program have been carefully considered. In terms of achievement, the typical gifted student can expect to score moderately higher (at about the 63rd percentile) on tests than comparable students who remain in heterogeneous classes (Kulik & Kulik, 1991). But the effects of separate class or school placement on measures of academic self-concept have been inconsistent; some researchers find them to be higher than those of students who remain in heterogeneous classes, whereas other researchers have found either no differences or declines (Hoge & Renzulli, 1993; Kulik & Kulik, 1991; Marsh & Craven, 2002).

Enrichment and Differentiated Instruction   Because of the potential negative effects of grade skipping, the limited availability of special classes and schools, and the fact that such classes and schools are not good options for some gifted and talented students, teachers may find themselves with one or two gifted and talented students in a regular classroom. A solution for meeting the special needs of these students (as well as those with disabilities) is a practice often referred to as *differentiated instruction*, a technique we have mentioned earlier. Basically, this means using different learning materials, instructional methods, assignments, and tests to accommodate differences in students' abilities, learning styles, prior knowledge, and cultural background (Benjamin, 2002; Gregory, 2003).

One scheme for delivering differentiated instruction to gifted and talented learners has been developed by Joseph Renzulli and Sally Reis (Reis & Renzulli, 1985; Renzulli & Reis, 1985: Renzulli, Gentry, & Reis, 2003). Based on their view that giftedness is a combination of above-average cognitive ability, creativity, and task commitment, Renzulli and Reis describe three levels of curriculum enrichment for gifted and talented learners:

Type I enrichment: Exploratory activities that are designed to expose students to topics, events, books, people, and places not ordinarily covered in the regular curriculum. The basic purpose of these activities is to stimulate new interests. Among the many suggestions Renzulli and Reis offer are having students view and write reports on films and videos (such as *The Eagle Has Landed: The Flight of Apollo 11*) and having local residents make presentations on their occupation or hobby.

Type II enrichment: Instructional methods and materials aimed at the development of such thinking and feeling processes as thinking creatively, classifying and analyzing data, solving problems, appreciating, and valuing.

Type III enrichment: Activities in which students investigate and collect data about a real topic or problem. For example, a student may decide to document the history of her school, focusing on such issues as changes in size, instructional materials and methods, and curriculum.

pause & reflect

Relatively little money is spent on programs for the gifted and talented compared with the amounts made available for the disabled. Defenders of this arrangement sometimes argue that because gifted students have a built-in advantage, we should invest most of our resources in services for the disabled. Do you agree or disagree? Why?

Numerous sites on the Internet are devoted to long-distance education, enrichment, and tutoring. You might explore the Global Network Academy (**www.gnacademy.org/**), which offers online courses in a wide range of areas. The web site of the Center for Collaborative Research in Education at the University of California, Irvine (**www.gse.uci.edu/CCRE/index.html**), contains information about online teaching and learning opportunities and various telementoring programs. The following Suggestions for Teaching provide further ideas for working with gifted and talented students.

Suggestions for Teaching in Your Classroom

Instructing Gifted and Talented Students

1 Consult with gifted and talented students regarding individual study projects, perhaps involving a learning contract.

JOURNAL ENTRY
Individual Study for Students Who Are Gifted and Talented

One of the most effective ways to deal with gifted students is to assign individual study projects. These may involve a contract approach, in which you consult with students on an individual basis and agree on a personal assignment that is to be completed by a certain date.

Such assignments should probably be related to some part of the curriculum. If you are studying Mexico, for example, a gifted student could devote free time to a special report on some aspect of Mexican life that intrigues him. In making these assignments, you should remember that even very bright students may not be able to absorb, organize, and apply abstract concepts until they become formal thinkers. Thus, until early middle school years, it may be preferable to keep these assignments brief rather than comprehensive.

To provide another variation of the individual study project, you could ask the gifted student to act as a research specialist and report on questions that puzzle the class. Still another individual study project is the creation of an open-ended, personal yearbook. Any time a gifted student finishes the assigned work, she might be allowed to write stories or do drawings for such a journal.

When possible, unobtrusive projects are preferable. Perhaps you can recall a teacher who rewarded the fast workers by letting them work on a mural (or the equivalent) covering the side board. If you were an average student, you can probably attest that the sight of the class "brains" having the time of their lives was not conducive to diligent effort on the part of the have-nots sweating away at their workbooks. Reward assignments should probably be restricted to individual work on unostentatious projects.

2 Encourage supplementary reading and writing.

JOURNAL ENTRY
Providing Gifted and Talented
Students with Opportunities for
Additional Reading and Writing

Encourage students to spend extra time reading and writing. A logical method of combining both skills is the preparation of book reports. It is perhaps less threatening to call them book *reviews* and emphasize that you are interested in personal reaction, not a précis or an abstract. Some specialists in the education of the gifted have suggested that such students be urged to read biographies and autobiographies. The line of reasoning here is that potential leaders might be inspired to emulate the exploits of a famous person. Even if such inspiration does not result, you could recommend life stories simply because they are usually interesting.

Other possibilities for writing are e-mail exchanges with other students, siblings at college, or friends in different areas. Or a student may write a review of a World Wide Web site that she has discovered. If the appropriate software and support are available, students could be encouraged to create home pages or web sites for themselves, either on a topic mutually selected with the teacher or on their personal interests (the latter would be much like a yearbook entry).

3 Have gifted students act as tutors.

Depending on the grade, subject, and personalities of those involved, gifted students might be asked to act occasionally as tutors, lab assistants, or the equivalent. Some bright students will welcome such opportunities and are capable of providing instruction in such a way that their peers do not feel self-conscious or humiliated. Others may resent being asked to spend school time helping classmates or may lack skills in interpersonal relationships. If you do decide to ask a gifted student to function as a tutor, it would be wise to proceed tentatively and cautiously.

USING TECHNOLOGY TO ASSIST EXCEPTIONAL STUDENTS

● Federal legislation has led to the development of various assistive technologies

There is perhaps no other place in education today where technology is making as significant an impact as in the field of special education, and this is largely due to the use of assistive technology. Mandated by IDEA for any need related to the learning or development of a child with a disability, **assistive technology** is defined in IDEA as "any item, piece of equipment, or product system, whether acquired commercially off the shelf, modified, or customized, that is used to increase, maintain, or improve functional capabilities of a child with a disability" ("Individuals with Disabilities," 1997, Section 602[1]).

Assistive technology tools may range from less expensive low-tech equipment such as adapted spoons, joysticks, taped stories, adaptive switches, head-pointing devices, captioned programming, and communication boards (message display devices that contain vocabulary choices from which the child can select an answer) to commercially developed high-tech devices such as screen magnifiers, speech synthesizers and digitizers, voice-recognition devices, touch screens, alternative computer keyboards, word prediction programs, and special reading software (Beck, 2002; Duhaney & Duhaney, 2000).

Technology for Students with Hearing Impairments

Hearing-impaired students can be assisted with technology tools in a number of ways, including closed captioning, audio amplification, and cochlear implants. Closed captioning (presenting spoken words as text on a screen) occurs most often in connection with television programs. But this technology can also be used in classrooms to help hearing-impaired students follow a teacher's lectures or explanations. A system called RAPIDTEXT allows 120–225 words per minute to be typed (using a stenographic keyboard) and sent to a student's computer monitor. Another way to accomplish the same goal is through audio amplification. The teacher wears a small microphone and transmitter whose signal is amplified and sent to a student who wears a lightweight receiver (Duhaney & Duhaney, 2000). A third option for students with severe to profound hearing loss is a cochlear implant. This system involves several external components (microphone, speech processor, transmitter, power pack) and a surgically implanted receiver-stimulator. Cochlear implants can also be combined with audio amplification systems (Moore & Teagle, 2002).

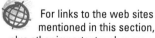 For links to the web sites mentioned in this section, plus other important web resources, go to the Weblinks section of the textbook web site.

The web site for Gallaudet University, a well-known school for the deaf in Washington, D.C., includes a page that describes its Technology Access Program (**tap.gallaudet.edu/**). This program examines technologies and services that eliminate communication barriers traditionally faced by the deaf and hard of hearing. It describes, for example, the current state of speech-to-text software (also known as speech recognition software). Another part of the Gallaudet web site is TecEds Reviews (**clerccenter2.gallaudet.edu/stg/**), a clearinghouse for technology evaluation.

Finally, a word of caution. As helpful as the preceding devices are, one thing they are not is a magic bullet. They cannot, for example, overcome students' lack of learning skills. A group of mainstreamed high school hearing-impaired students who were given class notes from a speech-to-text support service simply read them (which is what most non–hearing-impaired students would do) rather than using them in conjunction with other study methods (Elliott, Foster, & Stinson, 2002).

Technology for Students with Visual Impairments

Closed captioning and audio amplification are popular among deaf students; speech synthesizers and magnification devices offer similar liberating assistance to those who are visually impaired. With speech synthesis, the user can select a word, sentence, or chunk of information from any written or scanned text and hear it pronounced by a speech synthesizer. For example, the Kurzweil Reader scans printed material and converts it into high-quality speech. The Braille 'n Speak is a note taking system that also relies on speech synthesis. As students type on a seven-key keyboard, their input is converted into standard text that can either be read aloud or stored in the system's memory. In addition to devices that magnify the content of computer screens, head-mounted magnifiers allow students to see over various distances (Duhaney & Duhaney, 2000; Griffin, Williams, Davis, & Engleman, 2002).

Software programs called screen readers (such as Job Access with Speech, Windows-Eyes, and WinVision,) allow individuals with visual impairments to have the contents of a screen read to them by a speech synthesis program. The web sites of the National Federation of the Blind (**www.nfb.org/**) and the American Printing House for the Blind (**www.aph.org/**) describe screen readers and other software and hardware devices that are available for individuals with visual impairments.

Technology for Students with Orthopedic Impairments

For students who have physical limitations, pointing devices that are held in the mouth, attached to the head, or voice activated may provide the needed device control. Students with more limited fields of motion but acceptable fine motor skill may also benefit from condensed or mini keyboards that position the keys more closely together and require less strength to use. For students with less fine motor control, touch-sensitive expanded keyboards offer more space between keys and are often programmed to accept overlay plastic sheets for different applications or user needs (Duhaney & Duhaney, 2000). Free programs (called freeware) and inexpensive ones (called shareware) for helping individuals with physical and other disabilities more effectively use computers can be found at the Virtual Assistive Technology Center web site (**vatc.freeservers.com/**). Many of these programs are available for both Macintosh and Windows operating systems.

Technology for Students with Speech or Language Impairments

Technology can also help individuals with communication impairments. Using computer software with a speech synthesizer and expanded keyboard, Teris Schery and Lisa O'Connor (1997) demonstrated positive effects of computer training in vocabulary, early grammar skills, and social communication among toddlers with Down syndrome as well as young children with severe language and behavioral disabilities. In a small pilot study, they later discovered that parent volunteers briefly trained in using this software can be more effective than a professional speech pathologist. Computer programs designed to help students with speech or language impairments acquire language and communication skills can be found on the web sites of Apple Computer (**www.apple.com/disability/language/**) and the International Society for Augmentative and Alternative Communication (**www.isaac-online.org/**).

Technology for Students with Learning Disabilities

As we saw earlier in this chapter, learning disabled (LD) students typically have problems with reading, writing, and mathematics. But research has shown that the severity of these troubles can be reduced by using software programs designed for students with learning problems. For instance, in one study, LD students who responded to the demands of a computerized study guide (read a passage as many times as possible within a fifteen-minute period, respond silently to study guide questions at least twice, and then take a fifteen-item multiple-choice test) achieved higher scores than LD students who were not exposed to the program. In another study, a videodisc program helped LD students achieve higher scores on a test of math fractions. In a third study, students who worked on a hypermedia study guide for social studies scored higher on factual and inferential questions than students who experienced a lecture covering the same material (Maccini, Gagnon, & Hughes, 2002). Finally, software that allowed for a synchronized visual and auditory presentation of text helped college students with ADHD to read for longer periods of time with less stress and fatigue (Hecker, Burns, Elkind, Elkind, & Katz, 2002).

In the area of writing, there are many tools for students with learning disabilities that can help them—and other students—with basic sentence generation, transcription, and revision. Spelling, style, and grammar checkers can help raise student focus from mechanical demands and surface-level concerns to higher-level text cohesion and integration issues. Word prediction software can help students write more coherent and meaningful sentences by offering a choice of several words based on what the student has already written (Duhaney & Duhaney, 2000). Something as simple as an e-pal program (an electronic version of a pen pal) can improve certain aspects of LD students' writing. In one study (Stanford & Siders, 2001), sixth, seventh, and eighth graders with a learning disability either exchanged e-mails with college students, exchanged written letters with college students, or wrote to an imaginary pen pal. At the end of eight weeks, students in the e-pal group wrote longer and more complex letters than students in the other two groups. However, technology by itself does not improve the writing of LD students. Instead, sound instructional practices such as peer tutoring on the word-processed text raise the quality and number of student revisions and overall quality of their writing (MacArthur, 1994).

There are also tools for LD students to set writing goals, generate content, and plan and evaluate their writing (MacArthur, 1996). Personal data managers (such as a Palm Handheld computer), for instance, might help LD students record writing deadlines, remember important due dates, and plan their writing schedules (Bauer & Ulrich, 2002). Computerized sticky notes, outlining aids, and semantic webbing tools can also facilitate organization of their ideas prior to writing (Raskind, 1993). In addition, computer prompting programs can help students brainstorm and organize ideas and reflect on audience needs (Bonk & Reynolds, 1992).

Additional information about resources and teaching strategies for students with learning disabilities can be found on the web sites for LD OnLine (**www.ldonline .org/**) and the Division for Learning Disabilities of the Council for Exceptional Children (**www.teachingld.org/**). The former contains two potentially useful features. One is called Ask Dr. Silver, in which Larry Silver, a child and adolescent psychiatrist who specializes in treating children with LD or ADHD, answers questions. The other is Mentor Teacher of the Month (found on the Teacher's Homepage, **www.ldonline.org/teaching/index.html**), in which an experienced teacher shares ideas and strategies for teaching students with learning disabilities.

Technology for Gifted and Talented Students

Gifted students can also benefit from advances in instructional technology, such as distance education. Stanford University, for instance, has been experimenting with providing year-round accelerated instruction in mathematics, physics, English, and computer science to gifted high school students through the Education Program for Gifted Youth (EPGY) (Ravaglia, Alper, Rozenfeld, & Suppes, 1998; Ravaglia, Sommer, Sanders, Oas, & DeLeone, 1999). In addition to digitized lectures and on-line quizzes, students in EPGY can contact the instructors using e-mail, telephone project staff, attend discussion sessions at Stanford, and try out various physics experiments at home. Given all these supports, it is not surprising that students have done exceedingly well in this program (Tock & Suppes, 2002). The web site for EPGY can be found at **www-epgy.stanford.edu/**.

An online enrichment activity that can be used for any student, including the gifted and talented, is a web quest (see, for example, Ridgeway, Peters, & Tracy, 2002). This is an inquiry-oriented activity in which most or all of the information that students need is drawn from the Web. An excellent source of web quests is the WebQuest Page of San Diego State University (**webquest.sdsu.edu/**). Here you will find dozens of activities arranged by grade level and by subject matter within each grade level. For example, one of the English–language arts activities at the middle school level is, "Was It Murder? The Death of King Tutankhamun: The Boy King." A team of five students is given the following task and questions to answer:

 To review this chapter, see the ACE practice tests and PowerPoint slides on the textbook web site.

> Your team must gain as much knowledge about King Tut and the circumstances surrounding his death as possible. Your team consists of a medical examiner, a reporter, an archaeologist, a history professor, and a historian (optional). Each member of the team will visit a site and respond to the following questions:
>
> 1. How old was King Tut when he died?
> 2. Does the author suggest any foul play?

3. What information did you find concerning his death?
4. Who (if anybody) does the author suggest may have killed him?
5. Who succeeded Tut to the throne?
6. Is this site a reliable source? Explain.
7. What other "facts" are included about his death?

Resources for Further Investigation

● Ability Grouping

Additional discussions of ability grouping and alternatives to it can be found in a number of books and journal articles. For a comprehensive treatment of this topic, look at *Crossing the Tracks: How "Untracking" Can Save America's Schools* (1992), by Anne Wheelock. In Part 1, Wheelock describes the nature of tracking; its origins, prevalence, and negative effects; and alternative methods of organizing classrooms for the purpose of instruction. Part 2 describes how to organize and teach heterogeneous classrooms. Wheelock covers many of the same topics in *Alternatives to Tracking and Ability Grouping* (1994), but in far fewer pages (77 versus 285). The November 1995 issue of *Phi Delta Kappan* (Vol. 77, No. 3) contains several articles on tracking and its effects. For teachers who are committed to whole-class instruction, a useful source of ideas is *Teaching the Whole Class* (5th ed., 1998), by Betty Lou Leaver.

● Texts on the Education of Exceptional Children

The following books provide general coverage of the education of exceptional children: *Exceptional Children and Youth* (3rd ed., 2002), by Nancy Hunt and Kathleen Marshall; and *Educating Exceptional Children* (10th ed., 2003), by Samuel Kirk, James Gallagher, and Nicholas Anastasiow. A book that emphasizes both general and specific teaching techniques for students with learning problems is *Teaching Students with Learning Problems* (6th ed., 2001), by Cecil D. Mercer and Ann R. Mercer. Part 1, Foundations of Teaching, describes the general teaching skills that all teachers of students with special needs should possess. Part 2, Teaching Academic Skills, describes assessment and teaching techniques for improving language skills, reading, spelling, writing, mathematics, and study skills. A discussion of critical issues in special education can be found in *Critical Issues in Special Education* (2000), by James Ysseldyke, Bob Algozzine, and Martha Thurlow.

● Mainstreaming and Inclusion

In *Effective Teaching Strategies That Accommodate Diverse Learners* (2nd ed., 2002), Edward Kameenui and Douglas Carnine illustrate how various subjects (such as reading, writing, mathematics, science, social studies) can be effectively taught to groups of students who vary in cultural background, social class, and learning ability. Each chapter on teaching a particular subject matter is organized around six instructional principles whose effectiveness has been supported by research: Big Ideas, Conspicuous Strategies, Mediated Scaffolding, Primed Background Knowledge, Strategic Integration, and Judicious Review. *Successful Inclusive Teaching: Proven Ways to Detect and Correct Special Needs* (4th ed., 2003), edited by Joyce S. Choate, is a comprehensive treatment of how to accommodate special-needs students in the regular classroom. Part 1

covers the legal issues surrounding mainstreaming and inclusion, the characteristics of students with special needs, and basic principles of inclusive instruction. Part 2 describes how to use those basic principles to teach reading comprehension, language skills, writing, arithmetic, mathematical problem solving, science, and social studies. Part 3 covers classroom management.

The December 1994–January 1995, February 1996, and September 2000 issues of *Educational Leadership* are devoted to the pros and cons of inclusion and to ways of teaching students with special needs in the regular classroom. Edlaw, a national legal organization and publisher, supports a site that follows developments in IDEA and legal requirements for educators and administrators of special education programs. It can be found at **www.edlaw.net/**.

● Teaching Students with Mental Retardation

Specialized techniques for teaching students with mental retardation can be found in *Strategies for Teaching Students with Mild to Severe Mental Retardation* (1993), edited by Robert Gable and Steven Warren; and *Mental Retardation* (6th ed., 2002), by Mary Beirne-Smith, Richard Ittenbach, and James Patton.

Two excellent online sources of information about mental retardation and other types of disabilities are the Arc of the United States, a national organization on mental retardation (**TheArc.org/**); and the University of Kansas Special Education Department (**www.soe.ku.edu/sped/**). In particular, check the Disability Resources link on the University of Kansas site.

● Teaching Students with Learning Disabilities

The following books provide information about the nature of learning disabilities and how to teach students with learning disabilities: *Learning Disabilities: Theories, Diagnosis, and Teaching Strategies* (9th ed., 2003), by Janet Lerner; *Learning Disabilities: Characteristics, Identification, and Teaching Strategies* (5th ed., 2004) by William Bender; and *Differentiating Instruction for Students with Learning Disabilities* (2002), also by William Bender.

● Teaching Students with Emotional and Behavior Disorders

Information on the nature of behavior disorders and on how the regular classroom teacher can deal with such students can be found in *Characteristics of Emotional and Behavioral Disorders of Children and Youth* (7th ed., 2001), by James M. Kauffman; *Teaching Students with Behavior Disorders: Techniques and Activities for Classroom Instruction* (1995), by Patricia Gallagher; and *Strategies for Addressing Behavior Problems in the Classroom* (4th ed., 2002), by Mary Margaret Kerr and C. Michael Nelson.

● Teaching Gifted and Talented Learners

These books describe various techniques to use in instructing gifted and talented learners: *Handbook of Gifted Education* (3rd ed., 2003a), edited by Nicholas Colangelo and Gary Davis; *Curriculum Development and Teaching Strategies for Gifted Learners* (1996), by C. June Maker and Aleene B. Nielson; *Designing and Developing Programs for Gifted Students* (2003), edited by Joan Smutny; and *Special Populations in*

Gifted Education: Working with Diverse Learners (2003), by Jaime Castellano.

You should also visit the web sites of the National Association for Gifted Children (**www.nagc.org/**) and the National Research Center on the Gifted and Talented (**www.gifted.uconn.edu/nrcgt.html**).

Summary

1. Three early attempts at dealing with student variability were age-graded classrooms, ability grouping, and special class placement. Age-graded classrooms grouped students who were roughly the same age. Ability grouping sorted normal students into separate classes according to mental ability test scores. Special class placement was used to separate normal students from those with mental and physical disabilities.

2. Virtually all elementary schools and most middle and high schools use some form of ability grouping. At the middle and high school levels, the term *tracking* is commonly used.

3. The four currently popular approaches to ability grouping are between-class ability grouping, regrouping, the Joplin Plan, and within-class ability grouping. Within-class ability grouping is most frequently used in the elementary grades, while between-class ability grouping is most frequently used in the high school grades.

4. Ability grouping is based on the assumptions that intelligence is genetically determined, is reflected by an IQ score, and is unchangeable and that instruction is more effective with homogeneous groups of students.

5. There is no research support for between-class ability grouping and limited support for regrouping. Moderately positive results have been found for the Joplin Plan, as well as within-class ability grouping.

6. Students in low-ability groups often receive lower-quality instruction.

7. Allowing low-track students to take honors classes does not in itself result in more students moving into higher tracks.

8. In the light of research findings on ability grouping, educators may choose to discontinue the use of between-class ability grouping, use only within-class grouping and the Joplin Plan, or discontinue all forms of ability grouping.

9. The Education for All Handicapped Children Act (Public Law 94-142) was enacted in 1975 to ensure that students with disabling conditions receive the same free and appropriate education as nondisabled students. Since then, the law has been revised and expanded, and it is now known as the Individuals with Disabilities Education Act (IDEA).

10. Major provisions of IDEA include the right to a free and appropriate public education, an appropriate and valid preplacement evaluation, the development of an individualized education program (IEP), the education of students with disabilities in the least restrictive environment (also known as mainstreaming), and procedural safeguards.

11. In some school districts, mainstreaming has been extended to the point where students with disabilities are taught only in regular classrooms by regular and special education teachers. This practice is known as inclusion, or full inclusion.

12. The evidence on inclusion, although somewhat limited and inconsistent, indicates that the practice produces at least moderate benefits for some students with disabilities but has little beneficial effect on others.

13. Inclusion is likely to work best for students with disabilities for whom the regular classroom is an appropriate setting and in classrooms where the teacher uses instructional methods that are proven to be effective with a wide variety of learners.

14. The regular classroom teacher's responsibilities under IDEA may include participation in referral, assessment, preparation of the IEP, and implementation of the IEP.

15. Children with mild mental retardation score two or more standard deviations below the mean on a standardized test of intelligence and are likely to be mainstreamed for some part of the school day and week. They are likely to have a low tolerance for frustration, lack confidence and self-esteem, oversimplify matters, and have difficulty generalizing from one situation to another.

16. Students with learning disabilities account for more than half of all students with disabilities. They have a disorder in one or more of such basic psychological processes as perception, attention, memory, and metacognition, which leads to learning problems not attributable to other causes.

17. Using a discrepancy between a student's IQ score (average or above) and standardized achievement test score (one or more standard deviations below the mean) as a primary indicator of a learning disability does not appear to be useful.

18. Anywhere from 25 to 40 percent of children with a learning disability also have attention-deficit/hyperactivity disorder (ADHD). Children with ADHD may be inattentive, hyperactive, and impulsive, or all three, over an

extended period of time and in such different settings as home, school, and at play.

19. Students with ADHD may be treated with stimulant medication, psychological/educational programs, or a combination of the two.

20. The actual number of schoolchildren with serious emotional disturbance is unknown because of vague definitions of emotional disturbance and differences in interpretation of definitions, but it is estimated to be 3 to 5 percent of all school-age children.

21. Most classifications of disturbed behavior focus on aggressive behavior or withdrawn behavior.

22. Students who are gifted and talented excel in performing tasks that require intellectual, creative, artistic, or leadership ability.

23. Minorities are underrepresented in gifted and talented classes because standardized test scores are emphasized at the expense of other indexes.

24. The academic needs of students who are gifted and talented are usually met through accelerated instruction, placement in classes or schools for the gifted and talented, or classroom enrichment activities. Special classes and schools typically produce moderate achievement benefits but can also produce declines in academic self-concept.

25. A variety of adaptive technologies exist to help students with special needs. These include closed captioning, speech synthesis, voice recognition, screen magnifiers, special keyboards, writing tools, and distance education.

Key Terms

between-class ability grouping *(173)*
regrouping *(174)*
Joplin Plan *(174)*
within-class ability grouping *(174)*
individualized education program (IEP) *(179)*
least restrictive environment *(180)*

mainstreaming *(180)*
inclusion *(180)*
full inclusion *(180)*
multidisciplinary assessment team *(185)*
mental retardation *(186)*
learning disabilities *(190)*

attention-deficit/hyperactivity disorder (ADHD) *(192)*
emotional disturbance *(195)*
behavior disorder *(196)*
gifted and talented *(199)*
assistive technology *(204)*

7 Behavioral Learning Theory: Operant Conditioning

KEY POINTS

These key points will help you learn the important information in this chapter. To help you study, they also appear in the margins of the pages, next to the text where they are discussed.

Operant Conditioning

- Operant conditioning: voluntary response strengthened or weakened by consequences that follow
- Positive reinforcement: strengthen a target behavior by presenting a positive reinforcer after the behavior occurs
- Negative reinforcement: strengthen a target behavior by removing an aversive stimulus after the behavior occurs
- Punishment: weaken a target behavior by presenting an aversive stimulus after the behavior occurs
- Time-out: weaken a target behavior by temporarily removing a positive reinforcer after the behavior occurs
- Extinction: weaken a target behavior by ignoring it
- Spontaneous recovery: extinguished behaviors may reappear spontaneously
- Generalization: responding in similar ways to similar stimuli
- Discrimination: responding in different ways to similar stimuli
- Complex behaviors are shaped by reinforcing closer approximations to terminal behavior
- Fixed interval schedules: reinforce after regular time intervals
- Variable interval schedules: reinforce after random time intervals
- Fixed ratio schedules: reinforce after a set number of responses
- Variable ratio schedules: reinforce after a different number of responses each time

Educational Applications of Operant Conditioning Principles

- Skinner's approach to instruction: clear goals, logical sequencing of material, self-pacing
- Types of CBI programs include drill and practice, simulations, tutorials
- In general, CBI-taught students outscore conventionally taught students by a moderate amount
- Simulation programs have beneficial effect on science achievement
- ILS: comprehensive, self-paced learning system
- Behavior modification: shape behavior by ignoring undesirable responses, reinforcing desirable responses
- Premack principle: required work first, then chosen reward
- Token economy is a flexible reinforcement system
- Contingency contracting: reinforcement supplied after student completes mutually agreed-on assignment
- Time-out works best with disruptive, aggressive children
- Research unclear about strength of negative effects of corporal punishment

Using Computer-Based Instruction in Your Classroom

- Computers in school used mostly for word processing, drill, and as reference source
- Need to make informed choices of software
- CBI no substitute for high-quality teaching

ow that you are familiar with how students develop from preschool through high school, some of the major ways in which students differ from one another, and the main ways in which schools try to address student variability, it is time to examine what is perhaps the most fundamental and important aspect of schooling: the learning process. Because the primary reason that we have schools is to help children acquire the knowledge and skills that adults consider necessary for successful functioning in society, the instructional and curricular decisions that teachers make should be based on an understanding of how people learn. But as with most of the other topics in this text, learning is a complex phenomenon that has been studied from different perspectives.

Since 1879, when the first laboratory devoted to the scientific study of human behavior was opened in Leipzig, Germany, by Wilhelm Wundt, learning has been studied more extensively by more psychologists than any other aspect of human behavior. As a result, there are varied, seemingly conflicting opinions about how teachers should arrange learning activities in classrooms. Such differences of opinion are not necessarily a problem because different theories and the approaches to teaching that flow from them complement, rather than compete with, one another. Think of these different theories as something like a jigsaw puzzle. To see the entire picture, you need to have all the pieces, and you need to know how to put them together. We hope that you will have some sense of how to do that by the end of Part II.

This chapter is devoted to what is generally called behavioral learning theory. More precisely, the chapter describes a theory called operant conditioning and some of its implications. Operant conditioning focuses on the environmental factors that influence the types of behaviors people exhibit and the extent to which they are likely to exhibit those behaviors in the future. As you will see, this theory underlies many computer-based instructional applications. Subsequent chapters will examine the roles that other people and our own thought processes play in learning.

OPERANT CONDITIONING

To enhance your understanding of this chapter, read the Chapter Themes on the textbook site, accessible from **http://education.college.hmco.com/students.**

In 1913, with the publication of an article titled "Psychology as the Behaviorist Views It," the influential American psychologist John Watson argued that psychology would quickly lose credibility as a science if it focused on internal mental and emotional states that could not be directly observed or accurately measured. The solution was to study what could be directly observed and objectively and accurately measured: the external stimuli that people experienced and what people did in response—in a word, behavior.

From this point until the late 1960s, behavioral theories of one sort or another dominated the psychology of learning. Although they are considerably less popular today, they still offer many useful ideas for classroom teachers.

Basic Nature and Assumptions

● Operant conditioning: voluntary response strengthened or weakened by consequences that follow

Behavioral learning theories culminated in the work of B. F. Skinner. Skinner put together a theory that not only successfully combines many different ideas but also serves as the basis for a variety of applications to human behavior. Skinner's theory, **operant conditioning**, takes as its starting point that many of the voluntary responses of animals and humans are strengthened when they are reinforced (followed by a desirable consequence) and weakened when they are either ignored or punished. In this way, organisms learn new behaviors and when to exhibit them and "unlearn" existing behaviors. The term *operant conditioning* refers to the fact that organisms learn to "operate" on their environment (make a particular response) in order to obtain or avoid a particular consequence. Some psychologists use the term *instrumental* because the behavior is instrumental in bringing about the consequence.

Most of the experiments on which the principles of operant conditioning are based involved an ingenious apparatus that Skinner invented and is appropriately referred to as a Skinner box. This is a small enclosure that contains only a bar (or lever) and a small tray. Outside the box is a hopper holding a supply of food pellets that are dropped into the tray when the bar is pressed under certain conditions.

A hungry rat is placed in the box, and when in the course of exploring its new environment, the rat approaches and then presses the bar, it is rewarded with a food pellet. The rat then presses the bar more frequently than it did before being rewarded. If food pellets are supplied under some conditions when the bar is pushed down—for example, when a tone is sounded—but not under others, the rat learns to discriminate one situation from the other, and the rate of bar pressing drops noticeably when the tone is not sounded. If a tone is sounded that is very close in frequency to the original tone, the rat generalizes (treats the two tones as equivalent) and presses the bar at the same rate for both. But if the food pellets are not given after the rat presses the bar, that behavior stops, or is extinguished.

The Skinner box's prominent role in operant conditioning experiments reflects Skinner's view of psychology as a natural science. Several important assumptions underlie this view:

- *Assumption 1*. Underlying all natural sciences is the assumption that natural phenomena (such as weather patterns, earthquakes, and human behavior) may appear on the surface to be random but really operate according to set laws. What psychology needed, in Skinner's view, was the means by which a researcher could control the environment to observe the lawful and hence predictable influence of environmental factors on behavior.
- *Assumption 2*. A science develops most effectively when scientists study some phenomenon at its simplest, most fundamental level. What is learned at this level can then be used to understand more complex processes.
- *Assumption 3*. Principles of learning that arise from experiments with animals *should* apply to humans. Note the conditional phrasing of this sentence. Although Skinner accepted the usefulness of animal research, he was always careful to point out that such principles needed to be tested again at the human level.

• *Assumption 4.* A change in an organism's behavior pattern is the only basis for concluding that learning has occurred. Although admitting the existence of such internal processes as thoughts, motives, and emotions, Skinner had two objections to including them in his theoretical system. First, such processes have no place in the scientific study of learning because they cannot be directly observed or measured. Second, he believed that his experiments with rats in the Skinner box show that learning is caused not by internal processes but by the environmental consequences that follow behavior.

Basic Principles of Operant Conditioning

To repeat the basic idea behind operant conditioning: all behaviors are accompanied by certain consequences, and these consequences strongly influence (some might say determine) whether these behaviors are repeated and at what level of intensity. In general, the consequences that follow behavior are either pleasant and desirable or unpleasant and aversive. Depending on conditions that we will discuss shortly, these consequences either increase (strengthen) or decrease (weaken) the likelihood that the preceding behavior will recur under the same or similar circumstances.

When consequences strengthen a preceding behavior, *reinforcement* has taken place. When consequences weaken a preceding behavior, *punishment* and *extinction* have occurred. There are two forms of reinforcement and two forms of punishment. This section describes both forms of reinforcement, both forms of punishment, extinction, and several related principles that can be applied to aspects of human learning.

Positive Reinforcement   Although the term *positive reinforcement* may be unfamiliar to you, the idea behind it probably is not. If you can recall spending more time studying for a certain subject because of a compliment from the teacher or a high grade on an examination, you have experienced positive reinforcement. Specifically, **positive reinforcement** involves strengthening a target behavior—that is, increasing and maintaining the probability that a particular behavior will be repeated—by presenting a stimulus (called a *positive reinforcer*) immediately after the behavior has occurred. Praise, recognition, and the opportunity for free play are positive reinforcers for many (but not all) students.

pause & reflect

Operant conditioning holds that we learn to respond or not respond to certain stimuli because our responses are followed by desirable or aversive consequences. How many of your own behaviors can you explain in this fashion? Why, for example, are you reading this book and pondering these questions?

● Positive reinforcement: strengthen a target behavior by presenting a positive reinforcer after the behavior occurs

Students are likely to be motivated to learn if they are positively reinforced for completing a project or task. Awards and praise from the teacher and one's peers are strong positive reinforcers for many students.

The term *positive* as Skinner used it refers to the act of presenting a stimulus (think of positive as *adding* here); it does not refer to the pleasant nature of the stimulus itself. You will understand better why this distinction is very important as we consider the other form of reinforcement.

Negative Reinforcement   People frequently have difficulty understanding the concept of negative reinforcement, most often confusing it with punishment, so we will examine it carefully here. The goal of **negative reinforcement** is the same as positive reinforcement: to *increase* the strength of a particular behavior. The method, however, is different. Instead of supplying a desirable stimulus, *one removes an unpleasant and aversive stimulus* whenever a target behavior is exhibited. As you study this definition, pay special attention to the removing action. Just as positive refers to adding, negative refers to the act of *removing* a stimulus. By removing something unwanted, you encourage the student to learn new behaviors.

In everyday life, negative reinforcement occurs quite frequently. A child picks up his clothes or toys to stop his parents' nagging. A driver uses a seat belt to stop the annoying buzzer sound. Later in the chapter, we will describe how educators use negative reinforcement. We will also discuss its desirability relative to positive reinforcement.

Punishment   There are three procedures that reduce the likelihood that a particular behavior will be repeated. The first is **punishment,** also known as Type I punishment or presentation punishment. Punishment is defined by operant psychologists as the presentation of an aversive stimulus (such as scolding, paddling, ridiculing, or making a student write five hundred times "I will not chew gum in class") that reduces the frequency of a target behavior. From an operant perspective, you can claim to have punished someone else only if the target behavior is actually reduced in frequency. (Note that whether these methods of punishment do achieve their goal and are effective and whether they are ethical are other issues—ones that we will discuss later in this chapter.)

Many people confuse negative reinforcement with punishment. Both involve the use of an aversive stimulus, but the effects of each are opposite. Remember that negative reinforcement strengthens a target behavior, whereas punishment weakens or eliminates a behavior.

Time-Out   The second procedure that decreases the frequency of or eliminates a target behavior is another form of punishment, **time-out.** But instead of presenting an aversive stimulus, time-out *temporarily removes the opportunity to receive positive reinforcement.* (Time-out is sometimes called Type II punishment, or removal punishment.) For instance, a student who frequently disrupts classroom routine to get attention may be sent to sit in an empty room for five minutes. Removal from a reinforcing environment (as well as the angry tone of voice and facial expression that normally accompany the order to leave the classroom) is usually looked on as an aversive consequence by the individual being removed. An athlete who is suspended from competition is another example of this form of punishment.

Extinction   A third consequence that weakens undesired behavior is extinction. **Extinction** occurs when a previously reinforced behavior decreases in frequency, and eventually ceases altogether, because reinforcement is withheld. Examples of extinction include a mother's ignoring a whining child or a teacher's ignoring a student who spontaneously answers a question without waiting to be called on. Both extinction and time-out are most effective when combined with other consequences, such as positive reinforcement. To help yourself define and remember the distinguishing characteristics of positive reinforcement, negative reinforcement, punishment, and extinction, study Figure 7.1.

● Negative reinforcement: strengthen a target behavior by removing an aversive stimulus after the behavior occurs

● Punishment: weaken a target behavior by presenting an aversive stimulus after the behavior occurs

● Time-out: weaken a target behavior by temporarily removing a positive reinforcer after the behavior occurs

● Extinction: weaken a target behavior by ignoring it

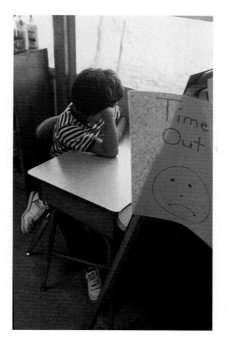

The time-out procedure recommended by behavior modification enthusiasts involves weakening an undesirable form of behavior (such as shoving on the playground) by temporarily removing positive reinforcement (by having the misbehaving student remain in a corner of the classroom for five minutes while the rest of the class continues to enjoy another activity).

Figure 7.1 Conditions That Define Reinforcement, Punishment, and Extinction

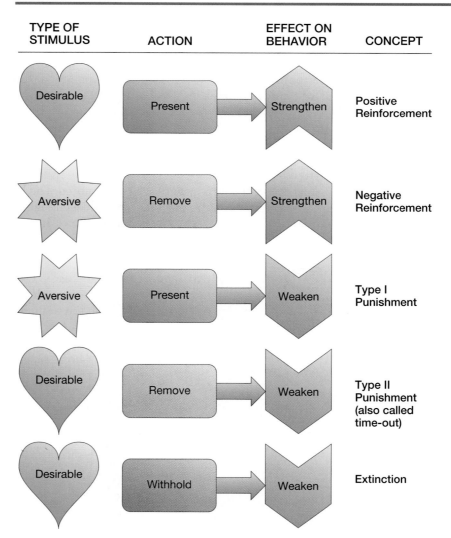

TYPE OF STIMULUS	ACTION	EFFECT ON BEHAVIOR	CONCEPT
Desirable	Present	Strengthen	Positive Reinforcement
Aversive	Remove	Strengthen	Negative Reinforcement
Aversive	Present	Weaken	Type I Punishment
Desirable	Remove	Weaken	Type II Punishment (also called time-out)
Desirable	Withhold	Weaken	Extinction

● Spontaneous recovery: extinguished behaviors may reappear spontaneously

Spontaneous Recovery   When used alone, extinction is sometimes a slow and difficult means of decreasing the frequency of undesired behavior because extinguished behaviors occasionally reappear without having been reinforced, an occurrence known as **spontaneous recovery**. Under normal circumstances, however, the time between spontaneous recoveries lengthens, and the intensity of the recurring behavior becomes progressively weaker. If the behavior undergoing extinction is not terribly disruptive and if the teacher (or parent, counselor, or supervisor) is willing to persevere, these episodes can sometimes be tolerated on the way to more complete extinction.

● Generalization: responding in similar ways to similar stimuli

Generalization   When an individual learns to make a particular response to a particular stimulus and then makes the same or a similar response in a slightly different situation, **generalization** has occurred. For example, students who were positively reinforced for using effective study skills in history go on to use those same skills in chemistry, social studies, algebra, and other subjects. Or, to use a less encouraging illustration, students ignore or question a teacher's every request and direction because they have been reinforced for responding that way to their parents at home. The less similar the new stimulus is to the original, however, the less similar the response is likely to be.

● Discrimination: responding in different ways to similar stimuli

Discrimination   When inappropriate generalizations occur, as in the preceding example, they can be essentially extinguished through discrimination training. In **discrimination** individuals learn to notice the unique aspects of seemingly similar situations (for example, that teachers are not parents, although both are adults) and to respond differently to each situation. Teachers can encourage this process by reinforcing only the desired behaviors (for instance, attention, obedience, and cooperation) and withholding reinforcement following undesired behaviors (such as inattention or disobedience).

Shaping   Up to now, we have not distinguished relatively simple learned behaviors from more complex ones. A bit of reflection, however, should enable you to realize that many of the behaviors human beings learn (such as playing a sport or writing a term paper) are complex and are acquired gradually. The principle of **shaping** best explains how complex responses are learned.

● Complex behaviors are shaped by reinforcing closer approximations to terminal behavior

In shaping, actions that move progressively closer to the desired *terminal behavior* (to use Skinner's term) are reinforced. Actions that do not represent closer approximations of the terminal behavior are ignored. The key to success is to take one step at a time. The movements must be gradual enough so that the person or animal becomes aware that each step in the sequence is essential. This process is typically called *reinforcing successive approximations to the terminal behavior*.

At least three factors can undermine the effectiveness of shaping:

- Too much positive reinforcement for early, crude responses may reduce the learner's willingness to attempt a more complex response.
- An expectation of too much progress too soon may decrease the likelihood of an appropriate response. If this results in a long period of nonreinforcement, what has been learned up to that point may be extinguished. For example, expecting a student to work industriously on a homework assignment for ninety minutes just after you have shaped forty-five minutes of appropriate homework behavior is probably too big a jump. If it is, the student may revert to her original level of performance owing to the lack of reinforcement.
- Delay in the reinforcement of the terminal behavior allows time for additional, unrelated behaviors to occur. When the reinforcement eventually occurs, it may strengthen one or more of the more recent behaviors rather than the terminal behavior.

Schedules of Reinforcement   If you have been reading this section on basic principles carefully, you may have begun to wonder if the use of operant conditioning principles, particularly positive reinforcement, requires you as the teacher to be present every time a desired response happens. If so, you might have some justifiable reservations about the practicality of this theory. The answer is yes, up to a point, but after that, no. As we have pointed out, when you are trying to get a new behavior established, especially if it is a complex behavior that requires shaping, learning proceeds best when every desired response is positively reinforced and every undesired response is ignored. This is known as a *continuous reinforcement* schedule.

Once the behavior has been learned, however, positive reinforcement can be employed on a noncontinuous, or intermittent, basis to perpetuate that behavior. There are four basic *intermittent reinforcement* schedules: fixed interval (FI), variable interval (VI), fixed ratio (FR), and variable ratio (VR). Each schedule produces a different pattern of behavior.

● Fixed interval schedules: reinforce after regular time intervals

Fixed Interval Schedule In this schedule, a learner is reinforced for the first desired response that occurs after a predetermined amount of time has elapsed (for example, five minutes, one hour, or seven days). Once the response has occurred and been reinforced, the next interval begins. Any desired behaviors that are made during an interval are ignored. The reinforced behavior occurs at a lower level during the early part of the interval and gradually rises as the time for reinforcement draws closer. Once the reinforcer is delivered, the relevant behavior declines in frequency and gradually rises toward the end of the next interval.

FI schedules of reinforcement occur in education when teachers schedule exams or projects at regular intervals. The grade or score is considered to be a reinforcer. As you are certainly aware, it is not unusual to see little studying or progress occur during the early part of the interval. However, several days before an exam or due date, the pace quickens considerably.

● Variable interval schedules: reinforce after random time intervals

Variable Interval Schedule If you would like to see a more consistent pattern of behavior, you might consider using a variable interval schedule. With a VI schedule, the length of time between reinforcements is essentially random but averages out to a predetermined interval. Thus, four successive reinforcements may occur at the following intervals: one week, four weeks, two weeks, five weeks. The average interval is three weeks. Teachers who give surprise quizzes or call on students to answer oral questions on the average of once every third day are invoking a variable interval schedule.

● Fixed ratio schedules: reinforce after a set number of responses

Fixed Ratio Schedule Within this schedule, reinforcement is provided whenever a predetermined number of responses are made. A rat in a Skinner box may be reinforced with a food pellet whenever it presses a lever fifty times. A factory worker may earn $20 each time he assembles five electronic circuit boards. A teacher may reinforce a student with praise for every ten arithmetic problems correctly completed. FR schedules tend to produce high response rates since the faster the learner responds, the sooner the reinforcement is delivered. However, a relatively brief period of no or few responses occurs immediately after the reinforcer is delivered.

● Variable ratio schedules: reinforce after a different number of responses each time

Variable Ratio Schedule Like a variable interval schedule, this schedule tends to eliminate irregularities in response rate, thereby producing a more consistent rate. This is accomplished through reinforcement after a different number of responses from one time to the next according to a predetermined average. If you decided to use a VR fifteen schedule, you might reinforce a desired behavior after twelve, seven, twenty-three, and eighteen occurrences, respectively (that is, after the twelfth, nineteenth, forty-second, and sixtieth desired behaviors). Because the occurrence of reinforcement is so unpredictable, learners tend to respond fairly rapidly for long periods of time. If you need proof, just watch people play the slot machines in gambling casinos.

EDUCATIONAL APPLICATIONS OF OPERANT CONDITIONING PRINCIPLES

How well do you understand reinforcement? Try this chapter's Netlab on the textbook web site, accessible from **http://education.college.hmco.com/students.**

In the late 1940s when Skinner's daughter was in elementary school, he observed a number of instructional weaknesses that concerned him. These included the excessive use of aversive consequences to shape behavior (students studying to avoid a low grade or embarrassment in the classroom), an overly long interval between students taking tests or handing in homework and getting corrective feedback, and poorly organized lessons and workbooks that did not lead to specific goals. Skinner became convinced that if the principles of operant conditioning were systematically applied to education, all such weaknesses could be reduced or eliminated.

That belief, which he then reiterated consistently until his death in 1990 (see, for example, Skinner, 1984), is based on four prescriptions that come straight from his laboratory research on operant conditioning:

● Skinner's approach to instruction: clear goals, logical sequencing of materials, self-pacing

1. Be clear about what is to be taught.
2. Teach first things first.
3. Allow students to learn at their own rate.
4. Program the subject matter.

This straightforward formulation became the basis for two educational applications: an approach to teaching that we now call computer-based instruction and a set of procedures for helping students learn appropriate classroom behaviors referred to as behavior modification. The next few sections will describe the nature of these applications and assess the extent to which they improve classroom learning.

Computer-Based Instruction

The Precursor: Skinner's Programmed Instruction   The key idea behind Skinner's approach to teaching is that learning should be shaped. Programs of stimuli (material to be learned) and consequences should be designed to lead students step by step to a predetermined end result. In the mid-1950s, Skinner turned this shaping approach into an innovation called **programmed instruction** (Morris, 2003).

When programmed materials were first made commercially available during the mid-1950s, they were designed to be presented to students in one of two ways: in book form or as part of teaching machines. The earliest teaching machines were simple mechanical devices. A program on a roll of paper was inserted in the machine, and the first statement or question was "framed" in a viewing window. (That is why the individual steps of a program are referred to as **frames.**) Today, programmed instruction in book format is very uncommon, and the early mechanical teaching machines have been supplanted by the personal computer because computers can do everything the books or the machine could do—and far more.

Programmers developed a program by defining precisely what was to be learned (the terminal behavior). They then arranged facts, concepts, and principles in a logical sequence so that students would be adequately prepared for each frame, or numbered problem, when they reached it. *Prompts* were periodically provided to draw out the desired response, and the step size (the knowledge needed to go from frame to frame) was made small enough so that reinforcement occurred with optimal frequency. Feedback about the correctness of the response was given immediately, and students worked through the program at their own pace.

Does Computer-Based Technology Aid Learning?   When desktop computers and the instructional programs that were created for them were introduced into public schools in the early 1980s, many educators and psychologists believed that students would learn significantly more through this medium than through traditional teacher-led, text-based instruction. This new approach to instruction was referred to as either **computer-based instruction (CBI)** or **computer-assisted instruction (CAI).**

Instructional programs designed for desktop computers generally fall into one of three categories:

● Types of CBI programs include drill and practice, simulations, tutorials

- **Drill-and-practice programs:** These programs provide students with sets of relatively simple exercises and problems, such as adding fractions and recognizing parts of speech, so they can practice knowledge and skills learned earlier.
- **Simulation programs:** Also called microworlds or problem-solving programs, these artificial environments mimic the real world in which students have to use previously learned knowledge to solve problems. A microworld program that we describe in more detail in a later chapter requires students to design a plant that will grow in the particular climate of each of five alien worlds.
- **Tutorial programs:** These programs mimic what a teacher does in class by teaching students new information and skills in a methodical, step-by-step approach. Showing students the steps involved in solving algebraic equations is an example of this type of program.

The research that has been done on the effectiveness of these varieties of CBI paints an interesting picture.

Research on the Effects of CBI   Computer-based instruction is such a widely researched topic that several authors from time to time have attempted to summarize what has been learned about one aspect or another of this matter. In the typical experiment, one group of students receives instruction either partly or entirely via computer while an equivalent group receives either conventional instruction (a text assignment supplemented by classroom lecture and discussion) or an alternative form of CBI. Here is a brief summary of the main findings from several of these analyses:

Computer-assisted instruction can help teachers shape new capabilities in students through the use of good-quality drill-and-practice, tutorial, and simulation programs.

● In general, CBI-taught students outscore conventionally taught students by a moderate amount

● Simulation programs have beneficial effect on science achievement

1. For various subject matters and age levels, students whose instruction was at least partly computer-based outscored students who received conventional instruction by fifteen percentile ranks (65th percentile versus 50th percentile) on measures of achievement, and they had more positive attitudes toward computers (Waxman, Connell, & Gray, 2002).

2. Students who worked on simulation programs in high school science classes outscored those who received conventional instruction by twenty-four percentile ranks on a science test (Christmann, Badgett, & Lucking, 1997).

3. Students who worked on simulation programs in general science and physics classes outscored students who received conventional instruction by twenty-six and eleven percentile ranks, respectively. No differences were found for chemistry and biology classes (Christmann & Badgett, 1999).

4. High school and college students who worked on simulation or tutorial programs outscored conventionally taught students by about fifteen percentile ranks on tests of science. But students who worked only on drill-and-practice programs scored slightly lower than conventionally taught students (Bayraktar, 2001/2002).

5. Students who worked on science simulations that included explanatory material and examples outscored those who worked with a pure simulation by about eighteen percentile ranks on tests of science content (Lee, 1999).

6. Students whose beginning reading skills (e.g., phonological awareness, word reading, text reading, reading/listening) were supported by CBI outscored students whose instruction was not computer-based on reading tests by about ten percentile ranks (Blok, Oostdam, Otter, & Overmaat, 2002). Interestingly, the findings of this review were about the same as reviews conducted ten to fifteen in recent years (providing verbal feedback, for example), their effect on the learning of beginning reading skills has remained fairly constant.

7. As we mentioned in earlier chapters, hypermedia is a program format that combines hypertext (a system of links that allow users to jump from one section of text to another or from one document to another in whatever order they desire) and multimedia (the combination of several forms of media, such as text, graphics, animation, sound, pictures, and video). Although hypermedia programs were expected to boost student learning greatly, their effects to date have been more modest. They appear to have no effect on student comprehension of information, and lower-ability students tend to be overwhelmed by the decision making such programs call for and by the need to keep track of which links one has visited. Hypermedia does, however, help higher-ability students search through lengthy and multiple information sources rapidly in order to locate target information (Dillon & Gabbard, 1998).

● ILS: comprehensive, self-paced learning system

Integrated Learning Systems   In recent years, some software packages have combined tutorial programs based on operant conditioning principles with programs that keep track over time of student performance and provide feedback to both the student and the teacher. These packages are called **integrated learning systems (ILS)** (Mazyck, 2002; Underwood, Cavendish, Dowling, Fogelman, & Lawson, 1996). Technology experts estimate that ILS may be used by as many as 25 percent of all school districts and, because of their high cost ($60,000 and up), account for about 50 percent of all technology-related expenditures by schools (Brush, Armstrong, Barbrow, & Ulintz, 1999; Mazyck, 2002).

Such systems present information in a more sequenced and comprehensive fashion than traditional CBI programs. Integrated learning systems can, in fact, cover the content for entire K–8 mathematics, reading, language arts, and science curricula. Some systems include an English language curriculum to address the needs of schools with high levels of limited-English-proficient students. Integrated learning systems allow students to go through tutorials at their own pace, administer tests, track student progress across grade levels, and present students with appropriate remediation or enrichment activities.

Research on the effectiveness of ILS has produced mixed results. A study conducted in England found that elementary grade students who used an ILS outscored non-ILS students in mathematics by 9 percent and that high school students outscored their non-ILS counterparts by 4.5 percent. There were no differences, however, in reading (Underwood et al., 1996). A large-scale study (over fifty schools) of third-grade students in Indiana found no differences between ILS and non-ILS groups on tests of mathematics, reading, and language arts (Estep, McInerney, Vockell, & Kosmoski, 1999/2000). A report issued by the North Central Regional Educational Laboratory (1999) noted that ILS users usually score better than non-ILS users on tests of the knowledge and skills taught by the program, but they do no better than non-ILS users on tests of transfer of learning to another context. Finally, an ILS-type system called Accelerated Math was tested on a group of fourth and fifth graders from a large urban school district (Ysseldyke, Kosciolek, Spicuzza, & Boys, 2003). Like other ILS programs, Accelerated Math created problem sets for students based on their achievement levels, scored the assignments, provided corrective feedback to the student and a report to the teacher, and provided further reports to the teacher on which students needed additional instruction, which were ready for a test, and how many objectives had been mastered. Compared with students who were exposed only to the district's regular math curriculum, Accelerated Math students had higher scores on two standardized math tests. Though modest, the difference was statistically significant.

Because ILS are not typically designed to accommodate individual differences, there have been calls to combine this technology with such proven instructional techniques as cooperative learning. Such an approach is likely to be especially useful among schools that have a high percentage of students who, because of their cultural background, have a high affinity for cooperative learning (Mazyck, 2002).

Evaluation of Computer-Based Instruction   How can we sum up the varieties of CBI or CAI that have evolved from operant conditioning principles? Overall, the research findings suggest that CBI is not the equivalent of a wonder drug, but when properly designed and used, can effectively supplement a teacher's attempts to present, explain, apply, and reinforce knowledge and skills. Simulation programs seem to be particularly useful for helping students understand scientific concepts and procedures.

These findings also reaffirm what we suggested in the opening chapter about good teaching being partly an art and partly a science. Whenever you as a teacher apply any psychological principle in your classroom, you will need to ask yourself: For whom is this instructional technique likely to be beneficial? With what materials? For what outcome? We will return to the issue of using CBI in your classroom at the end of this chapter.

Behavior Modification

Although applied in many ways, the term **behavior modification** basically refers to the use of operant conditioning techniques to (as the phrase indicates) modify behavior. Because those who use such techniques attempt to manage behavior by making rewards contingent on certain actions, the term *contingency management* is also sometimes used.

After Skinner and his followers had perfected techniques of operant conditioning in modifying the behavior of animals, they concluded that similar techniques could be used with humans. We will briefly discuss several techniques in this section that teachers may use to strengthen or weaken specific behaviors. Techniques applied in education to strengthen behaviors include shaping, token economies, and contingency contracts. Techniques that aim to weaken behaviors include extinction and punishment.

Many educators feel that operant conditioning presents a cold, dehumanizing picture of human learning and ignores the role of such factors as free will, motives, and creativity. Do you feel that way while reading this chapter? Do you think positive attributes of operant conditioning balance out possible negative aspects?

● Behavior modification: shape behavior by ignoring undesirable responses, reinforcing desirable responses

Shaping You may want to take a few minutes now to review our earlier explanation of shaping. Most attempts at shaping important classroom behaviors should include at least the following steps (Miltenberger, 2004; Walker, Shea, & Bauer, 2004):

1. Select the target behavior.
2. Obtain reliable baseline data (that is, determine how often the target behavior occurs in the normal course of events).
3. Select potential reinforcers.
4. Reinforce successive approximations of the target behavior each time they occur.
5. Reinforce the newly established target behavior each time it occurs.
6. Reinforce the target behavior on a variable reinforcement schedule.

To illustrate how shaping might be used, imagine that you are a third-grade teacher (or a middle or high school teacher) with a chronic problem: one of your students rarely completes more than a small percentage of the arithmetic (or algebra) problems on the worksheets you distribute in class, even though you know the student possesses the necessary skills. To begin, you decide that a reasonable goal would be for the student to complete at least 85 percent of the problems on a given worksheet. Next, you review the student's work for the past several weeks and determine that, on average, he completed only 25 percent of the problems per worksheet. Your next step is to select positive reinforcers that you know or suspect will work.

Reinforcers come in a variety of forms. Most elementary school teachers typically use such things as stickers, verbal praise, smiles, and classroom privileges (for example, feed the gerbil, clean the erasers). Middle school and high school teachers can use letter or numerical grades, material incentives (such as board games and computer games, as long as school policy and your financial resources allow it), and privately given verbal praise.

With certain reservations, public forms of recognition can also be used. The reservations include the following:

• Because many adolescents are acutely self-conscious, any public display of student work or presentation of awards should be made to several students at the same time to avoid possible embarrassment (Emmer, Evertson, & Worsham, 2003).
• Awards should be made without letter grades.
• Awards should be given with an awareness that public displays of recognition are not appropriate or comfortable for all cultures.

● Premack principle: required work first, then chosen reward

One popular shaping technique that has stood the test of time involves having students list favorite activities on a card. Then they are told that they will be able to indulge in one of those activities for a stated period of time after they have completed a set of instructional objectives. This technique is sometimes called the **Premack principle** after psychologist David Premack (1959), who first proposed it. It is also called *Grandma's rule* since it is a variation of a technique that grandmothers have used for hundreds of years ("Finish your peas, and you can have dessert").

Once you have decided on a sequence of objectives and a method of reinforcement, you are ready to shape the target behavior. For example, you can start by reinforcing the student for completing five problems (25 percent) each day for several consecutive days. Then you reinforce the student for completing five problems and starting a sixth (a fixed ratio schedule). Then you reinforce the student for six completed problems and so on. Once the student consistently completes at least 85 percent of the problems, you provide reinforcement after every fifth worksheet on the average (a variable ratio schedule).

Although you control the classroom environment while students are in school, this accounts for only about half of their waking hours. Accordingly, parents might supplement your efforts at shaping behavior. The first step in a home-based reinforcement program is obtaining the parents' and student's formal agreement to participate. Then you typically send home a brief note or form on a regular basis (daily, weekly) indicating whether the student exhibited the desired behaviors. For example, in response to the items "Was prepared for class" and "Handed in homework," you would circle "yes" or "no." In response to a homework grade or test grade, you would circle the appropriate letter or percentage correct designation. The parents are then responsible for providing the appropriate reinforcement or punishment (temporary loss of a privilege, for example). Home-based reinforcement programs are readily learned by parents and are effective in reducing undesired behaviors (e.g., Benoit, Edwards, Olmi, Wilczynski, & Mandal, 2001; Mackay, McLaughlin, Weber, & Derby, 2001). Overall, this procedure has been successful in both reducing disruptive classroom behavior and increasing academic performance (longer time on tasks and higher test scores, for example). Some studies suggest that it may not be necessary to target both areas, as improved academic performance often results in decreased disruptiveness (Kelley & Carper, 1988).

Token Economies　　A second technique used to strengthen behavior in the classroom, the **token economy,** was introduced first with people who had been hospitalized for emotional disturbances and then with students in special education classes. A token is something that has little or no inherent value but can be used to "purchase" things that do have inherent value. In society, money is our most ubiquitous token. Its value lies not in what it is made of but in what it can purchase—a car, a house, or a college education. By the same token (if you will excuse the pun), students can accumulate check marks, gold stars, or happy faces and "cash them in" at some later date for any of the reinforcers already mentioned. Moreover, such instructional activities as doing math worksheets, working at the computer, engaging in leisure reading, and playing academic games have proven to be effective reinforcers in token economies (Higgins, Williams, & McLaughlin, 2001).

● Token economy is a flexible reinforcement system

　　One reason for the development of the token economy approach was the limited flexibility of more commonly used reinforcers. Candies and cookies, for instance, tend to lose their reinforcing value fairly quickly when supplied continually. It is not always convenient to award free time or the opportunity to engage in a highly preferred activity immediately after a desired response. And social rewards may or may not be sufficiently reinforcing for some individuals. Tokens, however, can always be given immediately after a desirable behavior, can be awarded according to one of the four schedules mentioned earlier, and can be redeemed for reinforcers that have high reinforcing value.

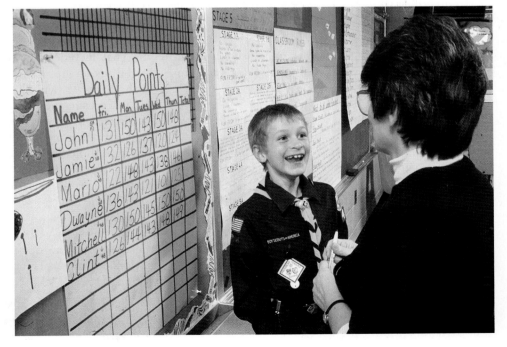

One useful method for positively reinforcing desired behavior is a token economy—supplying students with objects that have no inherent value but that can be accumulated and redeemed for more meaningful reinforcers.

Case in Print

Good Behavior Is a Rewarding Experience

*Although applied in many ways, the term **behavior modification** basically refers to the use of operant conditioning techniques to (as the phrase indicates) modify behavior. Because those who use such techniques attempt to manage behavior by making rewards contingent on certain actions, the term contingency management is also sometimes used. (p. 221)*

School Rewards Good Behavior

JANET SUGAMELI
The Detroit News, 12/29/03

NEW HAVEN — A positive behavior program implemented at Siefert Elementary last year now resonates outside the classroom.

Its impact is felt, for instance, at the bus stop and on the bus. A handful of volunteer staff members ride the bus to encourage the sort of behavior they expect inside the classroom and the school building.

"We were having some concerns about student behavior on the buses, so we wanted to make sure we had a safe environment for the students," Principal Lynda Holland said. "We want to make sure that the students know that when they are in the presence of an adult in the school setting, which starts when they get on the bus and ends when they get off the bus, their behavior should not be different. They must follow Siefert's expectations."

Fourth-grader Alexis Dynes said that, though she already follows the bus rules, "some kids act better when teachers come to the bus stop." She also enjoys seeing her teacher and other staff members at the stop.

"It's cool to have teachers ride with us," she said. "They get to see how we act on the bus. We act good. We talk to the people next to us, and we don't scream across the bus."

Though some students forget the rules, they are trying to be more conscientious about their behavior, she added.

Bus driver Patti Brohl is also a fan of the program.

"The students realize that we have positive reinforcement from all areas, not just in school," she said. "If they misbehave, there are consequences. There is total communication going on."

Having the teachers and principal at the bus stop or on the bus also makes her feel appreciated. "It makes us feel like we are a part of these children's education," Brohl said. "We start their morning off, because we are the first ones they communicate with."

Though Laura Chisholm typically accompanies her children to the bus stop each morning, she is even more at ease when she waves goodbye now.

"I've always accompanied (my children) because there are some occurrences that could happen because there are not a lot of parents (at the bus stop)," Chisholm said. "Now, the students have to take it upon themselves to make the right choice. For the most part, I see they are trying to make the right choices even when no one is looking."

The idea behind the positive behavior support program is simple. "If their behavior is good, they will be more focused and they will develop better academically and socially," Holland said. "The program focuses on a child's success instead of their weaknesses."

In a rural school of 535 students, most students use the district's transportation.

"We have the same expectations on the bus as we do in the school. All we are doing is reinforcing them," Holland said. They need to follow the three rules of positive behavior: "Be respectful, be responsible and be ready."

That includes following the appropriate behavior on the bus, on the playground, in lines, at the lunchroom, in the hallways, when arriving at school, in assemblies and when using the bathroom.

Under the program, two staff members are assigned to each of the nine bus drivers for the school. Those staff members give support to the driver, answer questions about the positive behavior program and periodically ride the bus to and from school. The staff also supplies the drivers with rewards to hand out for good behavior.

"Since we have been working cooperatively with the transportation department, it has reduced misbehaviors on the bus," Holland said.

Initially the principal turned her attention to the bus and bus stops after a parent voiced concern about inappropriate behavior.

"Our team thought since we are reinforcing the bus rules, we might as well reinforce the bus stop rules, too," she said. "Now, we call ourselves the bus-keteers."

Before the random visits, the upper elementary students helped create a bus video on proper behavior, including the right and wrong way to get on and off the bus. Those students receive Siefert Rocket Rewards, which buy them special privileges at school, to recognize their positive behavior each week.

First-grader Cassidy VanHaverbeck said she realizes how important it is to follow the rules on the bus.

"When you follow the rules, you get Rocket Rewards," she said. "I try to stand in line and put my hands down to the side, so I don't touch anybody."

Marcy Gerlach, the school's physical education teacher, said the most valuable part of the program is that the students know the staff and the bus drivers have a connection and work together.

"We are supportive of them and they are of us," she said.

The students are usually quite welcoming when the teachers arrive at a bus stop, since they come with rewards for those who behave properly.

"They think it's cool for the teachers to show up at the bus stop because they internalize it as 'the teachers care about 7us,' and that makes a more caring community," Gerlach said.

Bus stops can be a place of tension for students because they are not always supervised. "That's when they attempt good or bad," Chisholm said. "It's necessary for them to be rewarded for the good things that they do when they think no one is looking. They see that being good is the right choice."

Questions and Activities

1. Although the behavior modification program (essentially a token economy) implemented by the staff of Siefert Elementary School appeared to be successful in reducing undesired student behavior at bus stops and on the school bus, it had only been in effect for about a year. Do you think reinforcement programs like this one are likely to be successful over an extended period of time? Why or why not?

2. Behavior modification programs like the one at Siefert Elementary School provide positive reinforcers to students when they exhibit desired behaviors. Is there any reason that the behavior of teachers, administrators, and other staff members should not be reinforced by students when the occasion warrants? What might be the advantages (and disadvantages) of a reinforcement program that runs in both directions?

3. Critics of behavior modification programs argue that students are unlikely to exhibit desired behaviors when no one is around to observe and reinforce them. But the comment of one parent suggests this might not be the case. Identify the parent and what she said. Do you think the effect she noticed applies to many behavior management programs?

4. Lynda Holland, the principal of Siefert Elementary School, claims of her students, "If their behavior is good, they will be more focused and they will develop better academically and socially." Is this just wishful thinking, or is there research evidence to support her claim?

Token economies, especially when combined with classroom rules, appropriate delivery of reinforcers, and response cost (a concept we describe a bit later in the chapter), are effective in reducing such disruptive classroom behaviors as talking out of turn, being out of one's seat, fighting, and being off-task. Reductions of 50 percent or more in such behaviors are not uncommon. Token economies are also effective in improving academic performance in a variety of subject areas (Higgins et al., 2001; Kelhe, Bray, Theodore, Jenson, & Clark, 2000; Naughton & McLaughlin, 1995). Token economies have been used successfully with individual students, groups of students, entire classrooms, and even entire schools.

Some studies have shown that awarding tokens for group efforts is at least as effective as and possibly more effective than awarding them to individuals (Kelhe et al., 2000). Accordingly, token economies can be easily used in conjunction with the cooperative learning technique that will be described in detail in the chapter on instructional approaches. The Case in Print illustrates one token economy in action in a school system.

● Contingency contracting: reinforcement supplied after student completes mutually agreed-on assignment

Contingency Contracting   A third technique teachers use to strengthen behavior is **contingency contracting.** A contingency contract is simply a more formal method of specifying desirable behaviors and consequent reinforcement. The contract, which can be written or verbal, is an agreement worked out by two people (teacher and student, parent and child, counselor and client) in which one person (student, child, client) agrees to behave in a mutually acceptable way, and the other person (teacher, parent, counselor) agrees to provide a mutually acceptable form of reinforcement. For example, a student may contract to sit quietly and work on a social studies assignment for thirty minutes. When the student is done, the teacher may reinforce the child with ten minutes of free time, a token, or a small toy.

Contracts can be drawn up with all members of a class individually, with selected individual class members, or with the class as a whole. As with most other contracts, provisions can be made for renegotiating the terms. Moreover, the technique is flexible enough to incorporate the techniques of token economies and shaping. It is possible, for example, to draw up a contract that provides tokens for successive approximations to some target behavior (Bushrod, Williams, & McLaughlin, 1995).

Extinction, Time-Out, and Response Cost   The primary goal of behavior modification is to strengthen desired behaviors. Toward that end, techniques such as shaping, token economies, and contingency contracts are likely to be very useful. There will be times, however, when you have to weaken or eliminate undesired behaviors because they interfere with instruction and learning. For these occasions, you might consider some form of extinction. Research has demonstrated that extinction is effective in reducing the frequency of many types of problem behaviors (Miltenberger, 2004).

The most straightforward approach is to ignore the undesired response. If a student bids for your attention by clowning around, for instance, you may discourage repetition of that sort of behavior by ignoring it. It is possible, however, that classmates will not ignore the behavior but laugh at it. Such response-strengthening reactions from classmates will likely counteract your lack of reinforcement. Accordingly, you need to observe what happens when you try to extinguish behavior by not responding.

If other students are reinforcing a youngster's undesired behavior, you may want to apply the time-out procedure. Suppose a physically active third-grade boy seems unable to keep himself from shoving classmates during recess. If verbal requests, reminders, or warnings fail to limit shoving, the boy can be required to take a five-minute time-out period immediately after he shoves a classmate. He must sit alone in the classroom for that period of time while the rest of the class remains out on the playground. Time-out is an effective means of reducing or eliminating undesired behaviors, particularly those that are aggressive or disruptive, for both regular and mainstreamed children (Miltenberger, 2004; Walker et al., 2004). The rules for the procedure should be clearly explained, and after being sentenced to time-out (which should last no more than five minutes), a child should be given reinforcement for agreeable, helpful behavior—for example, "Thank you for collecting all the playground balls so nicely, Tommy."

● Time-out works best with disruptive, aggressive children

Another technique, **response cost,** is similar to time-out in that it involves the removal of a stimulus. It is often used with a token economy. With this procedure, a certain amount of positive reinforcement (for example, 5 percent of previously earned tokens) is withdrawn every time a child makes an undesired response. Anyone who has been caught exceeding the speed limit and been fined at least $50 can probably attest to the power of response cost as a modifier of behavior. As with extinction and time-out, research confirms that response cost helps reduce a variety of problem behaviors (such as getting off-task, not following directions, engaging in disruptive behavior) for a wide range of children (Miltenberger, 2004).

Punishment   Punishment is one of the most common behavior modification techniques, particularly when it takes the form of corporal punishment. It is also one of the most controversial. One factor that makes this issue controversial is that many parents (about 94 percent, according to one estimate) believe in corporal punishment and spank their children, while lobbying groups (such as End Physical Punishment of Children and the National Coalition to Abolish Corporal Punishment in the Schools) work to persuade state and federal officials to pass laws that outlaw the practice (Gershoff, 2002).

A second factor is that researchers have different views about what the existing research means. For example, Elizabeth Gershoff (2002) analyzed eighty-eight studies conducted over the past sixty years and concluded that corporal punishment was strongly associated with such negative behaviors and experiences as low internalization of moral rules, aggression, delinquent and antisocial behavior, low-quality parent-child relationships, and being the recipient of physical abuse. The definition of corporal punishment used by Gershoff was "the use of physical force with the intention of causing a child to experience pain but not injury for the purposes of correction or control of the child's behavior" (p. 540).

Gershoff's conclusions were challenged by Diana Baumrind, Robert Larzelere, and Philip Cowan (2002) on several grounds, one of which concerned the definition Gershoff chose to work from. These researchers argued that Gershoff's findings were due in part to the fact that the definition she used allowed her to include studies whose forms of punishment were more severe than most parents administer. Baumrind et al. advocated limiting the analysis to studies in which the form of corporal punishment used was the more common mild to moderate spanking. They defined spanking as a "subset of the broader category of corporal punishment that is a) physically non-injurious; b) intended to modify behavior; and c) administered with an opened hand to the extremities or buttocks" (p. 581). A reanalysis of those studies examined by Gershoff that were more consistent with this narrower definition produced a considerably weaker (but still positive) relationship between spanking and aggressive behavior. For this reason, as well as limitations in many of the studies, Baumrind et al. concluded that a blanket condemnation of spanking cannot be made on the basis of the existing research (although it may be made on other bases).

A final word of caution before leaving this topic. As Elizabeth Gershoff pointed out, the studies she reviewed were correlational in nature. That is, researchers simply sought to determine whether a relationship exists between corporal punishment and aggressive behaviors exhibited by children. Consequently, one cannot draw the conclusion from this research that spanking children *causes* them to be more aggressive. It is just as plausible, until additional research proves otherwise, that children who are inherently more aggressive than others cause their parents and other adults to administer more corporal punishment. Another possibility is that a third variable, such as inconsistent discipline, is responsible for both increased use of corporal punishment and aggressive behavior in children.

Corporal punishment is currently banned in twenty-seven states by either state law or state department of education regulation (National Coalition to Abolish Corporal Punishment in Schools, 2003). The remaining twenty-three states either explicitly permit schools to punish students physically or are silent on the matter. In states that allow corporal punishment, local school districts may regulate, but not prohibit, its use. Where states have not addressed the issue, local districts may regulate the use of corporal punishment or ban it altogether.

pause & reflect

Skinner argued that society too frequently uses aversive means to shape desired behavior (particularly punishment) rather than the more effective positive reinforcement. As you think about how your behavior has been shaped, would you agree or disagree? Why do you think we use punishment so frequently?

● Research unclear about strength of negative effects of corporal punishment

Take a Stand!

Positive Reinforcement Versus Punishment as a Classroom Management Tool

Common sense suggests that when one pedagogical technique is shown to be largely effective for achieving a particular objective and a second technique is shown to be largely ineffective, the former would be used by at least a sizable minority of teachers while the latter would be ignored by most. Well, common sense does not always prevail, particularly in the case of using positive reinforcement and punishment as classroom management tools. As we've documented on these pages, few teachers use positive reinforcement in their classrooms despite its demonstrated effectiveness in promoting desired behaviors. Various forms of punishment, which have numerous disadvantages, are more popular.

One reason for this contrary state of affairs undoubtedly has to do with the decline in popularity of operant conditioning theory in educational psychology textbooks and courses. It is not unusual these days for students in teacher-education programs to have learned little or nothing about operant conditioning principles and their classroom applications. As a result, many teachers fall into what is called the negative reinforcement trap. Here's how it works: A student's misbehavior instinctively elicits a punishing response from a teacher because punishment can be administered quickly and easily and often produces a rapid (albeit temporary) suppression of the undesired behavior. Let's say the teacher sends the offending student to the principal's office. Having obtained at least temporary relief, the teacher is now more inclined to send the next misbehaving student to the office. Now let's examine this situation from the student's perspective. Some students may misbehave because they find the work boring or, even worse, threatening because of a fear of failure. Sending such a student out of the room removes the student from a punishing environment. This is a form of negative reinforcement, which increases the likelihood that the student will engage in subsequent misbehavior.

The best way to deal with this problem is to avoid it in the first place by using a combination of effective teaching methods and positive reinforcement. In our Suggestions for Teaching section, we discuss several ways in which positive reinforcement can be used appropriately and effectively.

Have you seen the type of situation described here during your own schooling? What do you think about it? For more on this topic, go to the Take a Stand! section of the textbook web site.

Should You Use Behavior Modification? This may seem a strange question to ask given the number of pages we have just spent covering behavior modification methods. Obviously, we feel that the results of decades of research on these techniques justify their use by teachers. Nevertheless, there are criticisms of behavior modification that are not adequately addressed by research findings and that you should carefully consider.

One criticism is that many students, including those in the primary grades, will eventually catch on to the fact that they get reinforced only when they do what the teacher wants them to do. Some may resent this and misbehave out of spite. Others may weigh the amount of effort required to earn a favorable comment or a privilege and decide the reinforcer is not worth the trouble. Still others may develop a "What's in it for me?" attitude. That is, some students may come to think of learning as something they do only to earn an immediate reinforcer. The potential danger of using behavior modification over an extended period of time is that learning may come to an abrupt halt when no one is around to supply reinforcement (Kohn, 1993). (This point will be addressed in the chapter on social cognitive theory.)

A second major criticism is that behavior modification methods, because of their potential power, may lend themselves to inappropriate or even unethical uses. For example, teachers may shape students to be quiet and obedient because it makes their job easier, even though such behaviors do not always produce optimum conditions for learning.

In response to these criticisms, Skinner and other behavioral scientists (see Chance, 1993, and Maag, 2001, for example) argue that if we do not systematically use what we know about the effects of stimuli and consequences on behavior, we will leave things to chance. In an uncontrolled situation, some fortunate individuals will have a favorable chain of experiences that will equip them with desirable attitudes and skills, but others will suffer an unfortunate series of experiences that will lead to difficulties and disappointment. In a controlled situation, it may be possible to arrange experiences so that almost everyone acquires desirable traits and abilities. What behavioral psychologists seem to be saying is that educators could be accused of being unethical for not making use of an effective learning tool. The challenge, of course, is to use it wisely. The following Suggestions for Teaching in Your Classroom will give you additional ideas for putting operant conditioning principles into practice.

Applying Operant Conditioning in the Classroom

1 Remain aware that behavior is the result of particular conditions.

JOURNAL ENTRY
Checking on Causes of Behavior

Unlike the controlled environment of a Skinner box, many causes of behavior in a real-life classroom may not be observable or traceable. You might as well accept the fact, therefore, that quite often you are going to be a haphazard shaper of behavior. Nevertheless, there will be times when you and your students may benefit if you say to yourself, "Now, there have to be some causes for that behavior. Can I figure out what they are and do something about changing things for the better? Am I doing something that is leading to types of behavior that are making life difficult for some or all of us in the room?" When you are engaging in such speculations, keep in mind that reinforcement strengthens behavior. And check to see if you are inadvertently rewarding students for misbehavior (by calling attention to them, for example, or failing to reinforce those who engage in desirable forms of behavior).

EXAMPLES

- If you become aware that it takes a long time for your students to settle down at the beginning of a period and that you are reacting by addressing critical remarks specifically to those who dawdle the longest, ignore the dawdlers, and respond positively to those who are ready to get to work.

- Let's say that you have given students thirty minutes to finish an assignment. To your dismay, few of them get to work until almost the end of the period, and you find that you have to do a lot of nagging to hold down gossip and horseplay. When you later analyze why this happened, you conclude that you actually encouraged the time-killing behavior because of the way you set up the lesson. The next time you give a similar assignment, tell the students that as soon as they complete it, they can have class time to work on homework, a term project, or the equivalent and that you will be available to give help or advice to those who want it.

2 Use reinforcement, and use it appropriately to strengthen behaviors you want to encourage.

Why would we remind you to do something as obvious as reinforce behaviors you want students to acquire and exhibit in the future? Wouldn't you do that almost automatically? Well, we certainly hope so, but statistics suggest otherwise. A large team of researchers headed by Jon Goodlad (1984) observed the classroom behavior of 1,350 teachers and 17,163 students in thirty-eight schools from seven sections of the country. What they found may surprise you. Teachers' praise of student work occurred about 2 percent of the observed time in the primary grades and about 1 percent of the time in high school.

Once you have resolved to reinforce desired behavior systematically, you need to be sure that you do it appropriately. Although reinforcement is a simple principle that can be readily understood at an intuitive level, it has to be used in the right way to produce desired results. Paul Chance (1992) offers seven guidelines for the effective use of positive reinforcement:

JOURNAL ENTRY
Ways to Supply Reinforcement

- Use the weakest reward available to strengthen a behavior. In other words, do not use material rewards when you know that praise will be just as effective a reinforcer. Save the material rewards for that special behavior for which praise or other reinforcers may not be effective.
- When possible, avoid using rewards as incentives. What Chance means is not to get into the habit of automatically telling the student that if she does what you want, you will provide a specific reward. Instead, sometimes ask the student to do something (like work quietly or help another student), and then provide the reinforcer.

One of the basic principles of instruction derived from operant conditioning experiments is that teachers should provide elementary grade students with immediate reinforcement for correct responses.

- Reward at a high rate in the early stages of learning, and reduce the frequency of rewards as learning progresses.
- Reward only the behavior you want repeated. Although you may not realize it, students are often very sensitive to what is and is not being reinforced. If you decide that one way to encourage students to be more creative in their writing is to tell them not to worry about spelling and grammar errors, then do not be surprised to see many misspelled words and poorly constructed sentences. Or if you decide to reward only the three highest scorers on a test, reasoning that competition brings out the best in people, be prepared to deal with the fact that competition also brings out some of the worst in people (like cheating and refusing to help others).
- Remember that what is an effective reinforcer for one student may not be for another. For some students, comments such as "Very interesting point," "That's right," or "That was a big help" will strengthen the target behavior. But for others, something less overt, such as smiling encouragingly, may be just right.
- Set standards so that success is a realistic possibility for each student. Because classrooms are becoming increasingly diverse, you may have students whose English proficiency is limited or who have disabilities related to learning and intellectual functioning. One way to deal with such diversity is to reward students for making steady progress from whatever their baseline level of performance was at the beginning of the term.
- An often-mentioned goal of teachers is to have students become intrinsically motivated or to take personal pride and satisfaction in simply doing something well. You can use natural instructional opportunities to point this out—for example, explore with students how satisfying it is to write a clear and interesting story as they are writing.

3 Take advantage of knowledge about the impact of different reinforcement schedules to encourage persistent and permanent learning.

a. **When students first attempt a new kind of learning, supply frequent reinforcement. Then supply rewards less often.**

When students first try a new skill or type of learning, praise almost any genuine attempt, even though it may be inept. As they become more skillful, reserve your praise for especially good performances. Avoid a set pattern of commenting on student work. Make favorable remarks at unpredictable intervals.

b. If you want to encourage periodic spurts of activity, use a fixed interval schedule of reinforcement.

Occasionally, you will want to encourage students to engage in spurts of activity since steady output might be too demanding or fatiguing. In such cases, supply reinforcement at specified periods of time. For example, when students are engaging in strenuous or concentrated activity, circulate and provide praise and encouragement by following a set pattern that will bring you in contact with each student at predictable intervals.

 Give students opportunities to make overt responses, and provide prompt feedback.

a. Require students to make frequent, overt, and relevant responses.

The tendency of teachers is to talk, and for large chunks of time. Those who advocate a programmed approach to teaching recommend that teachers limit the amount of information and explanation they give to students and substitute opportunities for students to respond overtly. In addition, the responses should be directly related to the objectives. If your objectives emphasize the application of concepts and principles, then most of the responses students are asked to make should be about applications. The reason for this suggestion is that the delivery of corrective feedback and other forms of positive reinforcement can be increased when students make frequent responses, thereby accelerating the process of shaping.

EXAMPLES

- Instead of lecturing for twenty to thirty minutes at a time about the development of science and technology in the twentieth century, present information in smaller chunks, perhaps eight to ten minutes at a time, and then ask students to describe how an everyday product or service grew out of a particular scientific principle.

- Periodically ask students to summarize the main points of the material you presented over the past several minutes.

b. Provide feedback so that correct responses will be reinforced and students will become aware of and correct errors.

JOURNAL ENTRY
Ways to Supply Immediate
Feedback

Research clearly shows that students who study material about a topic, answer a set of questions about that material, and are then told whether their responses are correct and why score significantly higher on a subsequent test of that material than do students who receive no feedback. The difference was about three-fourths of a standard deviation, meaning that the average student who received no feedback scored at the 50th percentile, whereas the average student who received feedback scored at the 77th percentile. Here are a couple of examples of how you can provide timely and useful feedback to students (Bangert-Drowns, Kulik, Kulik, & Morgan, 1991).

EXAMPLES

- Immediately after students read a chapter in a text, give them an informal quiz on the key points you listed. Then have them pair off, exchange quizzes, and correct and discuss them.

- As soon as you complete a lecture or demonstration, ask individual students to volunteer to read to the rest of the class what they wrote about the points they were told to look for. Indicate whether the answer is correct; if it is incorrect or incomplete, ask (in a relaxed and nonthreatening way) for additional comments. Direct students to amend and revise their notes as they listen to the responses.

⑤ When students must struggle to concentrate on material that is not intrinsically interesting, use special forms of reinforcement to motivate them to persevere.

For a variety of reasons, some students may have an extraordinarily difficult time concentrating on almost anything. And, as we all know, to master almost any skill or subject, we have to engage in a certain amount of tedious effort. Accordingly, you may sometimes find it essential to use techniques of behavior modification to help students stick to a task. If and when that time comes, you might follow these procedures.

a. Select, with student assistance, a variety of reinforcers.

A behavior modification approach to motivation appears to work most successfully when students are aware of and eager to earn a payoff. Because students react differently to rewards and because any reward is likely to lose effectiveness if used to excess, it is desirable to list several kinds of rewards and permit students to choose. Some behavior modification enthusiasts (for example, Walker & Shea, 1999) even recommend that you make up a *reinforcement preference list* for each student. If you allow your students to prepare individual reinforcement menus themselves, they should be instructed to list school activities they really enjoy doing. It would be wise, however, to stress that the students' lists must be approved by you so that they will not conflict with school regulations or interfere with the rights of others. A student's reward menu might include activities such as reading a book of one's choice, working on an art or craft project, or viewing a videotape in another room.

A reinforcement menu can be used in conjunction with Grandma's rule (the Premack principle). Set up learning situations, particularly those that are not intrinsically appealing, by telling students that as soon as they finish their broccoli (for example, doing a series of multiplication problems), they can have a chocolate sundae (an item from their reinforcement menu).

 More ideas for your journal can be found in the Reflective Journal Questions on the textbook web site.

b. Establish, in consultation with individual students, an initial contract of work to be performed to earn a particular reward.

Once you have established a list of payoffs, you might consult with students (on an individual basis, if possible) to establish a certain amount of work that must be completed for students to obtain a reward selected from the menu. Refer to our chapter on instructional approaches for Robert Mager's suggestions for preparing specific objectives. To ensure that students will earn the reward, the first contract should not be too demanding. For example, it might be something as simple as, "Successfully spell at least seven out of ten words on a list of previously misspelled words," or "Correctly answer at least six out of ten questions about the content of a textbook chapter."

c. Once the initial reward is earned, establish a series of short contracts leading to frequent, immediate rewards.

The results of many operant conditioning experiments suggest that the frequency of reinforcement is of greater significance than the amount of reinforcement. Therefore, having students work on brief contracts that lead to frequent payoffs immediately after the task is completed is preferable to having them work toward a delayed, king-sized award.

USING COMPUTER-BASED INSTRUCTION IN YOUR CLASSROOM

We mentioned earlier that under the right conditions, computers can effectively supplement classroom instruction. If you are now thinking that you might like to use CBI in your own classroom, you should consider the multiple ways computers can be used and how you can get the most out of them for your own students.

Uses of Computers

Computer use in schools falls into one of three categories. The first use—the type you have read about in this chapter—is often called "the computer as tutor." In this mode, students consolidate information learned earlier through drill-and-practice programs, acquire new information and skills through tutorial programs, and solve problems through simulations and games (Table 7.1 notes the purpose and main features of these types of programs). For most drill-and-practice programs and some tutorial programs, this approach is consistent with behavioral theory because it presents information in a structured, step-by-step fashion with consistent feedback. The Center for Programmed Instruction maintains a web site (**www.centerforpi.com/**) that teaches you how to create tutorials and training programs through a series of self-paced, online tutorials. The Resources for Further Information section at the end of the chapter also lists several programs you may want to explore.

A second way in which computers are used is as a learning and problem-solving *tool.* Typical applications in this category include word processing, data analysis, production of graphic material, information organization, and searching the Web for information. This "computer as a learning tool" approach is more typical of the cognitive approaches to learning that are covered in following chapters.

The third use involves learning how to program computers to perform one type of activity or another (Grabe & Grabe, 2004).

● Computers in school used mostly for word processing, drill, and as reference source

There are both similarities and differences in the types of applications favored by elementary, middle school, and high school teachers. At all grade levels, word processing is the most frequently used application. For elementary teachers, drill-and-practice games for mathematics and language arts are the second most frequently used application. For middle and high school teachers, having students use the computer as a reference source is the most common use after word processing. Middle school teachers do this more often with CD-ROM software than with the World Wide Web, whereas the opposite pattern prevails among high school teachers (Becker, Ravitz, & Wong, 1999).

Getting the Most Out of Computer-Based Instruction

We would like to make two points about how you can optimize your use of computer-based instruction. First, recognize that out of the thousands of instructional programs that are on the market, most have such significant shortcomings in their design that they are not worth using. Thus, you will have to be an informed consumer either by conducting your own evaluations of instructional software (not as difficult a job as you might think) or consulting sources whose evaluations can be trusted. Here are the names and addresses of several web sites to help get you started:

● Need to make informed choices of software

Educational Products Information Exchange Institute: **www.epie.org/**
California Learning Resource Network: **clrn.org/home/**
Learning Resources and Technology: **lrt.ednet.ns.ca/**
Software Evaluation Form: **kathyschrock.net/1computer/**
World Village Educational Reviews: **www.worldvillage.com/softwarereviews/ educational.html**

 For quick links to web sites, go to the Weblinks section of the textbook site.

Table 7.1	Major Types of CBI Programs	
Type of Program	**Purpose**	**Main Features***
Drill and practice	Practice knowledge and skills learned earlier to produce fast and accurate responses	• Presents many problems, questions, and exercises. • Checks answers and provides feedback. • Provides cues when student is not sure of correct responses. • Keeps track of errors. • Adjusts difficulty level of problems and questions to the proficiency level of the student.
Tutorial	Teach new information (e.g., facts, definitions, concepts) and skills	• New material presented in linear or branching format. • Linear programs require all students to begin with first frame and work through subsequent frames in given sequence. Incorrect responses minimized by brief answers, small steps, and frequent prompts. • Branching programs allow students to respond to different sets of frames depending on correctness of responses. For incorrect responses, program provides supplementary material that attempts to reteach. • Dialogue programs mimic teacher-student interactions by presenting material, evaluating responses, and adjusting subsequent instruction by presenting either more difficult or easier material.
Problem-solving programs: Simulations and games	Teach new information and skills and provide an opportunity to apply what was learned in a meaningful context that would otherwise be unavailable because of cost, physical danger, and time constraints	• Student uses newly learned and existing information to solve a realistic problem. • Settings may be realistic (e.g., piloting a plane), historical/adventure (e.g., guiding a wagon train across the Oregon Trail), or imaginary (e.g., colonizing a new world). • Students practice creating and testing hypotheses on effects of different variables on achieving a goal.

*Not all programs contain all of the listed features.
SOURCES: Grabe & Grabe (2004).

● CBI no substitute for high-quality teaching

Second, as enthusiastic as you and others may be about the potential of CBI, recognize that it cannot substitute for high-quality classroom teaching. There is a set of skills all teachers need to master in order to integrate computers successfully in a classroom. As we noted early in this text and as Larry Cuban (1986) points out in a provocative book about the relationship between teachers and machines, successful teaching often depends on the ability of a live teacher to establish a positive emotional climate (by communicating interest, excitement, expectations, and caring), to monitor student actions and reactions (by "reading" students' verbal and nonverbal communications), and to orchestrate the sequence and pace of instructional events (by making additions, deletions, and modifications in lesson plans). This is one reason why Cuban (2001), in another provocative book, concludes that computers have been oversold as a means to raise teacher and student productivity. If one thinks of the computer as simply another tool to work with, then each type of computer program—drills, tutorials, simulations, integrated learning systems—requires teachers to plan learning activities, interact with students, provide encouragement and feedback, and design assessments. Although acquiring these skills may be a challenge, many teachers feel that being able to give their students meaningful access to such powerful learning tools is a significant reward (Grabe & Grabe, 2004).

 To review this chapter, see the ACE practice tests and PowerPoint slides on the textbook web site.

Resources for Further Investigation

● B. F. Skinner

In three highly readable volumes—*Particulars of My Life* (1976), *The Shaping of a Behaviorist* (1979), and *A Matter of Consequences* (1983)—B. F. Skinner describes his interests, aspirations, triumphs, and failures; the people and events that led him into psychology; and the forces that led him to devise operant conditioning. *The Technology of Teaching* (1968) is Skinner's most concise and application-oriented discussion of operant conditioning techniques related to pedagogy.

A highly readable summary and critical analysis of Skinner's brand of operant conditioning can be found in Robert Nye's *The Legacy of B. F. Skinner* (1992). According to Nye, "Two major thoughts accompanied the writing of this book: a growing sense of the importance of Skinner's work and the awareness that his ideas are often misjudged" (p. ix).

In *Walden Two* (1948), Skinner describes his conception of a utopia based on the application of science to human behavior. To get the full impact of the novel and of Skinner's ideas, you should read the entire book. However, if you cannot read the whole book at this time, Chapters 12 through 17, which describe the approach to child rearing and education at Walden Two, may be of special interest to you as a future teacher.

● Behavior Modification

If the possibilities of behavior modification seem attractive, you may wish to examine issues of the journals *Behavior Modification, Behavior Research and Therapy, Child Behavior Therapy, Journal of Applied Behavior Analysis*, and *Journal of Behavioral Education*. If you browse through the education and psychology sections of your college bookstore, you are likely to find a number of books on behavior modification. Or you might look for these titles in the library: *Classroom Management for Elementary Teachers* (2003), by Carolyn Evertson, Edmund Emmer, and Murray Worsham; *Classroom Management for Secondary Teachers* (2003), by Edmund Emmer, Carolyn Evertson, and Murray Worsham; and *Behavior Modification:*

What It Is and How to Do It (2003), by Garry Martin and Joseph Pear. And, as the title suggests, *Beyond Behavior Modification: A Cognitive-Behavioral Approach to Behavior Management in the School* (1998), by Joseph Kaplan, goes beyond the typical behavior modification book. It includes chapters on teaching students how to use self-management, social, problem-solving, and stress-management skills.

● Software Programs to Explore

The following are a few software programs whose excellence is generally recognized. They cover the range of drills, tutorials, simulations, and games:

Operation: Frog (Scholastic): allows students to simulate the dissection of a frog, complete with full graphics and video. Students can also "rebuild" the frog to practice locating its organs.

MathMagic (MindPlay Educational Software): offers an addition and subtraction drill program with an arcade game format, appropriate for elementary school students.

Oregon Trail (The Learning Company): enables students to experience the journey from Independence, Missouri, to Oregon as the pioneers did in 1865. Students are responsible for stocking a wagon, avoiding obstacles on the trail, making decisions about how to cross rivers and catch food, and so forth.

SimCity, SimCoaster, and Sim Theme Park (Electronic Arts): allow students to control a large number of variables in complex simulations. The simulations are challenging, but the extensive tutorials and touch of humor in the programs reduce the risk of frustration. Excellent for group work.

Where in the World Is Carmen Sandiego? (The Learning Company): requires students to interpret clues, put new or known facts (such as the location of cities) to use, and problem-solve creatively.

Summary

1. Operant conditioning is a theory of learning devised by B. F. Skinner. It focuses on how voluntary behaviors are strengthened (made more likely to occur in the future) or weakened by the consequences that follow them.

2. Operant conditioning assumes that human behavior is a natural phenomenon that can be explained by a set of general laws, that the best way to understand complex behaviors is to analyze and study the components that make them up, that the results of animal learning studies are potentially useful in understanding human learning, and that learning is the ability to exhibit a new behavior pattern.

3. Basic learning principles that derive from Skinner's work are positive reinforcement, negative reinforcement, punishment (Type I, or presentation punishment), time-out (Type II, or removal punishment), extinction, spontaneous recovery, generalization, and discrimination.

4. Positive reinforcement and negative reinforcement strengthen behaviors. Punishment, time-out, and extinction weaken target behaviors.

5. Complex behaviors can be learned by the reinforcement of successive approximations to the terminal (final) behavior and by the ignoring of nonapproximate behaviors, a process called shaping.

6. Once a new behavior is well established, it can be maintained at that level by the supplying of reinforcement on an intermittent schedule. The four basic schedules are fixed interval, variable interval, fixed ratio, and variable ratio.

7. One of the first educational applications of operant conditioning principles was programmed instruction. It involves presenting written material in small steps according to a predetermined sequence, prompting the correct response, and presenting positive reinforcement in the form of knowledge of results.

8. The early efforts in programmed instruction gave rise to computer-based instruction (CBI). The varieties of CBI include drill-and-practice programs, simulations, tutorials, and integrated learning systems.

9. In general, CBI has had a moderate positive effect on learning. In particular, simulation programs have had a positive effect on science achievement.

10. Integrated learning systems present an entire curriculum on computer, keep track of student performance, and provide feedback to the student and teacher. Research on the effectiveness of such systems is mixed.

11. Another application of operant conditioning principles is behavior modification. The goal of behavior modification is for the teacher to help students learn desirable behaviors by ignoring or punishing undesired behaviors and reinforcing desired ones. Techniques for achieving this goal include shaping, token economies, contingency contracts, extinction, and punishment.

12. Researchers disagree about the strength of the negative effects of corporal punishment, partly because of differences in how corporal punishment is defined.

13. Of the three main ways in which computers are used in schools—using the computer as a tutor, using the computer as a learning and problem-solving tool, and learning how to program computers—the first is most closely allied with the principles of operant conditioning.

14. To get the most out of computer-based instruction, teachers need to select good-quality programs and integrate their use of technology with effective teaching techniques.

Key Terms

operant conditioning *(212)*
positive reinforcement *(213)*
negative reinforcement *(214)*
punishment *(214)*
time-out *(214)*
extinction *(214)*
spontaneous recovery *(216)*
generalization *(216)*
discrimination *(216)*

shaping *(216)*
programmed instruction *(218)*
frames *(218)*
computer-based instruction *(CBI)* *(219)*
computer-assisted instruction (CAI) *(219)*
drill-and-practice programs *(219)*
simulation programs *(219)*

tutorial programs *(219)*
integrated learning systems (ILS) *(220)*
behavior modification *(221)*
Premack principle *(222)*
token economy *(223)*
contingency contracting *(226)*
response cost *(226)*

8 Information-Processing Theory

In the chapter on behavioral learning theory, we noted that operant conditioning emphasizes the role of external factors in learning. Behavioral psychologists focus on the nature of a stimulus to which a student is exposed, the response that the student makes, and the consequences that follow the response. They see no reason to speculate about what takes place in the student's mind before and after the response. The extensive Suggestions for Teaching in Your Classroom presented in the chapter on behavioral learning theory serve as evidence that conclusions and principles based on analyses of external stimuli, observable responses, and observable consequences can be of considerable value to teachers.

But cognitive psychologists, meaning those who study how the mind works and influences behavior, are convinced that it is possible to study nonobservable behavior, such as thought processes, in a scientific manner. Some cognitive psychologists focus on how people use what they know to solve different kinds of problems in different settings; their work will be discussed in the chapter on constructivist learning theory and problem solving. Many cognitive psychologists are especially interested in an area of study known as **information-processing theory,** which seeks to understand how people acquire new information, how they store information and recall it from memory, and how what they already know guides and determines what and how they will learn.

Information-processing theory became a popular approach to the study of learning because it provided psychologists with a framework for investigating the role of a variable that behaviorism had ignored: the nature of the learner. Instead of being viewed as relatively passive organisms that respond in fairly predictable ways to environmental stimuli, learners were now seen as highly active interpreters and manipulators of environmental stimuli. The stage was set for psychology to study learning from a broader and more complicated perspective—namely, as an *interaction* between the learner and the environment.

THE INFORMATION-PROCESSING VIEW OF LEARNING

● Information processing: how humans attend to, recognize, transform, store, retrieve information

Information-processing theory rests on a set of assumptions of which three are worth noting.

1. Information is processed in steps, or stages. The major steps typically are attending to a stimulus, recognizing it, transforming it into some type of mental representation, comparing it with information already stored in memory, assigning meaning to it, and acting on it in some fashion (Searleman & Herrmann, 1994). At an early processing stage, human beings *encode* information (represent it in thought) in somewhat superficial ways (as when they represent visual and auditory stimuli as true-to-life pictures and sounds) and at later stages in more meaningful ways (as when they grasp the gist of an idea or its relationship to other ideas).
2. There are limits on how much information can be processed at each stage. Although the absolute amount of information human beings can learn appears to be limitless, it must be acquired gradually.
3. The human information-processing system is interactive. Information already stored in memory influences and is influenced by perception and attention. We see what our prior experiences direct us to see, and, in turn, what we see affects what we know.

To preview this chapter's key ideas about information processing, see the Chapter Themes on the textbook web site, which you can reach from **http://education.college.hmco.com/students.**

Thus, according to the information-processing view, learning results from an interaction between an environmental stimulus (the *information* that is to be learned) and a learner (the one who *processes*, or transforms, the information). What an information-processing psychologist wants to know, for instance, is what goes on in a student's mind as a teacher demonstrates how to calculate the area of a triangle or as the student reads twenty pages of a social studies text or responds to test questions. In the sense that contemporary information processing emphasizes the use of existing knowledge schemes to interpret new information and build new knowledge structures, it can be considered a *constructivist* view of learning (Winne, 2001). (See the chapter on constructivism for a full description of the nature of the theory and the viewpoints most associated with it.)

We believe that you ought to read this chapter very carefully because the information-processing decisions you make affect when you learn, how much you learn, how well you learn—indeed, whether you learn at all. To give you an appreciation of the information-processing approach to learning and how it can help teachers and students do their jobs, the next section will describe several basic cognitive processes and their role in how people store and retrieve information. Later in the chapter we will describe research on selected learning tactics and discuss the nature of strategic learning.

A MODEL OF INFORMATION PROCESSING

Information-processing psychologists assume that people process new information in stages, that there are limits on how much information can be processed at each

Figure 8.1 A Model of Information Processing

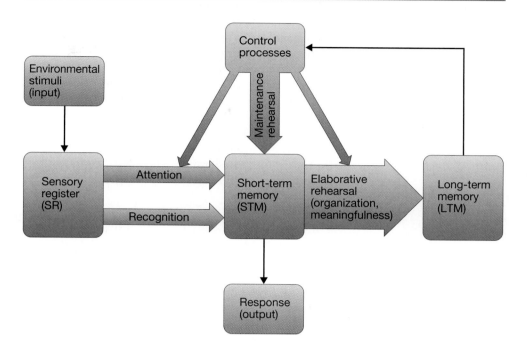

pause & reflect

Can you think of any personal experiences that illustrate one or more of the three memory stores? Have you recently, for instance, retrieved a long-dormant memory because of a chance encounter with an associated word, sound, or smell?

stage, and that previously learned information affects how and what people currently learn. Consequently, many psychologists think of information as being held in and transferred among three memory stores: a sensory register, a short-term store, and a long-term store. Each store varies as to the processes required to move information into and out of it, how much information it can hold, and for how long it can hold information. A symbolic representation of these memory stores and their associated processes appears in Figure 8.1. Called a *multi-store* model, it is based on the work of several theorists (for example, Atkinson & Shiffrin, 1968; Norman & Rumelhart, 1970).

Note that our use of the term *memory stores* is not meant to suggest specific locations in the brain where information is held; it is simply a metaphorical device for classifying different memory phenomena. Nevertheless, studies of neurological functioning using techniques like positron emission tomography (PET) scans (e.g., Haier, 2001) suggest that different types of tasks do activate different parts of the brain. For example, verbal memory tasks are correlated with heightened activity in the thalamus. Another interesting finding is that as people become more proficient at a task, activity decreases in the cortex, suggesting that the brain becomes more efficient at processing information with practice. But as interesting as findings like these are, research on neurological functioning during learning and memory tasks is in its infancy, and educators should be highly skeptical of "brain-based" educational materials and instructional methods (Jorgenson, 2003).

Shortly after the introduction of multi-store models, information-processing theorists divided themselves into two groups. In one camp are those who believe that a multi-store model is the best way to explain a variety of memory phenomena. In the other camp are those who favor a theoretically leaner, single-memory system. Although this debate has yet to be firmly resolved, the multi-store model is seen as having enough validity that it can be productively used to organize and present much of what is known about how humans store, process, and retrieve information from memory (Searleman & Herrmann, 1994; Spear & Riccio, 1994; Winne, 2001).

As shown in Figure 8.1, *control processes* govern both the manner in which information is encoded and its flow between memory stores. These processes include *recognition, attention, maintenance rehearsal, elaborative rehearsal* (also called *elaborative encoding*), and retrieval. Each control process is associated primarily with a particular memory store.

The control processes are an important aspect of the information-processing system for two reasons. First, they determine the quantity and quality of information that the learner stores in and retrieves from memory. Second, it is the learner who decides whether, when, and how to employ them. That the control processes are under our direct, conscious control will take on added importance when we discuss educational applications a bit later. Before we get to applications, however, we need to make you more familiar with the three memory stores and the control processes specifically associated with each of them.

The Sensory Register and Its Control Processes

The Sensory Register   A description of how human learners process information typically begins with environmental stimuli. Our sense receptors are constantly stimulated by visual, auditory, tactile, olfactory, and gustatory stimuli. These experiences are initially recorded in the **sensory register (SR),** the first memory store. It is called the sensory register because the information it stores is thought to be encoded in the same form in which it is originally perceived—that is, as raw sensory data.

● Sensory register: stimuli held briefly for possible processing

The purpose of the SR is to hold information just long enough (about one to three seconds) for us to decide if we want to attend to it further. Information not selectively attended to and recognized decays or disappears from the system. At the moment you are reading these words, for example, you are being exposed to the appearance of letters printed on paper, sounds in the place where you are reading, and many other stimuli. The sensory register might be compared to an unending series of instant-camera snapshots or videotape segments, each lasting from one to three seconds before fading away. If you recognize and attend to one of the snapshots, it will be "processed" and transferred to short-term memory.

● Recognition: noting key features and relating them to stored information

The Nature of Recognition   The process of **recognition** involves noting key features of a stimulus and relating them to already stored information. This process is interactive in that it depends partly on information extracted from the stimulus itself and partly on information stored in long-term memory. The ability to recognize a dog, for example, involves noticing those physical features of the animal that give it "dogness" (for example, height, length, number of feet, type of coat) and combining the results of that analysis with relevant information from long-term memory (such as that dogs are household pets, are walked on a leash by their owners, and are used to guard property).

To the degree that an object's defining features are ambiguous (as when one observes an unfamiliar breed of dog from a great distance) or a learner lacks relevant prior knowledge (as many young children do), recognition and more meaningful processing will suffer. Recognition of words and sentences during reading, for example, can be aided by such factors as clear printing, knowledge of spelling patterns, knowledge of letter sounds, and the frequency with which words appear in natural language. The important point to remember is that recognition and meaningful processing of information are most effective when we make use of all available sources of information (Driscoll, 2000).

One implication of this information-processing view is that elementary school students need more structured learning tasks than middle school or high school students. Because of their limited store of knowledge in long-term memory and narrow ability to relate what they do know logically to the task at hand, younger students should be provided with clear, complete, explicit directions and learning materials (see, for example, Doyle, 1983; Palmer & Wehmeyer, 2003).

The Impact of Attention   The environment usually provides us with more information than we can deal with at one time. From the multitude of sights, sounds, smells, and other stimuli impinging on us at a given moment, we notice and record in the sensory register only a fraction. At this point, yet another reduction typically occurs. We may process only one-third of the already-selected information recorded in the SR. We continually focus on one thing at the expense of something else. This selective focusing on a portion of the information currently stored in the sensory register is what we call **attention.**

As with any other human characteristic, there are individual differences in attention. Some people can concentrate on a task while they are surrounded by a variety of sights and sounds. Others need to isolate themselves in a private study area. Still others have difficulty attending under any conditions. What explains these differences? Again, information from long-term memory plays an influential role. According to Ulric Neisser, "Perceivers pick up only what they have schemata for, and willy-nilly ignore the rest" (1976, p. 79). In other words, we choose what we will see (or hear) by using our prior knowledge and experiences (i.e., schemata) to anticipate the nature of incoming information. Students daydream, doodle, and write letters rather than listen to a lecture because they anticipate hearing little of value. (In other words, the familiar statement, "I'll believe it when I see it," becomes "I'll see it when I believe it" from the perspective of information-processing theory.)

Moreover, these anticipatory schemata are likely to have long-lasting effects. If someone asked you now to read a book about English grammar, you might recall having been bored by diagramming sentences and memorizing grammatical rules in elementary school. If that was the case, you might not read the grammar text very carefully. A basic challenge for teachers is to convince students that a learning task will be useful, enjoyable, informative, and meaningful. Later in this chapter, we will present some ideas as to how this might be accomplished.

Short-Term Memory and Its Control Processes

Short-Term Memory   Once information has been attended to, it is transferred to **short-term memory (STM),** the second memory store. Short-term memory can hold about seven unrelated bits of information for approximately twenty seconds. Although this brief time span may seem surprising, it can be easily demonstrated. Imagine that you look up and dial an unfamiliar phone number and receive a busy signal. If you are then distracted by something or someone else for fifteen to twenty seconds, chances are you will forget the number. Short-term memory is often referred to as *working memory* since it holds information we are currently aware of at any given moment and is the place where various encoding, organizational, and retrieval processes occur.

Working memory is increasingly being viewed as a critical component in our information-processing system. In the view of one researcher, working memory capacity may be equivalent to Spearman's *g* factor (intelligence as a general mental capability) and "is more highly related to learning, both short-term and long-term, than is any other cognitive factor" (Kyllonen, 1996, p. 73). Two other researchers (Hambrick & Engle, 2003), noting that working memory capacity predicts performance in various comprehension and reasoning tasks, argue that working memory capacity is important when tasks require concentration and effort. In other words, the ability to attend to the relevant elements of the task at hand and ignore unimportant stimuli helps explain why some people learn more quickly and effectively than others. This view is supported by a study of how college students process textbook material. Those who scored higher than their peers on a test of working memory capacity were more likely to use demanding but effective cognitive processes (such as making predictions as they read and reflecting on their level of understanding) and recalled more information (Linderholm & van den Broek, 2002).

● Attention: focusing on a portion of currently available information

● Information in long-term memory influences what we attend to

● Short-term memory: about seven bits of information held for about twenty seconds

Rehearsal   A severe limitation of short-term memory is how quickly information disappears or is forgotten in the absence of further processing. This problem can be dealt with through *rehearsal*. Most people think of rehearsal as repeating something over and over either in silence or out loud. The usual purpose for such behavior is to memorize information for later use, although occasionally we simply want to hold material in short-term memory for immediate use (for example, to redial a phone number after getting a busy signal). Rehearsal can serve both purposes, but not in the same way. Accordingly, cognitive psychologists have found it necessary and useful to distinguish two types of rehearsal: maintenance and elaborative.

● Maintenance rehearsal: hold information for immediate use

Maintenance rehearsal (also called *rote rehearsal* or *repetition*) has a mechanical quality. Its only purpose is to use mental and verbal repetition to hold information in short-term memory for some immediate purpose. Although this is a useful and often-used capability (as in the telephone example), it has no effect on long-term memory storage.

● Elaborative rehearsal: use stored information to aid learning

Elaborative rehearsal (also called *elaborative encoding*) consciously relates new information to knowledge already stored in long-term memory. Elaboration occurs when we use information stored in long-term memory to add details to new information, clarify the meaning of a new idea, make inferences, construct visual images, and create analogies (King, 1992b). In these ways, we facilitate both the transfer of information to long-term memory and its maintenance in short-term memory. For example, if you wanted to learn the lines for a part in a play, you might try to relate the dialogue and behavior of your character to similar personal experiences you remember. As you strive to memorize the lines and actions, your mental "elaborations" will help you store your part in long-term memory so that you can retrieve it later.

Elaborative rehearsal, whereby information from long-term memory is used in learning new information, is the rule rather than the exception. Mature learners don't often employ maintenance rehearsal by itself. The decision to use one or the other, however, depends on the demands you expect the environment to make on you. If you need to remember things for future use, use elaborative rehearsal; if you want to keep something in consciousness just for the moment, use rote rehearsal.

It is important for you to keep in mind that younger children may not use rehearsal processes in the same way as more mature learners. Kindergarten students rarely engage in spontaneous rehearsal. By the age of seven, however, children typically use simple rehearsal strategies. When presented with a list of items, the average seven-year-old rehearses each word by itself several times. From the age of ten, rehearsal becomes more like that of an adult. Several items may be grouped together and rehearsed as a set.

So far, we have explained the effect of elaborative rehearsal in terms of relating new information to information already stored in long-term memory. That's fine as a very general explanation. But to be more precise, we need to point out that elaborative rehearsal is based on *organization* (as in the preceding example, where several items were grouped together on some basis and rehearsed as a set) and *meaningfulness* (as in the earlier example, where lines in a play were related to similar personal experiences).

Organization   Quite often the information we want to learn is complex and interrelated. We can simplify the task by organizing multiple pieces of information into a few "clumps," or "chunks," of information, particularly when each part of a chunk helps us remember other parts. The value of organizing material was illustrated by an experiment (Bower, Clark, Lesgold, & Winzenz, 1969) in which two groups of subjects were asked to learn 112 words in four successive lists but under different conditions. One group was given each of the four lists for four trials in the hierarchical or "blocked" arrangement displayed in Figure 8.2. The other group was given the same lists and the same hierarchical tree arrangement, but the words from each list were randomly arranged over the four levels of the hierarchy.

Figure 8.2 Hierarchical Arrangement of Words Produces Superior Recall

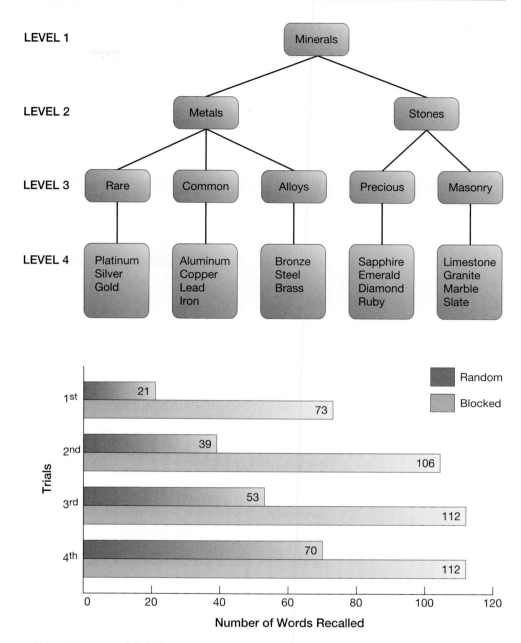

SOURCE: Bower et al. (1969).

● Organizing material reduces number of chunks, provides recall cues

As you can see, through the first three trials, the first group recalled more than twice as many words as the second and achieved perfect recall scores for the last two trials. The organized material was much easier to learn not only because there were fewer chunks to memorize but also because each item in a group served as a cue for the other items. When you decide to store pertinent material from this chapter in your long-term memory in preparation for an exam, you will find the job much easier if you organize what you are studying. To learn the various parts of the information-processing model under discussion, for instance, you might group the ideas being described under the various headings used in this chapter.

Meaningfulness The meaningfulness of new information that one is about to learn has been characterized as "potentially the most powerful variable for explaining the

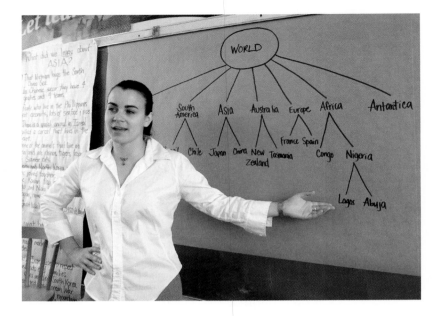

To help students encode information, teach them how to group objects and ideas according to some shared feature.

● Meaningful learning occurs when organized material is associated with stored knowledge

learning of complex verbal discourse" (Johnson, 1975, pp. 425–426). According to David Ausubel (Ausubel, Novak, & Hanesian, 1978), **meaningful learning** occurs when a learner encounters clear, logically organized material and consciously tries to relate the new material to ideas and experiences stored in long-term memory. To understand learning theory principles, for example, you might imagine yourself using them to teach a lesson to a group of students. Or you might modify a previously constructed flowchart on the basis of new information. The basic idea behind meaningful learning is that the learner actively attempts to associate new ideas to existing ones. As another example, many of the "Pause and Reflect" questions in this book are designed to foster meaningful encoding by getting you to relate text information to relevant prior experience.

Lev Vygotsky, the Russian psychologist we mentioned in the chapter on stage theories of development, emphasized the role of teachers, parents, siblings, and other kinds of expert tutors in meaningful learning. Vygotsky pointed out that some of what we learn about the world in which we live comes from direct, unfiltered contact with stimuli. Touch a hot stove, and you get burned. Insult or ridicule a friend, and you are likely to have one fewer friend at the end of the day. The limitation of this kind of learning, which Vygotsky called *direct* learning, is that one is likely to miss the general lesson or principle that underlies the event. Consequently, Vygotsky favored *mediated* learning. A mediator is an individual, usually older, more knowledgeable, and skilled, who selects stimuli to attend to, directs attention to certain aspects of the chosen stimulus, and explains why things are the way they are and why things are done in a certain way. Thus, parents explain to their children why it is not acceptable to hit or tease playmates, and teachers explain to students why it is necessary for them to learn how to use the concepts and rules of English grammar, plane geometry, and the like (Kozulin & Presseisen, 1995).

From a Vygotskian perspective, the main goal of instruction is to provide learners with the psychological tools they will need to engage in *self*-mediation. If individuals are to function effectively once they leave school, they have to learn how to look beyond the immediate situation and see how they can use new knowledge and skills in future situations. Psychologists refer to this process as transfer of learning; we will discuss it at length in the chapter on constructivism and problem solving.

This brief description of meaningfulness and its role in learning contains a strong implication for teaching in culturally diverse classrooms. You can foster meaningful learning for students from other cultures by pointing out similarities between ideas

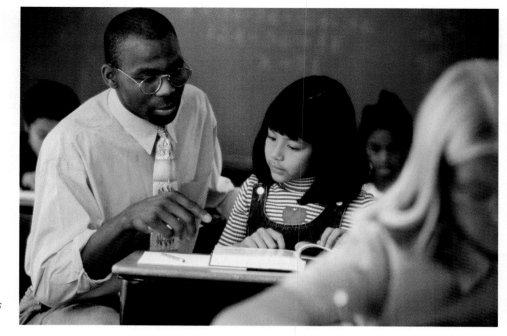

According to Russian psychologist Lev Vygotsky, meaningful learning is most likely to occur when a more knowledgeable and skilled individual explains to a less knowledgeable individual why things are the way they are, as when one points out the reasons behind various rules and procedures, the causes of different events, and the motives for people's behaviors.

presented in class and students' culture-specific knowledge. For example, you might point out that September 16 has the same significance to people of Mexican origin as July 4 has to U.S. citizens since the former date commemorates Mexico's revolution against and independence from Spain.

Visual Imagery Encoding   Generating mental images of objects, ideas, and actions is a particularly powerful form of elaborative encoding. Like pictures, images can be said to be worth a thousand words because they contain a wealth of information in a compact, organized, and meaningful format. Such notable individuals as Albert Einstein (physics), Michael Faraday (physics), Sir Francis Galton (anthropology and genetics), James D. Watson (biochemistry), and Joan Didion (literature) have described how mental imagery played a significant role in their thinking and problem-solving efforts (Shepard, 1978).

Research has consistently shown that directing students to generate visual images as they read lists of words or sentences, several paragraphs of text, or lengthy text passages produces higher levels of comprehension and recall as compared to students who are not so instructed. Also, text passages that contain many concrete words and phrases are more easily understood and more accurately recalled than passages that contain more abstract than concrete ideas (Clark & Paivio, 1991). In one study (Sadoski, Goetz, & Rodriguez, 2000), the beneficial effect of concreteness was obtained for several passage types (such as expository text, persuasive text, stories, and narratives). The more concrete the passage was, the more it was rated comprehensible by students, and students who read concrete passages recalled 1.7 times as much information as students who read abstract passages. As we will see later in the chapter, concreteness and visual imagery are an integral part of several effective study skills.

The theory that these findings support is Allan Paivio's dual coding theory (Clark & Paivio, 1991; Vekiri, 2002). According to the **dual coding theory,** concrete material (such as pictures of familiar objects) and concrete words (such as *horse, bottle, water*) are remembered better than abstract words (such as *deduction, justice, theory*) because the former can be encoded in two ways—as images and as verbal labels—whereas abstract words are encoded only verbally. This makes retrieval easier since a twice-coded item provides more potential retrieval cues than information that exists in only one form.

Before you go on to read about long-term memory, look at Table 8.1, which summarizes some important points about the control processes of short-term memory

Table 8.1	Implications for Instruction: How Findings About the Control Processes of Short-Term Memory Should Influence Your Teaching

Research Finding	Implications
Recognition involves relating a stimulus to information from long-term memory.	Compared with older students, elementary school students have less knowledge stored in long-term memory, and therefore they need structured learning tasks in which one step leads clearly to the next.
Attention is influenced by previous experience stored in long-term memory—we notice what we expect to be important.	Teachers should develop techniques for capturing students' attention and convincing them that the information being presented will be important to them.
Rehearsal prevents the quick disappearance of information from short-term memory. Most children do not begin to rehearse on their own until about age seven.	All children, especially younger ones, can benefit from being taught rehearsal techniques.
Organization of material into chunks makes it much easier to remember.	Teachers can aid students by presenting material in logical chunks and by showing students how to organize information on their own.
Meaningful learning occurs when the learner relates new information to prior ideas and experiences.	Teachers should mediate learning by relating new information to students' cultural knowledge and by helping students to learn techniques of self-mediation.
Visual imagery is easier to recall than abstractions.	Teachers should help students develop learning skills that incorporate visual imagery and other memory-aiding techniques.

and the implications for teachers. Later in the chapter, our Suggestions for Teaching in Your Classroom sections will help you put these ideas into practice.

Long-Term Memory

● Long-term memory: permanent storehouse of unlimited capacity

We have already referred in a general way to the third memory store, **long-term memory (LTM),** which is perhaps the most interesting of all. On the basis of neurological, experimental, and clinical evidence, most cognitive psychologists believe that the storage capacity of LTM is unlimited and that it contains a permanent record of everything an individual has learned, although some doubt exists about the latter point (see, for example, Schunk, 2004).

The neurological evidence comes from the work of Wilder Penfield (1969), a Canadian neurosurgeon who operated on more than one thousand patients who experienced epileptic seizures. To determine the source of the seizures, Penfield electrically stimulated various parts of the brain's surface. During this procedure, many patients reported vivid images of long-dormant events from their past. It was as if a neurological videotape had been turned on.

The experimental evidence, although less dramatic, is just as interesting, and it too has its origins in the early days of information-processing theory. In a typical memory study (such as Tulving & Pearlstone, 1966), subjects receive a list of nouns to learn. After giving subjects ample opportunity to recall as many of the words as possible, researchers provide retrieval cues—for instance, category labels such as "clothing," "food," or "animals." In many cases cued subjects quickly recall additional items. Experiments on how well people recognize previously seen pictures have produced some startling findings. Thirty-six hours after viewing over 2,500 pictures, a group of college students correctly identified an average of about 2,250, or 90 percent (Standing, Conezio, & Haber, 1970). In fact, it has been estimated that if 1 million pictures could be shown, recognition memory would still be 90 percent or better (Standing, 1973). Finally, psychiatrists and psychotherapists have reported many case histories of individuals who have been helped to recall seemingly forgotten events through hypnosis and other techniques (Erdelyi & Goldberg, 1979).

How Information Is Organized in Long-Term Memory   As you have seen, long-term memory plays an influential role throughout the information-processing system. The interests, attitudes, skills, and knowledge of the world that reside there influence what we perceive, how we interpret our perceptions, and whether we process information for short-term or long-term storage. In most instances, retrieval of information from long-term memory is extremely rapid and accurate, like finding a book in a well-run library. Accordingly, we can conclude that information in long-term memory must be organized. The nature of this organization is a key area in the study of memory. The insights it provides help to illuminate the encoding and retrieval processes associated with long-term memory.

● Information in long-term memory organized as schemata

Many cognitive psychologists believe that our store of knowledge in long-term memory is organized in terms of **schemata** (which is plural for *schema* and is related in meaning to Jean Piaget's *scheme*). A schema is typically defined as an abstract structure of information. It is abstract because it summarizes information about many different cases or examples of something, and it is structured because it represents how its own informational components are interrelated. Schemata give us expectations about objects and events (dogs bark, birds fly, students listen to their teachers and study industriously). When our schemata are well formed and a specific event is consistent with our expectation, comprehension occurs. When schemata are poorly structured or absent, learning is slow and uncertain (Bruning, Schraw, Norby, & Ronning, 2004; Schunk, 2004). The following example should make this notion of schemata more understandable.

For almost everyone raised in the United States, the word *classroom* typically calls to mind a scene that includes certain people (teacher, students), objects (desks, chalkboard, books, pencils), rules (attend to the teacher's instructions, stay in the classroom unless given permission to leave), and events (reading, listening, writing, talking, drawing). This is a generalized representation, and some classrooms may contain fewer or more of these characteristics. However, as long as students and teachers share the same basic classroom schema, each will generally know what to expect and how to

Because people interpret new information and experience on the basis of existing memory schemes, and because no two people's schemes are identical, each person is likely to represent the same idea or experience in a unique fashion.

behave in any classroom. It is when people do not possess an appropriate schema that comprehension, memory, and behavior problems arise.

This notion was first investigated during the early 1930s by Sir Frederick Bartlett (1932), an English psychologist. In one experiment, Bartlett had subjects read and recall a brief story, entitled "The War of the Ghosts," that was based on North American Indian folklore. Since Bartlett's subjects had little knowledge of Native American culture, they had difficulty accurately recalling the story; they omitted certain details and distorted others. The distortions were particularly interesting because they reflected an attempt to interpret the story in terms of the logic and beliefs of Western culture. Similar studies, conducted more recently with other kinds of reading materials, have reported similar results (Derry, 1996). The conclusion that Bartlett and other researchers have drawn is that remembering is not simply a matter of retrieving a true-to-life record of information. People often remember their *interpretations* or *constructions* of something read, seen, or heard. In addition, when they experience crucial gaps in memory, they tend to fill in these blanks with logical reconstructions of what they think must have been. People then report these reconstructions as memories of actual events (Derry, 1996).

These experiments and the Case in Print vividly demonstrate the interactive nature of memory. What we know influences what we perceive and how we interpret and store those perceptions. And because our memories of specific events or experiences are assembled, constructed, and sometimes reassembled by the brain over time, accurate and complete recall of information we once stored is not always possible. As a teacher, then, you should pay deliberate attention to how your students use their background knowledge, helping them to use it as accurately and completely as possible to process new information.

 Interested in finding out about your own memory? Go to the Netlabs section of this text's web site.

How Well Do We Remember What We Learn in School?   Conventional wisdom (which is often wrong, by the way) holds that much of the information that we learn in school is forgotten soon after a unit of instruction or course has ended. You may have felt the same way yourself on more than one occasion. But is this belief true? To answer this question, George Semb and John Ellis (1994) reviewed the results of fifty-six research articles published between 1930 and 1993. Their main findings are very consistent with the information-processing principles that you have read about and should at least partially reassure you that you haven't been wasting your time all these years:

- More than seven out of ten studies reported less than a 20 percent loss of what was learned when measured with a recognition task. Half of the studies reported less than a 20 percent loss of what was learned when measured with free recall.
- Subject matter that had a higher-than-average level of unfamiliar facts and associations (such as zoology, anatomy, and medical terminology) and for which students would have little relevant prior knowledge (such as electricity, mechanics, and linguistics) was associated with increased levels of forgetting.
- Most of the forgetting of information occurred within four weeks after the end of a unit of instruction. Additional declines in recall occurred more slowly.
- Less forgetting occurred among students who learned the material to a high level either by being required to achieve a high score on an exam before moving on to the next unit of instruction, having to teach it to less knowledgeable students, or taking advanced courses.
- Less forgetting occurred in classes where students were more actively involved in learning (as in a geography field trip where students had to observe, sketch, record, and answer questions).

● Students remember much of what they learn in school, especially if mastery and active learning are emphasized

The instructional implications that flow from these findings include an emphasis on mastery learning, peer tutoring, frequent testing with corrective feedback, and forms of instruction that actively involve students in learning. In addition, the Suggestions for Teaching in Your Classroom that begin on page 251 point out several ways in which you can help your students improve their information processing.

METACOGNITION

The discussion up to this point has focused on a general explanation of how people attend to, encode, store, and retrieve information. In a word, we have described some of the major aspects of thinking. During the past few decades, researchers have inquired into how much knowledge individuals have about their own thought processes and what significance this knowledge has for learning. The term that was coined to refer to how much we know of our own thought processes is *metacognition*. As we will see, it plays a very important role in learning.

The Nature and Importance of Metacognition

The notion of metacognition was proposed by developmental psychologist John Flavell (1976) to explain why children of different ages deal with learning tasks in different ways. For example, when seven-year-olds are taught how to remember pairs of nouns using both a less effective technique (simply repeating the words) and a more effective technique (imagining the members of each pair doing something together), most of these children will use the less effective technique when given a new set of pairs to learn. Most ten-year-olds, however, will opt to use the more effective method (Kail, 1990). The explanation for this finding is that the seven-year-old has not had enough learning experiences to recognize that some problem-solving methods are better than others. To the younger child, one means is as good as another. This lack of metacognitive knowledge makes true strategic learning impossible for young children.

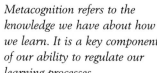 Metacognition: our own knowledge of how we think

One way to grasp the essence of metacognition is to contrast it with cognition. The term *cognition* is used to describe the ways in which information is processed—that is, the ways it is attended to, recognized, encoded, stored in memory for various lengths of time, retrieved from storage, and used for one purpose or another. **Metacognition** refers to our knowledge about those operations and how they might best be used to achieve a learning goal. As Flavell put it:

> I am engaging in metacognition . . . if I notice that I am having more trouble learning A than B; if it strikes me that I should double-check C before accepting it as a fact; if it occurs to me that I had better scrutinize each and every alternative in any multiple-choice type task situation before deciding which is the best one; if I become aware that I am not sure what the experimenter really wants me to do; if I sense that I had better make a note of D because I may forget it; if I think to ask someone about E to see if I have it right. Such examples could be multiplied endlessly. (1976, p. 232)

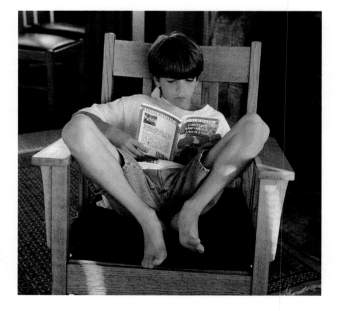

Metacognition refers to the knowledge we have about how we learn. It is a key component of our ability to regulate our learning processes.

Case in Print

"Remembering" Things That Never Were

People often remember their interpretations or constructions of something read, seen, or heard. In addition, when they experience crucial gaps in memory, people tend to fill in these blanks with logical reconstructions of what they think must have been. People then report these reconstructions as memories of actual events. (p. 248)

"Memory" Can Play Tricks, Researchers Discover Here

JOHN G. CARLTON
St. Louis Post-Dispatch 11/8/1998

A college student's smiling face flashed upon the giant screen inside Washington University's May Auditorium on Saturday afternoon.

She had just been telling an interviewer about the time she got lost in a large department store. It was back when she was 5 years old, the student had said, retelling the tale with remarkable detail and clarity.

But there was something she left out—an important fact that even the student didn't know until informed by a memory researcher.

It never really happened.

The smile slowly drained from the student's face. And as it did, a room full of scientists and psychotherapists sat riveted to the screen.

Like members of two sometimes-warring tribes, they gathered in St. Louis on Saturday searching for common ground in a rapidly shifting landscape.

The occasion was a conference sponsored by the St. Louis Psychoanalytic Institute and Washington University's department of psychology and school of social work.

It comes at a time when research has begun calling into question widely held assumptions about how memories are constructed.

Scientists at the University of Washington in Seattle, who made the videotape shown Saturday, and their colleagues around the world have demonstrated how easy it is to create "memories" of events that never actually occurred.

Others have shown that the way children are interviewed can drastically alter what they claim to remember and how much confidence they have in those memories.

Even more unsettling, they have shown that it can be nearly impossible to differentiate so-called false memories from recollections of actual events.

It may sound dry and academic, but the work—some of it done by participants at Saturday's conference—has enormous implications.

During the late 1980s and early 1990s, for example, teachers and day care providers were charged with sexually abusing children in a half-dozen high-profile cases around the country.

Prosecutors in those cases often relied heavily on testimony from children as young as 4 and 5 years old, whom jurors believed to be too young to lie.

That's what made one videotape so shocking.

Maggie Bruck, a professor of psychology at McGill University in Montreal, showed a videotape Saturday of a doctor examining a girl. After he completed his examination, the doctor measured the girl's wrist with a ribbon and tickled her foot with a stick.

The next day, the girl was asked to show on an anatomically correct doll how she had been examined. Her videotaped response: The doctor strangled her with the ribbon and inserted the stick into her genitals.

Bruck also played tapes of children subjected to repeated, suggestive questioning. After first answering an interviewer's questions truthfully, the tapes showed child after child changing their answers.

And it isn't only children who can be made to believe "memories" of events that never actually occurred.

Using suggestive interviewing techniques favored by some therapists, Elizabeth F. Loftus, a professor of psychology and law at the University of Washington, found she could make students "remember" things like getting lost in a department store.

Over time, students become more and more convinced that the events—which had been fabricated by researchers with the help of students' family members—had actually occurred.

In the same way, some patients have become convinced that they were sexually abused as children after being treated by therapists who used techniques such as hypnosis.

None of that research disputes the terrible reality of child sexual abuse, Loftus and other presenters said.

Such abuse occurs, and it is often corroborated when children speak out.

But the new research may prompt a re-examination of how abuse is investigated, and how certain interviewing techniques can result in innocent people being accused. It also underlines the fact that some memories of childhood abuse recovered by adults are inaccurate or unreliable.

Questions and Activities

1. Because people interpret experiences on the basis of their long-term memory schemes and, on occasion, add extraneous information to create a more meaningful and logical recollection, it is not surprising that disagreements occur about the details of an event. Teachers sometimes find themselves in such situations as, for example, when parents confront a teacher and demand to know why the teacher embarrassed their child in front of the rest of the class. The teacher is dumbfounded by the accusation and replies that she did no such thing. What might you do to avoid such confrontations by ensuring that you and your students have a common understanding of important or sensitive events?

2. What kinds of classroom situations are most likely to be interpreted differently and hence remembered differently by teachers and students?

3. If you plan to have students view a film or videotape as part of a lesson, you may be able to demonstrate the phenomenon of false memory. Two weeks after students have viewed the film or tape, and without prior warning, announce that a prize will be awarded to the student who recalls the most information from the film. Have students write down as much as they can recall of what they saw and heard. Then give them a list of all the ideas that actually occurred in the film. Have them compare both lists and make a tally of both how many actual ideas they recalled and how many ideas they recalled that had never appeared.

Suggestions for Teaching in Your Classroom

Helping Your Students Become Efficient Information Processors

1 Develop and use a variety of techniques to attract and hold attention, and give your students opportunities to practice and refine their skills in maintaining attention.

a. Be aware of what will capture your students' attention.

JOURNAL ENTRY
Techniques for Capturing Attention

The ability to capture your students' attention is affected by characteristics of the information itself and the learners' related past experiences. Learners are more likely to attend to things they expect to find interesting or meaningful. It is also true that human beings are sensitive to abrupt, sudden changes in their environment. Thus, anything that stands out, breaks a rhythm, or is unpredictable is almost certain to command students' attention.

EXAMPLES

- Print key words or ideas in extra-large letters on the board.
- Use colored chalk to emphasize important points written on the board.
- When you come to a particularly important part of a lesson, say, "Now really concentrate on this. It's especially important." Then present the idea with intensity and emphasis.
- Start off a lesson with unexpected remarks, such as, "Imagine that you have just inherited a million dollars and . . ."

JOURNAL ENTRY

Techniques for Maintaining Attention

b. To maintain attention, emphasize the possible utility of learning new ideas.

Although it is possible to overdo attempts at making the curriculum relevant, it never hurts to think of possible ways of relating school learning to the present and future lives of students. When students realize that the basic purpose of school is to help them adapt to their environment, they are more likely to pay close attention to what you are trying to do.

EXAMPLE

- Teach basic skills—such as arithmetic computation, arithmetic reasoning, spelling, writing, and reading—as part of class projects that relate to students' natural interests (for example, keeping records of money for newspaper deliveries; measuring rainfall, temperature, and wind speed; writing letters to local television stations to express opinions on or request information about television shows).

● Attention span can be increased with practice

c. Teach students how to increase their span of attention.

Remember that paying attention is a skill that many students have not had an opportunity to refine. Give your students plenty of opportunities to practice and improve their ability to maintain attention.

JOURNAL ENTRY

Techniques for Increasing Attention Span

EXAMPLES

- Institute games that depend on maintaining attention, such as playing Simon Says, keeping track of an object hidden under one of several boxes (the old shell game), or determining whether two pictures are identical or different. At first, positively reinforce students for all correct responses. Then reinforce only for improvements in performance. Remind students that their success is a direct result of how well they pay attention.
- Read a short magazine or newspaper story, and ask students to report who, what, where, when, and why.

2 **Point out and encourage students to recognize that certain bits of information are important and can be related to what they already know.**

Attention is one control process for the sensory register; the other is recognition. Sometimes the two processes can be used together to induce students to focus on important parts of material to be learned. Sometimes you can urge your students to recognize key features or familiar relationships on their own.

EXAMPLES

- Have students practice grouping numbers, letters, or classroom items according to some shared feature, such as odd numbers, multiples of five, letters with circles, or things made of wood.
- Say, "This math problem is very similar to one you solved last week. Does anyone recognize something familiar about this problem?"
- Say, "In this chapter, the same basic point is made in several different ways. As you read, try to recognize and write down as many variations on that basic theme as you can."
- Give students opportunities to express ideas in their own words and relate new knowledge to previous learning.

3 Use appropriate rehearsal techniques, including an emphasis on meaning and chunking.

JOURNAL ENTRY
Ways to Use Chunking to
Facilitate Learning

The power of chunking information into meaningful units was demonstrated in a study conducted with a single college student of average memory ability and intelligence (Ericsson, Chase, & Faloon, 1980). Over twenty months, he was able to improve his memory for digits from seven to almost eighty. Being a track and field buff, he categorized three- and four-digit groups as running times for imaginary races. Thus, 3,492 became "3 minutes and 49.2 seconds, near world record time." Number groups that could not be encoded as running times were encoded as ages. These two chunking techniques accounted for almost 90 percent of his associations.

The main purpose of chunking is to enhance learning by breaking tasks into small, easy-to-manage pieces. To a large degree, students who are ten and older can learn to do this for themselves if you show them how chunking works. In addition, you can help by not requiring students to learn more than they can reasonably handle at one time. If you have a list of fifty spelling words to be learned, it is far better to present ten words a day, five days in a row, during short study periods than to give all fifty at once. This method of presentation is called **distributed practice.** A description of the positive effect of distributed practice on classroom learning and an explanation of why educators do not make greater use of it have been offered by Frank Dempster (1988).

● Distributed practice: short study periods at frequent intervals

In distributed practice, it is usually necessary to divide the material into small parts, which seems to be the best way for students to learn and retain unrelated material (for example, spelling words). This approach makes use of the **serial position effect,** which is people's tendency to learn and remember the words at the beginning and end of a long list more easily than those in the middle. By using short lists, you in effect eliminate the hard-to-memorize middle ground.

● Serial position effect: tendency to remember items at beginning and end of a long list

Distributed practice may not be desirable for all learning tasks. If you ask students to learn roles in a play, short rehearsals might not be effective because students may have a difficult time grasping the entire plot. If you allow enough rehearsal time to run through a whole act, your students will be able to relate one speech to another and comprehend the overall structure of the play. When students learn by way of a few rather long study periods, spaced infrequently, psychologists call it **massed practice.**

You might also tell your students about the relative merits of distributed versus massed practice. Robert Bjork (1979) has pointed out that most students not only are unaware of the benefits of distributed study periods but also go to considerable lengths to block or mass the study time devoted to a particular subject, even when that tactic is a hindrance rather than a help.

4 Organize what you ask your students to learn, and urge older students to organize material on their own.

At least some items in most sets of information that you ask your students to learn will be related to other items, and you will find it desirable to call attention to interrelationships. The Bower et al. (1969) experiment described earlier in which one group of students was given a randomly arranged set of items to learn and another group was presented the same items in logically ordered groups illustrates the value of organization. By placing related items in groups, you reduce the number of chunks to be learned and also make it possible for students to benefit from cues supplied by the interrelationships between items in any given set. And by placing items in logical order, you help students grasp how information at the beginning of a chapter or lesson makes it easier to learn information that is presented later.

JOURNAL ENTRY
Organizing Information into
Related Categories

EXAMPLES

● If students are to learn how to identify trees, birds, rocks, or the equivalent, group items that are related (for example, deciduous and evergreen trees). Call attention to distinctive features and organizational schemes that have been developed.

- Print an outline of a chapter on the board, or give students a duplicated outline, and have them record notes under the various headings. Whenever you give a lecture or demonstration, print an outline on the board. Call attention to the sequence of topics, and demonstrate how various points emerge from or are related to other points.

5 Make what students learn more meaningful by presenting information in concrete, visual terms.

- Concrete analogies can make abstract information meaningful

To avoid blank stares and puzzled expressions from students when you explain an idea in abstract terms, try using representations that can more easily be visualized. Concrete analogies, for example, offer one effective way to add meaning to material. Consider someone who has no knowledge of basic physics but is trying to understand a passage about the flow of electricity through metal. For this person, statements about crystalline lattice arrays, free-floating electrons, and the effects of impurities will mean very little. However, such abstract ideas can be explained in more familiar terms. You might compare the molecular structure of a metal bar to a Tinker Toy arrangement, for example, or liken the effect of impurities to placing a book in the middle of a row of falling dominoes. Such analogies increase recall and comprehension (Royer & Cable, 1975, 1976).

JOURNAL ENTRY

Ways to Present Information Concretely

You should also consider using what are called graphical displays. These are visual-symbolic spatial representations of objects, concepts, and their relationships. Examples of graphical displays include diagrams, matrices, graphs, concepts maps, and charts.

According to Allan Paivio's dual coding theory, the use of graphical displays leads to higher levels of learning because they increase the concreteness of information, thereby allowing it to be encoded in memory in both a visual and a language format. Evidence from both cognitive and neuroscience research supports the idea that information can be stored in long-term memory in both visual and linguistic forms. Another theory, called the visual argument hypothesis, holds that graphical representations aid learning because the spatial arrangement of the items that make up the display allows for a visual form of chunking, thereby decreasing the demands on working memory. Support for the visual argument hypothesis comes from research that shows that students who are given graphic organizers are better able to integrate information and draw inferences about relationships than are students who are given plain text (Vekiri, 2002).

EXAMPLES

- When you explain or demonstrate, express complex and abstract ideas in several different ways. Be sure to provide plenty of examples.
- Use illustrations, diagrams, and concept maps to help students better understand basic concepts and how they relate to one another.
- Make sure the type of visual display used is consistent with the goal of a lesson. For example, when the goal is to understand a cause-and-effect relationship, diagrams that show relationships among objects or concepts should be used, but when the goal is to learn about changes over time, as in plant or animal growth, animation would be a better choice than a static display.

Metacognition is obviously a very broad concept. It covers everything an individual can know that relates to how information is processed. To get a better grasp of this concept, you may want to use the three-part classification scheme that Flavell (1987) proposed:

- *Knowledge-of-person variables:* for example, knowing that you are good at learning verbal material but poor at learning mathematical material, or knowing that information not rehearsed or encoded is quickly forgotten.
- *Knowledge-of-task variables:* for instance, knowing that passages with long sentences and unfamiliar words are usually harder to understand than passages that are more simply written.

- *Knowledge-of-strategy variables:* for example, knowing that one should skim through a text passage before reading it to determine its length and difficulty level.

Lev Vygotsky believed that children acquire metacognitive knowledge and skills most effectively through direct instruction, imitation, and social collaboration in the following way:

1. Children are told by more experienced and knowledgeable individuals what is true and what is false, what is right and what is wrong, how various things should and should not be done, and why. ("Jason, don't touch that stove. It's hot and will give you a painful burn if you touch it.")
2. As opportunities arise, children use this knowledge to regulate their own behavior (saying out loud, "Hot stove. Don't touch.") as well as the behavior of others. If you have ever seen young children play "House" or "School" and faithfully mimic the dictates of their parents or teacher, then you have seen this process at work.
3. Children regulate their own behavior through the use of inner speech.

Vygotsky's analysis strongly suggests that providing children with opportunities to regulate their own and others' behavior, as in peer tutoring, is an excellent way to help them increase their metacognitive knowledge and skills and to improve the quality of their learning. Later in this chapter, we describe one such program, reciprocal teaching. Programs like reciprocal teaching have produced high levels of learning, motivation, and transfer (Karpov & Haywood, 1998).

Recent research indicates significant differences in what younger and older children know about metacognition. What follows is a discussion of some of these differences.

Age Trends in Metacognition

Two reviews of research on metacognition (Duell, 1986; Kail, 1990) examined how students of different ages use memorization techniques and how well they understand what they are doing. Following are some of the key conclusions of the reviews:

- In terms of diagnosing task difficulty, most six-year-olds know that more familiar items are easier to remember than less familiar items and that a small set of items is easier to recall than a large set of items. What six-year-olds do not yet realize is that the amount of information they can recall immediately after they study it is limited.
- Similar findings have been obtained for reading tasks. Most second graders know that interest, familiarity, and story length influence comprehension and recall. However, they are relatively unaware of the effect of how ideas are sequenced, the introductory and summary qualities of first and last paragraphs, and the relationship between reading goals and tactics. Sixth graders, by contrast, are much more aware of the effects of these variables on comprehension and recall.
- Most young children know very little about the role their own capabilities play in learning. For example, not until about nine years of age do most children realize that their recall right after they study something is limited. Consequently, children through the third grade usually overestimate how much they can store in and retrieve from short-term memory. One likely reason for this developmental difference is that younger children base their prediction on irrelevant personal characteristics (such as, "I'm pretty smart"), whereas older children focus more on relevant task characteristics.
- There are clear developmental differences in how well students understand the need to tailor learning tactics to task demands. For example, four- and six-year-old children in one study cited by Robert Kail (1990) did not alter how much time they spent studying a set of pictures when they were told that a recognition test would follow either three minutes later, one day later, or one week later. Eight-year-olds did use that information to allocate less or more study time to the task.

- In terms of monitoring the progress of learning, most children younger than seven or eight are not very proficient at determining when they know something well enough to pass a memory test. Also, most first graders typically don't know what they don't know. When given multiple opportunities to study and recall a lengthy set of pictures, six-year-olds chose to study pictures they had previously seen and recalled as well as ones they hadn't. Third graders, by contrast, focused on previously unseen pictures.

The general conclusion that emerges from these findings is that the youngest school-age children have only limited knowledge of how their cognitive processes work and when to use them. Consequently, primary grade children do not systematically analyze learning tasks, formulate plans for learning, use appropriate techniques of enhancing memory and comprehension, or monitor their progress because they do not (some would say cannot) understand the benefits of doing these things. But as children develop and gain more experience with increasingly complex academic tasks, they acquire a greater awareness of metacognitive knowledge and its relationship to classroom learning. In this process, teachers can assist their students and guide them toward maximum use of their metacognitive knowledge. To help you understand how, the next section will discuss learning tactics and strategies.

 Insight into one's learning processes improves with age

HELPING STUDENTS BECOME STRATEGIC LEARNERS

With some effort and planning, a teacher can make logically organized and relevant lessons. However, this is only half the battle because students must then attend to the information, encode it into long-term memory, and retrieve it when needed. Getting students to use the attention, encoding, and retrieval processes discussed in the previous sections is not always easy. The sad fact is that most children and adults are inefficient learners (as evidenced, for example, by Bond, Miller, & Kennon, 1987; Brown, Campione, & Day, 1981; Covington, 1985; Peverly, Brobst, Graham, & Shaw, 2003; Selmes, 1987; Winne & Jamieson-Noel, 2002, 2003). Their attempts at encoding rarely go beyond rote rehearsal (for example, rereading a textbook chapter), simple organizational schemes (outlining), and various cueing devices (underlining or highlighting), and they have a poor sense of how well prepared they are to take a test.

Although evidence exists that students are more likely to use effective study skills as they get older (Schneider, Knopf, & Stefanek, 2002) and that some students behave strategically by using different learning skills for different tasks (Hadwin, Winne, Stockley, Nesbit, & Woszczyna, 2001), many do not do so either systematically or consistently. In one study (Schneider et al., 2002), 7 percent of twelve-year-olds used an effective organizing technique to learn and recall a set of pictures, but those same individuals used no discernible strategy for the same task at age eighteen. In another study (Hyönä, Lorch, & Kaakinen, 2002), only 20 percent of a group of college students noted text features that signaled transitions and important information (such as headings, topic sentences, and sentences that end paragraphs and sections), constructed a mental representation of the topic, and related it to earlier parts of the text.

One reason for this state of affairs is that students are rarely taught how to make the most of their cognitive capabilities. In one study, sixty-nine kindergarten through sixth-grade teachers gave strategy instruction only 9.5 percent of the time they were observed. Rationales for strategy use were given less than 1 percent of the time, and 10 percent of the teachers gave no strategy instructions at all. Moreover, the older the students were, the less

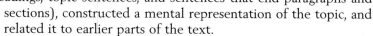

pause & reflect

Many teachers have said they would like to teach their students more about the nature and use of learning processes but they don't have time because of the amount of subject material they must cover. What can you do to avoid this pitfall?

likely they were to receive strategy instruction (Moely et al., 1992). A similar study of eleven middle school teachers eight years later produced the same findings. Teaching behaviors that reflected strategy instruction occurred only 9 percent of the time (Hamman, Berthelot, Saia, & Crowley, 2000).

Findings such as these are surprising, not to mention disappointing, since it is widely recognized that the amount of independent learning expected of students increases consistently from elementary school through high school and into college. The rest of this chapter will try to convince you that it need not be this way, at least for your students.

The Nature of Learning Tactics and Strategies

● Strategy: plan to achieve a long-term goal

A **learning strategy** is a general *plan* that a learner formulates for achieving a somewhat distant academic goal (like getting an A on the next exam). Like all other strategies, it specifies what will be done to achieve the goal, where it will be done, and when it will be done. A **learning tactic** is a specific *technique* (like a memory aid or a form of note taking) that a learner uses to accomplish an immediate objective (such as to understand the concepts in a textbook chapter and how they relate to one another).

● Tactic: specific technique that helps achieve immediate objective

As you can see, tactics have an integral connection to strategies. They are the learning tools that move you closer to your goal. Thus, they have to be chosen so as to be consistent with the goals of a strategy. If you had to recall verbatim the Preamble to the U.S. Constitution, for example, would you use a learning tactic that would help you understand the gist of each stanza or one that would allow for accurate and complete recall? It is surprising how often students fail to consider this point. Because understanding the different types and roles of tactics will help you better understand the process of strategy formulation, we will discuss tactics first.

Types of Tactics

Most learning tactics can be placed in one of two categories based on the tactic's primary purpose:

- *Memory-directed tactics*, which contain techniques that help produce accurate storage and retrieval of information
- *Comprehension-directed tactics*, which contain techniques that aid in understanding the meaning of ideas and their interrelationships (Levin, 1982)

Because of space limitations, we cannot discuss all the tactics in each category. Instead, we have chosen to discuss a few briefly that are either very popular with students or have been shown to be reasonably effective. The first two, rehearsal and mnemonic devices, are memory-directed tactics. Both can take several forms and are used by students of almost every age. The last two, self-questioning and note taking, are comprehension-directed tactics and are used frequently by students from the upper elementary grades through college.

● Rote rehearsal not a very effective memory tactic

Rehearsal   The simplest form of rehearsal—rote rehearsal—is one of the earliest tactics to appear during childhood, and almost everyone uses it on occasion. It is not a particularly effective tactic for long-term storage and recall because it does not produce distinct encoding or good retrieval cues (although, as discussed earlier, it is a useful tactic for purposes of short-term memory). The consensus among researchers (see, for example, Schlagmüller & Schneider, 2002; Schneider & Bjorklund, 1998) is that most five- and six-year-olds do not spontaneously rehearse but can be prompted to do so. Seven-year-olds sometimes use the simplest form of rehearsal. By eight years of age, youngsters start to rehearse several items together as a set instead of rehearsing single pieces of information one at a time. A slightly more advanced version, *cumulative rehearsal*, involves rehearsing a small set of items for several repetitions, dropping the item at the top of the list and adding a new one, giving the set several repetitions, dropping the item at the head of the set and adding a new one, rehearsing the set, and so on.

By early adolescence, rehearsal reflects the learner's growing awareness of the organizational properties of information. When given a list of randomly arranged words from familiar categories, thirteen-year-olds will group items by category to form rehearsal sets. This version of rehearsal is likely to be the most effective because of the implicit association between the category members and the more general category label. If at the time of recall the learner is given the category label or can generate it spontaneously, the probability of accurate recall of the category members increases significantly.

● Acronym: word made from first letters of items to be learned

● Acrostic: sentence made up of words derived from first letters of items to be learned

● Loci method: visualize items to be learned stored in specific locations

● Keyword method: visually link pronunciation of foreign word to English translation

Mnemonic Devices   A **mnemonic device** is a memory-directed tactic that helps a learner transform or organize information to enhance its retrievability. Such devices can be used to learn and remember individual items of information (a name, a fact, a date), sets of information (a list of names, a list of vocabulary definitions, a sequence of events), and ideas expressed in text. These devices range from simple, easy-to-learn techniques to somewhat complex systems that require a fair amount of practice. Because they incorporate visual and verbal forms of elaborative encoding, their effectiveness is due to the same factors that make imagery and category clustering successful: organization and meaningfulness.

Although mnemonic devices have been described and practiced for over two thousand years, they were rarely made the object of scientific study until the 1960s (see Yates, 1966, for a detailed discussion of the history of mnemonics). Since that time, mnemonics have been frequently and intensively studied by researchers, and there are several reviews of mnemonics research (for example, Bellezza, 1981; Carney & Levin, 2002; Levin, 1993; Snowman, 1986). Table 8.2 provides descriptions, examples, and uses of five mnemonic devices: rhymes, acronyms, acrostics, the loci method, and the keyword method.

● Mnemonic devices meaningfully organize information, provide retrieval cues

Why Mnemonic Devices Are Effective   Mnemonic devices work so well because they enhance the encodability and retrievability of information. First, they provide a context (such as acronyms, sentences, mental walks) in which apparently unrelated items can be organized. Second, the meaningfulness of material to be learned is enhanced through associations with more familiar meaningful information (for example, memory pegs or loci). Third, they provide distinctive retrieval cues that must be encoded with the material to be learned. Fourth, they force the learner to be an active participant in the learning process (Morris, 1977).

An example of these mnemonic benefits can be seen in a study conducted with college students (Rummel, Levin, & Woodward, 2003). You may find this study particularly relevant because the students used a variation of the keyword mnemonic to learn about a topic you covered in a previous chapter—theories of intelligence. Students assigned to the mnemonic condition were asked to read an eighteen-hundred-word passage that discussed the contributions of five psychologists to the measurement of intelligence and seven psychologists to the development of theories of intelligence. After each paragraph they encountered a mnemonic illustration that linked the theorist's surname to his major contribution. For example, after the paragraph about Charles Spearman, students saw a drawing of a man holding a "primary" hunting spear along with several specialized spears on the ground to represent Spearman's theory that intelligence is composed of one general and several specialized factors. Students assigned to the non-mnemonic condition encountered a summary sentence after each paragraph instead of an illustration. After reading the passage, all students were asked to write two short essays in which they compared and contrasted the work of each theorist and summarized the major aspects of each theory. They then took a three-column matching test in which they had to match each theorist's name with that person's major contribution and other information about that person's work. A second matching test was taken one week later. On the essay test,

| Table 8.2 | Five Types of Mnemonic Devices | | |

Mnemonic	Description	Example	Uses
Rhyme	The items of information that one wants to recall are embedded in a rhyme that may range from one to several lines. A rhyme for recalling the names of the first 40 U.S. presidents, for example, contains 14 lines.	• Thirty days hath September, April, June, and November • Fiddlededum, fiddlededee, a ring around the moon is $\pi \times d$. If a hole in your sock you want repaired, use the formula π r squared (to recall the formulas for circumference and area).	Recalling specific items of factual information
Acronym	The first letter from each to-be-remembered item is used to make a word. Often called the first-letter mnemonic.	• HOMES (for the names of the Great Lakes—Huron, Ontario, Michigan, Erie, Superior)	Recalling a short set of items, particularly abstract items, in random or serial order
Acrostic	The first letter from each to-be-remembered item is used to create a series of words that forms a sentence. The first letter of each word in the sentence corresponds to the first letters of the to-be-remembered items.	• Men Very Easily Make Jugs Serve Useful New Purposes (for the names of the 9 planets in our solar system—Mercury, Venus, Earth, Mars, Jupiter, Saturn, Uranus, Neptune, Pluto) • A Rat In The House May Eat The Ice Cream (to recall the spelling of the word *arithmetic*)	Recalling items, particularly abstract ones, in random or serial order
Method of loci	Generate visual images of and memorize a set of well-known locations that form a natural series (such as the furniture in and the architectural features of the rooms of one's house). Second, generate images of the to-be-learned items (objects, events, or ideas), and place each in a separate location. Third, mentally walk through each location, retrieve each image from where it was placed, and decode into a written or spoken message. *Loci* (pronounced *low-sigh*) is the plural of *locus*, which means "place."	• To recall the four stages of Piaget's theory: For sensorimotor stage, picture a car engine with eyes, ears, nose, and a mouth. Place this image in your first location (fireplace mantel). For preoperational stage, picture Piaget dressed in a surgical gown scrubbing up before an operation. Place this image in your second location (bookshelf). For concrete-operational stage, picture Piaget as a surgeon cutting open a piece of concrete. Place this image in your third location (chair). For formal-operational stage, picture Piaget as an operating room surgeon dressed in a tuxedo. Place this image in your fourth location (sofa).	Can be used by children, college students, and the elderly to recall lists of discrete items or ideas from text passages. Works equally well for free recall and serial recall, abstract and concrete items.
Keyword	Created to aid the learning of foreign language vocabulary, but is applicable to any task in which one piece of information has to be associated with another. First, isolate some part of the foreign word that, when spoken, sounds like a meaningful English word. This is the keyword. Then create a visual image of the keyword. Finally, form a compound visual image between the keyword and the translation of the foreign word.	• Spanish word *pato* (pronounced *pot-o*) means "duck" in English. Keyword is *pot*. Imagine a duck with a pot over its head or a duck simmering in a pot. • English psychologist Charles Spearman proposed that intelligence was composed of two factors—*g* and *s*. Keyword is "spear." Imagine a spear being thrown at a gas (for *g* and *s*) can.	For kindergarten through fourth grade, works best when children are given keywords and pictures. Can be used to recall cities and their products, states and their capitals, medical definitions, and famous people's accomplishments.

SOURCES: Atkinson (1975); Atkinson & Raugh (1975); Bellezza (1981); Carney, Levin, & Levin (1994); Raugh & Atkinson (1975); Yates (1966).

the two groups had equivalent scores for structural coherence and getting the chronological sequence correct, but the mnemonic students scored considerably higher on correctly associating each theorist's name with his major accomplishment. On the matching test, the mnemonic group outscored the non-mnemonic group by a wide margin for matching names and major facts on both the immediate test and the delayed test.

A second example comes from a study done in a fourth-grade classroom with five special education students (Mastropieri, Sweda, & Scruggs, 2000). Four of these students had a learning disability with speech or language impairment, and one had a learning disability with emotional disturbance. The teacher taught all the students in the class a variation of the keyword mnemonic to help them learn social studies facts and concepts (for instance, the meaning of the concept "charter" or the name of the continent from which explorers traveled to the New World). Although the students without disabilities performed well on a unit test (88.9 percent correct for information that was taught mnemonically versus 83.3 percent for information that was not taught mnemonically), the five students with disabilities benefited even more (75 percent correct versus 36.7 percent correct).

Why You Should Teach Students How to Use Mnemonic Devices   Despite the demonstrated effectiveness of mnemonic devices, many people argue against teaching them to students. They feel that students should learn the skills of critical thinking and problem solving rather than ways to recall isolated bits of verbatim information reliably. When factual information is needed, one can always turn to a reference source. Although we agree with the importance of teaching students to be critical thinkers and problem solvers, we feel this view is shortsighted for three reasons.

- It is very time-consuming to be constantly looking things up in reference books.
- The critique of mnemonic training ignores the fact that effective problem solving depends on ready access to a well-organized and meaningful knowledge base. Indeed, people who are judged to be expert in a particular field have an impressive array of factual material at their fingertips.
- Critics of mnemonics education focus only on the "little idea" that mnemonic usage aids verbatim recall of bits of information. The "big idea" is that students come to realize that the ability to learn and remember large amounts of information is an acquired capability. Too often students (and adults) assume that an effective memory is innate and requires high intelligence. Once they realize that learning is a skill, students may be more inclined to learn how to use other tactics and how to formulate broad-based strategies.

Self- and Peer Questioning   Because students are expected to demonstrate much of what they know by answering written test questions, self-questioning can be a valuable learning tactic. The key to using questions profitably is to recognize that different types of questions make different cognitive demands. Some questions require little more than verbatim recall or recognition of simple facts and details. If an exam is to stress factual recall, then it may be helpful for a student to generate such questions while studying. Other questions, however, assess comprehension, application, or synthesis of main ideas or other high-level information.

To ensure that students fully understood how to write comprehension-aiding questions, Alison King (1992b) created a set of question stems (see Table 8.3) that were intended to help students identify main ideas and think about how those ideas related to each other and to what the student already knew. When high school and college students used these question stems, they scored significantly better on tests of recall and comprehension of lecture material than did students who simply reviewed the same material. King (1994, 1998) also demonstrated that pairs of fourth- and fifth-grade students who were taught how to ask each other high-level questions and respond with elaborated explanations outperformed untrained students on tests

● Self-questioning improves comprehension, knowledge integration

Table 8.3	Self-Questioning Stems

What is a new example of . . . ?

How would you use . . . to . . . ?

What would happen if . . . ?

What are the strengths and weaknesses of. . . ?

What do we already know about. . . ?

How does . . . tie in with what we learned before?

Explain why . . .

Explain how . . .

How does . . . affect . . . ?

What is the meaning of . . . ?

Why is . . . important?

What is the difference between . . . and . . . ?

How are . . . and . . . similar?

What is the best . . . , and why?

What are some possible solutions to the problem of . . . ?

Compare . . . and . . . with regard to . . .

How does . . . cause . . . ?

What do you think causes . . . ?

SOURCE: From King, A. (1992b). "Facilitating Elaborative Learning Through Guided Student Generated Questioning," *Educational Psychologist*, 27(1), 111–126. Reprinted by permission of Lawrence Erlbaum Associates, Inc.

that measured both comprehension and the ability to integrate text information with prior knowledge.

Self-questioning is a highly recommended learning tactic because it has a two-pronged beneficial effect:

- It helps students to understand better what they read. In order to answer the kinds of question stems King suggested, students have to engage in such higher-level thinking processes as translating ideas into their own words (What is the meaning of . . . ? Explain why . . .), looking for similarities and differences (What is the difference between . . . and . . . ? How are . . . and . . . similar?), thinking about how ideas relate to one another (Compare . . . and . . . with regard to . . .) and to previously learned information (How does . . . tie in with what we learned before?), and evaluating the quality of ideas (What are the strengths and weaknesses of . . . ?). In short, answering high-level question stems leads to deeper processing of the reading material.
- It helps students to monitor their comprehension. If too many questions cannot be answered or if the answers appear to be too superficial, this provides clear evidence that the student has not achieved an adequate understanding of the passage.

Studies that have examined the effect of responding to question stems report very strong effects. The average student who responded to question stems while reading a passage scored at the 87th percentile on a subsequent teacher-made test, while the average student who did not answer questions scored only at the 50th percentile. Differences of this magnitude do not appear in research studies very often and, in this case, argue strongly for providing students with question stems and teaching them how to construct their own questions and answers (Rosenshine, Meister, & Chapman, 1996). Discussion of the conditions that underlie effective self-questioning instruction can be found in articles by Bernice Wong (1985), Zemira Mevarech and Ziva Susak (1993), and Alison King (2002).

Note Taking   As a learning tactic, note taking comes with good news and bad. The good news is that note taking can benefit a student in two ways. First, the process of taking notes while listening to a lecture or reading a text leads to better retention and comprehension of the noted information than just listening or reading does. For example, Andrew Katayama and Daniel Robinson (2000) found that college students who were given a set of partially completed notes for a text passage and told to fill in the blank spaces scored higher on a test of application than students who were given a complete set of notes. Second, the process of reviewing notes produces additional chances to recall and comprehend the noted material. The bad news is that we know very little about the specific conditions that make note taking an effective tactic.

This uncertainty as to what constitutes a good set of notes probably explains the results Alison King (1992a) obtained in a comparison of self-questioning, summarizing, and note taking. One group of students was given a set of question stems, shown how to generate good questions with them, and allowed to practice. A second group was given a set of rules for creating a good summary (identify a main idea or subtopic and related ideas, and link them together in one sentence), shown how to use them to create good summaries, and allowed to practice. A third group, however, was told simply to take notes as group members normally would in class. Both the self-questioning and summarizing groups scored significantly higher on an immediate and one-week-delayed retention test.

Conclusions Regarding Learning Tactics   On the basis of this brief review, we would like to draw two conclusions. One is that students need to be systematically taught how to use learning tactics to make connections among ideas contained in text and lecture, as well as between new and previously learned information. No one expects students to teach themselves to read, write, and compute. So why should they be expected to teach themselves how to use a variety of learning tactics?

The second conclusion is that learning tactics should not be taught as isolated techniques, particularly to high school students. If tactics are taught that way, most students probably will not keep using them for very long or recognize that as the situation changes, so should the tactic. Therefore, as we implied earlier, students should be taught how to use tactics as part of a broader learning strategy.

Using Learning Strategies Effectively

The Components of a Learning Strategy   As noted, a learning strategy is a plan for accomplishing a learning goal. It consists of six components: metacognition, analysis, planning, implementation of the plan, monitoring of progress, and modification. To give you a better idea of how to formulate a learning strategy of your own, here is a detailed description of each of these components (Snowman, 1986, 1987):

1. *Metacognition*. In the absence of some minimal awareness of how we think and how our thought processes affect our academic performance, a strategic approach to learning is simply not possible. At the very least, we need to know that effective learning requires an analysis of the learning situation, formulation of a learning plan, skillful implementation of appropriate tactics, periodic monitoring of our progress, and modification of things that go wrong. In addition, we need to know why each of these steps is necessary, when each step should be carried out, and how well prepared we are to perform each step. Without this knowledge, students who are taught one or more of the learning tactics mentioned earlier do not keep up their use for very long, nor do they apply the tactics to relevant tasks.

2. *Analysis*. To analyze the task and obtain relevant information, the strategic learner can play the role of an investigative journalist, asking questions that pertain to what, when, where, why, who, and how. In this way, the learner can identify important aspects of the material to be learned (what, when, where), understand the nature of the test that will be given (why), recognize relevant personal

● Taking notes and reviewing notes aid retention and comprehension

● Learning strategy components: metacognition, analysis, planning, implementation, monitoring, modification

Students can formulate strategic learning plans that identify and analyze the important aspects of a task. Then they can tailor these plans to their own strengths and weaknesses as learners.

learner characteristics (who), and identify potentially useful learning activities or tactics (how).

3. *Planning.* Once satisfactory answers have been gained from the analysis phase, the strategic learner then formulates a learning plan by hypothesizing something like the following: "I know something about the material to be learned (I have to read and comprehend five chapters of my music appreciation text within the next three weeks), the nature of the test criterion (I will have to compare and contrast the musical structure of symphonies that were written by Beethoven, Schubert, and Brahms), my strengths and weaknesses as a learner (I am good at tasks that involve identifying similarities and differences, but I have difficulty concentrating for long periods of time), and the nature of various learning activities (skimming is a good way to get a general sense of the structure of a chapter; mnemonic devices make memorizing important details easier and more reliable; note taking and self-questioning are more effective ways to enhance comprehension than simple rereading). Based on this knowledge, I should divide each chapter into several smaller units that will take no longer than thirty minutes to read, take notes as I read, answer self-generated compare-and-contrast questions, use the loci mnemonic to memorize details, and repeat this sequence several times over the course of each week."

4. *Implementation of the plan.* Once the learner has formulated a plan, each of its elements must be implemented *skillfully.* A careful analysis and a well-conceived plan will not work if tactics are carried out poorly. Of course, a poorly executed plan may not be entirely attributable to a learner's tactical skill deficiencies. Part of the problem may be a general lack of knowledge about what conditions make for effective use of tactics (as is the case with note taking).

5. *Monitoring of progress.* Once the learning process is under way, the strategic learner assesses how well the chosen tactics are working. Possible monitoring techniques include writing out a summary, giving an oral presentation, working practice problems, and answering questions.

6. *Modification.* If the monitoring assessment is positive, the learner may decide that no changes are needed. If, however, attempts to memorize or understand the learning material seem to be producing unsatisfactory results, the learner will need to reevaluate and modify the analysis. This will cause changes in both the plan and the implementation.

There are three points we would like to emphasize about the nature of a learning strategy. The first is that learning conditions constantly change. Subject matters have different types of information and structures, teachers use different instructional methods and have different styles, exams differ in the kinds of demands they make, and the interests, motives, and capabilities of students change over time. Accordingly, strategies must be *formulated* or constructed anew as one moves from task to task rather than *selected* from a bank of previously formulated strategies. The true strategist, in other words, exhibits a characteristic that is referred to as *mindfulness* (Alexander, Graham, & Harris, 1998). A mindful learner is aware of the need to be strategic, attends to the various elements that make up a learning task, and thinks about how to use the leaning skills he or she possesses to greatest effect.

The second point is that the concept of a learning strategy is obviously complex and requires a certain level of intellectual maturity. Thus, you may be tempted to conclude that although *you* could do it, learning to be strategic is beyond the reach of most elementary and high school students. Research evidence suggests otherwise, however. A study of high school students in Scotland, for example, found that some students are sensitive to contextual differences among school tasks and vary their approach to studying accordingly (Selmes, 1987). Furthermore, as we will show in the next section, research in the United States suggests that elementary school youngsters can be trained to use many of the strategy components just mentioned.

Finally, because strategic learners tailor their learning processes to the perceived demands of a task, teachers need to clearly convey to students such critical information as what tasks or parts of tasks (like certain parts of a reading assignment) are sufficiently important that they will test students on them and what form the tests will take. Students, in turn, need to accurately perceive those demands (Beishuizen & Stoutjesdijk, 1999). A study conducted in the Netherlands (Broekkamp, van Hout-Wolters, Rijlaarsdam, & van den Bergh, 2002 shows that this process occurs less frequently than one would desire. The study examined how twenty-two history teachers and their eleventh-grade students rated the importance of sections of an eight-thousand-word textbook passage on U.S. presidents. In brief, here is what the researchers found:

1. There was only limited agreement among teachers about which sections of the text students should focus on in preparation for a test.
2. There was only limited agreement among students as to which sections of the text were most important as well as between students and their teacher.

In other words, teachers had only limited success in communicating to students what parts of the passage were more important than others, and students were as apt to focus on the less important parts as the more important ones.

These findings suggest that teachers should provide students with clear and comprehensive information about the relative importance of various parts of a reading passage, instruct students in how to identify the important parts of a reading passage, and avoid dwelling on or overemphasizing aspects of a reading assignment that they have no intention of testing students on.

A major problem in training students to use learning strategies and tactics is getting the youngsters to spend the time and effort required. Suppose some students expressed a lack of interest, saying their own methods were just as effective (although you knew they were not). How would you convince these students otherwise?

Research on Learning Strategy Training Research clearly shows that training students to use various tactics and strategies is a worthwhile use of the teacher's time. Students who were trained to use a single mnemonic technique outperformed nontrained students by a wide margin on subsequent tests of memory (68th percentile versus 50th percentile, respectively). The effect was particularly noticeable among primary grade and low-achieving students. A similar advantage was found for students who had been taught to use a variety of tactics and were tested for memory and low-level comprehension (75th percentile versus the control group's 50th percentile). Although the weakest

Allow Students to Be Strategic Learners

In the financial world, it is illegal to engage in what is called insider trading. That is, an individual who receives important private information from an employee of a publicly traded company (such as news of a large drop in sales or the awarding of a major contract) is prohibited by law from buying or selling that company's stock or bonds until the information becomes public knowledge. Unfortunately, many teachers behave similarly with respect to students' preparations for exams. They believe, erroneously, that they should withhold such "insider" information as what content the test items will cover, what types of cognitive processes the test items will demand (for example, memorization, comprehension, application, analysis), what types of items will be on the test, and, in the case of essay questions, the criteria that will be used to grade the responses.

This approach is similar to telling students that you want them to go to a particular location in a town they have never been to but that you will not supply them with directions or a map. In defense of keeping students in the dark, teachers will often say that uncertainty motivates students to study hard. Further, some argue that making the nature and content of an exam too transparent invites "teaching to the test." When you hear such reasoning, we think there are three persuasive rebuttals you can make:

1. You can argue that the first step in being a strategic learner is to identify and analyze all those variables that could positively or negatively affect one's performance. Of those, none is more important than the nature of the task for which students will be held accountable. Without this information, students must resort to guessing—the antithesis of being a strategic learner.

2. If you follow the recommendation we make in our "Approaches to Instruction" chapter and carefully align your instructional objectives with the content you cover in class and the items on your tests, you can claim to be testing what you teach rather than teaching to the test.

3. You can point out that athletic coaches and instrumental music teachers are praised for having tests that are essentially transparent. That is, the way students are expected to perform on the field, court, or stage is made clear at the beginning, and the conditions under which they learn and practice are designed to be as similar to the "test" as possible.

So take a stand against this ill-informed practice and help students be strategic learners by telling them in clear, detailed terms what they need to know. We promise that you won't be breaking any laws by doing so.

How do you react to the arguments offered here? As you form your own position on this subject, you can find more information at the Take a Stand! section of the textbook web site.

● Reciprocal teaching: students learn comprehension skills by demonstrating them to peers

effect was found in studies where students were taught a general strategy rather than specific tactics, these students nevertheless performed significantly better than students who were left to their own devices (70th percentile versus 50th percentile, respectively) (Hattie, Biggs, & Purdie, 1996).

A particularly effective strategy training program, as we mentioned earlier, is the *reciprocal teaching* (RT) program of Annemarie Palincsar and Ann Brown (1984). As the title of this program indicates, students learn certain comprehension skills by demonstrating them to each other. Palincsar and Brown trained a small group of seventh graders whose reading comprehension scores were at least two years below grade level to use the techniques of summarizing, self-questioning, clarifying, and predicting to improve their reading comprehension. They chose these four methods because students can use them to improve *and* monitor comprehension.

During the early training sessions, the teacher explained and demonstrated the four methods while reading various passages. The students were then given gradually increasing responsibility for demonstrating these techniques to their peers, with the teacher supplying prompts and corrective feedback as needed. Eventually, each student was expected to offer a good summary of a passage, pose questions about important ideas, clarify ambiguous words or phrases, and predict upcoming events, all to be done with little or no intervention by the teacher. (This approach to strategy instruction is based on Vygotsky's zone of proximal development concept that we mentioned previously in the book.)

Palincsar and Brown found that the RT program produced two general beneficial effects. First, the quality of students' summaries, questions, clarifications, and predictions improved. Early in the program, students produced overly detailed summaries and many unclear questions. But in later sessions, concise summaries and questions dealing explicitly with main ideas were the rule. For example, questions on main ideas increased from 54 percent to 70 percent. In addition, the questions were increasingly stated in paraphrase form rather than as verbatim statements from the passage. Second, the RT-trained students, who had begun the sessions well below grade level, scored as high as a group of average readers on tests of comprehension (about 75 percent correct for both groups) and much better than a group taught how to locate information that might show up in a test question (75 percent correct versus 45 percent correct).

Subsequent research on the effectiveness of RT under both controlled and realistic conditions has continued to produce positive findings across a broad age spectrum (fourth grade through college). On the average, RT students have scored at the 62nd percentile on standardized reading comprehension tests (compared to the 50th percentile for the average control student) and at the 81st percentile rank on reading comprehension tests that were created by the experimenters (Alfassi, 1998; Carter, 1997; Rosenshine & Meister, 1994a).

In the following section, we offer several Suggestions for Teaching that will help your students become more strategic and efficient learners.

Suggestions for Teaching in Your Classroom

Helping Your Students Develop Their Metacognition and Learning Strategies

1 **Demonstrate a variety of learning tactics, and allow students to practice them.**

a. Teach students how to use various forms of rehearsal and mnemonic devices.

JOURNAL ENTRY
Ways to Teach Memory Tactics

At least two reasons recommend the teaching of rehearsal. One is that maintenance rehearsal is a useful tactic for keeping a relatively small amount of information active in short-term memory. The other is that maintenance rehearsal is one of a few tactics that young children can learn to use. If you do decide to teach rehearsal, we have two suggestions. First, remind young children that rehearsal is something that learners consciously decide to do when they want to remember things. Second, remind students to rehearse no more than seven items (or chunks) at a time.

Upper elementary grade students (fourth, fifth, and sixth graders) can be taught advanced forms of maintenance rehearsal, such as cumulative rehearsal, and forms of elaborative rehearsal, such as rehearsing sets of items that form homogeneous categories. As with younger students, provide several opportunities each week to practice these skills.

As you prepare class presentations or encounter bits of information that students seem to have difficulty learning, ask yourself if a mnemonic device would be useful. You might write up a list of the devices discussed earlier and refer to it often. Part of the value of mnemonic devices is that they make learning easier. They are also fun to make up and use. Moreover, rhymes, acronyms, and acrostics can be constructed rather quickly. You might consider setting aside about thirty minutes two or three times a week to teach mnemonics. First, explain how rhyme, acronym, and acrostic mnemonics work, and then provide examples of each (see Table 8.2). Once students understand how the mnemonic is supposed to work, have them construct mnemonics to learn various facts and concepts. You might offer a prize for the most ingenious mnemonic.

JOURNAL ENTRY
Ways to Teach Comprehension
Tactics

b. Teach students how to formulate comprehension questions.

We concluded earlier that self-questioning could be an effective comprehension tactic if students were trained to write good comprehension questions and given opportunities to practice the technique. We suggest you try the following instructional sequence:

1. Discuss the purpose of student-generated questions.
2. Point out the differences between knowledge-level questions and different types of comprehension-level questions (such as analysis, synthesis, and evaluation). An excellent discussion of these types can be found in the *Taxonomy of Educational Objectives, Handbook I: Cognitive Domain* (Bloom, Englehart, Furst, Hill, & Krathwohl, 1956).
3. Explain and illustrate the kinds of responses that should be given to different types of comprehension-level questions.
4. Provide students with a sample paragraph and a set of high-level question stems. Have students formulate questions and responses either individually or in pairs.
5. Provide corrective feedback.
6. Give students short passages from which to practice.
7. Provide corrective feedback (André & Anderson, 1978/1979, King, 1994).

c. Teach students how to take notes.

JOURNAL ENTRY
Teaching Students How to Take
Notes

Despite the limitations of research on note taking, mentioned earlier, three suggestions should lead to more effective note taking.

* Provide students with clear, detailed objectives for every reading assignment. The objectives should indicate what parts of the assignment to focus on and how that material should be processed (whether memorized verbatim, reorganized and paraphrased, or integrated with earlier reading assignments).
* Inform students that note taking is an effective comprehension tactic when used appropriately. Think, for example, about a reading passage that is long and for which test items will demand analysis and synthesis of broad concepts (as in "Compare and contrast the economic, social, and political causes of World War I with those of World War II"). Tell students to concentrate on identifying main ideas and supporting details, paraphrase this information, and record similarities and differences.
* Provide students with practice and corrective feedback in answering questions that are similar to those on the criterion test.

Research findings demonstrate that note taking in one form or another is an effective tactic for improving comprehension of text and lecture material. Consequently, students should be taught the basic principles that support effective note taking.

2 **Encourage students to develop their metacognitive knowledge and skills by thinking about the various conditions that affect how they learn and remember.**

The very youngest students (through third grade) should be told periodically that such cognitive behaviors as describing, recalling, guessing, and understanding mean different things, produce different results, and vary in how well they fit a task's demands. For older elementary school and middle school students, explain the learning process, and focus on the circumstances in which different learning tactics are likely to be useful. Then have students keep a diary or log in which they note when they use learning tactics, which ones, and with what success. Look for cases where good performance corresponds to frequent reported use of tactics, and positively reinforce those individuals. Encourage greater use of tactics among students whose performance and reported use of them are below average.

Although this same technique can be used with high school and college students, they should also be made aware of the other elements that make up strategic learning. Discuss the meaning of and necessity for analyzing a learning task, developing a learning plan, using appropriate tactics, monitoring the effectiveness of the plan, and implementing whatever corrective measures might be called for.

3 **Use such effective strategy training programs as reciprocal instruction, but be prepared to make adaptations to fit your particular circumstances.**

To stimulate your thinking with additional journal prompts, see the Reflective Journal Questions on the textbook web site.

As an instructional tool, RT has at least two positive characteristics: it is defined by a set of clear components and procedures, and it has been demonstrated to improve reading comprehension in numerous studies. But as a three-year study of seventeen elementary grade teachers demonstrated, you may encounter some obstacles to implementing a textbook version of RT that will cause you to make some modifications in how you use it (Hacker & Tenent, 2002).

In the study, only three teachers implemented RT as it is described in the literature. The remaining fourteen teachers felt compelled to implement a modified form of the technique because of the problems they encountered. Here are the main obstacles encountered by many of the teachers and their solutions:

1. *Strategy use problems:* Students' use of the four comprehension techniques of RT was infrequent or of low quality. For example, most of the questions posed by students were superficial and fact-oriented, predictions were not logical, and clarifying comments were rarely made.
   Solutions: Many teachers spent a great deal of time teaching students (through explicit instruction and modeling) how to formulate high-quality questions and tried to stimulate use of clarifying by having students identify words and sentences they did not understand.

2. *Dialogue problems:* Discussions among the students of the proper use of the four reading skills and the content of the reading passages were both limited and of low quality, largely due to their limited cooperative learning skills, but also because some students were shy about speaking in front of peers.
   Solutions: Using whole-class instruction and modeling, teachers taught students how to be good listeners, take turns talking, reach a consensus about the details and meaning of a passage, and give constructive feedback to one another.

3. *Scaffolding problems:* Because of the previously mentioned problems above with strategy use and dialogue, some teachers continued to provide a high level of support to students long beyond the point suggested by the literature on reciprocal teaching. The amount and duration of scaffolding were related to the age and reading ability of the students. Younger students and those with weaker reading skills required more scaffolding.
   Solutions: Teachers provided additional scaffolding through whole-class instruction; reading partnerships; modeling; allowing students more time to learn

the elements of RT; writing predictions, clarifications, and summaries; and direct instruction of group skills.

This study points to an interesting conclusion and lesson. The conclusion is that RT may well require more training, practice, and time than the literature suggests. The lesson, which echoes a basic theme of the first chapter of this book, is that even where a solid scientific basis exists for a particular technique, an effective implementation often requires those improvisational skills referred to as the art of teaching.

The next section describes several ways that you can use computer-based technology to improve your students' information-processing skills.

TECHNOLOGY AS AN INFORMATION-PROCESSING TOOL

Although computer-based technology may have had its roots in behavioral learning theory, as you saw in the chapter on that subject, current technology is more likely to reflect an information-processing perspective. The programs and devices described in this section influence how we access, filter, represent, and evaluate knowledge. As the limitations of human memory and the difficulty of creating learning strategies have been clarified, computer-based technology has been called on to help overcome these constraints and reduce the cognitive processing burden of complex tasks. For instance, technology might help someone better grasp an idea for a musical composition, see the structure of her writing plans, or watch chemical molecules react.

In this section, we will examine technological tools that help students formulate and represent knowledge, acquire important knowledge and skills from different subject areas, provide multiple representations of knowledge, and regulate their own thinking.

Tools to Represent Knowledge

● Computer-based technology helps students organize and represent ideas and comprehend text

One of the first knowledge representation tools, the Learning Tool, was developed in the 1980s (Kozma, 1987). This program was designed to help students organize, chunk, link, and use knowledge gathered from a variety of sources. Tools for outlining and mapping out one's ideas as well as taking notes were available in the Learning Tool to augment the limitations of human working memory. Its knowledge representation tools were designed to help students represent knowledge in multiple formats, organize and restructure knowledge, activate relevant prior knowledge, and efficiently retrieve information.

A current program that performs these functions is Inspiration (**www.inspiration. com/**). Inspiration allows learners to specify ideas in a variety of formats (outline, narrative text, pictorial, symbolic) and arrange and rearrange them in spatial displays known as *concept maps*. Considerable research documents the positive effect of concept mapping on students' recall and comprehension when compared with just reading text, especially for students with low verbal ability or low prior knowledge (see, for example, Novak, 1990, 1998; O'Donnell, Dansereau, & Hall, 2002; Romance & Vitale, 1999).

Technology Tools for Writing

Because of its flexibility, technology can be used in a variety of ways to make writing less threatening and to increase both the quantity and quality of students' writing. For schools that have a set of interconnected computers (called a local area network, or LAN), a technique called an Electronic Read Around can be used. Sitting at separate computers, each student writes on a topic the teacher gives. Each student then clicks on an icon representing another student's computer, reads what that student wrote, and provides feedback in a different font at the end of the document. This process is repeated until each student has read and commented on every other student's text. Students then use the comments to revise and edit their own pieces (Strassman & D'Amore, 2002).

One of the most important parts of the writing process is the prewriting phase. This is the point when authors generate, evaluate, and organize their ideas. For novice writers, which most students are, the prospect of having to do this entirely on one's own can be quite anxiety provoking. For many students it is comforting to have a friend available as a sounding board. This can be easily accomplished on a school's LAN through the use of online synchronous chats (basically, instant messaging). A student can share ideas in real time with one or more classmates on the topic they are writing about. Not only does this give students additional opportunities to write, but the chat writing doesn't have to follow the same grammatical conventions as formal writing assignments (Strassman & D'Amore, 2002).

For teachers who would like students to do more writing on computer, a major hindrance, obviously, is too few computers. A cost-effective way to solve this problem is for schools to invest in portable writing devices, such as the AlphaSmart 3000. Because six to eight of these devices can be purchased for the cost of one desktop computer, they are used in approximately 40 percent of U.S. schools. In one Boston-area school, every fourth grader was given an AlphaSmart for use in school and at home. In comparison to the end of the fall semester, when students had to share AlphaSmarts, by the end of the spring semester students were using their AlphaSmarts twice as often, and the quality of their writing (e.g., punctuation, grammar, spelling) had improved (Russell, Bebell, Cowan, & Corbelli, 2003). (If you wonder what these products look like, check the AlphaSmart web site at **www.alphasmart.com/**.)

The World Wide Web is yet another technology resource teachers can use to make writing more attractive to students. One approach that shows promise is the use of weblogs (commonly referred to as blogs). Weblogs can take the form of a personal journal in which the writer makes periodic entries for others to read, or they can be like bulletin boards in which the online audience responds both to what the author has written and to the comments of others (Weiler, 2003). To learn more about weblogs and how to start one, visit the Weblogs in Education site (**www.schoolblogs. com/**). Two other web sites that provide opportunities for collaborative writing projects are Kidforum (**www.kidlink.org/KIDFORUM/collaborative_writing.htm**) and Through Our Eyes (**www.kidlink.org/KIDPROJ/**).

 For quick links to web sites mentioned here, use the Weblinks section on the textbook site.

Technology Tools for Reading

As with writing, electronic support systems have been used to increase students' reading skills (see, for example, Llabo, 2002). In comparison to primary grade students who read a print version of a story, students who listened to a story from a CD-ROM storybook significantly increased their sight word vocabulary, reading level, and ability to retell the story accurately and completely (Matthew, 1996; McKenna, Cowart, & Watkins, 1997). When third graders had to read a CD-ROM story themselves but were able to use such other features as clicking on words and illustrations to obtain pronunciations and definitions, their retelling scores did not differ from those of children who read a print version, but they did score significantly higher on comprehension questions (Doty, Popplewell, & Byers, 2001).

Technology Tools for Science and Math

In mathematics and science, Marcia Linn (1992) and other prominent researchers have argued that students should spend less time manually calculating and plotting data and more time using technology to summarize and interpret data, look for trends, and predict relationships. To help teachers put this philosophy into practice,

Linn and others created the Web-based Inquiry Science Environment (WISE) Project (**wise.berkeley.edu/**). Based largely on constructivist learning principles and fifteen years of classroom research, the WISE web site contains a variety of science projects that teachers can adapt to local curricula and to state and national standards. The overarching goal of the WISE learning environment is to help students make connections among science ideas rather than learn by rote isolated facts whose relevance is not understood and that are soon forgotten. For each project, students have to locate relevant information on the Web, record and organize their findings in an electronic notebook, and participate in online discussions to refine their procedures and conclusions. The Houses in the Desert project, for example, requires pairs of middle school students to design a desert house that will be comfortable to live in. Using resources available on the Web, students have to, among other things, analyze the suitability of various materials for walls, roofs, and windows and perform a heat-flow analysis. The WISE site also allows students to compare climate data in a desert with climate data from their own community (Linn & Slotta, 2000).

CD-ROMs are another useful resource for science teachers. They can supply captivating animations of abstract microscopic events, video depictions of various chemical reactions, text information about potential hazards of these experiments, sample demonstrations and laboratory activities, and encyclopedias of teaching suggestions (Brooks & Brooks, 1996). DVDs (digital video discs or digital versatile discs, depending on whose article you read) should eventually supplant CD-ROMs because of their larger capacity (anywhere from 4.7 gigabytes to 17 gigabytes versus 650 megabytes for a CD-ROM), their ability to let the user search for and play particular parts of the program, and their ability to let the user navigate through the program by clicking on buttons with a remote control unit or a mouse that connects to the DVD player (Benedetto, 2000). In effect, with CD-ROMs, DVDs, and other technology, safety is no longer the overriding concern in a chemistry class. CD-ROMs and DVDs might also be used to study such large-scale phenomena as hurricanes or winter storm patterns.

For mathematics and physics, the Calculator-Based Laboratory (CBL) from Texas Instruments provides "a data-collection system that uses probes, such as temperature, light, and voltage probes, to gather data into a graphing calculator" (Nicol, 1997, p. 86). The current version is the CBL 2. CBLs convert information from sensors and probes into data that can be understood and graphed by the calculator. Students taking a math class might use this tool to represent and manipulate quadratic equations in algebra, visualize statistics and other information in geometry classes, and better understand derivatives and inequalities in calculus (Engebretsen, 1997; O'Neal, 2001).

Math teachers can also use CD-ROMs and the Web to help students understand the connections among math topics and to other disciplines. For example, data from the web site of the National Center for Health Statistics (**www.cdc.gov/nchs/**) on the number of births in the United States for various time periods can be used to teach such concepts as absolute and relative yearly increases and decreases. These same data can also be used to analyze the relationship between birthrates and other societal trends, such as immigration patterns. Connections between oscillating functions in math and the tides, planetary movements, and average monthly temperatures can be made with data from the web sites of the National Oceanic and Atmospheric Administration (**www.noaa.gov**) and the National Geophysical Data Center (**www.ngdc.noaa.gov**). These relationships can be made more concrete, and hence more meaningful, by using graphing calculators and spreadsheets to create graphic representations (Drier, Dawson, & Garofalo, 1999).

Technology Tools for Art and Music

As you may be aware, computer tools are also being used in the fine and performing arts. Art education, for instance, benefits from electronic tools like the draw and paint modules of AppleWorks and Microsoft Works that quickly erase or alter ideas.

Students can use these tools to mimic the branching, spiraling, and exploding structures of nature (as seen, for example, in trees, vines, and flowers) (Lach et al., 2003), and they can create abstract patterns by repeating, changing the horizontal and vertical orientation, and changing the alignment of a basic pattern (Yoerg, 2002). With these tools, students can also draw objects in two-point perspective (Patterson, 2002) and create stylized portraits by using shadows, contour lines, stippling, and cross-hatching (Mathes, 2002).

For the music classroom, there are tools such as digital oscilloscopes that help students understand relationships between pitch and wavelength. In addition, CD technology can be used to present graphical representations of notes as they are played, sections of which can be saved and compared to other verses of the same song or to other songs, thereby helping students understand themes and patterns in music. Moreover, computer tools such as a Musical Instrument Digital Interface (MIDI) allow students to compose at the keyboard, play a musical instrument and record it on a computer, and play one part of a multi-instrument piece while the program plays the other instruments (Peters, 2001; Reninger, 2000). Students can explore concepts of pitch, duration, sound combination, repetition, and melody and engage in the process of musical thinking.

Multimedia Tools

As mentioned in previous chapters, multimedia encyclopedias, databases, and libraries provide students with a wide variety of information resources. Multimedia tools offer multiple views (text, photographs, digitized video, animation, sound) on difficult concepts that can enrich student understanding of the topic. The use of multimedia tools is related to such information-processing concepts as meaningful learning, the dual coding of information, the use of visual imagery, and elaborative rehearsal (Mayer & Moreno, 2002). Like the mind, multimedia tools provide more than one way to retrieve or visit information; the richer or more dense the network or web of connections, the more likely one will comprehend the meaning.

Hypermedia Tools

Hypermedia technology exists when multimedia information can be nonsequentially accessed, examined, and constructed by users, thereby enabling them to move from one information resource to another while controlling which options to take (Grabe & Grabe, 2004). There are clear advantages to hypermedia, such as the richness of the network of ideas, the compact storage of information, the rapid nonlinear access to information, the flexible use of information, and learner control over the system. Not surprisingly, it has been suggested that hypermedia tools radically alter the way people read, write, compute, and perhaps even think (Yang, 2001).

A hypermedia science program that students are likely to find attractive is *Scholastic's The Magic School Bus Explores in the Age of the Dinosaurs*. Designed for first through fifth graders, the program allows students to explore multiple locations in different parts of the world (for example, Argentina, Arizona, Colorado, Tanzania, Mongolia) and in three prehistoric time periods (Triassic, Jurassic, and Cretaceous). The program offers a dozen games and activities that involve dinosaurs.

Research on Multimedia and Hypermedia Technology   One of the features of multimedia programs that supposedly contributes to their effectiveness as a learning tool is the use of animation. Drawing from the numerous studies that he and his associates have conducted on this topic, Richard Mayer (Mayer & Moreno, 2002) concludes that animation in multimedia programs produces gains in learning when on-screen text is presented next to the animation that it describes rather than somewhere else on the screen. Animation is even more effective when it is accompanied

● Multimedia and hypermedia programs that make appropriate use of animation and interactivity improve learning

by simultaneous, conversational narration rather than by text. Extraneous words, sounds, and video should be excluded. You can put these findings to practical use by using them to evaluate multimedia programs your school district already owns or is considering buying.

Another attractive feature of many multimedia and hypermedia programs is inter-activity. Interactive programs let children decide when to move to the next screen and the sequence in which they view information. Although many pro and con claims are made for interactivity, research evidence on its effects is just starting to appear.

In one study (Ricci & Beal, 2002), a group of first-grade children listened to and watched the story of the ugly duckling on a computer. They could move to the next page in the story at will by clicking on an arrow or produce additional animation and sound effects by clicking on any or all of the computer screen's "hotspots." They could, for example, click on a pond reed and see costumed ants march across the foreground accompanied by music. A second group of students passively watched and listened to the story as it appeared on the screen. A third group saw and heard on their own computer screens whatever was being produced by the children in the interactive group. A fourth group sat in front of a darkened computer screen and just listened to the story. Children in the first three groups scored higher than children in the fourth group on memory for story detail, comprehension, and ability to draw inferences. These results demonstrated that the interactivity feature had no detrimental effect on the story memory or inferential reasoning of children in group one despite the fact that some of them clicked on dozens of hotspots over the course of the story.

Effects of Technology on Metacognition

When students select topics and associated terms for a Web search and then evaluate the results, they are making decisions about what information to read, thinking about knowledge interrelationships, and engaging in extensive self-questioning and note taking (Gunn & Hepburn, 2003; Hoffman, Wu, Krajcik, & Soloway, 2003; MaKinster, Beghetto, & Plucker, 2002). When they create databases of related ideas or link information in multiple formats, they are making decisions and elaboratively encoding the information. These are important skills. But can computer-based instructional technology help students develop their metacognitive skills in addition to helping them learn content?

To answer this question, tools such as LOGO have been extensively explored for what they can offer in terms of student planning, error detection, comprehension monitoring, and other metacognitive skills. LOGO is a simple computer programming language that was designed to foster children's higher-order thinking and mathematical reasoning skills. Although initial studies were inconclusive, more research has found increases in metacognitive performance among elementary students when instructors mediate the learning environment (Lehrer, Lee & Jeong, 1999) or when students work in pairs or small groups (Clements & Nastasi, 1999). One study shows that simply having computers in the home or having access to them can promote metacognitive changes in the minds of preschool children (Fletcher-Flinn & Suddendorf, 1996). However, it is starting to become clear that computer environments *combined with* teacher guidance and explicit metacognitive training to plan, monitor, and evaluate learning seem to be the most effective means of developing children's self-regulatory skills and problem-solving strategies.

 To review this chapter, see the ACE practice tests and PowerPoint slides on the textbook web site.

Resources for Further Investigation

● The Nature of Information-Processing Theory

For more on information-processing theory and how it relates to teaching and learning, read Chapter 4 of *Learning Theories: An Educational Perspective* (4th ed., 2004), by Dale Schunk, and Chapters 2–5 of *Cognitive Psychology and Instruction* (4th ed., 2004), by Roger Bruning, Gregory Schraw, Monica Norby, and Royce Ronning.

Another source of information is *The Cognitive Psychology of School Learning* (1993), by Ellen Gagné, Carol Walker Yekovich, and Frank Yekovich. The goal of these authors is to help educators use information-processing theory and research to answer the questions, "What shall we teach?" and "How shall we teach?" Chapters 12 through 15 describe how to use this knowledge base to teach reading, writing, mathematics, and science, respectively.

● Memory Structures and Processes

Norman Spear and David Riccio describe various aspects of memory structures and processes in *Memory: Phenomena and Principles* (1994). As the title suggests, Alan Searleman and Douglas Herrmann cover the same ground, plus such additional topics as the role of social factors in memory, individual differences in memory, and changes in memory ability, in *Memory from a Broader Perspective* (1994). Alan Baddeley provides a basic account of memory phenomena, including a chapter on improving your memory, in *Essentials of Human Memory* (1999).

● Metacognition

If you would like to know more about the nature of metacognition and its role in learning and memory, take a look at *Applied Metacognition* (2002), edited by Timothy Perfect and Bennett Schwartz, and *Metacognition: Process, Function, and Use* (2002), edited by Patrick Chambres, Marie Izaute, and Pierre-Jean Marescaux. If teaching reading is going to be one of your future responsibilities, you may glean some useful ideas about the role of metacognition in reading from "Metacognition and Self-Regulated Comprehension," a chapter by Michael Pressley in *What Research Has to Say About Reading Instruction* (2002), edited by Alan Farstrup and S. Jay Samuels.

● Learning Tactics and Strategies

One of the most popular (and useful) memory improvement books available is *The Memory Book* (1974), by Harry Lorayne and Jerry Lucas. They explain why and how you should think up ridiculous associations, offer suggestions for using substitute words, provide techniques for learning foreign and English vocabulary, and describe ways to remember names and faces.

Drawing on research from the past twenty-five years, Janice Almasi examines the role of strategic processes in reading, explains why many students are not strategic readers, and describes how to design strategy instruction that enhances comprehension in *Teaching Strategic Processes in Reading* (2003).

Although written principally for college students and their instructors, *Learning to Learn: Making the Transition from Student to Life-Long Learner* (1998), by Kenneth A. Kiewra and Nelson F. DuBois, offers much of value to high school students and their teachers.

● Individual Differences in Memory

One of the most striking accounts of supernormal memory is provided by Alexander Luria, *The Mind of a Mnemonist: A Little Book About a Vast Memory* (1968). Luria describes his experiments and experiences over a period of almost thirty years with the man he refers to as S, who could recall nonsense material he had not seen for fifteen years. Charles Thompson, Thaddeus Cowan, and Jerome Frieman describe in *Memory Search by a Memorist* (1993) a series of studies done with Rajan Mahadevan, who earned a place in the *Guinness Book of World Records* by memorizing the first 31,811 digits of pi. Additional articles about people with unusually proficient memory capability can be found in *Memory Observed* (1982), edited by Ulric Neisser.

Robert Kail describes memory differences among normal children, as well as differences between normal and mentally retarded children in *The Development of Memory in Children* (1990). Also briefly discussed is the phenomenon of the idiot savants—individuals who are below average on all measures of ability except one, in which they far surpass almost all other individuals—and the reliability of children's eyewitness testimony. Leon Miller describes musical savants, individuals with mental retardation, who can perfectly reproduce musical passages on an instrument after one hearing, in *Musical Savants: Exceptional Skill in the Mentally Retarded* (1989).

Summary

1. Information-processing theory attempts to explain how individuals acquire, store, recall, and use information.

2. A popular model of information processing is composed of three memory stores and a set of control processes that determine the flow of information from one memory store to another. The memory stores are the sensory register, short-term memory, and long-term memory. The control processes are recognition, attention, maintenance rehearsal, elaborative rehearsal, and retrieval.

3. The sensory register holds information in its original form for one to three seconds, during which time we may recognize and attend to it further.

4. Recognition involves noticing key features of a stimulus and integrating those features with relevant information from long-term memory.

5. Attention is a selective focusing on a portion of the information in the sensory register. Information from long-term memory influences what we focus on.

6. Short-term memory holds about seven bits of information for about twenty seconds (in the absence of rehearsal). It is often called working memory because it is where various encoding, organizational, and retrieval processes occur. Working memory appears to be strongly related to proficiency of learning.

7. Information can be held in short-term memory indefinitely through the use of maintenance rehearsal, which is rote repetition of information.

8. Information is transferred from short-term memory to long-term memory by the linking of the new information to related information in long-term memory. This process is called elaborative rehearsal.

9. Elaborative rehearsal is based partly on organization. This involves grouping together, or chunking, items of information that share some important characteristic.

10. Elaborative rehearsal is also based on meaningfulness. Meaningful learning occurs when new information that is clearly written and logically organized is consciously related to information the learner currently has stored in long-term memory.

11. Long-term memory is thought by some psychologists to be an unlimited storehouse of information from which nothing is ever lost.

12. Many psychologists believe the information in long-term memory is organized in the form of schemata. A schema is a generalized abstract structure of information. When schemata are absent or crudely formed, learning and recall problems occur.

13. Contrary to popular belief, students remember much of the information they learn in school, especially if it was well learned to start with and if it was learned in a meaningful fashion.

14. Metacognition refers to any knowledge an individual has about how humans think and how those processes can be used to achieve learning goals.

15. Metacognition increases gradually with experience. This helps explain why junior high and high school students are more flexible and effective learners than primary grade students.

16. A learning strategy is a general plan that specifies the resources one will use, when they will be used, and how one will use them to achieve a learning goal.

17. Most students do not use strategic learning skills either systematically or consistently.

18. A learning tactic is a specific technique one uses to help accomplish an immediate task-related objective.

19. Most teachers provide little or no direct instruction to students in the formulation and use of strategies and tactics.

20. Learning tactics can be classified as memory directed or comprehension directed. The former are used when accurate storage and retrieval of information are important. The latter are used when comprehension of ideas is important.

21. Two types of memory-directed tactics are rehearsal and mnemonic devices. Because most forms of rehearsal involve little or no encoding of information, they are not very effective memory tactics. Because mnemonic devices organize information and provide built-in retrieval cues, they are effective memory tactics.

22. Popular mnemonic devices include rhymes, acronyms, acrostics, the loci method, and the keyword method.

23. Two effective comprehension tactics are self-questioning and note taking.

24. The components of a learning strategy are metacognition, analysis, planning, implementation, monitoring, and modification.

25. A new learning strategy must be created every time a learner's circumstances change. Middle and high school students are capable of learning how to formulate basic strategies, but teachers need to help students formulate good strategies by providing them with clear and useful information about the nature and demands of tests.

26. Learning strategy training raises the reading comprehension scores of both average and below-average readers.

27. Contemporary computer-based technology supports information processing by helping students to organize and mentally represent ideas, write more clearly, better comprehend text, interpret scientific and mathematical data, and understand musical patterns.

Key Terms

information-processing theory *(237)*
sensory register (SR) *(240)*
recognition *(240)*
attention *(241)*
short-term memory (STM) *(241)*
maintenance rehearsal *(242)*

elaborative rehearsal *(242)*
meaningful learning *(244)*
dual coding theory *(245)*
long-term memory (LTM) *(246)*
schemata *(247)*
metacognition *(249)*

distributed practice *(253)*
serial position effect *(253)*
massed practice *(253)*
learning strategy *(257)*
learning tactic *(257)*
mnemonic device *(258)*

9

Social Cognitive Theory

In the last two chapters, we have examined two very different descriptions of how learning occurs. Operant conditioning focuses exclusively on the role of observable, external events on learning new behaviors and strengthening or weakening existing ones. According to this theory, people are exposed to stimuli, they make some sort of response, and the reinforcing or punishing consequences that do or do not follow influence the probability that those responses will be made again. Consequently, operant conditioning requires that people make observable responses in order for others to conclude that learning has occurred. The strength of operant conditioning is the insight it provides about how environmental consequences affect learning. Its main weakness is that it offers no insights into what people do with that information.

Information-processing theory, on the other hand, focuses almost exclusively on the role of internal processes in learning. In this view, people are exposed to stimuli, and whether and how they attend to, encode, store, and retrieve that information influences what they know and can do. But information-processing theory has very little to say about how the social setting in which behavior occurs influences what people learn.

This chapter will examine a third approach that shares common ground with operant conditioning and information-processing theory but goes beyond both. Known initially as *social learning theory* and more recently as **social cognitive theory,** this explanation of learning was based on the premise that neither spontaneous behavior nor reinforcement was necessary for learning to occur. New behaviors could also be learned by observing and imitating a model. The current version of social cognitive theory incorporates elements of both operant conditioning and information processing, and it emphasizes how behavioral and personal factors interact with the social setting in which behavior occurs.

Albert Bandura (1986, 1997, 2001, 2002) is generally considered to be the driving force behind social cognitive theory. His goal is to explain how learning results from interactions among three factors: (1) personal characteristics, such as the various cognitive processes covered in the chapter on information processing as well as self-perceptions and emotional states; (2) behavioral patterns, and (3) the social environment, such as interactions with others. Bandura calls the process of interaction among these three elements **triadic reciprocal causation.** This impressive-sounding mouthful is not as difficult as it sounds. *Triadic* simply means having three elements, and *reciprocal* indicates that the elements influence one another. The entire term means that one's internal processes, behavior, and social environ-ment (the "triadic" part of the term) can affect one an-other (the "reciprocal" part) to produce learning (the "causation" part). To simplify our writing and your read-ing, we will refer to Bandura's triadic reciprocal causa-tion model as the triadic model.

Bandura and others (e.g., Schunk, 1998, 2000; Zimmer-man, 1990, 2000) are particularly interested in using so-cial cognitive theory to describe how people become *self-controlled* and *self-regulated* learners. Consequently, we'll begin our exploration of social cognitive theory by taking a more detailed look at the triadic model. Then we'll explain the meaning of and differences between self-control and self-regulation.

THE TRIADIC RECIPROCAL CAUSATION MODEL

To frame your thinking about this chapter, see the Chapter Themes on the textbook web site, accessible from **http://education.college.hmco. com/students.**

● Triadic reciprocal causation model: behavior is the result of interactions among personal characteristics, behavior, environmental factors

The triadic model holds that a person's behavior is always the result of interactions among personal characteristics, behavioral patterns, and environmental factors. Bandura and others describe these three elements as follows:

- *Personal characteristics* include mental and emotional factors such as goals and anxiety. They also include metacognitive knowledge, which (as you learned in the chapter on information-processing theory) refers to understanding of one's own cognitive processes, such as knowledge of the role of analysis, planning, and monitoring in learning. Personal characteristics further include *self-efficacy*, that is, be-liefs about one's ability to successfully carry out particular tasks. Self-efficacy is a concept we introduced in the chapter on age-level characteristics, and a later section of this chapter will discuss it in detail.
- *Behavioral patterns* include self-observation (such as using personal journals to note how various factors influence learning, motivation, and self-efficacy); self-evaluation; making changes in behavior to overcome or reduce perceptions of low self-efficacy, anxiety, and ineffective learning strategies; and creating productive study environments.
- *Environmental factors* refer to an individual's social and physical environment. They include such things as the nature of a task, reinforcing and punishing consequences, explanations and modeling of various skills by others, and verbal persuasion to exhibit particular behaviors.

As shown in Figure 9.1, Bandura portrays these relationships in a triangular arrangement with bidirectional arrows (Bandura, 1997; Zimmerman, 1990).

To grasp the interactive nature of the triadic model, consider the following three examples. The components of the model are represented by the letter *P* for personal characteristic, *B* for behavioral pattern, or *E* for environmental factor. In each example, notice how the elements influence one another.

1. Imagine a well-informed, outgoing individual who is liked and respected by many people and works in the sales department of a corporation. Because of his superior interpersonal skills, he considers running for city council. This person is likely to have a high level of self-efficacy for interpersonal relationships (P), which leads to a high level of successful sales (B) and the decision to campaign for public office (B). But it is also likely that this person's increasing proficiency at persuading others to adopt his point of view (B), the availability of successful

277

Figure 9.1 The Triadic Reciprocal Causation Model

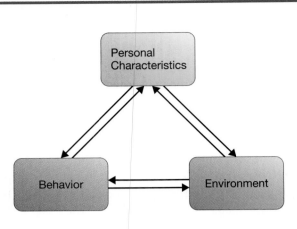

SOURCE: Bandura (1997).

models with whom the person identifies (E), and praise from other people regarding the person's skill at interpersonal relationships (E) will strengthen the person's perceived self-efficacy (P).

2. A student's high self-efficacy for mathematical problem solving (P) leads the student to work on mathematical problems (B) rather than painting a picture. The high self-efficacy also makes the student likely to persist in the face of difficulty (B). At the same time, the act of successfully working on mathematical tasks (B) raises the student's self-efficacy for solving mathematical problems (P).

3. A teacher introduces a new science topic by describing the theory and research that contributed to the current state of knowledge in this area (B). But when students show signs of confusion or boredom (E), thereby making the teacher uncomfortable and dissatisfied (P), the teacher tries a different approach (B).

As you can see, Bandura's social cognitive view of learning is broader than either Skinner's operant conditioning conceptualization or information-processing theory. Not only does Bandura acknowledge the role of internal cognitive and affective factors as well as a person's behavior in learning, but he also includes the impact of the social environment.

Bear in mind, however, that things do not operate as simply as Figure 9.1 suggests. As the activity and setting change, the strength of certain P-B-E connections can be expected to change. If, for example, you happen to be in a setting, like school, where rules and regulations place limits on behavior, the behavioral aspect of the model is likely to have less impact than if you are allowed more freedom of expression. Also, some relationships may be stronger than others at particular points in time (Schunk, 1998; Zimmerman, 1990).

Social cognitive theory assumes that people, and not environmental forces, are the predominant cause of their own behavior. Bandura uses the term **personal agency** to refer to the potential control we have over our own behavior, and he believes that our capacity for personal agency grows out of our skills of self-control and self-regulation.

SELF-CONTROL, SELF-REGULATION, AND SELF-EFFICACY

● Self-control: controlling one's behaviors in a particular setting in the absence of reinforcement or punishment

Self-control is the ability to control one's actions in the absence of external reinforcement or punishment. Some examples of self-control are inhibiting inappropriate behavior, rewarding oneself for acceptable behavior, and choosing to wait longer for

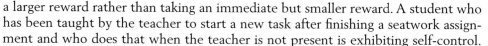

a larger reward rather than taking an immediate but smaller reward. A student who has been taught by the teacher to start a new task after finishing a seatwork assignment and who does that when the teacher is not present is exhibiting self-control.

● Self-regulation: consistently using self-control skills in new situations

Self-regulation involves the consistent and appropriate application of self-control skills to new situations. It is the product of interactions among the three components that make up Bandura's triadic model: personal characteristics, behavioral patterns, and environmental factors. Self-regulating individuals set their own performance standards, evaluate the quality of their performance, and reinforce themselves when their performance meets or exceeds their internal standards (Zimmerman, 1990, 2000). A teacher who modifies a particular day's lesson plan to capitalize on students' interest in a major news story, monitors students' reaction to the new lesson, compares her students' and her own performance against an internal standard, and rewards herself if she feels that standard has been met, is illustrating the essence of self-regulation.

Self-regulation is both a cyclical and a dynamic process. It is cyclical because the results of prior performance are used to guide and refine current efforts. It is dynamic because personal, behavioral, and environmental factors are constantly changing. Consequently, skilled self-regulated learners monitor their use of cognitive processes, their affective states, their environmental conditions, and the quality of their performance and make whatever modifications are called for in order to maximize the probability of achieving their goal (Zimmerman, 2000). We will examine the self-regulation cycle in more detail later in this chapter.

Self-regulation is a critically important capability for students to acquire for at least three reasons:

● Self-regulation is important because students are expected to become increasingly independent learners as they progress through school

1. As students get older, and especially when they get into the middle and high school grades, they are expected to assume greater responsibility for their learning than was the case in earlier grades, and so they receive less prompting and guidance from teachers and parents.

2. As students move through the primary, elementary, middle school, and high school grades, they have to learn and be tested over increasingly larger amounts of more complex material. With less parental and teacher supervision, the temptation to put studying off or do it superficially increases. Unfortunately, the damaging long-term consequences of poorly regulated academic behavior (low grades and diminished opportunities for higher education and employment) are not immediately apparent.

3. Because of the rapid pace of change in today's world, individuals increasingly need to be self-directed, autonomous learners not just during their school years, but over their lifetime (Zimmerman, 1990, 2002).

Should the development of self-regulated learning skills be left to parents and out-of-school experiences, or should this be a primary goal of our education system? If the latter, when should it begin?

Although the skills of self-control and self-regulation are important to academic success, some students are more successful than others in acquiring and using them. The characteristic that is most strongly related to and best explains differences in self-regulation is perceived self-efficacy, a concept we mentioned several times earlier in this chapter. In the next section, we further describe self-efficacy and its relationship to self-regulation.

The Role of Self-Efficacy in Self-Regulation

● Self-efficacy: how capable one feels to handle particular kinds of tasks

Unlike self-esteem, which we described in an earlier chapter as the overall, or global, evaluation that people make of themselves, **self-efficacy** refers to how capable or prepared we believe we are for handling particular kinds of tasks (Bandura, 1997, 2001, 2002). For example, a student may have a high level of self-efficacy for mathematical reasoning—a feeling that she can master any math task she might encounter in a particular course—but have a low level of self-efficacy for critical analysis of English literature.

Self-efficacy beliefs occupy a central role in social cognitive theory because of their widespread effects. They help influence whether people think optimistically or pessimistically, act in ways that are beneficial or detrimental to achieving goals, approach or avoid tasks, engage tasks with a high or low level of motivation, persevere for a short or lengthy period of time when tasks are difficult, and are motivated or demoralized by failure.

Bandura argues that self-efficacy is more influential than expected rewards or punishments or actual skills because it is based on a belief that one can or cannot produce the behaviors that are required to bring about a particular outcome. Students with the same level of mathematical skill may, for example, have different attitudes about mathematics and perform differently on tests of mathematical problem solving because of differences in their self-efficacy beliefs (Bandura, 2001; Zimmerman, 1990).

● Self-efficacy beliefs influence use of self-regulating skills

Students who believe they are capable of successfully performing a task are more likely than students with low levels of self-efficacy to use such self-regulating skills as concentrating on the task, creating strategies, using appropriate tactics, managing time effectively, monitoring their own performance, and making whatever adjustments are necessary to improve their future learning efforts. By contrast, students who do not believe they have the cognitive skills to cope with the demands of a particular subject are unlikely to do much serious reading or thinking about the subject or to spend much time preparing for upcoming tests. Such students are often referred to as lazy, inattentive, lacking initiative, and dependent on others. They often find themselves in a vicious circle as their avoidance of challenging tasks and dependence on others reduces their chances for developing self-regulation skills and a strong sense of self-efficacy (Bandura, 1997; Schunk, 1998).

Self-efficacy can be affected by one or more of several factors and, in turn, can affect one or more of several important self-regulatory behaviors (see Figure 9.2).

Factors That Affect Self-Efficacy   Four factors that affect self-efficacy are shown on the "Antecedents" side of Figure 9.2.

Figure 9.2 Antecedents and Effects of Self-Efficacy

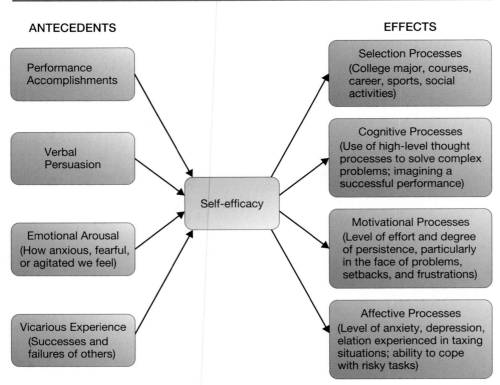

● Self-efficacy influenced by past performance, verbal persuasion, emotions, observing models

1. *Performance accomplishments.* One obvious way in which we develop a sense of what we can and cannot do in various areas is by thinking about how well we have performed in the past on a given task or a set of closely related tasks. If, for example, my friends are always reluctant to have me on their team for neighborhood baseball games, and if I strike out or ground out far more often than I hit safely, I will probably conclude that I just do not have whatever skills it takes to be a competitive baseball player. Conversely, if my personal history of performance in school includes mostly grades of A and consistent rank among the top ten students, my sense of academic self-efficacy is likely to be quite high.

2. *Verbal persuasion.* A second source of influence mentioned by Bandura—verbal persuasion—is also fairly obvious. We frequently try to convince a child, student, relative, spouse, friend, or coworker that he or she has the ability to perform some task at an acceptable level. Perhaps you can recall feeling somewhat more confident about handling some task (like college classes) after having several family members and friends express their confidence in your ability.

3. *Emotional arousal.* A third source of influence is more subtle. It is the emotions we feel as we prepare to engage in a task. Individuals with low self-efficacy for science may become anxious, fearful, or restless prior to attending chemistry class or to taking an exam in physics. Those with high self-efficacy may feel assured, comfortable, and eager to display what they have learned. Some individuals are acutely aware of these emotional states, and their emotions become a cause as well as a result of their high or low self-efficacy.

4. *Vicarious experience.* Finally, our sense of self-efficacy may be influenced by observing the successes and failures of individuals with whom we identify. This is what Bandura refers to as vicarious experience. If I take note of the fact that a sibling or neighborhood friend who is like me in many respects but is a year older has successfully adjusted to high school, I may feel more optimistic about my own adjustment the following year. We will have more to say a bit later in this chapter about the role of observing and imitating a model.

On the basis of your own experience, do you agree that personal experience is the most important factor affecting self-efficacy? What steps can you take to raise the probability that your students will experience more successes than failures?

Of these four factors, personal accomplishment is the most important because it carries the greatest weight. As important as it is to feel calm and be free of crippling fear or anxiety; to have parents, peers, and teachers express their confidence in us; and to have successful models to observe, actual failures are likely to override the other influences. In other words, our feelings, the comments of others, and the actions of models need to be confirmed by our own performance if they are to be effective contributors to self-efficacy.

Types of Behaviors Affected by Self-Efficacy Bandura has identified four types of behaviors that are at least partly influenced by an individual's level of self-efficacy. These are shown on the "Effects" side of Figure 9.2.

● Self-efficacy influences goals and activities, cognitive processes, perseverance, emotions

1. *Selection processes.* By the term *selection processes*, we mean the way the person goes about selecting goals and activities. Individuals with a strong sense of self-efficacy, particularly if it extends over several areas, are more likely than others to consider a variety of goals and participate in a variety of activities. They may, for example, think about a wide range of career options, explore several majors while in college, take a variety of courses, participate in different sporting activities, engage in different types of social activities, and have a wide circle of friends.

2. *Cognitive processes.* High self-efficacy individuals, compared with their low self-efficacy peers, tend to use higher-level thought processes (such as analysis, synthesis, and evaluation) to solve complex problems. Thus, in preparing a classroom report or a paper, low self-efficacy students may do little more than repeat a set of facts found in various sources; often this behavior stems from their belief that they are not capable of more. In contrast, high self-efficacy students often discuss similarities and differences, inconsistencies and contradictions, and make evaluations

A person's self-efficacy for a particular task is influenced primarily by past performance, but also by encouragement from others, emotional reactions, and observing others.

about the validity and usefulness of the information they have found. Another cognitive difference is that high self-efficacy people are more likely to visualize themselves being successful at some challenging task, whereas low self-efficacy individuals are more likely to imagine disaster. This leads to differences in the next category of behaviors—motivation.

3. *Motivational processes.* Those who rate their capabilities as higher than average can be expected to work harder and longer to achieve a goal than those who feel less capable. This difference should be particularly noticeable when individuals experience frustrations (poor-quality instruction, for example), problems (coursework being more difficult than anticipated), and setbacks (a serious illness).

4. *Affective processes.* Finally, when faced with a challenging task, the high self-efficacy individual is more likely to experience excitement, curiosity, and an eagerness to get started rather than the sense of anxiety, depression, and impending disaster that many low self-efficacy individuals feel.

Before leaving this discussion of self-efficacy, we would like to make one last point about its role in self-regulated behavior. As important as self-efficacy is, you should realize that other factors play a role as well. In addition to feeling capable of successfully completing a particular task, students also need to possess basic knowledge and skills, anticipate that their efforts will be appropriately rewarded, and value the knowledge, skill, or activity they have been asked to learn or complete (Schunk, 1998).

As we noted earlier, students (as well as adults) vary in how extensively and how well they regulate their thoughts, feelings, and behavior as they pursue goals. To help students with poorly developed self-regulation skills become better learners, you need to know what a well-formed self-regulatory system includes. In the next section we describe a system of self-regulatory processes that has been proposed by Barry Zimmerman (2000, 2002), a leading social cognitive theorist and researcher.

The Components of a Self-Regulatory System

Self-regulatory processes and their related beliefs can be grouped into one of three categories, each of which comes into play at different points in time in the course of pursuing a goal (see Figure 9.3). First are the *forethought* processes and self-beliefs that occur prior to beginning a task. Next are the *performance* processes that are activated during the course of a task. Third are the *self-reflection* processes that occur after a response or series of responses have been made. Because self-reflection influences subsequent forethought processes, this system is cyclical in nature. Consequently, Zimmerman (2000, 2002) refers to these processes as occurring in phases.

As you know from earlier chapters, children acquire their cognitive skills gradually. So in addition to describing the main self-regulatory processes that come into play at each phase, we will also note the developmental limitations you can expect to see if you teach primary grade children.

Forethought Phase The forethought phase is subdivided into the categories of task analysis and self-motivational beliefs. Task analysis includes the self-regulatory processes of *goal setting* and *strategic planning*. When setting goals, self-regulated learners do not just specify one or more long-term goals, especially those that take time to achieve. Instead, for each long-term goal they establish a series of near-term subgoals that are achievable and provide evidence of progress. For example, to accomplish the long-term goal of achieving a grade of A in physics, a self-regulating student will set subgoals that pertain to number of hours spent per week studying, working sample problems at the end of the textbook chapter, doing homework as accurately as possible, and seeking help when problems arise. As we pointed out in the chapter on information-processing theory, planning is a necessary self-regulatory skill because the circumstances under which one learns are constantly changing. Thus, self-regulated learners constantly assess themselves and the nature and demands of a learning task in order to select those methods that are most likely to lead to goal attainment.

- Self-regulated learners set goals, create plans to achieve those goals

As we also pointed out in the information-processing chapter, possessing these skills is of little value if one isn't motivated to use them. This is why the self-motivational beliefs category is part of this phase. Included here are self-efficacy beliefs, outcome expectations, intrinsic interest, and goal orientation. In the context of this discussion, self-efficacy pertains to how capable people believe themselves to be about using self-regulatory processes. Outcome expectations refer to what one believes will be the consequences of achieving a goal (such as praise, prestige, increased responsibility). Intrinsic interest can maintain motivation for self-regulated learning in situations where external rewards are either unavailable or unattractive. Goal orientations (which we discuss in the chapter on motivation) can be learning oriented or

Figure 9.3 Phases and Categories of the Self-Regulation Cycle

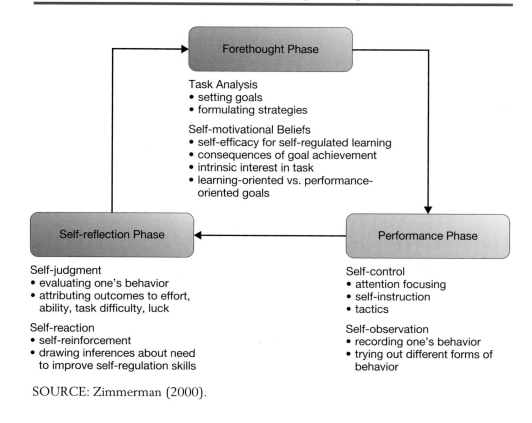

Forethought Phase

Task Analysis
- setting goals
- formulating strategies

Self-motivational Beliefs
- self-efficacy for self-regulated learning
- consequences of goal achievement
- intrinsic interest in task
- learning-oriented vs. performance-oriented goals

Self-reflection Phase

Self-judgment
- evaluating one's behavior
- attributing outcomes to effort, ability, task difficulty, luck

Self-reaction
- self-reinforcement
- drawing inferences about need to improve self-regulation skills

Performance Phase

Self-control
- attention focusing
- self-instruction
- tactics

Self-observation
- recording one's behavior
- trying out different forms of behavior

SOURCE: Zimmerman (2000).

performance oriented. Individuals who have a learning orientation are interested in learning primarily for its internal rewards (better understanding of the world in which one lives, increased competence) and are more apt to be motivated to use self-regulation processes than are performance-oriented individuals whose goal is to achieve a higher score or grade than others.

Developmental Limitations   In the forethought phase, young children are likely to be more limited than older children in their ability to do the following:

- Attend to a model, such as a teacher, for long periods of time
- Distinguish relevant model behaviors and verbalizations from less relevant ones
- Encode a model's behavior as generalized verbal guidelines
- Formulate and maintain well-defined long-term goals (Schunk, 2001

Performance Phase   This phase contains several self-regulatory processes, and again they divide into two categories: the self-control category and the self-observation category. Self-control processes help learners focus on the task and meaningfully process the information they are trying to learn. *Attention focusing*, for example, involves ignoring distractions, executing a task at a slower than normal pace, and not thinking about prior mistakes or failed efforts. *Self-instruction* involves describing to oneself, either silently or out loud, how to carry out the steps of a task or process. *Tactics* (or *task strategies*) include the many memory-directed and comprehension-directed techniques that we discussed in the chapter on information-processing theory.

○ Self-regulated learners focus on task, process information meaningfully, self-monitor

Self-observation processes, also known as self-monitoring, increase awareness of one's performance and the conditions that affect it. These processes include *self-recording* and *self-experimentation*. Two frequently used methods of self-recording are written journals and logbooks. When done consistently, self-recording can reveal desirable and undesirable behavioral patterns that correspond to particular environmental conditions, such as putting off homework or studying for an exam in favor of socializing with friends. The results of self-recording can lead learners to self-experimentation, or trying out different forms of behavior. For instance, a student might change the time and place of study or the techniques that are used to see whether these changes produce better results.

Developmental Limitations   For the performance phase, you can expect primary grade children to be limited in their ability to do the following:

- Ignore both external and internal distractions (such as self-doubts and thoughts of prior difficulties)
- Perform the steps of a task more slowly and deliberately in order to avoid making mistakes
- Provide themselves with verbal reminders of the steps needed to carry out a task
- Select appropriate tactics for a particular task (Schunk, 2001)

Self-Reflection Phase   As with the first two phases, this phase is composed of two categories, self-judgment and self-reaction, each of which involves two self-regulatory processes.

○ Self-regulated learners evaluate their performance, make appropriate attributions for success and failure, reinforce themselves

The first of the self-judgment processes is *self-evaluation*. Whenever we label our performance as good or bad, acceptable or unacceptable, satisfactory or unsatisfactory, we are engaging in self-evaluation. There are basically four ways in which students can make these self-evaluative judgments:

1. *Students can adopt what is called a mastery criterion.* This system uses a graded scale that was created by someone with extensive knowledge about the range of performances for that skill or topic; the scale ranges from novice to expert. By using a mastery criterion, learners know where they stand with respect to an absolute standard of performance and whether they are making progress with additional study and practice.

2. *Students can compare their current performance against their own previous performance.*
3. *Students can use a normative standard.* This involves comparing one's performance against the performances of others, such as classmates. Normative standards emphasize how one compares with others rather than one's absolute level of performance.
4. *Students can use a collaborative standard.* This method applies to situations in which an individual is part of a group effort. The student would make a positive self-evaluation if he or she had fulfilled those responsibilities identified as necessary for the group to succeed in its endeavor.

Causal attributions, which we also cover in our chapter on motivation, are the second self-judgment process. They involve ascribing a major cause to a behavior. A student's successes and failures can be attributed to effort, ability, task difficulty, and luck, among other factors. Students who attribute their successes to effort and ability, and their failures to insufficient effort, are more likely to engage in self-regulated learning behaviors than are students who attribute success to good luck or easy tasks and failure to bad luck or low ability.

The self-reaction category is composed of *self-satisfaction* and *adaptive inferences*. Self-satisfaction is the positive feeling we get when we know we have done a job well and achieved whatever goal or goals we established at the outset. Think of it as *self-reinforcement*, which is the label used for it in Figure 9.3. Adaptive inferences are the conclusions that learners draw about the need to improve their self-regulatory skills. Learners can, however, make defensive rather than adaptive inferences. These individuals see no need to improve their self-regulatory skills because they have little interest in the task at hand or feel incapable of developing the skills necessary to successfully carry out the task.

Developmental Limitations   For the self-reflection phase, expect primary grade children to be limited in their ability to do the following:

- Compare themselves to peers as a basis for judging their own capabilities. Young children's beliefs about their capabilities are more likely to be influenced by teacher feedback than by comparisons to peers' performance. For older students, the reverse is true.
- Make appropriate attributions for their successes and failures. In the primary grades the concepts of effort and ability are not clearly distinguished and so effort is viewed as the primary cause of success and failure. Older students, however, are more likely to ascribe success primarily to ability and failure primarily to insufficient ability.
- Accurately assess the level of their own capabilities. Primary grade children are likely to overestimate what they can do if they have learned only some aspects of a skill or if they use incorrect learning or problem-solving skills that accidentally produce an acceptable outcome. Conversely, young children can underestimate their competence when they are uncertain about the correctness of their responses (Schunk, 2001).

Now that we've laid out the basic structure of social cognitive theory and described its major focus (self-regulated behavior), we can turn our attention to how the concepts of self-regulation apply to classroom learning.

BECOMING A SELF-REGULATED LEARNER

What Is Self-Regulated Learning?

As we have suggested in the preceding sections, the concept of self-regulation can be directly applied to learning academic material in and out of classrooms. **Self-regulated**

● Self-regulated learning: thoughts, feelings, and actions purposely generated and controlled to maximize a learning outcome

learning refers to any thoughts, feelings, or actions that are purposely generated and controlled by a student to maximize learning of knowledge and skills for a given task and set of conditions (Paris & Paris, 2001; Schunk, 2001; Zimmerman, 2000). It includes the cognitive processes discussed in the chapter on information-processing theory, such as formulating strategies, attending to instructional material and directions, and using a variety of tactics to code, organize, and retrieve information. It also includes the use of metacognitive processes, such as analysis, planning, and self-monitoring, as well as other processes, beliefs, and affective states that will be discussed in this and later chapters, such as creating a comfortable and productive work environment, having positive beliefs about one's learning and problem-solving capabilities, placing a high value on learning, and feeling a sense of pride and satisfaction about one's efforts.

Not surprisingly, self-regulated learners are also referred to as either *self-directed* or *autonomous* learners. Because of its complexity, you can expect expertise in self-regulated learning (SRL) to develop gradually over many years. One estimate, based on research on the development of related skills, is that most students will need about 85 percent of the approximately twelve thousand hours they spend in school through twelfth grade in order to become highly proficient in SRL (Winne & Stockley, 1998).

An example of a self-regulating student is one who does the following:

- Prepares for an upcoming exam by studying for two hours each night for several nights instead of trying to cram all the studying into one or two nights (thereby applying the principle of distributed practice, discussed in the chapter on information-processing theory)
- Uses memory-directed tactics, such as mnemonic devices, to accurately store and recall information for test items that will demand verbatim recall
- Uses comprehension-directed tactics, such as concept maps and self-questioning, to deal with test items that will require comprehension, analysis, and synthesis of information
- Creates self-tests to monitor the effectiveness of study efforts, and takes some time off from studying if the results of a self-test are satisfactory

This chapter's Case in Print pinpoints the fact that many students still seem to lack SRL skills when they reach college.

Students who are self-regulated learners tend to achieve at high levels by using appropriate cognitive and metacognitive skills for particular tasks in the right way and at the right time.

T a k e   a   S t a n d !

Teach Students How to Be Self-Regulated Learners

A perennial complaint among educators is that many students lack the skills and knowledge to function as self-regulated learners. This is a strange complaint since everyone from politicians to parents endorses the goals of self-directed learning and lifelong learning. Like motherhood and apple pie, they are easy goals to endorse because nobody could be against them. But when it comes to putting one's resources where one's rhetoric is, much of this support disappears like the morning mist. The following reasons account for a large part of this inconsistency:

1. Many people (including teachers, parents, and students) believe that self-regulation is a natural process that students will figure out and master if they just work at it long and hard enough. This leads to the ubiquitous but mostly useless advice to "study harder."
2. School is thought of as a place where students acquire bodies of information about various subject matters and the so-called basic skills of reading, writing, and computing. There is simply not enough room in the curriculum to teach students how to be self-directed learners.
3. Teachers and administrators are held accountable for how well students score on state-mandated tests. Consequently,

school curricula and classroom instruction emphasize those skills and bodies of knowledge that relate most directly to state learning standards and test items, and SRL skills are either ignored or take a back seat.

If this situation is to change, everyone involved in education needs to realize that there is nothing more basic than learning how to be a self-regulated learner. These skills allow students to become proficient at reading, writing, and computing and to direct their learning long after they finish school. Consequently, SRL skills should be as much a part of the curriculum as the three Rs.

The place to start is the individual classroom. At the very least, you should teach students that a relationship exists between the cognitive processes they use and the outcomes they observe, how and when to use various learning tactics, how to determine if learning is proceeding as planned, and what to do if it is not.

What's your response to this argument? Is SRL so "basic" that teachers ought to teach it? On the textbook web site (accessible from **http://education. college.hmco.com/students**), you can find out more about this important issue.

How Students Become Self-Regulated Learners

What little students know about the nature and use of self-regulatory skills has usually been acquired through direct instruction (by teachers, parents, and peers) and trial-and-error learning. But there is another way to strengthen self-efficacy beliefs and learn how to use self-regulatory skills: observing and imitating the behavior of a skilled model. This form of learning is often referred to as **observational learning** or **modeling**.

The notion that learning occurs by watching and imitating the behavior of others has been acknowledged and valued for thousands of years. The Chinese philosopher Confucius (551–479 B.C.), for example, said, "By three methods we may learn wisdom: First, by reflection, which is noblest; second, by imitation, which is easiest; and third by experience, which is the bitterest." (Flaherty, 2002). During the mid-1700s, Edmund Burke (1729–1797), an English politician and political writer, noted, "It is by imitation, far more than by precept, that we learn everything; and what we learn thus, we acquire not only more efficiently, but more pleasantly. This forms our manners, our opinions, our lives." (Womersley, 1998).

Social cognitive theory, with its belief that the student's environment interacts with personal characteristics and behavior, has stressed the role of observational learning in schools.

Observational learning can play an especially strong role in the acquisition of self-regulatory skills. Specifically, evidence suggests that these skills are learned most efficiently and effectively when they are acquired according to the following four-level model: observation, emulation, self-control, self-regulation (Zimmerman, 2000, 2002; Zimmerman & Kitsantas, 2002). In the description that follows, note how the high levels of support and guidance (or scaffolding, to use the constructivist terminology) that are present for the observation and emulation levels are reduced at the self-control level and eliminated at the self-regulation level. Table 9.1 summarizes the cognitive and behavioral requirements of the learner and the source of the learner's motivation for each level.

● Self-regulation skills learned best in four-level process: observation, emulation, self-control, self-regulation

Observation　At the observation level, learners pick up the major features of a skill or strategy as well as performance standards, motivational beliefs, and values, by watching and listening as a model exhibits the skill and explains the reasons for his or her behavior: for example, a model who persists at trying to solve a problem and

Case in Print

Wanted: Self-Regulated Learners

Self-regulated learning refers to any thoughts, feelings, or actions that are purposely generated and controlled by a student to maximize learning of knowledge and skills for a given task and set of conditions. . . . Because of its complexity, you can expect expertise in self-regulated learning (SRL) to develop gradually over many years. One estimate, based on research on the development of related skills, is that most students will need about 85 percent of the approximately twelve thousand hours they spend in school through twelfth grade in order to become highly proficient in SRL. (p. 285–286)

Students Unprepared for Rigors of College

FREDREKA SCHOUTEN
Gannett News Service, 10/30/03

High school graduates in Nevada with at least a B average can win $10,000 college scholarships—enough to guarantee them free rides at any public university in the state.

But that ride has proved rough for many. Nearly one-third of the kids who get the scholarships, created to keep the state's most promising students in Nevada, have to take remedial classes when they start college.

They are not alone. Around the country, students, even those with stellar high school records, have discovered they don't have all the skills to survive in college. In Georgia, for instance, four out of 10 students who earn the popular Hope Scholarships to the state's university system lose the scholarship after they earn about 30 credits—roughly one year's worth of work—because they can't keep their grades up.

Student performance on college-admissions tests also point to possible grade inflation. Fifteen years ago, students with A averages accounted for 28 percent of SAT test takers, said Wayne Camara, who oversees research for the College Board.

Today, a whopping 42 percent of college-bound seniors have A averages, but they score no better on the college admissions tests than did "A" students a decade earlier.

Some education experts say the trend is a clear sign that high school teachers are handing out high grades for weak work. But many argue the real culprit is the typical high school course load. Students just aren't taking the rigorous math, science and writing classes in high school that they need to succeed in college and the workplace.

Only one in three 18-year-olds is even minimally prepared for college, according to a recent report by the Manhattan Institute, a New York–based think tank. The picture was even bleaker for minority students. Only 20 percent of blacks in the class of 2001 were college-ready.

Lack of preparation

Researchers defined minimum preparation as having a regular high school diploma—instead of merely passing the General Educational Development test—the GED—and taking at least four years of English, three years of math, and two years each of social studies, science and a foreign language in high school. They also counted students who performed at least at the basic level on a national reading test.

The preparation gap is particularly acute for graduates of inner-city and rural high schools, said Gary Henry, a Georgia State University professor who studies the Hope Scholarships.

Schools in those areas "can't hire really qualified math and science teachers so the course gets lowered to the level that the teacher is capable of teaching," he said.

"The students have no way of knowing whether the algebra class was decent. All they know is that they passed it."

Ivrekia Stanley thought her prospects were bright when she graduated from Forest Park High School in suburban Atlanta in 1999. Her 3.6 grade-point average earned her a Hope Scholarship and a ticket to college. But when she entered Georgia Perimeter College, a two-year community college, she had to take remedial classes in reading and math.

"You get very discouraged. You don't want to tell anybody you're in these classes," Stanley recalled. She said she kept telling herself, "I have a Hope Scholarship. I'm smarter than this."

But she said the classes taught her some lessons she hadn't learned in high school, like stopping to look up unfamiliar words in the dictionary and quickly determining the main point of a written passage.

This fall, the 22-year-old transferred to Georgia State, where she majors in criminal justice. She has a 3.8 grade-point average and has retained the Hope Scholarship.

40% lose scholarships

About 40 percent of Hope Scholars who entered Georgia schools as freshmen in fall 2000 failed to maintain the minimum 3.0 GPA in their first 30 credit hours of college work and lost the scholarships.

Statistics like those from Georgia have inspired officials in Nevada to set up strong mentoring programs to help their Millennium Scholarship recipients and students from the state's rural areas stay in school, said Barbara King, who oversees tutoring programs at the Reno campus of the University of Nevada.

King runs an Internet listserv for the students where she posts reminders about finding tutors and deadlines for dropping classes. She also tries to improve their study habits.

"I tell them to pay attention to repetition during lectures," King said. "The second time a professor says something, underline it. The third time, put a 'T' for 'test' next to it. It probably will be on the test."

Other King tips: Set aside two to three hours of study for every hour spent in class, keep that time commitment in mind when considering taking on a part-time job, and read the review questions at the end of a chapter first.

She advises students to try and answer those questions before tackling the reading assignment, because that will help pinpoint important material.

"We're not just assuming that because students got a 3.0 in high school that they come in here knowing what to do," King said.

Class choice important

Researchers say that when it comes to college success, what students study in high school is as important as their study skills.

Those who continue studying math for a fourth year in high school—taking classes such as trigonometry and calculus that are harder than second-year algebra—double their chances of earning a bachelor's degree, said Clifford Adelman, a U.S. Department of Education researcher who has examined thousands of high school and college transcripts.

His advice to parents: "Encourage your kids to be challenged in (high) school, and worry less about grades." Before granting merit-based scholarships like Hope, more states now demand that students demonstrate they passed rigorous classes in high school.

Under the Texas Grant program, which pays college tuition for financially needy students, eligible students must take the state's basic college-prep curriculum. That includes four years of English and three years of math, along with three years of science classes.

Starting with the high school freshman class of 2004, all Texas public high schools automatically will enroll students in the college-prep curriculum unless their parents or guardians formally object.

Questions and Activities

1. This article notes that many high school students in Nevada have to take remedial classes during their first year of college, and 40 percent of students in Georgia with state scholarships lose them after the first year of college because of low grades. Two explanations that were offered for students' difficulty in coping with the academic demands of college are grade inflation in high school and students' avoidance of rigorous math, science, and writing courses. A third, and more likely, explanation for students' lack of preparedness for college is poorly developed self-regulation skills. Explain why this factor, and not grade inflation or course taking, is likely to be the primary cause of so many students' academic difficulties in college.

2. One student quoted in the article, Ivrekia Stanley, said that despite her 3.6 grade-point average in high school, she had to take remedial math and reading courses at a community college, where she learned such valuable skills as looking up unfamiliar words in a dictionary and figuring out the main point of a passage. Do you think these basic SRL skills were not learned in high school because they weren't taught or because Ms. Stanley simply didn't learn them at the time? Try using your own high school experience and those of your friends to justify your answer.

3. The first sentence of the last section of the article states, "Researchers say that when it comes to college success, what students study in high school is as important as their study skills." The reporter backs up this claim with the finding by Clifford Adelman, a U.S. Department of Education researcher, that students who take four years of math in high school, and who take advanced math classes during their senior year, are twice as likely to graduate from college. Given what we said earlier in the book about how several plausible causal explanations can be generated from correlational data, come up with another explanation of the finding cited by Mr. Adelman.

Table 9.1	A Social Cognitive Model of Self-Regulated Skill Learning	
Level	**Main Requirement of the Learner**	**Source of Motivation**
Observation	Attend to actions and verbalizations of the model and discriminate relevant from irrelevant behaviors	Vicarious: note rewards received by the model and anticipate receiving similar rewards for exhibiting similar behavior
Emulation	Exhibit the general form of the modeled behavior	Direct: feedback from the model and/or others
Self-control	Learn to exhibit the modeled behavior automatically through self-directed practice (focus on the underlying rule or process that produces the behavior and compare the behavior with personal standards)	Self-satisfaction from matching the standards and behavior of the model
Self-regulation	Learn to adapt the behavior to changes in internal and external conditions (such as the reactions of others)	Self-efficacy beliefs; degree of intrinsic interest in the skill

SOURCES: Zimmerman (2000, 2002); Zimmerman & Kitsantas (2002).

expresses the belief that he or she is capable of solving the problem. What would motivate a student to observe and then try to emulate a model's behavior? At least four factors do so:

1. Students are more likely to closely attend to a model and retain what has been observed if they are unfamiliar with the task at hand or if they feel incapable of carrying out the task.
2. Students attend to models they admire, respect, and perceive as having knowledge, skills, and attributes that they themselves would like to have. The popular conception, by the way, that older children and adolescents look primarily to sports or music stars rather than family members as models is not supported by research. In response to the question "What persons are your personal model?," about 46 percent of a large sample (over one thousand) of European children and adolescents listed either their mother or father, and 31 percent listed a relative. Music and sports stars were named by only 15 percent and 12 percent of respondents, respectively (Bucher, 1997).
3. Students attend to models whose behavior they judge to be acceptable and appropriate. Thus, students will often model a peer's behavior.
4. Students are more likely to imitate a model's behavior if they see that the model is reinforced for exhibiting the behavior and anticipate that they will be similarly reinforced (Schunk, 2001). This type of reinforcement is referred to as **vicarious reinforcement.** A middle school student, for example, who observes an admired classmate being praised by the teacher for promptly completing an assignment may strive to work quickly and diligently on the next assignment in anticipation of receiving similar praise.

Emulation   At the emulation level, learners reproduce the general form of the model's behavior. Since learners rarely copy the exact behaviors of a model, the term *emulation* is used here instead of the word *imitation*. The learner's response can be refined by the model's use of guidance, feedback, and direct reinforcement (such as praise from the model). Social cognitive theorists identify four types of emulation

Social cognitive theory holds that one way students acquire self-regulated learning skills is by observing and imitating the behavior of admired models, such as teachers, siblings, and peers.

● People learn to inhibit or make responses by observing others

effects that result from observing models: inhibition, disinhibition, facilitation, and observational learning.

Inhibition occurs when we learn not to do something that we already know how to do because a model we are observing refrains from behaving in that way, is punished for behaving in that way, or does something different from what we intended to do. Consider the following example: A ten-year-old is taken to her first symphony concert by her parents. After the first movement of Beethoven's Fifth Symphony, she is about to applaud but notices that her parents are sitting quietly with their hands in their laps. She does the same.

Disinhibition occurs when we learn to exhibit a behavior that is usually disapproved of by most people because a model does the same without being punished. For example, a student attends his school's final football game of the season. As time expires, thousands of students run onto the field and begin tearing up pieces of turf to take home as a souvenir. Noticing that the police do nothing, the student joins in.

An early, and now classic, experiment on disinhibition was conducted by Bandura in the early 1960s (Bandura, Ross, & Ross, 1961). A child was seated at a table and encouraged to play with a toy. The model sat at a nearby table and either played quietly with Tinker Toys for ten minutes or played with the Tinker Toys for a minute and then played aggressively with an inflatable clown "Bobo" doll for several minutes, punching, kicking, and sitting on it and hitting it with a hammer. In a subsequent unstructured play situation, children who did not observe a model, as well as those who observed a nonaggressive model, displayed little aggression. By contrast, children exposed to the aggressive model behaved with considerably more aggression toward the Bobo doll and other toys.

Facilitation occurs whenever we are prompted to do something that we do not ordinarily do because of insufficient motivation rather than social disapproval. For example, a college student attends a lecture on reforming the American education system. Impressed by the lecturer's enthusiasm and ideas, the student vigorously applauds at the end of the presentation. As several members of the audience stand and applaud, the student stands as well.

The last of the four types of emulation effects, *true observational learning*, occurs when we learn a new behavioral pattern by watching and imitating the performance of someone else. A teenage girl learning how to hit a topspin forehand in tennis by watching her instructor do the same is an example of true observational learning.

pause & reflect

Can you recall a teacher you admired so much that you imitated some aspect of her behavior (either then or later)? How might you have the same effect on your students?

Self-Control   The self-control level is marked by the learner's being able to exhibit the modeled behavior in the absence of the model. Self-control is achieved through self-directed practice. The learner focuses on the underlying rule or process that produces the behavior and compares the behavior with personal standards. At this level, the learner's motivation comes from a sense of self-satisfaction at matching the standards and behavior of the model.

Self-Regulation   The self-regulation level is attained when learners can adapt the modeled behavior to changes in internal and external conditions (such as a low level of interest in a topic or negative reactions of others). The motivation for self-regulated behavior comes from one's perceived self-efficacy and degree of intrinsic interest in the modeled behavior.

Before leaving this description of SRL and examining some of the relevant research, we would like you to keep the following point in mind: self-regulation is possible only in an environment that allows students the opportunity to make choices. Teachers who specify in great detail what students will do, when they will do it, where they will do it, and how they will do it will see very little development and use of SRL processes (Schunk, 2004).

RESEARCH ON SOCIAL COGNITIVE THEORY

Although social cognitive theory offers a compelling explanation of learning, its value to teachers and others depends on the extent to which its concepts and their proposed relationships are supported by research findings. The research that we summarize in this section falls into two broad categories: correlational studies that have examined the relationships among self-efficacy, self-regulation, and achievement, and experimental studies that have examined the effect of modeling on self-efficacy, self-regulation, and achievement.

Relationships Among Self-Efficacy, Self-Regulation Processes, and Achievement

● Self-efficacy, self-regulation related to each other and to achievement

Social cognitive theory holds that self-efficacy and self-regulation processes should be positively related to each other and that both should be positively related to achievement. A number of studies, including the following, support these relationships.

- For eight- and nine-year-olds (but not for five-, six-, or seven-year-olds), self-efficacy for reading was positively and significantly related to reading comprehension (Chapman & Tunmer, 1995).
- Among an ethnically diverse sample of fifth, eighth, and eleventh graders, perceived self-efficacy for defining words and solving mathematical problems was significantly and positively related to the use of such self-regulatory processes as reviewing notes, seeking peer assistance, and organizing and transforming information (Zimmerman & Martinez-Pons, 1990).
- Seventh-grade students with higher levels of perceived self-efficacy for performing well on English and science assignments were more likely to use self-regulatory processes and earn higher scores on exams, quizzes, essays, and lab reports than were students with lower levels of perceived self-efficacy. Also, students who reported greater use of self-regulatory processes earned higher scores than did students who reported less use of self-regulatory processes (Pintrich & De Groot, 1990).
- High school students with higher levels of self-efficacy for learning how to solve geometry problems were more likely to report higher levels of self-monitoring

and persistence and to achieve higher test scores early in the semester than were students with lower levels of self-efficacy (Pokay & Blumenfeld, 1990).

- College students with higher levels of self-efficacy for writing were more likely to set higher goals, establish more stringent self-evaluative standards, and earn higher grades in a writing class than were classmates with lower levels of self-efficacy (Zimmerman & Bandura, 1994).
- College students who scored above the median on a class test reported greater use of self-regulatory processes prior to, during, and after the test than did lower-scoring students. Prior to the test, higher-scoring students reported greater use of goal setting and planning, organizing and transforming notes, and help seeking. During the test, they engaged more often in planning and reviewing of responses. After the test, they engaged more often in goal setting, planning, and monitoring. These students earned higher scores on both multiple-choice and essay items and reported higher levels of self-efficacy (Kitsantas, 2002).

Effects of Modeling on Self-Efficacy, Self-Regulation, and Achievement

In social cognitive theory, modeling is seen as an effective means for enhancing self-efficacy, teaching students how to use self-regulation skills, and increasing achievement, particularly when the observer is similar to the model or when the observer strongly identifies with the model (Schunk & Zimmerman, 1997). Support for the theory has come from a number of studies, particularly ones that focus on skills in mathematics and writing.

Improving Students' Mathematical Problem-Solving Skills   Mathematical problem-solving ability is a difficult skill for many students to master, and it has a prominent place in the curriculum (it is one of the three R's). For these reasons, it has often been studied by social cognitive researchers who are interested in the effects of modeling. The research we describe in this section is just a sample of what has appeared in the literature in the past several years.

Effect of Peer Models   A study conducted with ten-year-olds (Schunk & Hanson, 1985) tested the hypothesis that children become increasingly likely to attend to and emulate a model as the perceived similarity between the observer and the model increases. Children who were having difficulty learning to do subtraction-with-regrouping problems (also known as borrowing problems) were assigned to one of four groups. One group watched a videotape of a same-sex peer being taught how to solve such problems by a teacher. Because the peer model quickly solved a set of similar problems without making any errors, he/she was referred to as a mastery model. A second group also watched a videotape of a same-sex peer being taught by a teacher and then working on a set of similar problems. Because this model made mistakes at first but overcame them and then performed flawlessly, he/she was referred to as a peer coping model. The peer models in both groups verbalized the subtraction operations along with high self-efficacy statements. A third group watched a videotape of a teacher explaining and carrying out the subtraction operations. The fourth group did not view a model.

All the children were then given step-by-step written instructions in how to solve subtraction-with-regrouping problems. Because of the greater similarity between the students and the peer coping model, it was expected that students who observed such a model would perform better than students who observed a mastery model. Although there was no difference between the mastery and coping model groups on a posttest, both had significantly higher levels of self-efficacy for solving subtraction problems and solved significantly more problems correctly than did children who either observed the adult model or worked solely from written instructions.

● Observing a peer model improves students' self-efficacy for math problem solving and math problem-solving ability

Effect of Perceived Similarity in Learning Ability Another study that tested the similarity hypothesis (Schunk, Hanson, & Cox, 1987) did so by examining the effect of perceived similarity in learning ability (coping versus mastery) and gender (same sex versus opposite sex). Children in grades 4, 5, and 6 whose arithmetic achievement was below the 35th percentile were assigned to one of the following conditions: male mastery model, male coping model, female mastery model, female coping model. The mastery and coping models exhibited the same behaviors as the mastery and coping models in the study of ten-year-olds just described. The children in each group watched a videotape in which each of six fractions skills was modeled by a teacher and then performed by a peer under the supervision of the teacher. The teacher demonstrated how to do a problem and then asked the model to do a similar one. The model verbalized the procedure and was then told by the teacher that the solution was correct.

Students in all four groups were then given written instructions on each of six days that explained how to solve each of the six types of fractions problems they had seen the model solve. The students were then given several similar problems that they had to solve on their own. An adult was always present to answer questions. The main result was that children who observed a coping model, regardless of whether the model was male or female, reported significantly higher levels of self-efficacy for learning to solve fractions problems and solved significantly more problems correctly than did children who observed a mastery model.

Effect of Self-Modeling A further study (Schunk & Hanson, 1989) took the similarity hypothesis to its logical conclusion by having students use themselves as their model. Children in grades 4, 5, and 6 whose arithmetic achievement was below the 35th percentile were assigned to either a peer-model, self-model, peer-model + self-model, or no model condition. Children in the first and third groups watched a videotape in which each of six fractions skills was modeled by a teacher and then by three same-sex peers under the supervision of the teacher. The teacher demonstrated how to do a problem and then asked a model to do a similar one. The model verbalized the procedure and was then told by the teacher that the solution was correct.

Students in all four groups were then given written instructions for six days on how to solve different types of fractions problems (with an adult present to answer questions) and were videotaped working out similar problems at a chalkboard. After days 4, 5, and 6, children in the self-model and peer-model + self-model conditions watched the videotape of their performance from the previous day (thereby serving as their own model). Although there were no differences among the three modeling conditions, all three scored significantly higher than the no model condition on measures of self-efficacy for solving fractions problems and numbers of fractions problems solved correctly.

Effect of Learning-Goal Orientation Earlier in this chapter we outlined a set of self-regulatory processes that are activated either before a task is begun, during a task, or after the task has been completed. One process that comes into play prior to engaging a task and that is assumed to affect students' self-efficacy and performance is whether a student has a learning goal or a performance goal (Zimmerman, 2000). *Learning goals* focus on acquiring specific knowledge and skills, while *performance goals* focus just on completing the task. One study (Schunk, 1996) tested the effects of learning-goal orientation on learning six fractions skills (one per day for six days) for a group of average-achieving fourth-grade students.

Each day's lesson began with a statement from the teacher that established the goal. Students assigned to the learning-goal condition were told: "While you're working it helps to keep in mind what you're trying to do. You'll be trying to learn how to solve fractions problems where the denominators are the same and you have to add the numerators." Students assigned to the performance-goal condition were told: "While you're working it helps to keep in mind what you're trying to do. You'll be trying to solve fractions problems where the denominators are the same and you have to add the numerators." To ensure that the students in both groups understood the goal of each session (notice that their instructions differed by only a few words), the teacher asked them to repeat the instructions and indicate whether they had any questions. This was followed by a ten-minute explanation and demonstration by the teacher of the fractions skill the students would be learning that day, ten minutes of guided practice, and twenty-five minutes of independent practice. At the end of day 6, students judged their ability to solve fractions problems and indicated the extent to which they were pleased with their progress in learning fractions skills.

The main finding was that students in the learning-goal group exhibited a significantly higher level of self-efficacy for solving fractions problems—and solved significantly more problems correctly—than did the students in the performance-goal group. In addition, students in the learning-goal group had higher self-evaluation and self-satisfaction scores.

Improving Students' Writing Skills   Writing skills are also frequently used by researchers to investigate the effects of modeling. Writing is particularly important in the middle school years because writing tasks are more complex than in earlier years and play a larger role in classroom performance. Students who feel poorly prepared to carry out writing tasks tend to be more anxious about them and to spend less time on them (Klassen, 2002). As with the studies we summarized on mathematical problem solving, the research summarized next is just a sample.

Modeling for Strategy Development   As we noted earlier in the chapter, self-regulation skills make significant contributions to achievement, especially when students reach the middle school grades, and modeling can be an effective way to help students acquire these skills. In one study (Sexton, Harris, & Graham, 1998), six fifth- and sixth-grade students with learning disabilities who had poor writing skills were trained to use a self-regulation strategy to improve their writing of opinion essays. Following what was called the Self-Regulated Strategy Development (SRSD) model, the teacher helped students develop and activate relevant background knowledge, helped students learn and memorize a three-step writing strategy (think about who will read this, plan what to say, write and say more), modeled the strategy by thinking out loud, gradually shifted responsibility to the students for activating and using the strategy and making positive self-statements, and required students to independently plan, write, and revise an essay.

Immediately after instruction, the quality of most of the students' essays improved dramatically. Compared with their preinstruction essays, the ones they wrote now were longer, contained more elements, and were of higher quality. In percentage terms, the increases in quality scores ranged from 120 percent to 375 percent. In addition, there was objective evidence that the students used the strategy they had been taught in writing their essays. All six students expressed the belief that effort was largely responsible for their success or failure in writing, and four students showed a considerable increase in their belief in the importance of strategy use. But there were disappointing results as well. Three weeks after instruction, there were declines in the length and quality of the essays. In some cases, the scores were at the same level as before instruction. This latter finding suggests that relatively short-term interventions to help students improve writing, studying, problem solving, and so on should not be expected to work miracles. They will need to be supplemented by consistent long-term assistance.

Observing Weak and Strong Models   In another test of the model-observer similarity principle (Braaksma, Rijlaarsdam, & van den Bergh, 2002), eighth-grade students in a Dutch school who were classified as having either low, medium, or high verbal ability observed a weak peer model and a strong peer model write an argumentative passage.

Argumentative passages contain an opinion (such as "It is better to live in a city than in a village"), one or more supporting arguments (for example, a city offers more choices for shopping and going to school, cities are more conducive to personal growth, and there are more job opportunities in a city), one or more subordinate arguments (for example, cities are more conducive to personal growth because there is a wider range of people to meet and there are more cultural events to attend), and connective words like *because* and *and* that logically relate the supporting arguments to the opinion and the subordinate arguments to each other and to the supporting argument.

In the study, the weak models omitted critical aspects of an argumentative passage and produced passages that were less coherent than those produced by the strong models. Both weak and strong models verbalized their thought processes: planning what to write and then checking to make sure that it was complete and made sense. One group of students was asked to identify the model who performed less well and to explain why this was the less competent model. A second group was asked to identify which model performed better and to explain why this was the more competent model.

Low-verbal-ability students who were asked to identify and evaluate the weak model received higher scores on the argumentative passages they wrote than did low-verbal-ability students who either were asked to identify and evaluate the strong model or who just practiced writing argumentative passages. High-ability students who wrote argumentative passages after identifying and evaluating the strong model or who merely practiced writing argumentative passages received higher scores than did their peers who identified and evaluated the weak model. Both groups, in other words, seemed to respond better to models they perceived as similar to themselves.

Modeling Versus Practice   Most people have come to believe, partly because of their own experience and partly because of supporting research, that practice makes perfect. But one study (Couzijn, 1999) provides support for the contention of social cognitive theory that observing a model can be more effective than rote practice in helping students acquire new skills.

A group of ninth-grade students worked through a four-part self-instructional course on argumentative writing. After each part, they participated in one of the following four exercises: (a) working individually on writing exercises, (b) watching a videotape of two students of the same age doing writing exercises while thinking aloud, (c) watching a peer doing writing exercises while thinking aloud and then watching another peer verbally analyze the writer's passage, or (d) writing an argumentative passage and then observing a peer analyze the passage while thinking aloud. All students were then asked to write argumentative passages (e.g., "Do you think students should give grades to their teachers?") that were scored for putting the issue in context, text structure, argumentation structure, and presentation of argument (e.g., use of paragraphing, markers, and connectors).

As expected, students in groups (b), (c), and (d)—all the students exposed to modeling of one sort or another—produced better-quality argumentative passages than did students who simply practiced their writing.

Observation and Emulation   As we noted earlier in this chapter, Barry Zimmerman (2000) maintains that the learning of new skills, such as writing, occurs most effectively when it follows the sequence of observation, emulation, self-control, and self-regulation. One particular study (Zimmerman & Kitsantas, 2002) was designed to assess the observation and emulation steps of Zimmerman's model.

A group of undergraduates were taught a five-step strategy for combining a set of six to ten short sentences into one longer and more complex sentence. Then the students did one of the following things:

a. Watched a coping model work through several sets of sentences and receive praise for correctly using the five-step strategy

● Observing a peer model improves the quality of students' writing more than just practice in writing

b. Watched a coping model work through several sets of sentences but receive no feedback

c. Watched a mastery model work through several sets of sentences and receive praise for correctly using the five-step strategy

d. Watched a mastery model work through several sets of sentences but receive no feedback

e. Studied the sentences independently

During the second phase of the experiment, the students were given twelve additional sets of sentences on which to practice the five-step sentence-combining strategy. Half of the students received praise for those steps they performed correctly, while the other half received no praise.

During the third and final phase of the experiment, the students were tested for self-efficacy, writing skill, attributions, intrinsic interest, and self-satisfaction.

The results supported the authors' contention that writing (and other) skills are best learned when they follow the sequence of observation/emulation/self-control/self-regulation. During both the practice and posttest phases, students who observed the coping model wrote higher-quality sentences and had higher self-efficacy and intrinsic interest scores than did students who observed the mastery model or students who did not observe a model. Furthermore, students who did not observe a model but who received praise during the practice phase still performed more poorly on the posttest than did students who both observed a model (regardless of whether it was a coping model or a mastery model) and received praise. Thus, praise alone, while useful, is not as powerful as when it is combined with observation and imitation of a model.

Dale Schunk (2001) also describes the positive findings that numerous researchers have reported on these and other aspects of self-regulated learning, specifically the beneficial effects of goal setting, attributing success to persistent effort and ability, self-verbalizations, and self-monitoring in promoting self-efficacy and achievement.

Now that you are familiar with social cognitive theory and research, it is time to examine several Suggestions for Teaching derived from these principles and research findings.

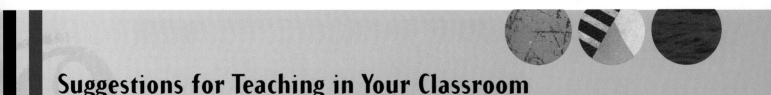

Suggestions for Teaching in Your Classroom

Applying Social Cognitive Theory in the Classroom

1 Use modeling techniques on a regular basis to teach a wide variety of skills.

If you plan to demonstrate the correct way to perform some skill or process, first make sure you have the attention of everyone in the class. Then, after explaining what you are going to do (perhaps noting particular points students should look for), demonstrate. Immediately after you demonstrate, have all the students in the class try out the new skill. For complex skills, have them write down the steps to follow before they try the activity on their own.

JOURNAL ENTRY
Modeling Desirable Skills

EXAMPLES

- Show primary grade students how to solve multiplication problems by first placing a large, colorful poster on a bulletin board with a diagram of the process. Explain the diagram and then demonstrate how to solve some simple problems. As soon as you finish, hand out a worksheet containing several simple problems similar to those you just demonstrated.

- Have students work on the problems for a specified period of time and then secure their attention once again and demonstrate on the board the correct procedure for solving each problem. Have students correct their own papers as you demonstrate, point out that they now know how to do multiplication problems, and praise them for learning the skill so rapidly.

- In a high school business class, follow a similar procedure when showing students how to set up a word processing program to type a form letter. Make sure everyone is paying attention. Demonstrate the correct procedure. Have students write down the steps they should follow to imitate your actions. Have them study the steps before setting up their own word processor. Have them reproduce the letter. Provide reinforcement to supplement their own satisfaction in having completed the task successfully.

2 **Include the development of self-regulated learning skills in your objectives and lesson plans.**

The research that we summarized clearly shows that SRL skills make a significant contribution to students' achievement. Consequently, their development should be included in your instructional objectives and lesson plans. You can help students become more effective self-regulated learners by incorporating the following elements into your classroom instruction (Ley & Young, 2001; Randi & Corno, 2000; Schunk, 2001).

a. Provide direct instruction in the various SRL skills that you want students to learn, including explanations of when to use those skills and why they aid learning.

JOURNAL ENTRY
Teaching Self-Regulated
Learning Skills

In all likelihood, you will want students to attain some degree of proficiency in goal setting, planning, use of cognitive skills, monitoring of one's actions and progress, self-evaluation, and self-reinforcement. When teaching planning skills, for example, point out that students who are good planners know the conditions under which they learn best and choose or arrange environments that eliminate or decrease distractions. To raise students' awareness of the value of a good learning environment, you can have them keep a log of how much time they spend

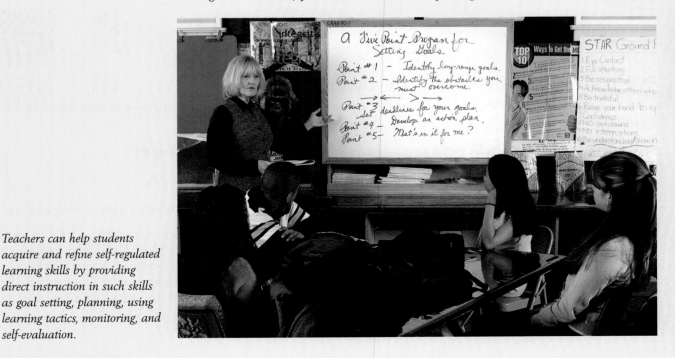

Teachers can help students acquire and refine self-regulated learning skills by providing direct instruction in such skills as goal setting, planning, using learning tactics, monitoring, and self-evaluation.

studying in various places and at various times, what internal and external distractions they experience, and how they deal with those distractions. On the basis of this information, they can draw conclusions about when and under what circumstances they best learn. To help students choose or create a hospitable learning environment, you can prepare and distribute a checklist of desirable features. Likely features would include: relatively quiet, well lit, well ventilated, comfortable furniture, away from other people, absence of a television set, and absence of alternative reading material like comic books or magazines.

Self-regulated learners commonly use many types of organizing tactics, which are among the cognitive skills that we mentioned in the chapter on information processing. You can help students appreciate the value of organizing skills by using such techniques as outlines, concept maps, previews, graphs, flowcharts, and tables as you teach, and by explaining how they are used and the ways in which they aid learning. To increase the probability that students will use such techniques themselves, teach them how to make outlines before they write essays, and show them how to create concept maps, graphs, flowcharts, and tables after they have read a section of text.

b. Model SRL skills, including the standards you use to evaluate your performance and reinforce yourself.

You can enhance the learning of SRL skills by having students observe and imitate what you and other skilled learners do. As noted, when you demonstrate a skill or process, you should first explain what you are going to do. At this stage, take time to describe why you are going to do it and how you will evaluate the quality of your performance. Then demonstrate the behavior, evaluate your performance, and, if you feel your behavior has met your standards, verbally administer some self-praise.

EXAMPLES

● The importance of modeling thought processes that are normally hidden from observation was noted by Margaret Metzger (1998), a high school English teacher. To help students better understand the process of literary interpretation and criticism, she recommended a procedure in which she led some students through a discussion of a story while the other students observed and took notes on the process.

c. Provide guided practice and corrective feedback for the SRL skills you want students to learn.

As we noted earlier in this chapter, self-observation or self-monitoring is an important SRL skill that plays a role at several points in the learning process. Self-regulating students are very proficient at monitoring their progress in meeting goals, the effectiveness of their learning strategies and tactics, and the quality of their achievements. They do this by comparing their performance both to internal standards and external feedback. Once you have explained and demonstrated self-monitoring, give students structured opportunities to practice this skill and provide feedback.

JOURNAL ENTRY
Helping Students Practice and
Refine Self-Regulated Learning
Skills

To familiarize students with the process of self-monitoring, you can require them to keep a log or journal in which they (a) state goals, (b) note how they prepare for and address the demands of projects, homework, and other tasks, and (c) assess the extent to which they have achieved one or more goals. Students could record, for example, how much time they spent on a task, the types of tactics they used, the number of problems they worked, and the extent to which they felt they understood the material.

External feedback should be constructive regardless of whether the basic message contains good news or bad news. On one hand, when you point out mistakes or omissions students have made on assignments and tests, focus on the cognitive processes students may have misused or omitted and provide suggestions for correcting such problems in the future. On the other hand, when the quality of a student's work has improved over time, point that out and relate it to one or more cognitive processes.

3 **Establish the foundation for self-regulated learning in kindergarten and the primary grades.**

JOURNAL ENTRY
Providing a Foundation for Self-Regulated Learning Skills in the Primary Grades

As we noted earlier, becoming a proficient self-regulated learner requires thousands of hours of instruction and experience spread over many years. Consequently, the foundation for SRL should be established in kindergarten and the primary grades. Observations of teachers in kindergarten through third grade (Perry, VandeKamp, Mercer, & Nordby, 2002) provide some insight as to how this might be accomplished. In general, teachers whose classrooms were rated as high-SRL classrooms emphasized student choice of activities, support in meeting academic challenges (a technique we referred to earlier in the book as scaffolding), and evaluation of self and classmates in a nonthreatening, mastery-oriented environment. Here are some specific examples of how SRL-oriented instruction was carried out.

EXAMPLES

- Prior to an oral reading of the story *The Three Little Pigs*, students were allowed to decide whether to track the text with their finger or their eyes.

- When a student had trouble decoding a word during an oral story reading, the teacher asked the other children in the group to suggest a solution. They then tried each suggestion to see which one worked.

- Students were asked to create an alternative story ending for *The Three Little Pigs*. To help them meet this challenge, the teacher allowed students to share their ideas with a classmate and, later, with the teacher. The teacher recorded each child's idea on chart paper so everyone in class could see everyone else's ideas.

- Kindergarten and first-grade children who had trouble writing out their ideas for a writing assignment were encouraged to start with drawings as a way to plan and organize their ideas.

- In preparation for student/parent–teacher conferences, students were asked to select samples of their work to share with parents and reflect on what they could do now that they could not do earlier in the school year.

- To help second-grade students choose and carry out a research topic, the teacher asked them to answer three questions: Am I interested in this topic? Can I find books about this topic? Can I read the books by myself, or will I need help from a friend or an adult?

4 **When teaching SRL skills, bear in mind the developmental limitations of younger students.**

If basic instruction in SRL skills is to begin as early as kindergarten, teachers need to acknowledge that because young children are more limited cognitively than older children, they will require more support and guidance. Dale Schunk (2001) suggests that teachers of primary and early elementary grade children do the following:

- Keep demonstrations and explanations of various skills and behaviors relatively short.
- As you or someone else models a skill, point out which aspects of the model's behaviors are more important than others.
- Set a series of short-term goals, each of which can be accomplished after a limited amount of instruction.
- Design your lessons to minimize interruptions and distractions and periodically tell students that you believe they are capable learners.
- Periodically remind students to carry out a task more slowly and think about the skills needed to complete the task.

- Provide verbal feedback about children's capabilities (e.g., "You're good at reading").
- Help students make appropriate attributions for success and failure by reminding them that effort is the primary cause of success and insufficient effort is the primary cause of failure. If you mention that ability also plays a role in performance, emphasize that ability is a set of learnable skills and not a fixed cognitive capacity.
- Provide students with clear guidelines for determining the appropriateness of their behavior and point out when they have and have not satisfied those guidelines.

5 Embed instruction in SRL in interesting and challenging classroom tasks.

Judi Randi and Lyn Corno (2000) suggest that if teachers want to teach their students SRL skills, they should embed their instruction in a classroom task that both illustrates and requires students to use SRL skills. One such task, which they describe in detail, is to analyze a story about a hero who has to undertake a dangerous journey and rely on personal resources in order to accomplish a goal. This is often called a journey tale. Two well-known examples from Greek literature are the *Odyssey* and *Jason and the Argonauts*. The students are then asked to draw parallels between the self-regulatory skills used by the story's hero and their own journeys as learners. For instance, just as Odysseus created a plan to escape from the Cyclops's cave, students should first think about the steps they will need to take to accomplish a goal.

6 Help students develop a sense of self-efficacy for SRL.

JOURNAL ENTRY
Ways to Help Students Develop Self-Efficacy for Self-Regulated Learning

As this chapter has suggested, self-efficacy, the belief that one can meet the demands of a particular task, is related to SRL in a reciprocal way. It contributes to the development of SRL skills and is also strengthened by their use. Students who are confident that they are capable of learning SRL skills are more likely than others to invest time and effort in self-regulation. In addition, students who believe that their SRL skills make them more effective learners are more likely to have higher levels of self-efficacy than students without such skills (Schunk & Miller, 2002). You can help students develop a strong sense of self-efficacy for SRL by emphasizing mastery of SRL skills, providing successful models of SRL with whom students identify, and by telling students you believe they are capable of being self-regulated learners. Here are a few suggestions for accomplishing this goal.

EXAMPLES

- For a variety of tasks, require students to set a moderately difficult near-term goal (such as receiving a grade of B+ on the next writing assignment) and specify how they intend to reach the goal. If the goal or the means to reach it is unrealistic (for instance, get a grade of A on all writing assignments for the school year) or too general (study harder for the next test), remind them that appropriate goals are specific, near-term, and moderately difficult and then have them write new goals and means.

- Have students practice self-monitoring by writing down the steps they took to accomplish a task and the effect each step had on achieving the goal

- Have a student who is popular with most classmates and possesses good SRL skills describe how he or she approaches tasks and prepares for exams. Another option is to create cooperative learning groups in which at least two of the students have strong SRL skills and require all students to verbalize the processes they use to cope with the demands of various parts of the task.

- When students exhibit improved performance on a task, remind them that this is due to their use of SRL skills and that they are better prepared than previously to cope with the demands of future classroom tasks.

See the textbook web site for additional suggestions for your journal.

USING TECHNOLOGY TO PROMOTE SELF-REGULATED LEARNING

As we noted earlier, teaching students to become proficient self-regulated learners will require thousands of hours of instruction spread over many years. With the many instructional responsibilities teachers have, you stand a better chance of contributing to this goal if you can use technology to supplement and reinforce your efforts. The studies we summarize in this section suggest that, with certain qualifications, this is a real possibility.

Modeling

Modeling, as we saw earlier in this chapter, is an effective way to help students acquire important SRL skills. But what if a teacher does not have sufficient time to perform this function or cannot always supply the modeling just when students need it? Might not a computer-based video model serve as an effective substitute? This was the driving question behind a study conducted with sixth-grade students (Pedersen & Liu, 2002).

The students, divided into three groups, worked on a computer-based hypermedia problem-solving simulation over the course of fifteen 45-minute class periods. Called *Alien Rescue*, the simulation had students play the role of scientists on an international space station whose mission was to rescue alien life forms. They encountered a ship that contained six species of aliens, survivors of a distant solar system that was destroyed by the explosion of a nearby star. The life-support system of the alien ship had been damaged, and its members were in suspended animation. The students' task was to figure out which planets or moons of our solar system might serve as suitable homes for each of the alien species by using existing databases and a simulation within the program that let them design and launch probes. They recorded their notes and solutions in an online notebook.

The students were assigned to one of three conditions:

- In the modeling condition, students watched video segments of an expert scientist solving the same problem for one of the alien species. At four points in the program the model explained what he was trying to accomplish and how he used various tools, such as the online notebook and the probe design room. He also modeled such cognitive processes as self-questioning, making connections, identifying missing information, forming hypotheses, and taking notes in a list format.
- In the direct instruction condition, students received the same information, but without modeling. The scientist explained the function of various tools and provided tips about how to work effectively (e.g., "If I were building a probe, I would use my mission statement to help me decide what to include on my probe").
- In the help condition, the scientist explained the function of various tools but provided no advice or modeling on how to use them.

Although the students in each group worked at their own computer, they were encouraged to share information with classmates and ask one another for help.

The students in the modeling condition significantly outscored those in the direct instruction and help conditions on several measures. They were more apt to take notes in list format, separate their notes into sections by topic, and consult their notes. They designed fewer probes, but this was expected because they spent more time thinking about and designing probes that were consistent with their mission statements. The modeling group also attained significantly higher scores than the other two groups for the quality of their problem solutions.

A follow-up study (Pedersen & Liu, 2002/2003), also done with sixth graders and using the same simulation and conditions, found that students in the modeling condition were more likely to transfer some of their problem-solving skills, such as asking

● Computer programs that include models can improve students' problem-solving skills

more appropriate questions and fewer inappropriate questions, to a similar problem (finding an alternative habitat for an endangered salamander) than were students in the direct instruction and help conditions.

Providing Metacognitive Feedback

As we noted earlier in the chapter, self-regulated learners monitor their thinking as they work through a task in order to ensure a high level of learning. Teachers and parents often help students develop and strengthen this skill by reminding them to think about key operations, such as appropriately defining the problem or issue at hand and recalling relevant prior knowledge. This type of support is often referred to as *metacognitive feedback*. The type of feedback students usually receive, called *results feedback*, takes the form of such cautionary and positive statements as "Try again," "Check once more," and "Very good, wonderful job!"

One study (Kramarski & Zeichner, 2001) compared computer-provided instruction and metacognitive feedback with computer-provided instruction and results feedback on eleventh graders' mathematical problem solving. As students in the metacognitive feedback group worked through the program, the computer would prompt them to think about the nature of the problem, the relevance of prior knowledge, and the use of appropriate problem-solving techniques by posing such questions as "What is the problem all about?," "What are the similarities and differences between the problem at hand and problems you have solved in the past?," and "What tactics or principles are appropriate for solving this problem and why?" Students in the results feedback group received comments such as "Think about it, you made a mistake," "Try again," "Check it once more," "Very good," and "Wonderful job!"

On a twenty-seven-item test that required students to explain the reasoning that led them to solve the problem as they did, students who received metacognitive feedback significantly outscored students who received results feedback. The explanations of the metacognitive feedback group were of a significantly higher quality (they included both algebraic formulas and verbal arguments) than the explanations of the results feedback group.

Providing Scaffolded Instruction

Earlier in the book we described Vygotsky's theory of cognitive development and his recommendation that teachers use various instructional aids, called scaffolds, to help students acquire the knowledge and self-regulatory skills that they would probably not otherwise acquire. But as busy as most classrooms are, it is not always possible for teachers to maximize the use of scaffolded instruction. Many advocates of computer-based instruction believe that computer programs that have various types of scaffolds built into them can accomplish what some teachers cannot. A study designed to assess that belief (Brush & Saye, 2001) examined the extent to which eleventh-grade students used the features of a hypermedia database called Decision Point! that contained both information about the civil rights movement in the United States during the 1960s and several types of scaffolds designed to encourage students to make optimal use of the database.

Each student was assigned to a four-person group. The students in each group were told to assume they were civil rights leaders in 1968 shortly after the assassination of Martin Luther King, Jr. They were asked to develop a solution to the following problem: What strategies should be used to continue pursuing the goal of the civil rights movement? Using the Decision Point! database, each group was assigned to gather relevant information on particular aspects of the civil rights movement (e.g., the legal system, desegregation, voting rights, the Student Non-Violent Coordinating Committee, and rejecting integration).

The Decision Point! database contained four types of scaffolds. The first was a set of interactive essays. Each essay provided an overview of an historical event, such as the March on Washington to secure voting rights for all African Americans, with hyperlinks to related documents within the database. If you have seen online encyclopedias in which certain names, places, events, and concepts of an essay are highlighted and linked to related documents, you can visualize how these interactive essays worked. The second scaffold was a set of recommended documents for each event. The program suggested that students first examine eight to ten recommended documents for an event before exploring any other information sources. The third scaffold was a student guide that provided categories that might be used by a professional historian to organize and synthesize information about an event (such as groups involved in the event, goals of each group, and strategies used by each group). The final scaffold was a journal in which students could note the effectiveness of their daily information-gathering strategies, the problems they had encountered, and the progress they had made toward completing the task. The purpose of the journal was to help students monitor their efforts.

Of the four scaffolds designed into the database, the interactive essays were used the most. Each group examined at least one of the essays, and two of the four groups read the essays for each event they were assigned. A third group examined all but one of the essays. The hyperlinks, however, were used much less frequently. Only 39 percent of the total number of documents available were accessed. Although students ignored most of the available documents, the ones they did examine were usually those recommended by the program. Consequently, this was felt to be a somewhat effective scaffold. Only two groups used the student guide scaffold to summarize their analyses for each event they were assigned to research. Moreover, the students' responses to this scaffold were judged to be inadequate. Most contained just a single phrase or sentence for each category. The student journals were used least of all. No group completed a journal for each day of data collection, and the entries were brief and superficial.

The results of this study provide limited support for embedding self-regulatory scaffolds in computerized databases. Students are most likely to use those scaffolds that they perceive to be most relevant to the successful completion of a task and ignore those that appear less relevant or require more time to complete than they have available. As the next set of studies indicate, it is also possible that students declined to use most of the scaffolds in the Decision Point! program because they lacked other self-regulatory qualities such as persistence and self-efficacy.

The Effect of Self-Regulated Learning Skills on Computer-Based Instruction

From the earliest days of computer-based instruction, the designers of instructional programs have disagreed over the issue of how much control to give students. Some programs offer students no choices; the program provides the same material to all students in the same sequence, under the same conditions, and at the same rate. Other programs allow students to choose which material they will examine, for how long, and in what sequence. Although the learner control option has been strongly promoted by many designers, research findings have been inconclusive. One reason for these mixed results is that the relative benefits of program versus learner control are likely to be partly a function of the level of students' SRL learning skills (Eom & Reiser, 2000; Young, 1996).

This hypothesis was tested with a group of seventh-grade students who received a computer-based lesson on the use of four techniques used in advertising: bandwagon, testimonials, transfer, and uniqueness (Young, 1996). The bandwagon technique tries to persuade people to buy a product by claiming that most people use it, thereby implying that nonusers are not as smart or up to date as everyone else. Testimonials are endorsements of a product by a well-known person. The transfer technique is similar to testimonials except that the famous person does not explicitly endorse the product but is simply associated with it. The uniqueness technique emphasizes how popular or special people will be by using the advertised product.

On the basis of their responses to an SRL questionnaire, the students were divided into high and low self-regulated learning skills (SRLS) groups. Half of each group was assigned to a program control (PC) condition in which the instructional events occurred in the same sequence for everybody. The other half of each group was assigned to a learner control (LC) condition in which students could decide what material they wanted to see, the sequence in which they wanted see it, and whether or not they wanted to review the instruction. The lesson for each condition consisted of two definitions (one a paraphrase of the other) of each advertising technique, one example and one nonexample, and two practice questions. The practice items presented an advertisement, and students were asked to indicate whether or not it was an example of a particular technique, such as a testimonial. This was followed by a review session in which students responded to multiple-choice questions similar to those they would encounter on the posttest.

As expected, students in the LC condition with high SRLS scores significantly outscored their low-SRLS peers on the posttest (73.2 percent correct versus 37 percent correct). But both high- and low-SRLS students scored at about the same level in the PC condition (64.7 percent correct versus 67.7 percent correct). Another interesting finding concerned the number of instructional elements students in the LC condition chose to view. Out of a maximum of twenty-four (two definitions, two examples, and two practice items per technique), both high- and low-SRLS students viewed only about ten items. Yet high-SRLS students in this condition achieved the highest average posttest score (73.2 percent correct).

A very similar study (Eom & Reiser, 2000) that used the same instructional materials and procedures was conducted a few years later with sixth- and seventh-grade students, and produced similar results. High self-regulators in the PC and LC conditions scored about the same on the posttest (65 percent and 58 percent, respectively). Low self-regulators in the PC condition achieved higher scores than did low self-regulators in the LC condition (66 percent and 37 percent, respectively). In addition, students in the PC condition, regardless of whether they were high or low self-regulators, spent significantly more time viewing the instructional materials, which may account for the generally higher posttest scores by those in the PC groups. As Young (1996) found, students in the LC condition viewed about 50 percent of the available twenty-four instructional events.

Taken together, these two studies strongly suggest that the use of computer programs that allow learner control should be limited to students who have acquired many of the self-regulatory skills described in this chapter. It also implies that if teachers want to use such programs, they should first help students acquire SRL skills.

The Effect of Self-Efficacy on Computer-Based Instruction

Use of the World Wide Web as an information-gathering and problem-solving resource is becoming increasingly popular in schools. But social cognitive theory suggests that successful use of the Web for this purpose will require high levels of self-efficacy and self-regulation because of the large number of independent decisions students must make. Since self-efficacy is task-specific, it stands to reason that the following types of self-efficacy will play a role in web-based instruction (WBI): self-efficacy for learning the subject matter, self-efficacy for using the Web, and, because WBI requires learners to locate and analyze information with little or no teacher guidance, self-efficacy for self-regulated learning. The effect of these forms of self-efficacy on achievement and Web use was investigated among high school sophomores in Korea (Joo, Bong, & Choi, 2000).

Before beginning the study, students were given measures of self-efficacy for SRL, academic self-efficacy, Internet self-efficacy, and cognitive strategy use. The students were then given worksheets for three topics (Common Diseases of the

● Computer programs that let students control access to information work best with those who have some self-regulatory skills

Organs in Our Body, Smoking and Health, Drugs and Prevention) that contained questions to be answered and blank tables to be completed. Each worksheet listed the addresses of web sites that were likely to contain useful information. The students were responsible for locating whatever information the site contained that would help them fill out the worksheet. In addition, they could use commercial search engines to identify other sites that contained relevant information. Following the third session, students took two tests: a written exam of multiple-choice and short-answer questions that covered the three topics and a performance test in which students had to access two web sites and locate information pertaining to given questions.

Several gender differences were found that are consistent with the research findings we described in the chapter "Understanding Student Differences." Female students scored significantly higher than male students on the self-efficacy for SRL and cognitive strategy use measures. The fact that the females also significantly outscored the males on the written exam suggests that higher levels of self-efficacy for SRL and greater use of SRL skills account for the finding that females typically earn higher grades than males. Consistent with research findings reported earlier in this chapter, self-efficacy for SRL was highly correlated with academic self-efficacy and strategy use. Finally, previous experience with computers and self-efficacy for SRL both related significantly to self-efficacy for Internet use, which in turn related significantly to performance on the Web search test.

Conclusions About Computer Technology and Self-Regulated Learning

The studies we have summarized, and many others, indicate that computer-based instructional programs can play a productive role in the development and support of students' SRL skills. They can provide students with concrete examples of self-regulation skills and explanations of how those skills relate to achieving a goal. They can support and strengthen the skill of self-monitoring by reminding students at critical points to think about the nature of the problem being solved, similar problems encountered in the past, and appropriate problem-solving tactics. They can also provide a variety of scaffolds.

In short, technology can do for SRL many of the things that teachers do, giving teachers more time to work individually with students who need additional help. But (and to repeat a point we made earlier in the book), the use of technology to promote SRL has its limits. Without teacher guidance and oversight, some students will profit from such open-ended tools as hypermedia simulations, databases, and the World Wide Web, while others will likely feel overwhelmed and confused. If you use these tools to promote SRL and other goals, one of the first things you will need to do is determine students' current levels of SRL ability and self-efficacy.

For help reviewing this chapter, look at the ACE practice tests and PowerPoint slides on the textbook web site.

Resources for Further Investigation

● Social Cognitive Theory

Albert Bandura's recent thoughts about social cognitive theory can be found in the first chapter ("Social Cognitive Theory: An Agentic Perspective") of volume 52 of the *Annual Review of Psychology* (2001).

● Self-Regulated Learning

The *Handbook of Self-Regulation* (2000), edited by Monique Boekaerts, Paul Pintrich, and Moshe Zeidner, contains numerous chapters on various aspects of self-regulation. The chapter by Barry Zimmerman, "Attaining Self-Regulation: A Social

Cognitive Perspective," provides a detailed treatment of his cyclical model of self-regulation.

Another excellent resource is *Self-Regulated Learning and Academic Achievement: Theoretical Perspectives* (2001), edited by Barry Zimmerman and Dale Schunk. Barry Zimmerman describes different theoretical approaches to the issue of SRL and academic achievement in his chapter, "Theories of Self-Regulated Learning and Academic Achievement: An Overview and Analysis." Mary McCaslin and Daniel Hickey describe SRL from a Vygotskyian perspective in their chapter, "Self-Regulated Learning and Academic Achievement: A Vygotskyian View."

Self-regulated learning is also referred to as self-directed learning. In *The Self-Directed Learning Handbook: Challenging Adolescent Students to Excel* (2002), Maurice Gibbons describes how middle and high school teachers can create a self-directed learning program for their classroom that ranges from trying out a few ideas to implementing a complete program. The end of the book contains a set of resources, labeled A–J, to help teachers design and implement a self-directed learning program.

● Self-Efficacy

Dale Schunk and Frank Pajares are coauthors of "The Development of Academic Self-Efficacy," a chapter in *Development of Achievement Motivation* (2002), edited by Allan Wigfield

and Jacquelynne Eccles. They discuss factors that affect the development of self-efficacy, gender and ethnic differences in self-efficacy, self-efficacy for learning and achievement, and research on self-efficacy.

Helping teachers enhance the self-efficacy and achievement of mainstreamed students with special learning needs (those with learning disabilities, mild mental retardation, and behavior disorders) is the goal of *Self-Efficacy: Raising the Bar for Students with Learning Needs* (2000), by Joanne Eisenberger, Marcia Conti-D'Antonio, and Robert Bertrando. All three authors have worked in the public school system for twenty-six to thirty-six years. Their book describes how to teach for self-efficacy and provides in two appendices a set of strategies and forms to supplement the instructional approach they describe.

Summary

1. Social cognitive theory was created by Albert Bandura to explain how an individual's personal characteristics, behavioral patterns, and environment interact to produce learning, a process Bandura called triadic reciprocal causation.

2. Personal characteristics include such things as metacognitive knowledge, self-efficacy beliefs, goals, and anxiety. Behavioral patterns include self-observation, self-evaluation, and changes made to overcome perceptions of low self-efficacy and improve learning strategies. The environment includes the types of tasks on which people work, the reinforcing and punishing consequences they receive for exhibiting various behaviors, and the explanations and modeling skills they get from others.

3. Social cognitive theory emphasizes that, through the use of self-control and self-regulation skills, people are the cause of and have control over their behavior, a process that Bandura calls personal agency.

4. Self-control is controlling one's actions in the absence of reinforcement or punishment. Self-regulation is the consistent and appropriate application of self-control skills to new situations.

5. It is important for students to acquire self-regulation skills for at least three reasons. First, as students progress through school they are expected to assume more responsibility for their learning and so receive less prompting and guidance from teachers and parents. Second, as they move from grade to grade the amount and complexity of material they have to learn and be tested over increases. Third, when they leave school they will have to cope with a world that changes at a rapid rate.

6. Individual differences in self-regulation are strongly related to the personal characteristic of self-efficacy. Self-efficacy is a belief about how capable or prepared individuals feel they are to meet the demands of particular types of tasks.

7. A person's level of self-efficacy is affected by past accomplishments, the persuasive comments of others, emotional

states such as anxiety or well-being, and observing the accomplishments of similar others with whom we identify.

8. Self-efficacy affects a person's choice of goals and activities, the cognitive processes one uses to meet the demands of various tasks, the amount and persistence of effort expended to accomplish a goal, especially in the face of obstacles, and the emotions one experiences while working on a task, such as excitement, curiosity, anxiety, and dread.

9. Self-regulation is a cyclical process that moves through three phases. These phases and some of their associated self-regulatory processes are: forethought (goal setting, planning, self-efficacy for self-regulated learning, beliefs about consequences of achieving a goal, intrinsic interest, and learning-oriented vs. performance-oriented goals), performance (attention focusing, self-instruction, learning tactics, recording one's behavior, trying out different forms of behavior), and self-reflection (evaluating one's behavior, making constructive attributions for success and failure, self-reinforcement, and drawing inferences about improving self-regulation skills).

10. Self-regulated learning occurs when a person purposely generates and controls thoughts, feelings, and actions to achieve a learning goal. Because of their complexity, self-regulation skills develop throughout one's school career.

11. Self-regulation skills are best learned according to the following four-step model: (a) observe a model who exhibits a skill and verbalizes performance standards and motivational beliefs, (b) emulate, or reproduce, the general form of the model's behavior, (c) exhibit the modeled behavior under similar conditions but without the model present, and (d) adapt the modeled behavior to different tasks, settings, and conditions. In general terms, models exhibit inhibited behaviors, disinhibited behaviors, facilitated behaviors, and new behaviors.

12. Correlational studies show that, as expected, self-efficacy and self-regulation processes are strongly related to each other and both are strongly related to achievement.

13. Modeling has been shown to be an effective means for helping students acquire the SRL skills and self-efficacy beliefs that contribute both to mathematical problem solving and to writing ability.

14. Technology is a useful tool for helping students acquire SRL skills. It can providing them with models they would not otherwise get to see, with metacognitive feedback, and with scaffolded instruction. But the strongest effects have been obtained with students who had already acquired some self-regulation skills and had a high level of self-efficacy for SRL.

Key Terms

social cognitive theory *(276)*
triadic reciprocal causation *(277)*
personal agency *(278)*

self-efficacy *(279)*
self-regulated learning *(285–286)*

observational learning/modeling *(287)*
vicarious reinforcement *(290)*

Constructivist Learning Theory, Problem Solving, and Transfer

Key Points continued on next page.

When you begin to teach, you may devote a substantial amount of class time to having students learn information discovered by others. But the acquisition of a storehouse of facts, concepts, and principles is only part of what constitutes an appropriate education. Students must also learn how to *find, evaluate,* and *use* what they need to know to accomplish whatever goals they set for themselves. In other words, students need to learn how to be effective problem solvers.

One justification for teaching problem-solving skills in *addition* to ensuring mastery of factual information is that life in technologically oriented countries is marked by speedy change. New products, services, and social conventions are rapidly introduced and integrated into our lifestyles. Microcomputers, the Internet, cellular telephones, anticancer drugs, and in vitro fertilization, to name just a few examples, are relatively recent innovations that significantly affect the lives of many people.

But change, particularly rapid change, can be a mixed blessing. Although new products and services such as those just mentioned can make life more convenient, efficient, and enjoyable, they can also make life more complicated and problematic. The use of robots to perform certain jobs, for example, promises increased efficiency and productivity (which contribute to our standard of living), but it also threatens the job security of thousands of workers. Advances in medical care promise healthier and longer lives, but they introduce a host of moral, ethical, legal, and economic problems.

The educational implication that flows from these observations is clear: if we are to benefit from our ability to produce rapid and sometimes dramatic change, our schools need to invest more time, money, and effort in teaching students how to be effective problem solvers. As Lauren Resnick, a past president of the American Educational Research Association, argues:

> We need to identify and closely examine the aspects of education that are most likely to produce ability to

Technology Tools for Knowledge Construction and Problem Solving

● Technology tools are available to help students construct knowledge, become better problem solvers

2000) found that 38 percent of job applicants lacked sufficient skills for the positions they sought. Rather than blaming "a 'dumbing down' of the incoming workforce," the authors attributed the problem to "the higher skills required in today's workplace" (p. 2).

Good problem solvers share two general characteristics: a well-organized, meaningful fund of knowledge and a systematic set of problem-solving skills. Historically, cognitive learning theories have been particularly useful sources of ideas for imparting both. In this chapter, then, we will examine the issue of meaningful learning from the perspective of a cognitive theory that we introduced previously in the book: constructivism. We will then go on to describe the nature of the problem-solving process and what you can do to help your students become better problem solvers. We will conclude by describing the circumstances under which learned capabilities are applied to new tasks, a process known as transfer of learning. ●

adapt in the face of transitions and breakdowns. Rather than training people for particular jobs—a task better left to revised forms of on-the-job training—school should focus its efforts on preparing people to be good *adaptive learners*, so that they can perform effectively when situations are unpredictable and task demands change. (1987, p. 18)

Resnick's argument, which echoes many others, is not without some justification. A survey by the American Management Association (Greenberg, Canzoneri, & Joe,

MEANINGFUL LEARNING WITHIN A CONSTRUCTIVIST FRAMEWORK

● Constructivism: creating a personal interpretation of external ideas and experiences

 To help yourself understand this chapter, see the Chapter Themes and Thought Questions on the textbook web site, accessible from **http://education.college. hmco.com/students.**

Constructivism, as you may recall, holds that meaningful learning occurs when people actively try to make sense of the world—when they construct an interpretation of how and why things are—by filtering new ideas and experiences through existing knowledge structures (referred to in previous chapters as schemes). For example, an individual who lives in a country that provides, for little or no cost, such social services as medical care, counseling, education, job placement and training, and several weeks of paid vacation a year is likely to have constructed a rather different view of the role of government in people's lives from someone who lives in a country with a more market-oriented economy. To put it another way, meaningful learning is the active creation of knowledge structures (such as concepts, rules, hypotheses, and associations) from personal experience. In this section, we'll take a brief look at an early constructivist-oriented approach to learning, examine the nature of the constructivist model, and then put it all in perspective by considering the limits as well as the advantages of the constructivist perspective.

Jerome Bruner and Discovery Learning: An Early Constructivist Perspective

Constructivist explanations of learning are not new. Over the past seventy-five years, they have been promoted by such notable scholars as John Dewey, Jean Piaget, Lev Vygotsky, and Jerome Bruner. One of Bruner's contributions from the 1960s was the concept of **discovery learning**.

Bruner argued that too much school learning takes the form of step-by-step study of verbal or numerical statements or formulas that students can reproduce on cue but are unable to use outside the classroom. When students are presented with such highly structured materials as worksheets and other types of drill-and-practice exercises, Bruner argues, they become too dependent on other people. Furthermore, they are likely to think of learning as something done only to earn a reward.

Instead of using techniques that feature preselected and prearranged materials, Bruner believes teachers should confront children with problems and help them seek solutions either independently or by engaging in group discussion. True learning, says Bruner, involves "figuring out how to use what you already know in order to go beyond what you already think" (1983, p. 183). Like Piaget, Bruner argues that conceptions that children arrive at on their own are usually more meaningful than those proposed by others and that students do not need to be rewarded when they seek to make sense of things that puzzle them.

● Bruner: discover how ideas relate to each other and to existing knowledge

Bruner does not suggest that students should discover every fact or principle or formula they may need to know. Discovery is simply too inefficient a process to be used that widely, and learning from others can be as meaningful as personal discovery. Rather, Bruner argues that certain types of outcomes—understanding the ways in which ideas connect with one another, the possibility of solving problems on our own, and how what we already know is relevant to what we are trying to learn—are the essence of education and can best be achieved through personal discovery.

Discovery learning is increasingly being done now with computer simulation programs and for the purpose of learning science concepts and skills: for instance, designing and conducting genetics experiments, creating graphs from experimental data, or determining the cause of the spread of an influenza epidemic. The effect of such programs has been inconsistent, probably because, as we saw in the chapter on social cognitive theory, many students do not have the self-regulation skills to cope with the demands of discovery learning. For the effects of simulations to be more uniformly beneficial in helping students discover science concepts, students need to have first learned how to generate hypotheses from gathered data, design experiments that allow for a valid test of one's hypotheses (learners have a tendency to design experiments that will confirm rather than disconfirm a hypothesis), interpret experimental data, and monitor the adequacy of their own reasoning processes (de Jong & van Joolingen, 1998).

Constructivism Today

Facets of Constructivism   Contemporary constructivist theory has several variations, two of which we will describe shortly. But despite their differences, all the variations incorporate the following four facets.

● Construction of ideas strongly influenced by student's prior knowledge

1. *To constructivists, as we mentioned earlier, meaningful learning is the active creation of knowledge structures from personal experience.* Each learner builds a personal view of the world by using existing knowledge, interests, attitudes, goals, and the like to select and interpret currently available information (Brooks & Brooks, 2001; Shapiro, 2002). As Rochel Gelman (1994) points out, this assumption highlights the importance of what educational psychologists call entering behavior—the previously learned knowledge and skill that students bring to the classroom.

    The knowledge that learners bring with them to a learning task has long been suspected of having a powerful effect on subsequent performance. In 1978, David Ausubel wrote on the flyleaf of his textbook, *Educational Psychology: A Cognitive View,* "If I had to reduce all of educational psychology to just one principle, I would say this: the most important single factor influencing learning is what the learner already knows. Ascertain this and teach him accordingly" (Ausubel, Novak, & Hanesian, 1978). Research findings appear to have borne out Ausubel's contention. A review of 183 studies (Dochy, Segers, & Buehl, 1999) concluded that a strong relationship exists between prior knowledge and performance. Almost all of the studies (91 percent) reported a positive effect of prior knowledge on performance, and in some circumstances most of the variation (60 percent) in students' scores on a test was a function of what learners knew about the topic prior to instruction.

2. *The essence of one person's knowledge can never be* totally *transferred to another person because knowledge is the result of a personal interpretation of experience, which is influenced by such factors as the learner's age, gender, race, ethnic background, and knowledge base.* When knowledge is transferred from one person to another, some aspects of it are invariably "lost in translation." The area of musical performance provides an apt illustration of this aspect of constructivism. Although a piano teacher can tell a student volumes about how and why a piece should be performed in a particular way, the teacher cannot tell the student everything. The interpretation of a composition is constructed from such factors as the performer's knowledge of the composer's personality and motives, the nature of the instrument or instruments for which the composition was written, and the nature of the music itself. Because performers assign different meanings to such knowledge, different (yet equally valid) interpretations of the same composition result. Think, for example, of the many different ways in which you have heard "The Star-Spangled Banner" sung. Although listeners may prefer one version over another, there is no one correct way to sing this song.

3. *Even though knowledge is personal, people often agree about what is true.* This third facet follows directly from the second. Does constructivism necessarily mean that everyone walks around with a personal, idiosyncratic view of the world and that consensus is impossible? A few minutes of reflection should tell you that the answer is no. And if you recall what you read in the chapter on cultural and socioeconomic diversity, you will recognize that the cultures and societies to which people belong channel and place limits on the views people have of the world around them. Consequently, individuals make observations, test hypotheses, and draw conclusions that are largely consistent with one another (Duffy & Cunningham, 1996; Hung, 2002).

   Of course, there are many instances when people cannot reconcile their views and so agree to disagree. For example, in January 2002, President George W. Bush signed into law the reauthorization of the Elementary and Secondary Education Act, more popularly known as No Child Left Behind (NCLB). Although everyone agrees on what the law requires (e.g., all children in grades 3 through 8 scoring at the proficient level or above on tests of math and reading/language arts by 2014, with negative consequences for schools and districts that fail to show progress toward these goals), there is sharp disagreement about the true purpose of this legislation and its likely effects on students and teachers. Some see it as an effective means of school reform while others see it as an attempt to undercut the autonomy and vitality of public education. In matters such as these, truth is where it always is for the constructivist: in the mind of the beholder.

4. *Additions to, deletions from, or modifications of individuals' knowledge structures come mainly from the sharing of multiple perspectives.* Systematic, open-minded discussions and debates are instrumental in helping individuals create personal views (Cobb & Bowers, 1999; Hay & Barab, 2001). As we have seen in previous chapters, scholars form and reform their positions on aspects of theory or research as a result of years of discussion and debate with colleagues. The debate between the Piagetians and the Vygotskians (discussed in the chapter on stage theories of development) is a good example of this facet of constructivism. Consequently, students need to be provided with conditions that allow them to share and discuss multiple perspectives on information and experiences.

● Construction of ideas aided by discussion and debate

Two Variations on a Constructivist Theme   One view of meaningful learning that we have described, Jean Piaget's, holds that it is the natural result of an intrinsic drive to resolve inconsistencies and contradictions—that is, always to have a view of the world that makes sense in the light of what we currently know. One contemporary variation of constructivism, **cognitive constructivism,** is an outgrowth of Piaget's ideas because it focuses on the cognitive processes that take place within individuals. In other words, an individual's conception of the truth of some matter (for example, both birds and airplanes can fly because they use the same aeronautical

● Cognitive constructivism emphasizes role of cognitive processes in meaningful learning

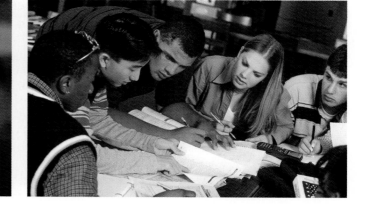

Most constructivist theories take one of two forms: cognitive constructivism or social constructivism. The former emphasizes the effect of one's cognitive processes on meaningful learning while the latter emphasizes the effect of other people's arguments and points of view on meaningful learning.

● Social constructivism emphasizes role of culture and social interaction in meaningful learning

principles) is based on her ability, with teacher guidance, to assimilate information effectively into existing schemes and develop new schemes and operations (the process Piaget called accommodation) in response to novel or discrepant ideas (Fosnot, 1996; Windschitl, 2002).

The constructivist variation known as **social constructivism** holds that meaningful learning occurs when people are explicitly taught how to use the psychological tools of their culture (like language, mathematics, diagrams, and approaches to problem solving) and are then given the opportunity to use these tools in authentic, real-life activities to create a common, or shared, understanding of some phenomenon. Students are encouraged to engage in open-ended discussion with peers and the teacher about such things as the meaning of terms and procedures, the relationships among ideas, and the applicability of knowledge to specific contexts. This process is often referred to by social constructivists as *negotiating meaning*. This view has its roots in the writings of such individuals as the psychologist Lev Vygotsky and the educational philosopher John Dewey (Perkins, 1999; Shapiro, 2002; Windschitl, 2002).

Although the cognitive and social constructivist perspectives emphasize different aspects of learning, they are not incompatible. The cognitive approach does not deny the value of learning in group activities, and the social approach does not deny the value of working independently of others. As one constructivist observed, "learning is an act of both individual interpretation and negotiation with other individuals" (Windschitl, 2002, p. 142). For example, people who play musical instruments in an orchestra practice both in a group and by themselves because some things are best learned in isolation (aspects of technique, such as breathing, fingering, or bowing) and others are best learned as part of the orchestra (discussing how various techniques best express the composer's intent). In athletics, too, certain skills are practiced alone while others are practiced with others (Anderson, Greeno, Reder, & Simon, 2000). Both perspectives also subscribe to the belief that "learning is an active process that is student-centered in the sense that, *with the teacher's help*, learners select and transform information, construct hypotheses, and make decisions" (Chrenka, 2001, p. 694).

Table 10.1 summarizes the characteristics of cognitive and social constructivism and the basic instructional approaches that flow from each of these variations. The main conditions that support an individual's attempt to construct personally meaningful knowledge are detailed in the next section.

● Constructivism aided by cognitive apprenticeship, realistic tasks, multiple perspectives

Conditions That Foster Constructivism   The fostering conditions that constructivists typically mention include a cognitive apprenticeship between student and teacher, a use of realistic problems and conditions, and an emphasis on multiple perspectives.

Cognitive Apprenticeship   The first condition, that of a cognitive apprenticeship, was illustrated in the chapter on information-processing theory when we described the reciprocal teaching program of Annemarie Palincsar and Ann Brown (1984). Its main feature is that the teacher models a cognitive process that students are to learn and then gradually turns responsibility for executing the process over to students as

Table 10.1	Cognitive and Social Constructivist Approaches to Learning and Teaching	
Approach	**Basic Characteristics**	**Instructional Implications**
Cognitive constructivism	• Existing knowledge schemes and operations are modified by the addition (assimilation) of new ideas that are judged to be related. New knowledge schemes and operations are created (accommodation) to adapt to ideas and procedures that are inconsistent with existing schemes. • Assimilation and accommodation processes assumed to be innate and supported by opportunities to interact with peers and the physical environment.	• Teacher challenges students' current conceptions by presenting new ideas that do not quite fit (inducing disequilibrium) • Students work individually and together to construct new, more effective schemes. • Emphasis is on constructing personal meaning by developing new schemes.
Social constructivism	• Learning initially occurs in the presence of and is influenced by more knowledgeable others. • The knowledge and skills that are acquired through the guidance of others are connected to existing schemes and gradually internalized, allowing the learner to become increasingly self-regulated and independent.	• Teacher helps students through scaffolded instruction to construct ideas using realistic, open-ended tasks. • Under teacher guidance, students work collaboratively to construct new conceptions. • Emphasis is on constructing and internalizing shared meaning.

● Scaffolding: provide student with enough help to complete a task; gradually decrease help as student becomes able to work independently

they become more skilled. As you may recall from our earlier discussions, providing such environmental supports as modeling, hints, leading questions, and suggestions, and then gradually removing them as the learner demonstrates increased competence is called *scaffolding*. Cognitive apprenticeships also occur in less formal circumstances, as when a child joins an existing peer group (like a play group), at first mostly watches what the other children do, and then gradually, with little explicit direction from the others, participates in one or more aspects of the task.

Situated Learning   The second condition, often called **situated learning** (or situated cognition), is that students be given learning tasks set in realistic contexts. A realistic context is one in which students must solve a meaningful problem by using a variety of skills and information. The rationale for this condition is twofold:

1. Learning is more likely to be meaningful (related to previously learned knowledge and skills) when it is embedded in a realistic context (Duffy & Cunningham, 1996; Hung, 2002).
2. Traditional forms of classroom learning and instruction, which are largely decontextualized in the sense that what students learn is relevant only to taking tests and performing other classroom tasks, leads to a condition that has been referred to as **inert knowledge.** That is, students fail to use what they learned earlier (such as mathematical procedures) to solve either real-life problems (such as calculating the square footage of the walls of a room in order to know how many rolls of wallpaper to buy) or other school-related problems because they don't see any relationship between the two (Perkins, 1999). But as we point out later in this chapter when we discuss transfer of learning, some have argued that too strong an emphasis on situated cognition may create the same kind of problem (Bereiter, 1997).

An example of situated learning would be to use the game of baseball as a vehicle for middle school or high school students to apply aspects of science, mathematics, and sociology. Students could be asked to use their knowledge of physics to explain how pitchers are able to make the ball curve left or right or drop down as it approaches home plate. They could be asked to use their mathematical skills to figure out how far home runs travel. They could also be asked to read about the Negro Leagues and Jackie Robinson and discuss why it took until the late 1940s for major league baseball to begin integration. The Case in Print provides real-life examples of how teachers have put the concept of situated learning into practice.

A more formal way of implementing situated learning is to use problem-based learning (PBL) (Hung, 2002). Unlike a traditional approach to instruction in which students first learn a body of knowledge and then use that knowledge to solve problems, PBL presents students with complex, authentic problems (such as creating a water management plan for the desert southwest) and requires them to identify and locate the information they need to solve the problem. In other words, students decide what they need to know in order to solve the problem (Angeli, 2002; Soderberg & Price, 2003; Uyeda, Madden, Brigham, Luft, & Washburne, 2002). In our chapter on approaches to instruction we describe how PBL can be used with computer-based technology. In the Resources for Further Investigation section of this chapter, we describe a web site that provides information about PBL, directions for designing PBL units, and model problems.

Multiple Perspectives The third condition fostering constructivism is that students should view ideas and problems from multiple perspectives. The rationale, again, is twofold: most of life's problems are multifaceted, and the knowledge base of experts is a network of interrelated ideas. The complex process of becoming an effective teacher is a good example of the need for multiple perspectives. As we mentioned at the beginning of the book, being an effective teacher requires the mastery of many skills and disciplines so that classroom problems (such as why a particular student does not perform up to expectations) can be analyzed and attacked from several perspectives.

The following section provides an example of a constructivist-oriented teaching lesson, and Table 10.2 notes the major characteristics of a constructivist classroom.

An Example of Constructivist Teaching A fifth-grade teacher wanted his students to understand that the mathematical concept of pi expresses the relationship

Table 10.2	Characteristics of a Constructivist Classroom

- Teaching and learning start from a student's current understanding of a subject. Therefore, a teacher's first task is to determine the completeness and accuracy of what students currently know about key topics.

- Teachers help students create realistic learning experiences that will lead students to elaborate on and restructure current knowledge. Teachers believe that meaningful learning involves discovering, questioning, analyzing, synthesizing, and evaluating information.

- Students frequently engage in complex, meaningful, problem-based activities whose content and goals are negotiated with the teacher.

- Students have frequent opportunities to debate and discuss substantive issues.

- A primary goal of instruction is for students to learn to think for themselves. Consequently, teachers use a variety of indirect teaching methods, such as modeling the thinking processes they want students to use; providing prompts, probes, and suggestions; providing heuristics (a topic discussed later in this chapter); and using technology to organize and represent information.

- Students engage in such high-level cognitive processes as explaining ideas, interpreting texts, predicting phenomena, and constructing arguments based on evidence.

- In addition to assessing student learning with written exams, teachers also require students to write research reports, make oral presentations, build models, and engage in problem-solving activities.

- Student progress is assessed continually rather than just at the end of a unit and the end of a semester.

- Subject-matter disciplines and their knowledge bases are seen as continually undergoing revision.

SOURCES: Brooks & Brooks (2001); Gabler, Schroeder, & Curtis (2003); Windschitl (2002).

Constructing Real Learning Experiences

The fostering conditions that constructivists typically mention include a cognitive apprenticeship between student and teacher, a use of realistic problems and conditions, and an emphasis on multiple perspectives. . . . The second condition, often called situated learning (or situated cognition), is that students be given learning tasks set in realistic contexts. A realistic context is one in which students must solve a meaningful problem by using a variety of skills and information. (p. 313–314)

All-USA Teacher Team: Changing Lives
One Class at a Time

TRACEY WONG BRIGGS
USA Today 10/14/99

In rural Alaska, science teacher Steven Jacquier's high school students feed alcohol to pregnant mice.

After the students see the deformed fetuses that develop, they hold clinics to spread the message in their Eskimo villages, where fetal alcohol syndrome is a major problem.

In Walnut, Calif., Suzanne Middle School teacher Alan Haskvitz had his social studies students rewrite voting instructions because they couldn't understand them. Their changes were used by Los Angeles County.

And in Newnan, Ga., seventh- and eighth-graders who have arrived at Fairmont Alternative School through the juvenile court system can experience the other side of the bench as judges, lawyers, bailiffs and jurors through a school judicial system Carmella Williams Scott created to turn criminal thinkers into critical thinkers.

For their success at unlocking student minds and making a difference in their lives, Jacquier, Haskvitz and Scott, along with 13 other individual teachers and four teaching teams, have been named to USA TODAY's All-USA Teacher First Team as representatives of all outstanding teachers. . . .

"These stellar teachers inspire their students to be the best they can be, academically. They also teach lessons of empowerment, responsibility and community," says Tom Curley, president and publisher of *USA Today*. "By honoring them, we recognize what they're doing is building a better future."

The teachers unlock minds in a variety of situations, from Jacquier, who travels to three remote Eskimo villages in western Alaska each year to teach science in 12-week modules; to Suzanne Taffet-Romano, who transforms Long Island children with autism from non-communicators to students who read and tell jokes.

Among the 20 First Team members, 10 teach elementary school, two teach middle school and six teach high school. Scott teaches at an alternative middle/high school, and Taffet-Romano teaches at the Rosemary Kennedy School for students with cognitive disorders in Wantagh, N.Y.

Science of Discovery

The First Team represents a diversity of outstanding teaching, but there is also a strong scientific bent. Nearly half either teach science or are noted for how well they incorporate science into the curriculum:

- Myron Blosser's molecular genetics students not only design original research but also order their supplies and maintain thousands of dollars' worth of lab equipment at Harrisonburg (Va.) High. That's real science—and real life, Blosser says.
- Edna Waller led school and community efforts to establish two wetland areas and nature trails on the grounds of Magnolia Park Elementary School, bordering Gulf Islands National Seashore in Ocean Springs, Miss. The outdoor labs draw students not just into the science of the wetlands but also into the history and economics of Ocean Springs, which relies on the shrimping industry. "It makes a connection to them to real life," Waller says.
- Sylvia Dee Shore trains her Clubview Elementary third-graders to monitor water quality and work on water conservation in Columbus, Ga. In five years, Shore's River Kids Network has spread to 17 schools and more than 1,000 students statewide. "They truly believe they're making a difference, and they are," Shore says.
- Susan Roberts Bradburn has fourth- to sixth-graders research science exhibits to present to other classes and finds they work harder to finish their schoolwork correctly so they have more time for their mobile museum projects. "It's like I've just

found this secret," says Bradburn, who teaches at West Marion (N.C.) Elementary School.

- Tina Cross has involved students in writing $179,000 worth of grants for Carver High in Columbus, Ga. "I don't think there's a student in the magnet program who hasn't been involved in a grant," says senior Phillip Moore, 17.

The process teaches students larger lessons about going after what they want, Cross says. "They know where the equipment comes from and what it takes to get it."

Teamwork

Four of the 20 First Team slots this year went to teams of teachers who collaborate:

- In Bio/Geo, a biology/geometry course dubbed "math and science get wet and muddy," Sandra Duck Eidson and Lela Whelchel's students at West Hall High in Oakwood, Ga., teamed up to build DNA models and monitor creek water quality.

    "It taught me to think about getting other people's opinions instead of just my own," says Justin Woodsmall, 17.
- Craig Yager and Lise Blumenthal tap parent and grandparent volunteers, student teachers, professors and others to help teach the Fifth Grade Flock at Whittier Elementary School in Boulder, Colo.
- The "Zoo School" faculty in Lincoln, Neb., encourages students to pursue their own interests and share their expertise. "We are a community of learners," science teacher Sara Leroy-Toren says.
- And the four-member Tiger Team at Andrew Jackson Middle School in Cross Lanes, W. Va., builds interdisciplinary units around subjects such as the Native American experience and World War II that help eighth-graders understand the dangers of intolerance.

    "When the World War II unit is done, student behavior changes. They become more tolerant and see hate and prejudice in a different light," math teacher Karen McNeer says.

First Teamers run student-centered classrooms that foster individual and community growth in ways not found in any textbook:

- Jody Solmonson introduces her fifth-graders at Bear Valley Elementary in Anchorage to Shakespeare, atomic structure and the physics of energy loss, often through activities that encourage them to forge their own way. True accomplishment is the only path to self-esteem, Solmonson says: "You can't give it. You can only earn it. You set up challenges that they can overcome."
- Linda Chelman welcomes students with special needs in to her second-grade class at Jefferson Elementary in Franklin, Mass. Beyond designing activities using different talents to reinforce the same concept, she uses inclusion to build a sense of community. Twice a week, Chelman gathers her students in a circle to talk about problem-solving strategies and how to include other students. "Students have to realize that we're all different, but we're all alike," she says.
- And Spanish teacher Maria Garcia-Rameau opens up the entire Latin world to students at Scarborough High in Houston, many of whom don't think beyond Mexico, say former student Brett Millican, 30. Millican credits his high school Spanish with opening the door to his Coast Guard career, in which he has served on cutters off Florida and Puerto Rico.

Questions and Activities

1. What principles of constructivist learning theory are reflected in the instructional activities of those teachers who were named to *USA Today*'s All-USA First Team?

2. What other field-based projects can you think of that would accomplish the same objectives as the projects described in this story? Describe where you would take students, what you would have them do, and what you would hope to accomplish.

3. Some of the projects described in this story required students to visit such field sites as wetlands, rivers, and creeks and to conduct projects that benefited such other groups as municipal governments. How would you respond to a parent who believed that students were learning less because of decreased classroom time?

between the circumference of a circle and its diameter. On the first day of school he gave students writing tablets divided into three columns. He told them that over the next three weeks they were to identify circular objects of all sizes outside of school and measure how many inches each one was across its center and around its perimeter (he purposely avoided using the terms diameter and circumference at this point). The first measurement was to be recorded in the first column of the tablet and the second measurement in the second column. Over the next three weeks the students measured all manner of round things (such as coins, tires, and dishes), all the time wondering why they were doing this project and what the teacher's explanation would be. When the class met on the day of the project's deadline, the students were both surprised and disappointed that the teacher did not offer an explanation. Instead, he had the students look over their two columns of numbers and said, "Now tell me what you can see that is interesting about these two sets of numbers."

Gradually, the students noticed that the measurements of the circumference were always larger than the measurements of the diameter. He then asked, "How much bigger are the numbers in the second column, the distance around the circle, in relation to the numbers in the first column, the distance across the circle?" Once again, students wondered when the teacher would simply tell them the answer. But with a bit of coaxing, students began to guess, until one girl realized that the answer to the question could be gained by dividing the larger number by the smaller one. The students did so, recorded their answers in the third column of their tablet, and were astounded to realize that the answer was always the same (3.14) regardless of the size of the circles.

In a much more meaningful way than would have occurred had the students simply memorized that pi is the ratio of the circumference of a circle to its diameter, the students learned, as one put it, "No matter how big a circle is, the distance around it is always a little more than three times the distance across it." They also learned that discovering ideas is fun and that mathematics has a basis in the real world (Funk, 2003).

The essence of a constructivist-oriented lesson is to provide students with realistic problems that cannot be solved with their current level of understanding and, by allowing them to interact mainly among themselves, to work out new understandings. It's important to emphasize the social nature of this approach. The experiences and ideas of others become springboards for further experimentation and discussion. This approach also emphasizes the role of the teacher as artist. Because a teacher does not know beforehand what questions students will ask or what solutions they will propose, the teacher's questions and suggestions cannot be scripted in advance. They have to be generated on the spot, and they have to further the point of the lesson most of the time.

● Constructivist-oriented teaching encourages creating new views; uses scaffolding, realistic tasks, and class discussion

Putting Constructivism in Perspective   Although constructivism has much to offer teachers, like any other theory, it does have its limitations, and there may be problems with its implementation (see Matthews, 2002, for example, for a discussion of constructivism's weaknesses and limitations). Here are a few you should keep in mind:

- Because of constructivism's emphasis on guiding rather than telling, accepting different perspectives on issues and solutions to problems, modifying previous conceptions in the light of new information, and creating an atmosphere that encourages active participation, it is almost impossible to create highly detailed lesson plans. Much of what teachers do depends on how students respond. Teaching from this perspective will place a premium on your teacher-as-artist abilities.
- Teaching from a constructivist perspective is more time-consuming and places higher demands on learners as compared to a typical lecture format (de Jong & van Joolingen, 1998; Perkins, 1999).
- Constructivism is not the only orientation to learning and teaching that you will ever need (nor is any other theory, for that matter). You need to know which theory

or approach best fits which purposes and circumstances. Sometimes memorization of factual information is essential, and sometimes an instructional objective can be accomplished more efficiently (and just as effectively) with a clear and well-organized lecture (Airasian & Walsh, 1997).

Can you recall a class in which the instructor used constructivist techniques? What did the instructor do? How did you react? Was the learning outcome more meaningful than for other classes?

The extent to which teachers engage in constructivist teaching practices is determined in large part by how completely they accept its underlying principles (e.g., knowledge is temporary, knowledge is the result of discussions among students and between students and the teacher, students have input into the curriculum, learning is grounded in real-life tasks and settings to make it relevant to students' lives). Teachers who believe that they, and not the students, should decide what gets learned and how, and that their primary responsibility is to prepare students for high-stakes tests, are less likely to use a constructivist approach (Haney & McArthur, 2002).

Assuming you do accept some constructivist principles, there are many techniques you can use to foster meaningful learning within a constructivist framework. Several computer-based approaches are described at the end of this chapter. One that does not rely on computer technology but is particularly well suited to developing, comparing, and understanding different points of view is the classroom discussion (Brookfield & Preskill, 1999; Brown & Renshaw, 2000; Rabow, Charness, Kipperman, & Radcliffe-Vasile, 1994). Because this format also allows students to deal with realistic problems that are often complex and ambiguous and to exercise cognitive skills taught by the teacher, it is an excellent general-purpose method for helping students construct a meaningful knowledge base. It is also an effective way to improve the quality of students' writing. A study of discussion-based approaches to literature instruction in middle and high school classrooms (involving almost one thousand students) found that higher levels of discussion-based instruction about reading assignments were associated with more abstract and elaborated reports, analyses, and essays based on the readings (Applebee et al., 2003).

Let's turn our attention to some specific Suggestions for Teaching that describe how to use discussion and other techniques to emphasize meaningful learning in your classroom.

Suggestions for Teaching in Your Classroom

Using a Constructivist Approach to Meaningful Learning

1 **Arrange the learning situation so that students are exposed to different perspectives on a problem or an issue.**

JOURNAL ENTRY
Ways to Arrange for Discovery to Take Place

This is the crux of the discovery approach and the constructivist view of learning. The basic idea is to *arrange* the elements of a learning task and *guide* student actions so that students discover, or construct, a personally meaningful conception of a problem or issue (as opposed to someone else's conception). In some cases, you may present a topic that is a matter of opinion or that all students are sure to know something about. In other cases, you might structure the discussion by exposing all participants to the same background information.

a. Ask students to discuss familiar topics or those that are matters of opinion.

EXAMPLES

● "What are some of the techniques that advertising agencies use in television commercials to persuade us to buy certain products?"

● "What do you think is the best book you ever read, and why do you think so?"

b. Provide necessary background information by asking all students to read all or part of a book, take notes on a lecture, view a film, conduct library research, or conduct research on the Internet.

EXAMPLES

● After the class has read *Great Expectations,* ask, "What do you think Dickens was trying to convey when he wrote this novel? Was he just trying to tell a good story, or was he also trying to get us to think about certain kinds of relationships between people?"

● "After I explain some of the principles of electrical currents, I'm going to ask you to suggest rules for connecting batteries in series and in parallel. Then we'll see how well your rules work."

2 **Structure discussions by posing a specific question, presenting a provocative topic-related issue, or asking students to choose topics or subtopics.**

JOURNAL ENTRY
Questions That Are Likely to
Stimulate Productive Classroom
Discussion

It is important to structure a discovery session by giving students something reasonably specific to discuss; otherwise, they may simply engage in a disorganized and desultory bull session. You might supply direction in the following ways:

a. In some cases, encourage students to arrive at conclusions already reached by others.

Thousands of books provide detailed answers to such questions as, "What is human about human beings? How did they get that way? How can they be made more so?" But constructivists believe that answers mean more when they are constructed by the individual, not supplied ready-made by others. As you look over lesson plans, therefore, you might try to put together some questions for students to answer by engaging in discussion rather than by reading or listening to what others have already discovered. In searching for such topics, you might take into account the techniques that Bruner described. Here is a list of those techniques, together with an example of each one. In your Reflective Journal you might describe similar applications that you could use when you begin to teach. Keep in mind that students often acquire a deeper understanding of ideas and issues when they have had appropriate previous experience:

● *Emphasize contrast.* In an elementary school social studies unit on cultural diversity, say, "When you watch this film on Mexico, look for customs and ways of living that differ from ours. Then we'll talk about what these differences are and why they may have developed."

● *Stimulate informed guessing.* In a middle school unit on natural science, you might say, "Suppose we wanted to figure out some kind of system to classify trees so that we could later find information about particular types. What would be the best way to do it?" After students have developed a classification scheme, show them schemes that specialists have developed.

● *Encourage participation.* In a high school political science class, illustrate the jury system by staging a mock trial. (Note that the use of a simulation satisfies the constructivist criterion of realistic tasks and contexts.)

● *Stimulate awareness.* In a high school English class, ask the students to discuss how the author developed the plot.

b. In other cases, present a controversial topic for which there is no single answer.

Discussions might center on provocative issues about which there are differences of opinion. One caution here is to avoid topics (such as premarital sex or legalized abortion) that parents may not want discussed in school, either because they are convinced it is their prerogative to discuss them with their children or because they feel that students may be pressured to endorse your opinion because you assign grades. You should not avoid controversy, but neither should you go out of your way to agitate students and their parents.

Another caution is to avoid selecting issues that provoke more than they instruct. You may be tempted to present a highly controversial topic and then congratulate yourself at the end of the period if most students engaged in heated discussion. But if they simply argued enthusiastically about something that had nothing to do with the subject you are assigned to teach, you cannot honestly claim to have arranged an instructive exchange of ideas.

A final caution relates to a characteristic of formal thought that we described in the chapter on stage theories of development: there may be a tendency for secondary school students to engage in unrestrained theorizing when they first experience the thrill of being able to deal with hypotheses and possibilities. Thus, you may have to remind some students to take into account realities when they discuss controversial issues involving tangled background circumstances or conflicts of interest.

EXAMPLES

- In a middle school science class, ask students to list arguments for and against attempting to alter the genetic code of human beings.
- In a high school political science class, ask students to list arguments for and against democratic forms of government.

③ If time is limited and if only one topic is to be covered, ask students to form a circle and have an all-class discussion.

You may sometimes wish to have the entire class discuss a topic. Such discussions are most likely to be successful if all students have eye contact with one another. The simplest way to achieve this is to ask all students to form a circle. Next, invite responses to the question you have posed. As students make remarks, serve more as a moderator than as a leader. Try to keep the discussion on the topic, but avoid directing it toward a specific predetermined end result. If one or more students tend to dominate the discussion, say something like, "Kim and Carlos have given us their ideas. Now I'd like to hear from the rest of you." If an aggressive student attacks or belittles something that a classmate says, respond with something like, "It's good to *believe* in a point of view, but let's be friendly as we listen to other opinions. This is supposed to be a discussion, not an argument or a debate."

Factors that lead to successful or unsuccessful discussions are often idiosyncratic, but there are certain procedures you might follow to increase the likelihood of success.

a. Ask questions that stimulate students to apply, analyze, synthesize, and evaluate.

When you first structure a discussion session, but also when it is under way, take care to ask questions likely to elicit different points of view. If you ask students to supply information (for example, "When did Charles Dickens write *Great Expectations?*"), the first correct response will lead to closure. You may end up asking a series of questions leading to brief answers—the equivalent of a program or a fill-in exam. When you seek to encourage students to construct personally meaningful interpretations of the issues or to develop skills as deductive thinkers, it is preferable to ask questions likely to tap higher levels of thinking.

JOURNAL ENTRY
Ways to Supervise Discussion Sessions

EXAMPLES

- "You just learned how to calculate the area of a circle. Think of as many different ways as you can of how you might be able to use that bit of knowledge if you were a do-it-yourself home-owner." (Application)

- "Last month we read a novel by Dickens; this month we read a play by Shakespeare. What are some similarities in the way each author developed the plot of his story?" (Synthesis)

b. Allow sufficient time for initial responses, and then probe for further information (if appropriate).

Recent research has found that many teachers fail to allow enough time for students to respond to questions. Quite often, instructors wait only one second before repeating the question, calling on another student, or answering the question themselves. When teachers wait at least three seconds after asking a question, students are more likely to participate; their responses increase in frequency, length, and complexity; and their achievement improves. There are changes in teacher behavior as well. As a function of waiting longer, teachers ask more complex questions and have higher expectations for the quality of students' responses (Ormrod, 2004).

One possible explanation for improved student recitation when teachers wait longer for a response is that reflective thinkers have an opportunity to figure out what they want to say. But even impulsive thinkers probably welcome a few more seconds of thinking time. It seems logical to expect that snap answers will be more superficial than answers supplied after even a few seconds of reflection.

In addition to giving students ample time to make an initial response, you should encourage them to pursue an idea. If it seems appropriate, probe for further information or clarification of a point by asking students who give brief or incomplete answers to explain how or why they arrived at a conclusion or to supply additional comments.

EXAMPLE

- "Well, Keesha, I'm sure a gardener might sometimes need to figure the area of a circle, but can you give a more specific example? If you can't think of one right away, put up your hand as soon as you can describe a specific situation where it would help to know the area of a circular patch of lawn or soil."

c. When selecting students to recite, use techniques likely to sustain steady but nonthreatening attention. At the same time, guard against the temptation to call primarily on bright, articulate, assertive students.

The way you moderate student contributions may not only determine how successful the discussion will be; it may also influence how students feel about themselves and each other. Jacob Kounin (1970) points out that when a teacher first names a student and then asks a question, the rest of the class may tend to turn its attention to other things. The same tendency to tune out may occur if a teacher follows a set pattern of calling on students (for example, by going around a circle). To keep all the students on their toes, you might ask questions first and then, in an unpredictable sequence, call on those who volunteer to recite, frequently switching from one part of the room to another. Guard against the temptation to call primarily on students you expect to give good or provocative answers. Repeatedly ignoring students who may be a bit inarticulate or unimaginative may cause them and their classmates to conclude that you think they are incompetent. These students may then lose interest in and totally ignore what is taking place.

4 Use guided experiences to satisfy both constructivist principles and state learning standards.

JOURNAL ENTRY
Techniques for Satisfying
Constructivist Principles and
State Learning Standards

Because constructivism is strongly student-centered and emphasizes high-level outcomes, it is sometimes perceived as being incompatible with the need for teachers to prepare students for high-stakes tests that are based on state learning standards. But through the use of guided experiences, teachers can do both. The trick is to embed standards in learning experiences that students care about. Geoffrey Caine, Renate Nummela Caine, and Carol McClintic (2002) describe how this was done for eighth-grade classes studying the U.S. Civil War.

To satisfy state learning standards, students needed to learn such things as the nature of slavery, the causes of the war, important dates and the sequence of events, major battles, and significant individuals who affected the course of the war. The first step was to teach students how to listen to one another and express disagreements in a nonjudgmental way. An introductory event was then used to spark students' interest in the topic. They were read a story about a woman who disguised herself as a man, enlisted in the Union Army, and worked as a coal handler on a canal boat. They were then shown a short segment from the motion picture *Gettysburg* in which Confederate soldiers marched directly into withering cannon and rifle fire. The last part of the introduction involved telling students that over four hundred women disguised themselves as men and participated in the war and that the fifty-one thousand soldiers who were killed during the three-day battle of Gettysburg exceeded the number of U.S. soldiers who were killed during the entire Vietnam War. When invited to raise questions, the students wanted to know such things as why women fought in the war, how it was that nobody knew they were women, why the North and South went to war, and why soldiers would walk into enemy gunfire.

The students were assigned to groups based on the similarity of the questions they raised and were told to seek answers from library resources, the Internet, and interviews with war veterans. The teachers used the subsequent reports each group made to the class and the discussions that followed to ensure that such standards-related issues as the different groups involved in the war and the nature of slavery were introduced and discussed.

5 If abundant time is available and if a controversial or subdivided topic is to be discussed, divide the class into groups of about five.

JOURNAL ENTRY
Techniques for Arranging Small-
Group Discussions

A major limitation of any kind of discussion is that only one person can talk at a time. You can reduce this difficulty by dividing the class into smaller groups before asking them to exchange ideas. A group of about five seems to work best. If only two or three students are interacting with one another, the exchange of ideas may be limited. If there are more than five, not all members will be able to contribute at frequent intervals.

Raymond Brown and Peter Renshaw (2000) describe an approach to small-group classroom discussion based on the following five principles derived from Vygotsky's sociocultural theory of cognitive development:

1. Students should present their ideas with sufficient clarity that other students can distinguish relevant from irrelevant ideas.
2. Relevant ideas can be rejected by others only if their validity can be questioned on the basis of past experience or logical reasoning.
3. Ideas that contradict one another or that belong to mutually exclusive points of view must be resolved through group argument.
4. All members understand and agree that the group will strive to reach consensus on an issue by each member actively contributing to arguments that lead to a solution.
5. The group will present its arguments to the other members of the class.

THE NATURE OF PROBLEM SOLVING

As with most of the other topics covered in this book, an extensive amount of theorizing and research on problem solving has been conducted over the years. We will focus our discussion on the types of problems that students are typically required to deal with, the cognitive processes that play a central role in problem solving, and various approaches to teaching problem solving in the classroom.

Let's begin by asking what we mean by the terms *problem* and *problem solving*. Most, if not all, psychologists would agree that "a problem is said to exist when one has a goal and has not yet identified a means for reaching that goal" (Gagné et al., 1993, p. 211). **Problem solving,** then, is the identification and application of knowledge and skills that result in goal attainment (Martinez, 1998). Although this definition encompasses a wide range of problem types, we will focus on three types that students frequently encounter both in school and out.

Three Common Types of Problems

In the first category are the well-structured problems of mathematics and science—the type of problems that students from kindergarten through middle school are typically required to solve. **Well-structured problems** are clearly formulated, can be solved by recall and application of a specific procedure (called an *algorithm*), and result in a solution that can be evaluated against a well-known, agreed-on standard (Hamilton & Ghatala, 1994)—for example:

$$5 + 8 =$$
$$732 - 485 =$$
$$8 + 3x = 40 - 5x$$

What constitutes a problem to be solved varies with the age and experience of the learner and the nature of the problem itself (Martinez, 1998). The second of the mathematical examples is likely to be a genuine problem for some first or second graders who are used to seeing subtraction exercises arrayed vertically (minuend on top, subtrahend beneath, horizontal line under the subtrahend). Fifth graders, however, who have had experience with arithmetic assignments in a variety of formats, would be able to retrieve and use the correct algorithm automatically. Because the

> • Well-structured problems: clearly stated, known solution procedures, known evaluation standards

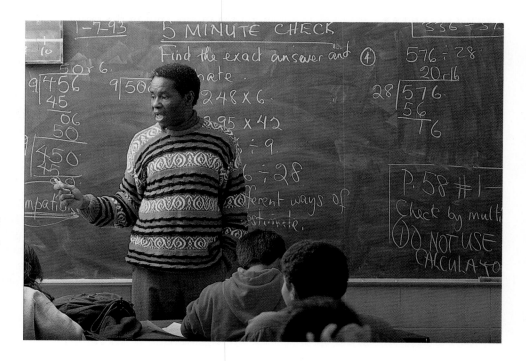

Well-structured problems have a clear structure, can be solved by using a standard procedure, and produce solutions that can be evaluated against an agreed-on standard. They are the type of problem that students are asked to solve most frequently.

fifth graders know the means to reach their goal, they do not face a problem-solving task according to our definition, but just a type of exercise or practice.

In the second category are the ill-structured problems often encountered in everyday life and in disciplines such as economics or psychology. **Ill-structured problems** are more complex, provide few cues pointing to solution procedures, and have less definite criteria for determining when the problem has been solved (Hamilton & Ghatala, 1994). Examples of ill-structured problems are how to identify and reward good teachers, how to improve access to public buildings and facilities for persons with physical disabilities, and how to increase voter turnout for elections.

The third category includes problems that are also ill structured but differ from the examples just mentioned in two respects. First, these problems tend to divide people into opposing camps because of the emotions they arouse. Second, the primary goal, at least initially, is not to determine a course of action but to identify the most reasonable position. These problems are often referred to as **issues** (Ruggiero, 1988, 2004). Examples of issues are capital punishment, gun control, and nondenominational prayer in classrooms. Beginning with the freshman year in high school, students usually receive more opportunities than in earlier grades to deal with ill-structured problems and issues.

● Ill-structured problems: vaguely stated, unclear solution procedures, vague evaluation standards

● Issues: ill-structured problems that arouse strong feelings

Helping Students Become Good Problem Solvers

Despite the differences that exist among well-structured problems, ill-structured problems, and issues, recent theory and research suggest that good problem solvers employ the same general approach when solving one or another of these problem types (see, for example, Bransford & Stein, 1993; Gagné et al., 1993; Krulik & Rudnick, 1993; Nickerson, 1994; Pretz, Naples, & Sternberg, 2003; Ruggiero, 1988, 2004). This approach consists of five steps or processes:

1. Realize that a problem exists.
2. Understand the nature of the problem.
3. Compile relevant information.
4. Formulate and carry out a solution.
5. Evaluate the solution.

Well-structured problems may call only for the implementation of steps 2, 4, and 5, but the other two problem types require all five steps. We will discuss each of these steps in the next few pages, along with some specific techniques that you can use to help your students become good problem solvers.

Step 1: Realize That a Problem Exists   Most people assume that if a problem is worth solving, they won't have to seek it out; it will make itself known. Like most other assumptions, this one is only partly true. Well-structured problems are often thrust on us by teachers, in the form of in-class exercises or homework, or by supervisors at work. Ill-structured problems and issues, however, often remain hidden from most people. It is a characteristic of good problem solvers that they are more sensitive to the existence of problems than most of their peers (Pretz et al., 2003).

● Problem finding depends on curiosity, dissatisfaction with status quo

The keys to problem recognition, or *problem finding* as it is sometimes called, are curiosity and dissatisfaction. You need to question why a rule, procedure, or product is the way it is or to feel frustrated or irritated because something does not work as well as it might. The organization known as Mothers Against Drunk Driving, for example, was begun by a woman who, because her daughter had been killed in a traffic accident by a drunk driver, was dissatisfied with current, ineffective laws. This organization has been instrumental in getting state legislatures to pass laws against drunk driving that mandate more severe penalties. As another example, John Bransford and Barry Stein (1993) mention a business that was able to eliminate the generation of 120 tons of paper per year by taking a critical look at its record-keeping procedure.

Problem finding does not come readily to most people, possibly because schools emphasize solving well-structured problems and possibly because most people have a natural tendency to assume that things work as well as they can. Like any other cognitive process, however, problem recognition can improve with instruction and practice. Students can be sensitized in a number of ways to the absence or flaws and shortcomings of products, procedures, rules, or whatever else. We will make some specific suggestions about improving problem recognition and the other problem-solving processes a bit later in Suggestions for Teaching in Your Classroom: Teaching Problem-Solving Techniques.

Step 2: Understand the Nature of the Problem   The second step in the problem-solving process is perhaps the most critical. The problem solver has to construct an *optimal* representation, or understanding, of the nature of a problem or issue. The preceding sentence stresses the word *optimal* for two reasons. First, most problems can be expressed in a number of ways. Written problems, for example, can be recast as pictures, equations, graphs, charts, or diagrams. Second, because the way we represent the problem determines the amount and type of solution-relevant information we recall from long-term memory, some representations are better than others. For obvious reasons, problem-solving researchers often refer to this process as **problem representation** or **problem framing**.

● Problem framing depends on knowledge of subject matter, familiarity with problem types

To achieve an optimal understanding of a problem, an individual needs two things: a high degree of knowledge of the subject matter (facts, concepts, and principles) on which the problem is based and familiarity with that particular type of problem. This background will allow the person to recognize important elements (words, phrases, and numbers) in the problem statement and patterns of relationships among the problem elements. This recognition will activate one or more solution-relevant schemes from long-term memory. It is this level of knowledge of subject matter and problem types that distinguishes the high-quality problem representations of the expert problem solver from the low-quality representations of the novice. Experts typically represent problems in terms of one or more basic patterns or underlying principles, whereas novices focus on limited or superficial surface features of problems.

To give you a clearer idea of the nature and power of an optimal problem representation, consider the following situation. When novices are given a set of physics problems to solve, they sort them into categories on the basis of some noticeable feature. For example, they group together all problems that involve the use of an inclined plane, or all the ones that involve the use of pulleys, or all those that involve friction. Then novices search their memory for previously learned information. The drawback to this approach is that although two or three problems may involve the use of an inclined plane, their solutions may depend on the application of different laws of physics. Experts, in contrast, draw on their extensive and well-organized knowledge base to represent groups of problems according to a common underlying principle, such as conservation of energy or Newton's third law (Gagné et al., 1993; Pretz et al., 2003).

An important aspect of the problem-solving process is the ability to activate relevant schemes (organized collections of facts, concepts, principles, and procedures) from long-term memory when they are needed. The more relevant and powerful the activated scheme is, the more likely it is that an effective problem solution will be achieved. But as many observers of education have pointed out, acquiring this ability is often easier said than done. John Bransford argues that standard educational practices produce knowledge that is *inert*. As mentioned earlier in the chapter, inert knowledge can be accessed only under conditions that closely mimic the original learning context (Bransford, Sherwood, Vye, & Rieser, 1986). Richard Feynman, a Nobel Prize–winning physicist, made the same observation in describing how his classmates at the Massachusetts Institute of Technology failed to recognize the application of a previously learned mathematical formula: "They didn't put two and two together. They didn't even know what they 'knew.' I don't know what's the matter

● Inert knowledge due to learning isolated facts under limited conditions

with people: they don't learn by understanding; they learn by some other way—by rote, or something. Their knowledge is so fragile!" (1985, p. 36). To overcome this limitation of inert and fragile knowledge, teachers need to present subject matter in a highly organized fashion, and students need to learn more about the various conditions under which their knowledge applies.

Step 3: Compile Relevant Information　　For well-structured problems that are relatively simple and familiar (such as arithmetic drill problems), this step in the problem-solving process occurs simultaneously with problem representation. In the process of defining a problem, we very quickly and easily recall from long-term memory all the information needed to achieve a solution. As problems and issues become more complex, however, we run into two difficulties: the amount of information relevant to the solution becomes too great to keep track of mentally, and there is an increasing chance that we may not possess all the relevant information. As a result, we are forced to compile what we know in the form of lists, tables, pictures, graphs and diagrams, and so on and to seek additional information from other sources.

The key to using oneself as an information source is the ability to accurately retrieve from long-term memory information that will aid in the solution of the problem. We need to think back over what we have learned in other somewhat similar situations, make a list of some other form of representation of those ideas, and make a judgment as to how helpful that knowledge might be. Techniques for ensuring accurate and reliable recall were discussed in the chapter on information-processing theory.

In addition to relying on our own knowledge and experience to solve problems, we can draw on the knowledge and experience of friends, colleagues, and experts. The main purpose of soliciting the views of others about solutions to problems and positions on issues is to identify the reasons and evidence those people offer in support of their positions. This skill of asking questions and analyzing responses is quite useful in debates and classroom discussions of controversial issues.

Step 4: Formulate and Carry Out a Solution　　When you feel you understand the nature of a problem or issue and possess sufficient relevant information, you are ready to attempt a solution. The first step is to consider which of several alternative approaches is likely to be most effective. The literature on problem solving mentions quite a few solution strategies. Because these solution strategies are very general in nature—they can apply to different kinds of problems in different content areas and offer only a general approach to solving a problem—they are referred to as heuristics (Martinez, 1998). We will discuss six **heuristics** that we think are particularly useful.

* *Study worked examples.*　This approach may strike you as so obvious that it hardly merits attention, but it is worth mentioning for two reasons. First, obvious solution strategies are the ones that are most often overlooked. Second, it is a very effective solution strategy (see, for example, Sweller, Merriënboer, & Paas, 1998). The beneficial effect is thought to be due to the learners' acquisition of a general problem schema. To get the most out of this heuristic, use multiple examples and different formats for each problem type and encourage learners to explain to themselves the problem-solving strategy illustrated by the examples (Atkinson, Derry, Renkl, & Wortham, 2000).

  Of course, students vary in how much they know about the subject matter on which the problems are based, and students with more prior knowledge do better on problem-solving tests when they are given problem-solving instruction and practice than when they are given worked examples to study (Atkinson et al., 2000). For these reasons, a good procedure to use with all students is something called backward fading. *Backward fading* is basically a combination of studying worked examples, working backward, and practice in solving problems. First, a completely worked-out example (such as one that requires three steps to complete)

Want to test your own problem-solving process? See the Netlabs on the textbook web site, accessible from **http://education.college.hmco. com/students.**

● Studying worked examples is an effective solution strategy

is provided. Then a similar problem is presented with only the first two steps worked out. The last step has to be completed by the learner. A third problem provides the solution to the first step and requires the learner to determine the solution for steps two and three. Finally, the fourth problem requires the learner to solve all three steps. Compared with peers who saw ordinary worked examples and practiced solving problems, a group of college students who were exposed to the backward fading procedure scored significantly better on problems that were both similar to and different from the practice problems (Atkinson, Renkle, & Merrill, 2003).

● Solve simpler version of problem first; then transfer process to harder problem

- *Work on a simpler version of the problem.* This is another common and very effective approach. Geometry offers a particularly clear example of working on a simpler problem. If you are having difficulty solving a problem of solid geometry (which involves three dimensions), work out a similar problem in plane geometry (two dimensions) and then apply the solution to the three-dimensional example (Nickerson, 1994; Polya, 1957). Architects and engineers employ this approach when they construct scaled-down models of bridges, buildings, experimental aircraft, and the like. Scientists do the same thing by creating laboratory simulations of real-world phenomena.

● Break complex problems into manageable parts

- *Break the problem into parts.* The key to this approach is to make sure you break the problem into manageable parts. Whether you can do this will depend largely on how much subject-matter knowledge you have. The more you know about the domain from which the problem comes, the easier it is to know how to break a problem into logical, easy-to-handle parts.

  At least two benefits result from breaking a problem into parts: it reduces the amount of information you have to keep in short-term memory to a manageable level, and the method used to solve one part of the problem can often be used to solve another part. Bransford and Stein (1993) use the following example to illustrate how this approach works.

  Problem: What day follows the day before yesterday if two days from now will be Sunday?

  1. What is today if two days from now will be Sunday? (Friday)
  2. If today is Friday, what is the day before yesterday? (Wednesday)
  3. What day follows Wednesday? (Thursday)

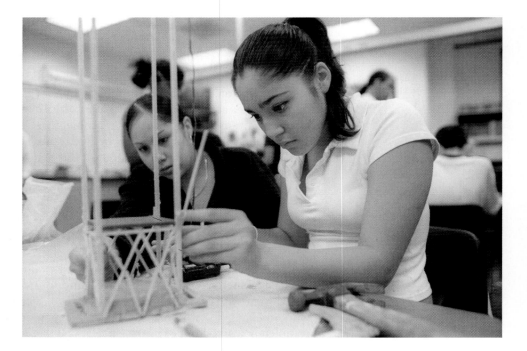

To figure out the solution to a problem, good problem solvers often work first on a simpler version of the problem.

● Work backward when goal is clear but beginning state is not

● Solve a similar problem and then apply the same method

● Create an external representation of the problem

• *Work backward.* This is a particularly good solution strategy to use whenever the goal is clear but the beginning state is not. Bransford and Stein (1993) offer the following example. Suppose you arranged to meet someone at a restaurant across town at noon. When should you leave your office to be sure of arriving on time? By working backward from your destination and arrival time (it takes about ten minutes to find a parking spot and walk to the restaurant; it takes about thirty minutes to drive to the area where you would park; it takes about five minutes to walk from your office to your car), you would more quickly and easily determine when to leave your office (about 11:15) than if you had worked the problem forward.

• *Solve an analogous problem.* If you are having difficulty solving a problem, possibly because your knowledge of the subject matter is incomplete, it may be useful to think of a similar problem about a subject in which you are more knowledgeable. Solve the analogous problem, and then use the same method to solve the first problem. In essence, this is a way of making the unfamiliar familiar.

   Although solving analogous problems is a very powerful solution strategy, it can be difficult to employ, especially for novices. In our previous discussion of understanding the problem, we made the point that novices represent problems on the basis of superficial features, whereas experts operate from knowledge of underlying concepts and principles. The same is true of analogies. Novices are more likely than experts to use superficial analogies (Gick, 1986).

• *Create an external representation of the problem.* This heuristic is doubly useful because it also aids in problem framing. Many problems can be represented as pictures, equations, graphs, flowcharts, and the like. The figures in the next Suggestions for Teaching section illustrate how a pictorial or symbolic form of representation can help one both understand and solve the problem (Martinez, 1998).

Step 5: Evaluate the Solution The last step in the problem-solving process is to evaluate the adequacy of the solution. For relatively simple, well-structured problems where the emphasis is on producing a correct response, two levels of evaluation are available:

● Evaluate solutions to well-structured problems by estimating or checking

• The problem solver can ask whether, given the problem statement, the answer makes sense. For example, if the problem reads $75 \times 5 = ?$ and the response is 80, a little voice inside the problem solver's head should say that the answer cannot possibly be right. This signal should prompt a reevaluation of the way the problem was represented and the solution procedure that was used (for example, "I misread the times sign as a plus sign and added when I should have multiplied").
• The problem solver can use an alternative algorithm (a fixed procedure used to solve a problem) to check the accuracy of the solution. This is necessary because an error in carrying out an algorithm can produce an incorrect response that is in the ballpark. For example, a common error in multiple-column subtraction problems is to subtract a smaller digit from a larger one regardless of whether the small number is in the minuend (top row) or the subtrahend (bottom row) (Mayer, 1987), as in

$$\begin{array}{r} 522 \\ -\ 418 \\ \hline 116 \end{array}$$

   Since this answer is off by only 12 units, it "looks right." The flaw can be discovered, however, by adding the answer to the subtrahend to produce the minuend.

   The evaluation of solutions to ill-structured problems is likely to be more complicated and time-consuming for at least two reasons. First, the evaluation should occur both before and after the solution is implemented. Although many flaws and omissions can be identified and corrected beforehand, some will slip through. There is much to be learned by observing the effects of our solutions. Second, because these problems are

pause & reflect

Critics of American education argue that students are poor problem solvers because they receive little systematic instruction in problem-solving processes. How would you rate the instruction you received in problem solving? In terms of the five steps discussed on the preceding pages, which ones were you taught? What can you do to ensure that your students become good problem solvers?

complex, often involving a dozen or more variables, some sort of systematic framework should guide the evaluation. Vincent Ruggiero suggests a four-step procedure (1988, pp. 44–46):

1. Ask and answer a set of basic questions. Imagine, for example, that you have proposed a classroom incentive system (a token economy, perhaps) to enhance student motivation. You might ask such questions as, How will this program be implemented? By whom? When? Where? With what materials? How will the materials be obtained?

2. Identify imperfections and complications. Is this idea, for example, safe, convenient, efficient, economical, and compatible with existing policies and practices?

3. Anticipate possible negative reactions from other people. For instance, might parents or the school principal object?

4. Devise improvements.

The next section contains guidelines and examples that will help you improve the problem-solving skills of your students.

Suggestions for Teaching in Your Classroom

Teaching Problem-Solving Techniques

1 Teach students how to identify problems.

Because the notion of finding problems is likely to strike students as an unusual activity, you may want to introduce this skill in gradual steps. One way to start is to have students list different ways in which problems can be identified. Typical responses are to scan newspaper and magazine articles, observe customer and employee behavior in a store, watch traffic patterns in a local area, and interview local residents, including, for instance, teachers, business owners, police, clergy, or government officials. A next step is to have students carry out these suggested activities in order to gain an understanding of the status quo and to find out how people identify problems. They may learn, for example, that a principal periodically has lunch with a teacher in order to learn of conditions that decrease the teacher's effectiveness.

2 Teach students how to represent problems.

Problem representation involves transforming the words that express a problem to an internal representation of those words. To do this, students must understand the concepts embedded in the problem statement and the relationships among those concepts. Consequently, the ability to construct a good representation of a problem is based on a command of the subject matter surrounding the problem and familiarity with the particular type of problem.

● Comprehension of subject matter critical to problem solving

As the work of Jerome Bruner and David Ausubel indicates, students need to acquire a genuine understanding of many of the associations, discriminations, concepts, and rules of a discipline before they can effectively solve problems in that subject-matter area. Too often, students are taught to state principles on cue, but they reveal by further responses that they do not understand what they are saying. The recommendations we make in this book about presenting information in an organized fashion and in meaningful contexts will go a long way toward helping students understand the subject matter on which problems are based; see the specific suggestions in the chapter on information-processing theory and the chapter on approaches to instruction.

The classic illustration of what can occur when information is not learned meaningfully was given over a century ago by William James in his *Talks to Teachers:*

> A friend of mine, visiting a school, was asked to examine a young class in geography. Glancing at the book, she said: "Suppose you should dig a hole in the ground, hundreds of feet deep, how should you find it at the bottom—warmer or colder than on top?" None of the class replying, the teacher said: "I'm sure they know, but I think you don't ask the question quite rightly. Let me try." So, taking the book, she asked: "In what condition is the interior of the globe?" and received the immediate answer from half the class at once: "The interior of the globe is in a condition of igneous fusion." (1899, p. 150)

If these students had genuinely understood concepts and principles regarding the composition of the earth (such as the relationship between igneous fusion and heat), instead of having simply memorized meaningless phrases, they would have been able to answer the original question.

Once you are satisfied that students meaningfully understand the elements of a problem, you can demonstrate methods to represent those elements and how they interrelate. One frequent recommendation is to use visual forms of problem representation (concept maps, Venn diagrams, flowcharts, and drawings, for example). Visual representations of ideas foster comprehension because of their concreteness. The following two examples illustrate how a Venn diagram (a set of intersecting circles) and a flow diagram can represent a particular type of problem.

EXAMPLE PROBLEM

The government wants to contact all druggists, all gun store owners, and all parents in a town without contacting anyone twice. Based on the following statistics, how many people must be contacted?

Druggists	10
Gun store owners	5
Parents	3,000
Druggists who own gun stores	0
Druggists who are parents	7
Gun store owners who are parents	3

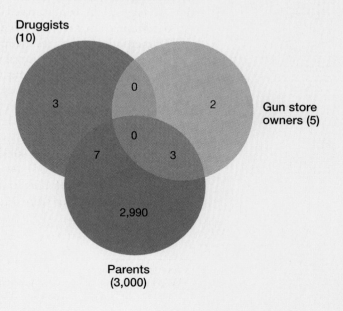

Druggists (10)

Gun store owners (5)

Parents (3,000)

Solution Using Venn Diagram

As the Venn diagram illustrates, the total number of people who must be contacted is 2,990 + 7 + 3 + 3 + 2 = 3,005 (adapted from Whimbey & Lochhead, 1999, p. 104).[1]

EXAMPLE PROBLEM

Sally loaned $7.00 to Betty. But Sally borrowed $15.00 from Estella and $32.00 from Joan. Moreover, Joan owes $3.00 to Estella and $7.00 to Betty. One day the women got together at Betty's house to straighten out their accounts. Which woman left with $18.00 more than she came with?

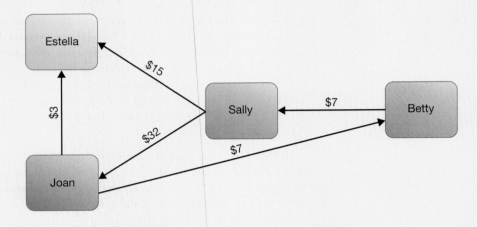

Solution Using Flow Diagram

Verbal reasoning problems that describe transactions can take the form of a flow diagram, as shown here. From the diagram, it is clear that Estella left with $18.00 more than she came with (adapted from Whimbey & Lochhead, 1999, p. 128).

③ Teach students how to compile relevant information.

Good problem solvers start with themselves when compiling information to solve a problem or evidence to support a position on an issue. They recognize the importance of recalling earlier-learned information (metacognitive knowledge) and are adept at doing so (cognitive skill). Poor problem solvers, by contrast, lack metacognitive knowledge, cognitive skills, or both. If their deficiency is metacognitive, they make little or no effort to recall solution-relevant memories, even when the information was recently learned, because they do not understand the importance of searching long-term memory for potentially useful knowledge. Even if a student poor in problem solving recognizes the value of searching long-term memory for relevant information, he may still be handicapped because of inadequate encoding and retrieval skills.

To minimize any metacognitive deficiency, make sure your instruction in problem-solving methods emphasizes the importance of retrieving and using previously learned knowledge. To minimize retrieval problems, make sure you recall and implement the Suggestions for Teaching in Your Classroom sections that we offered in the chapter on information-processing theory.

If a student does not possess all the relevant information needed to work out a solution or analyze an issue, you will have to guide her toward individuals and sources that can help. In referring students to individuals, select people who are judged to be reasonably knowledgeable about the subject, are careful thinkers, and are willing to share their ideas (Ruggiero, 1988, 2004). As an example, consider the issue of whether certain books (such as the novels *Catcher in the Rye*, by J. D. Salinger, and *Tom Sawyer*, by Mark Twain) should be banned from a school's reading list. In interviewing a knowledgeable

---

[1] Excerpts and diagrams in this section are from "Solution Using Venn Diagram," adapted from A. Whimbey and J. Lochead, *Problem Solving and Comprehension*, Sixth Edition (Mahwah, NJ: Lawrence Erlbaum Associates, Inc., Publishers), pp. 104, 128. © 1999 reprinted by permission.

person, students might ask questions like the following because they allow some insight into the individual's reasoning process and the evidence used to support his position:

- What general effects do you think characters in novels who rebel against adult authority have on a reader's behavior?
- Are certain groups of people, such as middle and high school students, likely to be influenced by the motives and actions of such characters? Why do you think so?
- Does a ban on certain books violate the authors' right to free speech?
- Does a book ban violate the principle of academic freedom? Why?
- Is it the proper role of a school board to prevent or discourage students from exposure to certain ideas during school hours?

If a reasonably informed person is not available, recognized authorities can often be interviewed by phone. If a student chooses this tactic, Ruggiero suggests calling or writing in advance for an appointment, preparing questions in advance, and asking permission to tape-record the interview.

Obviously, in addition to or in lieu of personal interviews, students can find substantial information in a good library. For example, you can steer them toward books by recognized authorities, research findings, court cases, and interviews with prominent individuals in periodicals. Although the Internet potentially contains a vast amount of information on any topic, warn students about using material gathered there indiscriminately. As with any other medium, there are more and less reliable sources, and only material from reputable sources should be gathered. One additional benefit is that an extra layer of problem-solving activity is introduced when students must decide how to gather and evaluate online information.

 Check the Reflective Journal Questions on the textbook web site for ideas to address in your journal writing.

④ Teach several methods for formulating problem solutions.

Previously, we mentioned six methods for formulating a problem solution: study worked examples, work on a simpler version of the problem, break the problem into parts, work backward, solve an analogous problem, and create an external representation of the problem. At the end of the chapter, under Resources for Further Investigation, we recommend several recently published books on problem solving that, taken together, provide numerous examples of each method. We encourage you to check out one or more of those references and other sources as demonstrations of worked problems and as opportunities for you to practice your own problem-solving skills so that you will be well prepared to teach each of these six methods.

⑤ Teach students the skills of evaluation.

Solutions to well-structured problems are usually evaluated through the application of an estimating or checking routine. Such procedures can be found in any good mathematics text. The evaluation of solutions to ill-structured problems and analyses of issues, however, is more complex and is less frequently taught. Ruggiero (1988, 2004) discusses the following ten habits and skills as contributing to the ability to evaluate complex solutions and positions:

- Being open-minded about opposing points of view.
- Selecting proper criteria of evaluation. Violations of this skill abound. A current example is the use of standardized achievement test scores to evaluate the quality of classroom instruction.
- Understanding the essence of an argument. To foster this skill, Ruggiero recommends that students be taught how to write a *précis*, which is a concise summary of an oral argument or a reading passage.
- Evaluating the reliability of sources.
- Properly interpreting factual data (for example, recognizing that an increase in a state's income tax rate from 4 to 6 percent is an increase not of 2 percent but of 50 percent).

- Testing the credibility of hypotheses. On the basis of existing data, hypotheses can range from highly improbable to highly probable.
- Making important distinctions (for instance, between preference and judgment, emotion and content, appearance and reality).
- Recognizing unstated assumptions (for example, that because two events occur close together in time, one causes the other; that what is clear to us will be clear to others; that if the majority believes something, it must be true).
- Evaluating the validity and truthfulness of one's arguments (by, for example, checking that conclusions logically follow from premises and that conclusions have not been influenced by such reasoning flaws as either-or thinking, overgeneralizing, or oversimplifying).
- Recognizing when evidence is insufficient.

All of these ten skills can be modeled and taught in your classroom.

TRANSFER OF LEARNING

Throughout this chapter and preceding ones, we have indicated that classroom instruction should be arranged in such a way that students independently apply the knowledge and problem-solving skills they learn in school to similar but new situations. This capability is the main goal of problem-solving instruction and is typically valued very highly by educators (De Corte, 2003; Haskell, 2001). Referred to as **transfer of learning**, it is the essence of being an autonomous learner and problem solver. In this section, we will examine the nature of transfer and discuss ways in which you can help bring it about.

The Nature and Significance of Transfer of Learning

The Theory of Identical Elements   During the early 1900s, it was common practice for high school students and colleges to require that students take such subjects as Latin, Greek, and geometry. Because they were considered difficult topics to learn, mastery of them was expected to improve a student's ability to memorize, think, and reason. These enhanced abilities were then expected to facilitate the learning of less difficult subjects. The rationale behind this practice was that the human mind, much like any muscle in the body, could be exercised and made stronger. A strong mind, then, would learn things that a weak mind would not. This practice, known as the *doctrine of formal discipline*, constituted an early (and incorrect) explanation of transfer (Barnett & Ceci, 2002; Haag & Stern, 2003).

In 1901, Edward Thorndike and Robert Woodworth proposed an alternative explanation of how transfer occurs. They argued that the degree to which knowledge and skills acquired in learning one task can help someone learn another task depends on how similar the two tasks are (if we assume that the learner recognizes the similarities). The greater the degree of similarity is between the tasks' stimulus and response elements (as in riding a bicycle and riding a motorcycle), the greater the amount of transfer will be. This idea became known as the **theory of identical elements** (Cox, 1997).

● Early view of transfer based on degree of similarity between two tasks

Positive, Negative, and Zero Transfer   In time, however, other psychologists (among them Ellis, 1965; Osgood, 1949) identified different types of transfer and the conditions under which each type prevailed. A useful distinction was made among positive transfer, negative transfer, and zero transfer (Ormrod, 2004).

● Positive transfer: previous learning makes later learning easier

The discussion up to this point has been alluding to **positive transfer,** defined as a situation in which prior learning aids subsequent learning. According to Thorndike's

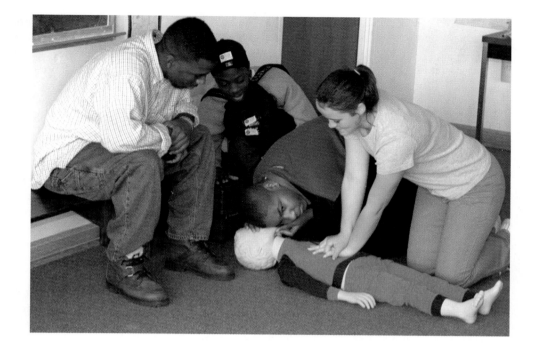

If teachers want students to apply what they learn in the classroom in other settings in the future, they should create tasks and conditions that are similar to those that students will encounter later.

analysis, positive transfer occurs when a new learning task calls for essentially the same response that was made to a similar, earlier-learned task. The accomplished accordion player, for instance, probably will become a proficient pianist faster than someone who knows how to play the drums or someone who plays no musical instrument at all, all other things being equal. Similarly, the native English speaker who is also fluent in French is likely to have an easier time learning Spanish than is someone who speaks no foreign language.

● Negative transfer: previous learning interferes with later learning

Negative transfer is defined as a situation in which prior learning interferes with subsequent learning. It occurs when two tasks are highly similar but require different responses. A tennis player learning how to play racquetball, for example, may encounter problems at first because of a tendency to swing the racquetball racket as if it were a tennis racket. Primary grade children often experience negative transfer when they encounter words that are spelled alike but pronounced differently (as in "I will *read* this story now since I *read* that story last week").

Zero transfer is defined as a situation in which prior learning has no effect on new learning. It can be expected when two tasks have different stimuli and different responses. Learning to conjugate Latin verbs, for example, is not likely to have any effect on learning how to find the area of a rectangle.

Specific and General Transfer   The preceding description of positive transfer, although useful, is somewhat limiting because it is unclear whether transfer from one task to another is due to specific similarities or to more general similarities. Psychologists (as described by Ellis, 1978) decide whether transfer is due to specific or general factors by setting up learning tasks such as the following for three different but equivalent groups of learners.

	Initial Task	Transfer Task
Group 1	Learn French	Learn Spanish
Group 2	Learn Chinese	Learn Spanish
Group 3	Learn Spanish	

● Specific transfer due to specific similarities between two tasks

If on a Spanish test, group 1 scores higher than group 2, the difference is attributed to **specific transfer** of similarities between French and Spanish (such as vocabulary, verb conjugations, and sentence structure). If groups 1 and 2 score the same but

● General transfer due to use of same cognitive strategies

both outscore group 3, the difference is attributed to nonspecific transfer, or **general transfer,** of similarities between the two tasks since Chinese shares no apparent specific characteristics with French or Spanish. In this case, it is possible that learners use cognitive strategies—such as imagery, verbal elaboration, and mnemonic devices—when learning a foreign language and that these transfer to the learning of other foreign languages. Such nonspecific transfer effects have also been demonstrated for other classroom tasks, such as problem solving and learning from text (Ellis, 1978; Royer, 1979).

Support for specific transfer, as well as for the identical elements theory, comes from a study of college students in Germany who had taken either French or Latin when they were in seventh grade as their second foreign language. At the time of the study, these students were enrolled in an intensive beginners' course in Spanish. On a written test that required the students to translate a passage into Spanish, those who had taken French (which, like Spanish, is a Romance language) several years earlier made significantly fewer grammar and vocabulary errors than did students who had taken Latin (Haag & Stern, 2003).

● Near transfer: previously learned knowledge and skills used relatively soon on highly similar task

● Far transfer: previously learned knowledge and skills used much later on dissimilar tasks and under different conditions

Near and Far Transfer   Another common distinction, similar to the specific-general distinction, is based on the perceived similarity of the original learning task to the transfer task. **Near transfer** refers to situations in which the knowledge domains are highly similar, the settings in which the original learning and transfer tasks occur are basically the same, and the elapsed time between the two tasks is relatively short. **Far transfer** occurs when the knowledge domains and settings are judged to be dissimilar and the time between the original learning and transfer tasks is relatively long (Barnett & Ceci, 2002). Thus, using math skills one acquired over the past several weeks to solve the problems at the end of the current chapter in a textbook is an example of near transfer. Using those same skills several years later to determine which of several investment options is most likely to produce the highest rate of return is an example of far transfer.

You may have noticed our use of such imprecise and subjective terms as "highly similar," "basically the same," "relatively long," and "judged to be dissimilar." This is for a good reason. At present, there is no way to precisely measure the similarity between a learning task and a transfer task. The best we can do is identify the major dimensions that two tasks share (such as subject matter, physical setting, time between two tasks, and the conditions under which each is performed) and subjectively decide that the two dimensions are sufficiently similar or dissimilar to warrant the label *near transfer* or *far transfer.* Sometimes this approach produces a high degree of agreement, but at other times one person's far transfer is another person's near transfer (Barnett & Ceci, 2002).

Contemporary Views of Specific/Near and General/Far Transfer

Gavriel Salomon and David Perkins (1989) combine aspects of specific and near transfer and general and far transfer under the labels *low-road transfer* and *high-road transfer,* respectively.

● Low-road transfer: previously learned skill automatically applied to similar current task

Low-Road Transfer   Low-road transfer refers to a situation in which a previously learned skill or idea is almost automatically retrieved from memory and applied to a highly similar current task. For example, a student who has mastered the skill of two-column addition and correctly completes three-column and four-column addition problems with no prompting or instruction is exhibiting low-road transfer. Another example is a student who learns how to tune up car engines in an auto shop class and then almost effortlessly and automatically carries out the same task as an employee of an auto repair business. As you may have suspected, low-road transfer is basically a contemporary version of Thorndike and Woodworth's identical elements theory (Cox, 1997).

Two conditions need to be present for low-road transfer to occur:

1. Students have to be given ample opportunities to practice using the target skill.
2. Practice has to occur with different materials and in different settings. The more varied the practice is, the greater is the range of tasks to which the skill can be applied.

If, for example, you want students to be good note takers, give them instruction and ample practice at taking notes from their biology, health, and English textbooks. Once they become accomplished note takers in these subjects, they will likely apply this skill to other subjects in an almost automatic fashion. The auto mechanic who has learned to change the spark plugs in a Chrysler, a Toyota, and a Mercedes-Benz should be able to do the same job as efficiently in a Ford, a Buick, or a Nissan.

In essence, what we are describing is the behavioral principle of generalization. Because the transfer task is similar in one or more respects to the practice task and tends to occur in similar settings, low-road transfer is similar to specific and near transfer. To understand how people transfer prior knowledge and skills over longer time periods to new situations that look rather different from the original task, we need to explore the nature of high-road transfer.

● High-road transfer: formulate rule from one task and apply to related task

High-Road Transfer   **High-road transfer** involves the conscious, controlled, somewhat effortful formulation of an "abstraction" (that is, a rule, a schema, a strategy, or an analogy) that allows a connection to be made between two tasks. For example, an individual who learns to set aside a certain number of hours every day to complete homework assignments and study for upcoming exams formulates the principle that the most efficient way to accomplish a task is to break it down into small pieces and work at each piece according to a set schedule. As an adult, the individual uses this principle to deal successfully with complex tasks at work and at home.

As another example, imagine a student who, after much observation and thought, has finally developed a good sense of what school is and how one is supposed to behave there. This student has developed a school schema. Such a schema would probably be made up of actors (teachers and students), objects (desks, chalkboards, books, pencils), and events (reading, listening, writing, talking, drawing). Because this is an idealized abstraction, actual classrooms may contain fewer or greater numbers of these characteristics in varying proportions. Even so, with this schema, a student could walk into any instructional setting (another school classroom, a training seminar, or a press briefing, for example) and readily understand what was going on, why it was going on, and how one should behave. Of course, with repeated applications of schemata, rules, strategies, and the like, the behaviors become less conscious and more automatic. What was once a reflection of high-road transfer becomes low-road transfer.

For help remembering the key terms introduced in this chapter, you may want to use the interactive Flashcards on the textbook web site.

Several researchers (e.g., Bereiter, 1997; Salomon & Perkins, 1989) refer to this deliberate, conscious, effortful formulating of a general principle or schema that can be applied to a variety of different-looking but fundamentally similar tasks as *mindful abstraction*. The *mindful* part of the phrase indicates that the abstraction must be thought about and fully understood for high-road transfer to occur. That is, people must be aware of what they are doing and why they are doing it. This is essentially training in metacognition. Recall our earlier discussion in this chapter of inert knowledge and Richard Feynman's observations of how his classmates at the Massachusetts Institute of Technology failed to recognize the application of a previously learned mathematical formula because it was initially learned for use only in that course. Carl Bereiter (1997) argues that when learning is too strongly situated in a particular context, as in the case of Feynman's MIT classmates, high-road transfer is impeded.

Teaching for Low-Road and High-Road Transfer   As we noted at the beginning of this section, transfer of previously learned knowledge and skill to new tasks and

Take a Stand!

If You Want Transfer, Then Teach for Transfer

From the elementary grades through graduate school, you will find teachers who believe that it is perfectly acceptable to provide students with basic explanations and examples of concepts and procedures during classroom instruction, and then test them on their ability to answer more advanced questions or solve more difficult problems. Their intuitively appealing rationale is that if the students are paying attention in class, carefully reading the textbook, and diligently doing the assigned homework, they will be able to make the jump from the simpler, lower-level classroom examples to the more difficult and advanced test items.

We hope you have learned from the discussion of transfer in this chapter that

nothing could be further from the truth. Students have to be exposed to the same types of concepts, problems, and procedures during instruction that they will be held accountable for on an exam, and they may even have to be prompted on the exam to use the knowledge they were taught. In other words, *if you want transfer, then teach for transfer.* If you expect it to occur spontaneously, like so many other teachers, you will be disappointed most of the time.

What are your own experiences with teachers who expect transfer to occur automatically? To investigate this subject further, see the Take a Stand! section of the textbook web site.

settings is a goal that is high on almost every teacher's list. Yet one study of classroom activity found that only 7 percent of tasks required students to use information they had learned previously (Bennett, Desforges, Cockburn, & Wilkinson, 1984). Perhaps most teachers feel they simply don't know how to teach for transfer. That need not be your fate. The following guidelines (based on Cox, 1997; De Corte, 2003; Halpern, 1998; Salomon & Perkins, 1989) should produce greater levels of both low-road and high-road transfer:

1. Provide students with multiple opportunities for varied practice to help them develop a rich web of interrelated concepts.
2. Give students opportunities to solve problems that are similar to those they will eventually have to solve, and establish conditions like those they will eventually face.
3. Teach students how to formulate for a variety of tasks general rules, strategies, or schemes that they can use in the future with a variety of similar problems.
4. Give students cues that will allow them to retrieve from memory earlier-learned information that can be used to make current learning easier.
5. Teach students to focus on the beneficial effects of creating and using rules and strategies to solve particular kinds of problems.

● Low-road and high-road transfer produced by varied practice at applying skills, rules, memory retrieval cues

TECHNOLOGY TOOLS FOR KNOWLEDGE CONSTRUCTION AND PROBLEM SOLVING

Previously in the book, we noted that one way in which computers are used in schools is as learning and problem-solving tools. This use of computer-based technology supports a constructivist approach to learning and is often called learning *with* computers (Jonassen, 2000; Jonassen, Howland, Moore, & Marra, 2003). Students learn with computers when computers support knowledge construction, exploration, learning by doing, learning by conversing, and learning by reflecting.

● Technology tools are available to help students construct knowledge, become better problem solvers

David Jonassen (Jonassen, 2000; Jonassen et al., 2003) uses the term *mindtools* to refer to computer applications that lend themselves to these types of activities. Mindtools include databases, semantic networks (concept mapping programs), spreadsheets, expert systems (artificial intelligence), microworlds, search engines, visualization tools, hypermedia, and computer conferencing. Rather than using computer programs just to present and represent information, which is what drill and tutorial programs do, mindtools allow learners to construct, share, and revise knowledge in more open-ended environments. In effect, learners become producers, designers, and "authors of knowledge" (Lehrer, 1993). In the sections that follow, we briefly examine applications of computer-based technology that support the constructivist view of learning.

Multimedia Simulations

A basic principle of constructivism is that meaningful learning involves learning by doing, as opposed to learning just by reading and/or listening. Since actual hands-on experience is not always feasible, computer-based simulation programs can be used as the next best thing. But learning by doing, particularly in the absence of instructor guidance, or scaffolding, has been criticized as being inefficient because of the large number of mistakes that students make.

One study (Mayer, Mautone, & Prothero, 2002) tested this contention by examining the effect of different types of instructor scaffolding on undergraduate students' performance in a multimedia geology simulation. The simulation places students on an unknown planet and requires them to identify the geological features (such as canyons, mountain ridges, craters, or islands) that are present on a certain part of the planet's surface. The catch is that the students cannot directly see these features but have to infer their existence by creating what are called profile lines. Profile lines provide information about distance, elevation of the target feature, and the surrounding area. Students then use this information to visualize the unknown feature. This process is analogous to geologists' using sonar waves to identify underground or underwater features. In the study, the students were given either written instructions, a verbal explanation of how to use a strategy summary sheet for identifying each geologic feature, pictorial sketches of each feature, or both the summary sheet and the sketches.

Students who received either sketches of the features they were asked to identify or both sketches and guidance about which steps to take in drawing and interpreting profile lines identified more features than did students who received just written instructions. The authors likened this effect to the positive effect of providing students with worked examples. These results suggest that simulations will work best when accompanied by careful and appropriate scaffolding.

The learning-by-doing feature of multimedia simulation programs attains perhaps its fullest expression in virtual reality environments. By wearing a head-mounted display and earphones and being able to physically move through the environment by walking around a room, learners feel as if they are actually "in" the environment in which the simulation occurs. For this reason, virtual reality environments are also called high-immersion environments. By contrast, standard multimedia simulations, in which students sit in front of a computer screen and explore an environment by moving the computer's mouse, are considered to be low-immersion environments. Because of virtual reality's high-immersion features, it is thought to produce higher levels of motivation and learning than the standard multimedia simulation. Of the few experimental tests of this claim, one was conducted by Roxana Moreno and Richard Mayer (2002).

The simulation used in this study took undergraduate students to five alien planets, each of which had a different climate, and required them to design a plant (choosing from various roots, stems, and leaves) that would grow well under the prevailing conditions. They were given prompts and feedback by the computer in the form of either speech or on-screen text. Students in the high-immersion condition wore a head-mounted display and earphones and explored each planet's environment by walking around the room in which the experiment was conducted. Students in the low-immersion condition sat in front of a computer wearing headphones (to hear the spoken feedback) and navigated around each environment by using the mouse.

Although students in the high-immersion condition rated the experience as being more lifelike and involving, their performance on tests of retention (the number of types of roots, stems, and leaves recalled) and transfer (designing plants for conditions that were different from those on the five planets) was equivalent to that of students in the low-immersion condition. Because there is as yet very little research on the relative benefits of virtual reality, it is too soon to conclude that this technology has no place in the classroom. For now, however, educators can feel comfortable using less expensive computer-based multimedia simulation since it appears to produce the same effects on learning and transfer.

Computer-Supported Intentional Learning Environments

Marlene Scardamalia and Carl Bereiter (1996, p. 10) ask us to "imagine a network of networks—people from schools, universities, cultural institutions, service organizations, businesses—simultaneously building knowledge within their primary groups while advancing the knowledge of others. We might call such a community network a knowledge-building society." Since the 1980s these researchers have developed and tested aspects of such a network with the Computer-Supported Intentional Learning Environments (CSILE) project (Scardamali & Bereiter, 1991).

The CSILE project is built around the concept of intentional learning (Scardamalia & Bereiter, 1991). In an intentional learning environment, students learn how to set goals, generate and interrelate new ideas, link new knowledge to old, negotiate meaning with peers, and relate what they learned to other tasks. The product of these activities, like the product of any scientific inquiry, is then made available to other students.

The CSILE project allows students to create informational links, or "notes," in several ways (for example, text notes, drawings, graphs, pictures, timelines, and maps). CSILE also contains designated "cooperation" icons that encourage students to reflect on how their work links to others, as well as idea browsing and linking tools for marking notes that involve or intend cooperation. Using this database system, students comment on the work of others, read responses to their hypotheses, or search for information posted by their peers under a particular topic title. For instance, a search for the word *whales* would call up all the work of students who assigned that word as a keyword in their CSILE contributions. In such a decentralized, free-flowing environment, no longer must the teacher initiate all discussion and coordinate turn taking (Hewitt, 2002; Scardamalia & Bereiter, 1991, 1996). Jim Hewitt (2002) describes how a sixth-grade teacher used CSILE to gradually transform his instructional approach from being teacher directed and task centered to being collaborative and knowledge centered.

Studies show that students who use CSILE perform better on standardized language and reading tests, ask deeper questions, are more elaborate and coherent in their commentaries, demonstrate more mature beliefs about learning, and engage in discussions that are more committed to scientific progress (Scardamalia & Bereiter, 1996). The availability of a cooperation icon seems to foster greater peer commenting and cooperative efforts (Scardamalia & Bereiter, 1991), and students who make more conceptual progress with CSILE tend to be more problem- than fact-oriented (Oshima, Scardamalia, & Bereiter, 1996).

A version of CSILE for the Web, called Knowledge Forum, is also available. The goal of Knowledge Forum is to have students mimic the collaborative knowledge-building process that characterizes the work of expert learners. Consequently, students must label their contribution to a communal database topic prior to posting it by using such labels as *My Theory, I Need to Understand, New Information, This Theory Cannot Explain, A Better Theory,* and *Putting Our Knowledge Together.* So, if in the course of helping to build a knowledge base about human vision, a student wrote, "I need to understand why we have two eyes instead of one or three," another member of this community could post a New Information note that discussed the relationship between binocular vision and depth perception. The resulting knowledge base would then be subject to modifications and additions from others. You can obtain more information about Knowledge Forum at **www.knowledgeforum.com/**.

Learning Through Collaborative Visualization

As indicated in previous chapters, the emergence of computer networks has fostered global scientific data collection and sharing. Now, less skilled young learners can be apprenticed into fields like meteorology and environmental science through social interaction with experts and peers in a learning community. Many science projects illustrate how to embed learning in real-world contexts by having students collect such data as rainfall, wind speed, and environmental pollutants, and share findings with peers. Such projects exemplify both the situated learning and social constructivist ideas outlined earlier in this chapter.

One such project was called Learning Through Collaborative Visualization (CoVis). One of the primary goals of CoVis was to foster project-based science learning, or "collaboratories" (Edelson et al., 1996, p. 158), which use computer networks so that students can access practicing environmental scientists and scientific tools. The belief was that science is learned through participation and "learning-in-doing," not through preparation by someone else. The project included e-mail, news group discussions, listservs (Internet sites where individuals exchange information and ask questions about a specific topic), remote screen sharing, and communication with peers and scientists using both video and audio conferencing. Students' collaborative investigations might include such topics as weather forecasting, ozone depletion trends, global warming, and severe storms. Unlike conventional instruction, CoVis used computer visualization tools to represent real-time data (for example, temperature as color, wind as vectors, and atmospheric pressure as contours).

Research on CoVis revealed mixed success with the telecommunications tools, as some were easier and more practical to use than others (Gomez, Fishman, & Pea, 1998). This research also indicated that teachers need assistance in developing assessment devices for student work, and students may need some help adapting to this new type of learning environment. Case studies also found dramatic differences in adaptation and inventive use of CoVis between low- and high-socioeconomic schools (Shrader, Lento, Gomez, & Pea, 1997).

Although the CoVis program ended in 1998, its web site (**www.covis.nwu.edu/**) serves as an archive for CoVis materials. Research on ideas spawned by CoVis is now being conducted by the Center for Learning Technologies in Urban Schools (**www.letus.org/**). You can download a visualization program called WorldWatcher from the web site of the GEODE Initiative (**www.worldwatcher.nwu.edu/**), which grew out of CoVis.

Jasper Woodbury and Anchored Instruction

Another project that attempts to foster constructivist principles while overcoming the inert knowledge problem comes from a group of researchers at Vanderbilt University called the Cognition and Technology Group at Vanderbilt (CTGV). For more than a decade, CTGV researchers have devised and tested an interesting set of instructional materials that incorporate constructivist principles based on ideas of anchored instruction. **Anchored instruction** involves creating tasks that situate and focus student learning in interesting real-world contexts with many subproblems or issues (for example, making a business plan for the dunking booth at a school's fun fair; Barron et al., 1995). Anchoring problems in a larger context helps students gain a meaningful understanding of the problems and perceive both critical aspects of problems and different points of view (CTGV, 1990).

The Adventures of Jasper Woodbury is a videodisc-based series designed to promote mathematical problem solving, reasoning, and effective communication among middle school students using anchored instruction. There are three stories for each of four topics (complex trip planning, statistics and business plans, geometry, and algebra) in the series. Each story is a fifteen- to twenty-minute adventure that involves Jasper Woodbury and other characters. At the end of each story, the characters are faced with a problem that students must solve before they are allowed to see how the characters in the video solved the problem. Each episode was designed to be consistent with the learning standards recommended by the National Council of Teachers of Mathematics (CTGV, 1993).

In the course of solving the problem posed in the video, students become involved in activities such as generating subgoals, identifying relevant information,

This chapter argues that if teachers want transfer, they should teach for transfer. Go to the Adventures of Jasper Woodbury web site and read the summaries of the adventures for any of the subject areas. Are these materials likely to produce transfer? Why?

cooperating with others, discussing the advantages and disadvantages of possible solutions, and comparing perspectives (CTGV, 1992a, 1992b). Information about the twelve adventures, the theory behind the Jasper series, research findings, and how the videodiscs can be ordered can be found on the Jasper Woodbury web site (**www.peabody.vanderbilt.edu/projects/funded/jasper/**).

A study of nineteen fifth-grade classrooms that had adopted a constructivist orientation to teaching mathematics reported strong positive effects for those classrooms that used Jasper. Students who worked with the program outscored their non-Jasper peers on the Problem Solving and Data Interpretation, Mathematics Concepts and Estimation, and Mathematics Computation subtests of the Iowa Tests of Basic Skills, with the largest difference occurring on the Problem Solving and Data Interpretation subtest (Hickey, Moore, & Pellegrino, 2001).

The beneficial effects of the Jasper experience can be increased by exposing students to related material and experiences prior to their working on the problems. Before students in a sixth-grade class watched the "Rescue at Boone's Meadow" story (about an attempt to rescue an injured eagle from a remote area), two members of the local Audubon Society brought a wounded bald eagle to class and discussed the habitat, way of life, and locations of eagles. This was followed by two days of related activities on eagles. In comparison to a group of sixth graders who engaged in an unrelated activity for those three days, the students in the experimental group recalled more information from the story and were more likely to consider alternative rescue options (Arthurs, DeFranco, & Young, 1999).

Because it is based on constructivist learning principles, the Jasper Woodbury series was designed to be a collaborative problem-solving activity. The benefits of working with other students versus working alone were tested on a group of academically talented sixth graders who viewed the "Journey to Cedar Creek" episode (Barron, 2000). Students who worked in groups of three scored significantly higher than students who worked alone on measures of general planning, subproblem planning, and solutions to subproblems. As a test of near transfer, all students then worked individually on a similar version of the "Cedar Creek" episode. Students who initially worked in teams achieved significantly higher scores than students who worked alone on general planning and subproblem solutions, though not on subproblem planning.

Despite these positive findings, students do not always formulate effective solutions to the problems. The most frequent error students made in solving Jasper problems is overlooking such important solution elements as expenses, amount of time needed to carry out the plan, and the degree of risk incurred by the plan. If you use the Jasper series, you should be prepared to model for students how to analyze such complex problems and formulate an appropriate solution plan (Vye et al., 1997).

The CTGV researchers have extended their anchored instruction research to create a videodisc-based Scientists in Action series meant to help students experience and better understand actual science work (Sherwood, Petrosino, Lin, & Cognition and Technology Group at Vanderbilt, 1998). This series differs from the Jasper Woodbury series in several ways:

- Challenges are posed at several points during the course of the story rather than at the end. When the video resumes, students can compare their solutions to what the scientists on the video actually did.
- While some of the information needed to solve the problem is presented in the video, much of it is available in ancillary materials (such as topographic maps and actual data from experiments on water quality) that the characters in the video refer to.
- There are links to other curriculum areas, especially social issues related to science.
- The stories are designed so that the hypothesis most students are expected to generate will be wrong (such as the source of river pollution). The video then

provides additional data that allows students to revise their original hypothesis. This procedure is used to mimic more closely the way science is done in the real world.

For more information on the four episodes that make up this series, visit the Scientists in Action web site (**peabody.vanderbilt.edu/projects/funded/sia/**).

A third project by this group, the Little Planet Literacy Series, is a multimedia program that also uses anchored instruction to support children's decoding, writing, and recording of their own books (Secules, Cottom, Bray, & Miller, 1997). The Little Planet series can be purchased from Sunburst Technology. The company's web site (**www.sunburst.com/littleplanet/**) contains information about the series and its cost.

Use the Weblinks section of the textbook web site for convenient links to sites mentioned in this section.

Constructivist-Oriented Web Sites

Dozens of web sites provide constructivist-oriented inquiry and problem-solving activities for students of all ages. In this section, we briefly describe five of them to give you an idea of what is available.

National Geographic offers an Xpeditions web site (**www.nationalgeographic.com/xpeditions/**) that has numerous resources and activities to help students learn about geographic concepts and issues. In "A Reason for the Season," students are given basic information about the rotation of the earth around the sun, the tilt in the earth's axis, the summer and winter solstices, and the autumnal and vernal equinoxes, and they are then challenged to figure out why the seasons change. The site includes teacher-tested lesson plans sorted by geography standard and grade level.

ThinkQuest (**www.thinkquest.org/**) is an international academic competition for students aged nine to nineteen. Students work in teams in one of three age divisions to research a topic in science, mathematics, literature, the social sciences, or the arts, and publish their findings as a web site that teachers and students around the world can use.

Educational Web Adventures (**www.eduweb.com/portfolio/adventure.php**) offers adventures that deal with the visual arts, the performing arts, natural history, earth and space science, engineering and technology, history, people and cultures, and economics. For example, "Jefferson's West" is an interactive role-playing game in which middle grade students journey westward with Lewis and Clark. Students explore, collect plants and animals, and trade with native tribes for cultural objects.

The Web-based Inquiry Science Environment (WISE), created by Marcia Linn, a leading math and science education researcher, can be visited at **wise.berkeley.edu**. WISE is free and uses such visualization tools as diagrams, graphs, photographs, and simulations to help students in grades 4–12 better understand scientific concepts. According to the site: "In WISE, students work on exciting inquiry projects on topics such as genetically modified foods, earthquake prediction, and the deformed frogs mystery. Students learn about and respond to contemporary scientific controversies through designing, debating, and critiquing solutions—all on the World Wide Web!"

For help in reviewing this chapter, see the ACE practice tests and the PowerPoint slides on the textbook web site.

As part of the Supportive Inquiry-Based Learning Environment (SIBLE) Project, researchers at Northwestern University have created a set of five software tools called Progress Portfolio that help students document and reflect on their progress as they work through computer- and web-based science simulations and explorations. These tools allow students to save and print information that is currently on their computer screen, annotate their work with "sticky notes," create worksheet-like pages, organize work into folders or tables, and present work in a PowerPoint-like slide show. The Progress Portfolio program can be downloaded from the Progress Portfolio web site (**www.progressportfolio.northwestern.edu/general/index.html**).

Resources for Further Investigation

● Constructivism

Bruce Marlow and Marilyn Page discuss the nature of constructivism and how to create a constructivist classroom in *Creating and Sustaining the Constructivist Classroom* (1998). In a section of the preface titled "How This Book Is Different from Others," they state: "There is much written about theories of constructivism and the connection to superior learning results; however, there is no consolidated discussion of the foundations, results, and practical issues of constructivism. Additionally, there are few guidelines to help new or experienced teachers create and sustain a constructivist classroom. Our book does both" (p. x).

Jacqueline Grennon Brooks and Martin G. Brooks discuss the call for constructivism in education, describe five guiding principles (with several examples of classroom applications), and describe how to create a constructivist classroom setting in their fairly brief (127 pages) and readable book, *In Search of Understanding: The Case for Constructivist Classrooms* (2001).

Constructivist Strategies: Meeting Standards and Engaging Adolescent Minds (2001), by Chandra Foote, Paul Vermette, and Catherine Battaglia, summarizes the theoretical basis for constructivism; discusses how school issues and practices, such as block scheduling, classroom management, cooperative learning, higher-order thinking, culturally relevant teaching, and multiple intelligences theory, relate to constructivism; notes concerns, problems, and misunderstandings about constructivist teaching practices; and provides model lessons and unit plans.

For ideas about how to teach social studies from a constructivist perspective, see the January 1998 issue (vol. 62, no. 1) of *Social Education*.

Given the importance of interpersonal interaction to the constructivist position and the flexibility of classroom discussions as an instructional tool, you might want to read either or both of the following books. *William Fawcett Hill's Learning Through Discussion* (1994), by Jerome Rabow, Michelle Charness, Johanna Kipperman, and Susan Radcliffe-Vasile, is a compact book (67 pages) that nevertheless provides a wealth of practical information on how to structure and run discussion groups in the classroom. *Discussion as a Way of Teaching* (1999), by Stephen Brookfield and Stephen Preskill, provides the same information but also includes chapters on the use of discussion in culturally diverse classrooms and across genders.

The application of constructivist theory to secondary classrooms is discussed in *Constructivist Methods for the Secondary Classroom* (2003), by Ina Claire Gabler, Michael Schroeder, and David Curtis. This book includes three chapters on the directed discussion method, the exploratory discussion method, and the reflective discussion method.

● Problem-Solving Processes

Problem Finding, Problem Solving, and Creativity (1994), edited by Mark Runco, contains thirteen chapters that cover various aspects of problem solving. Several chapters discuss the often overlooked topic of problem finding.

In *Reasoning and Problem Solving: A Handbook for Elementary School Teachers* (1993), Stephen Krulik and Jesse Rudnick discuss the nature of higher-order thinking skills, present a general approach to problem solving, provide steps teachers should follow when teaching problem solving, and offer hands-on materials and resources for problem-solving instruction.

In *The Art of Thinking* (7th ed., 2004), Vincent Ruggiero describes a four-part model for helping students become better thinkers and problem solvers. The chapters that describe each part ("Be Aware," "Be Creative," "Be Critical," "Communicate Your Ideas") are clearly written and contain a wealth of suggestions for classroom use.

In *Learning to Solve Problems: A Constructivist Perspective* (2003), David Jonassen, Jane Howland, Joi Moore, and Rose Marra describe how technology can be used from a constructivist perspective to foster meaningful learning and problem solving. Included are chapters on learning from the Internet, use of such video-based technologies as television, camcorders, and videodiscs, learning with hypermedia, and exploring microworlds and virtual realities.

The Illinois Mathematics and Science Academy, a high school for gifted and talented students, also houses a Center for Problem-Based Learning. The web site for the Center (www2.imsa.edu/programs/pbl/cpbl.html) provides a tutorial introduction to PBL, a comparison between PBL and more traditional teaching methods, instructions on how to design a PBL unit, and model problems.

● Transfer of Learning

A comprehensive account of transfer can be found in *Transfer of Learning* (2001), by Robert E. Haskell. Part I discusses the nature of transfer of learning, and Part II explains what makes transfer of learning work.

Summary

1. The constructivist view of learning holds that meaningful learning occurs when people use existing knowledge schemes and the viewpoints of others to interpret the world around them.

2. During the 1960s, Jerome Bruner proposed a constructivist view of learning that relied on giving students realistic problems for which they had to discover appropriate solutions. Contemporary approaches to discovery learning frequently use computer simulation programs to help students grasp basic concepts and skills.

3. The major aspects of constructivism are that meaningful learning occurs when people actively construct personal knowledge structures, that only part of a teacher's understanding of some concept or issue can be transferred to students through direct instruction, that the knowledge structures of different people have much in common,

and that the formation and changing of knowledge structures come mainly from peer interaction.

4. A cognitive constructivist view, like that of Piaget, focuses on how individuals' cognitive processes influence the view of the world they construct.

5. A social constructivist view, like that of Vygotsky, focuses on how social processes influence the view of reality that students construct.

6. Three conditions that support constructivism are a cognitive apprenticeship between teacher and student, the use of realistic learning tasks (situated learning), and exposure to multiple perspectives.

7. The situated learning condition can be met by using a problem-based approach to learning.

8. The classroom discussion is an instructional technique that teachers can use to support a constructivist view of meaningful learning, for it allows students to share different perspectives of realistic problems.

9. A problem exists when a learner has a goal but no means for reaching the goal. Problem solving involves identifying and using knowledge and skills that result in achieving one's goal.

10. What constitutes a problem will vary with the age and experience of the learner, as well as the nature of the problem itself.

11. The types of problems that students most often come into contact with are well-structured problems, ill-structured problems, and issues. Well-structured problems are clearly stated and can be solved by applying previously learned procedures, and their solutions can be accurately evaluated. Ill-structured problems are often vaguely stated, they cannot always be solved by applying previously learned procedures, and their solutions cannot always be evaluated against clear and widely accepted criteria. Issues are like ill-structured problems, but with two differences: they arouse strong emotions that tend to divide people into opposing camps, and they require that one determine the most reasonable position to take before working out a solution.

12. A general problem-solving model is composed of five steps: realize that a problem exists, understand the nature of the problem, compile relevant information, formulate and carry out a solution, and evaluate the solution.

13. The keys to realizing that a problem exists are to be curious about why things are the way they are and to be dissatisfied with the status quo.

14. Understanding the nature of a problem, also known as problem representation or problem framing, requires a high level of knowledge about the subject matter surrounding the problem and familiarity with the particular type of problem.

15. A problem solver can compile relevant information by searching long-term memory, retrieving solution-relevant information, and representing that information as lists, tables, pictures, graphs, diagrams, and so on. In addition, friends, colleagues, and experts can be tapped for information.

16. A problem solver can formulate solutions by studying worked examples, working on a simpler version of the problem, breaking the problem into parts, working backward, solving an analogous problem, or creating an external representation of the problem.

17. A problem solver can evaluate solutions for well-structured problems by estimating or checking. To evaluate solutions for ill-structured problems, the problem solver can answer a set of basic questions that deal with who, what, where, when, why, and how; identify imperfections and complications; anticipate possible negative reactions; and devise improvements.

18. Transfer of learning occurs when students apply knowledge and skills learned at one point in time and in a particular context to similar but different problems and tasks at a later point in time.

19. An early view of transfer was based on Thorndike and Woodworth's theory of identical elements. This theory holds that transfer of learning is a function of how many elements two tasks have in common. The greater the similarity is, the greater is the degree of transfer.

20. Positive transfer occurs when a new learning task is similar to a previously learned task and calls for a similar response. Negative transfer occurs when a new learning task is similar to a previously learned task but calls for a different response. Zero transfer occurs when previously learned information or skills are so dissimilar to new information or skills that they have no effect on how quickly the latter will be learned.

21. Positive transfer that is due to identifiable similarities between an earlier-learned task and a current one is referred to as specific transfer. Positive transfer that is due to the formulation, use, and carryover of cognitive strategies from one task to another is referred to as general transfer.

22. Near transfer occurs when the knowledge and skills that are acquired for a particular task are used relatively soon after for a highly similar task. Far transfer occurs when the knowledge and skills that are acquired for a particular task are used much later for another task that is dissimilar in appearance and represents a different knowledge domain.

23. A current view of specific transfer is called low-road transfer. This kind of transfer is produced by giving students many opportunities to practice a skill in different settings and with different materials.

24. A current view of general transfer is called high-road transfer. This kind of transfer is produced by teaching students how to formulate a general rule, strategy, or schema that can be used in the future with a variety of problems that are fundamentally similar to the original.

25. Students' knowledge construction and problem-solving skills can be improved through a wide variety of computer applications, many of which involve collaboration on learning projects.

Key Terms

discovery learning *(310)*
cognitive constructivism *(312)*
social constructivism *(313)*
situated learning *(314)*
inert knowledge *(314*
problem solving *(324)*
well-structured problems *(324)*
ill-structured problems *(325)*

issues *(325)*
problem representation, problem
    framing *(326)*
heuristics *(327)*
transfer of learning *(334)*
theory of identical elements *(334)*
positive transfer *(334)*
negative transfer *(335)*

zero transfer *(335)*
specific transfer *(335)*
general transfer *(336)*
near transfer *(336)*
far transfer *(336)*
low-road transfer *(336)*
high-road transfer *(337)*
anchored instruction *(341)*

11 Approaches to Instruction

These key points will help you learn the important information in this chapter. To help you study, they also appear in the margins of the pages, next to the text where they are discussed.

Devising and Using Objectives

- Goals are broad, general statements of desired educational outcomes
- Instructional objectives specify observable, measurable student behaviors
- Taxonomy: categories arranged in hierarchical order
- Cognitive taxonomy: knowledge, comprehension, application, analysis, synthesis, evaluation
- Taxonomy of affective objectives stresses attitudes and values
- Psychomotor taxonomy outlines steps that lead to skilled performance
- Most test questions stress knowledge, ignore higher levels of cognitive taxonomy
- Mager: state specific objectives that identify act, define conditions, state criteria
- Gronlund: state general objectives, list sample of specific learning outcomes
- Objectives work best when students are aware of them

The Behavioral Approach to Teaching: Direct Instruction

- Direct instruction: focus on learning basic skills, teacher makes all decisions, keep students on-task, emphasize positive reinforcement
- Direct instruction involves structured, guided, and independent practice
- Direct instruction helps students learn basic skills

The Cognitive Approach to Teaching: Facilitating Meaningful and Self-Directed Learning

- Information-processing approach: design lessons around principles of meaningful learning, teach students how to learn more effectively
- Tell students what you want them to learn, why, and how they will be tested
- Present organized and meaningful lessons
- Present new information in small chunks
- Constructivist approach: students discover how to be autonomous, self-directed learners
- Meaningful learning aided by exposure to multiple points of view
- Technology supports a cognitive approach to instruction by helping students code, store, and retrieve information

The Humanistic Approach to Teaching: Student-Centered Instruction

- Maslow: help students develop their potential by satisfying their needs
- Rogers: establish conditions that allow self-directed learning
- Humanistic approach addresses needs, values, motives, self-perceptions
- Japanese classrooms marked by humanistic orientation, high scores on international math and science test

The Social Approach to Teaching: Teaching Students How to Learn from Each Other

- Competitive reward structures may decrease motivation to learn
- Cooperative learning characterized by heterogeneous groups, positive interdependence, promotive interaction, individual accountability

Key Points continued on next page.

This chapter is concerned with helping you answer two questions: What are my objectives? (or What do I want students to know and be able to do after I complete a unit of instruction?) and How can I help students achieve those objectives? The ordering of these two questions is not arbitrary. Instructional planning should always begin with a description of what you want students to know and be able to do some weeks, or even months, after the beginning of an instructional unit.

To appreciate why, suppose that you follow the common practice of many teachers and prepare lesson plans by examining texts and other curriculum materials in order to devise an instructional sequence. Probably your first inclination is to concentrate on what is going to happen tomorrow and to put off thinking about what is going to happen two weeks or a month ahead when the time comes to evaluate what students have learned. You might reason that there is no point in thinking about tests until it is time to prepare tests. Quite a few teachers operate in such a one-thing-at-a-time way, and you are probably familiar with the results: disorganized lessons, lectures, and assignments, followed by exams that may not have much to do with what you think you were supposed to have learned.

You can avoid falling into that common trap by concentrating at the very beginning on what you want your students to be able to do at the end of a unit of study. If you decide in advance what you want your students to achieve, you can prepare lessons that logically lead to a particular result and also use evaluation techniques efficiently designed to determine what level of achievement has occurred.

Once you have a clear idea of what you are trying to accomplish with your students, you can consider how you are going to help get them there. Here is where you can use your knowledge of learning and motivation. After all, if the goal of teaching is to help students acquire and use a variety of knowledge and skills, what better way to do

- Cooperative learning effects likely due to stimulation of motivation, cognitive development, meaningful learning
- Low- and average-ability students in mixed-ability groups outperform peers in homogeneous groups on problem-solving tests; high-ability students in homogeneous groups score slightly higher than peers in mixed-ability groups
- Successful technology applications are embedded in an active social environment

that than to use approaches and techniques that are consistent with what is known about how people learn and the conditions under which they learn best?

The theories that underlie the approaches to instruction described in this chapter emphasize different aspects of the learning process, and each has been supported by research. Thus, no one theory is sufficiently comprehensive and powerful that you can rely exclusively on it as a guide for designing classroom instruction. To work effectively with the diversity of students you will almost certainly encounter, you will need to use a variety of instructional approaches and techniques. For some objectives and students, you may want to use a highly structured approach that is consistent with the principles of behavioral and social learning theories. For other objectives, you may want to focus on helping students develop more effective learning and problem-solving skills. You may also want students to work productively in groups and respond to you and to learning in positive ways and develop positive feelings about themselves as students. And you will probably also want to integrate computer-based technology with one or more of these approaches.

In the next section, we will introduce you to the concept of instructional objectives. We will distinguish between goals and objectives, describe organizational schemes called taxonomies that help you decide what you want your students to learn, and describe methods for preparing and using objectives. ●

DEVISING AND USING OBJECTIVES

Contrasting Objectives with Educational Goals

- Goals are broad, general statements of desired educational outcomes

One way to help you understand the nature of instructional objectives is to contrast them with something with which they are often confused: educational goals. Goals are relatively broad statements of what political and educational leaders would like to see schools accomplish. Perhaps the best-known set of educational goals were those in the U.S. government's Goals 2000 program. Signed into law in 1994, Goals 2000 listed eight goals that the government hoped to achieve by the year 2000. (The current status of the Goals 2000 program is described on a web site maintained by the U.S. Department of Education. It can be found at **www.ed.gov/G2K/index. html**.) Although a few of the goals were stated in measurable terms ("At least 90 percent of all students will graduate from high school"), others were much vaguer in their wording, such as these:

 To preview this chapter's central concepts, see the Chapter Themes on the textbook web site, accessible from **http://education.college.hmco. com/students.**

- Students will acquire the thinking skills that will allow them to become responsible citizens, independent learners, and productive workers.
- All adults will be sufficiently literate, knowledgeable, and skilled to compete in a global economy and behave as responsible citizens.

Unfortunately, statements of this sort do not provide very useful guidelines for teachers charged with the responsibility for achieving the goals. What exactly is meant by "thinking skills" or being "sufficiently literate, knowledgeable, and skilled"? And will these terms mean the same thing to every teacher? Thinking skills, for example, could be interpreted to mean everything from memorization to problem solving.

- Instructional objectives specify observable, measurable student behaviors

Instructional objectives, in contrast to these broad educational goals, specify the kinds of observable and measurable student behaviors that make it possible for the underlying goals to be achieved. To give teachers both a common vocabulary and a system for writing different kinds of objectives, psychologists have created organizational schemes called taxonomies.

Taxonomies of Objectives

Awareness of the vagueness of educational goals stimulated a group of psychologists who specialized in testing to seek a better way to describe educational objectives. After experimenting with various ways to prepare lists of objectives that would be more useful to teachers than vaguely worded sets of goals, the test specialists decided to develop taxonomies of educational objectives.

● Taxonomy: categories arranged in hierarchical order

A **taxonomy** is a classification scheme with categories arranged in hierarchical order. Because goals of education are extremely diverse, the decision was made to prepare taxonomies in three areas, or *domains:* cognitive, affective, and psychomotor. The taxonomy for the **cognitive domain** stresses knowledge and intellectual skills; the taxonomy for the **affective domain** concentrates on attitudes and values; and that for the **psychomotor domain** focuses on physical abilities and skills.

Taxonomy for the Cognitive Domain   The taxonomy for the cognitive domain was prepared by Benjamin S. Bloom, Max D. Englehart, Edward J. Furst, Walker H. Hill, and David R. Krathwohl (1956). It consists of six hierarchically ordered levels of instructional outcomes: knowledge, comprehension, application, analysis, synthesis, and evaluation. The taxonomy is described as a hierarchy because it was reasoned that comprehension relies on prior mastery of knowledge or facts, application depends on comprehension of relevant ideas, and so on through the remaining levels. An abridged outline of the taxonomy for the cognitive domain follows:

Taxonomy of Educational Objectives: Cognitive Domain

● Cognitive taxonomy: knowledge, comprehension, application, analysis, synthesis, evaluation

1.00 *Knowledge.* Remembering previously learned information, such as facts, terms, procedures, and principles.

2.00 *Comprehension.* Grasping the meaning of information by putting it into one's own words, drawing conclusions, or stating implications.

3.00 *Application.* Applying knowledge to actual situations as in taking principles learned in math and applying them to laying out a baseball diamond or applying principles of civil liberties to current events.

4.00 *Analysis.* Breaking down objects or ideas into simpler parts and seeing how the parts relate and are organized. For example, discussing how the public and the private sectors differ or detecting logical fallacies in an argument.

5.00 *Synthesis.* Rearranging component ideas into a new whole. For example, planning a panel discussion or writing a comprehensive term paper.

6.00 *Evaluation.* Making judgments based on internal evidence or external criteria. For example, evaluating a work of art, editing a term paper, or detecting inconsistencies in the speech of a politician.

Taxonomy for the Affective Domain   In addition to arranging instructional experiences to help students achieve cognitive objectives, virtually all teachers are interested in encouraging the development of attitudes and values. To clarify the nature of such objectives, a taxonomy for the affective domain was prepared (Krathwohl, Bloom, & Masia, 1964). Affective objectives are more difficult to define, evaluate, or encourage than cognitive objectives because they are often demonstrated in subtle or indirect ways. Furthermore, certain aspects of value development are sometimes considered to be more the responsibility of parents than of teachers. Finally, because values and attitudes involve a significant element of personal choice, they are often expressed more clearly out of school than in the classroom. The complete taxonomy for the affective domain stresses out-of-school values as much as, if not more than, in-school values.

The following abridgment concentrates on the kinds of affective objectives you are most likely to be concerned with as a teacher. You will probably recognize, though, that there is not much you can do to influence substantially the kinds of objectives described in the higher levels of the taxonomy because they represent a crystallization of values formed by experiences over an extended period of time.

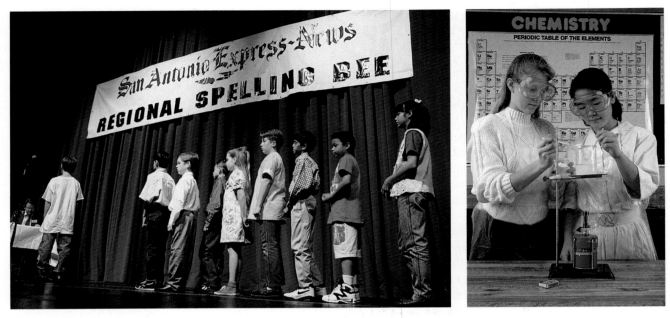

The taxonomy of objectives for the cognitive domain calls attention to the fact that instructional outcomes can range from such basic capabilities as verbatim recall and comprehension to such higher-level capabilities as application of knowledge and skill, analysis of complex ideas into their component parts, synthesis of different ideas into an integrated whole, and evaluation of the quality of ideas.

● Taxonomy of affective objectives stresses attitudes and values

● Psychomotor taxonomy outlines steps that lead to skilled performance

Taxonomy of Educational Objectives: Affective Domain

1.0 *Receiving (attending).* Willingness to receive or attend.
2.0 *Responding.* Active participation indicating positive response or acceptance of an idea or policy.
3.0 *Valuing.* Expressing a belief or attitude about the value or worth of something.
4.0 *Organization.* Organizing various values into an internalized system.
5.0 *Characterization by a value or value complex.* The value system becomes a way of life.

Taxonomy for the Psychomotor Domain   Cognitive and affective objectives are important at all grade levels, but so are psychomotor objectives. Regardless of the grade level or subject you teach, at some point you are likely to want to help your students acquire physical skills of various kinds. In the primary grades, for example, you will want your students to learn how to print legibly. And in many subjects in middle school and high school, psychomotor skills (for example, driving a car, playing a violin, adjusting a microscope, manipulating a computer keyboard, operating a power saw, throwing a pot) may be essential. Recognition of the importance of physical skills prompted Elizabeth Simpson (1972) to prepare a taxonomy for the psychomotor domain. An abridged version of the taxonomy follows:

Taxonomy of Educational Objectives: Psychomotor Domain

1.0 *Perception.* Using sense organs to obtain cues needed to guide motor activity.
2.0 *Set.* Being ready to perform a particular action.
3.0 *Guided response.* Performing under the guidance of a model.
4.0 *Mechanism.* Being able to perform a task habitually with some degree of confidence and proficiency. For example, demonstrating the ability to get the first serve in the service area 70 percent of the time.
5.0 *Complex or overt response.* Performing a task with a high degree of proficiency and skill. For example, typing all kinds of business letters and forms quickly with no errors.
6.0 *Adaptation.* Using previously learned skills to perform new but related tasks. For example, using skills developed while using a word processor to do desktop publishing.
7.0 *Origination.* Creating new performances after having developed skills. For example, creating a new form of modern dance.

Why Use Taxonomies?   Using these taxonomies will help you avoid two common instructional failings: ignoring entire classes of outcomes (usually affective and psycho-motor) and overemphasizing the lowest level of the cognitive domain. According to Benjamin S. Bloom, organizer and driving force of the team that prepared the first taxonomy,

● Most test questions stress knowledge, ignore higher levels of cognitive taxonomy

> After the sale of over one million copies of the *Taxonomy of Educational Objectives—Cognitive Domain* [Bloom et al., 1956] and over a quarter of a century of use of this domain in preservice and in-service teacher training, it is estimated that over 90% of test questions that U.S. public school students are *now* expected to answer deal with little more than information. Our instructional material, our classroom teaching methods, and our testing methods rarely rise above the lowest category of the Taxonomy—knowledge. (1984, p. 13)

The next section describes how you can write and profitably use objectives.

Ways to State and Use Objectives

Many psychologists have offered suggestions for writing and using objectives, but the following discussion is limited to recommendations made by two of the most influential writers on the subject: Robert F. Mager and Norman E. Gronlund.

Mager's Recommendations for Use of Specific Objectives   With the publication of a provocative and unorthodox little treatise titled *Preparing Instructional Objectives* (1962, 1997), Mager sparked considerable interest in the use of objectives. Mager emphasizes the importance of objectives by pointing out that

> if you don't know where you're going, the best-made maps won't help you get there. . . . Without a way to communicate your instructional objectives to others:
>
> • You wouldn't be able to decide which instructional content and procedures would help you to accomplish your objectives.
> • You wouldn't be able to create measuring instruments (tests) that tell you whether your students had become competent enough to move on.
> • And your students wouldn't be able to decide for themselves when to stop practicing. (1997, p. vi)

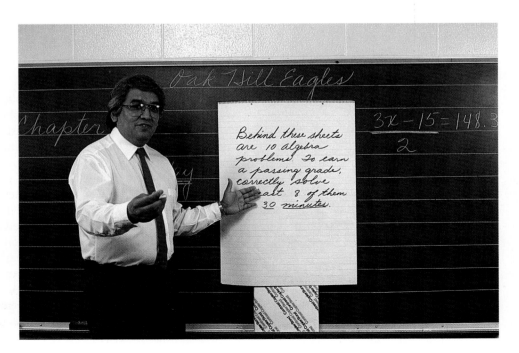

Mager recommends that teachers use objectives that identify the behavioral act that indicates achievement, define conditions under which the behavior is to occur, and state the criterion of acceptable performance.

Mager then offers these suggestions for writing **specific objectives** of instruction:

● Mager: state specific objectives that identify act, define conditions, state criteria

1. Describe what you want learners to be doing when demonstrating achievement, and indicate how you will know they are doing it.
2. In your description, identify and name the behavioral act that indicates achievement, define the conditions under which the behavior is to occur, and state the criterion of acceptable performance.
3. Write a separate objective for each learning performance.

Here are some examples of the types of objectives Mager recommends:

Correctly solve at least seven addition problems consisting of three two-digit numbers within a period of three minutes.

Correctly answer at least four of the five questions on the last page of story booklet 16 in the Reading Comprehension series of booklets.

Given pictures of ten trees, correctly identify at least eight as either deciduous or evergreen.

Correctly spell at least 90 percent of the words on the list handed out last week.

Given a computer and word processing program, set it up to type a business letter (according to the specifications provided) within two minutes.

Note that the criterion of acceptable performance can be stated as a time limit, a minimum number of correct responses, or a proportion of correct responses.

Mager's proposals were widely endorsed immediately after the publication of *Preparing Instructional Objectives*, but in time it became apparent that the very specific kinds of objectives he recommended were most useful in situations where students were asked to acquire knowledge of factual information or to learn simple skills. Norman E. Gronlund concluded that a different type of objective was more appropriate for more complex and advanced kinds of learning.

Gronlund's Recommendations for Use of General Objectives   Gronlund (2004) has developed a two-step procedure for writing a more general type of objective:

1. Examine what is to be learned with reference to lists of objectives such as those included in the three taxonomies. Use such lists to formulate **general objectives** of instruction that describe types of behavior students should exhibit in order to demonstrate what they have learned.
2. Under each general instructional objective, list up to five *specific learning outcomes* that provide a representative sample of what students should be able to do when they have achieved the general objective. Each learning outcome should begin with an *action verb* (such as *explain* or *describe*) that names the particular action the student is expected to take.

● Gronlund: state general objectives, list sample of specific learning outcomes

To see how Gronlund's method differs from Mager's, imagine you are teaching an educational psychology course and you want to write objectives that reflect an understanding of the four stages of Piaget's theory of cognitive development. Figure 11.1 compares objectives you might develop using Gronlund's approach with objectives that follow Mager's method.

Gronlund gives several reasons for beginning with general objectives. First, most learning activities are too complex to be described in terms of a specific objective for every learning outcome, as Mager proposed. Second, the kind of specific objective Mager advocated may tend to cause instructors and students to concentrate on memorizing facts and mastering simple skills. As indicated earlier, these types of behaviors are at the lowest levels of the taxonomies of objectives. Third, specific objectives can restrict the flexibility of the teacher. Gronlund's objectives allow performance criteria to be kept separate from the objective so a teacher can revise performance standards as needed without having to rewrite the objective.

pause & reflect

One criticism of writing objectives is that it limits the artistic side of teaching, locking teachers into a predetermined plan of instruction. Can you respond by recalling a teacher who provided objectives but was still enthusiastic, flexible, and inventive?

Figure 11.1 Types of Objectives: Gronlund's and Mager's Approaches Compared

Topic: Piaget's Theory of Cognitive Development

Gronlund's Approach	**Mager's Approach**
General objective	**Specific objectives**

Gronlund's Approach	Mager's Approach
General objective The student will understand the characteristics of Piaget's four stages of cognitive development.	**Specific objectives** Given a list of Piaget's four stages of cognitive development, the student, within twenty minutes, will describe in his or her own words two problems that students at each stage should and should not be able to solve.
Specific learning outcomes, stated with action verbs *Describe* in his or her own words the type of thinking in which students at each stage can and cannot engage.	Given a videotape of kindergarteners presented with a conservation-of-volume problem, the student will predict the response of 90 percent of the students.
Predict behaviors of students of different ages.	Given a videotape of fifth-grade students presented with a class inclusion problem, the student will predict the response of 90 percent of the students.
Explain why certain teaching techniques would or would not be successful with students of different ages.	Given eight descriptions of instructional lessons, two at each of Piaget's four stages, the student will be able to explain in each case why the lesson would or would not succeed.

This feature is useful if the same behavior is to be evaluated several times over the course of a unit of instruction, with successively higher levels of performance required. A fourth and final reason is that general objectives help keep you aware that the main target of your instructional efforts is the general outcome (such as comprehension, application, or analysis).

To illustrate the differences between general objectives and specific outcomes, Gronlund has prepared lists of phrases and verbs that can be used in writing each type of objective for each of the levels of all three taxonomies of educational objectives. These lists can be found in Appendix C of Gronlund's *Writing Instructional Objectives for Teaching and Assessment* (2004) and in Appendix G of Linn and Gronlund's *Measurement and Assessment in Teaching* (2000).

Aligning Assessment with Objectives and Instruction

Deciding in advance what you want your students to achieve by drawing from the various levels of the taxonomies and formulating instructional methods to help them master those objectives will be a largely wasted effort if you fail to recognize that the tests you create must also fit those objectives and methods.

As we discuss in the chapter on assessment, there are several types of classroom assessment methods, each of which is most useful for measuring only *certain* outcomes. Multiple-choice, short-answer, and true-false tests are useful for measuring mastery of basic factual knowledge. For objectives that emphasize the comprehension, analysis, and synthesis levels of Bloom's Taxonomy, essay questions that call for students to summarize, compare, and contrast would be more useful. For objectives that reflect a constructivist orientation, paper-and-pencil tests are likely to be much less useful than requiring students to solve a complex problem, create a product over an extended period of time, or work productively with a small group of peers on a project. (This type of testing, called performance assessment, is discussed in the chapters on assessment and testing.)

Here's a small example of how things can go wrong if you don't align your tests with both your objectives and your instructional methods. If you tell students that you want them to organize information into logical structures, integrate ideas into broad themes, and make connections with knowledge learned elsewhere, and then

 Need guidance in preparing lesson plans that align objectives, activities, and assessment? Check the sample lesson plans and template on this book's web site (accessible from **http://education.college.hmco. com/students**).

teach them how to think along those lines but load your tests with short-answer and multiple-choice items that require rote memorization, don't be surprised when students simply memorize facts. From their perspective, the content and level of the test items are the real objectives.

One final comment about alignment. In the first paragraph of this section, we referred to the tests you *create* rather than the tests you *use*. These two terms imply a subtle but important distinction. The best way to ensure alignment of objectives, teaching approach, and assessment is for you to be the creator of the assessment. If you use a test that somebody else has designed, such as a standardized test, it is almost a certainty that some of the items will not match your objectives or instructional approach.

Evaluations of the Effectiveness of Objectives

Do students learn more when their teachers provide them with clearly written objectives? The answer is yes, but only under certain conditions. Reviews of research on the effectiveness of objectives (for example, Faw & Waller, 1976; Klauer, 1984; Melton, 1978) lead to the following conclusions:

● Objectives work best when students are aware of them

1. Objectives seem to work best when students are aware of them, treat them as directions to learn specific sections of material, and feel they will aid learning.
2. Objectives seem to work best when they are clearly written and the learning task is neither too difficult nor too easy.
3. Students of average ability seem to profit more from being given objectives than do students of higher or lower ability.
4. Objectives lead to an improvement in intentional learning (what is stressed as important) but to a decline in incidental learning (not emphasized by the teacher). General objectives of the type that Gronlund recommended seem to lead to more incidental learning than do specific objectives of the type that Mager recommended.

As we mentioned at the beginning of the chapter, once you have decided what it is you want your students to learn, you need to decide which approaches you will use to help them achieve those objectives. Our use of the term *approaches* is deliberate. To repeat what we said at the beginning of the chapter, different approaches to instruction are based on different theories of learning and motivation, and given the complexity of the learning process and the diversity of learners in most classrooms, no one theory can be used for all instructional purposes and for all students. So as you read through the next several sections, try to imagine how you might use each approach over the course of a school year.

pause & reflect

Based on this chapter and your own experience, do you agree that writing objectives and providing them to students are worthwhile uses of a teacher's time? If so, what steps will you take to make writing objectives a standard part of your professional behavior?

THE BEHAVIORAL APPROACH TO TEACHING: DIRECT INSTRUCTION

For behavioral psychologists, learning means acquiring new behaviors, and new behaviors are learned because of the role that external stimuli play. Thus, a behavioral approach to teaching involves arranging and implementing those conditions that make it highly likely that a desired response will occur in the presence of a particular stimulus (such as reading a sentence fluently, accurately using the correct mathematical operations when faced with a long-division problem, and giving the correct English translation to a paragraph written in Spanish). Perhaps the most popular approach to teaching that is based on behavioral theory is direct instruction.

The Nature of Direct Instruction

The underlying philosophy of **direct instruction** (sometimes called *explicit teaching*) is that if the student has not learned, the teacher has not effectively taught. This approach calls for the teacher to keep students consistently engaged in learning basic skills and knowledge through the design of effective lessons, corrective feedback, and opportunities for practice. It is most frequently used in the teaching of basic skills (for example, reading, mathematical computation, writing) and subject matter (for example, science, social studies, foreign language vocabulary) in the primary and elementary grades. It is also used to teach remedial classes at the middle school and high school levels. It is felt to be most useful for young learners, slow learners, and all learners when the material is new and difficult to grasp at first. Although there are several variations of direct instruction, the following represents a synthesis of descriptions offered by George Adams and Sigfried Engelmann (1996), Bruce Joyce and Marsha Weil (2004), Barak Rosenshine (1987), and Barak Rosenshine and Carla Meister (1994b).

The main characteristics of direct instruction include:

1. Focusing almost all classroom activity on learning basic academic knowledge and skills. Affective and social objectives, such as improved self-esteem and learning to get along with others, are either de-emphasized or ignored.
2. Having the teacher make all instructional decisions, such as how much material will be covered at one time, whether students work individually or in groups, and whether students work on mathematics during the morning and social studies during the afternoon.
3. Keeping students working productively toward learning new academic knowledge and skills (usually called being on-task) as much as possible.
4. Maintaining a positive classroom climate by emphasizing positive reinforcement and avoiding the use of aversive consequences.

The goal of direct instruction is to have students master basic skills. Advocates of this method believe that students who mislearn information require substantially more time and effort to relearn concepts than would have been the case had they learned them correctly in the first place.

For obvious reasons, direct instruction is a highly structured approach to teaching and is often referred to as *teacher-directed* or *teacher-led instruction*.

The Components of Direct Instruction

Bruce Joyce and Marsha Weil (2004) identify five general components, or phases, that make up direct instruction: orientation, presentation, structured practice,

● Direct instruction: focus on learning basic skills, teacher makes all decisions, keep students on-task, emphasize positive reinforcement

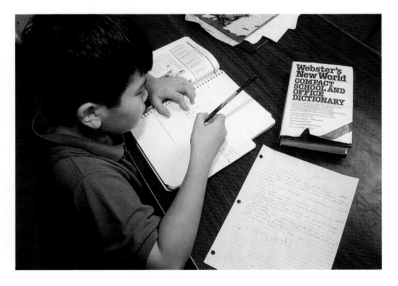

Teachers who subscribe to direct instruction emphasize efficient learning of basic skills through the use of structured lessons, positive reinforcement, and extensive practice.

guided practice, and independent practice. These components are not derived just from theory. They reflect the techniques that effective teachers at all grade levels have been observed to use.

JOURNAL ENTRY
Using a Direct Instruction Approach

Orientation   During the orientation phase, the teacher provides an overview of the lesson, explains why students need to learn the upcoming material, relates the new subject either to material learned during earlier lessons or to their life experience, tells students what they will need to do to learn the material, and tells students what level of performance they will be expected to exhibit.

Presentation   The presentation phase initially involves explaining, illustrating, and demonstrating the new material. As with all other forms of instruction based on operant conditioning, the lesson is broken down into small, easy-to-learn steps to ensure mastery of each step in the lesson sequence. Numerous examples of new concepts and skills are provided, and, consistent with social learning theory, the teacher demonstrates the kind of response students should strive for (such as a particular pronunciation of foreign vocabulary, a reading of a poem or story, the steps in mathematical operations, or how to analyze a novel for theme, character, or setting). To assist comprehension, and where appropriate, material can be presented pictorially (for example, slides, videotapes, on computer) or graphically (as a concept map, or a timeline, or in table form). At the first sign of difficulty, the teacher gives additional explanations.

The last step of the presentation phase is to evaluate students' understanding. This is typically done through a question-and-answer session in which the questions call for specific answers as well as explanations of how students formulated their answers. Some sort of system is used to ensure that all students receive an equal opportunity to respond to questions. Throughout the lesson, efforts are made to stay on-task and avoid nonproductive digressions.

Structured, Guided, and Independent Practice   The last three phases of the direct instruction model all focus on practice, although with successively lower levels of assistance. Joyce and Weil (2004) refer to these three phases as *structured practice, guided practice*, and *independent practice*. Because the level of teacher assistance is gradually withdrawn, you may recognize this progression as an attempt to apply the behavioral principle of shaping. You may also recognize it as the constructivist principle of scaffolding.

Structured practice involves the greatest degree of teacher assistance. The teacher leads the entire class through each step in a problem or lesson so as to minimize incorrect responses. Visual displays, such as overhead transparencies, are commonly used during structured practice as a way to illustrate and help students recall the components of a lesson. As the students respond, the teacher reinforces correct responses and corrects errors.

During guided practice, students work at their own desks on problems of the type explained and demonstrated by the teacher. The teacher circulates among the students, checking for and correcting any errors.

When students can correctly solve at least 85 percent of the problems given to them during guided practice, they are deemed ready for independent practice. At this point, students are encouraged to practice on their own either in class or at home. Although the teacher continues to assess the accuracy of the students' work and provide feedback, it is done on a more delayed basis.

• Direct instruction involves structured, guided, and independent practice

Getting the Most Out of Practice

Joyce and Weil (2004) offer the following suggestions to help make practice effective:

1. Shape student learning by systematically moving students from structured practice to guided practice to independent practice.
2. Schedule several relatively short but intense practice sessions, which typically produce more learning than fewer but longer sessions. For primary grade students,

several five- to ten-minute sessions scattered over the day are likely to produce better results than the one or two thirty- to forty-minute sessions that middle school or high school students can tolerate.

3. Carefully monitor the accuracy of students' responses during structured practice to reinforce correct responses and correct unacceptable responses. The reason for this suggestion comes straight out of operant conditioning research. As you may recall from the chapter on behavioral learning theory, Skinner found that new behaviors are learned most rapidly when correct responses are immediately reinforced and incorrect responses are eliminated. When a learner makes incorrect responses that are not corrected, they become part of the learner's behavioral repertoire and impede the progress of subsequent learning.

4. To ensure the high degree of success that results in mastery of basic skills, students should not engage in independent practice until they can respond correctly to at least 85 percent of the examples presented to them during structured and guided practice.

5. Practice sessions for any lesson should be spread over several months. The habit of some teachers of not reviewing a topic once that part of the curriculum has been covered usually leads to a lower quality of learning. Once again, distributed practice produces better learning than massed practice.

6. Space practice sessions close together during structured practice but further and further apart for guided practice and independent practice.

Effectiveness of Direct Instruction

George Adams and Sigfried Engelmann (1996) conducted a review of thirty-seven studies of direct instruction and reported strong effects. On average, direct instruction students scored at the 81st percentile on an end-of-unit exam, whereas their conventionally taught peers scored at the 50th percentile.

● Direct instruction helps students learn basic skills

More recent studies of direct instruction have been done in urban schools that enroll high percentages of minority students and students of low socioeconomic status (SES). These studies have produced positive but more modest results. For example, a version of direct instruction called the BIG Accommodation model (because instruction is organized around "big ideas") was implemented in a California middle school that served high-poverty neighborhoods. After one year, the percentage of seventh- and eighth-grade students who were reading at the fifth-grade level or lower declined, while the percentage reading at the sixth- and seventh-grade or higher levels increased. Similar results were obtained for math achievement scores. In percentage terms, the most dramatic increase occurred among limited-English-proficient learners. Before the program was implemented, only 10 percent scored at grade level (seventh-grade or above) on reading and math tests. One year later that figure rose to about 36 percent. The largest gains in grade equivalent scores were made by white (2.1), Native American (1.7), and Latino (1.6) students (Grossen, 2002).

Using Technology to Support Behavioral Approaches to Instruction

The computer-based approach to instruction that uses behavioral learning principles emphasizes specific performance objectives, breaking learning down into small steps, shaping student success, using immediate feedback and consistent rewards, and predefining assessment techniques. Learning is viewed much like an industrial assembly line: information is transferred efficiently from a computer program to a waiting student.

Most of the drill-and-practice computer-assisted instruction tools and integrated learning systems mentioned in the chapter on behavioral learning theory fit within this framework (Mazyck, 2002; Ysseldyke et al., 2003), as would multimedia technology if used simply to embellish a lecture with new pictures or sounds. Although this approach to the use of technology in instruction may be perceived as rote, boring, and dehumanizing, it can prove valuable if you are interested in accurate and efficient learning of basic facts and skills.

THE COGNITIVE APPROACH TO TEACHING: FACILITATING MEANINGFUL AND SELF-DIRECTED LEARNING

The focus of cognitive learning theories is the mind and how it works. Hence, cognitive psychologists are primarily interested in studying those mental processes that expand our knowledge base and allow us to understand and respond to the world differently. In this section, we will lay out two approaches to instruction that are based on different forms of cognitive theory: information processing and constructivism. The information-processing approach to teaching involves implementing those conditions that help students effectively transfer information from the "outside" (a text or lecture, for example) to the "inside" (the mind), while the constructivist approach focuses on providing students opportunities to create their own meaningful view of reality.

The Nature and Elements of an Information-Processing Approach

As we noted previously in the book, information-processing theory focuses on how human beings interpret and mentally manipulate the information they encounter. Research shows that, for information to be meaningfully learned, it must be attended to, its critical features must be noticed, and it must be coded in an organized and meaningful way so as to make its retrieval more likely (Joyce & Weil, 2004; Marx & Winne, 1987; Pressley, Woloshyn, & Associates, 1995).

The approach to teaching that flows from information-processing theory has two main parts. First, design lessons and gear teaching behaviors to capitalize on what is known about the learning process. As you will see, this part of the information-processing approach has much in common with the behavioral approach that we just covered. Both approaches direct you to structure the classroom environment in a certain way (and to use some of the same tactics) to improve the effectiveness and efficiency of learning. Second—and this is what makes the information-processing approach unique—make students aware of how they learn and how they can use those processes to improve their classroom performance. Following are several suggestions for helping students become more effective processors of classroom instruction.

Communicate Clear Goals and Objectives   In previous chapters, we pointed out that motivation for learning is highest when students can relate new information to what they already know and to out-of-school experiences. The ability to make these links is what makes learning in general, and school learning in particular, meaningful. The first question that students ask themselves when they take a new course, encounter a new topic, or are asked to learn a new skill is, "Why do I have to learn this?"

Unfortunately, many teachers seem unaware of the need to explain clearly to students the immediate and larger purposes of learning most of a school's curriculum. Seymour Sarason (1993), who has written extensively and persuasively about the problems of education (including teacher education) and the need for reform, notes that "although that kind of question occurs to every child, I have never heard a student ask that question out loud, just as I have never observed a teacher address the issue" (p. 224). But some teachers do recognize the value of communicating clear goals. Margaret Metzger (1996), a veteran high school teacher, notes that teachers

● Information-processing approach: design lessons around principles of meaningful learning, teach students how to learn more effectively

JOURNAL ENTRY

Using an Information-Processing Approach to Instruction

have to convince students that what they learn in school is important and relevant to their lives outside school, both now and in the future.

● Tell students what you want them to learn, why, and how they will be tested

At the beginning of each lesson, tell students what you want them to accomplish, why you think it's important that they learn this knowledge or skill, and how you are going to assess their learning. If you intend to use paper-and-pencil tests, tell them what content areas will be covered, what kinds of questions you will include (in terms of the levels of Bloom's Taxonomy), and how many of each type of question will be on the test. Without this information, students will be unable to formulate a rational approach to learning and studying since they will be forced to guess about these features. They may, for example, take your general directive to "learn this material for the test" as a cue to memorize, when you expected them to be able to explain ideas in their own words. If you intend to use performance measures, tell students the conditions under which they will have to perform and what criteria you will use to judge their performance.

Use Attention-Getting Devices   Information-processing theory holds that material not attended to is not processed, and material that is not processed is not stored in memory. Consequently, you should use (but not overuse) a variety of attention-getting devices. The suggestion we just made to explain the purpose of a lesson, what students will be held accountable for learning, and how student learning will be assessed will likely capture the attention of some students. But once you are into a lesson, you may need to gain and maintain students' attention repeatedly.

The first Suggestions for Teaching in Your Classroom section (Helping Your Students Become Efficient Information Processors) in the chapter on information-processing theory mentioned a few devices for capturing students' attention. Here are several more:

- Orally emphasize certain words or phrases by raising or lowering your voice.
- Use dramatic gestures.
- Underline key words and phrases that you write on a chalkboard or whiteboard.
- When discussing the work of important people, whether in science, math, social studies, or history, dress up to look like the person and speak as you think the person might have spoken.

Emphasize Organization and Meaningfulness   Research studies have repeatedly found that students learn and recall more information when it is presented in an

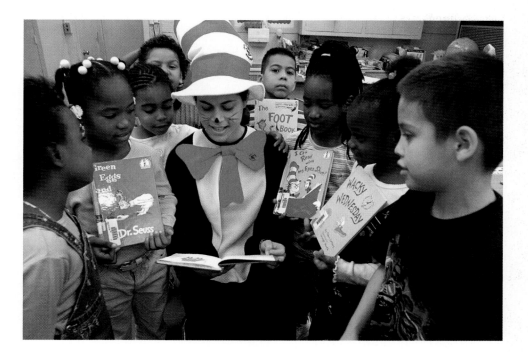

One implication of the information-processing approach to instruction is to use attention-getting devices since information not attended to will not be learned.

● Present organized and meaningful lessons

organized format and a meaningful context. Information is organized when the components that make it up are linked together in some rational way. If you teach high school physics, you can organize material according to major theories or basic principles or key discoveries, depending on your purpose. For history, you can identify main ideas and their supporting details or describe events as a chain of causes and effects. Just about any form of organization would be better than having students memorize names, dates, places, and other facts as isolated fragments of information.

A popular method for organizing and spatially representing the relationships among a set of ideas is *concept mapping*. This technique involves specifying the ideas that make up a topic and indicating with lines how they relate to one another. Figure 11.2 is a particularly interesting example of both organized knowledge and a constructivist view of learning. (We will take a further look at this latter angle when we discuss constructivist approaches.)

As we pointed out in the chapter on information-processing theory, meaningful learning results in richer and more stable memory representations and occurs more

Figure 11.2 Two Concept Maps Constructed from Identical Concepts

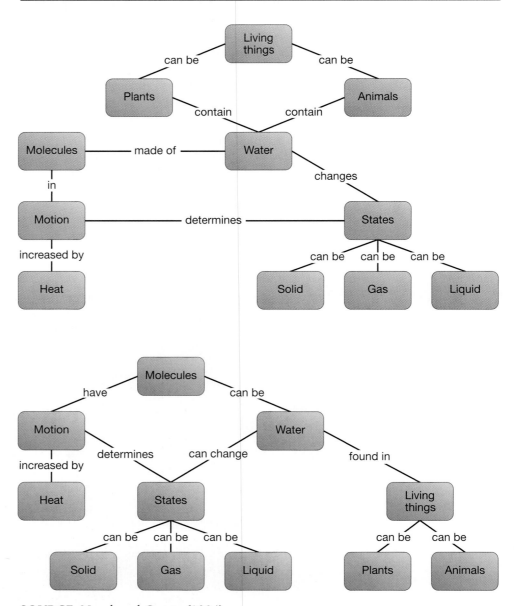

SOURCE: Novak and Gowin (1984).

readily when information can be related to familiar ideas and experiences. Several techniques are known to facilitate meaningful learning:

- Using some form of overview or introduction that provides a meaningful context for new material
- Using concrete examples and analogies to illustrate otherwise abstract ideas
- Using visually based methods of representing information, such as maps, graphs, three-dimensional models, and illustrations
- Stressing practical applications and relationships to other subjects (you may recall from a previous chapter that this tactic is used to help adolescent girls remain interested in science)

Present Information in Learnable Amounts and Over Realistic Time Periods

When students struggle to master the information they are expected to learn, the problem sometimes arises simply from an excess of information being presented to them at once—that is, from too great an external demand. At other times, the student's working (short-term) memory is strained because of the nature of the task itself: for instance, if the task has several components that all have to be monitored. By taking the nature of the task into consideration, you can judge how much information to expect your students to learn in a given time.

For tasks where a set of discrete elements must be learned in a one-at-a-time fashion, such as learning foreign language vocabulary or the symbols of chemical elements, the demand on working memory and comprehension is low because the elements are independent. Learning the meaning of one word or symbol has no effect on learning any of the others. As long as the external load on working memory is kept reasonable by limiting the number of words or symbols that students have to learn at any time, learning problems should be minimal.

Other tasks make greater demands on working memory because their elements interact. Learning to produce and recognize grammatically correct utterances ("The cat climbed up the tree" versus "Tree the climbed cat up the") is a task that places a higher demand on working memory because the meaning of all the words must be considered simultaneously in order to determine if the sentence makes sense. For such tasks, keeping the amount of information that students are required to learn at a low level is critically important because it leaves the student with sufficient working memory to engage in schema construction (Sweller et al., 1998).

● Present new information in small chunks

One instructional recommendation that flows from this analysis is the same as one of the recommendations for direct instruction: break lessons into small, manageable parts and don't introduce new topics until you have evidence that students have learned the presented material. A second recommendation is to build into lessons opportunities for students to write about, discuss, and use the ideas they are learning. By monitoring the accuracy of their responses, you will also have the information you need to judge whether it is time to introduce new ideas. Finally, arrange for relatively short practice sessions spread over several weeks rather than one or two long practice sessions because distributed practice leads to better learning than massed practice.

Facilitate Encoding of Information into Long-Term Memory High-quality learning rarely occurs when students adopt a relatively passive orientation. As we pointed out in the chapter on information-processing theory, many students do little more than read assigned material and record ideas in verbatim form. They spend little time thinking about how ideas within topics and between topics relate to one another or to concepts they have already learned. One reason is that many students simply do not know what else to do with information. Another reason is that teachers do little to support the kind of encoding that results in more meaningful forms of learning. Recall the study we mentioned that found that primary grade through middle school teachers provided students with suggestions for processing information less than 10 percent of the time and explanations for the suggestions they did give less than 1 percent of the time. To help your students encode information for more effective storage in and retrieval from long-term memory, incorporate the following techniques into your classroom instruction:

- Present information through such different media as pictures, videotape, audiotape, live models, and manipulation of physical objects.
- Use lots of examples and analogies (to foster elaboration).
- Prompt students to elaborate by asking them to put ideas in their own words, relate new ideas to personal experience, and create their own analogies.

Practice What You Preach   As we pointed out in discussing social learning theory, a great deal of learning takes place by observing and imitating a model. Because teachers are generally perceived by students as being competent, in a high-status occupation, and having power, their behaviors are likely to be noticed and imitated. This is especially true when the behaviors that teachers model are important to a student's classroom success. If you are convinced that how students process information plays a major role in how well they learn that information, then you should clearly and explicitly demonstrate how to analyze a task, formulate a learning plan, use a variety of learning tactics (such as mnemonics, summarizing, self-questioning, note taking, concept mapping), monitor the effectiveness of those tactics, and make changes when the results are unsatisfactory.

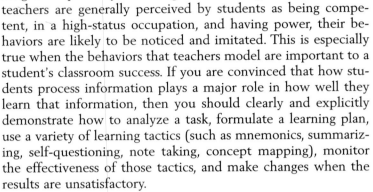

In the chapter on information-processing theory, we noted that elementary grade teachers rarely give students instruction in how to process information effectively. One reason is that teacher-education programs typically provide little or no coursework on this subject. Is this true of your program? What can you do when you teach to make full use of information-processing principles?

The Nature and Elements of a Constructivist Approach

In previous chapters, we noted that the essence of constructivist theory is that people learn best by creating their own understanding of reality. Using such characteristics as existing knowledge, attitudes, values, and experiences as filters, people interpret current experience in a way that seems to make sense to them at the time. As Figure 11.2 demonstrates, by constructing two different concept maps from an identical set of concepts, knowledge can be organized in any number of ways, and the scheme one creates will reflect one's purpose or focal point. Thus, some students understand that the Jane Austen novel *Sense and Sensibility* is as much a satire of the paternalistic class system of 1800s England as it is a love story, while other students see it only as a love story, and a boring one at that. The goal of constructivist-oriented teaching, then, is to provide a set of conditions that will lead students to construct a view of reality that both makes sense to them and addresses the essence of your objectives (Delgarno, 2001).

A brief description of four of the more prominent elements that help define a constructivist-oriented classroom follows. Although two of these elements reflect a social constructivist orientation, bear in mind that the goal of both cognitive and social constructivism is the same: to help students become more effective thinkers and problem solvers by helping them construct richer and more meaningful schemes. A social constructivist orientation simply gives greater weight to the role of social interaction in this process.

JOURNAL ENTRY

Using a Constructivist Approach to Instruction

Provide Scaffolded Instruction Within the Zone of Proximal Development   To review quickly what we said previously in the book, the zone of proximal development is the difference between what a learner can accomplish without assistance and what can be accomplished with assistance. As an example, consider the case of a youngster who has been given her first bicycle. Because the child has no experience with balancing herself on a two-wheeled bike, her parents know she will fall quite a few times before learning how to balance, steer, and pedal at the same time. To avoid injury and loss of motivation, one parent holds the bike upright and helps the child steer in a straight line while she figures out how to monitor her balance and make the necessary adjustments. This is done initially at very low speeds with the parent firmly holding the frame of the bike. Gradually, the child is allowed to pedal faster and the parent loosens his grip on the bike. Eventually, the parent does little more than run alongside the bike, and then he withdraws altogether.

This common example illustrates two related points about teaching from a constructivist perspective: instruction should demand more than what a student is capable of doing independently and, because of these demands, instruction should be scaffolded. That is, teachers should provide just enough support, through such devices as explanations, modeling, prompting, offering clarifications, and verifying the accuracy of responses, that the learner can successfully complete the task. As students indicate that they have begun to internalize the basic ideas and procedures of the lesson, the scaffolding is gradually withdrawn (Brooks & Brooks, 2001; Shapiro, 2003).

Provide Opportunities for Learning by Discovery   By its very nature, constructivism implies the need to let students discover things for themselves. But what things? According to Jerome Bruner, whose pioneering work we mentioned in the chapter on constructivist learning theory, the process of discovery should be reserved for those outcomes that allow learners to be autonomous and self-directed. These include understanding how ideas connect with one another, knowing how to analyze and frame problems, asking appropriate questions, recognizing when what we already know is relevant to what we are trying to learn, and evaluating the effectiveness of our strategies. The case we cited in the previous chapter of the first-grade teacher who wanted her students to understand the importance of using a standardized measuring instrument is a good example of how these outcomes can be learned by guided discovery.

● Constructivist approach: students discover how to be autonomous, self-directed learners

Foster Multiple Viewpoints   Given the basic constructivist premise that all meaningful learning is constructed and that everyone uses a slightly different set of filters with which to build his or her view of reality, what we refer to as knowledge is actually a consensus of slightly different points of view. Thus, another element of a constructivist approach to teaching is to help students understand that different views of the same phenomena exist and that they can often be reconciled to produce a broader understanding.

● Meaningful learning aided by exposure to multiple points of view

In the chapter on constructivism, we described how classroom discussions can be used for this purpose. Computer-based technology, such as e-mail, as well as regular mail, can be used to increase both the number and the diversity of individuals with whom students can interact. In one elementary classroom, students from a small

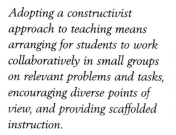

Adopting a constructivist approach to teaching means arranging for students to work collaboratively in small groups on relevant problems and tasks, encouraging diverse points of view, and providing scaffolded instruction.

town in Indiana exchanged stories, letters, and photographs with a similar classroom of students from Northern Ireland. This exchange awakened students to differences between them that ranged from the trivial (dates are written differently in Europe) to the significant (differences in car ownership by families and the constant presence of army patrols carrying loaded weapons) (Duffy & Cunningham, 1996).

The technique of cooperative learning is another way to expose students to peers who may have different views about the "right" way to do something or the "truth" of some matter and help them forge a broader understanding that is acceptable to all members of the group. Consider, for example, a group of college students who, as part of a science methods course, were asked to figure out how to generate electricity for a home using windmills, with the condition that batteries could not be used. Some members of the group were stumped because they couldn't figure out how to supply the house with a constant supply of electricity in the absence of a battery (which is just a particular type of energy-storage device). Their inability to solve this problem was due to their narrow conception of an energy storage device—the kinds of batteries that are used to power such things as toys, flashlights, and cars. But other members of the group maintained that the function of a battery could be performed by any device that stored energy, such as a spring or a tank of hot water, thereby helping the rest of the group to see a different and broader truth (Brooks & Brooks, 2001). In the last major section of this chapter, we describe cooperative learning in considerable detail.

Emphasize Relevant Problems and Tasks   Can you recall completing a class assignment or reading a chapter out of a textbook that had no apparent relevance to anything that concerned you? Not very interesting or exciting, was it? Unfortunately, too many students perceive too much of schooling in that light. One constructivist remedy is to create interest and relevance by posing problems or assigning tasks that are both challenging and realistic (see our Case in Print for an illustration of how one teacher accomplishes this goal). A basic purpose for emphasizing problems and tasks that are relevant to the lives of students is to overcome the problem of inert knowledge, mentioned in our chapter on constructivism. Constructivists believe that the best way to prepare students to function effectively in real-life contexts is to embed tasks in contexts that come as close as possible to those of real life (Delgarno, 2001; Duffy & Cunningham, 1996).

Problems can be challenging either because the correct answer is not immediately apparent or because there is no correct answer. The ill-structured problems and issues that we described previously are, by their nature, challenging and realistic and do not have solutions that everyone perceives as being appropriate and useful. But if you assign students an ill-structured task to investigate, pose it in such a way that they will see its relevance. For example, instead of asking high school students to debate the general pros and cons of laws that restrict personal freedoms, have them interview their community's mayor, chief of police, business owners, and peers about the pros and cons of laws that specify curfews for individuals under a certain age and that prohibit such activities as loitering and the purchase of alcohol and tobacco. Because many adolescents consider themselves mature enough to regulate their own behavior, analyzing and debating laws that are intended to restrict certain adolescent behaviors is likely to produce a fair amount of disequilibrium.

Encourage Students to Become Self-Directed Learners   According to constructivist and humanistic theory (which we discuss later in this chapter), students should, under the right circumstances, be able to direct more of their learning than they typically do. Although you may think that school-age children simply don't have the emotional maturity and cognitive skills necessary for such an endeavor, a program for eighth graders in Radnor, Pennsylvania, called Soundings has illustrated its feasibility (Brown, 2002). The program is built around a set of questions that students have identified as being of interest and importance to them. Students then help the teacher develop the curriculum, study methods, and assessments.

In line with humanistic theory, the first goal of every school year is the development of safe and trusting relationships among students and between the students and the teacher. This goal is accomplished by pairs of students interviewing each other and introducing the other student to the class, students interviewing the teacher, and the use of cooperative games. Then the teachers, who act as coordinators of the students' efforts, train students to ask meaningful and insightful questions (for example, "Why do we eat breakfast?" "Who decided which foods would be breakfast foods?" "Do people in all cultures eat the same foods for breakfast?") that flow from two general questions: "What questions and concerns do you have about yourself?" and "What questions and concerns do you have about the world?"

Working in small groups, students examine their own questions as well as those of their classmates, identify common questions that will be the subject of a large-group discussion, and write their questions on large sheets that are posted on a wall and viewed by the other students in class. After viewing all the lists and discussing common themes and their importance, the students create a prioritized list of themes to study throughout the year (such as violence in our culture, medical issues affecting our lives, and surviving alien environments). Students then develop a timeline for studying the selected topics, block out time periods on the calendar, and join a small group that is interested in one of the topics.

The Challenges to Being a Constructivist Teacher

Constructivist-oriented approaches to teaching run counter to the dominant didactic approach in which the teacher transmits established, accumulated knowledge to students through lecture and demonstration and students incorporate that knowledge largely through drill-and-practice exercises. Consequently, teachers interested in adopting a constructivist approach will have to successfully negotiate a set of challenges that Mark Windschitl (2002) describes as conceptual, pedagogical, cultural, and political.

The conceptual challenge is to fully understand the theoretical foundation on which constructivism rests and reconcile current pedagogical beliefs with constructivist beliefs. This involves, for example, understanding the difference between cognitive and social constructivism and such concepts as cognitive apprenticeship, scaffolding, situated learning, and negotiated meaning. A solid grasp of constructivist theory will also help teachers avoid misconceptions: for instance, that direct instruction can never be used, that students must always be physically and socially active to learn, that all ideas and interpretations offered by students are equally valid, and that constructivist teaching avoids rigorous assessment practices.

The pedagogical challenge has several facets:

- Constructivist teachers need to understand how different students think, how complete each student's knowledge is about a subject, how accurate that knowledge is, and how aware students are about the state of their own knowledge.
- Teachers must know how to use a variety of methods to support understanding during problem-based activities. These methods include modeling; providing prompts, probes, and suggestions that differ in their explicitness; providing problem-solving rules of thumb; and using technology to organize and represent information.
- Teachers must guide students to choose meaningful projects or issues to investigate that are sufficiently complex, intellectually challenging, and related to the theme of the particular subject under study.
- Teachers have to teach students how to work productively in collaborative activities (an issue we take up a bit later in this chapter) even though some students may be uninterested in or even opposed to working with others.
- Teachers need to have a deep enough understanding of a subject to be able to guide students who become puzzled by an observation to an explanation (as in the case of students who wonder why seedlings grow taller under weaker light than under stronger light).

Case in Print

Constructing Meaningful Learning Tasks

Can you recall completing a class assignment or reading a chapter out of a textbook that had no apparent relevance to anything that concerned you? Not very interesting or exciting, was it? Unfortunately, too many students perceive too much of schooling in that light. One constructivist remedy is to create interest and relevance by posing problems or assigning tasks that are both challenging and realistic. . . . A basic purpose for emphasizing problems and tasks that are relevant to the lives of students is to overcome the problem of inert knowledge, mentioned in our chapter on constructivism. (p. 364)

Top Teacher Thrives on Unorthodox

ELAINE RIVERA
Washington Post, 11/6/03

Arlington County science teacher Laurie Sullivan may be Virginia's 2004 Teacher of the Year, but she'll be the first to tell you that she wasn't quite the stellar student herself.

"There were some things I didn't get right away," said Sullivan, who teaches math and science at Barrett Elementary School. "So I can empathize with the student who doesn't get it at first. If I can think of another way of teaching them, I will."

Spend time with Sullivan, and it becomes clear that her empathy for students who learn differently comes from the fact that she herself thinks differently. With her quirky sense of humor and vision, she finds usefulness in things others might not.

Take the elongated cardboard boxes in which her bookcases had been packed two years ago. Most people would have thrown out them out. Not Sullivan. She kept them, knowing that she would find use for them at some point. "I don't throw anything away," she said.

Last week, she found the perfect use for the boxes. "These are going to be our ramps for racing cans," she said excitedly, referring to her fifth-grade class's current science experiment with speed, mass and weight.

"I don't think I was ever traditional," she added, almost sheepishly.

Sullivan's non-traditional teaching style has captivated students, colleagues and supervisors over the last 10 years and led to her being named the state's top teacher Oct. 24 in Richmond.

"She has all the qualities of a great teacher," said Barrett Principal Terry Bratt. "She gets the students interested right away, and she gets them to persevere." Sullivan's ability to keep students engaged and tuned in, Bratt said, is "better than all the highly paid actors on television."

But Bratt and Sullivan know that teaching is not about entertaining but about ensuring that kids learn.

"I want it to be always, 'Why are we learning this? How does it apply to what's going on outside of the classroom?'" Sullivan said about her goal to teach children how the physical world works.

During her fifth-grade class, it was clear that her students were engaged. Sullivan posed this science problem to them: Which of the assorted-size cans would roll down the ramp fastest?

"The hypothesis can be: Will the biggest or the smallest go fastest?" volunteered 10-year-old Christian Rodriguez.

The class was broken up into five teams, each armed with a cardboard ramp, tape to mark the starting line and stopwatches.

Sullivan was attempting to teach her students about "rotational inertia," as well as how to use a stopwatch, how to make a fair test and how to record and interpret data. The end result was that several of the students reached the correct conclusion—it's the weight, not the size of an object, that determines its speed.

"She fascinates me," said Ronald Velez, 10, one of the first students to figure out that the lighter the contents in the can, the faster it will go (beef broth defeated the beans). "She can always give me a science fact, and she always helps me out when I have questions."

Fifth-grader Roxana Hernandez said Sullivan "treats us so nice, and we all learn a lot from her. She made me like science."

Rodriguez offered Sullivan his own kind of compliment: "Her room might be messy, but cool things are in it."

As it nears time for the students' next class, they stop and look at the flowers, balloons, congratulatory cards and articles about their favorite teacher that have been piled on a table—stuff that may one day be used in another unique classroom lesson.

Questions and Activities

1. Teacher Laurie Sullivan is described by the author of this article as having a nontraditional teaching style. Educational psychologists would describe her as having a constructivist teaching style. How is her approach consistent with constructivist learning theory?

2. How would you respond to someone who argued that in the time it took to carry out and set up the racing cans experiment, Laurie Sullivan could have taught her students two to three times as much information using more direct methods?

3. Besides her nontraditional teaching methods, what other qualities does Laurie Sullivan have that warranted her selection as Virginia's Teacher of the Year?

- Last, constructivist teachers need to know how to use a wide range of alternative assessment devices, such as interviews, observations, student journals, peer reviews, research reports, art projects, the building of physical models, and participation in plays, debates, and dances.

The cultural challenge pertains to the implicit classroom norms that govern the behavior of teachers and students. As noted, the dominant approach to instruction is a didactic one in which established facts and procedures are transmitted from an expert (the teacher) to novices (students). The classroom culture that flows from this model is one in which teachers talk most of the time while students sit, are quiet, attentive, do seatwork, and take tests. A constructivist classroom, on the other hand, is characterized by inquiry, collaboration among students, using the teacher as a resource, explaining points of view and solutions to problems to others, and attempting to reach consensus about answers and solutions. The major challenge for teachers is to recognize that their beliefs about what constitutes an ideal classroom are likely to have been shaped by their experiences as students in traditional classrooms.

The political challenge is to convince those who control the curriculum and influence teaching methods (principally school board members, administrators, other teachers, and parents) that constructivist teaching will satisfy state learning standards, is consistent with the content of high-stakes tests, and will help students meaningfully learn the key ideas that underlie various subjects. Should you run into this problem, you might cite a research study or two that supports constructivist teaching. For example, third graders in Germany whose teachers used a constructivist approach scored higher on a test of mathematical word problems and at the same level on a test of arithmetic computation problems as third graders whose teachers used the traditional direct transmission approach (Staub & Stern, 2002).

The technology section that follows presents some additional ideas for embedding learning in realistic settings.

Using Technology to Support Cognitive Approaches to Instruction

As educators begin to understand and address cognitive learning theories, the focus of computer technology is shifting from remediating learner skill deficiencies and rehearsing basic skills to finding ways to help the learner build, extend, and amplify new knowledge (Grabe & Grabe, 2004; Jonassen et al., 2003).

Helping Students Process Information   An information-processing approach to instruction uses technology to minimize the cognitive demands of a task; help learners form schemas, or patterns, of information; extend or augment thinking in new directions; and supply information overviews and memory cues (Grabe & Grabe, 2004). The programs for outlining and note taking mentioned in the chapter on information-processing theory are consistent with this approach, as are electronic encyclopedias

● Technology supports a cognitive approach to instruction by helping students code, store, and retrieve information

367

(for example, Grolier's Multimedia Encyclopedia), hypermedia databases that contain conceptual resources like timelines, information maps, and overviews, and concept mapping software like Inspiration that helps students organize their knowledge and ideas (Delgarno, 2001).

Discovery and Exploratory Environments   Computers are not just tools to transmit or represent information for the learner; they also provide environments that allow for discoveries and insights. In such an **exploratory environment,** students might explore exciting information resources on the Web, enter simulations or microworlds like LEGO-LOGO, browse and rotate objects in a hypermedia or web database, and use imaging technologies to explore inaccessible places (such as underwater canyons or planet surfaces).

For instance, the Geometric Supposer is an exploratory tool that students can use to construct, manipulate, and measure different geometric figures and relationships. High school juniors and seniors who used the Geometric Supposer for an academic year in their plane geometry course achieved significantly higher scores on a geometry test than a comparable group that covered the same topics without the aid of any computer programs (Funkhouser, 2002/2003). Another exploratory tool, GenScope, was designed to help students better understand the principles of genetics. High school students in technical biology and general life science courses who used the GenScope program performed significantly better than did students in classes without the program on a test of genetic reasoning (Hickey, Kindfield, Horwitz, & Christie, 2003).

Microcomputer-based laboratory (MBL) equipment, mentioned in an earlier chapter, allows students to make predictions, test hypotheses, and interpret the results. MBLs and other devices that create exploratory environments enable students to try out many potential solution paths and problem-solving strategies without fear of being wrong, while learning how to solve problems. There are now, for example, exploratory modeling programs for learning how to analyze water samples, track the movement of stars, investigate the effects of floods or logging on an ecosystem, and analyze the effects of different environmental factors on heart rate (Grabe & Grabe, 2004; Jonassen et al., 2003).

Guided Learning   Although students can use modeling programs and simulations to plan experiments, take measurements, analyze data, and graph findings, there is still a need for teacher scaffolding and guidance in support of the learning process (Delgarno, 2001). In these **guided learning** environments, teachers might help students set goals, ask questions, encourage discussions, and provide models of problem-solving processes. In technology environments for social studies, for instance, Lee Ehman and his colleagues found that the teachers who were most successful at fostering problem solving provided a sense of structure, or metacognitive guidance, for their students (Ehman, Glenn, Johnson, & White, 1992). Such teachers provided a clear road map of the unit at the beginning, clear expectations and sequencing of activities, continued reinforcement and guidance, teacher modeling, opportunities for students to practice problem-solving steps, reflection on learning, and regular checking and sharing of student progress. (Note how this approach combines elements of the behavioral and social cognitive approaches.)

One guided learning environment, the Higher Order Thinking Skills program (HOTS), focuses on higher-order thinking skills among at-risk youth in grades 4 through 8 (Pogrow, 1990, 1999). HOTS was designed around active learning, Socratic questioning, and reflection activities in using computers. Instead of the rote computer-based drills that these students would normally receive, they are prompted to reflect on their decision-making process while using computer tools. Teachers do not give away the answers but instead draw out key concepts by questioning students or telling them to go back and read the information on the computer screen. The developer of HOTS, Stanley Pogrow, calls this "controlled floundering," or leading stu-

For direct links to the HOTS site and others mentioned in this chapter, go to the Weblinks section of this book's web site.

dents into frustration so that they have to reflect on the information on the screen to solve a problem. In effect, the learning dialogues and conversations between the teacher and student are the keys to learning here, not student use of the computer, since small-group discussion allows students to compare strategies and reflect on those that work.

Pogrow (1999) reports that students in the HOTS program record year-to-year gains that are twice those of the national average on standardized tests of reading and math and three times those of control groups on tests of reading comprehension. Approximately 15 percent of HOTS students make the honor roll of their school. Gains in self-concept, as well as in thinking skills, have also been reported (Eisenman & Payne, 1997). Additional information on the HOTS program can be found at **www.hots.org/**.

Problem- and Project-Based Learning   Another way to implement constructivist trends in education is to use technology for problem-based learning (PBL), an instructional method that requires learners to develop solutions to real-life problems. Computer-based problem-solving programs typically provide students with story problems, laboratory problems, or investigation problems. Story problem programs are usually tutorials and are very much like the math story problems you probably encountered in school. Laboratory problems are typically simulations of laboratory science problems, such as chemistry or biology. Investigation problems are set in realistic environments (microworlds) and may involve such varied subject areas as astronomy, social studies, environmental science, and anthropology (Jonassen et al., 2003). When using PBL with technology, students can plan and organize their own research while working collaboratively with others.

Although PBL has its roots in medical and business school settings, it has been successfully adapted to the elementary, middle school, and high school grades. Problem-solving programs that are based on constructivist principles and are most likely to foster meaningful learning will do the following:

- Encourage students to be active learners, engaging in such behaviors as making observations, manipulating objects, and recording the results of their manipulations
- Encourage students to reflect on their experiences and begin to construct mental models of the world
- Provide students with complex tasks that are situated in real-world settings
- Require students to state their learning goals, the decisions they make, the strategies they use, and the answers they formulate
- Require students to work in cooperative groups in which there is a considerable amount of social interaction (Hung, 2002; Jonassen et al., 2003)

In addition to PBL, science educators are advocating the use of technology within project-based learning. Project-based learning provides structure by giving students a project or a problem, along with project goals and deadlines. Ronald Marx, Phyllis Blumenfeld, Joseph Krajcik, and Elliot Soloway (1997) identified the following key components of project-based science:

- Driving questions (for example, instead of asking what the atmosphere of Mars is like, one should ask, "What kinds of environments could be built on Mars for humans to survive?")
- Feasible real-world investigations (for example, "Is this lake dying?")
- Tangible products (such as multimedia documents, posters, and group presentations)
- Group collaboration (for example, sharing and negotiating ideas, drawing on expertise of others, and extending the thinking of group members)
- The use of technology tools (to visualize dynamic relationships like cloud cover at night, collect data on a stream or lake, or publish student work on the Web)

However, Marx et al. (1997) also admit that there are concerns and problems with these projects, such as the time required for deep exploration of ideas, meeting existing curriculum standards, balancing classroom management concerns with student exploration, designing proper assessments, and a lack of teacher training on how to scaffold instruction and effectively use technology tools.

Situated Learning   As you may recall from the chapter on constructivism, situated learning, or situated cognition, is the concept that knowledge is closely linked to the environment in which it is acquired. The more true to life the task is, the more meaningful the learning will be. Technology can play a key role in providing access to a wide variety of real-world learning situations. For instance, computer-based instructional technology like CSILE, WISE, the GLOBE Program, and the WEB Project can apprentice students into real-life learning and problem-solving settings by providing access to authentic data and the tools to manipulate the data (Hung, 2001).

One project that embodied the concept of situated learning was conducted with elementary grade students in a Northern Ireland school and a Republic of Ireland school. Called the Author-on-Line Project, students in both schools read a book called *The Cinnamon Tree* by Aubrey Flegg and wrote a book report. The students then posted their reports on a portion of the Northern Ireland Network for Education web site. As new reports appeared, they were read by all of the students and discussed. At this point, the author got involved by posting his reactions to each student's report. The students discussed his comments in class and, either individually or in small groups, composed a response. At one point the author adopted the persona of the book's main character, a thirteen-year-old girl, thereby giving the students the rather unique opportunity to interact with a fictional character (Clarke & Heaney, 2003). The senior author of this book can attest to the authentic and situated nature of this experience, as it parallels the exchanges he has with his editor.

Simulations are another effective way to implement situated learning. In one study, students in a tenth-grade biology class were divided into control and experimental groups. The control group learned about microorganisms through the traditional classroom/laboratory method. The experimental group learned the same material through classroom teaching, laboratory experiments, and a computer-based simulation. The simulation, called "The Growth Curve of Microorganisms," allowed the students to perform multiple experiments in a short period of time to gauge how factors such as the initial number of organisms, the temperature range, and the amount of nutrients affected the population growth. On a test of science process skills, significant differences in favor of the experimental group were found for students in Piaget's concrete operational stage. They achieved higher scores on tests of measurement, classification, graph communication, interpreting data, and designing an experiment. No significant differences between the two groups were found for students in the formal operational stage (Huppert, Lomask, & Lazarowitz, 2002).

THE HUMANISTIC APPROACH TO TEACHING: STUDENT-CENTERED INSTRUCTION

The **humanistic approach** pays particular attention to the role of noncognitive variables in learning, specifically, students' needs, emotions, values, and self-perceptions. It assumes that students will be highly motivated to learn when the learning material is personally meaningful, when they understand the reasons for their own behavior, and when they believe that the classroom environment supports their efforts to learn, even if they struggle. Consequently, a humanistic approach to teaching strives to help students better understand themselves and to create a supportive classroom atmosphere that activates the inherent desire all human beings have to learn and fulfill their potential (Groeben, 1994; Maslow, 1987; Rogers, 1983).

The relevance of a humanistic approach to teaching may not be immediately apparent to everyone, but it is easy to support. First, we've known for some time that learning is as much influenced by how students feel about themselves as by the cognitive skills they possess. When students conclude that the demands of a task are beyond their current level of knowledge and skill (what we referred to in a previous chapter as a low sense of self-efficacy), they are likely to experience such debilitating emotions as anxiety and fear. Once these negative self-perceptions and emotions are created, the student has to divert time and energy from the task at hand to figuring out how to deal with them. And the solutions that students formulate are not always appropriate. Some may, for instance, decide to reduce their efforts and settle for whatever passing grade they can get. Others may give up entirely by cutting class, not completing homework assignments, and not studying for tests. A considerable amount of research from the health field has shown that people are more likely to use positive methods of coping with the stress of illness and disease when they perceive their environment to be *socially supportive*. The small amount of comparable research that exists on classroom learning suggests a similar outcome (Boekarts, 1993; Ryan & Patrick, 2001).

Second, this approach has the implicit support of teachers and parents. High on their list of desired educational outcomes is for students to develop positive feelings about themselves and about learning and to perceive school as a place where they will be supported in their efforts to develop new knowledge and skills.

Pioneers of the Humanistic Approach

The humanistic approach to teaching was proposed during the 1960s principally by Abraham Maslow, Carl Rogers, and Arthur Combs.

Maslow: Let Children Grow   Abraham Maslow's approach to the study of human behavior was unique for its time (1960s). While most of his colleagues studied the psychological processes of people who were having problems dealing with the demands and stresses of everyday life (as Sigmund Freud had done), Maslow decided that more could be learned by studying the behavior of especially well-adjusted people, whom he referred to as *self-actualizers*. Self-actualizers, be they children, adolescents, or adults, have an inherent need for experiences that will help them fulfill their potential.

In Chapter 15 of *Toward a Psychology of Being* (1968), Maslow describes forty-three basic propositions that summarize his views (a more detailed outline of Maslow's view is presented in the chapter on motivation). Some of the most significant of these propositions are as follows:

- Each individual is born with an essential inner nature.
- This inner nature is shaped by experiences and unconscious thoughts and feelings, but it is not *dominated* by such forces. Individuals control much of their own behavior.
- Children should be allowed to make many choices about their own development.
- Parents and teachers play a significant role in preparing children to make wise choices by satisfying their physiological, safety, love, belonging, and esteem needs, but they should do this by helping and letting children grow, not by attempting to shape or control the way they grow.

● Maslow: help students develop their potential by satisfying their needs

Rogers: Learner-Centered Education   Carl Rogers was a psychotherapist who pioneered a new approach to helping people cope more effectively with their problems. He called it *client-centered* (or *nondirective*) therapy, to stress the fact that the client, rather than the therapist, should be the central figure and that the therapist was not to tell the patient what was wrong and what should be done about it.

As he practiced this person-centered approach, Rogers came to the conclusion that he was most successful when he did not attempt to put up a false front of any kind; when he established a warm, positive, acceptant attitude toward his clients; and when he was able to sense their thoughts and feelings. Rogers concluded that these conditions set the stage for successful experiences with therapy because clients became more self-accepting and aware of themselves. Once individuals acquired these qualities, they were inclined and equipped to solve personal problems without seeking the aid of a therapist (1967).

● Rogers: establish conditions that allow self-directed learning

In addition to functioning as a therapist, Rogers served as a professor. Upon analyzing his experiences as an instructor, he concluded that the person-centered approach to therapy could be applied just as successfully to teaching. He thus proposed the idea of **learner-centered education:** that teachers should try to establish the same conditions as do person-centered therapists. Rogers argues (1980) that the results of learner-centered teaching are similar to those of person-centered therapy: students become capable of educating themselves without the aid of direct instruction from teachers.

Combs: The Teacher as Facilitator   Arthur Combs assumed that "all behavior of a person is the direct result of his field of perceptions at the moment of his behaving" (1965, p. 12). From this assumption, it follows that the way a person perceives herself or himself is of paramount importance and that a basic purpose of teaching is to help each student develop a positive self-concept. He observed, "The task of the teacher is not one of prescribing, making, molding, forcing, coercing, coaxing, or cajoling; it is one of ministering to a process already in being. The role required of the teacher is that of facilitator, encourager, helper, assister, colleague, and friend of his students" (1965, p. 16).

Combs elaborated on these points by listing six characteristics of good teachers:

1. They are well informed about their subject.
2. They are sensitive to the feelings of students and colleagues.
3. They believe that students can learn.
4. They have a positive self-concept.
5. They believe in helping all students do their best.
6. They use many different methods of instruction. (1965, pp. 20–23)

Taken together, the observations of Maslow, Rogers, and Combs lead to a conception of education in which teachers trust pupils enough to permit them to make many choices about their own learning. At the same time, teachers should be sensitive to the social and emotional needs of students, empathize with them, and respond positively to them. Finally, teachers should be sincere, willing to show that they too have needs and experience positive feelings about themselves and what they are doing.

Teaching from a Humanistic Orientation

● Humanistic approach addresses needs, values, motives, self-perceptions

Teachers who adopt a humanistic orientation seek to create a classroom atmosphere in which students believe that the teacher's primary goal is to understand the student's needs, values, motives, and self-perceptions and to help the student learn. This atmosphere is established primarily by the teacher's expressing genuine interest in and acceptance of the student and valuing the contribution each student makes to the progress of the class. The teacher avoids giving the impression that he or she would like the student better if only the student dressed more appropriately, had a more positive attitude toward learning, associated with a different group of peers, and so on. In this kind of setting, students will be more inclined to discuss openly their feelings about and problems with learning and related issues. The teacher is then in a position to help students figure out better approaches to their schoolwork and relationships with others. The teacher does not tell students what to do but guides them to the correct action. Because the students' perceptions and decisions are the central focus, this approach is often referred to as either *student-directed* or *nondirective* (Joyce & Weil, 2004; Tomlinson, 2002).

pause & reflect

Can you recall any teachers who practiced humanistic techniques? Did you like these teachers? Did you feel you learned as much from them as from other teachers? Would you model yourself after such teachers?

To illustrate this approach, consider the case of a student who is unhappy about a poor grade on a test. The instinctive reaction of most teachers would be to explain how to study and prepare for the next test. The humanistically oriented teacher instead asks the student to describe his interest in the subject matter, how capable a learner the student feels himself to be, how well the student understands the subject, under what conditions the student studies, whether the student feels the teacher's instruction to be clear and well organized, and so on. To help students understand their feelings and the role they play in learning, the teacher may disclose some of her own feelings. For example, the teacher may tell this hypothetical student, "When I've had a bad day and feel as if I've let my students down, I sometimes question my ability as a teacher. Is that how you feel?" Once these self-perceptions have been raised and clarified, the teacher encourages the student to suggest a solution to the problem (Joyce & Weil, 2004).

The Humanistic Model

According to Bruce Joyce and Marsha Weil (2004), the nondirective model is made up of the following components:

JOURNAL ENTRY
Using a Humanistic Approach to Instruction

1. *Defining the helping situation.* The topic that the student wants to discuss is identified, and the student is told that he or she is free to express any and all feelings that relate to the topic.

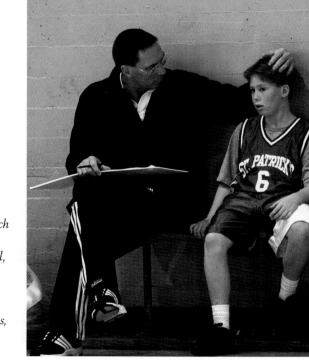

Adopting a humanistic approach to teaching means identifying and meeting students' physical, social, emotional, and intellectual needs, as well as helping students understand how their perceptions, emotions, and behaviors affect their achievement.

2. *Exploring the problem.* If the teacher has been able to establish the atmosphere of trust just described, it is assumed that students will be willing to describe the problem and any associated feelings. The teacher does not attempt to diagnose the student's problem but seeks to understand the situation as the student experiences it and then reflects this understanding back to the student. The teacher functions more as a resource, facilitator, and guide than as a director.

3. *Developing insight.* The student uses the information gained from exploring the problem to understand how various perceptions, emotions, beliefs, and behaviors cause various effects (such as a belief that one lacks ability, leading to incomplete homework assignments and lack of interest in the subject, or a need for affiliation leading to more socializing than studying).

4. *Planning and decision making.* The teacher helps the student identify alternative behaviors and how they will be carried out.

5. *Integration.* The student reports on actions taken, their effects, and plans for future actions.

Research on Aspects of Humanistic Education

As we noted previously, Maslow believed that children's academic and personal growth is enhanced when various needs are met. One of those needs, belonging, has been the subject of considerable research. Belonging, which is also referred to as relatedness and sense of community, means the desire to get support from and be accepted by teachers and classmates and to have opportunities to participate in classroom planning, goal setting, and decision making.

According to some motivational theorists, belonging is one of three basic psychological needs (autonomy and competence are the other two) essential to human growth and development. Yet the need to belong receives less attention from educators than autonomy or competence does. One possible reason for this discrepancy is the belief that students' emotional needs are best met at home and in other out-of-school groups. This attitude does a disservice to students for two reasons: teachers play an important role in helping to satisfy the need to belong (a point we elaborate on in the following), and research has uncovered positive relationships between satisfaction of the need to belong and the following school-related outcomes (Anderman, 2002; Osterman, 2000):

- Increased intrinsic motivation to learn
- A strong sense of competence
- A heightened sense of autonomy
- A stronger sense of identity
- The willingness to conform to classroom rules and norms
- Positive attitudes toward school, class work, and teachers
- Higher expectations of success
- Lower levels of anxiety
- Being supportive of others
- Higher levels of achievement

Feelings of rejection or exclusion from the group are associated with the following negative outcomes (Anderman, 2002; Osterman, 2000):

- Higher levels of stress and health problems
- Behavior problems in school
- Lower interest in school
- Lower achievement
- Dropping out of school

Two studies offer persuasive evidence of the positive effect that a humanistic classroom environment can have on a variety of student behaviors. The first piece of evidence comes from an unusual source: an analysis of why Japanese students outscore U.S. students after fourth grade on an internationally normed standardized test of mathematics and science (the Third International Mathematics and Science Study). After observing ten science lessons taught in five Japanese public schools, Marcia Linn, Catherine Lewis, Ineko Tsuchida, and Nancy Butler Songer (2000) attributed the difference in part to a classroom atmosphere that Abraham Maslow and Carl Rogers would have endorsed.

● Japanese classrooms marked by humanistic orientation, high scores on international math and science test

In addition to emphasizing cognitive development, elementary education in Japan also places a high value on children's social and ethical development. This is done by such tactics as (1) giving children various classroom responsibilities so they feel a valued part of the school, (2) emphasizing such qualities as friendliness, responsibility, and persistence, and (3) communicating to students that teachers value their presence in the classroom and the contributions they make. By fourth grade, Japanese children have been steeped in a school culture that emphasizes responsibility to the group, collaboration, and kindness. In addition, Linn et al. found that almost every lesson began with an activity that was designed to spark the students' interest in the topic by connecting it to either their personal experiences or to previous lessons. The positive emotional attachment to school and the commitment to the values of hard work and cooperation that this approach produces are thought to play a strong role in how well students learn mathematics and science lessons.

The second piece of evidence (Ryan & Patrick, 2001) comes from a study of eighth-grade classroom environments and their effects on students. The environment created by each teacher was described along four lines:

1. Teacher support (students' perceptions of how strongly teachers valued and established personal relationships with them)
2. Promoting interaction among classmates (e.g., allowing students to share ideas, work together in small groups, give help during individual seatwork)
3. Promoting mutual respect and social harmony among classmates
4. Promoting performance goals (emphasizing competition and relative ability comparisons among classmates)

Each of these components was related to several outcome measures, including the four listed in Figure 11.3. The figure uses plus and minus signs to show the significant associations that the researchers reported. Notice that the first three environmental components—the ones that humanistic educators would favor—tended to increase desirable outcomes and decrease undesirable ones. The fourth, however—stressing competition and performance goals—raised students' off-task and disruptive behavior and decreased students' confidence in being able to interact with the teacher.

Figure 11.3 Results of the Ryan and Patrick Study of Eighth-Grade Classrooms

Environment Created by Teacher	Outcomes			
	Self-efficacy for interacting with teacher	Self-efficacy for academic performance	Use of self-regulated learning skills	Off-task and diruptive behavior
Teacher support for students	+		+	−
Promoting interaction among classmates	+			
Promoting mutual respect and harmony		+	+	
Promoting performance goals	−			+

+ means significant increase; − means significant decrease.
Desirable outcomes indicated in blue, undesirable in red.

The results of these two studies on classroom atmosphere have strong implications for teachers in urban areas whose classrooms have a high percentage of minority students. African American students who were bused to school or were attending an urban school reported weaker feelings of belonging than students who were attending neighborhood or suburban schools (Anderman, 2002). But African American students in urban schools who said they liked going to school described their relationship with their teacher as a supportive and caring one (Baker, 1999). This suggests that teachers who take a humanistic approach can offset some of the negative emotions experienced by many minority students and help produce the positive outcomes we have just described.

Using Technology to Support Humanistic Approaches to Instruction

Using technology to support a humanistic approach to teaching may seem like a contradiction in terms. But educational technology is becoming more learner centered in both its design and its use. As we move from the relatively passive and predetermined approach of computer-assisted instruction of the 1960s and 1970s, learning with technology is now best viewed as a learner-centered process involving peers, teachers, experts, and other learning resources (Bonk, Hay, & Fischler, 1996; Sandholtz, Ringstaff, & Dwyer, 1997).

The learner-centered psychological principles from the American Psychological Association (American Psychological Association, 1997), mentioned in the first chapter of this book, focus on helping learners meaningfully construct and represent their knowledge, creating challenging and novel learning environments that help students link new information to old, achieving complex learning goals, and building thinking and reasoning strategies. They also emphasize fostering curiosity and intrinsic motivation, nurturing social interaction and interpersonal relationships, recognizing individual differences in learning, and setting appropriately high and challenging learning standards and goals. Technology can help achieve all of these goals.

Learner-centered technology tools can link concepts to everyday experiences, guide students in the problem-solving process, encourage learners to think more deeply, facilitate unique knowledge construction, and provide opportunities for social interaction and dialogue. For example, graphing calculators, hand-held computers, and microcomputer laboratory equipment allow students to depict data collected from a polluted stream or pond. Prompts embedded in a word processing program encourage reflection on one's report about that environmental problem. Finally, computer conferencing on the Web allows these same students

Take a Stand!

The Perennial Relevance of Humanistic Theory

As you know from reading this section, humanistic approaches to learning and teaching were formulated during the 1960s and 1970s. What you probably don't know is that they were every bit as popular at that time as, say, constructivist theories are today. But humanistic theories gradually fell from favor and eventually almost disappeared from sight. By the late 1980s, many textbooks had either drastically cut back or eliminated coverage of them, fewer papers on humanistic topics were delivered at major conferences, and fewer conceptual and research articles appeared in journals.

The reasons for the decline appeared to be threefold. First, information-processing theory, social cognitive theory, and constructivism ignited a torrent of research that promised, more than noncognitive conceptualizations, dramatic gains in achievement. Second, the humanistic theorists and researchers who came after Maslow, Rogers, and Combs were not of the same stature and did not have the same impact on the field. Third, concerns about students' emotions, needs, and values seemed to many people to be frivolous,

if not irrelevant, at a time when American students appeared to be inferior to earlier generations of students as well as to students from other countries in terms of standardized test scores. Teachers and students were urged to get back to basics!

In recent years, however, humanistic theory has staged something of a comeback. Current conceptualizations of classroom instruction recognize that students' needs and self-perceptions are every bit as important to understanding and improving classroom learning as the quality of their thinking. The research we have described on the effects of belongingness, teacher support, and social harmony among students exemplifies this trend. So if someone tries to convince you that humanistic theories are dead, tell them that humanistic approaches to education never die; they just hang around waiting to be acknowledged.

What are your thoughts about humanistic education? Will you use its principles in your classroom? Explore the debate about humanistic teaching at the Take a Stand! section of this book's web site.

to engage in discussions about their findings with same-age peers far beyond their own classroom. A key strength of emerging technology environments is that they place the responsibility for learning in the hands of learners, thereby enabling them to ask personally relevant questions, pursue needed knowledge, and generally be more self-directed.

THE SOCIAL APPROACH TO TEACHING: TEACHING STUDENTS HOW TO LEARN FROM EACH OTHER

Classroom tasks can be structured so that students are forced to compete with one another, work individually, or cooperate with one another to obtain the rewards that teachers make available for successfully completing these tasks. Traditionally, competitive arrangements have been assumed to be superior to the other two in increasing motivation and learning. But reviews of the research literature by David Johnson and Roger Johnson (Johnson & Johnson, 1995; Johnson, Johnson, & Smith, 1995) found cooperative arrangements to be far superior in producing these benefits. In this section, we will describe cooperative, competitive, and individual learning arrangements; identify the elements that make up the major approaches to cooperative learning; and examine the effect of cooperative learning on motivation, achievement, and interpersonal relationships. We would also like to point out that cooperative learning methods are fully consistent with social constructivism because they encourage inquiry, perspective sharing, and conflict resolution.

Types of Classroom Reward Structures

Competitive Structures Competitive goal structures are those in which one's grade is determined by how well everyone else in the group performs (a reward structure that is typically referred to as *norm referenced*). The traditional practice of grading on the curve predetermines the percentage of A, B, C, D, and F grades regardless of the actual distribution of test scores. Because only a small percentage of students in any group can achieve the highest rewards and because this accomplishment must come at some other students' expense, competitive goal structures are characterized by *negative interdependence*. Students try to outdo one another, view classmates' failures as an advantage, and come to believe that the winners deserve their rewards because they are inherently better (Johnson & Johnson, 1998; Johnson, Johnson, & Holubec, 1994; Johnson et al., 1995).

pause & reflect

Have you ever experienced a competitive reward structure in school? Were your reactions positive or negative? Why? Would you use it in your own classroom? How and when?

Some researchers have argued that competitive reward structures lead students to focus on ability as the primary basis for motivation. This orientation is reflected in the question, "Am I smart enough to accomplish this task?" When ability is the basis for motivation, competing successfully in the classroom may be seen as relevant to self-esteem (since nobody loves a loser), difficult to accomplish (since only a few can succeed), and uncertain (success depends on how everyone else does). These perceptions may cause some students to avoid challenging subjects or tasks, give up in the face of difficulty, reward themselves only if they win a competition, and believe that their own successes are due to ability, whereas the successes of others are due to luck (Ames & Ames, 1984; Covington, 2000).

● Competitive reward structures may decrease motivation to learn

Individualistic Structures Individualistic goal structures are characterized by students working alone and earning rewards solely on the quality of their own efforts. The success or failure of other students is irrelevant. All that matters is whether the student meets the standards for a particular task (Johnson et al., 1994, 1995). For example, thirty students working by themselves at computer terminals are functioning in an individual reward structure. According to Carole Ames and Russell Ames (1984), individual structures lead students to focus on task effort as the primary basis for motivation (as in "I can do this if I try"). Whether a student perceives a task as difficult depends on how successful she has been with that type of task in the past.

Cooperative Structures   Cooperative goal structures are characterized by students working together to accomplish shared goals. What is beneficial for the other students in the group is beneficial for the individual and vice versa. Because students in cooperative groups can obtain a desired reward (such as a high grade or a feeling of satisfaction for a job well done) only if the other students in the group also obtain the same reward, cooperative goal structures are characterized by *positive interdependence*. Also, all groups may receive the same rewards, provided they meet the teacher's criteria for mastery. For example, a teacher might present a lesson on map reading, then give each group its own map and a question-answering exercise. Students then work with each other to ensure that all know how to interpret maps. Each student then takes a quiz on map reading. All teams whose average quiz scores meet a preset standard receive special recognition (Johnson & Johnson, 1998; Joyce & Weil, 2004; Slavin, 1995). In the Suggestions for Teaching: Motivating Students to Learn section in the chapter on motivation, we describe two particular cooperative learning techniques: Student Teams–Achievement Divisions and Jigsaw.

Cooperative structures lead students to focus on effort and cooperation as the primary basis of motivation. This orientation is reflected in the statement, "We can do this if we try hard and work together." In a cooperative atmosphere, students are motivated out of a sense of obligation: one ought to try, contribute, and help satisfy group norms (Ames & Ames, 1984). William Glasser points out that student motivation and performance tend to be highest for such activities as band, drama club, athletics, the school newspaper, and the yearbook, all of which require a team effort (Gough, 1987).

pause & reflect

Have you ever experienced a cooperative reward structure in school? Were your reactions positive or negative? Why? Would you use it in your own classroom? How and when?

Elements of Cooperative Learning

Over the past thirty years, different approaches to cooperative learning have been proposed by different individuals. The three most popular are those of David Johnson and Roger Johnson (Johnson et al., 1994), Robert Slavin (1994, 1995), and Shlomo Sharan and Yael Sharan (Sharan, 1995; Sharan & Sharan, 1999). To give you a general sense of what cooperative learning is like and to avoid limiting you to any one individual's approach, the following discussion is a synthesis of the main features of each approach.

Group Heterogeneity   The size of cooperative-learning groups is relatively small and as heterogeneous as circumstances allow. The recommended size is usually four to five students. At the very least, groups should contain both males and females and students of different ability levels. If possible, different ethnic backgrounds and social classes should be represented as well.

Group Goals/Positive Interdependence   A specific goal, such as a grade or a certificate of recognition, is identified for the group to attain. Students are told that they will have to support one another because the group goal can be achieved only if each member learns the material being taught (in the case of a task that culminates in an exam) or makes a specific contribution to the group's effort (in the case of a task that culminates in a presentation or a project).

Promotive Interaction   This element is made necessary by the existence of positive interdependence. Students are shown how to help one another overcome problems and complete whatever task has been assigned. This may involve episodes of peer tutoring, temporary assistance, exchanges of information and material, challenging of one another's reasoning, feedback, and encouragement to keep one another highly motivated. *Promotive* means simply that students promote each other's success.

Individual Accountability   This feature stipulates that each member of a group has to make a significant contribution to achieving the group's goal. This may be satisfied by requiring the group to achieve a minimal score on a test, having the group's test score be the sum or average of each student's quiz scores, or having each member be responsible for a particular part of a project (such as doing the research and writing for a particular part of a history report).

- Cooperative learning characterized by heterogeneous groups, positive interdependence, promotive interaction, individual accountability

Interpersonal Skills   Positive interdependence and promotive interaction are not likely to occur if students do not know how to make the most of their face-to-face interactions. And you can safely assume that the interpersonal skills most students possess are probably not highly developed. As a result, they have to be taught such basic skills as leadership, decision making, trust building, clear communication, and conflict management. The conflict that arises over differences of opinion, for example, can be constructive if it is used as a stimulus to search for more information or to rethink one's conclusions. But it can destroy group cohesion and productivity if it results in students' stubbornly clinging to a position or referring to one another as "stubborn," "dumb," or "nerdy."

Equal Opportunities for Success   Because cooperative groups are heterogeneous with respect to ability and their success depends on positive interdependence, promotive interaction, and individual accountability, it is important that steps be taken to ensure that all students have an opportunity to contribute to their team. You can do this by awarding points for degree of improvement over previous test scores, having students compete against comparable members of other teams in a game- or tournament-like atmosphere, or giving students learning assignments (such as math problems) that are geared to their current level of skill.

Team Competition   This may seem to be an odd entry in a list of cooperative-learning components, especially in the light of the comments we already made about the ineffectiveness of competition as a spur to motivation and learning. But we're not being contradictory. The main problem with competition is that it is rarely used appropriately. When competition occurs between well-matched teams, is done in the absence of a norm-referenced grading system, and is not used too frequently, it can be an effective way to motivate students to cooperate with each other.

Does Cooperative Learning Work?

The short answer to this question is yes. In the vast majority of studies, forms of cooperative learning have been shown to be more effective than noncooperative reward structures in raising the levels of variables that contribute to motivation, raising achievement, and producing positive social outcomes.

Effect on Motivation   Because a student's sense of self-esteem can have a strong effect on motivation, this variable has been examined in several cooperative-learning studies. The results are encouraging yet confusing. Slavin (1995) found that in eleven of fifteen studies, cooperative learning produced bigger increases in some aspect of self-esteem (general self-esteem, academic self-esteem, social self-esteem) than the noncooperative method with which it was compared. But these effects were not consistent across studies. Some researchers reported increases in academic self-esteem or social self-esteem, but others found no effect. Adding to the confusion is the conclusion that Johnson and Johnson (1995) drew that cooperative learning consistently produces higher self-efficacy scores than do competitive or individualistic conditions.

Such inconsistencies may reflect weaknesses in the self-esteem instruments that were used (self-ratings are not always accurate), weaknesses in the designs of the studies (many cooperative-learning studies last anywhere from a few days to a few weeks, yet changes in self-esteem happen slowly), or differences in specific cooperative-learning programs. Perhaps future research will clarify this issue.

Another way in which cooperative learning contributes to high levels of motivation is in the proacademic attitudes that it fosters among group members. Slavin (1995) cites several studies in which students in cooperative-learning groups felt more strongly than did other students that their groupmates wanted them to come to school every day and work hard in class.

Probably because of such features as promotive interaction and equal opportunities for success, cooperative learning has been shown to have a positive effect on motivation-inducing attributions. That is, students in cooperative-learning groups were more likely to attribute success to hard work and ability than to luck (Slavin, 1995).

A strong indicator of motivation is the actual amount of time students spend working on a task. Most studies have found that cooperative-learning students spend significantly more time on-task than do control students (Johnson et al., 1995; Slavin, 1995).

Effect on Achievement   Slavin (1995) examined several dozen studies that lasted four or more weeks and used a variety of cooperative-learning methods. Overall, students in cooperative-learning groups scored about one-fourth of a standard deviation higher on achievement tests than did students taught conventionally. This translates to an advantage of ten percentile ranks (60th percentile for the average cooperative-learning student versus 50th percentile for the average conventionally taught student). But the beneficial effect of cooperative learning varied widely as a function of the particular method used. The best performances occurred with two techniques called Student Teams–Achievement Divisions and Teams-Games-Tournaments. (Both are described in the chapter on motivation.) The cooperative-learning features that seem to be most responsible for learning gains are group goals and individual accountability.

David Johnson, Roger Johnson, and Karl Smith (1995) also reviewed much of the cooperative-learning literature but drew a somewhat different conclusion. They found that the test scores of students in the cooperative-learning groups were about two-thirds of a standard deviation higher than the test scores of students in competitive or individualistic situations. This translates to an advantage of twenty-five percentile ranks (75th versus 50th). It's not clear why Slavin's analysis produced a somewhat lower estimate of the size of the advantage produced by cooperative learning. It may be due in part to differences in the studies that each cited; Slavin focused on studies lasting at least four weeks. It may also be due to differences in the cooperative techniques that various researchers used.

In addition to achievement outcomes, researchers have also assessed the impact of cooperative learning on problem solving. Given the complex nature of problem solving and the multiple resources that a cooperative group has at its disposal, one would logically expect cooperative learning to have a positive effect on this outcome as well. This hypothesis was confirmed by Zhining Qin, David Johnson, and Roger Johnson (1995). After reviewing forty-six studies, they concluded that students of all age levels (elementary, secondary, college, adult) who worked cooperatively outscored students who worked competitively. The average student in a cooperative group solved more problems correctly than 71 percent of the students who worked competitively.

Effect on Social Relationships   In most studies, students exposed to cooperative learning were more likely than students who learned under competitive or individualistic conditions to name a classmate from a different race, ethnic group, or social class as a friend or to label such individuals as "nice" or "smart." In some studies, the friendships that were formed were deemed to be quite strong. A similar positive effect was found for students with mental disabilities who were mainstreamed. Furthermore, the cooperation skills that students learn apparently transfer. Cooperative-learning students were more likely than other students to use the cooperative behaviors they were taught when they worked with new classmates (Johnson & Johnson, 1995; Slavin, 1995).

In sum, students who learn cooperatively tend to be more highly motivated to learn because of increased self-esteem, the proacademic attitudes of groupmates, appropriate attributions for success and failure, and greater on-task behavior. They also score higher on tests of achievement and problem solving and tend to get along better with classmates of different racial, ethnic, and social class backgrounds. This last outcome should be of particular interest if you expect to teach in an area marked by cultural diversity.

Why Does Cooperative Learning Work?

When researchers attempt to explain the widespread positive effects that are typically found among studies of cooperative learning, they usually cite one or more of the following explanations (Slavin, 1995).

● Cooperative learning effects likely due to stimulation of motivation, cognitive development, meaningful learning

Motivational Effect   The various features of cooperative learning, particularly positive interdependence, are highly motivating because they encourage such achievement-oriented behaviors as trying hard, attending class regularly, praising the efforts of others, and receiving help from one's groupmates. Learning is seen as an obligation and a valued activity because the group's success is based on it and one's groupmates will reward it.

Cognitive-Developmental Effect   According to Lev Vygotsky, collaboration promotes cognitive growth because students model for each other more advanced ways of thinking than any would demonstrate individually. According to Jean Piaget, collaboration among peers hastens the decline of egocentrism and allows the development of more advanced ways of understanding and dealing with the world.

Cognitive Elaboration Effect   As we saw in the previous discussion of information-processing theory, new information that is elaborated (restructured and related to existing knowledge) is more easily retrieved from memory than is information that is not elaborated. A particularly effective means of elaboration is explaining something to someone else.

Teachers' Use of Cooperative Learning

JOURNAL ENTRY
Using a Social Approach
to Instruction

As we have seen, cooperative learning is a topic about which much has been written and much research has been done. But until recently, no one had tried to assess the extent to which teachers actually use it and in what form. To fill that gap in the literature, Laurence Antil, Joseph Jenkins, Susan Wayne, and Patricia Vadasy (1998) interviewed twenty-one teachers from six elementary schools to assess the extent to which they used cooperative learning methods. All of the teachers claimed they were familiar with cooperative learning through preservice learning, student teaching, graduate classes, workshops, or other teachers. Seventeen of the teachers said they used it every day in a typical week. Most reported being attracted to cooperative learning because it enabled them to address both academic and social learning goals within a single approach. But just because teachers say they use cooperative learning, they aren't necessarily using it as it was intended.

Antil et al. argued that for an instructional approach to merit the label *cooperative learning*, it must include at least the conditions of positive interdependence and individual accountability. A more stringent definition would call for the inclusion of promotive interaction, group heterogeneity, and the development of interpersonal skills. Only five of the twenty-one teachers met the two-feature criterion, and only one reported using all five features. For example, instead of creating heterogeneous groups by putting students of different ability levels together, some teachers used random assignment, allowed students to select their teammates, or allowed students who sat near one another to form groups. Similar results were obtained from a study of 216 highly rated elementary and middle school teachers. Their actual use of such critical components as individual accountability, positive interdependence, and development of interpersonal skills was significantly less than what they would have preferred (Lopata, Miller, & Miller, 2003).

Why do teachers follow the spirit but not the letter of the cooperative learning model? Antil et al. offer several possibilities:

- Perhaps teachers find the models too complicated and difficult to put into practice. For example, in Slavin's model, individual accountability involves keeping a running log of students' weekly test scores, computing individual averages and improvement scores, totaling scores for each team based on members' improvement scores, and assigning group rewards.
- Teachers don't really believe the researchers' claims that certain elements of cooperative learning are essential for improved learning, perhaps because their classroom experience has led them to believe otherwise.
- Teachers interpret the research as providing suggestions or guidelines rather than prescriptions that must be followed, leaving them free to construct personal adaptations.
- Researchers rarely explicitly state that the demonstrated benefits of cooperative learning will occur only when certain conditions are met.

Another possibility not mentioned by Antil et al. is based on studies of how teachers implement other instructional tools such as reciprocal teaching. Sometimes, unexpected and unfavorable classroom conditions force teachers into making alterations and compromises they might not make under more favorable circumstances (Hacker & Tenent, 2002).

Do teachers' adaptations of the cooperative learning approaches advocated by researchers lead to inferior outcomes? Unfortunately, that's a question that has no definitive answer at this point, since there is little research on how effective cooperative learning is when some of its defining elements are omitted. But the following study, which looked at the effects of group heterogeneity on problem solving, suggests that you should stay as close as circumstances permit to the original features of cooperative learning.

Noreen Webb, Kariane Nemer, Alexander Chizhik, and Brenda Sugrue (1998) looked at seventh- and eighth-grade students who had been given three weeks of instruction on electricity concepts (such as voltage, resistance, and current) and electric circuits and who were judged as being either low ability, low-medium ability, medium-high ability, or high ability. These students were assigned to either homogeneous or heterogeneous groups and then allowed to work collaboratively to solve a hands-on physics test (create a circuit by using batteries, bulbs, wires, and resistors). Low-ability and low-medium-ability students who worked in heterogeneous groups (that is, groups that included either a medium-high or high-ability student) outscored their peers in homogeneous groups on both the hands-on test and a subsequent paper-and-pencil test that students took individually. The difference was attributed to the active involvement of the lower-ability students in the problem-solving

The Thought Questions and Reflective Journal Questions on the textbook web site can help you think about the issues raised in this chapter.

process. In response to the more relevant and accurate comments made by the high-ability students, the lower-ability students made and defended suggestions, asked questions, and paraphrased other students' suggestions.

A follow-up analysis of the performance of the top 25 percent of this sample was done to examine the effect of placing the highest-ability students in either homogeneous or heterogeneous groups (Webb, Nemer, & Zuniga, 2002). As in the original study, students were classified as either being low, low-medium, medium-high, or high ability on the basis of preexperiment test scores. High-ability students who worked in homogeneous groups (with just other high-ability students) earned significantly higher scores on the hands-on and paper-and-pencil tests than high-ability students who worked in groups that contained either medium-high or low-medium students. But the performance of high-ability students in homogeneous groups was only slightly lower when they worked in groups that contained the lowest-ability students.

Now that you have read about the behavioral, cognitive, humanistic, and social approaches to instruction, you should take a few minutes to study Table 11.1. It summarizes the basic emphases of each approach and allows you to compare them for similarities and differences.

● Low- and average-ability students in mixed-ability groups outperform peers in homogeneous groups on problem-solving tests; high-ability students in homogeneous groups score slightly higher than peers in mixed-ability groups

Table 11.1	Behavioral, Cognitive, Humanistic, and Social Approaches to Instruction
Behavioral (direct instruction)	Teacher presents information efficiently. Student accepts all information transmitted by teacher and textbook as accurate and potentially useful. Emphasis is on acquiring information in small units through clear presentations, practice, and corrective feedback and gradually synthesizing the pieces into larger bodies of knowledge.
Cognitive (information processing)	Teacher presents and helps students to process information meaningfully. Student accepts all information transmitted by teacher and textbook as accurate and potentially useful. Emphasis is on understanding relationships among ideas, relationships between ideas and prior knowledge, and on learning how to control one's cognitive processes effectively.
Cognitive (constructivist)	Teacher helps students to construct meaningful and adaptive knowledge structures by requiring them to engage in higher levels of thinking such as classification, analysis, synthesis, and evaluation; providing scaffolded instruction within the zone of proximal development; embedding tasks in realistic contexts; posing problems and tasks that cause uncertainty, doubt, and curiosity; exposing students to multiple points of view; and allowing students the time to formulate a consensus solution to a task or problem.
Humanistic	Teacher creates a classroom environment that addresses students' needs, helps students understand their attitudes toward learning, promotes a positive self-concept in students, and communicates the belief that all students have value and can learn. Goal is to activate the students' inherent desire to learn and grow.
Social	Teacher assigns students to small, heterogeneous groups and teaches them how to accomplish goals by working together. Each student is accountable for making a significant contribution to the achievement of the group goal. Because of its emphasis on peer collaboration, this approach is consistent with a social constructivist view of learning.

Using Technology to Support Social Approaches to Instruction

Social Constructivist Learning   While the cognitive constructivist looks to find tools to help the child's mind actively construct relationships and ideas, the social constructivist looks as well for tools that help children negotiate ideas and findings in a community of peers. For instance, some point out that it is not just the quality of a computer simulation or microworld that determines the degree to which students will become more like expert scientists; rather, the social activities and talk between students and teachers in that environment are also central to student learning (Roschelle, 1996). This contention is supported by a large number of studies. An analysis of the results from 122 studies found that students whose computer-based instruction took place in the context of small-group learning outscored students who worked alone at a computer by about six percentile ranks on individual tests of achievement. When the performance of the group as a whole was compared with that of students who worked alone, the difference increased to about twelve percentile ranks. In addition, students who worked on computer-based projects with other students exhibited more self-regulated learning behavior, greater persistence, and more positive attitudes toward group work and classmates as compared with students who worked on computers alone (Lou, Abrami, & d'Apollonia, 2001).

If you are wondering why small groups outperform individuals on computer-based learning tasks, this next study provides some insight. Eight-year-old students who worked with a peer on a computer-based task exhibited two to three times as many interactions per minute as did students who worked together on other activities (6.8 interactions per minute for computer tasks, 2.9 interactions per minute for creative activities, and 2.1 interactions per minute for other school activities). For the students who worked on a computer-based task, 89 percent of their interactions were about how to do the task, while 9 percent of their comments were emotional statements (most of which were positive, as in, "That's a nice drawing!"). For the students who worked on creative and other school activities, about 60 percent of their comments were task related, and about 10 percent were emotional statements. Most of the rest of the comments for both groups were not school related (Svensson, 2000). This study suggests that working with classmates on computer-based tasks produces a very high level of on-task behavior. As a teacher, you might attempt to foster rich conversations and collaborations among your students by incorporating computer networks, online information services, e-mail, discussion groups, bulletin boards, chat lines, collaborative web sites and pages, or electronic newsletters and journals.

Cooperative and Collaborative Learning   Cooperative learning is fairly well structured, with assigned roles, tasks, and procedures to help students learn material covered in a classroom setting; a related concept, **collaborative learning,** allows the students themselves to decide on their roles and use their individual areas of expertise to help investigate problems (Marx et al., 1997). As noted throughout this book, with the emergence of the World Wide Web and telecommunications technologies that enable students to publish and share their work internationally, there is no shortage of cooperative and collaborative learning opportunities (Burns, 2002). Networking technologies can be used for many cooperative and collaborative tasks—for example:

- Collecting data for group science projects (Riel & Fulton, 2001)
- Sharing video and text messages and ideas with peers and experts in a multimedia bulletin board (Woolsey & Bellamy, 1997)
- Interacting with scientists in the field (Riel & Fulton, 2001)
- Explaining theories and findings from excavations of simulated archaeological or geological sites (Woolsey & Bellamy, 1997)
- Gathering and sharing data on current events in one's community (for example, the weather; Bonk et al., 1996; Dede, 1996)
- Designing hypermedia "metastacks" that visually depict how all student hypermedia projects relate to one another (Scholten & Whitmer, 1996)

Successful technology applications are embedded in an active social environment

- Practicing reading and writing in a foreign language (Greenfield, 2003; LeLoup & Ponterio, 2003)
- Giving peer and expert feedback on art, music, and writing assignments (Sherry & Billig, 2002)
- Mentoring by adult experts in such subjects as math, science, and writing (Riel & Fulton, 2001)
- Communicating with students in other countries (LeLoup & Ponterio, 2003)

One test of computer-mediated collaborative learning compared how well pairs of undergraduates versus students working alone solved an ill-defined problem. All students first learned a four-step problem-solving procedure similar to the one we outlined in the chapter on constructivist learning theory. The students logged on to a web site and followed the instructions provided by an animated cartoon. After demonstrating that they understood each step in the procedure, the students were given a problem and asked to provide answers to the following statements:

- Define the overall problem environment and write a problem statement.
- List and categorize the data that are relevant for solving this problem.
- List as many solutions as possible that meet your criteria.
- List additional criteria and select the best possible solution for this problem scenario.

Students who worked in pairs used the web site to exchange synchronous messages (the equivalent of instant messaging) about the nature of the problem, relevant data, and possible solutions. Results showed that the students who worked in pairs had significantly higher problem-solving scores and spent significantly more time on the task (Uribe, Klein, & Sullivan, 2003).

As you review this chapter, check the ACE practice tests and the PowerPoint slides on the textbook web site.

As noted in previous chapters, the emergence of computer networking technologies is creating many interesting opportunities for students to enter into virtual communities with peers from other schools and countries and share and discuss various data and ideas. Students who participate in the GLOBE Program (**www.GLOBE.gov/**), for example, collaborate with students from around the world on environmental science projects (Riel & Fulton, 2001). The WEB Project (**www.webproject.org/**) allows students to interact with and receive feedback from adult experts about works in progress. Art and music students, for example, get suggestions from artists, multimedia designers, musicians, and composers (Sherry & Billig, 2002). Last, the 4Directions Project (**www.4directions.org**), which we mentioned in our chapter on cultural and socioeconomic diversity, allows Native American students in ten states to interact with one another and adult experts. They can, for example, discuss research ideas and career options with Native American professionals (Allen, Resta, & Christal, 2002).

Resources for Further Investigation

• Instructional Objectives

If you would like to read Robert Mager's complete description of his recommendations for writing specific objectives, peruse his brief paperback *Preparing Instructional Objectives* (1997). Norman Gronlund explains his approach to using objectives in *Writing Instructional Objectives for Teaching and Assessment* (7th ed., 2004) and in *Measurement and Assessment in Teaching* (2000), which he coauthored with Robert Linn.

To accommodate the growth in understanding of such cognitive processes as metacognition and self-regulated learning, Robert Marzano proposes a new cognitive domain taxonomy that incorporates and adds to the taxonomy created by Benjamin Bloom and his associates in *Designing a New Taxonomy of Educational Objectives* (2001).

• Direct Instruction

In *Research on Direct Instruction: 25 Years Beyond DISTAR* (1996), Gary Adams and Siegfried Engelmann cover the origins of Direct Instruction (by capitalizing the term *Direct Instruction*, Adams and Engelmann seek to distinguish the original and highly structured approach that Engelmann devised in 1964 from the more generic approach we described in this chapter), its features, myths about its nature, and a review of research results on its effects. Appendix A provides a list of Direct Instruction programs for reading, language arts, writing, spelling, mathematics, and science.

Introduction to Direct Instruction (2004), by Nancy Marchand-Martella, Timothy Slocum, and Ronald Martella, covers the history and nature of Direct Instruction and its application to various school subjects.

● The Cognitive Approach to Instruction

In *Cognitive Strategy Instruction That Really Improves Children's Academic Performance* (1995), Michael Pressley, Vera Woloshyn, and others describe how to use information-processing principles to design cognitive strategy instruction for beginning reading, reading comprehension, vocabulary, spelling, writing, mathematics, science, and learning facts.

Scaffolding Student Learning: Instructional Approaches and Issues (1997), edited by Kathleen Hogan and Michael Pressley, contains five chapters that describe and illustrate with actual classroom examples how to use scaffolding for a variety of instructional outcomes.

Implementing problem-based learning in kindergarten through eighth-grade classrooms is described by Ann Lambros in *Problem-Based Learning in K–8 Classrooms: A Teacher's Guide to Implementation* (2002).

The Geometric Supposer program can be purchased from the Center for Educational Technology (CET), a nonprofit organization located in Israel, or from Amazon.com. A description of the program can be found on the CET web site at **www.cet.ac.il/math-international/software5.htm**. Information about the GenScope program, which you can download for free, can be found at **genscope.concord.org/**.

● The Humanistic Approach to Instruction

William W. Purkey and John M. Novak describe a humanistic approach to teaching called "invitational learning" in *Inviting*

School Success: A Self-Concept Approach to Teaching, Learning, and Democratic Practice (1996). If you would like to sample a variety of descriptions and interpretations of humanistic education, examine *Readings in Values Clarification* (1973), edited by Howard Kirschenbaum and Sidney B. Simon, or *Humanistic Education Sourcebook* (1975), edited by Donald A. Read and Sidney B. Simon.

● Cooperative Learning

The New Circles of Learning: Cooperation in the Classroom and School (1994), by David W. Johnson, Roger T. Johnson, and Edythe Johnson Holubec, is a brief (105 pages) and readable description of the basic elements of the authors' version of cooperative learning. In *Cooperative Learning* (1995), Robert E. Slavin describes the cooperative learning techniques that he favors, analyzes the research evidence that supports their use, and provides detailed directions on how to use them. Lynda Baloche provides numerous examples of how to use cooperative learning techniques in *The Cooperative Classroom: Empowering Learning* (1998).

The Teacher's Sourcebook for Cooperative Learning (2002), by George Jacobs, Michael Power, and Loh Wan Inn, provides a wealth of practical suggestions for implementing cooperative learning in the classroom. Part I describes how to implement the various principles of cooperative learning, Part II answers frequently asked questions, and Part III lists print resources and web sites devoted to cooperative learning.

Summary

1. Goals are broad, general statements of desired educational outcomes. Because of their general language, they mean different things to different people and cannot be precisely measured.

2. The vagueness of such goals stimulated psychologists to specify educational outcomes as specific, clearly stated objectives and to organize objectives as taxonomies in each of three domains: cognitive, affective, and psychomotor.

3. The taxonomy for the cognitive domain that Bloom and several associates prepared is composed of six levels: knowledge, comprehension, application, analysis, synthesis, and evaluation.

4. The taxonomy for the affective domain that Krathwohl and several associates prepared is composed of five levels: receiving, responding, valuing, organization, and characterization by a value or value complex.

5. The taxonomy for the psychomotor domain that Simpson prepared is composed of seven levels: perception, set, guided response, mechanism, complex or overt response, adaptation, and origination.

6. Most teachers use test questions that measure knowledge-level objectives, largely ignoring higher-level cognitive outcomes.

7. Mager states that well-written objectives should specify what behaviors the learner will exhibit to indicate mastery, the conditions under which the behavior will be exhibited, and the criteria of acceptable performance.

8. Gronlund believes that complex and advanced kinds of learning do not lend themselves to Mager-type objectives. Complex outcomes are so broad in scope that it is impractical to ask students to demonstrate everything they have learned. Instead, Gronlund suggests that teachers first state a general objective and then specify a sample of related specific outcomes.

9. Objectives must be consistent with the instructional approach one uses and the types of tests one creates.

10. Objectives work best when students are aware of them and understand their intent, they are clearly written, and they are provided to average students for tasks of average difficulty. Objectives often increase intentional learning but may decrease incidental learning.

11. Direct instruction is an approach derived from behavioral learning theory. Lessons are broken down into small steps, the teacher models the desired behavior, material is presented in a variety of formats, students are given extensive opportunities to practice, and feedback is given consistently.

12. An information-processing approach to teaching is based on knowledge of how information is meaningfully processed and attempts to teach students how to be self-directed

learners. Teachers should communicate their goals clearly, use attention-getting devices, present information in organized and meaningful ways, present information in relatively small chunks over realistic time periods, use instructional techniques that facilitate encoding of information in long-term memory, and model effective learning processes.

13. A constructivist approach to teaching is based on the view that meaningful learning occurs when students are encouraged and helped to create the knowledge schemes that produce a broad understanding of ideas and lead to self-directed learning. Key elements of the constructivist approach include scaffolded instruction within a student's zone of proximal development, learning by discovery, exposure to multiple points of view, and use of relevant and realistic problems and tasks.

14. Teachers who opt to use a constructivist approach will likely face conceptual, pedagogical, cultural, and political challenges.

15. A humanistic approach to teaching assumes all students will be motivated to learn if the classroom environment satisfies their basic needs, strengthens their self-concept, provides assistance in learning new ideas and skills, and allows them to direct their learning experiences.

16. A social approach to learning focuses on teaching students how to learn from one another in a cooperative environment. For students to be able to work together successfully, the following conditions are necessary: heterogeneous groups, achievement of group goals by having students help one another to achieve individual goals, holding each student responsible for making a significant contribution to the group goal, development of interpersonal skills, giving each student an opportunity to succeed, and allowing for competition among teams. Cooperative learning is successful because it raises the motivation levels of students, promotes cognitive growth, and encourages meaningful learning.

17. Research on the effects on problem solving of homogeneous versus mixed-ability groups suggests that teachers should implement all the defining features of cooperative learning rather than just one or two.

18. Technology tools can be used to support behavioral, information-processing, learner-centered, and social approaches to instruction.

Key Terms

instructional objectives *(348)*
taxonomy *(349)*
cognitive domain *(349)*
affective domain *(349)*
psychomotor domain *(349)*

specific objectives *(352)*
general objectives *(352)*
direct instruction *(355)*
exploratory environment *(368)*

guided learning *(368)*
humanistic approach *(370)*
learner-centered education *(372)*
collaborative learning *(384)*

12 Motivation

KEY POINTS

These key points will help you learn the important information in this chapter. To help you study, they also appear in the margins of the pages, next to the text where they are discussed.

The Behavioral View of Motivation

- Behavioral view of motivation: reinforce desired behavior
- Extrinsic motivation occurs when learner does something to earn external reward
- Intrinsic motivation occurs when learner does something to experience inherently satisfying results
- Excessive use of external rewards may lead to temporary behavior change, materialistic attitudes, decreased intrinsic motivation
- Intrinsic motivation enhanced when reward provides positive feedback, is available to all who qualify
- Intrinsic motivation undermined by forcing students to compete for limited supply of rewards
- Give rewards sparingly, especially on tasks of natural interest

The Social Cognitive View of Motivation

- Social cognitive view of motivation: observe and imitate admired models; raise self-efficacy
- Self-efficacy affects choice of goals, expectations of success, attributions for success and failure

Other Cognitive Views of Motivation

- Cognitive development view of motivation: strive for equilibration; master the environment
- Need for achievement revealed by desire to attain goals that require skilled performance
- High-need achievers prefer moderately challenging tasks

- Low-need achievers prefer very easy or very hard tasks
- Unsuccessful students attribute success to luck, easy tasks; failure, to lack of ability
- Successful students attribute success to effort, ability; failure, to lack of effort
- Students with incremental beliefs tend to have mastery goals and are motivated to meaningfully learn, improve skills
- Students with entity beliefs tend to have performance goals and are motivated to get high grades, avoid failure
- Personal interest marked by intrinsic desire to learn that persists over time; situational interest is context dependent and short term
- Often difficult to arouse cognitive disequilibrium
- Need for achievement difficult to assess on basis of short-term observations
- Faulty attributions difficult to change

The Humanistic View of Motivation

- People are motivated to satisfy deficiency needs only when those needs are unmet
- Self-actualization depends on satisfaction of lower needs, belief in certain values
- When deficiency needs are not satisfied, person likely to make bad choices
- Encourage growth choices by enhancing attractions, minimizing dangers
- Teachers may be able to satisfy some deficiency needs but not others

The Role of Self-Perceptions in Motivation

- Self-esteem is global judgment we make of self; self-concept is judgment we make of self in

---

Teaching is very much like putting together a puzzle. You first have to identify the pieces and then figure out how to construct them into a meaningful whole. This book is designed to help you identify the relevant pieces that make up the effective teaching puzzle and give you some ideas for using them in a coordinated fashion. In Part I, for example, you learned the importance of understanding how students develop socially, emotionally, and cognitively; what students are like at different ages; and how they differ from one another. In Part II, you were introduced to those pieces of the puzzle that pertain to the learning process and how different views of learning can be used to guide the type of instruction you provide. The puzzle pieces in this part deal with the importance of establishing a classroom environment that will motivate students to learn and of maintaining that positive atmosphere over time.

In this chapter, we address the question of why students strive (or don't strive) for academic achievement— that is, what motivates students? The importance of motivation was vividly pointed out by Larry Cuban, a Stanford University professor of education who returned to teach a high school class for one semester after a sixteen-year absence. Of this experience, he says, "If I wanted those students to be engaged intellectually, then every day—and I *do* mean *every* day—I had to figure out an angle, a way of making connections between whatever we were studying and their daily lives in school, in the community, or in the nation" (1990, pp. 480–481).

The senior author of this book remembers an instance from his days as a school psychologist that reinforces Cuban's observation. A teacher referred a ten-year-old student for testing and possible placement in a special education class (this was before the advent of inclusive classrooms) because the student's classroom performance, particularly in math, was very poor. On almost every test and homework assignment he received grades of F or D. Two pieces of evidence led to the conclusion

Key Points continued on next page.

specific domains; self-efficacy is our belief in ability to carry out a specify action
● Academic self-concept and achievement can positively affect each other
● Design instruction to improve both academic self-concept and achievement

Motivating Students with Technology
● Technology can be used to support both extrinsic and intrinsic motivation
● Technology increases intrinsic motivation by making learning more interesting and meaningful

that this student suffered more from lack of motivation than from intellectual deficits. First, his score on an individually administered intelligence test was average. Second, and most significant, he made pocket money in the evenings by keeping score for several bowling teams at the neighborhood bowling alley. Obviously, there was nothing wrong with this student's ability to learn or with his arithmetic skills!

Motivation can be defined as the selection, persistence, intensity, and direction of behavior (Elliot & Covington, 2001). In practical terms, motivation is simply the willingness of a person to expend a certain amount of effort to achieve a particular goal under a particular set of circumstances. Nevertheless, many teachers have at least two major misconceptions about motivation that prevent them from using this concept with maximum

effectiveness. One misconception is that some students are unmotivated. Strictly speaking, that is not an accurate statement. As long as a student chooses goals and expends a certain amount of effort to achieve them, he is, by definition, motivated. What teachers really mean is that students are not motivated to behave in the way teachers would like them to behave. In other words, their motivation is negatively, rather than positively, oriented. The second misconception is that one person can directly motivate another. This view is inaccurate because motivation comes from within a person. What you *can* do, with the help of the various motivation theories discussed in this chapter, is create the circumstances that *influence* students to do what you want them to do (Keane & Shaughnessy, 2002).

Many factors determine whether the students in your classes will be motivated or not motivated to learn. You should not be surprised to discover that no single theoretical interpretation of motivation explains all aspects of student interest or lack of it. Different theoretical interpretations do, however, shed light on why some students in a given learning situation are more likely to want to learn than others. Furthermore, each theoretical interpretation can help you develop techniques for motivating students in the classroom. ●

THE BEHAVIORAL VIEW OF MOTIVATION

 To structure your study of this chapter, see the Chapter Themes on the textbook web site, accessible from **http://education. college.hmco.com/students**.

Earlier in the text we noted that some psychologists explain learning from a theoretical perspective that focuses exclusively on the effects of observable stimuli, responses, and consequences on our propensity to exhibit particular behaviors. This approach is called operant conditioning, and its application to motivation has focused on the effect of reinforcement.

The Effect of Reinforcement

In the chapter on behavioral learning theory, we discussed Skinner's emphasis on the role of reinforcement in learning. After demonstrating that organisms tend to repeat actions that are reinforced and that behavior can be shaped by reinforcement, Skinner developed the technique of programmed instruction to make it possible for students to be reinforced for every correct response. Supplying the correct answer—and being informed by the program that it *is* the correct answer—motivates the student to go on to the next frame, and as the student works through the program, the desired terminal behavior is progressively shaped.

Following Skinner's lead, many behavioral learning theorists devised techniques of behavior modification. Students are motivated to complete a task by being promised a reward of some kind. Many times, the reward takes the form of praise or a grade.

● Behavioral view of motivation: reinforce desired behavior

Sometimes it is a token that can be traded in for some desired object, and at other times the reward may be the privilege of engaging in a self-selected activity.

Operant conditioning interpretations of learning help reveal why some students react favorably to particular subjects and dislike others. For instance, some students may enter a required math class with a feeling of delight, while others may feel that they have been sentenced to prison. Skinner suggests that such differences can be traced to past experiences. He would argue that the student who loves math has been shaped to respond that way by a series of positive experiences with math. The math hater, in contrast, may have suffered a series of negative experiences.

Limitations of the Behavioral View

Although approaches to motivation based on positive reinforcement are often useful, you should be aware of the disadvantages that can come from overuse or misuse of such techniques. Most of the criticisms of the use of reinforcement as a motivational incentive stem from the fact that it represents **extrinsic motivation**. That is, the learner decides to engage in an activity (such as participate in class, do homework, study for exams) to earn a reward that is not inherently related to the activity (such as receive praise from the teacher, earn a high grade, or enjoy the privilege of doing something different). By contrast, students under the influence of **intrinsic motivation** study a subject or acquire a skill because it produces such inherently positive consequences as becoming more knowledgeable, competent, and independent.

Although extrinsic motivation is widespread in society (individuals are motivated to engage in many activities because they hope to win certificates, badges, medals, public recognition, prizes, or admiration from others), this approach has at least three potential dangers (Covington, 2002; Kohn, 1999):

1. Changes in behavior may be temporary. As soon as the extrinsic reward has been obtained, the student may revert to such earlier behaviors as studying inconsistently, turning in poor-quality homework, and disrupting class with irrelevant comments and behaviors.
2. Students may develop a materialistic attitude toward learning. They may think (or say), "What tangible reward will I get if I agree to learn this information?" If the answer is "none," they may decide to make little or no effort to learn it.
3. Giving students extrinsic rewards for completing a task may lessen whatever intrinsic motivation they may have for that activity.

This last disadvantage, which is referred to as the *undermining effect*, has been extensively investigated by researchers. It appears that giving students rewards may indeed decrease their intrinsic motivation for a task, but only under certain conditions. Under other conditions, external rewards may enhance intrinsic motivation. Figure 12.1 summarizes recent research on this subject. Notice, in particular, that intrinsic motivation falls when students must compete for a limited supply of rewards. In contrast, intrinsic motivation rises when the reward consists of positive verbal feedback and is available to all who meet the standard.

Making students compete against each other for limited rewards (the "grading on the curve" practice we first mentioned in our discussion of Erik Erikson's psychosocial theory of development) is particularly damaging to intrinsic motivation because of its impact on self-worth. Whether intended or not, children in our society base their sense of self-worth on their accomplishments. When we artificially limit opportunities to attain the highest level of accomplishment, intrinsic motivation declines in an effort to protect one's sense of worth (Covington, 2002).

Taken as a whole, these results strongly suggest that teachers should avoid the indiscriminate use of rewards for influencing classroom behavior, particularly when an

Margin notes

● Extrinsic motivation occurs when learner does something to earn external reward

● Intrinsic motivation occurs when learner does something to experience inherently satisfying results

pause & reflect

What percentage of your behavior do you think stems from intrinsic motivation? From extrinsic motivation? Is it possible to change this ratio? How?

● Excessive use of external rewards may lead to temporary behavior change, materialistic attitudes, decreased intrinsic motivation

● Intrinsic motivation enhanced when reward provides positive feedback, is available to all who qualify

● Intrinsic motivation undermined by forcing students to compete for limited supply of rewards

● Give rewards sparingly, especially on tasks of natural interest

Figure 12.1 Conditions Determining Effect of External Rewards on Intrinsic Motivation

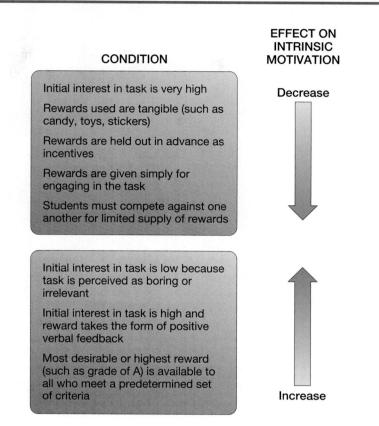

CONDITION

EFFECT ON INTRINSIC MOTIVATION

Initial interest in task is very high

Rewards used are tangible (such as candy, toys, stickers)

Rewards are held out in advance as incentives

Rewards are given simply for engaging in the task

Students must compete against one another for limited supply of rewards

Decrease

Initial interest in task is low because task is perceived as boring or irrelevant

Initial interest in task is high and reward takes the form of positive verbal feedback

Most desirable or highest reward (such as grade of A) is available to all who meet a predetermined set of criteria

Increase

SOURCES: Cameron (2001); Cameron, Banko, & Pierce (2001); Covington (2002); Deci, Koestner, & Ryan (2001); Elliot & Covington (2001).

activity seems to be naturally interesting to students. Instead, rewards should be used to provide students with information about their level of competence on tasks they have not yet mastered and to encourage them to explore topics for which their initial interest is low.

THE SOCIAL COGNITIVE VIEW OF MOTIVATION

● Social cognitive view of motivation: observe and imitate admired models; raise self-efficacy

Social cognitive theorists, such as Albert Bandura, Dale Schunk, and Barry Zimmerman, emphasize two factors that strongly influence motivation to learn: (a) the models to which people are exposed, and (b) people's sense of self-efficacy, or how capable they believe they are to handle a particular task.

Power of Persuasive Models

One factor that positively affects students' self-efficacy and motivation to learn certain behaviors is the opportunity to see other people exhibiting those behaviors and to observe the consequences that occur. Social cognitive theorists refer to this as observation, imitation, and vicarious reinforcement. As we pointed out in discussing social cognitive theory in an earlier chapter, *vicarious* reinforcement means that we expect to receive the same reinforcer that we see someone else get for exhibiting a particular behavior.

A student who observes an older brother or sister reaping benefits from earning high grades may strive to do the same with the expectation of experiencing the same

When students admire and identify with classmates who are positively reinforced for their behavior, the observing students' self-efficacy and motivation to exhibit the same behavior may be strengthened.

or similar benefits. A student who notices that a classmate receives praise from the teacher after acting in a certain way may decide to imitate such behavior to win similar rewards. A student who identifies with and admires a teacher may work hard partly to please the admired individual and partly to try becoming like that individual. Both vicarious reinforcement and direct reinforcement can raise an individual's sense of self-efficacy for a particular task, which, in turn, leads to higher levels of motivation.

The Importance of Self-efficacy

● Self-efficacy affects choice of goals, expectations of success, attributions for success and failure

An individual's sense of self-efficacy can affect motivation to learn through its influence on the learning goal one chooses, the outcome one expects, and the reasons one gives to explain successes and failures.

Choice of Learning Goal   Analyses of learning goals suggest that a student may choose a task mastery goal, a performance-approach goal, a performance-avoidance goal, or a combination of task mastery and performance-approach goals (Elliot & Thrash, 2001; Harackiewicz, Barron, Pintrich, Elliot, & Thrash, 2002; Pintrich & Schunk, 2002; Urdan & Midgley, 2001; Urdan, Ryan, Anderman, & Gheen, 2002).

- *Task mastery goals* involve doing what is necessary to learn meaningfully the information and skills that have been assigned. Students with high levels of self-efficacy choose this goal more often than do students with low levels of self-efficacy. In pursuit of task mastery goals, high-efficacy students will use a variety of encoding techniques, do more organizing of information to make it meaningful, review and practice more frequently, monitor their understanding more closely, formulate more effective learning strategies, and treat mistakes as part of learning.
- *Performance-approach goals* involve demonstrating to teachers and peers one's superior intellectual ability by outperforming most others in class. If the best way to accomplish this goal is to do assignments neatly and exactly according to directions, or to memorize large amounts of information to get a high grade on a test without necessarily understanding the ideas or how they relate to one another, then these tactics will be used. Students who adopt performance-approach goals

often do well on tests, but they are less likely than students who adopt mastery goals to develop a strong interest in various subjects. On the other hand, students who choose these goals tend to have high levels of self-efficacy.

- *Performance-avoidance goals* involve reducing the possibility of failure so as not to appear less capable than other students. Students can reduce their chances of failure by avoiding novel and challenging tasks or by cheating. They can also engage in *self-handicapping behaviors,* such as putting off homework or projects until the last minute, studying superficially for an exam, and getting involved in many in-school and out-of-school nonacademic activities. The purpose of self-handicapping is to be able to blame poor performance on the circumstances rather than on one's ability. Students most likely to choose performance-avoidance goals are boys and those with low grades and low academic self-efficacy.

Teachers may unwittingly encourage self-handicapping behaviors, even in students whose sense of self-efficacy is at least adequate, by using a norm-referenced grading system. Because students are compared with one another to determine the top, middle, and low grades, this system encourages students to attribute their grades to a fixed ability. Students who have doubts about their ability are then more likely to engage in self-handicapping behaviors (Urdan, Midgley, & Anderman, 1998).

Outcome Expectations   A second way in which self-efficacy can affect motivation is in terms of the outcomes that students expect. Those with high levels of self-efficacy more often expect a positive outcome. As a result, they tend to be more willing to use the more complex and time-consuming learning skills and to persist longer in the face of difficulties. (It is possible, however, for a student to have a relatively high level of self-efficacy but expect a relatively low grade on a test because the student believes the teacher is prejudiced or grades unfairly.) Those with lower levels of self-efficacy are more likely to expect a disappointing outcome, tend to use simpler learning skills, and are likely to give up more quickly when tasks demand greater cognitive efforts (Pintrich & Schunk, 2002).

Attributions   A third way in which self-efficacy influences motivation is through the reasons students cite to explain why they succeeded or failed at a task. Those with a high level of self-efficacy for a subject are likely to attribute failure to insufficient effort (and so vow to work harder the next time) but credit their success to a combination of ability and effort. Their low-self-efficacy peers are likely to explain their failures by saying that they just don't have the ability to do well in this subject, but they will chalk their successes up to an easy task or luck. As we point out a bit further on in this chapter, this latter attribution pattern undercuts motivation (Pintrich & Schunk, 2002).

OTHER COGNITIVE VIEWS OF MOTIVATION

In addition to social cognitive theorists, researchers who take other cognitive approaches to learning have done extensive studies of motivation. The views described in this section emphasize how the following five characteristics affect students' intrinsic motivation to learn: the inherent need to construct an organized and logically consistent knowledge base, one's expectations for successfully completing a task, the factors that one believes account for success and failure, one's beliefs about the nature of cognitive ability, and one's interests.

You should also be aware that intrinsic motivation for school learning is fairly well developed by about nine years of age (fourth grade) and becomes increasingly stable through late adolescence. Thus, it is important to develop intrinsic motivation in students in the primary grades as well as to identify students with low levels of academic motivation (Gottfried, Fleming, & Gottfried, 2001).

Cognitive Development and the Need for Conceptual Organization

The cognitive development view is based on Jean Piaget's principles of equilibration, assimilation, accommodation, and schema formation, which we discussed in the chapter on stage theories of development. Piaget proposes that children possess an inherent desire to maintain a sense of organization and balance in their conception of the world (equilibration). A sense of equilibration may be experienced if a child assimilates a new experience by relating it to an existing scheme, or the child may accommodate by modifying an existing scheme if the new experience is too different.

● Cognitive development view of motivation: strive for equilibration; master the environment

In addition, individuals will repeatedly use new schemes because of an inherent desire to master their environment. This explains why young children can, with no loss of enthusiasm, sing the same song, tell the same story, and play the same game over and over and why they repeatedly open and shut doors to rooms and cupboards with no apparent purpose. It also explains why older children take great delight in collecting and organizing almost everything they can get their hands on and why adolescents who have begun to attain formal operational thinking will argue incessantly about all the unfairness in the world and how it can be eliminated (Stipek, 2002).

The Need for Achievement

Have you ever decided to take on a moderately difficult task (like take a course on astronomy even though you are a history major and have only a limited background in science) and then found that you had somewhat conflicting feelings about it? On the one hand, you felt eager to start the course, confident that you would be pleased with your performance. But on the other hand, you also felt a bit of anxiety because of the small possibility of failure. Now try to imagine the opposite situation. In reaction to a suggestion to take a course outside your major, you refuse because the probability of failure seems great, while the probability of success seems quite small.

● Need for achievement revealed by desire to attain goals that require skilled performance

In the early 1960s, John Atkinson (1964) proposed that such differences in achievement behavior are due to differences in something called the *need for achievement*. Atkinson described this need as a global, generalized desire to attain goals that require some degree of competence. He saw this need as being partly innate and partly the result of experience. Individuals with a high need for achievement have a stronger expectation of success than they do a fear of failure for most tasks and therefore anticipate a feeling of pride in accomplishment. When given a choice,

● High-need achievers prefer moderately challenging tasks

high-need achievers seek out moderately challenging tasks because they offer an optimal balance between challenge and expected success. By contrast, individuals with a low need for achievement avoid such tasks because their fear of failure greatly outweighs their expectation of success, and they therefore anticipate feelings of shame. When faced with a choice, they typically choose either relatively easy tasks

● Low-need achievers prefer very easy or very hard tasks

because the probability of success is high or very difficult tasks because there is no shame in failing to achieve a lofty goal. Atkinson's theory was an early version of what is currently called *expectancy-value theory*. An individual's level of motivation for a particular task is governed by that person's expectation of success and the value placed on that success (Wigfield & Eccles, 2002b).

Atkinson's point about taking fear of failure into account in arranging learning experiences has been made by William Glasser in *Choice Theory in the Classroom* (2001) and *The Quality School* (1998). Glasser argues that for people to succeed at life in general, they must first experience success in one important aspect of their lives. For most children, that one important part should be school. Erik Erikson made the same point by maintaining that the primary psychosocial task for school-age children is to successfully resolve the issue of industry versus inferiority.

Explanations of Success and Failure: Attribution Theory

Some interesting aspects of success and failure are revealed when students are asked to explain why they did or did not do well on some task. The four most commonly given reasons stress ability, effort, task difficulty, and luck. To explain a low score on a math test, for example, different students might make the following statements:

"I just have a poor head for numbers." (lack of ability)
"I didn't really study for the exam." (lack of effort)
"That test was the toughest I've ever taken." (task difficulty)
"I guessed wrong about which sections of the book to study." (luck)

Because students *attribute* success or failure to the factors just listed, research of this type contributes to what is referred to as **attribution theory**. We have already touched on this topic in discussing self-efficacy.

- **Unsuccessful students attribute success to luck, easy tasks; failure, to lack of ability**

Students with long histories of academic failure and a weak need for achievement typically attribute their success to easy questions or luck and their failures to lack of ability. Ability is a stable attribution (that is, people expect its effect on achievement to be pretty much the same from one task to another), while task difficulty and luck are both external attributions (in other words, people feel they have little control over their occurrence). Research has shown that stable attributions, particularly ability, lead to expectations of future success or failure, and internal attributions (those under personal control) lead to pride in achievement or to shame following failure. Because low-achieving students attribute failure to low ability, they see future failure as more likely than future success. In addition, ascribing success to factors beyond one's control diminishes the possibility of taking pride in achievement and placing a high value on rewards. Consequently, satisfactory achievement and reward may have little effect on the failure-avoiding strategies that poor students have developed over the years (Elliott & Bempechat, 2002).

- **Successful students attribute success to effort, ability; failure, to lack of effort**

Success-oriented students (high-need achievers), in contrast, typically attribute success to ability and effort and failure to insufficient effort. Consequently, failure does not diminish expectancy of success, feelings of competence, or reward attractiveness for these students. They simply resolve to work harder in the future. This attribution pattern holds even for academically gifted students who might be expected to focus on ability because they excel at most tasks and are well aware of their superior capabilities. Citing effort as a factor in their success or failure is thought to be more motivating than citing just ability because effort is a modifiable factor that allows one to feel in control of one's destiny (Dai et al., 1998).

The typical attribution pattern of high-achieving students highlights an important point: both effort and ability should be credited with contributing to one's success. Students who attribute their success mostly to effort may conclude that they have a low level of ability because they have to work harder to achieve the same level of performance as others (Tollefson, 2000).

pause & reflect

Do you fit the pattern of most successful students, attributing success to effort and ability and failure to lack of effort? If so, how did you get this way? Is there anything you can draw from your own experiences to help students develop this pattern?

Beliefs About the Nature of Cognitive Ability

Children's motivation for learning is affected by their beliefs about the nature of ability. During the primary and elementary grades, children create and refine their conception of ability. By the time they reach middle school, most children start to think of themselves and others as belonging to particular categories in terms of ability.

Changes in Beliefs About Ability   According to Carol Dweck (2002a, 2002b), a leading theorist and researcher on this subject, noticeable changes in children's ability conceptions occur at two points in time: between seven and eight years of age and between ten and twelve years of age. Compared with kindergarten and early primary grade children, seven- and eight-year-olds are more likely to do the following:

- Show an increased interest in the concept of ability and take greater notice of peer behaviors that are relevant to achievement comparisons
- Distinguish ability from such other characteristics as social skills, likability, and physical skills and believe that the same person can have different levels of ability for different academic skills (such as reading, writing, and mathematics)
- Think of ability as a more internal and less observable characteristic that is defined normatively (that is, by comparing oneself to others)
- Think of ability as a characteristic that is stable over time and can therefore be used to make predictions about future academic performance
- Engage in self-criticism related to ability and compare their performance with that of others

Compared with seven- and eight-year-olds, ten- to twelve-year-old children are more likely to do the following:

- Distinguish between effort and ability as factors in performance. Consequently, some are more likely to say of two students who receive the same grade on a test or assignment that the one who exerted more effort has less ability.
- Evaluate their academic ability more accurately, although more begin to underestimate their ability.
- Think of ability as being both a stable characteristic and a fixed capacity that explains the grades they currently receive and will receive in the future. It is not uncommon to hear older children and adolescents talk about peers who do or do not have "it" (Anderman & Maehr, 1994). Consequently, students who believe their ability in a particular subject is below average seek to avoid additional courses in that subject. Girls, especially high-achieving ones, are more likely than boys to adopt this view of ability, and this may partly explain their greater reluctance to take advanced science and math classes in high school.
- Value performance goals (getting the highest grade possible) over learning goals (making meaningful connections among ideas and how they relate to the world outside of school).

Why these changes occur, and why they occur in some individuals but not others, is not entirely known, but comparing the performance of a student to the performance of every other student in a class to determine who gets which grades (the practice of grading on the curve that we mentioned earlier) is suspected of playing a major role. One casualty of this belief, as we've indicated, is motivation for learning.

Types of Beliefs About Ability   According to the work of Dweck (2002a) and others (e.g., Quihuis, Bempechat, Jiminez, & Boulay, 2002), students can be placed into one of three categories based on their beliefs about the nature of cognitive ability:

1. *Entity theorists*. Some students subscribe solely to what is called an entity theory because they talk about intelligence as if it were a thing, or an entity, that has fixed characteristics.
2. *Incremental theorists*. Other students subscribe solely to what is called an incremental theory, believing that intelligence can be improved gradually by degrees or increments as they refine their thinking skills and acquire new ones. Entity and incremental theorists hold to their respective views for all subjects.
3. *Mixed theorists*. Students in this third group subscribe to both entity and incremental theories depending on the subject. A mixed theorist may, for example, be an entity theorist for math but an incremental theorist for science and English, while the opposite (or some other) pattern may prevail for another student.

● Students with incremental beliefs tend to have mastery goals and are motivated to meaningfully learn, improve skills

Students with incremental beliefs tend to be motivated to acquire new and more effective cognitive skills and are said to have *mastery goals*. They seek challenging

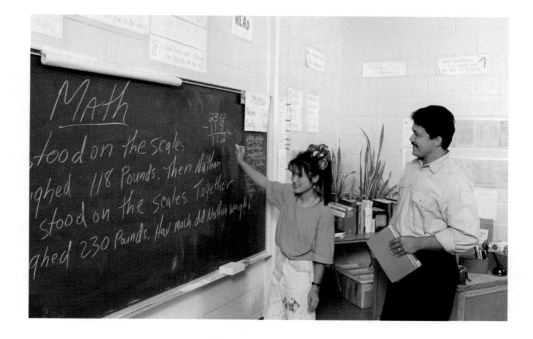

Students who believe that intelligence is a collection of cognitive skills that can be refined are likely to adopt mastery goals and attribute failure to insufficient effort, whereas students who believe that intelligence is an unchangeable capacity are likely to adopt performance goals and attribute failure to low ability.

● Students with entity beliefs tend to have performance goals and are motivated to get high grades, avoid failure

tasks and do not give up easily because they see obstacles as a natural part of the learning process. They often tell themselves what adults have told them for years: "Think carefully," "Pay attention," and "Try to recall useful information that you learned earlier." They seem to focus on the questions, "How do you do this?" and "What can I learn from this?" Errors are seen as opportunities for useful feedback. Not surprisingly, they are more likely than entity theorists to attribute failure to insufficient effort and ineffective learning skills.

Students who believe that intelligence is an unchangeable entity are primarily motivated to appear smart to others by getting high grades and praise and by avoiding low grades, criticism, and shame. Such students are said to have *performance goals*. When confronted with a new task, their initial thought is likely to be, "Am I smart enough to do this?" They may forgo opportunities to learn new ideas and skills if they think they will become confused and make mistakes, and they tend to attribute failure to low ability rather than insufficient effort.

However, among students who subscribe to the entity theory, there is a difference between those with high confidence in their ability and those with low confidence. High-confidence entity theorists are likely to demonstrate such mastery-oriented behaviors as seeking challenges and persisting in the face of difficulty. Those with low confidence, in contrast, may be more interested in avoiding failure and criticism—even after achieving initial success—than in continuing to be positively reinforced for outperforming others. Because of their anxiety over the possibility of failure, these low-confidence entity theorists are less likely than students who have an incremental view of ability to exhibit subsequent motivation for a task (Rawsthorne & Elliot, 1999). If avoidance is not possible, they become discouraged at the first sign of difficulty. This, in turn, produces anxiety, ineffective problem solving, and withdrawal from the task (as a way to avoid concluding that one lacks ability and thereby maintain some self-esteem). According to attribution theory, entity theorists should continue this pattern since success is not attributed to effort, but failure is attributed to low ability.

The Effect of Interest on Intrinsic Motivation

Interest can be described as a psychological state that involves focused attention, increased cognitive functioning, persistence, and emotional involvement (Ainley, Hidi, & Berndorff, 2002; Hidi & Ainley, 2002; Renninger & Hidi, 2002; Schraw & Lehman,

2001). A person's interest in a topic can come from personal and/or situational sources:

● Personal interest marked by intrinsic desire to learn that persists over time; situational interest is context-dependent and short-term

- *Personal interest* (also referred to as individual or topic interest) is characterized by an intrinsic desire to understand a topic, a desire that persists over time and is based on preexisting knowledge, personal experience, and emotion.
- *Situational interest* is more temporary and is based on context-specific factors, such as the unusualness of information or its personal relevance. For example, baseball teams that qualify for the League Championship or World Series after many years of not doing so (think Chicago Cubs or Boston Red Sox) often spark temporary interest in the players and the games among people who live in those cities. Similarly, people who buy a company's stock often become interested, albeit temporarily, in the company's activities.

The degree of personal interest a student brings to a subject or activity has been shown to affect intrinsic motivation for that task. Such students pay greater attention to the task, stay with it for a longer period of time, learn more from it, and enjoy their involvement to a greater degree (Schraw & Lehman, 2001).

It is possible, of course, that situational interest in a topic can grow into a personal interest. Consider, for example, a high school student who knows nothing of how information is stored in and retrieved from memory but learns about it when she has to read a chapter on memory in her psychology textbook. Fascinated with the description of various forms of encoding and retrieval cues because of her own problems with being able to recall information for tests accurately, she searches for additional books and articles on the topic and even thinks about majoring in psychology in college (Renninger & Hidi, 2002; Schraw & Lehman, 2001).

Factors That Influence Personal Interest   A long-term interest in a particular subject or activity may be influenced by one or more of the following factors (Bergin, 1999; Hidi, 2001; Hidi & Ainley, 2002; Schraw & Lehman, 2001):

- *Ideas and activities that are valued by one's culture or ethnic group.* As we discussed in the chapter on cultural diversity, culture is the filter through which groups of people interpret the world and assign values to objects, ideas, and activities. Thus, inner-city male youths are likely to be strongly interested in playing basketball and following the exploits of professional basketball players, whereas a rural midwestern male of the same age is likely to be interested in fishing and hunting.
- *The emotions that are aroused by the subject or activity.* Students who experience extreme math anxiety, for example, are less likely to develop a strong interest in math-related activities than those who experience more positive emotions.
- *The degree of competence one attains in a subject or activity.* People typically spend more time pursuing activities that they are good at than activities at which they do not excel.
- *The degree to which a subject or activity is perceived to be relevant to achieving a goal.* As noted in the chapter on approaches to instruction, many students fail to perceive such relevance, partly because teachers rarely take the time to explain how a topic or lesson may affect students' lives.
- *Level of prior knowledge.* People are often more interested in topics they already know something about than in topics they know nothing about.
- *A perceived hole in a topic that the person already knows a good deal about.* A person who considers himself to be well informed about the music of Mozart would likely be highly interested in reading the score of a newly discovered composition by Mozart.

Factors That Influence Situational Interest   Some of the factors that spark a spontaneous and short-term interest in a topic or activity include (Bergin, 1999; Hidi, 2001; Hidi & Ainley, 2002; Schraw & Lehman, 2001; Schraw, Flowerday, & Lehman, 2001):

- *The opportunity to engage in hands-on activities.*
- *A state of cognitive conflict or disequilibrium.* Teachers can sometimes spark students' interest in a topic by showing or telling them something that is discrepant with a current belief. Consider, for example, a high school class on government. The teacher has a lesson planned on government spending and wants to avoid the usual lack of interest that this topic produces. One tactic would be to ask students if they believe that the money they contribute to social security from their part-time jobs (or the full-time jobs they will eventually have) is placed in an account with their name on it, where it remains until they become eligible for benefits in their midsixties. Most will probably believe something like that. The teacher could then tell them that the contributions they make today are actually used to pay the benefits of current retirees and that their social security benefits will come from the social security taxes levied on a future generation of workers.
- *Well-written reading material.* Texts and other written materials that are logically organized and engaging are rated as more interesting by students and produce higher levels of comprehension than more poorly written material.
- *The opportunity to work on a task with others.* As we saw earlier in the book, cooperative arrangements are highly motivating and produce high levels of learning.
- *The opportunity to observe influential models.*
- *The teacher's use of novel stimuli.*
- *The teacher's use of games and puzzles.*

These findings have a number of clear instructional implications. Given that some students may develop a strong interest in a topic as a result of a classroom activity or assignment and that this initial interest may grow into a personal interest and the adoption of mastery goals, a general recommendation is for teachers to do what constructivist learning theory implies: involve students in a variety of subject matters and meaningful activities (Hidi & Harackiewicz, 2000). Our Case in Print illustrates how one Detroit-area school uses personal and situational interest to motivate primary grade students to write. The section of Suggestions for Teaching in Your Classroom offers further recommendations.

Limitations of Cognitive Views

Cognitive Development   Although cognitive development theory, with its emphasis on people's need for a well-organized conception of the world, can be useful as a means for motivating students, it has a major limitation: it is not always easy or even possible to induce students to experience a cognitive disequilibrium sufficient to stimulate them to seek answers. This is particularly true if an answer can be found only after comparatively dull and unrewarding information and skills are mastered. (How many elementary school students, for example, might be expected to experience a self-impelled urge to learn English grammar or acquire skill in mathematics?) You are likely to gain some firsthand experience with the difficulty of arousing cognitive disequilibrium the first time you ask students to respond to what you hope will be a provocative question for class discussion. Some students may experience a feeling of intellectual curiosity and be eager to clarify their thinking, but others may stare out the window or surreptitiously do homework for another class.

● Often difficult to arouse cognitive disequilibrium

Need for Achievement   Perhaps the major problem that teachers have in using Atkinson's theory of need for achievement is the lack of efficient and objective instruments for measuring its strength. Although you could probably draw reasonably accurate conclusions about whether a student has a high or low need for achievement by watching that student's behavior over time and in a variety of situations, you may not be in a position to make extensive observations. And the problem with short-term observations is that a student's achievement orientation may be affected by more or less chance circumstances.

● Need for achievement difficult to assess on basis of short-term observations

Taking an Interest in Learning

Interest can be described as a psychological state that involves focused attention, increased cognitive functioning, persistence, and emotional involvement. . . . A person's interest in a topic can come from personal and/or situational sources: Personal interest (also referred to as individual or topic interest) is characterized by an intrinsic desire to understand a topic, a desire that persists over time and is based on preexisting knowledge, personal experience, and emotion. Situational interest is more temporary and is based on context-specific factors, such as the unusualness of information or its personal relevance. (p. 397–398)

Fairy Tales Come to Life at School in Birmingham

JANET SUGAMELI
The Detroit News, 12/29/03

BIRMINGHAM — Donning a long, shimmering green skirt, a pink ribbon sweater and a party hat trimmed with faux fur, Celia Hoag, 6, took a sip from her cup at her classroom's fairy tale tea.

"The tea tasted like punch and I liked it," the 6-year-old announced. "A tea is sort of like a party with a whole bunch of tables."

"I pretended I was drinking tea, even though it was red," added first-grader Isabella Wesner.

The special event at Quarton Elementary wrapped up the first-grade fairy tale unit. Fairy tales are part of the literature curriculum at the school, opening up lessons in reading, writing and even science.

"A lot of these kids have heard these stories before, but they are realizing how the story is set up," said first-grade teacher Eileen McKinney. "We are taking it apart for them to help them understand how the story is made and how it comes together. At the end of that, they are able to write their own fairy tale. And they have come up with some amazing things."

First-grader Caroline Wade wrote a story about a unicorn.

"Once upon a time a princess wanted a unicorn," Caroline wrote. "A witch came and told her if she gives her money she would give her a unicorn. After that the unicorn was able to get her money back and the princess lived happily ever after."

McKinney said she teaches her students seven steps to writing a fairy tale: how to begin a fairy tale, how to end a fairy tale, the setting, the characters, magical events, good versus evil and a lesson to be learned.

"Once they learn all that, they can write their own fairy tale," she said.

Audrey Belf, 6, has started a fairy tale whose main characters are a witch and a queen.

"The witch turned the queen into a cat and the witch turned herself into a frog," Audrey said. "They were arguing and that's why we turned her into a cat."

During the unit, Celia said she learned a lot about fairy tales.

"All of the fairy tales have a problem," she said. "They take place in a castle, forest, a town or a village. There are magical events, too, like foxes can wear clothes and a frog can turn into a prince."

"What makes a fairy tale is it starts with 'Once upon a time' and it ends with 'happily ever after'," said Perry Kaplan. "It's not a true story."

Each school day over the course of three weeks, McKinney and the other first-grade teachers at the school read fairy tales to the students. With each story, pupils either wrote something or made an art project such as Cinderella's slippers or a Pinocchio, she said.

"We try to keep it not quite so girly because we have boys in the class too," she said. "We do 'Jack and the Beanstalk' and 'The Frog Prince' or 'Three Little Pigs.'"

To tie in science, the teachers bring in projects that relate to the fairy tales.

"As one of the home projects, the students had to use materials to make the beds of the three bears," she said. "One was hard, another soft and one was just right to go along with that part of my science curriculum.

"We also teach them why the wolf was able to blow down two of the pigs' houses. They do the puff test after building a puffing machine. They test different objects to see if each is puff-proof. Then we take them one step forward and they learn the word *absorb* and so they learn what is waterproof."

Fairy tales are familiar to students, and using them as a frame of reference helps them learn the curriculum.

"And they solve moral dilemmas," McKinney said. "Like, should the wolf have blown down those houses and should he have gone to jail? We have a lesson to learn in the end and the kids will tell you what is right."

Parent Nancy Hoag said she has noted how the unit has enhanced her daughter's understanding of reading and writing.

"We've been reading fairy tales for years, but now she is excited about reading them by herself," she said.

"The unit plays up to what kids are interested in, and it's exciting and current for them," Hoag said. "This has even been exciting for the whole family because we were all able to get involved. We went to the library to get more books and she even wanted to read them to her little sister."

Questions and Activities

1. According to this chapter, interest in learning is influenced by several individual and situational factors. Review the lists of these factors and then identify which factors were probably operating in the classroom situation described in this article.

2. Explain how the approach to motivation taken by the teachers at Quarton Elementary School is consistent with a constructivist view of learning.

3. In addition to teaching students about the structure of fairy tales, the teachers in this story included lessons in art and science. If you wanted to, how could you also incorporate lessons in arithmetic?

A student might do well on a first exam in a course, for example, because the teacher gave in-class time for study and happened to offer advice at a crucial point during the study period. The high score on that test might inspire the student to work for an A in that class. But if that exam happened to be scheduled the day after a two-week bout with the flu, the student might not be well prepared and could end up with a C or D grade. Such a poor performance might cause the student to forget about the A and concentrate instead on obtaining a C.

● Faulty attributions difficult to change

Attribution Theory and Beliefs About Ability   The major implication of the idea that faulty attributions are at least partly responsible for sabotaging students' motivation for learning is to teach students to make more appropriate attributions. But this is likely to be a substantial undertaking requiring a concerted, coordinated effort. One part of the problem in working with students who attribute failure to lack of ability is that ability tends to be seen as a stable factor that is relatively impervious to change. The other part of the problem is that the same students often attribute their success to task difficulty and luck, two factors that cannot be predicted or controlled because they are external and random. Ideas about how to teach students to make more appropriate attributions for success and failure can be found in *Enhancing Motivation: Change in the Classroom* (1976), by Richard deCharms.

An additional limitation is that attribution training is not likely to be fully effective with elementary school children. For them, two individuals who learn the same amount of material are equally smart despite the fact that one person has to work twice as long to achieve that goal. Older children and adolescents, however, have a better grasp of the concept of efficiency; they see ability as something that influences the amount and effectiveness of effort (Stipek, 2002).

Now that you are familiar with some of the approaches to motivation, it is time to consider Suggestions for Teaching in Your Classroom that show how these ideas can be converted into classroom practice.

Motivating Students to Learn

1 **Use behavioral techniques to help students exert themselves and work toward remote goals.**

JOURNAL ENTRY
Using Behavior Modification
Techniques to Motivate

Techniques you might use for this purpose were described in the chapter on behavioral and social learning theories. They include verbal praise, shaping, modeling, symbolic reinforcers (smile faces, stars, and the like), and contingency contracting.

a. Give praise as positive reinforcement, but do so effectively.

Think about the times when you've been praised for a job well done, particularly when you weren't sure about the quality of your work. In all likelihood, it had a strong, maybe even dramatic, effect on your motivation. That being the case, you might think that effective positive reinforcement in the form of verbal praise is a common occurrence in the classroom. But you would be wrong. Extensive observations of classroom life reveal that verbal praise is rarely given (Goodlad, 1984) and is often given in ways that limit its effectiveness (Brophy, 1981). Jere Brophy recommends that teachers use praise in the following ways:

- As a spontaneous expression of surprise or admiration. ("Why, Juan! This report is really excellent!")
- As compensation for criticism or as vindication of a prediction. ("After your last report, Lily, I said I knew you could do better. Well, you have done better. This is really excellent.")
- As an attempt to impress all members of a class. ("I like the way Nguyen just put his books away so promptly.")
- As a transition ritual to verify that an assignment has been completed. ("Yes, Maya, that's very good. You can work on your project now.")
- As a consolation prize or as encouragement to students who are less capable than others. ("Well, Josh, you kept at it, and you got it finished. Good for you!")

In an effort to help teachers administer praise more effectively, Brophy drew up the guidelines for effective praise listed in Table 12.1.

b. Use other forms of positive reinforcement.

In addition to verbal praise, you can make use of such other forms of positive reinforcement as modeling, symbolic reinforcers, and contingency contracts.

EXAMPLES

- Arrange for students to observe that classmates who persevere and complete a task receive a reinforcer of some kind. (But let this occur more or less naturally. Also, don't permit students who have finished an assignment to engage in attention-getting or obviously enjoyable self-chosen activities; those who are still working on the assignment may become a bit resentful and therefore less inclined to work on the task at hand.)

- Draw happy faces on primary grade students' papers, give check marks as students complete assignments, write personal comments acknowledging good work, and assign bonus points.

- Develop an individual reward menu, or contract, with each student based on the Premack principle (Grandma's rule), which we discussed earlier in the book. After passing a spelling test at a particular level, for example, each student might be given class time to work on a self-selected project.

- When making use of such motivational techniques, you might do your best to play down overtones of manipulation and materialism. Point out that rewards are used in almost all forms of endeavor to induce people to work toward a goal. Just because someone does something to earn a reward does not mean that the activity should never be indulged in for intrinsic reasons. For example, athletes often compete to earn the reward of being members of the best team, but they still enjoy the game.

Table 12.1	Guidelines for Effective Praise

Effective Praise	**Ineffective Praise**
1. Is delivered contingently	1. Is delivered randomly or unsystematically
2. Specifies the particulars of the accomplishment.	2. Is restricted to global positive reactions
3. Shows spontaneity, variety, and other signs of credibility; suggests clear attention to the student's accomplishment	3. Shows a bland uniformity, which suggests a conditional response made with minimal attention
4. Rewards attainment of specified performance criteria (which can include effort criteria, however)	4. Rewards mere participation, without consideration of performance process or outcomes
5. Provides information to students about their competence or the value of their accomplishments	5. Provides no information at all or gives students information about their status
6. Orients students toward better appreciation of their own task-related behavior and thinking about problem solving	6. Orients students toward comparing themselves with others and thinking about competing
7. Uses students' own prior accomplishments as the context for describing new accomplishments	7. Uses the accomplishments of peers as the context for describing students' present accomplishments
8. Is given in recognition of noteworthy effort or success at tasks that are difficult (for *this* student)	8. Is given without regard to the effort expended or the meaning of the accomplishment (for *this* student)
9. Attributes success to effort and ability, implying that similar successes can be expected in the future	9. Attributes success to ability alone or to external factors such as luck or easy task
10. Leads students to expend effort on the task because they enjoy the task or want to develop task-relevant skills	10. Leads students to expend effort on the task for external reasons—to please the teacher, win a competition or reward, etc.
11. Focuses students' attention on their own task-relevant behavior	11. Focuses students' attention on the teacher as an external authority figure who is manipulating them
12. Fosters appreciation of and desirable attributions about task-relevant behavior after the process is completed	12. Intrudes into the ongoing process, distracting attention from task-relevant behavior

SOURCE: Brophy (1981).

2 **Make sure that students know what they are to do, how to proceed, and how to determine when they have achieved goals.**

Many times students do not exert themselves in the classroom because they say they don't know what they are supposed to do. Occasionally, such a statement is merely an excuse for goofing off, but it may also be a legitimate explanation for lack of effort. Recall that knowing what one is expected to do is important information in the construction of a learning strategy. You should use the techniques described in the chapter "Approaches to Instruction" to take full advantage of the values of instructional objectives. In terms of motivation, objectives should be clear, understood by all members of the class, and attainable in a short period of time.

JOURNAL ENTRY
Ways to Arrange Short-Term Goals

For reasons illustrated by behavioral theorists' experiments with different reinforcement schedules, students are more likely to work steadily if they are reinforced at frequent intervals. If you set goals that are too demanding or remote, lack of reinforcement during the early stages of a unit may derail students, even if they started out with good intentions. Whenever you ask students to work toward a demanding or remote goal, try to set up a series of short-term goals.

EXAMPLE

● One way to structure students' learning efforts is to follow the suggestions offered by Raymond Wlodkowski for drawing up a personal contract. He recommends that such a contract should contain four elements. A sample contract from Wlodkowski (1978, p. 57) is presented here, with a description of each element in brackets.

Date _____

1. Within the next two weeks I will learn to multiply correctly single-digit numbers ranging between 5 and 9, for example, 5×6, 6×7, 7×8, 8×9, 9×5. [What the student will learn]
2. When I feel prepared, I will ask to take a mastery test containing 50 problems from this range of multiplication facts. [How the student can demonstrate learning]
3. I will complete this contract when I can finish the mastery test with no more than three errors. [The degree of proficiency to be demonstrated]
4. My preparation and study will involve choosing work from the workbook activities, number games, and filmstrip materials. [How the student will proceed]

Signed _____

3 **Encourage low-achieving students to attribute success to a combination of ability and effort and failure to insufficient effort.**

Should you decide to try to alter the attributions of a student who is having difficulty with one or more subjects, here are three suggestions based on an analysis of twenty attribution training studies (Robertson, 2000):

- Make sure the student has the ability to succeed on a task before telling the student to attribute failure to insufficient effort. Students who try hard but lack the cognitive skills necessary for success are likely to become convinced not only that they lack the ability but that they will never become capable of success on that type of task.
- Tell students that having the ability for a subject is the same as knowing how to formulate and use a learning strategy for that subject. Thus, success is attributable to an appropriate strategy (which is controllable) while failure is attributable to insufficient effort at formulating the strategy (also controllable).
- Combine attribution training with strategy instruction for students who don't understand the relationship between strategy use and success and failure.

4 **Encourage students to think of ability as a set of cognitive skills that can be added to and refined, rather than as a fixed entity that is resistant to change, by praising the processes they use to succeed.**

JOURNAL ENTRY

Ways to Promote an Incremental View of Intelligence

The work that Carol Dweck (2002a, 2002b) has done on students' beliefs about ability clearly shows that those who adopt an entity view (ability as a fixed capacity) are more likely to develop a maladaptive approach to learning than are students who adopt an incremental view (ability as a modifiable collection of skills). One way to help students develop incremental rather than entity beliefs is to praise them for their effort and use of effective skills rather than for their ability after doing well on a task.

Many parents and teachers believe they are strengthening a student's motivation for learning by praising their ability with such comments as, "You did very well on this test; you certainly are smart" or "You're really good at this." Dweck's research shows that this type of praise encourages students to develop entity beliefs that impede their motivation. A better alternative is to offer what Dweck calls process praise. Examples of process praise are: "That's a really high score; you must have worked really hard at these problems"; "Now that you've mastered this skill, let's go on to something a bit harder that you can learn from"; and "You did a fine job on this paper because you started early and used the writing skills we practiced in class."

5 **Encourage students to adopt appropriate learning goals.**

As we noted earlier, students may adopt task mastery goals, performance-approach goals, or performance-avoidance goals. To briefly review, students who have task mastery goals are motivated to use effective learning tactics to acquire new knowledge and skills even if it means an occasional disappointing performance. Students who adopt performance-approach goals, on the other hand, are principally motivated to outscore others on exams and assignments in order to demonstrate their ability. Students who adopt performance-avoidance goals are principally motivated to avoid failure and appear less capable than their peers by engaging in such behaviors as self-handicapping, avoiding novel and challenging tasks, and cheating. The problem with performance-approach goals is that they suppress intrinsic interest in tasks and encourage students to equate failure with low ability. Performance-avoidance goals have many obvious problems, including the reinforcement of low self-efficacy and stunted intellectual growth. To help students maintain high levels of motivation and achievement, you should establish conditions that encourage the adoption of mastery goals (Midgley et al., 2002).

a. Help students develop mastery learning goals.

The following suggestions (Urdan & Midgley, 2001) were designed with middle school students in mind but are just as applicable to both lower and higher grades:

- Group students by topic, interests, or their own choice rather than by ability.
- Use a variety of assessment techniques (discussed in a later chapter) rather than just one, and make the top grade potentially achievable by all students by evaluating performance according to a predetermined set of criteria.
- Provide students with feedback about their progress rather than feedback about how they scored relative to the rest of the class.
- Recognize students who demonstrate progress rather than focus just on students who have achieved the highest grades.
- Provide students with opportunities to choose what projects they will do, what electives they will take, and for how long they wish to study a particular subject rather than have these decisions made exclusively by administrators and teachers.
- Treat mistakes as a part of learning, encourage students to take academic risks, and allow students to redo work that does not meet some minimum satisfactory standard.
- Provide students with complex and challenging tasks that require comprehension and problem solving rather than tasks that require little more than rote learning and verbatim recall.
- Use cross-age tutoring, peer tutoring, and enrichment activities with students who are falling behind rather than grade retention.
- Use cooperative-learning methods rather than competition. Because so much has been written about the use of cooperative-learning techniques and their demonstrated effectiveness in raising motivation and learning, we discuss this recommendation in more detail next.

b. Use cooperative-learning methods.

As we pointed out in previous chapters, cooperative-learning methods have proven effective in increasing motivation for learning and self-esteem, redirecting attributions for success and failure, fostering positive feelings toward classmates, and increasing performance on tests of comprehension, reasoning, and problem solving (Johnson & Johnson, 1995; Johnson et al., 1995; Slavin, 1995). Accordingly, you may want to try one or more of the cooperative learning techniques described by David Johnson and Roger Johnson (Johnson et al.,1994) and Robert Slavin (1995). To familiarize you with these methods, we will briefly describe the Student Teams–Achievement Divisions (STAD) method that Slavin and his associates at Johns Hopkins University devised.

STAD is one of the simplest and most flexible of the cooperative-learning methods, having been used in grades 2 through 12 and in such diverse subject areas as math, language arts, social studies, and science. As with other cooperative-learning methods, students are assigned to four- or five-member groups, with each group mirroring the makeup of the class in terms of ability, background, and gender. Once these assignments are made, a four-step cycle is initiated:

1. *Teach.* The teaching phase begins with the presentation of material, usually in a lecture-discussion format. Students should be told what it is they are going to learn and why it is important.
2. *Team study.* During team study, group members work cooperatively with teacher-provided worksheets and answer sheets.
3. *Test.* Each student *individually* takes a quiz. Using a scoring system that ranges from 0 to 30 points and reflects degree of individual improvement over previous quiz scores, the teacher scores the papers.
4. *Recognition.* Each team receives one of three recognition awards, depending on the average number of points the team earned. For example, teams that average 15 to 19 improvement points receive a GOODTEAM certificate, teams that average 20 to 24 improvement points receive a GREAT-TEAM certificate, and teams that average 25 to 30 improvement points receive a SUPERTEAM certificate.

The cooperative learning method Teams-Games-Tournaments is similar to STAD except that students compete in academic tournaments instead of taking quizzes.

Another popular cooperative learning technique, Jigsaw, was created by Elliott Aronson. The class is divided into groups of about five or six, each group works on the same project, and each member of a group is solely responsible for a particular part of the project. For a project on energy consumption in the United States, for example, one student of each group may be responsible for researching and reporting to the other group members on how the price of oil is determined. Another student in each group may report on the factors that determine the size and efficiency of automobiles, still another on the status of alternative energy sources, and so on. To control for the fact that some students may not listen attentively to or may criticize the reports of others in the group because of preexisting animosities (Maria thinks Brandon is a jerk because he insulted her friend last week), they are reminded that they will be taking an exam based on the content of each person's report. So it is in Maria's interest to lay aside her dislike of Brandon because he is the only source of part of the information she will be tested on. Before reporting to the other members of their group, the students from each group with identical assignments get together to share information, discuss ideas, and rehearse their presentations. They are referred to as the "expert" group. Research on Jigsaw shows improvements in listening, interpersonal relationships, and achievement when compared with traditional instruction (Aronson, 2002).

6 **Maximize factors that appeal to both personal and situational interest.**

a. **Find out what your students' interests are, and design as many in-class and out-of-class assignments as possible around those interests.**

b. **Try to associate subjects and assignments with pleasurable rather than painful experiences by using such techniques as cooperative learning and constructivist approaches to teaching, as well as providing students with the information-processing tools they need to master your objectives.**

c. **Link new topics to information students are already likely to have or provide relevant background knowledge in creative yet understandable ways.**

d. **Select reading materials that are logically organized and written in an engaging style.**

7 **Try to make learning interesting by emphasizing activity, investigation, adventure, social interaction, and usefulness.**

More than thirty years ago, May Seagoe suggested an approach to motivation that is based on students' interests and is consistent with many of the motivation theories and technology tools mentioned in this chapter. Among the "points of appeal that emerge from studies of specific interests," she lists the following:

> (a) the opportunity for overt bodily activity, for manipulation, for construction, even for observing the movement of animals and vehicles of various sorts; (b) the opportunity for investigation, for using mental ingenuity in solving puzzles, for working problems through, for creating designs, and the like; (c) the opportunity for adventure, for vicarious experiences in make believe, in books, and in the mass media; (d) the opportunity for social assimilation, for contacts with others suitable to the maturity level of the child (ranging from parallel play to discussion and argument), for social events and working together, for human interest and humanitarianism, and for conformity and display; and (e) the opportunity for use of the new in real life, making the new continuous with past experience and projecting it in terms of future action. (1970, p. 25)

One approach that incorporates most or all of these features, and that can be used with preschool and primary grade children, is the project approach. Lillian Katz and Sylvia Chard (2000) define a project as an in-depth study of a particular topic that one or more children undertake, extends over a period of days or weeks, and involves children seeking answers to questions that they formulate by themselves or in consultation with the teacher. Projects may involve an initial discussion that captures the students' interest (for example, discussing how a house is built); dramatic play; drawing, painting, and writing; group discussions; field trips; construction activities; and investigation activities. As many researchers (e.g., Collier, 1999) have noted, class projects for all grade levels can be designed to make use of various forms of technology. Because projects are based on children's natural interests and involve a wide range of activities, they are more likely to be intrinsically motivating.

Diane Curtis (2002) describes a fifth-grade project that helped students fulfill state curriculum standards in social studies, math, writing, and technology. Building on their interest in architecture, the students completed a project on several of the major memorial buildings in Washington, DC (such as those honoring Presidents Washington, Jefferson, and Lincoln). They gathered information from books, the World Wide Web, and architects about the memorials, drew computer models of them, created a timeline of construction, and researched the contributions of Jefferson and others to the writing of the U.S. Constitution. This was followed by a field trip to the U.S. capital and a presentation of their work to community members.

One potential drawback to the use of projects is the amount of time they take. To help teachers overcome that barrier, several web sites offer project-based pro-

May Seagoe found that students respond with interest to school situations that are active, investigative, adventurous, social, and useful. Having members of a fifth-grade class play the roles of state government officials is an activity that includes almost all these features.

grams that contain curriculum materials, assignments, resources, and experts. See, for example:

http://www.jasonproject.org/
http://www.learner.org/jnorth/
http://www.thinkquest.org/
http://quest.classroom.com/

For quick links to web sites mentioned here, use the Weblinks section of the textbook site.

As you think about how you are going to organize your lesson plans for each day and each period, you might ask yourself: "Are there ways that I can incorporate activity, investigation, adventure, social interaction, and usefulness into this presentation?" "Are there projects that I can assign to students, particularly as cooperative groups, that incorporate most of these features?" Here are some examples of techniques you might use.

ACTIVITIES

JOURNAL ENTRY
Ways to Make Learning Active

- Have several students go to the board. Give a rapid-fire series of problems to be solved by those at the board as well as those at their desks. After five problems, have another group of students go to the board, and so on.

- Think of ways to move out of the classroom legitimately every now and then. Teach geometry, for instance, by asking the class to take several balls of string and lay out a baseball diamond on the side lawn of the school.

INVESTIGATIONS

JOURNAL ENTRY
Ways to Promote Investigation

- In elementary grade classrooms (and in some middle school and high school classrooms), set up a variety of learning centers with themes such as library, games, social science, cultural appreciation, and computer use, and organize these with intriguing displays and materials. For example, your social science center could be stocked with maps, charts, and documents. Your computer center might include educational software such as CD-ROMs and database programs; student-created publications made with desktop publishing or word processing programs; a computer with Internet access; and lists of appropriate and interesting online sites.

- In middle school and high school classrooms, you might arrange centers that pertain to different aspects of a single subject. In a science class, for example, you might have an appreciation center stressing aesthetic aspects of science, a display center calling attention to new developments in the field, a library center consisting of attractive and provocative books, and so on.

ADVENTURES

JOURNAL ENTRY
Ways to Make Learning Seem Adventurous

- Occasionally, use techniques that make learning entertaining and adventurous. Such techniques might be particularly useful when you introduce a new topic. You might employ devices used by advertisers and the creators of Sesame Street, for instance. Use intensity, size, contrast, and movement to attract attention. Make use of color, humor, exaggeration, and drama to introduce a new unit. Take students by surprise by doing something totally unexpected.

- The night before you introduce a new unit, redecorate part of the room. Then ask the class to help you finish it.

- Arrange a "Parade of Presidents" in which each student selects a president of the United States and presents a State of the Union message to the rest of the class, with the rest of the class taking the part of members of Congress.

- Hand out a duplicated sheet of twenty questions based on articles in each section of a morning newspaper. Students compete against themselves to discover how many of the questions they can answer in the shortest period of time. Typical questions: "Why is the senator from Mississippi upset?" "Who scored the most points in the UCLA–Notre Dame basketball game?" "What city suffered widespread flood damage?"

SOCIAL INTERACTIONS

JOURNAL ENTRY
Ways to Make Learning Social

- Have students pair off and ask each other questions before an exam. Do the same with difficult-to-learn material by suggesting that pairs cooperate—for example, in developing mnemonic devices or preparing flashcards—to help each other master information.

- Organize an end-of-unit extravaganza in which individuals and groups first present or display projects and then celebrate by having refreshments.

JOURNAL ENTRY
Ways to Make Learning Useful

USEFULNESS

- Continually point out that what is being learned can be used outside class. Ask students to keep a record of how they use in real life what they learn in class.

- Develop exercises that make students aware that what they are learning has transfer value. Have students in an English class write a job application letter, for instance; have math students balance a checkbook, fill out an income tax form, or work out a yearly budget; have biology students think about ways they can apply what they have learned to avoid getting sick.

THE HUMANISTIC VIEW OF MOTIVATION

For interactive Netlabs on motivation, go to this book's web site.

Abraham Maslow earned his Ph.D. in a psychology department that supported the behaviorist position. After he graduated, however, he came into contact with Gestalt psychologists (a group of German psychologists whose work during the 1920s and 1930s laid the foundation for the cognitive theories of the 1960s and 1970s), prepared for a career as a psychoanalyst, and became interested in anthropology. As a result of these various influences, he came to the conclusion that American psychologists who endorsed the behaviorist position had become so preoccupied with overt behavior and objectivity that they were ignoring other important aspects of human existence (hence, the term *humanistic* to describe his views). When Maslow observed the behavior of especially well-adjusted persons—or *self-actualizers,* as he called them—he concluded that healthy individuals are motivated to seek fulfilling experiences.

Maslow's Theory of Growth Motivation

Maslow describes seventeen propositions, discussed in Chapter 1 of *Motivation and Personality* (1987), that he believes would have to be incorporated into any sound theory of *growth motivation* (or *need gratification*). Referring to need gratification as the most important single principle underlying all development, he adds that "the single, holistic principle that binds together the multiplicity of human motives is the tendency for a new and higher need to emerge as the lower need fulfills itself by being sufficiently gratified" (1968, p. 55).

Maslow elaborates on this basic principle by proposing a five-level hierarchy of needs. *Physiological* needs are at the bottom of the hierarchy, followed in ascending order by *safety, belongingness and love, esteem,* and *self-actualization* needs (see Figure 12.2). This order reflects differences in the relative strength of each need. The lower a need is in the hierarchy, the greater is its strength, because when a lower-level need is activated (as in the case of extreme hunger or fear for one's physical safety), people will stop trying to satisfy a higher-level need (such as esteem or self-actualization) and focus on satisfying the currently active lower-level need (Maslow, 1987).

- People are motivated to satisfy deficiency needs only when those needs are unmet

The first four needs (physiological, safety, belongingness and love, and esteem) are often referred to as **deficiency needs** because they motivate people to act only when they are unmet to some degree. Self-actualization, by contrast, is often called a **growth need** because people constantly strive to satisfy it. Basically, **self-actualization** refers to the need for self-fulfillment—the need to develop all of one's potential talents and capabilities. For example, an individual who felt she had the capability to write novels, teach, practice medicine, and raise children would not feel self-actualized until she had accomplished all of these goals to some minimal degree. Because it is at the top of the hierarchy and addresses the potential of the whole person, self-actualization is discussed more frequently than the other needs.

Figure 12.2 Maslow's Hierarchy of Needs

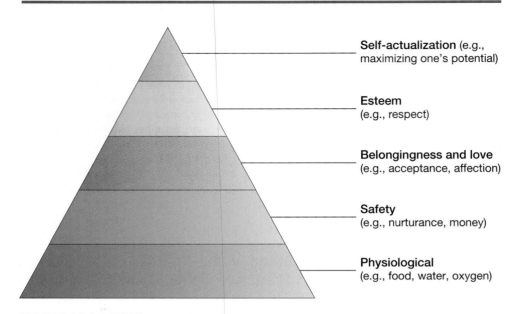

SOURCE: Maslow (1943).

● Self-actualization depends on satisfaction of lower needs, belief in certain values

Maslow originally felt that self-actualization needs would automatically be activated as soon as esteem needs were met, but he changed his mind when he encountered individuals whose behavior did not fit this pattern. He concluded that individuals whose self-actualization needs became activated and met held in high regard such values as truth, goodness, beauty, justice, autonomy, and humor (Feist & Feist, 2001).

In addition to the five basic needs that compose the hierarchy, Maslow describes cognitive needs (such as the needs to know and to understand) and aesthetic needs (such as the needs for order, symmetry, or harmony). Although not part of the basic hierarchy, these two classes of needs play a critical role in the satisfaction of basic needs. Maslow maintains that such conditions as the freedom to investigate and learn, fairness, honesty, and orderliness in interpersonal relationships are critical because their absence makes satisfaction of the five basic needs impossible. (Imagine, for example, trying to satisfy your belongingness and love needs or your esteem needs in an atmosphere characterized by dishonesty, unfair punishment, and restrictions on freedom of speech.)

pause & reflect

Maslow states that for individuals to be motivated to satisfy self-actualization needs, deficiency needs have to be satisfied first. Has this been true in your experience? If not, what was different?

Implications of Maslow's Theory

The implications of Maslow's theory of motivation for teaching are provocative. One down-to-earth implication is that a teacher should do everything possible to see that the lower-level needs of students are satisfied so that students are more likely to function at the higher levels. Students are more likely to be primed to seek satisfaction of the esteem and self-actualization needs, for example, if they are physically comfortable, feel safe and relaxed, have a sense of belonging, and experience self-esteem. William Glasser (1998), whose ideas we mentioned earlier in this chapter, states that low-achieving students have told him they would like to get better grades but don't make more of an effort because, in their eyes, teachers don't care about them or what they do.

● When deficiency needs are not satisfied, person likely to make bad choices

Only when the need for self-actualization is activated is a person likely to choose wisely when given the opportunity. Maslow emphasizes this point by making a distinction between *bad choosers* and *good choosers*. When some people are allowed

Theorists like Abraham Maslow, who argue that deficiency needs such as belongingness and self-esteem must be satisfied before students will be motivated to learn, call attention to the importance of positive teacher-student relationships in the classroom.

freedom to choose, they seem to make wise choices consistently. Most people, however, frequently make self-destructive choices. An insecure student, for example, may choose to attend a particular college more on the basis of how close it is to home than on the quality of its academic programs.

Growth, as Maslow sees it, is the result of a never-ending series of situations offering a free choice between the attractions and dangers of safety and those of growth. If a person is functioning at the level of growth needs, the choice will ordinarily be a progressive one. Maslow adds, however, that "the environment (parents, therapists, teachers) . . . can help by making the growth choice positively attractive and less dangerous, and by making the regressive choice less attractive and more costly" (1968, pp. 58–59). This point can be clarified by a simple diagram Maslow uses to illustrate a situation involving choice (1968, p. 47).

Enhance the dangers		Enhance the attraction
Safety	⟵ Person ⟶	**Growth**
Minimize the attractions		Minimize the dangers

● Encourage growth choices by enhancing attractions, minimizing dangers

This diagram emphasizes that if you set up learning situations that impress students as dangerous, threatening, or of little value, they are likely to play it safe, make little effort to respond, or even try to avoid learning. If, however, you make learning appear appealing, minimize pressure, and reduce possibilities for failure or embarrassment, your students are likely to be willing, if not eager, to do an assigned task.

Limitations of Maslow's Theory

Although Maslow's speculations are thought provoking, they are also sometimes frustrating. You may conclude, for instance, that awareness of his hierarchy of needs will make it possible for you to do an excellent job of motivating your students, only to discover that you don't know exactly how to apply what you have learned. Quite often, you may not be able to determine precisely which of a student's needs are unsatisfied. Even if you *are* quite sure that a student lacks interest in learning because he feels unloved or insecure, you may not be able to do much about it. A girl who feels that her parents do not love her or that her peers do not accept her may not respond to your efforts. And if her needs for love, belonging, and esteem are not satisfied, she is less likely to be in the mood to learn.

● Teachers may be able to satisfy some deficiency needs but not others

Then again, there will be times when you can be quite instrumental in helping to satisfy certain deficiency needs. The development of self-esteem, for example, is closely tied to successful classroom achievement for almost all students. Although you may not be able to feed students when they are hungry or protect them from physical danger, you can always take steps to help them learn more effectively.

THE ROLE OF SELF-PERCEPTIONS IN MOTIVATION

Current interest in the effects of self-perceptions on school motivation and achievement runs high and seems to have been prompted by such developments as a better understanding of the nature of self-concept and self-esteem, Albert Bandura's introduction of the self-efficacy concept, advances in the measurement of self-perceptions, and the consistent finding of a positive relationship among self-perceptions, motivation, and school achievement. Much of this interest can be traced to ideas published during the 1960s and 1970s by psychologists such as Abraham Maslow, Carl Rogers, and Arthur Combs. These individuals stressed that how students see and judge themselves and others play an important part in determining how motivated they are and how much they learn.

In the next section we focus on the relationship of academic self-concept to motivation and learning. As we noted earlier in the book, self-concept is somewhat different from self-esteem, self-efficacy, and self-definition. Table 12.2 offers a quick review of these terms.

● Self-esteem is global judgment we make of self; self-concept is judgment we make of self in specific domains; self-efficacy is our belief in ability to carry out a specify action

Table 12.2	Comparing Self-Description, Self-Esteem, Self-Concept, and Self-Efficacy	
Type of Self-Perception	**Major Characteristics**	**Examples**
Self-description	• The largely nonevaluative picture people have of themselves.	• "I am a sixth-grader." • "I am five feet one inches tall." • "My favorite subject is history."
Self-esteem (Self-worth)	• The global evaluative judgments people make of themselves. • Self-description describes who you are; self-esteem indicates how you feel about that identity.	• "I am a good person." • "I am happy with myself the way I am." • "I feel inferior to most people."
Self-concept	• The evaluative judgments people make of their competence in specific areas or domains and their associated feelings of self-worth. • Past-oriented. • For older students, self-concepts may be hierarchically arranged. For example, academic self-concept = verbal self-concept + mathematical self-concept + science self-concept, etc.	• "I'm pretty good at sports." • "I have always done well in math." • "My academic skills are about average." • "I get tongue-tied when I have to speak in public."
Self-efficacy	• The beliefs people have about their ability to carry out a specific course of action. • Future-oriented.	• "I believe I can learn how to use a computer program." • "I don't think I'll ever figure out how to solve quadratic equations." • "I'm sure I can get at least a B in this course."

SOURCES: Bong & Skaalvik (2003); Harter (1999); Kernis (2002); Marsh & Hattie (1996); Schunk & Pajares (2002).

The Role of Academic Self-Concept in Motivation and Learning

Over the years, researchers have consistently found a moderately positive relationship (called a correlation) between measures of academic self-concept and school achievement. Students who score relatively high on measures of academic self-concept tend to have higher-than-average grades. But correlation does not imply causation. The fact that students with high academic self-concept scores tend to have high grades is not sufficient grounds for concluding that high academic self-concept causes high achievement. It is just as plausible that high achievement causes increased academic self-concept or that increases in both variables are due to the influence of a third variable. Recent work on the relationship between academic self-concept and achievement has begun to shed some light on what causes what.

On the basis of their own research with children in grades 2, 3, and 4, and the research of others, Frédéric Guay, Herbert Marsh, and Michel Boivin (2003) propose the causal explanation depicted in Figure 12.3. These researchers maintain that academic self-concept and achievement have what are called reciprocal effects. That is, not only does prior achievement affect children's academic self-concept, but the current strength of a child's academic self-concept influences subsequent achievement. In addition, prior achievement has a significant positive relationship with subsequent achievement and prior self-concept has a significant positive relationship with subsequent self-concept.

Although the role of motivation was not directly tested in this study, related research suggests that the effect of academic self-concept on subsequent achievement is likely to be influenced by motivation. So a student with a strong academic self-concept for, say, social studies is likely to be highly motivated to take additional courses in that subject and use effective learning skills, which produce higher levels of achievement. At the same time, high levels of achievement strengthen the student's academic self-concept, which supports a high level of motivation, which supports high levels of achievement, and so on.

The instructional implication that flows from this research is fairly clear: teachers should design instructional programs that are aimed directly at improving both academic self-concept and achievement. The former can be accomplished by, for example, pointing out to students how well they have learned certain skills and bodies of knowledge, and the latter can be accomplished by teaching students the information-processing and self-regulation skills we discussed in the chapters on information-processing theory and social cognitive theory.

- Academic self-concept and achievement can positively affect each other

- Design instruction to improve both academic self-concept and achievement

Limitations of the Self-Perceptions Approach

One problem with using students' views of themselves as a way of influencing their motivation and learning is the lack of useful, commercially prepared measures of self-efficacy and academic self-concept. Most of the available instruments assess global self-concept or global self-esteem. But the narrower the measure of self-perception

Figure 12.3 Relationship Between Academic Self-Concept and Achievement

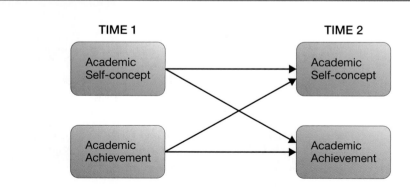

SOURCE: Adapted from Guay, Marsh, & Boivin (2003).

Take a Stand!

Increase Motivation by Maintaining High Self-Worth

There is no getting around the fact that classrooms are competitive places, largely because students know they are there to develop certain competencies and that some are better equipped to do so than others. Consequently, the decisions students make that affect their motivation to learn revolve around creating and maintaining a sense of self-worth. When a student pays attention to and imitates the behavior of high-achieving models, strives to develop high levels of self-efficacy in various subject areas, selects task mastery goals, attributes success and failure to appropriate combinations of effort and ability, believes that intellectual ability can be learned and refined, and strives to satisfy growth needs, the student is driven by the need to feel good about him- or herself (self-esteem or self-worth).

The leading proponent of this view, Martin Covington, points out that students who believe they are less capable than others (in terms of acquiring the academic competencies demanded by parents,

teaches, and society at large) will be less motivated to strive for high levels of achievement because of the increased risk of failure, and they will be more motivated to engage in such self-protective behaviors as reducing effort and self-handicapping.

You can establish the conditions that lead to high levels of motivation by following the many suggestions made in this and other chapters. In particular (and we know we have raised this issue before), do not turn your classroom into a cutthroat, survival-of-the-fittest contest for a limited supply of As, Bs, awards, and praise. Instead, help students acquire the skills they need to meet the learning standards established by you, your school district, and your state. Remember, your primary role in the classroom is to teach, not to sort.

Do you agree with the argument that teachers should "teach, not sort"? How will you apply your beliefs in your classroom? To delve further into this issue, see the Take a Stand! section of the textbook web site.

is (such as math self-concept, science self-concept, and reading self-concept), the better it predicts motivation and achievement. One solution to this limitation is to prepare the same kinds of instruments that researchers use. This is not as difficult as it might seem. Some researchers use a relatively small set of questions ("How good are you at math?" "If you were to rank all the students in your math class from the worst to the best, where would you put yourself?" "Compared to your other school subjects, how good are you at math?") and ask students to rate themselves on a 7-point scale that may range from "not at all good" to "very good" (Stipek, 2002).

Another problem is that whatever success you may have in changing a student's self-esteem and academic self-concept is likely to be slow in coming. This conclusion follows from two others. One is that changes in self-perception are best made by helping students become more effective learners than by constantly telling them they should feel good about themselves. The second conclusion is that learning how to use the cognitive skills that result in meaningful learning takes time because of their complexity and the doubts that some students will have about their ability to master these skills.

Now that you are familiar with approaches to motivation based on humanistic theories and on self-perceptions, consider the additional Suggestions for Teaching in Your Classroom that follow.

Students who have a strong academic self-concept often are more highly motivated and earn higher grades than students with weaker academic self-concepts.

Satisfying Deficiency Needs and Strengthening Self-Perceptions

1 Make learning inviting to students.

JOURNAL ENTRY
Ways to Invite Students to Learn

Motivation researchers (e.g., Purkey & Novak, 1996; Tomlinson, 2002) maintain that students care about learning when they are invited to learn. Teachers extend such invitations when they do the following:

- Meet Maslow's safety and belonging needs. Examples of meeting students' safety and belonging needs include never ridiculing a student for lack of knowledge or skills or letting other students do the same, praising students when they do well and inquiring about possible problems when they do not, relating lessons to students' interests, and learning students' names as quickly as possible.
- Provide opportunities for students to make meaningful contributions to their classroom. Examples here include having students help classmates master instructional objectives through short-term tutoring or cooperative learning arrangements and inviting students to use personal experiences and background as a way to broaden a lesson or class discussion. One classroom teacher created overhead transparencies of students' work for use as an instructional tool; this gave students the sense that they were a contributing part of a community (Gilness, 2003).
- Create a sense of purpose for the material students are required to learn. As we pointed out in the "Approaches to Instruction" chapter, students rarely ask "Why do I have to learn this?" (although it is uppermost in their minds), and teachers rarely offer an explanation without being prompted. One way to create purpose for a reading lesson is to engage the students in a discussion of an issue they are interested in that is at the heart of a story or novel they are about to read.
- Allow students to develop a sense of power about their learning. Students who believe that the knowledge and skills they are learning are useful to them now (using history as a tool for thinking about the present, for example), who know what constitutes good-quality work and believe themselves capable of producing it, and who know how to set goals and meet them are more likely than other students to believe they are in control of their learning.
- Create challenging tasks for students. Students who work hard, who feel they are being stretched, yet who succeed more often than not, are more likely to enjoy learning and to approach future tasks with increased motivation than are students whose work is routine and consistently at a low level of difficulty.

2 Direct learning experiences toward feelings of success in an effort to encourage an orientation toward achievement, high self-esteem, and a strong sense of self-efficacy and academic self-concept.

To feel successful, an individual must first establish goals that are neither so low as to be unfulfilling nor so high as to be impossible and then be able to achieve them at an acceptable level.

a. Make use of objectives that are challenging but attainable and, when appropriate, that involve student input.

JOURNAL ENTRY
Ways to Encourage Students to
Set Their Own Objectives

Although you will have primary responsibility for choosing the learning objectives for your students, you can use this process to heighten motivation by inviting your students to participate in selecting objectives or at least in thinking along with you as you explain why the objectives are worthwhile. This will tend to shift the emphasis from extrinsic to intrinsic motivation.

To help students suggest appropriate objectives, you may want to use the techniques recommended by Robert Mager (discussed in the chapter "Approaches to Instruction"). You might assist your students in stating objectives in terms of a time limit, a minimum number of correct responses, a proportion of correct responses, or a sample of actions.

EXAMPLES

- "How many minutes do you think you will need to outline this chapter? When you finish, we'll see that film I told you about."

- "George, you got six out of ten on this spelling quiz. How many do you want to try for on the retest?"

b. Help students master your objectives.

JOURNAL ENTRY
Ways to Help Students
Master Objectives

As you have seen, a student's past accomplishments on a particular task influence his or her self-efficacy and academic self-concept. Consequently, you should do whatever you can to help students achieve at an acceptable level. One important recommendation for helping students become better learners was made earlier: teach them how to create and use learning strategies. Another suggestion that will help them get the most out of their strategies is to assign moderately difficult tasks and provide the minimum amount of assistance necessary to complete the task successfully (think of Vygotsky's zone of proximal development and the concept of scaffolding).

See the Reflective Journal Questions on the textbook web site for additional journal ideas.

Many of the motivational techniques we have suggested in this chapter can be enhanced by the appropriate use of technology. To conclude the chapter, we discuss research on the link between technology and motivation, and we survey a number of kinds of technology that have been shown to be useful.

MOTIVATING STUDENTS WITH TECHNOLOGY

Extrinsic Versus Intrinsic Motivation

Previously in this chapter, we contrasted the behavioral, or extrinsic, approach to motivation with various cognitive, or intrinsic, approaches. Our goal was not to demonstrate that one approach is inherently superior to the other but to point out how and when both approaches can profitably be used to support classroom learning. A parallel situation exists with regard to the motivating effects of technology. Behavioral psychologists, for example, argue that students who work on computer-based drill-and-practice programs are motivated by the immediate feedback they receive and the steady progress they make. Cognitive psychologists argue that involving students in fantasy environments or authentic tasks that are directed to audiences beside the teacher is intrinsically motivating because such programs and tasks give students a sense of confidence, personal responsibility, and control over their own learning (Hewitt, 2002; Hickey et al., 2001; Moreno & Mayer, 2002).

Despite the differences in these two approaches to motivation, they are not mutually exclusive. Some of the most innovative and effective technological aids to learning combine both approaches. For example, the Jasper Woodbury series, which we mentioned in the chapter on constructivist learning theory, tries to engage intrinsic motivation by giving students control over and responsibility for how they collect, analyze, and use the data presented by the program and by embedding the task in a realistic context. The accompanying extrinsic rewards include class announcements of accomplishments, student demonstrations of problem-solving strategies,

● Technology can be used to support both extrinsic and intrinsic motivation

teacher praise for correct problem solutions, and feedback and encouragement from peers in other schools about one's problem solutions (Barron, 2000; Cognition and Technology Group at Vanderbilt, 1996). Other types of extrinsic rewards that can be used in conjunction with other technology-based approaches to learning include membership in multimedia clubs, special computer events and fairs for parents or the community, and certificates of recognition.

Using Technology to Increase Motivation to Learn

Now that we've established that computer-based technology can accommodate extrinsic and intrinsic approaches to motivation, we can look at whether it does, in fact, increase students' motivation to learn.

Critics of computer-based learning argue that any observed increases in student motivation are likely to be short term and due largely to the novelty of the medium. But several studies have demonstrated that the use of computer-based instruction increases students' intrinsic motivation and performance:

● Technology increases intrinsic motivation by making learning more interesting and meaningful

- Diana Cordova and Mark Lepper (1996) found that rich fantasy contexts, personalization, and provision for student choice within children's software not only foster intrinsic motivation and deeper engagement in learning but also boost the amount that students learn, their perceived level of competence, and their levels of aspiration.

- Another study looked at Malaysian middle school students who were considered to be at risk because of low self-efficacy and motivation. These students were taught how to use CD-ROMs and the Internet to locate information for various subjects. They then became the "technology experts" for projects that were assigned to their respective cooperative learning group. Over the school year, these students became more interested in their schoolwork, were more willing to work on class assignments, and increased their participation in class discussions (Gan, 1999).

- Eighth graders who were judged to be candidates for dropping out of school because of academic and social problems received two weeks of instruction on the Bill of Rights. Those who were given a chance to create and present a multimedia project on the subject scored better on tests of both subject matter and attitudes toward learning than peers who engaged in traditional classroom projects (Woodul, Vitale, & Scott, 2000).

- High school seniors working in cooperative learning groups created PowerPoint presentations about poets of the Romantic period. (PowerPoint is a software program from Microsoft that allows users to create slide shows that combine text, graphics, motion, sounds, and video.) Compared with previous classes, this group showed a much higher level of motivation for learning about this subject matter (Marr, 2000).

- Some students in one Nevada school were so motivated by their semester-long multimedia project on water use in their state that they came to school as early as 6 A.M. to work on it and stayed after 4 P.M. Students also conducted additional field studies to verify their work and spent weekends checking out possible sites for videotaping (Ebert & Strudler, 1996).

- High school students in Israel who were learning to use the LEGO/LOGO program exhibited the same enthusiasm for learning as did the Nevada students. LOGO is a computer programming language for moving objects in space, and LEGO is a set of plastic blocks, sensors, gears, and motors. With these components, the students designed and built such objects as robots, cars, and cranes. According to the researchers, "The laboratory became a second home to the pupils. They came to work on their projects during breaks and free hours, and even after school" (Doppelt & Barak, 2002, p. 26).

Computer-based or augmented programs are often used to improve students' literacy skills and motivation for reading and writing. For example, a technology-enhanced summer program designed to help low-achieving inner-city middle school children improve their reading and writing skills produced noticeable improvements in motivation. Students used data gathering tools (Web searches, multimedia encyclopedias, content-specific software), data management tools (programs for note taking and creating charts and graphs), and presentation tools (word processing programs, web page design programs, and PowerPoint) to complete inquiry projects and present the results to an audience of parents, peers, and siblings. As the students shared their efforts with one another and noticed the impact of such features as computer graphics, web pages, PowerPoint slide shows, and videotaped interviews, they quickly and eagerly revised their own projects to incorporate one or more of these features (Owens, Hester, & Teale, 2002).

A survey of elementary grade teachers who published students' writing projects on a classroom web site revealed a similar motivating effect. Students were more inclined to complete their projects and do high-quality work when they knew it would be seen by a wider audience (Karchmer, 2001). According to one fourth-grade teacher:

> Before the Internet, my children did not write as much, as writing without a purpose was not fulfilling. We have a purpose now and that makes the work more interesting for the children. They are really proud to see their work on the Internet. . . . I believe the students are being more careful with their language arts skills. Their errors are pretty easy to see, and they do not seem to have any problem with changing them. In paper and pencil writing, it is very difficult to get them to change what they are writing. (p. 459)

A second-grade teacher noted that technology had a strong motivating effect on students with weaknesses in certain skills:

> Technology levels the playing field somewhat. For example, writing and handwriting are easier, art applications/scanning/photos make illustration easier, and so on. . . . A student in last year's class had handwriting that was generally illegible, and he would do nearly anything to avoid writing—sharpen pencils, count pages in his spiral notebook, watch his neighbors, etc. He became very anxious during writing time. When he was able to use a computer, he was able to create stories and reports. He was very proud of his work and began to enjoy it. (p. 459)

 To review this chapter, see the ACE practice tests and PowerPoint slides on the textbook web site.

E-mail is often used to heighten student interest and motivation through pen pal projects that link students in different countries or locales or to coordinate interschool projects. Celeste Oakes (1996) described how she used e-mail with her first-grade class in Nevada to correspond with students in Alaska, ask questions of space shuttle astronauts, collaboratively write stories with students from other schools, and write letters to Santa Claus. Rebecca Sipe (2000) described a project in which her preservice teacher education undergraduates corresponded with tenth-grade English students, who helped the preservice students formulate realistic classroom beliefs and practices. Dean Blase (2000) arranged for his middle school class in Cincinnati to exchange e-mail messages about the meaning of a novel with students from Vermont, Massachusetts, and Texas. Carole Duff (2000) described how female high school students use e-mail to get career advice, academic guidance, and personal support from a professional woman mentor. In any of these projects, it is critical to have icebreaking activities, goals that relate to key objectives, and ground rules for collaboration (for example, time length, targeted deadlines, final project guidelines, and plans for culminating activities).

Resources for Further Investigation

● Surveys of Motivational Theories

In a basic survey text, *Motivation to Learn: From Theory to Practice* (4th ed., 2002), Deborah Stipek discusses reinforcement theory, social cognitive theory, intrinsic motivation, need for achievement theory, attribution theory, and perceptions of ability. In Appendix 2-A, she presents a rating form and scoring procedure for teachers to use in identifying students who may have motivation problems. Appendix 3-A is a self-rating form that teachers can use to keep track of how often they provide rewards and punishments.

Another well-written basic survey text is *Motivation in Education: Theory, Research, and Applications* (2nd ed., 2002), by Paul Pintrich and Dale Schunk. The last three chapters of this book discuss teacher and classroom influences on motivation, the role of schools in motivation, and sociocultural influences on motivation.

An interesting collection of articles on intrinsic and extrinsic motivation can be found in *Intrinsic and Extrinsic Motivation: The Search for Optimal Motivation and Performance* (2000), edited by Carol Sansone and Judith Harackiewicz. This volume discusses the effects of rewards on intrinsic motivation, the advantages and disadvantages of performance goals versus mastery goals, and the role of interest in learning.

● Cognitive Views of Motivation

Development of Achievement Motivation (2002c), edited by Allan Wigfield and Jacquelynne Eccles, contains thirteen chapters written by leading researchers on various aspects of cognitive approaches to motivation. Each of the first three parts is organized around a question that a typical student might ask: "Can I Do This Activity?" (Chapters 1–3), "Do I Want to Do This Activity, and Why?" (Chapters 4–9), and "What Do I Need to Do to Succeed?" (Chapters 10 and 11). Part Four, "Motivation and Instruction," contains two chapters that address instructional practices that are likely to positively influence students' motivation.

● Motivational Techniques for the Classroom

Powerful Classroom Management Strategies: Motivating Students to Learn (2000), by Paul R. Burden, is based on research and what is considered to be best practice. Each chapter contains one or more brief sections called "Teachers in Action" that were written by practicing teachers to describe techniques they use for motivating students. Techniques for motivating students from diverse cultural backgrounds are described by Margery Ginsberg and Raymond Wlodkowski in *Creating Highly Motivating Classrooms for All Students* (2000).

Steve Sugar and Kim Komoski Sugar describe how to motivate K–8 students through the use of classroom games in *Primary Games* (2002). Part One describes how games can promote learning, as well as how to select an appropriate game, develop game content, and set up and run a game. Part Two describes twenty-five games, such as Letter Bingo, Math Bingo, Knowledge Golf, and Scavenger Hunt. Part Three is a set of four appendices that help you find the right game for various purposes.

Basic information about motivation and ideas on how to affect student motivation can be found on the Web. The KidSource web site has a page titled "Student Motivation to Learn" (accessible from **www.kidsource.com/kidsource/pages/ ed.k12.html**). It discusses the factors that influence the development of motivation, the advantages of intrinsic motivation, how motivation to learn can be fostered in the school setting, and what can be done to help unmotivated students. For ideas on how to motivate students to learn math, visit the web page titled "Mathematics and Motivation: An Annotated Bibliography" at the following site: **mathforum.com/~sarah/ Discussion.Sessions/biblio.motivation.html/**.

As we noted earlier in the book, the quality of instructional software ranges from abysmal to excellent. In volume 82, number 8, of *Phi Delta Kappan* (2001), Selma Wasserman describes her own efforts in creating a high-quality CD-ROM to supplement an eleventh-grade social studies curriculum, lists several criteria that teachers can use when considering the purchase of a CD-ROM, and provides guidelines for teachers who may wish to create their own CD-ROM.

Summary

1. Motivation is the willingness to expend a certain amount of effort to achieve a particular goal under a particular set of circumstances.

2. The behavioral (operant conditioning) view of motivation is based on the desire of students to obtain a positive reinforcer for exhibiting a particular behavior or behavior pattern.

3. A potential limitation of operant conditioning theory is its emphasis on extrinsic sources of motivation. The learner is motivated to attain a goal in order to receive a reward that is not inherently related to the activity. This may produce only temporary changes in behavior, a materialistic attitude toward learning, and an undermining of whatever intrinsic motivation a student may have for a particular task.

4. Intrinsic motivation can be undermined by extrinsic reinforcement when initial interest in a task is high, the rewards are tangible, the rewards are promised in advance as an incentive to exhibit the desired behavior, the reward is given just for engaging in an activity, and students have to compete with one another for a limited supply of rewards.

5. Extrinsic rewards may enhance intrinsic motivation when initial interest in a task is low because it is seen as boring or irrelevant; when initial interest in a task is high and reward involves positive verbal feedback; and when the highest level of reward is potentially available to all who qualify.

6. The social cognitive view of motivation is based largely on giving students the opportunity to observe and imitate the behavior of models they admire and enhancing students' self-efficacy for particular tasks.

7. A student's level of self-efficacy—how capable one believes one is to perform a particular task—affects motivation by affecting the learning goals that are chosen, the outcome the student expects, and the attributions the student makes for success and failure.

8. Students may choose a task mastery goal, a performance-approach goal, a performance-avoidance goal, or a combination of the first two. Students who choose task mastery goals use meaningful learning strategies and treat mistakes as part of learning. Students who choose performance-approach goals are motivated to demonstrate superior ability by outperforming others. Students who choose performance-avoidance goals are motivated to avoid the possibility of failure so as not to appear less capable than others; they may also engage in self-handicapping behaviors so that they have an excuse for poor performance.

9. High self-efficacy students generally expect a positive outcome for tasks they take on. Low self-efficacy students are more likely than students with high self-efficacy to expect negative academic outcomes.

10. The cognitive development view holds that people are inherently motivated by a need to achieve equilibration by overcoming inconsistencies or contradictions between what they know and what they experience.

11. Atkinson proposes that people are motivated by a need for achievement, which is a general desire to attain goals that require some degree of competence. Individuals with a high need to achieve have a greater expectation of success than they do a fear of failure. They prefer moderately difficult tasks because such tasks provide an optimal balance between the possibility of failure and the expectation of success. Individuals with a low need to achieve are dominated by a fear of failure. Consequently, they prefer either very easy tasks (because success is assured) or very difficult tasks (because there is no shame in failing to do well at them).

12. Research on attribution theory has found marked differences between high achievers and low achievers. High achievers attribute success to ability and effort and failure to insufficient effort. Low achievers attribute success to luck or easiness of the task and failure to lack of ability.

13. Compared with younger children, seven- and eight-year-olds show greater awareness of the concept of ability, distinguish ability from other characteristics, think of ability as an internal capability that is stable over time, and are more likely to compare their performance to those of their peers.

14. Compared with seven- and eight-year-olds, ten- to twelve-year-old children are more likely to distinguish between ability and effort, evaluate their ability accurately, think of ability as a stable and fixed characteristic, and be concerned with getting the highest grade.

15. Some students are less motivated than others because they subscribe to what Dweck calls an entity theory of cognitive ability. Because they believe that intelligence is a fixed capacity, they are primarily interested in getting high grades and appearing smart to others and tend to avoid challenging tasks if uncertain of success. Students who subscribe to an incremental theory tend to pursue more meaningful learning opportunities because they think of intelligence as something that can be improved through experience and corrective feedback.

16. Level of interest in a subject is related to intrinsic motivation for that subject. In some instances, students have a preexisting interest in a subject (personal interest), but in other instances, interest grows out of involvement with the subject (situational interest). Students with a personal interest in a topic or subject are more likely to be intrinsically motivated to learn about that topic or subject.

17. Personal interest in a subject may be influenced by such factors as the student's own emotions, degree of competence attained, relevance to a goal, and level of prior knowledge.

18. Situational interest in a subject may be influenced by such factors as hands-on activities, a state of cognitive disequilibrium, well-written material, the opportunity to work with others, and observing influential models.

19. One limitation of the cognitive development view is that teachers may not always find it possible to induce a sense of disequilibrium in students.

20. A problem with need-for-achievement theory is the lack of instruments with which to measure that need and the unreliability of short-term observations.

21. A limitation of attribution theory and beliefs about ability is the difficulty of changing students' faulty attribution patterns and beliefs about the nature of cognitive ability.

22. Maslow's humanistic view of motivation is based on the idea that a person must satisfy a hierarchical sequence of deficiency needs (physiological, safety, belongingness and love, and esteem) before satisfying the growth need for self-actualization.

23. A limitation of the humanistic view is that the teacher may not always find it possible to identify a student's unmet deficiency needs or to satisfy them once they are identified.

24. The relationship between a student's academic self-concept and achievement is reciprocal. That is, not only does academic self-concept influence motivation for learning a particular subject, which influences achievement, but prior achievement has a positive effect on both motivation and academic self-concept.

25. Technology tools such as hypermedia, multimedia, simulations, problem-solving programs, and telecommunications have been shown to have a beneficial effect on students' motivation to learn because they make learning interesting and meaningful.

Key Terms

extrinsic motivation *(390)*

intrinsic motivation *(390)*

attribution theory *(395)*

deficiency needs *(409)*

growth need *(409)*

self-actualization *(409)*

13

Classroom Management

These key points will help you learn the important information in this chapter. To help you study, they also appear in the margins of the pages, next to the text where they are discussed.

Authoritarian, Permissive, and Authoritative Approaches to Classroom Management

● Authoritative approach to class-room management superior to permissive and authoritarian approaches

Preventing Problems: Techniques of Classroom Management

● Ripple effect: group response to a reprimand directed at an individual

● Teachers who show they are "with it" head off discipline problems

● Being able to handle overlapping activities helps maintain class-room control

● Teachers who continually interrupt activities have discipline problems

● Keeping entire class involved and alert minimizes misbehavior

● Identify misbehavers; firmly specify constructive behavior

● Well-managed classroom: students complete clear assignments in busy but pleasant atmosphere

● Effective teachers plan how to handle classroom routines

● During first weeks, have students complete clear assignments under your direction

● Manage behavior of adolescents by making and communicating clear rules and procedures

Suggestions for Teaching in Your Classroom: Techniques of Classroom Management

● Establish, call attention to, and explain class rules the first day

● Establish a businesslike but supportive classroom atmosphere

Techniques for Dealing with Behavior Problems

● Use supportive reactions to help students develop self-control

● Give criticism privately; then offer encouragement

● I-message: tell how you feel about an unacceptable situation

● Determine who owns a problem before deciding on course of action

Suggestions for Teaching in Your Classroom: Handling Problem Behavior

● Be prompt, consistent, reasonable when dealing with misbehavior

Violence in American Schools

● Incidents of crime and serious violence occur relatively infrequently in public schools

● Male aggressiveness due to biological and cultural factors

● Middle school and junior high boys with low grades may feel trapped

● Misbehavior of high school students may reveal lack of positive identity

● Classroom disruptions can be significantly reduced by various approaches

● Violence less likely when school-wide programs teach students constructive ways to handle conflicts

B y now you have no doubt begun to realize what we pointed out at the beginning of the book: teaching is a complex enterprise. It is complex for the following reasons:

- Students vary in their physical, social, emotional, cognitive, and cultural characteristics.
- Learning occurs gradually and only with extensive and varied practice.
- Different students learn at different rates.
- Systematic preparations have to be made to ensure that students master the objectives that teachers lay out.
- Different students, or groups of students, are often working on different tasks at any point in time.
- Student behaviors are somewhat unpredictable.
- Students are motivated to learn (or not learn) by different factors.
- Learning can be measured and evaluated in a variety of ways.

If not managed properly, an endeavor as complex as teaching can easily become chaotic. When that happens, students are likely to become confused, bored, uninterested, restless, and perhaps even disruptive. But a well-managed classroom is not what many people think: students working silently at their desks (or in front of their computers), speaking only when spoken to, and providing verbatim recitations of what the teacher and textbook said. Such a classroom is incompatible with the contemporary views of learning and motivation described in the preceding chapters. If some of your goals are for students to acquire a meaningful knowledge base, become proficient problem solvers, and learn how to work productively with others, then you have to accept the idea that these goals are best met in classrooms that are characterized by a fair amount of autonomy, physical movement, and social interaction (Emmer & Stough, 2001).

To help you accomplish these goals *and* keep student behavior within manageable bounds, we describe in this chapter a general approach to classroom management that is related to an effective parenting style, various techniques that you can use to prevent behavior problems from occurring, and a set of techniques for dealing with misbehavior once it has occurred. In addition, we analyze the issue of school violence and summarize approaches to reducing its frequency. ●

AUTHORITARIAN, PERMISSIVE, AND AUTHORITATIVE APPROACHES TO CLASSROOM MANAGEMENT

To set a good foundation for understanding this chapter, refer to the Chapter Themes on the textbook web site, accessible from **http://education.college.hmco. com/students**.

You may recall from the chapter on age-level characteristics that Diana Baumrind (1971, 1991a) found that parents tend to exhibit one of four styles in managing the behavior of their children: authoritarian, permissive, authoritative, or rejecting-neglecting. The first three of these styles have been applied to a teacher's actions in the classroom. We will quickly review Baumrind's categories and then take a brief look at how teachers' approaches to management can be characterized by these styles too.

Authoritarian parents establish rules for their children's behavior and expect them to be blindly obeyed. Explanations of why a particular rule is necessary are almost never given. Instead, rewards and punishments are given for following or not following rules. *Permissive* parents represent the other extreme. They impose few controls. They allow their children to make many basic decisions (such as what to eat, what to wear, when to go to bed) and provide advice or assistance only when asked. *Authoritative* parents provide rules but discuss the reasons for them, teach their children how to meet them, and reward children for exhibiting self-control. Authoritative parents also cede more responsibility for self-governance to their children as the children demonstrate increased self-regulation skills. This style, more so than the other two, leads to children's internalizing the parents' norms and maintaining intrinsic motivation for following them in the future.

You can probably see the parallel between Baumrind's work and classroom management. Teachers who adopt an authoritarian style are likely to have student compliance rather than autonomy as their main goal ("Do what I say because I say so") and make heavy use of rewards and punishments to produce that compliance. Teachers who adopt a permissive style are likely to rely heavily on students' identifying with and respecting them as their main approach to classroom management ("Do what I say because you like me and respect my judgment"). Teachers who adopt an authoritative style are likely to have as their main goal students who can eventually regulate their own behavior. By explaining the rationale for classroom rules and adjusting those rules as students demonstrate the ability to govern themselves appropriately, authoritative teachers hope to convince students that adopting the teacher's norms for classroom behavior as their own will lead to the achievement of valued academic goals ("Do what I say because doing so will help you learn more"). The students of authoritative teachers better understand the need for classroom rules and tend to operate within them most of the time (McCaslin & Good, 1992).

Two studies support the extension of Baumrind's parenting styles to classroom teachers. In one, middle school students who described their teachers in terms that reflect the authoritative style (for example, the teacher sets clear rules and explains the penalty for breaking them, trusts students to carry out certain tasks independently, treats all students fairly, does not criticize students for not having the right answer, and has high expectations for academic achievement and behavior) scored

● Authoritative approach to classroom management superior to permissive and authoritarian approaches

higher on measures of motivation, prosocial behavior, and achievement than did students who described their teacher in more authoritarian terms (Wentzel, 2002). The other study demonstrated that a teacher's decision to either support student autonomy or be more controlling of what students do in class is very much a function of the environment in which they work. When teachers have curriculum decisions and performance standards imposed on them for which they will be held accountable and when they feel that students are not highly motivated to learn, their intrinsic motivation for teaching suffers. This lowered intrinsic motivation, in turn, leads them to be less supportive of student autonomy and more controlling (Pelletier, Séguin-Lévesque, & Legault, 2002).

The next part of this chapter will describe guidelines you might follow to establish and maintain an effective learning environment.

PREVENTING PROBLEMS: TECHNIQUES OF CLASSROOM MANAGEMENT

Kounin's Observations on Group Management

Interest in the significance of classroom management was kindled when Jacob Kounin wrote a book titled *Discipline and Group Management in Classrooms* (1970). Kounin noted that he first became interested in group management when he reprimanded a college student for blatantly reading a newspaper in class. Kounin was struck by the extent to which the entire class responded to a reprimand directed at only one person, and he subsequently dubbed this the **ripple effect**. Chances are you can recall a situation when you were diligently working away in a classroom and the teacher suddenly became quite angry at a disruptive classmate. If you felt a bit tense after the incident (even though your behavior was blameless) and tried to give the impression that you were a paragon of student virtue, you have had personal experience with the ripple effect.

● Ripple effect: group response to a reprimand directed at an individual

Would you use the ripple effect deliberately? Why or why not?

Once his interest in classroom behavior was aroused, Kounin supervised a series of observational and experimental studies of student reactions to techniques of teacher control. In analyzing the results of these various studies, he came to the conclusion that the following classroom management techniques appear to be most effective:

● Teachers who show they are "with it" head off discipline problems

1. *Show your students that you are "with it."* Kounin coined the term **withitness** to emphasize that teachers who prove to their students that they know what is going on in a classroom usually have fewer behavior problems than teachers who appear to be unaware of incipient disruptions. An expert at classroom management will nip trouble in the bud by commenting on potentially disruptive behavior before it gains momentum. An ineffective teacher may not notice such behavior until it begins to spread and then perhaps hopes that it will simply go away.

At first glance Kounin's suggestion that you show that you are with it might seem to be in conflict with operant conditioning's prediction that nonreinforced behavior will disappear. If the teacher's reaction is the only source of reinforcement in a classroom, ignoring behavior may cause it to disappear. In many cases, however, a misbehaving student gets reinforced by the reactions of classmates. Therefore, ignoring behavior is much less likely to lead to extinction of a response in a classroom than in controlled experimental situations.

JOURNAL ENTRY
Learning to Deal with Overlapping Situations

2. *Learn to cope with overlapping situations.* When he analyzed videotapes of actual classroom interactions, Kounin found that some teachers seemed to have one-track minds. They were inclined to deal with only one thing at a time, and this way of proceeding caused frequent interruptions in classroom routine. One primary

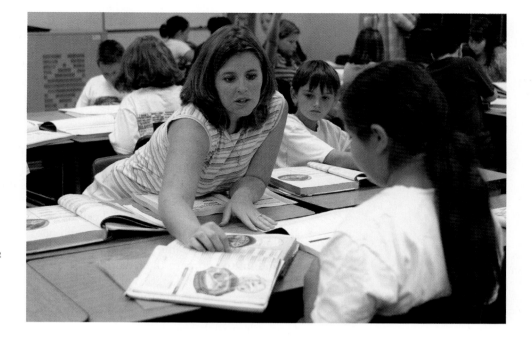

Jacob Kounin found that teachers who were "with it" could deal with overlapping situations, maintained smoothness and momentum in class activities, used a variety of activities, kept the whole class involved, and had few discipline problems.

● Being able to handle overlapping activities helps maintain classroom control

---

JOURNAL ENTRY
Learning to Handle Momentum

● Teachers who continually interrupt activities have discipline problems

---

JOURNAL ENTRY
Ways to Keep the Whole Class Involved

grade teacher whom Kounin observed, for example, was working with a reading group when she noticed two boys on the other side of the room poking each other. She abruptly got up, walked over to the boys, berated them at length, and then returned to the reading group. By the time she returned, however, the children in the reading group had become bored and listless and were tempted to engage in mischief of their own.

Kounin concluded that withitness and skill in handling overlapping activities seemed to be related. An expert classroom manager who is talking to children in a reading group, for example, might notice two boys at the far side of the room who are beginning to scuffle with each other. Such a teacher might in midsentence tell the boys to stop and make the point so adroitly that the attention of the children in the reading group does not waver.

3. *Strive to maintain smoothness and momentum in class activities.* This point is related to the previous one. Kounin found that some teachers caused problems for themselves by constantly interrupting activities without thinking about what they were doing. Some teachers whose activities were recorded on videotape failed to maintain the thrust of a lesson because they seemed unaware of the rhythm of student behavior (that is, they did not take into account the degree of student inattention and restlessness but instead moved ahead in an almost mechanical way). Others flip-flopped from one activity to another. Still others would interrupt one activity (for example, a reading lesson) to comment on an unrelated aspect of classroom functioning ("Someone left a lunch bag on the floor"). There were also some who wasted time dwelling on a trivial incident (making a big fuss because a boy lost his pencil). And a few teachers delivered individual, instead of group, instruction ("All right, Charlie, you go to the board. Fine. Now, Rebecca, you go to the board"). All of these types of teacher behavior tended to interfere with the flow of learning activities.

4. *Try to keep the whole class involved, even when you are dealing with individual students.* Kounin found that some well-meaning teachers had fallen into a pattern of calling on students in a predictable order and in such a way that the rest of the class served as a passive audience. Unless you stop to think about what you are doing during group recitation periods, you might easily fall into the same trap. If you do, the "audience" is almost certain to become bored and may be tempted to engage in troublemaking activities just to keep occupied.

Some teachers, for example, call on students to recite by going around a circle, or going up and down rows, or following alphabetical order. Others call on a child first and then ask a question. Still others ask one child to recite at length (read an entire page, for example). All of these techniques tend to spotlight one child in predictable order and cause the rest of the class members to tune out until their turn comes. You are more likely to maintain interest and limit mischief caused by boredom if you use techniques such as the following:

- Ask a question, and after pausing a few seconds to let everyone think about it, pick out someone to answer it. With subsequent questions, call on students in an unpredictable order so that no one knows when he or she will be asked to recite. (If you feel that some students in a class are very apprehensive about being called on, even under relaxing circumstances, you can either ask them extremely easy questions or avoid calling on them at all.)
- If you single out one child to go to the board to do a problem, ask all other students to do the same problem at their desks, and then choose one or two at random to compare their work with the answers on the board.
- When dealing with lengthy or complex material, call on several students in quick succession (and in unpredictable order) and ask each to handle one section. In a primary grade reading group, for example, have one child read a sentence; then pick someone at the other side of the group to read the next sentence and so on.
- Use props in the form of flashcards, mimeographed sheets, or workbook pages to induce all students to respond to questions simultaneously. Then ask students to compare answers. One ingenious elementary school teacher whom Kounin observed had each student print the ten digits on cards that could be inserted in a slotted piece of cardboard. She would ask a question such as "How much is 8 and 4?" and then pause a moment while the students arranged their answers in the slots and then say, "All show!")

5. *Introduce variety, and be enthusiastic, particularly with younger students.* After viewing videotapes of different teachers, Kounin and his associates concluded that some teachers seemed to fall into a deadly routine much more readily than others. They followed the same procedure day after day and responded with the same, almost reflexive comments. At the other end of the scale were teachers who introduced variety, responded with enthusiasm and interest, and moved quickly to new activities when they sensed that students either had mastered or were satiated by a particular lesson. It seems logical to assume that students will be less inclined to sleep, daydream, or engage in disruptive activities if they are exposed to an enthusiastic teacher who varies the pace and type of classroom activities.

6. *Be aware of the ripple effect.* When criticizing student behavior, be clear and firm, focus on behavior rather than on personalities, and try to avoid angry outbursts. If you take into account the suggestions just made, you may be able to reduce the amount of student misbehavior in your classes. Even so, some behavior problems are certain to occur. When you deal with these, you can benefit from Kounin's research on the ripple effect. On the basis of observations, questionnaires, and experimental evidence, he concluded that "innocent" students in a class are more likely to be positively impressed by the way the teacher handles a misbehavior if the following conditions exist:

- The teacher identifies the misbehaver and states what the unacceptable behavior is. ("Jorge! Don't flip that computer disk at Jamal.")
- The teacher specifies a more constructive behavior. ("Please put the computer disk back in the storage box.")
- The teacher explains why the deviant behavior should cease. ("If the computer disk gets broken or dirty, no one else will be able to use it, and we'll have to try to get a new one.")

● Keeping entire class involved and alert minimizes misbehavior

● Identify misbehavers; firmly specify constructive behavior

- The teacher is firm and authoritative and conveys a no-nonsense attitude. ("All infractions of classroom rules will result in an appropriate punishment—no ifs, ands, or buts.")
- The teacher does not resort to anger, humiliation, or extreme punishment. Kounin concluded that extreme reactions did not seem to make children behave better. Instead, anger and severe reprimands upset them and made them feel tense and nervous. ("Roger, I am deeply disappointed that you used obscene language in your argument with Michael. Such behavior is simply unacceptable in my classroom.")
- The teacher focuses on behavior, not on personality. (Say, "Ramona, staring out the window instead of reading your textbook is unacceptable behavior in my classroom" rather than "Ramona, you're the laziest student I have ever had in class.")

University of Texas Studies of Group Management

Stimulated by Kounin's observations, members of the Research and Development Center for Teacher Education at the University of Texas at Austin instituted a series of studies on classroom management. The basic procedure followed in most studies was to first identify very effective and less effective teachers by using a variety of criteria (often stressing student achievement) and then analyze in detail classroom management techniques that very effective teachers used. In some studies (for example, Brophy, 1979; Good, 1982), basic characteristics of well-managed classrooms were described. They can be summarized as follows:

● Well-managed classroom: students complete clear assignments in busy but pleasant atmosphere

1. Students know what they are expected to do and generally experience the feeling that they are successful doing it.
2. Students are kept busy engaging in teacher-led instructional activities.
3. There is little wasted time, confusion, or disruption.
4. A no-nonsense, work-oriented tone prevails, but at the same time there is a relaxed and pleasant atmosphere.

These conclusions relate to information presented in earlier chapters. The first point can be interpreted as supporting the use of instructional objectives that are stated in such a way that students know when they have achieved them. The next three points stress student productivity under teacher guidance and a no-nonsense, work-oriented atmosphere. These outcomes are more likely when teachers use procedures that behavioral and cognitive psychologists have recommended.

Another set of studies carried out by the Texas researchers led to two recent books on group management—one for elementary school teachers (Evertson, Emmer, & Worsham, 2003) and the other for secondary school teachers (Emmer, Evertson, & Worsham, 2003). You may wish to examine the appropriate book for your grade level (complete titles and names of authors are given in Resources for Further Information at the end of this chapter), but for now we will provide the following summary of basic keys to management success stressed in both volumes:

● Effective teachers plan how to handle classroom routines

1. On the first day with a new class, very effective teachers clearly demonstrate that they have thought about classroom procedures ahead of time. They have planned first-day activities that make it possible for classroom routine to be handled with a minimum of confusion. They also make sure students understand why the procedures are necessary and how they are to be followed.
2. A short list of basic classroom rules is posted or announced (or both), and students are told about the penalties they will incur in the event of misbehavior.

● During first weeks, have students complete clear assignments under your direction

3. During the first weeks with a new group of students, effective teachers have students engage in whole-group activities under teacher direction. Such activities are selected to make students feel comfortable and successful in their new classroom.

4. After the initial orientation period is over, effective teachers maintain control by using the sorts of techniques that Kounin described: they show they are with it, cope with overlapping situations, maintain smoothness and momentum, and avoid ignoring the rest of the class when dealing with individual students.

5. Effective teachers give clear directions, hold students accountable for completing assignments, and give frequent feedback.

Managing the Middle, Junior High, and High School Classroom

Most of the classroom management techniques and suggestions we have discussed so far are sufficiently general that they can be used in a variety of classroom settings and with primary through secondary grade students. Nevertheless, teaching preadolescents and adolescents is sufficiently different from teaching younger students that the management of the middle school, junior high, and high school classroom requires a slightly different emphasis and a few unique practices.

Classroom management has to be approached somewhat differently in the secondary grades (and in those middle schools where students change classes several times a day) because of the segmented nature of education for these grades. Instead of being in charge of the same twenty-five to thirty students all day, most junior high or high school teachers (and some middle school teachers) are responsible for as many as five different groups of twenty-five to thirty students for about fifty minutes each. This arrangement results in a wider range of individual differences, a greater likelihood that these teachers will see a wide range of behavior problems, and a greater concern with efficient use of class time.

Because of the special nature of adolescence, relatively short class times, and consecutive classes with different students, middle school, junior high, and high school teachers must concentrate their efforts on preventing misbehavior. Edmund Emmer, Carolyn Evertson, and Murray Worsham (2003), in *Classroom Management for Secondary Teachers*, discuss how teachers can prevent misbehavior by carefully organizing the classroom environment, establishing clear rules and procedures, and delivering effective instruction.

According to Emmer and his associates, the physical features of the classroom should be arranged to optimize teaching and learning. They suggest an environment in

Because middle school, junior high, and high school students move from one teacher to another every fifty minutes or so, it is important to establish a common set of rules that govern various activities and procedures and to clearly communicate the reasons for those rules.

which (1) the arrangement of the seating, materials, and equipment is consistent with the kinds of instructional activities the teacher favors; (2) high-traffic areas, such as the teacher's desk and the pencil sharpener, are kept free of congestion; (3) the teacher can easily see all students; (4) frequently used teaching materials and student supplies are readily available; and (5) students can easily see instructional presentations and displays.

In too many instances, teachers spend a significant amount of class time dealing with misbehavior rather than with teaching and learning, either because students are never told what is expected of them or because rules and procedures are not communicated clearly. Accordingly, Emmer and associates suggest that classroom rules be specifically stated, discussed with students on the first day of class, and, for seventh, eighth, and ninth grades, posted in a prominent place. Sophomores, juniors, and seniors should be given a handout on which the rules are listed. A set of five to eight basic rules should be sufficient. Some examples of these basic rules follow:

> Bring all needed materials to class.
> Be in your seat and ready to work when the bell rings.
> Respect and be polite to all people.
> Do not talk or leave your desk when someone else is talking.
> Respect other people's property.
> Obey all school rules.

You may also want to allow some degree of student participation in rule setting. You can ask students to suggest rules, arrange for students to discuss why certain classroom rules are necessary, and perhaps allow students to select a few rules. This last suggestion should be taken up cautiously, however. Because middle school and secondary teachers teach different sets of students, having a different set of rules for each class is bound to cause confusion for you and hard feelings among some students. You may find yourself admonishing a student for breaking a rule that applies to a different class, and some students will naturally want to know why they cannot do something that is allowed in another class.

In addition to rules, various procedures need to be formulated and communicated. Procedures differ from rules in that they apply to a specific activity and are usually directed at completing a task rather than completing a behavior. To produce a well-run classroom, you will need to formulate efficient procedures for beginning-of-the-period tasks (such as taking attendance and allowing students to leave the classroom), use of materials and equipment (such as the encyclopedia, dictionary, and pencil sharpener), learning activities (such as discussions, seatwork, and group work), and end-of-the-period tasks (such as handing in seatwork assignments, returning materials and equipment, and making announcements).

Much of what Jacob Kounin, Carolyn Evertson, and Edmund Emmer mention in relation to the characteristics of effective instruction has been described in previous chapters. For example, they recommend that short-term (daily, weekly) and long-term (semester, annual) lesson plans be formulated and coordinated, that instructions and standards for assignments be clear and given in a timely manner, that feedback be given at regular intervals, and that the grading system be clear and fairly applied. As the next section illustrates, technology can help you carry out these tasks efficiently and effectively.

● Manage behavior of adolescents by making and communicating clear rules and procedures

Technology Tools for Classroom Management

A large part of classroom management involves such routine tasks as taking attendance, completing forms, maintaining student records, tracking student progress, and settling disputes. Although effectively carrying out such tasks is part of what makes a classroom well managed, they can be both tedious and time-consuming. Fortunately, technology tools now exist to help teachers keep records of student progress, organize teaching notes, create lesson plans and timelines, send individualized

For direct links to sites mentioned in the text, go to the Weblinks section of this book's web site.

notes to students, update attendance records, and generate electronic study guides (McNally & Etchison, 2000). Computer technology can help teachers create test question banks and individual tests (including alternate forms), as well as record, calculate, and graph student grades (Cardwell, 2000). Moreover, teachers can employ database, word processing, and spreadsheet files to maintain class rosters, develop seating charts, create professional-looking handouts and worksheets, and note missing student work (McNally & Etchison, 2000).

The web site of Myschoolonline.com (**www.myschoolonline.com/golocal/**) allows you to access the web sites of school districts around the country and their ideas about technology use and classroom management. You can also create your own electronic web-based gradebook and access it from any computer that is connected to the Internet.

Centralized Information Systems   The tools mentioned so far are designed for a single teacher's use in a single classroom. Centralized student information systems are designed to be used by all teachers in a school. With such systems, teachers can take attendance for their own records and have that information simultaneously transferred to a central administration computing system. In return, teachers have automatic access to this information as well as that related to student special needs, test results, and other pertinent data. Centralized information systems allow teachers and administrators more efficiently to access records of infractions and action taken, and any notes, photos, or other information that might aid them with difficult decisions regarding student behavioral problems (Telem, 2001; Thorn, 2001; Trefny, 2002).

Integrated Learning Systems   The message of the first section of this chapter is that an ounce of prevention is worth a pound of cure. In other words, clear classroom rules, good classroom management practices, and effective instruction are likely to prevent more instances of classroom disruption than heavy-handed, arbitrary punishment. And as we mentioned in the chapter on operant conditioning, an integrated learning system may be a useful tool for helping teachers achieve this goal. These systems, which are also referred to as curriculum courseware and management systems, provide a type of individualized instruction. They adjust the difficulty level and content of lessons to each student's pattern of progress, allow students to progress at their own rate, and provide teachers with continuous assessment reports that are keyed to state and professional organization learning standards.

In addition to keeping teachers continually updated on students' progress, these reports can be used to group students according to strengths and weaknesses for additional classroom instruction (Herr, 2000). As one fifth-grade teacher said, "Thanks to the management system, I clearly became more of a facilitator of learning, rather than the 'sage on the stage.' It did not replace my role as teacher; it simply made my job easier and expanded my role in ways I never thought possible" (Herr, 2000, p. 4).

New Classroom Roles for Teachers   What happens to the classroom management duties of teachers when schools adopt technology? Carolyn Keeler's (1996) study of thirteen elementary classrooms engaged in a schoolwide computer implementation project revealed that students were more on-task, self-managed, and engaged than before. As technology tools provided greater insight into student thought processes, the teachers became more interested in individual students and their progress. Given the perceived improvements in student motivation and behavior, as well as increases in student responsibility for their own learning, these teachers stated that they would most likely not return to the instructional techniques that they used earlier. In effect, technology significantly changed the teaching-learning environment of this school.

John Mergendoller (1996) argues that although many technology tools and ideas simplify everyday tasks, they also create new and more difficult managerial and instructional roles for teachers. "American teachers," he wrote, "will need to become experts in the management of complex classroom social interactions and the scaffolding of individual student learning" (p. 45). As schools combine various technology tools and systems, your classroom management procedures and disciplinary decisions will no doubt be highly complex yet, at the same time, vitally important to student success.

The following Suggestions for Teaching will help you become an effective manager of student behavior in the classroom.

Suggestions for Teaching in Your Classroom

Techniques of Classroom Management

1 Show you are confident and prepared the first day of class.

The first few minutes with any class are often crucial. Your students will be sizing you up, especially if they know you are a new teacher. If you act scared and unsure of yourself, you will probably be in for trouble. Even after years of experience, you may find that confronting a roomful of strange students for the first time is a bit intimidating. You will be the center of attention and may feel the equivalent of stage fright. To switch the focus of attention and begin identifying your students as individuals rather than as a threatening audience, you might consider using this strategy. Hand out four-by-six-inch cards as soon as everyone is seated, and ask your students to write down their full name, the name they prefer to be called, what their hobbies and favorite activities are, and a description of the most interesting experience they have ever had. (For primary grade students who are unable to write, substitute brief oral introductions.)

As they write, you will be in a position to make a leisurely scrutiny of your students as individuals. Recognizing that you are dealing with individuals should reduce the tendency to feel threatened by a group. Perhaps you have read about singers who pick out a single sympathetic member of the audience and sing directly to that person. The sea of faces as a whole is frightening; the face of the individual is not. Even if you are not bothered by being the center of attention, you might still consider using this card technique to obtain information that you can use to learn names rapidly and to individualize instruction. Whatever you do during the first few minutes, it is important to give the impression that you know exactly what you are doing. The best way to pull that off is to be thoroughly prepared.

2 Think ahead about how you plan to handle classroom routine, and explain basic procedures the first few minutes of the first day.

JOURNAL ENTRY

Planning How to Handle Routines

The Texas researchers found that very effective teachers demonstrated from the first moment with a new group of students that they knew how to handle the details of their job. They also conveyed the impression that they expected cooperation. To demonstrate that you are a confident, competent instructor, you should plan exactly how you will handle classroom routines. You will pick up at least some ideas about the details of classroom management during student-teaching experiences, but it might be worth asking a friendly experienced teacher in your school for advice about tried-and-true procedures that have worked in that particular school. (You might also read one of the books on classroom management recommended at the end of this chapter in Resources for Further Investigation.)

Try to anticipate how you will handle such details as taking attendance, assigning desks, handing out books and materials, permitting students to go to the restroom during class, and so forth. If you don't plan ahead, you will have to come up with an improvised policy on the spur of the moment, and that policy might turn out to be highly inefficient or in conflict with school regulations.

③ Establish class rules, call attention to them, and explain why they are necessary.

• Establish, call attention to, and explain class rules the first day

Very effective teachers observed by the Texas researchers demonstrated an authoritative approach to classroom management by explaining class rules the first day of school. Some teachers list standard procedures on a chart or bulletin board; others simply state them the first day of class. Either technique saves time and trouble later because all you have to do is refer to the rule when a transgression occurs. The alternative to this approach is to interrupt the lesson and disturb the whole class while you make a hurried, unplanned effort to deal with a surprise attack. Your spur-of-the-moment reaction may turn out to be clumsy and ineffective.

When you introduce rules the first day, take a positive, nonthreatening approach. If you spit rules out as if they were a series of ultimatums, students may feel you have a chip on your shoulder, which the unwritten code of the classroom obligates them to try knocking off. One way to demonstrate your good faith is to invite the class to suggest necessary regulations and explain why they should be established. Whatever your approach, encourage understanding of the reasons for the rules. You can make regulations seem desirable rather than restrictive if you discuss why they are needed. Reasonable rules are much more likely to be remembered and honored than pronouncements that seem to be the whims of a tyrant.

EXAMPLES

• "During class discussion, please don't speak out unless you raise your hand and are recognized. I want to be able to hear what each person has to say, and I won't be able to do that if more than one person is talking."

• "During work periods, I don't mind if you talk a bit to your neighbors. But if you do it too much and disturb others, I'll have to ask you to stop."

• "If you come in late, go to your desk by walking along the side and back of the room. It's disturbing—and not very polite—to walk between people who are interacting with each other."

④ Begin class work the first day with an instructional activity that is clearly stated and can be completed quickly and successfully.

When selecting the very first assignment to give to a new class, refer to the suggestions for preparing instructional objectives proposed by Robert Mager and Norman Gronlund (see the chapter "Approaches to Instruction"), and arrange a short assignment that students can complete successfully before the end of the period. Clearly specify what is to be done, and perhaps state the conditions and criteria for determining successful completion. In addition, mention an activity (such as examining the assigned text) that students should engage in after they have completed the assignment. In the elementary grades, you might give a short assignment that helps students review material covered in the preceding grade. At the secondary level, pick out an initial assignment that is short and interesting and does not depend on technical knowledge.

EXAMPLES

• "Your teacher from last year told me that most of you were able to spell all of the words on the list I am going to read. Let's see if you can still spell those words. If you have trouble with certain ones, we can work together to come up with reminders that will help you remember the correct spelling."

- "The first chapter in our natural science text for this fall is about birds. I want you to read the first ten pages, make a list of five types of birds that are described, and prepare your own set of notes about how to recognize them. At 10:30, I am going to hold up pictures of ten birds, and I want you to see if you can correctly identify at least five of them."

- In a high school history class, ask students to write a brief description of a movie they have seen that depicted historical events. Then ask them to indicate whether they felt the film interpretation was accurate.

5 **During the first weeks with a new group of students, have them spend most of their time engaging in whole-class activities under your direction.**

The very effective teachers observed by the Texas researchers followed the strategy just described, which makes sense when you stop to think about it. You can't expect students to adjust to the routine of a new teacher and classroom in just a few days. Accordingly, it would be wise to make sure students have settled down before asking them to engage in relatively unstructured activities like discovery learning. Furthermore, group discussions or cooperative-learning arrangements usually work out more successfully when the participants have a degree of familiarity with one another and a particular set of background factors (such as a chapter in a textbook). Thus, during the first weeks with a new class, prepare instructional objectives that ask students to complete assignments under your direction. Postpone using the other techniques just mentioned until later in the report period.

6 **Give clear instructions, hold students accountable for carrying them out, and provide frequent feedback.**

All three of these goals can be achieved by making systematic use of instructional objectives (as described in the chapter "Approaches to Instruction") and by putting into practice the model of instruction described throughout this book.

7 **Continually demonstrate that you are competent, well prepared, and in charge.**

As students work at achieving instructional objectives, participate in group discussions, or engage in any other kind of learning activity, show them that you are a competent classroom manager. Arrange periods so that there will be a well-organized transition from one activity to the next, maintain smoothness and momentum, and don't waste time. Use a variety of teaching approaches so that you please most of your students at least some of the time. Show you are with it by being alert for signs of mischief or disruptive behavior, and handle such incidents quickly and confidently by using the techniques described later in this chapter.

8 **Be professional but pleasant, and try to establish a businesslike but supportive classroom atmosphere.**

- Establish a businesslike but supportive classroom atmosphere

If you establish classroom routines in a competent fashion and keep your students busy working to achieve clearly stated instructional objectives, you should be able to establish a no-nonsense, productive atmosphere. At the same time, you should strive to make your room an inviting and pleasant place to be. Keep in mind the points made in previous chapters regarding the importance of self-esteem, self-efficacy, and interpersonal relationships. Put yourself in the place of students thrust into a strange classroom with an unfamiliar instructor. Try to identify with your students so that you can appreciate how they feel if they do or say something embarrassing or have difficulty with class work.

One of the best ways to get students to respond positively to you and make them feel welcome in your classroom is to learn their names as quickly as possible (even if you have five sections of secondary school students to teach). To accomplish this feat, refer to the cards mentioned in point 1. Use the information that students have provided, perhaps supplemented by your own notes or sketches about distinctive physical and facial features, to establish associations between names and faces. Before and after every class period the first few days, flip through your pile of cards, try to picture the appearance of the students, and practice using their names. Refer to the description of mnemonic devices in the chapter on information-processing theory. Once you have learned a student's name, use it as often as possible to maintain the memory trace. Greet students by name as they come in the door, use their names when asking them to recite or carry out some task, and speak to them personally when you hand back assignments.

Another way to make students feel at home in your classroom is to try establishing a feeling of class spirit and tolerance for differences in behavior, dress, and beliefs (Osterman, 2003). One way to do this is to have a brief sharing period—similar to the sharing time you may remember from your kindergarten days—at the beginning of each period. Invite students to describe recent interesting experiences they have had or to give announcements about extracurricular activities. If a member of the class is injured in an accident or suffers a lengthy illness, buy a get-well card and have every member of the class sign it before sending it off.

TECHNIQUES FOR DEALING WITH BEHAVIOR PROBLEMS

If you follow the procedures just discussed, you should be able to establish a well-managed classroom. Even if you do everything possible to prevent problems from developing, however, you are still likely to have to deal with disruptive behavior. Therefore, techniques for handling disruptive behavior, the extent of disciplinary problems, and some of the factors that lead to misbehavior are topics that merit attention.

Influence Techniques

In *Mental Hygiene in Teaching* (1959), Fritz Redl and William Wattenberg describe a list of behavior management interventions called *influence techniques*. This list was modified by James Walker, Thomas Shea, and Anne Bauer in *Behavior Management: A Practical Approach for Educators* (2004). In the following sections and subsections, based on the ideas of both sets of individuals, we will offer specific examples roughly reflecting a least-direct to most-direct ordering. Some of these examples are also drawn from personal experience and from reports by students and teachers. You might use the Journal Entries to pick out or devise techniques that seem most appropriate for your grade level or that you feel comfortable about.

The value of these techniques is that they appeal to self-control and imply trust and confidence on the part of the teacher. However, they may become ineffective if they are used too often, and that is why we describe so many different techniques. The larger your repertoire is, the less frequently you will have to repeat your various gambits and ploys.

Planned Ignoring   As we pointed out in the chapter on behavioral learning theory, you might be able to extinguish inappropriate attention-seeking behaviors by merely ignoring them. Such behaviors include finger snapping, body movements, book dropping, hand waving, and whistling. If you plan to use this technique, make sure the student is aware that he is engaging in the behavior and that the behavior does not interfere with the efforts of other students.

Example

- Carl has recently gotten into the habit of tapping his pencil on his desk as he works on an assignment as a way to engage you in a conversation that is unrelated

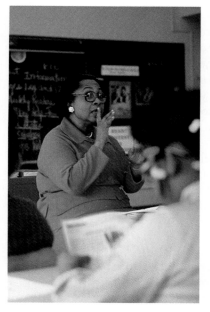

Signals such as staring at a misbehaving student or putting a finger to one's lips are examples of the influence techniques suggested by Redl and Wattenberg.

JOURNAL ENTRY

Signals to Use to Nip Trouble in the Bud

● Use supportive reactions to help students develop self-control

to the work. The next several times Carl does this, do not look at him or comment on his behavior.

Signals   In some cases, a subtle signal can put an end to budding misbehavior. The signal, if successful, will stimulate the student to control herself. (Note, however, that this technique should not be used too often and that it is effective only in the early stages of misbehavior.)

Examples

- Clear your throat.
- Stare at the offender.
- Stop what you are saying in midsentence and stare.
- Shake your head (to indicate no).
- Say, "Someone is making it hard for the rest of us to concentrate" (or the equivalent).

Proximity and Touch Control   Place yourself close to the misbehaving student. This makes a signal a bit more apparent.

Examples

- Walk over and stand near the student.
- With an elementary grade student, it sometimes helps if you place a gentle hand on a shoulder or arm.

Interest Boosting   If the student seems to be losing interest in a lesson or assignment, pay some additional attention to the student and the student's work.

Example

- Ask the student a question, preferably related to what is being discussed. (Questions such as, "Ariel, are you paying attention?" or "Don't you agree, Ariel?" invite wisecracks. *Genuine* questions are preferable.) Go over and examine some work the student is doing. It often helps if you point out something good about it and urge continued effort.

Humor   Humor is an excellent all-around influence technique, especially in tense situations. However, remember that it should be *good*-humored humor—gentle and benign rather than derisive. Avoid irony and sarcasm.

Example

- "Shawn, for goodness sake, let that poor pencil sharpener alone. I heard it groan when you used it just now."

Perhaps you have heard someone say, "We're not laughing at you; we're laughing *with* you." Before you say this to one of your students, you might take note that one second grader who was treated to that comment unhinged the teacher by replying, "I'm not laughing."

Helping over Hurdles   Some misbehavior undoubtedly occurs because students do not understand what they are to do or lack the ability to carry out an assignment.

Examples

- Try to make sure your students know what they are supposed to do.
- Arrange for students to have something to do at appropriate levels of difficulty.
- Have a variety of activities available.

Program Restructuring   At the beginning of this book, we noted that teaching is an art because lessons do not always proceed as planned and must occasionally be changed in midstream. The essence of this technique is to recognize when a lesson or activity is going poorly and to try something else.

JOURNAL ENTRY
Using Alternative Activities to
Keep Students on Task

Examples

- "Well, class, I can see that many of you are bored with this discussion of the pros and cons of congressional term limits. Let's turn it into a class debate instead, with the winning team getting 50 points toward its final grade."
- "I had hoped to complete this math unit before the Christmas break, but I can see that most of you are too excited to give it your best effort. Since today is the last day before the break, I'll postpone the lesson until school resumes in January. Let's do an art project instead."

Antiseptic Bouncing   Sometimes a student will get carried away by restlessness, uncontrollable giggling, or the like. If you feel that this is nonmalicious behavior and due simply to lack of self-control, ask the student to leave the room. (You may have recognized that antiseptic bouncing is virtually identical to the *time-out* procedure described by behavior modification enthusiasts.)

Examples

- "Nancy, please go down to the principal's office and sit on that bench outside the door until you feel you have yourself under control."
- Some high schools have "quiet rooms": supervised study halls that take extra students any time during a period, no questions asked.

Physical Restraint   Students who lose control of themselves to the point of endangering other members of the class may have to be physically restrained. Such restraint should be protective, not punitive; that is, don't shake or hit. This technique is most effective with younger children; such control is usually not appropriate at the secondary level.

Example

- If a boy completely loses his temper and starts to hit another child, lead him gently but firmly away from the other students, or sit him in a chair, and keep a restraining hand on his shoulder.

Direct Appeals   When appropriate, point out the connection between conduct and its consequences. This technique is most effective if done concisely and infrequently.

Examples

- "We have a rule that there is to be no running in the halls. Scott forgot the rule, and now he's down in the nurse's office having his bloody nose taken care of. It's too bad Mr. Harris opened his door just as Scott went by. If Scott had been walking, he would have been able to stop in time."
- "If everyone would stop shouting, we'd be able to get this finished and go out to recess."

Criticism and Encouragement   On those occasions when it is necessary to criticize a particular student, do so in private if possible. When public criticism is the only possibility, do your best to avoid ridiculing or humiliating the student. Public humiliation may cause the child to resent you or hate school, to counterattack, or to withdraw. Because of the ripple effect, it may also have a negative impact on innocent students (although nonhumiliating public criticism has the advantage of setting an example for other students). One way to minimize the negative aftereffects of criticism is to tack on some encouragement in the form of a suggestion as to how the backsliding can be replaced by more positive behavior.

● Give criticism privately; then
offer encouragement

Examples

- If a student doesn't take subtle hints (such as stares), you might say, "LeVar, you're disturbing the class. We all need to concentrate on this." It sometimes adds punch if you make this remark while you are writing on the board or helping some other student.

- Act completely flabbergasted, as though the misbehavior seems so inappropriate that you can't comprehend it. A kindergarten teacher used this technique to perfection. She would say, "Adam! Is that you?" (Adam has been belting Lucy with a shovel.) "I can't believe my eyes. I wonder if you would help me over here." Obviously, this gambit can't be used too often, and the language and degree of exaggeration have to be altered a bit for older students. But indicating that you expect good behavior and providing an immediate opportunity for the backslider to substitute good deeds can be very effective.

Defining Limits   In learning about rules and regulations, children go through a process of testing the limits. Two-year-olds particularly, when they have learned how to walk and talk and manipulate things, feel the urge to assert their independence. In addition, they need to find out exactly what the house rules are. (Does Mommy *really* mean it when she says, "Don't take the pots out of the cupboard"? Does Daddy *really* mean it when he says, "Don't play with that hammer"?) Older children do the same thing, especially with new teachers and in new situations. The technique of defining limits includes not only establishing rules (as noted earlier) but also enforcing them.

Examples

- Establish class rules, with or without the assistance of students, and make sure the rules are understood.
- When someone tests the rules, show that they are genuine and that there *are* limits.

Postsituational Follow-Up   Classroom discipline occasionally has to be applied in a tense, emotion-packed atmosphere. When this happens, it often helps to have a postsituational discussion—in private if an individual is involved, with the whole class if it was a groupwide situation.

Examples

- In a private conference: "Leila, I'm sorry I had to ask you to leave the room, but you were getting kind of carried away."
- "Well, everybody, things got a bit wild during those group work sessions. I want you to enjoy yourselves, but we practically had a riot going, didn't we? And that's why I had to ask you to stop. Let's try to hold it down to a dull roar tomorrow."

Marginal Use of Interpretation   Analysis of behavior can sometimes be made while it is occurring rather than afterward. The purpose here is to help students become aware of potential trouble and make efforts to control it.

Example

- To a restless and cranky prelunch class, you might say, "I know that you're getting hungry and that you're restless and tired, but let's give it all we've got for ten minutes more. I'll give you the last five minutes for some free visiting time."

I-Messages

JOURNAL ENTRY
Using I-Messages

● I-message: tell how you feel about an unacceptable situation

In *Teacher and Child*, Haim Ginott offers a cardinal principle of communication: "Talk to the situation, not to the personality and character" (1972, p. 84). Instead of making derogatory remarks about the personalities of two boys who have just thrown bread at each other, Ginott suggests that as a teacher you deliver an **I-message** explaining how you feel. Don't say, "You are a couple of pigs"; say, "I get angry when I see bread thrown around. This room needs cleaning." According to Ginott, guilty students who are told why a teacher is angry will realize the teacher is a real person, and this realization will cause them to strive to mend their ways.

Ginott offers several examples of this cardinal principle of communication in Chapter 4 of *Teacher and Child*. And in Chapter 6 he offers some observations on discipline:

- Seek alternatives to punishment.
- Try not to diminish a misbehaving student's self-esteem.
- Try to provide face-saving exits.

Despite the fact that Ginott's work is over thirty years old, its usefulness is demonstrated by the fact that his ideas appear regularly in recent books and articles on classroom management (for instance, Cangelosi, 2004; DiGiulio, 2000; Palmer, 2001).

Problem Ownership and Active Listening

● Determine who owns a problem before deciding on course of action

In *TET: Teacher Effectiveness Training* (1974), Thomas Gordon suggests that teachers try to determine who owns a problem before they decide how to handle that problem. If a student's misbehavior (such as disrupting the smooth flow of instruction with inappropriate comments or joking remarks) results in the teacher's feeling annoyed, frustrated, or angry at not being able to complete a planned lesson, the teacher owns the problem and must respond by doing something to stop the disruptive behavior. But if a student expresses anger or disappointment about some classroom incident (getting a low grade on an exam), that student owns the problem.

JOURNAL ENTRY
Speculating About
Problem Ownership

Gordon suggests that failure to identify problem ownership may cause teachers to intensify difficulties unwittingly, even as they make well-intended efforts to diminish them. If a student is finding it difficult to concentrate on schoolwork because her needs are not satisfied, the situation will not be ameliorated if the teacher orders, moralizes, or criticizes. According to Gordon, such responses act as roadblocks to finding solutions to student-owned problems because they tend to make the student feel resentful and misunderstood.

The preferred way to deal with a student who owns a problem is to use what Gordon calls **active listening.** The listener is *active* in the sense that interest is shown and the talker is encouraged to continue expressing feelings; the listener does *not* actively participate by interpreting, explaining, or directing. The listener *does* respond, however, by recognizing and acknowledging what the student says.

For teacher-owned problems—those that involve misbehavior that is destructive or in violation of school regulations—Gordon agrees with Ginott that I-messages are appropriate. Instead of ordering, threatening, moralizing, using logic, offering solutions, or commenting on personal characteristics, teachers should explain why they are upset. Proof of the effectiveness of I-messages takes the form of anecdotes reported in *TET* and provided by teachers who used the technique successfully. A principal of a continuation school for dropouts, for example, reported that a group of tough boys responded very favorably when he told them how upset he became when he saw them break some bottles against the school wall.

pause & reflect

Ginott and Gordon both recommend that when responding to misbehavior, teachers speak to the behavior and not the character of the student. How often have you seen this done? If it strikes you as a good approach, what steps will you take to use it as often as possible with your own students?

Active listening and I-messages are popular tactics for helping students understand and manage the emotional reactions that are a part of disagreements and conflicts. A high school assistant principal, for example, arranged a series of five large posters on one wall of her office and named it the "Conflict Wall." The first poster provided a definition of conflict. The second poster listed steps that can be taken to reduce or eliminate one's anger. Poster three encouraged the use of I-messages. Poster four listed typical behaviors that escalate a conflict. The last poster described the use of active listening techniques (Phillips, 1997). Active listening was one of several components of a conflict resolution program that was made part of all subject-matter instruction in the K–12 curriculum of the Montgomery County (Maryland) school system. For example, seventh-grade language arts students were asked to show how active listening on the part of the characters of a short story might have changed the story's outcome (Jeweler & Barnes-Robinson, 1999).

Some practical suggestions for handling problem behavior appear in the following Suggestions for Teaching in Your Classroom.

Handling Problem Behavior

1 Have a variety of influence techniques planned in advance.

You may save yourself a great deal of trouble, embarrassment, and strain if you plan ahead. When first-year teachers are asked which aspects of teaching bother them most, classroom control is almost invariably near the top of the list. Perhaps a major reason is that problems of control frequently erupt unexpectedly, and they often demand equally sudden solutions. If you lack experience, your shoot-from-the-hip reactions may be ineffective. Initial attempts at control that are ineffective tend to reinforce misbehavior, and you will find yourself trapped in a vicious circle. You can avoid this sort of trap if you devise specific techniques ahead of time. Being familiar with several of the techniques mentioned in the preceding section will prepare you for the inevitable difficulties that arise.

If you find yourself forced to use prepared techniques too often, some self-analysis is called for. How can you prevent so many problems from developing? Frequent trouble is an indication that you need to work harder at motivating your class. Also, check on your feelings when you mete out punishment. Teachers who really like students and want them to learn consider control techniques a necessary evil and use them only when they will provide a better atmosphere for learning. If you find yourself looking for trouble or perhaps deliberately luring students into misbehaving, or if you discover yourself gloating privately or publicly about an act of punishment, stop and think. Are you using your power to build up your ego or giving vent to personal frustration rather than paying attention to your students' needs?

2 Be prompt, consistent, and reasonable.

● Be prompt, consistent, reasonable when dealing with misbehavior

No attempt to control behavior will be effective if it is remote from the act that provokes it. If a troublemaker is to comprehend the relationship between behavior and counterreaction, one must quickly follow the other. Don't postpone dealing with misbehaving students or make vague threats to be put into effect sometime in the future (such as not permitting the students to attend an end-of-the-year event). By that time, most students will have forgotten what they did wrong. They then feel

Teachers who excel at classroom management have at their disposal a variety of influence techniques that they consistently and immediately apply to prevent or deal with misbehavior. In each case, they use a technique that is appropriate to the severity of the misbehavior.

resentful and persecuted and may conclude that you are acting out of sheer malice. A frequent reaction is more misbehavior in an urge to get even. (In such situations, guilty students are not likely to remember that you are the one doing the evening up.) However, retribution that is too immediate and applied when a student is still extremely upset may also be ineffective. At such times, it is often better to wait a bit.

Being consistent about classroom control can save a lot of time, energy, and misery. Strictness one day and leniency the next, or roughness on one student and gentleness with another, invite all students to test you every day just to see whether this is a good day or a bad day or whether they can get away with something more frequently than others do. Establishing and enforcing class rules is an excellent way to encourage yourself to be consistent.

Harshness in meting out retribution encourages, rather than discourages, more extreme forms of misbehavior. If students are going to get into a lot of trouble for even a minor offense, they will probably figure they should get their money's worth. Several hundred years ago in England, all offenses—from picking pockets to murder—were punishable by death. The petty thief quickly became a murderer; it was a lot easier (and less risky) to pick the pocket of a dead man and, since the punishment was the same, eminently more sensible. The laws were eventually changed to make punishment appropriate to the degree of the offense. Keep this in mind when you dispense justice.

JOURNAL ENTRY
Being Prompt, Consistent, and Reasonable in Controlling the Class

3 Avoid threats.

If at all possible, avoid a showdown in front of the class. In a confrontation before the whole group, you are likely to get desperate. You may start out with a "Yes, you will"–"No, I won't" sort of duel and end up making a threat on the spur of the moment. Frequently, you will not be able to make good on the threat, and you will lose face. It's far safer and better for everyone to settle extreme differences in private. When two people are upset and angry with each other, they look silly at best and completely ridiculous at worst. You lose a great deal more than a student does when this performance takes place in front of the class. In fact, a student may actually gain prestige by provoking you successfully.

Perhaps the worst temptation of all is to try getting back at the entire class by making a blanket threat of a loss of privilege or detention. It hardly ever works and tends to lead to a united counterattack by the class. One elementary school teacher had the reputation of telling her students at least once a year that they would not be allowed to participate in the Spring Play-Day if they didn't behave. By the time students reached this grade, they had been tipped off by previous students that she always made the threat but never carried it out. They behaved accordingly.

4 Whenever you have to deal harshly with a student, make an effort to reestablish rapport.

JOURNAL ENTRY
Ways to Reestablish Rapport

If you must use a drastic form of retribution, make a point of having a confidential conference with your antagonist as soon as possible. Otherwise, she is likely to remain an antagonist for the rest of the year. It's too much to expect chastised students to come to you of their own volition and apologize. You should set up the conference and then explain that the punishment has cleared the air as far as you are concerned. You shouldn't be surprised if a recalcitrant student doesn't respond with signs or words of gratitude. Perhaps some of the causes of misbehavior lie outside school, and something you did or said may have been merely the last straw. Even if you get a sullen reaction, at least indicate your willingness to meet punished students more than halfway.

At the elementary level, you can frequently make amends simply by giving the child some privilege—for example, passing out paper or being hall monitor at recess. One teacher made it a point to praise a child for some positive action shortly after a severe reprimand.

5 **If you decide that a problem is owned by a student, try to help the student solve the problem by using active listening.**

As we noted earlier, when a student experiences a problem (such as feeling upset about an argument with a friend or feeling anxious about an upcoming exam) that interferes with the student's classroom performance but does not interfere with the teacher's ability to instruct, the student owns the problem. Thomas Gordon (1974) believes that it is a mistake for teachers to tell such students that they must or should change their attitude and behavior, because this suggests that there is something wrong with the student and that he or she is at fault for having the problem. Instead, he suggests active listening, as in the following example:

STUDENT: *"It's just that I don't know what kind of a test you're going to give and I'm afraid it'll be an essay type."*
TEACHER: *"Oh, you're worried about the kind of test we are going to have."*
STUDENT: *"Yes, I don't do well on essay tests."*
TEACHER: *"I see, you feel you can do better on objective tests."*
STUDENT: *"Yeah, I always botch up essay tests."*
TEACHER: *"It'll be a multiple-choice test."*
STUDENT: *"What a relief! I'm not so worried now." (Gordon, 1974, p. 69)*

6 **When you have control, ease up some.**

It is extremely difficult, if not impossible, to establish a controlled atmosphere after allowing anarchy. Don't make the mistake of thinking you will be able to start out without any control and suddenly take charge. It may work, but in most cases you will have an armed truce or a cold war on your hands. It is far better to adopt the authoritative approach of starting out on the structured side and then easing up a bit after you have established control.

7 **Follow the advice of a master teacher.**

Margaret Metzger is a veteran high school English teacher whose sensible and practical views on modeling and clearly communicating one's goals to students were mentioned in earlier chapters. She has also written, in the form of an open letter to new teachers, an insightful and compelling distillation of her experiences in learning the art of classroom management (Metzger, 2002). Metzger's recommendations for managing the behavior of adolescents also illustrate a point we have made in previous chapters: successful teachers formulate practices that are consistent with, if not inspired by, research-based findings. Although we offer a summary of Metzger's recommendations, this is an article we urge you to read in its entirety and refer to repeatedly during your first few years of teaching.

Metzger divides her suggestions into two lists: "simple principles of survival," created during her early years of teaching, and "more complex principles," which grew out of her experiences during her middle teaching years. Here in summary form are both lists.

SIMPLE PRINCIPLES OF SURVIVAL

1. *Use a light touch.* Don't immediately resort to a highly aversive technique to control students' behavior. Instead, try such simpler methods as whispering instead of yelling, using humorous statements, changing locations, talking to students privately, calling students by name, smiling a lot, and ignoring some infractions.
2. *Let students save face.* Instead of describing a student's misbehavior and issuing a reprimand, which takes time and interrupts the flow of a lesson, indicate that you've noticed the misbehavior and use such quick and somewhat humorous phrases as "It's a good thing I like you," "Here's the deal: I'll pretend I didn't see

that, and you never do it again," "Consider yourself scolded," "Am I driving you over the edge?" and "That's inappropriate."

3. *Insist on the right to sanity.* To avoid becoming a burnout candidate, don't try to address all misbehaviors. Instead, make a list of possible classroom infractions and rank them. Decide which behaviors have to be addressed immediately, which can wait until some later time, and which can be ignored. Margaret Metzger, for example, decided to ignore students who came late to class. She was often so busy trying to get the class under way (returning papers, talking with students about makeup work) that she wasn't always in a position to notice who arrived late.

4. *Get help.* Learn who among the school staff (administrators, guidance counselors, truant officer, other teachers) are able and willing to help you solve certain discipline problems.

5. *Get out of the limelight.* This is Metzger's way of saying that you shouldn't feel as if you have to actively lead the class all period, every period. Learn to make appropriate use of student presentations, seatwork, movies, and group work.

MORE COMPLEX PRINCIPLES

1. *Ask questions.* Teachers often assume, incorrectly, that they have all the information they need to understand why one or more students misbehaved. Rather than make this assumption, take the time to ask students for an explanation. As Metzger says, "Sometimes you feel you have already spent too much time on the disruptive students. Frankly, you don't want to talk to them. Too bad. Do it" (p. 80). Administrators, other teachers, and the students' parents can also be useful sources of information.

2. *Give adult feedback.* If students are engaging in behaviors that you find disruptive or that indicate a serious underlying problem, don't mince words. Tell them directly. Here are two examples offered by Metzger:

   • "Your posture, your mumbling under your breath, and your tardiness all show disrespect. If you hate this class, you should talk to me about it. If you like this class, you should know that you are giving misleading signals." (p. 80)
   • "You have complained about everything we have done for the past two months. I now see you as a constant whiner. You probably don't want to give this impression, and it's getting on my nerves. So for the next two months, let's have a moratorium on complaining. You can start whining again in January. Does this seem fair?" (p. 80)

3. *Respect the rights of the whole class.* Try to remember that most of your students follow the rules and are just as deserving of your attention as those who do not.

4. *Ask students to do more.* This echoes a suggestion we have made several times in earlier chapters. Often the best-behaved classes are those in which the work is interesting, relevant to students' lives, and challenging.

5. *Bypass or solve perennial problems.* There will always be students who forget to bring a pencil or book to class. Rather than erupt every time this problem arises, take steps to eliminate it. For several dollars a year, you can buy a supply of pencils and allow students to borrow one for class. For students who forget to bring their book, you could keep a few extra copies on hand. To ensure that students return at the end of class what they have borrowed, you may need to require that they leave with you something they will not leave the classroom without, such as a shoe or a watch.

JOURNAL ENTRY
Techniques for Becoming an
Expert Classroom Manager

Metzger also advises teachers to reflect on themselves as a factor in classroom management by asking the following questions: "Does race or gender influence my response? Does this interaction remind me of another one? What from my background is being triggered? Am I tired, grouchy, or distracted? What else is going on in my life?

Who is watching? Is the problem mine or the student's? Has the student hit some raw nerve in me? Why am I threatened by the behavior? Why do I lack resilience on this matter? Am I being inflexible? Am I being authoritative or authoritarian?" (pp. 81–82).

Metzger ends her article with a copy of a twenty-five-point memo that she gives to all students at the beginning of each semester and that reflects her philosophy of classroom management. Read it.

If you would like to compare your current understanding of classroom management against the views of a veteran middle school teacher, take the brief six-item quiz created by Kim Chase (2002) that appears in the December 2002 issue of *Phi Delta Kappan*.

 For additional ideas for your journal writing, see the Reflective Journal Questions on the textbook web site.

VIOLENCE IN AMERICAN SCHOOLS

How Safe Are Our Schools?

You have probably read or heard reports about the frequency of crime in the United States, particularly among juveniles. According to figures compiled by the Office of Juvenile Justice and Delinquency Prevention (Lynch, 2002), thirty-six of every one thousand juveniles (those between the ages of twelve and eighteen) in 1998, acting either alone or with other juveniles, committed a serious violent crime. The good news about this figure is that it represents a large decrease from the peak year of 1991, when the rate was ninety-one per thousand.

● Incidents of crime and serious violence occur relatively infrequently in public schools

Since the kinds of behaviors one observes in schools tend to reflect trends in society at large, it is natural that a certain amount of violent behavior occurs on school grounds and during school hours. However, schools are still relatively safe places. One basis for that claim is that the most common types of school-based conflicts fall into a few time-honored categories: verbal harassment (name calling, insults, teasing), verbal arguments, and physical fights (hitting, kicking, scratching, and pushing). Most of the fights do not involve serious injury or violations of law (DeVoe et al., 2003). Second, a recent government report found relatively low levels of violence and crime (DeVoe et al., 2003). Here are the main findings from that report:

- From July 1, 1999, through June 30, 2000, sixteen school-age students (ages five through nineteen) were murdered at school. This figure is less than 1 percent of the 2,124 youth homicides recorded for that one-year period.
- In 2001, 161,000 students between ages twelve and eighteen were the victims at school of such nonfatal violent crimes as rape, sexual assault, robbery, and aggravated assault. By contrast, almost twice as many (290,000) of these crimes occurred away from school. Between 1992 and 2001, the rate of nonfatal violent crimes at school decreased from forty-eight per thousand students to twenty-eight per thousand students.
- The percentage of high school students who were threatened or injured with a weapon within a twelve-month period between 1993 and 2001 remained constant at about 8 percent.
- The percentage of students ages twelve through eighteen who reported being bullied increased from 5 percent in 1999 to about 8 percent (7 percent for girls, 9 percent for boys) in 2001.
- The percentage of students ages twelve through eighteen who reported avoiding one or more places at school for their own safety decreased from 9 percent in 1995 to 5 percent in 2001.
- The percentage of teachers threatened with injury by a student decreased from 12 percent during the 1993–1994 school year to 9 percent during the 1999–2000

school year. The percentage of teachers who were physically attacked during that same time period remained constant at about 4 percent. During the 1999–2000 school year, three times as many elementary grade teachers (6 percent) as secondary grade teachers (2 percent) were physically attacked by students.

- During the 1999–2000 school year, there were more occurrences of violence and crime in middle and high schools than in elementary schools, more in larger schools (more than a thousand students) than in smaller (less than three hundred students) schools, and more among males than among females.

These findings suggest that overall crime rates in schools are decreasing, that students feel increasingly safe at school, and that most teachers and students are likely to be physically safe in their own classrooms and school buildings. Nevertheless, school violence can occur in any school and at any time. Accordingly, you should be aware of the various explanations of school violence and the steps that can be taken to reduce its frequency.

Analyzing Reasons for Violence

Biological Factors   The research just cited noted that the level of violence was highest in middle and high schools and among male students. One of the clear-cut gender differences that has been repeatedly supported by consistent evidence is that males are more aggressive than females (Bloomquist & Schnell, 2002; Connor, 2002). Although the cause of this difference cannot be traced precisely, it is likely due in part to one or more of the following neurological, hormonal, and physiological factors: an overactive behavioral activation system and an underactive behavioral inhibition system (both of which are located in the frontal lobes of the brain), below-average levels of neurotransmitters, higher than average levels of testosterone, elevated levels of lead in the bloodstream, and a higher tolerance for pain (Bloomquist & Schnell, 2002; Connor, 2002).

● Male aggressiveness due to biological and cultural factors

Gender-Related Cultural Influences   As noted in the discussion of age-level characteristics in an earlier chapter, there is evidence that young girls in our society are encouraged to be dependent and to be eager to please adults, while young boys are encouraged to assert their independence (Carter, 1987; Lancey, 2002). Furthermore, it appears that boys are more likely than girls to be reinforced by aggressive and antisocial peers for assertive and illegal forms of behavior (Bloomquist & Schnell, 2002). These gender-related cultural influences may partly account for the fact that boys are more likely than girls to engage in such overt aggressive behaviors as fighting, bullying, robbery, and sexual assault and, particularly in the later elementary and middle school years, such covert aggressive behaviors as stealing, lying, vandalism, and setting fires. Girls, on the other hand, are more likely than boys to engage in what is called relational aggression—the withholding or termination of friendships and other social contacts, and spreading rumors in order to hurt another girl's feelings (Bloomquist & Schnell, 2002; Connor, 2002).

The same reasoning may well apply to disruptive behavior in the classroom. A boy who talks back to the teacher or shoves another boy in a skirmish in the cafeteria is probably more likely to draw a favorable response from peers than is a girl who exhibits the same behavior. This cultural difference adds to the physiological factors that predispose boys to express frustration and hostility in physical and assertive ways.

Academic Skills and Performance   Boys also seem more likely than girls to experience feelings of frustration and hostility in school. For a variety of reasons (more rapid maturity, desire to please adults, superiority in verbal skills), girls earn higher grades, on the average, than boys do. A low grade almost inevitably arouses feelings of resentment and anger. In fact, any kind of negative evaluation is a very direct threat to a student's self-esteem. Thus, a middle school, junior high, or high school boy who has received an unbroken succession of low grades and is unlikely to graduate may experience extreme frustration and anger. Even poor students are likely to be aware that their chances of getting a decent job are severely limited by the absence of a high school diploma.

● Middle school and junior high boys with low grades may feel trapped

Older high school boys can escape further humiliation by dropping out of school, but middle school and junior high boys cannot legally resort to the same solution, which may partially explain why, as of 2001, the crime rate at school or on the way to school is about 25 percent higher among sixth, seventh, and eighth graders than among high school students (DeVoe et al., 2003).

Interpersonal Cognitive Problem-Solving Skills Children who get along reasonably well with their peers do so in part because they are able to formulate realistic plans to satisfy their social goals and can think of several possible solutions to interpersonal problems. The former skill is referred to as *means-ends thinking*, and the latter is called *alternative solution thinking*. Students who are deficient in these two interpersonal cognitive problem-solving skills are more likely than others to show an inability to delay gratification, have difficulty making friends, have emotional blow-ups when frustrated, show less sympathy to others in distress, and exhibit verbal and physical aggression (Shure, 1999). This chapter's Case in Print describes how one school district attempted to increase means-end thinking and alternative solution thinking among its students.

Psychosocial Factors Other explanations of disruptive classroom behavior are supplied by Erik Erikson's and James Marcia's observations on identity, which we discussed in the chapter on stage theories of development. A teenager who has failed to make a clear occupational choice, is confused about gender roles, or does not experience acceptance "by those who count" may exhibit what Erikson called a negative identity. Instead of striving to behave in ways that parents and teachers respond to positively, negative-identity teenagers may deliberately engage in opposite forms of behavior (Lowry, Sleet, Duncan, Powell, & Kolbe, 1995).

● Misbehavior of high school students may reveal lack of positive identity

This hypothesis has been supported by a study of two thousand middle and high school students. Those classified as having a diffusion identity status (no serious thought given or commitment made to occupational and gender roles) were much more likely than adolescents classified as having an achievement status to exhibit behaviors characteristic of both a conduct disorder and attention-deficit/hyperactivity disorder (Adams et al., 2001).

School Environment So far we have mentioned the role of biological, gender-related cultural, academic, cognitive, and psychosocial factors in school violence. Each of these explanations places the responsibility for violent behavior largely or entirely on the individual. Other explanations focus instead on schools that are poorly designed and do not meet the needs of their students. Violent behavior, in this view, is seen as a natural (though unacceptable) response to schools that are too large, impersonal, and competitive; that do not enforce rules fairly or consistently; that use punitive ways of resolving conflict; and that impose an unimaginative, meaningless curriculum on students (Lowry et al., 1995; Bloomquist & Schnell, 2002).

pause & reflect

Do you agree with the argument that school violence can be caused by a nonmeaningful, unimaginative curriculum? If so, what can you do to make the subjects you teach lively, interesting, and useful?

Reducing School Violence and Misbehavior

Classroom Interventions Since most teachers work with two dozen or more students, some of whom have a disability, and typically have no assistance, classroom interventions that are designed to prevent misbehavior and keep small disruptions from escalating into serious problems need to be both effective and easy to implement.

Case in Print

Fighting the Urge to Fight

Children who get along reasonably well with their peers do so in part because they are able to formulate realistic plans to satisfy their social goals and can think of several possible solutions to interpersonal problems. The former skill is referred to as means-ends thinking, and the latter is called alternative solution thinking. Students who are deficient in these two interpersonal cognitive problem-solving skills are more likely than others to show an inability to delay gratification, have difficulty making friends, have emotional blow-ups when frustrated, show less sympathy to others in distress, and exhibit verbal and physical aggression. (p. 445)

Kids Learn Anger Management

JANET SUGAMELI
The Detroit News, 1/12/04

WASHINGTON TOWNSHIP — A puppet show helped teach 7-year-old Bobby Bilsky healthy ways to avoid violence.

If someone is teasing him, for instance, "I can say, 'Can you stop being mean to me and don't do it again,'" said Bobby, a first-grader at Indian Hills Elementary School.

The puppet show, a part of the Don't Strike Back health program offered by St. Joseph's Mercy Hospital of Macomb, is for elementary-age children. Last week, first-graders in the Romeo school district learned what to do when anger and stress build inside.

Two puppets acted out a scenario dealing with teasing and bullying when one student is called a "baby" in the lunchroom. The health staff periodically stopped the show to highlight the different elements and explain what anger looks like.

"Anger is not just an innate behavior in us," said St. Joseph nurse Tammy Fletcher. "We have to get it through their heads that bullying is not appropriate behavior."

"And that there are consequences to their decisions," added School Health Coordinator Flavia Scarsella.

St. Joseph's school health program received a grant from the Four County Community Foundation to purchase the puppets, stage and Don't Strike Back materials. The foundation serves the northeast corner of Oakland County, the southeast corner of Lapeer County, the southwest corner of St. Clair County and the northwest corner of Macomb County.

Janet Bauer, executive director of the group, said the grant came from the Healthy Seniors/Healthy Youth Fund, which supports programs to reduce violence and aid conflict resolution among youth.

"Our Youth Advisory Committee's recent survey of seventh-, ninth- and 11th-graders identified harassment and peer pressure among the top five problems in area schools," she said. "We believe working with elementary-aged students will help improve their conflict resolution and life skills for the rest of their lives."

Scarsella also noted that district administrators have voiced their interest in anti-bullying programs like this one.

Along with the puppet theater presentation, Scarsella and her team added scientific experiments to illustrate anger management for elementary school children. The program is tailored to certain grade levels. So far, Romeo is the first public school to offer the program. In coming weeks, other districts will pick it up, trying to comply with state legislation promoting anti-bullying campaigns.

Included in the elementary curriculum in the Romeo district are lessons on anger management and bullying. Indian Hills Principal Bob Smith said the St. Joseph's Mercy program was in line with what was already being enforced in the classroom.

"We're really trying to promote alternative ways to recognize and deal with anger at an early age. It's OK to be angry. It's part of human nature," he said. "We're just teaching the students early intervention on tips to control their anger."

During the presentation, the students learn that emotions resulting from anger are normal, but actions need to be controlled.

"There are a million times in your life people will frustrate or disappoint you. To say to [the children] that they shouldn't feel that way will only have them bottle it up inside," Fletcher said.

As part of their experiments, the water is poured into a sponge named "Sponge Bob" each time a student verbalizes a situation that makes him or her upset. Eventually Sponge Bob is oversaturated, which is supposed to illustrate stress.

"Sponge Bob tried to absorb everybody's anger, and he just couldn't handle it," Scarsella said to the students. "He is dripping out the stress."

In another experiment, students saw different ways children deal with stress. Three air-filled balloons illustrated popping, flying out of control and letting air out little by little.

"Letting it out one little bit at a time is better than letting it build . . . because then you might go a little crazy," Scarsella said to students. "It's not good to feel out of control because then you feel yucky afterwards."

Taylor Weaver, 7, said the balloon presentation made the most impact.

"I liked the balloon part because if you're really mad you know how to let it out," she said.

In another portion of the program, Scarsella held out a remote control. She told the students when they feel angry or upset, they need to pretend they can turn it off, change the channels, rewind or even lower the volume.

"You need to have a remote control inside you to control your behavior," Scarsella said.

"Sometimes when you say you're just kidding, you already have hurt someone's feelings," Fletcher said.

When the program was over, Caitlin Sabath said she was impressed with the resolution in the puppet show.

"If people are being mean to each other, you can just talk it over," the 7-year-old said.

Questions and Activities

1. Given what you know about the cognitive characteristics of primary and elementary grade children, do you believe that using puppet shows and concrete analogies to teach students anger management skills is a good idea? Why?

2. Janet Bauer, the executive director of the group that created the anger management program described in this article, maintains that providing children with conflict resolution skills will help them more appropriately cope with the harassment and peer pressure that is prevalent among middle and high school students. Do you believe this is a realistic expectation? Use what you learned from this and other chapters to justify your answer.

Some experts on school violence argue that impersonal and punitively oriented schools produce higher-than-average levels of school violence.

● Classroom disruptions can be significantly reduced by various approaches

One such intervention, which has been shown to work with mainstreamed students with a behavior disorder as well as regular students, combines two classroom management techniques mentioned earlier in this chapter, three behavior modification techniques that we described in our chapter on operant conditioning, and a reinforcement contingency that allows the other students in the class to be rewarded when the target students exhibit desired behaviors (Kehle et al., 2000). The components of this program include the following:

- *Classroom rules.* A relatively short list of five or six rules is posted where all students can see it. These rules are stated in a positive manner, are measurable, and specify basic expected behavior (for example, "Raise your hand if you need to leave your seat or the room," "Wait for permission to speak," and "Keep hands and feet to yourself").
- *Teacher movement.* The teacher circulates among the students to detect problem behaviors and reinforce desired behaviors.
- *Reinforcement.* Target students who exhibit desired behavior should be reinforced immediately, as frequently as possible, in an enthusiastic manner, and with eye contact.
- *Token economy.* As soon as the target students have followed all class rules for a specified period of time, they are awarded points. After a certain number of points have been accumulated, they can be redeemed for a tangible reinforcer. Among the tangible reinforcers are several highly desired objects (such as stickers or sports trading cards) called mystery motivators. When the student has accumulated enough points to redeem them for a tangible reinforcer, he spins an arrow that is attached to the center of a cardboard circle. The circle is divided into pie-shaped segments, each of which contains the name of a particular reinforcer. One segment is labeled "mystery motivator." Whichever segment the arrow lands on is the reinforcer the student receives. If the arrow lands on the mystery motivator segment, the student withdraws a slip of paper from an envelope that contains the names of several highly desirable reinforcers.
- *Response cost.* Students can lose points as a consequence of not following any of the posted rules.
- *Group contingency.* To keep the other students from feeling resentful toward the reinforced students and to capitalize on the power of peer pressure, something called a dependent group contingency is applied. When the target students receive their mystery motivator, the rest of the students in the class receive the same reward.

This intervention has produced declines in the frequency of disruptive behavior (such as making noises, talking out of turn, and wandering around the classroom) of as much as 50 percent (Kehle et al., 2000).

A very different approach to classroom management is called Judicious Discipline (Landau & Gathercoal, 2000). This program teaches students that they have both rights and responsibilities with respect to their behavior. That is, they are free to behave in various ways provided their behaviors do not threaten the safety, health, or academic well-being of classmates. To help students determine the appropriateness of their behavior, they are taught to ask themselves three questions that have to do with time, place, and manner: "Is this the appropriate time for what is happening? Is this the appropriate place for what I am doing? Is this the best manner?" The principles behind this approach and its application are reinforced during class meetings, during which the teacher and students discuss problems that have occurred and how they can be addressed. The guidelines for class meetings include the following:

- At least some of the topics are suggested by students.
- The students and teacher sit in a circle so that everyone has eye contact.
- Students' names are never used during a class meeting; just the issue or issues are discussed.

- Although all students attend class meetings, no student is obligated to actively participate.
- Immediately following the meeting, the teacher and students take a few minutes to record their thoughts in a journal.

Research on Judicious Discipline shows that it is associated with decreases in dropout rates, violence, and referrals to the principal's office, and increases in daily attendance.

Schoolwide Programs to Reduce Violence and Improve Discipline Although classroom interventions like the ones described in the previous section can make life less threatening and more enjoyable for individual teachers and their students, they do not address disruptive behavior elsewhere in a school and may conflict with other teachers' procedures. Consequently, some educators have designed violence-reduction programs that can be implemented throughout an entire school. This section describes three such approaches.

Unified Discipline In a program called Unified Discipline (Algozzine & White, 2002; White, Algozzine, Audette, Marr, & Ellis, 2001), teachers, administrators, and other school personnel create a uniform approach to managing disruptive behavior. The goal of Unified Discipline is to create a consensus around the following program elements:

- *Attitudes.* The school staff agree that all students can improve their behavior, that learning to manage one's behavior is an important part of an education, that corrections for misbehavior should be administered in a professional manner, and that becoming angry with students for misbehaving undermines a teacher's instructional effectiveness.
- *Expectations.* The school staff agree to the rules for student behavior and to use the program's correction procedures in the same way whenever a student breaks a rule.
- *Rules.* The rules that govern student behavior are typically divided into categories. One school, for example, created a three-level system. Class III rules pertained to such behaviors as physically assaulting another person, bringing a weapon to school, and selling drugs, tobacco, or alcohol. Class II rules pertained to behaviors such as fighting, ignoring adult requests, and vandalism. Class I rules pertained to behaviors such as disrupting others and using inappropriate language. The rules that govern classroom behavior have to be, of course, appropriate to the students' grade level. One group of kindergarten through second-grade teachers decided that students had to follow all teacher directions promptly, speak in an appropriate voice, keep body parts to themselves, and stay in their assigned places. Teachers in grades 3 through 5 decided that students had to follow all teacher directions promptly, stay on-task, be prepared for class, raise their hand to be recognized, and respect the rights and property of others.
- *Correction procedures.* As with rules, correction procedures vary somewhat by grade level. In the lower grades of one school, a first offense results in the teacher's putting a green ticket in a pocket with the student's name on it. The pocket is stapled to a posterboard. A second offense results in a yellow ticket. At the third offense, the student receives a red ticket and has to sit in an exclusion area of the classroom for several minutes. For a fourth offense, the student gets a blue ticket and is sent to another room for a time-out of about twenty minutes. In the upper grades, students receive a verbal correction for a first offense, a loss of privilege for a second offense, and a time-out for a third offense. For students of all ages, teachers respond to infractions by stating the misbehavior, stating the rule that was violated, stating the consequence, and encouraging the student to follow the rule in the future.

Take a Stand!

Show Zero Tolerance for Zero Tolerance Policies

Zero tolerance policies mandate specific, nonnegotiable punishments, usually suspension from school, for specific offenses. These policies are typically aimed at curbing such serious offenses as fighting, sexual harassment, or bringing weapons or drugs to school. They are extremely popular, with as many as 75 percent of all schools having such policies. But, as we have pointed out many times in this book, popular ideas or practices are not always good ones. We believe that zero tolerance policies have more disadvantages than advantages and simply give the appearance that serious problems are being addressed. Here are several reasons why we believe educators should not support such policies:

- The same punishment is handed out for violations that seem to be the same but that involve very different behaviors and motives. Under the terms of a zero tolerance antidrug policy, do we really want to expel from school both the child who shares a zinc cough drop with a classmate and the child who brings marijuana to school?
- Zero tolerance policies do not teach students those behaviors that will produce positive reinforcement. This is why Skinner was adamantly opposed to the use of punishment as a means of modifying students' behavior.
- They result in more students being expelled from school than would otherwise be the case. For some students, being banished from an environment that they find aversive is positively reinforcing and encourages them to continue to exhibit those behaviors that produce suspension.
- Many research studies have failed to find a relationship between such policies and significant reductions in school violence.
- In some cases in which students were automatically expelled from school, extenuating circumstances should have led to a different decision.
- More often than not, courts will support an administrator's decision to suspend a student where the circumstances warrant, making zero tolerance policies redundant.

What are your views of zero tolerance policies? Have you seen them applied in your community? To explore this issue further, go to the Take a Stand! section of the textbook web site.

- *Roles.* The principal's role is to support teachers when they follow the Unified Discipline procedures and, for the most serious offenses, make decisions about consequences based on a student's needs, history, and the circumstances surrounding the misbehavior (a refreshing change from the mindless uniform punishments dictated by "zero tolerance" policies). The teachers' role is to support the principal and not engage in second-guessing with other teachers, students, or parents.

In one elementary school, the Unified Discipline program resulted in a 20 percent decrease in referrals of students to the principal's office during the first year and decreases of 50 percent or more in subsequent years, fewer violations of classroom rules, and increases in the amount of time students spent on-task (Algozzine & White, 2002).

Peer Mentoring Another approach that some schools have taken to reducing school violence and misbehavior is to create a positive school environment. For example, Crystal City High School in Crystal City, Missouri, has used a peer mentoring program to meet the safety, belongingness, and esteem needs of Maslow's theory that we discussed in previous chapters. Junior and senior students who meet the school's criteria for grade-point average, attendance, citizenship, and trustworthiness are eligible to volunteer to mentor one or two freshmen. Mentors participate in discussions of issues facing young high school teens, are trained in team-building and basic counseling skills, and are told when it is appropriate to involve the school counselor. Meetings between mentors and mentees take place about once every three weeks and cover such topics as participation in classroom discussions, study skills, problems with students or teachers, and problems at home. Mentors also provide tutoring and help with homework.

The effect of this program on the overall school climate was quite noticeable to the faculty. Previously, as in many other high schools, there was constant tension between individual students and groups of students. Suspensions were a common occurrence. After the mentor program had been in effect for several years, an atmosphere of cooperation, friendliness, and being at ease became the norm. Between 1994–1995 and 1998–1999, out-of-school suspensions decreased by 40 percent, the dropout rate declined to 3 percent, and average daily attendance improved to 93 percent. As older students became concerned about the welfare of their mentees, the hazing of freshmen became rare. The popularity of the program is such that over 95 percent of freshmen participate and over 60 percent of juniors and seniors apply to be mentors.

One approach to reducing school violence is to train students to mediate disputes between other students.

● Violence less likely when school-wide programs teach students constructive ways to handle conflicts

If you were a primary or elementary grade teacher and had to choose between a program like Don't Strike Back (described in the Case in Print) and a peer mediation program like the Resolving Conflict Creatively Program, which one would you choose? Why?

Of those who become mentors, 100 percent said they would volunteer to do it again (Stader & Gagnepain, 2000).

Resolving Conflict Creatively Program   A somewhat different approach to decreasing physical violence, particularly between students, is the Resolving Conflict Creatively Program (RCCP), created by Linda Lantieri in 1985. The goal of the program is to teach students how to use nonviolent conflict resolution techniques in place of their more normal and more violent methods. Students are trained by teachers to monitor the school environment (such as the playground, the cafeteria, and hallways) for imminent or actual physical confrontations between students. For example, picture two students who are arguing about a comment that struck one as an insult. As the accusations and counteraccusations escalate, one student threatens to hit the other. At that moment, one or two other students who are wearing T-shirts with the word *mediator* printed across the front and back intervene and ask if the two students would like help in resolving their problem. The mediating students may suggest that they all move to a quieter area where they can talk. The mediators then establish certain ground rules, such as each student gets a turn to talk without being interrupted and name calling is not allowed.

RCCP was designed as a primary prevention program. This means that all students, even those not prone to violence, are taught how to prevent disagreements from becoming violent confrontations. In schools where the program has been implemented, teachers have noted less physical violence in their classrooms, fewer insults and verbal putdowns, and greater spontaneous use of conflict resolution skills (Lantieri, 1995).

Nevertheless, educators noticed that the program did not produce desirable results with all students. So during the 1997–1998 school year, an intervention component was added for children who exhibit behaviors that are associated with violent behavior in later years. School counselors and RCCP-trained teachers, working with groups of fifteen to twenty children, engaged the students in activities that were designed to increase a sense of social responsibility (caring and cooperative behaviors, for example) and develop such interpersonal skills as active listening. The capstone of this thirty-week program is the social action project. The group has to decide on and implement a community service project, such as fixing dinner for a family in need of assistance, making Easter baskets for the mentally disabled residents of a nearby center, or collecting books and art materials for a children's hospital. An evaluation of this new component reported improvements in listening skills, anger management skills, ability to share with others, relationships with teachers and students, self-esteem, and attitudes towards school (Lantieri, 1999). RCCP has been adopted by four hundred schools in the United States and by schools in Brazil, England, and Puerto Rico (Roerden, 2001).

Additional information about RCCP, the states and school districts in which it has been implemented, and whom to contact can be found on the following web site: **www.esrnational.org/about-rccp.html**.

Using Technology to Keep Students in School

As we pointed out previously, students who exhibit poor academic performance and believe that their teachers don't care about them are prone to engage in disruptive and violent behavior. They are also at risk for dropping out of school. In 2000, 10.9 percent of sixteen- to twenty-four-year-olds were classified as dropouts (were out of school and had not earned a diploma or alternative credential). The percentages for white, black, and Hispanic youth were 6.9 percent, 13.1 percent, and 27.8 percent, respectively (U.S. Department of Education, 2001b). Although these dropout rates have steadily fallen over the past twenty-five years, some believe that creative uses of technology may cause them to fall even faster. Here are a few examples of how some schools have used technology to reduce student absenteeism and the dropout rate:

- The Hueneme School District in Hueneme, California, created a "smart classroom" to help retain students who are at risk of dropping out. Students in this program got experience in computerized robotics, computer-aided manufacturing, desktop publishing, and aeronautics and pneumatic technology. Average daily attendance for this program was close to 100 percent (Cardon & Christensen, 1998).

- The Azusa Unified School District in Azusa, California, made extensive use of an integrated learning system to encourage student attendance and retention. Students spent four class periods each day working at their computer terminals on English, reading, social studies, mathematics, and science. By the end of the program's second year, the average daily attendance was 96 percent, and 93 percent of students remained in the program from one year to the next (Cardon & Christensen, 1998).

- Virtual high schools (high school courses and entire four-year programs that are available on the Web) are a recent development that may help students with high absentee rates—such as the children of migrant workers, students whose school districts don't offer desired courses, and students who are home-schooled—to take courses and complete their schooling. The virtual high school programs in eight states are described by Lottie Joiner (2002).

Although computer-based technology can be used in a number of creative ways to combat the problems of low achievement, disruptive behavior, absenteeism, and dropping out of school, we don't want to leave you with the impression that these are relatively simple problems for which technology is an all-purpose solution. We have, after all, spent this entire book showing you that school learning and instruction are complex phenomena. Technology is but a tool. And as with any other tool, its effectiveness is largely determined by how well educators understand its strengths and its limitations and how it can best be used in combination with other resources to serve various purposes.

To review this chapter, see the ACE practice tests and PowerPoint slides at the textbook web site.

Resources for Further Investigation

● Classroom Management

Although the second edition of *Mental Hygiene in Teaching*, by Fritz Redl and William Wattenberg, was published in 1959, its clear, concise, and well-organized analysis of influence techniques remains useful. Many of the techniques it describes have been used by teachers for years and will continue to be used as long as an instructor is asked to supervise a group of students. Recent textbooks that mention some of Redl and Wattenberg's ideas include *Elementary Classroom Management: Lessons from Research and Practice* (3rd ed., 2003), by Carol Weinstein and Andrew Mignano, Jr.; *Behavior Management: A Practical Approach for Educators* (8th ed., 2004), by James Walker, Thomas Shea, and Anne Bauer; and *Principles of Classroom Management: A Professional Decision-Making Model* (4th ed., 2004), by James Levin and James F. Nolan.

Other recent analyses of classroom management techniques can be found in *Relationship-Driven Classroom Management* (2003), by John Vitto; *Classroom Management for Elementary Teachers* (6th ed., 2003), by Carolyn Evertson, Edmund Emmer, and Murray Worsham; and *Classroom Management for Secondary Teachers* (6th ed., 2003), by Edmund Emmer, Carolyn Evertson, and Murray Worsham.

Discussions of classroom management that emphasize particular approaches or techniques can also be found. For instance, James Cangelosi emphasizes the use of methods that foster student cooperation in *Classroom Management Strategies: Gaining and Maintaining Students' Cooperation* (5th ed., 2004); and William Purkey and David Strahan emphasize the use of invitational learning in *Inviting Positive Classroom Discipline* (2002). In *Making Good Choices* (2003), Richard Curwin discusses the issue of classroom management from the perspective of teaching students to take personal responsibility for their actions. The book is directed at those who teach children from nine through fifteen years of age. *Common-Sense Classroom Management* (2002), by Jill Lindberg and April Swick, is a brief (ninety-five pages), readable, practical book written by a special education teacher (Lindberg) and an elementary grade teacher (Swick). Each chapter includes a brief discussion of how to deal with students who have been mainstreamed. Online resources for classroom management include Teacher Talk, a web site maintained by the Indiana University Center for Adolescent and Family Studies at **education.indiana.edu/cas/tt/tthmpg.html**. The site is a journal with articles on many topics, including coverage of classroom management. In particular, it includes a self-survey to help you determine your classroom management style. The survey can be found at **www.education.indiana.edu/cas/tt/v1i2/what.html.**

Teachnet.com (**www.teachnet.com/**) is another resource with tips for classroom management. Use the site's How-To area to find information on classroom management techniques.

Teachers Helping Teachers provides postings by teachers about particular topics, including classroom management. Many of these first-person comments are insightful and relevant to most beginning teachers. The site can be found at **www.pacificnet.net/~mandel/ClassroomManagement.html.**

The Educator's Reference Desk web site (**www.eduref.org/**) contains a classroom management page that will link you to an archive of resources, over twelve Internet sites, and a classroom management chatboard.

The classroom management page of the web site of the Jefferson County, Tennessee, Schools (**http://jc-schools.net/tutorials/classroom/management.htm**) is a comprehensive and practical resource that offers suggestions on five classroom management skills: creating plans that coordinate classroom procedures, materials, and schedules; communicating with students and parents; monitoring student behavior; being a classroom coach; and acting consistently.

● School Violence

A comprehensive approach to school violence interventions can be found in *School Violence Intervention: A Practical Handbook* (1997), edited by Arnold P. Goldstein and Jane Close Conoley. Eleven of its twenty chapters discuss student-oriented interventions, school-oriented interventions, and system-oriented interventions.

Ready-to-Use Conflict Resolution Activities for Elementary Students (2002), by Beth Teolis, is, as the title suggests, a collection of activities that elementary grade teachers can use to help students avoid conflicts and peacefully resolve those that do occur. The book is organized into four sections: Conflict-Resolution for Educators, Building the Groundwork for Conflict-Resolution, Conflict-Resolution Activities for Your Classroom, and Conflict-Resolution Activities for Your School. The activities for sections 2–4 specify an objective, materials needed, and directions.

Summary

1. Just as parents adopt an authoritarian, permissive, authoritative, or rejecting-neglecting approach to raising children, teachers adopt approaches to managing the behavior of students. The authoritative approach, which revolves around explaining the rationale for classroom rules and adjusting those rules as students demonstrate the ability for self-governance, produces the highest level of desirable student behavior.

2. Kounin, one of the early writers on classroom management, identified several effective classroom management techniques. He emphasized being aware of the ripple effect, cultivating withitness, coping with overlapping activities, maintaining the momentum of a lesson, keeping the whole class involved in a lesson, using a variety of instructional techniques enthusiastically, focusing on the misbehavior of students rather than on their personalities, and suggesting alternative constructive behaviors.

3. Researchers at the University of Texas found that in well-managed classrooms, students know what they are expected to do and do it successfully, are kept busy with teacher-designated activities, and exhibit little confusion or disruptive behavior. Such classrooms are marked by a work-oriented yet relaxed and pleasant atmosphere.

4. Classroom management can be made easier by using technology tools to carry out such tasks as test construction, record keeping, developing seating arrangements, analyzing space utilization, and monitoring student work. Software programs exist that teach students how to resolve conflicts nonviolently. These techniques continue to be valuable in today's classrooms.

5. Redl and Wattenberg proposed a set of behavior management methods in 1959 called influence techniques that were designed to help teachers deal with classroom misbehavior.

6. Ginott suggests that teachers use I-messages when responding to misbehavior. These are statements that indicate to students how the teacher feels when misbehavior occurs. The aim is to comment on the situation rather than on the personality and character of the student.

7. Gordon recommends that teachers determine who owns a problem and use active listening when the student owns the problem.

8. Despite reports in the media about school-based crime and violence, classrooms and school buildings are relatively safe environments.

9. Possible explanations for misbehavior and violence, particularly among boys at the middle school, junior high, and high school levels, include neurological factors, high levels of the male sex hormone testosterone, a culture that encourages male aggression and independence, feelings of resentment and frustration over low levels of achievement, lack of interpersonal problem-solving skills, and difficulty in establishing a positive identity.

10. Other explanations for school violence focus on the characteristics and atmosphere of schools that are so large that they seem impersonal, emphasize competition, do not enforce rules fairly or consistently, use punishment as a primary means of resolving conflict, and offer a curriculum perceived as unimaginative and meaningless.

11. Steps that classroom teachers can take to reduce school violence include using approaches that combine basic classroom management and behavior modification techniques

and teaching students how to monitor and regulate their behavior.

12. Schoolwide programs that may reduce violence and improve behavior include Unified Discipline, in which teachers and other school personnel adopt consistent rules and correction procedures and support one another in implementing them; peer mentoring programs, in which older students are trained in mentoring younger ones; and the Resolving Conflict Creatively Program, in which students mediate disputes between other students to prevent physical violence.

13. Some school districts have been able to reduce their absenteeism and dropout rates by getting students interested in using technological aids to learning.

Key Terms

ripple effect *(424)*   I-message *(437)*   active listening *(438)*
withitness *(424)*

14 Assessment of Classroom Learning

KEY POINTS

These key points will help you learn the important information in this chapter. To help you study, they also appear in the margins of the pages, next to the text where they are discussed.

The Role of Assessment in Teaching

- Measurement: assigning numbers or ratings according to rules to create a ranking
- Evaluation: making judgments about the value of a measure
- Summative evaluation: measure achievement; assign grades
- Formative evaluation: monitor progress; plan remedial instruction
- Tests can positively affect many aspects of students' learning
- Moderate testing produces more learning than no testing or infrequent testing

Ways to Measure Student Learning

- Written tests measure degree of knowledge about a subject
- Selected-response tests objectively scored and efficient but usually measure lower levels of learning and do not reveal what students can do
- Short-answer tests easy to write but measure lower levels of learning
- Essay tests measure higher levels of learning but are hard to grade consistently
- Performance tests measure ability to use knowledge and skills to solve realistic problems, create products
- Performance tests may vary in degree of realism
- Rubrics increase objectivity and consistency of scoring, align instruction with assessment, communicate teachers' expectations, help students monitor progress
- Performance tests pose several challenges for teachers
- Reliability and validity of performance tests not yet firmly established

Ways to Evaluate Student Learning

- Norm-referenced grading: compare one student to others
- Norm-referenced grading based on absence of external criteria
- Norm-referenced grading can be used to evaluate advanced levels of learning
- Criterion-referenced grading: compare individual performance to stated criteria
- Criterion-referenced grades provide information about strengths and weaknesses
- Mastery approach: give students multiple opportunities to master goals at own pace

Improving Your Grading Methods: Assessment Practices to Avoid

- Be aware of and avoid faulty measurement and grading practices

Technology for Classroom Assessment

- Digital portfolio: collection of work that is stored and illustrated electronically
- Special rubrics available to assess digital portfolios and presentations

Suggestions for Teaching in Your Classroom: Effective Assessment Techniques

- Necessary to obtain a representative sample of behavior when testing
- Table of specifications helps ensure an adequate sample of content, behavior
- Elementary grade students tested as much for diagnostic, formative evaluation purposes as for summative purposes
- Rating scales and checklists make evaluations of performance more systematic
- Item analysis tells about difficulty, discriminating power of multiple-choice items

 arlier parts of this book discuss three major aspects of the teacher's role: understanding student differences and how to address them properly, understanding the learning process and how to use that knowledge to formulate effective approaches to instruction, and establishing a positive learning environment by influencing motivation to learn and creating an orderly classroom. Now we turn to assessing performance, which is an equally significant aspect of the teacher's role. Virtually everyone connected with public schools, from students to teachers and administrators to state education officials to members of the U.S. Congress, is keenly interested in knowing how much and how well students have learned.

In this and the next chapter, we describe a twofold process for assessing student learning: using teacher-made measures to assess mastery of the teacher's specific objectives and using professionally prepared standardized tests to measure the extent of a student's general knowledge base and aptitudes. Although the items that make up teacher-made and standardized assessments can be very similar, if not identical, these two types of assessment differ significantly in their construction, the conditions under which they are administered, and the purposes for which they are used. In short, standardized tests are designed to highlight where students, classrooms, schools, and districts stand with respect to one another in terms of general levels of performance in various skills and subject areas. Period. Think of this as assessment *of* learning. Teacher-made assessments, by contrast, are designed to highlight students' strengths and weaknesses, give students timely feedback about the effectiveness of their study habits, and provide teachers with timely information that can help them make more effective instructional decisions. These assessments may or may not look like traditional "tests." Think of them as assessment *for* learning (Stiggins, 2002).

THE ROLE OF ASSESSMENT IN TEACHING

A list of chapter themes is available at this book's web site, accessible from **http://education.college.hmco.com/students.**

Assessing student learning is something that every teacher has to do, and usually quite frequently. Written tests, book reports, research papers, homework exercises, oral presentations, question-and-answer sessions, science projects, and artwork of various sorts are just some of the ways in which teachers measure student learning, with written tests accounting for about 33 percent of a typical student's course grade (Stiggins, 2001a). One elementary teacher estimated that on average, students take a written test once every twelve days (Barksdale-Ladd & Thomas, 2000). It is no surprise, then, that the typical teacher can spend about one-third of class time engaged in one or another type of assessment activity (McTighe & Ferrara, 1998).

Assessing student learning is a task that most teachers dislike and few do well. One reason is that many have little or no in-depth knowledge of assessment principles (Guskey, 2003; Mertler, 2000; Stiggins, 2002; Trevisan, 2002), largely because most states do not require prospective teachers to demonstrate competence in assessment in order to obtain a teaching license (Guskey, 2003). Another reason is that the role of assessor is seen as being inconsistent with the role of teacher (or helper). In fact, well-designed classroom assessment schemes contribute to student achievement (Popham, 2003; Stiggins, 2002; Trevisan, 2002). Moreover, teachers with more training in assessment use more appropriate assessment practices than do teachers with less training (McMillan, Myran, & Workman, 2002).

A basic goal of this chapter is to help you understand how to use knowledge about assessment to reinforce, rather than work against, your role as teacher. Toward that end, we will begin by defining what we mean by the term *assessment* and by two key elements of this process: *measurement* and *evaluation*.

What Is Assessment?

Broadly conceived, classroom assessment involves two major types of activities: collecting information about how much knowledge and skill students have learned (measurement) and making judgments about the adequacy or acceptability of each student's level of learning (evaluation). Both aspects of classroom assessment can be accomplished in a number of ways. The most common way that teachers determine how much learning has occurred is to have students take exams, respond to oral questions, do homework exercises, write papers, solve problems, create products, and make oral presentations. Teachers can then evaluate the scores from those activities by comparing them either to one another or to an absolute standard (such as an A equals 90 percent correct). In this chapter, we will explain and illustrate the various ways in which you can measure and evaluate student learning with assessments that you create and administer regularly (Airasian, 2001; Nitko, 2004).

● Measurement: assigning numbers or ratings according to rules to create a ranking

Measurement   For educational purposes, **measurement** is defined as the assignment of either numbers (such as the score from a traditional paper-and-pencil test) or a rating (such as the designation "excellent" or "exceeds standards" from a performance assessment) to certain attributes of people according to a rule-governed system. For example, we can measure someone's level of typing proficiency by counting the number of words the person accurately types per minute or someone's level of mathematical reasoning by counting the number of problems correctly solved. For an oral presentation, we might measure the quality by using a guide called a scoring rubric. In a classroom or other group situation, the rules that are used to assign the numbers or provide the rating ordinarily create a ranking that reflects how much of the attribute different people possess (Airasian, 2001; Nitko, 2004).

● Evaluation: making judgments about the value of a measure

Evaluation   **Evaluation** involves using a rule-governed system to make judgments about the value or worth of a set of measures (Airasian, 2001; Nitko, 2004). What does it mean, for example, to say that a student answered eighty out of one hundred earth science questions correctly? Depending on the rules that are used, it could mean that the student has learned that body of knowledge exceedingly well and is ready to progress to the next unit of instruction or, conversely, that the student has significant knowledge gaps and requires additional instruction.

Why Should We Assess Students' Learning?

This question has several answers. We will use this section to address four of the most common reasons for assessment: to provide summaries of learning, monitor learning progress, diagnose specific strengths and weaknesses in an individual's learning, and motivate further learning.

Summative Evaluation   The first, and probably most obvious, reason for assessment is to provide to all interested parties a clear, meaningful, and useful summary or accounting of how well a student has met the teacher's objectives. When testing is done for the purpose of assigning a letter or numerical grade, it is often called **summative evaluation** since its primary purpose is to sum up how well a student has performed over time and at a variety of tasks.

- Summative evaluation: measure achievement; assign grades

Formative Evaluation   A second reason for assessing students is to monitor their progress. The main things that teachers want to know from time to time are whether students are keeping up with the pace of instruction and are understanding all of the material that has been covered so far. For students whose pace of learning is either slower or faster than average or whose understanding of certain ideas is faulty, you can introduce supplementary instruction (a workbook or a computer-based tutorial program), remedial instruction (which may also be computer based), or within-class ability grouping (recall that we discussed the benefits of this arrangement in the chapter "Accommodating Student Variability"). Because the purpose of such assessment is to facilitate, or form, learning and not to assign a grade, it is usually called **formative evaluation**.

- Formative evaluation: monitor progress; plan remedial instruction

Formative evaluations are conducted more or less continuously during an instructional unit, using both formal and informal assessment techniques. Periodic quizzes, homework assignments, in-class worksheets, oral reading, responding to teacher

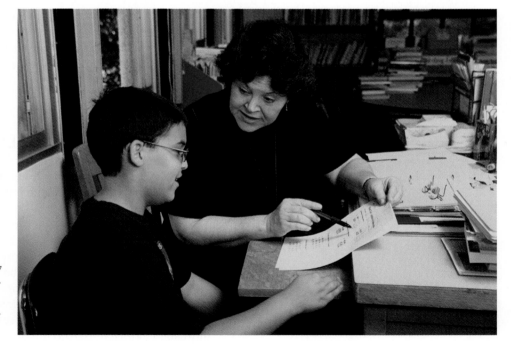

Classroom assessments serve several purposes. They provide information about the extent to which students have acquired the knowledge and skills that have recently been taught, they indicate whether students are understanding and keeping up with the pace of instruction, they may identify the particular cause of a student's learning difficulties, and they help students effectively regulate their study efforts.

questions, and behavioral observations are all examples of formative evaluation if the results are used to generate timely feedback about what students have learned, what the source of any problems might be, and what might be done to prevent small problems from becoming major ones later in the year. Unlike summative evaluation, which is a one-time event conducted only after instruction is finished, formative evaluation has a more dynamic, ongoing, interactive relationship with teaching. The results of formative assessments affect instruction, which affects subsequent performance, and so on.

Diagnosis   A third reason for assessing students follows from the second. If you discover a student who is having difficulty keeping up with the rest of the class, you will probably want to know why in order to determine the most appropriate course of action. This purpose may lead you to construct an assessment (or to look for one that has already been made up) that will provide you with specific diagnostic information.

● Tests can positively affect many aspects of students' learning

Effects on Learning   A fourth reason for assessment of student performance is that it has potentially positive effects on various aspects of learning and instruction. As Terence Crooks (1988) points out, classroom assessment guides students' "judgment of what is important to learn, affects their motivation and self-perceptions of competence, structures their approaches to and timing of personal study (e.g., spaced practice), consolidates learning, and affects the development of enduring learning strategies and skills. It appears to be one of the most potent forces influencing education" (p. 467).

Proof of Crooks's contention that classroom testing helps students consolidate their learning (despite students' arguments to the contrary) was examined by Robert Bangert-Drowns, James Kulik, and Chen-Lin Kulik (1991). They analyzed the results of forty studies conducted in actual classrooms and drew the following conclusions:

● Moderate testing produces more learning than no testing or infrequent testing

- Students who were tested more frequently (six or seven tests over the course of a semester) scored about one-fourth of a standard deviation higher on a final exam than did students who were tested less frequently. (See the chapter on standardized tests for a discussion of standard deviations.) This translated to an advantage of nine percentile ranks for the more frequently tested students.
- The advantage was even larger (twenty percentile ranks) when students who were tested several times were compared with students who were never tested.
- As students took more tests over the course of a semester, they generally scored higher on a final exam, but the increases became successively smaller for each additional test. The benefit of taking multiple tests seemed to peak by the sixth or seventh test.

WAYS TO MEASURE STUDENT LEARNING

Just as measurement can play several roles in the classroom, teachers have several ways to measure what students have learned. Which type of measure you choose will depend, of course, on the objectives you have stated. For the purposes of this discussion, objectives can be classified in terms of two broad categories: knowing *about* something (for example, that knots are used to secure objects, that dance is a form of social expression, that microscopes are used to study things too small to be seen by the naked eye) and knowing *how to do* something (for example, tie a square knot, dance the waltz, operate a microscope). Measures that attempt to assess the range and accuracy of someone's knowledge are usually called *written tests*. And measures that attempt to assess how

pause & reflect

Over the past ten to twelve years, you have taken probably hundreds of classroom tests. What types of tests best reflected what you learned? Why?

well somebody can do something are often referred to as *performance tests*. Keep in mind that both types have a legitimate place in a teacher's assessment arsenal. Which type is used, and to what extent, will depend on the purpose or purposes you have for assessing students. In the next two sections, we will briefly examine the nature of both types.

Written Tests

● Written tests measure degree of knowledge about a subject

As we indicated at the beginning of this chapter, teachers spend a substantial part of each day assessing student learning, and much of this assessment activity involves giving and scoring some type of written test. Most written tests are composed of one or more of the following categories and item types: *selected response* (multiple-choice, true-false, and matching, for example) and *constructed response* (short-answer and essay). They are designed to measure how much people know about a particular subject. In all likelihood, you have taken hundreds of these types of tests in your school career thus far.

In the next couple of pages, we will briefly describe the main features, advantages, and disadvantages of each test. As you read, bear in mind that what we said about the usefulness of both written and performance tests applies here as well. No one type of written test will be equally useful for all purposes. You are more likely to draw correct inferences about students' capabilities by using a variety of selected- and constructed-response items.

Selected-Response Tests Selected-response tests are so named because the student reads a relatively brief opening statement (called a stem) and selects one of the provided alternatives as the correct answer. Selected-response tests are typically made up of multiple-choice, true-false, or matching items. Quite often all three item types are used in a single test. Although guidelines exist for writing selected-response items (see, for example, the thirty-one guidelines for writing multiple-choice items discussed by Haladyna, Downing, & Rodriguez, 2002), many of these guidelines have not been validated by research. Hence, test-item writing is currently as much an art as a science.

Characteristics Selected-response tests are sometimes called "objective" tests because they have a simple and set scoring system. If alternative b of a multiple-choice item is keyed as the correct response and the student chose alternative d, the student is marked wrong regardless of how much the teacher wanted the student to be right. Selected-response tests are typically used when the primary goal is to assess what might be called *foundational knowledge*. This is the basic factual information and cognitive skills that students need in order to do such high-level tasks as solve problems and create products (Stiggins, 2001b).

Advantages A major advantage of selected-response tests is efficiency: a teacher can ask many questions in a short period of time. Another advantage is ease and reliability of scoring. With the aid of a scoring template (such as a multiple-choice answer sheet that has holes punched out where the correct answer is located), many tests can be quickly and uniformly scored. Moreover, there is some evidence that selected-response tests, when well written, can measure higher-level cognitive skills as effectively as constructed-response tests (Martinez, 1999; Nitko, 2004).

● Selected-response tests are objectively scored and efficient but usually measure lower levels of learning and do not reveal what students can do

Disadvantages Because items that reflect the lowest level of Bloom's Taxonomy (verbatim knowledge) are the easiest to write, most teacher-made tests (and many standardized tests as well) are composed almost entirely of knowledge-level items (a point we made initially in the chapter "Approaches to Instruction"). As a result, students focus on verbatim memorization rather than on meaningful learning. Another disadvantage is that although we get some indication of what students know, such tests reveal nothing about what students can do with that knowledge. A third disadvantage is that heavy or exclusive use of selected-response tests leads students to believe that learning is merely the accumulation of universally agreed upon facts (Martinez, 1999; Nitko, 2004).

Short-Answer Tests   As their name implies, short-answer tests require a brief written response from the student.

Characteristics   Instead of *selecting* from one or more alternatives, the student is asked to *supply* from memory a brief answer consisting of a name, word, phrase, or symbol. Like selected-response tests, short-answer tests can be scored quickly, accurately, and consistently, thereby giving them an aura of objectivity. They are primarily used for measuring foundational knowledge.

Advantages   Short-answer items are relatively easy to write, so a test, or part of one, can be constructed fairly quickly. They allow for either broad or in-depth assessment of foundational knowledge since students can respond to many items within a short space of time. Because students have to supply an answer, they have to recall, rather than recognize, information.

● Short-answer tests are easy to write but measure lower levels of learning

Disadvantages   Short-answer tests have the same basic disadvantages as selected-response tests. Because short-answer items ask only for short verbatim answers, students are likely to limit their processing to that level, and these items provide no information about how well students can use what they have learned. In addition, unexpected but plausible answers may be difficult to score.

Essay Tests   Essay items require students to organize a set of ideas and write a somewhat lengthy response to a broad question.

Characteristics   The student is given a somewhat general directive to discuss one or more related ideas according to certain criteria. An example of an essay question is, "Compare operant conditioning theory and information-processing theory in terms of basic assumptions, typical research findings, and classroom applications."

Advantages   Essay tests reveal how well students can recall, organize, and clearly communicate previously learned information. When well written, essay tests call on such higher-level abilities as analysis, synthesis, and evaluation. Because of these demands, students are more likely to try to meaningfully learn the material on which they are tested (Martinez, 1999; Nitko, 2004).

● Essay tests measure higher levels of learning but are hard to grade consistently

Disadvantages   Consistency of grading is likely to be a problem. Two students may have essentially similar responses yet receive different letter or numerical grades because of differences in vocabulary, grammar, and style. These test items are also very time-consuming to grade. And because it takes time for students to formulate and write responses, only a few questions at most can be given (Martinez, 1999; Nitko, 2004). But recent developments in essay scoring by computer programs may eliminate or drastically reduce these disadvantages in the near future (Myers, 2003).

Constructing a Useful Test   Understanding the characteristics, advantages, and disadvantages of different types of written tests, and knowing how to write such test items, are necessary but not sufficient conditions for creating an instructionally useful test. James Popham (2003), a noted measurement scholar, maintains that a useful classroom test has the following five attributes:

- *Significance.* The test measures worthwhile skills (such as the last four levels of Bloom's Taxonomy—application, analysis, synthesis, and evaluation) and substantial bodies of important knowledge.

- *Teachability.* Effective instruction can help students acquire the skills and knowledge measured by the test.
- *Describability.* The skills and knowledge measured by the test can be described with sufficient clarity that they make instructional planning easier.
- *Reportability.* The test produces results that allow a teacher to identify areas of instruction that were probably inadequate.
- *Nonintrusiveness.* The test does not take an excessive amount of time away from instruction.

Performance Tests

In recent years, many teachers, learning theorists, and measurement experts have argued that the typical written test should be used far less often than it is because it reveals little or nothing of the depth of students' knowledge and how students use their knowledge to work through questions, problems, and tasks. These individuals argue that because we are living in a more complex and rapidly changing world than was the case a generation ago, schools can no longer be content to hold students accountable just for how well they can learn, store, and retrieve information in more or less verbatim form. Instead, we need to teach and assess students for such capabilities as how well they can frame problems, formulate and carry out plans, generate hypotheses, find information that is relevant to the solution to a problem, and work cooperatively with others because those are the types of skills that are necessary to cope successfully with the demands of life after school in the twenty-first century (Cunningham, 2001; Eisner, 1999).

 For direct links to these and other web sites, go to the Weblinks section of the textbook web site.

In addition, the learning standards of such professional groups as the National Council of Teachers of Mathematics (**www.standards.nctm.org/**), the National Council for the Social Studies (**www.socialstudies.org/standards/**), the National Council of Teachers of English (**www.ncte.org/about/over/standards/**), and the National Research Council (**www.nap.edu/catalog/4962.html**) call for students to develop a sufficiently deep understanding of subject matter that they can demonstrate their knowledge in socially relevant ways. One way to address these concerns is to use performance tests.

● Performance tests measure ability to use knowledge and skills to solve realistic problems, create products

What Are Performance Tests? **Performance tests** require students to use a wide range of knowledge and skills over an extended period of time to complete a task or solve a problem under more or less realistic conditions. At the low end of the realism spectrum, students may be asked to construct a map, interpret a graph, or write an essay under highly standardized conditions. Everyone in the class completes the same task in the same amount of time and under the same conditions. At the high end of the spectrum, students may be asked to conduct a science experiment, produce a painting, or write an essay under conditions that are similar to those of real life. For example, students may be told to produce a compare-and-contrast essay on a particular topic by a certain date, but the resources students choose to use, the number of revisions they make, and when they work on the essay are left unspecified. When performance testing is conducted under such realistic conditions, it is also called **authentic assessment** (Gronlund, 2003; Janesick, 2001; Nitko, 2004).

Perhaps the clearest way to distinguish between traditional paper-and-pencil tests (like multiple-choice tests) and performance tests is to say that the former measure how much students know, whereas the latter measure what students can do with what they know. In the sections that follow, we will first define four different types of performance tests and then look at their most important characteristics.

Types of Performance Tests There are four ways in which the performance capabilities of students are typically assessed: direct writing assessments, portfolios, exhibitions, and demonstrations.

Direct Writing Assessments These tests ask students to write about a specific topic ("Describe the person whom you admire the most, and explain why you admire that

Performance tests assess how well students complete a task under realistic conditions.

person") under a standard set of conditions. Each essay is then scored by two or more people according to a set of defined criteria.

Portfolios   A **portfolio** contains one or more pieces of a student's work, some of which demonstrate different stages of completion. For example, a student's writing portfolio may contain business letters; pieces of fiction; poetry; and an outline, rough draft, and final draft of a research paper. Through the inclusion of various stages of a research paper, both the process and the end product can be assessed. Portfolios can also be constructed for math and science, as well as for projects that combine two or more subject areas.

Either the student alone or the student in consultation with the teacher decides what is to be included in the portfolio. The portfolio is sometimes used as a showcase to illustrate exemplary pieces, but it also works well as a collection of pieces that represent a student's typical performances. In its best and truest sense, the portfolio functions not just as a housing for these performances but also as a means of self-expression, self-reflection, and self-analysis for an individual student (Hebert, 2001; LaBoskey, 2000).

Exhibitions   Exhibitions involve just what the label suggests: a showing of such products as paintings, drawings, photographs, sculptures, videotapes, and models. As with direct writing assessments and portfolios, the products a student chooses to exhibit are evaluated according to a predetermined set of criteria.

Demonstrations   In this type of performance testing, students are required to show how well they can use previously learned knowledge or skills to solve a somewhat unique problem (such as conducting a scientific inquiry to answer a question, interpreting a graph, or diagnosing the cause of a malfunctioning engine and describing the best procedure for fixing it) or perform a task (such as reciting a poem, performing a dance, or playing a piece of music). Figure 14.1 shows a performance item for graph interpretation, the partially correct response of a student, and the corrective feedback offered by two classmates.

Characteristics of Performance Tests   Performance tests are different from traditional written tests in that they require the student to make an active response, are more like everyday tasks, contain problems that involve many variables, are closely related to earlier instructional activities, use scoring guides that clearly specify the criteria against which responses will be evaluated, emphasize formative evaluation, and are probably more responsive to cultural diversity.

Emphasis on Active Responding   As we pointed out previously, the goal of performance testing is to gain some insight into how competently students can carry out various tasks. Consequently, such tests focus on processes (that is, the underlying skills that go into a performance), products (an observable outcome such as a speech or a painting), or both. For example, a speech teacher may be interested in assessing how well students use gestures, pauses, and changes in voice pitch and volume; the accuracy and comprehensiveness of the content of their speeches; or both (Linn & Gronlund, 2000). An instrumental music teacher may want to know if students can apply their knowledge of music technique and theory to use the correct fingering and dynamics when playing a woodwind or piano (Clark, 2002).

● Performance tests may vary in degree of realism

Degree of Realism   Although performance tests strive to approximate everyday tasks, not every test needs to be or can be done under the most realistic circumstances. How realistic the conditions should be depends on such factors as time, cost, availability of equipment, and the nature of the skill being measured. Imagine, for example, that you are a third-grade teacher and one of your objectives is that students will be able to determine how much change they should receive after making a purchase

Figure 14.1 Example of a Performance Assessment: Interpreting a Graph

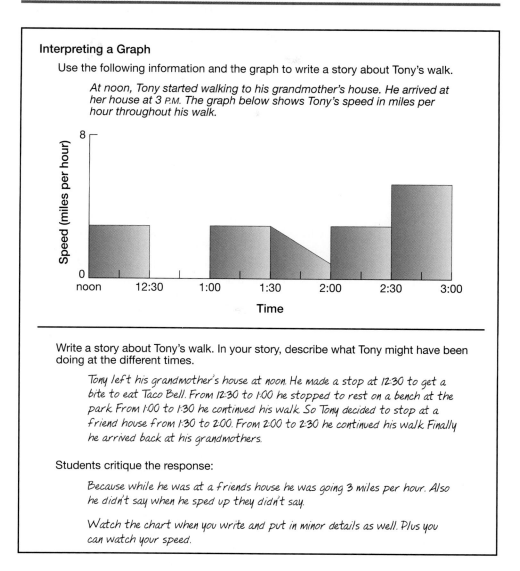

Interpreting a Graph

Use the following information and the graph to write a story about Tony's walk.

At noon, Tony started walking to his grandmother's house. He arrived at her house at 3 P.M. The graph below shows Tony's speed in miles per hour throughout his walk.

Write a story about Tony's walk. In your story, describe what Tony might have been doing at the different times.

Tony left his grandmother's house at noon. He made a stop at 12:30 to get a bite to eat Taco Bell. From 12:30 to 1:00 he stopped to rest on a bench at the park. From 1:00 to 1:30 he continued his walk. So Tony decided to stop at a friend house from 1:30 to 2:00. From 2:00 to 2:30 he continued his walk. Finally he arrived back at his grandmothers.

Students critique the response:

Because while he was at a friends house he was going 3 miles per hour. Also he didn't say when he sped up they didn't say.

Watch the chart when you write and put in minor details as well. Plus you can watch your speed.

SOURCE: Parke and Lane (1997).

in a store. If this is a relatively minor objective or if you do not have a lot of props available, you might simply demonstrate the situation with actual money and ask the students to judge whether the amount of change received was correct. If, however, you consider this to be a major objective and you have the props available, you might set up a mock store and have each student make a purchase using real money (Gronlund, 2003).

An example of a task that is realistic in content and intellectual demands but not in its setting (it takes place in the classroom) is "Read All About It!" Playing the roles of newspaper staff writers and editorial board members, students put together a special series for their local newspaper that compares and contrasts the five major wars in which the United States was involved during the 1900s (World War I, World War II, Korean War, Vietnam War, and Persian Gulf War). Writing assignments include feature articles, opinion columns, and letters to the editor. Editorial responsibilities include story editor, photo editor, mockup editor, layout editor, and copyeditor (Moon, 2002).

Emphasis on Complex Problems   To assess how well students can use foundational knowledge and skills in a productive way, the questions and problems they are given should be sufficiently open-ended and ill structured (Stiggins, 2001b). The problems contained in The Adventures of Jasper Woodbury program that we described in earlier chapters are good examples of complex and somewhat ill-structured tasks. They have several interrelated parts, provide few cues as to how the problem might be solved, and contain some uncertainty about what constitutes an appropriate solution.

Close Relationship Between Teaching and Testing   All too often students walk out of an exam in a state of high frustration (if not anger) because the content and format of the test seemed to have little in common with what was covered in class and the way in which it was taught. It's the old story of teaching for one thing and testing for something else. Performance testing strives for a closer match between teaching and testing. Often a performance assessment can be a variation or extension of a task used during instruction. For example, the mock store assessment mentioned earlier could follow an instructional activity in which students practiced making change.

This close relationship between assessment and instruction is not automatic, however; the teacher must deliberately establish it. For example, if in giving an oral book report, a student is expected to speak loudly and clearly enough for everyone to hear, speak in complete sentences, stay on the topic, and use pictures or other materials to make the presentation interesting, the student needs to be informed of these criteria, and classroom instruction should be organized around them. One proponent of performance testing cited the old farm adage "You don't fatten the cattle by weighing them" to make this point. He then went on to note, "If we expect students to improve their performance on these new, more authentic measures, we need to engage in 'performance-based instruction' on a regular basis" (McTighe, 1996/1997, p. 7).

By the same token, the assessment of students' performances should be limited to just the criteria emphasized during instruction (Nitko, 2004; Taylor, 2003). One reason that proponents of performance testing push for this feature is that it has always been a standard part of successful programs in sports, the arts, and vocational education. Football coaches, for example, have long recognized that if they want their quarterback to know when during a game (the equivalent of a final exam) to attempt a pass and when not to, they must provide him with realistic opportunities to practice making this particular type of decision. Perhaps you recall our mentioning in the chapter on constructivist learning theory that realistic and varied practice are essential if students are to transfer what they learn in an instructional setting to an applied setting.

pause & reflect

Have you ever taken any kind of performance assessment as a student? Did you feel that it accurately reflected what you had learned? To what extent would you use performance measures for such academic subjects as writing, math, science, and social studies? Why?

● Rubrics increase objectivity and consistency of scoring, align instruction with assessment, communicate teachers' expectations, help students monitor progress

Use of Scoring Rubrics   A **rubric** is a scoring guide that specifies the capabilities students should exhibit (also known as content standards), describes the qualitative levels or categories into which the responses will be sorted (also known as performance standards), and specifies how the responses will be scored (as separate elements or holistically). For writing tasks, which are probably the most common performance measures, some commonly used content criteria are clarity of purpose, organization, voice, word choice, grammatical usage, and spelling (Arter & McTighe, 2001). An example of a scoring rubric for an oral report is provided in Table 14.1.

Creating and using scoring rubrics, and providing them to students at the beginning of a task, is highly desirable for at least three reasons:

1. They increase the objectivity, consistency, and efficiency of scoring.
2. They help teachers match their instructional activities to the demands of the performance measure, the goal we discussed in the previous section.

3. By providing students with verbal descriptions and examples of the desired performance or product, teachers clearly communicate to students the types of behaviors that represent the range from unacceptable to exceptional performance and help students better monitor their progress and make productive changes in the quality of their work (Arter & McTighe, 2001; Whittaker, Salend, & Duhaney, 2001). Students with learning disabilities are likely to experience the greatest benefit from being given a scoring rubric and being shown how to use it (Jackson & Larkin, 2002).

As we noted in the chapter on information-processing theory, planning and monitoring are two components of strategic learning. Thus, if you want to help students be strategic learners, provide them with the measurement conditions that make that behavior possible. Although this type of preparation is unfortunately not a common part of everyday classroom testing, it is typically used in the performing arts, the studio arts, athletics, and vocational education.

Bear in mind, however, that scoring rubrics have their limitations. Although the rubrics used by two teachers to score writing samples may have some of the same content standards (such as clarity of purpose, organization, and grammar), they may differ as well (for instance, in the presence or absence of idea development, use of detail, and figurative use of language) because there are different ways to define good writing. Thus, any one rubric is not likely to represent the domain of writing fully and may provide few or no opportunities for scorers to reward certain desirable writing skills (Mabry, 1999).

Use of Formative Evaluation Earlier, we pointed out that tests can be used as a source of feedback to help students improve the quality of their learning efforts. Because many real-life performances and products are the result of several feedback and revision cycles, performance testing often includes this feature as well. As anyone who has ever done any substantial amount of writing can tell you (and we are no exception), a satisfactory essay, story, or even personal letter is not produced in one attempt. Usually, there are critical comments from oneself and others and subsequent attempts at another draft. If we believe that the ability to write well, even among people who do it for a living, is partly defined by the ability to use feedback

Table 14.1	Scoring Rubric for a Group Oral Presentation			
Level	**Content**	**Audiovisual Components**	**Group Members**	**Audience Members**
Excellent	Accurate, specific, research based, retold in own words	Are unique, add to presentation quality of materials used, are neat, present clear message	Each member is equally involved in presentation and is well informed about the topic	Maintain eye contact with presenters, ask many questions
Good	Less detailed, lacking depth, limited number of sources used	Support topic but do not enhance presentation; some attempts at originality, clear message	Most members are active; most members are informed about the topic	Some members of the audience not attending; questions are limited or off the topic
Minimal	Limited information, general, strays from topic, not presented in own words	Inappropriate, no originality, detract from presentation, message is confusing	One or two members dominate; some members do not seem well prepared or well informed	Audience is not attending; no questions asked or questions are off the topic

SOURCE: Montgomery (2000).

Take a Stand!

Practice Assessment for Learning

The classroom assessments that teachers devise are among the most powerful influences on the quality of students' learning, largely due to their effect on self-efficacy, interest, and the types of learning strategies that students construct. Whether these assessments have positive or negative effects on students depends on how they are constructed and the purpose for which they are primarily intended.

As we have noted in this and other chapters, classroom assessments can be used both to sum up what students have learned (summative evaluation) and to provide information about the effectiveness of instruction and students' specific strengths and weaknesses (formative evaluation). All too often, unfortunately, formative assessment tends to be overshadowed by the summative type. Many teachers are more concerned with giving students grades than with using information gained from assessment to improve their instruction. Although both types of assessment are legitimate, we encourage you to emphasize formative assessment because of its potential to positively shape students' learning.

To ensure that assessments serve as a positive force for learning, we believe teachers should take the following steps:

- Make sure that you are knowledgeable about, understand, and use the basic measurement concepts and practices described in this chapter. Don't fall into the trap that so many teachers have fallen into of treating classroom assessment as a necessary evil.

- Recognize that the most accurate and useful assessments of learning are composed of multiple and varied measures. Use the full range of assessments (written tests, performance tests, checklists, rating scales) available to you.

- Align the content of your assessments with your objectives, and fully inform students about the content and demands of your assessments.

- Finally, use the results to help you work even more productively with your students.

Have you been in classes where formative evaluation was downplayed in favor of summative evaluation? What did you think of that? For more on this issue, see the Take a Stand! section of the textbook web site.

profitably, why should this be any different for students (Stiggins, 2001a)? Some specific forms of formative assessment are dress rehearsals, reviews of writing drafts, and peer response groups (Gronlund, 2003).

Responsiveness to Cultural Diversity Traditional written tests have been criticized over the years for being culturally biased. That is, they are thought to underestimate the capabilities of many ethnic minority students, as well as students of low socioeconomic status, because they rely on a narrow range of item types (mainly selected response) and on content that mostly reflects the experiences of the majority culture. This criticism is based in large part on the constructivist view of learning: that meaningful learning occurs within a cultural context with which one is familiar and comfortable. If this is so, say the critics, then tests should be more consistent with the cultural context in which learning occurs. Performance tests have been promoted as a way to assess more fairly and accurately the knowledge and skills of all students, and particularly minority

students, because of their realism (including group problem solving) and closer relationship between instruction and assessment (Hood, 1998; Lee, 1998).

Much research on this issue remains to be done, but there is some evidence to support the arguments of the critics. In one study (Supovitz & Brennan, 1997), white, black, and Hispanic first- and second-grade students either took a standardized test of language arts or constructed a language arts portfolio. While the white students significantly outscored the black and Hispanic students on the standardized test, the gap for the portfolio assessment was smaller by about half. In another study (Supovitz, 1998), white, black, and Hispanic fourth graders took either an open-ended paper-and-pencil science test or a science performance test. Although the score of the white students on the paper-and-pencil exam was higher than the scores of the black and Hispanic students, there was no difference among the three groups on the performance assessment. Within groups, white students performed better on the paper-and-pencil measures than on the performance measures, and the black and Hispanic students scored higher on the performance measures.

Some Concerns About Performance Assessment   There is no question that alternative assessment methods have excited educators and will be used with increasing frequency. But some of the same features that make these new assessment methods attractive also create problems that may or may not be solvable. For example, a study of performance assessments used by twenty-nine seventh- and eighth-grade teachers in Ontario, Canada (Hargreaves, Earl, & Schmidt, 2002), turned up several problems.

One problem was the amount of time required by these tests. Because the goal of performance assessments is to reveal what students can and cannot do with the knowledge they acquire, they take more time to construct, administer, and score than standard tests. And writing anecdotal comments, conferencing with individual students, and reading through and grading portfolios takes time away from other aspects of instruction. One teacher interviewed by the researchers used the colorful metaphor of "portfolio prison" to denote situations in which one has to give up other activities (such as accompanying students on a field trip) in order to help slower students complete their portfolios. Another problem is that it was harder to explain to parents the relationship between how such tests are often scored (e.g., "meets the standard," "satisfactory performance") and the letter grades on students' report cards.

A third problem involved adopting new responsibilities. With traditional tests, the teacher's primary responsibilities are to provide effective instruction for the subject matter that makes up the curriculum and to determine the extent to which students have acquired that knowledge. The student's primary responsibility is to be prepared to demonstrate that knowledge in whatever way the teacher deems appropriate. Teachers typically spend little time helping students prepare for tests. When using alternative assessments, a teacher becomes more of a collaborator and facilitator than a gatekeeper. The assessment criteria are clear and communicated at the outset of instruction, and the assessment tasks are taken directly from the instructional activities.

● Performance tests pose several challenges for teachers

The last problem concerned the radically different purposes of traditional standardized tests and performance tests. Standardized tests are typically used to satisfy the summative evaluation purpose of testing. They are given at the end of the academic year and are used solely to rank and compare students, schools, and school districts. Performance-based classroom tests, on the other hand, lend themselves to the formative evaluation purpose of testing. They are given periodically to provide teachers, students, and parents with relevant information about the current level of student learning and to generate ideas about how performance might be improved. The challenge for the teachers in this study was not to let the school district's preoccupation with high-stakes tests (those on which poor performance has significant consequences for students, teachers, and administrators) crowd out their use of performance-based tests for formative evaluation purposes.

● Reliability and validity of performance tests not yet firmly established

In addition, there are questions about the reliability (consistency of performance) and validity (how accurately the test measures its target) of performance measures (see, for example, Bachman, 2002). In one study (Shavelson & Baxter, 1992), fifth- and sixth-grade students' scores on three science investigations were very inconsistent from task to task, thereby producing a relatively low level of a form of reliability known as *internal consistency*. Thus, to get a clear picture of whether a student understands the use of basic scientific principles, understands how to do scientific projects of a particular type, or can complete only the particular science project that is contained in the assessment, a number of tasks may be needed.

In another study (Herman, Gearhart, & Baker, 1993), samples of students' classroom writing that were included in their portfolios were scored higher than a narrative they wrote in thirty minutes under standardized conditions (an example of a direct writing assessment). The researchers could not determine which writing sample was a better estimate of students' writing ability. A second problem was that overall portfolio scores were substantially higher than the aggregate scores of the individual items that made up the portfolio, truly a case of the whole being greater than the sum of its parts.

Some performance assessments are, however, proving to be valid measures of achievement. The Work Sampling System is a performance assessment that uses checklists, portfolios, and summary reports to measure seven areas of development (personal/social, language/literacy, mathematical thinking, scientific thinking, social studies, the arts, physical development) of kindergarten and primary grade children. In one study (Meisels, Bickel, Nicholson, Xue, & Atkins-Burnett, 2001), it was shown to be a valid measure of achievement by virtue of its moderate to high correlations with a standardized achievement test.

Those Who Can, Perform

In recent years, many teachers, learning theorists, and measurement experts have argued that the typical written test should be used far less often than it is because it reveals little or nothing of the depth of students' knowledge and how students use their knowledge to work through questions, problems, and tasks. . . . One way to address these concerns is to use performance tests. (p. 461)

Teachers Look for New Ways to Measure Learning

DALE SINGER
St. Louis Post-Dispatch 1/26/98

Congratulations! You've been invited to Joe's birthday party along with Stephanie and Andrea and will get some of those terrific chocolate-chunk cookies baked by his grandmother.

But there's one problem: You have 15 cookies for four partygoers. What is the best way to share?

In the past, second-graders faced with this question on a test would be able to choose the right answer from a set of possibilities. As tests move away from multiple choice in favor of judging how well students can solve problems—and describe how they came up with their answers—cooking up the proper response is more difficult.

As teachers discovered in a recent workshop, devising properly phrased questions—ones that fairly and accurately test what they are designed to test—isn't so easy either.

"I left that meeting feeling kind of frustrated," said Melanie Avery, a teacher at Robinson School in Kirkwood, who came up with the cookie question along with Judith Joerding, a second-grade teacher at Airport School in the Ferguson-Florissant district. "I felt we needed to go back and really rethink that question and make sure we are addressing the higher-level thinking that performance assessment is supposed to address."

"When Melanie and I got together and designed the task," Joerding added, "we wanted the children to use problem-solving skills. The world they're going to live in won't necessarily have one correct answer. They're going to need different ways and strategies to solve a problem."

Cookies, Clay and Marshmallows

Before such thinking became popular, anyone faced with the cookie dilemma probably would have had choices like this:

(a) 3 cookies each.
(b) 4 cookies each.
(c) 5 cookies each.
(d) 3 3/4 cookies each.

Students who came up with the right answer—in this case (d), if the goal was to make sure each person had an equal cookie ration—didn't necessarily know how to divide 15 by four. They could have guessed or used real-life substitutes like clay or marshmallows to eliminate some wrong options.

As new tests are born, students in Missouri will have to do more than simply fill in a correct answer. They'll have to explain how they got there and why they think their choice is right. The change is designed to show how they can turn the basic knowledge they have into real problem-solving skills instead of simply the ability to take tests.

"You could really psych out the test," said Bill Foster about the multiple-choice variety. Foster is director of professional development schools at the School of Education of the University of Missouri at St. Louis. "If you'd memorized a lot, you could easily pick out the answer. It's like bench engineers who are surprised by new graduates who don't know how to approach a problem and come up with a creative solution. They know a lot of facts and theories, but they don't know how to use them."

Foster and Mike Fulton, an assistant to the superintendent of the Pattonville School District for planning and assessment, are helping develop the techniques needed to test such skills. Their Show-Me Classroom Performance Assessment Project brings together teachers from across Missouri, under a grant from the Department of Elementary and Secondary Education, to devise ways to determine how well students are learning what the state's education standards demand.

"We want them to think in ways so that if they can do these kind of activities," Fulton said, "they should be able to do well on the test."

Bake More Cookies

That's where Joe and his birthday cookies come in. Avery, Joerding and other teachers met on a recent Saturday at Holman Middle School, 11055 St. Charles Rock Road in St. Ann, to go over questions they had devised earlier and the answers their students had given in the classroom. Responses didn't always match expectations.

For example, the cookie question was phrased this way:

"Now you will need to figure out a way to share the cookies among the FOUR of you."

Even though they knew elementary division, few students used precision to give each child 3¾ cookies. Most used more creative solutions, like giving Joe extra cookies because he was the guest of honor; or letting Joe's mother share the feast, giving each person three cookies; or baking more cookies so that the bigger batch would let everyone share equally.

Such answers may be resourceful, but the teachers had to determine whether they really responded to the question. They also had to determine what grade to give each response, based on a four-point scale, with each level responding to certain criteria.

Matching each answer to a grade was slippery work, but for such tests to be meaningful when they are given to a large group of students, both the questions and the grading scale must be uniformly understood.

"You have to make sure you come up with tasks where the question you ask is not phrased in a way that will allow confusion," said Foster. "It's not fair to students to have them guessing what you want. It should be clear to them the kind of thing you are looking for."

Creativity Within Limits

Teachers also wanted to make sure students had room to use their imaginations to come up with different ways to reach their conclusion, within the proper limits. Creativity doesn't mean anything goes; there may not be just one right answer, but students' responses have to fit what the question is asking and what skills the test is trying to assess.

Questions and Activities

1. Performance-based assessment has the advantage of requiring students to demonstrate both their understanding of information and their ability to use it to solve problems. But what are the disadvantages of this testing format? Can they be reduced or overcome? How?

2. For students to do well on a performance-based test, they have to be able to recognize that previously learned information is relevant to the problem they are working on and to retrieve that information accurately from memory or a reference source. This is essentially a problem of transfer of learning (which we discussed in the chapter on constructivist learning theory and problem solving). What should teachers do to maximize the probability that transfer will occur when students take performance-based tests?

3. The teachers mentioned in this article discovered that writing good performance-based assessment items is not necessarily an easy task. Because some amount of specialized knowledge about assessment is necessary to write good test items and because you will be responsible some day for creating both paper-and-pencil and performance tests, you might think about how you will acquire the knowledge and skill that helps one produce good tests. If your program offers a classroom measurement course that is not required, you would be wise to consider adding it to your electives.

Finally, we have a word about keeping things in perspective. Like most other new ideas, performance assessment has been vigorously debated as *the* solution to the shortcomings and distortions of traditional tests. The truth, of course, is almost always somewhere in between. As we have pointed out in previous chapters and in numerous ways, *nothing works for everyone all the time or under all circumstances*. Writing portfolios, for example, do not engage all students. As one middle school student rather dramatically put it: "I would rather shovel coal in hell than put together another one of these portfolios" (Spalding, 2000, p. 762).

Despite these problems, the Case in Print illustrates why performance tests have become so popular among educators, including primary grade teachers.

WAYS TO EVALUATE STUDENT LEARNING

Once you have collected all the measures you intend to collect—for example, test scores, quiz scores, homework assignments, special projects, ratings of products and performances, and laboratory experiments—you will have to give the data some sort of value (the essence of evaluation). As you probably know, this is most often done by using an A to F grading scale. There are two general ways to approach this task. One approach is comparisons among students. Such forms of evaluation are called norm-referenced since students are identified as average (or normal), above average, or below average. An alternative approach is called criterion-referenced because performance is interpreted in terms of defined criteria. Although both approaches can be used, we favor criterion-referenced grading for reasons we will mention shortly.

Norm-Referenced Grading

A **norm-referenced grading** system assumes that classroom achievement will naturally vary among a group of heterogeneous students because of differences in such characteristics as prior knowledge, learning skills, motivation, and aptitude (to be discussed in the chapter on standardized tests). Under ideal circumstances (hundreds of scores from a diverse group of students), this variation produces a bell-shaped, or "normal," distribution of scores that ranges from low to high, has few tied scores, and has only a very few low scores and only a very few high scores. For this reason, norm-referenced grading procedures are also referred to as "grading on the curve."

● Norm-referenced grading: compare one student to others

The Nature of Norm-Referenced Grading   Course grades, like standardized test scores, are determined through a comparison of each student's level of performance to the normal, or average, level of other, similar students in order to reflect the assumed differences in amount of learned material. The comparison may be to all other members of the student's class that year, or it may be to the average performance of several classes stretching back over several years. It is probably better for teachers to use a broad base of typical student performance made up of several classes as grounds for comparison than to rely on the current class of students. Doing so avoids two severe distorting effects: when a single class contains many weak students, those with more well-developed abilities will more easily obtain the highest grades; and when the class has many capable students, the relatively weaker students are virtually predestined to receive low or failing grades (Gronlund, 2003; Kubiszyn & Borich, 2003; Nitko, 2004).

The basic procedure for assigning grades on a norm-referenced basis involves just a few steps:

1. Determine what percentage of students will receive which grades. If, for example, you intend to award the full range of grades, you may decide to give A's to the top 15 percent, B's to the next 25 percent, C's to the middle 35 percent, D's to the next 15 percent, and F's to the bottom 10 percent.
2. Arrange the scores from highest to lowest.
3. Calculate which scores fall in which category, and assign the grades accordingly.

Many other arrangements are also possible. How large or small you decide to make the percentages for each category will depend on such factors as the nature of the students in your class, the difficulty of your exams and assignments, and your own sense of what constitutes appropriate standards. Furthermore, a norm-referenced approach does not necessarily mean that each class will have a normal distribution of grades or that anyone will automatically fail. For example, it is possible for equal numbers of students to receive A's, B's, and C's if you decide to limit your grading system to just those three categories and award equal numbers of each grade. A norm-referenced approach simply means that the grading symbols being used indicate one student's level of achievement relative to other students.

● Norm-referenced grading based on absence of external criteria

Proponents of norm-referenced grading typically point to the absence of acceptable external criteria for use as a standard for evaluating and grading student performance. In other words, there is no good way to determine externally how much learning is too little, just enough, or more than enough for some subject. And if there is no amount of knowledge or set of behaviors that all students must master, then grades may be awarded on the basis of relative performance among a group of students (Gronlund, 2003).

Strengths and Weaknesses of Norm-Referenced Grading   There are at least two circumstances under which it may be appropriate to use norm-referenced measurement and evaluation procedures:

● Norm-referenced grading can be used to evaluate advanced levels of learning

1. *Evaluating advanced levels of learning.* You might, for example, wish to formulate a two-stage instructional plan in which the first stage involves helping all students master a basic level of knowledge and skill in a particular subject. Performance at this stage would be measured and evaluated against a predetermined standard (such as 80 percent correct on an exam). Once this has been accomplished, you could supply advanced instruction and encourage students to learn as much of the additional material as possible. Because the amount of learning during the second stage is not tied to a predetermined standard and it will likely vary because of differences in motivation and learning skills, a norm-referenced approach to grading can be used at this stage. This situation also fits certain guidelines for the use of competitive reward structures (discussed in the chapter "Approaches to Instruction") since everyone starts from the same level of basic knowledge.

2. *Selection for limited-enrollment programs.* Norm-referenced measurement and evaluation are also applicable in cases where students with the best chances for success are selected for a limited-enrollment program from among a large pool of candidates. One example is the selection of students for honors programs who have the highest test scores and grade-point averages (Gronlund, 2003).

The main weakness of the norm-referenced approach to grading is that there are few situations in which the typical public school teacher can appropriately use it. Either the goal is not appropriate (as in mastery of certain material and skills by all students or diagnosis of an individual student's specific strengths and weaknesses), or the basic conditions cannot be met (classes are too small or homogeneous, or both). When a norm-referenced approach is used in spite of these weaknesses, communication and motivation problems are often created.

Consider the example of a group of high school sophomores having a great deal of difficulty mastering German vocabulary and grammar. The students may have been underprepared, the teacher may be doing a poor job of organizing and explaining the material, or both factors may be at work. The top student averages 48 percent correct on all of the exams, quizzes, and oral recitations administered during the term. That student and a few others with averages in the high 40s will receive the A's. Although these fortunate few may realize their knowledge and skills are incomplete, others are likely to conclude falsely that these students learned quite a bit about the German language since a grade of A is generally taken to mean superior performance.

At the other extreme, we have the example of a social studies class in which most of the students are doing well. Because the students were well prepared by previous teachers, used effective study skills, were exposed to high-quality instruction, and were strongly motivated by the enthusiasm of their teacher, the final test averages ranged from 94 to 98 percent correct. And yet the teacher who uses a norm-referenced scheme would assign at least A's, B's, and C's to this group. Not only does this practice seriously damage the motivation of students who worked hard and performed well, but it also miscommunicates to others the performance of students who received B's and C's (Airasian, 2001).

pause & reflect

Have you ever taken a class that was graded "on the curve"? Did you feel that your grade accurately reflected how much you had learned? If not, why was the grade too low or too high?

Norm-referenced grading systems should rarely, if ever, be used in schools since there are few circumstances that warrant their use and they are likely to depress the motivation of all but the highest-scoring students.

● Criterion-referenced grading: compare individual performance to stated criteria

● Criterion-referenced grades provide information about strengths and weaknesses

Criterion-Referenced Grading

A **criterion-referenced grading** system permits students to benefit from mistakes and improve their level of understanding and performance. Furthermore, it establishes an individual (and sometimes cooperative) reward structure, which fosters motivation to learn to a greater extent than other systems.

The Nature of Criterion-Referenced Grading   Under a criterion-referenced system, grades are determined by the extent to which each student has attained a defined standard (or criterion) of achievement or performance. Whether the rest of the students in the class are successful or unsuccessful in meeting that criterion is irrelevant. Thus, any distribution of grades is possible. Every student may get an A or an F, or no student may receive these grades. For reasons we will discuss shortly, very low or failing grades may occur less frequently under a criterion-referenced system.

A common version of criterion-referenced grading assigns letter grades on the basis of the percentage of test items answered correctly. For example, you may decide to award an A to anyone who correctly answers at least 85 percent of a set of test questions, a B to anyone who correctly answers 75 to 84 percent, and so on down to the lowest grade. To use this type of grading system fairly, which means specifying realistic criterion levels, you would need to have some prior knowledge of the levels at which students typically perform. You would thus be using normative information to establish absolute, or fixed, standards of performance. However, although both norm-referenced and criterion-referenced grading systems spring from a normative database (that is, from comparisons among students), only the former system uses those comparisons to directly determine grades.

Strengths and Weaknesses of Criterion-Referenced Grading   Criterion-referenced grading systems (and criterion-referenced tests) have become increasingly popular in recent years primarily because of the following advantages:

- Criterion-referenced tests and grading systems provide more specific and useful information about student strengths and weaknesses than do norm-referenced grading systems. Parents and teachers are more interested in knowing that a student received an A on an earth science test because she mastered 92 percent of the objectives for that unit than they are in knowing that she received an A on a test of the same material because she outscored 92 percent of her classmates.
- Criterion-referenced grading systems promote motivation to learn because they hold out the promise that all students who have sufficiently well-developed learning skills and receive good-quality instruction can master most of a teacher's objectives (Gronlund, 2003). The motivating effect of criterion-referenced grading systems is likely to be particularly noticeable among students who adopt mastery goals (which we discussed in our chapter on motivation) since they tend to use grades as feedback for further improvement (Covington, 2000).

One weakness of the criterion-referenced approach to grading is that the performance standards one specifies (such as a grade of A for 90 percent correct) are arbitrary and may be difficult to justify to parents and colleagues. (Why not 87 percent correct for an A? Or 92 percent?) A second weakness is that although a teacher's standards may appear to be stable from one test to another (90 percent correct for an A for all tests), they may in reality fluctuate as a result of unnoticed variation in the difficulty of each test and the quality of instruction (Gronlund, 1998).

Finally, we would like to alert you to a characteristic of criterion-referenced evaluation that is not a weakness but is an unfortunate fact of educational life that you may have to address. In a variety of subtle and sometimes not so subtle ways, teachers are discouraged from using a criterion-referenced approach to grading because it tends to produce higher test scores and grades than a norm-referenced approach does. The reason for the higher scores is obvious and quite justified. When test items are based solely on the specific instructional objectives that teachers write and when those objectives are clear and provided to students, students know what they need to learn and what they need to do to meet the teacher's objectives. Also, because students' grades depend only on how well they perform, not how well their classmates perform, motivation for learning tends to be higher. The result is that students tend to learn more and score higher on classroom tests. So why should this happy outcome be a cause for concern? Because individuals who are not well versed in classroom measurement and evaluation may believe that the only reason large numbers of students achieve high grades is that the teacher has lower standards than other teachers. Consequently, you may find yourself in a position of having to defend the criteria you use to assign grades. As Tom Kubiszyn and Gary Borich point out, "It is a curious fact of life that everyone presses for excellence in education, but many balk at marking systems that make attainment of excellence within everyone's reach" (2003, pp. 219–220).

● Mastery approach: give students multiple opportunities to master goals at own pace

A Mastery Approach   A particular criterion-referenced approach to grading is often referred to as a mastery approach because it allows students multiple opportunities to learn and demonstrate their mastery of instructional objectives. This approach stems in large part from the work of John Carroll (1963) and Benjamin Bloom (1968, 1976) on the concept of *mastery learning*. The basic idea behind mastery learning is that most students can master most objectives if they are given good-quality instruction and sufficient time to learn and are motivated to continue learning (see, for example, Gentile & Lalley, 2003).

In a mastery approach, tests are used for formative as well as summative evaluation purposes. Thus, students whose scores indicate deficiencies in learning are given additional instruction and a second chance to show what they have learned. Although pedagogically sound, this approach is often criticized on the grounds that life outside of school often does not give people a second chance. Surgeons and pilots, for example, are expected to do their jobs without error each and every time (Guskey, 2003). In our view, this criticism is flawed because it is shortsighted and involves an apples and oranges comparison. First, even surgeons and pilots made mistakes they were allowed to correct. Surgeons made their mistakes on cadavers and pilots on flight simulators. Second, schooling is about helping students acquire the knowledge and skills they need to move from novices to experts and become self-directed learners. Life outside of school, on the other hand, frequently involves competition among individuals who are, or are expected to be, equally proficient.

If you are interested in using a mastery approach, the following suggestions can be adapted for use at any grade level and any subject area:

JOURNAL ENTRY
Trying a Mastery Approach to Grading

1. Go through a unit of study, a chapter of a text, or an outline of a lecture, and pick out what you consider to be the most important points—that is, the points you wish to stress because they are most likely to have later value or are basic to later learning.

2. List these points in the form of a goal card (a list of the major concepts and skills that should be acquired by the end of an instructional unit), instructional objectives (as described by Robert Mager, 1997, or Robert Linn and Norman Gronlund, 2000), key points, or the equivalent. If appropriate, arrange the objectives in some sort of organized framework, perhaps with reference to the relevant taxonomy of educational objectives (see the chapter "Approaches to Instruction").

3. Distribute the list of objectives at the beginning of a unit. Tell your students that they should concentrate on learning those points and that they will be tested on them.

4. Consider making up a study guide in which you provide specific questions relating to the objectives and a format that students can use to organize their notes.
5. Use a variety of instructional methods and materials to explain and illustrate objectives-related ideas.
6. Make up exam questions based on the objectives and the study guide questions. Try to write several questions for each objective.
7. Arrange these questions into at least two (preferably three) alternate exams for each unit of study.
8. Make up tentative criteria for grade levels for each exam and for the entire unit or report period (for example, A for not more than one question missed on any exam; B for not more than two questions missed on any exam; C for not more than four questions missed on any exam).
9. Test students either when they come to you and indicate they are ready or when you determine they have all had ample opportunity to learn the material. Announce all exam dates in advance, and remind students that the questions will be based only on the objectives you have mentioned. Indicate the criteria for different grade levels, and emphasize that any student who fails to meet a desired criterion on the first try will have a chance to take an alternate form of the exam.
10. Grade and return the exams as promptly as possible, go over questions briefly in class (particularly those that caused problems for more than a few students), and offer to go over exams individually with students. Allow for individual interpretations, and give credit for answers you judge to be logical and plausible, even if they differ from the answers you expected.
11. Schedule alternate exams, and make yourself available for consultation and tutoring the day before. (While you are giving alternate exams, you can administer the original exam to students who were absent.)
12. If students improve their score on the second exam but still fall below the desired criterion, consider a safety valve option: invite them to provide you with a completed study guide (or the equivalent) when they take an exam the second time, or give them an open-book exam on the objectives they missed to see whether they can explain them in terms other than those of a written examination. If a student fulfills either of these options satisfactorily, give credit for one extra answer on the second exam.
13. To supplement exams, assign book reports, oral reports, papers, or some other kind of individual work that will provide maximum opportunity for student choice. Establish and explain the criteria you will use to evaluate these assignments, but stress that you want to encourage freedom of choice and expression. (Some students will thrive on free choice; others are likely to feel threatened by open-ended assignments. To allow for such differences, provide specific directions for those who need them and general hints or a simple request that "original" projects be cleared in advance for the more independent thinkers.) Grade all reports Pass or Do Over, and supply constructive criticism on those you consider unsatisfactory. Announce that all Do Over papers can be reworked and resubmitted within a certain period of time. Have the reports count toward the final grade—for example, three reports for an A, two for a B, one for a C. (In addition, students should pass each exam at the designated level.) You might also invite students to prepare extra papers to earn bonus points to be added to exam totals.

This basic technique will permit you to work within a traditional A to F framework, but in such a way that you should be able, without lowering standards, to increase the proportion of students who do acceptable work. An example of a mastery-oriented, criterion-referenced approach to grading appears in Figure 14.2.

Figure 14.2 Page from a Teacher's Grade Book and Instructions to Students: A Mastery Approach

Instructions for Determining Your Grade in Social Studies

Your grade in social studies this report period will be based on three exams (worth 20 points each) and satisfactory completion of up to three projects.

Here are the standards for different grades:

A—Average of 18 or more on three exams, plus three projects at Pass level
B—Average of 16 or 17 on three exams, plus two projects at Pass level
C—Average of 14 or 15 on three exams, plus one project at Pass level
D—Average of 10 to 13 on three exams
F—Average of 9 or less on three exams

Another way to figure your grade is to add together points as you take exams. This may be the best procedure to follow as we get close to the end of the report period. Use this description of standards as a guide:

A—At least 54 points, plus three projects at Pass level
B—48 to 53 points, plus two projects at Pass level
C—42 to 47 points, plus one project at Pass level
D—30 to 41 points
F—29 points or less

If you are not satisfied with the score you earn on any exam, you may take a different exam on the same material in an effort to improve your score. (Some of the questions on the alternate exam will be the same as those on the original exam; some will be different.) Projects will be graded P (Pass) or DO (Do Over). If you receive a DO on a project, you may work to improve it and hand it in again. You may also submit an extra project, which may earn up to 3 points of bonus credit (and can help if your exam scores fall just below a cutoff point). As you take each exam and receive a Pass for each project, record your progress on this chart.

First Exam		Second Exam		Third Exam		Project 1	Project 2	Project 3	Extra Project	Grade
1st Try	2nd Try	1st Try	2nd Try	1st Try	2nd Try					

Teacher's Grade Book

Name	1st Exam 1st Try	1st Exam 2nd Try	2nd Exam 1st Try	2nd Exam 2nd Try	3rd Exam 1st Try	3rd Exam 2nd Try	Exam Total Points	Project 1	Project 2	Project 3	Extra Project	Grade
Adams, Ann	16	18	17	18	18			P	P	P		
Baker, Charles	13	14	14		18	14		P				
Cohen, Matthew	14	16	15	16	17			P	P			
Davis, Rebecca	19		19		20			P	P	P		
Evans, Deborah	16	18	17	18	18			P	P	P		
Ford, Harold	18	16	17		15			P	P			
Grayson, Lee	10	13	12	14	12	15		P				
Hood, Barbara	16		17		15			P	P			
Ingalls, Robert	16	18	16		15			P	P			
Jones, Thomas	14	14	12	16	15			P	P			
Kim, David	18		19		19			P	P	P		
Lapine, Craig	14	16	18		16			P	P	P		
Moore, James	17		17		17			P	P	P		
Nguyen, Tuan	17	18	19		16	17		P	P	P		
Orton, John	10	10	11		9							
Peck, Nancy	14		15		14			P				
Quist, Ann	16	18	17	18	18			P	P	P		
Richards, Mary	16		17		15			P	P			
Santos, Maria	13		15		14			P				
Thomas, Eric	15	16	18	17	15			P	P			
Wong, Yuen	14		15		16			P				
Vernon, Joan	14	14	13	14	12	14		P				
Zacharias, Saul	16	18	17		16	19		P	P	P		

IMPROVING YOUR GRADING METHODS: ASSESSMENT PRACTICES TO AVOID

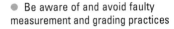

● Be aware of and avoid faulty measurement and grading practices

Earlier in this chapter, we noted that the typical teacher has little systematic knowledge of assessment principles and as a result may engage in a variety of inappropriate testing and grading practices. We hope that the information in this chapter will help you become more proficient at these tasks. (In addition, we strongly encourage you to take a course in classroom assessment if you have not already done so.) To reinforce what you have learned here, we will describe some of the more common inappropriate testing and grading practices that teachers commit. The following list is based largely on the observations of Thomas Haladyna (1999), Thomas Guskey (2002), John Hills (1991), and Anthony Nitko (2004).

1. *Worshiping averages.* Some teachers mechanically average all scores and automatically assign the corresponding grade, even when they know an unusually low score was due to an extenuating circumstance. Allowances can be made for physical illness, emotional upset, and the like; students' lowest grade can be dropped, or they can repeat the test on which they performed most poorly. Although objectivity in grading is a laudatory goal, it should not be practiced to the extent that it prevents you from altering your normal procedures when your professional judgment indicates an exception is warranted.

   Another shortcoming of this practice is that it ignores measurement error. No one can construct the perfect test, and no person's score is a true indicator of knowledge and skill. Test scores represent estimates of these characteristics. Accordingly, giving a student with an average of 74.67 a grade of D when 75 is the minimum needed for a C pretends the test is more accurate than it really is. This is why it is so important to conduct an item analysis of your tests. If you discover several items that are unusually difficult, you may want to make allowances for students who are a point or two from the next highest grade (and modify the items if you intend to use them again). We describe a simple procedure for analyzing your test items in the next Suggestions for Teaching section.

2. *Using zeros indiscriminately.* The sole purpose of grades is to communicate to others how much of the curriculum a student has mastered. When teachers also use grades to reflect their appraisal of a student's work habits or character, the validity of the grades is lessened. This occurs most dramatically when students receive zeros for assignments that are late (but are otherwise of good quality), incomplete, or not completed according to directions and for exams on which they are suspected of cheating. This is a flawed practice for two reasons:

   - First, and to repeat what we said in point 1, there may be good reasons that projects and homework assignments are late, incomplete, or different from what was expected. You should try to uncover such circumstances and take them into account.
   - Second, zeros cause communication problems. If a student who earns grades in the low 90s for most of the grading period is given two zeros for one or more of the reasons just mentioned, that student could easily receive a D or an F. Such a grade is not an accurate reflection of what was learned.

pause & reflect

Because students in American schools feel considerable pressure to obtain high grades, a significant number of them feel driven to cheat. What might you do to reduce your students' tendency to cheat?

If penalties are to be given for work that is late, incomplete, or not done according to directions and for which there are no extenuating circumstances, they should be clearly spelled out far in advance of the due date, and they should not seriously distort the meaning of the grade. For students suspected of cheating, for example, a different form of the exam can be given.

3. *Providing insufficient instruction before testing.* For a variety of reasons, teachers occasionally spend more time than they had planned on certain topics. In an effort to "cover the curriculum" prior to a scheduled exam, they may significantly increase the pace of instruction or simply tell students to read the remaining material on their own. The low grades that typically result from this practice will unfortunately be read by outsiders (and this includes parents) as a deficiency in students' learning ability when in fact they more accurately indicate a deficiency in instructional quality.

4. *Teaching for one thing but testing for another.* This practice takes several forms. For instance, teachers may provide considerable supplementary material in class through lecture, thereby encouraging students to take notes and study them extensively, but base test questions almost entirely on text material. Or if teachers emphasize the text material during class discussion, they may take a significant number of questions from footnotes and less important parts of the text. A third form of this flawed practice is to provide students with simple problems or practice questions in class that reflect the knowledge level of Bloom's Taxonomy but to give complex problems and higher-level questions on a test. Remember what we said earlier in this book: if you want transfer, then teach for transfer.

5. *Using pop quizzes to motivate students.* If you recall our discussion of reinforcement schedules, you will recognize that surprise tests represent a variable interval schedule and that such schedules produce a consistent pattern of behavior in humans under certain circumstances. Being a student in a classroom is not one of those circumstances. Surprise tests produce an undesirable level of anxiety in many students and cause others simply to give up. If you sense that students are not sufficiently motivated to read and study more consistently, consult the chapter "Motivation" for better ideas on how to accomplish this goal.

6. *Keeping the nature and content of the test a secret.* Many teachers scrupulously avoid giving students any meaningful information about the type of questions that will be on a test or what the test items will cover. The assumption that underlies this practice is that if students have been paying attention in class, have been diligently doing their homework, and have been studying at regular intervals, they will do just fine on a test. But they usually don't—and the main reason can be seen in our description of a learning strategy (see the chapter on information-processing theory). A good learning strategist first analyzes all of the available information that bears on attaining a goal. But if certain critical information about the goal is not available, the rest of the strategy (planning, implementing, monitoring, and modifying) will suffer.

7. *Keeping the criteria for assignments a secret.* This practice is closely related to the previous one. Students may be told, for example, to write an essay on what the world would be like if all diseases were eliminated and to give their imagination free rein in order to come up with many original ideas. But when the papers are graded, equal weight is given to spelling, punctuation, and grammatical usage. If these aspects of writing are also important to you and you intend to hold students accountable for them, make sure you clearly communicate that fact.

8. *Shifting criteria.* Teachers are sometimes disappointed in the quality of students' tests and assignments and decide to change the grading criteria as a way to shock students into more appropriate learning behaviors. For example, a teacher may have told students that mechanics will count for one-third of the grade on a writing assignment. But when the teacher discovers that most of the papers contain numerous spelling, punctuation, and grammatical errors, she may decide to let mechanics determine half of the grade. As we indicated before, grades should not be used as a motivational device or as a way to make up for instructional oversights. There are far better ways to accomplish these goals.

9. *Combining apples and oranges.* Students' grades are supposed to indicate how much they have learned in different subject-matter areas. When factors like effort and

ability are combined with test scores, the meaning of a grade becomes unclear. Consequently, measurement experts routinely recommend that teachers base students' grades solely on how well they have performed on written and performance tests. Assessments of effort and ability should be reported separately (Gronlund, 2003). Nevertheless, many teachers do not follow this recommendation. A survey of just over nine hundred third- through fifth-grade teachers revealed that 36 percent factored a student's level of effort into a grade either quite a bit, extensively, or completely, and 47 percent used a student's ability level to help determine a grade either quite a bit, extensively, or completely. Many high school teachers engage in this practice as well (McMillan et al., 2002).

A number of technological formats and products have been developed to make the task of classroom assessment easier, more informative, and less prone to error. The next section describes several of these formats and products.

TECHNOLOGY FOR CLASSROOM ASSESSMENT

At the beginning of this chapter, we mentioned that assessment activities can account for about one-third of a teacher's time. This large investment in time is partly due to the importance of assessment in both teaching and learning, but it is also related to the fact that many assessment activities involve time-consuming methods of creating, administering, and scoring tests and analyzing and recording scores. Fortunately, computer-based technology now allows for the efficient creation of test-item banks, assembling of examinations, maintaining of student records, and generation of reports (Cardwell, 2000).

Test-item banks are large collections of test items that publishers often supply with particular textbooks or that teachers can construct themselves using the database programs in Microsoft Works or AppleWorks. They can store information regarding date of entry, author, references, type of item (for example, true-false), cognitive skill addressed, and item difficulty; thus, they are an efficient way to generate one or more forms of a classroom test.

A web site that will help you create online tests is FunBrain (**www.funbrain. com/**). Ken Cardwell (2000), a Redmond, Oregon, teacher who has described his experiences in creating and using online tests, recommends this site for accessing ready-made tests or making your own.

Small wireless computers (referred to as either palm-sized or hand-held computers) can also be used to make evaluation more efficient. If both teacher and students have palm-sized computers, the teacher can electronically distribute PalmSheets, a digital version of paper worksheets, and collect them from students. The data from these worksheets can then be uploaded to a database where they can be extensively analyzed (McIntire, 2002; Soloway et al., 2001). Another hand-held application lets K–3 teachers automatically create running records (observational assessments) (McIntire, 2002). You can obtain more information about classroom use of hand-held computers at the web site of the Center for Highly Interactive Computing in Education at the University of Michigan (**palm.hice-dev.org/**).

Electronic Gradebooks and Grading Programs

Electronic gradebooks can store records of student test performance, compute test averages and cumulative averages, weight scores, note students with particular scores or characteristics, and print grade reports with standard as well as specific student comments. Edward Vockell and Douglas Fiore (1993) found that speed, accuracy, customizability, and organization are the key advantages of these systems. However, they also admit that there can be distinct disadvantages to electronic gradebooks, such as

Go to the Weblinks section of the textbook site for convenient links to recommended web sites.

incorrect data entry, system impersonality, and inflexibility with absent students and special situations. Three electronic gradebooks that you may want to examine are Gradebook2 (**www.gradebook.com/solutions/pro_gb2.htm**), 1st Class Gradebook (**www.1st-class-software.com/**), and Grade Busters (**www.gradebusters.com/**). For more flexibility in electronic record keeping, you may want to consider regular database and spreadsheet programs, which will allow you to tailor assessment records to your specific needs (Vockell & Fiore, 1993). A networked database can compile all teachers' grades and automatically create an electronic report card (McNally & Etchison, 2000).

Computerized grading programs are very popular with teachers because they are designed to be consistent with the point-based grading systems that are used by most middle and high school teachers. These programs can scan and mark students' choices to selected-response test items (true-false, matching, multiple-choice) and allow teachers to track, summarize, and present student performance in a variety of ways. But the efficiency and seeming objectivity of such programs mask a serious potential drawback: they can lead to unfair assignment of grades when used uncritically. The challenge of accurately assigning grades usually involves more than just mathematical precision.

To demonstrate the complex nature of grading and why professional judgment should supplement the use of computerized grading programs, consider the example offered by Thomas Guskey (2002) in Table 14.2.

The table represents a group of seven students, each of whom has been graded using three methods: calculating the simple average of all scores, calculating the median or middle score, and calculating the average, but with the lowest score deleted. Using the simple arithmetic average produces a grade of C for all students despite the differences in their grade pattern. Student 1, for example, started slowly but gradually improved. Student 2 exhibited the opposite pattern. Student 3's performance was consistently around the average. Student 4 failed the first two unit tests but scored near or at the top for the last three. Student 5 exhibited the opposite pattern from student 4. Student 6 had an unexcused absence for the first test and was given a score of zero, but scored near or at the top for the last 4 tests. Student 7 had virtually perfect scores for the first 4 tests, but was caught cheating on the last one and received a score of zero. If giving all seven students the same grade strikes you as inappropriate, note that using the median score or the average with the lowest score deleted produces grades that range from A through C, and that students 4 and 5 could receive either an A, B, or C, depending on which method is used.

Table 14.2	Summary Grades Tallied by Three Different Methods										
Student	**Unit 1**	**Unit 2**	**Unit 3**	**Unit 4**	**Unit 5**	**Avg Score**	**Grade**	**Median Score**	**Grade**	**Delete Lowest**	**Grade**
1	59	69	79	89	99	79	C	79	C	84	B
2	99	89	79	69	59	79	C	79	C	84	B
3	77	80	80	78	80	79	C	80	B	79.5	B
4	49	49	98	99	100	79	C	98	A	86.5	B
5	100	99	98	49	49	79	C	98	A	86.5	B
6	0	98	98	99	100	79	C	98	A	98.8	A
7	100	99	98	98	0	79	C	98	A	98.8	A

Grading Scale: 90–100% = A; 80–89% = B; 70–79% = C; 60–69% = D; 59% or lower = F.

SOURCE: Guskey, 2002.

Our purpose here is not to tell you which of these methods to use, since that will depend on other information teachers typically have about student capabilities and teachers' beliefs about the appropriateness of different grading methods, but to remind you that computerized grading books should not be allowed to substitute for a teacher's professional judgment in awarding grades.

Technology-Based Performance Assessment

As you may recall from our earlier discussion, performance assessments give students the opportunity to demonstrate how well they can use the knowledge and skills that were the focus of an instructional unit to carry out realistic and meaningful tasks. Computer-based technology is an excellent vehicle for this purpose. For example, simulations are likely to be more effective than traditional paper-and-pencil tests for determining how well students understand and can carry out the process of scientific inquiry (for example, planning an investigation, collecting data, organizing and analyzing the data, forming conclusions, and communicating findings). A web-based simulation that lends itself to the assessment of scientific inquiry is the GLOBE environmental science education program. Students who participate in GLOBE collect environmental data at a local site and submit it to a scientific database on the Web. About four thousand schools from countries around the world participate in this program. Teachers could use the GLOBE database to assess how well students analyze and interpret climate data by having them use a set of climate-related criteria (such as temperature at different altitudes, amount of sunshine, and amount of snow) to determine in which of several cities the next Winter Olympics should be held (Means & Haertel, 2002).

Technology tools like hypermedia, with text, audio, video, and graphics components, also offer opportunities for students to demonstrate their ability to solve real-world problems in a number of content areas. Ivan Baugh (1994), for instance, notes that students investigating concepts such as biomes and ecosystems could (1) construct hypermedia stacks such as encyclopedias and pictorial atlases on CD-ROM, (2) record narrative voice-overs for such segments, (3) use telecommunications to exchange information with people living near those environments, (4) use videodiscs to provide illustrations of food chains in action, (5) digitize videotape taken from the local environment, (6) type environmental reports, newspapers, and brochures in a word processor, and (7) create brief replayable movies about the different locales that link to other hypermedia or word processing documents.

Digital Portfolios

What Is a Digital Portfolio? Terry Wiedmer (1998, p. 586) defines a **digital portfolio** as "a purposeful collection of work, captured by electronic means, that serves as an exhibit of individual efforts, progress, and achievements in one or more areas." In their digital portfolios, students can create, store, and manage various products and processes that they want to document and perhaps showcase. From smallest to largest storage capacity and flexibility, the contents of a digital portfolio can be stored on a floppy disk, a zip disk, a CD-R disk (can be written on just once), a CD-RW disk (rewritable, like floppy disks), a DVD-R disk (can contain movie clips in addition to text, graphics, and pictures), a DVD-RW disk, or a web site. One advantage to putting a portfolio on a web site is that it can be accessed from any computer that has a web browser and Internet connection (Siegle, 2002).

Digital portfolios (also called electronic portfolios) are similar in purpose to the more traditional portfolios, but they extend beyond paper versions because they can include sound effects, audio and video testimonials, voice-over explanations of a student's thinking process as a project is worked on, and photographs of such products as drawings, paintings, and musical compositions (Siegle, 2002).

● Digital portfolio: collection of work that is stored and illustrated electronically

The Components and Contents of Digital Portfolios   Because the purposes for having students construct a digital portfolio (such as to assign grades, assess students' strengths and weaknesses, evaluate a program or curriculum) are not always the same, the portfolio structure will vary somewhat across teachers and school districts. But some components, such as those in the list that follows, are frequently recommended (for instance, Barrett, 1998; Goldsby & Fazal, 2001; Janesick, 2001; Niguidula, 1997) and should always be seriously considered for inclusion:

- The goals the student was attempting to achieve
- The guidelines that were used to select the included material
- Work samples
- Teacher feedback
- Student self-reflection
- The criteria that were used to evaluate each entry
- Examples of good-quality work

Just as the general components of a digital portfolio may vary, so may the particular media that are used. Following are some specific examples of the types of media a student may use and information that would be represented by each medium (Barrett, 2000; Gatlin & Jacob, 2002; Janesick, 2001; O'Lone, 1997; Siegle, 2002):

- *Digitized pictures and scanned images*: photos of the student and/or objects he or she has created, artwork, models, science experiments over time, fax exchanges with scientists, spelling tests, math work, self-assessment checklists
- *Documents*: electronic copies of student writing, reflection journals, publications, copies of web pages created, and teacher notes and observations
- *Audio recordings*: persuasive speeches, poetry readings, rehearsals of foreign language vocabulary, readings of select passages, self-evaluations, interviews or voice notes regarding the rationale for work included
- *Video clips*: short videos showing the student or teams of students engaged in science experiments and explaining their steps, or showing student performances in physical education or the performing arts
- *Multimedia presentations*: QuickTime movies of interdisciplinary projects

Creating Digital Portfolios   Portfolios can be created by using one of two types of software programs. One option is to purchase generic portfolio templates such as the Grady Profile (**www.aurbach.com/**). The second option is to purchase authoring programs such as HyperStudio (**www.hyperstudio.com/**), Final Cut Express (**www.apple.com/finalcutexpress/**), and Macromedia Authorware (**www.macromedia.com/software/authorware/**), which give students total freedom to design their own portfolios. Helen Barrett (2000) discusses the advantages and disadvantages of eight types of portfolio authoring tools.

Advantages and Disadvantages of Digital Portfolios   The main advantage of a digital portfolio is the ability of students to explain in text and narration why they gave their portfolio its particular content and form. It is very important that each student portfolio submission be linked to self-reflections about why the item was selected, since "without time for reflection, the digital portfolio might be no different from a paper portfolio filed away in a locked cabinet" (Niguidula, 1997, p. 28). Using this opportunity for self-reflection, students can demonstrate what they know, how they came to know it, how their knowledge increased and evolved, and what they have accomplished with that knowledge.

However, many of the same disadvantages that occur when computers are used for other purposes apply to the creation and use of digital portfolios. Because portfolios are personal documents, access to them needs to be restricted. This is typically done with passwords, which, as you probably know, are easily forgotten. Second, portfolios that are stored on a school's server (basically a large-capacity computer) can be altered or destroyed by hackers. Third, work that is not saved while working on a portfolio can be lost if the computer crashes. Finally, if your school's computers are not relatively new, they will probably lack the capability to create (or "burn") a CD or DVD. In that case, separate CD-RW or DVD-RW machines (called "burners") will have to be purchased at anywhere from $100 to $300 apiece.

Rubrics for Digital Portfolios and Presentations   With all the information a digital portfolio might contain, how can a classroom teacher fairly and efficiently assess student learning? First, electronic writing, just like paper-based compositions, can be assessed holistically in a general impression rating. It can also be analyzed with specific criteria such as whether the work is insightful, well organized, clear, focused, relevant, sequentially flowing, persuasive, inspirational, and original (see Arter & McTighe, 2001; Bonk & Cummings, 1998). There are also rubrics for analyzing the quality of a portfolio that has been posted to a web site. One uses a four-point scale (exceeds requirements, meets requirements, close to meeting standards, clearly does not meet standards) to assess the design and aesthetics of the web site, the web site's usability, and the presence and clarity of the portfolio's contents (Goldsby & Fazal, 2001). The web site **www.4teachers.org/** contains, among other things related to technology, a tool called RubiStar that provides templates for creating rubrics for several types of digital products.

- Special rubrics available to assess digital portfolios and presentations

Performance and Portfolio Assessment Problems

We would be remiss not to point out the problems often associated with technology-based performance and portfolio assessment. High-quality performance assessments require multiple assessments (for both formative and summative purposes), extensive time, electronic equipment, careful planning, and continued modification (McGrath, 2003). Electronic portfolios can become large, complex, and time-consuming to grade fairly and thus can overload teachers with work (Moersch & Fisher, 1995).

Staff development and teacher training are additional barriers to effective use of performance assessment and digital portfolios. But with proper training, teachers may begin to find ways in which technology-based school and classroom assessment plans are practical, cost-effective, and qualitatively better than traditional assessments.

The following Suggestions for Teaching should help you properly implement the assessment concepts and research findings presented in this chapter.

Suggestions for Teaching in Your Classroom

Effective Assessment Techniques

1 **As early as possible in a report period, decide when and how often to give tests and other assignments that will count toward a grade, and announce tests and assignments well in advance.**

If you follow the suggestions for formulating objectives presented in the chapter "Approaches to Instruction," you should be able to develop a reasonably complete master plan that will permit you to devise a course outline even though you have only limited experience with teaching or with a particular text or unit of study. In doing so, you will have not only a good sense of the objectives you want your students to achieve but also the means by which achievement will be assessed.

Before the term starts is a good time to block out the number of tests you will give in that term. Recall that research cited earlier has shown that students who take six or seven tests per term (two or three per grading period) learn more than students who are tested less frequently or not at all. Don't assume, however, that if giving three tests per grading period is good, then giving five or six tests is better. A point of diminishing returns is quickly reached after the fourth test.

If you announce at the beginning of a report period when you intend to give exams or set due dates for assignments, you not only give students a clear idea of what they will be expected to do, but you also give yourself guidelines for arranging lesson plans and devising, administering, and scoring tests. (If you will be teaching elementary students, it will be better to announce exams and assignments for a week at a time rather than providing a long-range schedule.)

For the most part, it is preferable to announce tests well in advance. Pop quizzes tend to increase anxiety and tension and force students to cram on isolated sections of a book on a day-by-day and catch-as-catch-can basis. Simple homework assignments or the equivalent are more likely to encourage more careful and consistent study than pop quizzes. When tests are announced, be sure to let students know exactly what material they will be held responsible for, what kinds of questions will be asked, and how much tests will count toward the final grade. As we noted in the Take a Stand! feature for the chapter on information-processing theory, and as others have pointed out (for example, Guskey, 2003), students need complete information about the content and nature of tests if they are to function strategically. In addition, research indicates that students who are told to expect (and who receive) an essay test or a multiple-choice test score slightly higher on an exam than students who do not know what to expect or who are led to expect one type of test but are given another type (Lundeberg & Fox, 1991).

For term papers or other written work, list your criteria for grading the papers (for example, how much emphasis will be placed on style, spelling and punctuation, research, individuality of expression). In laboratory courses, most students prefer a list of experiments or projects and some description of how they will be evaluated (for example, ten experiments in chemistry, fifteen drawings in drafting, five paintings in art, judged according to posted criteria).

JOURNAL ENTRY
Announcing Exams and Assignments

For students to effectively plan how they will master your objectives, they need to know as early as possible how many tests they will have to take, when the tests will occur, what types of items each test will contain, and what content they will be tested on.

2 **Prepare a content outline or a table of specifications of the objectives to be covered on each exam, or otherwise take care to obtain a systematic sample of the knowledge and skill acquired by your students.**

The more precisely and completely goals are described at the beginning of a unit, the easier and more efficient assessment (and teaching) will be. The use of a clear outline will help ensure an adequate sample of the most significant kinds of behavior.

When the time comes to assess the abilities of your students, you can't possibly observe and evaluate all relevant behavior. You can't listen to more than a few pages of reading by each first grader, for example, or ask high school seniors to answer questions on everything discussed in several chapters of a text. Because of the limitations imposed by large numbers of students and small amounts of time, your evaluation will have to be based on a sample of behavior—a three- or four-minute reading performance and questions covering points made in only a few sections of text material assigned for an exam. It is therefore important to try to obtain a representative, accurate sample.

Psychologists who have studied measurement and evaluation often recommend that as teachers prepare exams, they use a **table of specifications** to note the types and numbers of test items to be included so as to ensure thorough and systematic coverage. You can draw up a table of specifications by first listing along the left-hand margin of a piece of lined paper the important topics that have been covered. Then insert appropriate headings from the taxonomy of objectives for the cognitive domain (or for the affective or psychomotor domain, if appropriate) across the top of the page. An example of such a table of specifications for some of the information discussed in this chapter is provided in Figure 14.3. A computer spreadsheet program such as Microsoft Excel is an ideal tool for creating a table of specifications. Doing your work on the computer gives you the ability to save and modify it for future use.

Test specialists often recommend that you insert in the boxes of a table of specifications the percentage of test items that you intend to write for each topic and each type of objective. This practice forces you to think about both the number and the relative importance of your objectives before you start teaching or writing test items. Thus, if some objectives are more important to you than others, you will have a way of ensuring that these are tested more thoroughly. If, however, a test is going

- Necessary to obtain a representative sample of behavior when testing

- Table of specifications helps ensure an adequate sample of content, behavior

Figure 14.3 Example of a Table of Specifications for Material Covered in This Chapter

Topic	Objectives					
	Knows	Comprehends	Applies	Analyzes	Synthesizes	Evaluates
Nature of measurement and evaluation						
Purposes of measurement and evaluation						
Types of written tests						
Nature of performance tests						

to be brief and emphasize all objectives more or less equally, you may wish to put a check mark in each box as you write questions. If you discover that you are overloading some boxes and that others are empty, you can take steps to remedy the situation. The important point is that by taking steps to ensure that your tests cover what you want your students to know, you will be increasing the tests' validity.

For reasons to be discussed shortly, you may choose not to list all of the categories in the taxonomy for all subjects or at all grade levels. Tables of specifications that you draw up for your own use therefore may contain fewer headings across the top of the page than the table illustrated in Figure 14.3.

JOURNAL ENTRY
Using a Table of Specifications

3 **Consider the purpose of each test or measurement exercise in the light of the developmental characteristics of the students in your classes and the nature of the curriculum for your grade level.**

In addition to considering different uses of tests and other forms of measurement when you plan assessment strategies, you should think about the developmental characteristics of the students you plan to teach and the nature of the curriculum at your grade level. As noted in the discussion of Jean Piaget's theory early in this book, there are significant differences among preoperational, concrete operational, and formal thinkers. Furthermore, because primary grade children are asked to master a curriculum that is substantially different from the curriculum upper elementary and secondary school students are expected to learn, different forms of measurement should be used at each level.

● Elementary grade students tested as much for diagnostic, formative evaluation purposes as for summative purposes

Primary grade children are asked to concentrate on learning basic skills, and their progress—or lack of it—will often be apparent even if they are not asked to take tests. A second grader who has difficulty decoding many longer unfamiliar words, for instance, will reveal that inability each time she is asked to read. Upper elementary grade and middle school students are asked to improve and perfect their mastery of skills in reading, writing, and arithmetic and also to study topics in the sciences, social studies, and other subjects. Since their success in dealing with many subjects, learning materials, and tests often depends on reading ability, you may have to create tests to diagnose weaknesses and chart improvement (a formative evaluation function) as well as to establish grades.

At the secondary level, testing is done largely to assign grades and to determine if students are sufficiently prepared to take more advanced courses (as in Algebra I, Algebra II). Consequently, as you create a table of specifications for a particular instructional unit, you want to make sure that you have identified all of the important concepts and skills for that unit and that your test items cover most, if not all, of the levels of Bloom's Taxonomy.

4 **Decide whether a written test or a performance test is more appropriate.**

JOURNAL ENTRY
Using Different Types of Test Items

As you think about which types of questions to use in a particular situation, consider the student characteristics and curriculum differences noted earlier. In the primary grades, you may not use any written tests in the strict sense. Instead, you might ask your students to demonstrate skills, complete exercises (some of which may be similar to completion tests), and solve simple problems (often on worksheets). In the upper elementary and middle school grades, you may need to use or make up dozens of measurement instruments since many subjects must be graded. Accordingly, it may be necessary to make extensive use of completion, short-answer, and short-essay items that can be printed on the board or on paper. If you find it impossible or impractical to make up a table of specifications for each exam, at least refer to instructional objectives or a list of key points as you write questions. At the secondary level, you might do your best to develop some sort of table of specifications for exams not only to ensure measurement of objectives at various levels of the taxonomy but also to remind yourself to use different types of items.

In certain elementary and middle school subjects and in skill or laboratory subjects at the secondary level, performance tests may be more appropriate than written

● Rating scales and checklists make evaluations of performance more systematic

tests. At the primary grade level, for instance, you may be required to assign a grade in oral reading. In a high school home economics class, you may grade students on how well they produce a garment or a soufflé. In a woodshop class, you may base a grade on how well students construct a piece of furniture. In such cases, you can make evaluations more systematic and accurate by using rating scales and checklists and by attempting to equate (or at least take into account) the difficulty level of the performance to be rated.

To evaluate a product such as a garment or piece of furniture, you might use a checklist that you devised and handed out at the beginning of a course. Such a checklist should state the number of possible points that will be awarded for various aspects of the project—for example, accuracy of measurements and preparation of component parts, neatness of assembly, quality of finishing touches, and final appearance. To evaluate a performance, you might use the same approach, announcing beforehand how heavily you intend to weigh various aspects of execution. In music, for instance, you might note possible points to be awarded for tone, execution, accuracy, and interpretation. For both project and performance tasks, you might multiply the final score by a difficulty factor. (You have probably seen television coverage of Olympic events in which divers and gymnasts have their performance ratings multiplied by such a difficulty factor.)

5   **Make up and use a detailed answer key or rubric.**

a. Evaluate each answer by comparing it to the key or rubric.

JOURNAL ENTRY
Preparing a Detailed Key

One of the most valuable characteristics of a test is that it permits comparison of the permanently recorded answers of all students to a fixed set of criteria. A complete key or rubric not only reduces subjectivity; it can also save you much time and trouble when you are grading papers or defending your evaluation of questions.

For short-answer, true-false, matching, or multiple-choice questions, you should devise your key as you write and assemble the items. With planning and ingenuity, you can prepare a key that will greatly simplify grading. For essay questions, you should also prepare answers as you write the questions. If you ask students to write answers to a small number of comprehensive essay questions, you are likely to maximize the consistency of your grading process by grading all answers to the first question at one sitting, then grading all answers to the second question, and so on. However, if a test consists of eight or ten short-essay items (which can usually be answered in a half-hour or so), you would have to do too much paper shuffling to follow such a procedure. One way to speed up the grading of short-essay exams (so that you can evaluate up to thirty tests in a single session of forty minutes or so) is to use plus or minus grading. If you use a point scale to grade short-essay answers, you will spend an agonizing amount of time deciding just how much a given answer is worth. But with practice, you should be able to write short-essay questions and answers (on your key) that can be graded plus or minus.

To maintain consistency when scoring exams, teachers should use a scoring key for selected-response and short-answer items and a rubric for essay items.

To develop skill in writing such questions, make up a few formative quizzes that will not count toward a grade. Experiment with phrasing questions that require students to reveal that they either know or don't know the answer. Prepare your key as you write the questions. When the time comes to grade papers, simply make a yes or no decision about the correctness of each answer. With a felt-tip pen, make a bold check over each satisfactory answer on an exam, and tally the number of checks when you have read all the answers. (Counting up to eight or ten is obviously a lot quicker and easier than adding together various numbers of points for eight or ten answers.) Once you have developed skill in writing and evaluating short-essay questions that can be graded plus or minus, prepare and use summative exams. If you decide to use this type of exam, guard against the temptation to write items that measure only knowledge. Use a table of specifications, or otherwise take steps to write at least some questions that measure skills at the higher levels of the taxonomy for the cognitive domain.

b. Be willing and prepared to defend the evaluations you make.

You will probably get few complaints if you have a detailed key and can explain to the class when exams are returned how each answer was graded. To a direct challenge about a specific answer to an essay or short-essay question, you might respond by showing complainers an answer that received full credit and inviting them to compare it with their own.

Perhaps the best way to provide feedback about responses to multiple-choice questions is to prepare a feedback booklet. As you write each multiple-choice question, also write a brief explanation as to why you feel the answer is correct and why the distracters are incorrect. If you follow this policy (which takes less time than you might expect), you can often improve the questions as you write your defense of the answer. If you go a step further (described in the next point), you can obtain information to use in improving questions after they have been answered. This is a good policy to follow with any exam, multiple choice or otherwise.

6 **During and after the grading process, analyze questions and answers in order to improve future exams.**

JOURNAL ENTRY
Analyzing Test Items

If you prepare sufficient copies of feedback booklets for multiple-choice exams, you can supply them to all students when you hand back scored answer sheets (and copies of the question booklets). After students have checked their papers and identified and examined questions that were marked wrong, invite them to select up to three questions that they wish to challenge. Even after they read your explanation in the feedback booklet, many students are likely to feel that they selected a different answer than you did for logical and defensible reasons. Permit them to write out a description of the reasoning behind their choices. If an explanation seems plausible, give credit for the answer. If several students chose the same questions for comment, you have evidence that the item needs to be revised. (It's also possible that the information reflected in the item was not directly related to your objectives or was poorly taught.)

If you follow the procedure of supplying feedback booklets, it is almost essential to prepare at least two forms of every exam. After writing the questions, arrange them into two tests. Make perhaps half of the questions the same and half unique to each exam. (If you have enough questions, you might prepare three forms.) If you teach multiple sections, give the first form to period 1, the next form to period 2, and thereafter use the forms in random order. This procedure will reduce the possibility that some students in later classes will have advance information about most of the questions on the test. (Having two or more forms also equips you to use a mastery approach.)

If you find that you do not have time to prepare feedback booklets, you might invite students to select three answers to defend as they record their choices when taking multiple-choice exams. This will supply you with information about ambiguous questions, even though it will not provide feedback to students. It may also provide you with useful information about how well the items were written.

● Item analysis tells about difficulty, discriminating power of multiple-choice items

Turning back to multiple-choice questions, you may also want to use simple versions of item-analysis techniques that measurement specialists use to analyze and improve this type of item. These techniques will allow you to estimate the difficulty level and discriminating power of each item. Discriminating power is the ability of a test item to distinguish students who have learned that piece of information from students who have not. To do so, try the following steps:

1. Rank the test papers from highest score to lowest score.
2. If you have 50 or more, select approximately the top 30 percent, and call this the upper group. Select approximately the bottom 30 percent, and call this the

lower group. Set the middle group of papers aside. If you have 30–40 students, split the scores in the middle and create upper and lower groups. If you have fewer than 30 students, you have too few to conduct an item analysis (Nitko, 2004).

3. For each item, record the number of students in the upper group and in the lower group who selected the correct answer and each distracter as follows (the correct answer has an asterisk next to it):

Item 1 Alternatives	A	B*	C	D	E
Upper group	0	6	3	1	0
Lower group	3	2	2	3	0

4. Estimate the item difficulty by calculating the percentage of students who answered the item correctly. The difficulty index for the preceding item is 40 percent ($8/20 \times 100$). Note that the smaller the percentage is, the more difficult the item is.

5. Estimate the item discriminating power by subtracting the number in the lower group who answered the item correctly from the number in the upper group, and divide by one-half of the total number of students included in the item analysis. For the preceding example, the discrimination index is 0.40 ($6 - 2 \div 10$). When the index is positive, as it is here, it indicates that more students in the upper group than in the lower group answered the item correctly. A negative value indicates just the opposite.

As you can see, this type of item analysis is not difficult to do, nor is it likely to be very time-consuming. It is important to remember, however, that the benefits of item analysis can quickly be lost if you ignore certain limitations. One is that you will be working with relatively small numbers of students. Therefore, the results of item analysis are likely to vary as you go from class to class or from test to test with the same class. Because of this variation, you should retain items that a measurement specialist would discard or revise. In general, you should retain multiple-choice items whose difficulty index lies between 50 and 90 percent and whose discrimination index is positive (Gronlund, 2003). Another limitation is that you may have objectives that everyone must master. If you do an effective job of teaching these objectives, the corresponding test items are likely to be answered correctly by nearly every student. These items should be retained rather than revised to meet arbitrary criteria of difficulty and discrimination.

To review this chapter, see the ACE practice tests and PowerPoint slides on the textbook web site. You may also want to try the interactive Flashcards for glossary terms.

Resources for Further Investigation

● Suggestions for Constructing Written and Performance Assessments

For specific suggestions on ways to write different types of items for paper-and-pencil tests of knowledge and on methods for constructing and using rating scales and checklists to measure products, performances, and procedures, consult one or more of the following books: *Assessment of Student Achievement* (7th ed., 2003), by Norman Gronlund; *Classroom Assessment: What Teachers Need to Know* (3rd ed., 2002), by W. James Popham; *Student-Involved Classroom Assessment* (3rd ed., 2001b), by Richard Stiggins; and *Educational Assessment of Students* (4th ed., 2004), by Anthony Nitko.

Jeffrey Smith, Lisa Smith, and Richard De Lisi offer an approach to assessment that flows logically and naturally from teachers' instructional activities; hence the title of their book, *Natural Classroom Assessment* (2001). This book is also note-

worthy for its open, conversational, and humorous writing style.

Elizabeth Hebert discusses how to create and evaluate student portfolios in *The Power of Portfolios* (2001). Guidelines for using informal assessment methods (such as observational checklists and rating scales), performance tests, and selected-response and essay tests can be found in *Informal Classroom Assessment Strategies for Teachers* (2003), by George Taylor.

● Scoring Rubrics for Performance Tests

If you use performance tests, you will need to know how to construct and use scoring rubrics. The following two books can help you do that. *Scoring Rubrics in the Classroom* (2001), by Judith Arter and Jay McTighe, describes how to construct scoring rubrics for various performance tasks. Numerous examples are provided in the section titled "Resource: Rubrics

Galore." *Understanding Scoring Rubrics: A Guide for Teachers* (2002), edited by Carol Boston, contains eight chapters written by measurement specialists on various aspects of rubric construction and use. The last section of this book provides a list of eleven online resources, nine of which were current as of February 2, 2004. (The site for the ERIC Clearinghouse on Assessment and Evaluation has been closed, and the Staff Room for Ontario's Teachers can now be found at **www.quadro.net/ ~ecoxon/Reporting/rubrics.htm**.)

The web site of the organization Relearning by Design (**www.relearning.org/**) contains a Resources page on which you can either view or download a variety of materials and references on classroom assessment, portfolios, rubrics, and grading. Another part of the site, the CCA Curriculum Bank, allows you to search, download, and adapt curriculum units designed by educators in New Jersey school districts.

● Writing Higher-Level Questions

As Benjamin Bloom and others point out, teachers have a disappointing tendency to write test items that reflect the lowest level of the taxonomy: knowledge. To avoid this failing, carefully read Part 2 of *Taxonomy of Educational Objectives: The Classification of Educational Goals, Handbook I: Cognitive Domain* (1956), edited by Benjamin Bloom, Max Englehart, Edward Furst, Walker Hill, and David Krathwohl. Each level of the taxonomy is clearly explained and followed by several pages of illustrative test items.

● Analyzing Test Items

Anthony Nitko discusses item-analysis procedures for multiple-choice and performance tests in Chapter 14 (pp. 313–320) of *Educational Assessment of Students* (4th ed., 2004). For both types of tests, there are procedures for assessing both the difficulty and the discriminating power of each item. A discussion of item-analysis procedures can also be found in Chapter 10 of *Educational Testing and Measurement: Classroom Application and Practice* (7th ed., 2003), by Tom Kubiszyn and Gary Borich.

Question Mark Computing, based in Great Britain, produces a software program that can help teachers generate high-quality test items. Information on the software can be found at **www.questionmark.com/uk/home.htm**.

● Classroom Grading

For detailed information on how to construct an accurate and fair grading system, examine *Transforming Classroom Grading* (2000), by Robert J. Marzano, and *Developing Grading and Reporting Systems for Student Learning* (2001), by Thomas Guskey and Jane Bailey.

● Something Different

In *Using Assessments to Teach for Understanding: A Casebook for Educators* (2002), edited by Judith Shulman, Andrea Whittaker, and Michele Lew, fifteen teachers provide brief accounts of the classroom assessment problems they encountered and how they dealt with them.

Summary

1. Classroom assessment, which involves the measurement and evaluation of student learning, accounts for about one-third of a teacher's class time.

2. Measurement involves ranking individuals according to how much of a particular characteristic they possess. Evaluation involves making judgments about the value or worth of a set of measures.

3. Teachers give tests and assign grades to communicate to others how well students have mastered the teacher's objectives, find out if students are keeping up with and understanding the learning material, diagnose students' strengths and weaknesses, and positively affect students' approaches to studying.

4. Research indicates that students who take four to six exams a term learn more than students who take fewer or no exams.

5. Written tests are used to measure how much knowledge people have about some topic. Test items can be classified as selected response (multiple-choice, true-false, matching), and constructed response (short-answer and essay).

6. Selected-response tests are efficient to administer and score but tend to reflect the lowest level of the cognitive domain taxonomy and provide no information about what students can do with the knowledge they have learned. They may also lead students to believe that learning is just the accumulation of factual knowledge.

7. Short-answer tests measure recall, rather than recognition, of information and allow for comprehensive coverage of a topic, but they have the same disadvantages as selected-response tests.

8. Essay tests measure such high-level skills as analysis, synthesis, and evaluation but are difficult to grade consistently, are time-consuming to grade, and allow only limited coverage of material. In the near future, essay scoring by computer may reduce these disadvantages.

9. Performance tests measure how well students use basic knowledge to perform a particular skill or produce a particular product under somewhat realistic conditions.

10. Performance tests are characterized by active responding, realistic conditions, complex problems, a close relationship between teaching and testing, use of scoring rubrics, and use of test results for formative evaluation purposes.

11. Rubrics are beneficial for both teachers and students. They help teachers assess student performances more objectively, consistently, and efficiently and align instructional activities with the demands of the performance measure. They help students understand the teacher's expectations, monitor their progress, and make improvements in their work.

12. Performance tests present such challenges to teachers as increased time for assessment, explaining to parents how performance test scores translate to letter grades, spend-

ing more time helping students prepare for and pass tests, and not letting the summative evaluation purpose of standardized tests crowd out the formative evaluation purpose of performance tests.

13. It has not yet been completely demonstrated that student performances and products can be measured reliably (consistently) and validly (accurately).

14. When grades are determined according to a norm-referenced system, each student's level of performance is compared to the performance of a group of similar students. A norm-referenced scheme is used by those who feel that external criteria for determining the adequacy of performance are unavailable.

15. In a criterion-referenced grading system, each student's level of performance is compared to a predetermined standard.

16. A mastery approach to criterion-referenced measurement and evaluation, which is based on the concept of mastery learning, allows students multiple opportunities to pass tests.

17. The potential benefits of measurement and evaluation activities can be undermined by any one of several inappropriate testing and grading practices.

18. Classroom assessment can be made easier through the use of such technological products and formats as test-item banks, electronic gradebooks, simulation programs, and digital portfolios.

19. To be sure that the number of various types of items on a test is consistent with your instructional objectives, prepare a table of specifications.

20. For primary and elementary grade students, the formative evaluation purpose of tests should be emphasized at least as much as the summative purpose.

21. Item-analysis procedures exist to determine the difficulty and discriminating power of multiple-choice items.

Key Terms

measurement *(456)*
evaluation *(456)*
summative evaluation *(457)*
formative evaluation *(457)*

performance tests *(461)*
authentic assessment *(461)*
portfolio *(462)*
rubric *(464)*

norm-referenced grading *(470)*
criterion-referenced grading *(472)*
digital portfolio *(480)*
table of specifications *(484)*

15 Understanding and Using Standardized Tests

KEY POINTS

These key points will help you learn the important information in this chapter. To help you study, they also appear in the margins of the pages, next to the text where they are discussed.

Standardized Tests

- Standardized tests: items presented and scored in standard fashion; results reported with reference to standards
- Basic purpose of standardized test is to obtain accurate, representative sample of some aspect of a person
- Standardized test scores used to identify strengths and weaknesses, plan instruction, select students for programs
- Reliability: similarity between two rankings of test scores obtained from the same individual
- Validity: how accurately a test measures what users want it to measure
- Content validity: how well test items cover a body of knowledge and skill
- Predictive validity: how well a test score predicts later performance
- Construct validity: how accurately a test measures a theoretical attribute
- Meaningfulness of standardized test scores depends on representativeness of norm group
- Formal testing of young children is inappropriate because of rapid developmental changes
- Achievement tests measure how much of a subject or skill has been learned
- Diagnostic achievement tests designed to identify specific strengths and weaknesses
- Competency tests determine if potential graduates possess basic skills
- Aptitude tests measure predisposition to develop additional capabilities in specific areas

- Norm-referenced tests compare one student with others
- Criterion-referenced tests indicate degree of mastery of objectives
- Percentile rank: percentage of scores at or below a given point
- Standard deviation: degree of deviation from the mean of a distribution
- z score: how far a raw score is from the mean in standard deviation units
- T score: raw score translated to a scale of 1–100 with a mean of 50
- Stanine score: student performance indicated with reference to a 9-point scale based on normal curve

Using Standardized Tests for Accountability Purposes: High-Stakes Testing

- High-stakes testing: using test results to hold students and educators accountable for achievement
- NCLB requires annual testing in math and reading, annual progress for all students, public reports
- High-stakes tests expected to improve clarity of goals, quality control, teaching methods, and student motivation
- High-stakes tests criticized because of structural limitations, misinterpretation/misuse of results, narrow view of motivation, adverse side effects
- Research on effects of high-stakes testing limited and inconsistent

Standardized Testing and Technology

- Web sites of state departments of education, private companies provide services that help prepare students for state assessments
- Computer-adaptive testing: computers determine sequence and difficulty level of test items

Because standardized assessment of scholastic aptitude and achievement is such a popular practice in the United States (as well as in many other countries), this chapter will focus on the nature of standardized tests, how they are used to assess student variability, and how these test results can be employed in putting together effective instructional programs for students. As you will see, the use of standardized tests is truly a double-edged sword: it has the potential to harm students as well as help them. ●

STANDARDIZED TESTS

Nature of Standardized Tests

To guide your study of this chapter, see the Chapter Themes on the textbook web site, accessible from **http://education. college.hmco.com/students.**

The kinds of assessment instruments described in this chapter are typically referred to as **standardized tests**, although the term *published tests* is sometimes used (because they are prepared, distributed, and scored by publishing companies or independent test services). You have almost certainly taken several of these tests during your academic career, and so you are probably familiar with their appearance and general characteristics. They are called standardized tests for the following reasons:

- They are designed by people with specialized knowledge and training in test construction.
- Every person who takes the test responds to the same items under the same conditions.
- The answers are evaluated according to the same scoring standards.
- The scores are interpreted through comparison to the scores obtained from a group (called a norm group) that took the same test under the same conditions or (in the case of some achievement tests) through comparison to a predetermined standard.

● Standardized tests: items presented and scored in standard fashion; results reported with reference to standards

The basic purpose of giving a standardized test is to obtain an *accurate and representative sample* of how much of some characteristic a person possesses (such as knowledge of a particular set of mathematical concepts and operations). The benefit of getting an accurate measure from a test is obvious. When standardized tests are well designed, they are likely to be more accurate measures of a particular characteristic than nonstandardized tests. Standardized tests measure a *sample* of the characteristic since a comprehensive measure would be too expensive, time-consuming, and cumbersome to administer (Walsh & Betz, 2001).

● Basic purpose of standardized test is to obtain accurate, representative sample of some aspect of a person

Prevalence of Standardized Testing

No one knows for certain how many students are tested in a given year or how many tests the typical student takes because comprehensive and unambiguous data are not available. (If a student takes an achievement battery that covers four subjects, does that count as one test or four?) Nevertheless, some numbers are available. According to the National Board of Educational Testing and Public Policy (Clarke, Madaus, Horn, & Ramos, 2001), approximately 147 million standardized tests are administered annually to public school students. Of this total, about 51 million are administered as part of state-mandated assessment programs, 85 million are given as part of district-level programs, and 11 million are given to special populations. Whatever the actual figure is for the number of tests given annually, it seems accurate to say that American schools engage in a substantial amount of standardized testing.

Uses of Standardized Tests

● Standardized test scores used to identify strengths and weaknesses, plan instruction, select students for programs

Historically, educators have used standardized test scores, particularly achievement tests, for a variety of instructionally related purposes. Teachers, guidance counselors, and principals have used test data to identify general strengths and weaknesses in student achievement, inform parents of their child's general level of achievement, plan instructional lessons, group students for instruction, and recommend students for placement in special programs. To cite just one example, when a child moves to a different school, it is highly desirable for those in the new school to have some idea as to what the child knows about basic subjects. Standardized achievement tests do an effective job of providing information about the mastery of general subject matter and skills and thus can be used for planning, grouping, placement, and instructional purposes.

When properly used, standardized test scores can keep parents, students, and educators aware of a student's general level of achievement, and they can help teachers and administrators make decisions about placing students in special programs.

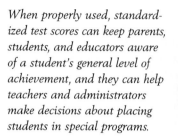

If you are like most other people, you took a variety of standardized tests throughout your elementary and high school years. Do you think that those tests adequately reflected what you had learned and were capable of learning and therefore were always used in your best interest? What can you do to increase the chances you will use test scores to help *your* students fulfill their potential?

When you read the test profiles that report how students in your classes have performed on standardized tests, you will get a general idea of some of your students' strengths and weaknesses. If certain students are weak in particular skill areas and you want to help them overcome those weaknesses, test results *may* give you *some* insights into possible ways to provide remedial instruction. If most of your students score below average in certain segments of the curriculum, you will know that you should devote more time and effort to presenting those topics and skills to the entire class. You can and should, of course, supplement what you learn from standardized test results with your own tests and observations in order to design potentially effective forms of remedial or advanced instruction.

Criteria for Evaluating Standardized Tests

Like most other things, standardized tests vary in quality. To use test scores wisely, you need to be an informed consumer—to know what characteristics distinguish well-constructed from poorly constructed tests. Four criteria are widely used to evaluate standardized tests: reliability, validity, normed excellence, and examinee appropriateness. Each of these criteria will be explained individually.

Reliability   A basic assumption that psychologists make about human characteristics (such as intelligence and achievement) is that they are relatively stable, at least over short periods of time. For most people, this assumption seems to be true. Thus, you should be able to count on a test's results being consistent, just as you might count on a reliable worker to do a consistent job time after time. This stability in test performance is known as **reliability**. You can think of reliability as the extent to which test scores are free of measurement errors that arise from such factors as test anxiety, making correct guesses, vaguely worded items, and unclear scoring procedures (Pitoniak & Royer, 2001). It is one of the most important characteristics of standardized tests and can be assessed in a number of ways.

   To illustrate the importance of reliability, imagine that you wish to form cooperative learning groups for mathematics. Because these types of groups should be composed of five to six students who differ on a number of characteristics, including

● Reliability: similarity between two rankings of test scores obtained from the same individual

achievement, you use the students' most recent scores from a standardized mathematics test to assign two high, medium, and low achievers to each group. One month later, the children are retested, and you now find that many of those who scored at the top initially (and whom you thought were very knowledgeable about mathematics) now score in the middle or at the bottom. Conversely, many students who initially scored low now have average or above-average scores. What does that do to your confidence in being able to form heterogeneous groups based on scores from this test? If you want to be able to differentiate among individuals consistently, you need to use an instrument that performs consistently.

Psychologists who specialize in constructing standardized tests assess reliability in a variety of ways:

- *Test-retest reliability.* Psychologists administer the same test to the same people on two occasions and measure the extent to which the rankings change over time.
- *Alternate-form reliability.* Psychologists administer two equivalent forms of a test to the same group of students at the same time and compare the results.
- *Split-half reliability.* Psychologists administer a single test to a group of students, create two scores by dividing the test in half, and measure the extent to which the rankings change from one half to the other. This method gauges the internal consistency of a test.

Regardless of which method is used to assess reliability, the goal is to create two rankings of scores and see how similar the rankings are. This degree of consistency is expressed as a correlation coefficient (abbreviated with a lowercase r) that ranges from 0 to 1. Well-constructed standardized tests should have correlation coefficients of about 0.95 for split-half reliability, 0.90 for test-retest reliability, and 0.85 for alternate-form reliability (Kubiszyn & Borich, 2003). Bear in mind, however, that a particular test may not report all three forms of reliability and that reliabilities for subtests and for younger age groups (kindergarten through second grade) are likely to be lower than these overall figures.

● Validity: how accurately a test measures what users want it to measure

Validity   A second important characteristic of a test is that it accurately measures what it claims to measure. A reading comprehension test should measure just that—nothing more, nothing less. Whenever we speak of a test's accuracy in this sense, we are referring to its **validity**.

Because most of the characteristics we are interested in knowing something about (such as arithmetic skills, spatial aptitude, intelligence, and knowledge of the American Civil War) are internal and hence not directly observable, tests are indirect measures of those attributes. Therefore, any test-based conclusions we may draw about how much of a characteristic a person possesses, or any predictions we may make about how well a person will perform in the future (on other types of tests, in a job, or in a specialized academic program, for example), are properly referred to as *inferences.* So when we inquire about the validity of a test by asking, "Does this test measure what it claims to measure?" we are really asking, "How accurate are the inferences that I wish to draw about the test taker?" (See, for example, Messick, 1989.)

The degree to which these inferences can be judged accurate, or valid, depends on the type and quality of the supporting evidence that we can muster. Three kinds of evidence that underlie test-based inferences are content validity evidence, predictive validity evidence, and construct validity evidence.

● Content validity: how well test items cover a body of knowledge and skill

Content Validity Evidence   This kind of evidence rests on a set of judgments about how well a test's items reflect the particular body of knowledge and skill (called a *domain* by measurement specialists) about which we want to draw inferences. If a test on the American Civil War, for example, contained no items on the war's causes, its great battles, or the years it encompassed, some users might be hesitant to call someone who had achieved a high score knowledgeable about this topic. Then again, other users might not be nearly so disturbed by these omissions (and the inference

A standardized test that is considered to be valid measures what it claims to measure and allows educators to make reasonably accurate predictions about how well students are likely to perform academically in the near future.

that would be drawn from the test score) if they considered such information to be relatively unimportant.

● Predictive validity: how well a test score predicts later performance

Predictive Validity Evidence   This evidence allows us to make probabilistic statements about how well students will behave in the future ("Based on his test scores, there is a strong likelihood that Yusef will do well in the creative writing program next year"). Many colleges, for example, require students to take the American College Testing Program (ACT) or the Scholastic Assessment Test (SAT) and then use the results (along with other information) to predict each prospective student's grade-point average at the end of the first year. All other things being equal, students with higher test scores are expected to have higher grade-point averages than students with lower test scores and thus stand a better chance of being admitted.

● Construct validity: how accurately a test measures a theoretical attribute

Construct Validity Evidence   This evidence indicates how accurately a test measures a theoretical description of some internal attribute of a person. Such attributes—for example, intelligence, creativity, motivation, and anxiety—are called *constructs* by psychologists.

   To illustrate the nature of construct validity, we will use a hypothetical theory of intelligence called the Perfectly Valid theory. This theory holds that highly intelligent individuals should have higher-than-average school grades now and in the future, demonstrate superior performance on tasks that involve abstract reasoning, and be able to distinguish worthwhile from nonworthwhile goals. They may or may not, however, be popular among their peers. If the Perfectly Valid theory is accurate and if someone has done a good job of constructing an intelligence test based on this theory (the Smart Intelligence Test), people's scores on the Smart Test should vary in accordance with predictions derived from the Perfectly Valid theory. We should see, for example, a strong, positive relationship, or correlation, between intelligence quotient (IQ) scores and grade-point average but no relationship between IQ scores and measures of popularity. As more and more of this type of evidence is supplied, we can feel increasingly confident in drawing the inference that the Smart Intelligence Test is an accurate measure of the Perfectly Valid theory of intelligence.

Normed Excellence   For a test score to have any meaning, it has to be compared to some yardstick, or measure of performance. Standardized tests use the performance of a norm group as the measure against which all other scores are compared. A **norm group** is a sample of individuals carefully chosen so as to reflect the larger population of students for whom the test is intended. In many cases, the larger population consists of all elementary school children, all middle school children, or all high school children in the United States.

● Meaningfulness of standardized test scores depends on representativeness of norm group

The norm group must closely match the larger population it represents on such major demographic variables as age, sex, race, ethnic group, region of country, family income, and occupation of head of household. These variables are considered major because they are strongly associated with differences in school performance. If, for example, the U.S. Census Bureau reports that 38 percent of all Hispanic American males between the ages of six and thirteen live in the southwestern region of the country, a good test constructor testing in the Southwest will try to put together a norm group that contains the same percentage of six- to thirteen-year-old Hispanic American males.

As you might suspect, problems of score interpretation arise when the major demographic characteristics of individuals who take the test are not reflected in the norm group. Suppose you were trying to interpret the score of a fourteen-year-old African American male on the EZ Test of Academic Achievement. If the oldest students in the norm group were twelve years of age and if African American children were not part of the norm group, you would have no way of knowing if your student's score was below average, average, or above average, compared to the norm.

Examinee Appropriateness   Because developing a standardized test is a substantial undertaking that requires a considerable investment of money, time, and expertise, most tests of this type are designed for nationwide use. But the curriculum in school districts in different types of communities and in different sections of the country varies to a considerable extent. Therefore, it is important to estimate how appropriate a given test is for a particular group of students. When you are estimating the content validity of a test, you should pay attention not only to how well the questions measure what they are supposed to measure, but also to whether they are appropriate in terms of level of difficulty and the vocabulary and characteristics of your students.

● Formal testing of young children is inappropriate because of rapid developmental changes

For example, the administration of readiness tests to preschool and kindergarten children to determine whether they are ready to begin school or should be promoted to first grade has been heavily criticized on the basis of examinee appropriateness. A major problem with the use of tests for the making of admission and retention decisions in the early grades is their low reliability. Young children change physically, socially, emotionally, and intellectually so rapidly that many of them score very differently when retested six months later (Bjorklund, 2000).

Types of Standardized Tests

In this section we will examine two major categories of standardized tests—achievement tests and aptitude tests—each of which has several varieties. We will also examine two approaches to the interpretation of test scores: norm referenced and criterion referenced.

● Achievement tests measure how much of a subject or skill has been learned

Achievement Tests   One type of standardized test that you probably took during your elementary school years was the **single-subject achievement test**, designed to assess how much you had learned—that is, achieved—in a particular basic school subject. The very first standardized test you took was probably designed to evaluate aspects of reading performance. Then at intervals of two years or so, you probably worked your way tensely and laboriously through **achievement batteries** designed to assess your performance in reading as well as math, language, and perhaps other subjects. During your high school years, you may have taken one or more achievement batteries that evaluated more sophisticated understanding of basic reading-writing-arithmetic skills, as well as course content in specific subjects.

At some point during your elementary school years, you may also have been asked to take a **diagnostic test**, a special type of single-subject achievement test intended to identify the source of a problem in basic subjects and perhaps in study skills as well.

● Diagnostic achievement tests designed to identify specific strengths and weaknesses

Depending on when and where you graduated from high school, you may have been asked to take a **competency test** a few months before the end of your senior year. Competency tests came into use in the mid-1970s when it was discovered that many graduates of American high schools were unable to handle basic skills. In many school districts, therefore, students are asked to prove that they are competent in reading, writing, and arithmetic before they are awarded diplomas.

● Competency tests determine if potential graduates possess basic skills

You may have earned some of your college credits by taking the College-Level Examination Program, a **special-purpose achievement test.** Depending on the state in which you choose to teach, you may be required to take and pass another special-purpose achievement test, the National Teacher Examination, before being granted a teaching certificate.

Aptitude Tests   An aptitude is an underlying predisposition to respond to some task or situation in a particular way; it makes possible the development of more advanced capabilities (Snow, 1992). The word *aptitude* is derived from the Middle English *apte*, which meant "to grasp" or "to reach" and is related to the French *à propos*, which means "appropriate," "fitting," or "suited to a purpose."

For several decades, aptitudes have come to be identified entirely with cognitive predispositions, and **aptitude tests**, designed to indicate the level of knowledge and skill a student could acquire with effective instruction, have become increasingly common. Thus, there are now a number of somewhat general tests of **scholastic aptitude** (the cognitive skills deemed most likely to predict a student's ability to cope with academic demands), like the familiar SAT, and many specific tests of aptitude, such as tests of musical aptitude, mechanical aptitude, and spatial relations.

● Aptitude tests measure predisposition to develop additional capabilities in specific areas

However, Richard Snow (1992) argues for a broader conception of aptitude that also includes affective and motivational predispositions. In his scheme, which we find attractive, such characteristics of people as extroversion, conformity, independence, production of mental images, attention span, beliefs, and fear of failure would also be considered aptitudes because they are fairly broad and stable predispositions to respond to tasks in certain ways.

Further, some contemporary psychologists argue that we should stop trying to distinguish between aptitude (or ability) and achievement and should abandon the view that one's ability is the cause of one's achievement. Robert Sternberg (1998), for example, notes that the items that appear in various mental ability tests (such as vocabulary, reading comprehension, verbal analogies, arithmetic problem solving, and determining similarities) are often the focus of classroom instruction and are the same types of items that appear on many achievement tests. Second, he notes that achievement test scores are as good predictors of ability test scores as ability test scores are predictors of achievement test scores. Rather than thinking of such aptitudes as verbal reasoning, mathematical reasoning, spatial orientation, and musical aptitude as largely inherited capabilities that are responsible for the level of expertise one develops in a particular area, he prefers to think of aptitudes as various forms of *developing* expertise.

● Norm-referenced tests compare one student with others

Norm-Referenced Tests   Most of the achievement and aptitude tests just described are referred to as **norm-referenced tests** since performance is evaluated with reference to norms—the performance of others—established when the final form of the test was administered to the sample of students who made up the standardization group. After taking an achievement battery in the elementary grades, for example, you were probably told that you had performed as well on reading comprehension questions as 80 percent (or whatever) of all of the students who took the test. If you take the Graduate Record Examination (GRE), you will be told how far from the average score of 500 you are (in terms of a score to be described shortly). Thus, you will learn just where you stand in a distribution of scores arranged from lowest to highest. Tests that are constructed according to norm-referenced criteria tend to cover a broad range of knowledge and skill but have relatively few items for each topic or skill tested. But in the last twenty-five years or so, an alternative approach to reporting achievement scores has been developed: the criterion-referenced method.

● Criterion-referenced tests indicate degree of mastery of objectives

Criterion-Referenced Tests   A different approach to reporting achievement test scores is used by **criterion-referenced tests**. When a test is scored in this manner, an individual's performance is not compared with the performance of others. Instead, students are evaluated according to how well they have mastered specific objectives in various well-defined skill areas. Because of this feature, you may find criterion-referenced tests more useful than norm-referenced tests in determining who needs how much additional instruction in what areas (provided, of course, that the test's objectives closely match your own).

The criterion-referenced approach is intended to reduce overtones of competition and emphasize mastery of objectives at a rate commensurate with students' abilities.

Tests that have criterion-referenced scoring systems tend to cover less ground than norm-referenced tests but contain more items for the objectives they do assess. Because norm-referenced and criterion-referenced scoring systems provide different types of information about student achievement, many testing companies provide both types of scores.

A relatively new development in criterion-referenced testing has occurred in several states. In an attempt to counter some of the disadvantages of traditional norm-referenced standardized testing, states such as Vermont and Kentucky have begun to rely partly or entirely on performance-based measures in their statewide assessment systems. We will offer some examples from these new tests later in this chapter.

Do you prefer norm-referenced or criterion-referenced tests? Why? Can you describe circumstances in which a norm-referenced test would be clearly preferable to a criterion-referenced test, and vice versa?

Interpreting Standardized Test Scores

Scores on the most widely used standardized tests are typically reported on student profile forms that summarize and explain the results. Although most profiles contain sufficient information to make it possible to interpret scores without additional background, you should know in advance about the kinds of scores you may encounter, particularly since you may be asked to explain scores to students as well as to their parents.

Grade Equivalent Scores   The **grade equivalent score** interprets test performance in terms of grade levels. A student who makes a grade equivalent score of 4.7 on an achievement test, for example, got the same number of items right on this test as the average fourth grader in the standardization group achieved by the seventh month of the school year.

The grade equivalent score was once widely used at the elementary level, but because it may lead to misinterpretations, it is not as popular as it once was. One problem with grade equivalent scores is the tendency to misinterpret a score above a student's actual grade level as an indication that the student is capable of consistently working at that level. This kind of assumption might lead parents or perhaps teachers themselves to consider accelerated promotion. Remember that although such scores may show that a student did somewhat better on the test than the average student a grade or two above her, they do not mean that the student tested has acquired knowledge of all the skills covered in the grade that she would miss if she skipped a grade.

● Percentile rank: percentage of scores at or below a given point

Percentile Ranks   Probably the most widely used score for standardized tests is the **percentile rank**. This score indicates the percentage of students who are at and below a given student's score. It provides specific information about relative position.

Students earning a percentile rank of 87 did as well as or better than 87 percent of the students in the particular normative group being used. They did not get 87 percent of the questions right—unless by coincidence—and this is the point parents are most likely to misunderstand. Parents may have been brought up on the percentages grading system, in which 90 or above was A, 80 to 90 was B, and so on down the line. If you report that a son or daughter has a percentile rank of 50, some parents are horror-struck or outraged, not understanding that the child's score on this test is average, not a failure. In such cases, the best approach is to emphasize that the percentile rank tells the percentage of cases at or below the child's score. You might also talk in terms of a hypothetical group of 100; for example, a child with a percentile rank of 78 did as well as or better than 78 out of every 100 students who took the test.

Although the percentile rank gives simple and direct information on relative position, it has a major disadvantage: the difference in achievement among students clustered around the middle of the distribution is often considerably less than the difference among those at the extremes. The reason is that *most* scores are clustered around the middle of most distributions of large groups of students. The difference in raw score (number of items answered correctly) between students at percentile ranks 50 and 51 may be 1 point. But the difference in raw score between the student ranked 98 and one ranked 97 may be 10 or 15 points because the best (and worst) students scatter toward the extremes. This quality of percentile ranks means that ranks on different tests cannot be averaged. To get around that difficulty, standard scores are often used.

● Standard deviation: degree of deviation from the mean of a distribution

Standard Scores   Standard scores are expressed in terms of a common unit: the **standard deviation**. This statistic indicates the degree to which scores in a group of tests (a distribution) differ from the average, or mean. (The *mean* is the arithmetical average of a distribution and is calculated by adding all scores and dividing the total by the number of scores.) The standard deviation is most valuable when it can be related to the normal probability curve. Figure 15.1 shows a normal probability curve indicating the percentage of cases to be found within three standard deviations above and below the mean. The horizontal axis indicates the score, ranging from low on the left to high on the right; the vertical axis represents the number of cases

Figure 15.1 Normal Probability Curve

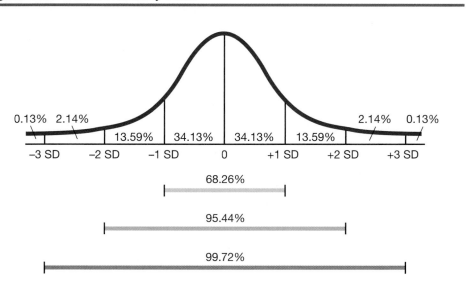

corresponding to each score. Notice, for example, that more than 68 percent of the cases fall between +1 SD (one standard deviation above the mean) and −1 SD (one standard deviation below the mean).

As you can see from the figure, the normal probability curve, or **normal curve** as it is usually known, is a mathematical concept that depicts a hypothetical bell-shaped distribution of scores. Such a perfectly symmetrical distribution rarely, if ever, occurs in real life. However, since many distributions of human characteristics and performance closely *resemble* the normal distribution, it is often assumed that such distributions are typical enough to be treated as "normal." Thus, information that mathematicians derive for the hypothetical normal distribution can be applied to the approximately normal distributions that are found when human attributes are measured. When very large numbers of students are asked to take tests designed by specialists who go to great lengths to cancel out the impact of selective factors, it may be appropriate to interpret the students' scores on such tests with reference to the normal curve.

For purposes of discussion, and for purposes of acquiring familiarity with test scores, it will be sufficient for you to know about two of the standard scores that are derived from standard deviations. One, called a **z score**, tells how far a given raw score is from the mean in standard deviation units. A z score of −1.5, for example, would mean that the student was 1.5 standard deviation units below the mean. Because some z scores (such as the one in the example just given) are negative and involve decimals, **T scores** are often used instead. T scores range from 0 to 100 and use a pre-selected mean of 50 to get away from negative values. Most standardized tests that use T scores offer detailed explanations, either in the test booklet or on the student profile of scores, of how they should be interpreted. In fact, many test profiles adopt the form of a narrative report when explaining the meaning of all scores used.

To grasp the relationship among z scores, T scores, and percentile ranks, examine Figure 15.2. The diagram shows each scale marked off below a normal curve. It supplies information about the interrelationships of these various scores, provided that the distribution you are working with is essentially normal. In a normal distribution, for example, a z score of +1 is the same as a T score of 60 or a percentile rank of 84; a z score of −2 is the same as a T score of 30 or a percentile rank of about 2. (In addition,

● z score: how far a raw score is from the mean in standard deviation units

● T score: raw score translated to a scale of 1–100 with a mean of 50

Figure 15.2 Relationship Among z Scores, T Scores, and Percentile Ranks

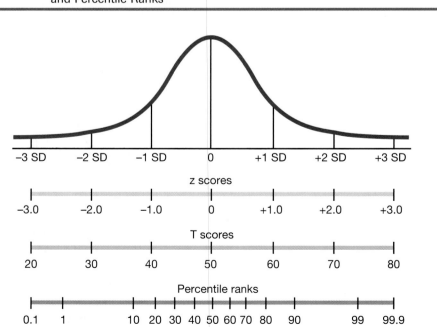

notice that the distance between the percentile ranks clustered around the middle is only a small fraction of the distance between the percentile ranks at the ends of the distribution.)

Stanine Scores   During World War II, U.S. Air Force psychologists developed a statistic called the **stanine score** (an abbreviation of "standard nine-point scale"). The name reflects the fact that this is a type of standard score, and it divides a population into nine groups. Each stanine is one-half of a standard deviation unit, as indicated in Figure 15.3.

When stanines were introduced on test profiles reporting the performance of public school children on standardized tests, they were often used to group students. (Students in stanines 1, 2, and 3 would be placed in one class; those in 4, 5, and 6 in another class; and so on.) For the reasons given in the chapter "Accommodating Student Variability" and later in this chapter, such ability grouping has become a highly controversial issue in American schools. Consequently, stanine scores are now used just to indicate relative standing. They are easier to understand than z scores or T scores since any child or parent can understand that stanines represent a 9-point scale with 1 as the lowest, 5 as the average, and 9 as the highest. Furthermore, unlike percentile ranks, stanine scores can be averaged. When it is desirable to have more precise information about relative standing, however, percentile ranks may be more useful, even though they cannot be averaged.

Local and National Norms   Percentile ranks and stanines are often used when local norms are prepared. As noted in our earlier description of how standardized tests are developed, the norms used to determine a student's level of performance are established by asking a representative sample of students to take the final form of the test. Inevitably, there will be differences between school systems (in texts used and the time during a school year or years when certain topics are covered, for instance). Accordingly, some test publishers report scores in terms of local as well as national norms. Each student's performance is thus compared not only with the performance of the members of the standardization group but also with the performance of all students in the same school system.

Earlier, we pointed out that standardized tests can be used in several ways to support the instructional goals of a school and a teacher. When teachers fully understand the characteristic being measured; reliable, valid, and well-normed tests are readily available; and teachers know how to interpret test results appropriately,

● Stanine score: student performance indicated with reference to a 9-point scale based on normal curve

For help in learning the new terms introduced in this chapter, you may want to use the glossary Flashcards on the textbook web site.

pause & reflect

If you had to tell parents about the results of a standardized test, which type of score could you explain most clearly: raw score, percentile rank, z score, T score, or stanine score? Which do you think would be most informative for parents? For you? If you do not understand these tests completely, what can you do about this situation?

Figure 15.3 Percentage of Cases in Each Stanine (with Standard Deviation Units Indicated)

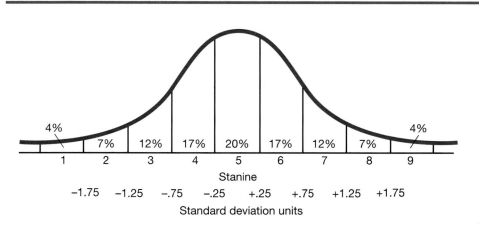

this strategy for assessing individual differences can work quite well, particularly when it is supplemented with teacher observations and informal assessments. Effective remedial reading and math programs, for example, are based to a large extent on scores from diagnostic reading and math tests. But when tests are used for purposes other than those for which they were designed, misuses occur, and inappropriate decisions and controversy often result. In the next section, we'll take a look at the widespread and controversial practice of high-stakes testing: using standardized test scores to hold students, teachers, and administrators accountable for academic achievement.

USING STANDARDIZED TESTS FOR ACCOUNTABILITY PURPOSES: HIGH-STAKES TESTING

The Push for Accountability in Education

In 1983, the National Commission on Excellence in Education published a report titled *A Nation at Risk: The Imperative for Educational Reform.* The report painted a bleak picture of the quality of education in the United States. It noted, for example, that about 13 percent of all seventeen-year-olds were judged to be functionally illiterate, that standardized test scores had generally fallen below levels achieved twenty-five years earlier, and that many seventeen-year-olds were judged as being deficient in such higher-order thinking skills as drawing inferences from written material and writing a persuasive essay. To justify the amount of money being spent on education and to improve student outcomes, the report called for standardized tests to be used as a way of documenting students' achievement and spurring educators to focus on raising achievement in such basic areas as reading, math, and science.

Subsequent standardized test data, such as scores from the National Assessment of Educational Progress and the Third International Mathematics and Science Study, and reports on the numbers of students who were being promoted from grade to grade despite poor reading, writing, and math skills, reinforced the perception that American students were poorly educated and had fallen behind students in many other countries. (For alternative interpretations of these findings, see Bracey, 2002, 2003, and Berliner & Biddle, 1995.) State legislatures and state departments of education responded by mandating the establishment of learning standards, the administration of standardized tests to determine how well those standards are being met, and, in some cases, mechanisms for rewarding or punishing students, teachers, and administrators for acceptable or unacceptable scores.

● High-stakes testing: using test results to hold students and educators accountable for achievement

Because standardized test scores, either by themselves or in conjunction with other data, are being used to determine whether students get promoted to the next grade or graduate from high school, whether teachers and administrators receive financial rewards or demotions, and whether school districts receive additional state funds or lose their accreditation, this practice is commonly referred to as **high-stakes testing**, and it has swept the nation. If you are in a teacher education program, you are likely to have firsthand experience with high-stakes testing through the Praxis series of exams or something similar. Created by the Educational Testing Service, Praxis exams are given by many colleges and universities to determine eligibility for entrance to teacher education programs and by states to determine eligibility for licensure.

The Federal Initiative: No Child Left Behind (NCLB)

In December 2001, the U.S. Congress passed legislation proposed by President George W. Bush to implement testing of students in reading and mathematics in all public schools that receive federal funds. This legislation, a reauthorization of the Elementary and Secondary Education Act (ESEA), is commonly known as the No

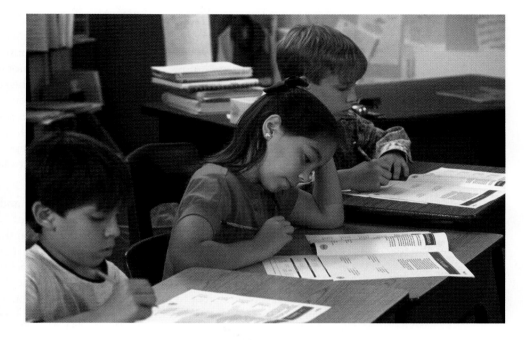

To hold students accountable for learning certain subjects and skills at acceptable levels and to improve the quality of education, all states annually administer standardized achievement tests in several subject areas. These tests are linked to state learning standards.

Child Left Behind (NCLB) Act. In addition to the accountability programs that states themselves put into place over the past several years, states and their school districts must now also adhere to the requirements of NCLB. You can read and download a copy of NCLB at the Department of Education's web site (**www.ed.gov/policy/elsec/leg/esea02/index.html**).

Features of NCLB   The No Child Left Behind Act has three main requirements (Commission on Instructionally Supportive Assessment, 2002; Linn, 2003; Linn, Baker, & Betebenner, 2002; Neill, 2003; Olson, 2003a):

● NCLB requires annual testing in math and reading, annual progress for all students, public reports

- *Testing.* Annual testing of all students in grades 3 through 8 in math and reading/language arts and at least one assessment of students in grades 9 through 12 in the same two subjects. By 2007, states must also administer a science assessment at least once to students in grades 3 through 5, 6 through 9, and 10 through 12. Decisions about test format, length, and item type have been left to each state. Vermont's assessment program, for example, includes mathematics problem-solving portfolios, writing portfolios, and science performance tasks in addition to the more familiar selected-response items (Vermont Department of Education, 2004). Kentucky's program also includes writing portfolios as well as open-ended questions that require students to explain the reasoning behind their answers in reading, science, social studies, mathematics, and the humanities (Kentucky Department of Education, 2004).

- *Adequate Yearly Progress (AYP).* By 2014, all students must score at least at the "proficient" level (as defined by each state) of their state assessment in reading/language arts and math. To ensure that this goal is met, states must demonstrate each year that a certain additional percentage of all students have met that goal. This feature is referred to as adequate yearly progress, or AYP. Adequate yearly progress must be demonstrated by all groups of students, including racial and ethnic minorities, students of low socioeconomic status (SES), students with limited English proficiency, and students with disabilities.

  The original wording of NCLB stated that schools would fail to meet the AYP requirement if too many students in *any* of the subgroups just mentioned failed to score at the minimally acceptable level (usually called "proficient" or "meets expectations") or if fewer than 95 percent of eligible students in all subgroups were tested. Because of complaints from many school districts, the

U.S. Department of Education in early 2004 amended the 95 percent assessment requirement, so that schools can meet the law if they average a 95 percent participation rate over two or three years ("White House Is Easing Up," 2004).

Schools that fail to meet the AYP requirement not only must use different instructional approaches and programs, but the ones they choose have to be shown to be effective by scientific research. If scores in a particular school do not improve after two years, students can transfer to other public schools. If there is no improvement after three years, the school's staff and curriculum may be replaced.

- *Reporting.* States and school districts must issue report cards to parents and the general public that describe how every group of students has performed on the annual assessment.

Our Case in Print describes how several schools and districts in the St. Louis metropolitan area are coping with the requirements of NCLB.

Although NCLB mandates that students be tested in the areas of reading/language arts and math (and eventually science) and that they perform at a particular level, it has been left up to the states to decide which aspects of those subjects will be tested and how different levels of performance will be defined. This does not mean that states have free rein to do whatever they please; each state has an accountability plan for meeting the requirements of NCLB that has been approved by the federal government. States are free to amend these plans in the future, but changes have to be approved by the U.S. Department of Education. For example, Michigan's proposal to not test students with limited English proficiency that have been enrolled in U.S. schools for less than three years was not approved. Instead, Michigan will give these students reading and math tests that use a simpler level of English than the regular state exams (Olson, 2003a).

State assessment plans can be quite different from one another. For example, Iowa plans to use two commercially published norm-referenced tests to measure student progress while Nebraska will use a combination of state and local assessments. Pennsylvania originally planned to use state and local assessments, but ultimately decided to use just state tests because of the cost and interpretive difficulties associated with using different types of tests (Olson, 2003a).

Problems with Implementing NCLB   No Child Left Behind is a law that is both complex and has high stakes attached to it. Consequently, problems with its implementation, both potential and actual, have been noted. Here are a few of them:

- Because establishing high standards decreases the probability of meeting the AYP requirement as well as the ultimate requirement of proficiency by all students in 2014, states may be tempted to weaken both their content and performance standards (Commission on Instructionally Supportive Assessment, 2002).
- Setting the cut score that determines whether or not a student has reached the proficiency level is based on the judgment of educators and carries significant consequences. If the score is set too low, a state's accountability plan may not pass federal muster. If it is set too high, the school may have a difficult time demonstrating AYP. This difference in defining the standard for proficiency probably accounts for a good part of the difference between low- and high-scoring states. For example, in 2001 the percentage of students who scored at the proficient level in math ranged from a low of 7 percent in Louisiana to a high of 92 percent in Texas. It is rather unlikely that the quality of instruction in Texas is that much better than the quality of instruction in Louisiana (Linn et al., 2002).
- The freedom that states have to establish their own performance standards has led to large disparities in the percentage of schools in different states that have met the requirement of AYP. For example, only 13 percent of schools in Kansas failed to make adequate yearly progress, while in Delaware the failure rate was 57 percent, and in Florida the failure rate was 87 percent (Robelen, 2003).

Because public education has many stakeholders (teachers, administrators, students, parents, legislators, and business leaders, for example) who differ in terms of their education-related attitudes, values, and ideals, the advent of high-stakes testing programs and the NCLB law has sparked a veritable flood of pro and con arguments. In the next two sections we summarize the major arguments that support and are critical of high-stakes testing.

Arguments in Support of High-Stakes Testing Programs

● High-stakes tests expected to improve clarity of goals, quality control, teaching methods, and student motivation

High-stakes testing programs receive support because of their potential and actual beneficial effects on goal clarity, quality control, teaching skills and methods, and student motivation.

Goal Clarity   A major responsibility of teachers and a contributing factor to effective teaching is the ability to clearly communicate one's educational goals. A state's content and performance standards can help teachers clarify their goals and more clearly communicate those goals to students and parents (Clarke, Abrams, & Madaus, 2001; Falk, 2002).

Improved Quality Control   NCLB and the state assessment programs that preceded it were implemented as a means to more closely monitor the quality of teaching and learning and to provide incentives for educators to make improvements. Here are a few ways in which high-stakes tests are thought to bring about improved quality control:

- Because high-stakes tests require results to be reported for groups of students that have traditionally been underserved (e.g., racial and ethnic minorities, students with disabilities and limited English proficiency), educators now monitor their academic progress as closely as they monitor the progress of regular students (Cizek, 2001a; Linn, 2003).
- States have markedly increased their collection of achievement data and improved the quality of their programs (Cizek, 2001a).
- Standardized tests with high stakes attached to them are an objective, efficient, and equitable way to hold teachers and students accountable for achieving a common set of standards (Clarke, Abrams, & Madaus, 2001).

Beneficial Effects for Teaching   High-stakes testing programs can have a beneficial effect on teaching in a number of ways:

- High-stakes tests have stimulated the designers of professional development seminars and workshops to emphasize teaching skills that are curriculum relevant and result oriented (Cizek, 2001a).
- Teachers are becoming more knowledgeable about the nature and uses of standardized testing (Cizek, 2001a).
- Motivated by the prospect of financial bonuses and helping their school district maintain its accreditation, teachers will search for and use more effective instructional methods and focus on material described in the standards (Clarke, Abrams, & Madaus, 2001).
- Well-conceived learning standards deal with significant outcomes (e.g., asking questions and solving problems), reflect how students normally learn (actively in meaningful contexts), and are appropriate for the students' developmental stage. Standards that reflect these concerns are likely to lead educators to use inquiry forms of learning, embed lessons in meaningful contexts, and use various performance-based assessments as well as paper-and-pencil assessments (Falk, 2002).
- NCLB does not specify a particular type of assessment instrument that schools have to use for determining AYP in math and reading. While most states will use a standardized test devised either by their departments of education or an outside testing company, some have indicated they will use locally constructed tests

Case in Print

Is NCLB Leaving Schools Behind?

In December 2001, the U.S. Congress passed legislation proposed by President George W. Bush to implement testing of students in reading and mathematics in all public schools that receive federal funds. This legislation, a reauthorization of the Elementary and Secondary Education Act (ESEA), is commonly known as the No Child Left Behind (NCLB) Act. In addition to the accountability programs that states themselves put into place over the past several years, states and their school districts must also now adhere to the requirements of NCLB. (p. 502–503)

Those That Fail to Meet Standards Find Roadblocks to Remedies

ALEXA AGUILAR
St. Louis Post-Dispatch 9/3/03

As Illinois schools navigate the maze of federal school reform law, many local educators point to more roadblocks than success stories.

For example, last month, 18 schools in six Metro East–area districts landed on the state's list of schools that failed to make state goals on standardized tests. They must offer their students the option of transferring to higher-performing schools.

But one-school districts such as Venice are having trouble finding welcoming arms.

Many Venice parents have expressed interest in sending their children to nearby Madison, but that's a no-go, because Madison schools are also on the list. So are Brooklyn schools. Interim Venice Superintendent Ron Ganschinietz has been trying to find a school that will take the district's students.

"We are certainly hearing often from downstate districts who are having trouble because of distance issues or because all of their neighborhood school districts are also on the list," said Naomi Greene, spokeswoman for the Illinois State Board of Education.

"But you can't just throw up your hands and say, 'Well, we can't find anybody,'" Greene added. If a school can't find a transfer option, then it must offer services like tutoring.

Transfers and tutoring are two of the remedies prescribed in the federal No Child Left Behind Act for schools that fail to meet yearly academic goals. The act, signed into law last year, requires that every child be proficient in reading and math by the 2013–14 school year.

The law lets each state decide the meaning of proficiency in those areas, so standards vary widely.

In Florida, 87 percent of schools did not meet annual goals. In Kansas, 13 percent missed the goals.

About half of Missouri's 2,055 schools—including most middle and high schools—failed to meet yearly progress goals, the state's educators said Tuesday. Many of the schools that did not meet the standards earned recognition last year for outstanding performance on state tests.

The paradox is rooted in how the federal law requires each state to measure progress on standardized tests. The law holds districts and schools accountable not only for how all third-graders perform, for example, but also for how they perform in groups based on race, income, special education needs and limited ability to speak English. In addition, at least 95 percent of students in each group must take the tests each year.

If any one group fails to make adequate progress, the whole school falls short.

Superintendents such as Brent Clark in the Belleville high school district point to that aspect of the law when they are asked to accept students from districts that have failed to meet state goals. Clark turned down a request for East St. Louis high schoolers to attend Belleville high schools. Clark said it would not be fair for Belleville taxpayers to pay for out-of-district students because the federal law provides no financial incentives.

And by accepting students from low-performing schools, Clark said, he would place his own schools in danger of landing on the list next year.

"It would be virtually impossible to get them to perform adequately on the tests in just one year," Clark said. "It's not just here. What I'm facing is a nationwide problem."

John Lawrence, superintendent of schools in Troy, Mo., and president of the American Association of School Administrators, said he fears that the federal law may lead to the unintended perception that some students are hurting the rest of a school or district. "That's wrong," he said.

The situation will only get worse, school officials predict. More and more schools are expected to appear on the list as they try to meet a federal goal that many educators say is unattainable.

In Cahokia, 15 pupils asked to transfer into Penniman Elementary, despite its label of failing. The district has an open-transfer policy that was in place long before No Child Left Behind, aimed at accommodating parents' needs.

Penniman may be a desired option for many parents because it actually met and exceeded standards this year after an intensive effort by teachers armed with a new curriculum and backed by a new principal. But because the law requires a school to make progress for two years in a row, Penniman is still labeled as a school that failed.

"By the chart, we are a failing school," said principal Jeff Burkett. "But you tell me we are a failing school with all the great things that are going on here."

Last week, neat rows of students walked down bright hallways decorated with signs urging success. Cathy Yates' third-grade class was busy. Yates said she begins teaching Illinois learning standards from the first day to prepare her pupils for the state test. It paid off last year when third-graders made a 46 percent gain, and 90 percent met or exceeded standards.

"Our success does not come from those scores," Yates said. "But we know the expectations, and I start on day one."

Burkett said the trade-off is that teachers have to forsake creative units they might otherwise plan.

"We can't do a dinosaur unit or a log-cabin unit," Burkett said. "Whether we agree with it or not, that's the hand we were dealt."

Questions and Activities

1. The dilemma faced by the Venice, Illinois, school district is one faced by many rural school districts that are composed of one or two schools and repeatedly fail to meet NCLB's adequate yearly progress requirement. The financial stress that results from students transferring to nearby districts or receiving tutoring if a transfer is not possible may bring about a small school district's demise. Of necessity, the students would then be absorbed into neighboring districts. Does this strike you as a desirable outcome?

2. As the article and the text point out, NCLB allows each state to create its own definition of proficiency in math and reading. What are the pros and cons of this provision? If you were writing such a law, would you have chosen this option, or would you have imposed a uniform standard on all states?

3. The article points out that many schools in Missouri did not meet NCLB's adequate yearly progress requirement, yet had performed well in previous years on the state's test. One explanation that was offered to explain the discrepancy is that

NCLB requires yearly progress for *all* subgroups of students and virtually all students in those groups must take the tests. Can you think of any other factors that might produce such a discrepancy?

4. Penniman Elementary School experienced a significant increase in the percentage of third-grade students meeting or exceeding state standards because teachers closely aligned their instruction to those standards and avoided lessons (such as a dinosaur unit) that were unrelated to state standards. Proponents of high-stakes testing would applaud this outcome while critics would probably describe it as an undesirable side effect. Where do you stand on this issue, and what arguments would you use to support your position?

5. Interview several teachers at different grade levels to learn what they think of high-stakes testing programs. Make a note of the techniques they use to address the demands of such testing programs.

instead of or in addition to state-mandated tests. The benefit to teachers in those states is that locally produced tests are more likely to provide them with diagnostically useful information that they can use to improve students' achievement (Clarke, Abrams, & Madaus, 2001; Neill, 2003).

- Teachers may collaborate with one another more often because NCLB mandates annual testing in grades 3 through 8 and threatens schools with sanctions if adequate yearly progress is not made (Winkler, 2003).

Beneficial Effects for Students   High-stakes tests may motivate students to improve their study skills and work harder to avoid the embarrassment and disruption of academic progress that comes from being retained in a grade or not being allowed to graduate from high school (Clarke, Abrams, & Madaus, 2001).

Arguments Critical of High-Stakes Testing Programs

● High-stakes tests criticized because of structural limitations, misinterpretation/misuse of results, narrow view of motivation, adverse side effects

High-stakes testing programs are frequently criticized because they do not adhere to a rigorous set of assessment guidelines like those promoted by the American Educational Research Association (2000) and because they are subject to misuse and misinterpretation. In this section we summarize these criticisms in terms of structural limitations, the way test scores are interpreted, the motivational basis on which these programs rest, and undesirable side effects.

Structural Limitations   High-stakes testing programs are perceived to be more of a hindrance than an aid to educators because of the nature of the components that make them up and how those parts fit together.

- For the sake of objectivity, efficiency, and cost, state assessments are often narrow in scope, limited in range, and shallow in depth. They favor selected-response items, are limited in the subjects they cover, do not assess any given topic in great depth, and mostly assess what students know rather than what they can do with what they know (Clarke, Abrams, & Madaus, 2001; Goldberg, 2004). For example, under realistic conditions many writing projects pass through the stages of planning, drafting, revising, editing, and publishing. But because efficiency is highly valued in the construction of high-stakes tests, many writing tests assess only a student's ability to create a draft (Schuster, 2004).
- State assessments that are narrow in scope, limited in range, and shallow in depth may not provide teachers with the type of diagnostic information they need to improve the effect of their instruction. Telling a teacher that a student's score was in the "Needs Improvement" category on a reading test does not help that teacher make the next reading lesson more effective (Camilli, 2003; Cizek, 2003; Clarke, Abrams, & Madaus, 2001; Neill, 2003; Popham, 2003). Teachers would be better served if they were told which standards a student has or has not mastered and if the standards were described with sufficient clarity that teachers could draw reasonably accurate inferences about how to remediate the student's weaknesses.
- A test's content, and the learning standards on which the test is based, do not necessarily reflect the knowledge and skills that the majority of people value the most and believe are most important for students to learn (Goldberg, 2004).
- States frequently adopt far more content standards than teachers can cover and students can master, and they are often worded so generally that it is difficult to be certain about the precise content or skill in question (Clarke, Abrams, & Madaus, 2001; Popham, 2003).
- The abstract paper-and-pencil items that make up the bulk of state assessments may confuse many third graders who are either in Piaget's preoperational stage or the early part of the concrete operational stage (Gould, 2003).
- Standardized tests, as well constructed as they may be, are subject to measurement error. Although the negative effect of measurement error on accurate decision making can be decreased by measuring achievement in different ways, most assessment programs use just a single type of test (Clarke, Abrams, & Madaus, 2001; Gulek, 2003).
- The stated goal of accountability programs—to improve the quality of classroom teaching and the level of student achievement—cannot be accomplished by programs that rely largely or exclusively on standardized test scores. The conditions under which teaching and learning occur must also be assessed, and professional

development initiatives designed to help teachers be more effective must be provided (Camilli, 2003; Cizek, 2003; Linn, 2003).

- If you think of education in terms of inputs (teacher and student characteristics, resources, physical environment), processes (instructional and learning processes), and outputs (student knowledge and skills), the main focus of high-stakes testing programs is the output. Although NCLB requires that failing students receive remedial instruction and, if necessary, be allowed to transfer to a different school, the main thrust of the law is to drive school improvement by the imposition of output standards and accountability. High-stakes systems tend to ignore the contributions of input and process variables, or what might be called opportunity to learn. If, for example, students are not given sufficient time to learn, if the classroom and school environments are chaotic and threatening to the students' well-being, if classroom instruction is dull and unresponsive to individual differences, and if students have low levels of self-efficacy for learning and poor self-regulated learning skills, this diminished opportunity to learn is likely to result in a failing test performance (Starratt, 2003).

Misinterpretation and Misuse of Test Results   Although high-stakes testing programs do a reasonably good job of assessing mastery of certain learning standards, they do not, because they were not designed to, measure the general quality of a school or an individual teacher's effectiveness. Nevertheless, when faced with district and state report cards that rank schools, many people will draw the intuitively appealing but incorrect inference that high test scores equal good schools and teachers, that low scores equal poor-quality schools and teachers, and that rewarding or punishing schools and teachers on the basis of test scores is appropriate (Camilli, 2003; Cochran-Smith, 2003; Vogler & Kennedy, 2003).

A One-Size-Fits-All Approach to Motivation   High-stakes testing programs are based on a limited and simplistic view of motivation. Whether intended or not, the use of rewards and punishments to improve educational outcomes represents a behavioral view of motivation (Clarke, Abrams, & Madaus, 2001). But if you go back to and quickly review our chapter on motivation, you will see that many factors influence an individual's willingness and ability to master learning standards and perform well on standardized assessments. Among these factors are the opportunity to observe and imitate the behavior of appropriate models, self-efficacy for accomplishing particular tasks, the goals one chooses to pursue, level of achievement motivation, the attributions one makes for success and failure, beliefs about the nature of ability, interests, the extent to which one's deficiency and growth needs are satisfied by the classroom and school environment, and academic self-concept. And as we pointed out in other chapters, the values students have about education (which are strongly influenced by parents and peer groups) and the sophistication of their learning skills will also affect their motivation to learn.

For some students, the prospect of gaining rewards and avoiding punishment may be sufficient incentive to work harder. But students who suffer from low self-efficacy, the adoption of avoidance goals, low levels of achievement motivation, maladaptive attributions, inappropriate beliefs about ability, an environment that does not satisfy deficiency needs, a poor academic self-concept, and poorly developed learning skills will likely see learning standards and high-stakes tests as obstacles they cannot overcome regardless of the rewards and punishments.

Undesirable Side Effects   Critics of high-stakes testing argue that the rewards and punishments associated with high-stakes testing programs may produce one or more of the following undesirable side effects.

- Concern with rankings and the rewards and punishments attached to state assessment programs leads many teachers to provide students with intensive test

A possible negative effect of high-stakes testing programs is that teachers may spend more time preparing students for the test and less time on topics and subjects that are not covered by the test.

preparation. While this practice may raise scores, it often comes at the expense of meaningful learning (Goldberg, 2004). Consequently, there is often little transfer to other tests that purport to measure the same knowledge and skills.

For example, one study found that scores on a statewide assessment increased almost every year for seven years in reading and math. In the eighth year, a new test of similar reading and math skills was introduced. Scores in both areas fell dramatically and then rose in subsequent years (Linn, 2000). In another study, 83 percent of students in a Pittsburgh elementary school scored above the national norm on the reading test of the Iowa Test of Basic Skills (a standardized achievement test). But on the reading test of the state assessment, only 26 percent scored within the top two proficiency levels (Yau, 2002). The phenomenon that both studies highlight is sometimes referred to as WYTIWYG: what you test is what you get. In other words, high-stakes assessments lead teachers to focus on preparing students for a particular type of test and, as a result, there is little carryover to other tests that measure the same or similar skills.

- Many educators fear that the press to meet the demands of NCLB and other state assessment goals will result in more time spent strengthening students' basic math and reading/language arts skills at the expense of time for such subjects as art, music, and foreign languages. While there is no broad-based evidence at this point that such curriculum narrowing has occurred, there are individual cases. In one low-scoring Massachusetts school district, reading was dropped for the spring semester to accommodate test preparation activities for English/language arts and mathematics (Vogler & Kennedy, 2003). In addition, administrators admit having considered cutting back on certain courses, and research indicates that teachers do spend more time on subjects for which they are held accountable for students' performance (Manzo, 2003).

- A similar fear has been expressed about the fate of certain forms of instruction. For example, inquiry-based science education has been praised because it emphasizes hands-on science activities as opposed to the traditional reading about science in textbooks and watching the teacher conduct an occasional experiment. But because of the pressure to have students perform well on state-mandated assessments, science educators fear that the amount of time devoted to science instruction will be reduced in favor of test preparation activities, and the instruction that does occur will emphasize drill-and-practice activities because they fit the demands of high-stakes tests (Jorgenson & Vanosdall, 2002).

- To avoid the negative sanctions mandated by NCLB for schools whose students continue to score poorly for several years in a row, states are likely to propose the lowest-level content and performance standards that the federal government will accept (Linn, 2003).

- As high-stakes testing programs have proliferated, so have reports of cheating by teachers and administrators (echoing research, summarized earlier in the book, suggesting that most people are susceptible to cheating under the right circumstances). Educators have been accused of such infractions as giving slow students extra time on timed tests, suggesting answers to students, changing students' answers, directly teaching specific portions of a test, and allowing students to have access to dictionaries and thesauruses on writing tests. In one survey, about 35 percent of teachers said they had either engaged in unethical test-related practices or had seen others engaging in them (Cizek, 2001b). Administrators have been accused of publishing inaccurate graduation and enrollment data to make their school districts look better than they actually are. In one case, a school district claimed that 51 percent of the class of 2002 graduated, but an independent investigation claimed that only 39 percent graduated. The size of another school's freshman class decreased by two-thirds over four years, yet the school reported no dropouts (Goldberg, 2004).

- States that make promotion contingent on achieving a passing score are likely to have higher dropout rates than states that have no such requirement (Clarke, Abrams, & Madaus, 2001; Gayler, Chudowsky, Kober, & Hamilton, 2003; Neill, 2003; Sirotnik, 2002).

Research on the Effects of High-Stakes Testing

● Research on effects of high-stakes testing limited and inconsistent

Given all the argument about the effects of high-states testing, actual research on this subject is vital. But because these programs have been in existence for a relatively short time, the research on their effects is limited, the results are inconsistent, and the implications have been hotly debated. In addition, some of the evidence is merely anecdotal. Nevertheless, we will summarize for you what has been reported about the effects these programs appear to have on student achievement, student motivation, teachers' behavior, classroom instruction, and the dropout rate.

Effect on Achievement At this point, only a few studies have examined whether the adoption of performance standards and high-stakes consequences leads to higher levels of student achievement. Not surprisingly, researchers disagree about how best to analyze and interpret the data.

One approach (e.g., Amrein & Berliner, 2002, 2003) examined how well fourth- and eighth-grade students in certain states performed on the math and reading tests of the National Assessment of Educational Progress (NAEP) prior to and after the introduction of high-stakes tests. If NAEP scores in these states increased more than the NAEP national average, high-stakes testing was considered to have had a positive effect. But if scores increased less than the national average, high-stakes testing was considered to have had a negative effect. These researchers reported that NAEP scores increased at a faster rate than the national average in four states and at a slower rate than the national average in eight states. Thus the overall effect seemed to be negative.

Another approach (e.g., Braun, 2004; Raymond & Hanushek, 2003; Rosenshine, 2003), which used the same data, compared students in states with high-stakes consequences to students from states with low or no consequences. On the NAEP math and reading tests, these researchers found statistically significant average gains in favor of the high-stakes testing states. These gains, they argued, could not be accounted for just on the basis of test preparation and exclusion of students with disabilities or limited English proficiency. It was also pointed out that this advantage was not found in all high-stakes states and that future research would be needed to determine if the finding is reliable and, if it is, why it occurs in some states but not others.

Effect on Motivation Some evidence suggests that the presence of high stakes motivates some students to work harder. Among Massachusetts high school students who failed that state's high-stakes test the first time they took it, about two-thirds said they were now working harder and paying more attention in class, and almost 75 percent said that missing too much school was a major reason for failing the test (Cizek, 2003).

In 1996, the Chicago Public Schools instituted a high-stakes testing program that required third, sixth, and eighth graders to pass the reading and mathematics sections of the Iowa Test of Basic Skills in order to be promoted to the next grade. During the school year leading up to the test, students could receive extra help both before school and through an after-school program. Students who failed the test were required to attend a summer program before they could retake the test and be promoted for the fall semester. Those who failed the second test were retained.

An analysis of 102 low-achieving students (Roderick & Engel, 2001) revealed that the program affected different students in different ways. About 53 percent of the students reported greater attention to class work, increased academic expectations and support from their teachers, and greater effort both in and out of class. The students interpreted the higher expectations and support from teachers as evidence that the teachers cared about them and wanted them to succeed. A second and much smaller group (about 9 percent) also worked hard to prepare for the test but received most of their support outside of school from parents and other family members. A third group of students, about 35 percent of the sample, expressed concern about passing the test and was aware of the before- and after-school help that was available but did not take advantage of it. The fourth and smallest group of students (about 4 percent) wasn't worried about passing the test and wasn't considered by teachers to be at risk of failing.

To examine the relationship between effort and test performance, students from the first three groups were reassigned to one of the following categories: Substantial Work Effort Either in or out of School, No Substantial Work Effort, or Substantial Home or Skill Problems. Of the 53 students in the Substantial Work Effort group, 57 percent passed the test in June, 23 percent passed in August, and 20 percent were retained. Of the 28 students in the No Substantial Work Effort group, 11 percent passed in June, 25 percent passed in August, and 64 percent were retained. Of the 17 students in the Substantial Home or Skill Problems group, 12 percent passed in June, 47 percent passed in August, and 41 percent were retained.

These findings clearly show, as have other interventions mentioned in previous chapters, that no single policy or approach will work for all students because classroom learning is an extremely complex phenomenon that is only partly under the teacher's control. Although the threat of retention was sufficient to motivate some students to work harder and take advantage of the additional resources that were provided, it had a much smaller effect on students with serious learning skill deficits and/or problems at home and students who simply declined to put forth more effort. Retaining students who fall into these latter two groups is likely to cause them to become even more disengaged and eventually drop out of school. Obviously, an alternative to retention is required to motivate these students and raise their achievement levels.

Effect on Teachers   At the beginning of our chapter on classroom management, we noted that the students of teachers who exhibited an authoritative style were likely to be more intrinsically motivated and self-regulating than the students of teachers who exhibited authoritarian or permissive styles. Recent evidence (Pelletier et al., 2002) shows that a teacher's decision to either support student autonomy or be more controlling of what students do in class is very much a function of the environment in which the teacher works. When teachers have curriculum decisions and performance standards imposed on them (as is often the case in states with high-stakes testing programs) and when they feel that students are not highly motivated to learn, their intrinsic motivation for teaching suffers. This lowered intrinsic motivation, in turn, leads them to be less supportive of student autonomy and more controlling.

For at least some teachers, however, anecdotal evidence from Vermont and Virginia (Winkler, 2003) suggests that state assessments can have a beneficial effect. Some teachers said that their states' content and performance standards stimulated them to use more forms of instruction than they had previously. In an attempt to get as many students as possible to score at the proficiency level, teachers were doing more individualized planning and using different materials and methods with different students. This is the concept of differentiated instruction that we mentioned in previous chapters. One teacher said that her classroom test construction skills had improved because she tried to write items that accurately reflected her state's learning standards.

Effect on Instruction   The Boston Arts Academy is a relatively new public high school whose curriculum emphasizes the fine and performing arts and that enrolls many at-risk minority students. Because the state's high-stakes test, the Massachusetts Comprehensive Assessment System (MCAS), doesn't reflect either the talents these students possess (such as portraying the motivations and feelings of characters in a play) or their developing capabilities (such as needing extensive time, consultations, and several rewrites to produce an acceptable paper), these students are more likely than students at other Boston high schools to fail the MCAS and be denied a diploma. Consequently, the school hired the Princeton Review to provide MCAS test preparation classes, hired an extra math teacher to bolster students' math skills, and did not hire a badly needed full-time music teacher.

The headmaster of the Boston Arts Academy stated that the test coaching helped students improve their MCAS scores over previous years. Besides allowing them to become more comfortable with the testing procedure, the coaching taught students to distinguish between good and bad options on multiple-choice questions, to read the questions to a literary passage before reading the passage itself, and to make educated guesses. What it did not do was make students better readers; help them appreciate literature in a deeper way; lead them to explore works of fiction, nonfiction, or history; or teach them how to generate the energy, organization, interests, and hard work that are necessary for the successful completion of long-term projects (Nathan, 2002).

Effect on the Dropout Rate   The question of whether high-stakes exams, particularly high school exit exams, increase the dropout rate (currently about 5 percent of all high school students) is a difficult one to answer definitively. Not only is the research limited, it is inconclusive because states define and count dropouts differently, and it is difficult for researchers to isolate the effect of a high-stakes test from other factors that may also be playing a role. Nevertheless, an expert panel convened by the Center for Education Policy reviewed the existing literature and concluded that the weight of the evidence currently supports the claim that exit exams cause more students to drop out of school than would otherwise be the case (Gayler et al., 2003).

Recommendations for Improving High-Stakes Testing

If NCLB and state-mandated assessment programs are to fulfill their goals of improving the quality of instruction and raising achievement levels, they will have to be implemented in such a way that all stakeholders believe they are being treated fairly. On this score, NCLB appears to be off to a rocky start. At present, about a dozen state legislatures have either introduced bills to opt out of certain requirements of NCLB, passed resolutions expressing their dissatisfaction with its requirements, or requested a waiver from the Department of Education.

pause & reflect

Critics of high-stakes testing suggest that teachers try to persuade policymakers to change the worst aspects of such programs. They recommend steps like these: speak out at school board meetings; organize a letter-writing campaign to the school board and legislators; assemble a delegation to visit legislators; write letters to the local newspaper; set up a workshop on the abuses of high-stakes testing. How many of these activities are you willing to engage in? Why?

The most strenuous objection of the states is that NCLB amounts to an unfunded mandate. That is, the government requires states to implement the law's requirements but has not, in their view, provided sufficient funds to defray the costs of its implementation (Dobbs, 2004). While political leaders complain about funding, educators argue that the goal of having all students be proficient in math and reading/language arts by 2014 is unrealistic and will bring about the demise of fundamentally sound schools (Archer, 2003). Still others argue that most accountability programs have adopted the wrong focus. Kenneth Sirotnik (2002), for example, believes that a more useful accountability system is one that holds policymakers accountable for the effects of their high-stakes accountability systems. In his view, an accountability system that focuses exclusively on the test scores of students, classes, schools, and districts—ignoring wide disparities in educational opportunity because of differences in funding and facilities—is an irresponsible system.

In response to the many criticisms of high-stakes testing programs, five professional organizations (the American Association of School Administrators, the National Association of Elementary School Principals, the National Association of Secondary School Principals, the National Education Association, and the National Middle School Association) created a commission of nationally recognized experts in assessment and instruction to provide recommendations for meeting the annual testing, AYP, and reporting requirements of NCLB in such a way that positive outcomes are more likely than negative ones. They produced the following nine recommendations for state assessment systems:

1. Each state should adopt only those content standards that represent the most important knowledge and skills that students need to learn. This will help states avoid having more standards than teachers can cover, students can master, and test makers can assess. Having a more modest set of standards also allows educators, students, and parents to get feedback about performance for each standard instead of a single score summed over hundreds of standards.

2. A state's content standards should clearly describe exactly what is being assessed so teachers can create lessons that directly address those standards. Phrases like "express and interpret information and ideas," for example, should be translated into more precise language.

3. Scores on a state assessment should be reported on a standard-by-standard basis for each student, school, and district.

4. States should provide school districts with additional assessment procedures to assess those standards that the required assessment does not cover.

5. States should monitor the curricula of school districts to ensure that instruction addresses all content standards and subjects, not just those assessed by the required state test.

6. State assessments should be designed so that all students have an equal opportunity to demonstrate which of the state's standards they have mastered. This includes providing accommodations and alternative assessments for students with disabilities and those who are limited in their English proficiency.

7. All tests should satisfy the Standards for Educational and Psychological Testing of the American Educational Research Association and similar test quality guidelines.

8. Teachers and principals should receive professional development training that helps them use test results to optimize children's learning.

9. States should continually seek to improve the quality of their assessments (Commission on Instructionally Supportive Assessment, 2002).

Several years ago, Robert Linn, a prominent expert in educational measurement, wrote the following:

> As someone who has spent his entire career doing research, writing, and thinking about educational testing and assessment issues, I would like to conclude by summarizing a compelling case showing that the major uses of tests for student and school accountability during the past 50 years have improved education and student learning in dramatic ways. Unfortunately, this is not my conclusion. Instead, I am led to conclude in most cases that instruments and technology have not been up to the demands that have been placed on them by high-stakes accountability. . . . The unintended negative effects of the high-stakes accountability uses often outweigh the intended positive effects. (Linn, 2000, p. 14)

If the preceding recommendations are taken seriously by policymakers at the state and national levels, then perhaps Robert Linn and others will express a more favorable opinion of the effects of high-stakes testing several years from now.

Take a Stand!

Healing the Patient: Using the Medical Model to Guide Educational Accountability

Almost everybody, including educators, accepts the contention that educators should be held accountable for their efforts. Indeed, every person should be accountable in some fashion to others. What is, and should be, vigorously debated is the way in which accountability is defined and practiced. We believe that the accountability systems of many states are less effective than they could be because their primary focus is on identifying and punishing substandard performance rather than identifying and remediating the causes of those weaknesses.

We agree with measurement expert Gregory Cizek, who argues that if high-stakes programs are to be more widely embraced by educators, students, and parents, they should mimic the assessment approach that physicians use in their practices. Medical tests tend to be diagnostic in nature because of the detailed level at which they report results. A typical analysis of a blood sample, for example, provides information on the levels of more

than twenty elements (e.g., blood sugar, sodium, potassium, calcium, protein, HDL cholesterol, LDL cholesterol, and triglyceride). Abnormal results are then followed by specific recommendations for treatment. The patient isn't accused of being inferior and charged twice the doctor's normal fee as a penalty for having "failing" test scores.

Consequently, a reasonable stand for teachers to take regarding high-stakes testing programs is that they should be constructed to provide detailed information about students' strengths and weaknesses, and these results should serve as a basis for additional instruction. In addition, professional development workshops and seminars should be provided, focusing on how teachers can help students learn the knowledge and skills that are assessed.

Would you agree with using a medical model for high-stakes testing? What can you do in your own school to promote this view of testing? To explore this issue further, see the Take a Stand! section of the textbook web site.

STANDARDIZED TESTING AND TECHNOLOGY

Given the prevalence of standardized testing and the large amount of money that schools spend on testing programs, it is not too surprising that technology tools exist for a wide range of assessment formats, including the standard true-false, multiple-choice, and fill-in-the-blank questions, as well as alternative assessments such as essay writing, debate forums, simulations, and electronic exhibitions of student work. As we discuss in this section, technology can be used in all phases of testing, including preparing students for standardized tests, administering tests, and scoring students' responses.

Using Technology to Prepare Students for Assessments

For students to perform well on standardized tests, they need to have a clear understanding of the standards for which they will be held accountable and the types of items that will be used to assess those standards. Toward that end, many states provide web-based resources to help students become familiar with and prepare for state assessments. On the web sites of state departments of education, students, teachers, and parents can read or download copies of their states' content and performance standards, study examples of the types of items that will appear on the test, and, in some cases, take practice tests. In addition, some states (Indiana, Georgia, and Texas, for example) either already provide or have plans to provide item banks linked to state standards that teachers can use to construct tests, quizzes, and homework assignments (Olson, 2003b).

● Web sites of state departments of education, private companies provide services that help prepare students for state assessments

Some states and school districts also make available the online test preparation services of private, for-profit companies. The Princeton Review, for example, has a 130,000-question test bank that school districts can use to create online practice tests that are aligned with their states' standards for grades 3–12. A company called Smarthinking (**www.smarthinking.com**) provides tutoring through online instructors (called "e-structors") and digital whiteboards. Students can correspond with tutors in real time or submit questions and assignments and get a response within twenty-four hours. The digital whiteboard is used by students to demonstrate their understanding of concepts and skills (such as English grammar or mathematical problem solving), and also by the tutor, who adds comments and corrections.

On the web site of TestU (**www.testu.com/**), students take a diagnostic pretest and are then provided with individualized courses in various aspects of math and language arts. Teachers receive diagnostic reports that analyze students' responses to test questions. A teacher in an Orlando, Florida, school who used the TestU service

To explore web sites mentioned in this chapter, go to the Weblinks section of the textbook site.

In coming years, it is likely that increasing numbers of students will take high-stakes and other standardized tests on a computer.

was convinced that it helped his students improve their scores on that state's high-stakes test, the Florida Comprehensive Assessment Test (Borja, 2003).

Using Technology to Assess Mastery of Standards

A number of technology-based approaches to assessing students' mastery of standards are either being evaluated or are currently being used. Indiana, for example, is pilot testing online English and algebra exams for high school students, and Oregon allows schools to administer state reading and math tests online for grades 3, 5, 8, and 10. Although online assessments are less expensive than paper-and-pencil versions, there are some hurdles to overcome before they are likely to be used on a widespread basis:

- It is costly to buy and maintain enough computers to test large groups of students. One high school in Indiana, for example, had to close four computer labs for a month to test every student.
- Schools need to have a plan for dealing with interruptions due to a faulty computer or a power loss.
- In situations where students can opt for the online or paper-and-pencil version of a test, schools need to be able to convince all concerned that the test-taking experience is equivalent for both groups (Olson, 2003b).

One advantage that computer-based testing has over paper-and-pencil tests is the ability to use novel items to assess certain skills. For example, a computer screen could display the Periodic Table of Elements with a question mark in five of the cells and the five elements that belong in those cells above the table. The student would have to drag each element to its correct location and then drop it (release the mouse button). Another possibility is to provide students with a set of concepts and have them depict how they relate to one another by constructing a concept map. A third example is to have students edit a passage by selecting sentence rewrites from a list of alternatives on a drop-down menu (Zenisky & Sireci, 2002). Another advantage is the ability to get scores and detailed reports at any time, from immediately after a test is completed to a few days later (Olson, 2002; Russo, 2002).

Among the more innovative suggestions is the use of intelligent tutoring systems. These systems provide computer-based, self-paced instruction in a subject and then assess whether or not the knowledge and skills that relate to particular state standards have been mastered. By analyzing the student's pattern of correct and incorrect responses, the computer decides whether to present new material or remedial instruction (Chudowsky & Pellegrino, 2003).

National testing services have shown an interest in using technology to grade essay exam questions since human judgment on national and state tests is fairly subjective, and human time is costly. The first of these so-called automated essay scoring programs, called Project Essay Grade (PEG), has demonstrated that it can rate student essays as well as or better than humans. According to its creator, Ellis Page (2003), this tool evaluates such complex and important writing variables as content, organization, style, and creativity, in addition to mechanics and document length. In one experiment, the scores assigned by PEG to more than a thousand essays from the Praxis exam (taken mostly by teacher education students applying for teacher certification) were compared with the scores given by six human judges. PEG's ratings were more similar to the judges' ratings than the judges' ratings were similar to each other's. Computer scoring is not only quicker and more economical, but apparently it is more accurate and consistent than human ratings (Page, 2003).

Although programs like PEG are used mostly at the college and graduate school levels, they are also being tried out in grades K–12 for scoring essay-type constructed-response questions (Elliot, 2003). Indiana is pilot testing the scoring program used by the Educational Testing Service to assess high school students' essay responses on an English exam (Olson, 2003b). Given the millions of essays rated each year by the

Educational Testing Service alone and the addition of essay writing to the SATs and GREs, computer-rated essays may soon become commonplace in standardized testing.

Computer Adaptive Testing

● Computer adaptive testing: computers determine sequence and difficulty level of test items

Technology has also shaped the way tests are put together and administered. Instead of subjecting every student to the same sequence of test items, **computer adaptive testing (CAT)** allows students to take tests that are geared to their own ability level. When a student begins a test in the CAT format, the computer selects an item that matches his or her estimated ability. If the student responds correctly, the computer selects a slightly more difficult item. An incorrect response results in an easier item. After each correct or incorrect response, the computer estimates the student's ability. The test ends when the computer determines that it has reached the limits of the student's knowledge (Latu & Chapman, 2002; Olson, 2002).

The major advantages of CAT are a reduction in the number of proctors needed, fewer scoring errors, tests that are only as long as they need to be for each examinee, and greater test security. The major disadvantages are increased test anxiety and confusion for those not familiar or comfortable with taking a test on a computer and high test-taking fees because of the high cost involved in developing and implementing such a system (Latu & Chapman, 2002).

The CAT format is being used by the Department of Defense to administer the Armed Services Vocational Aptitude Battery and by the Educational Testing Service for the Graduate Record Examination (Drasgow, 2002). A group of eighth-grade students in Taiwan had strong positive responses to taking a science test in CAT format (Wang & Chuang, 2002).

In an interesting turn of events, several states that had intended to use CAT to meet the requirements of NCLB had to change course. The reason is that NCLB requires that students be evaluated only according to the expectations for their grade level. Taking a test that contains items that are either easier or harder than what is normal for a grade level, as in the case of computer adaptive tests, is considered "out-of-level" testing and is not allowed. States are free to use CAT for other purposes. South Dakota, which had planned to use CAT for NCLB purposes, will instead provide it as a voluntary option to satisfy other accountability goals (Trotter, 2003).

In the next section we offer several Suggestions for Teaching that will help you and your students appropriately use standardized tests and interpret the scores from them.

Suggestions for Teaching in Your Classroom

Using Standardized Tests

1 **Before you give a standardized test, emphasize that students should do their best.**

For maximum usefulness, scores on standardized tests should be as accurate a representation of actual ability as possible.

Accordingly, the day before a standardized test is scheduled, tell your students that they should do their best. Emphasize that the scores will be used to help them improve their school performance and will provide useful feedback to you about the quality of your instruction. If you're thinking about ignoring this suggestion because you don't believe that students will score significantly higher on a standardized test in response to a simple pep talk, you might want to reconsider. Research has shown that students who have a positive attitude toward learning and test taking score higher on tests than do students whose attitudes are less positive or negative (Brown & Walberg, 1993; Gulek, 2003).

2 Before your students take a standardized test, give them specific suggestions for taking such tests.

JOURNAL ENTRY
Explaining Test-Taking Skills

You may be able partly to reduce the anxiety and tension that are almost inevitable under formal testing conditions by giving some test-taking hints in advance. Robert Linn and Norman Gronlund (2000) note the following tips that might be stressed (depending on the type of test and the grade level of the student):

1. Listen to or read directions carefully.
2. Listen to or read test items carefully.
3. Set a pace that will allow time to complete the test.
4. Bypass difficult items and return to them later.
5. Make informed guesses rather than omit items.
6. Eliminate as many alternatives as possible on multiple-choice items before guessing.
7. Follow directions carefully when marking the answer sheet (for example, be sure to darken the entire space).
8. Check to be sure the item number and answer number match when marking an answer.
9. Check to be sure the appropriate response is marked on the answer sheet.
10. Go back and check the answers if time permits. (p. 466)

3 Examine the test booklet and answer sheet in advance so that you are familiar with the test.

Ideally you might take the test yourself so that you become thoroughly familiar with what your students will be doing. If there are any aspects of recording answers that are especially tricky or if the test contains unfamiliar terminology, you might mention these when you give your test-taking skills presentation or when you hand out examination booklets and answer sheets. Knowledge of test vocabulary and terminology has been found to have a significant effect on students' performance on high-stakes tests (Gulek, 2003).

4 Be cautious when interpreting scores, and always give the student the benefit of the doubt.

JOURNAL ENTRY
Interpreting Test Scores

The profiles or reports you will receive a few weeks after a test has been administered will contain information that is potentially beneficial to you and your students. If misused or misinterpreted, however, the information is potentially harmful. Misinterpretations of scores can lead to complaints by parents. Therefore, as you examine the scores, concentrate on ways you can make positive use of the results.

For example, if a student's test scores are lower than you expected them to be, examine them to discover areas of weakness but guard against thinking, "Well, I guess he had me fooled. He's not as sharp as I thought he was. Maybe I had better lower his grades a notch on the next report card." There are many reasons a student may not do well on a test (for example, anxiety, fatigue, illness, worry about some home or school interpersonal situation), and scores may not be an accurate reflection of current capability. Thus, whenever there is a discrepancy between test scores and observed classroom performance, always assume that the more favorable impression is the one to use as an indication of general capability. Try to use indications of below-average performance in constructive ways to help students overcome inadequacies.

⑤ Do your best to control the impact of negative expectations.

As you peruse student test scores, do your best to resist the temptation to label or categorize students, particularly those who have a consistent pattern of low scores. Instead of succumbing to thoughts that such students are incapable of learning, you might make an effort to concentrate on the idea that they need extra encouragement and individualized attention. Use the information on test profiles to help them overcome their learning difficulties, not to justify fatalistically ignoring their problems.

⑥ Be prepared to offer parents clear and accurate information about their children's test scores.

 To spur your reflections about standardized tests, see the Thought Questions and Reflective Journal Questions on the textbook web site.

For a variety of reasons, misconceptions about the nature of standardized tests are common. As a result, many parents do not fully understand what their children's scores mean. Parent-teacher conferences are probably the best time to correct misconceptions and provide some basic information about the meaning of standardized test scores. In an unobtrusive place on your desk, you might keep a brief list of points to cover as you converse with each parent. In one way or another, you should mention that test scores should be treated as *estimates* of whatever was measured (achievement, for example). There are two reasons for representing test scores in this fashion:

- Tests do not (indeed, they cannot) assess everything that students know or that makes up a particular capability. Standardized achievement tests, for example, tend to cover a relatively broad range of knowledge but do not assess any one topic in great depth. Therefore, students may know more than their scores suggest.
- All tests contain some degree of error because of such factors as vaguely worded items, confusing directions, and low motivation on the day the test is administered.

Remember that a student's test score reflects the extent to which the content of that test has been mastered at about the time the test was taken. A student may have strengths and weaknesses not measured by a particular test, and because of changes in such characteristics as interests, motives, and cognitive skills, test scores can change, sometimes dramatically. The younger the student is and the longer the interval is between testings (on the same test), the greater is the likelihood that a test score will change significantly.

What a test score means depends on the nature of the test. If your students took an intelligence or a scholastic aptitude test, point out that such tests measure the current status of those cognitive skills that most closely relate to academic success. Also mention that IQ scores are judged to be below average, average, or above average on the basis of how they compare to the scores of a norm group. You might use personal wealth as an analogy to illustrate this last point. Whether someone is considered poor, financially comfortable, or wealthy depends on how much money everyone else in that person's reference group possesses. A net worth of $100,000 is considered wealthy in some circles and barely adequate in others.

If you are discussing achievement test scores, make sure you understand the differences among diagnostic tests, norm-referenced tests, and criterion-referenced tests:

- Scores from a diagnostic achievement test can be used to discuss a student's strengths and weaknesses in such skills as reading, math, and spelling.
- Scores from a norm-referenced achievement test can be used to discuss general strengths and weaknesses in one or more content areas. For achievement tests that provide multiple sets of norms, start your interpretation at the most local level (school norms, ideally) since they are likely to be the most meaningful to parents, and then move to a more broad-based interpretation (district, state, or national norms).
- Scores from a criterion-referenced achievement test can be used to discuss how well a student has mastered the objectives on which the test is based. If

there is a close correspondence between the test's objectives and your own objectives as a teacher, the test score can be used as an indicator of how much the student has learned in class.

To review this chapter, see the ACE practice tests and PowerPoint slides on the textbook web site.

The instructional decisions you make in the classroom will be *guided* but not dictated by the test scores. Many parents fear that if their child obtains a low score on a test, she will be labeled a slow learner by the teacher and receive less attention than higher-scoring students do. This is a good opportunity to lay such a fear to rest in two ways. First, note that test scores are but *one* source of information about students. You will also take into account how well they perform on classroom tests, homework assignments, and special projects, as well as in classroom discussions. Second, emphasize that you are committed to using test scores not to classify students but to help them learn.

Resources for Further Investigation

● Technical and Specialized Aspects of Testing

For more information about standardized tests and how to use the information they provide appropriately, consult one or more of these books: *Psychological Testing* (1997), by Anne Anastasi and Susan Urbina; *Measurement and Assessment in Teaching* (2000), by Robert Linn and Norman Gronlund; *Tests and Assessment* (2001), by W. Bruce Walsh and Nancy Betz; and *Essentials of Standardized Achievement Testing* (2002), by Thomas Haladyna.

For information about issues surrounding the testing of minority students, examine *Assessment and Instruction of Culturally and Linguistically Diverse Students with or At-Risk of Learning Problems: From Research to Practice* (1997), by Virginia Gonzalez, Rita Brusca-Vega, and Thomas Yawkey.

Volume 71, number 1 (Spring, 2001), of *Review of Educational Research* contains an article by Mary Pitoniak and James Royer that examines the measurement, legal, and social policy issues of providing testing accommodations to students with disabilities.

The web site of the National Board on Educational Testing and Public Policy (**www.bc.edu/research/nbetpp/reports.html**) contains downloadable reports, statements, and monographs on various aspects of educational testing.

● References for Evaluating Standardized Tests

To obtain the information necessary for evaluating standardized tests, examine *The Fifteenth Mental Measurements Yearbook* (2003), edited by Barbara Plake and James Impara. You may have to check earlier editions of *Mental Measurements*

Yearbook for information on a specific test since there are far too many tests available to review in a single edition.

The American Psychological Association provides a Code of Fair Testing Practices at **www.apa.org/science/fairtestcode.html**. The Code is also available at the site of the National Board on Educational Testing and Public Policy, mentioned earlier.

The National Center for Fair and Open Testing (more commonly known as FairTest) is an advocacy group whose goal is the development of fair, open, and educationally sound standardized tests. Its home page can be found at **www.fairtest.org/**. By following the link to "K–12 Testing," you can find additional information and publications on standardized testing and accountability.

● High-Stakes Testing

Two excellent analyses of the high-stakes testing issue can be found in *High Stakes: Testing for Tracking, Promotion, and Graduation* (1999) by Jay Heubert and Robert Hauser, and *The Unintended Consequences of High-Stakes Testing* (2003), by M. Gail Jones, Brett Jones, and Tracy Hargrove.

The web site of the Center for Performance Assessment (**www.makingstandardswork.com/**) provides links to the learning standards of all fifty states.

● Computer-Based Testing

An examination of several issues that pertain to computer-based testing can be found in *Practical Considerations in Computer-Based Testing* (2002), by Cynthia Parshall, Judith Spray, John Kalohn, and Tim Davey.

Summary

1. Standardized tests are designed by people with specialized training in test construction, are given to everyone under the same conditions, are scored the same for everyone, and are interpreted with reference to either a norm group or a set of predetermined standards.

2. The purpose of giving a standardized test is to obtain an accurate and representative sample of some characteristic of a person, since it is impractical to measure that characteristic comprehensively.

3. Standardized tests are typically used to identify students' strengths and weaknesses, inform parents of their child's general level of achievement, plan instructional lessons, and place students in special groups or programs.

4. One of the most important characteristics of a standardized test is its reliability—the similarity between two rankings of test scores obtained from the same individuals.

5. Another important characteristic of standardized tests is validity. A valid test accurately measures what its users intend it to measure and allows us to draw appropriate inferences about how much of some characteristic the test taker possesses. Three types of evidence that contribute to accurate inferences are content validity evidence, predictive validity evidence, and construct validity evidence.

6. A third important characteristic of a standardized test is its norm group—a sample of students specially chosen and tested so as to reflect the population of students for whom the test is intended. The norm group's performance becomes the standard against which scores are compared.

7. Standardized achievement tests measure how much has been learned about a particular subject. The major types of achievement tests are single subject, batteries, diagnostic, competency, and special purpose.

8. Diagnostic tests identify specific strengths and weaknesses in basic learning skills.

9. Competency tests measure how well high school students have acquired such basic skills as reading, writing, and computation.

10. Aptitude tests estimate an individual's predisposition to acquire additional knowledge and skill in specific areas with the aid of effective instruction.

11. Tests that use a norm-referenced scoring system compare an individual's score to the performance of a norm group.

12. Tests that use a criterion-referenced scoring system judge scores in terms of mastery of a set of objectives.

13. Percentile rank indicates the percentage of scores that are at or below a person's score.

14. A z score is a standard score that indicates how far in standard deviation units a raw score is from the mean.

15. A T score is a standard score based on a scale of 1 to 100, with a mean of 50.

16. A stanine score indicates in which of nine normal-curve segments a person's performance falls.

17. Perceived deficiencies and lack of accountability in education during the 1980s led to the development of state-wide testing programs.

18. The practice of using standardized test scores to determine promotion to the next grade, graduation from high school, additional state funding, job security for teachers and administrators, and school accreditation is called high-stakes testing. Although high-stakes tests are given in every state and are related to learning standards, little is known about their effects on student achievement.

19. The federal government became involved in high-stakes testing in 2001 when the Congress passed the No Child Left Behind (NCLB) Act. The goal of NCLB is to have all students score at least at the proficient level in math and reading/language arts on state-administered tests by 2014.

20. NCLB has three main features. First, all states are required to administer annual high-stakes tests in math and reading/language arts to students in grades 3 through 8. Science assessments must be given by 2007. The format of the tests, the type of items used, and the length of the tests is decided by each state. Second, states must demonstrate every year that a certain additional percentage of all students, including students in such subgroups as racial and ethnic minorities, low-income, limited English proficiency, and special education, have scored at the proficient level or higher. This feature is known as adequate yearly progress, or AYP. Third, states and school districts must publish yearly reports that describe how every group of students performed on the annual assessment.

21. Proponents of high-stakes testing argue that it will have a number of beneficial effects: greater goal clarity, improved quality control, improvements in teaching skills and methods, and increased motivation among students.

22. Critics of high-stakes testing argue that it will have adverse effects because of structural limitations (such as assessments that are narrow in scope, limited in range, and shallow in depth), misinterpretation/misuse of test results, a narrow approach to motivation (essentially a behavioral one), and undesirable side effects (such as excessive time devoted to test preparation and decreased time for nontested subjects).

23. The research on high-stakes testing is limited, inconsistent, and strongly debated.

24. Technology can aid in preparing students for standardized tests and in administering and scoring the tests.

Key Terms

standardized tests *(492)*
reliability *(493)*
validity *(494)*
norm group *(496)*
single-subject achievement test *(496)*
achievement batteries *(496)*
diagnostic test *(497)*
competency test *(497)*

special-purpose achievement test *(497)*
aptitude tests *(497)*
scholastic aptitude *(497)*
norm-referenced tests *(497)*
criterion-referenced tests *(498)*
grade equivalent score *(498)*
percentile rank *(499)*

standard deviation *(499)*
normal curve *(500)*
z score *(500)*
T score *(500)*
stanine score *(501)*
high-stakes testing *(502)*
computer adaptive testing (CAT) *(517)*

16 Becoming a Better Teacher by Becoming a Reflective Teacher

As you know from personal experience, some teachers are much more effective than others. Take a moment, and think back to as many teachers as you can remember. How many of them were really outstanding in the sense that they established a favorable classroom atmosphere, were sensitive to the needs of students, and used a variety of techniques to help you learn? How many of them did an adequate job but left you bored or indifferent most of the time? How many of them made you dread entering their classrooms because they were either ineffective teachers or insensitive or even cruel in dealing with you and your classmates?

Chances are you remember just a few outstanding teachers and had at least one who was incompetent or tyrannical (and perhaps several of them). You probably know from your experiences as a student that ineffective or vindictive teachers are often dissatisfied with them-selves and with their jobs. It seems logical to assume a circular relationship in such cases: unhappy teachers often do a poor job of instruction; teachers who do a poor job of instruction are likely to be unhappy.

If you hope to be an effective teacher who enjoys life in the classroom (most of the time), you must be well prepared and willing to work. You will need a wide variety of skills, sensitivity to the needs of your students, and awareness of many instructional techniques. Each chapter in this book was written to help you acquire these various skills, sensitivities, and techniques. In addition, you will need to develop the reflective attitudes and abilities that help you formulate thoughtful instructional goals and plans, implement those plans, observe their effects, and judge whether your goals were met. This chapter offers some suggestions you might use to enhance such attitudes and abilities. ●

IMPROVING YOUR TEACHING AND REFLECTION SKILLS

To aid your professional development, go to this textbook's web site (accessible from **http://education.college.hmco. com/students**) and explore the Weblinks section. See especially the links to professional organizations and publications.

Scholars who study instructional processes (e.g., Freiberg, 2002; Howard & McColskey, 2001; Protheroe, 2002) often note that effective teachers know how to coordinate a diverse array of instructional elements (such as planning, lesson design, time management, classroom management, instructional methods, student motivation, and assessment techniques) and adapt them to differences in student needs, materials, and purposes. Their insights highlight the point that to be consistently effective, you will need to observe and analyze what you do in the classroom and use different approaches with different groups of students. In essence, you will be conducting formative evaluations of yourself. Barbara Howard and Wendy McColskey (2001), who helped develop a teacher evaluation system for the state of North Carolina, describe formative teacher evaluation as a structure for individual professional growth that uses self-assessment, goal setting, feedback from peers, and portfolio development. In the sections that follow, we will explore these and other techniques.

Student Evaluations and Suggestions

In many respects, students are in a better position to evaluate teachers than anyone else. They may not always be able to analyze *why* what a teacher does is effective or ineffective (even an experienced expert observer might have difficulty doing so), but they know, better than anyone else, whether they are responding and learning. Furthermore, students form their impressions after interacting with a teacher for hundreds or thousands of hours. Most principals or other adult observers may watch a teacher in action for only a few minutes at a time. It therefore makes sense to pay attention to and solicit opinions from students.

As a matter of fact, it will be virtually impossible for you to ignore student reactions. Every minute that school is in session, you will receive student feedback in the form of attentiveness (or lack of it), facial expressions, restlessness, yawns, sleeping, disruptive behavior, and the like. If a particular lesson arouses either a neutral or a negative reaction, this should signal to you that you need to seek a better way to present the same material in the future. If you find that you seem to be spending much of your time disciplining students, it will be worth your while to evaluate why and to find other methods.

In addition to informally analyzing the minute-by-minute reactions of your students, you may find it helpful to request more formal feedback. After completing a unit, you might say, "I'd like you to tell me what you liked and disliked about the way this unit was arranged and give me suggestions for improving it if I teach it again next year."

A more comprehensive and systematic approach is to distribute a questionnaire or evaluation form and ask students to record their reactions anonymously. You might use a published form or devise your own. In either case, a common format is to list a series of statements and ask students to rate them on a five-point scale. Some of the published forms use special answer sheets that make it possible to tally the results electronically. Many rating-scale evaluation forms have some disadvantages, however:

- Responses may not be very informative unless you can compare your ratings to those of colleagues. If you get an overall rating of 3.5 on "makes the subject matter interesting," for example, you won't know whether you need to work on that aspect of your teaching until you discover that the average rating of other teachers of the same grade or subject was 4.2.
- Published evaluation forms may not be very helpful unless all other teachers use the same rating scale. Fortunately, this may be possible in school districts that use a standard scale to obtain evidence for use in making decisions about retention, tenure, and promotion.

- Many rating scales are subject to a *leniency problem*. Students tend to give most teachers somewhat above-average ratings on most traits. Although leniency may soothe a teacher's ego, wishy-washy responses do not provide the information needed to improve pedagogical effectiveness.

To get around the leniency problem and to induce students to give more informative reactions, forced-choice ratings are often used. Figure 16.1 shows a forced-choice rating form, the Descriptive Ranking Form for Teachers, developed by Don Cosgrove (1959). This form is designed to let teachers know how students perceive their skill in

Figure 16.1 Descriptive Ranking Form for Teachers

Set a ———	Always on time for class [3]
———	Pleasant in class [2]
———	Very sincere when talking with students [4]
———	Well-read [1]
Set b ———	Contagious enthusiasm for subject [4]
———	Did not fill up time with trivial material [3]
———	Gave everyone an equal chance [2]
———	Made clear what was expected of students [1]
Set c ———	Classes always orderly [3]
———	Enjoyed teaching class [4]
———	Friendliness did not seem forced [2]
———	Logical in thinking [1]
Set d ———	Encouraged creativity [4]
———	Kept course material up to date [1]
———	Never deliberately forced own decisions on class [2]
———	Procedures well thought out [3]
Set e ———	Authority on own subject [1]
———	Friendly attitude toward students [4]
———	Marked tests very fairly [3]
———	Never criticized in a destructive way [2]
Set f ———	Good sense of humor [4]
———	Spaced assignments evenly [3]
———	Students never afraid to ask questions in class [2]
———	Well-organized course [1]
Set g ———	Accepted students' viewpoints with open mind [2]
———	Increased students' vocabulary by own excellent usage [1]
———	Students always knew what was coming up next day [3]
———	Students willingly worked for teacher [4]
Set h ———	Always knew what he or she was doing [3]
———	Appreciated accomplishment [4]
———	Did not ridicule wrong answers [2]
———	Well informed in all related fields [1]
Set i ———	Always had class material ready [3]
———	Covered subject well [1]
———	Encouraged students to think out answers [4]
———	Rules and regulations fair [2]
Set j ———	Always managed to get things done on time [3]
———	Course had continuity [1]
———	Made material significant [4]
———	Understood problems of students [2]

SOURCE: Cosgrove (1959).

four areas of performance: (1) knowledge and organization of subject matter, (2) adequacy of relations with students in class, (3) adequacy of plans and procedures in class, and (4) enthusiasm in working with students. If you decide to use this form, omit the numbers in brackets that follow each statement when you prepare copies for distribution to students. On your own copy of the form, write in those numbers, and use them to prepare your score in each of the four categories.

First, direct your students to rank the phrases in each set from 1 ("most like you") to 4 ("least like you"). Then calculate your index of effectiveness in each category of the Descriptive Ranking Form for Teachers by assigning a score of 4 to the phrase in each group that is ranked 1, a score of 3 to the phrase marked 2, and so on. Add together the scores for all phrases identified by the parenthetical number 1, and do the same for the other sets of phrases. The cluster of phrases that yields the highest score is perceived by your students to be your strongest area of teaching; the cluster that yields the lowest score is considered to be your weakest. A total of 30 points for all phrases indicated by the parenthetical number 1, for example, means that you ranked high in category 1 (knowledge and organization of subject matter). If, however, you get only 12 points for phrases identified by the parenthetical number 4, you will need to work harder at being enthusiastic when working with students.

For teachers who adopt a constructivist approach and value students' perceptions of how well constructivist learning principles are implemented in the classroom, the survey instrument in Figure 16.2 may prove useful. Called the Constructivist Learning Environment Survey (CLES) (Taylor & Fraser, 1998; Taylor, Fraser, & Fisher, 1997), it was designed especially for science teachers. But except for items 6–10, the items are sufficiently general that they can be used for other subject areas.

One way to use the CLES is to administer it at the beginning of the school year to establish a baseline and then again in the middle of the year and at the end. Since the students will not have experienced your approach to instruction at the beginning of the year, have them answer on the basis of their experiences in last year's class. A high school teacher who administered the CLES in September and June found that scores on all the scales increased (that is, shifted toward the constructivist end). The largest increases occurred in the Learning About the World, Learning to Speak Out, and Learning to Communicate scales (Johnson, 2000).

Peer and Self-Assessment Techniques

Classroom Observation Schedules   Although your students can supply quite a bit of information that can help you improve your teaching, they cannot always tell

Figure 16.2 The Constructivist Learning Environment Survey

Learning about the world	Almost Always	Often	Sometimes	Seldom	Almost Never
In this class . . .					
1 I learn about the world outside of school.	5	4	3	2	1
2 My new learning starts with problems about the world outside of school.	5	4	3	2	1
3 I learn how science can be part of my out-of-school life.	5	4	3	2	1
In this class . . .					
4 I get a better understanding of the world outside of school.	5	4	3	2	1
5 I learn interesting things about the world outside of school.	5	4	3	2	1

Continued

Figure 16.2 The Constructivist Learning Environment Survey—Cont'd

Learning about science	Almost Always	Often	Sometimes	Seldom	Almost Never
In this class . . .					
6 I learn that science has changed over time.	5	4	3	2	1
7 I learn that science is influenced by people's values and opinions.	5	4	3	2	1
In this class . . .					
8 I learn about the different sciences used by people in other cultures.	5	4	3	2	1
9 I learn that modern science is different from the science of long ago.	5	4	3	2	1
10 I learn that science involves <u>inventing</u> theories.	5	4	3	2	1

Learning to speak out	Almost Always	Often	Sometimes	Seldom	Almost Never
In this class . . .					
11 It's OK for me to ask the teacher "why do I have to learn this?"	5	4	3	2	1
12 It's OK for me to question the way I'm being taught.	5	4	3	2	1
13 It's OK for me to complain about activities that are confusing.	5	4	3	2	1
In this class . . .					
14 It's OK for me to complain about anything that prevents me from learning.	5	4	3	2	1
15 It's OK for me to express my opinion.	5	4	3	2	1

Learning to learn	Almost Always	Often	Sometimes	Seldom	Almost Never
In this class . . .					
16 I help the teacher to plan what I'm going to learn.	5	4	3	2	1
17 I help the teacher to decide how well I am learning.	5	4	3	2	1
18 I help the teacher to decide which activities are best for me.	5	4	3	2	1
In this class . . .					
19 I help the teacher to decide how much time I spend on activities.	5	4	3	2	1
20 I help the teacher to decide which activities I do.	5	4	3	2	1

Learning to communicate	Almost Always	Often	Sometimes	Seldom	Almost Never
In this class . . .					
21 I get the chance to talk to other students.	5	4	3	2	1
22 I talk with other students about how to solve problems.	5	4	3	2	1
23 I explain my ideas to other students.	5	4	3	2	1
In this class . . .					
24 I ask other students to explain their ideas.	5	4	3	2	1
25 Other students listen carefully to my ideas.	5	4	3	2	1

SOURCE: Taylor & Fraser (1998); Taylor, Fraser, & Fisher (1997). Permission to reproduce the CLES granted personally to the author by Peter Taylor.

you about technical flaws in your instructional technique. This is especially true with younger students. Accordingly, you may wish to submit to a detailed analysis by a colleague of your approach to teaching.

One of the simplest classroom observation instruments to create and use is the checklist. Figure 16.3 contains a set of six relatively brief checklists that reflect many of the topics discussed in this book. You can adopt this instrument as is or modify it to suit your circumstances (such as your grade level and your state's learning standards) to help you evaluate your effectiveness in several important areas.

Figure 16.3 Examples of Classroom Observation Checklists

1. Characteristics of a Good Learning Environment

____ Samples of exemplary work are displayed.

____ Criteria charts, rubrics, or expectations are visible.

____ There is evidence of students making choices.

____ Furniture arrangements allow for individual, small-group, and whole-class work.

____ Written expectations for behavior and subject matter are displayed.

____ There are a variety of materials and activities to address different learning styles.

____ There are discussions that involve many different students and points of view.

2. Characteristics of Good Teaching

____ Content and standards are being explicitly taught.

____ A variety of instructional strategies are integrated into all lessons.

____ Individual progress is monitored.

____ There are interventions for students not demonstrating mastery.

____ A variety of assessment techniques are used.

____ There is evidence of staff development impact.

3. Patterns of Teacher Behavior

____ Gender and racial equity are observed in interactions with students.

____ There is recognition and positive reinforcement of effort as well as achievement.

____ Students are treated as individuals.

4. Characteristics of Student Learning

____ Students communicate ideas clearly, orally and in writing.

____ Students plan and organize their own work.

____ Students use a variety of resources.

____ Students create new products and ideas.

____ Students use prior knowledge to solve problems.

____ Students collaborate with peers and adults on projects, drafts, and investigations.

5. Questions to Ask Students Who Are On-Task

____ What are you learning?

____ Why do you need to know this information?

____ How is this like other things you've learned?

____ What will this help you do in the future?

____ What do you do if you get stuck?

____ How do you know if your work is good enough?

____ If you want to make your work better, do you know how to improve it?

____ Do you talk about your work with your parents or other adults?

6. Observing Individual Students Who Are Not On-Task

____ What is the student doing while others are learning?

____ Where is the student sitting?

____ How often does the teacher make contact with the student?

____ What is the nature of the interactions?

Ask the Student:

____ What do you think this lesson is about?

____ What would help you understand this better?

____ What would make it more interesting?

____ What do you do if you don't understand something?

____ How do you get help?

SOURCE: L. Schmidt (2003).

Soliciting comments about the effectiveness of one's teaching methods from students and colleagues and reflecting on these comments is an excellent way to become a better teacher.

Another useful observation instrument can be found in an article by Donna Sobel, Sheryl Taylor, and Ruth Anderson in the July/August 2003 issue (Vol. 35, No. 6) of *Teaching Exceptional Children.* Called the Diversity-Responsive Teaching Observation Tool, it was created for a Colorado school district with a broad diversity of students. The instrument contains three sections and focuses on how well teachers address diversity as well as exhibit appropriate classroom instruction and classroom management behaviors. Because the form is too lengthy to reproduce here, we encourage you to consult the article in which it appears if you think you might want to have a colleague use it to evaluate your teaching.

Audiotaped Lessons   If it is not possible for you to team up with a colleague, you might consider trying to accomplish the same goal through the use of audiotape. Your first step should be to decide which classes or parts of classes you want to record, for how long, and on what day of the week. The goal should be to create a representative sample of the circumstances under which you teach. Then you should inform your students that you intend to tape-record a sample of your lessons over a period of several weeks to study and improve your instructional methods and that you will protect their confidentiality by not allowing anyone else but you to listen to the tapes. Then you can analyze the tapes according to categories like those in Figure 16.1 and any others that might be of interest.

A first-year high school teacher decided after analyzing an audiotape of one of her lessons that she needed to wait longer for students to respond to high-level questions, give students more opportunities to ask questions, give students more feedback, use specific praise, review and integrate previous concepts with new lessons, and stop saying "OK" and "all right." Impressed with these insights, she continued to tape-record and analyze her lessons, and at the end of the year was nominated for an award as the district's best new teacher (Freiberg, 2002).

Videotaped Lessons   Allowing yourself to be videotaped as you teach and then analyzing your actions later can be a valuable learning experience because it often reveals (even more clearly than audiotape) discrepancies between the instructional beliefs you espouse and how you put those beliefs into practice. Think of it as putting into practice the old saying, "Actions speak louder than words." The potential of videotaped lessons to reveal these discrepancies and produce major shifts in teaching behavior was illustrated in a study (Wedman, Espinosa, & Laffey, 1999) of eleven individuals whose teaching experience ranged from none to twenty-two years.

The participant with twenty-two years of experience, a primary grade teacher who had never had her teaching observed, claimed to have a student-centered philosophy. She believed that teachers should provide students with opportunities to explore and experiment. But her videotaped lessons revealed a strong teacher-directed, teacher-centered approach. She selected all the material and activities for the students and provided few opportunities for student expression, exploration, or questioning. As a result of reviewing and discussing her videotaped lessons, she began to look for ways to be more student centered and to emphasize inquiry rather than information dissemination as her approach to student learning.

Because videotaping is more intrusive than audiotaping, teachers are often concerned that the natural flow of classroom events will be disrupted. Experience has shown, however, that both students and teachers quickly lose their self-consciousness and treat the camera as just part of the background. As with audiotaped lessons, make sure your students are informed of what will occur and why and how you will keep the results confidential (Lonoff, 1997).

Reflective Lesson Plans   You may want to try something called reflective lesson plans (Ho, 1995). To do so, follow these four steps:

1. Divide a sheet of paper in half. Label the left-hand side "Lesson Plan." Label the right-hand side "Reflective Notes."
2. On the lesson plan side, note relevant identifying information (fourth period English, January 23, 9:00 A.M.; honors algebra; fourth-grade social studies), the objectives of the lesson, the tasks that are to be carried out in chronological order, the materials and equipment that are to be used, and how much time has been allotted for this lesson.
3. On the reflective notes side, as soon as possible after the lesson, write your thoughts about the worth of the objective that underlies the lesson, the adequacy of the materials, and how well you performed the basic mechanics of teaching.
4. Make changes to the lesson plan based on your analysis of the reflective notes.

Guided Reflection Protocol   A technique that is somewhat less structured than the reflective lesson plan is the guided reflection protocol (McEntee et al., 2003). After choosing one or more teaching episodes that you would like to examine, try to answer as honestly as possible the following four questions:

1. *What happened?* The main requirement of this step is simply to describe the incident as fully as possible. Note, for instance, when and where the incident occurred, who was involved, and what occurred just prior to, during, and immediately after the incident. Avoid analysis and interpretation.
2. *Why did it happen?* If you've provided enough context in answering the first question, you should be able to identify the events that produced the incident.
3. *What might it mean?* Note the conditional wording of this question. Using the word *might* instead of *does* is intended to help you realize that there are usually several possible interpretations of the meaning of an incident. A teacher who reprimands a class for not finishing an assignment on time may, for example, need to examine the clarity of her objectives, the amount of time she budgets for the completion of assignments, the ability of students to use their time productively, or her ability to cope with administrative pressure to cover the curriculum in time for an upcoming high-stakes test.
4. *What are the implications for my practice?* Consider what you might do differently in a similar situation in the light of how you answered the first three questions.

Developing a Reflective Journal   Seymour Sarason (1993), who has written extensively about schooling and school reform, points out what may seem obvious but is often missed in practice: every teacher should be an expert in both subject matter and how children learn in classrooms. The goal, and the challenge, is to figure out how to present the subject matter so that students understand it, remember it, and use it. To do that, you must constantly prepare, observe, and reflect on how closely your instructional practices relate to theory and research and produce the desired outcome (Heath, 2002). The Reflective Journal that we mentioned at the beginning of the book is intended to help you begin that process in a systematic way. Now we will give you more detailed suggestions for keeping such a journal.

We recommend that you develop a Reflective Journal for two basic purposes: (1) to serve as a repository of instructional ideas and techniques that you have either created from your own experiences or gleaned from other sources and (2) to give yourself a format for recording your observations and reflections on teaching. These two purposes can be separate from each other or, if you choose, related to each other in a cycle of reflectivity that we will describe. As you read this section, refer to Figure 16.4 for an illustration of how a journal page might look.

The form your Reflective Journal takes will probably change over the years to reflect your experiences and changing needs. But to begin, we suggest that you organize your first journal around the marginal notes in each chapter that are labeled "Journal Entry." Use the Journal Entries as just what their name implies: page headings in your Reflective Journal. To allow room for both the expansion of your teaching ideas and the inclusion of your ongoing reflections, you might purchase a three-ring binder so that you can add and drop pages. Alternatively, you might want to create your Reflective Journal as computer files, which would give you unlimited capacity for interaction and expansion.

Figure 16.4 Sample Page for Your Reflective Journal

Journal Entry: *Ways to Teach Comprehension Tactics*
Source: *"Information-Processing Theory"*

Ideas for Instruction

Note: All the ideas you list here will pertain to the particular journal entry/instructional goal for this journal page.

- *Customized suggestions for teaching—those points, principles, activities, and examples taken from the text and the Suggestions for Teaching that are most relevant to your own situation.*

- *Ideas generated from past experiences as a student.*

- *Ideas provided by professional colleagues.*

- *Ideas collected from student-teaching experiences.*

- *Ideas gathered from methods textbooks.*

Reflections: Questions and "Restarter" Suggestions for Instruction

Reflective Question (to focus observation of my teaching and my students' learning): *Do my students have difficulty understanding the meaning of what they read or of what I present in class?*

(Record your ongoing reflections, observations, and analytic notes about your instruction and your students' learning of this topic here. If necessary, you may need to "jump-start" or reorient your instruction. One possible idea follows.)

Suggested Action: *Schedule a series of sessions on how to study. Explain the purpose of various comprehension tactics, and provide opportunities for students to practice these skills on material they have been assigned to read. Give corrective feedback.*

Under each heading, you can develop a two-part page or multipage entry. As illustrated in the top half of Figure 16.4, the first part should contain your own teaching ideas, custom-tailored from the Suggestions for Teaching sections of the chapters of this book and from personal experience and other sources to fit the grade level and subjects you expect to teach.

To illustrate, let's use a Journal Entry from the chapter on information-processing theory, "Ways to Teach Comprehension Tactics":

- Search your memory for techniques that your past teachers used. Did your fifth-grade teacher, for instance, have a clever way of relating new information to ideas that you had learned earlier in order to make the new information easier to understand? Describe the technique so you will remember to try it yourself. Did a high school teacher have an ingenious way of displaying the similarities and differences among a set of ideas? Exactly how did she or he do it?

- After you exhaust your own recollections, ask roommates or classmates if they can remember any successful ways that their teachers made learning easier.

- Examine the examples given in the text section where the Journal Entry appears. Which ones seem most appropriate for the grade level and subject you will be teaching? Jot them down. Do any of the examples suggest variations you can think of on your own? Write them down before you forget them.

- Add ideas that you pick up in methods classes or during your student-teaching experience. If you see a film in a methods class that shows how a teacher helps students understand a particular point, describe it in your journal. If your master teacher uses a successful technique to clarify difficult-to-understand material, record it.

If you follow some or all of these suggestions for using the Journal Entries, you will have a rich source of ideas to turn to when you discover that your students seem confused and anxious because of poor comprehension and you find yourself wondering if there is anything you can do about it.

With this part of the journal under way, you should feel reasonably well prepared when you first take charge of a class. But given the complexity of classroom teaching, lessons or techniques that looked good on paper do not always produce the intended effect. This is the point at which you need to reflect on and analyze what you are doing and how you might bring about improvements. On the bottom half of your journal page, or on a new page, write in question form what the nature of the problem seems to be. Then try to identify the cause (or causes) of the problem and at least one possible solution. You can use this suggestion to get restarted or headed in a new direction with your teaching. If, for example, some of your students still have difficulty comprehending what they read despite the comprehension-enhancing techniques that you embedded into your lessons, you might reread the chapter on information-processing theory, as well as other articles and books on information processing, and decide that your students really need systematic instruction in how to use various comprehension-directed learning tactics.

Using a Portfolio with Your Journal   Middle school teacher Linda Van Wagenen used a personal portfolio along with a Reflective Journal to analyze and improve the quality of her instruction (Van Wagenen & Hibbard, 1998). She compiled a portfolio of her efforts to achieve certain teaching goals and used that to examine her effectiveness. She judged her first two efforts at analysis to be unsatisfactory because they were largely descriptive; they emphasized what she had done and ignored what effects those efforts had on her students (self-assessment), what she thought about the quality of her own instruction (self-evaluation), or what she planned to do next (self-regulation). Her third attempt focused on ways to motivate students to improve their performance in persuasive and expository writing. She identified a set of steps that would help her understand the problem and

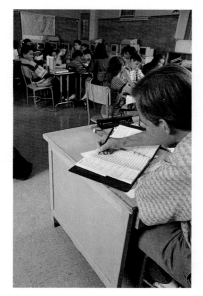

Research has shown that keeping a personal journal about one's teaching activities and outcomes helps teachers improve their effectiveness because it forces them to focus on what they do, why they do it, and what kinds of results are typically obtained.

produce improvements. Evidence of her successes and failures made up the portfolio. In addition, she kept a Reflective Journal because she felt it would help her stay focused on finding a solution to the problem and would stimulate attempts at self-evaluation and self-regulation. The result of this third attempt was judged to be much more useful than either of her first two efforts. In addition to addressing the question, "What did I do?" she also addressed the questions, "What did I learn?" and "Now what will I do?"

In thinking about the contents of your own portfolio, you might want to start with the following list of items (Drake & McBride, 2000; Hurst, Wilson, & Cramer, 1998; Lyons, 1999):

1. Title page
2. A table of contents
3. A statement of your educational philosophy, which may include the reasons that you chose teaching as a career
4. A résumé
5. A statement of your teaching goals
6. Example(s) of a lesson plan, keyed to state standards
7. Examples of learning activities (especially those that contain innovative ideas)
8. Samples of students' work
9. Photographs and videotapes
10. Letters of recommendation
11. Teaching evaluations
12. Samples of college work
13. An autobiography
14. Reflections about how teaching (or student teaching) has contributed to your growth as a person and a teacher
15. Official documents (transcripts, teaching certificates, test scores)

To stimulate your thinking about reflective teaching techniques and how you can apply them to your own practice, see the Thought Questions and Reflective Journal Questions on the textbook web site.

The Case in Print describes a portfolio type of Reflective Journal that some teacher education programs require their students to compile and that students are using to demonstrate to potential employers their readiness to teach.

Are Reflective Techniques Effective?

The answer to this question depends very much on the type of evidence one chooses to examine and the characteristics of the teachers who participated in studies on reflection. There are, for example, many positive anecdotes about the benefits of reflection on the quality of one's teaching. Lynn Streib, a primary grade teacher, had this to say about journal writing:

> Keeping a journal has been a realistic way for me to learn about, inquire into, collect data about, and enhance my practice as well as to learn about and plan for the children. Although writing in my journal each day takes time, it is economical and is the genre most compatible with my style of writing, my way of teaching, and my way of thinking.
>
> Since 1980, I have kept some kind of journal. . . . I continue to keep a journal for a variety of reasons. First and most important, it helps me with my teaching. When used in certain ways, the journal allows me to look closely at the curriculum. As I teach, I wonder how my thinking and my students' thinking evolve over time. I wonder what I have valued and what the children are interested in and value. Lesson plans don't tell me this, but the journal does. My journal is a place for planning, for raising questions, for figuring things out, and for thinking. (Streib, 1993, pp. 121–122)

The findings from experiments, on the other hand, have generally found that reflective activities produced little discernible effect on the quality of subsequent teaching behavior (Cornford, 2002). According to Ian Cornford (2002), these negative outcomes are largely due to flawed research designs. He believes that for reflection to be effective, teachers need to possess two qualities: broad and in-depth knowledge of the classroom as a teaching-learning environment and strong critical thinking skills. Many of the studies on reflection mentioned by Cornford were conducted with teachers who appeared to lack these qualities, and he was unable to find any studies that first tried to teach critical thinking skills before assessing the effect of reflection. The validity of Cornford's conclusion is supported by the fact that the few positive findings he did locate involved studies done with experienced teachers. For example, teachers with more than three years' experience who learned reflective skills in college were more satisfied with their jobs and had better teacher-student relationships than teachers who had no college training in reflection.

Cornford's analysis also receives support from a study of the effect of self-assessment on the type of instructional talk used by nine experienced elementary school teachers who were teaching reading (Roskos, Boehlen, & Walker, 2000). Much of the instructional talk exhibited by reading teachers involves a social function in that its purpose is to maintain the flow of instruction and provide direction (for example, restating students' comments, providing reinforcement, directing attention, and commenting on students' ideas). Instructional talk that is directed more to the conceptual basis of reading (such as tapping background knowledge, stimulating memory of relevant experiences, suggesting decoding techniques, and defining a concept) occurs much less frequently. For five weeks, the teachers' daily interactions with students in a reading clinic were videotaped and analyzed by both the teachers and researchers with an instrument (The Instructional Talk Analysis Tool) that assessed how frequently the preceding two categories of teacher talk occurred.

One of the major findings of this study is that the Talk Analysis Tool scores generated by the teachers did not match those of the researchers. The teachers saw themselves using social and conceptual talk in about equal proportions, whereas the researchers' analysis showed the split to be about 60/40 in favor of social language. This finding may have been due to the teachers' not having totally mastered the scoring rules of the Talk Analysis Tool, or it may have stemmed from the teachers' seeing and hearing what they wanted to believe.

The other major finding is that the way the teachers described their instructional behavior changed over the five-week period. Early on, most of their comments were evaluations of either their use of social and conceptual talk or their students' reading behaviors. These evaluative comments gradually subsided while comments about the *instructional effects* of their talk increased. Thus, at least for experienced teachers who can engage in some degree of critical thinking, viewing and analyzing one's actions seems to positively affect how one thinks about and interprets them.

The discrepancy in the preceding study between teachers' self-assessment and the assessment made of them by the researchers suggests that teachers may want to supplement self-assessment with forms of assessment that involve colleagues. Elementary and high school teachers in Hong Kong who participated in a study of peer coaching found it to be a beneficial experience (Lam, Yim, & Lam, 2002). Four or five teachers first met to discuss how a certain unit would be taught. The lesson plan was then tried out by one teacher while the others observed. The teachers then met to discuss the strengths and weaknesses of the lesson. In general, teachers felt the coaching experience improved their teaching and their ability to communicate with one another and said they would participate in the experience again.

USING TECHNOLOGY FOR REFLECTION

Throughout this book, we have described how you can use various technology tools to help your students become more effective learners. Now it's time to consider how you can use such technologies as the World Wide Web, videotape, and

Starting a Reflective Journal Now Pays Off in the Future

Seymour Sarason (1993), who has written extensively about schooling and school reform, points out what may seem obvious but is often missed in practice: every teacher should be an expert in both subject matter and how children learn in classrooms. The goal, and the challenge, is to figure out how to present the subject matter so that students understand it, remember it, and use it. To do that, you must constantly prepare, observe, and reflect on how closely your instructional practices relate to theory and research and produce the desired outcome (Heath, 2002). The Reflective Journal . . . is intended to help you begin that process in a systematic way. (p. 529–530)

Portfolios Give Prospective Teachers an Edge When They Interview for Jobs

VALERIE SCHREMP
St. Louis Post-Dispatch 12/14/97

Katherine Karoby, professor of education at Webster University, often tells a story about a student who showed up to a job interview with a teaching portfolio in her lap. The principal asked, "How would you teach reading in the second grade?"

"I would tell you," said the student, "But I would like to show you." She pulled a videotape from her portfolio, pulled in a VCR cart, popped in the tape, pressed play and got the job.

Karoby and the employed teacher are not alone in their testimony. Colleges, student teachers and even the Missouri Department of Elementary and Secondary Education are also praising portfolios. Teacher portfolios may contain videotapes, photos of bulletin boards and sample lesson plans.

The portfolios accomplish three things: they show the state Board of Education that a school is producing worthy teachers; they give students a record of growth over their college careers; and they show what a teacher can do.

Starting in fall 1998, Missouri will require education colleges to start portfolio programs. Every five years, to ensure the quality of an education program, the state will examine randomly selected portfolios from at least 10 percent of a program's students.

"Before, we focused on things like making sure institutions offered appropriate courses and hours," said Mike Lucas, head of certification for the Missouri Department of Elementary and Secondary Education. "Just because a student takes courses for x number of hours doesn't mean the individual has the competency to teach."

Several of Missouri's 34 teacher-educating colleges have already launched portfolio programs. So have Illinois colleges, though the state board does not require them.

Fontbonne College required this year's freshmen education students to begin portfolios. It even sells oversized, three-ring binders in its school bookstore as "start-up kits." Webster University wants to put portfolios on CD-ROM.

The University of Missouri at St. Louis, which placed 450 student teachers last year, uses portfolios to help grade students in education classes. Kathie Heywood, associate dean for academic affairs, said the education professors at first doubted the value of the portfolios. They feared students would put only their best pieces in them, presenting a false picture.

So they encourage students to include examples from the science lesson gone awry, or the behavior management plan that just didn't cut it in a high school class. That way, professors can help students correct their work or advise them not to go into teaching.

When students start looking for jobs, they can put together a professional portfolio, full of their best pieces to show off on interviews.

Principals notice. Phillip Silsby, principal of Belleville West High School, has seen just a few portfolios but called them effective. This year, he hired a counselor who had a portfolio of newspaper clips about a career education program she started at another school.

Jim Schwab, principal of Carollton Oaks Elementary in the Pattonville School District, says about one out of three applicants comes into an interview with a portfolio. "I look through them more out of courtesy than anything," he said. "But if two people come in with equal interviewing skills and equal credentials, a portfolio would certainly give them an edge."

One teacher interviewed at the school a couple of years ago, toting what Schwab called an impressive portfolio, full of creative ideas and projects. "That definitely put her over the top," he said. He hired her to teach third grade.

1. This article describes how prospective teachers are using portfolios to demonstrate their teaching skills to prospective employers. If this technique impresses you, start now to create your own portfolio. Save assignments from different classes, particularly those that required several steps to complete. As this article indicates, you can include video-tapes, photographs, and newspaper articles, as well as the traditional written format.

2. In addition to using portfolios as a job-seeking technique, you can use them to practice reflective teaching. Think about how you can combine the Reflective Journal described in this chapter with a portfolio.

multimedia and hypermedia programs to help you think about and improve your own teaching skills.

Discussion Forums and Chatrooms

A major source of frustration for teachers is the limited intellectual and social contact they have with one another (Sarason, 1993). Certainly during school hours, there are few opportunities for teachers to engage in meaningful discussions about teaching and learning. And after school, many teachers are either busy grading papers and making lesson plans or are at home with their families. Computer-based technologies can help break down this sense of isolation by providing forums for teachers to discuss instructional ideas and problems from any location and at any time.

You can begin that process now by using the World Wide Web to discuss ideas and field experiences with peers in this country and others. Later, when you have a full-time teaching position, you can use the Web to discuss such issues as teaching philosophy and common classroom problems and their solutions and to explore relevant resources. Numerous web sites have been designed for K–12 teachers and contain discussion forums or chatrooms (or both). Here are five you might consider using:

 For direct links to these and other web sites, use the Weblinks at the textbook site.

- The Connect page of ALPS, Harvard's Teacher Lab (**learnweb.harvard.edu/alps/bigideas/q5.cfm**)
- The New Teachers Online page of Teachers Network.org (**www.teachersnetwork.org/ntol/**)
- The Interactive Forums page of the International Education and Resource Network (**foro.iearn.org/**)
- The Teacher2Teacher page of Teachnet.com (**www.teachnet.com/t2t/**)
- The Teachers Helping Teachers Guestbook page of Teachers Helping Teachers (**www.pacificnet.net/~mandel/guestbook.html**)

Multimedia Case-Based Instruction

In addition to online conferencing, educational researchers and teacher education programs are using multimedia and hypermedia programs that feature case-based learning formats that encourage new models of teaching, learning, and assessment among both preservice and practicing teachers (Abell, Bryan, & Anderson, 1998; Baker, 2000; Hughes, Packard, & Pearson, 2000; Stephens, Leavell, & Fabris, 1999).

These materials contain video-based stories to provide a context or situation for teacher reflection and introduce a more constructivist teaching orientation. Tools are provided for selecting and displaying problem cases and situations, recording preliminary case solutions, browsing through expert commentary and supplemental case information, exploring library materials for case solutions and alternative cases, and provoking student reflection. And with technology's replay capabilities, a preservice teacher like you could use these multimedia cases to identify key instructional decisions in planning or conducting a lesson. After watching a video sequence a second or third time for critical teaching decisions, you might post some reflection notes or compare that situation to another. Perhaps more important, such tools are not only useful for individual exploration; they also promote rich conversations among teachers.

One set of such materials (Baker, 2000) focuses on the reading and writing of an elementary grade student over the course of a school year. Each videotape segment shows the student either reading or writing with classmates or the teacher. The book that the student reads from and the student's written products can be easily read from the videotape. The video segments can be arranged in such a way that one can track the student's performance either over time or across subject-matter areas.

One study (Abell et al., 1998) focused on science education undergraduates who viewed video cases of first graders learning about eggs and seeds. The experience produced significant changes in the future teachers' beliefs about the capabilities of six-year-olds. According to one undergraduate:

> My expectations for a first grade science lesson have really changed after viewing the Seeds and Eggs lesson. The first graders are able to handle hands-on a lot better than I thought they would. I thought the teacher would mainly do all of the talking and experimenting. I saw these students, even though they are young, being able to conduct and observe experiments on their own. I thought they would misbehave if there was not a lot of supervision. This class really surprised me at how well behaved and under control they were. (p. 505)

How will you use reflective teaching in your own career? To prompt your thinking, read the PowerPoint slides and try the ACE practice tests at the textbook web site.

Resources for Further Investigation

● Reflective Teaching

Among the many recently published books on reflection in teaching, several are worth examining: *Reflective Planning, Teaching, and Evaluation: K–12* (3rd ed., 2002), by Judy Eby, Adrienne Herrell, and James Hicks; *Reflective Teaching: Professional Artistry Through Inquiry* (3rd ed., 2001), by James Henderson; *At the Heart of Teaching: A Guide to Reflective Practice* (2003), by Grace Hall McEntee, Jon Appleby, JoAnne Dowd, Jan Grant, Simon Hole, and Peggy Silva; *Becoming a Reflective Educator* (2nd ed., 2000), by Timothy Reagan, Charles Case, and John Brubacher; and *Reflective Practice to Improve Schools* (2001), by Jennifer York-Barr, William Sommers, Gail Ghere, and Jo Montie. Each book defines reflective teaching, discusses how it contributes to one's professional growth, and describes several techniques to facilitate reflection. The Henderson book discusses how teachers can integrate five forms of inquiry into their reflections in order to facilitate John Dewey's goal of democratic living. The authors of *At the Heart of Teaching* either are or were public school teachers. The York-Barr et al. book has separate chapters on individual reflection,

reflection with partners, reflection in small groups, and school-wide reflection.

A book that has an unusual format is *Reports from the Classroom: Cases for Reflection* (1995), by Sarah Huyvaert. It presents thirty-two case reports, each written by a practicing classroom teacher. Each report describes a classroom incident between the teacher and a student, the teacher and an administrator, or the teacher and another teacher. Following the incident, the teacher reflects on how the incident was handled (sometimes well, but sometimes not).

● Teachers' Portfolios

So You Have to Have a Portfolio? A Teacher's Guide to Preparation and Presentation (2nd ed., 2004), by Robert Wyatt III and Sandra Looper, describes different types of portfolios, their purposes, and how to collect data for an appropriate portfolio presentation.

The Career Advancement Portfolio (2000), by Beverly Irby and Genevieve Brown, discusses how to create a professional portfolio for the purpose of career advancement.

Glossary

accommodation The process of creating or revising a scheme to fit a new experience. (*See* **scheme**)

achievement batteries Sets of tests designed to assess performance in a broad range of subjects.

active listening A way of dealing with a problem-owning student by showing interest and encouraging the talker to continue expressing feelings.

Adaptation The process, described by Piaget, of creating a good fit or match between one's conception of reality and one's real-life experiences. (*See* **accommodation; assimilation**)

adolescent egocentrism The introspective, inward turning of a high school student's newly developed powers of thought, with a tendency to project one's self-analysis onto others. (*See* **egocentrism**)

adventure learning A type of learning wherein students might participate in real-life expeditions, virtual field trips, historical reenactments, and local adventures in their community, typically in structured activities with students from other schools.

affective domain taxonomy A classification of instructional outcomes that concentrates on attitudes and values.

anchored instruction Method of embedding important information or skills in authentic problem-solving situations and meaningful contexts for prolonged student exploration. (*See* **inert knowledge; situated learning**)

aptitude tests Tests intended to give educators some idea of the level of knowledge and skill a student could acquire with effective instruction.

assimilation The process of fitting new experience into an existing scheme. (*See* **scheme**)

assistive technology Any item, device, or piece of equipment, from low-tech equipment such as taped stories to more sophisticated technologies such as voice-recognition and speech-synthesis devices, that is used to increase, maintain, or improve the functional abilities of persons with disabilities.

attention The selective focusing on a portion of the information currently stored in the sensory register. (*See* **sensory register**)

attention-deficit/hyperactivity disorder (ADHD) A disorder that begins in childhood; is marked by abnormally high levels of impulsive behavior, distractibility, and motor activity; and leads to low levels of learning.

attribution theory A body of research into the ways that students explain their success or failure, usually in terms of ability, effort, task difficulty, and luck.

authentic assessment (*See* **performance tests**)

authoritarian parents Parents who make demands and wield power without considering their children's point of view.

authoritative parents Parents who provide models of competence to be imitated, based on confidence in their own abilities.

B

behavior disorder (*See* **emotional disturbance**)

behavior modification The use of operant conditioning techniques to modify behavior, generally by making rewards contingent on certain actions. Also called *contingency management*. (*See* **operant conditioning**)

between-class ability grouping Assigning students of similar learning ability to separate classes based on scores from standardized intelligence or achievement tests.

C

cognitive apprenticeship A relationship in which help and guidance are provided by a mentor or expert practitioner to a learner, enabling him or her to master a task and gradually participate in a culture or community. (*See* **telementoring**)

cognitive constructivism A form of constructivist learning theory that emphasizes the role of assimilation and accommodation in constructing an understanding of the world in which one lives. (*See* **accommodation; assimilation; constructivism**)

cognitive domain taxonomy A classification scheme of instructional outcomes that stresses knowledge and intellectual skills, including comprehension, application, analysis, synthesis, and evaluation. Also called *Bloom's taxonomy*.

collaborative learning Activities for which groups of learners use and combine their individual talents and areas of expertise to investigate problems, negotiate ideas, generate knowledge, and design products. (*See* **cooperative learning**)

competency test A test to determine a student's ability to handle basic subjects.

computer adaptive testing (CAT) A testing technique in which a computer program adapts the difficulty of questions to the ability level of the examinee based on his or her responses, thereby resulting in a reduction in test length and greater efficiency.

computer-assisted instruction (CAI) (*See* **computer-based instruction**)

computer-based instruction (CBI) Teaching methods that use interactive software as an aid to learning.

computer conferencing An online discussion group, typically organized by topic, that can provide students with access to information, viewpoints, and communities beyond the boundaries of their classrooms.

concept mapping   A technique for identifying and visually representing on paper the ideas that comprise a section of text and the ways in which they relate to each other.

conservation   The recognition that certain properties stay the same despite a change in appearance or position.

constructivism   The view that meaningful learning is the active creation of knowledge structures rather than a mere transferring of objective knowledge from one person to another.

contingency contracting   A behavior-strengthening technique that specifies desirable behaviors and consequent reinforcement.

cooperative learning   An approach that uses small heterogeneous groups for purposes of mutual help in the mastery of specific tasks.

criterion-referenced grading   A system in which grades are determined on the basis of whether each student has attained a defined standard of achievement or performance.

criterion-referenced tests   Tests in which students are evaluated according to how well they have mastered specific objectives in various well-defined skill areas.

cultural pluralism   A set of tenets based on three principles: (1) every culture has its own internal coherence, integrity, and logic; (2) no culture is inherently better or worse than another; and (3) all persons are to some extent culture-bound.

culture   A description of the ways a group of people perceives the world; formulates beliefs; evaluates objects, ideas, and experiences; and behaves.

D

decentration   The ability to think of more than one quality of an object or problem at a time. (*See* **perceptual centration**)

deficiency needs   The first four levels (physiological, safety, belongingness or love, and esteem) in Maslow's hierarchy of needs, so called because these needs cause people to act only when they are unmet to some degree.

depression   An emotional disorder characterized by self-deprecation, crying spells, and suicidal thoughts, afflicting between 7 and 28 percent of all adolescents.

diagnostic test   A single-subject achievement test intended to identify the source of a problem in basic subjects and perhaps in study skills. (*See* **single-subject achievement test**)

digital portfolio   A multimedia collection of student work that documents individual expertise, achievement, accomplishments, and growth in one or more areas over extended periods of time. Also called *electronic portfolio*.

direct instruction   An approach to instruction that emphasizes the efficient acquisition of basic skills and subject matter through lectures and demonstrations, extensive practice, and corrective feedback.

discovery learning   A teaching strategy that encourages children to seek solutions to problems either on their own or in group discussion.

discrimination   A process in which individuals learn to notice the unique aspects of seemingly similar situations and thus learn different ways of responding.

distributed practice   The practice of breaking up learning tasks into small, easy-to-manage pieces that are learned over several relatively brief sessions.

drill-and-practice programs   Computer programs that help students practice skills and learn factual information.

dual coding theory   A theory of elaboration that states that concrete objects and words are remembered better than abstract information because they are coded in memory as both visual images and verbal labels, whereas abstract words are only encoded verbally.

E

early-maturing boy   A boy whose early physical maturation typically draws favorable adult responses and promotes confidence and poise, thus contributing to leadership and popularity with peers. (*See* **late-maturing boy**)

early-maturing girl   A girl whose early physical maturation typically makes her socially out of step with her peers. (*See* **late-maturing girl**)

educational psychology   The branch of psychology that specializes in understanding how different factors affect the classroom behavior of both teachers and students.

egocentrism   Difficulty in taking another person's point of view, a characteristic typical of young children.

elaborative rehearsal   A process that consciously relates new information to knowledge already stored in long-term memory. Also called *elaborative encoding*. (*See* **long-term memory**)

electronic portfolio   (*See* **digital portfolio**)

emotional disturbance   An emotional condition in which inappropriate aggressive or withdrawal behaviors are exhibited over a long period of time and to a marked degree, adversely affecting a child's educational performance.

empirical learning   The use of noticeable characteristics of objects and events to form spontaneous concepts; a form of learning typical of young children.

epigenetic principle   The notion that a child's personality develops as the ego progresses through a series of interrelated stages, much as the human body takes shape during its fetal development.

equilibration   The tendency to organize schemes to allow better understanding of experiences. (*See* **scheme**)

ethnic group   A collection of people who identify with one another on the basis of such characteristics as ancestral origin, race, religion, language, values, political or economic interests, and behavior patterns.

evaluation   In assessment, the use of a rule-governed system to make judgments about the value or worth of a set of measures.

exploratory environments Electronic environments that provide students with materials and resources to discover interesting phenomena and construct new insights; for example, computer simulations. Also called *discovery environments*. (*See* **discovery learning**)

extinction The weakening of a target behavior by ignoring it.

extrinsic motivation A form of incentive based on a system of rewards not inherent in a particular activity. (*See* **intrinsic motivation**)

F

far transfer The ability to use knowledge and skills learned at an earlier point in time in a particular context to help one learn new information or solve a problem in a very different context at a much later point in time.

field-dependent style A learning style in which a person's perception of and thinking about a task or problem are strongly influenced by such contextual factors as additional information and other people's behavior.

field-independent style A learning style in which a person's perception of and thinking about a task or problem are influenced more by the person's knowledge base than by the presence of additional information or other people's behavior.

foreclosure status An adolescent identity status marked by the unquestioning endorsement of parents' goals and values.

formative evaluation A type of assessment that monitors a student's progress in order to facilitate learning rather than assign a grade.

frames The individual steps in a teaching program. (*See* **programmed instruction**)

full inclusion The practice of eliminating pullout programs (those outside the classroom) and providing regular teachers with special training so as to keep special needs students in regular classrooms. Also called *inclusion*.

G

gender bias The tendency of teachers to respond differently to male and female students when there is no educationally sound reason for doing so.

gender roles Sets of behaviors typically identified with either males or females in a society; young children's awareness of these roles shows up clearly in the different toys and activities that boys and girls prefer.

generalization The learned ability to respond in similar ways to similar stimuli.

general objectives Objectives that use the three taxonomies (cognitive, affective, and psychomotor) to describe types of behavior that would demonstrate a student's learning. (*See* **affective domain taxonomy; cognitive domain taxonomy; psychomotor domain taxonomy**)

general transfer A situation in which prior learning aids subsequent learning due to the use of similar cognitive strategies.

gifted and talented student A student who shows unusual ability in any of a variety of ways and who may require services not ordinarily provided by his or her school.

grade equivalent score A measurement that interprets test performance in terms of grade levels.

growth need A yearning for personal fulfillment that people constantly strive to satisfy. (*See* **self-actualization**)

growth spurt The rapid and uneven physical growth that besets adolescents during the middle school years.

guided learning Environments where teachers, experts, or more knowledgeable peers support student inquiry by helping students set plans and goals, ask questions, discuss issues, solve problems, and reflect on strategies and solutions. Also called *guided discovery learning*. (*See* **cognitive apprenticeship; constructivism**)

H

heuristics General approaches to solving problems, such as studying worked examples and breaking problems into parts, that can be applied to different subject areas.

high-road transfer A situation involving the conscious, controlled, somewhat effortful formulation of an "abstraction" (that is, a rule, a schema, a strategy, or an analogy) that allows a connection to be made between two tasks.

high-stakes testing The use of standardized test results to make such significant decisions as whether students get promoted to the next grade or graduate from high school, whether teachers and administrators receive financial rewards or demotions, and whether school districts receive additional state funds or lose their accreditation.

humanistic approach An approach to instruction that emphasizes the effect of student needs, values, motives, and self-perceptions on learning.

hypermedia A technology that combines multimedia and hypertext so that the learner can nonsequentially access and explore interesting and important information resources. (*See* **hypertext; multimedia**)

hypertext A system of linking text in a nonlinear way, thereby enabling users to jump from one section of text to another section of the same document or to other documents, often through pressing highlighted or "hot" words.

I

IDEA Acronym for the Individuals with Disabilities Education Act (originally called the Education for All Handicapped Children Act), the principal federal law governing the education of children with disabilities.

identity A relatively stable conception of where and how one fits into a society that is strongly influenced by the perception of one's physical appearance, the goals one establishes and achieves, and recognition from significant others in the environment.

identity achievement status An adolescent identity status marked by self-chosen commitments with respect to at least some aspects of identity.

identity diffusion status An adolescent identity status marked by the avoidance of choices pertaining to jobs, roles, or values and the readiness to change one's position in response to negative or positive feedback.

identity status A style or approach that adolescents adopt to deal with such identity-related issues as career goal, gender-role orientation, and religious beliefs. James Marcia identified four identity statuses: identity diffusion, moratorium, foreclosure, and identity achievement.

ill-structured problems Vaguely stated problems with unclear solution procedures and vague evaluation standards. (*See* **well-structured problems**)

I-message A first-person statement by a teacher that emphasizes the teacher's feelings about a situation rather than his or her feelings about the students.

impulsive A learning style in which students respond relatively quickly to questions or tasks for which there is no obvious correct answer or solution.

inclusion An extension of the least restrictive environment provision of IDEA in which students with disabilities are placed in regular classrooms for the entire school day and receive some instruction and support from a special education teacher. (*See also* **full inclusion**)

individualized education program (IEP) A written statement describing an educational program designed to meet the unique needs of a child with a particular disability.

inert knowledge Information, typically memorized verbatim, that is unconnected, lacking in context, and not readily accessible for application to real-world tasks. (*See* **anchored instruction; drill-and-practice programs; meaningful learning; situated learning**)

information-processing theory An area of study that seeks to understand how people acquire, store, and recall information and how their current knowledge guides and determines what and how they will learn.

instructional objectives Statements written by teachers that specify the knowledge and skills students should be able to exhibit after a unit of instruction.

integrated learning systems (ILS) Computer-based instructional systems that provide sequenced and self-paced learning activities to students in many different content areas as well as appropriate remediation or enrichment activities.

Intelligence The ability of an individual to use a variety of cognitive and noncognitive capabilities to formulate goals, logically work toward achieving those goals, and adapt to the demands of the environment.

Internet *See* **World Wide Web**.

interpersonal reasoning The ability to understand the relationship between motives and behavior among a group of people.

intrinsic motivation A form of incentive inherent in a particular activity, such as the positive consequence of becoming more competent or knowledgeable. (*See* **extrinsic motivation**)

irreversibility The inability of a young child to mentally reverse physical or mental processes, such as pouring water from a tall, thin glass back into a short, squat one.

issues Ill-structured problems that arouse strong feelings. (*See* **ill-structured problems**)

J

Joplin Plan An ability grouping technique that combines students of different grade levels according to their standardized test scores. (*See* **regrouping**)

L

late-maturing boy A boy whose delayed physical maturation typically causes inferiority feelings and leads to bossy and attention-getting behavior. (*See* **early-maturing boy**)

late-maturing girl A girl whose delayed physical maturation typically makes her more poised than others her age and elicits praise from elders, thus conferring leadership tendencies. (*See* **early-maturing girl**)

learner-centered education An educational philosophy in which the teacher helps guide students to construct knowledge meaningfully and monitor their own learning by emphasizing student choice, responsibility, challenge, intrinsic motivation, and ownership of the learning process.

learning disabilities Problems in otherwise mentally fit students who are unable to respond to certain aspects of the curriculum presented in regular classrooms because of disorders in one or more basic psychological processes.

learning strategy A general plan that a learner formulates for achieving a somewhat distant academic goal.

learning style A consistent tendency or preference to respond to a variety of intellectual tasks and problems in a particular fashion.

learning tactic A specific technique that a learner uses to accomplish an immediate learning objective.

least restrictive environment A requirement (under the 1994 Code of Federal Regulations governing the implementation of IDEA) that disabled children be provided with education in the least restrictive setting possible, usually by including them in regular classrooms. (*See* **mainstreaming**)

long-term memory (LTM) Storehouse of permanently recorded information in an individual's memory.

loss of voice The tendency of adolescent females to suppress their true beliefs about issues and either claim that they have no opinion or state what they think others want to hear because of socialization practices.

low-road transfer A situation in which a previously learned skill or idea is almost automatically retrieved from memory and applied to a highly similar current task. (*See* **high-road transfer**)

M

mainstreaming The policy of placing students with disabilities in regular classes.

maintenance rehearsal A rather mechanical process that uses mental and verbal repetition to hold information in short-term memory for some immediate purpose. Also called *rote rehearsal* or *repetition*. (*See* **short-term memory**)

massed practice An approach to learning that emphasizes a few long, infrequently spaced study periods.

mastery learning An approach that assumes most students can master the curriculum if certain conditions are established: (1) sufficient aptitude, (2) sufficient ability to understand instruction, (3) a willingness to persevere, (4) sufficient time, and (5) good-quality instruction.

meaningful learning Learning that occurs when new information or activities are made relevant by relating them to personal interests and prior experiences or knowledge.

measurement The assignment of numbers to certain attributes of objects, events, or people according to a rule-governed system.

melting pot A term referring to the assimilation of diverse ethnic groups into one national mainstream.

mental retardation A condition in which learning proceeds at a significantly slow rate, is limited to concrete experiences, and is accompanied by difficulty functioning in social environments.

metacognition Knowledge about the operations of cognition and how to use them to achieve a learning goal.

microcomputer-based laboratory (MBL) A microcomputer with attached sensors and probes that can quickly represent such data as temperature or speed in multiple ways in order to help students explore concepts, test hypotheses, and repair scientific misconceptions.

microworld A computer scenario intended to foster cognitive development and overcome misconceptions by allowing students the chance to explore relationships among variables or concepts and build personal models of how things work.

mnemonic device A memory-directed tactic that helps a learner transform or organize information to enhance its retrievability.

morality of constraint Piaget's term for the moral thinking of children up to age ten or so, in which they hold sacred rules that permit no exceptions and make no allowance for intentions. Also called *moral realism*.

morality of cooperation Piaget's term for the moral thinking of children age eleven or older, based on flexible rules and considerations of intent. Also called *moral relativism*.

moratorium status An adolescent identity status marked by various kinds of identity crises, often involving experimentation and restless searching.

multicultural education An approach to learning and teaching that seeks to foster an understanding of and mutual respect for the values, beliefs, and practices of different cultural groups.

multidisciplinary assessment team A group of people involved in determining the nature of a child's disability, typically consisting of a school psychologist, guidance counselor, classroom teacher, school social worker, school nurse, learning disability specialist, physician, and psychiatrist.

multimedia The combination of several forms of media such as text, graphics, animation, sound, images, and video that teachers can use to enrich student understanding and address various student learning styles, preferences, and impairments. (*See* **dual coding theory; hypermedia**)

N

near transfer The ability to use knowledge and skills learned at an earlier point in time in a particular context to help one learn new information or solve a problem in a very similar context and soon after the original learning.

negative reinforcement A way of strengthening a target behavior by removing an aversive stimulus after a particular behavior is exhibited. (*See* **positive reinforcement**)

negative transfer A situation in which one's prior learning interferes with subsequent learning. (*See* **positive transfer**)

normal curve The bell-shaped distribution of scores that tends to occur when a particular characteristic is measured in thousands of people.

norm group A sample of individuals carefully chosen to reflect the larger population of students for whom a test is intended.

norm-referenced grading A system of grading that assumes classroom achievement will vary among a group of heterogeneous students because of such differences as prior knowledge, learning skills, motivation, and aptitude, and so compares the score of each student to the scores of other students in order to determine grades.

norm-referenced tests Tests in which individual performance is evaluated with reference to the performance of a norm group.

O

observational learning/modeling That part of the triadic reciprocal causation model of social cognitive theory that describes the role of observing and imitating the behavior of models in learning new capabilities.

operant conditioning The theory of behavior developed by B. F. Skinner, based on the fact that organisms respond to their environments in particular ways to obtain or avoid particular consequences.

organization The tendency to systematize and combine processes into coherent general systems.

overgeneralization A phenomenon of early language development in which preschool children consistently misapply such grammatical rules as adding "ed" and "s" to the ends of words to make them plural.

P

peer tutoring An approach to learning that involves the teaching of one student by another, based on evidence that a child's cognitive growth benefits from exposure to alternative cognitive schemes.

percentile rank A score that indicates the percentage of students who are at or below a given student's achievement level, providing specific information about relative position.

perceptual centration The tendency to focus attention on only one characteristic of an object or aspect of a problem or event at a time.

performance tests Assessment devices that attempt to gauge how well students can use basic knowledge and skill to perform complex tasks or solve problems under more or less realistic conditions. Also called *performance-based assessment* and *authentic assessment*.

permissive parents   Parents who make few demands on their children and fail to discourage immature behavior, thus reflecting their own tendency to be disorganized, inconsistent, and lacking in confidence.

personal agency   The idea that people are the primary cause of their own behavior rather than environmental forces.

play behavior   Kinds of free play observed in preschool children and described by Mildred Parten as consisting of six types: unoccupied, solitary, onlooker, parallel, associative, and cooperative.

portfolio   A collection of one or more pieces of a person's work, some of which typically demonstrate different stages of completion.

positive reinforcement   A way of strengthening a target behavior (increasing and maintaining the probability that a particular behavior will be repeated) by supplying a positive stimulus immediately after a desired response. (*See* **negative reinforcement**)

positive transfer   A situation in which prior learning aids subsequent learning, when, for example, a new learning task calls for essentially the same response that was made to a similar earlier-learned task. (*See* **negative transfer**)

Premack principle   A shaping technique that allows students to indulge in a favorite activity after completing a set of instructional objectives. Also called *Grandma's rule*. (*See* **shaping**)

problem-based learning (PBL)   An instructional method that requires learners to develop solutions to authentic and complex problems through problem analysis, hypothesis generation, collaboration, reflection, and extensive teacher coaching and facilitation.

problem representation/problem framing   The process of finding ways to express a problem so as to recall the optimal amount of solution-relevant information from long-term memory. (*See* **long-term memory**)

problem solving   The identification and application of knowledge and skills that result in goal attainment.

programmed instruction   A method of instruction developed by B. F. Skinner that presents specially designed written material to students in a predetermined sequence.

project-based learning   An approach to teaching and learning that attempts to motivate students through collaborative investigations of real-world problems that result in tangible products.

psychological androgyny   An acquired sense of gender that combines traditional masculine and feminine traits.

psychomotor domain taxonomy   A classification of instructional outcomes that focuses on physical abilities and skills.

psychosocial moratorium   A period of identity development marked by a delay of commitment, ideally a time of adventure and exploration having a positive, or at least neutral, impact on the individual and society.

punishment   A method of weakening a target behavior by presenting an aversive stimulus after the behavior occurs.

R

recognition   A cognitive process that involves noting key features of a stimulus and relating them to previously stored information in an interactive manner.

reflective   A learning style in which students collect and analyze information before offering an answer to a question or a solution to a problem.

reflective teaching   A way of teaching that blends artistic and scientific elements through thoughtful analysis of classroom activity.

regrouping   A form of ability grouping that brings together students of the same age, ability, and grade but from different classrooms, for instruction in a specific subject, usually reading or mathematics.

rejecting-neglecting parents   Parents who make no demands on their children, provide no structure at home, and do not support their children's goals, activities, and emotional needs.

reliability   Consistency in test results, related to the assumption that human characteristics are relatively stable over short periods of time.

response cost   The withdrawal of previously earned positive reinforcers as a consequence of undesirable behavior, often used with a token economy. (*See* **token economy**)

ripple effect   The extent to which an entire class responds to a reprimand directed at only one student.

role confusion   Uncertainty as to what behaviors will elicit a favorable reaction from others.

rubric   A scoring guide used in performance assessment that helps define and clarify levels of student performance from poor to exemplary.

S

scaffolding   Supporting learning during its early phases through such techniques as demonstrating how tasks should be accomplished, giving hints to the correct solution to a problem or answer to a question, and providing leading questions. As students become more capable of working independently, these supports are withdrawn.

schemata   Plural for *schema*, an abstract information structure by which our store of knowledge is organized in long-term memory. *Schemas* is another plural form. (*See* **long-term memory**)

scheme   An organized pattern of behavior or thought that children formulate as they interact with their environment, parents, teachers, and agemates.

scholastic aptitude   The cognitive skills that most directly relate to and best predict the ability to cope with academic demands. Often used as a synonym for *intelligence*.

scientific concepts   A term coined by Russian psychologist Lev Vygotsky to denote such psychological tools as language, formulas, rules, and symbols that are learned mostly with the aid of formal instruction.

self-actualization The movement toward full development of a person's potential talents and capabilities.

self-concept The evaluative judgments people make of themselves in specific areas, such as academic performance, social interactions, athletic performance, and physical appearance.

self-description The way people describe themselves to others, using statements that are largely nonevaluative.

self-efficacy The degree to which people believe they are capable or prepared to handle particular tasks.

self-esteem The overall or general evaluation people make of themselves. Also called self-worth.

self-fulfilling prophecy The tendency of students to achieve the levels expected of them by their teachers. Also called the *Pygmalion effect* (*See* **teacher expectancy effect**)

self-image A mental self-portrait composed of a self-description, self-esteem, and self-concept. (*See* **self-concept; self-description; self-esteem**)

self-regulated learning The conscious and purposeful use of one's cognitive skills, feelings, and actions to maximize the learning of knowledge and skills for a given task and set of conditions.

self-reinforcement A situation in which the individual strives to meet personal standards and does not depend on or care about the reactions of others.

sensory register (SR) The primary memory store that records temporarily (for one to three seconds) an incoming flow of data from the sense receptors.

serial position effect The tendency to learn and remember words at the beginning and end of a list more easily than those in the middle.

sexually transmitted diseases (STDs) Contagious diseases, such as HIV/AIDS, gonorrhea, and herpes, that are spread by sexual contact.

shaping Promoting the learning of complex behaviors by reinforcing successive approximations to the terminal behavior.

short-term memory (STM) The second temporary memory store, which holds about seven bits of information for about twenty seconds. (Also called *working memory*)

simulation programs Highly individualized and flexible programs that allow learners to test hypotheses, display knowledge, repair errors in thinking, and solve problems in an artificial environment that imitates the real world.

single-subject achievement test A test designed to assess learning or achievement in a particular basic school subject, such as reading or mathematics.

situated learning The idea that problem-solving skills, cognitive strategies, and knowledge are closely linked to the specific context or environment in which they are acquired; hence, the more authentic, or true to life, the task, the more meaningful the learning. Also called *situated cognition*. (*See* **cognitive apprenticeship; inert knowledge; teleapprenticeship**)

social class An individual's or a family's relative standing in society, determined by such factors as income, occupation, education, place of residence, types of associations, manner of dress, and material possessions.

social cognitive theory An explanation of how people learn to become self-regulated learners through the interactive effects of their personal characteristics, behaviors, and social reinforcement. (*See* **triadic reciprocal causation**)

social constructivism A form of constructivist learning theory that emphasizes how people use such cultural tools as language, mathematics, and approaches to problem solving in social settings to construct a common or shared understanding of the world in which they live. (*See* **constructivism**)

socioeconomic status (SES) A quantifiable level of social standing, determined by the federal government on the basis of a person's income, occupation, and education. (*See* **social class**)

special-purpose achievement test A test to determine specific qualifications, such as the College-Level Examination Program or the National Teacher Examination.

specific objectives Objectives that specify the behavior to be learned, the conditions under which it will be exhibited, and the criterion for acceptable performance.

specific transfer A situation in which prior learning aids subsequent learning because of specific similarities between two tasks.

spontaneous concepts A term coined by Russian psychologist Lev Vygotsky to denote the facts, concepts, and rules that young children acquire as a natural consequence of engaging in everyday activities.

spontaneous recovery The reappearance of a seemingly extinguished behavior. (*See* **extinction**)

standard deviation A statistic that indicates the degree to which scores in a group of tests differ from the average or mean.

standardized tests Assessment tools designed by people with specialized knowledge and applied to all students under the same conditions.

stanine score A statistic reflecting a division of a score distribution into nine groups, with each stanine being one-half of a standard deviation unit.

styles of mental self-government theory A theory of learning style formulated by Robert Sternberg that is based on the different functions and forms of civil government. The theory describes thirteen styles that can vary in terms of function, form, level, scope, and learning.

summative evaluation Testing done for the purpose of assigning a letter or numerical grade to sum up a student's performance at a variety of tasks over time.

T

table of specifications A table used in exam preparation that notes types and numbers of included test items, ensuring systematic coverage of the subject matter.

taxonomy A classification scheme with categories arranged in hierarchical order.

teacher expectancy effect   The tendency of students to behave in ways they think the teacher expects them to behave. Also called *self-fulfilling prophecy*; *Pygmalion effect*.

teaching as an art   A way of teaching that involves intangibles such as emotions, values, and flexibility.

teaching as a science   A way of teaching based on scientific methods such as sampling, control, objectivity, publication, and replication.

telementoring   The use of networking technologies by experts, mentors, instructors, and peers to demonstrate ideas, pose questions, offer insights, and provide relevant information that can help learners build new knowledge and effectively participate in a learning community.

theoretical learning   Learning how to use psychological tools across a range of settings and problem types to acquire new knowledge and skills.

theory of identical elements   The theory that a similarity between the stimulus and response elements in two different tasks accounts for transfer of learning from one task to the other. (*See* **transfer of learning**)

theory of mind   The ability, typically developed by children around the age of four, to be aware of the difference between thinking about something and experiencing that same thing and to predict the thoughts of others.

theory of multiple intelligences   A theory formulated by Howard Gardner that describes intelligence as being composed of eight, mostly independent capabilities.

time-out   A procedure that weakens a target behavior by temporarily removing the opportunity for the behavior to be rewarded.

token economy   A behavior-strengthening technique that uses items of no inherent value to "purchase" other items perceived to be valuable.

transfer of learning   A student's ability to apply knowledge and problem-solving skills learned in school to similar but new situations.

triadic reciprocal causation   The conceptual foundation of social cognitive theory, which specifies that learned capabilities are the product of interactions among an individual's personal characteristics, behaviors, and social environment. (*See* **social cognitive theory**)

triarchic theory of intelligence   A theory formulated by Robert Sternberg that describes intelligence as being composed of practical, creative, and analytical components.

T score   A standardized test score that ranges from 0 to 100 and uses a preselected mean of 50 to avoid negative values. (*See* **z score**)

tutorial programs   Programs that attempt to teach facts, definitions, concepts, and other new material to students in either a step-by-step or a more individualized, branching approach.

two-way bilingual (TWB) education   An approach to bilingual education in which instruction is provided to all students in both the minority language and the majority language. Also called *bilingual immersion* or *dual language*.

V

validity   The extent to which a test measures what it claims to measure.

vicarious reinforcement   A situation in which the observer anticipates receiving a reward for behaving in a given way because someone else has been so rewarded.

W

well-structured problems   Clearly formulated problems with known solution procedures and known evaluation standards. (*See* **ill-structured problems**)

within-class ability grouping   A form of ability grouping that involves the division of a single class of students into two or three groups for reading and math instruction.

withitness   An attribute of teachers who prove to their students that they know what is going on in a classroom and as a result have fewer discipline problems than teachers who lack this characteristic.

World Wide Web   A global system of interconnected computers that provides access to a wide variety of data in different formats. Also called *the Internet*; *the Web*; *WWW*.

Z

zero transfer   A situation in which prior learning has no effect on new learning.

zone of proximal development (ZPD)   Vygotsky's term for the difference between what a child can do on his or her own and what can be accomplished with some assistance.

z score   A standardized test score that tells how far a given raw score differs from the mean in standard deviation units. (*See* **T score**)

References

Abell, S. K., Bryan, L. A., & Anderson, M. A. (1998). Investigating preservice elementary science teacher reflective thinking using integrated media case-based instruction in elementary science teacher preparation. *Science Education, 82*(4), 491–510.

Abma, J. C., & Sonenstein, F. L. (2001). *Sexual activity and contraceptive practices among teenagers in the United States, 1988 and 1995.* Hyattsville, MD: National Center for Health Statistics. Retrieved January 2, 2002, from http://www.cdc.gov/nchs/data/series/sr_23/sr23_21.pdf.

Abrami, P. C., Lou, Y., Chambers, B., Poulsen, C., & Spence, J. C. (2000). Why should we group students within-class for learning? *Educational Research and Evaluation, 6*(2), 158–179.

Access to technology. (2003, May 8). *Education Week, 22*(35), 54–57.

Adams, G. L., & Engelmann, S. (1996). *Research on direct instruction: 25 years beyond DISTAR.* Seattle, WA: Educational Ahievement Systems.

Adams, G. R., Munro, B., Doherty-Poirer, M., Munro, G., Peterson, A. R., & Edwards, J. (2001). Diffuse-avoidance, normative, and informational identity styles: Using identity theory to predict maladjustment. *Identity, 1*(4), 307–320.

Adelson, J. (1972). The political imagination of the young adolescent. In J. Kagan & R. Coles (Eds.), *Twelve to sixteen: Early adolescence.* New York: Norton.

Adelson, J. (1986). *Inventing adolescence: The political psychology of everyday schooling.* New Brunswick, NJ: Transaction Books.

Adey, P. S., Shayer, M., & Yates, C. (2001). *Thinking science* (3rd ed.). London: Nelson Thornes.

Ainley, M., Hidi, S., & Berndorff, D. (2002). Interest, learning, and the psychological processes that mediate their relationship. *Journal of Educational Psychology, 94*(3), 545–561.

Airasian, P. W. (2001). *Classroom assessment* (4th ed.). Boston: McGraw-Hill.

Airasian, P. W., & Walsh, M. E. (1997). Constructivist cautions. *Phi Delta Kappan, 78*(6), 444–449.

Alasker, F. D., & Olweus, D. (2002). Stability and change in global self-esteem and self-related affect. In T. M. Brinthaupt & R. P. Lipka (Eds.), *Understanding early adolescent self and identity: Applications and interventions* (pp. 193–223). Albany, NY: State University of New York Press.

Alexander, P. A., Graham, S., & Harris, K. R. (1998). A perspective on strategy research: Progress and prospects. *Educational Psychology Review, 10*(2), 129–154.

Alfassi, M. (1998). Reading for meaning: The efficacy of reciprocal teaching in fostering reading comprehension in high school students in remedial reading classes. *American Educational Research Journal, 35*(2), 309–332.

Algozzine, B., & White, R. (2002). Preventing problem behaviors using schoolwide discipline. In B. Algozzine & P. Kay (Eds.), *Preventing problem behaviors: A handbook of successful prevention strategies* (pp. 85–103). Thousand Oaks, CA: Corwin Press.

Allen, N., Christal, M., Perrot, D., Wilson, C., Grote, B., & Earley, M. A. (1999). Native American schools move into the new millennium. *Educational Leadership, 56*(7), 71–74.

Allen, N., Resta, P. E., & Christal, M. (2002). Technology and tradition: The role of technology in Native American schools. *TechTrends, 46*(2), 50–55.

Allington, R. L., & McGill-Franzen, A. (1995). Flunking: Throwing good money after bad. In R. L. Allington & S. A. Walmsley (Eds.), *No quick fix: Rethinking literacy programs in America's elementary schools.* New York: Teachers College Press.

Allison, B. N., & Schultz, J. B. (2001). Interpersonal identity formation during early adolescence. *Adolescence, 36*(143), 509–523.

Almasi, J. F. (2003). *Teaching strategic processes in reading.* New York: Guilford Press.

Alson, A. (2002/2003). The minority student achievement network. *Educational Leadership, 60*(4), 76–78.

American Association of University Women. (1999). *Gender gaps: Where schools still fail our children.* New York: Marlowe & Company.

American Association on Mental Retardation. (2002). *The AAMR definition of mental retardation.* Retrieved January 16, 2004, from http://161.58.153.187/Policies/faq_mental_retardation.shtml.

American Educational Research Association. (2000). *AERA position statement concerning high-stakes testing in preK–12 education.* Retrieved January 2, 2002, from http://www.aera.net/about/policy/stakes.html.

American Psychiatric Association. (2000). *Diagnostic and Statistical Manual of Mental Disorders* (4th edition, Text Revision). Washington, DC: Author.

American Psychological Association. (1997). *Learner-centered psychological principles: A framework for school redesign and reform.* Retrieved January 2, 2002, from http://www.apa.org/ed/lcp.html.

Ames, C., & Ames, R. (1984). Systems of student and teacher motivation: Toward a qualitative definition. *Journal of Educational Psychology, 76*(4), 535–556.

Ames, N. L., & Miller, E. (1994). *Changing middle schools: How to make schools work for young adolescents.* San Francisco: Jossey-Bass.

Amiram, R., Bar-Tal, D., Alona, R., & Peleg, D. (1990). Perception of epistemic authorities by children and adolescents. *Journal of Youth and Adolescence, 19*(5), 495–510.

Amrein, A. L., & Berliner, D. C. (2002, March 28). High-stakes testing, uncertainty, and student learning. *Education Policy Analysis Archives, 10*(18). Retrieved February 6, 2004 from http://epaa.asu.edu/epaa/v10n18/.

Amrein, A. L., & Berliner, D. C. (2003). The effects of high-stakes testing on student motivation and learning. *Educational Leadership, 60*(5), 32–38.

Anastasi, A., & Urbina, S. (1997). *Psychological testing* (7th ed.). Upper Saddle River, NJ: Prentice Hall.

Anderman, E. M. (2002). School effects on psychological outcomes during adolescence. *Journal of Educational Psychology, 94*(4), 795–809.

Anderman, E. M., & Maehr, M. L. (1994). Motivation and schooling in the middle grades. *Review of Educational Research, 64*(2), 287–309.

Anderson, J. R., Greeno, J. G., Reder, L. M., & Simon, H. A. (2000). Perspectives on learning, thinking, and activity. *Educational Researcher, 29*(4), 11–13.

André, M. E. D. A., & Anderson, T. H. (1978/1979). The development and evaluation of a self-questioning study technique. *Reading Research Quarterly, 14*(4), 605–623.

Andrews, K., & Marshall, K. (2000). Making learning connections through telelearning. *Educational Leadership, 58*(2), 53–56.

Angeli, C. (2002). Teachers' practical theories for the design and implementation of problem-based learning. *Science Education International, 13*(3), 9–15.

Angeli, C., & Cunningham, D. J. (1998). Bubble Dialogue: Tools for supporting literacy and mind. In C. J. Bonk, & K. S. King (Eds.), *Electronic collaborators: Learner-centered technologies for literacy, apprenticeship, and discourse* (pp. 81–101). Mahwah, NJ: Erlbaum.

Antil, L. R., Jenkins, J. R., Wayne, S. K., & Vadasy, P. F. (1998). Cooperative learning: Prevalence, conceptualizations, and the relation between research and practice. *Review of Educational Research, 35*(3), 419–454.

Applebee, A. N., Langer, J. A., Nystrand, M., & Gamoran, A. (2003). Discussion-based approaches to developing understanding: Classroom instruction and student performance in middle and high school English. *American Educational Research Journal, 40*(3), 685–730.

Appleton, N. (1983). *Cultural pluralism in education.* New York: Longman.

Archer, J. (2003, November 19). Survey: Administrators vexed by mandates. *Education Week, 23*(12), 3.

Archer, S. L. (1991). Identity development, gender differences in. In R. M. Lerner, A. C. Peterson, & J. Brooks-Gunn (Eds.), *Encyclopedia of adolescence.* New York: Garland Publishing.

Armstrong, T. (1994). *Multiple intelligences in the classroom.* Alexandria, VA: Association for Supervision and Curriculum Development.

Arnold, M. L. (2000). Stage, sequence, and sequels: Changing conceptions of morality, post-Kohlberg. *Educational Psychology Review, 12*(4), 365–383.

Aronson, E. (2002). Building empathy, compassion, and achievement in the Jigsaw classroom. In J. Aronson (Ed.), *Improving academic achievement: Impact of psychological factors on education* (pp. 209–225). San Diego, CA: Academic Press.

Arter, J., & McTighe, J. (2001). *Scoring rubrics in the classroom.* Thousand Oaks, CA: Corwin Press.

Arthurs, E. M., DeFranco, T. C., & Young, M. F. (1999). An examination of the impact of tuning students' attention to information in a mathematics problem on their problem-solving performance. *Journal of Educational Computing Research, 20*(4) 345–363.

Ash, C. (2000). *Voices of a new century: Students' perspectives on the achievement gap.* Chicago: North Central Regional Educational Laboratory. Retrieved July 23, 2003, from http://www.msanetwork.org/.

Astington, J. W. (1998). Theory of mind goes to school. *Educational Leadership, 56*(3), 46–48.

Atkinson, J. W. (1964). *An introduction to motivation.* Princeton, NJ: Van Nostrand.

Atkinson, R. C. (1975). Mnemotechnics in second language learning. *American Psychologist, 30*(2), 821–828.

Atkinson, R. C., & Raugh, M. R. (1975). An application of the mnemonic keyword method to the acquisition of a Russian vocabulary. *Journal of Experimental Psychology: Human Learning and Memory, 104*(2), 126–133.

Atkinson, R. C., & Shiffrin, R. M. (1968). Human memory: A proposed system and its control processes. In K. W. Spence & J. T. Spence (Eds.), *The psychology of learning and motivation* (Vol. 2). New York: Academic Press.

Atkinson, R. K., Derry, S. J., Renkl, A., & Wortham, D. (2000). Learning from examples: Instructional principles from the worked examples research. *Review of Educational Research, 70*(2), 181–214.

Atkinson, R. K., Renkl, A., & Merrill, M. M. (2003). Transitioning from studying examples to solving problems: Effects of self-explanation prompts and fading worked-out steps. *Journal of Educational Psychology, 95*(4), 774–783.

Ausubel, D. P., Novak, J. D., & Hanesian, H. (1978). *Educational psychology: A cognitive view* (2nd ed.). New York: Holt, Rinehart & Winston.

Azar, B. (2002). The "science of learning" moves mainstream. *Monitor on Psychology, 33*(8), 60–62.

Bachman, L. F. (2002). Alternative interpretations of alternative assessments: Some validity issues in educational performance assessments. *Educational Measurement: Issues and Practice, 21*(5), 5–18.

Baddeley, A. D. (1999). *Essentials of human memory.* East Sussex, ENGLAND: Psychology Press.

Bae, Y., Choy, S., Geddes, C., Sable, J., & Snyder, T. (2000). *Trends in educational equity of girls and women.* Washington, DC: National Center for Educational Statistics. Retrieved January 2, 2002, from http://nces.ed.gov/pubs2000/2000030.pdf.

Bailey, S. M. (1996). Shortchanging girls and boys. *Educational Leadership, 53*(8), 75–79.

Baker, E. (2000). Case-based learning theory: Implications for software design. Journal of *Technology and Teacher Education, 8*(2), 85–95.

Baker, J. A. (1999). Teacher-student interaction in urban at-risk classrooms: Differential behavior, relationship quality, and student satisfaction with school. *The Elementary School Journal, 100*(1), 57–70.

Baker, K. (1998). Structured English immersion: Breakthrough in teaching limited-English-proficient students. *Phi Delta Kappan, 80*(3), 199–204.

Balk, D. E. (1995). *Adolescent development.* Pacific Grove, CA: Brooks/Cole.

Baloche, L. A. (1998). *The cooperative classroom: Empowering learning.* Upper Saddle River, NJ: Prentice-Hall.

Bandura, A. (1986). *Social foundations of thought and action: A social cognitive theory.* Englewood Cliffs, NJ: Prentice-Hall.

Bandura, A. (1997). *Self-efficacy: The exercise of control.* New York: W. H. Freeman.

Bandura, A. (2001). Social cognitive theory: An agentic perspective. In S. T. Fiske, D. L. Schacter, & C. Zahn-Waxler (Eds.), *Annual Review of Psychology, 52*(1), 1–26.

Bandura, A. (2002). Social cognitive theory in cultural context. *Applied Psychology, 51*(2), 269–290.

Bandura, A., Ross, D., & Ross, S. (1961). Transmission of aggression through imitation of aggressive models. *Journal of Abnormal and Social Psychology, 63*(3), 575–582.

Bangert-Drowns, R. L., Kulik, J. A., & Kulik, C-L, C. (1991). Effects of frequent classroom testing. *Journal of Educational Research, 85*(2), 89–99.

Bangert-Drowns, R. L., Kulik, C-L. C., Kulik, J. A., & Morgan, M. (1991). The instructional effect of feedback in test-like events. *Review of Educational Research, 61*(2), 213–238.

Banks, J. A. (1993). The canon debate, knowledge construction, and multicultural education. *Educational Researcher, 22*(5), 4–14.

Banks, J. A. (1994). Transforming the mainstream curriculum. *Educational Leadership, 51*(8), 4–8.

Banks, J. A. (2001). *Cultural diversity and education: Foundations, curriculum, and teaching* (4th ed.). Boston: Allyn & Bacon.

Banks, J. A. (2002). *An introduction to multicultural education* (3rd ed.). Boston: Allyn & Bacon.

Banks, J. A. (2003). *Teaching strategies for ethnic studies* (7th ed.). Boston: Allyn & Bacon.

Barksdale-Ladd, M. A., & Thomas, K. F. (2000). What's at stake in high-stakes testing: Teachers and parents speak out. *Journal of Teacher Education, 51*(5), 384–397.

Barnett, S. M., & Ceci, S. J. (2002). When and where do we apply what we learn?: A taxonomy for far transfer. *Psychological Bulletin, 128*(4), 612–637.

Barrett, H. C. (1998). Strategic questions: What to consider when planning for electronic portfolios. *Learning and Leading with Technology, 26*(2), 6–13.

Barrett, H. C. (2000). Create your own electronic portfolio. *Learning and Leading with Technology, 27*(7), 14–21.

Barron, B. (2000). Problem solving in video-based microworlds: Collaborative and individual outcomes of high-achieving sixth-grade students. *Journal of Educational Psychology, 92*(2), 391–398.

Barron, B., Vye, N., Zech, L., Schwartz, D., Bransford, J., Goldman, S., Pelligrino, J., Morris, J., Garrison, S., & Kantor, R. (1995). Creating contexts for community-based problem solving: The Jasper challenge series. In C. A. Hedley, P. Antonacci, & M. Rabinowitz (Eds.), *Thinking and literacy: The mind at work* (pp. 47–71). Hillsdale, NJ: Erlbaum.

Bartlett, F. C. (1932). *Remembering*. London: Cambridge University Press.

Bauer, A. M., & Ulrich, M. E. (2002). "I've got a palm in my pocket." Using handheld computers in an inclusive classroom. *Teaching Exceptional Children, 35*(2), 18–22,

Baugh, I. W. (1994). Hypermedia as a performance-based assessment tool. *The Computing Teacher, 21*(6), 14–17.

Baumrind, D. (1971). Current patterns of parental authority. *Developmental Psychology Monographs, 4*(1, Pt. 2), 1–103.

Baumrind, D. (1991a). Parenting styles and adolescent development. In R. M. Lerner, A. C. Peterson, & J. Brooks-Gunn (Eds.), *Encyclopedia of adolescence*. New York: Garland Publishing.

Baumrind, D. (1991b). The influence of parenting style on adolescent competence and substance abuse. *Journal of Early Adolescence, 11*(1), 56–95.

Baumrind, D., Larzelere, R. E., & Cowan, P. A. (2002). Ordinary physical punishment: Is it harmful? Comment on Gershoff (2002). *Psychological Bulletin, 128*(4), 580–589.

Bay, J. M., Bledsoe, A. M., & Reys, R. E. (1998). State-ing the facts: exploring the United States. *Mathematics Teaching in the Middle School, 4*(1), 8–14.

Bayraktar, S. (2001/2002). A meta-analysis of the effectiveness of computer-assisted instruction in science education. *Journal of Research on Technology in Education, 34*(2), 173–188.

Beaumont, C., de Valenzuela, J. S., & Trumbull, E. (2002). Alternative assessment for transitional readers. *Bilingual Research Journal, 26*(2), 241–268.

Beck, A. T. (1972). *Depression: Causes and treatment*. Philadelphia: University of Pennsylvania Press.

Beck, J. (2002). Emerging literacy through assistive technology. *Teaching Exceptional Children, 35*(2), 44–48.

Becker, H. J., Ravitz, J. L., & Wong, Y. (1999). *Teacher and teacher-directed student use of computers and software*. Retrieved January 2, 2002, from http://www.crito.uci.edu/tlc/findings/computeruse/.

Bee, H. L., Boyd, D. (2004). *The developing child* (10th ed.). Boston: Allyn & Bacon.

Beilin, H., & Pufall, P. B. (Eds.). (1992). *Piaget's theory: Prospects and possibilities*. Hillsdale, NJ: Erlbaum.

Beirne-Smith, M, Ittenbach, R. F., & Patton, J. R. (2002). *Mental retardation* (6th ed.). Upper Saddle River, NJ: Merrill Prentice Hall.

Beiser, M., Erickson, D., Fleming, J. A. E., & Iacono, W. G. (1993). Establishing the onset of psychotic illness. *American Journal of Psychiatry, 150*(9), 1349–1354.

Beishuizen, J. J., & Stoutjesdijk, E. T. (1999). Study strategies in a computer assisted study environment. *Learning and Instruction, 9*(3), 281–301.

Bell, L. I. (2002/2003). Strategies that close the gap. *Educational Leadership, 60*(4), 32–34.

Bellezza, F S. (1981). Mnemonic devices: Classification, characteristics, and criteria. *Review of Educational Research, 51*(2), 247–275.

Bender, W. N. (2002). *Differentiating instruction for students with learning disabilities*. Thousand Oaks, CA: Corwin Press.

Bender, W. N. (2004). *Learning disabilities: Characteristics, identification, and teaching strategies* (5th ed.). Boston: Allyn & Bacon.

Benedetto, S. (2000). DVD video: A primer for educators. *Syllabus, 14*(1), 46–49.

Ben-Hur, M. (1998). Mediation of cognitive competencies for students in need. *Phi Delta Kappan, 79*(9), 661–666.

Benjamin, A. (2002). *Differentiated instruction: A guide for middle and high school teachers*. Larchmont, NY: Eye on Education.

Bennett, C. I. (2003). *Comprehensive multicultural education: Theory and practice* (5th ed.). Boston: Allyn & Bacon.

Bennett, L. & Pye, J. (2000). Using the internet for reflective journals in elementary teacher preparation. *Journal of Social Studies Research, 24*(2), 21–30.

Bennett, N., Desforges, C., Cockburn, A., & Wilkinson, B. (1984). *The quality of pupil learning experiences*. Hillsdale, NJ: Erlbaum.

Benoit, D. A., Edwards, R. P., Olmi, D. J., Wilczynski, S. M., & Mandal, R. M. (2001). Generalization of a positive treatment package for child noncompliance. *Child and Family Behavior Therapy, 23*(2), 19–32.

Bereiter, C. (1997). Situated cognition and how to overcome it. In D. Kirshner & J. A. Whitson (Eds.), *Situated cognition: Social, semiotic, and psychological perspectives* (pp. 281–300). Mahwah, NJ: Erlbaum.

Bergin, D. A. (1999). Influences on classroom interest. *Educational Psychologist, 34*(2), 87–98.

Berk, L. E. (1994). Why children talk to themselves. *Scientific American, 271*(5), 78–83.

Berko, J. (1958). The child's learning of English morphology. *Word, 14*(1–2), 150–177.

Berliner, D. C. (1992b). Redesigning classroom activities for the future. *Educational Technology, 32*(10), 7–13.

Berliner, D. C. (2002). Educational research: The hardest science of all. *Educational Researcher, 31*(8), 18–20.

Berliner, D. C., & Biddle, B. J. (1995). *The manufactured crisis: Myths, fraud, and the attack on America's public schools*. Reading, MA: Addison-Wesley.

Berliner, D. C., & Calfee, R. C. (Eds.).(1996). *Handbook of educational psychology*. New York: Simon & Schuster Macmillan.

Berliner, D. C., & Casanova, U. (1996). *Putting research to work in your school*. Arlington Heights, IL: IRI/Skylight Training and Publishing.

Biemiller, A. (1993). Lake Woebegon revisited: On diversity and education. *Educational Researcher, 22*(9), 7–12.

Billig, S. H. (2000). Research on K–12 school-based service-learning: The evidence builds. *Phi Delta Kappan, 81*(9), 658–664.

Bilsker, D., & Marcia, J. E. (1991). Adaptive regression and ego identity. *Journal of Adolescence, 14*(1), 75–84.

Bjork, R. A. (1979). Information processing analysis of college teaching. *Educational Psychologist, 14*, 15–23.

Bjorklund, D. F. (2000). *Children's thinking* (3rd ed.). Belmont, CA: Wadsworth/Thomson Learning.

Blase, D. W. (2000). A new sort of writing: E-mail in the E-nglish classroom. *English Journal, 90*(2), 47–51.

Block, J. H., Efthim, H. E., & Burns, R. B. (1989). *Building effective mastery learning schools*. New York: Longman.

Blok, H., Oostdam, R., Otter, M. E. & Overmaat, M. (2002). Computer-assisted instruction in support of beginning reading instruction: A review. *Review of Educational Research, 72*(1), 101–130.

Bloom, B. S. (1968). Learning for mastery. *Evaluation Comment, 1*(2), 1–12.

Bloom, B. S. (1976). *Human characteristics and school learning*. New York: McGraw-Hill.

Bloom, B. S. (1984). The two sigma problem: The search for methods of group instruction as effective as one-to-one tutoring. *Educational Researcher, 13*(6), 4–16.

Bloom, B. S., Englehart, M. B., Furst, E. J., Hill, W. H., & Krathwohl, D. R. (Eds.). (1956). *Taxonomy of educational objectives. The classification of educational goals. Handbook I Cognitive domain*. New York: McKay.

Bloomquist, M. L., & Schnell, S. V. (2002). *Helping children with aggression and conduct problems: Best practices for intervention*. New York: Guilford Press.

Boekarts, M. (1993). Being concerned with well-being and with learning. *Educational Psychologist, 28*(2), 149–167.

Boekaerts, M., Pintrich, P. R., & Zeidner, M. (Eds.). (2000). *Handbook of self-regulation*. San Diego: Academic Press.

Bond, C. L., Miller, M. J., & Kennon, R. W. (1987). Study skills: Who is taking the responsibility for teaching? *Performance & Instruction, 26*(7), 27–29.

Bong, M., & Skaalvik, E. (2003). Academic self-concept and self-efficacy: How different are they really? *Educational Psychology Review, 15*(1), 1–40.

Bonk, C. J., & Cummings, J. A. (1998). A dozen recommendations for placing the student at the center of Web-based instruction. *Educational Media International, 35*(2), 82–89.

Bonk, C. J., & Cunningham, D. J. (1998). Searching for learner-centered, constructivist, and sociocultural components of collaborative educational learning tools. In C. J. Bonk & K. S. King (Eds.), *Electronic collaborators: Learner-centered technologies for literacy, apprenticeship, and discourse* (pp. 25–50). Mahwah, NJ: Erlbaum.

Bonk, C. J., Hay, K. E., & Fischler, R. B. (1996). Five key resources for an electronic community of elementary student weather forecasters. *Journal of Computing in Childhood Education, 7*(1/2), 93–118.

Bonk, C. J., & Reynolds, T. H. (1992). Early adolescent composing within a generative-evaluative computerized prompting framework. *Computers in Human Behavior, 8*(1), 39–62.

Bonk, C. J., & Sugar, W. A. (1998). Student role play in the World Forum: Analyses of an Arctic learning apprenticeship. *Interactive Learning Environments, 6*(1–2), 1–29.

Boonstra, H. (2002). Teen pregnancy: Trends and lessons learned. *The Guttmacher Report on Public Policy, 5*(1), 7–10. Retrieved June 27, 2003, from http://www.agi-usa.org/pubs/journals/gr050107.html.

Borja, R. R. (2003, May 8). Prepping for the big test. *Education Week, 22*(35), 22–24, 26.

Bornas, X., Servera, M., & Llabrés, J. (1997). Preventing impulsivity in the classroom: How computers can help teachers. *Computers in the Schools, 13*(1–2), 27–40.

Boston, C. (Ed.). (2002). *Understanding scoring rubrics: A guide for teachers.* College Park, MD: ERIC Clearinghouse on Assessment and Evaluation.

Bower, G. H., Clark, M. C., Lesgold, A. M., & Winzenz, D. (1969). Hierarchical retrieval schemes in recall of categorized word lists. *Journal of Verbal Learning and Verbal Behavior, 8*(3), 323–343.

Bowman, D. H. (2002). National survey puts ADHD incidence near 7 percent. *Education Week, 21*(38), 3.

Boyer, E. L. (1983). *High school.* New York: Harper & Row.

Braaksma, M. A. H., Rijlaarsdam, G., & van den Bergh, H. (2002). Observational learning and the effects of model-observer similarity. *Journal of Educational Psychology, 94*(2), 405–415.

Bracey, G. W. (2002). The 12th Bracey report on the condition of public education. *Phi Delta Kappan, 84*(2), 135–1150.

Bracey, G. W. (2003). The 13th Bracey report on the condition of public education. *Phi Delta Kappan, 85*(2), 148–164.

Branch, C. W., & Boothe, B. (2002). The identity status of African Americans in middle adolescence: A replication and extension of Forbes and Ashton (1998). *Adolescence, 37*(148), 815–821.

Bransford, J., Sharp, D. M., Vye, N. J., Goldman, S. R., Hasselbring, T. S., Goin, L., O'Banion, K., Liverois, J., Saul, E., & The Cognition and Technology Group at Vanderbilt (1996). MOST environments

for accelerating literacy development. In S. Vosniadou, E. De Corte, R. Glaser, & H. Mandl (Eds.), *International perspectives on the design of technology-supported learning environments* (pp. 223–255). Mahwah, NJ: Erlbaum.

Bransford, J. D., Sherwood, R., Vye, N., & Rieser, J. (1986). Teaching thinking and problem solving: Research foundations. *American Psychologist, 41*(10), 1078–1089.

Bransford, J. D., & Stein, B. S. (1993). *The ideal problem solver* (2nd ed.). New York: W. H. Freeman.

Braun, C. (1976). Teacher expectations: Sociopsychological dynamics. *Review of Educational Research, 46*(2), 185–213.

Braun, H. (2004, January 5). Reconsidering the impact of high-stakes testing. *Education Policy Analysis Archives, 12*(1). Retrieved February 6, 2004, from http://epaa.asu.edu/epaa/v12n1/.

Breton, J-J., Boyer, R., Bilodeau, H., Raymond, S., Joubert, N., & Nantel, M-A. (2002). Is evaluative research on youth suicide programs theory-driven? The Canadian experience. *Suicide and Life-Threatening Behavior, 32*(2), 176–190.

Brewer, D. J., Rees, D. I., & Argys, L. M. (1995). Detracking America's schools: The reform without cost? *Phi Delta Kappan, 77*(3), 210–215.

Broekkamp, H., van Hout-Wolters, B. H. A. M., Rijlaarsdam, G., & van den Bergh, H. (2002). Importance in instructional text: Teachers' and students' perceptions of task demands. *Journal of Educational Psychology, 94*(2), 260–271.

Brookfield, S. D., & Preskill, S. (1999). *Discussion as a way of teaching.* San Francisco: Jossey-Bass.

Brooks, H. B., & Brooks, D. W. (1996). The emerging role of CD-ROMs in teaching chemistry. *Journal of Science Education and Technology, 5*(3), 203–215.

Brooks, J. G., & Brooks, M. G. (2001). *In search of understanding: The case for constructivist classrooms.* Upper Saddle River, NJ: Merrill Prentice Hall.

Brophy, J. E. (1979). Teacher behavior and its effects. *Journal of Educational Psychology, 71*(6), 733–750.

Brophy, J. E. (1981). Teacher praise: A functional analysis. *Review of Educational Research, 51*(1), 5–32.

Brophy, J. E. (1983). Research on the self-fulfilling prophecy and teacher expectations. *Journal of Educational Psychology, 75*(5), 631–661.

Brophy, J. E., & Alleman, J. (1991). Activities as instructional tools: A framework for analysis and evaluation. *Educational Researcher, 20*(4), 9–23.

Brophy, J. E., & Evertson, C. M. (1976). *Learning from teaching.* Boston: Allyn & Bacon.

Brown, A. L., Campione, J. C., & Day, J. D. (1981). Learning to learn: On training stu-

dents to learn from text. *Educational Researcher, 10*(2), 14–24.

Brown, D. F. (2002). Self-directed learning in an 8th grade classroom. *Phi Delta Kappan, 60*(1), 54–58.

Brown, J. S., Collins, A., & Duguid, P. (1989). Situated cognition and the culture of learning. *Educational Researcher, 18*(1), 32–42.

Brown, R. (1973). *A first language: The early stages.* Cambridge, MA: Harvard University Press.

Brown, R. A. J., & Renshaw, P. D. (2000). Collective argumentation: A sociocultural approach to reframing classroom teaching and learning. In H. Cowie & G. van der Aalsvoort (Eds.), *Social interaction in learning and instruction* (pp. 52–66). Amsterdam: Pergamon.

Brown, S. M., & Walberg, H. J. (1993). Motivational effects on test scores of elementary students. *Journal of Educational Research, 86*(3), 133–136.

Bruner, J. S. (1983). *In search of mind: Essays in autobiography.* New York: Harper & Row.

Bruning, R. H., Schraw, G. J., Norby, M. M., & Ronning, R. R. (2004). *Cognitive psychology and instruction* (4th ed.). Upper Saddle River, NJ: Merrill Prentice Hall.

Brush, T. A., Armstrong, J., Barbrow, D., & Ulintz, L. (1999). Design and delivery of integrated learning systems: Their impact on student achievement and attitudes. *Journal of Educational Computing Research, 21*(4), 475–486.

Brush, T., & Saye, J. (2001). The use of embedded scaffolds with hypermedia-supported student-centered learning. *Journal of Educational Multimedia and Hypermedia, 10*(4), 333–356.

Bryant, D. P., Vaughn, S., Linan-Thompson, S., Ugel, N., Hamff, A., & Hougen, M. (2000). Reading outcomes for students with and without reading disabilities in general education middle-school content area classes. *Learning Disability Quarterly, 23*(4), 238–252.

Bucher, A. A. (1997). The influence of models in forming moral identity. *International Journal of Educational Research, 27*(7), 619–627.

Burch, C. B. (1993). Teachers vs. professors: The university's side. *Educational Leadership, 51*(2), 68–76.

Burchinal, M. R., Peisner-Feinberg, E., Pianta, R., & Howes, C. (2002). The development of academic skills from preschool through second grade: Family and classroom predictors of developmental trajectories. *Journal of School Psychology, 40*(5), 415–436.

Burden, P. R. (2000). Powerful classroom management strategies: *Motivating students to learn.* Thousand Oaks, CA: Corwin.

Bureau of Labor Statistics. (2003). Most 16- to 18-year-old students work in school year and summer. *Monthly Labor Review: The Editor's Desk.* Retrieved December 12,

2003 from http://ww.bls.gov/news.release/nlsyth.toc.htm.

Burns, M. (2002). From compliance to commitment: Technology as a catalyst for communities of learning. *Phi Delta Kappan, 84*(4), 295–302.

Burtch, J. A. (1999). Technology is for everyone. *Educational Leadership, 56*(5), 33–34.

Bushrod, G., Williams, R. L., & McLaughlin, T. F. (1995). An evaluation of a simplified daily report system with two kindergarten pupils. *B.C. Journal of Special Education, 19*(1), 35–43.

Caine, G., Caine, R. N., & McClintic, C. (2002). Guiding the innate constructivist. *Educational Leadership, 60*(1), 70–73.

Calderón, M. E., & Minaya-Rowe, L. (2003). *Designing and implementing two-way bilingual programs.* Thousand Oaks, CA: Corwin Press.

Callahan, C. M., & McIntire, J. A. (1994). *Identifying outstanding talent in American Indian and Alaska native students.* Washington, DC: U. S. Department of Education, Office of Educational Research and Improvement.

Cameron, J. (2001). Negative effects of reward on intrinsic motivation—A limited phenomenon: Comment on Deci, Koestner, & Ryan (2001). *Review of Educational Research, 71*(1), 29–42.

Cameron, J., Banko, K. M., & Pierce, W. D. (2001). Pervasive negative effects of rewards on intrinsic motivation: The myth continues. *Behavior Analyst, 24*(1), 1–44.

Camilli, G. (2003). Comment on Cizek's "more unintended consequences of high-stakes testing." *Educational Measurement: Issues and Practice, 22*(1), 36–39.

Campbell, L. (1997). How teachers interpret MI theory. *Educational Leadership, 55*(1), 14–19.

Canady, R. L., & Hotchkiss, P. R. (1989). It's a good score! Just a bad grade. *Phi Delta Kappan, 71*(1), 68–71.

Cangelosi, J. S. (2004). *Classroom management strategies: Gaining and maintaining students' cooperation* (5th ed.). New York: Wiley.

Cardon, P. L., & Christensen, K. W. (1998). Technology-based programs for drop-out prevention. *Journal of Technology Studies, 24*(1), 50–54.

Cardwell, K. (2000). Electronic assessment. *Learning and Leading with Technology, 27*(7), 22–26.

Carney, R. N., & Levin, J. R. (2000). Mnemonic instruction, with a focus on transfer. *Journal of Educational Psychology, 92*(4), 783–790.

Carney, R. N., & Levin, J. R. (2002). Pictorial illustrations still improve students' learning from text. *Educational Psychology Review, 14*(1), 5–26.

Carney, R. N., Levin, J. R., & Levin, M. E. (1994). Enhancing the psychology of memory by enhancing memory of psychology. *Teaching of Psychology, 21*(3), 171–174.

Carroll, J. B. (1963). A model of school learning. *Teachers College Record, 64*(8), 723–733.

Carter, C. J. (1997). Why reciprocal teaching? *Educational Leadership, 54*(6), 64–68.

Carter, D. B. (1987). The role of peers in sex role socialization. In D. B. Carter (Ed.), *Current conceptions of sex roles and sex typing.* New York: Praeger.

Case, R. (1975). Gearing the demands of instruction to the developmental capacities of the learner. *Review of Educational Research, 45*(1), 59–88.

Case, R. (1999). Conceptual development in the child and in the field: A personal view of the Piagetian legacy. In E. K. Scholnick, K. Nelson, S. A. Gelman, & P. H. Miller (Eds.), *Conceptual development: Piaget's legacy.* Mahwah, NJ: Erlbaum.

Castellani, J., & Jeffs, T. (2001). Emerging reading and writing strategies using technology. *TEACHING Exceptional Children, 33*(5), 60–67.

Castellano, J. A. (Ed.). (2003). *Special populations in gifted education: Working with diverse learners.* Boston: Allyn & Bacon.

Center for Applied Linguistics. (2003). *Directory of two-way bilingual immersion programs in the U.S.* Retrieved August 23, 2003, from http://www.cal.org/twi/directory.

Centers for Disease Control. (2002a). *Trends in sexual risk behaviors among high school students—United States, 1991–2001.* MMWR, 51(38), 856–859. Retrieved June 27, 2003, from http://www.cdc.gov/mmwr/preview/mmwrhtml/mm5138a2.htm.

Centers for Disease Control. (2002b). Suicide as a leading cause of death, by age, race, and sex (2000). *National Vital Statistics Report, 50*(16). Retrieved June 27, 2003, from http://www.cdc.gov/nchs/fastats/suicide.htm.

Centers for Disease Control (2003). *Unintentional injuries/violence, 2001 United States. Youth risk behavior surveillance system.* Retrieved June 27, 2003, from http://apps.nccd.cdc.gov/YRBSS/ListV.asp?site1=XX&Cat=1.

Chambres, P., Izaute, M., & Marescaux, P-J. (Eds.). (2002). *Metacognition: Process, function, and use.* Boston, MA: Kluwer Academic.

Chance, P. (1992). The rewards of learning. *Phi Delta Kappan, 74*(3), 200–207.

Chance, P. (1993). Sticking up for rewards. *Phi Delta Kappan, 74*(10), 787–790.

Chapman, J. W., & Tunmer, W. E. (1995). Development of young children's reading self-concepts: An examination of emerging subcomponents and their relationships with reading achievement. *Journal of Educational Psychology, 87*(1), 154–167.

Character Education Partnership. (2000). *Eleven principles of effective character education.* Retrieved January 2, 2002, from http://www.character.org/.

Chase, K. (2002). The brilliant inventiveness of student misbehavior: Test your classroom management skills. *Phi Delta Kappan, 84*(4), 327–328, 330.

Checkley, K. (1997). The first seven . . . and the eighth: A conversation with Howard Gardner. *Educational Leadership, 55*(1), 8–13.

Choate, J. S. (Ed.). (2003). *Successful inclusive teaching: Proven ways to detect and correct special needs* (4th ed.). Boston: Allyn & Bacon.

Chrenka, Lynn. (2001). Misconstructing constructivism. *Phi Delta Kappan, 82*(9), 694–695.

Christmann, E., & Badgett, J. (1999). A comparative analysis of the effects of computer-assisted instruction on student achievement in differing science and demographical areas. *Journals of Computers in Mathematics and Science Teaching, 18*(2), 135–143.

Christmann, E., Badgett, J., & Lucking, R. (1997). Microcomputer-based computer-assisted instruction within differing subject areas: A statistical deduction. *Journal of Educational Computing Research, 16*(3), 281–296.

Chudowsky, N., & Pellegrino, J. W. (2003). Large-scale assessments that support learning: What will it take? *Theory into Practice, 42*(1), 75–83.

Cicchetti, D., & Toth, S. L. (1998). The development of depression in children and adolescents. *American Psychologist, 53*(2), 221–241.

Cizek, G. J. (2001a). More unintended consequences of high-stakes testing. *Educational Measurement: Issues and Practices, 20*(4), 19–27.

Cizek, G. J. (2001b). Cheating to the test. *Education Matters, 1*(1), 41–47.

Cizek, G. J. (2003). Rejoinder. *Educational Measurement: Issues and Practice, 22*(1), 40–44.

Clark, J. M., & Paivio, A. (1991). Dual coding theory and education. *Educational Psychology Review, 3*(3), 149–210.

Clark, R. E. (2002). Performance assessment in the arts. *Kappa Delta Pi Record, 39*(1), 29–32.

Clarke, L., & Heaney, P. (2003). Author On-Line: Using asynchronous computer conferencing to support literacy. *British Journal of Educational Psychology, 34*(1), 57–66.

Clarke, M., Abrams, L., & Madaus, G. (2001). The effects and implications of high-stakes achievement tests for adolescents. In T. Urdan & F. Pajares (Eds.), *Adolescence and education. Vol. 1: General issues in the education of adolescents* (pp. 201–229). Greenwich, CT: Information Age Publishing.

Clarke, M., Madaus, G., Horn, C., & Ramos, M. (2001, April). The marketplace for educational testing. *NBETPP Statements, 2*(3), 1–12. Retrieved February 10, 2004, from http://www.bc.edu/research/nbetpp/reports.html#statements.

Clawson, M. A., & Robila, M. (2001). Relations between parenting style and children's play behavior. Issues in education. *Journal of Early Education and Family Review, 8*(3), 13–19.

Clements, D. H., & Nastasi, B. K. (1999). Metacognition, learning, and educational computer environments. *Information Technology in Childhood Education Annual,* 5–38.

Clements, P., & Seidman, E. (2002). The ecology of middle grades schools and possible selves. In T. M. Brinthaupt & R. P. Lipka (Eds.), *Understanding early adolescent self and identity: Applications and interventions* (pp. 133–164). Albany, NY: State University of New York Press.

Cobb, P., & Bowers, J. (1999). Cognitive and situated learning perspectives in theory and practice. *Educational Researcher, 28*(2), 4–15.

Cochran-Smith, M. (2003). The unforgiving complexity of teaching: Avoiding simplicity in the age of accountability. *Journal of Teacher Education, 54*(1), 3–5.

Cognition and Technology Group at Vanderbilt. (1990). Anchored instruction and its relationship to situated cognition. *Educational Researcher, 19*(6), 2–10.

Cognition and Technology Group at Vanderbilt. (1992a). The Jasper series: A generative approach to improving mathematical thinking. In K. Sheingold, L. G. Roberts, & S. M. Malcolm (Eds.), *This year in school science 1991: Technology for teaching and learning.* Washington, DC: American Association for the Advancement of Science.

Cognition and Technology Group at Vanderbilt. (1992b). The Jasper series as an example of anchored instruction: Theory, program description, and assessment data. *Educational Psychologist, 27*(3), 291–315.

Cognition and Technology Group at Vanderbilt. (1993). Anchored instruction and situated cognition revisited. *Educational Technology, 33*(3), 52–70.

Cognition and Technology Group at Vanderbilt. (1994). Multimedia environments for developing literacy for at-risk students. In B. Means (Ed.), *Technology and educational reform: The reality behind the promise* (pp. 23–56). San Francisco, CA: Jossey-Bass.

Cognition and Technology Group at Vanderbilt. (1996). Looking at technology in context: A framework for understanding technology and education research. In D. C. Berliner & R. C. Calfee (Eds.), *Handbook of educational psychology* (pp. 807–840). New York, NY: Simon & Schuster.

Colangelo, N., & Davis, G. A. (Eds.).(2003a). *Handbook of gifted education* (3rd ed.). Boston: Allyn & Bacon.

Colangelo, N., & Davis, G. A. (2003b). Introduction and overview. In N. Colangelo & G. A. Davis (Eds.), *Handbook of gifted education* (3rd ed., pp. 3–10). Boston: Allyn & Bacon.

Collier, C. (1999). Project-based student technology competencies. *Learning and Leading with Technology, 27*(3), 50–53.

Colten, M. E., & Gore, S. (Eds.). (1991). *Adolescent stress.* New York: Aldine de Gruyter.

Combs, A. W. (1965). *The professional education of teachers.* Boston: Allyn and Bacon.

Commission on Instructionally Supportive Assessment. (2002, March). *Implementing ESEA's testing provisions.* Retrieved February 9, 2004, from http://www.nea.org/accountability/images/02eseatesting.pdf.

Conger, J. J., & Galambos, N. L. (1997). *Adolescence and youth* (5th ed.). New York: Longman.

Connor, D. F. (2002). *Aggression and antisocial behavior in children and adolescents: Research and treatment.* New York: Guilford Press.

Cooper, H. (1979). Pygmalion grows up: A model for teacher expectation, communication, and performance influence. *Review of Educational Research, 49*(3), 389–410.

Cooper, H., & Dorr, N. (1995). Race comparisons on need for achievement: A meta-analytic alternative to Graham's narrative review. *Review of Educational Research, 65*(4), 438–508.

Corbett, D., & Wilson, B. (2002). What urban students say about good teaching. *Educational Leadership, 60*(1), 18–22.

Cordova, D. I., & Lepper, M. R. (1996). Intrinsic motivation and the process of learning: Beneficial effects of contextualization, personalization, and choice. *Journal of Educational Psychology, 88*(4), 715–730.

Cornford, I. (2002). Reflective teaching: Empirical research findings and some implications for teacher education. *Journal of Vocational Education and Training, 54*(2), 219–235.

Cosgrove, D. J. (1959). Diagnostic ratings of teacher performance. *Journal of Educational Psychology, 50*(5), 200–204.

Cotterall, S., & Cohen, R. (2003). Scaffolding for second language writers: Producing an academic essay. *ELT Journal, 57*(2), 158–166.

Couzijn, M. (1999). Learning to write by observation of writing and reading processes: Effects on learning and transfer. *Learning and Instruction, 9*(2), 109–142.

Covington, M. V. (1985). Strategic thinking and the fear of failure. In J. W. Segal, S. F. Chipman, & R. Glaser (Eds.), *Thinking and learning skills* (Vol. 1). Hillsdale, NJ: Erlbaum.

Covington, M. V. (2000). Goal theory, motivation, and school achievement: An integrative review. In S. T. Fiske, D. L. Schacter, & C. Zahn-Waxler (Eds.), *Annual review of psychology* (Vol. 51, pp. 171–200). Palo Alto, CA: Annual Reviews.

Covington, M. V. (2002). Rewards and intrinsic motivation: A needs-based developmental perspective. In F. Pajares & T. Urdan (Eds.), *Academic motivation of adolescents* (pp. 169–192). Greenwich, CT: Information Age Publishing.

Cox, B. D. (1997). The rediscovery of the active learner in adaptive contexts: A developmental-historical analysis of transfer of training. *Educational Psychologist, 32*(1), 41–55.

Crain, W. (2000). *Theories of development: Concepts and applications* (4th ed.). Upper Saddle River, NJ: Prentice-Hall.

Cramer, P. (2001). Identification and its relation to identity development. *Journal of Personality, 69*(5), 667–688.

Crooks, T. J. (1988). The impact of classroom evaluation practices on students. *Review of Educational Research, 58*(4), 438–481.

Cruickshank, D. R. (1990). *Research that informs teachers and teacher educators.* Bloomington, IN: Phi Delta Kappa Educational Foundation.

Cuban, L. (1986). *Teachers and machines: The classroom use of technology since 1920.* New York: Teachers College Press.

Cuban, L. (1990). What I learned from what I had forgotten about teaching: Notes from a professor. *Phi Delta Kappan, 71*(6), 479–482.

Cuban, L. (2001). *Oversold and underused: Computers in the classroom.* Cambridge, MA: Harvard University Press.

Cummins, J. (1999). Alternative paradigms in bilingual education research. *Educational Researcher, 28*(7), 26–32,41.

Cunningham, D. J. (2001, April). *Fear and loathing in the information age.* Paper presented at the annual meeting of the American Educational Research Association, Seattle, WA.

Curtis, D. (2002). The power of projects. *Educational Leadership, 60*(1), 50–53.

Curwin, R. L. (2003). *Making good choices.* Thousand Oaks, CA: Corwin Press.

Dai, D. Y., Moon, S. M., & Feldhusen, J. F. (1998). Achievement motivation and gifted students: a social cognitive perspective. *Educational Psychologist, 33*(2/3), 45–63.

Daiute, C. (1985). Issues in using computers to socialize the writing process. *Educational Communication and Technology, 33*(1), 41–50.

Damon, W., & Hart, D. (1988). *Self-understanding in childhood and adolescence.* New York: Cambrdige University Press.

Darling-Hammond, L., & Falk, B. (1997). Using standards and assessments to support student learning. *Phi Delta Kappan, 79*(3), 190–199.

Darling-Hammond, L., & Youngs, P. (2002). Defining "highly qualified teachers": What does "scientifically-based research" actually tell us? *Educational Researcher, 31*(9), 13–25.

Dasen, P., & Heron, A. (1981). Cross-cultural tests of Piaget's theory. In H. C. Triandis &

A. Heron (Eds.), *Handbook of cross-cultural psychology, developmental psychology* (Vol. 4). Boston: Allyn & Bacon.

DeBell, M., & Chapman, C. (2003). *Computer and internet use by children and adolescents in 2001.* Washington, DC: National Center for Educational Statistics. Retrieved January 5, 2004, from http://nces.ed.gov/pubsearch/pubsinfo.asp?pubid=2004014.

deCharms, R. (1976). *Enhancing motivation: Change in the classroom.* New York: Irvington.

Deci, E. L., Koestner, R., & Ryan, R. M. (2001). Extrinsic rewards and intrinsic motivation in education: Reconsidered once again. *Review of Educational Research, 71*(1), 1–27.

De Corte, E. (2003). Transfer as the productive use of acquired knowledge, skills, and motivations. *Current Directions in Psychological Science, 12*(4), 142–146.

Dede, C. (1996). The evolution of distance education: Emerging technologies and distributed learning. *The American Journal of Distance Education, 10*(2), 4–36.

de Jong, T., & van Joolingen, W. R. (1998). Scientific discovery learning with computer simulations of conceptual domains. *Review of Educational Research, 68*(2), 179–201.

Delgarno, B. (2001). Interpretations of constructivism and consequences for computer assisted learning. *British Journal of Educational Technology, 32*(2), 183–194.

Dempster, F. N. (1988). The spacing effect: A case study in the failure to apply the results of psychological research. *American Psychologist, 43*(8), 627–634.

Denbo, S. J. (2002). Institutional practices that support African American student achievement. In S. J. Denbo & L. M. Beaulieu (Eds.), *Improving schools for African American students* (pp. 55–71). Springfield, IL: Charles C. Thomas.

Derry, S. J. (1996). Cognitive schema theory in the constructivist debate. *Educational Researcher, 31*(3/4), 163–174.

DeVoe, J. F., Peter, K., Kaufman, P., Ruddy, S. A., Miller, A. K., Planty, M., Snyder, T. D., & Rand, M. R. (2003, October). *Indicators of school crime and safety: 2003* NCES2004-004/NCJ 201257. U.S. Departments of Education and Justice: Washington, DC. Retrieved December 3, 2003, from www.ojp.usdoj.gov/bjs/.

DeVries, R. (1997). Piaget's social theory. *Educational Researcher, 26*(2), 4–17.

DiGiulio, R. (2000). *Positive classroom management* (2nd ed.). Thousand Oaks, CA: Corwin.

Dill, E. M., & Boykin, A. W. (2000). The comparative influence of individual, peer tutoring, and communal learning contexts of the text recall of African American children. *Journal of Black Psychology, 26*(1), 65–78.

Dillon, A., & Gabbard, R. (1998). Hypermedia as an educational technology:

A review of the quantitative research literature on learner comprehension, control, and style. *Review of Educational Research, 68*(3), 322–349.

Dobbs, M. (2004, February 19). More states are fighting 'No Child Left Behind' law. *Washington Post,* p. A3.

Dochy, F., Segers, M., & Buehl, M. M. (1999). The relation between assessment practices and outcomes of studies: The case of research on prior knowledge. *Review of Educational Research, 69*(2), 145–186.

Doherty, R. W., Hilberg, R. S., Epaloose, G., & Tharp, R. G. (2002). Standards performance continuum: Development and validation of a measure of effective pedagogy. *Journal of Educational Research, 96*(2), 78–89.

Donahue, P. L., Finnegan, R. J., Lutkus, A. D., Allen, N. L., & Campbell, J. R. (2001). *The nation's report card: Fourth-grade reading 2000.* Washington, DC: National Center for Educational Statistics. Retrieved January 2, 2002, from http://nces.ed.gov/nationsreportcard/pubs/main2000/2001499.asp.

Donovan, C. A., & Smolkin, L. B. (2002). Children's genre knowledge: An examination of K–5 students' performance on multiple tasks providing differing levels of scaffolding. *Reading Research Quarterly, 37*(4), 428–465.

Doppelt, Y., & Barak, M. (2002). Pupils identify key aspects and outcomes of a technological learning environment. *The Journal of Technology Studies, 28*(1), 22–28.

Dornbusch, S. M., & Kaufman, J. G. (2001). The social structure of the American high school. In T. Urdan & F. Pajares (Eds.), *Adolescence and education. Volume 1* (pp. 61–91). Greenwich, CT: Information Age Publishing.

Doty, D. E., Popplewell, S. R., & Byers, G. O. (2001). Interactive CD-ROM storybooks and young readers' reading comprehension. *Journal of Research on Computing in Education, 33*(4), 374–384.

Doyle, W. (1983). Academic work. *Review of Educational Research, 53*(2), 159–200.

Drake, F. D., & McBride, L. W. (2000). The summative teaching portfolio and the reflective practitioner of history. *The History Teacher, 34*(1), 41–60.

Drasgow, F. (2002). The work ahead: A psychometric infrastructure for computerized adaptive tests. In C. N. Mills, M. T. Potenza, J. J. Fremer, & W. C. Ward (Eds.), *Computer-based testing* (pp. 1–10). Mahwah, NJ: Erlbaum.

Drier, H. S. (2001). Conceptualization and design of Probability Explorer. *TechTrends, 45*(2), 2–24.

Drier, H. S., Dawson, K. M., & Garofalo, J. (1999). Not your typical math class. *Educational Leadership, 56*(5), 21–25.

Driscoll, M. P. (2000). *Psychology of learning for instruction* (2nd ed.). Boston: Allyn & Bacon.

Duell, O. K. (1986). Metacognitive skills. In G. D. Phye & T. Andre (Eds.), *Cognitive classroom learning.* Orlando, FL: Academic Press.

Duff, C. (2000). Online mentoring. *Educational Leadership, 58*(2), 49–52.

Duffy, T. M., & Cunningham, D. J. (1996). Constructivism: Implications for the design and delivery of instruction. In D. Jonassen (Ed.), *Handbook of research for educational communications and technology* (pp. 170–198). New York: Macmillan Library Reference.

Dugger, W. E., Jr. (2001). Standards for technological literacy. *Phi Delta Kappan, 82*(7), 513–517.Duhaney, L. M., & Duhaney, D. C. (2000). Assistive technology: Meeting the needs of learners with disabilities. *International Journal of Instructional Media, 27*(4), 393–401.

Dunn, R., & Dunn, K. (1992). *Teaching elementary students through their individual learning styles.* Boston: Allyn & Bacon.

Dunn, R., & Dunn, K. (1993). *Teaching secondary students through their individual learning styles.* Boston: Allyn & Bacon.

Dusek, J. B. (1996). *Adolescent development and behavior* (3rd ed.). Upper Saddle River, NJ: Prentice-Hall.

Dweck, C. S. (2002a). The development of ability conceptions. In A Wigfield & J. S. Eccles (Eds.), *Development of achievement motivation* (pp. 57–88). San Diego, CA: Academic Press.

Dweck, C. S. (2002b). Messages that motivate: How praise molds students' beliefs, motivation, and performance (in surprising ways). In J. Aronson (Ed.), *Improving academic achievement* (pp. 37–59). San Diego, CA: Academic Press.

Dyer, P. C., & Binkney, R. (1995). Estimating cost effectiveness and educational outcomes: Retention, remediation, special education, and early intervention. In R. L. Allington & S. A. Walmsley (Eds.), *No quick fix: Rethinking literacy programs in America's elementary schools.* New York: Teachers College Press.

Eakin, S. S. (1997). Educators on the edge: Spreading the wise use of technology. *Technos, 6*(3), 15–22.

Eberstadt, M. (2003). The child-fat problem. *Policy Review, 117,* 3–19.

Ebert, E., & Strudler, N. (1996). Improving science learning using low-cost multimedia. *Learning and Leading with Technology, 24*(1), 23–26.

Eby, J. W., Herrell, A., & Hicks, J. L. (2002). *Reflective planning, teaching, and evaluation: K–12.* Upper Saddle River, NJ: Merrill Prentice Hall.

Edelson, D. C., Pea, R. D., & Gomez, L. (1996). Constructivism in the collaboratory. In B. G. Wilson (Ed.), *Constructivist learning environments: Case studies in instructional design* (pp. 151–164). Englewood Cliffs, NJ: Educational Technology Publications.

Ehman, L. H., Glenn, A. D., Johnson, V., & White, C. S. (1992). Using computer databases in student problem solving: A study of eight social studies teachers' classrooms. *Theory and Research in Social Education, 20*(2), 179–206.

Eisenberger, J., Conti-D'Antonio, M., & Bertrando, R. (2000). *Self-efficacy: Raising the bar for students with learning needs.* Larchmont, NY: Eye on Education.

Eisner, E. W. (1999). The uses and limits of performance assessment. *Phi Delta Kappan, 80*(9), 658–660.

Eisner, E. W. (2002). What can education learn from the arts about the practice of education? *Journal of Curriculum and Supervision, 18*(1), 4–16.

Eisenman, G., & Payne, B. D. (1997). Effects of the higher order thinking skills program on at-risk young adolescents' self-concept, reading achievement, and thinking skills. *Research in Middle Level Education Quarterly, 20*(3), 1–25.

Elkind, D. (1968). Cognitive development in adolescence. In J. F. Adams (Ed.), *Understanding adolescence.* Boston: Allyn & Bacon.

Elkind, D. (1989). Developmentally appropriate practice: Philosophical and practical implications. *Phi Delta Kappan, 71*(2), 113–117.

Elliot, A. J., & Covington, M. V. (2001). Approach and avoidance motivation. *Educational Psychology Review, 13*(2), 73–92.

Elliot, A. J., & Thrash, T. M. (2001). Achievement goals and the hierarchical model of achievement motivation. *Educational Psychology Review, 13*(2), 139–156.

Elliot, S. (2003). IntelliMetric™: From here to validity. In M. D. Shermis & J. C. Burstein (Eds.), *Automated essay scoring* (pp. 71–86). Mahwah, NJ: Erlbaum.

Elliott, J. G., & Bempechat, J. (2002). The culture and contexts of achievement motivation. In J. Bempechat & J. G. Elliott (Eds.), *New Directions for Child and Adolescent Development, No. 96. Learning in culture and context: Approaching the complexities of achievement motivation in student learning* (pp. 7–26). San Francisco, CA: Jossey-Bass.

Elliott, L., Foster, S., & Stinson, M. (2002). Student study habits using notes from a speech-to-text support service. *Exceptional Children, 69*(1), 25–40.

Ellis, A. K. (2001). *Teaching, learning, and assessment together: The reflective classroom.* Larchmont, NY: Eye on Education.

Ellis, H. C. (1965). *The transfer of learning.* New York: Macmillan.

Ellis, H. C. (1978). *Fundamentals of human learning, memory, and cognition* (2nd ed.). Dubuque, IA: William C. Brown.

Elrich, M. (1994). The stereotype within. *Educational Leadership, 51*(8), 12–15.

Emmer, E. T., Evertson, C. M., & Worsham, M. E. (2003). *Classroom management for secondary teachers* (6th ed.). Boston: Allyn & Bacon.

Emmer, E. T., & Stough, L. M. (2001). Classroom management: A critical part of educational psychology, with implications for teacher education. *Educational Psychologist, 36*(2), 103–112.

Engebretsen, A. (1997). Visualizing least-square lines of best fit. *Mathematics Teacher, 90*(5), 405–408.

Eom, W., & Reiser, R. A. (2000). The effects of self-regulation and instructional control on performance and motivation in computer-based instruction. *International Journal of Instructional Media, 27*(3), 247–260.

Erdelyi, M. H., & Goldberg, B. (1979). Let's now sweep repression under the rug: Towards a cognitive psychology of repression. In J. Kihlstrom & F. Evans (Eds.), *Functional disorders of memory.* Hillsdale, NJ: Erlbaum.

Ericsson, K. A., Chase, W. G., & Faloon, S. (1980). Acquisition of a memory skill. *Science, 208*(4448), 1181–1182.

Erikson, E. H. (1963). *Childhood and society* (2nd ed.). New York: Norton.

Erikson, E. H. (1968). *Identity: Youth and crisis.* New York: Norton.

Estep, S. G., McInerney, W. D., Vockell, E., & Kosmoski, G. (1999–2000). An investigation of the relationship between integrated learning systems and academic achievement. *Journal of Educational Technology Systems, 28*(1), 5–19.

Evans, R. I. (1967). *Dialogue with Erik Erikson.* New York: Harper & Row.

Evertson, C. M., Emmer, E. T., & Worsham, M. E. (2003). *Classroom management for elementary teachers* (6th ed.). Boston: Allyn & Bacon.

Fabes, R. A., Martin, C. L., & Hanish, L. D. (2003). Young children's play qualities in same-, other-, and mixed-sex peer groups. *Child Development, 74*(3), 921–932.

Fabris, M. E. (1992/1993). Using multimedia in the multicultural classroom. *Journal of Educational Technology Systems, 21*(2), 163–171.

Falk, B. (2002). Standard-based reforms: Problems and possibilities. *Phi Delta Kappan, 83*(8), 612–620.

Faw, H. W., & Waller, T. G. (1976). Mathemagenic behaviors and efficiency in learning from prose materials. *Review of Educational Research, 46*(4), 691–720.

Fehrenbach, C. R. (1994). Cognitive styles of gifted and average readers. *Roeper Review, 16*(4), 290–292.

Feigenbaum, P. (2002). Private speech: Cornerstone of Vygotsky's theory of the development of higher psychological processes. In D. Robbins & A. Stetsenko (Eds.), *Voices within Vygotsky's non-classical psychology: Past, present, and future* (pp. 161–174). New York: Nova Science.

Feiman-Nemser, S. (2003). What new teachers need to learn. *Educational Leadership, 60*(8), 25–29.

Feinberg, R. C. (2002). *Bilingual education: A reference handbook.* Santa Barbara, CA: ABC-CLIO.

Feist, J., & Feist, G. J. (2001). *Theories of personality* (5th ed). Dubuque, IA: McGraw-Hill.

Feynman, R. P. (1985). *"Surely you're joking, Mr. Feynman."* New York: Norton.

Feyten, C. M., Macy, M. D., Ducher, J., Yoshii, M., Park, E., Calandra, B., & Meros, J. (2002). *Teaching esl/efl with the internet.* Upper Saddle River, NJ: Merrill Prentice Hall.

Field, T., Diego, M., & Sanders, C. (2001). Adolescent depression and risk factors. *Adolescence, 36*(143), 491–498.

Fitzgerald, J. (1995). English-as-a-second-language learners' cognitive reading processes: A review of the research in the United States. *Review of Educational Research, 65*(2), 145–190.

Flaherty, P. (2002). *The scout law: Quotes for life.* Iowa City, IA: Penfield Books.

Flavell, J. H. (1976). Metacognitive aspects of problem solving. In L. B. Resnick (Ed.), *The nature of intelligence.* Hillsdale, NJ: Erlbaum.

Flavell, J. H. (1987). Speculations about the nature and development of metacognition. In F. E. Weinert & R. H. Kluwe (Eds.), *Metacognition, motivation, and understanding.* Hillsdale, NJ: Erlbaum.

Flavell, J. H., Miller, P. A., & Miller, S. A. (2002). *Cognitive development* (4th ed.). Upper Saddle River, NJ: Prentice Hall.

Fletcher-Flinn, C. M., & Suddendorf, T. (1996). Do computers affect 'the mind'? *Journal of Educational Computing Research, 15*(2), 97–112.

Flieller, A. (1999). Comparison of the development of formal thought in adolescent cohorts aged 10 to 15 years (1967–1996 and 1972–1993). *Developmental Psychology, 35*(4), 1048–1058.

Flinders, D. J. (1989). Does the "art of teaching" have a future? *Educational leadership, 46*(8), 16–20.

Foote, C. J., Vermette, P. J., & Battaglia, C. F. (2001). *Constructivist strategies: Meeting standards and engaging adolescent minds.* Larchmont, NY: Eye on Education.

Forbes, S., & Ashton, P. (1998). The identity status of African Americans in middle adolescence: A replication and extension of Watson & Protinsky (1991). *Adolescence, 33*(132), 845–849.

Forgrave, K. E. (2002). Assistive technology: Empowering students with learning disabilities. *Clearing House, 75*(3), 122–126.

Fosnot, C. T. (1996). Constructivism: A psychological theory of learning. In C. T. Fosnot (Ed.), *Constructivism: Theory, perspectives, and practice.* New York: Teachers College Press.

Fox, N. E., & Ysseldyke, J. E. (1997). Implementing inclusion at the middle school level: Lessons from a negative example. *Exceptional Children, 64*(1), 81–98.

Freedman, K., & Liu, M. (1996). The importance of computer experience, learning processes, and communication patterns in multicultural networking. *Educational Technology Research and Development, 44*(1), 43–59.

Freiberg, H. J. (2002). Essential skills for new teachers. *Educational Leadership, 59*(6), 56–60.

Fuchs, D., Fuchs, L. S., Mathes, P. G., & Simmons, D. C. (1997). Peer-assisted learning strategies: Making classrooms more responsive to diversity. *American Educational Research Journal, 34*(1), 174–206.

Funk, C. (2003). James Otto and the pi man: A constructivist tale. *Phi Delta Kappan, 85*(3), 212–214.

Funkhouser, C. (2002/2003). The effects of computer-augmented geometry instruction on student performance and attitudes. *Journal of Research on Technology in Education, 35*(2), 163–175.

Furth, H. G. (1970). *Piaget for teachers.* Englewood Cliffs, NJ: Prentice-Hall.

Gable, R. A., & Warren, S. F. (Eds.). (1993). *Strategies for teaching students with mild to severe mental retardation.* Baltimore, MD: Paul H. Brookes.

Gabler, I. C., Schroeder, M., & Curtis, D. H. (2003). *Constructivist methods for the secondary classroom.* Boston: Allyn & Bacon.

Gaffney, J. S., & Anderson, R. C. (1991). Two-tiered scaffolding: Congruent processes of teaching and learning. In E. H. Hiebert (Ed.), *Literacy in a diverse society: Perspectives, practices, and policies* (pp. 141–156). New York: Teachers College Press.

Gage, N. L., & Berliner, D. C. (1998). *Educational psychology* (6th ed.). Boston: Houghton Mifflin.

Gagné, E. D., Yekovich, C. W., & Yekovich, F. R. (1993). *The Cognitive psychology of school learning* (2nd ed.). New York: HarperCollins.

Gallagher, J. J. (2003). Issues and challenges in the education of gifted students. In N. Colangelo & G. A. Davis (Eds.), *Handbook of gifted education* (3rd ed., pp. 11–23). Boston: Allyn & Bacon.

Gallagher, P. A. (1995). *Teaching students with behavior disorders: Techniques and activities for classroom instruction.* (2nd ed.). Denver: Love.

Gallimore, R., & Tharp, R. (1990). Teaching mind in society: Teaching, schooling, and literate discourse. In L. C. Moll (Ed.), *Vygotsky and education: Instructional implications and applications of sociohistorical psychology.* Cambridge, England: Cambridge University Press.

Gan, S. (1999). Motivating at-risk students through computer-based cooperative learning activities. *Educational Horizons, 77*(3), 151–156.

Gantner, M. W. (1997). Lessons learned from my students in the barrio. *Educational Leadership, 54*(7), 44–45.

García, E. (2002). *Student cultural diversity: Understanding and meeting the challenge* (3rd ed.). Boston: Houghton Mifflin.

Garcia, J. (1993). The changing image of ethnic groups in textbooks. *Phi Delta Kappan, 75*(1), 29–35.

Gardner, H. (1999). *Intelligence reframed: Multiple intelligences for the 21st century.* New York: Basic Books.

Gardner, H., & Hatch, T. (1989). Multiple intelligences go to school. *Educational Researcher, 18*(8), 410.

Garland, A. F., & Zigler, E. (1993). Adolescent suicide prevention: Current research and social policy implications. *American Psychologist, 48*(2), 169–182.

Garrison, J. W. (1997). *Dewey and eros: Wisdom and desire in the art of teaching.* New York: Teachers College Press.

Gatlin, L., & Jacob, S. (2002). Standards-based digital portfolios: A component of authentic assessment for preservice teachers. *Action in Teacher Education, 23*(4), 35–41.

Gayler, K., Chudowsky, N., Kober, N., & Hamilton, M. (2003, August). *State high school exit exams put to the test.* Retrieved February 18, 2004, from http://www.cep-dc.org/.

Gelman, R. (1994). Constructivism and supporting environments. In D. Tirosh (Ed.), *Implicit and explicit knowledge: An educational approach.* Norwood, NJ: Ablex.

Genesee, F., & Cloud, N. (1998). Multilingualism is basic. *Educational Leadership, 55*(6), 62–65.

Gentile, J. R., & Lalley, J. P. (2003). *Standards and mastery learning.* Thousand Oaks, CA: Corwin Press.

Gentry, M., Gable, R. K., & Rizza, M. G. (2002). Students' perceptions of classroom activities: Are there grade-level and gender differences? *Journal of Educational Psychology, 94*(3), 539–544.

Gershoff, E. T. (2002). Corporal punishment by parents and associated child behaviors and experiences: A meta-analytic and theoretical review. *Psychological Bulletin, 128*(4), 539–579.

Gersten, R. (1999). The changing face of bilingual education. *Educational Leadership, 56*(7), 41–45.

Gersten, R., & Brengelman, S. U. (1996). The quest to translate research into classroom practice: The emerging knowledge base. *Remedial and Special Education, 17*(2), 67–74.

Gersten, R., Fuchs, L. S., Williams, J. P., & Baker, S. (2001). Teaching reading comprehension strategies to students with learning disabilities: A review of research. *Review of Educational Research, 71*(2), 279–320.

Gibbons, M. (2002). *The self-directed learning handbook: Challenging adolescents to excel.* San Francisco, CA: Jossey-Bass.

Gick, M. L. (1986). Problem-solving strategies. *Educational Psychologist, 21*(1,2), 99–120.

Gilberg, C. (2001). Epidemiology of early onset schizophrenia. In H. Remschmidt (Ed.), *Schizophrenia in children and adolescents* (pp. 43–59). New York: Cambridge University Press.

Gillespie, C. W., & Beisser, S. (2001). Developmentally appropriate LOGO computer programming with young children. *Information Technology in Childhood Education Annual,* 229–245.

Gilligan, C. (1979). Women's place in man's life cycle. *Harvard Educational Review, 49*(4), 431–446.

Gilligan, C. (1982). *In a different voice: Psychological theory and women's development.* Cambridge, MA: Harvard University Press.

Gilligan, C. (1987). Adolescent development reconsidered. In C. E. Irwin, Jr. (Ed.), *Adolescent social behavior and health.* San Francisco: Jossey-Bass.

Gilligan, C. (1988). Exit-voice dilemmas in adolescent development. In C. Gilligan, J. Ward, J. Taylor, & B. Bardige (Eds.), *Mapping the moral domain: A contribution of women's thinking to psychological theory and education.* Cambridge, MA: Harvard University Press.

Gilness, J. (2003). How to integrate character education into the curriculum. *Phi Delta Kappan, 85*(3), 243–245.

Ginott, H. (1965). *Between parent and child.* New York: Macmillan.

Ginott, H. (1972). *Teacher and child.* New York: Macmillan.

Ginott, H., G., Ginott, A., & Goddard, H. W. (2003). *Between parent and child* (Revised and updated). New York: Three Rivers Press.

Ginsburg, H. P., & Opper, S. (1988). *Piaget's theory of intellectual development* (3rd ed.). Englewood Cliffs, NJ: Prentice-Hall.

Ginsberg, M. B., & Wlodkowski, R. J. (2000). *Creating highly motivating classrooms for all students.* San Francisco: Jossey-Bass.

Gipson, J. (1997). Girls and computer technology: Barrier or key? *Educational Technology, 37*(2). 41–43.

Glasser, W. (1998). *The quality school: Managing students without coercion* (Rev. ed.). New York: HarperPerennial.

Glasser, W. (2001). *Choice theory in the classroom* (Rev. ed.). New York: Quill.

Goldberg, M. F. (2004). The test mess. *Phi Delta Kappan, 85*(5), 361–366.

Goldsby, D., & Fazal, M. (2001). Now that your students have created web-based digital portfolios, how do you evaluate them? *Journal of Technology and Teacher Education, 9*(4), 607–616.

Goldstein, A. P., & Conoley, J. C. (Eds.). (1997). *School violence intervention: A practical handbook.* New York: Guilford Press.

Gollnick, D. A., & Chinn, P. C. (2002). *Multicultural education in a pluralistic society* (6th ed.). Upper Saddle River, NJ: Merrill.

Golub, J. N. (1994). *Activities for the interactive classroom*. Urbana, IL: National Council of Teachers of English.

Gomez, L. M., Fishman, B. J., & Pea, R. D. (1998). *The CoVis project: Building a large scale science education testbed*. Interactive Learning Environments.

Gonzalez, V., Brusca-Vega, R., & Yawkey, T. (1997). *Assessment and instruction of culturally and linguistically diverse students with or at-risk of learning problems: From research to practice*. Boston: Allyn & Bacon.

Good, T. (1982). *Classroom research: What we know and what we need to know* (R&D Report No. 9018). Austin, TX: University of Texas, Research and Development Center for Teacher Education.

Good, T. L., & Brophy, J. (1995). *Contemporary educational psychology* (5th ed.). New York: Longman.

Good, T. L., & Nicholls, S. L. (2001). Expectancy effects in the classroom: A special focus on improving the reading performance of minority students in first-grade classrooms. *Educational Psychologist, 36*(2), 113–126.

Good, J. M., & Whang, P. A. (2002). Encouraging reflection in preservice teachers through response journals. *Teacher Educator, 37*(4), 254–267.

Goodlad, J. I. (1984). *A place called school*. New York: McGraw-Hill.

Gordon, P. R., Rogers, A. M., Comfort, M., Gavula, N., & McGee, B. P. (2001). A taste of problem-based learning increases achievement of urban minority middle-school students. *Educational Horizons, 79*(4, 171–175.

Gordon, S., & Gilgun, J. F. (1987). Adolescent sexuality. In V. B. van Hasselt & M. Hersen (Eds.), *Handbook of adolescent psychology*. New York: Pergamon Press.

Gordon, T. (1974). *TET: Teacher effectiveness training*. New York: McKay.

Gorski, P. C. (2001). *Multicultural education and the internet: Intersections and integrations*. New York: McGraw-Hill.

Goswami, U. (Ed.).(2002). *Blackwell handbook of childhood cognitive development*. Malden, MA: Blackwell.

Gottfried, A. E., Fleming, J. S., & Gottfried, A. W. (2001). Continuity of academic intrinsic motivation from childhood through late adolescence: A longitudinal study. *Journal of Educational Psychology, 93*(1), 3–13.

Gough, P. B. (1987). The key to improving schools: An interview with William Glasser. *Phi Delta Kappan, 69*(9), 656 662.

Gould, F. (2003). Testing third-graders in New Hampshire. *Phi Delta Kappan, 84*(7), 507–513.

Gould, M. S., & Kramer, R. A. (2001). Youth suicide prevention. *Suicide and Life-Threatening Behavior, 31*(1), 6–31.

Gould, S. J. (1981). *The mismeasure of man*. New York: Norton.

Grabe, M., & Grabe, C. (2004). *Integrating technology for meaningful learning* (4th ed.). Boston: Houghton Mifflin.

Graham, S., & Taylor, A. Z. (2002). Ethnicity, gender, and the development of achievement values. In A. Wigfield & J. S. Eccles (Eds.), *Development of achievement motivation* (pp. 121–146). San Diego, CA: Academic Press.

Graue, M. E., & DiPerna, J. (2000). Redshirting and early retention: Who gets the "gift of time" and what are its outcomes? *American Educational Research Journal, 37*(2), 509–534.

Greenberg, E. R., Canzoneri, C., & Joe, A. (2000). *2000 AMA survey on workplace testing: Basic skills, job skills, psychological measurement*. Retrieved January 2, 2002, from http://www.amanet.org/research/pdfs/psych.pdf.

Greenfield, R. (2003). Collaborative e-mail exchange for teaching secondary ESL: A case study in Hong Kong. *Language Learning and Technology, 7*(1), 46–70.

Greenwald, E. A., Persky, H. R., Campbell, J. R., & Mazzeo, J. (1999). *NAEP 1998 writing: Report card for the nation and the states*. Washington, DC: National Center for Educational Statistics. Retrieved January 2, 2002, from http://nces.ed.gov/pubsearch/pubsinfo.asp?pubid=1999462.

Gregory, G. H. (2003). *Differentiated instructional strategies in practice*. Thousand Oaks, CA: Corwin Press.

Gregory, G. H., & Chapman, C. (2002). *Differentiated instructional strategies: One size doesn't fit all*. Thousand Oaks, CA: Corwin Press.

Gresham, F. M., & MacMillan, D. L. (1997). Social competence and affective characteristics of students with mild disabilities. *Review of Educational Research, 67*(4), 377–415.

Griffin, H. C., Williams, S. C., Davis, M. L., & Engleman, M. (2002). Using technology to enhance cues for children with low vision. *Teaching Exceptional Children, 35*(2), 36–42.

Grigorenko, E. L., Jarvin, L., & Sternberg, R. J. (2002). School-based tests of the triarchic theory of intelligence: Three settings, three samples, three syllabi. *Contemporary Educational Psychology, 27*(2), 167–208.

Groeben, N. (1994). Humanistic models of human development. In T. Husen & T. N. Postlewhaite (Eds.), *International encyclopedia of education* (2nd ed., Vol. 5, pp. 2689–2692). New York: Pergamon.

Gronlund, N. E. (1959). *Sociometry in the classroom*. New York: Harper & Row.

Gronlund, N. E. (1998). *Assessment of student achievement* (6th ed.). Boston: Allyn & Bacon.

Gronlund, N. E. (2003). *Assessment of student achievement* (7th ed.). Boston: Allyn & Bacon.

Gronlund, N. E. (2004). *Writing instructional objectives for teaching and assessment* (7th ed.). Upper Saddle River, NJ: Merrill Prentice Hall.

Grossen, B. J. (2002). The BIG Accommodation model: The direct instruction model for secondary schools. *Journal of Education for Students Placed At Risk, 7*(2), 241–263.

Gruber, E., & Vonèche, J. J. (Eds.). (1977). *The essential Piaget: An interpretive reference and guide*. New York: Basic Books.

Guay, F., Marsh, H. W., & Boivin, M. (2003). Academic self-concept and academic achievement: Developmental perspectives on their causal ordering. *Journal of Educational Psychology, 95*(1), 124–136.

Guild P. (1994). The culture/learning style connection. *Educational Leadership, 51*(8), 16–21.

Gulek, C. (2003). Preparing for high-stakes testing. *Theory into Practice, 42*(1), 42–50.

Gunn, H., & Hepburn, G. (2003). Seeking information for school purposes on the internet. *Canadian Journal of Learning and Technology, 29*(1), 67–88.

Guralnick, M. J. (1986). The peer relations of young handicapped and nonhandicapped children. In P. S. Strain, M. J. Guralnick, & H. M. Walker (Eds.), *Children's social behavior Development, assessment, and modification*. Orlando, FL: Academic Press.

Gurian, M., & Henley, P. (2001). *Boys and girls learn differently!: A guide for teachers and parents*. San Francisco: Jossey-Bass.

Guskey, T. R. (2002). Computerized gradebooks and the myth of objectivity. *Phi Delta Kappan, 83*(10), 775–780.

Guskey, T. R. (2003). How classroom assessments improve learning. *Educational Leadership, 60*(5), 6–11.

Guskey, T. R., & Bailey, J. M. (2001). *Developing grading and reporting systems for student learning*. Thousand Oaks, CA: Corwin Press.

Gutek, G. L. (1992). *Education and schooling in America* (3rd ed.). Boston: Allyn & Bacon.

Gutiérrez, K. D., & Rogoff, B. (2003). Cultural ways of learning: Individual traits or repertories of practice. *Educational Researcher, 32*(5), 19–25.

Haag, L., & Stern, E. (2003). In search of the benefits of learning Latin. *Journal of Educational Psychology, 95*(1), 174–178.

Haberman, M., & Dill, V. (1993). The knowledge base on retention vs. teacher ideology: Implications for teacher preparation. *Journal of Teacher Education, 44*(5), 352–360.

Hacker, D. J., & Tenent, A. (2002). Implementing reciprocal teaching in the classroom: Overcoming obstacles and making modifications. *Journal of Educational Psychology, 94*(4), 699–718.

Hadwin, A. F., Winne, P. H., Stockley, D. B., Nesbit, J. C., & Woszczyna, C. (2001). Context moderates students' self-reports about how they study. *Journal of Educational Psychology, 93*(3), 477–487.

Haier, R. J. (2001). PET studies of learning and individual differences. In J. L. McClelland & R. S. Siegler (Eds.), *Mechanisms of cognitive development: Behavioral and neural perspectives* (pp. 123–145). Mahwah, NJ: Erlbaum.

Haladyna, T. (1999). *A complete guide to student grading.* Boston: Allyn & Bacon.

Haladyna, T. M. (2002). *Essentials of standardized achievement testing: Validity and accountability.* Boston: Allyn & Bacon.

Haladyna, T. M., Downing, S. M., & Rodriguez, M. C. (2002). A review of multiple-choice item-writing guidelines for classroom assessment. *Applied Measurement in Education, 15*(3), 309–334.

Hallfors, D., Vevea, J. L., Iritani, B., Cho, H., Khatapoush, S., & Saxe, L. (2002). Truancy, grade point average, and sexual activity: A meta-analysis of risk indicators for youth substance abuse. *Journal of School Health, 72*(5), 205–211.

Hallinan, M. T. (1994). Tracking: From theory to practice. *Sociology of Education, 67*(2), 79–91.

Halpern, D. F. (1997). Sex differences in intelligence: Implications for education. *American Psychologist, 52*(10), 1091–1102.

Halpern, D. F. (1998). Teaching critical thinking for transfer across domains. *American Psychologist, 53*(4), 449–455.

Halpern, D. F., & Ikier, S. (2002). Causes, correlates, and caveats: Understanding the development of sex differences in cognition. In A. McGillicuddy-De Lisi & R. De Lisi(Eds.), *Biology, society, and behavior: The development of sex differences in cognition* (pp. 3–19). Westport, CT: Ablex.

Halpern, D. F., & LaMay, M. L. (2000). The smarter sex: A critical review of sex differences in intelligence. *Educational Psychology Review, 12*(2), 229–246.

Hambrick, D. Z., & Engle, R. W. (2003). The role of working memory in problem solving. In J. E. Davidson & R. J. Sternberg (Eds.), *The psychology of problem solving* (pp. 176–205). Cambridge, ENGLAND: Cambridge University Press.

Hamilton, R., & Ghatala, E. (1994). *Learning and instruction.* New York: McGraw-Hill.

Hamman, D., Berthelot, J., Saia, J., & Crowley, E. (2000). Teachers' coaching of learning and its relation to students' strategic learning. *Journal of Educational Psychology, 92*(2), 342–348.

Haney, J. J., & McArthur, J. (2002). Four case studies of prospective science teachers beliefs concerning constructivist teaching practices. *Science Education, 86*(6), 783–802.

Hansgen, R. D. (1991). Can education become a science? *Phi Delta Kappan, 72*(9), 689–694.

Harackiewicz, J. M., Barron, K. E., Pintrich, P. R., Elliot, A. J., & Thrash, T. M. (2002). Revision of achievement goal theory: Necessary and illuminating. *Journal of Educational Psychology, 94*(3), 638–645.

Harding, C. G., & Snyder, K. (1991). Tom, Huck, and Oliver Stone as advocates in Kohlberg's just community: Theory-based strategies for moral-based education. *Adolescence, 26*(102), 319–330.

Hardy, C. L., Bukowski, W. M., & Sippola, L. K. (2002). Stability and change in peer relationships during the transition to middle-level school. *Journal of Early Adolescence, 22*(2), 117–142.

Hargreaves, A., Earl, L., & Schmidt, M. (2002). Perspectives on alternative assessment reform. *American Educational Research Journal, 39*(1), 69–95.

Harris, J. (1998). Curriculum-based telecollaboration. *Leading and Learning with Technology, 26*(1), 6–15.

Harter, S (1990). Self and identity development. In S. S. Feldman & G. R. Elliot (Eds.), *At the threshold: The developing adolescent* (pp. 352–387). Cambridge, MA: Harvard University Press.

Harter, S. (1999). *The construction of the self: A developmental perspective.* New York: Guilford.

Harter, S., Waters, P. L., & Whitesell, N. R., (1997). Lack of voice as a manifestation of false self-behavior among adolescents: The school setting as a stage upon which the drama of authenticity is enacted. *Educational Psychologist, 32*(3), 153–174.

Hartshorne, H., & May, M. A. (1929). *Studies in service and self-control.* New York: Macmillan.

Hartshorne, H., & May, M. A. (1930a). *Studies in deceit.* New York: Macmillan.

Hartshorne, H., & May, M. A. (1930b). *Studies in the organization of character.* New York: Macmillan.

Hartup, W. W. (1989). Social relationships and their developmental significance. *American Psychologist, 44*(2), 120–126.

Haskell, R. E. (2001). *Transfer of learning: Cognition, instruction, and reasoning.* San Diego, CA: Academic Press.

Hatch, T. (1997). Getting specific about multiple intelligences. *Educational Leadership, 54*(6), 26–29.

Hattie, J., Biggs, J., & Purdie, N. (1996). Effects of learning skills interventions on student learning: A meta-analysis. *Review of Educational Research, 66*(2), 99–136.

Haver, J. J. (2003). *Structured English immersion: A step-by-step guide for K–6 teachers and administrators.* Thousand Oaks, CA: Corwin Press.

Hay, K. E., & Barab, S. A. (2001). Constructivism in practice: A comparison and contrast of apprenticeship and constructionist learning environments. *The Journal of the Learning Sciences, 10*(3), 281–322.

Healy, L., & Hoyles, C. (2001). Software tools for geometrical problem solving: Potentials and pitfalls. *International Journal of Computers for Mathematical Learning, 6*(3), 235–256.

Heath, I. A. (1996). The social studies video project: A holistic approach for teaching linguistically and culturally diverse students. *The Social Studies, 87*(3), 106–112.

Heath, M. (2002). Electronic portfolios for reflective self-assessment. *Teacher Librarian, 30*(1), 19–23.

Hebert, E. A. (2001). *The power of portfolios.* San Francisco: Jossey-Bass.

Hecker, L., Burns, L., Elkind, J., Elkind, K., & Katz, L. (2002). Benefits of assistive reading software for students with attention disorders. *Annals of Dyslexia, 52,* 243–272.

Heidemann, S., & Hewitt, D. (1992). *Pathways to play.* St. Paul, MN: Redleaf Press.

Henderson, J. G. (Ed.).(2001). *Reflective teaching: Professional artistry through inquiry.* Upper Saddle River, NJ: Merrill Prentice Hall.

Herman, J. L., Gearhart, M., & Baker, E. L. (1993). Assessing writing portfolios: Issues in the validity and meaning of scores. *Educational Assessment, 1*(3), 201–224.

Herr, P. (2000). The changing role of the teacher: How management systems help facilitate teaching. *T.H.E. Journal, 28*(4), 28–34.

Hersh, R. H., Paolitto, D. P., & Reimer, J. (1979). *Promoting moral growth: From Piaget to Kohlberg.* New York: Longman.

Hetherington, E. M., & Parke, R. D. (1993). *Child psychology: A contemporary viewpoint* (4th ed.). New York: McGraw-Hill.

Heubert, J. P., & Hauser, R. M. (1999). *High stakes: Testing for tracking, promotion, and graduation.* Washington, DC: National Academy Press.

Heward, W. L. (2003). *Exceptional children: An introduction to special education* (7th ed.). Upper Saddle River, NJ: Merrill Prentice Hall.

Hewitt, J. (2002). From a focus on tasks to a focus on understanding: The cultural transformation of a Toronto classroom. In T. Koschmann, R. Hall, & N. Miyake (Eds.), *CSCL2: Carrying forward the conversation* (pp. 11–41). Mahwah, NJ: Erlbaum.

Hickey, D. T., Kindfield, A. C. H., Horwitz, P., & Christie, M. T. (2003). Integrating curriculum, instruction, assessment, and evaluation in a technology-supported genetics learning environment. *American Educational Research Journal, 40*(2), 495–538.

Hickey, D. T., Moore, A. L., & Pellegrino, J. W. (2001). The motivational and academic consequences of elementary mathematics environments: Do constructivist innovations and reforms make a difference? *American Educational Research Journal, 38*(3), 611–652.

Hidi, S. (2001). Interest, reading, and learning: Theoretical and practical considerations. *Educational Psychology Review, 13*(3), 191–209.

Hidi, S., & Ainley, M. (2002). Interest and adolescence. In F. Pajares & T. Urdan (Eds.),

Academic motivation of adolescents (pp. 247–275). Greenwich, CT: Information Age Publishing.

Hidi, S., & Harackiewicz, J. M. (2000). Motivating the academically unmotivated: A critical issue for the 21st century. *Review of Educational Research, 70*(2), 151–179.

Hiebert, J., Gallimore, R., & Stigler, J. W. (2002). A knowledge base for the teaching profession: What would it look like and how can we get one? *Educational Researcher, 31*(5), 3–15.

Higgins, J. W., Williams, R. L., & McLaughlin, T. F. (2001). The effects of a token economy employing instructional consequences for a third-grade student with learning disabilities: A case study. *Education and Treatment of Children, 24*(1), 99–106.

Hill, J. P. (1987). Research on adolescents and their families: Past and prospect. In C. E. Irwin, Jr. (Ed.), *Adolescent social behavior and health.* San Francisco: Jossey-Bass.

Hills, J. R. (1991). Apathy concerning grading and testing. *Phi Delta Kappan, 72*(7), 540–545.

Ho, B. (1995). Using lesson plans as a means of reflection. *ELT Journal, 49*(1), 66–70.

Hoegh, D. G., & Bourgeois, M. J. (2002). Prelude and postlude to the self: Correlates of achieved identity. *Youth & Society, 33*(4), 573–594.

Hoffer, T. B. (1992). Middle school ability grouping and student achievement in science and mathematics. *Educational Evaluation and Policy Analysis, 14*(3), 205–227.

Hoffman, J. L., Wu, H-K., Krajcik, J. S., & Soloway, E. (2003). The nature of middle school learners' science content understandings with the use of on-line resources. *Journal of Research in Science Teaching, 40*(3), 323–346.

Hoffman, M. L. (1980). Moral development in adolescence. In J. Adelson (Ed.), *Handbook of adolescent psychology.* New York: Wiley.

Hogan, K., & Pressley, M. (Eds.). (1997). *Scaffolding student learning: Instructional approaches and issues.* Cambridge, MA: Brookline Books.

Hoge, R. D., & Renzulli, J. S. (1993). Exploring the link between giftedness and self-concept. *Review of Educational Research, 63*(4), 449–465.

Holman, L. J. (1997). Meeting the needs of Hispanic immigrants. *Educational Leadership, 54*(7), 37–38.

Hood, S. (1998). Culturally responsive performance-based assessment: Conceptual and psychometric considerations. *Journal of Negro Education, 67*(3), 187–196.

Houston, W. R., & Williamson, J. L. (1992/1993). Perceptions of their preparation by 42 Texas elementary school teachers compared with their responses as student teachers. *Teacher Education and Practice, 8*(2), 27–42.

Howard, B. B., & McColskey, W. H. (2001). Evaluating experienced teachers. *Educational Leadership, 58*(5), 48–51.

Howard, B. C., McGee, S., Shin, N., & Shia, R. (2001). The triarchic theory of intelligence and computer-based inquiry learning. *Educational Technology Research and Development, 49*(4), 49–69.

Howe, C. K. (1994). Improving the achievement of Hispanic students. *Educational Leadership, 51*(8), 42–44.

Howe, N., Rinaldi, C. M., Jennings, M., & Petrakos, H. (2002). "No! the lambs can stay out because they got cozies": Constructive and destructive sibling conflict, pretend play, and social understanding. *Child Development, 73*(5), 1460–1473.

Hrabowski, F. A., III. (2002/2003). Raising minority achievement in science and math. *Educational Leadership, 60*(4), 44–48.

Hughes, F. P. (1999). *Children, play, and development* (3rd ed.). Boston: Allyn & Bacon.

Hughes, F. P., & Noppe, L. D. (1991). *Human development across the life span.* New York: Macmillan.

Hughes, J. E., Packard, B. W-L., & Pearson, P. D. (2000). The role of hypermedia cases on preservice teachers' views on reading instruction. *Action in Teacher Education, 22*(2A), 24–38.

Hung, D. (2001). Theories of learning and computer-mediated instructional technologies. *Education Media International, 38*(4), 281–287.

Hung, D. (2002). Situated cognition and problem-based learning: Implications for learning and instruction with technology. *Journal of Interactive Learning Research, 13*(4), 393–414.

Huppert, J., Lomask, S. M., & Lazarowitz, R. (2002). Computer simulations in high school: Students' cognitive stages, science process skills and academic achievement in microbiology. *International Journal of Science Education, 24*(8), 803–821.

Hurst, B., Wilson, C., & Cramer, G. (1998). Professional teaching portfolios: Tools for reflection, growth, and advancement. *Phi Delta Kappan, 79*(8), 578–582.

Huyvaert, S. (1995). *Reports from the classroom: Cases for reflection.* Boston: Allyn & Bacon.

Hyönä, J., Lorch, R. F., Jr., & Kaakinen, J. K. (2002). Individual differences in reading to summarize expository text: Evidence from eye fixations. *Journal of Educational Psychology, 94*(1), 44–55.

Individual with Disabilities Education Act Amendments of 1997 (1997, June). Retrieved September 15, 2003, from http://frwebgate.access.gpo.gov/cgi-bin/useftp.cgi?IPaddress=162.140.64.21&filename=publ17.105&directory=/diskc/wais/data/105_cong_public_laws.

International Society for Technology in Education. (2000). *National Educational Technology Standards for Students: Connecting Curriculum and Technology.* Eugene, OR: Author.

Irby, B. J., & Brown, G. (2000). *The career advancement portfolio.* Thousand Oaks, CA: Corwin Press.

Jackson, A. W., & Davis, G. A. (2000). *Turning points 2000: Educating adolescents in the 21st century.* New York: Teachers College Press.

Jackson, C. W., & Larkin, M. J. (2002). Rubric: Teaching students to use grading rubrics. *Teaching Exceptional Children, 35*(1), 40–45.

Jackson, D. B. (2003). Education reform as if student agency mattered: Academic microcultures and student identity. *Phi Delta Kappan, 84*(8), 579–585.

Jackson, J. F. (1999). What are the real risk factors for African American children? *Phi Delta Kappan, 81*(4), 308–312.

Jackson, S., & Bosma, H. (1990). Coping and self in adolescence. In H. Bosma & S. Jackson (Eds.), *Coping and self-concept in adolescence.* New York: Springer-Verlag.

Jacobs, G. M., Power, M. A., & Inn, L. W. (2002). *The teacher's sourcebook for cooperative learning.* Thousand Oaks, CA: Corwin Press.

James, W. (1899). *Talks to teachers on psychology: And to students on some of life's ideals.* New York: Holt.

Janesick, V. J. (2001). *The assessment debate: A reference handbook.* Santa Barbara, CA: ABC-CLIO.

Jensen, L. A., Arnett, J. J., Feldman, S. S., & Cauffman, E. (2002). It's wrong, but everybody does it: Academic dishonesty among high school and college students. *Contemporary Educational Psychology, 27*(2), 209–228.

Jeweler, S., & Barnes-Robinson, L. (1999). Curriculum from a conflict-resolution perspective. *Kappa Delta Pi Record, 35*(3), 112–114.

Jimerson, S. R. (2001). Meta-analysis of grade retention research: Implications for practice in the 21st century. *School Psychology Review, 30*(3), 420–437.

Jimerson, S. R., & Kaufman, A. M. (2003). Reading, writing, and retention: A primer on grade retention research. *The Reading Teacher, 56*(7), 622–635.

Jimerson, S. R., Anderson, G. E., & Whipple, A. D. (2002). Winning the battle and losing the war: Examining the relation between grade retention and dropping out of high school. *Psychology in the Schools, 39*(4), 441–457.

Jobe, D. A. (2002/2003). Helping girls succeed. *Educational Leadership, 60*(4), 64–66.

Johnson, J., Farkas, S., & Bers, A. (1997). *What American teenagers really think about their schools: A report from Public Agenda.* New York: Public Agenda.

Johnson, D. W., & Johnson, R. T. (1995). Cooperative learning and nonacademic outcomes of schooling: The other side of the report card. In J. E. Pedersen, & A. D. Digby (Eds.), *Secondary schools and cooperative learning* (pp. 81–150). New York: Garland Publishing.

Johnson, D. W., & Johnson, R. T. (1998). Cultural diversity and cooperative learning. In J. W. Putnam (Ed.), *Cooperative learning and strategies for inclusion* (2nd ed.). Baltimore, MD: Brookes Publishing.

Johnson, D. W., Johnson, R. T., & Holubec, E. J. (1994). *The new circles of learning: Cooperation in the classroom and school.* Alexandria, VA: Association for Supervision and Curriculum Development.

Johnson, D. W., Johnson, R. T., & Smith, K. A. (1995). Cooperative learning and individual student achievement in secondary schools. In J. E. Pedersen, & A. D. Digby (Eds.), *Secondary schools and cooperative learning* (pp. 3–54). New York: Garland Publishing.

Johnson, K. E. (2000). Constructive evaluations. *Science Teacher, 67*(2), 38–41.

Johnson, R. E. (1975). Meaning in complex learning. *Review of Educational Research, 45*(3), 425–460.

Joiner, J. L. (2002). A virtual tour of virtual schools. *American School Board Journal, 189*(9), 50–52.

Jonassen, D. H. (2000). *Computers as mindtools for schools: Engaging critical thinking* (2nd ed.). Upper Saddle River, NJ: Merrill Prentice Hall.

Jonassen, D. H., Howland, J., Moore, J., & Marra, R. M. (2003). *Learning to solve problems with technology: A constructivist perspective* (2nd ed.). Upper Saddle River, NJ: Merrill Prentice Hall.

Jones, A., & Selby, C. (1997). The use of computers for self-expression and communication. *Journal of Computing in Childhood Education, 8*(2/3), 199–214.

Jones, M. G., Jones, B. D., & Hargrove, T. Y. (2003). *The unintended consequences of high-stakes testing.* Lanham, MD: Rowman & Littlefield.

Joo, Y-j, Bong, M., & Choi, H-j. (2000). Self-efficacy for self-regulated learning, academic self-efficacy, and internet self-efficacy in web-based instruction. *Educational Technology Research and Development, 48*(2), 5–17.

Jorgenson, O. (2003). Brain scam? Why educators should be careful about embracing 'brain research.' *The Educational Forum, 67*(4), 364–369.

Jorgenson, O., & Vanosdall, R. (2002). The death of science? What we risk in our rush toward standardized testing and the three r's. *Phi Delta Kappan, 83*(8), 601–605.

Jovanovic, J., & King, S. S. (1998). Boys and girls in the performance-based science classroom: Who's doing the performing?

American Educational Research Journal, 35(3), 477–496.

Juvonen, J. (2000). The social functions of attributional face-saving tactics among early adolescents. *Educational Psychology Review, 12*(1), 15–32.

Joyce, B., & Weil, M. (with Calhoun, E.). (2000). *Models of teaching* (6th ed.). Boston: Allyn & Bacon.

Kagan, J. (1964a). *Developmental studies of reflection and analysis.* Cambridge, MA: Harvard University Press.

Kagan, J. (1964b). Impulsive and reflective children. In J. D. Krumboltz (Ed.), *Learning and the educational process.* Chicago: Rand McNally.

Kail, R. (1990). *The development of memory in children* (3rd ed.). San Francisco: Freeman.

Kail, R. V. (2001). *Children and their development* (2nd ed.). Upper Saddle River, NJ: Prentice Hall.

Kalbaugh, P., & Haviland, J. M. (1991). Formal operational thinking and identity. In R. M. Lerner, A. C. Peterson, & J. Brooks-Gunn (Eds.), *Encyclopedia of adolescence.* New York: Garland Publishing.

Kameenui, E. J., & Carnine, D. W. (2002). *Effective teaching strategies that accommodate diverse learners* (2nd ed.). Upper Saddle River, NJ: Merrill Prentice Hall.

Kamii, C. (2000). *Young children reinvent arithmetic: Implications of Piaget's theory* (2nd ed). New York: Teachers College Press.

Kaplan, E. B. (1999). "It's going good": Inner-city Black and Latino adolescents' perceptions about achieving an education. *Urban Education, 34*(2), 181–213.

Kaplan, J. S. (1998). *Beyond behavior modification: A cognitive-behavioral approach to behavior management in the school* (3rd ed.). Austin, TX: Pro-Ed.

Karchmer, R. A. (2001). The journey ahead: Thirteen teachers report how the internet influences literacy and literacy instruction in their K–12 classrooms. *Reading Research Quarterly, 36*(4), 442–466.

Karniol, R., Gabay, R., Ochion, Y., & Harari, Y. (1998). Is gender or gender-role orientation a better predictor of empahthy in adolescence? *Sex Roles, 39*(1–2), 45–59.

Karpov, Y. V., & Bransford, J. D. (1995). L. S. Vygotsky and the doctrine of empirical and theoretical learning. *Educational Psychologist, 30*(2), 61–66.

Karpov, Y. V., & Haywood, H. C. (1998). Two ways to elaborate Vygotsky's concept of mediation. *American Psychologist, 53*(1), 27–36.

Katayama, A. D., & Robinson, D. H. (2000). Getting students "partially" involved in note-taking using graphic organizers. *The Journal of Experimental Education, 68*(2), 119–133.

Katz, L. G., & Chard, S. C. (2000). *Engaging children's minds: The project approach* (2nd ed.). Stamford, CT: Ablex Publishing.

Kauffman, J. M. (2001). *Characteristics of emotional and behavioral disorders of children and youth* (7th ed.). Upper Saddle River, NJ: Merrill Prentice Hall.

Kavale, K. A. (2002). Mainstreaming to full inclusion: From orthogenesis to pathogenesis of an idea. *International Journal of Disability, Development and Education, 49*(2), 201–214.

Keane, G., & Shaughnessy, M. F. (2002). An interview with Robert J. Sternberg: The current "state of the art." *Educational Psychology Review, 14*(3), 313–330.

Keeler, C. M. (1996). Networked instructional computers in the elementary classroom and their effect on the learning environment: A qualitative evaluation. *Journal of Research on Computing in Education, 28*(3), 329–345.

Kehle, T. J., Bray, M. A., Theodore, L. A., Jenson, W. R., & Clark, E. (2000). A multicomponent intervention designed to reduce disruptive classroom behavior. *Psychology in the Schools, 37*(5), 475–481.

Kelley, M. L., & Carper, L. B. (1988). Home-based reinforcement procedures. In J. C. Witt, S. N. Elliott, & F. M. Gresham (Eds.), *Handbook of behavior therapy in education.* New York: Plenum Press.

Kelly, M., & Moag-Stahlberg, A. (2002). Battling the obesity epidemic. *Principal, 81*(5), 26–29.

Kentucky Department of Education (2004). *Commonwealth accountability testing system.* Retrieved from http://www.education.ky.gov/KDE/Administrative+Resources/Testing+and+Reporting+/CATS/default.htm.

Kernis, M. H. (2002). Self-esteem as a multifaceted construct. In T. M. Brinthaupt & R. P. Lipka (Eds.), *Understanding early adolescent self and identity: Applications and interventions* (pp. 57–87). Albany, NY: State University of New York Press.

Kerr, M. M., & Nelson, C. M. (2002). *Strategies for addressing behavior problems in the classroom* (4th ed.). Upper Saddle River, NJ: Merrill Prentice Hall.

Ketterlinus, R. D., & Lamb, M. E. (1994). *Adolescent problem behaviors: Issues and research.* Hillsdale, NJ: Erlbaum.

Kiewra, K. A., & DuBois, N. F. (1998). *Learning to learn: Making the transition from student to life-long learner.* Boston: Allyn & Bacon.

Kinard, B., & Bitter, G. G. (1997). Multicultural mathematics and technology: The hispanic math project. *Using Technology in the Classroom, 13*(2), 77–88.

King, A. (1992a). Comparison of self-questioning, summarizing, and notetaking-review as strategies for learning from lectures. *American Educational Research Journal, 29*(2), 303–323.

King, A. (1992b). Facilitating elaborative learning through guided student-generated questioning. *Educational Psychologist, 27*(1), 111–126.

King, A. (1994). Guiding knowledge construction in the classroom: Effects of teaching children how to question and how to explain. *American Educational Research Journal, 31*(2), 338–368.

King, A. (1998). Transactive peer tutoring: Distributing cognition and metacognition. *Educational Psychology Review, 10*(1), 57–74.

King, A. (2002). Structuring peer interaction to promote high-level cognitive processing. *Theory into Practice, 41*(1), 33–39.

Kirk, S. A., Gallagher, J. J., & Anastasiow, N. J. (2003). *Educating exceptional children* (10th ed.). Boston: Houghton Mifflin.

Kirschenbaum, H., & Simon, S. B. (Eds.). (1973). *Readings in values clarification.* Minneapolis: Winston.

Kitsantas, A. (2002). Test preparation and performance: A self-regulatory analysis. *Journal of Experimental Education, 70*(2), 101–113.

Klassen, R. (2002). Writing in early adolescence: A review of the role of self-efficacy beliefs. *Educational Psychology Review, 14*(2), 173–203.

Klauer, K. (1984). Intentional and incidental learning with instructional texts: A meta-analysis for 1970–1980. *American Educational Research Journal, 21*(2), 323–339.

Knapp, M. S., & Shields, P. M. (1990). Reconceiving academic instruction for the children of poverty. *Phi Delta Kappan, 71*(10), 753–758.

Knapp, M. S., Shields, P. M., & Turnbull, B. J. (1995). Academic challenge in high-poverty classrooms. *Phi Delta Kappan, 76*(10), 770–776.

Koch, M. (1994). No girls allowed. *Technos, 3*(3), 14–19.

Kohlberg, L. (1963). The development of children's orientations toward a moral order: 1. Sequence in the development of moral thought. *Vita Humana, 6*(1–2), 11–33.

Kohlberg, L. (1969). Stage and sequence: The cognitive-developmental approach to socialization. In D. A. Goslin (Ed.), *Handbook of socialization theory and research.* Chicago: Rand McNally.

Kohlberg, L. (1976). Moral stages and moralization: The cognitive-developmental approach. In T. Lickona (Ed.), *Moral development and behavior: Theory, research, and social issues.* New York: Holt, Rinehart & Winston.

Kohlberg, L. (1978). Revisions in the theory and practice of moral development. In W. Damon (Ed.), *New directions for child development: Moral development* (No. 2). San Francisco: Jossey-Bass.

Kohn, A. (1993). Rewards versus learning: A response to Paul Chance. *Phi Delta Kappan, 74*(10), 783–787.

Kohn, A. (1999). *Punished by rewards: The trouble with gold stars, incentive plans, A's, praise, and other bribes.* Boston: Houghton Mifflin.

Kontos, G., & Mizell, A. P. (1997). Global village classroom: The changing roles of teachers and students through technology. *TechTrends, 42*(5), 17–22.

Kordaki, M., & Potari, D. (2002). The effect of area measurement tools on student strategies: The role of a computer microworld. *International Journal of Computers for Mathematical Learning, 7*(1), 65–100.

Kosunen, T., & Mikkola, A. (2002). Building a science of teaching: How objectives and reality meet in Finnish teacher education. *European Journal of Teacher Education, 25*(2/3), 135–150.

Kounin, J. S. (1970). *Discipline and group management in classrooms.* New York: Holt, Rinehart & Winston.

Kozma, R. B. (1987). The implications of cognitive psychology for computer-based learning tools. *Educational Technology, 27*(11), 20–25.

Kozma, R. B. (1991). Learning with media. *Review of Educational Research, 61*(2), 179–211.

Kozulin, A., & Presseisen, B. Z. (1995). Mediated learning experience and psychological tools: Vygotsky's and Feuerstein's perspectives in a study of student learning. *Educational Psychologist, 30*(2), 57–75.

Kramarski, B., & Zeichner, O. (2001). Using technology to enhance mathematical reasoning: Effects of feedback and self-regulation learning. *Educational Media International, 38*(2/3), 77–82.

Krashen, S. (1999). What the research really says about structured English immersion: A reply to Keith Baker. *Phi Delta Kappan, 80*(9), 705–706.

Krathwohl, D. R., Bloom, B. S., & Masia, B. B. (1964). *Taxonomy of educational objectives. Handbook II: Affective domain.* New York: McKay.

Kroger, J. (1996). *Identity and adolescence: The balance between self and other* (2nd ed.). New York: Routledge.

Krulik, S., & Rudnick, J. A. (1993). *Reasoning and problem solving: A handbook for elementary school teachers.* Boston: Allyn & Bacon.

Kubiszyn, T., & Borich, G. (2003). *Educational testing and measurement: Classroom application and practice* (7th ed.). New York: Wiley.

Kuhn, D. (1997). Constraints or guideposts? Developmental psychology and science education. *Review of Educational Research, 67*(1), 141–150.

Kuhn, D. (1999). A developmental model of critical thinking. *Educational Researcher, 28*(2), 16–26, 46.

Kulik, J. A. (2003). Grouping and tracking. In N. Colangelo & G. A. Davis (Eds.), *Handbook of gifted education* (3rd ed., pp. 268–281). Boston: Allyn & Bacon.

Kulik, J. A., & Kulik, C.-L. C. (1991). Ability grouping and gifted students. In N. Colangelo & G. A. Davis (Eds.), *Handbook of gifted education.* Boston: Allyn & Bacon.

Kulik, C.-L., Kulik, J. A., & Bangert-Drowns, R. L. (1990). Effectiveness of mastery learning programs. *Review of Educational Research, 60*(2), 265–299.

Kyllonen, P. C. (1996). Is working memory capacity Spearman's g? In I. Dennis & P. Tapsfield (Eds.), *Human abilities: Their nature and measurement.* Mahwah, NJ: Erlbaum.

LaBoskey, V. K. (2000). Portfolios here, portfolios there . . . Searching for the essence of "educational portfolios." *Phi Delta Kappan, 81*(8), 590–595.

Lach, C., Little, E., & Nazzaro, D. (2003). From all sides now: Weaving technology and multiple intelligences into science and art. *Learning and Leading with Technology, 30*(6), 32–35, 59.

Laczko-Kerr, I., & Berliner, D. C. (2003). In harm's way: How undercertified teachers hurt their students. *Educational Leadership, 60*(8), 34–39.

Ladson-Billings, G. (1994). What we can learn from multicultural education research. *Educational Leadership, 51*(8), 22–26.

Ladson-Billings, G. (2002). But that's just good teaching! The case for culturally relevant pedagogy. In S. J. Denbo & L. M. Beaulieu (Eds.), *Improving schools for African American students* (pp. 95–102). Springfield, IL: Charles C. Thomas.

Lam, S., Yim, P., & Lam, T. W. (2002). Transforming school culture: Can true collaboration be inititated? *Educational Research, 44*(2), 181–195.

Lambros, A. (2002). *Problem-based learning in K–8 classrooms: A teacher's guide to implementation.* Thousand Oaks, CA: Corwin Press.

Lancey, D. F. (2002). Cultural constraints on children's play. In J. L. Roopnarine (Ed.), *Conceptual, social-cognitive, and contextual issues in the fields of play* (pp. 53–60). Westport, CT: Ablex.

Landau, B. M., & Gathercoal, P. (2000). Creating peaceful classrooms: Judicious Discipline and class meetings. *Phi Delta Kappan, 81*(6), 450–452, 454.

Lantieri, L. (1995). Waging peace in our schools: Beginning with the children. *Phi Delta Kappan, 76*(5), 386–388.

Lantieri, L. (1999). Hooked on altruism: Developing social responsibility in at-risk youth. *Reclaiming Children and Youth, 8*(2), 83–87.

Latu, E., & Chapman, E. (2002). Computerised adaptive testing. *British Journal of Educational Technology, 33*(5), 619–622.

Lazear, D. G. (1992). *Teaching for multiple intelligences.* Bloomington, IN: Phi Delta Kappa Educational Foundation.

Leadbeater, B. (1991). Relativistic thinking in adolescence. In R. M. Lerner, A. C. Peterson & J. Brooks-Gunn (Eds.), *Encyclopedia of adolescence*. New York: Garland Publishing.

Leaver, B. L. (1998). *Teaching the whole class* (5th ed.). Dubuque, IA: Kendall/Hunt.

Lee, C. D. (1998). Culturally responsive pedagogy and performance-based assessment. *Journal of Negro Education, 67*(3), 268–279.

Lee. J. (1999). Effectiveness of computer-based instructional simulation: A meta-analysis. *International Journal of Instructional Media, 26*(1), 71–85.

Lee, J. (2002). Racial and ethnic achievement gap trends: Reversing the progress toward equity? *Educational Researcher, 31*(1), 3–12.

Lefrançois, G. R. (2001). *Of children: An introduction to child and adolescent development* (9th ed.). Belmont, CA: Wadsworth/ Thomson Learning.

Lehrer, R. (1993). Authors of knowledge: Patterns of hypermedia design. In S. Lajoie & S. Derry (Eds.), *Computers as cognitive tools* (pp. 197–227). Hillsdale, NJ: Erlbaum.

Lehrer, R., Lee, M., & Jeong, A. (1999). Reflective teaching of LOGO. *Journal of the Learning Sciences, 8*(2), 245–289.

LeLoup, J., & Ponterio, R. (2003). Tele-collaborative projects: Monsters.com? *Language Learning and Technology, 7*(2), 6–11.

Leming, J. S. (1993). In search of effective character education. *Educational Leadership, 51*(3), 63–71.

Lerner, J. W. (2003). *Learning disabilities: Theories, diagnosis, and teaching strategies* (9th ed.). Boston: Houghton Mifflin.

Lessow-Hurley, J. (2000). *The foundations of dual langauage instruction*. New York: Longman.

Levin, J., & Nolan, J. F. (2004). *Principles of classroom management: A professional decision-making model* (4th ed.). Boston: Allyn & Bacon.

Levin, J. R. (1982). Pictures as prose-learning devices. In A. Flammer & W. Kintsch (Eds.), *Advances in psychology: Vol. 8. Discourse processing*. Amsterdam: North-Holland.

Levin, J. R. (1993). Mnemonic strategies and classroom learning: A 20-year report card. *Elementary School Journal, 94*(2), 235–244.

Levine, D. U., & Levine, R. F. (1996). *Society and education* (9th ed.). Boston: Allyn & Bacon.

Lewis, L., Parsad, B., Carey, N., Bartafi, N., Farris, E., & Smerdon, B. (1999, January). *Teacher quality: A report on the preparation and qualifications of public school teachers*. U.S. Department of Education, National Center for Education Statistics. Retrieved January 2, 2002, from http://nces.ed.gov/ pubsearch/pubsinfo.asp?pubid=1999080.

Ley, K., & Young, D. B. (2001). Instructional principles for self-regulation. *Educational Technology Research and Development, 49*(2), 93–103.

Leyser, Y., Frankiewicz, L. E., & Vaughn, R. (1992). Problems faced by first-year teachers: A survey of regular and special educators. *Teacher Educator, 28*(1), 36–45.

Li, J. (2002). Learning models in different cultures. In J. Bempechat & J. G. Elliott (Eds.), *Learning in culture and context: Vol. 96. New directions for child and adolescent development* (pp. 45–63). San Francisco: Jossey-Bass.

Liben, L. S., Bigler, R. S., & Krogh, H. R. (2002). Language at work: Children's gendered interpretations of occupational titles. *Child Development, 73*(3), 810–828.

Lickona, T. (1976). Research on Piaget's theory of moral development. In T. Lickona (Ed.), *Moral development and behavior: Theory, research, and social issues*. New York: Holt, Rinehart & Winston.

Lickona, T. (1998). A more complex analysis is needed. *Phi Delta Kappan, 79*(6), 449–454.

Light, P., & Littleton, K. (1999). *Social processes in children's learning*. Cambridge, England: Cambridge University Press.

Lindberg, J. A., & Swick, A. (2002). *Common-sense classroom management*. Thousand Oaks, CA: Corwin Press.

Linderholm, T., & van den Broek, P. (2002). The effects of reading purpose and working memory capacity on the processing of expository text. *Journal of Educational Psychology, 94*(4), 778–784.

Linn, M C. (1992). Science education reform: Building on the research base. *Journal of Research in Science Teaching, 29*(8), 821–840.

Linn, M. C., Lewis, C., Tsuchida, I., & Songer, N. B. (2000). Beyond fourth-grade science: Why do U.S. and Japanese students diverge? *Educational Researcher, 29*(3), 4–14.

Linn, M. C., & Slotta, J. D. (2000). WISE science. *Educational Leadership, 58*(2), 29–32.

Linn, R. L. (2000). Assessments and accountability. *Educational Researcher, 29*(2), 4–16.

Linn, R. L. (2003). Accountability: Responsibility and reasonable expectations. *Educational Researcher, 32*(7), 3–13.

Linn, R. L., Baker, E. L., & Betebenner, D. W. (2002). Accountability systems: Implications of requirements of the No Child Left Behind Act of 2001. *Educational Researcher, 31*(6), 3–16.

Linn, R. L., & Gronlund, N. E. (2000). *Measurement and assessment in teaching* (8th ed.). Upper Saddle River, NJ: Merrill.

Liu, M. (1994). Hypermedia assisted instruction and second language learning: A semantic-network-based approach. *Computers in the Schools, 10*(3/4); 293–312.

Livson, N., & Peskin, H. (1980). Perspectives on adolescence from longitudinal research. In J. Adelson (Ed.), *Handbook of adolescent psychology*. New York: Wiley.

Llabo, L. D. (2002). Computers, kids, and comprehension: Instructional practices that make a difference. In C. C. Block,

L. B. Gambrell, & M. Pressley (Eds.), *Improving comprehension instruction: Rethinking research, theory, and classroom practice* (pp. 275–289). San Francisco: Jossey-Bass.

Lloyd, L. (1999). Multi-age classes and high ability students. *Review of Educational Research, 69*(2), 187–212.

Lockwood, A. (1978). The effects of values clarification and moral development curricula on school age subjects: A critical review of recent research. *Review of Educational Research, 48*(3), 325–364.

Lonoff, S. (1997). Using videotape to talk about teaching. *ADE Bulletin, 118*, 10–14.

Lopata, C., Miller, K. A., & Miller, R. H. (2003). Survey of actual and preferred use of cooperative learning among exemplar teachers. *Journal of Educational Research, 96*(4), 232–239.

Lorayne, H., & Lucas, J. (1974). *The memory book*. New York: Ballantine Books.

Losey, K. M. (1995). Mexican American students and classroom interaction: An overview and critique. *Review of Educational Research, 65*(3), 283–318.

Lou, Y., Abrami, P. C., & d'Apollonia, S. (2001). Small group learning and individual learning with technology: A meta-analysis. *Review of Educational Research, 71*(3), 499–521.

Lou, Y., Abrami, P. C., & Spence, J. C. (2000). Effects of within-class grouping on student achievement: An exploratory model. *Journal of Educational Research, 94*(2), 101–112.

Loveless, T. (1998). The tracking and ability grouping debate. *Fordham Report, 2*(8). Retrieved January 2, 2002, from http:// www.edexcellence.net/library/track.html.

Loveless, T. (1999). Will tracking reform promote social equity? *Educational Leadership, 56*(7), 28–32.

Lowry, R., Sleet, D., Duncan, C., Powell, K, & Kolbe, L. (1995). Adolescents at risk for violence. *Educational Psychology Review, 7*(1), 7–39.

Lundeberg, M. A., & Fox, P. W. (1991). Do laboratory findings on test expectancy generalize to classroom outcomes? *Review of Educational Research, 61*(1), 94–106.

Luria, A. R. (1968). *The mind of a mnemonist: A little book about a vast memory*. New York: Ballantine Books.

Lynch, J. P. (2002, October). Trends in juvenile violent offending: An analysis of victim survey data. *Juvenile Justice Bulletin*. Retrieved December 3, 2003, from www .ojjdp.ncjrs.org/pubs/delinq.html#191052

Lyons, N. (1999). How portfolios can shape emerging practice. *Educational Leadership, 56*(8), 63–65.

Maag, J. W. (2001). Rewarded by punishment: Reflections on the disuse of positive reinforcement in schools. *Exceptional children, 67*(2), 173–186.

Mabry, L. (1999). Writing to the rubric: Lingering effects of traditional standardized testing on direct writing assessment. *Phi Delta Kappan, 80*(9), 673–679.

MacArthur, C. (1994). Peers + word processing + strategies = a powerful combination for revising student writing. *Teaching Exceptional Children, 27*(1), 24–29.

MacArthur, C. A. (1996). Using technology to enhance the writing processes of students with learning disabilities. *Journal of Learning Disabilities, 29*(4), 344–354.

MacArthur, C. A. (1998a). Word processing with speech synthesis and word prediction: Effects on the dialogue journal writing of students with learning disabilities. *Learning Disability Quarterly, 21*(2), 151–166.

MacArthur, C. A. (1998b). From illegible to understandable: How word prediction and speech synthesis can help. *Teaching Exceptional Children, 30*(6), 66–71.

Maccini, P., Gagnon, J. C., & Hughes, C. A. (2002). Technology-based practices for secondary students with learning disabilities. *Learning Disability Quarterly, 25*(4), 247–261.

Macedo, D. (2000). The illiteracy of English-only literacy. *Educational Leadership, 57*(4), 62–67.

MacKay, A. P., Fingerhut, L. A., & Duran, C. R. (2000). *Health, United States, 2000. Adolescent health chartbook.* Hyattsville, MD: National Center for Health Statistics. Retrieved January 2, 2002, from http://www.cdc.gov/nchs/data/hus/hus00cht.pdf.

Mackay, S., McLaughlin, T. F., Weber, K., & Derby, K. M. (2001). The use of precision requests to decrease noncompliance in the home and neighborhood: A case study. *Child and Family Behavior Therapy, 23*(2), 43–52.

MacKinnon, J. L., & Marcia, J. E. (2002). Concurring patterns of women's identity status, attachment styles, and understanding of children's development. *International Journal of Behavioral Development, 26*(1), 70–80.

MacMillan, D. L., Gresham, F. M., & Forness, S. R. (1996). Full inclusion: An empirical perspective. *Behavioral Disorders, 21*(2), 145–159.

Mager, R. F. (1962). *Preparing instructional objectives.* Palo Alto, CA: Fearon.

Mager, R. F. (1997). *Preparing instructional objectives* (3rd ed.). Atlanta, GA: The Center for Effective Performance.

Maher, F. A., & Ward, J. V. (2002). *Gender and teaching.* Mahwah, NJ: Erlbaum.

Maker, C. J., & Nielson, A. B. (1996). *Curriculum development and teaching strategies for gifted learners* (2nd ed.). Austin, TX: Pro-Ed.

MaKinster, J. G., Beghetto, R. A., & Plucker, J. A. (2002). Why can't I find Newton's third law? Case studies of students' use of the web as a science resource. *Journal of Science Education and Technology, 11*(2), 155–172.

Maloch, B., Fine, J., & Flint, A. S. (2002/2003). Trends in teacher certification and literacy. *Reading Teacher, 56*(4), 348–350.

Manzo, K. K. (2003, November 15). Arts, foreign languages getting edged out. *Education Week, 23*(10), 3.

Marchand-Martella, N. E., Slocum, T. A. & Marchand, R. C. (2004). *Introduction to direct instruction.* Boston: Allyn & Bacon.

Marcia, J. E. (1966). Development and validation of ego identity status. *Journal of Personality and Social Psychology, 3*(5), 551–558.

Marcia, J. E. (1967). Ego identity status: Relationship to change in self-esteem, "general adjustment," and authoritarianism. *Journal of Personality, 35*(1), 119–133.

Marcia, J. E. (1980). Identity in adolescence. In J. Adelson (Ed.), *Handbook of adolescent psychology.* New York: Wiley.

Marcia, J. E. (1991). Identity and self-development. In R. M. Lerner, A. C. Peterson, & J. Brooks-Gunn (Eds.), *Encyclopedia of adolescence.* New York: Garland Publishing.

Marcia, J. E. (1999). Representational thought in ego identity, psychotherapy, and psychosocial developmental theory. In I. E. Sigel (Ed.), *Development of mental representation: theories and application* (pp. 391–414). Mahwah, NJ: Erlbaum.

Marcia, J. E. (2001). A commentary on Seth Schwartz's review of identity theory and research. *Identity, 1*(1), 59–65.

Marlow, B. A., & Page, M. L. (1998). *Creating and sustaining the constructivist classroom.* Thousand Oaks, CA: Corwin Press.

Marr, P. M. (2000). Grouping students at the computer to enhance the study of British literature. *English Journal, 90*(2), 120–125.

Marsh, H. W., & Craven, R. G. (2002). The pivotal role of frames of reference in academic self-concept formation: The "big fish-little pond" effect. In F. Pajares & T. Urdan (Eds.), *Academic motivation of adolescents* (pp. 83–123). Greenwich, CT: Information Age Publishing.

Marsh, H. W., & Hattie, J. (1996). Theoretical perspectives on the structure of self-concept. In B. A. Bracken (Ed.), *Handbook of self-concept* (pp. 38–90). New York: Wiley.

Marsh, R. S., & Raywid, M. A. (1994). How to make detracking work. *Phi Delta Kappan, 76*(4), 314–317.

Marsh, H. W., & Yeung, A. S. (1998). Longitudinal structural equation models of academic self-concept and achievement: Gender differences in the development of math and English constructs. *American Educational Research Journal, 35*(4), 705–738.

Martin, G., & Pear, J. (2003). *Behavior modification: What it is and how to do it* (7th ed.). Upper Saddle River, NJ: Prentice Hall.

Martin, K. A. (1996). *Puberty, sexuality, and the self: Boys and girls at adolescence.* New York: Routledge.

Martinez, M. E. (1998). What is problem solving? *Phi Delta Kappan, 79*(8), 605–609.

Martinez, M. E. (1999). Cognition and the question of test item format. *Educational Psychologist, 34*(1), 207–218.

Marx, R. W., Blumenfeld, P. C., Krajcik, J. S., & Soloway, E. (1997). Enacting project-based science. *The Elementary School Journal, 97*(4), 341–358.

Marx, R. W., & Winne, P. H. (1987). The best tool teachers have—their students' thinking. In D. C. Berliner & B. V. Rosenshine (Eds.), *Talks to teachers.* New York: Random House.

Marzano, R. J. (2000). *Transforming classroom grading.* Alexandria, VA: Association for Supervision and Curriculum Development.

Marzano, R. J. (2001). *Designing a new taxonomy of educational objectives.* Thousand Oaks, CA: Corwin Press.

Marzano, R. J., Pickering, D. J., & Pollock, J. E. (2001). *Classroom instruction that works: Research-based strategies for increasing student achievement.* Alexandria, VA: Association for Supervision and Curriculum Development.

Maslin, J. E., & Nelson, M. E. (2002). Peering into the future: Students using technology to create literacy products. *Reading Teacher, 55*(7), 628–631.

Maslow, A. H. (1943). A theory of human motivation. *Psychological Review, 50*(4), 370 396.

Maslow, A. H. (1968). *Toward a psychology of being* (2nd ed.). Princeton, NJ: Van Nostrand.

Maslow, A. H. (1987). *Motivation and personality* (3rd ed.). New York: Harper & Row.

Mastropieri, M. A., Sweda, J., & Scruggs, T. E. (2000). Putting mnemonic strategies to work in an inclusive classroom. *Learning Disabilities Research and Practice, 15*(2), 69–74.

Mathes, L. (2002). Theme and variation: The Crosshatch portrait. *Arts & Activities, 131*(2), 32–33, 70,74.

Matthew, K. I. (1996). The impact of CD-ROM storybooks on children's reading comprehension and reading attitude. *Journal of Educational Multimedia and Hypermedia, 5*(3/4), 379–394.

Matthews, C. E., Binkley, W., Crisp, A., & Gregg, K. (1998). Challenging gender bias in fifth grade. *Educational Leadership, 55*(4), 54–57.

Matthews, M. R. (2002). Constructivism and science education: A further appraisal. *Journal of Science Education and Technology, 11*(2), 121–134.

Mayer, R. E. (1987). Learnable aspects of problem solving: Some examples. In D. E. Berger, K. Pezdek, & W. P. Banks (Eds.), *Applications of cognitive psychology: Problem solving, education, and computing.* Hillsdale, NJ: Erlbaum.

Mayer, R. E. (2001). *Multimedia learning.* Cambridge, England: Cambridge University Press.

Mayer, R. E., Mautone, P., & Prothero, W. (2002). Pictorial aids for learning by doing in a multimedia geology simulation game. *Journal of Educational Psychology, 94*(1), 171–185.

Mayer, R. E., & Moreno, R. (2002). Animation as an aid to multimedia learning. *Educational Psychology Review, 14*(1), 87–99.

Mazyck, M. (2002). Integrated learning systems and students of color: Two decades of use in K–12 education. *TechTrends, 46*(2), 33–39.

McCaslin, M., & Good, T. L. (1992). Compliant cognition: The misalliance of management and instructional goals in current school reform. *Educational Researcher, 21*(3), 4–17.

McCaslin, M., & Hickey, D. T. (2001). Self-regulated learning and academic achievement: A Vygotskyian view, In B. J. Zimmerman & D. H. Schunk (Eds.), *Self-regulated learning and academic achievement: Theoretical perspectives* (pp. 227–252). Mahwah, NJ: Erlbaum.

McConnell, S. R., & Odom, S. L. (1986). Sociometrics: Peer-referenced measures and the assessment of social competence. In P. S. Strain, M. J. Guralnick, & H. M. Walker (Eds.), *Children's social behavior: Development, assessment, and modification.* Orlando, FL: Academic Press.

McDevitt, T. M., & Ormrod, J. E. (2002). *Child development and education.* Upper Saddle River, NJ: Merrill Prentice Hall.

McEntee, G. H., Appleby, J., Dowd, J., Grant, J., Hole, S., & Silva, P. (2003). *At the heart of teaching: A guide to reflective practice.* New York: Teachers College Press.

McGrath, D. (2003). Rubrics, portfolios, and tests, oh my! *Learning and Leading with Technology, 30*(8), 42–45,

McIntire, T. (2002). Assessment on the fly. *Technology & Learning, 23*(4), 30, 32.

McKenna, M. C., Cowart, E., & Watkins, J. (1997, December). *Effects of talking books on the growth of struggling readers in second grade.* Paper presented at the meeting of the National Reading Conference, Scottsdale, AZ.

McKenzie, W. (2002). *Multiple intelligences and instructional technology: A manual for every mind.* Eugene, OR: International Society for Technology in Education.

McLeskey, J., & Waldron, N. L. (2002). School change and inclusive schools: Lessons learned from practice. *Phi Delta Kappan, 84*(1), 65–72.

McLoyd, V. C. (1998). Socioeconomic disadvantage and child development. *American Psychologist, 53*(2), 185–204.

McMillan, J. H., Myran, S., & Workman, D. (2002). Elementary teachers' classroom assessment and grading practices. *Journal of Educational Research, 95*(4), 203–213.

McNally, L., & Etchison, C. (2000). Streamlining classroom management. *Learning and Leading with Technology, 28*(2), 6–9, 12.

McTighe, J. (1996/1997). What happens between assessments? *Educational Leadership, 54*(4), 6–12.

McTighe, J., & Ferrara, S. (1998). *Assessing learning in the classroom.* Washington, DC: National Education Association.

McVarish, J., & Solloway, S. (2002). Self-evaluation: Creating a classroom without unhealthy competitiveness. *Educational Forum, 66*(3), 253–260.

Means, B., & Haertel, G. (2002). Technology supports for assessing science inquiry. In National Research Council (Ed.), *Technology and assessment: Thinking ahead* (pp. 12–25). Washington, DC: National Academy Press.

Means, B., & Knapp, M. S. (1991). Introduction: Rethinking teaching for disadvantaged students. In B. Means, C. Chelemer, & M. S. Knapp (Eds.), *Teaching advanced skills to at-risk students.* San Francisco: Jossey-Bass.

Meier, N. (1999). A fabric of half-truths: A response to Keith Baker on structured English immersion. *Phi Delta Kappan, 80*(9), 704, 706.

Meisels, S. J., Bickel, D. D., Nicholson, J., Xue, Y., & Atkins-Burnett, S. (2001). Trusting teachers' judgments: A validity study of a curriculum-embedded performance assessment in kindergarten to grade 3. *American Educational Research Journal, 38*(1), 73–95.

Meisels, S. J., & Liaw, F-R. (1993). Failure in grade: Do retained students catch up? *Journal of Educational Research, 87*(2), 69–77.

Melton, R. F. (1978). Resolution of conflicting claims concerning the effect of behavioral objectives on student learning. *Review of Educational Research, 48*(2), 291–302.

Mendoza, J. I. (1994). On being a Mexican American. *Phi Delta Kappan, 76*(4), 293–295.

Mercer, C. D., & Mercer, A. R. (2001). *Teaching students with learning problems* (6th ed.). Upper Saddle River, NJ: Merrill Prentice Hall.

Mergendoller, J. R. (1996). Moving from technological possibility to richer student learning: Revitalized infrastructure and reconstructed pedagogy. *Educational Researcher, 25*(8), 43–46.

Mertler, C. A. (2000). Teacher-centered fallacies of classroom assessment validity and reliability. *Mid-Western Educational Researcher, 13*(4), 29–35.

Messick, S. (1989). Meaning and values in test validation: The science and ethics of assessment. *Educational Researcher, 18*(2), 5–11.

Metz, K. E. (1995). Reassessment of developmental constraints on children's science instruction. *Review of Educational Research, 65*(2), 93–127.

Metzger, M. (1996). Maintaining a life. *Phi Delta Kappan, 77*(5), 346–351.

Metzger, M. (1998). Teaching reading: Beyond the plot. *Phi Delta Kappan, 80*(3), 240–246, 256.

Metzger, M. (2002). Learning to discipline. *Phi Delta Kappan, 84*(1), 77–84.

Mevarech, Z., & Susak, Z. (1993). Effects of learning with cooperative-mastery method on elementary students. *Journal of Educational Research, 86*(4), 197–205.

Meyer, C. A. (1992). What's the difference between authentic and performance assessment? *Educational Leadership, 49*(8), 39–40.

Meyer, M. S. (2000). The ability-achievement discrepancy: Does it contribute to our understanding of learning disabilities? *Educational Psychology Review, 12*(3), 315–337.

Midgley, C. (2001). A goal theory perspective on the current status of middle level schools. In T. Urdan & F. Pajares (Eds.), *Adolescence and education: Vol. 1. General issues in the education of adolescents* (pp. 33–59). Greenwich, CT: Information Age Publishers.

Midgley, C., Middleton, M. J., Gheen, M. H., & Kumar, R. (2002). Stage-environment fit revisited: A goal theory approach to examining school transitions. In C. Midgley (Ed.), *Goals, goal structures, and patterns of adaptive learning* (pp. 109–142). Mahwah, NJ: Erlbaum.

Miller, L. K. (1989). *Musical savants: Exceptional skill in the mentally retarded.* Hillsdale, NJ: Erlbaum.

Miller, P. H. (2002). *Theories of developmental psychology* (4th ed.). New York: Worth.

Miltenberger, R. G. (2004). *Behavior modification: Principles and procedures.* Belmont, CA: Wadsworth/Thomson Learning.

Mistler-Jackson, M., & Songer, N. B. (2000). Student motivation and internet technology: Are students empowered to learn science? *Journal of Research in Science Teaching, 37*(5), 459–479.

Mitchell, J. J. (1990). *Human growth and development: The childhood years.* Calgary, Alberta: Detselig Enterprises Ltd.

Mock, D. R., & Kauffman, J. M. (2002). Preparing teachers for full inclusion: Is it possible? *The Teacher Educator, 37*(3), 202–215.

Moely, B. E., Hart, S. S., Leal, L., Santulli, K. A., Rao, N., Johnson, T., & Hamilton, L. B. (1992). The teacher's role in facilitating memory and study strategy development in the elementary school classroom. *Child Development, 63*(3), 653–672.

Moersch, C., & Fisher III, L. M. (1995). Electronic portfolios—some pivotal questions. *Learning and Leading with Technology, 23*(2), 10–14.

Mohnsen, B., & Mendon, K. (1997). Electronic portfolios in physical education. *Strategies, 11*(2), 13–16.

Moll, L. C. (Ed.). (1990). *Vygotsky and education: Instructional implications and applications of sociohistorical psychology.* New York: Cambridge University Press.

Montgomery, K. (2000). Classroom rubrics: Systematizing what teachers do naturally. *The Clearing House, 73*(6), 324–328.

Moon, T. R. (2002). Using performance assessment in the social studies classroom. *Gifted Child Today, 25*(3), 53–59.

Mooney, C. G. (2000). *Theories of childhood.* St. Paul, MN: Redleaf Press.

Moore, J. A., & Teagle, H. F. B. (2002). An introduction to cochlear implant technology, activation, and programming. *Language, Speech, and Hearing Services in the Schools, 33*(3), 153–161.

Mora, J. K., Wink, J., & Wink, D. (2001). Dueling models of dual language instruction: A critical review of the literature and program implementation guide. *Bilingual Research Journal, 25*(4), 435–460.

Moreno, R., & Mayer, R. E. (2002). Learning science in virtual reality multimedia environments: Role of methods and media. *Journal of Educational Psychology, 94*(3), 598–610.

Morgan, H. (1997). *Cognitive styles and classroom learning.* Westport, CT: Praeger.

Morris, E. K. (2003). B. F. Skinner: A behavior analyst in educational psychology. In B. J. Zimmerman & D. H. Schunk (Eds.), *Educational psychology: A century of contributions* (pp. 229–250). Mahwah, NJ: Erlbaum.

Morris, P. (1977). Practical strategies for human learning and remembering. In M. J. A. Howe (Ed.), *Adult learning.* New York: Wiley.

Moshavi, D. (2001). "Yes and . . .": Introducing improvisational theatre techniques to the management classroom. *Journal of Management Education, 25*(4), 437–449.

Mullis, I. V. S., Martin, M. O., Gonzalez, E., O'Connor, K. M., Chrostowski, S. J., Gregory, K. D., Garden, R. A., & Smith, T. A. (2001). *Mathematics benchmarking report TIMSS 1999–eighth grade.* Chestnut Hill, MA: Boston College. Retrieved January 2, 2002, from http://www.timss.org/timss1999b/publications.html.

Murpy, B. C., & Eisenberg, N. (2002). An integrative examination of peer conflict: Children's reported goals, emotions, and behavior. *Social Development, 11*(4), 534–557.

Murray, B. (2002). Wanted: Politics-free, science-based education. *Monitor on Psychology, 33*(8), 52–54.

Myers, M. (2003). What can computers contribute to a K–12 writing program? In M. D. Shermis & J. C. Burstein (Eds.), *Automated essay scoring* (pp. 3–20). Mahwah, NJ: Erlbaum.

Nagy, P., & Griffiths, A. K. (1982). Limitations of recent research relating Piaget's theory to adolescent thought. *Review of Educational Research, 52*(4), 513–556.

Nakhleh, M. B. (1994). A review of microcomputer-based labs: How have they affected science learning? *Journal of Computers in Mathematics and Science Teaching. 13*(4), 368–381.

Narvaez, D. (2002). Does reading moral stories build character? *Educational Psychology Review, 14*(2), 155–172.

Nathan, L. (2002). The human face of the high-stakes testing story. *Phi Delta Kappan, 83*(8), 595–600.

National Board for Professional Teaching Standards. (2003, May 30). *What teachers should know and be able to do: The five core propositions of the national board.* Retrieved October 23, 2003, from http://www.nbpts.org/about/coreprops.cfm.

National Center for Health Statistics. (2002). *Health, United States, 2002.* Hyatsville, MD: Author.

National Coalition to Abolish Corporal Punishment in Schools. (2003). *U.S.: Statistics on corporal punishment by state and race.* Retrieved November 11, 2003, from www.stophitting.com/disatschool/statesBanning.php.

National Commission on Excellence in Education. (1983). *A nation at risk: The imperative for educational reform.* Washington, DC: U.S. Department of Education.

National Research Council. (1996). *National science education standards.* Washington, DC: National Academy Press.

Naughton, C. C., & McLaughlin, T. F. (1995). The use of a token economy system for students with behaviour disorders. *B.C. Journal of Special Education, 19*(2/3), 29–38.

Neill, M. (2003). High stakes, high risk. *American School Board Journal, 190*(2), 18–21.

Neisser, U. (1976). *Cognition and reality.* San Francisco: Freeman

Neisser, U. (1982). *Memory observed.* San Francisco: Freeman.

Newman, B. M., & Newman, P. R. (2003). *Development through life: A psychosocial approach* (8th ed.). Belmont, CA: Wadsworth/Thomson Learning.

Newman, F., & Holzman, L. (1993). *Lev Vygotsky: Revolutionary scientist.* London: Routledge.

Nicholson, J., Gelpi, A., Young, S., & Sulzby, E. (1998). Influences of Gender and Open-Ended Software on first graders' collaborative composing activities on computers. *Journal of Computing in Childhood Education, 9*(1), 3–42.

Nickerson, R. S. (1994). The teaching of thinking and problem solving. In R. J. Sternberg (Ed.), *Thinking and problem solving.* San Diego, CA: Academic Press.

Nicol, M. P. (1997). How one physics teacher changed his algebraic thinking. *The Mathematics Teacher, 90*(2), 86–89.

Nieto, S. (2002/2003). Profoundly multicultural questions. *Educational Leadership, 60*(4), 6–10.

Nieto, S. (2004). *Affirming diversity: The sociopolitical context of multicultural education* (4th ed.). Boston: Allyn & Bacon.

Niguidula, D. (1997). Picturing performance with digital portfolios. *Educational Leadership, 55*(3), 26–29.

Nitko, A. J. (2004). *Educational asssessment of students* (4th ed.). Upper Saddle River, NJ: Merrill Prentice Hall.

Norman, D. A., & Rumelhart, D. E. (1970). A system for perception and memory. In D. A. Norman (Ed.), *Models of human memory.* New York: Academic Press.

North Central Regional Educational Laboratory. (1999). *Critical issue: Using technology to improve student achievement.* Retrieved January 2, 2002, from http://www.ncrel.org/sdrs/ areas/issues/methods/technlgy/te800.htm/.

Novak, J. D. (1990). Concept mapping: A useful tool for science education. *Journal of Research in Science Teaching, 27*(10), 937–949.

Novak, J. D. (1998). *Learning, creating, and using knowledge: Concept maps as facilitative tools in schools and corporations.* Mahwah, NJ: Erlbaum.

Novak, J. D., & Gowin, D. B. (1984). *Learning how to learn.* Cambridge, England: Cambridge University Press.

Novak, M. (1971). Rise of unmeltable ethnics. In M. Friedman (Ed.), *Overcoming middle class rage.* Philadelphia: Westminster Press.

Nye, R. D. (1992). *The legacy of B. F. Skinner.* Pacific Grove, CA: Brooks/Cole.

Oakes, C. (1996). First grade online. *Learning and Leading with Technology, 24*(1), 37–39.

Oakes, J. (1985). *Keeping track: How schools structure inequality.* New Haven: Yale University Press.

Oakes, J., & Wells, A. S. (1998). Detracking for high student achievement. *Educational Leadership, 55*(6), 38–41.

Ochse, R., & Plug, C. (1986). Cross-cultural investigation of the validity of Erikson's theory of personality development. *Journal of Personality and Social Psychology, 50*(6), 1240–1252.

O'Donnell, A. M., Dansereau, D. F., & Hall, R. H. (2002). Knowledge maps as scaffolds for cognitive processing. *Educational Psychology Review, 14*(1), 71–86.

Office of the Federal Register. (1994). *Code of Federal Regulations 34. Parts 300 to 399.* Washington, DC: Author.

Ogbu, J. U. (1992). Understanding cultural diversity and learning. *Educational Researcher, 21*(8), 5–14.

Okagaki, L. (2001). Triarchic model of minority children's school achievement. *Educational Psychologist, 36*(1), 9–20.

O'Lone, D. J. (1997). Student information system software: Are you getting what you expected? *NASSP Bulletin, 81*(585), 86–93.

Olson, A. (2002). Technology solutions for testing. *The School Administrator, 59*(4), 20–23.

Olson, D. R., & Torrance, N. (Eds.). (1996). *Handbook of education and human development*. Cambridge, MA: Blackwell.

Olson, L. (2003a, June 18). All states get federal nod on key plans. *Education Week*, 22(41), 1, 20–21

Olson, L. (2003b, May 8). Legal twists, digital turns. *Education Week*, 22(35), 11–16.

O'Neal, J. (2001). Y=mx+b really is found in real-life situations. *Ohio Journal of School Mathematics*, 43,18–20.

Ormrod, J. E. (2004). *Human learning* (4th ed.). Upper Saddle River, NJ: Prentice Hall.

Ornstein, A. C., & Levine, D. U. (2003). *Foundations of education* (8th ed.). Boston: Houghton Mifflin.

Osgood, C. E. (1949). The similarity paradox in human learning: A resolution. *Psychological Review*, 56(3), 132–143.

Oshima, J., Scardamalia, M., & Bereiter, C. (1996). Collaborative learning processes associated with high and low conceptual progress. *Instructional Science*, 24(1), 125–155.

Osterman, K. F. (2000). Students' need for belonging in the school community. *Review of Educational Research*, 70(3), 323–367.

Osterman, K. F. (2003). Preventing school violence. *Phi Delta Kappan*, 84(8), 622–623, 627.

O'Sullivan, C. Y., Reese, C. M., & Mazzeo, J. (1997). *NAEP 1996 science: Report card for the nation and the states*. Washington, DC: National Center for Educational Statistics. Retrieved January 2, 2002, from http://nces.ed.gov/pubsearch/pubsinfo.asp?pubid=97497.

Overton, W. F., & Byrnes, J. P. (1991). Cognitive development. In R. M. Lerner, A. C. Peterson, & J. Brooks-Gunn (Eds.), *Encyclopedia of adolescence*. New York: Garland Publishing.

Owens, R. F., Hester, J. L., & Teale, W. H. (2002). Where do you want to go today? Inquiry-based learning and technology integration. *The Reading Teacher*, 55(7), 616–625.

Owings, W. A., & Kaplan, L. S. (2001). Standards, retention, and social promotion. *NASSP Bulletin*, 85(629), 57–66.

Padilla, A. M., & Gonzalez, R. (2001). Academic performance of immigrant and U.S.-born Mexican heritage students: Effects of schooling in Mexico and bilingual/English language instruction. *American Educational Research Journal*, 38(3), 727–742.

Page, E. B. (2003). Project essay grade: PEG. In M. D. Shermis & J. C. Burstein (Eds.), *Automated essay scoring* (pp. 43–54). Mahwah, NJ: Erlbaum.

Page, M. S. (2002). Technology-enriched classrooms: Effects on students of low socioeconomic status. *Journal of Research on Technology in Education*, 34(4), 389–409.

Palincsar, A., & Brown, A. L. (1984). Reciprocal teaching of comprehension-fostering and comprehension-monitoring activities. *Cognition and Instruction*, 1(2), 117–175.

Palmer, J. (2001). Conflict resolution: Strategies for the elementary classroom. *The Social Studies*, 92(2), 65–68.

Palmer, S. B., & Wehmeyer, M. L. (2003). Promoting self-determination in early elementary school: Teaching self-regulated problem-solving and goal-setting skills. *Remedial and Special Education*, 24(2), 115–126.

Panchaud, C., Singh, S., Feivelson, D., & Darroch, J. E. (2000). Sexually transmitted diseases among adolescents in developed countries. *Family Planning Perspectives*, 32(1), 24–32,45. Retrieved January 2, 2002, from http://www.agi-usa.org/ pubs/ journals/3202400.html.

Paris, S. G., & Paris, A. H. (2001). Classroom applications of research on self-regulated learning. *Educational Psychologist*, 36(2), 89–101.

Parke, C. S., & Lane, S. (1997). Learning from performance assessments in math. *Educational Leadership*, 54(6), 26–29.

Parshall, C. G., Spray, J. A., Kalohn, J. C., & Davey, T. (2002). *Practical considerations in computer-based testing*. New York: Springer-Verlag.

Parten, M. B. (1932). Social participation among preschool children. *Journal of Abnormal and Social Psychology*, 27(3), 243–269.

Patterson, B. (2002). Creating two-point perspective on the computer. *Arts & Activities*, 131(4), 52.

Patterson, G. R., DeBaryshe, B. D., & Ramsey, E. (1989). A developmental perspective on antisocial behavior. *American Psychologist*, 44(2), 329–335.

Pea, R. D. (1985). Beyond amplification: Using the computer to reorganize mental functioning. *Educational Psychologist*, 21(4), 167–182.

Pedersen, S., & Liu, M. (2002). The effects of modeling expert cognitive strategies during problem-based learning. *Journal of Educational Computing Research*, 26(4), 353-380.

Pedersen, S., & Liu, M. (2002/2003). The transfer of problem-solving skills from a problem-based learning environment: The effect of modeling an expert's cognitive processes. *Journal of Research on Technology in Education*, 35(2), 303–320.

Pellegrini, A. D., & Bjorklund, D. F. (1997). The role of recess in children's cognitive performance. *Educational Psychologist*, 32(1), 35–40.

Pelletier, L. G., Séguin-Lévesque, C., & Legault, L. (2002). Pressure from above and pressure from below as determinants of teachers' motivation and teaching behaviors. *Journal of Educational Psychology*, 94(1), 186–196.

Peltier, G. L. (1991). Why do secondary schools continue to track students? *The Clearing House*, 64(4), 246–247.

Peña, C. M., & Alessi, S. M. (1999). Promoting a qualitative understanding of physics. *Journal of Computers in Mathematics and Science Teaching*, 18(4), 439–457.

Penfield, W. (1969). Consciousness, memory, and man's conditioned reflexes. In K. Pribram (Ed.), *On the biology of learning*. New York: Harcourt Brace Jovanovich.

Perfect, T. J., & Schwartz, B. L. (Eds.). (2002). *Applied metacognition*. New York: Cambridge University Press.

Perkins, D. (1999). The many faces of constructivism. *Educational Leadership*, 57(3), 6–11.

Perkins, D., Tishman, S., Ritchhart, R., Donis, K., & Andrade, A. (2000). Intelligence in the wild: A dispositional view of intellectual traits. *Educational Psychology Review*, 12(3), 269–293.

Perkins, D. F., & Hartless, G. (2002). An ecological risk-factor examination of suicide ideation and behavior of adolescents. *Journal of Adolescent Research*, 17(1), 3–26.

Perrone, V. (1991). *A letter to teachers: Reflections on schooling and the art of teaching*. San Francisco: Jossey-Bass.

Perry, N. E., VandeKamp, K. O., Mercer, L. K., & Nordby, C. J. (2002). Investigating teacher-student interactions that foster self-regulated learning. *Educational Psychologist*, 37(1), 5–15.

Peters, G. D. (2001). Transformations: Technology and the music industry. *Teaching Music*, 9(3), 20–25.

Peterson, A. C. (1988). Adolescent development. In M. R. Rosenzweig & L. W. Porter (Eds.), *Annual review of psychology* (Vol. 39, pp. 583–607). Palo Alto, CA: Annual Reviews.

Peterson, A. C., Compas, B. E., Brooks-Gunn, J., Stemmler, M., Ey, S., & Grant, K. E. (1993). Depression in adolescence. *American Psychologist*, 48(2), 155–168.

Peterson, A. C., & Taylor, B. (1980). The biological approach to adolescence. In J. Adelson (Ed.), *Handbook of adolescent psychology*. New York: Wiley.

Peverly, S. T., Brobst, K. E., Graham, M., & Shaw, R. (2003). College adults are not good at self-regulation: A study on the relationship of self-regulation, note taking, and test taking. *Journal of Educational Psychology*, 95(2), 335–346.

Pewewardy, C. (2002). Learning styles of American Indian/Alaska Native students: A review of the literature and implications for practice. *Journal of American Indian Education*, 41(3), 22–56.

Phillips, P. (1997). The conflict wall. *Educational Leadership*, 54(8), 43–44.

Piaget, J. (1932). *The moral judgement of the child* (M. Gabain, Trans.). New York: Harcourt Brace.

Piaget, J. (1952a). *The language and thought of the child*. London: Routledge & Kegan Paul.

Piaget, J. (1952b). *The origins of intelligence in children*. New York: International Universities Press.

Piaget, J. (1965). *The moral judgment of the child* (M. Gabain, Trans.). Glencoe, IL: Free Press. (Original work published 1932.)

Piaget, J., & Inhelder, B. (1956). *The child's conception of space.* London: Routledge & Kegan Paul.

Piaget, J., & Inhelder, B. (1969). *The psychology of the child.* New York: Basic Books.

Piechowski, M. M. (1997). Emotional giftedness: The measure of intrapersonal intelligence. In N. Colangelo & G. A. Davis (Eds.), *Handbook of gifted education* (2nd ed.). Boston: Allyn & Bacon.

Pintrich, P. R., & De Groot, E. V. (1990). Motivational and self-regulated learning components of classroom academic performance. *Journal of Educational Psychology, 82*(1), 33–40.

Pintrich, P. R., & Schunk, D. H. (2002). *Motivation in education: Theory, research, and applications* (2nd ed.). Upper Saddle River, NJ: Merrill Prentice Hall.

Pitoniak, M. J., & Royer, J. M. (2001). Testing accommodations for examinees with disabilities: A review of psychometric, legal, and social policy issues. *Review of Educational Research, 71*(1), 53–104.

Plake, B. S., & Impara, J. C. (Eds.). (2003). *The fifteenth mental measurements yearbook.* Lincoln, NE: University of Nebraska Press.

Pleydon, A. P., & Schner, J. G. (2001). Female adolescent friendships and delinquent behavior. *Adolescence, 36*(142), 189–205.

Pogrow, S. (1990). A Socratic approach to using computers with at-risk students. *Educational Leadership, 47*(5), 61–66.

Pogrow, S. (1999). Systematically using powerful learning environments to accelerate the learning of disadvantaged students in grades 4–8. In C. M. Reigeluth (Ed.), *Instructional design theories and models, Vol. II: A new paradigm of instructional theory.* Mahwah, NJ: Erlbaum.

Pokay, P., & Blumenfeld, P. C. (1990). Predicting achievement early and late in the semester: The role of motivation and use of learning strategies. *Journal of Educational Psychology, 82*(1), 41–50.

Pollard, D. S. (1993). Gender, achievement, and African-American students' perceptions of their school experience. *Educational Psychologist, 28*(4), 341–356.

Polya, G. (1957). *How to solve it* (2nd ed.). Princeton, NJ: Princeton University Press.

Pomerantz, E. M. (2002). Making the grade but feeling distressed: Gender differences in academic performance and internal distress. *Journal of Educational Psychology, 94*(2), 396–404.

Popham, W. J. (2002). *Classroom assessment: What teachers need to know* (3rd ed.). Boston: Allyn & Bacon.

Popham, W. J. (2003). The seductive allure of data. *Educational Leadership, 60*(5), 48–51.

Porter, A. C., & Brophy, J. (1988). Synthesis of research on good teaching: Insights from the work of the Institute for Research on Teaching. *Educational Leadership, 45*(8), 74–85.

Porter, R. P. (2000). The benefits of English immersion. *Educational Leadership, 57*(4), 52–56.

Portes, P., Dunham, R., & Del Castillo, K. (2000). Identity formation and status across cultures: Exploring the cultural validity of Erikson's theory. In A. L. Comunian & U. Gielen (Eds.), *International Perspectives on Human Development* (pp. 449–459). Lengerich, Germany: Pabst Science Publishers.

Premack, D. (1959). Toward empirical behavior laws: 1. Positive reinforcement. *Psychological Review, 66*(4), 219–233.

Pressley, M. (2002). Metacognition and self-regulated comprehension. In A. E. Farstrup & S. Jay Samuels (Eds.), *What research has to say about reading instruction* (3rd ed., pp. 291–309). Newark, DE: International Reading Association.

Pressley, M., Woloshyn, V., & Associates. (1995). *Cognitive strategy instruction that really improves children's strategy instruction* (2nd ed.). Cambridge, MA: Brookline Books.

Pretz, J. E., Naples, A. J., & Sternberg, R. J. (2003). Recognizing, defining, and representing problems. In J. E. Davidson & R. J. Sternberg (Eds.), *The psychology of problem solving* (pp. 3–30). Cambridgek, England: Cambridge University Press.

Protheroe, N. (2002). Improving instruction through teacher observation. *Principal, 82*(1), 48–51.

Purdie, N., & Hattie, J. (1996). Cultural differences in the use of strategies for self-regulated learning. *American Educational Research Journal, 33*(4), 845–871.

Purdie, N., Hattie, J., & Carroll, A. (2002). A review of the research on interventions for attention deficit hyperactivity disorder: What works best? *Review of Educational Research, 72*(1), 61–99.

Purkey, W. W., & Novak, J. M. (1996). *Inviting school success: A self-concept approach to teaching, learning, and democratic practice* (3rd ed.). Belmont, CA: Wadsworth.

Purkey, W. W., & Strahan, D. B. (2002). *Inviting positive classroom discipline.* Westerville, OH: National Middle School Association.

Qin, Z., Johnson, D. W., & Johnson, R. T. (1995). Cooperative versus competitive efforts and problem solving. *Review of Educational Research, 65*(2), 129–143.

Quenneville, J. (2001). Tech tools for students with learning disabilities: Infusion into inclusive classrooms. *Preventing School Failure, 45*(4), 167–170.

Quihuis, G., Bempechat, J., Jiminez, N. V., & Boulay, B. A. (2002). Implicit theories of intelligence across domains: A study of meaning making in adolescents of Mexican descent. In J. Bempechat & J. G. Elliott (Eds.), *New Directions for Child and Adolescent Development, No. 96. Learning in culture and context: Approaching the complexities of achievement motivation in student learning* (pp. 87–100). San Francisco: Jossey-Bass.

Rabow, J., Charness, M. A., Kipperman, J., & Radcliffe-Vasile, S. (1994). *William Fawcett Hill's learning through discussion* (3rd ed.). Thousand Oaks, CA: Sage.

Raison, J., Hanson, L. A., Hall, C., & Reynolds, M. C. (1995). Another school's reality. *Phi Delta Kappan, 76*(6), 480–482.

Ramirez-Valles, J., Zimmerman, M. A., & Juarez, L. (2002). Gender differences of neighborhood and social control processes: A study of the timing of first intercourse among low-achieveing, urban, African American youth. *Youth & Society, 33*(3), 418–441.

Randi, J., & Corno, L. (2000). Teacher innovations in self-regulated learning. In M. Boekaerts, P. R. Pintrich, & M. Zeidner (Eds.), *Handbook of self-regulation* (pp. 651–685). San Diego: Academic Press.

Raskind, M. (1993). Assistive technology and adults with learning disabilities: A blueprint for exploration and advancement. *Learning Disability Quarterly, 16*(3), 185–196.

Ratner, C. (1991). *Vygotsky's sociohistorical psychology and its contemporary applications.* New York: Plenum Press.

Raudenbush, S. W. (1984). Magnitude of teacher expectancy effects on pupil IQ as a function of the credibility of expectancy induction: A synthesis of findings from 18 experiments. *Journal of Educational Psychology, 76*(1), 85–97.

Raudenbush, S. W., Rowan, B., & Cheong, Y. F. (1993). Higher order instructional goals in secondary schools: Class, teacher, and school influences. *American Educational Research Journal, 30*(3), 523–553.

Raugh, M. R., & Atkinson, R. C. (1975). A mnemonic method for learning a second-language vocabulary. *Journal of Educational Psychology, 67*(1), 1–16.

Ravaglia, R., Alper, T., Rozenfeld, M., & Suppes, P. (1998). Successful pedagogical applications of symbolic computation. In N. Kajler (Ed.), *Computer-human interaction in symbolic computation* (pp. 61–88). New York: Springer-Verlag.

Ravaglia, R., Sommer, R., Sanders, M., Oas, G., & DeLeone, C. (1999). Computer-based mathematics and physics for gifted remote students. *Proceedings of the International Conference on Mathematics/Science Education and Technology*, pp. 405–410. Retrieved January 15, 2004, from http://www.epgy-stanford.edu/research/index.html?papers.

Rawsthorne, L. J., & Elliot, A. J. (1999). Achievement goals and intrinsic motivation: A meta-analytic review. *Personality and Social Psychology Review, 3*(4), 326–344.

Raymond, M. E., & Hanushek, E. A. (2003). High-stakes research. *Education Next, 3*(3), 48–55.

Rea, A. (2001). Telementoring: An A+ initiative. *Education Canada, 40*(4), 28–29.

Read, D. A., & Simon, S. B. (Eds.). (1975). *Humanistic education sourcebook.* Englewood Cliffs, NJ: Prentice-Hall.

Reagan, T. G., Case, C. W., & Brubacher, J. W. (2000). *Becoming a reflective educator* (2nd ed.). Thousand Oaks, CA: Corwin Press.

Redl, F., & Wattenberg, W. W. (1959). *Mental hygiene in teaching* (2nd ed.). New York: Harcourt Brace Jovanovich.

Reese, C. M., Miller, K. E., Mazzeo, J., & Dossey, J. A. (1997). *NAEP 1996 mathematics report card for the nation and the states.* Washington, DC: National Center for Educational Statistics. Retrieved January 2, 2002, from http://nces.ed.gov/pubsearch/pubsinfo.asp?pubid=97488.

Reid, C., Romanoff, B., & Algozzine, R. (2000). An evaluation of alternative screening procedures. *Journal for the Education of the Gifted, 23*(4), 378–396.

Reis, S. M., & Renzulli, J. S. (1985). *The secondary triad model.* Mansfield Center, CT: Creative Learning Press.

Reninger, R. D. (2000). Music education in a digital world. *Teaching Music, 8*(1), 24–31.

Renninger, K. A., & Hidi, S. (2002). Student interest and achievement: Developmental issues raised by a case study. In A. Wigfield & J. S. Eccles (Eds.), *Development of achievement motivation* (pp. 173–195). San Diego, CA: Academic Press.

Renzulli, J. S. (2002). Expanding the conception of giftedness to include co-cognitive traits and promote social capital. *Phi Delta Kappan, 84*(1), 33–40, 57–58.

Renzulli, J. S., & Reis, S. M. (1985). *The schoolwide enrichment model.* Mansfield Center, CT: Creative Learning Press.

Renzulli, J. S., Gentry, M., & Reis, S. M. (2003). *Enrichment clusters: A practical plan for real-world, student-driven learning.* Mansfield Center, CT: Creative Learning Press.

Resnick, L. B. (1987). Learning in school and out. *Educational Researcher, 16*(9), 13–20.

Rest, J., Narvaez, D., Bebeau, M. J., & Thoma, S. J. (1999). *Postconventional moral thinking: A Neo-Kohlbergian Approach.* Mahwah, NJ: Erlbaum.

Reynolds, T. H., & Bonk, C. J. (1996). Creating computerized writing partner and keystroke recording tools with macro-driven prompts. *Educational Technology Research and Development, 44*(3), 83–97.

Ricci, C. M., & Beal, C. R. (2002). The effect of interactive media on children's story memory. *Journal of Educational Psychology, 94*(1), 138–144.

Richardson, V. (Ed.).(2001). *Handbook of research on teaching* (4th ed.). Washington, DC: American Educational Research Association.

Ridgeway, V. G., Peters, C. L., & Tracy, T. S. (2002). Out of this world: Cyberspace, literacy, and learning. In C. C. Block, L. B.

Gambrell, & M. Pressley (Eds.), *Improving comprehension instruction: Rethinking research, theory, and classroom practice.* San Francisco: Jossey-Bass.

Riel, M. (1993). Global Education through learning circles. In L. Harasim (Ed.), *Global Networks* (pp. 221–236). Cambridge, MA: MIT Press.

Riel, M. (1996). Cross-classroom collaboration: Communication and education. In T. Koschmann (Ed.), *CSCL: Theory and practice* (pp. 187–207). Mahwah, NJ: Erlbaum.

Riel, M., & Fulton, K. (2001). The role of technology in supporting learning communities. *Phi Delta Kappan, 82*(7), 518–523.

Robelen, E. W. (2003, September 3). State reports on progress vary widely. *Education Week, 23*(1), 1, 37.

Robertson, A. (2001, Sept/Oct). CASE is when we learn to think. *Primary Science Review, 69,* 20–22.

Robertson, J. S. (2000). Is attribution training a worthwhile classroom intervention for K–12 students with learning difficulties? *Educational Psychology Review, 12*(1), 111–134.

Robins, K. N., Lindsey, R. B., Lindsey, D. B., & Terrell, R. D. (2002). *Culturally proficient instruction.* Thousand Oaks, CA: Corwin Press.

Robledo, M. M., & Cortez, J. D. (2002). Successful bilingual education programs: Development and dissemination of criteria to identify promising and exemplary practices in bilingual education at the national level. *Bilingual Research Journal, 26*(1), 1–21.

Roderick, M. (1995, December). *Grade retention and school dropout: Policy debate and research questions* (Research Bulletin No. 15). Bloomington, IN: Center for Evaluation, Development, and Research.

Roderick, M., & Engel, M. (2001). The grasshopper and the ant: motivational responses of low-achieving students to high-stakes testing. *Educational Evaluation and Policy Analysis, 23*(3), 197–227.

Rodney, L. W., Crafter, B., Rodney, H. E., & Mupier, R. M. (1999). Variables contributing to grade retention among African American adolescent males. *Journal of Educational Research, 92*(3), 185–190.

Roerden, L. (2001). The resolving conflict creatively program. *Reclaiming Children and Youth, 10*(1), 24–28.

Roeser, R. W., & Lau, S. (2002). On academic identity formation in middle school settings during early adolescence: A motivational contextual perspective. In T. M. Brinthaupt & R. P. Lipka (Eds.), *Understanding early adolescent self and identity: Applications and interventions* (pp. 91–131). Albany, NY: State University of New York Press

Rogers, C. R. (1967). Learning to be free. In C. R. Rogers & B. Stevens (Eds.), *The problem of being human.* Lafayette, CA: Real People Press.

Rogers, C. R. (1980). *A way of being.* Boston: Houghton Mifflin.

Rogers, C. R. (1983). *Freedom to learn for the 80's.* Columbus, OH: Merrill.

Rogoff, B. (1990). *Apprenticeship in thinking: Cognitive development in social context.* New York: Oxford University Press.

Rogoff, B., & Chavajay, P. (1995). What's become of research on the cultural basis of cognitive development? *American Psychologist, 50*(10), 859–877.

Rohrbeck, C. A., Ginsburg-Block, M. D., Fantuzzo, J. W., & Miller, T. R. (2003). Peer-assisted learning interventions with elementary school students: A meta-analytic review. *Journal of Educational Psychology, 95*(2), 240–257.

Roller, C. M. (2002). Accommodating variability in reading instruction. *Reading & Writing Quarterly, 18*(1), 17–38.

Rolón, C. A. (2002/2003). Educating Latino students. *Educational Leadership, 60*(4), 40–43.

Romance, N. R., & Vitale, M. R. (1999). Concept mapping as a tool for learning: Broadening the framework for student-centered instruction. *College Teaching, 47*(2), 74–79.

Rop, C. (1998). Breaking the gender barrier in the physical sciences. *Educational Leadership, 55*(4), 58–60.

Roschelle, J. (1996). Computer support for knowledge-building communities. In T. Koschmann (Ed.), *CSCL: Theory and practice* (pp. 209–248). Mahwah, NJ: Erlbaum.

Rosenshine, B. V. (1987). Explicit teaching. In D. C. Berliner & B. V. Rosenshine (Eds.), *Talks to teachers* (pp. 75–92.). New York: Random House.

Rosenshine, B. (2003, August 4). High-stakes testing: Another analysis. *Education Policy Analysis Archives, 11*(24). Retrieved February 6, 2004, from http://epaa.asu.edu/epaa/v11n24/.

Rosenshine, B., & Meister, C. (1994a). Reciprocal teaching: A review of the research. *Review of Educational Research, 64*(4), 479–530.

Rosenshine, B. V., & Meister, C. (1994b). Direct Instruction. In T. Husen & T. N. Postlewhaite (Eds.), *International encyclopedia of education* (2nd ed., Vol. 3, pp. 1524–1530). New York: Pergamon.

Rosenshine, B., Meister, C., & Chapman, S. (1996). Teaching students to generate questions: A review of the intervention studies. *Review of Educational Research, 66*(2), 181–221.

Rosenthal, R. (1985). From unconscious experimenter bias to teacher expectancy effects. In J. B. Dusek (Ed.), *Teacher expectations.* Hillsdale, NJ: Erlbaum.

Rosenthal, R. (2002). The Pygmalion effect and its mediating mechanisms. In J. Aronson (Ed.), *Improving academic achievement* (pp. 26–36). San Diego: Academic Press.

Rosenthal, R., & Jacobson, L. (1968). *Pygmalion in the classroom*. New York: Holt, Rinehart, & Winston.

Roskos, K., Boehlen S., & Walker, B. J. (2000). Learning the art of instructional conversations: The influence of self-assessment on teachers' instructional discourse in a reading clinic. *The Elementary School Journal, 100*(3), 229–252.

Ross, D. D., Bondy, E., & Kyle, D. W. (1993). *Reflective teaching for student empowerment*. New York: Macmillan.

Rothstein, R. (1998). Bilingual education: The controversy. *Phi Delta Kappan, 79*(9), 672–678.

Rothstein-Fisch, C., Greenfield, P. M., & Trumbull, E. (1999). Bridging cultures with classroom strategies. *Educational Leadership, 56*(7), 64–67.

Rowan, B. (1994). Comparing teachers' work with work in other occupations: Notes on the professional status of teaching. *Edcuational Reseracher, 23*(6), 4–17.

Royer, J. M. (1979). Theories of the transfer of learning. *Educational Psychologist, 14*, 53–72.

Royer, J. M., & Cable, G. W. (1975). Facilitated learning in connected discourse. *Journal of Educational Psychology, 67*(1), 116 123.

Royer, J. M., & Cable, G. W. (1976). Illustrations, analogies, and facilitative transfer in prose learning. *Journal of Educational Psychology, 68*(2), 205–209.

Royer, J. M., Tronsky, L. N., Chan, Y., Jackson, S. J., & Marchant, H., III. (1999). Math-fact retrieval as the cognitive mechanism underlying gender differences in math test performance. *Contemporary Educational Psychology, 24*(3), 181–266.

Rubado, K. (2002). Empowering students through multiple intelligences. *Reclaiming Children and Youth, 10*(4), 233–235.

Rubin, K. H., Maioni, T. L., & Hornung, M. (1976). Free play behavior in middle- and lower-class preschoolers: Parten and Piaget revisited. *Child Development, 47*(2), 414 419.

Rubin, L. J. (1985). *Artistry in teaching*. New York: Random House.

Ruder, S. (2000). We teach all. *Educational Leadership, 58*(1), 49–51.

Ruggiero, V. R. (1988). *Teaching thinking across the curriculum*. New York: Harper & Row.

Ruggiero, V. R. (2004). *The art of thinking: A guide to critical and creative thought* (7th ed.). New York: Pearson Longman.

Ruhland, S. K., & Bremer, C. D., (2002). Professional development needs of novice career and technical educational teachers. *Journal of Career and Technical Education, 19*(1), 18–31.

Rummel, N., Levin, J. R., & Woodward, M. M. (2003). Do pictorial mnemonic text-learning aids give students something

worth writing about? *Journal of Educational Psychology, 95*(2), 327–334.

Runco, M. A. (Ed.). (1994). *Problem finding, problem solving, and creativity*. Norwood, NJ: Ablex.

Ruopp, R., Gal, S., Drayton, B., & Pfister, M. (Eds.). (1993). *LabNet: Toward a community of practice*. Hillsdale, NJ: Erlbaum.

Russell, M., Bebell, D., Cowan, J., & Corbelli, M. (2003). An AlphaSmart for each student: Do teaching and learning change with full access to word processors? *Computers and Composition, 20*(1), 51–76.

Russo, A. (2002). Mixing technology and testing. *The School Administrator, 59*(4), 6–12.

Rutledge, M. (1997). Reading the subtext on gender. *Educational Leadership, 54*(7), 71–73.

Ryan, A. M., & Patrick, H. (2001). The classroom social environment and changes in adolescents' motivation and engagement during middle school. *American Educational Research Journal, 38*(2), 437–460.

Rycek, R. F., Stuhr, S. L., & McDermott, J. (1998). Adolescent egocentrism and cognitive functioning during late adolescence. *Adolescence, 33*(132), 745–749.

Saban, A. (2002). Toward a more intelligent school. *Educational Leadership, 60*(2), 71–73.

Sadker, M. P., & Sadker, D, M. (1994). *Failing at fairness: How America's schools cheat girls*. New York: Charles Scribner's Sons.

Sadker, M. P, & Sadker, D. M. (2000). *Teachers, schools, and society* (5th ed.). Boston: McGraw-Hill.

Sadoski, M., Goetz, E. T., & Rodriguez, M. (2000). Engaging texts: Effects of concreteness on comprehensibility, interest, and recall in four text types. *Journal of Educational Psychology, 92*(1), 85–95.

Salmon, M., & Akaran, S. E. (2001). Enrich your kindergarten program with a cross-cultural connection. *Young Children, 56*(4), 30–32.

Salomon, G. (1988). AI in reverse: Computer tools that turn cognitive. *Journal of Educational Computing Research, 4*(2), 123–139.

Salomon, G., Globerson, T., & Guterman, E. (1989). The computer as a zone of proximal development: Internalizing reading-related metacognitions from a reading partner. *Journal of Educational Psychology, 81*(4), 620–627.

Salomon, G., & Perkins, D. N. (1989). Rocky roads to transfer: Rethinking mechanisms of a neglected phenomenon. *Educational Psychologist, 24*(2), 113–142.

Saltzman, J. (2003, July 20). Reinstating two-way bilingual ed is hailed. *The Boston Globe* (Globe West section), p. 1

Sameroff, A., & McDonough, S. C. (1994). Educational implications of developmental transitions: Revisiting the 5- to 7-year shift. *Phi Delta Kappan, 76*(3), 189–193.

Sanders, J. S. (1985). Here's how you can help girls take greater advantage of school computers. *American School Board Journal, 172*(4), 37–38.

Sanders-Phillips, K. (1989). Prenatal and postnatal influences on cognitive development. In G. L. Berry & J. K. Asamen (Eds.), *Black students: Psychosocial issues and academic achievement* (pp. 18–39). Newbury Park, CA: Sage.

Sandholtz, J. H., Ringstaff, C., & Dwyer, D. C. (1997). *Teaching with technology: Creating student-centered classrooms*. New York: Teachers College Press.

Sansone, C., & Harackiewicz, J. M. (Eds.). (2000). *Intrinsic and extrinsic motivation: The search for optimal motivation and performance*. San Diego: Academic Press.

Sapon-Shevin, M. (1996). Full inclusion as disclosing tablet: Revealing the flaws in our present system. *Theory into Practice, 35*(1), 35–41.

Saracho, O. N. (2001). Cognitive style and kindergarten pupils' preferences for teachers. *Learning and Instruction, 11*(3), 195–209.

Sarason, S. B. (1993). *The case for change: Rethinking the preparation of educators*. San Francisco: Jossey-Bass.

Scales, P. (1993). How teachers and education deans rate the quality of teacher preparation for the middle grades. *Journal of Teacher Education, 44*(5), 378–383.

Scardamalia, M., & Bereiter, C. (1991). Higher levels of agency for children in knowledge building: A challenge for the design of new knowledge media. *Journal of the Learning Sciences, 1*(1), 37–68.

Scardamalia, M. & Bereiter, C. (1996). Computer support for knowledge-building communities. In T. Koschmann (Ed.), *CSCL: Theory and practice* (pp. 249–268). Mahwah, NJ: Erlbaum.

Scarr, S., Weinberg, R. A., & Levine, A. (1986). *Understanding development*. San Diego, CA: Harcourt Brace Jovanovich.

Schery, T., & O'Connor, L. (1997). Language intervention: Computer training for young children with special needs. *British Journal of Educational Technology, 28*(4), 271–279.

Schifter, D. (1996). A constructivist perspective on teaching and learning mathematics. *Phi Delta Kappan, 77*(7), 492–499.

Schlaefli, A., Rest, J. R., & Thoma, S. J. (1985). Does moral education improve moral judgment? A meta-analysis of intervention studies using the Defining Issues Test. *Review of Educational Research, 55*(3), 319–352.

Schlagmüller, M., & Schneider, W. (2002). The development of organizational strategies in children: Evidence from a microgenetic longitudinal study. *Journal of Experimental Child Psychology, 81*(3), 298–319.

Schmidt, L. (2003). Getting smarter about supervising instruction. *Principal, 82*(4), 24–28.

Schmidt, P. (2003, November 28). The label 'Hispanic' irks some, but also unites. *Chronicle of Higher Education, 50*(14), A9.

Schneider, W., & Bjorklund, D. F. (1998). Memory. In W. Damon, D. Kuhn, & R. S. Siegler (Eds.), *Handbook of child psychology: Cognition, perception, and language* (Vol. 2, pp. 467–521). New York: Wiley.

Schneider, W., Knopf, M, & Stefanek, J. (2002). The development of verbal memory in childhood and adolescence: Findings from the Munich longitudinal study. *Journal of Educational Psychology, 94*(4), 751–761.

Scholten, B., & Whitmer, J. (1996). Hypermedia projects. *Learning and Leading with Technology, 24*(3), 59–62.

Schraw, G., Flowerday, T., & Lehman, S. (2001). Increasing situational interest in the classroom. *Educational Psychology Review, 13*(3), 211–224.

Schraw, G., & Lehman, S. (2001). Situational interest: A review of the literature and directions for future research. *Educational Psychology Review, 13*(1), 23–52.

Schunk, D. H. (1987). Peer models and children's behavioral change. *Review of Educational Research, 57*(2), 149–174.

Schunk, D. H. (1996). Goal and self-evaluative influences during children's cognitive skill learning. *American Educational Research Journal, 33*(2), 359–382.

Schunk, D. H. (1998). Teaching elementary students to self-regulate practice of mathematical skills with modeling. In D. H. Schunk & B. J. Zimmerman (Eds.), *Self-regulated learning: From teaching to self-reflective practice* (pp. 137–159). New York: Guilford Press.

Schunk, D. H. (2001). Social cognitive theory and self-regulated learning. In B. J. Zimmerman & D. H. Schunk (Eds.), *Self-regulated learning and academic achievement: Theoretical perspectives* (pp. 125–151). Mahwah, NJ: Erlbaum.

Schunk, D. H. (2004). *Learning theories: An educational perspective* (4th ed.). Upper Saddle River, NJ: Merrill Prentice Hall.

Schunk, D. H., & Hanson, A. R. (1985). Peer models: Influence on children's self-efficacy and achievement. *Journal of Educational Psychology, 77*(3) 313–322.

Schunk, D. H., & Hanson, A. R. (1989). Self-modeling and children's cognitive skill learning. *Journal of Educational Psychology, 81*(2), 155–163.

Schunk, D. H., Hanson, A. R., & Cox, P. D. (1987). Peer model attributes and children's achievement behaviors. *Journal of Educational Psychology, 79*(1), 54–61.

Schunk, D. H., & Miller, S. D. (2002). Self-efficacy and adolescents' motivation. In F. Pajares & T. Urdan (Eds.), *Academic motivation of adolescents* (pp. 29–52). Greenwich, CT: Information Age Publishing.

Schunk, D. H., & Pajares, F. (2002). The development of academic self-efficacy. In A. Wigfield & J. Eccles (Eds.), *The development of achievement motivation* (pp. 16–31). San Diego: Academic Press.

Schunk, D. H., & Zimmerman, B. J. (1997). Social origins of self-regulatory competence. *Educational Psychologist, 32*(4), 195–208.

Schuster, E. H. (2004). National and state writing tests: The writing process betrayed. *Phi Delta Kappan, 85*(5), 375–378.

Schvaneveldt, P. L., Miller, B. C., Berry, E. H., & Lee, T. R. (2001). Academic goals, achievement, and age at first sexual intercourse: Longitudinal, bidirectional influences. *Adolescence, 36*(144), 767–787.

Schweinhart, L. J., Weikart, D. P., & Hohmann, M. (2002). the High/Scope preschool curriculum: What is it? Why use it? *Journal of At-Risk Issues, 8*(1), 13–16.

Seagoe, M. V. (1970). *The learning process and school practice.* Scranton, PA: Chandler.

Seagoe, M. V. (1975). *Terman and the gifted.* Los Altos, CA: Kaufmann.

Searleman, A., & Herrmann, D. (1994). *Memory from a broader perspective.* New York: McGraw-Hill.

Secules, T., Cottom, C., Bray, M., & Miller, L. (1997). Creating schools for thought. *Educational Leadership, 54*(6), 56–60.

Seifert, K. L, & Hoffnung, R. J. (2000). *Child and adolescent development* (5th ed.). Boston: Houghton Mifflin.

Seligman, M. E. P. (1975). *Helplessness: On depression, development, and death.* San Francisco: Freeman.

Selman, R. L. (1980). *The growth of interpersonal understanding: Developmental and clinical analyses.* New York: Academic Press.

Selmes, I. (1987). *Improving study skills.* London: Hodder and Stoughton.

Semb, G. B., & Ellis, J. A. (1994). Knowledge taught in school: What is remembered? *Review of Eductional Research, 64*(2), 253–286.

Sexton, M., Harris, K. R., & Graham, S. (1998). Self-regulated strategy development and the writing process: Effects on essay writing and attributions. *Exceptional Children, 64*(3), 295–311.

Shapiro, A. (2002). The latest dope on research (about constructivism): Part I: Different approaches to constructivism—what it's all about. *International Journal of Educational Reform, 11*(4), 347–361.

Shapiro, A. (2003). The latest dope on research (about constructivism): Part II: On instruction and leadership. *International Journal of Educational Reform, 12*(1), 62–77.

Sharan, S. (1995). Group investigation: Theoretical foundations. In J. E. Pedersen & A. D. Digby (Eds.), *Secondary schools and cooperative learning* (pp. 251–277). New York: Garland.

Sharan, Y., & Sharan, S. (1999). Group investigation in the cooperative classroom. In S. Sharan (Ed.), *Handbook of cooperative learning methods* (pp. 97–114). Westport, CT: Greenwood Press.

Shavelson, R. J., & Baxter, G. P. (1992). What we've learned about assessing hands-on science. *Educational Leadership, 49*(8), 20–25.

Shayer, M. (1997). Piaget and Vygotsky: A necessary marriage for effective eductional interventions. In L. Smith, J. Dockrell, & P. Tomlinson (Eds.), *Piaget, Vygotsky, and beyond.* London: Routledge.

Shayer, M. (1999). Cognitive acceleration through science education II: Its effects and scope. *International Journal of Science Education, 21*(8), 883–902.

Shepard, R. N. (1978). Externalization of mental images and the act of creation. In B. S. Randhawa & W. E. Coffman (Eds.), *Visual learning, thinking, and communication.* New York: Academic Press.

Sherry, L., & Billig, S. H. (2002). Redefining a "virtual community of learners." *TechTrends, 46*(1), 48–51.

Shepard, L. A. (2000). The role of assessment in a learning culture. *Educational Researcher, 29*(7), 4–14.

Sherwood, R. D., Petrosino, A. J., Lin, X., & Cognition and Technology Group at Vanderbilt. (1998). Problem-based macro contexts in science instruction: Design issues and applications. In B. J. Fraser & K. G. Tobin (Eds.), *International handbook of science education, Part I* (pp. 349–362). Dordrecht, Netherlands: Kluwer.

Shrader, G., Lento, E., Gomez, L., & Pea, R. (1997). *Inventing interventions: Cases from CoVis–An analysis by SES.* Paper presented at the Annual meeting of the American Educational Research Association, Chicago, IL. (ERIC Document Reproduction Service No. ED 412 115)

Shulman, J. H., Whittaker, A., & Lew, M. (Eds.). (2002). *Using assessments to teach for understanding: A casebook for educators.* New York: Teachers College Press.

Shure, M. B. (1999, April). Preventing violence the problem-solving way. *Juvenile Justice Bulletin.* Retrieved January 2, 2002, from http//ojjdp.ncjrs.org/pubs/violvict .html.

Siegel, M. A., & Kirkley, S. E. (1998). Adventure learning as a vision of the digital learning environment. In C. J. Bonk & K. S. King (Eds.), *Electronic collaborators: Learner-centered technologies for literacy, apprenticeship, and discourse* (pp. 341–364). Mahwah, NJ: Erlbaum.

Siegle, D. (2002). Creating a living portfolio: Documenting student growth with electronic portfolios. *Gifted Child Today, 25*(3), 60–63.

Siegler, R. S. (1996). *Emerging minds: The process of change in children's thinking*. New York: Oxford University Press.

Siegler, R. S. (1998). *Children's thinking* (3rd ed.). Upper Saddle River, NJ: Prentice Hall.

Sigelman, C. K., & Shaffer, D. R. (1991). *Lifespan human development*. Pacific Grove, CA: Brooks Cole.

Sikula, J. (Ed.).(1996). *Handbook of research on teacher education* (2nd ed.). New York: Simon & Schuster.

Simon, S. (2002). The CASE approach for pupils with learning difficulties. *School Science Review, 83*(305), 73–79.

Simpson, E. J. (1972). *The classification of educational objectives: Psychomotor domain*. Urbana, IL: University of Illinois Press.

Singer, A. (1994). Reflections on multiculturalism. *Phi Delta Kappan, 76*(4), 284–288.

Singer, D. G., & Revenson, T. A. (1996). *A Piaget primer: How a child thinks* (rev. ed.). New York: Plume.

Singham, M. (1998). The canary in the mine: The achievement gap between Black and White students. *Phi Delta Kappan, 80*(1), 9–15.

Singham, M. (2003). The achievement gap: Myths and reality. *Phi Delta Kappan, 84*(8), 586–591.

Singletary, T. J., & Jordan, J. R. (1996). Exploring the globe. *The Science Teacher, 63*(3), 36–39.

Sipe, R. B. (2000). Virtually being there: Creating authentic experiences through interactive exchanges. *English Journal, 90*(2), 104–111.

Sirotnik, K. A. (2002). Promoting responsible accountability in schools and education. *Phi Delta Kappan, 83*(9), 662–673.

Sistek-Chandler, C. (2002). Enhancing literacy skills through technology. *Converge, 5*(6), 20–22.

Skinner, B. F. (1948). *Walden two*. New York: Macmillan.

Skinner, B. F. (1968). *The technology of teaching*. New York: Appleton-Century-Crofts.

Skinner, B. F (1976). *Particulars of my life*. New York: Knopf.

Skinner, B. F (1979). *The shaping of a behaviorist*. New York: Knopf.

Skinner, B. F (1983). *A matter of consequences*. New York: Knopf.

Skinner, B. F. (1984). The shame of American education. *American Psychologist, 39*(9), 947–954.

Skrtic, T. M., Sailor, W., & Gee, K. (1996). Voice, collaboration, and inclusion. *Remedial and special education, 17*(3), 142–157.

Slavin, R. E. (1989). PET and the pendulum: Faddism in education and how to stop it. *Phi Delta Kappan, 79*(10), 752–758.

Slavin, R. E. (1994). Student teams-achievement divisions. In S. Sharan (Ed.), *Handbook of cooperative learning methods* (pp. 3–19). Westport, CT: Greenwood Press.

Slavin, R. E. (1995). *Cooperative learning: Theory, Research, and Practice* (2nd ed.). Boston: Allyn & Bacon.

Sleeter, C. E., & Grant, C. A. (2003). *Making choices for multicultural education* (4th ed.). New York: John Wiley & Sons.

Smelter, R. W., Rasch, B. W., & Yudewitz, G. J. (1994). Thinking of inclusion for all special needs students? Better think again. *Phi Delta Kappan, 76*(1), 35–38.

Smilansky, S. (1968). *The effects of sociodramatic play on disadvantaged preschool children*. New York: Wiley.

Smith, C. L. (2003, August 12). *Internet or web? There's a difference*. Retrieved August 12, 2003, from http: www.cnn.com/2003/TECH/ptech/08/12/popsci.special.internet/index.html.

Smith, D. D. (2004). *Introduction to special education* (5th ed.). Boston: Allyn & Bacon.

Smith, J. K., Smith, L. F., & De Lisi, R. (2001). *Natural classroom assessment*. Thousand Oaks, CA: Corwin Press.

Smutny, J. F. (Ed.). (2003). *Designing and developing programs for gifted students*. Thousand Oaks, CA: Corwin Press.

Snow, R. E. (1986). Individual differences and the design of educational programs. *American Psychologist, 41*(10), 1029–1039.

Snow, R. E. (1992). Aptitude testing: Yesterday, today, and tomorrow. *Educational Psychologist, 27*(1), 5–32.

Snowman, J. (1986). Learning tactics and strategies. In G. D. Phye & T. Andre (Eds.), *Cognitive classroom learning: Understanding, thinking, and problem solving*. New York: Academic Press.

Snowman, J. (1987, October). *The keys to strategic learning*. Paper presented at the annual meeting of the Mid-Western Educational Research Association, Chicago, IL.

Sobel, D. M., Taylor, S. V., & Anderson, R. E. (2003). Shared accountability: Encouraging diversity—responsive teaching in an inclusive classroom. *Teaching Exceptional Children, 35*(6), 46–54.

Soderberg, P., & Price, F. (2003). An examination of problem-based teaching and learning in population genetics and evolution using EVOLVE, a computer simulation. *International Journal of Science Education, 25*(1), 35–55.

Soldier, L. L. (1989). Cooperative learning and the Native American student. *Phi Delta Kappan, 71*(2), 161–163.

Soldier, L. L. (1997). Is there an 'Indian' in your classroom? Working successfully with urban Native American students. *Phi Delta Kappan, 78*(8), 650–653.

Soloway, E., Norris, C., Curtis, M., Jansen, R., Krajcik, J., Marx, R., Fishman, B., & Blumenfeld, P. (2001). Making palm-sized computers the PC of choice for K–12. *Learning and Leading with Technology, 28*(7), 32–34, 56–57.

Sorell, G. T., & Montgomery, M. J. (2001). Feminist perspectives on Erikson's theory: Their relevance for contemporary identity development research. *Identity, 1*(2), 97–128.

Spalding, E. (2000). Performance assessment and the new standards project: A story of serendipitous success. *Phi Delta Kappan, 81*(10), 758–764.

Spear, N. E., & Riccio, D. C. (1994). *Memory: Phenomena and principles*. Boston: Allyn & Bacon.

Spear-Swerling, L., & Sternberg, R. J. (1998). Curing our 'epidemic' of learning disabilities. *Phi Delta Kappan, 79*(5), 397–401.

Spitz, H. H. (1999). Beleaguered Pygmalion: A history of the controversy over claims that teacher expectancy raises intelligence. *Intelligence, 27*(3), 199–234.

Sprinthall, N. A., Sprinthall, R. C. (1987). *Educational psychology; A developmental approach* (4th ed.). New York: Random House.

Sprinthall, N. A., Sprinthall, R. C., & Oja, S. N. (1998). *Educational psychology: A developmental approach* (7th ed.). New York: McGraw-Hill.

Stader, D., & Gagnepain, F. G. (2000). Mentoring: The power of peers. *American Secondary Education, 28*(3), 28–32.

Standing, L. (1973). Learning 10,000 pictures. *Quarterly Journal of Experimental Psychology, 25*(2), 207–222.

Standing, L., Conezio, J., & Haber, R. (1970). Perception and memory for pictures: Single trial learning of 2500 visual stimuli. *Psychonomic Science, 19*(2), 73–74.

Stanford, P., & Siders, J. A. (2001). E-pal writing! *Teaching Exceptional Children, 34*(2), 21–25.

Starratt, R. J. (2003). Opportunity to learn and the accountability agenda. *Phi Delta Kappan, 85*(4), 298–303.

Staub, F. C., & Stern, E. (2002). The nature of teachers' pedagogical content beliefs matters for students' achievement gains: Quasi-experimental evidence from elementary mathematics. *Journal of Educational Psychology, 94*(2), 344–355.

Stefanakis, E. H. (2002). *Multiple intelligences and portfolios*. Portsmouth, NH: Heinemann.

Steinberg, L. (1996). *Beyond the classroom: Why school reform has failed and what parents need to do*. New York: Simon & Schuster.

Steinberg, L. (2002). *Adolescence* (6th ed.). New York: McGraw-Hill.

Steinberg, L., & Morris, A. S. (2001). Adolescent development. In S. T. Fiske, D. L. Schacter, & C. Zahn-Waxler (Eds.), *Annual Review of Psychology* (pp. 83–110). Stanford, CA: Annual Reviews.

Stephens, L., Leavell, J. A., & Fabris, M. E. (1999). Producing video-cases that enhance instruction. *Journal of Technology and Teacher Education, 7*(4), 291–301.

Sternberg, R. J. (1985). *Beyond IQ: A triarchic theory of human intelligence.* New York: Cambridge University Press.

Sternberg, R. J. (1994). Allowing for thinking styles. *Educational Leadership, 52*(3), 36–40.

Sternberg, R. J. (1996). Matching abilities, instruction, and assessment: Reawakening the sleeping giant of ATI. In I. Dennis & P. Tapsfield (Eds.), *Human abilities: Their nature and measurement* (pp. 167–181). Mahwah, NJ: Erlbaum.

Sternberg, R. J. (1997a). What does it mean to be smart? *Educational Leadership, 54*(6), 20–24.

Sternberg, R. J. (1997b). *Thinking styles.* New York: Cambridge University Press.

Sternberg, R. J. (1997c). Technology changes intelligence: Societal implications and soaring IQ's. *Technos, 6*(2), 12–14.

Sternberg, R. J. (1998). Abilities are forms of developing expertise. *Educational Researcher, 27*(3), 11–20.

Sternberg, R. J. (2002a). Intelligence is not just inside the head: The theory of successful intelligence. In J. Aronson (Ed.), *Improving academic achievement* (pp. 227–244). San Diego, CA: Academic Press.

Sternberg, R. J. (2002b). Raising the achievement of all students: Teaching for successful intelligence. *Educational Psychology Review, 14*(4), 383–393.

Sternberg, R. J. (2003). Construct validity of the theory of successful intelligence. In R. J. Sternberg, J. Lautrey, & T. I. Lubart (Eds.), *Models of intelligence: International perspectives* (pp. 55–77). Washington, DC: American Psychological Association.

Sternberg, R. J., Ferrari, M., Clinkenbeard, P., & Grigorenko, E. L. (1996). Identification, instruction, and assessment of gifted children: A construct validation of a triarchic model. *Gifted Child Quarterly, 40*(3), 129–137.

Sternberg, R. J., & Grigorenko, E. L. (2001). A capsule history of theory and research on styles. In R. J. Sternberg & L. Zhang (Eds.), *Perspectives on thinking, learning, and cognitive styles* (pp. 1–21) Mahwah, NJ: Lawrence Erlbaum.

Sternberg, R. J., & Spear-Swerling, L. (1996). *Teaching for thinking.* Washington, DC: American Psychological Association.

Sternberg, R. J., Torff, B., & Grigorenko, E. (1998). Teaching for successful intelligence raises school achievement. *Phi Delta Kappan, 79*(9), 667–671.

Steubing, K. K., Fletcher, J. M., LeDoux, J. M., Lyon, G. R., Shaywitz, S. E., & Shaywitz, B. A. (2002). Validity of IQ-discrepancy classifications of reading disabilities: A meta-analysis. *American Educational Research Journal, 39*(2), 469–518.

Stevens, R. J., & Slavin, R. E. (1995), The cooperative elementary school: Effects on students' achievement, attitudes, and social relations. *American Educational Research Journal, 32*(2), 321–351.

Stiggins, R. J. (2001a). The unfulfilled promise of classroom assessment. *Educational Measurement: Issues and Practice, 20*(3), 5–15.

Stiggins, R. J. (2001b). *Student-involved classroom assessment* (3rd ed.). Upper Saddle River, NJ: Merrill Prentice Hall.

Stiggins, R. J. (2002). Assessment crisis: The absence of assessment FOR learning. *Phi Delta Kappan, 83*(10), 758–765.

Stinson, N., Jr. (2003, August). Working toward our goal: Eliminating racial and ethnic disparities in health. *Closing the Gap,* 1–2. Retrieved January 6, 2004, from http://www.omhrc.gov/OMH/sidebar/archivedctg.htm.

Stipek, D. (2002). *Motivation to learn: Integrating theory and practice* (4th ed.). Boston: Allyn & Bacon.

Strassman, B. K., & D'Amore, M. (2002). The write technology. *Teaching Exceptional Children, 34*(6), 28–31.

Streib, L. Y. (1993). Visiting and revisiting the trees. In M. Cochran-Smith & S. L. Lytle (Eds.), *Inside/outside: Teacher research and knowledge.* New York: Teachers College Press.

Sugar, S., & Sugar, K. K. (2002). *Primary games: Experiential learning activities for teaching children K–8.* San Francisco: Jossey-Bass.

Suomala, J., & Alajaaski, J. (2002). Pupils' problem-solving processes in a complex computerized learning environment. *Journal of Educational Computing Research, 26*(2), 155–176.

Supovitz, J. A. (1998). Gender and racial/ethnic differences on alternative science assessments. *Journal of Women and Minorities in Science and Engineering. 4*(2 & 3), 129–140.

Supovitz, J. A., & Brennan, R. T. (1997). Mirror, mirror on the wall, which is the fairest test of all? An examination of the equitability of portfolio assessment relative to standardized tests. *Harvard Educational Review, 67*(3), 472–506.

Susman, E. J. (1991). Stress and the adolescent. In R. M. Lerner, A. C. Peterson, & J. Brooks-Gunn (Eds.), *Encyclopedia of adolescence.* New York: Garland Publishing.

Svensson, A-K. (2000). Computers in school: Socially isolating or a tool to promote collaboration? *Journal of Educational Computing Research, 22*(4), 437–453.

Swanson, C. B. (2004). *Who graduates? Who doesn't? A statistical portrait of public high school graduation, class of 2001.* Washington, DC: The Urban Institute. Retrieved March 10, 2004, from www.urban.org/url.cfm?ID=410934.

Swanson, H. L., & Hoskyn, M. (1998). Experimental intervention research on students with learning disabilities: A meta-analysis of treatment outcomes. *Review of Educational Research, 68*(3), 277–321.

Swartz, A. (2003, August). Strengthening the community: Academic partnerships for research. *Closing the Gap,* 17–19. Retrieved January 6, 2004, from http://www.omhrc.gov/OMH/sidebar/archivedctg.htm.

Sweeting, H., & West, P. (2001). Being different: Correlates of the experience of teasing and bullying at age 11. *Research Papers in Education: Policy & Practice, 16*(3), 225–246.

Sweller, J., van Merriënboer, J. J. G., & Paas, F. G. W. C. (1998). Cognitive architecture and instructional design. *Educational Psychology Review, 10*(3), 251–296.

Tappan, M. B. (1998). Sociocultural psychology and caring pedagogy: Exploring Vygotsky's "hidden curriculum." *Educational Psychologist, 33*(1), 23–33.

Tauber, R. T., & Mester, C. S. (1994). *Acting lessons for teachers: Using performance skills in the classroom.* Westport, CT: Praeger.

Taylor, D., & Lorimer, M. (2002/2003). Helping boys succeed. *Educational Leadership, 60*(4), 68–70.

Taylor, G. R. (2003). *Informal classroom assessment strategies for teachers.* Lanham, MD: Scarecrow Press.

Taylor, P. C., & Fraser, B. J. (1998). *The constructivist learning environment survey: Mark 2.* Perth, Australia: Science and Mathematics Education Centre, Curtin University of Technology.

Taylor, P. C., Fraser, B. J., & Fisher, D. L. (1997). Monitoring constructivist classroom learning environments. *International Journal of Educational Research, 27*(4), 293–301,

Telem, M. (2001). Computerization of school administration: Impact on the principal's role—A case study. *Computers & Education, 37*(3–4), 345–362.

Teolis, B. (2002). *Ready-to-use conflict resolution activities for elementary students.* Paramus, NJ: The Center for Applied Research in Education.

Tharp, R. G., Estrada, P., Dalton, S. S., & Yamauchi, L. A. (2000). *Teaching transformed: Achieving excellence, fairness, inclusion, and harmony.* Boulder, CO: Westview Press.

Thoma, S. J. (1986). Estimating gender differences in the comprehension and preference of moral issues. *Developmental Review, 6*(2), 165–180.

Thomas, V. G. (2000). Learner-centered alternatives to social promotion and retention: A talent development approach. *Journal of Negro Education, 69*(4), 323–337.

Thomas, W. P., & Collier, V. P. (1997/1998). Two languages are better than one. *Educational Leadership, 55*(4), 23–26.

Thomas, W. P., & Collier, V. P. (1999). Accelerated schooling for English language learners. *Educational Leadership, 56*(7), 46–49.

Thompson, C. P., Cowan, T. M., & Frieman, J. (1993). *Memory search by a memorist.* Hillsdale, NJ: Erlbaum.

Thompson, M. S., DiCerbo, K. E., Mahoney, K., & MacSwan, J. (2002, January 25). ¿Exito en California? A validity critique of language program evaluations and analysis of English learner test scores. *Education Policy Analysis Archives, 10*(7). Retrieved January 26, 2004 from http://epaa.asu.edu/epaa/v10n7/.

Thorn, C. A. (2001). Knowledge management for educational information systems: What is the state of the field? *Educational Analysis Policy Archives, 9*(47). Retrieved February 22, 2004, from http://epaa.asu.edu/epaa/v9n47/.

Thorndike, R. L., Hagen, E. P., & Sattler, J. M. (1986). *The Stanford-Binet intelligence scale-IV.* Chicago: Riverside Publishing.

Thorndike, E. L., & Woodworth, R. S. (1901). The influence of improvement in one mental function upon the efficiency of other functions. *Psychological Review, 8,* 247–261.

Toch, T. (2003). *High schools on a human scale.* Boston: Beacon Press.

Tock, K., & Suppes, P. (2002, June 23). *The high dimensionality of students' individual differences in performance in EPGY's k6 computer-based mathematics curriculum.* Retrieved January 15, 2004, from http://www.epgy-stanford.edu/research/index.html?trajectories.html.

Tollefson, N. (2000). Classroom applications of cognitive theories of motivation. *Educational Psychology Review, 12*(1), 63–83.

Tomlinson, C. A. (2002). Invitations to learn. *Educational Leadership, 60*(1), 6–10.

Trefny, B. (2002). A guide to student information systems. *Technology & Learning, 23*(2), 54.

Trevisan, M. S. (2002). The states' role in ensuring assessment competence. *Phi Delta Kappan, 83*(10), 766–771.

Triandis, H. C. (1986). Toward pluralism in education. In S. Modgil, G. K. Verma, K. Mallick, & C. Modgil (Eds.), *Multicultural education: The interminable debate.* London: Falmer.

Trotter, A. (2003, May 8). A question of direction. *Education Week, 22*(35), 17–18, 20–21.

Trumper, R., & Gelbman, M. (2000). Investigating electromagnetic induction through a microcomputer-based laboratory. *Physics Education, 35*(2), 90–95.

Trumper, R., & Gelbman, M. (2002). Using MBL to verify Newton's second law and the impulse-momentum relationship with an arbitrary changing force. *School Science Review, 83*(305), 135–139.

Tudge, J. R. H., & Rogoff, B. (1989). Peer influences on cognitive development:

Piagetian and Vygotskian perspectives. In M. H. Bornstein & J. S. Bruner (Eds.), *Interaction in human development.* Hillsdale, NJ: Erlbaum.

Tudge, J., & Scrimsher, S. (2003). Lev S. Vygotsky on education: A cultural-historical, interpersonal, and individual approach to development. In B. J. Zimmerman & D. H. Schunk (Eds.), *Educational psychology: A century of contributions.* Mahwah, NJ: Erlbaum.

Tudge, J. R. H., & Winterhoff, P. A. (1993). Vygotsky, Piaget, and Bandura: Perspectives on the relations between the social world and cognitive development. *Human Development, 36*(2), 61–81.

Tukey, L. (2002). Differentiation. *Phi Delta Kappan, 84*(1), 63–64, 92.

Tulving, E., & Pearlstone, Z. (1966). Availability vs. accessibility of information in memory for words. *Journal of Verbal Learning and Verbal Behavior, 5*(4), 381–391.

Tuttle, H. G. (1997). Electronic portfolios tell a personal story. *MultiMedia Schools, 4*(1), 32–37.

Umar, K. B. (2003, August). Disparities persist in infant mortality: Creative approaches work to close the gap. *Closing the Gap,* 4–5. Retrieved January 6, 2004, from http://www.omhrc.gov/OMH/sidebar/archivedctg.htm.

Underwood, J., Cavendish, S., Dowling, S., Fogelman, K., & Lawson, T. (1996). Are integrated learning systems effective learning support tools? In M. R. Kibby & J. R. Hartley (Eds.), *Computer assisted learning: Selected contributions for the CAL 95 symposium.* Oxford, England: Elsevier Science.

Urdan, T., & Midgley, C. (2001). Academic self-handicapping: What we know, what more there is to learn. *Educational Psychology Review, 13*(2), 115–138.

Urdan, T., Midgley, C., & Anderman, E. M. (1998). The role of classroom goal structure in students' use of self-handicapping strategies. *American Educational Research Journal, 35*(1), 101–122.

Urdan, T., Ryan, A. M., Anderman, E. M., & Gheen, M. H. (2002). Goals, goal structures, and avoidance behaviors. In C. Midgley (Ed.), *Goals, goal structures, and patterns of adaptive learning* (pp. 55–83). Mahwah, NJ: Lawrence Erlbaum.

Uribe, D., Klein, J. D., & Sullivan, H. (2003). The effect of computer-mediated collaborative learning on solving ill-defined problems. *Educational Training, Research and Development, 51*(1), 5–19.

U.S. Bureau of the Census (2000). *National population projections I. Summary Files: Projections of the total resident population by 5-year age groups, race, and Hispanic origin with special age categories.* Retrieved January 2, 2002, from http://www.census.gov/population/www/projections/natsum-T3.html/.

U.S. Bureau of the Census. (2001). *Table H7. Women 15 to 44 years old who have ever had a child in the last year and children ever born per 1,000 women, by age and place of birth: June 1994, 1995, 1998 and 2000.* Retrieved September 15, 2003, from http://www.census.gov/population/socdemo/fertility/.

U.S. Bureau of the Census. (2002). *Table 1. People and families in poverty by selected characteristics: 2000 and 2001.* Retrieved September 15, 2003, from http://www.census.gov/hhes/www/poverty/poverty01.

U.S. Department of Education. (2001a). *To assure the free appropriate public education of all children with disabilities. Twenty-third annual report to Congress on the implementation of the Individuals with Disabilities Education Act.* Retrieved [add date], from www.ed.gov/offices/OSERS/OSEP/.

U.S. Department of Education. (2001b). *The condition of education 2001.* Washington, DC: U.S. Government Printing Office. Retrieved January 2, 2002, from http://nces.ed.gov/pubsearch/pubsinfo.asp?id=2001072.

U.S. Office of Immigration Statistics. (2003). *2002 yearbook of immigration statistics.* Retrieved September 15, 2003, from http://www.immigration.gov/graphics/shared/aboutus/statistics/ybpage.

Uyeda, S., Madden, J., Brigham, L. A., Luft, J. A., & Washburne, J. (2002). Solving authentic science problems. *The Science Teacher, 69*(1), 24–29.

Vallecorsa, A. L., deBettencourt, L. U., & Zigmond, N. (2000). *Students with mild disabilities in general education settings.* Upper Saddle River, NJ: Merrill Prentice Hall.

Valli, L.(1993). Teaching before and after professional preparation: The story of a high school mathematics teacher. *Journal of Teacher Education, 44*(2), 107–118.

van Laar, C. (2000). The paradox of low academic achievement but high self-esteem in African American students: An attributional account. *Educational Psychology Review, 12*(1), 33–62.

Van Wagenen, L., & Hibbard, K. M. (1998). Building teacher portfolios. *Educational Leadership, 55*(5), 26–29.

Vartanian, L. R. (2000). Revisiting the imaginary audience and personal fable constructs of adolescent egocentrism: A conceptual review. *Adolescence, 35*(140), 639–661.

Vasquez, J. A. (1990). Teaching to the distinctive traits of minority students. *The Clearing House, 63*(7), 299–304.

Vekiri, I. (2002). What is the value of graphical displays in learning? *Educational Psychology Review, 14*(3), 261–312.

Vermont Department of Education. (2004). *Vermont's framework of standards and learning opportunities.* Retrieved March 3, 2004 from http://www.state.vt.us/educ/new/html/pubs/framework.html.

Vitto, J. M. (2003). *Relationship-driven class-*

room management. Thousand Oaks, CA: Corwin Press.

Vitz, P. C. (1990). The use of stories in moral development: New psychological reasons for an old educational method. *American Psychologist, 45*(6), 709–720.

Vockell, E. L., & Fiore, D. J. (1993). Electronic gradebooks: What current programs can do for teachers. *The Clearing House, 66*(3), 141–145.

Vogler, K. E., & Kennedy, R. J., Jr. (2003). A view from the bottom: What happens when your school system ranks last? *Phi Delta Kappan, 84*(6), 446–448.

Volman, M., & van Eck, E. (2001). Gender equity and information technology in education: The second decade. *Review of Educational Research, 71*(4), 613–634.

Vondracek, F. W., Schulenberg, J., Skorikov, V., Gillespie, L. K., & Wahlheim, C. (1995). The relationship of identity status to career indecision during adolescence. *Journal of Adolescence, 18*(1), 17–30.

Vye, N. J., Goldman, S. R., Voss, J. F., Hmelo, C., Williams, S., & Cognition and Technology Group at Vanderbilt. (1997). Complex mathematical problem solving by individuals and dyads. *Cognition and Instruction, 15*(4), 435–484.

Vygotsky, L. S. (1986). *Thought and language* (A. Kozulin, Trans.). Cambridge, MA: MIT Press. (Original work published 1934)

Wadsworth, B. J. (1996). *Piaget's theory of cognitive and affective development* (5th ed.). White Plains, NY: Longman.

Walberg, H. J. (1990). Productive teaching and instruction: Assessing the knowledge base. *Phi Delta Kappan, 71*(6), 470 478.

Walker, J. E., & Shea, T. M. (1999). *Behavior management: A practical approach for educators* (7th ed.). Upper Saddle River, NJ: Merrill.

Walker, J. E., Shea, T. M., & Bauer, A. M. (2004). *Behavior management: A practical approach for educators* (8th ed.). Upper Saddle River, NJ: Merrill Prentice Hall.

Wallace-Broscious, A., Serafica, F. C., & Osipow S. H. (1994). Adoelscent career development: Relationships to self-concept and identity status. *Journal of Research on Adolescence, 4*(1), 127–149.

Walsh, W. B., & Betz, N. E. (2001). *Tests and assessment* (4th ed.). Upper Saddle River, NJ: Merrill Prentice Hall.

Wang, A. C., & Chuang, C. (2002). Applicable adaptive testing models for school teachers. *Education Media International, 39*(1), 55–59.

Wang, M. C., Haertel, G. D., & Walberg, H. J. (1993). Toward a knowledge base for school learning. *Review of Educational Research, 63*(3), 249–294.

Wasserman, S. (2001). Curriculum enrichment with computer software: Adventures in the trade. *Phi Delta Kappan, 82*(8), 592–597.

Waterman, A. S. (1988). Identity status theory and Erikson's theory: Communalities and differences. *Developmental Review, 8*(2), 185–208.

Waterman, A. S., & Archer, S. L. (1990). A life-span perspective on identity formation: Developments in form, function, and process. In P. B. Baltes, D. L. Featherman, & R. M. Lerner (Eds.), *Life-span development and behavior* (Vol. 10, pp. 30–57). Hillsdale, NJ: Erlbaum.

Watson, J. B. (1913). Psychology as the behaviorist views it. *Psychological Review, 20,* 158–177.

Watson, M. F., & Protinsky, H. (1991). Identity status of black adolescents: An empirical investigation. *Adolescence, 26*(104), 963–966.

Wasserman, S. (1999). Shazam! you're a teacher: Facing the illusory quest for certainty in classroom practice. *Phi Delta Kappan, 80*(6), 464–468.

Waxman, H. C., Connell, M. L., & Gray, J. (2002, December). *A quantitative synthesis of recent research on the effects of teaching and learning with technology on student outcomes* (NCREL Report). Naperville, IL: North Central Regional Educational Laboratory.

Wayne, A. J., & Youngs, P. (2003). Teacher characteristics and student achievement gains: A review. *Review of Educational Research, 73*(1), 89–122.

Weah, W., Simmons, V. C., & Hall, M. (2000). Service-learning and multicultural/multiethnic perspectives: From diversity to equity. *Phi Delta Kappan, 81*(9), 673–675.

Webb, N. M., Nemer, K. M., Chizhik, A. W., & Sugrue, B. (1998). Equity issues in collaborative group assessment: Group composition and performance. *American Educational Research Journal, 35*(4), 607–651.

Webb, N. M., Nemer, K. M., & Zuniga, S. (2002). Short circuits of superconductors? Effects of group composition on high-achieving students' science assessment performance. *American Educational Research Journal, 39*(4), 943–989.

Wechsler, D. (1975). Intelligence defined and undefined: A relativistic appraisal. *American Psychologist, 30*(2), 135–139.

Wechsler, D. (1997). *Wechsler adult intelligence scale-III.* New York: Psychological Corporation.

Wechsler, D. (2003). *Wechsler intelligence scale for children-IV.* New York: Psychological Corporation.

Wedman, J. M., Espinosa, L. M., & Laffey, J. M. (1999). A process for understanding how a field-based course influences teachers' beliefs and practices. *Teacher Educator, 34*(3), 189–214.

Weiler, G. (2003). Using weblogs in the classroom. *English Journal, 92*(5), 73–75.

Weiner, I. B. (1975). Depression in adolescence. In F. F Flach & S. C. Draghi (Eds.), *The nature and treatment of depression.* New York: Wiley.

Weinert, F. E., & Hany, E. A. (2003). The stability of individual differences in intellectual development: Empirical evidence, theoretical problems, and new research questions. In R. J. Sternberg, J. Lautrey, & T. I. Lubart (Eds.), *Models of intelligence: International perspectives* (pp. 169–181). Washington, DC: American Psychological Association.

Weinstein, C. S., & Mignano, A. J., Jr. (2003). *Elementary classroom management: Lessons from research and practice* (3rd ed.). Boston: McGraw-Hill.

Weiss, R. P. (2000). Howard Gardner talks about technology. *Training & Development, 54*(9), 52–56.

Wentzel, K. R. (2002). Are effective teachers like good parents? Teaching styles and student adjustment in early adolescence. *Child Development, 73*(1), 287–301.

Wertsch, J. V. (1998). *Mind as action.* New York: Oxford University Press.

Wertsch, J. V., & Tulviste, P. (1996). L. S. Vygotsky and contemporary developmental psychology. In H. Daniels (Ed.), *An introduction to Vygotsky.* New York: Routledge.

Westerman, D. A. (1991). Expert and novice teacher decision making. *Journal of Teacher Education, 42*(4), 292–305.

Wheatley, G. H. (1991). Constructivist perspectives on science and mathematics learning. *Science Education, 75*(1), 9–21.

Wheelock, A. (1992). *Crossing the tracks: How "untracking" can save America's schools.* New York: New Press.

Wheelock, A. (1994). *Alternatives to tracking and ability grouping.* Arlington, VA: American Association of School Administrators.

Whimbey, A., & Lochhead, J. (1999). *Problem solving and comprehension* (6th ed.). Mahwah, NJ: Erlbaum.

White, R., Algozzine, B., Audette, R., Marr, M. B., & Ellis, E. D., Jr. (2001). Unified Discipline: A school-wide approach for managing problem behavior. *Intervention in School and Clinic, 37*(1), 3–8.

White House is easing up on federal requirement for testing in schools. (2004, March 30). *St. Louis Post-Dispatch,* p. A4.

Whittaker, C. R., Salend, S. J., & Duhaney, D. (2001). Creating instructional rubrics for inclusive classrooms. *Teaching Exceptional Children, 34*(2), 8–13.

Wicks-Nelson, R., & Israel, A. C. (2003). *Behavior disorders of childhood* (5th ed.). Upper Saddle River, NJ: Prentice-Hall.

Wiedmer, T. L. (1998). Digital portfolios: Capturing and demonstrating skills and levels of performance. *Phi Delta Kappan, 79*(8), 586–589.

Wigfield, A., Battle, A., Keller, L. B., & Eccles, J. S. (2002). Sex differences in motivation, self-concept, career aspiration, and career choice: Implications for cognitive development. In A. McGillicuddy-De Lisi & R. De Lisi(Eds.), *Biology, society, and behavior: The development of sex differences in cognition* (pp. 93–124). Westport, CT: Ablex.

Wigfield, A., & Eccles, J. S. (2002a). Students' motivation during the middle school years. In J. Aronson (Ed.), *Improving academic achievement* (pp. 159–184). San Diego, CA: Academic Press.

Wigfield, A., & Eccles, J. S. (2002b). The development of competence beliefs, expectancies for success, and achievement values from childhood through adolescence. In A. Wigfield & J. S. Eccles (Eds.), *Development of achievement motivation* (pp. 91–120). San Diego: Academic Press.

Wigfield, A., & Eccles, J. (Eds.). (2002c). *Development of achievement motivation.* San Diego, CA: Academic Press.

Wiles, J., & Bondi, J. (2001). *The new American middle school* (3rd ed.). Upper Saddle River, NJ: Merrill Prentice-Hall.

Williams, J. P., Lauer, K. D., Hall, K. M., Lord, K. M., Gugga, S. S., Bak, S-J., Jacobs, P. R., & deCani, J. S. (2002).Teaching elementary school students to identify story themes. *Journal of Educational Psychology, 94*(2), 235–248.

Willig, A. C. (1985). A meta-analysis of selected studies on the effectiveness of bilingual education. *Review of Educational Research, 55*(3), 269–318.

Wilson, S. M., Floden, R. E., & Ferrini-Mundy, J. (2002). Teacher preparation research: An insider's view from the outside. *Journal of Teacher Education, 53*(3), 190–204.

Windschitl, M. (2002). Framing constructivism in practice as the negotiation of dilemmas: An analysis of the conceptual, pedagogical, cultural, and political challenges facing teachers. *Review of Educational Research, 72*(2), 131–175.

Windschitl, M., & Sahl, K. (2002). Tracing teachers' use of technology in a laptop computer school: The interplay of teacher beliefs, social dynamics, and institutional culture. *American Educational Research Journal, 39*(1), 165–206.

Winkler, A. M. (2003). The power of the A word. *American School Board Journal, 190*(6), 22–24.

Winne, P. H. (2001). Self-regulated learning viewed from models of information processing. In B. J. Zimmerman & D. H. Schunk (Eds.), *Self-regulated learning and academic achievement: Theoretical perspectives* (2nd ed., pp. 153–189). Mahwah, NJ: Erlbaum.

Winne, P. H., & Jamieson-Noel, D. (2002). Exploring students' calibration of self reports about study tactics and achievement. *Contemporary Educational Psychology, 27*(4), 551–572.

Winne, P. H., & Jamieson-Noel, D. (2003). Self-regulating studying by objectives for learning: Students' reports compared to a model. *Contemporary Educational Psychology, 28*(3), 259–276.

Winne, P. H., & Stockley, D. B. (1998). Computing technologies as sites for developing self-regulated learning. In D. H. Schunk & B. J. Zimmerman (Eds.), *Self-regulated learning: From teaching to reflective practice* (pp. 107–136). New York: Guilford Press.

Winner, E. (1997). Exceptionally high intelligence and schooling. *American Psychologist, 52*(10), 1070–1081.

Witkin, H. A., Moore, C. A., Goodenough, D. R., & Cox, P. W. (1977). Field-dependent and field-independent cognitive styles and their educational implications. *Review of Educational Reswearch, 47*(1), 1–64.

Wlodkowski, R. J. (1978). *Motivation and teaching: A practical guide.* Washington, DC: National Education Association.

Wlodkowski, R. J., & Ginsberg, M. B. (1995).A framework for culturally responsive teaching. *Educational Leadership, 53*(1), 17–21.

Womersley, D. (Ed.). (1998). *Edmund Burke: A philosophical enquiry into the origin of our ideas of the sublime and beautiful, and other pre-revolutionary writings.* London, England: Penguin Books.

Wong, B. Y. L. (1985). Self-questioning instructional research: A review. *Review of Educational Research, 55*(2), 227–268.

Woods, P. (1996). *Researching the art of teaching: Ethnography for educational use.* New York: Routledge.

Woodul, III, C. E., Vitale, M. R., & Scott, B. J. (2000). Using a cooperative multimedia learning environment to enhance learning and affective self-perceptions of at-risk students in grade 8. *Journal of Educational Technology Systems, 28*(3), 239–252.

Woolsey, K., & Bellamy, R. (1997). Science education and technology: Opportunities to enhance student learning. *The Elementary School Journal, 97*(4), 385–399.

Wuthrick, M. A. (1990). Blue jays win! Crows go down in defeat! *Phi Delta Kappan, 71*(7), 553–556.

Wyatt, R. L., III, & Looper, S. (2004). *So you have to have a portfolio? A teacher's guide to preparation and presentation.* Thousand Oaks, CA: Corwin Press.

Wynn, R. L., & Fletcher, C. (1987). Sex role development and early educational experiences. In D. B. Carter (Ed.), *Current conceptions of sex roles and sex typing.* New York: Praeger.

Yager, R. E. (2000). The constructivist learning model. *Science Teacher, 67*(1), 44–45.

Yang, S. C. (2001). Synergy of constructivism and hypermedia from three constructivist perspectives: Social, semiotic, and cognitive. *Journal of Educational Computing Research, 24*(4), 321–361.

Yates, F. A. (1966). *The art of memory.* London: Routledge & Kegan Paul.

Yau, R. (2002). High-achieving elementary schools with large percentages of low-income African American students: A review and critique of the current research. In S. J. Denbo & L. M. Beaulieu (Eds.), *Improving schools for African American students* (pp. 193–217). Springfield, IL: Charles C. Thomas.

Yoerg, K. (2002). Painting patterns with pixels. *Arts & Activities, 131*(4), 50–51.

Yonezawa, S., Wells, A. S., & Serna, I. (2002). Choosing tracks: "Freedom of choice" in detracking schools. *American Educational Research Journal, 39*(1), 37–67.

York-Barr, J., Sommers, W. A., Ghere, G. S., & Montie, J. (2001). *Reflective practice to improve schools.* Thousand Oaks, CA: Corwin Press.

Young, J. D. (1996). The effect of self-regulated learning strategies on performance in learner controlled computer-based instruction. *Educational Technology Research and Development, 44*(2), 17–27.

Ysseldyke, J. E., & Algozzine, B., & Thurlow, M. L. (2000). *Critical issues in special education.* (3rd ed.). Boston: Houghton Mifflin.

Ysseldyke, J., Kosciolek, S., Spicuzza, R., & Boys, C. (2003). Effects of a learning information system on mathematics achievement and classroom structure. *Journal of Educational Research, 96*(3), 163–173.

Zeichner, K. M., & Liston, D. P. (1996). *Reflective teaching: An introduction.* Mahwah, NJ: Erlbaum.

Zeldin, A. L., & Pajares, F. (2000). Against the odds: Self-efficacy beliefs of women in mathematical, scientific, and technological careers. *American Educational Research Journal, 37*(1), 215–246.

Zellermayer, M., Salomon, G., Globerson, T., & Givon, H. (1991). Enhancing writing-related metacognitions through a computerized writing partner. *American Educational Research Journal, 28*(2), 373–391.

Zenisky, A., & Sireci, S. G. (2002). Technological innovations in large-scale assessment. *Applied Measurement in Education, 15*(4), 337–362.

Zhang, L., & Sternberg, R. J. (2001). Thinking styles across cultures: Their relationships with student learning. In R. J. Sternberg & L-f. Zhang (Eds.), *Perspectives on thinking, learning, and cognitive styles* (pp. 197–226). Mahwah, NJ: Erlbaum.

Zigmond, N., Jenkins, J., Fuchs, L. S., Deno, S., Fuchs, D., Baker, J. N., Jenkins, L., & Couthino, M. (1995). Special education in restructured schools: Findings from three multi-year studies. *Phi Delta Kappan, 76*(7), 531–540.

Zimmerman, B. J. (1990). Self-regulating academic learning and achievement: The emergence of a social cognitive perspective. *Educational Psychology Review, 2*(2), 173–200.

Zimmerman, B. J. (2000). Attaining self-regulation: A social cognitive perspective. In M. Boekaerts, P. R. Pintrich, & M. Zeidner

(Eds.), *Handbook of self-regulation* (pp. 13–39). San Diego: Academic Press.

Zimmerman, B. J. (2001). Theories of self-regulated learning and academic achievement: An overview and analysis. In B. J. Zimmerman & D. H. Schunk (Eds.), *Self-regulated learning and academic achievement: Theoretical perspectives* (pp. 1–37). Mahwah, NJ: Erlbaum.

Zimmerman, B. J. (2002). Achieving self-regulation: the trial and triumph of adolescence. In F. Pajares & T. Urdan (Eds.), *Academic motivation of adolescents* (pp. 1–27). Greenwich, CT: Information Age Publishing.

Zimmerman, B. J., & Bandura, A. (1994). Impact of self-regulatory influences on writing course attainment. *American Educational Research Journal, 31*(4), 845–862.

Zimmerman, B. J., & Kitsantas, A. (2002). Acquiring writing revision and self-regulatory skill through observation and emulation. *Journal of Educational Psychology, 94*(4), 660–668.

Zimmerman, B. J., & Martinez-Pons, M. (1990). Student differences in self-regulated learning: Relating grade, sex, and giftedness to self-efficacy and strategy use. *Journal of Educational Psychology, 82*(1), 51–59.

Zuo, L., & Cramond, B. (2001). An examination of Terman's gifted children from the theory of identity. *Gifted Child Quarterly, 45*(4), 251–259.

Author/Source Index

Subject Index

Text Credits

Text Credits

Ch. 1
p. 12 *Case in Print:* "Dedication, Innovation Add Up to Prize for Teacher" by Alexa Aguilar, *St. Louis Post-Dispatch*, November 15, 2003. Reprinted by permission of the St. Louis Post-Dispatch, copyright 2003;
p. 19 *Table 1.1:* Reprinted with permission from National Education Technology Standards for Students Connecting Curriculum and Technology.

Ch. 2
p. 54 *Table 2.3:* Lickona, Thomas, (1998). "A more complex analysis is needed." Phi Delta Kappan, 79(6), 449–454. Reprinted by permission of Phi Delta Kappa International and the author;
p. 60 *Case in Print:* "Reading, Writing, and Character Education" by Carolyn Bower, *St. Louis Post-Dispatch*, November 28, 2003. Reprinted by permission of the St. Louis Post-Dispatch, copyright 2003.

Ch. 3
p. 90 *Case in Print:* "Middle Ground" by Carolyn Bower, *St. Louis Post-Dispatch*, May 29, 2002. Reprinted by permission of the St. Louis Post-Dispatch, copyright 2002.

Ch. 4
p. 113 *Table 4.2:* Sternberg, R. J., "What Does It Mean to be Smart?", *Educational Leadership*, 54(6), 20–24. Reprinted by permission;
p. 117 *Table 4.3:* Adapted from R. J. Sternberg, *Educational Leadership*, 52(3), 1994, 36–40;
p. 124 *Case in Print:* "Girl-Powered" by Carolyn Bower, *St. Louis Post-Dispatch*, December 1, 2000. Reprinted with permission of the *St. Louis Post-Dispatch*, Copyright 2000.

Ch. 5
p. 142 *Case in Print:* "Minority Students Trail in Suburbs" by Connie Langland and Alletta Emeno, *Philadelphia Inquirer*, December 14, 2003. Reprinted with permission by The Philadelphia Inquirer;
p. 147 Student-Teacher dialog excerpt, from M. Elrich, "The Stereotype Within," in *Educational Leadership*, 31 (8), 1994, pp. 12–15;
p. 159 Excerpt J. I. Mendoza, "On Being Mexican American," in Phi Delta Kappan, 76(40), 1994, pp. 293–295.

Ch. 6
p. 182 *Case in Print:* "Study Finds Special Ed Disparities" by Linda Perlstein, *Washington Post*, December 18, 2003. © 2003, The Washington Post, reprinted with permission.

Ch. 7
p. 224 *Case in Print:* "School Rewards Good Behavior" by Janet Sugameli, *The Detroit News*, December 29, 2003. Reprinted with permission from The Detroit News.

Ch. 8
p. 243 *Figure 8.2:* From G. H. Bower, M. C. Clark, A. M. Lesgold, and D. Winzenz, "Hierarchical Retrieval Schemes in Recall of Categorized Word Lists." *Journal of Verbal Learning and Verbal Behavior*, 1969, 8(3), 1969, 323–343. Copyright 1969 by Academic Press. Reproduced by permission of the publisher and the authors;
p. 250 *Case in Print:* "'Memory' Can Play Tricks, Researchers Discover Here" by John G. Carlton, *St. Louis Post-Dispatch*, November 8, 1998. Reprinted with permission of the *St. Louis Post-Dispatch*, Copyright 1998;
p. 261 *Table 8.3:* From King A. (1992), "Facilitating elaborative learning through guided student-generated questioning." *Educational Psychologist*, 27 (1), 111–126. Reprinted by permission of Lawrence Erlbaum Associates, Inc.

Ch. 9
p. 278 *Figure 9.1:* From A. Bandura, Self-efficacy: The exercise of control (New York: W. H. Freeman and Company, 1997);

p. 283 *Figure 9.3:* Reprinted from B. J. Zimmerman, "Attaining self-regulation: A social cognitive perspective," in M. Boekaerts, P. R. Pintrich, & M. Zeidner (Eds.), *Handbook of Self-Regulation*, pp. 13–39. Copyright ©2000, with permission from Elsevier;

p. 288 *Case in Print:* "Students Unprepared for Rigors of College" by Fredreka Schouten, Gannett News Service, October 30, 2003. *USA Today.* Copyright 10/30/2003. Reprinted with permission.

Ch. 10

p. 316 *Case in Print:* "All-USA Teacher Team: Changing Lives One Class at a Time" by Tracy Wong Briggs, *USA Today*, October 14, 1999. *USA Today.* Copyright October 14, 1999. Reprinted with permission;

p. 331 *Venn Diagram:* "Solution Using Venn Diagram," adapted from A. Whimbey and J. Lockhead, *Problem Solving and Comprehension*, Sixth Edition, (Mahway, N. J.: Lawrence Erlbaum 1999), pp. 104, 128. Reprinted by permission;

p. 332 *Flow Diagram:* "Solution Using Flow Diagram," adapted from A. Whimbey and J. Lockhead, *Problem Solving and Comprehension*, Sixth Edition, (Mahway, N. J.: Lawrence Erlbaum 1999), pp. 104, 128. Reprinted by permission.

Ch. 11

p. 360 *Figure 11.2:* Source: Novak, J. D. & Gowin, D. B. (1984). *Learning How to Learn.* Cambridge, England: Cambridge University Press. Reprinted by permission;

p. 366 *Case in Print:* "Top Teacher Thrives on Unorthodox" by Elaine Rivera, *Washington Post*, November 6, 2003. ©2003, The Washington Post, reprinted with permission.

Ch. 12

p. 400 *Case in Print:* "Fairy Tales Come to Life at School" by Janet Sugameli, *The Detroit News*, December 29, 2003. Reprinted with permission from The Detroit News;

p. 403 *Table 12.1:* J. E. Brophy, "Teacher Praise: A Functional Analysis," *Review of Educational Research*, 51, No. 1 (1981), 532. Copyright ©1981. American Educational Research Association, Washington D.C. Used with permission;

p. 413 *Figure 12.3:* F. Guay, H. Marsh, & M. Boivin, "Academic self-concept and academic achievement: Developmental perspectives on their causal ordering," in *Journal of Educational Psychology*, 95(1), pp. 124–136. Copyright © by the American Psychological Association. Reprinted with permission.

Ch. 13

pp. 441–443 Adapted excerpts from M. Metzger, "Learning to discipline," Phi Delta Kappan, 84(1), pp. 77–84. English teacher at Brookline Height School in Massachusetts;

p. 446 *Case in Print:* "Kids Learn Anger Management" by Janet Sugameli, *The Detroit News*, January 12, 2004. Reprinted with permission from The Detroit News.

Ch. 14

p. 463 *Figure 14.1:* From C. S. Parke & S. Lane, "Example of a Performance Assessment: Interpreting a Graph," "Learning from performance assessments in math," in *Educational Leadership*, 54 (6), 1997, pp.26–29. Reprinted by permission;

p. 465 *Table 14.1:* From K. Montgomery, "Classroom rubrics: Systematizing what teachers do naturally." *The Clearing House*, 73 (6), 2000, pp. 324–328. Reprinted with permission of the Helen Dwight Reid Educational Foundation. Published by Heldref Publications, 1319 Eighteenth St., NW, Washington, DC 20036-1802. Copyright © 2000;

p. 468 *Case in Print:* "Teachers Look for New Ways to Measure Learning" by Dale Singer, *St. Louis Post-Dispatch*, January 26, 1998. Reprinted by permission of the St. Louis Post-Dispatch, copyright 1998;

p. 479 *Table 14.2:* From "Computerized Gradebooks and the Myth of Objectivity" by Thomas R. Guskey. Phi Delta Kappan, 83(10), 2002, pp. 775–780. Reprinted with permission of the author.

Ch. 15

p. 505 *Case in Print:* "Those That Fail to Meet Standards Find Roadblocks to Remedies" by Alexa Aguilar, in *St. Louis Post-Dispatch*, September 3, 2003. Reprinted by permission of the St. Louis Post-Dispatch, copyright 2003.

Ch. 16

p. 527 *Figure 16.3:* From L. Schmidt, "Getting smarter about supervising instruction," in *Principal*, 82(4), 2003, pp. 24–28. Reprinted with permission. Copyright 2003 National Association of Elementary School Principals. All rights reserved;

p. 534 *Case in Print:* "Portfolios Give Prospective Teachers an Edge When They Interview for Jobs" by Valerie Schremp, *St. Louis Post-Dispatch*, December 14, 1997. Reprinted with permission of the *St. Louis Post-Dispatch*, Copyright 1997.

Photo Credits

Chapter 1: p. 2, David Young-Wolff/PhotoEdit; p. 5, Flash!Light/Stock Boston; p. 8, Bob Daemmrich/Bob Daemmrich Photography; p. 10, Bill Bachman/PhotoEdit; p. 15, Ken Whitmore/Getty Images.

Chapter 2: p. 28, Stewart Cohen/Index Stock Imagery; p. 34, Paul Conklin/PhotoEdit; p. 39, Flash!Light/Stock Boston; p. 48, left, Susie Fitzhugh; p. 48, right, David Young Wolff/PhotoEdit; p. 51, David Young Wolff/PhotoEdit; p. 59, Myrleen Ferguson/PhotoEdit.

Chapter 3: p. 70, Susie Fitzhugh; p. 77, Geoffrey Biddle; p. 80, left, David M. Grossman/Photo Researchers, Inc.; p. 80, right, Junebug Clark/Photo Researchers, Inc.; p. 82, David Young Wolff/PhotoEdit; p. 86, Susie Fitzhugh; p. 88, Elizabeth Crews; p. 93, Adamsmith/Getty Images; p. 96, Richard Hutchings/PhotoEdit.

Chapter 4: p. 105, Ray Scott/The Image Works; p. 108, Will Hart/PhotoEdit; p. 111, left, David Young Wolff/PhotoEdit; p. 111, right, Laura Druskis/Stock Boston; p. 115, left, Susie Fitzhugh; p. 115, right, Erika Stone; p. 123, Bob Daemmrich/Bob Daemmrich Photography.

Chapter 5: p. 139, Steve Skjold/Skjold Photographs; p. 142, Catherine Karnow/Corbis; p. 154, John Elk/Stock Boston; p. 155, David Young Wolff/PhotoEdit; p. 160, Felicia Martinez/PhotoEdit; p. 165, Bob Daemmrich/Stock Boston.

Chapter 6: p. 174, Don and Pat Valenti; p. 179, Bill Aron/PhotoEdit; p. 185, Michael Newman/PhotoEdit; p. 191, Laura Dwight; p. 196, Frank Siteman/Stock Boston; p. 201, Bob Daemmrich/The Image Works.

Chapter 7: p. 213, Lawrence Migdale/Stock Boston; p. 214, Bob Daemmrich/The Image Works; p. 219, Bob Daemmrich/PhotoEdit; p. 223, Jim Pickerell/Stock Boston; p. 230, Susie Fitzhugh.

Chapter 8: p. 244, Michael Newman/PhotoEdit; p. 245, Jim Cummins/Getty Images; p. 247, Jeff Greenberg/PhotoEdit; p. 249, Elizabeth Crews; p. 263, Rick Friedman/Black Star; p. 267, Rhoda Sidney/Stock Boston.

Chapter 9: p. 282, Paul Barton/Corbis; p. 286, Michael Newman/PhotoEdit; p. 291, Laura Dwight; p. 298, Michael Newman/PhotoEdit.

Chapter 10: p. 313, left, Joel Gordon; p. 313, right, Will & Deni McIntyre/Photo Researchers, Inc.; p. 324, Seth Resnick/Stock Boston; p. 328, Susie Fitzhugh; p. 335, Steve Skjold/Skjold Photographs.

Chapter 11: p. 350, left and right, Robert Finken/Index Stock Imagery; p. 351, Bob Daemmrich/Bob Daemmrich Photography; p. 355, Bob Daemmrich/Stock Boston; p. 359, Jeff Greenberg/PhotoEdit; p. 363, Steve Skjold/Skjold Photographs; p. 373, Cindy Charles/PhotoEdit.

Chapter 12: p. 392, Michael Newman/PhotoEdit; p. 397, Blair Seitz/Photo Researchers, Inc.; p. 407, Richard Hutchings/PhotoEdit; p. 411, John Lei/Stock Boston; p. 414, David Young Wolff/PhotoEdit.

Chapter 13: p. 425, Bob Daemmrich/Bob Daemmrich Photography; p. 428, David Young Wolff/PhotoEdit; p. 435, Junebug Clark/Photo Researchers, Inc.; p. 439, Bill Aron/PhotoEdit; p. 447, Richard Hutchings/PhotoEdit; p. 451, Elizabeth Crews.

Chapter 14: p. 457, Mary Kate Denny/PhotoEdit; p. 462, Steve Skjold/Skjold Photographs; p. 472, Bob Daemmrich/Bob Daemmrich Photography; p. 483, Michael Newman/PhotoEdit; p. 486, Bill Aron/PhotoEdit.

Chapter 15: p. 493, Don Stevenson/Index Stock Imagery; p. 495, Spencer Grant/PhotoEdit; p. 503, Bob Daemmrich/The Image Works; p. 510, Peter Hvizdak/The Image Works; p. 516, PhotoDisc Green/Getty Images.

Chapter 16: p. 528, Mary Kate Denny/PhotoEdit; p. 531, Michael Newman/PhotoEdit.

Correlation Chart for INTASC Principles and Standards

INTASC:

The following chart compares the content of *Psychology Applied to Teaching* with the ten principles and related standards published by the Interstate New Teacher Assessment and Support Consortium (INTASC). See Chapter 1 of the text for a discussion of INTASC. A more detailed version of this chart is available at the textbook web site, which you can access from http://education.college.hmco.com/students.

INTASC Principles and Standards	Psychology Applied to Teaching
1. Subject Matter Expertise *The teacher understands the central concepts, tools of inquiry, and structures of the discipline(s) he or she teaches and can create learning experiences that make these aspects of subject matter meaningful for students.*	Chapter 1, The Nature and Values of Science, pp. 5–6
	Chapter 8: Meaningfulness, pp. 243–245; How Information Is Organized in Long-Term Memory, pp. 247–248; Suggestions for Teaching no. 5, p. 253
	Chapter 10: Facets of Constructivism, pp. 311–312
2. Learning and Development *The teacher understands how children learn and develop, and can provide learning opportunities that support their intellectual, social, and personal development.*	Chapter 2: Entire chapter, pp. 22–66
	Chapter 3: Entire chapter, pp. 67–102
	Chapter 7: Entire chapter, pp. 211–236
	Chapter 8: Entire chapter, pp. 237–275
	Chapter 9: Entire chapter, pp. 276–308
	Chapter 10: Entire chapter, pp. 309–346
	Chapter 11: Entire chapter, pp. 347–387
3. Diverse Learners *The teacher understands how students differ in their approaches to learning and creates instructional opportunities that are adapted to diverse learners.*	Chapter 4: Entire chapter, pp. 103–132
	Chapter 5: Entire chapter, pp. 133–170
	Chapter 6: Entire chapter, pp. 171–210
4. Instructional Strategies *The teacher understands and uses a variety of instructional strategies to encourage students' development of critical thinking, problem solving, and performance skills.*	Chapter 7: Entire chapter, pp. 211–236
	Chapter 8: Entire chapter, pp. 237–275
	Chapter 9: Entire chapter, pp. 276–308
	Chapter 10: Entire chapter, pp. 309–346
	Chapter 11: Entire chapter, pp. 347–387
5. Motivation and Classroom Management *The teacher uses an understanding of individual and group motivation and behavior to create a learning environment that encourages positive social interaction, active engagement in learning, and self-motivation.*	Chapter 11: Entire chapter, pp. 347–387
	Chapter 12: Entire chapter, pp. 388–421
	Chapter 13: Entire chapter, pp. 422–454